To Rod Feldmann

best wishes and regards

M. O. Woelbone
10-17-88

CENOZOIC MAMMALS
OF NORTH AMERICA

CENOZOIC MAMMALS OF NORTH AMERICA

Geochronology and Biostratigraphy

Edited by
Michael O. Woodburne

UNIVERSITY OF CALIFORNIA PRESS
Berkeley • Los Angeles • London

University of California Press
Berkeley and Los Angeles, California

University of California Press, Ltd.
London, England

Library of Congress Cataloging in Publication Data

Cenozoic mammals of North America.

Includes bibliographies and indexes.
Contents: Introduction / M. O. Woodburne—Principles, classification, and
recommendations / M. O. Woodburne—Mammal ages, stages, and zones / M. O.
Woodburne—[etc.]
1. Mammals, Fossil. 2. Paleontology—Cenozoic. 3. Paleontology—
North America. 4. Geology, Stratigraphic—Cenozoic. 5. Geology—North
America. I. Woodburne, Michael O.
QE881.C46 1987   569′.097   86–7135
ISBN 0–520–05392–3 (alk. paper)

Printed in the United States of America

1 2 3 4 5 6 7 8 9

CONTENTS

Preface   *M. O. Woodburne*   *vii*

Contributors   *xi*

Definitions   *xiii*

Introduction   *M. O. Woodburne*   *1*

1. Principles, Classification, and Recommendations   *9*

    M. O. Woodburne

2. Mammal Ages, Stages, and Zones   *18*

    M. O. Woodburne

3. First North American Land Mammal Ages of the Cenozoic Era   *24*

    J. D. Archibald*

4. Eocene (Wasatchian through Duchesnean) Biochronology of North America   *77*

    R. M. West*

5. The Chadronian, Orellan, and Whitneyan North American Land Mammal Ages   *118*

    R. J. Emry*

6. Faunal Succession and Biochronology of the Arikareean through Hemphillian Interval (Late Oligocene through Earliest Pliocene Epochs) in North America   *153*

    R. H. Tedford*

7. The North American Quaternary Sequence   *211*

    E. L. Lundelius, Jr.*

8. Biochronology of the Microtine Rodents of the United States   *236*

    C. A. Repenning

* Chairman of a committee of contributors, a list of whom appears at the beginning of the volume.

9. Mammalian Chronology and the Magnetic Polarity Time Scale   *269*

    E. H. Lindsay*

10. A Prospectus of the North American Mammal Ages   *285*

    M. O. Woodburne

Indexes   *291*

    Systematic Index   *293*

    Subject Index   *309*

PREFACE

"How old is it?" The subject of this query can be the age of a fossil mouse, a geologic event, or a statement that attempts to link the two. These considerations epitomize the aims and orientation of this book. Effective communication concerning age requires language that is reasonably precise as to what is meant by "old" or "age"; it also requires that the particular interval of time at issue—in this case the Cenozoic Era (the last 60 + million years)—be divisible into segments useful to the discussion and that these segments be recognizable and distinguishable from one another on the basis of certain criteria, in this case, fossil mammals.

Fossil animals, including mammals, have long been used to distinguish intervals of geologic time as part of the scientific discipline known as geochronology. In fact, fossils were the first, and still are one of the most effective, means of recognizing temporal intervals in stratigraphic sections of nonmarine rocks and correlating the rocks from one area to another.

Paleontological correlation began in earnest with the work of William Smith (1815), and since that time increasingly refined biostratigraphic studies have been utilized to propose correlation of rock sequences, either continuously exposed from place to place or isolated from other outcrops, on a purely objective basis. Thus, inspection of certain stratigraphic sequences can show that new forms of life occur in intervals below which they were previously unknown, that these new occurrences can be found in other sequences as well, and that correlations between them (on those bases) can be proposed. This is, in fact, what Smith was doing on a purely objective basis, without the knowledge that the observed changes were due to evolutionary processes.

Refinements in correlation by means of fossils commonly rely on small morphological changes that are now interpreted to be the result of progressive (and thus time-sequential) changes in evolutionary lineages. Nevertheless, correlations can be, and often are, proposed on the basis of objectively observed changes in the biological content of strata, because the stratigraphic record necessary to demonstrate the evolutionary development of the new taxon commonly is lacking. Such proposals of correlation are especially forceful when found to be internally consistent with respect to a diverse array of various geologically "instantaneous" data, such as radioisotopic, magnetostratigraphic, or certain lithostratigraphic information.

Whether these other data are available or not, the effectively irreversible nature of evolutionary processes (either "gradual" or " punctuational") as now understood supports the hypothesis that biological novelties appear only once, that each has a unique temporal duration, and that their new occurrence in the stratigraphic record is a defensible basis for correlation. It is obvious, in short, that fossils have a temporal significance that can be applied directly to the rocks in which they occur. Homotaxy (see Definitions) can be taken as a first hypothesis in correlation, and with due respect for the astute cautions of T. H. Huxley (1862) that similarity of biological content in rock strata might be due to biofacies rather than to temporal factors, increasingly abundant cross-checks of biochronologic correlations from other data sets have tended to diminish (but not eliminate) Huxley's concern.

Why should one be concerned with distinguishing geologic time on the basis of fossil mammals? First, each biological discipline has developed a chronological scheme based on, and subdivided by, events that are relevant to important evolutionary changes or advances unique to that discipline and can be discerned with respect to them. Second, inasmuch as all biological systems proceed at their own rate and develop their own patterns, it is unlikely that subdivisions of a unit of time based on one discipline will coincide with subdivisions based on events important to other disciplines. Third, the system of temporal subdivisions based on patterns of change displayed by fossil mammals still is the most widely important biologically based scheme for assessing correlations between nonmarine rocks of any area, including North America. Finally, rocks bearing fossil mammals are usefully (but in relatively small numbers) interbedded with rocks that contain fossil marine organisms with a potential, if not always actual, worldwide distribution. It has been possible, therefore, to develop an interdisciplinary network of data (now augmented by a growing set of radioisotopic ages and magnetic polarity correlations) with which locally achieved and important fossil mammal-bearing successions of each of the world's continents can be related to successions of the others (although generally with less precision than is possible on the basis of the local paleontologically based temporal divisions).

Thus, refinements in the basic correlations involving fossil mammals, and the relation of these correlations to invertebrate, plant, radioisotopic, and magnetic polarity chronologies, can only enhance the local, regional, and worldwide study of evolutionary, distributional, and chronological patterns displayed by fossil mammals. In addition, earth scientists interested in other disciplines (general stratigraphy, geologic history, succession of fossil floras, invertebrate biostratigraphy, etc.) will be able to compare more accurately those events important for their own work with the fossil mammal chronology, and vice versa. Each time a body of information is updated, for the interested observer the task of becoming his or her own "expert" with respect to those data becomes easier. As an example, the debate concerning early man's role in the extinction of the Pleistocene mammal megafauna (large-sized animals) in North America includes comparison with the extinction pattern (and its timing) displayed on other continents. Such comparisons are only as valid as the refined and upgraded correlations achieved in each area, including North America.

With respect to fossil mammals, these considerations are part of the discipline of vertebrate paleontology; thus, vertebrate paleontologists usually are geochronologists. Their main task as geochronologists is to perform basic biostratigraphic studies, that is, to carefully note the stratigraphic position of fossils found in sediments.

The vertebrate paleontologist also must describe and identify the fossils and assess their evolutionary relationships, thereby allowing the interpretatively and operationally unique temporal properties of the fossils to be fitted into a well-documented physical framework. The age-significant information derived therefrom thus can be applied to other geologic data contained in the sediments: the "age" of a mouse can be related directly to the "age" of another geologic event,[1] for example, whether it is a volcanic ash, an unconformity, evidence of uplift, subsidence, beginning or ending of a certain geochemical, magnetic polarity, or paleoecological regime.

To be effective in these endeavors, however, it is necessary that mammalian vertebrate paleontologists communicate well and precisely about the intervals of time being utilized so that the information is useful not only among themselves but to other members of the geochronologic community as well. As will become abundantly clear from this volume, the basic scheme in use in North America is a system of mammal ages, and comparable entities are found elsewhere throughout the world (Savage and Russell 1983). All aim toward a common goal: communicating effectively and with increasing precision about intervals of the Cenozoic Era, as recognized on the basis of the evolution and dispersal of fossil mammals. As will be seen below, a number of improvements in this regard have been made, and the beginnings of a more refined zonal scheme for much of the Cenozoic mammal record in North America has been recently accomplished.

The impetus for the present work was the annual meeting in 1973 of the Geological Society of America, in Dallas, Texas. There a symposium on the topic "Vertebrate Paleontology as a Discipline in Geochronology" was convened chaired by D. E. Savage (Savage and McKenna 1974). The rationale for that symposium was to bring together articles by relevant specialists to update the means by which North American paleontologists, especially, distinguish segments of geologic time based on fossil mammals which lived during the Cenozoic Era.

This was particularly important inasmuch as the original statement on characterization and recognition of the North American mammal ages had been presented in 1941 (Wood et al. 1941) but was long out of print. Many of the taxonomic bases for recognition of the mammal ages required upgrading, not only because of taxonomic revisions but also because of advances in knowledge. Some of the applications by Wood and his colleagues of principles expressed in their 1941 work

---

[1] Burial of the once-living mouse is in itself a geologic event.

have been called into question (e.g., Savage 1962), but the general sequence of mammal ages has proven viable and has been used by essentially all subsequent workers. At the same time, many refinements in basic stratigraphic as well as paleontological data have developed since 1941. If the system of mammal ages is to continue to be effective—and, most important, no other generally applicable scheme has been proposed as a replacement—it is now critical and more than timely to present a modern synthesis of these data and to indicate the format under which additional refinements will be made.

Syntheses for other areas include Simpson (1940), Marshall et al. (1983, 1984) for South America; Thenius (1959) and Savage and Russell (1983) for global treatments; and Rich and Thompson (1982) and Woodburne et al. (1985) for Australasia. The African record has been summarized by Maglio and Cooke (1978), primarily from an evolutionary point of view, and the Pleistocene of North America has been addressed by Kurten and Anderson (1980).

This volume concerns North America and the mammal age subdivisions of the Cenozoic Era there. The chapters herein conform to a grouping roughly comparable to the standard Cenozoic epochs. Each was written by one or more knowledgeable persons, group efforts being under the nominal direction of a "chairman." The authors were charged with discussing the means by which the mammal ages can be recognized and refined, the means by which the boundaries between them can be defined, and, where possible, the means by which they can be integrated with other disciplines. The aim is to provide a state-of-the-art summary of where we are now and where we might go from here.

In addition to the contributors to the volume, I thank the following individuals (listed alphabetically) for helping with illustrative material: Linda Bobbitt, Robert Hicks, Karoly Fogassy, and Glenn Thomas (University of California, Riverside). *Mammalian Paleofaunas of the World* by D. E. Savage and D. L. Russell (1983) was an invaluable source of recent literature both within and beyond North America.

I dedicate this book to the memory of William Smith, Henry Fairfield Osborn, and the others who have followed in their path.

Riverside, California   M. O. W.
January 26, 1986

CONTRIBUTORS

J. David Archibald
> Department of Biology, San Diego State University, San Diego, California 92182

Philip R. Bjork
> Museum of Geology, South Dakota School of Mines and Technology, Rapid City, South Dakota 57701

Craig C. Black
> Natural History Museum of Los Angeles County, Los Angeles, California 90007

Thomas M. Bown
> Paleontology and Stratigraphy Branch, U.S. Geological Survey, Denver, Colorado 80025

Robert F. Butler
> Department of Geosciences, University of Arizona, Tucson, Arizona 85721

C. S. Churcher
> Department of Zoology, University of Toronto, Canada M5S 1A1

William A. Clemens
> Department of Paleontology, University of California, Berkeley, California 94720

Mary R. Dawson
> Section of Vertebrate Fossils, Carnegie Museum of Natural History, Pittsburgh, Pennsylvania 15213

Theodore Downs
> Division of Earth Sciences, Natural History Museum of Los Angeles County, Los Angeles, California 90007

Robert J. Emry
> Department of Paleobiology, National Museum of Natural History, Smithsonian Institution, Washington, D.C. 20560

Robert W. Fields
> Department of Geology, University of Montana, Missoula, Montana 59801

John J. Flynn
> Department of Geological Sciences, Rutgers University, New Brunswick, New Jersey 08903

Theodore Galusha*
> Department of Vertebrate Paleontology, American Museum of Natural History, New York, New York 10024

Philip D. Gingerich
> Museum of Paleontology, The University of Michigan, Ann Arbor, Michigan 48104

David J. Golz
> Department of Geology, California State University, Sacramento, California 95819

C. R. Harington
> National Museum of Canada, Ottawa, Canada K1A 0M8

---

* Deceased: 2 August, 1979

Noye M. Johnson
> Department of Earth Sciences, Dartmouth College, Hanover, New Hampshire 03755

David W. Krause
> Department of Anatomical Sciences, State University of New York, Stony Brook, New York 11794

Leonard Krishtalka
> Section of Vertebrate Fossils, Carnegie Museum of Natural History, Pittsburgh, Pennsylvania 15213

Jason A. Lillegraven
> Department of Geology, The University of Wyoming, Laramie, Wyoming 82071

Everett H. Lindsay
> Department of Geosciences, University of Arizona, Tucson, Arizona 85721

Ernest L. Lundelius, Jr.
> Department of Geological Sciences, University of Texas, Austin, Texas 78712

J. Reid Macdonald
> Rapid City, South Dakota 57701

Malcolm C. McKenna
> Department of Vertebrate Paleontology, American Museum of Natural History, New York, New York 10024

Neil D. Opdyke
> Department of Geology, University of Florida, Gainesville, Florida 32611

John W. Rensberger
> Burke Memorial Museum, University of Washington, Seattle, Washington 98105

Charles A. Repenning
> Paleontology and Stratigraphy Branch, U.S. Geological Survey, Denver, Colorado 80025

Kenneth D. Rose
> Department of Cell Biology and Anatomy, Johns Hopkins University School of Medicine, Baltimore, Maryland 21205

Loris S. Russell
> Vertebrate Paleontology Department, Royal Ontario Museum, Toronto, Ontario M5S 2C6

Gerald E. Schultz
> Department of Geosciences, West Texas State University, Canyon, Texas 79015

Holmes A. Semken
> Department of Geology, University of Iowa, Iowa City, Iowa 52242

Morris F. Skinner
> Department of Vertebrate Paleontology, American Museum of Natural History, New York, New York 10024

Richard K. Stucky
> Section of Vertebrate Fossils, Carnegie Museum of Natural History, Pittsburgh, Pennsylvania 15213

Beryl E. Taylor
> Department of Vertebrate Paleontology, American Museum of Natural History, New York, New York 10024

Richard H. Tedford
> Department of Vertebrate Paleontology, American Museum of Natural History, New York, New York 10024

William D. Turnbull
> Department of Geology, Field Museum of Natural History, Chicago, Illinois 60605

S. David Webb
> Florida State Museum, University of Florida, Gainesville, Florida 32611

Robert M. West
> Carnegie Museum of Natural History, Pittsburgh, Pennsylvania 15213

David P. Whistler
> Division of Earth Sciences, Natural History Museum of Los Angeles County, Los Angeles, California 90007

Michael O. Woodburne
> Department of Earth Sciences, University of California, Riverside, California 92521

Richard J. Zakrzewksi
> Department of Earth Sciences and Sternberg Memorial Museum, Fort Hays State University, Hays, Kansas 67601

DEFINITIONS

These few definitions are provided as an aid to understanding the materials presented herein. They are in alphabetical order, following primarily the Stratigraphic Code of the North American Commission on Stratigraphic Nomenclature (1983; NASC in subsequent notation), Hedberg (1976), and the *Glossary of Geology* (Bates and Jackson 1980).

Age. A statement about the antiquity of a fossil organism; "The position of anything in the geologic time scale; e.g., 'the rocks of Miocene age'" (Bates and Jackson 1980, p. 9). Formally, the lowest-ranking unit of the hierarchy of units of geochronologic (geologic time) classification; equivalent in rank to, and based on, a chronostratigraphic stage.

Allochthonous. "Formed or produced elsewhere than in its present place; of foreign origin, or introduced." (Bates and Jackson 1980, p. 15).

Assemblage-zone. A biozone characterized by the association of three or more taxa (NASC, p. 862). In some cases the ranges of the taxa are not specified (Hedberg 1976, p. 50). An interval-zone is based on only two taxa (see below).

Autochthonous. "Formed or produced in the place where now found." (Bates and Jackson 1980, p. 43).

Biochron. An interval of geologic time based on the "duration of organic characters" (Williams 1901, p. 579.), for example, the time when a certain fauna, genus, or species lived.

Biochronologic unit. "A division of time distinguished on the basis of biostratigraphic or objective paleontologic data" (Bates and Jackson 1980, p. 65).

Biochronology. "*Geochronology* based on the relative dating of geologic events by biostratigraphic or paleontologic methods or evidence" (Bates and Jackson 1980, p. 65).

Biostratigraphic unit. A unit of rocks based on a described stratigraphic array (vertically and laterally) of biologic (fossil) data.

Biostratigraphy. The discipline of describing the stratigraphic range (vertically and laterally) of fossil remains in rock strata; the organization of strata into units based on their fossil content (see Hedberg 1976, p. 48).

Biozone. The fundamental biostratigraphic unit (NASC, p. 863), including those entities designated below as "X"-zone. Although a biozone commonly is of shorter temporal duration than a stage, such is not necessarily the case (biozone of Reptilia). In contrast to a chronozone, in which the defining and characterizing criteria (in this case, fossils) are interpreted to have chronological significance and can be used in correlation, a biozone is a descriptive unit.

Chron. Formally, a geochronologic unit comparable in rank to, and derived from, a chronozone. Neither the chron nor the chronozone is proscribed as to duration, in spite of being listed usually as the lowest geochronologic and chronostratigraphic units, respectively (see chap. 1). Confusingly, a chron also is a unit of the Magnetic Polarity time scale of the North American Stratigraphic Code (1983). It represents an interval of time based on the duration of a period of magnetic polarity, established by a polarity chronozone.

Chronological. Having to do with recognizing or discriminating intervals of Earth history.

Chronostratigraphic unit. "A body of rock strata that is unified by having been formed during a specific interval of geologic time. It represents all of the rocks formed during a certain time span of Earth history, and only the rock formed during that time span; . . . [it] is bounded by isochronous surfaces" (Hedberg 1976, p. 67).

Chronostratigraphy. "The element of stratigraphy that deals with the *age* of strata and their *time* relations" (Hedberg 1976, p. 66).

Chronozone. A unit of chronostratigraphic classification, the duration of which is not proscribed even though it is portrayed as being the lowest-ranking unit of that classification; for fossil mammals, usually based on a biozone. It is a material record of the stratigraphic range of a taxon or taxa interpreted to be temporally significant which, when replicated in strata of other places, is considered to demonstrate a correlation between them; when unambiguously defined, it is the primary means of precise correlation based on biological information. The chronozone forms the material base for the chron of geochronologic classification.

Concurrent range-zone. An assemblage-zone in which the interval is characterized by two or more taxa and defined as being between the lowest stratigraphic occurrence of one taxon and the highest stratigraphic occurrence of another (NASC, p. 863).

Correlation. A general statement of similarity or identity between two objects or entities. The term is used here to denote correspondence in time or age of rocks, faunas, local faunas, mammal ages, stages, or zones, for example, Hedberg's chronocorrelation (1976, p. 14).

Fauna. In this case, an assemblage of fossil vertebrates of specific taxonomic composition obtained from a number of geographically diverse sites.

Faunule. Reserved here for associations of taxa interpreted directly or intentionally for their ecological significance.

Geochron. An interval of time based on the stratigraphic record, usually the interval of time represented by the deposition of a body of strata, rock formation, and so forth.

Geochronologic unit. An interval of geologic time equivalent to the corresponding chronostratigraphic unit.

Geochronology. The discipline of discerning and ordering events or other phenomena of Earth history with respect to geologic time.

Homotaxy. "The similarity in separate regions of the serial arrangement or succession of strata of comparable compositions or of included fossils. The term is derived from *homotaxis,* proposed by Huxley (1892) to emphasize that similarity in succession does not

prove age equivalence of comparable units" (NASC, p. 851).

Interval-zone. A body of strata between the specified and documented lowest and/or highest occurrences of two taxa (NASC 1983, p. 862).

Lineage-zone. An interval-zone in which the interval corresponds to the lowest stratigraphic occurrences in an evolutionary lineage (NASC, p. 862).

Lithologic unit. See **Lithostratigraphic unit**.

Lithology. The discipline of describing and analyzing the composition of rock specimens on the basis of mineralogical composition, color, grain size (e.g., Bates and Jackson 1980, p. 364); also, a general term for rock composition.

Lithostratigraphic unit. ". . . a defined body of sedimentary, extrusive igneous, metasedimentary, or metavolcanic strata which is distinguished and delimited on the basis of lithic characteristics and stratigraphic position" (NASC, p. 855, in part).

Lithostratigraphy. "that element of stratigraphy which is concerned with the organization of strata into units based on their lithologic character" (Hedberg 1976, p. 8).

Local fauna. An assemblage of fossil vertebrates of specific taxonomic composition recovered from one or a few sites that are closely spaced stratigraphically and geographically.

Ma. Megannum; one million years in the radioisotopic time scale. Thus, for example, 10 Ma refers to the ten-million-year level of that time scale.

Magnetic polarity chron. A part "of geologic time during which the Earth's magnetic field had a characteristic polarity or sequence of polarities. These units correspond to the time spans represented by polarity chronozones, e.g., Gauss Normal Polarity Chronozone" (NASC, p. 870). The units can also receive numerical designations, for example, magnetic polarity chron 29N.

Mammal age. Geochronologic unit based on an association of fossil mammals considered to represent a particular interval of geologic time, originally informal in that it was not based on a chronostratigraphic stage (Wood et al. 1941). It is similar to an assemblage-zone, in which ranges of taxa are not specified (e.g., Hedberg 1976, p. 50). At present, some mammal ages can be considered to be formal units as they are based on stages of the same name and extent (e.g., Wasatchian, Clarkforkian; chaps. 2, 3, and 4).

M.Y. (or m.y.). A segment of geologic time one million years in duration, or something that happened ten million years ago (without reference to a given point or set of points on the radioisotopic time scale).

Oppel-zone. An assemblage-zone composed of more than two taxa and with boundaries based on two or more first and/or last occurrences of characteristic taxa (NASC, p. 863).

Range-zone. An interval-zone based on the lowest and highest stratigraphic occurrences of a single taxon (NASC, p. 862).

Stage. Lowest-ranking unit in the hierarchy of chrono-stratigraphic classification; a material unit that forms the base for a geochronologic age (e.g., Hedberg 1976).

Stratigraphy. The discipline (usually) of studying the properties and relationships of stratified (layered) rocks; the arrangement of strata.

REFERENCES

Bates, R. L., and J. A. Jackson. 1980. Glossary of geology. Falls Church, Va.: American Geological Institute.

North American Commission on Stratigraphic Nomenclature. 1983. North American stratigraphic code. Amer. Assoc. Petrol. Geol. 67:841–875.

Hedberg, H. D., ed. 1976. International stratigraphic guide. New York: John Wiley & Sons.

Huxley, T. H. 1862. The anniversary address. Qtly. J. Geol. Soc. London 18:xl–liv.

Williams, H. S. 1901. The discrimination of time values in geology. J. Geol. 9:570–585.

Wood, H. E., II, R. W. Chaney, J. Clark, E. H. Colbert, G. L. Jepsen, J. B. Reeside, Jr., and C. Stock. 1941. Nomenclature and correlation of the North American continental Tertiary. Bull. Geol. Soc. Amer. 52:1–48.

INTRODUCTION

Michael O. Woodburne

HISTORICAL BACKGROUND

To a large degree, this book began in 1937 (Wood et al. 1941, pp. 3–8). At its annual meeting that year, the Vertebrate Paleontology Section of the Paleontological Society charged certain of its members to describe the criteria by which temporal intervals of the Cenozoic Era could be recognized on the basis of fossil mammals. The great sequences of tilted, uplifted, and eroded strata of the western United States had yielded a wealth of fossils in the late nineteenth and early twentieth century, and H. F. Osborn and W. D. Matthew of the American Museum of Natural History had begun to construct bio-stratigraphies of Tertiary mammals with the ultimate aim of basing interpretative time-stratigraphic (chronostratigraphic) zonations on them, which was comparable in philosophy to procedures being followed by European marine stratigraphers of the time (Osborn 1929; for a review, see Tedford 1970). But the momentum of Osborn's project was lost, and the practice of compiling detailed biostratigraphies was deemphasized between 1920 and 1940 in North America as paleontologists turned to biological pursuits. Dissatisfaction also had arisen from the fact that if the name of the name bearer of the zone or unit changed as a result of taxonomic revision, so did the name of the zone. A system was desired which would eliminate this problem.

A scheme of Provincial (for North America) Mammal Ages was proposed (Wood et al. 1941; see Savage 1951 for Quaternary Mammal Ages to supplement those of Wood et al.). These mammal ages were intended to represent divisions of the Cenozoic Era based on characteristic groups of fossil mammals whose temporal relationships and overall stage of evolution were thought to be indicative of a particular interval of geologic time. Superpositional relationships were noted to the extent that rocks containing fossils of one mammal age might be found to occur above or below rocks with fossils of another mammal age, but stratigraphic details in the tradition of Osborn and Matthew were not developed consistently. Attention was given to first and last occurrences, "index fossils" were noted, and characterizing assemblages were listed. The resulting system is a biochronology, even if not thus explicitly stated by Wood et al.; the units are *biochrons* in the terminology of H. S. Williams (1901) as they are based on biological rather than lithologic criteria.

In spite of the relatively loose characterization originally given and subsequently maintained for mammal ages, the profession has been "saved" by the fact that mammals do indeed evolve and disperse rapidly (e.g., Savage 1977, pp. 432–435). Mammal ages are, in fact, operationally valuable in characterizing, recognizing, and correlating within and between intervals of time during the Cenozoic Era.

Some comment has been generated by a confusing aspect of the procedures followed in many cases by Wood et al. (see Savage 1962; McKenna 1965; Tedford 1970; Emry 1973). The confusion arises from the fact that whereas the mammal ages were characterized by biological criteria, their duration in time often was set by the temporal span (geochron) of the rock unit on which the age was based, for example, "Torrejonian age—new provincial time term, based on the Torrejon formation" (Wood et al. 1941, p. 9). In stated terms, at least, the advances made since the time of William Smith were lost. The practice of maintaining the age-significant paleontological information separately from the rocks with which the fossils were associated was not followed by Wood et al. Strict adherence to the operations they utilized would have resulted in subsequent refinements in correlation and discussion of boundaries between mammal ages, requiring that the interval of time under discussion be determined from the geochron of the rock unit on which the mammal age had been based, regardless of whether or not paleontological evidence was found throughout the strata (see also McKenna 1965). Fortunately, Wood et al. also noted that "the ages are not necessarily coextensive with their types, and the precise limits between successive ages are intended to be somewhat flexible and may presumably be modified in the light of later discoveries" (1941, p. 6). Later discoveries and refinements are what we are concerned with in this volume, based on the working hypothesis that paleontological information is of primary importance in this regard; it is aided but infrequently (limited samples, biofacies problems) superseded in importance by other data sets.

SUBSEQUENT REFINEMENTS

As noted above, Osborn and Matthew (Osborn 1929) had begun constructing biostratigraphies of fossil mammals as a basis for chronostratigraphic correlation. Biostratigraphy is critical not only for making improvements and refinements of the present mammal ages but also for developing traditional chronostratigraphic hierarchies. Savage (1955) thus nominated two mammalian stages (for California), devised with a philosophical and procedural approach amenable to the characterization of chronostratigraphic units. He developed a biostratigraphy, tested it for consistency at a number of localities, showed that the lower (Cerrotejonian) stage occurred—by correlation at least—superpositionally below the upper (Montediablan) stage, and interpreted the characteristic fossil assemblages of each stage to have temporal, rather than biofacies, significance.

Later workers (Rensberger 1971; Fisher and Rensberger 1972; Lindsay 1972) developed smaller-than-stage-level zonations based on closely observed and interpreted (for species' limits) stratigraphies. Those of Rensberger were concurrent range-zones, whereas those of Lindsay were assemblage-zones but with more than usual attention paid to biostratigraphic ranges of taxa (see Definitions). Both were developed in such a way as to allow proposed (Rensberger) and potential (Lindsay) time correlations (see also Woodburne 1977). In both Rensberger and Lindsay, characteristic fossil assemblages were given for zonal sequences. Rensberger and Fisher and Rensberger made the additional necessary step and defined boundaries for their zones. The zones thus had established limits. Until now, these are among the only defined chronostratigraphic units in the recent literature of mammalian geochronology in North America. As noted herein, further examples of zonal subdivision of strata (of Paleocene and Eocene age in Wyoming) are provided by P. D. Gingerich and his colleagues, and the importance of defining, versus characterizing, these biochronologic intervals continues to be stressed. (See also chap. 8 for a zonal division of the late Tertiary and Quaternary epochs.)

It is, of course, critical to define boundaries between units whenever possible, because only this will allow us to determine whether or not, or to what extent, there are gaps or overlaps between units or whether they are isochronous. One of the stated aims of Wood et al. was to devise a scheme of North American mammal ages of "purely temporal significance based on North American mammal-bearing units" (1941, p. 1) and "to cover all of Tertiary time" (p. 6). As shown in the following chapters, certain advances have been made toward achieving this goal.

One of our reviewers pointed out the need for a definite hierarchy of geochronologic units and terms for mammalian correlation and suggested that these should be brought into line with comparable units of other disciplines, as expressed in American "codes" (NASC 1983) and international "guides" (Hedberg 1976) in recent years. Because of the disinclination of most North American vertebrate paleontologists to operate within the framework of formal chronostratigraphic hierarchies and units (for reasons cited above), achievement of this desirable aim has been slow. If treatments presented here reflect a consensus, however, it appears that North American mammalian vertebrate paleontologists have accepted this challenge, that detailed biostratigraphies are being developed and biological bases for defining unit boundaries are being sought, and that the discipline of mammalian chronostratigraphy is being brought into line with chronostratigraphy for other organisms. To further this aim is one of the major objectives of this volume, and an assessment of the degree to which this challenge has been met is taken up in chapter 2.

TEMPORAL INTERVALS, CALIBRATION, AND MAMMAL AGES

Whether large or small, temporal subdivisions based on paleontological data form an ordinal chronology in which the intervals are not necessarily of equal duration. This differs from an interval chronology, such as a radio-isotopic time scale, in which the intervals are equal. The equal interval chronology may seem more orderly and more appealing, and some workers have proposed that paleontologically based chronologies be replaced with radioisotopic ones. Because it is not possible to obtain isotopic ages for all sedimentary sequences, because the plus or minus ($\pm$) factor common to all radioisotopic ages causes severe problems in discrimination even in relatively young rocks (see below), and because it still is important and useful to have a chronology for fossil mammals based on their biological aspects (evolution, dispersal, etc.), vertebrate paleontologists continue with the investigations we describe here.

As a recognition of the utility of the existing mammal age chronology, one of the pioneering applications of the then newly developed potassium-argon (K-Ar) method of radioisotopic dating was tested against the relative age framework based on mammal age hierarchies in North America (Evernden et al. 1964). The two schemes were found to order the rocks in a generally compatible fashion, and those with even a passing acquaintance with recent literature can certify that K-Ar "dates" appear with a rapidity that surpasses the ability of most to absorb them, much less assess their validity.

"Absolute dates" are appealing, if only for reasons of simplicity and universal comprehension. Because there is a tendency for those who use these dates to accept them at face value, a few cautionary remarks are in order. Potassium-argon (or any other) determinations are relatively expensive to obtain, so the general public often is presented with numbers that derive from a single analysis of a single sample. Depending on the analytical variables, these numbers obtain various degrees of reliability, commonly expressed as a $\pm$ factor, for example, 22.4 ± 2.9 Ma. Sometimes no qualifying $\pm$ factor is given, leaving the reader to wonder whether the probable "error" ranges from plus or minus 2 percent to 5 percent or even greater, as shown by 20.1 ± 8.9 Ma (examples from column XIV, fig. 2, Woodburne 1975; these two "dates" were obtained from the same site by different investigators and analyzed separately at the same facility). The point is that users of "absolute dates" should be aware of (1) their value, (2) the difference between precision and accuracy, (3) what the plus or minus figure

really means, and (4) the geologic history of the rock from which the sample was obtained, who dated it, and on the basis of what mineral species (see Dalrymple and Lanphere 1969, pp. 100–120, for general theory). Bernor, Woodburne, and Van Couvering (1980, pp. 34–36) discuss a very abundantly "dated" succession of late Miocene age in Iran and the confusion that occurs as a result of different mineral species being used as well as these "dates" being determined by a number of investigators. They also indicate an instance in which a fossiliferous succession at Samos, Greece, was "dated" at about 9 Ma, whereas the evolutionary grade of the fauna is more consistent with a prorated "age" of about 7 Ma (pp. 45–46). Miller and Morton (1980, pp. 13–18) also discuss the effect of dates that are obtained from different mineral species (in this case, on basement rocks that have experienced thermal resetting of various "clocks") and also point out the subjective aspect of determining $\pm$ factors (p. 9).

Another matter that requires particular attention is the sometimes casual designation of radioisotopic dates as "absolute." Even if one sets aside the question of whether the decay constants by which radioisotopic ages are calculated actually are "constant," there is yet no assurance that a radioisotopic year is exactly of the same duration as the calendar year we experience. The problem is exacerbated (although perhaps not meaningfully for practitioners of mammalian paleontology) by evidence that suggests the rotation of the Earth has slowed measurably since its origin (calendar years thus becoming progressively longer, whereas radioisotopically calculated years should be staying the same). The notion that "radioisotopic time" is "real time" has not been substantiated (nor has the definition of "real time"), and casual translation from one concept to the other is inappropriate to the purposes of this book. For these reasons, a distinction is made here between Ma (millions of years in the radioisotopic time scale) versus m.y. (a more abstract consideration of temporal duration not necessarily tied to a particular locus, or particular loci, of the radioisotopic time scale; see Definitions).

To what purpose is the "date" being put? To roughly determine a sequence of strata or to calculate rates of deposition or evolution? "Dates" of 20 Ma can have a total error range of at least 1 Ma; for "dates" of 60 Ma, the comparable error range can be at least as large as 3 Ma. Thus, depending on the amount of estimated (stated) or assumed (not stated) error in a "date," an age "assignment" for three samples of 19, 20, or 21 Ma could easily reflect the same geologic event, as could samples assigned "ages" of 58, 60, or 62 Ma. The point is that when zonal boundaries, datum levels, or other events are arrayed sequentially with respect to a radioisotopic million-year scale, as is commonly done, and when intervals are only 1 Ma apart, a closely spaced cluster of events ("dates") could all pertain to the same point in time. In such cases, their graphic separation may exemplify the principle of misplaced concreteness. The K-Ar dates used in these chapters have been recalculated as necessary to reflect revisions in the "standard" decay constants used in making such determinations (Steiger and Jaeger 1977).

As discussed in Woodburne (1977, pp. 232–233), zonations based on fossil mammals (as well as on other organisms; e.g., Kauffman 1970, pp. 656–664) are capable of subdividing the rock record much more finely than radioisotopic analysis. Both authors report examples where individual species can be interpreted as having arisen at intervals of 0.3 Ma or less. When part of a biostratigraphic matrix, an array of many species—each having origination rates on the order of 0.1 to 0.3 Ma and originating at random (or at least independently during the total duration represented by the array)—can describe a pattern that theoretically can represent and discriminate very small temporal intervals, that is, distinctly less than 0.1 to 0.3 Ma.

Partly for that reason, certain mammalian paleontologists have concerned themselves with attempting to subdivide the Cenozoic Era into levels more refined than mammal ages (examples above, and others are presented in the following chapters). It is important that future workers follow some of the leads indicated here and give defining, as well as characterizing, criteria for these subdivisions. Only then will it be possible to formulate a chronological hierarchy with clearly recognizable subdivisions having mutually exclusive, nonoverlapping, directly sequential boundaries. Examples in this volume indicate that defining criteria can range from evolutionary first appearances to local or regional dispersal first occurrences, each with its own set of constraints. Certainly, refinement of the geologic column and precision in communication can only be enhanced if the boundaries between the intervals are defined as precisely as possible.

MAMMAL AGES AND MAGNETIC POLARITY CHRONOLOGIES

Another advance since 1941 is the application of magnetostratigraphic practices to nonmarine rocks and the development of patterns of magnetic polarity reversals that can be correlated to the Magnetic Polarity Time Scale. Once a correlation of a local sequence has been achieved, with first approximations commonly being accomplished with the aid of other age-significant information, it is then possible to correlate the associated fossil mammals to the magnetic polarity time scale as well. The younger part of this time scale (0–5 Ma) is generally well calibrated by directly associated K-Ar ages, but much of it from 5 to 65 Ma (and older) is "dated" by assumptions as to spreading rates of the seafloor, which yield the magnetic patterns on which this time scale is based. Paleontologically determined ages of the oldest sediments that immediately overlie portions of the seafloor also contribute to its calibration. As materials amenable to radioisotopic analysis are frequently present in nonmarine strata, however, one result of the development of magnetic polarity stratigraphies for nonmarine rocks is to help calibrate the oceanic portion of the magnetic polarity time scale.

Because reversals of the Earth's magnetic field are nominally instantaneous geologically, boundaries between the events or chrons are considered to be isochronous. The development and application of magnetostratigraphic practices certainly have revolutionized the development of global, as well as local, correlation frameworks, various segments of which (with some notable exceptions) are 1 m.y. or less in duration. Mammalian chronostratigraphy is one beneficiary of this revolution, in spite of the generally more episodic mode of accumulation of the nonmarine, versus marine, stratigraphic record. At best, detailed and useful integrations have been developed between mammalian and magnetic polarity stratigraphies. At worst, it still can be very important to know that a fossil sample occurs in rocks that either are or are not of the same polarity as—and thus the sample is or is not potentially correlative with—rocks that contain another fossil sample (see also chap. 9).

A few cautionary notes are in order, however. Directly or by extrapolation, calibration of the magnetic polarity time scale is derived from radiochronometric methods. The discussion above concerning the systematic errors inherent in the K-Ar system, for instance, indicates that whereas the polarity reversals may be geologically instantaneous, determination of the ages of the reversals is systematically inaccurate to the same degree as is any other aspect of the geologic time scale when measured by such chronometric systems.

One clear misapplication of the results of magnetic polarity stratigraphy (but one that is not unique to the discipline) is the tendency for investigators to interpolate ages to points in the magnetic polarity sequence that lie between, and extrapolate ages to points that lie above or below, points that have been calibrated by whatever means. Such interpolations or extrapolations assume a steadiness of sedimentary accumulation that recent studies (Sadler 1981, Dingus and Sadler 1982) have shown to be highly improbable. "An interpolated age inherits not only the uncertainties [±] factor of the original determinations, but also an additional uncertainty due to the probable incompleteness of the [stratigraphic] section" (Sadler 1981, p. 583). Clearly, interpolated ages must be less precise than the "calibrations" by which they are bounded, so that, at best, the practice of making interpolated or extrapolated age assessments must be accomplished with great care and the clear realization of how accurate such an assessment actually may be. Again, unless carefully qualified, numbers assume an aura of concreteness, if for no other reason than their simplicity.

EUROPEAN CENOZOIC EPOCHS AND MAMMAL AGES

The epochs into which Lyell (1833) and others subdivided the Tertiary and Quaternary periods in Europe were generally based on the degree to which fossil (mostly invertebrate) organisms resembled living taxa. Strata with a fauna of a given degree of "modernness" were correlated with others and ascribed to a given epoch. The epochs so characterized and referrals so made were clearly in general terms. Epoch boundaries were not defined, which has provided numerous opportunities for debate ever since. With modern stratigraphic studies, incorporating information derived from pelagic invertebrates and plants as well as radioisotopic and magnetic polarity analysis, a certain censensus has been reached as to what rocks are of "Miocene," versus "Pliocene," age, for example, and what is the span of time that accrues to the various epochs (see Berggren and Van Couvering 1974, Berggren et al. 1985). Unanimity is not yet achieved, however, and many still mourn the near-extinction of the Pliocene Epoch as more and more time and space has been consumed by the Miocene. This example illustrates that generally applicable but loosely defined concepts, even if reassessed in modern times (Stanley, Addicott, and Chinzei 1980) must "float" and suffer readjustments relative to locally stabler references.

It must be clear to all that whereas the epoch terms of Lyell and others were based almost entirely on marine rocks and fossils in Western Europe and the Mediterranean region, the use of such terms with respect to intervals of time recognized on the basis of nonmarine mammals, even in the Old World, is achieved only by various kinds of extrapolation, such as physical interfingering of marine and nonmarine strata or radioisotopic analysis of interbedded volcanic rocks. The common application of epoch names to many mammal-bearing successions is tenuous and is useful only for the purpose of general,

and generalized, communication, not only for European sequences but for those of North America as well.

ORGANIZATION AND SCOPE

To establish the basis for the chapters that follow, the volume opens with a statement of principles and recommendations (chap. 1) and a synopsis and appraisal of the results that have been achieved (chap. 2). Chapters 3 through 7 discuss, in sequence, progressively later fossil mammal subdivisions of the Cenozoic Era (chaps. 7, 8, and 9 focus on essentially the same temporal interval, the Quaternary Period, from different points of view). They are of generally similar format, with variations to suit individual needs. In each of these chapters, the mammal ages pertinent to the interval are introduced, original characterization is discussed, and new information is presented with regard to both stratigraphic data and updated taxonomic names of the mammals concerned.

Thus, for the Paleocene Epoch (chap. 3), the basic stratigraphic relations of the type sequences for each mammal age are discussed, original and refined biological characterizations are given, and discussions are presented as to how the mammal ages of the Paleocene can be correlated to develop a regional composite that demonstrates their successive, nonoverlapping relationships. Local, finer-scale zonations are reported as examples of potential directions for future refinements. Special problems are presented, that is, the nature and recognition of the Cretaceous-Tertiary boundary and the Paleocene-Eocene boundary, the latter involving intercontinental correlations to type sections in the Old World. Magnetic polarity stratigraphy (to be more fully considered in chap. 9) is important to the correlation of mammal-bearing units of Paleocene age, so this is discussed here as are those instances where mammal-bearing strata are interbedded with rocks that have been aged by radioisotopic means.

The general format of chapter 4 is similar to that for the Paleocene Epoch. The boundary between mammal ages attributed to the Eocene Epoch versus those assigned to the Oligocene is discussed here. There are fewer internal zonations as compared to chapter 3, which reflects the status of those endeavors, although some subages, stages, substages, and zones have been proposed. There are more radioisotopic, but fewer magnetic polarity, data for North American strata correlated with the Eocene Epoch than for those correlated with the Paleocene. At its beginning, the Eocene Epoch was blessed with a major overland intercontinental dispersal between the New World and Old World and (in California) at its end, with intertongued nonmarine and marine strata. It is thus possible to establish a framework to relate much of the North American land mammal record in the Eocene Epoch with correlative strata in the Old World, something not so easily accomplished for the Paleocene Epoch.

The Oligocene Epoch (chap. 5) began with another strong intercontinental overland dispersal between the New and Old worlds, so this can be used to tie together the North American and European sequences, at least at the beginning. There are, however, a number of problems: assessment of some North American samples as either Duschesnean or Chadronian; whether the Duschesnean Land Mammal Age correlates best with European strata of Eocene or Oligocene age (or in part both); how to correlate rock and faunal units (and the nomenclature each carries) in the classical Nebraska and South Dakota districts in North America; and the question of recognizing the Whitneyan-Arikareean Mammal Age boundary and whether or not this corresponds to the boundary between the Oligocene and Miocene epochs. Radioisotopic data are relatively sparse, but magnetic polarity information is developing, as are proposals for chronostratigraphic zonations.

The chronofaunal character of North American "Oligocene" faunas, wherein the general structure and partition of the ecosystem is relatively stable and changes within are relatively minor, is emphasized here. This pattern begins the overall structure seen in many faunal units correlated with the Miocene and Pliocene epochs, where endemic changes are likely to be relatively unspectacular, if progressive. This leads to the practice of defining mammal age boundaries at points where (relatively few) new entries—presumably immigrants from elsewhere—occur in the fossil record. Important events are thus usually allochthonous rather than autochthonous in origin.

Mammal ages now referred to the Miocene Epoch are discussed in chapter 6 (fossils from the early part of the Arikareean Land Mammal Age probably are correlative with taxa attributed to the Oligocene Epoch). Fossils of Miocene age are among the most abundantly and widely distributed in North America. This also is a time when on the East, Gulf, and West coasts there was extensive interfingering of nonmarine and marine strata, allowing useful integration of the chronological systems of both environments. This, plus recognition of a few, but regionally important, intercontinental dispersals between the New and Old worlds allows increasingly refined comparison of the patterns being developed in the various regions.

Not only are rocks and faunas attributed to the Miocene Epoch well developed in North America but the stratigraphic relations between the various units are among the most complex, both locally and in region to region comparison. This is borne out by the extensive and detailed summary of biostratigraphic/lithostratigraphic relations in terms of the major depositional districts of the continent. Much of this is based on unpublished work developed during the past forty years by personnel of the American Museum of Natural History, with the result that mammal ages of the Miocene Epoch in North America and the local faunas comprising them are more thoroughly revised than those of any other single chapter.

Faunas attributed to the Pliocene and Pleistocene epochs are discussed in chapters 7, 8, and 9 from three different perspectives. Chapter 7 presents the basic mammal age framework, advances, and innovations made since 1941. Treatment here is deliberately succinct. The subject is so vast and the data so voluminous that a treatment fully exploring all topics could easily exceed in length the book by Kurtén and Anderson (1980). One of the important advances with respect to geochronology and biochronology of this interval has been developed in recent years by C. A. Repenning and Oldrich Fejfar. This work is summarized in chapter 8. Based on a theory of successive microtine rodent introductions from an Asian parent population, a sequence of immigrations in North America and Europe holds promise of making possible a much more refined correlation between the two areas for the Pliocene and Pleistocene epochs based on fossil mammals than heretofore possible. Repenning's work is augmented by chapter 9, which presents a modern view of the development and application of magnetic polarity reversals to nonmarine strata. (Although the method is now being applied to Cenozoic rocks of all ages, it first was developed and tested in those of Quaternary age and has special relevance to chaps. 7 and 8, which is clearly demonstrated by examples used in these chapters.) Chapter 10 ends the volume with sparse text woven around an overall correlation chart that summarizes what has been accomplished.

This volume has a number of limitations. It cannot pretend to solve many important problems concerning the relationship of mammalian biochronology to other disciplines. For example, the relationships between the North American continental mammal succession and succession based on fossil plants must be determined by careful inspection of pertinent literature (Axelrod 1958, Evernden and James 1964). Only recently have plant stage-ages been proposed (Wolfe 1966, 1971, 1972; Wolfe and Hopkins 1967; Wolfe et al. 1966), and these bear little, if any correspondence to mammalian chronologies. Previous attempts at ordering the fossil plant record into a chronological scheme involved the development, migration, and one-by-the-other replacement of "Geofloras" (e.g., Axelrod 1958). Temporal interpretations could be proposed for a given suite of plants depending on the relationship between their geographic (latitudinal) location, geofloral affinity, and inferences as to the altitude at which the suite lived. Age assignments usually were given with respect to Cenozoic epochs or mammal ages, but a distinctive, plant-based chronology was not proposed. MacGinitie (1962) has advocated caution regarding the above procedures, and Wolfe and co-workers (cited above) have proposed a new scheme based on the evolution of the plants themselves rather than on changes in their areal distribution.

As to marine chronologies in various districts of North America, Tedford and others (this volume) portray the important relationships between the Miocene mammal and invertebrate successions in the East Coast and West Coast regions. Golz (1976) has also summarized them for Eocene strata of the West Coast. Woodburne (1975) shows a reasonable alignment of late Cenozoic invertebrate microfaunal, invertebrate megafaunal, mammal age data, and radioisotopic evidence for California based on literature available up to that time. Beyond these examples, there are few important marine-nonmarine interdigitations that can independently align chronologies of these different data bases, so that additional attempts rely largely on either an indirect world-wide framework that synthesizes microfossil marine, megafossil marine, and land mammal relationships (see Berggren 1972; Berggren and Van Couvering 1974; Berggren et al. 1978, 1985) or extrapolations based on radioisotopic evidence. Thus, the interdisciplinary potential is best for rocks and faunas of late Eocene and Miocene age in North America. Alignments attempted for other parts of the time scale are based on evidence that is not directly related to fossil mammals or is extrapolated by radioisotopic evidence from one chronology to the other, with a resolving power that generally is poorer than the potential of the biologically based disciplines.

This book, then, will focus on what it can do best: describe and discuss temporal intervals for the Cenozoic Era based on fossil mammals. For more detailed local proposals and problems as to the relationships between the mammalian and other chronologies, it is necessary to consult the pertinent literature. Much of it is readily available, and some of the more important works have been cited in these pages. As for the mammals, it is to be hoped that what has been assembled here is sufficient to give a reasonable idea of the state-of-the-art in fossil

mammal geochronology and to provide a useful basis for encouraging further progress.

REFERENCES

Axelrod, D. I. 1958. Evolution of the Madro-Tertiary geoflora. Bot. Rev. 24 (7):433–509.

Berggren, W. A. 1972. A Cenozoic time-scale—Some implications for regional geology and palaeobiogeography. Lethaia 5:195–215.

Berggren, W. A., and J. A. Van Couvering. 1974. The Late Neogene: Biostratigraphy, geochronology and paleoclimatology of the last 15 million years in marine and continental sequences. Palaeogeogr., palaeoclimatol., Palaeoecol. 16:1–216.

Berggren, W. A., M. C. McKenna, J. Hardenbol, and J. D. Obradovich. 1978. Revised Paleogene polarity time scale. J. Geol. 86:67–81.

Berggren, W. A., D. V. Kent, J. J. Flynn, and J. A. Van Couvering. 1985. Cenozoic geochronology. Bull. Geol. Soc. Amer. 96:1407–1418.

Bernor, R. L., M. O. Woodburne, and J. A. Van Couvering. 1980. A contribution to the chronology of some Old World Miocene faunas based on hipparionine horses. Geobios 13:25–59.

Butler, R. F., and E. H. Lindsay. 1985. Mineralogy of magnetic minerals and revised magnetic polarity stratigraphy of continental sediments, San Juan Basin, New Mexico. J. Geol. 94:535–554.

Dalrymple, G. B., and M. A. Lanphere. 1969. Potassium-argon dating: principles, techniques, and applications to geochronology. San Francisco: W. H. Freeman and Company.

Dingus, L., and P. M. Sadler. 1982. The effects of stratigraphic completeness on estimates of evolutionary rates. Syst. Zool. 31, 4:400–412.

Emry, R. J. 1973. Stratigraphy and preliminary biostratigraphy of the Flagstaff Rim area, Natrona County, Wyoming. Smithsonian Contrib. Paleobiol. 25:1–20.

Evernden, J. F., and G. T. James. 1964. Potassium-argon dates and the Tertiary floras of North America. Amer. J. Sci. 262:945–974.

Evernden, J. F., D. E. Savage, G. H. Curtis, and G. T. James. 1964. Potassium-argon dates and the Cenozoic mammal chronology of North America. Amer. J. Sci. 262:145–198.

Fisher, R. V., and J. M. Rensberger. 1972. Physical stratigraphy of the John Day Formation, central Oregon. Univ. Calif. Publ. Geol. Sci. 101:1–95.

Golz, D. J. 1976. Eocene artiodactyla of southern California. Nat. Hist. Mus. Los Angeles Co. Sci. Bull. 26:1–85.

Huxley, T. H. 1862. The anniversary address. Qtrly. J. Geol. Soc. London 18:xl–liv.

Kauffman, E. G. 1970. Population systematics, radiometrics, and zonation—A new biostratigraphy. Proc. No. Amer. Paleont. Conv., Pt. F, pp. 612–666.

Kurtén, B., and E. Anderson. 1980. Pleistocene mammals of North America. New York: Columbia University Press.

Lindsay, E. H. 1972. Small mammals from the Barstow Formation, California. Univ. Calif. Publ. Geol. Sci. 93:1–104.

Lyell, C. 1833. Principles of geology, vol. 3. 1st ed. London: John Murray.

MacGinitie, H. D. 1962. The Kilgore flora. Univ. Calif. Publ. Geol. Sci. 35 (2):67–158.

McKenna, M. C. 1965. Stratigraphic nomenclature of the Miocene Hemingford group, Nebraska. Amer. Mus. Novitates, no. 2228, pp. 1–21.

Maglio, V. J., and H. B. S. Cooke, eds. 1978. Evolution of African mammals. Cambridge, Mass.: Harvard University Press.

Marshall, L. G., A. Berta, R. Hoffstetter, R. Pascual, O. Reig, M. Bombin, and A. Mones. 1984. Mammals and stratigraphy: geochronology of the mammal-bearing Quaternary of South America. Palaeovert. Mem. Extraordinaire: 1–76.

Marshall, L. G., R. Hoffstetter, and R. Pascual. 1983. Mammals and stratigraphy: Geochronology of the continental mammal-bearing Tertiary of South America. Palaeovertebrata. Mem. Extraordinaire: 1–93.

Miller, F. G., and D. M. Morton. 1980. Potassium-argon geochronology of the eastern Transverse Ranges and southern Mojave Desert, southern California. U.S. Geol. Surv. Prof. Paper 1152, pp. 1–30.

Osborn, H. F. 1929. The titanotheres of ancient Wyoming, Dakota, and Nebraska. U.S. Geol. Surv. Monograph 55(1): 1–701.

Rensberger, J. M. 1971. Entoptychine pocket gophers (Mammalia, Geomyoidea) of the early Miocene John Day Formation, Oregon. Univ. Calif. Publ. Geol. Sci. 90:1–209.

Rich, P. V., and E. M. Thompson. 1982. The fossil vertebrate record of Australasia. Clayton, Victoria, Australia: Monash University Offset Printing Unit.

Sadler, P. M. 1981. Sediment accumulation rates and the completeness of stratigraphic sections. J. Geol. 89:569–584.

Savage, D. E. 1951. Late Cenozoic vertebrates of the San Francisco Bay region. Univ. Calif. Publ. Geol. Sci. 28:215–314.

———. 1955. Nonmarine lower Pliocene sediments in California: A geochronologic-stratigraphic classification. Univ. Calif. Publ. Geol. Sci. 31:1–26.

———. 1962. Cenozoic geochronology of the fossil mammals of the Western Hemisphere. Rev. Mus. Argent. Cienc. Nat. 8:53–67.

———. 1975. Cenozoic—The primate episode. In Approaches to primate paleobiology, ed. F. S. Szalay, pp. 2–26. Contrib. Primat., vol. 5. Basel: S. Karger.

———. 1977. Aspects of vertebrate paleontological stratigraphy and geochronology. In Concepts and methods of biostratigraphy, eds. E. G. Kauffman and J. E. Hazel, pp. 427–442. Stroudsburg, Pa.: Dowden, Hutchison, and Ross.

Savage, D. E. and M. C. McKenna. 1974. Symposium: Vertebrate paleontology as a discipline in geochronology, I, II, III. Geology 2 (2):83–84.

Savage, D. E. and D. E. Russell. 1983. Mammalian paleofaunas of the world. New York: Addison-Wesley.

Simpson, G. G. 1940. Review of the mammal-bearing Tertiary of South America. Proc. Amer. Philos. Soc. 83:649–709.

Smith, W. 1815. Memoir to the map and delineation of the strata of England and Wales with a part of Scotland. London: Cary.

Stanley, S. M., W. O. Addicott, and K. Chinzei. 1980. Lyellian curves in paleontology: Possibilities and limitations. Geology 8:422–426.

Steiger, R. H., and E. Jager. 1977. Subcommission on geochronology: Convention on the use of decay constants in geo- and cosmo-chronology. Earth Planet. Sci. Letters 36:359–362.

Tedford, R. H. 1970. Principles and practices of mammalian geochronology in North America. Proc. No. Amer. Paleont. Conv. Pt. F, pp. 666–703.

Thenius, E. 1959. Tertiär, II Teil: Wirbeltierfaunen. In Handbuch der stratigraphischen geologie, Bd. III, ed. F. Lotze. Stuttgart: Enke Verlag.

Williams, H. S. 1901. The discrimination of time-values in geology. J. Geol. 9:570–585.

Wolfe, J. A. 1966. Tertiary plants from the Cook Inlet region, Alaska. U.S. Geol. Surv. Prof. Paper 398-B, pp. B1-B32.

———. 1971. Tertiary climatic fluctuations and methods of analysis of Tertiary floras. Palaeogeogr., Palaeoclimatol., Palaeoecol. 39:27–57.

———. 1972. An interpretation of Alaskan Tertiary floras. In Floristics and paleofloristics of Asia and eastern North America. Amsterdam: Elsevier.

Wolfe, J. A., and D. M. Hopkins. 1967. Climatic changes recorded by Tertiary land floras in northwestern North America. In Tertiary correlations and climatic changes in the Pacific, pp. 67–76, 11th Pacific Science Congress.

Wolfe, J. A., D. M. Hopkins, and E. B. Leopold. 1966. Tertiary stratigraphy and paleobotany of the Cook Inlet region, Alaska. U.S. Geol. Surv. Prof. Paper 298A, pp. A1–A29.

Wood, H. E., II, R. W. Chaney, J. Clark, E. H. Colbert, G. L. Jepsen, J. B. Reeside, Jr., and C. Stock. 1941. Nomenclature and correlation of the North American continental Tertiary. Bull. Geol. Soc. Amer. 52:1–48.

Woodburne, M. O. 1975. Cenozoic stratigraphy of the Transverse Ranges and adjacent areas, southern California. Geol. Soc. Amer. Spec. Paper 162, pp. 1–91.

———. 1977. Definition and characterization in mammalian chronostratigraphy. J. Paleont. 51 (2):220–234.

Woodburne, M. O., R. H. Tedford, M. Archer, W. D. Turnbull, M. Plane, and E. L. Lundelius. 1985. Biochronology of the continental mammal record of Australia and New Guinea. So. Australia Dept. Mines and Energy Spec. Publ. 5, pp. 347–363.

1

PRINCIPLES, CLASSIFICATION, AND RECOMMENDATIONS

Michael O. Woodburne

This work differs from other treatments of North American fossil mammal biostratigraphy and biochronology in the degree of attention paid to stratigraphic information. In contrast to the emphasis of Wood et al. (1941), much of the work reported here reflects a growing trend among mammalian paleontologists to acquire detailed biostratigraphic data in the manner emphasized by Osborn and Matthew, rather than avoiding, intentionally or not, problems concerned with determination of boundaries between units, their proper definition as well as characterization, and detailed assessment of the security of correlation from place to place.

This is not to minimize the proper importance of other advances that have developed during the past decades relative to mammalian paleontology such as increased attention to taphonomic analysis, paleoecological reconstructions, faunal development, structure, and turnover, changes in adaptive patterns through time, and utilization of cladistic methodology in phyletic analysis, much of which is dependent on the development of the biochronologic record. Many of those same advances have affected other aspects of paleontology during recent years. What is strikingly different for mammalian paleontology is that its practitioners now see it as being amenable to modern stratigraphic procedures, concepts, and classification (see also Savage 1977).

As discussed above, mammal ages were historically, and operationally primarily still are (see below), informal geochronologic units that have no chronostratigraphic base; that is, mammal ages usually (and until recently) have not been based on formally established stages. As is documented in this volume, however, this situation is

changing. It is now possible, more than ever before, to entertain substantive discussions of fossil mammal biostratigraphy and chronostratigraphy in terms of the various stratigraphic guides, codes, principles, and procedures that have been developed through the years in other paleontological disciplines and to develop comparable units based on fossil mammals.

Certain working principles with regard to the development of temporal intervals based on fossil mammals are briefly summarized below. Some have been alluded to above and some or all may be already understood by most readers, but they are mentioned here for the sake of completeness. The kinds of biostratigraphic and chronostratigraphic units useful to mammalian paleontology will be noted, and recommendations for the successful application of the principles and utilization of stratigraphic units will be made. The North American Stratigraphic Code (NASC; North American Commission on Stratigraphic Nomenclature 1983) is derived from, and partly encompasses and partly departs from, earlier works (see references cited therein) but is largely consonant with proposals of the International Stratigraphic Guide (ISG; Hedberg 1976). These two works will be extensively referred to here as recent statements on these topics.

PRINCIPLES AND CLASSIFICATION

Inasmuch as fossil mammals are almost completely restricted in occurrence to association with sedimentary, extrusive, ash-flow, or air-fall volcanic rocks, their study is governed by the principles of Superposition, Original Horizontality, and Original Continuity of sedimentary strata formulated in 1669 by Nicholas Steno. Another fundamental concept for the study of fossil mammals is the Principle of Paleontological Correlation, attributed to William Smith (e.g., 1815, 1817). "Biologic remains contained in, or forming, strata are uniquely important in stratigraphic practice . . . they provide the means of defining and recognizing material units based on fossil content (biostratigraphic units)" (NASC, p. 849), comparable to the material lithostratigraphic units, defined, characterized, and recognized on the basis of lithologic content. Biostratigraphic units are interpretive units only to the degree that species limits require interpretation, as discussed more fully below. It also can be objectively determined that fossilized remains of each organism have a unique stratigraphic range, and correlations can be proposed on this basis without an understanding of evolutionary theory. This is, in fact, what Smith and his colleagues were doing.

With the addition of the theory of evolution, however, fossilized remains of once-living organisms have an even greater temporal significance: " . . . The irreversibility of organic evolution makes it possible to partition enclosing strata temporally . . . " (NASC, p. 849), to recognize a given interval of time from place to place, and to propose a correlation based thereon. In so doing, one leaves the material, and effectively descriptive, biostratigraphic unit (some interpretation is still involved in species recognition) and enters into a discussion of still material (based on fossils contained within particular strata) but interpretive (as to the paleontological data being temporally significant) chronostratigraphic units. This operation affirms the direct relationship between biostratigraphy and chronostratigraphy, although chronostratigraphic units also can be devised and extended on any kind of time-significant information. Berry (1966) has termed the temporally significant association of fossil taxa (on which zonal recognition and correlation is based) a *congregation*, effectively equivalent to a unique suite of taxa with overlapping (concurrent) ranges. As suggested below, there is little difference between the Oppel-zone and concurrent range-zone as recognized by recent stratigraphic guides and codes, and neither the NASC nor the ISG uses a comparable term for the primary unit used for purposes of correlation. Nevertheless, it is clear that certain kinds of biozones (ISG, NASC) can serve as the basis of chronostratigraphic zones (chronozone; ISC, NASC), the temporal spans of which reflect the scope of the equivalent biozones. Although there is no hierarchy of biostratigraphic units and chronozones are considered to have no explicit rank,

there is a definite hierarchy of other chronostratigraphic units (and the equivalent geochronologic units based thereon; see table 1.1).

Among the units of most interest to mammalian paleontologists are biozones, chronozones, stages, and ages. (This is evident in the discussions in this work.) Under any system of classification, however, their task is clear: to carefully describe and identify the taxonomic affinities of the fossils found in stratigraphic sequences, to document the stratigraphic ranges of the fossil taxa so identified, and to decide which criteria are most likely to yield unambiguous results in correlation. It is then necessary to (1) define the unit to be devised; (2) present a characterization by which it may be recognized should the defining criterion be absent; (3) evaluate the utility of the unit by determining the extent to which it can be found (i.e., replicated) in other stratigraphic sequences; (4) determine by cross-checks with other zonations or information from other time-significant data sets that the unit does, in fact, have isochronous boundaries; (5) determine its relationship to superjacent and subjacent units and their mutual boundaries; and (6) develop a formal proposal for the unit in accordance with recommendations presented by the NASC or the ISG.

Essentially all these steps can be accomplished on an objective basis. The most subjective part of the operation occurs in certain aspects of species discrimination (discussed below), and among the more controversial proposals is suggesting that unit boundaries should be defined on a single taxon (Woodburne 1977). The alternate point of view, that unit definition must involve a number of taxa, with a potentially "fuzzy" boundary as

TABLE 1.1
Hierarchy of chronostratigraphic and geochronologic units (after ISG, table 2)

Chronostratigraphic	Geochronologic
Eonothem	Eon
Erathem	Era
System	Period
Series	Epoch
Stage	Age
Chronozone	Chron

Note: Chronozones may be based on biostratigraphic units (e.g., certain kinds of biozones). Chronozones and chrons are not proscribed as to duration, for example, a chronozone (of dubious utility) could contain one or more stages. Hierarchical ranking thus ends with Stage/Age.

a result, and that single-taxon definitions are effectively "index fossils," has been expressed recently by Savage and Russell (1983, p. 4). This topic also is discussed further, below.

Biostratigraphic units are commonly referred to as various kinds of zones. The ISG recognizes a greater number of biostratigraphic zones than does the present NASC, but both are in implicit agreement that carefully describing the presence and distribution of fossil taxa in rock strata (and defining biostratigraphic zones based thereon) is essential to stratigraphic analysis. For those interested in chronostratigraphy, biostratigraphic zones of any name must be based on detailed information of the stratigraphic ranges of fossil taxa. In the best cases, these taxa are unambiguously categorized as (1) morphotypes of species (Murphy, Matti, and Walliser 1981), (2) species themselves, or (3) uniquely recognizable taxa of any rank which show an abrupt allochthonous intrusion into the stratigraphic record which is determined to have been instantaneous (within the ability of stratigraphers to resolve very short increments of geologic time).

When the first and second categories are developed within the context of lineages of organisms, they are interval-zones of the NASC and lineage-zones of the ISG (see Definitions); the third category is an interval-zone when the interval under discussion is bounded by successive allochthonous events, which generally are considered to offer one of the best assurances of reliable time correlation on a biostratigraphic basis (ISG, p. 59). Note that interval-zones of the NASC include all kinds of range-zones as well as the interval-zones of the ISG. It also is pointed out that "in practice, the assurance [of reliable time correlation in terms of the above-mentioned zones] may be lessened by uncertainty on evolutionary courses and by the subjectivity of taxonomic identification and morphologic differentiation" (ibid.). This is an important observation. The problem is not unique to interval- or range-zones, however; it affects all aspects of biostratigraphy. I thus stress the above use of "unambiguously defined . . . morphotypes . . . species . . . [or] uniquely recognizable allochthonous [taxa]."

It is obvious that boundaries based on species will not be isochronous if different species definitions are applied by various workers. Most mammalian paleontologists in North America adhere to a species concept that approximates that of neomammalogists, that is, a species is an actually or potentially interbreeding population of individuals, most of which show an "average" or "central" morphology but some of which, usually at the population periphery, show a discernible deviation from

the "norm." Neomammalogists see this "bell-shaped curve" with respect to a horizontal line (time component essentially zero) and plot the contents of the curve above that line. If species overlap in morphology, it usually is represented by an overlap in one end or the other of each species' population curve (fig. 1.1). Lacking an actual test for interbreeding, the decision as to where to place the boundary between the two species usually is somewhat arbitrary (presence of a certain morphology, a stated abundance of such a morphology, etc.), but unless that decision is universally accepted and consistently applied, investigator 1 may assign individual X to species A, whereas investigator 2 may assign individual X to species B. This may pose few problems for many neontological or paleobiological studies and is recognized as an artifact of allopatric speciation; species are expected to intergrade, particularly if their origin has been relatively recent.

When the presence of a species (shown by—and named on the basis of—individual specimens in a fossil population) is inconsistently applied, the lateral shift in species boundaries of the neontologist becomes a change in the vertical (stratigraphic) position of those species in the fossil record. The ambiguities in vertical position of species boundaries thus translate directly into equally vague temporal boundaries of chronostratigraphic units based thereon (fig. 1.2). Precision in correlation suffers. The problem is important but not insoluble. (See Murphy, Matti, and Walliser [1981], for a discussion of the situation and the very workable solution proposed.)

The problem is that under "paleopopulational" considerations, species distinctions assume a statistical aspect. Walliser (1964) uses

the relative abundance of two morphs [or varieties] to separate a lineage into two chronological subspecies. This approach emphasizes classifying all varieties of a species together at each stratigraphic level and selecting the level where one variety becomes dominant as the lower boundary of the taxon. Its advantages are that the species are classified in the same ways as a neontologist would classify them and the relationship between the varieties is emphasized. The disadvantage is that the [stratigraphic] ranges of the individual varieties are not expressed by this classification and nomenclature. (Murphy, Matti, and Walliser 1981, p. 749)

Klapper and Murphy (1975) used an alternative approach, one that emphasized the ranges of the varieties in the classification applied to them. All specimens of a morph, or variety, in the sample which had the morphology central to a particular species were classified with that species, regardless of abundance in the sample.

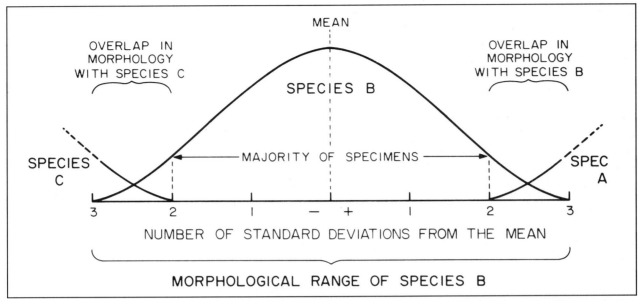

Fig. 1.1. Idealized representation of morphological range of Species B at the present time, showing that the morphology of most specimens falls within ± two standard deviations of the mean for the population. A few specimens at each end of the range of Species B overlap in morphology with populations of Species A and C, respectively.

The advantages of [that classification are] . . . that the ranges of recognizable varieties are expressed in the nomenclature of the classification and morphs in all samples may be identified even though the size of the sample is statistically insignificant. However, this classification may place contemporaneous members of the same population in different taxa, thereby obscuring the biologic relationship between them. The use of different methods by different workers makes biostratigraphic synthesis difficult or impossible because the same named taxa will have different ranges which depend on the purpose of the author . . . (Murphy, Matti, and Walliser 1981, p. 749)

These authors assume that all intergrading morphs (varieties) "occurring at a single horizon belong to the same species and, therefore, should have the same name" (ibid.). If species boundaries are defined at the first occurrence of a specified morph (or variety), the various morphs (or varieties) are formally described, and their stratigraphic limits are specified wherever possible, two aims can be effectively achieved at once.

Presume, as in this example, that a two-species lineage consists of several morphs (or varieties) and that the stratigraphic ranges of some are mutually exclusive but many overlap (fig. 1.3). Each morph is informally named using a Greek letter. Species A is defined on the first stratigraphic occurrence of morph alpha. "All morphs from alpha through zeta are morphs of [Species A], but only morph delta characterizes the species" (ibid.). The presence of Species A is, however, indicated

by the presence of morphs alpha, beta, and delta, that is, based on the experience and perspectives of the worker, these are more characteristic of Species A than are certain other morphs. Species B is defined as beginning with the first stratigraphic presence of morph nu but is overlapped stratigraphically by morphs alpha, beta, gamma, epsilon, and zeta. In addition to those overlapping morphs, Species A (defined on nu) contains morphs theta, kappa, and lambda, which begin, and range, later than the preceding morphs.

The point is that two species can be recognized as uniquely containing a number of varieties (or morphs); some morphs are shared between them, preserving the more or less bell-shaped curve as one population progressively shifts to another and, therefore, preserving as much as possible of the neontological perspective on species definition. The consanguinity of the two species is thus reflected in the fossil record, which is capable of portraying both gradual and iterative (= "punctuational") regimes (see ibid.). At the same time, chronostratigraphically important novelties are capable of documentation within very close limits, the beginning of Zone B being defined on the first stratigraphic occurrence of Species B, morph nu, with some of the overlapping morphs still being present at that stratigraphic level. "The identity of the morphs will be clear in most cases." Problems of correlation, beginning with original definition, will be simplified in that the presence of a single

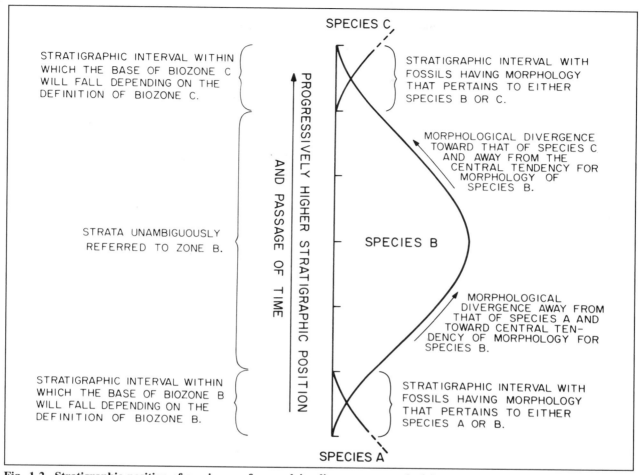

Fig. 1.2. Stratigraphic position of specimens of an evolving lineage composed of Species A, B, and C, showing intervals of overlap in morphology between Species A and B and B and C, respectively. Departure of the curved line from the vertical axis denotes relative abundance of specimens with the morphology that defines Species B. Specimens with morphs that are characteristic of Species B or Species A and C, respectively, could have different abundance curves (suggested in fig. 1.3).

specimen of the defining morph (in this case, η) is sufficient to demonstrate the presence of Species B (see fig. 1.3). Species definitions that require the presence of a certain percentage of a given morphology for the species to be recognized will be less precisely applicable from place to place because of inhomogeneities in sampling results. Imprecision in species definition translates directly into imprecision in locating the stratigraphic position of the species and, hence, imprecision in establishing the stratigraphic position of zones based on such species (e.g., fig. 1.2). It is also clear that in any system purporting to define species, the lineage must be well known (i.e., study of it must be taxonomically mature), "otherwise the boundaries between parts of the lineage cannot be specified" (ibid.).

This appears to be a very workable solution to a

vexing problem. The various statistical solutions to taxonomic allocation of morphologically diverse samples (effectively bimodal or polymodal) of fossil rodents of the John Day Formation (Rensberger 1971, Fisher and Rensberger 1972) could have been handled by the above approach. Similarly, the older presence of morphs (morphologies) in the Barstow Formation (Barstovian Mammal Age) included by Lindsay (1972) in *Tamias ateles* which are similar to—and could have been named as—morphs of *Ammospermophilus fossilius* from Clarendonian-aged strata about 1 Ma younger in the Cuyama Badlands district of southern California (Woodburne 1977, p. 231) represent mammalian examples that reflect many aspects of the situation described by Murphy and his colleagues (1981) and would have been amenable to a comparable solution. It is thus conceivable that either

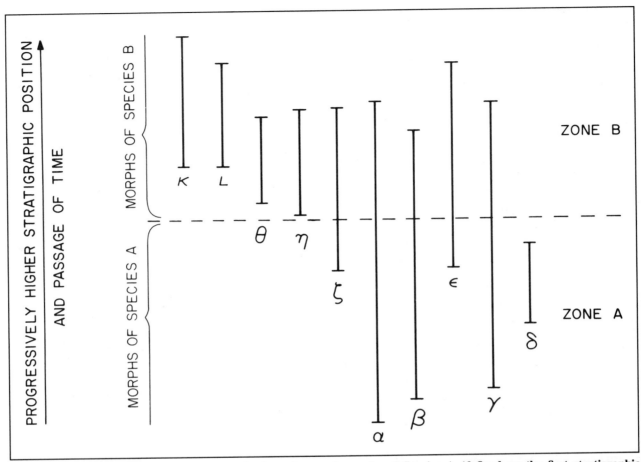

Fig. 1.3. Chart showing stratigraphic distribution of several morphs of Species A (defined on the first stratigraphic occurrence of specimens of morph α) and morphs of Species B (defined on the first stratigraphic occurrence of specimens of morph η). (Modified from Murphy, Matti, and Walliser 1981, fig. 4.)

this approach, or another somewhat similar to it, can be devised which will serve the interests of zoological and chronostratigraphic taxonomic nomenclature in mammalian vertebrate paleontology. For fossil mammals, the stratigraphic first occurrence of an unambiguously recognizable morphological feature could be used to define a species in a manner similar to the treatment of morphs (above), even if not labeled a morph. At the same time, there seems to be little hope for resolving the situation of requiring changes in zonal or unit names to reflect taxonomic revisions. If mammalian paleontologists and stratigraphers wish to bring their disciplines into line with the methodology utilized by students of other groups of fossil organisms, this kind of nomenclatural revision will have to be sustained (NASC, p. 863; ISG, p. 65).

The NASC addresses two additional zone categories, assemblage-zones (see Definitions) and abundance-zones. The latter is of no general importance for time correlation and will not be considered further here. Two

types of assemblage-zone are listed by the NASC: the assemblage-zone of the ISG, where ranges of the component taxa are not detailed, and the so-called Oppel-zones, or concurrent range-zones. The last two are treated separately by the ISG, with the concurrent range-zone considered to be more rigorous in "definition" (the presence of all, or most, taxa with overlapping ranges named in the "definition" is required to identify the zone in other places, i.e., correlation, whereas strict reliance on the presence of all, or at least a large number, of the "defining" criteria is not required to propose correlation under the Oppel-zone). In fact, the distinction between these two zones is difficult to demonstrate or maintain, however, as is also clear from the discussions in the ISG (pp. 55–58). Their merging by the NASC thus seems warranted (p. 863). In any case, definitions that involve several taxa are certain to be ambiguous (Murphy 1977, Woodburne 1977) and must actually be considered "characterizations." Nevertheless, it is important to recognize the discussions in the ISG (e.g., p. 56) which point to the principle of the joint occurrence of several taxa with overlapping ranges having long been considered important when proposing temporal correlations from place to place.

Both the NASC and the ISG agree that to be usefully established, the above kinds of zones require stratotypes, and it is certainly implicit, if not explicit, that judgment as to the kind of zone being established, the degree and fidelity with which it is replicated in other places, demonstrated or evaluated independence from facies control, and so forth, is required for correlation to be proposed (see also ISG, p. 63). Correlations also have the best chance of being unambiguous when "base defines boundary," or when the base of the succeeding unit defines the top of that below. By now, most stratigraphic paleontologists are well aware of the many cases of upward extensions in stratigraphic range of taxa (as well as a much fewer number of downward range extensions), and it has become commonplace to define only the base of a given unit paleontologically, leaving its top to be defined by the base of the next succeeding unit. Once correlation has been established, the unit may be designated as a chronozone, no matter whether it is based on biostratigraphic (biozone) or other criteria, and it is important to clearly separate the two by their prefixes (descriptive = bio-; descriptive and interpretative = chrono-).

Mammal Ages, Stages, and Zones

The present situation with respect to mammal chronostratigraphy in North America is one characterized by evolution. The system of biochrons, or mammal ages, remains intact for most situations, and as indicated in the following chapters, these have been refined since first established in 1941. Some stages and a few chronozones have been proposed. Although the situation is hopeful with respect to eventual application throughout the Cenozoic Erathem, at this time it appears that, even with additional improvements of mammal ages, there will be a similar range of chronostratigraphic and geochronologic diversity for some time to come. It is clear that more refinements will be attempted, however, and that assistance will come from the growing application of magnetic polarity stratigraphy as well as the now-traditional use of various chronometric systems (particularly K-Ar and fission-track analyses). At the same time, paleontologically based zonations now are subdividing, and will continue to subdivide, the Cenozoic geologic time scale more precisely than any other stratigraphic or chronometric system.

RECOMMENDATIONS

As is evident from the above discussion, it is recommended that mammalian stratigraphers continue to avail themselves of detailed analysis of the mammal-bearing stratigraphic record, search for replicable and unambiguously defined, as well as characterized, biostratigraphically based chronostratigraphic units, and pursue methods that ensure that use of the traditional zoological binomial nomenclature serves both paleobiologist and chronostratigrapher.

Some concluding (not necessarily final) remarks about definition versus characterization. It is clear to me, at least, that biostratigraphic units and chronostratigraphic units based thereon should be defined on a single taxon, whether it is (1) a local introduction (possible example of punctuated or iterative evolution), (2) a more regional allochthonous first occurrence, or (3) based on a local evolutionary first occurrence. Each situation involves considerations of species discrimination and dispersal rates from the point of origin to places where the new taxon is "first" observed in the (there) local stratigraphic record. Numerous examples (see Savage and Russell 1983, pp. 6–8, for some) indicate beyond reasonable doubt that mammal species are capable of very rapid (= "geologically instantaneous") dispersals, so in the case of (1) or (2), it is quite possible that the local stratigraphic record will have no prior evidence of the newly immigrant species. In those cases, discrimination of the new species' morphology from previous ones should be relatively easy and involve effectively no statistical aspects (i.e., boundary discrimination should be a simple presence or absence situation). Lower boundaries of biozones, chronozones, chrons, stages, or ages based on such new occurrences should be theoretically and operationally isochronous away from the stratotype, assuming that the distal sequences that contain the defining criterion survive cross-checks from other data sets and that there are no important stratigraphic hiatuses at or just below the point where the new taxon is considered to first appear. In (3), where the record is interpreted to portray the gradual transition from a preceding to a succeeding species, the situation may become involved with solutions comparable to those proposed by Murphy, Matti, and Walliser (1981) or otherwise necessarily become part of concerns regarding the extent to which precision in taxonomy relates to accuracy in assignment of chronostratigraphic boundaries and qualitative versus quantitative species (and hence boundary) definitions (e.g., Woodburne 1977).

In contrast to the views of Savage (1977) and Savage and Russell (1983), it is my belief that multiple-taxon "definitions" of boundaries still are essentially characterizations. The voluntary statement that such boundaries may admit to a "fuzziness" of about 1 m.y. duration (Savage 1977) supports the point I am trying to make. In other words, chronostratigraphic units may be characterized by the joint simultaneous occurrence of several taxa, and the lower boundary of the unit may be approximated by the joint presence of a smaller number of these taxa. Depending on the degree of biostratigraphic rigor necessary to develop the antecedent biozone, such constructs may be concurrent range-zones or Oppel-zones (ISG, NASC). "However, with *more* than two taxons named as diagnostic of the zone, the matter of boundaries becomes increasingly complex. . . . [If] a concurrence of [many, e.g., two or more] taxons is necessary for recognition of the zone, the extent of the concurrent range might be so much reduced both vertically and horizontally over that of any of the individual taxons as to make its time span and geographic extent extremely small" (ISG, p. 56). The point of this is that any zone or chronostratigraphic unit can be recognized on the basis of its characteristic co-occurring taxa. Thoughtful estimations of the degree to which the available record in a distant locality approaches in time the actual lower boundary of the unit in the boundary stratotype depends on subjective analysis of the available information (what other taxa are present; what morphologies of those specimens suggest that they pertain to more primitive, versus more advanced, subdivisions of the species involved or, with respect to an allochthonous first appearance, the degree to which the available fossil morphology approaches or conforms to that of the earliest, i.e., stratigraphically lowest, segments of the original newly derived population in its type area or section).

This is a subset of the situation that arises with an evolutionary first occurrence, taken as an "evolutionarily gradual" situation. If such an occurrence can be demonstrated, or reliably inferred to have taken place, there is thus at least one point in the rock record where that development may be replicated, observed, or studied. An evolutionary first occurrence (by definition, a relatively local phenomenon) retains a fundamental degree of stratigraphic and morphological control that does not accrue to the "punctuated" allochthonous, or more distantly allochthonous (first appearance datum), events.

Those who reject such proposals on the basis, for example, of despairing of finding the defining "criterion" in all potentially correlative sections admit this is the common situation with respect to units that are characterized but not rigorously defined (as above). In such instances, one can propose correlations with degrees of certainty which depend on other time-significant data,

but one must concede that the base of the unit is not determinable. Correlation is therefore made to an interval somewhere within that displayed and represented in the unit stratotype. This is exactly what mammalian paleontologists now encounter whenever they utilize characterizations only of chronostratigraphic units or multiple "definitions" of their bases. Giving a single-taxon definition to a chronostratigraphic unit at least should supply it with a single, unambiguously documented boundary stratotype (stratotype definitions involving two or more taxa cannot be unambiguous inasmuch as the congruent first occurrence of more than a single taxon in a stratigraphic section must be a result of extrinsic factors that have removed part of the local sequence or otherwise affected its fidelity). Whether or not one despairs of being able to closely correlate a given sequence "back" to the original stratotype, development of an interpretatively evolutionary first occurrence sets the stage for the best (replicable) control for the lower boundary of the chronostratigraphic unit and most closely approaches the basis for believing that the lower boundary of the unit is at least potentially synchronous throughout its extent. Repetition of a detailed zonal sequence over a wide geographic area will give credence to its utility. For instance, Klapper and Murphy (1974) report the presence of the same sequence of five or six conodont zones in rocks of Silurian and Devonian age in Nevada, the Carnic Alps, and Bohemia.

As will be seen from the discussions in this volume, mammalian paleontologists appear to be relinquishing, to some extent, what may be described as their former distrust of a detailed stratigraphic record and supporting the idea that it is possible to develop useful, biostratigraphically based chronostratigraphic zonations. Further developments in this regard should be vigorously pursued. Utilization of single-taxon boundaries in chronostratigraphic units will allow the potential for isochroneity in correlation to have been built in at the beginning of the operation. Only thereby will the full potential of paleontologically based chronostratigraphic units be realized and will they be placed in a position to effectively lead other age-significant data sets in defeating, or strongly diminishing, the ever-present specter of diachroneity in correlation.

REFERENCES

Berry, W. B. N. 1966. Zones and zones—with exemplifications from the Ordovician. Amer. Assoc. Petrol. Geol. Bull. 50:1487–1500.

Fisher, R. V., and J. M. Rensberger. 1972. Physical stratigraphy of the John Day Formation, central Oregon. Univ. Calif. Publ. Geol. Sci. 101:1–96.

Hedberg, H. D., ed. 1976. International stratigraphic guide. International Subcommission on Stratigraphic Classification. New York: John Wiley & Sons.

Klapper, G., and M. A. Murphy. 1974. Silurian-lower Devonian conodont sequence in the Roberts Mountains Formation of central Nevada. Univ. Calif. Publ. Geol. Sci. 111:1–62.

Lindsay, E. H. 1972. Small mammals from the Barstow Formation, California. Univ. Calif. Publ. Geol. Sci. 93:1–104.

Murphy, M. A. 1977. On chronostratigraphic units. J. Paleont. 51:123–219.

Murphy, M. A., J. C. Matti, and O. H. Walliser. 1981. Biostratigraphy and evolution of the *Ozarkodina remscheidensis-Eognathodous sulcatus* lineage (lower Devonian) in Germany and central Nevada. J. Paleont. 55 (4):747–772.

North American Commission on Stratigraphic Nomenclature (1982). 1983. North American stratigraphic code. Amer. Assoc. Petrol. Geol. Bull. 65 (5):841–875.

Rensberger, J. M. 1971. Entoptychine pocket gophers (Mammalia, Geomyoidea) of the early Miocene John Day Formation, Oregon. Univ. Calif. Publ. Geol. Sci. 90:1–209.

Savage, D. E. 1977. Aspects of vertebrate paleontological stratigraphy and geochronology. In Concepts and methods of biostratigraphy, eds. E. G. Kauffman and J. E. Hazel, pp. 427–442. Stroudsburg, Pa.: Dowden, Hutchison, and Ross.

Savage, D. E., and D. E. Russell. 1983. Mammalian paleofaunas of the world. Reading, Mass.: Addison-Wesley.

Smith, W. 1815. Memoir to the map and delineation of the strata of England and Wales with a part of Scotland. London: Cary.

———. 1817. Stratigraphical system of organized fossils with reference to the specimens of the original collection in the British Museum explaining their state of preservation and their use in identifying the British strata. London.

Steno, N. 1669. De solido intra solidum naturaliter contento dissertationis prodomus. Florence.

Walliser, O. H. 1964. Conodonten des Silurs. Abh. Hess. Landeasamtes Bodenforsch 41.

Wood, H. E., II, R. W. Chaney, J. Clark, E. H. Colbert, G. L. Jepsen, J. B. Reeside, and C. Stock. 1941. Nomenclature and correlation of the North American continental Tertiary. Bull. Geol. Soc. Amer. 52:1–48.

Woodburne, M. O. 1977. Definition and characterization in mammalian chronostratigraphy. J. Paleont. 51 (2): 220–234.

2

MAMMAL AGES, STAGES, AND ZONES

Michael O. Woodburne

As indicated in chapter 1 and in the chapters following, the system of mammal ages still is intact in North American stratigraphic practice. Moreover, these units are being refined and strengthened. At the same time, a growing number of chronostratigraphic stages have been proposed for various sequences. These are reviewed in this chapter. I also review temporal intervals not designated as stages or chronozones but devised according to criteria amenable to the establishment of such entities, that is, the subages of the Blancan and Irvingtonian mammal ages discussed in chapter 7 and the microtine rodent immigration events by which the Blancan, Irvingtonian, and Rancholabrean mammal ages are subdivided in chapter 8. Magnetic polarity subdivision of strata attributed to the Oligocene Series and faunal partition of those strata attributed to the Miocene Series also are discussed (see also the Introduction).

Chronostratigraphic stages based on fossil mammals are now known for strata deposited during all or part of the Clarkforkian, Wasatchian, and Clarendonian mammal ages. In order of nomination, Savage (1977) proposed the Cerrotejonian and Montediablan stages for mammal-bearing strata in northern and southern California, a geographic range of nearly three hundred miles. These units correlate with at least part of the Clarendonian Mammal Age (see chap. 6). The taxonomic content of these stages was expanded by James (1963); as yet, none of their boundaries have been defined.

Savage (1977) proposed the Wasatchian Stage (see chap. 10), utilizing information developed since 1941 regarding the stratigraphic ranges of taxa originally or subsequently shown to be important for the recognition of the Wasatchian Mammal Age. He also proposed that, based on his work and that of others, the Wasatchian Stage could be recognized in North America, Europe, England, and China and that the European Sparnacian Stage (or substage, e.g., Savage and Russell 1977) is incorporated within the Wasatchian Stage. Thus, the Wasatchian, being based on a chronostratigraphic stage, also can be said to be represented by an age in the formal sense of that category.

The lower limit of the Wasatchian Stage was defined on the basis of fourteen genera[1] (Savage 1977, p. 439), and Savage pointed out that the beginning of the Wasatchian in that respect is "fuzzy" and could fluctuate within as much as one million years. As noted above, such a "definition" is, in my opinion, really a characterization (Woodburne 1977). That its application could result in a "boundary" one million years in duration is not surprising.

Savage did not define the top of the Wasatchian Stage as being on the base of the next overlying stage (there is none at the moment) but essentially paved the way for the recognition of such a stage (lowest joint occurrence of 13 North American taxa[2]) and extended the upper limit of the Wasatchian Stage into Eurasia based on the highest stratigraphic record of *Hyraco-*

---

[1] *Hyracotherium, Coryphodon, Haplomylus, Pelycodus, Apatemys, Didelphodus, Palaeosinopa, Prototomus, Viverravus, Miacis, Pachyaena, Hyopsodus, Homogalax, Diacodexis.*

[2] *Anaptomorphus, Smilodectes, Uintanius, Washakius, Hemiacodon, Mesonyx, Uintatherium, Palaeosyops, Orohippus, Helaletes, Trogosus, Leptotomus, Homacodon.* See chap. 4 for a slightly different list.

therium, Esthonyx, Palaeosinopa, Meniscotherium, and *Coryphodon* (taxa recognized in North America as well). The stage that caps the Wasatchian will be of different composition in North America, Europe, and Asia because the faunal interchange recognized by the Wasatchian Stage ceased thereafter, at least for the duration of the Eocene epoch. At the same time, Savage nominated the *Lambdotherium* Concurrent Range-Zone within the upper part of the Wasatchian Stage, stabilizing a unit previously known informally as the *Lambdotherium* "zone." (See Stucky [1984] for refinements of the temporal range of this zone.)

Rose (1981) revived, defined, and characterized the Clarkforkian Mammal Age and nominated it as a chronostratigraphic stage. The Clarkforkian Stage-Age is defined by the stratigraphic first occurrence of Rodentia (*Paramys*), although coimmigrants *Esthonyx, Coryphodon,* and *Haplomylus* also appear simultaneously. As suggested above, the apparent simultaneous introduction of several taxa probably is due to the influence of one or more yet undetermined extrinsic factors, but there may have been an extensive immigration of taxa into North America at about this time, possibly, in part, from Asia (Archibald et al., chap. 3). The top of the Clarkforkian Stage is formed by the base of the Wasatchian, which can be defined on the first occurrence of either *Diacodexis* or *Pelycodus,* both of which are common and widespread (Rose 1981, pp. 24–25). Note that use of one or the other of these taxa would be a single-taxon definition and thus different from that of Savage (1977). (See chap. 3 for other details concerning the Clarkforkian Stage.)

In addition to the *Lambdotherium* Concurrent Range-Zone, other zonal constructs are the *Meniscomys, Entoptychus-Gregorymys,* and *Mylagaulodon* concurrent range-zones of the John Day Formation, correlates in Nebraska and South Dakota of, in part, Arikareean and Hemingfordian age (Fisher and Rensberger 1972; see also chap. 6), and the *Cupidinimus nebraskensis, Pseudadjidaumo stirtoni, Copemys longidens,* and *Copemys russelli* assemblage-zones of Barstovian age in California (Lindsay 1972). The units of Fisher and Rensberger have defined boundaries, whereas those of Lindsay (1972) are characterized only. To date, those latter assemblage-zones, even though based on taxa with well-documented stratigraphic ranges (in contrast to assemblage-zones of the ISG [p. 50]), have yet to be recorded beyond the limits of the Barstow Formation of California. (See also, Introduction.)

More recently, Gingerich and colleagues (see chaps. 3 and 4) have devised zonal schemes for the Paleocene and Eocene strata of the Fort Union and Willwood

formations of the Bighorn Basin, Wyoming. These were originally based on species of primates, primarily, *Pronothodectes, Plesiadapis,* and *Pelycodus.* The fossil-bearing strata were divided into thirteen zones, two for that portion of the Torrejonian Mammal Age represented in the Bighorn Basin, five for the Tiffanian Mammal Age, one for the Clarkforkian, and five for the Wasatchian. The limits of each zone were nominally based on the stratigraphic range of a species of fossil primate. Rose (1981) proposed two more zones for strata of Tiffanian to Clarkforkian age based on evolutionary first occurrences of defining taxa.

Archibald et al. (chap. 3) propose three interval-zones for the Puercan Mammal Age, three for the Torrejonian, five lineage-zones, and a single interval-subzone for the Tiffanian, and one subzone and two lineage-zones for the Clarkforkian. Some of these are provisional only, all have defined boundaries, and essentially all have been developed with the aid of magnetic polarity data.

Schankler (1980) criticized Gingerich's interval-zones for the Willwood Formation as being arbitrarily bounded or equivocal in that certain species (e.g., *Pelycodus jarrovii* and *P. abditus*) have overlapping ranges. It also appears, contrary to statements by Gingerich (1975, p. 144), that the limits of some zones are not coextensive with the species that define them. In three instances, naming species are portrayed as branching into two derivative species within the zone that bears the ancestor's name (ibid., fig. 1). In any case, Schankler proposed to substitute the primate zonation with divisions that reflect major biotic events (biohorizons) based on immigrations and extinctions and recognized three divisions of the Willwood Formation. The stratigraphically lowest, the *Haplomylus-Ectocion* Range-Zone, is based on the concurrent ranges of thirteen species that become extinct at its upper limit (Biohorizon B), shortly after which certain immigrant species also occur. A stratigraphically lower biohorizon (Biohorizon A) reflects extinction of eight species, the joint occurrence of which also defines the lower part of the *Haplomylus-Ectocion* Range-Zone. Biohorizon A closely precedes the immigration of seven species, and forms the basis of dividing the *Haplomylus-Ectocion* Range-Zone into a lower and upper part. The interval between Biohorizon B and Biohorizon C (based on nine immigrant species) is known as the *Bunophorous* Interval-Zone. Only one taxon, *Bunophorous,* is new in the zone that bears its name (the genus actually first appears slightly below the zone). The *Bunophorous* Interval-Zone is thus not based on a suite of concurrent ranges, but rather, reflects a part of the section that is barren of novelties, in contrast to units below and above. The lower limit of the overlying unit, the *Heptodon* Range-Zone, is based on the immigrant species of Biohorizon C, defined on the concurrent ranges of *Heptodon* and *Vulpavus canavus,* and subdivided into three parts based on various immigrant taxa. The boundary between the Middle and Upper *Heptodon* Range-Zone is based on the first occurrence of *Lambdotherium,* and therefore should include the *Lambdotherium* Concurrent Range-Zone of Savage (1977).

As for other strata of Wasatchian age, mammal faunas of the Willwood Formation have been referred to mammal age subdivisions known as Graybullian, Lysitean, and Lostcabinian (now Sandcouleean, as well; see chaps. 4 and 10). The *Haplomylus-Ectocion* Range-Zone and the *Bunophorous* Interval-Zone contain taxa previously referrred to the Sandcouleean and Graybullian Subages, the lower and middle *Heptodon* Range-Zone corresponds to units correlated with the Lysitean Subage, and the upper *Heptodon* Range-Zone is a general correlate of units referred to the Lostcabinian Subage. Although work still is in progress, preliminary evidence suggests it will be possible to extend at least part of the *Haplomylus-Ectocion* Range-Zone to fossil-bearing strata of the Willwood Formation of the Clark's Fork Basin several miles to the north (chap. 4). The lower and middle parts of the *Heptodon* Range-Zone can be correlated with faunas from the Lysite member of the Wind River Formation, in the Wind River Basin about one hundred miles to the south, and the upper part of the *Heptodon* Range-Zone can be correlated with the fauna from the Lost Cabin member of that formation as well (Schankler 1980, p. 109). Thus, it appears that this zonation of the Willwood Formation of the Bighorn Basin has regional significance.

In conjunction with a program to develop a magnetic polarity stratigraphy for fossiliferous strata of the White River Group, D. R. Prothero and colleagues (Prothero 1982; Prothero, Denham, and Farmer 1982, 1983) suggested that twenty newly proposed biostratigraphic datums may be isochronous throughout North Dakota, South Dakota, Wyoming, Nebraska, and Colorado (see chap. 10). These datums, which represent twelve first appearance and eight extinction events, occur in an interval of late Chadronian to early Whitneyan age, calibrated by magnetic polarity stratigraphy as having been about 2.5 m.y. long. In only a few cases (usually involving rare taxa) were the biostratigraphic and magnetic polarity data in conflict, and especially for those first occurrences that appear to have been evolutionary first occurrences, isochroneity within the limits of the system (magnetic polarity interval, duration approximately less than 1 m.y.) is suggested. Prothero (pers. commun., 1984) has

proposed concurrent range-zones for this sequence—one for the late Chadronian Mammal Age, three for the Orellan, and one for the early Whitneyan. When published, this framework could materially advance chronological resolution within those mammal ages, and it is to be hoped that zonations will be devised for those parts of the Oligocene sequence not yet covered. At the same time, the zonations based on fossil mammals subdivide the associated successions of Oligocene strata more finely than can be accomplished by magnetostratigraphic evidence, so the ultimate test of isochroneity of these zones will come from their replication in other areas.

As shown in chapter 6, stratigraphic sequences and mammalian faunas of approximately Miocene age are among the most diverse and complexly interrelated in the Cenozoic record of North America. The Cerrotejonian and Montediablan stages—of approximately Clarendonian age—have been mentioned above, as have the concurrent range-zones of the John Day Formation (plus other correlatives) and the assemblage-zones of the Barstow Formation. Regional provincialism is a problem for the Miocene Epoch which has not been so forcefully displayed in older parts of the Cenozoic record. Thus, faunas that can be most readily correlated to those of the Barstovian stratotype in California are found west of the Great Plains, whereas Barstovian faunal equivalents of the Great Plains province (the essentially correlative Valentinian "Mammal Age") are more easily recognized from Nebraska southeast to the Gulf Coast province. The relative abundance of immigrant or other newly appearing taxa from the Arikareean through Hemphillian mammal ages allows the establishment of a greater number of defined subdivisions of these mammal ages (and thereby the establishment of the mammal ages themselves) than has been possible heretofore. In fact, the data developed in chapter 6 approach the maximum chronological refinements possible for mammal ages consistent with modern methodologies. A logical next step would be to develop the necessary taxonomic and stratigraphic documentation to transform these mammal ages and their subdivisions into interval-zones and to assess the degree to which their boundaries are isochronous, possibly by the application of magnetostratigraphic data, as has been attempted for the strata attributed to the Oligocene Series. However, for the Miocene Series, as well as for the Oligocene, further refinements would require the development of new, and/or a wider application of presently proposed, zonal schemes, all or most of which probably would ultimately prove to subdivide the rock record more finely than is possible on the basis of magnetic polarity or radioisotopic data.

The Blancan Mammal Age now represents nearly

all of the Pliocene Epoch in North America. This is interesting in that both this mammal age and its European correlate, the Villafranchian, have long been considered at least partly of Pleistocene age; many proponents of subdividing the Blancan in North America did so on the illogical basis that if some boundary of the Blancan could not be made to coincide with the beginning of the Pleistocene, some boundary within it should. Ironically, the Blancan/Irvingtonian boundary falls at, or very close to, the base of the Pleistocene as now recognized.

Two subdivisions of the Blancan Mammal Age are reported in chapter 7. The Rexroadian, technically an early Blancan Subage, begins with the immigration of several European taxa, including certain arvicoline rodents that lack cement on the reentrant angles of their cheek teeth (i.e., *Nebraskomys*, *Pliopotamys*, *Ophiomys*, and *Pliolemmus*). The stratigraphic ranges of these taxa are commented on below.

The late Blancan, or Senecan, Subage is characterized by the first appearance of *Synaptomys* bog lemmings (subgenera *Plioctomys* and *Metaxomys*) as well as microtine rodents that have cement in the reentrant angles of their cheek teeth (*Ondatra* and *"Mimomys" monohani*). With the aid of magnetic polarity studies (see chap. 9), the Rexroadian/Senecan boundary appears to be very close to, if not at, the boundary between the Gauss and Matuyama chrons of the magnetic polarity time scale, calibrated at about 2.5 Ma. The late Blancan also witnessed the arrival of several South American edentates (*Glossotherium*, *Glyptotherium*, *Kraglievichia*, *Dasypus*) and rodents (*Neochoerus*, *Erethizon*) as the Panamanian land bridge was established at about 3.0 Ma (e.g., fig. 10.1a).

Although agreement on which Italian sequence represents the best Pleistocene stratotype—and analysis of that stratotype—is still not concluded, it appears that the Pleistocene Epoch began at about 1.7 Ma. Integration of mammal-bearing successions with magnetic polarity data (chap. 9) suggests that the Irvingtonian Mammal Age began about that time (1.9 Ma), even though some of the criteria that could define that point (first occurrence of *Lepus*) still are subject to some debate.

One important development during the past decade or so is the realization that attempts to integrate chronologies based on fossil mammals with those based on glacial fluctuations lead to dubious results and that Period or other unit boundaries should not be based on climatic criteria, as commonly attempted for the Pleistocene Epoch in earlier literature. In addition to problems of diachroneity (cooling should begin earlier at the poles or in higher elevations than at the equator or at lower eleva-

tions), it is even more difficult to develop a uniquely useful time scale based on climatic events than to do the same thing on the basis of magnetic polarity stratigraphy. (See chap. 9 for further discussion of the latter topic.)

Setting the *Lepus* problem aside, the Irvingtonian Mammal Age records the presence of a number of new taxa. Some of those are considered to identify the base of the Sappan Subage (*Ondatra*, cf. *annectens*, *Microtus* [*Allophaiomys*], *Mictomys* [*Kentuckyomys*]). It is possible that a "Cudahayan" Subage of the Irvingtonian could be based on the first occurrence of a greater diversity of microtine rodents, including, for example, *Microtus paroperarius*, *Pitymys meadensis*, *Ondatra annectans* (see also fig. 10.1).

The Sheridanian Subage, which follows the Senecan, is recognized on the basis of the presence of *Ondatra nebraskensis*, *Microtus pennsylvanicus*, *Microtus* (*Pedomys*) *ochrogaster*, and *Smilodon fatalis*. Mammal faunas that correlate with the Sheridanian Subage apparently postdate the beginning of the Brunhes Normal Magnetic Polarity Chron and are thus younger than about 0.7 Ma. (For more details, see chaps. 7, 8, and 10.)

No subdivisions are proposed in chapter 7 for the Rancholabrean Mammal Age, which appears to have begun about 0.3 m.y. ago. The beginning of this mammal age is difficult to recognize, however, in part because of differences of opinion about the time at which *Bison*, one of the most important definitions of the Rancholabrean Mammal Age as originally proposed (Savage 1951), entered and spread throughout North America. Another problem is that few Rancholabrean faunal sites are superposed, which hinders documentation of clinal or evolutionary polarity in stratigraphic analysis. Faunas of later Rancholabrean age lived within the time range susceptible to radiocarbon analysis and can be organized chronologically by that means. In contrast to other parts of the Cenozoic Era, the Rancholabrean Mammal Age is not aided by magnetic polarity analysis inasmuch as all of Rancholabrean time is contained within the Brunhes Normal Magnetic Polarity Chron.

Another perspective on the Blancan-Rancholabrean mammal ages is presented in chapter 8, where nine subdivisions of that interval (and one for the late Hemphillian Mammal Age) are proposed on the basis of immigration and evolution of microtine rodents. The data are compiled with respect to a chronological network that includes lithostratigraphic, radioisotopic, and tephrochronologies. Correlation is proposed between the North American record and that of the Old World inasmuch as the dispersal events that mark much of the record in one area have counterparts in the other. The results are mostly consistent with proposals in chapter 7, but they are somewhat more detailed.

One immigration event is proposed for the late Hemphillian Mammal Age (numbering follows that of chap. 8):

1. 6.7 Ma: Immigration of *Promimomys*. Evolution of *Propliophenacomys*.

Five immigration/evolution events are proposed for the Blancan Mammal Age:

2. 4.8 Ma: Immigration of *Mimomys* (*Ophiomys*) and (*Cosomys*) and *Nebraskomys*. Evolution of *Pliophenacomys*.
3. 4.25 Ma: Endemic evolution of *Nebraskomys rexroadensis*, *Pliolemmus antiquus*, and especially of *Pliophenacomys finneyi*, *Mimomys* (*Ophiomys*) *mcknighti-taylori*, *Mimomys* (*Cosomys*) *primus*, and *Mimomys* (*Ogmodontomys*) *poaphagus*.
4. 3.7 Ma: Immigration of *Pliopotamys*. Continued evolution of *Mimomys*, *Pliophenacomys*, and *Nebraskomys*.
5. 3.2 Ma: Endemic evolution of *Mimomys* (*Cosomys*) *primus*, *Mimomys* (*Ophiomys*) *taylori-parvus*, *M.(O.) meadensis*, *Pliopotamys minor*, and *Pliophenacomys primaevus-osborni*.
6. 2.6 Ma: Immigration of *Synaptomys* subgenera (*Synaptomys*) and (*Mictomys*). Evolution of *Synaptomys* (*Mictomys*) *landesi*, *Ondatra idahoensis*, *Mimomys* (*Ogmodontomys*) *monohani*, *Mimomys* (*Ophiomys*) *parvus*, and *Pliophenacomys osborni*.

Two immigration events are proposed for the Irvingtonian Mammal Age:

7. 1.9 Ma: Immigration of *Proneofiber*, *Microtus*, *Phenacomys*, and *Allophaiomys*. Evolution of *Synaptomys* (*Mictomys*) *kansasensis*, *Synaptomys* ("*Metaxyomys*") *anzaensis*, and *Ondatra annectens*.
8. 0.85 Ma: Immigration of *Clethrionomys*, and *Pitymys*. Evolution of *Synaptomys* (*Synaptomys*) *cooperi*, *Synaptomys* (*Mictomys*) *meltoni*, *Neofiber leonardi*, *Pedomys llanensis*, *Allophaiomys guildayi*, *Atopomys texensis*, and *Atopomys salvelinus*.

Two immigration events are proposed for the Ranchola-brean Mammal Age:

9. 0.40 Ma: Immigration of *Microtus pennsylvanicus*, *M. mexicanus*, and *M. montanus*. Evolution of

Synaptomys (*Synaptomys*) *australis*, *Synaptomys* (*Mictomys*) *borealis*, *Pedomys ochrogaster*, and *Ondatra nebraskensis*.

10. 0.15 Ma: Immigration of *Dicrostonyx*, *Lemr.ius*, *Lagurus*, and several new species of *Microtus*.

Note that this arrangement gives a finer subdivision of the Blancan Mammal Age than is reported in chapter 7. Further, the Senecan Subage of the Blancan which is proposed in chapter 7 is comparable to the interval between events (6) and (7), but some of the taxa listed as restricted to that interval are considered to be older (*Mictomys*) here than in chapter 7 (Irvingtonian), and others assigned to that interval in chapter 7 (*Metaxomys*) are considered in chapter 8 to pertain to the next younger interval. In part, these differences probably reflect different taxonomic interpretations. It is clear, nevertheless, that in combining data presented in both chapters 7 and 8 there is strong potential to develop what could be a combination of range-zones, lineage-zones, and interval-zones to more precisely identify small-scale temporal intervals of this segment of geologic time than has been possible before on the basis of fossil mammals.

It is fitting that the final remarks in this chapter are addressed to the application of the magnetic polarity time scale to nonmarine strata. This work, pioneered by Neil Opdyke, Everett Lindsay, Noye Johnson, and colleagues, has revolutionized many mammalian correlations for the Cenozoic Era and aided tremendously in the developing network of lithostratigraphic, biostratigraphic, chronometric, tephrochronologic, and, now, magnetostratigraphic analysis. (See chap. 9 for further discussion of magnetic polarity stratigraphy.)

It is important to point out, nevertheless, that the initial correlation of a local magnetic polarity stratigraphy to the magnetic polarity time scale must be achieved by identifying the generally relevant part of that time scale with the aid of radioisotopic or biochronologic means and that many of the zonations being developed on the basis of fossil mammals more finely subdivide the available rock record than is possible by magnetostratigraphic analysis for many parts of the time scale. But it is often important merely to know that a particular fossil sample occurs in rocks that are normally or reversely (with respect to modern polarity) magnetized. That information alone can aid in evaluating whether a given sample, or unit, is a possible correlate of another, and the potential for worldwide correlation of events important to the history of mammals, even within the variable resolution of the Magnetic Polarity Time Scale, where the various chrons or subdivisions are not all of the same duration, definitely enhances the application of mammalian bio- and chronostratigraphy and the integration of the mammalian chronological scheme with those schemes based on other disciplines.

Stratigraphically long (both in thickness and in time) nonmarine sequences that were deposited more or less continuously traditionally have been thought to be rare in the North American Cenozoic record. Examples cited in chapter 9 and elsewhere in this volume make it clear, however, that these sequences are not so rare in rocks older than Miocene, and for those of Miocene and younger age, a sufficient number of long sequences exist to allow the development of fossiliferous magnetic polarity reference sections important for correlation. In fact, the magnetic polarity time scale, originally developed on marine seafloor data and involving assumptions about spreading rates so as to "date" parts of the reversal pattern, is now being tested and calibrated against nonmarine sequences in North America. This is possible because of the common presence in these nonmarine rocks of materials amenable to radioisotopic or tephrochronologic analysis.

The continued integration of data pertaining to, and cooperation by specialists of, magnetic polarity stratigraphy, mammalian biostratigraphy, and Cenozoic chronometry and tephrochronology can only lead to the increased enhancement of the significance of all disciplines and to the development of an increasingly refined chronostratigraphic framework for mammalian paleontology for the Cenozoic record of North America. This is an endeavor well worth pursuing.

REFERENCES

Fisher, R. V., and J. M. Rensberger. 1972. Physical stratigraphy of the John Day Formation, central Oregon. Univ. Calif. Publ. Geol. Sci. 101:1–96.

Gingerich, P. D. 1975. New North American Plesiadapidae (Mammalia, primates) and a biostratigraphic zonation of the middle and upper Paleocene. Contrib. Mus. Paleont. Univ. Mich. 24 (13):135–148.

Hedberg, H. D., ed. 1976. International stratigraphic guide. International Subcommission on Stratigraphic Classification. New York: John Wiley & Sons.

James, G. T. 1963. Paleontology and nonmarine stratigraphy of the Cuyama Valley Badlands, California. Univ. Calif. Publ. Geol. Sci. 45:1–145.

Lindsay, E. H. 1972. Small mammals from the Barstow Formation, California. Univ. Calif. Publ. Geol. Sci. 93:1–104.

North American Commission on Stratigraphic Nomenclature (1982). 1983. North American stratigraphic code. Amer. Assoc. Petrol. Geol. Bull. 65 (5):841–875.

Prothero, D. R. 1982. How isochronous are mammalian biostratigraphic events? Proc. Third No. Amer. Paleont. Conv. 2:405–409.

Prothero, D. R., C. R. Denham, and H. G. Farmer. 1982. Oligocene calibration of the magnetic polarity time scale. Geology 10:650–653.

———. 1983. Magnetostratigraphy of the White River Group and its implications for Oligocene geochronology. Palaeogeogr., Palaeoclimatol., Palaeoecol. 42:151–166.

Robinson, P. 1966. Fossil Mammalia of the Huerfano Formation, Eocene of Colorado. Peabody Mus. Nat. Hist. Yale Univ. Bull. 21:1–95.

Rose, K. D. 1981. The Clarkforkian land-mammal age and mammalian faunal composition across the Paleocene-Eocene boundary. Univ. Mich. Papers Paleont., no. 26, pp. 1–197.

Savage, D. E. 1951. Late Cenozoic vertebrates of the San Francisco Bay region. Univ. Calif. Publ. Geol. Sci. 28:215–314.

———. 1955. Nonmarine lower Pliocene sediments in California: A geochronologic-stratigraphic classification. Univ. Calif. Publ. Geol. Sci. 31:1–26.

———. 1977. Aspects of vertebrate paleontological stratigraphy and geochronology. In Concepts and methods of biostratigraphy, eds. E. G. Kauffman and J. E. Hazel, pp. 427–442. Stroudsburg, Pa.: Dowden, Hutchison, and Ross.

Savage, D. E., and D. E. Russell. 1977. Comments on mammalian paleontologic stratigraphy and geochronology: Eocene stages and mammal ages of Europe and North America. In Faunes de Mammiferes du Paleogene d'Eurasie, Colloique international CNRS, Montpellier, 1976. Geobios, mem. spec. no. 1, pp. 47–56.

Schankler, D. M. 1980. Faunal zonation of the Willwood Formation in the central Bighorn Basin, Wyoming. In Early Cenozoic paleontology and stratigraphy of the Bighorn Basin, Wyoming, ed. P. D. Gingerich, pp. 99–114. Univ. Mich. Papers Paleont., no. 24.

Stucky, R. K. 1984. The Wasatchian-Bridgerian Land Mammal Age boundary (early to middle Eocene) in western North America. Ann. Carnegie Mus. 53:347–382.

Woodburne, M. O. 1977. Definition and characterization in mammalian chronostratigraphy. J. Paleont. 51 (2):220–234.

3

FIRST NORTH AMERICAN LAND MAMMAL AGES OF THE CENOZOIC ERA

J. David Archibald

Philip D. Gingerich

Everett H. Lindsay

William A. Clemens

David W. Krause

Kenneth D. Rose

INTRODUCTION AND METHODOLOGY

The Paleocene continental sediments of the western interior of North America preserve the world's most complete and most thoroughly studied record of early Cenozoic mammal evolution. In this chapter, we examine this record. Our examination updates and amplifies earlier ones, specifically, the Wood committee's work (Wood et al. 1941) on the first four North American Land Mammal Ages of the Cenozoic Era—the Puercan, the Torrejonian, the Tiffanian, and the Clarkforkian. For purposes of brevity, we will refer to these as "mammal ages." The Wood committee recognized a fifth mammal age, the Dragonian, between the Puercan and Torrejonian mammal ages. Van Valen (1978) later proposed another, the Mantuan, preceding the Puercan Mammal Age. We consider the Dragonian Mammal Age to be part of the Torrejonian and the Mantuan Mammal Age to be part of the Puercan (see below, for discussion of Torrejonian and Puercan mammal ages).

Although we do not discuss at great length the Paleocene Epoch per se, earlier work on North American mammalian faunas now regarded as Paleocene in age had a significant influence on the global recognition of this epoch. In 1874, Schimper proposed the Paleocene Epoch in Europe based on fossil plants. The concept of this epoch, however, began to take form in the late nineteenth and early twentieth century. At that time, vertebrate paleontologists began to discover and describe mammalian faunas in the western United States which seemed to be more archaic than faunas of undisputed Eocene age but at the same time were probably not latest Cretaceous in age. Nevertheless, the Paleocene Epoch was not formally recognized by the U.S. Geological Survey until 1939 (D. E. Russell 1967). By the time the Wood committee's results were published in 1941, the Paleocene Epoch was more widely accepted in North America than in Europe.

The Wood committee correlated the beginning of the Paleocene Epoch with the beginning of the Puercan Mammal Age and the end of the Paleocene Epoch with the end of the Clarkforkian Mammal Age. As discussed below, the former correlation is still followed, but more recent correlations (Rose 1980, 1981a) suggest that the Clarkforkian Mammal Age straddles the Paleocene-Eocene epochal boundary. The last section of this chapter, concerning intercontinental correlations, discusses the correlation of the Clarkforkian Mammal Age.

Only a few concepts and comments on terminology are noted here, as these matters are treated fully elsewhere in this volume. We are concerned with two basic types of units: the mammal "age" and the mammal "zone" (including subzone). The zone is treated as a subdivision of a mammal age. In general, we have attempted to follow the North American Stratigraphic Code (NASC; 1983) and the International Stratigraphic Guide (ISG; Hedberg 1976) in defining or redefining and characterizing these ages and zones. There is only one conceptual difference to keep in mind. We consider mammal ages and mammal zones to be a type of biochronologic unit, a unit that is not used by the NASC and is only briefly considered by the ISG. Such units are characterized by faunal content (see below for definitions). On a local or regional scale, stratigraphic position plays the key role in establishing the relative position of faunas independent of the fossil content. For broader correlations, faunal comparison remains the primary method. Within the limits of resolution now possible, we assume the boundaries of our biochronologic units to be synchronous. This does not mean that we regard such boundaries to be instantaneous, as is the case for a geochronologic unit, but rather that the biochronologic units can be used as approximations of geochronologic age. Finally, it must be noted that because these ages (and zones) are based on faunal content that in many instances cannot be defined with precision in type sections (specifically, first appearances), for the most part these units cannot yet be regarded as stages. This is, of course, one of the goals for the future.

The four mammal ages we discuss all differ in historical development; however, their defining and characterizing criteria are similar. This is not true for the zonations within these mammal ages. Three different types of zones are used in subdividing them. Both the Puercan and Torrejonian mammal ages are subdivided into three zones, all of which are defined and limited by the successive appearances of unrelated taxa, although some of the appearances do require a personal judgment with regard to taxonomic usage (i.e., differentiation of *Taeniolabis taoensis* from an unnamed species of the genus and a similar separation of *Periptychus* from *Carsioptychus;* see appropriate sections for further comment). Zones such as these are recognized by both the NASC and the ISG as one type of interval-zone.

The second type of zone is recognized for all five of the Tiffanian zones and for the oldest two Clarkforkian zones (but see the discussion of the Clarkforkian concerning its oldest zone, which is partly Tiffanian in age and which we have divided into two interval-subzones). These seven zones conform to the concept of a range-zone according to the ISG and to a type of interval-zone according to the NASC. Both codes are in agreement in calling these taxon-range-zones, or, more specifically,

lineage-zones, since the successive lowest appearances defining each of the zones form a presumed phylogenetic lineage. The final type of zone is represented by the youngest of the three zones in the Clarkforkian Mammal Age and is referred to as an abundance-zone by the NASC and an acme-zone by the ISG.

For consistency, we will follow the ISG terminology and refer to our three types of zones as interval-zones, lineage-zones, and acme-zones. Ideally, the use of interval-zones (*sensu* ISG) throughout would be preferred because these zones are less subjective than lineage-zones, which rely more heavily on a given paleontologist's taxonomic biases, and than acme-zones, which are potentially more influenced by various paleoecological factors and are more questionable units in attempts at faunal correlation.

The ISG suggests several options for naming and subsequent usage of zonal names. We have chosen the admittedly more cumbersome, but more precise, style of including the name of the commencing taxon and the closing taxon for both the interval- and lineage-zones. Thus, the oldest zone in the Puercan Mammal Age is the *Peradectes/Ectoconus* Interval-Zone, and the oldest in the Tiffanian Mammal Age is the *Plesiadapis praecursor/P. anceps* Lineage-Zone. If these zones are accepted and used elsewhere, we suggest that they be explicitly and fully written out before being abbreviated or shortened in whatever manner may be chosen. It is important to specify that unless otherwise indicated, the above method of naming zones, along with the method of defining the zones described below, does not change the sense of previously recognized zones. For informal, shorthand purposes, each zone is also referred to by an abbreviation of the mammal age(s) in which it occurs plus a subscript number indicating its sequence within the given mammal age. Thus, the above two zones are also known informally as the Pu1 interval-zone and the Ti1 lineage-zone, or simply Pu1 and Ti1, respectively. Specific peculiarities of several of the zones are discussed under their respective mammal ages.

For each of the four mammal ages and thirteen of the fourteen zones (and 2 subzones) discussed in this chapter, we provide a standardized definition and characterization. A formal definition is not given for the fourteenth zone, the *Phenacodus-Ectocion* Acme-Zone. The definitions for all four mammal ages and for the remaining thirteen zones (and 2 subzones) are based on the appearance of a single taxon. The characterizations for all of the ages and zones consist of five parts: (1) "first appearances" for taxa that appear for the first time within a mammal age or zone but not necessarily in the oldest faunas of that mammal age or zone; (2) "last appearances" for taxa that appear for the last time within a mammal age or zone but not necessarily in the youngest faunas of that mammal age or zone; (3) "index fossils" for taxa restricted to a mammal age or zone; (4) "characteristic fossils" for all taxa (not just common taxa) that occur within a mammal age or zone but do not belong to one of the three preceding categories; and (5) taxa that are recognized before and after a given mammal age or zone but not within it. This last category is utilized to emphasize potential problems with sampling or taxonomy or both.

The lack of a consistent and up-to-date systematics hampers efforts to achieve a widely applicable biochronology (and biostratigraphy) based on mammals (see also Savage and Russell 1983). We have generally used the most recent systematic reviews, although there are a number of exceptions discussed in the appropriate mammal age or zone. For most usages in this chapter, the genus is the lowest taxonomic level considered.

In addition to definitions, characterizations, and discussions for each of the mammal ages and zones, we have provided two figures and two tables to augment the text. Figure 3.1 is a map of western North America which shows the approximate locations from which most Puercan through Clarkforkian mammalian faunas were recovered. Numbers shown are clusters of localities occurring in particular regions. These are the same numbers used in figure 3.2 (in pocket) showing the biochronologic correlation of all localities. The same numbers are also employed in tables 3.1 and 3.2, which identify, respectively, localities and taxa recovered from these localities.

Figure 3.2 is a correlation of Puercan through Clarkforkian faunas clustered according to geographic and/or geologic features, usually depositional basins. These sections are ordered from left to right in an approximately south to north and west to east pattern with two miscellaneous occurrences shown on the far right. Although the accompanying key is essentially self-explanatory, a few additional comments are in order. The approximate geochronologic ages and epochal and magnetic chronal boundaries are basically after Berggren et al. (1985). Placement of the boundaries for mammal ages and zones relative to the above units is for the most part estimated by means of correlation to magnetostratigraphic sections.

For some sections, within Clark's Fork and Bighorn basins, for example, one can place the biochronologically defined mammal ages and zones into a biochronostratigraphic context utilizing stratigraphic placement in conjunction with magnetostratigraphy. Such correlations provide a limited degree of confidence to chronostratigraphic and geochronologic assignments for some sec-

tions. This is not currently possible for many of the sections shown in figure 3.2, and thus a given portion of a formation should *not* be assumed to correlate across the chart to a given mammal age or zone (e.g., the lowermost portion of the Hoback Formation should *not* be assumed to be latest Torrejonian in age).

In some instances we lack or have only poorly known superposed faunas straddling mammal age and zonal boundaries. Thus, even approximate correlations of these biochronologic units to each other and to geochronologic and magnetochronologic units are equivocal. Such "gaps" in our knowledge of these biochronologic units are indicated in figure 3.2 (under the heading, "Zones"). Slanted lines for some zonal boundaries on the left margin do not imply diachroneity; these are simply the result of differences in thickness of some of the magnetostratigraphic columns compared to the relative durations of the magnetochronologic scale. Many of the stratigraphic sections shown are discussed in the text. More information regarding stratigraphic and faunal information can be obtained from the references listed under each major region in table 3.1.

As noted previously, tables 3.1 and 3.2 provide locality and taxonomic information, respectively. Table 3.1 is arranged according to the sections shown in figure 3.2. The localities or clusters of localities identified in figures 3.1 and 3.2 are listed in the table in numerical order. For clarification in some instances, localities listed under a single number are further subdivided using letter designations. The abbreviation in parentheses following a given locality is the zone to which the fauna from the locality is referred. References follow each of the major sections listed, and each reference is coded by number to the appropriate locality or localities. Although not complete, the references are extensive. The choice to include a reference was often influenced by how well the fauna(s) has been studied. Thus, the more poorly known, or less studied, faunas included all or most references, whereas the inclusion of references for better-studied faunas was somewhat more selective. The major categories of included references are faunal studies and revisions, major taxonomic studies, minor taxonomic papers relevant to faunal analysis, biostratigraphic-magnetostratigraphic studies, and stratigraphic papers germane to faunal interpretation. For completeness, many localities have been listed in the table even though these are not discussed in the text.

Table 3.2 is a faunal list (to the generic level) for the Puercan through Clarkforkian mammal ages. Unless they significantly alter a biochronologic range, most taxa questionably identified by authors are excluded or are included with a query. Most unpublished faunal accounts

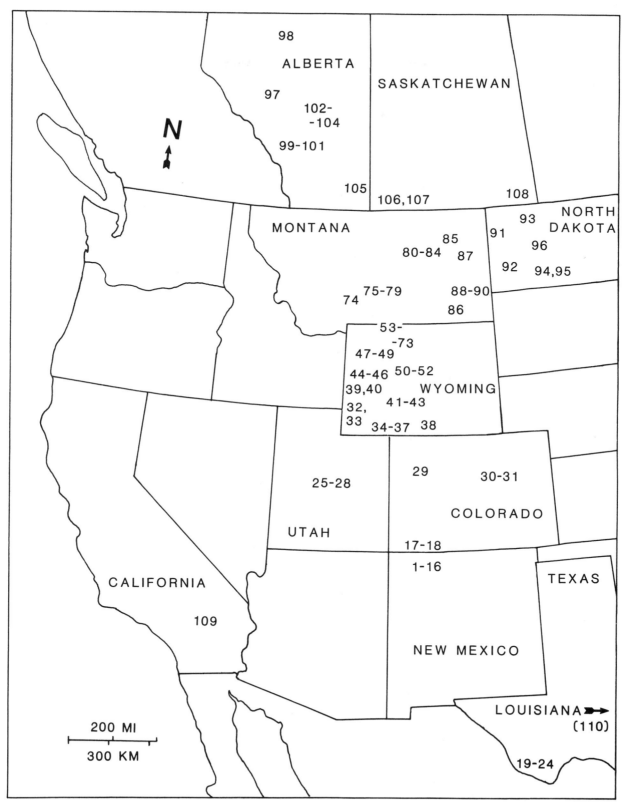

Fig. 3.1. Puercan through Clarkforkian mammal localities in the United States and Canada. The numbered localities are the same as those used in the correlation chart in fig. 3.2 and in tables 3.1 and 3.2. See table 3.1 for references and the Introduction for further comments.

TABLE 3.1
Localities of the Puercan, Torrejonian, Tiffanian, and Clarkforkian North American Land Mammal Ages

Localities are numbered approximately from west to east and from south ot north and agree with the numbers used in figs. 3.1 and 3.2 (in pocket), and table 3.2. Taxa in table 3.2 which are recorded as occurring at localities listed under a given number do not necessarily occur at all localities listed under that number. See introduction and methodology for further comments.

San Juan Basin, New Mexico

1	West Fork of Gallegos Canyon – includes Sinclair and Granger Loc. 4 (Pu3?).
2	*Ectoconus* zone, De-na-zin (= Barrel Spring Arroyo) and Alamo washes (Pu2).
3	*Taeniolabis* zone, De-na-zin (= Barrel Spring Arroyo) and Alamo washes (Pu3).
4	*Periptychus* site, De-na-zin Wash (= Barrel Spring Arroyo) (To1?).
5	Lower Kutz Canyon sites (To1).
6	West Kutz Canyon sites (low to high) – a. Bob's Jaw, b. Taylor Mound, c. Big Pocket (= KU Loc. 13), d. Bab's Basin, and others (To2).
7	South Kutz Canyon sites – O'Neill *Pantolambda,* Coprolite Point, and others (To3).
8	Animas River Valley (incl. Cedar Hill) (To2–3).
9	Lower Kimbetoh Arroyo – Black Toe, Black Stripe, plus others (Pu2?).
10	Upper Kimbetoh Arroyo – a. Head of Kimbetoh Arroyo, b. Dick's Dig (To1).
11	KU Loc. 9 (= Little Pocket) (To3).
12	Lower Betonnie-Tsosie Arroyo – Mammalon Hill, plus others (Pu2?).
13	Upper Betonnie-Tsosie Arroyo – Powerline (To1).
14	*Deltatherium* zone, Arroyo Torreon – lower part Sinclair and Granger Loc. 10 (To2).
15	*Pantolambda* zone, Arroyo Torreon – upper part Sinclair and Granger Loc. 10, Sinclair and Granger Loc. 11, microsite of Tsentas (To3).
16	Type area of Cope's "Puercan marls" (To2 or 3).
17	Mason Pocket near Tiffany (Ti4).
18	Bayfield and others (Ti5).

References: Archibald et al. (1983*a*): 2, 3, 9, 12; Archibald et al. (1983*b*): 9, 12; Butler et al (1977): 2, 3; Conroy (1981): 6, 15; Cope (1875, 1877, 1885, 1888, plus 55 others, see Matthew, 1937, for most): various localities; Gazin (1968): 15; Gingerich (1983): 17; Granger (1917): 6–8, 17, 18; Granger and Simpson (1929): 3, 12, 14, 15; Lindsay et al. (1978, 1981): 2–4, 6–15; Lucas (1984): 1; MacIntyre (1966): 6c, 11, 12, 14, 15; Matthew (1897, 1937): 2, 3, 9, 12, 14, 15; Matthew and Granger (1921): 3, 14, 15, 17, 18, Osborn and Earle (1895); Reynolds (1936): 12; Rigby (1981): 12; Rigby and Lucas (1977): 12; D. E. Russell (1967): 2, 3, 6c, 9, 12, 14, 15, 17, 18, plus others?; Schoch (1981): 2?, 3, 9, 12; Schoch and Lucas (1981*a*): 5, 6; (1981*b*): 11?; Simpson (1935*a,b,c*): 17, 18; Simpson (1936*a*): 3, 12; (1955 in Simons 1960): 18?; (1959): 16; Sinclair and Granger (1914): 1–4, 9–16; Sloan (1981): 3, 6, 9, 11, 12; Taylor (1981): 5–7; Taylor and Butler (1980): 6a–d, 7, 14, 15; Tomida (1981): 5–7, 14, 15; Tsentas (1981): 14, 15; Van Valen (1978): 3, 6a?, 9, 12, 14, 15, 17; (1980): 15; R. Wilson (1951, 1956*b*): 6c; R. Wilson (1956*a*): 11, 14, 15; R. Wilson (1956*c*): 3, 11.

Big Bend, Texas

19	Schiebout-Reeves Quarry (West Tornillo Flats) (Ti1).
20	Eastern Tornillo Flats Washing Site (Ti3?).
21	Ray's Bone Bed and Annex (Ti3).
22	Joe's Bone Bed (Ti5).
23	New Taeniodont Site (Ti-Cf).
24	Southwall (Cf-Wa).

References: Gingerich (1976): 21, 22; Rapp et al. (1983): 19–24; Rose (1981*a*): 23, 24; D. E. Russell (1967); Schiebout (1974): 19–24; Schoch (1986): 20–24; J. A. Wilson (1965, 1967).

Wasatch Plateau, Utah

25	Gas Tank Hill Local Fauna (= Flagstaff Peak) (Pu2?).
26	Wagonroad (= lower part Loc. 4 of Gazin) (Pu3?).

27   Dragon (= upper part Loc. 4 of Gazin) (To1).
28   Dragon (= Loc. 2 of Gazin) (To1).

References: Archibald et al. (1983a): 25, 26; Gazin (1938, 1939): 28; Gazin (1941b): 26–28; Robison (1980): 25–28; D. E. Russell (1967): 25–28; Schoch (1986): 26; Spieker (1960): 25; Tomida (1981): 26–28; Tomida (1982): 28; Tomida and Butler (1980): 26–28; Van Valen (1978): 25–28.

Plateau Valley, Piceance Creek Basin, Colorado

29   Plateau Valley (Cf1?).

References: Gingerich (1976, 1977, 1978); Gingerich and Childress (1983); Jepsen (1940); Krause (1980); Patterson (1933, 1936, 1937, 1939, 1949); Patterson and Simons (1958); Patterson and West (1973); Rose (1977, 1981a); D. E. Russell (1967); Simons (1960); R. C. Wood (1967).

Denver Basin, Colorado

30   Littleton Local Fauna – a. Alexander and b. South Table Mtn. localities (Pu1).
31   Corral Bluffs, Jimmy Camp Ck., West Bijou Ck. 1 (Pu2?–3?).

References: Brown (1943): 30b, 31; Gazin (1941a, 1963): 30b, 31; Middleton (1982): 30a; Middleton (1983): 30a, b, 31; D. E. Russell (1967): 30b, 31.

Fossil Basin—Washakie Basin, Wyoming

32   Little Muddy Creek (Ti1).
33   Twin Creek (Ti3).
34   Big Multi (Cf2).
35   UW loc. V77009–10, 77012, 77014, 78055 (To3?).
36   UW loc. V77005–08, 77013, 77015–16, 77061 (Ti4).
37   UW loc. V76008, 77059–60, 78052–54 (Ti5).
38   Swain Quarry (To3?).

References: Gazin (1956a, 1969): 32, 33; Gingerich (1983): 36, 37; Krause (1980): 34; Rigby (1980): 38; Rose (1981a): 34; D. E. Russell (1967): 33; Sloan (1981): 34, 38; Winterfeld (1982): 35–37.

LaBarge Creek, Green River Basin, Wyoming

39   Chappo Type Locality (= Chappo–17) (Ti3).
40   Buckman Hollow Locality (= Chappo–1 and 12) (Cf2).

References: Dorr and Gingerich (1980): 39, 40; Gazin (1942, 1956c): 40; Gingerich (1983): 39; Gingerich and Childress (1983b): 40; Krause (1980): 40; Rose (1981a): 40; D. E. Russell (1967): 40.

Bison Basin, Wyoming

41   Saddle Locality (Ti2).
42   Ledge Locality, Saddle Annex, West End (Ti3).
43   *Titanoides* Locality (Ti5).

References: Gazin (1956b): 41–43; Gingerich (1983): 41–43; MacIntyre (1966): 41; D. E. Russell (1967): 41–43; Van Valen (1978): 41.

TABLE 3.1
Localities of the Puercan, Torrejonian, Tiffanian, and Clarkforkian North American Land Mammal Ages—*Continued*

Hoback Basin, Wyoming

44   Battle Mountain (Ti3).
45   Dell Creek (Ti5).
46   UM-Sub-Wy localities 7, 10, 20 (Cf2).

References: Dorr (1952): 45, 46; Dorr (1958, 1978): 44–46; Dorr and Steidtmann (1970): 45; Dorr et al. (1977): 45; Gingerich (1982b): 45; Gingerich (1983): 44, 45; Rose (1981): 46; D. E. Russell (1967): 44, 45.

Togwotee Pass (N.W. Wind River Basin), Wyoming

47   Love Quarry (Ti3).
48   "Low Locality," "Rohrer Locality" (Ti6-Cf1?).
49   Other localities (Cf2).

References: McKenna (1972, 1980): 47–49; Rose (1981a): 48, 49; Rose and Krause (1982): 48.

Shotgun (northern Wind River Basin), Wyoming

50   Keefer Hill (= Twin Buttes (Ti1).
51   West side of Shotgun Butte (Cf2?).
52   "Malcolm's Locality" (= ? the Badwater Locality) (Ti4).

References: Gazin (1971): 50, 51?; Gingerich (1976): 50, 51?, 52; Holtzman and Wolberg (1977): 50?, 52; Keefer (1961): 50, 51; Krause and Gingerich (1983): 50; Krishtalka et al. (1975): 52; MacIntyre (1966): 50; McGrew and Patterson (1962): 50; Middleton (1982): 50; Patterson and McGrew (1962): 50; Rose (1975): 50, 52; D. E. Russell (1967): 50–52; Van Valen (1966): 50.

Clark's Fork—Bighorn Basins, Wyoming and Montana
Northwest of Polecat Bench

53   Cub Creek (To3).
54   Seaboard Well (Ti3).
55   a. Princeton Quarry, b. Schaff Quarry, c. Fossil Hollow, d. Brice Canyon, e. Fritz Quarry, f. Jepsen Valley (Ti5).
56   a. Little Sand Coulee (Cf1), b. various UM localities (includes 52a?) (Cf1), c. Bear Creek (Cf1), d. various UM localities (Ti6).
57   a. *Franimys* Hill, b. Phil's Hill, c. Paint Creek, d. Krause Quarry, e. Holly's Microsite, f. various other localities (Cf2).
58   a. Granger Mountain, b. Rainbow Valley, c. various UM localities (Cf3).

Between Polecat Bench and Powell, Wyoming

59   Mantua Lentil (Pu1).
60   Rock Bench Quarry (To3).
61   UM locality 263 (Ti2).
62   Various UM localities (Ti3).
63   Airport Locality, Long Draw Quarry (Ti4).
64   Various UM localities (Ti5).
65   Various UM localities (Cf1).
66   Various UM localities (Cf2).
67   Various UM localities (Cf3).

TABLE 3.1

Localities of the Puercan, Torrejonian, Tiffanian, and Clarkforkian North American Land Mammal Ages—*Continued*

South and East of Powell, Wyoming

68 Leidy Quarry (Pu1).
69 a. Cedar Point Quarry, b. Jepsen Quarry (Ti3).
70 Lower Sand Draw, Witter (= Croc. Tooth) Quarry, Divide Quarry, Sand Draw Anthill Locality (Ti4).
71 a. Middle Sand Draw, b. Sunday Locality (Ti5).
72 a. Foster Gulch (= Cleopatra Reservoir Quarry), b. Rough Gulch, c. Upper Sand Draw (Cf2).
73 a. Ries Locality, b. Foster Gulch Oil Well no. 1, (Cf).

References: Archibald (1982): 59; Bown and Gingerich (1973): 60; Butler et al. (1981): 55, 58–67; Gingerich (1976): 53, 54, 55a, b, c, 56a, c, 57c, 60, 68, 69a, b, 70, 71a, 72a, b, c; Gingerich (1978): 53; Gingerich (1980a): 69a; Gingerich (1982b): 55c; Gingerich (1983): 63, 69a; Gingerich and Rose (1979): 72b; Gingerich et al. (1980): 53, 54, 55a, b, c, d, e, f, 63, 68, 70, 71a, b; Jepsen (1930a): 57c; Jepsen (1930b): 55a, 56c, 59, 60; Jepsen (1937): 56c; Jepsen (1940): 55a, 59, 60; Jepsen and Woodburne (1969): 55a; Korth (1984): 56c; Krause (1980): 56b, 57c, e, 58c, 65; McKenna (1961): 56c; Middleton (1982, 1983): 59; Rose (1975): 55a, b, e, 57c, 60, 69a, 70, 72a; Rose (1978): 70; Rose (1979): 55f; Rose (1981a): 55a, b, e, f, 56b, c, 57a, b, c, d, e, 58a, b, c, 60, 65–67, 69a, 72a, b, 73a, b; Rose (1981b): 55a, 60, 65–67, 69a; Rose and Krause (1982): 55d, 66, 67, 70; D. E. Russell (1967): 55a, 56c, 60; Schoch and Lucas (1981b): 60; Simons (1960): 60, 69a; Simpson (1928, 1929a, 1929b): 56c; Simpson (1937c): 58a, c; Sinclair and Granger (1912): 72b; Sloan (1969): 59; Sloan and Van Valen (1965): 59; Van Valen (1978): 59, 60, 68, 69a; Van Valen and Sloan (1966): 56c; West (1973): 69a; (1976): 60, 69a; A. E. Wood (1962): 57a; R. C. Wood (1967): 56a, b, 58a, c, 66.

Crazy Mountain Basin and Vicinity, Montana

74 Bangtail Locality (Ti1).
75 Gidley Quarry (= Locality 4) (To3).
76 Silberling Quarry (= Locality 1) (To3).
77 Douglass Quarry (= Locality 63) (Ti1).
78 Scarritt Quarry (= Locality 56) (Ti2).
79 Locality 11 and Locality 13 (= Melville Locality) (Ti3).

References: Douglass (1908): 76; Gidley (1915, 1923): 75; Gingerich (1975a): 77; Gingerich (1976): 77, 79; Gingerich (1983): 78; Gingerich et al. (1983): 74; Krause and Gingerich (1983): 77; Rose (1981): 75, 76, 78; D. E. Russell (1967): 75, 76, 78; Schoch (1986): 76, 77; Simons (1960): 77; Simpson (1935d): 75, 76, 79; Simpson (1936a): 78; Simpson (1937a): 75–79; Simpson (1937b): 78; Sloan (1981): 75; Van Valen (1978): various localities; West (1971): 77.

Eastern Montana and North Dakota (Missouri River Drainage and Powder River and Williston Basins)

80 McKeever Ranch localities (Pu1).
81 Horsethief Canyon localities (To1?).
82 Hell's Hollow Local Fauna (including Worm Coulee #1) (Pu1).
83 a. Garbani Quarry, b. Biscuit Butte, c. Biscuit Springs, d. Yellow Sand Hill localities (Pu3?).
84 Mosquito Gulch localities (To1?).
85 Purgatory Hill (Pu3?).
86 Olive (Ti4).
87 Circle (Ti4).
88 Bechtold Site (Pu3?).
89 Medicine Rocks 1, Mehling Site (To3).
90 White Site, 7-UP Butte, Highway Blowout (Ti2).
91 Type of *Titanoides primaevus* near Buford, Williams Co.; McKenna's *Titanoides* material, McKenzie Co.; skull of *T. primaevus,* Williams Co.; all N. Dakota (Ti3?–5?).
92 Wannagan Creek Quarry (Ti4).
93 Donnybrook (To or Ti).
94 Lloyd and Hares Site (= Heart Butte) (To or Ti).

TABLE 3.1
Localities of the Puercan, Torrejonian, Tiffanian, and Clarkforkian North American Land Mammal Ages—*Continued*

95   a. Judson, b. Brisbane (Ti3).
96   Riverdale (Ti4?).

References: Archibald (1981): 82; Archibald (1982): 80–84; Archibald and Clemens (1984): 80, 82; Archibald et al. (1982): 80, 82, 85; Archibald et al. (1983*a*): 83a, d; Clemens (1974): 83a; Clemens (pers. observ.): 88; Gingerich (1976): 89, 90; Gingerich (1983): 95a, b; Holtzman (1978): 91–96; Holtzman and Wolberg (1977): 87, 95b; Johnston and Fox (1984): 83a; Middleton (1982, 1983): 82; Novacek (1977): 83a, c, d; Novacek and Clemens (1977): 83a; Rose (1975): 86, 87, 89; Rose (1981*b*): 95a, b; D. E. Russell (1967): 85–87, other in N. Dak.; Simons (1960): 91; Sloan (1970): 89, 90; Sloan (1981): 85; Van Valen (1978): 85; Van Valen and Sloan (1965): 85; Wolberg (unpubl. 1978).

Alberta and Saskatchewan

97   Saunders Creek (Ti1?).
98   Swan Hill Site 1 (Ti4).
99   Alberta Core Hole 66–1 (= Balzac West) (Pu2?).
100   a. Calgary 2E, b. Calgary 7E (To3).
101   a. Cochrane I, b. Cochrane II (Ti1).
102   Ericksons Landing (and L. S. Russell's "Red Deer" (1929)?) (Ti3).
103   UADW–1 and UADW–2 (Ti3).
104   Canyon Ski Quarry (Ti4).
105   Police Point (Ti3?).
106   RAV W–1 (Pu2?).
107   Pine Cree Park (Pu2?).
108   Roche Percée (Ti4).

References: Fox (1968): 99; Fox (1983*b*, 1984*a–d*): 103; Gingerich (1982*a*): 101; Johnston and Fox (1984): 99, 106; Krause (1977): 108; Krause (1978): 98, 100a, 101b, 102–105, 108; Krause and Gingerich (1983): 101; Krishtalka (1973): 105; Matthew (1914): 102; Rose and Krause (1982): 108; Novacek (1977): 101b; D. E. Russell (1967): 97, 100–102; L. S. Russell (1926): 100a; (in Rutherford, 1927): 101; L. S. Russell (1929): 100a, b, 101a, b, 102; L. S. Russell (1932, 1958): 100a, 101a, b; L. S. Russell (1948): 97; L. S. Russell (1967): 98; L. S. Russell (1974): 107; Simons (1960): 97; Simpson (1927): 102; Van Valen (1978): 98, 99.

Miscellaneous sites

109   Laudate (California (To2?).
110   Junior Oil Company Beard No. 1 well (Louisiana) (To2?).

References: McKenna (1960): 109; D. E. Russell (1967): 109, 110; Simpson (1932): 110.

and faunal lists are not included in the table or in our faunal lists. Such faunal data are discussed in the text, however, where germane. Higher taxa are listed only as an aid in locating genera and species in the table and do not reflect any particular author's systematic views. Genera within a given family are listed biochronologically in the table and alphabetically in the faunal lists in the text. Following the genus are the zones in which it occurs and the localities at which it is found. The localities are identified by the same numbers used in the previous figures and table. Association of a taxon and a specific number does not necessarily mean the taxon occurs at all localities listed under a given number. Rather than completely duplicating references for the localities listed in table 3.1 and the taxa listed in table 3.2, we felt that locality lists were of greater concern in this volume. Thus, it is necessary to consult the references listed in table 3.1 for additional taxonomic details. Unless indicated otherwise, all taxa listed in table 3.2 and discussed in the text have been reported in the literature or are in press except where noted (e.g., theses and dissertations).

TABLE 3.2
Temporal Ranges for Puercan Through Clarkforkian Mammals

Arrows indicate ranges earlier than the Puercan or later than the Clarkforkian mammal ages. Symbols as follows: taxon known from zone (X), questionably known (?), not known (O). See table 3.1 for localities (diagonal line between localities indicates occurrence at one or more of the localities).

Taxon	L+ Pul Pu2 Pu3 Tol To2 To3 Ti1 Ti2 Ti3 Ti4 Ti5 Ti6 Cf1 Cf2 Cf3 W+	Localities (and References)
MULTITUBERCULATA		
Neoplagiaulacidae		
Mesodma	◀---X---X---X---O---O---X---O---O---X---X	3?, 12, 20, 30, 36, 38, 52, 59, 60, 75, 80, 82, 83a, 85, 86, 95b, 103, 105, 106, 108.
Neoplagiaulax	?◀---O---X---X---O---O---X---X---X---X---X	6c, 11, 12, 20, 22, 32, 36, 38, 41, 45, 47, 55a, 69a, 75–78, 85–87, 95a, b, 103, 105, 106, 108, 109?.
Ectypodus	X---O---O---X---X---X---X---X---X---X---O---O---X---X---▶	6c, 15?, 17, 20, 22, 32, 34, 36, 38, 41, 45, 47, 52, 55a, 57a-e, 58c, 69a?, 74, 75, 86, 87, 95b, 101b, 106, 108.
Parectypodus	X---X---X---X---X---O---O---X---O---X---O---O---X---O---▶	6c, 11, 12, 14/15, 20, 22, 28, 38, 55a, 58c, 75, 76, 85, 87, 95a, b, 98, 100a?, 105, 106.
Mimetodon	X---X---O---X---X---X	6c, 11, 20, 22, 50, 55a, 60?, 75, 103, 108.
Xanoclomys	X	38.
?Neoplagiaulacidae		
Xyronomys	X---O---O---O---X	38, 106.
Ptilodontidae		
Kimbetohia	X---X	12, 85.
Ptilodus	X---O---X---X---X---X---X---X---X	12, 14, 19, 20, 22, 28, 32, 35, 36, 38, 39, 41, 44, 50, 52, 60, 69a, 75–78, 87, 93a, b, 96, 101b, 103, 105, 108.
Prochetodon	X---X---X---X---X---X	40, 47?, 55a, 56b, d, 57a-d, 58c, 95a, 108.
Cimolodontidae		
Cimolodon	◀---O---O ---?	12?.
Anconodon	X---X---X---X	6c, 41, 50?, 60, 75–77, 98, 100a, 101a, b.
Eucosmodontidae		
Stygimys	◀---X---X---X---O---O---X	9/12, 59, 60, 75, 76, 82, 85, 100b?, 106.
Acheronodon	X	82.
Eucosmodon	X---X---X---X---X ---?	3, 6, 8, 11, 12, 14/15, 50?.
Microcosmodon	X---O---O---O---O---X---O---X---X---X---O---X---X	34, 52, 55a, 56b, 57a-e, 87, 95b, 103, 105, 106, 108.
Pentacosmodon	X	55a.
Neoliotomus	X---X---X---X---O---▶	29, 55a, 56b, d, 57a-d, 65.
Taeniolabididae		
Catopsalis	◀---X---X---X---X---X---X	3, 9/12, 14/15, 28, 30, 50, 59, 60, 82, 100a, b.
Taeniolabis	X---X	1, 3, 26?, 83a, 85, 88?, 106.
Family indet.		
Cimexomys	◀---X---X---X	59, 82, 85, 106.
Taxon	L+ Pul Pu2 Pu3 Tol To2 To3 Ti1 Ti2 Ti3 Ti4 Ti5 Ti6 Cf1 Cf2 Cf3 W+	Localities (and References)

TABLE 3.2
Temporal Ranges for Puercan Through Clarkforkian Mammals—*Continued*

Taxon	L + Pu1 Pu2 Pu3 To1 To2 To3 Ti1 Ti2 Ti3 Ti4 Ti5 Ti6 Cf1 Cf2 Cf3 W +	Localities (and References)
MARSUPIALIA		
Didelphidae		
Peradectes	X---X---X---O---O---X---X---X---X---X---X---O ---?---X---X---▶	3, 12, 17, 34?, 37?–39, 41, 50, 52, 55a, 56c, 57a-e, 58a-c, 59, 67, 69a, 82, 85, 87, 95b, 103, 105.
Mimoperadectes	?---▶	58c.
PROTEUTHERIANS		
Leptictidae		
Prodiacodon	X---O---X---X ---?---X ---?---O---X---O---O ---? ---?---▶	6c, 14/15, 38, 41, 47?, 55a, 57?a-e, 58?a-c, 67?, 75, 83a, c, d, 85, 101b?.
Myrmecoboides	X---X---O---X---O---X	38, 60, 69a, 74, 75.
Palaeoryctidae		
Procerberus	◀---X---O---X	59, 82, 85.
Cimolestes	◀---O---X---X	3, 12.
Acmeodon	X---X---X---O---O---X	6, 15, 28, 35, 38, 87.
Palaeoryctes	X---X---O---O---X---O---X---O---O---X---X	6c, 14/15, 35, 38, 55a?, 57a-d, 58c, 69a?, 87, 95a, b.
Avunculus	X	75.
Stilpnodon	X	75.
Gelastops	X---X---O---X	35, 38, 50, 60, 75, 76, 103.
Pararyctes	?---X---X	41, 95b, 101b, 103, 105.
Aaptoryctes	X	45, 55c.
Pantolestidae		
Pantomimus	?	38?.
Leptonysson	X	75.
Paleotomus	X---X---X---X---O---X	38, 45, 69a, 77, 78.
Propalaeosinopa	X---X---X---X---X---X	36–39, 47, 75–78, 87, 95a, b, 96, 102, 103, 105.
Bisonalveus	X---X---X	41, 69a, 77, 87, 95b, 103.
Palaeosinopa	X---X---X---X---X---X---▶	36, 45, 56b, c, d, 57a-d, 58a-c, 67, 72a?, 87.
Pentacodontidae		
Aphronorus	X---O---X---X---O ---?	28, 32, 35, 50?, 60, 74–76, 77?, 93?, 103?.
Pentacodon	X---X	6, 8, 11, 14, 15.
Coriphagus	X---X	6, 11, 14, 60, 75, 76.
Protentomodon	X	56c.
Apatemyidae		
Jepsenella	X	38, 60, 75.
Unuchinia	X---X---O---X	55a, 78, 95a, b.
Labidolemur	X---X---O---O---O---X---O---▶	17, 57e, 69a.
Apatemys	X---X---X---▶	56c, 57a-e, 58a-c, 67.
Mixodectidae		
Dracontolestes	X	28.
Mixodectes	X---X	6, 7, 11, 14, 15, 38.
Eudaemonema	X	60, 75, 76.
Taxon	L + Pu1 Pu2 Pu3 To1 To2 To3 Ti1 Ti2 Ti3 Ti4 Ti5 Ti6 Cf1 Cf2 Cf3 W +	Localities (and References)

TABLE 3.2
Temporal Ranges for Puercan Through Clarkforkian Mammals—*Continued*

Taxon	L+ Pu1 Pu2 Pu3 To1 To2 To3 Ti1 Ti2 Ti3 Ti4 Ti5 Ti6 Cf1 Cf2 Cf3 W+	Localities (and References)
INSECTIVORA		
Erinaceidae		
Cedrocherus	X	69a.
Litolestes	X---X---X	55a, 87, 103.
Leipsanolestes	X---X---X---▶	34?, 49, 56c, 57e, 58?a-c, 67?.
Erinaceomorpha, *incertae sedis*		
Mckennatherium	X---X---O---X---O---X	32, 35, 38, 47, 60, 75, 103.
Diacodon	?---O---O---O ---?	50?, 55a?, 101b?.
Litocherus	X---X---X---X	36, 37, 39, 41–44, 47?, 69a, 78, 95a, b, 103, 105.
Diacocherus	X---X---X---X---X---X---X	36, 37, 45, 55a, 56b, c, d, 57a-e, 58a-c, 67, 69a, 103.
Nyctitheriidae		
Leptacodon	?---O---O---X---X---X---X---X---X---O ---? ---?---▶	17, 36–38, 47, 55a, 56d?, 57e?, 58?a-c, 60?, 67?, 69a, 74, 75, 77, 78, 85, 95a?, b, 98, 101b, 103, 105.
Pontifactor	?---O---▶	34?.
Plagioctenodon	?---O---▶	57e?.
?INSECTIVORA		
Xenacodon	X	17.
DERMOPTERA		
Plagiomenidae		
Elpidophorus	X---O---X---X	47, 69a, 76, 78, 87, 102, 103.
Planetetherium	X ---?	49, 56c.
Plagiomene	X---X---▶	57f, 58a-c, 67.
Worlandia	X---X---▶	57e, 58a-c, 67.
PRIMATES		
Paromomyidae		
Purgatorius	?◀---O---X---X	83a, d, 85,106.
Palaechthon	X---X---X---X	6, 15, 28?, 38, 74–76.
Paromomys	X---O---X---X	6?, 10?, 35, 38, 60, 75, 76, 101b.
Talpohenach	X	6.
Torrejonia	X---X	6, 15.
Palenochtha	X---X	38, 50, 60, 75.
Plesiolestes	X---X---X	41, 50, 60.
Ignacius	X---O---X---X---X---X---O---O---X---X---▶	17, 36, 39, 45, 47, 57a-e, 58c, 60, 69a, 78, 86?, 87?, 95a, b, 103, 105, 108.
Navajovius	X---X---X	17, 20–22, 87?.
Micromomys	X---X---X---O---O---O---O---▶	55a, 103, 108.
Phenacolemur	X---X---X---X---X---▶	22, 29?, 34, 48, 49, 55a, 56b, c, 57a-e, 58a-c, 67.
Tinimomys	X---O---▶	34, 57e.
Plesiadapidae		
Pronothodectes	X ---?	32?, 35, 53, 60, 75, 89, 100a, 101b?.
Nannodectes	X---X---X---X---X	17, 22, 32, 36, 37, 41, 42, 50, 74, 77, 95b.
Taxon	L+ Pu1 Pu2 Pu3 To1 To2 To3 Ti1 Ti2 Ti3 Ti4 Ti5 Ti6 Cf1 Cf2 Cf3 W+	Localities (and References)

TABLE 3.2
Temporal Ranges for Puercan Through Clarkforkian Mammals—*Continued*

Taxon	L+ Pu1 Pu2 Pu3 To1 To2 To3 Ti1 Ti2 Ti3 Ti4 Ti5 Ti6 Cf1 Cf2 Cf3 W+	Localities (and References)
Plesiadapis	X---X---X---X---X---X---X---X---X	29, 33, 34, 36, 37, 39–45, 47–52, 54, 55a, b, 56b, c, 57a-e, 58a-c, 63, 69a, 70, 72a, b, 76, 77–79, 86, 87, 90, 95a, b, 96, 98, 102, 103, 105, 108.
Chiromyoides	X---X---X---X---X---X	17, 21, 22, 34, 36, 37, 39, 45, 55b, 56c, d, 57a-d, 70, 72a, b.
Saxonellidae		
Saxonella	X	103.
Carpolestidae		
Elphidotarsius	X---X---O---X	50, 60, 75, 89, 101b.
Carpodaptes	X---X---X---X	17, 36, 39, 47, 50, 52, 69a, 78, 79, 86, 87, 95a, 98, 103–105, 108.
Carpolestes	X---X---X---X---X	34, 37, 40, 45, 49, 55a, b, e, 56b, c, d, 57c, e, 58a-c, 67, 70, 72a.
Picrodontidae		
Draconodus	X	28.
Picrodus	X---X---X---X---O---X	37, 38, 41, 50, 60, 69a, 74–76, 101b, 103.
Zanycteris	X---X	17, 47.
PRIMATES?		
Microsyopidae		
Niptomomys	X---X---▶	34, 57?a-e, 58a-c, 67.
Microsyops	X---X---▶	57a-d, 58a-c, 67.
CONDYLARTHRA		
Arctocyonidae		
Ragnarok	◀---X	59, 68, 80.
Protungulatum	◀---X---O---X	80, 82, 85.
Baioconodon	X---X---X	3, 30b, 106.
Eoconodon	X---X---X	2?, 3, 9/12, 59, 85, 106?.
Platymastus	X	12.
Carcinodon	X	106, 107.
Oxyclaenus	X---X---X	2?, 3, 9/12, 26, 28, 106.
Loxolophus	X---X---X---O---X	1, 2?, 3, 9/12, 13?, 25, 26?, 28, 31, 38, 106.
Desmatoclaenus	X---X---X---O---O---O---X	1, 2?, 3, 9/12, 26, 28, 41.
Mimotricentes	X---O---X---X---X---X---X---X---X---X	2?, 6, 8, 9?, 11, 12, 14, 15, 16, 21, 22, 28, 32, 38, 41, 42, 47,50, 52, 55a, 56d?, 60, 69a, 75–77, 78?, 87.
Thangorodrim	X	85.
Chriacus	X---X---X---X---X---X---X---X---O---O---O ---? ---?---▶	6, 11, 14, 15, 17, 28, 32, 35, 36, 38, 41, 42, 44, 52, 57a-d, 58?a-e, 60?, 67?, 69a, 77, 85, 100a?, 101b, 103.
Goniacodon	X---X---X---X	6, 14, 15, 26, 28, 38, 60.
Triisodon	X---X	5, 6, 14.
Prothryptacodon	?---X	15?, 38, 75, 76, 99.
Deuterogonodon	X---X	6, (& Simpson's 1935 loc. 25).
Deltatherium	X---X	6, 7, 8, 11, 14.
Taxon	L+ Pu1 Pu2 Pu3 To1 To2 To3 Ti1 Ti2 Ti3 Ti4 Ti5 Ti6 Cf1 Cf2 Cf3 W+	Localities (and References)

TABLE 3.2
Temporal Ranges for Puercan Through Clarkforkian Mammals—*Continued*

Taxon	L + Pu1 Pu2 Pu3 To1 To2 To3 Ti1 Ti2 Ti3 Ti4 Ti5 Ti6 Cf1 Cf2 Cf3 W +	Localities (and References)
Stelocyon	X	53.
Arctocyon	X---X---X---X---X---X	8, 15, 22, 33, 36–39, 41–43, 50, 55a, 60, 69a, 75, 77, 87, 95a.
Colpoclaenus	X	50.
Thryptacodon	X---X---X---X---X---O---X---X---X---▶	17, 33, 36, 37, 39–45, 47, 55a, 56b, c, 57a-e, 58a-c, 67, 69a, 73b?, 77, 78, 86, 87, 95a, b.
Lambertocyon	X---X---X---O---X	29, 36, 37.
Mesonychidae		
Microclaenodon	X---X	6, 14, 60.
Dissacus	X---X---O---X---X---X---X---O---X---X---X---▶	14, 15, 17, 37–40, 42, 49, 55a, 56b, c, 57a-e, 58a-c, 60, 67, 69a, 72b, 75, 76, 78.
Ankalagon	X	15.
Periptychidae		
Mimatuta	◀---X	59, 68, 80, 82.
Earendil	X	59.
Maiorana	X	59.
Escatepos	X	12.
Oxyacodon	X---X	2, 3, 9, 12, 25, 26, 83a, d, 85.
Conacodon	X---X	2?, 3?, 9, 12, 31.
Gillisonchus	X---X	1, 2?, 3, 9, 12.
Hemithlaeus	X---X	2?, 3, 9/12.
Ectoconus	X---X	2?, 3, 9/12, 25, 26.
Carsioptychus	X---X	1, 2?, 3, 9, 12, 26, 31.
Haploconus	X---X---X---X---X	6, 11, 14, 16, 26, 28, 38.
Anisonchus	X---X---X---X---X---X	2?, 3, 5, 6, 9, 11, 12, 14, 15, 25, 26, 28, 35, 38, 50, 60, 75, 85, 106, 109, 110.
Tinuviel	X	85.
Periptychus	X---X---X---X---O---X---X	4–7, 8, 10, 11, 13–17, 19, 20, 21, 28, 38, 50.
Hyopsodontidae		
Oxyprimus	◀---X	59, 82, 85.
Litomylus	X---O---X---O---X---X---X---X---X	14/15, 28, 32, 35, 36, 38, 41, 42, 47, 50?, 52?, 60, 75, 77, 87, 106.
Haplaletes	X---O---O---X---O---X---X---X---X	22, 26, 38, 41, 43–45, 60, 75, 85, 87, 95a, b.
Dorraletes	X---O---X	39, 45, 95a.
Aletodon	X---X---X---O---X---X---X	17, 29, 34?, 37, 39, 44, 49, 57a-d, 58a-c, 67, 69a, 95b.
Utemylus	X	17.
Phenacodaptes	X---X---O---X	36, 37, 52, 55a, 56c?.
Haplomylus	X---X---X---▶	29?, 46, 49, 56b, c, 57a-e, 58a-c, 67.
Apheliscus	X---X---X---▶	34?, 40, 48, 49, 56b, 57a-d, 58a-c, 67.
Hyopsodus	X---▶	58c.
Taxon	L + Pu1 Pu2 Pu3 To1 To2 To3 Ti1 Ti2 Ti3 Ti4 Ti5 Ti6 Cf1 Cf2 Cf3 W +	*Localities (and References)*

TABLE 3.2
Temporal Ranges for Puercan Through Clarkforkian Mammals—*Continued*

Taxon	L + Pu1 Pu2 Pu3 To1 To2 To3 Ti1 Ti2 Ti3 Ti4 Ti5 Ti6 Cf1 Cf2 Cf3 W +	Localities (and References)
Mioclaenidae		
Bubogonia	X	106.
Choeroclaenus	X---X	2/3/9/12.
Bomburia	X---X	2/3/9/12.
Protoselene	X---O---X---X---X---O---X---X	6, 7, 11, 12, 14, 15, 21, 28, 41?, 47.
Promioclaenus	X---X---O---X---X---X---X---X	2/3/9/12, 6, 7?, 11, 14, 15, 19, 32, 38, 41, 42, 47, 50, 60, 75, 76.
Ellipsodon	X---O---X	3, 6, 14, 26?, 38.
Litaletes	X---O---X	28, 60, 75.
Mioclaenus	X---X---X	5?, 6, 8, 11, 14, 15, 109?.
Phenacodontidae		
Tetraclaenodon	X---X	6, 7, 8, 11, 14, 15, 16, 35, 38, 60, 76, 94?, 100a, 109?.
Ectocion	X---X---X---X---X---X---X---X---X---▶	21, 22, 29, 34, 36, 37, 39–44, 47, 49, 50, 52, 55a, 56b, d, 57a-e, 58a-c, 67, 72a?, b, 73a, b, 87, 95a, b, 96, 101a, b, 103, 105.
Phenacodus	X---X---X---X---X---X---X---X---X---▶	17, 19, 20–22, 29, 33, 34, 36, 37, 39–44, 46–49, 51, 52, 55a, 56b, c, 57a-e, 58a-c, 67, 72a, b, 73b, 95a, b, 96, 102?.
Prosthecion	X	29.
NOTOUNGULATA		
Arctostylopidae		
Arctostylops	X---O---O---X---X	49, 55a, 57a-e, 58a-c, 67.
TILLODONTIA		
Esthonychidae		
Esthonyx	?---X---X---X---▶	29, 34, 48, 49, 57a-e, 58a-c, 65, 67, 73a.
PANTODONTA		
Pantolambdidae		
Pantolambda	X ---?	8, 15, 50?, 60?, 75, 94?.
Caenolambda	X---X	41, 42, 69a, 97?.
Titanoideidae		
Titanoides	X---X---X---X---X---O ---?	21, 29, 43, 55a, 69a, 77, 78, 86, 91, 95a, b, 96, 103.
Cyriacotheriidae		
Cyriacotherium	X---X---X---X ---?---X---X	48, 55a, d, 57a-d, 58a-c, 67, 70, 103, 108.
Barylambdidae		
Barylambda	X---X---X---O---X---X ---?---▶	21, 24, 29, 40, 55a, 63.
Haplolambda	X---X---O---X	17, 29, 55a.
Coryphodontidae		
Coryphodon	X---X---X---▶	29, 46, 49, 56b, 57a-e, 58a-c, 65, 67, 72a, 73a, b.
DINOCERATA		
Uintatheriidae		
Probathyopsis	X---X---X---X---X---▶?	29, 34, 40, 46, 55a, 56b, d, 57a-d, 58a-c, 67, 72b.
Taxon	L + Pu1 Pu2 Pu3 To1 To2 To3 Ti1 Ti2 Ti3 Ti4 Ti5 Ti6 Cf1 Cf2 Cf3 W +	Localities (and References)

TABLE 3.2
Temporal Ranges for Puercan Through Clarkforkian Mammals—*Continued*

Taxon	L+	Pu1	Pu2	Pu3	To1	To2	To3	Ti1	Ti2	Ti3	Ti4	Ti5	Ti6	Cf1	Cf2	Cf3	W+	Localities (and References)
TAENIODONTIA																		
Conoryctidae																		
Onychodectes			X	X														2?, 3, 9, 12, 26.
Conoryctella					X	X												5, 6, 28.
Conoryctes						X	X											6, 60, 75, 76.
Huerfanodon						X												11?, 60.
Stylinodontidae																		
Wortmania			X	X														2?, 3, 9, 12.
Psittacotherium						X	X	X	O	X	O	?						6, 14/15, 16, 20–23, 38, 76, 77.
Ectoganus												X	X	X	X	X	▶	29, 40, 55a?, 56b?, c, d?, 57a-d, 58a-c, 67, 73a, b.
CREODONTA																		
Hyaenodontidae																		
Prolimnocyon						?	O	O	O	O	O	O	O	O	O	O	▶	38.
Oxyaenidae																		
Tytthaena								X										69a.
Dipsalodon												X	?	O	X	?		29, 49, 55a, 58a-c?, 67.
Oxyaena												X	X	X	X	X	▶	49, 55a?, 56b, d, 57a-e, 58a-c, 67.
Palaeonictis															X			58c.
CARNIVORA																		
Didymictidae																		
Protictis					X	X	X	X	X	X	X	X						6, 7, 8?, 11, 14, 15, 28, 37, 39, 41, 45, 47, 50, 55a-c, 60, 69a, 70, 75–77, 86, 95a, b, 103.
Bryanictis						X												60, 75, 76.
Intyrictis						X												15, 38.
Didymictis												X	X	X	X	X	▶	34, 45, 48, 49, 55a, 56b, 57a-e, 58a-c, 67, 72a, b.
Viverravidae																		
Simpsonictis						X	O	?										38?, 41, 60, 75.
Raphictis								X										69a.
Viverravus												X	O	X	X	X	▶	34?, 40?, 49, 55a?, 56b, c?, 57a-e, 58a-c, 67.
Family indet.																		
Ictidopappus		?	O	O	O	X												12?, 75.
?Miacidae																		
Uintacyon														X	X	▶		57a-e, 58a-c, 67.
RODENTIA																		
Ischyromyidae																		
Acritoparamys													X	O	O	▶		56c.
Apatosciuravus													X	X	X	▶		34?, 49?, 56b, 57e, f, 58c.
Paramys													X	X	X	▶		40, 49, 56b, 57a-e, 58a-c, 67, 72b, 73b.
Franimys													X	O	▶			57f.
PALAEANODONTA																		
Epoicotheriidae																		
Amelotabes											X							70.
Metacheiromyidae																		
Propalaeanodon												X						55a.
Palaeanodon														X	X	▶		57c, 58a-c, 67.
Family *incertae sedis*																		
Melaniella										X								103.
Taxon	L+	Pu1	Pu2	Pu3	To1	To2	To3	Ti1	Ti2	Ti3	Ti4	Ti5	Ti6	Cf1	Cf2	Cf3	W+	Localities (and References)

PUERCAN MAMMAL AGE

Introduction

The concept of the Puercan Mammal Age, like that of the Torrejonian Mammal Age, grew out of work done in the San Juan Basin, New Mexico, beginning in the late nineteenth century. The history of this work is discussed more fully in the introduction to the Torrejonian Mammal Age. It is sufficient to note here that the "type locality" of the Puercan Mammal Age in the "Rio Puerco area" (near Cuba, New Mexico) as recognized by Wood et al. (1941) is, in fact, Torrejonian in age.

In 1959, Simpson reported the occurrence of Torrejonian fossils from the type area of the "Puerco" Formation near Cuba, New Mexico. He further noted that the "Puerco" and "Torrejon" formations could not be differentiated based on lithologic criteria and suggested that the Nacimiento Formation of Gardner (1910) be used in a restricted sense to replace these two "formations."

Wood et al. (1941) noted that the "most typical and only fossiliferous exposures" of the Puercan Mammal Age are "the escarpment running from northwest of Ojo Alamo about 25 miles to Arroyo Eduardo, east of Kimbetoh." Since about 1959, these exposures have also been recognized as yielding the type Puercan fauna (Simpson 1959). For purposes of discussion, these exposures will be divided into the De-na-zin (= Barrel Spring Arroyo) and Alamo washes, West Fork of Gallegos Canyon, Kimbetoh Arroyo, and Betonnie-Tsosie Arroyo.

The only correlative of the type Puercan assemblage recognized by Wood et al. is what we will formally term the "Mantua Lentil Local Fauna" from the Fort Union (= Polecat Bench) Formation, Wyoming (Jepsen 1940). Mantua is still retained in the Puercan Mammal Age by most authors (but see Van Valen 1978), although it is now known to be older than the type Puercan assemblage (*sensu* Simpson 1959) of the San Juan Basin. The evidence for this correlation is based on the stage of evolution of the mammals, the demonstrable superposition of type Puercan-like local faunas over Mantua-like local faunas in northeastern Montana, and faunal and magnetostratigraphic correlation between type Puercan-like local faunas in Montana and the type Puercan fauna of New Mexico (see below for further comments).

The number of new Puercan localities has increased greatly since Wood et al. Faunas referable to the Puercan Mammal Age have been reported from the North Horn Formation, Utah (Gazin 1941*b*; Tomida and Butler 1980; Robison 1980, pers. comm. to JDA 1984), the Denver Formation, Colorado (Gazin 1941; Middleton 1983, pers. comm. to JDA 1984), the Tullock Formation, Montana (Van Valen and Sloan 1965; Clemens 1974; Novacek 1977; Van Valen 1978; Archibald 1982), and the Ravenscrag Formation, Saskatchewan (Johnston 1980, Johnston and Fox 1984). Other small collections or single specimens of Puercan (or possible Puercan) age have also been reported from Wyoming (Leidy Quarry: Van Valen 1978), Montana (Bechtold Locality: Clemens and Simmons, pers. observ. 1984), Alberta (Alberta Core Hole 66–1: ?Torrejonian; Fox 1968; Van Valen 1978; Johnston and Fox 1984), and Saskatchewan (Pine Cree Park: L. S. Russell 1974; Van Valen 1978; Johnston and Fox 1984).

Lancian/Puercan Boundary

Our knowledge of pre-Cenozoic North American mammal faunas has been greatly augmented since the conclusions of Wood et al. were published in 1941. The Wood committee noted the occurrence of the latest Cretaceous Lance fauna and its equivalents but refrained from naming a formal "time term." L. S. Russell (1964, 1975) proposed a series of Upper Cretaceous "stages," for including a Lancian "stage," Late Cretaceous terrestrial faunas from North America. As pointed out by Clemens et al. (1979), Russell's "stages" lack the "rigorous definition and precision of biostratigraphic stages, but have a genesis and character similar to the Cenozoic 'land mammal ages' currently used in North America." Although we know considerably more about the Lancian fauna than was available to the Wood committee (Clemens 1964, 1966, 1973; Sloan and Van Valen 1965; Lillegraven 1969; Van Valen 1978; Archibald 1982), we are still unable to clearly define a beginning for this age because sediments containing Lancian faunas are underlain by poorly fossiliferous or marine rocks.

Fortunately, this is not the case for the boundary of the Lancian with the younger Puercan Mammal Age. As discussed below, the Puercan Mammal Age can be characterized by the appearance of a host of new taxa, although there are very few appearances of taxa in the earliest Puercan faunas (Archibald 1981, 1982). The only new genus to appear at the very beginning of the Puercan is the didelphid *Peradectes* (see remarks on this taxon under the *Peradectes/Ectoconus* Interval-Zone). Several new species also occur in earliest Puercan faunas; these are *Mesodma garfieldensis*, *Acheronodon garbani* (known only from a single tooth), *Catopsalis alexanderi*, *Ragnarok engdahli*, and *Mimatuta minuial*. Of these taxa, only *Peradectes pusillus*, *Catopsalis alexanderi*, and *Mimatuta minuial* are known from more than a single local fauna (Van Valen 1978; Archibald 1982; Middleton 1982, 1983).

There are two potentially confusing topics regarding the recognition of the Lancian/Puercan boundary which require further comment. The first concerns the possibility of an additional mammal age between the Lancian and Puercan mammal ages, the so-called Bugcreekian Mammal Age (Sloan, pers. comm. to JDA 1984) representing the faunas from the Bug Creek sequence in northeastern Montana first described by Sloan and Van Valen in 1965. (As noted above, we reject a second additional mammal age, the "Mantuan," preferring to include it in the Puercan Mammal Age; see below for further discussion.) Archibald (1982) used stratigraphic position to argue that the Bug Creek sequence is a lateral equivalent to characteristic Lancian localities that also occur near the top of the Hell Creek Formation, and thus the faunal differences are due mostly to facies differences. Accordingly, in northeastern Montana, Archibald referred the Bug Creek sequence to the Bug Creek faunal-facies, the characteristic Lancian localities to the Hell Creek faunal-facies, and both of these to the Lancian Mammal Age. More recently, Dingus, Clemens, and Fastovsky (pers. comm. 1984) have found evidence to suggest that part or all of the Bug Creek sequence, although Lancian in age, may be younger than known typical Lancian localities. But until differences in time (and biostratigraphy) can be demonstrated more clearly between typical Lancian localities and part or all of the Bug Creek sequence, it is best to treat these as facies differences and not recognize a separate "Bugcreekian" age. This seems the more prudent approach given the problems (discussed below) of recognizing zonation within the type Puercan faunas of the San Juan Basin and its faunal equivalents.

The second topic, although also pertaining to the Bug Creek sequence, is of much broader scope and involves an assessment of the degree of precision in the correlation of the Lancian/Puercan boundary with the Cretaceous/Tertiary boundary. "Cretaceous" and "Tertiary" are units founded on analyses of the evolution of the marine faunas of Western Europe. Usually, the boundary is placed at a level recording the extinction of ammonites, many lineages of foraminiferans, and some other marine organisms. In coarse-scaled analyses, these extinctions often are presented as being massive, instantaneous, global events, but studies of higher stratigraphic resolution (e.g., Voight 1981, Ward 1984) suggest much less precipitous patterns of change during the transition from the Cretaceous to the Tertiary Period.

In western North America, sections containing interdigitating marine and nonmarine rocks that provide a direct basis for correlation of a Cretaceous/Tertiary boundary, characterized by changes in the marine biota,

with the evolution of the terrestrial biota have yet to be found. In the past, recognition of the Cretaceous/Tertiary boundary in continental sections was based on the assumption that the extinctions of dinosaurs and those lineages of marine organisms used to define the Cretaceous/Tertiary boundary in Europe were precisely contemporaneous events. Studies of the magnetostratigraphy of some marine and terrestrial sections provide limited support for this view through demonstration that the pertinent extinctions of marine or terrestrial organisms occurred during magnetic polarity chron 29R. The duration of this chron is usually given as about five hundred thousand years. It must be stressed that this estimate is based on radiometric age determinations with uncertainties of at least ± one million years and on assumptions concerning constancy of seafloor spreading rates (see Dingus 1984 for further discussion of time resolution).

One of the following three operational definitions is used in common stratigraphic practice to identify the Cretaceous/Tertiary boundary in terrestrial deposits in western North America: (1) the stratigraphically highest record of dinosaurian remains, (2) the base of the first lignite overlying the stratigraphically highest record of dinosaurs (Brown 1952), or (3) extinction of *Aquilapollenites* or other palynological taxa (Tschudy 1970). In the southern part of the area where faunas of Lancian and Puercan mammal ages have been recognized (i.e., San Juan Basin, Wasatch Plateau, Denver Basin), the first or third operational definitions usually are employed. Farther north, in areas of deposition of the "Fort Union" lignites and coals, the second or third is utilized. Fine stratigraphic scaling is needed to even begin analyses of faunal or floral change on biologically significant time scales, yet these three operational definitions delimit geochronologically different interpretations of the placement of the Cretaceous/Tertiary boundaries (Archibald 1982, Archibald and Clemens 1982).

The issue of the degree of precision with which the Cretaceous/Tertiary boundary (still imprecisely defined on the basis of changes in the Western European marine biota) could be recognized in North American terrestrial deposits was brought to a head by Smit and van der Kaars (1984) who suggested that the Bug Creek Anthills Locality is within a Paleocene channel that cut down into Cretaceous sediments. Clearly, one of their purposes was to demonstrate that the Bug Creek faunal sequence is compatible with the catastrophic asteroid scenario for latest Cretaceous extinctions. This interpretation and its supposed consequences have been shown incorrect on several counts. Archibald (1984, in press) demonstrated that the stepwise extinctions within this sequence do not support catastrophic scenarios whether the Bug Creek

Anthills fauna is Cretaceous in age or not; Clemens (pers. observ. 1984) reported the discovery of a new Bug Creek-like locality demonstrably within uppermost Hell Creek sediments; Fastovsky (pers. comm. to WAC 1984) and Sloan (1985) have demonstrated that the sedimentological setting of Bug Creek Anthills is different from that reported by Smit and van der Kaars and does not clearly demonstrate either a Cretaceous or Paleocene age for the site, although a Cretaceous age is most strongly supported by the available evidence.

The relevance of the preceding comments to mammalian biochronology and biostratigraphy is that the assignment of the faunas from the Bug Creek sequence to either the Late Cretaceous or Paleocene Epoch is immaterial relative to their assignment to the Lancian or Puercan Mammal Age. There is certainly no reason that mammal ages should be concordant with any other time boundary, whether era, period, or epoch boundaries. This is the case with the Clarkforkian Mammal Age, which straddles the Paleocene/Eocene boundary (Rose 1981a), and also for other North American mammal ages relative to other epochs of the Cenozoic Era. The concordance of the Lancian/Puercan and the Late Cretaceous/Paleocene boundaries in North America probably has some biological reality because of the considerable extinctions that occurred preceding, at, and following these boundaries, but such concordance is not required by any theoretical constraints.

Definition and Characterization

We define the Puercan Mammal Age to include faunas that occur during the time between the first appearance of the didelphid marsupial, *Peradectes,* and the first appearance of the periptychid condylarth, *Periptychus.*

Wood et al. (1941) noted that the following taxa first appeared in the Puercan Mammal Age: *Anisonchus,* Condylarthra, Creodonta, *Eucosmodon, Oxyclaenus,* Taeniodonta, Taligrada. The genera in this list are still known to appear in the Puercan, although not at the earliest sites referable to this age. Of the four orders listed as first appearances, only the Taeniodonta retains a usage similar to that of Wood et al. (Schoch 1986, pers. com. to JDA 1984). This order is still considered to appear in the Puercan Mammal Age but, again, not at the earliest sites. Assuming that Wood et al. followed Matthew's (1937) concept of the Condylarthra, Creodonta, and Taligrada, the Puercan representatives of the Condylarthra were included in the Hyopsodontidae, the Creodonta were represented by the Arctocyonidae, and the Taligrada by the Periptychidae. The Taligrada is no

longer recognized, while the Hyopsodontidae, Arctocyonidae, and Periptychidae are now placed either within the Condylarthra (e.g., Romer 1966) or within various other orders (McKenna 1975, Szalay 1977). Representatives of the Arctocyonidae and the Periptychidae are now known to have appeared in the latest Cretaceous Lancian Mammal Age (Sloan and Van Valen 1965, Van Valen 1978), and representatives of the Hyopsodontidae also may have appeared in the same mammal age if *Oxyprimus* is referable to this family (Archibald 1982).

In addition to first appearances, the Wood et al. report (1941) identified the following "index fossils" that were thought to be restricted to the Puercan Mammal Age: *Carsioptychus, Conacodon, Ectoconus, Eoconodon, Loxolophus, Onychodectes, Oxyacodon, Taeniolabis,* and *Wortmania.* Of these genera, only *Loxolophus* is now known from other than Puercan localities. *Loxolophus spiekeri* (Gazin 1938) is recognized in the Dragon Local Fauna of the Torrejonian Mammal Age (Van Valen 1978, Tomida and Butler 1980). *Carsioptychus* was considered a subgenus of *Periptychus* by Van Valen. As discussed in the section on the Torrejonian Mammal Age, this referral is not accepted here. Van Valen also reported a species of *Oxyacodon* from the Torrejonian, but Archibald et al. (1982) indicated that the specimen on which this species was based is referable to *Mixodectes.* We follow Russell (1980) in questionably retaining *Claenodon* as a synonym of *Arctocyon,* rather than placing both of these genera in synonymy with *Arctocyonoides* as done by Van Valen. Although not necessarily endorsing all other synonymies suggested by Van Valen, we use the following because they represent the most recent views: *Loxolophus* includes *Protogonodon; Mimotricentes* includes *Tricentes* (in part?); and *Chriacus* includes *Spanoxyodon, Tricentes* (in part?), and *Metachriacus.* Similarly, in this as well as in discussions of later mammal ages, we follow the recent taxonomic review of Novacek et al. (1985) for erinaceomorph insectivores.

A combined biochronologic-magnetostratigraphic correlation of Puercan local faunas from the Nacimiento Formation, San Juan Basin, New Mexico (Butler and Lindsay 1985), the North Horn Formation, Wasatch Plateau, Utah (Tomida and Butler 1980), and the Tullock Formation, northeastern Montana (Archibald et al. 1982), indicates that Puercan mammals first occur in sediments of reversed polarity and last occur in sediments of normal polarity. We interpret that the Puercan begins sometime during magnetic polarity chron 29R and ends within, or possibly at the end of, magnetic polarity chron 29N (Butler and Lindsay, 1985).

An updated list of first and last appearances, index

fossils, and characteristic fossils for the Puercan follows. Occurrences for these taxa are given in table 3.2.

First appearances: *Anisonchus, Chriacus, Desmatoclaenus, Ectypodus, Ellipsodon, Eucosmodon, Goniacodon, Haplaletes, Haploconus,* cf. *Ictidopappus, Leptacodon*(?), *Litomylus, Loxolophus, Microcosmodon, Mimotricentes, Oxyclaenus, Parectypodus, Peradectes, Prodiacodon, Promioclaenus, Protoselene, Ptilodus, Xyronomys.*

Last appearances: *Cimexomys, Cimolestes, Cimolodon*(?), *Mimatuta, Oxyprimus, Procerberus, Protungulatum, Purgatorius, Ragnarok.*

Index fossils: *Acheronodon, Baioconodon, Bomburia, Bubogonia, Carcinodon, Carsioptychus, Choeroclaenus, Conacodon, Earendil, Ectoconus, Eoconodon, Escatepos, Gillisonchus, Hemithlaeus, Kimbetohia, Maiorana, Onychodectes, Oxyacodon, Platymastus, Taeniolabis, Thangorodrim, Tinuviel, Wortmania.*

Characteristic fossils: *Catopsalis, Mesodma, Neoplagiaulax*(?), *Stygimys.*

Zonation

We recognize three interval-zones within the Puercan Mammal Age. From oldest to youngest, they are the *Peradectes/Ectoconus* Interval-Zone (Pu1), the *Ectoconus/Taeniolabis taoensis* Interval-Zone (Pu2), and the *Taeniolabis taoensis/Periptychus* Interval-Zone (Pu3). The most questionable aspects of this tripartite division concern the latter two interval-zones; they will be considered together.

Peradectes/Ectoconus Interval-Zone (Pu1)

As noted previously, Van Valen (1978) recognized the Mantuan as a separate mammal age. This suggestion has not found wide acceptance, however. Van Valen's Mantuan is essentially equivalent to the *Peradectes/Ectoconus* Interval-Zone, which we define to include faunas that occur during the time between the first appearance of *Peradectes* and the first appearance of *Ectoconus.*

Discussion of the *Peradectes/Ectoconus* Interval-Zone is complicated by taxonomic issues surrounding *Peradectes.* Archibald (1982) followed Clemens (unpublished data in Archibald 1982) in treating the Puercan genus, *Thylacodon,* as a junior synonym of the Tiffanian and younger genus, *Peradectes.* Recently, Krishtalka and Stucky (1983) suggested this synonymy may not be correct. This is a taxonomic issue that has yet to be resolved (Clemens, pers. observ. 1984). The primary reason for naming this interval-zone for *Peradectes* is

that it is the only known genus that first appears in it. Further, this genus also is present in the three geographic regions where this interval-zone can be recognized.

The *Peradectes/Ectoconus* Interval-Zone is represented by the following: Mantua Lentil Local Fauna and Leidy Quarry, Bighorn Basin, northern Wyoming; Hell's Hollow Local Fauna and McKeever Ranch localities, northeastern Montana; and Littleton Local Fauna, Denver Basin, central Colorado. *Peradectes* is abundant in the Hell's Hollow Local Fauna but is much rarer in the other faunas. The Mantua Lentil Local Fauna was the first discovered representative of this interval-zone and may be the richest local fauna within it. However, the Littleton Local Fauna rivals the Mantua Lentil Local Fauna in the quality of preservation, if not in richness of specimens, whereas the sites in northeastern Montana are within the most complete biostratigraphic context. Until all these local faunas are fully published and compared, it seems imprudent to designate one over the other as the type.

The Mantua Lentil Local Fauna was first reported by Jepsen (1930*b*), at which time he described some of the taxa. Later, he provided a more detailed description for some of the multituberculates (1940). The only other major description of mammals from this local fauna has been provided by Van Valen's (1978) abbreviated description of a number of new condylarths. Additional references to taxa in the Mantua Lentil Local Fauna can be found in Sloan and Van Valen (1965), D. E. Russell (1967), Archibald (1982), and Middleton (1983). Van Valen (1978) also reported another locality, Leidy Quarry, in the southern Bighorn Basin, that is referable to the *Peradectes/Ectoconus* Interval-Zone. Leidy Quarry yielded two new species of condylarths that, according to Van Valen, belong to the genera *Ragnarok* and *Mimatuta.*

The Hell's Hollow Local Fauna and the small fauna from the McKeever Ranch localities in northeastern Montana were described by Archibald (1982). He informally used the terms "pre-mantuan" for the Hell's Hollow Local Fauna and "mantuan" for the McKeever Ranch localities to indicate probable faunal correlations with Mantua Lentil. The use of these terms might lead to confusion and thus should be dropped, although the implied correlations remain valid.

The Hell's Hollow Local Fauna appears to be older than the Mantua Lentil Local Fauna based on the presence of the multituberculates *Stygimys* aff. *S. kuszmauli* and *Cimexomys minor,* the proteutherian *Procerberus formicarum,* and the condylarths *Protungulatum* cf. *P. donnae, Ragnarok harbichti*(?), *Oxyprimus erikseni,* and *Mimatuta morgoth* at Hell's Hollow. These taxa are known from Lancian sites such as Harbicht Hill but are absent from Mantua Lentil (Van Valen 1978, Archibald 1982). Taxa present at Mantua Lentil but absent from Hell's Hollow include the multituberculates *Mesodma ambigua* and *Stygimys gratus,* a different species of the proteutherian *Procerberus,* and the condylarths *Eoconodon copanus, Ragnarok nordicum, Oxyprimus galadrielae* and *O. putorius,* "*Oxyacodon*" *josephi, Maiorana noctiluca, Mimatuta minuial,* and *Earendil undomiel.* Taxa in common between these two local faunas are the multituberculates *Catopsalis alexanderi* and *Cimexomys hausoi* and the marsupial *Peradectes pusillus.* The McKeever Ranch localities are much less rich than Hell's Hollow, but the probable joint occurrence of the condylarths *Ragnarok nordicum* and *Mimatuta minuial* at both McKeever and Mantua Lentil suggest these faunas could be contemporaneous (Jepsen 1940; Van Valen 1978; Archibald 1982; Middleton 1982; Archibald et al. 1982).

The Littleton Local Fauna is the name that has been applied by Middleton (unpublished data and pers. comm. to Archibald 1984) to material collected from South Table Mountain (Gazin 1941*a*) and the Alexander Locality, Denver Basin, central Colorado. Middleton's unpublished analysis of the mammalian fauna suggests that the Littleton Local Fauna is slightly younger than the Mantua Lentil Local Fauna but older than the type Puercan faunas of the San Juan Basin.

Of the three geographic regions in which the *Peradectes/Ectoconus* Interval-Zone can be recognized, only the local faunas in northeastern Montana have been correlated to the magnetic polarity time scale. In this region, the Hell's Hollow Local Fauna lies within a reversed magnetozone that probably represents magnetic polarity chron 29R (Archibald et al. 1982). It is probable that this entire interval-zone lies within magnetic polarity chron 29R as the oldest portion of the *Ectoconus/ Taeniolabis taoensis* Interval-Zone (the next highest interval-zone) within the San Juan Basin appears to lie just above the shift from reversed to normal polarity which is correlated with the change from magnetic polarity chron 29R to 29N.

Occurrences for the taxa listed below are given in table 3.2.

First appearances: *Baioconodon, Eoconodon, Peradectes.*

Last appearances: *Mimatuta, Oxyprimus, Ragnarok.*

Index fossils: *Acheronodon, Earendil, Maiorana,* "*Oxyacodon*" *josephi.*

Characteristic fossils: *Catopsalis, Cimexomys, Mesodma, Procerberus, Protungulatum, Stygimys.*

Taxa absent but known before and after Pu1: *Cimolestes, Cimolodon*(?), *Neoplagiaulax*(?), *Purgatorius*(?).

(Note that *Kimbetohia* would appear here except that earlier reports of this taxon from the Lancian Mammal Age of Wyoming [Clemens 1973] are incorrect according to pers. obser. of DWK.)

Ectoconus/Taeniolabis taoensis (Pu2) and *Taeniolabis taoensis/Periptychus* (Pu3) Interval-Zones

One of the more difficult problems regarding the Puercan Mammal Age has been the inability to clearly identify zones within the type Puercan Mammal Age of San Juan Basin and then to extend this zonation beyond the limits of this basin. Accordingly, the following definitions of these two interval-zones are offered with the caution that substantial revision may be required. We define the *Ectoconus/Taeniolabis taoensis* Interval-Zone to include faunas that occur during the time between the first appearance of *Ectoconus* and the first appearance of *Taeniolabis taoensis.* Similarly, we define the *Taeniolabis taoensis/Periptychus* Interval-Zone to include faunas that occur between the first appearance of *Taeniolabis taoensis* and the first appearance of *Periptychus.*

In 1892, Wortman recognized two faunal zones for Puercan assemblages within what are now called De-na-zin and Alamo washes (see Osborn and Earle 1895, Sinclair and Granger 1914). The formalization of these zones was accomplished by subsequent workers (Sinclair and Granger 1914, Matthew 1937). These zones are the lower "*Ectoconus* zone" (= "*Hemithlaeus* zone" of Van Valen [1978]) and the upper "*Taeniolabis* zone." There is little doubt that they are superposed within De-na-zin and Alamo washes and thus represent some difference in time. However, the slight faunal differences are probably due more to subtle ecological variation than to any marked difference in age (Lindsay et al. 1981). This view is strengthened by the absence of the multituberculate *Taeniolabis* in the other two major collecting areas for the type Puercan fauna, Kimbetoh and Betonnie-Tsosie arroyos. For this reason, the faunas from these two arroyos have been assigned to the lower "*Ectoconus* zone." Further complications arise because this "zone" in De-na-zin Wash may not be as fossiliferous as sites in Kimbetoh and Betonnie-Tsosie arroyos. Another collecting area for Puercan mammals lies northwest of De-na-zin and Alamo washes in the West Fork of Gallegos Canyon. Lucas (1984) recently described the small collection of mammals from this area. He argued that based on the presence of *Taeniolabis,* what we term the *Taeniolabis taoensis/Periptychus* Interval-Zone is present in the West Fork of Gallegos Canyon and that the *Ectoconus/Taeniolabis taoensis* Interval-Zone is absent.

The discovery of new local faunas and the reanalysis of previously discovered local faunas referable to the middle and/or late portion of the Puercan Mammal Age may eventually provide a securer basis for subdividing the middle and late portions of the Puercan. None of these analyses, however, are as yet published. Further, the available evidence suggests additional complications in simply extending the concepts of these two interval-zones beyond the San Juan Basin. Until these two interval-zones can be recognized more confidently outside of De-na-zin and Alamo washes, we recommend that (1) the *Ectoconus/Taeniolabis taoensis* and *Taeniolabis taoensis/Periptychus* interval-zones, considered formally, be restricted to De-na-zin and Alamo washes, and (2) in other parts of the San Juan Basin and in other regions, these two interval-zones be used provisionally and that this be indicated by the use of a question mark, that is, *Ectoconus/Taeniolabis taoensis* Interval-Zone(?) and *Taeniolabis taoensis/Periptychus* Interval-Zone(?) or Pu2(?) and Pu3(?).

In only two of the other four regions outside of San Juan Basin which have yielded middle and/or late Puercan assemblages does there appear to be a possibility that both the Pu2 and Pu3 interval-zones are present. These assemblages are from the Denver Formation, Colorado, and the North Horn Formation, Utah. Middleton (1983, pers. comm. to JDA 1984) has suggested that the vertical distribution of several condylarths in his Corral Bluffs section of the Denver Formation, Denver Basin, Colorado, lends meager support to the superposition of the Pu3 over the Pu2 interval-zone. It should be noted that the multituberculate *Taeniolabis* has not been recovered from sites in the Denver Basin. The possible occurrence of these two interval-zones in the North Horn Formation is suggested by some unpublished work by Robison (1980, pers. comm. to JDA 1984). Robison has a series of localities that appear to be older than the Wagonroad Local Fauna of Utah (Gazin 1941*b*, Tomida and Butler 1980). Among his supporting data are the absence of *Taeniolabis* from his new assemblage and its presence in the Wagonroad Local Fauna. He has named his new assemblage the Gas Tank Hill Local Fauna after the discovery locality of Gas Tank Hill (Van Valen 1978; = Flagstaff Peak Locality in Spieker 1960 and D. E. Russell 1967).

The two other major collecting regions in northeastern Montana and southwestern Saskatchewan have yielded assemblages that appear to be temporal correlatives of only one or the other of the interval-zones present in the type Puercan fauna of the San Juan Basin.

Although these faunas are middle to late Puercan in age, a more precise correlation to either Pu2 or Pu3 must be regarded with skepticism at least until the faunas from northeastern Montana have been fully described.

The first of these middle to late Puercan correlatives consists of several local faunas from the Tullock Formation, northeastern Montana. The Purgatory Hill Local Fauna was the first Puercan fauna in Montana to be discovered and briefly described (Van Valen and Sloan 1965, Van Valen 1978). Sloan (1970) assigned the Purgatory Hill Local Fauna a late Puercan age (the *Taeniolabis taoensis/Periptychus* Interval-Zone[?]) based in part on the presence of *Taeniolabis* at Purgatory Hill. The Garbani Local Fauna, located to the west of Purgatory Hill, appears to be correlative. It was collected from a series of localities occurring in a single channel complex (Archibald 1982); it is richer than Purgatory Hill, but most of the fauna has not been published (Clemens 1974; Novacek 1977; Novacek and Clemens 1977; Archibald et al. 1982).

The second important Puercan correlative occurs in southwestern Saskatchewan. The fauna from this site, RAV W-1, has recently been described (Johnston 1980, Johnston and Fox 1984). Johnston and Fox argue that RAV W-1 is older than, or very early within, the *Ectoconus/Taeniolabis taoensis* Interval-Zone(?) (= *Hemithlaeus* zone of these authors), even though a species of *Taeniolabis* is present. They argue that the species from the RAV W-1 and the Garbani local faunas are the same and that this species is more primitive than *Taeniolabis taoensis* from the type Puercan assemblage of the San Juan Basin. Based on stronger evidence from condylarths, Johnston and Fox (1984) argue for this earlier age, at least for RAV W-1 if not for Garbani Local Fauna. Analysis of new material of *Taeniolabis* from the Bechtold Site in southeastern Montana by N. B. Simmons (pers. com. to WAC 1984) indicates the presence of at least one species distinct from *T. taoensis*. Thus, the presence of *Taeniolabis* outside of the San Juan Basin should not necessarily, for the present, at any rate, be assumed to indicate that such sites are correlatives of the *Taeniolabis taoensis/Periptychus* Interval-Zone. To emphasize the possible specific differences between specimens referred to *Taeniolabis* from within and from outside the San Juan Basin, the name of the species from that basin is included in the zonal name.

Based on the preceding comments, we assign the various local faunas, localities, and regions as follows: (1) *Ectoconus/Taeniolabis taoensis* and *Taeniolabis taoensis/Periptychus* interval-zones—De-na-zin and Alamo washes, Nacimiento Formation, San Juan Basin, New Mexico; (2) *Ectoconus/Taeniolabis taoensis* Interval-

Zone(?) and/or *Taeniolabis taoensis/Periptychus* Interval-Zone(?)—Corral Bluffs, Denver Formation, Colorado (assignment of the associated West Bijou Creek-1 to one or the other of these interval-zones is uncertain); (3) *Ectoconus/Taeniolabis taoensis* Interval-Zone(?)—Kimbetoh and Betonnie-Tsosie arroyos, Nacimiento Formation, San Juan Basin, New Mexico; Gas Tank Hill Local Fauna, North Horn Formation, Utah; RAV W-1 Local Fauna, Ravenscrag Formation, Saskatchewan; (4) *Taeniolabis taoensis/Periptychus* Interval-Zone(?)—West Fork of Gallegos Canyon, Nacimiento Formation, San Juan Basin, New Mexico; Wagonroad Local Fauna, North Horn Formation, Utah; and, questionably, Purgatory Hill, Garbani, and associated local faunas, Tullock Formation, Montana, and the Bechtold Site, Ludlow Formation, Montana.

Magnetostratigraphic data do not contradict, but also do not offer significant support for, the recognition of the Pu2 and Pu3 interval-zones. A revised magnetostratigraphic correlation by Butler and Lindsay (1985) for the San Juan Basin indicates that both the Pu2 and Pu3 interval-zones occur in sediments of normal polarity interpreted as magnetic polarity chron 29N. A similar interpretation is given for sediments of normal polarity that yield the Wagonroad Local Fauna, Utah (Tomida and Butler 1980), and the Purgatory Hill Local Fauna, Montana (Archibald et al. 1982).

Because of the difficulties in sorting out middle and late Puercan faunas, tabulations of first and last appearances and index and characteristic fossils are very speculative. In addition, the "type" *Ectoconus/Taeniolabis taoensis* Interval-Zone in De-na-zin Wash is relatively unfossiliferous. Mammals from both this interval-zone and the *Taeniolabis taoensis/Periptychus* Interval-Zone are in need of systematic revision; the first major collections made in the type and surrounding areas do not have adequate provenience data. The most recent attempt to correlate mammals (only condylarths) according to the equivalent of interval-zones was done by Van Valen (1978). We offer the following update and expansion of his tabulation, but we emphasize that it should be used with caution, especially for the San Juan Basin. An asterisk denotes mammals known from the San Juan Basin but not necessarily limited to that region. Occurrences for the taxa listed below are given in table 3.2.

Ectoconus/Taeniolabis taoensis Interval-Zone(?) (Pu2 [?]).

First appearances: *Anisonchus, Bomburia*, Carsioptychus*, Choeroclaenus*, Conacodon*, Desmatoclaenus*, Ectoconus*, Ectypodus, Eucosmodon*, Gilli-* *sonchus*, Haploconus, Hemithlaeus*, cf. Ictiodopappus, Kimbetohia*, Litomylus, Loxolophus*, Microcosmodon, Mimotricentes*, Onychodectes*, Oxyacodon*, Oxyclaenus*, Parectypodus*, Promioclaenus*, Protoselene*, Ptilodus*, Purgatorius unio, Taeniolabis* n. sp., *Wortmania*, Xyronomys.*

Last appearances: none.

Index fossils: *Bubogonia, Carcinodon, Escatepos, Platymastus*.*

Characteristic fossils: *Baioconodon, Catopsalis*, Cimexomys, Cimolestes*, Eoconodon*, Mesodma*, Neoplagiaulax*, Peradectes(?)*, Purgatorius, Stygimys.*

Taxa absent but known before and after Pu2?: *Procerberus, Protungulatum.*

Taeniolabis taoensis/Periptychus Interval-Zone(?) (Pu3[?]).

First appearances: *Chriacus, Ellipsodon*, Goniacodon, Haplaletes, Leptacodon(?), Prodiacodon, Promioclaenus, Tinuviel.*

Last appearances: *Baioconodon, Bomburia*, Carsioptychus*, Choeroclaenus*, Cimexomys, Cimolestes*, Cimolodon(?)*, Conacodon*, Ectoconus*, Eoconodon*, Gillisonchus*, Hemithlaeus*, Kimbetohia, Onychodectes*, Oxyacodon*, Peradectes*, Procerberus, Protungulatum, Purgatorius, Taeniolabis* n. sp., *Wortmania*.*

Index fossils: *Taeniolabis taoensis*, Thangorodrim.*

Characteristic fossils: *Anisonchus, Catopsalis*, Desmatoclaenus, Eucosmodon*, Haploconus, Loxolophus*, Mesodma, Neoplagiaulax, Oxyclaenus*, Parectypodus, Peradectes*, Promioclaenus*, Stygimys.*

Taxa absent but known before and after Pu3(?): *Ectypodus*, cf. *Ictidopappus, Litomylus, Microcosmodon, Mimotricentes, Protoselene, Ptilodus, Xyronomys.*

TORREJONIAN MAMMAL AGE

Introduction

The initial concept of the Torrejonian Mammal Age included only the *Pantolambda* zone of Osborn and Matthew (1909). As was correctly interpreted by them, the early pantodont, *Pantolambda*, was never a very common mammal during its "life zone." Sinclair and Granger (1914) recognized two faunal zones, a lower *Deltatherium* and an upper *Pantolambda*, in the Torrejonian interval. These two zones were later questioned by Matthew (1937) and other workers, largely because neither *Deltatherium* nor *Pantolambda* were abundant enough to warrant much confidence in their stratigraphic range.

Until 1959, Puercan and Torrejonian fossils from the San Juan Basin were reported from the "Puerco" and "Torrejon" formations. These formations were the definitive basis for the Puercan and Torrejonian "Provincial mammal ages" of Wood et al. (1941). However, it was recognized early (Sinclair and Granger 1914) that those formations were identified only on the basis of paleontological criteria. In 1949 and 1950, G. G. Simpson, G. O. Whitaker, and others made a thorough search for mammals from exposures near Cuba Mesa, south of Cuba, New Mexico, where Cope (1875) had defined the Puerco Formation. Simpson (1959) reported the presence of definitive Torrejonian fossils from levels about 100 to 125 ft. (30–38 m) above the base (and higher) in strata identified as the type section of the "Puercan marls" of the west tip of Cuba Mesa. He concluded that the Puerco Formation of Cope and later workers, or at least the upper five-sixths of it, belong to the Torrejon Formation. He emphasized that the "Puerco" and "Torrejon" formations should be abandoned, as they were not defined (or differentiated) on lithologic criteria. He suggested that the Nacimiento Formation of Gardner (1910) be redefined and limited to include strata in the San Juan Basin which had previously been assigned to the Puerco and Torrejon formations and that the concept of Puercan and Torrejonian faunas be retained for separate and distinctive biochronologic units within the Nacimiento Formation. Those suggestions have been followed since 1959 and are endorsed here.

The concept of the Torrejonian Mammal Age has been substantially modified since the work of Wood et al. (1941). Between the Puercan and Torrejonian mammal ages, the Wood committee recognized a third, the "Dragonian" Mammal Age, based solely on the "Dragon local fauna" from the North Horn Formation, Utah. As discussed below, the Dragonian Mammal Age is now recognized as the first interval-zone within a redefined Torrejonian Mammal Age. One definite correlative of the Dragonian Mammal Age is now known from the San Juan Basin, New Mexico (Tomida 1981), and possible correlatives occur in the Tullock Formation, northeastern Montana (Archibald 1982; Clemens, pers. observ. 1984). Wood et al. recognized two correlatives of their Torrejonian Mammal Age, "Lebo and Rock Bench." "Lebo" clearly refers to Simpson's (1937a) Crazy Mountain Field, Montana, which is now considered to include Torrejonian and Tiffanian local faunas. "Rock Bench" Quarry on Polecat Bench in the Bighorn Basin, Wyoming, is still one of the major quarry samples of Torrejonian age. In addition to the local faunas noted above, other Torrejonian sites are now known from the Goler Formation, California (McKenna 1960, West 1976); the Porcupine Hills Formation, Alberta (Russell 1958, Krause 1978); and the Fort Union Formation of Washakie (Rigby 1981) and Fossil (Gazin 1969) basins, Wyoming.

Puercan/Torrejonian Boundary

The beginning of the Torrejonian Mammal Age is recognized by the appearance of the periptychid, *Periptychus carinidens*. *Periptychus* is a distinctive member of Torrejonian faunas, including the Dragon Local Fauna of Utah on which the Dragonian Mammal Age was founded (Wood et al. 1941). Tomida and Butler (1980) established the magnetic polarity sequence in the North Horn Formation, Utah, showing the magnetic polarity sequence and biostratigraphic limits of the Dragon Local Fauna and the (Puercan) Wagonroad Local Fauna. Thus limited and correlated with the magnetic polarity sequence in the San Juan Basin (Lindsay et al. 1978), Tomida and colleagues were able to search the "Dragonian" interval and characterize its faunal content (Tomida 1981). It now appears that the Dragonian faunal interval is better assigned to the early Torrejonian Mammal Age because the Dragonian assemblage is dominated by Torrejonian mammals, including *Periptychus*. Further, the paleomagnetic data suggest that the Dragonian assemblage temporally overlaps assemblages in the San Juan Basin which, based on faunal data, are assigned to the Torrejonian Mammal Age.

Two species of *Carsioptychus*, *C. coarctatus* and *C. matthewi*, are recorded from Puercan sites in the Nacimiento Formation, San Juan Basin. As noted in the Puercan section, Van Valen (1978) considered *Carsioptychus* to be a subgenus of *Periptychus*. No reasons were given for this action, however. We treat these taxa as separate genera. *Carsioptychus* differs from *Periptychus* in a number of ways, especially in premolar cusp development, occlusal outline, and the distinctive posterior inclination of the premolars in *Carsioptychus*. *C. matthewi* is more than 10 percent larger than *C. coarctatus* (Simpson 1936a), and the former species could be ancestral to *Periptychus carinidens*. Thus, the Puercan/Torrejonian boundary in the San Juan Basin may be identified by an evolutionary event—the appearance of *Periptychus* in sediments overlying those bearing the possible ancestor, *Carsioptychus*.

The lowest stratigraphic occurrence of *Periptychus carinidens* in the San Juan Basin is in the De-na-zin Wash (= Barrel Springs Arroyo) section where Sinclair and Granger (1914, p. 307) reported *Periptychus* from a level 173 ft. (53 m) above the *Taeniolabis* zone. This level is about 150 ft. (46 m) above the highest stratigraphic occurrence of diagnostic Puercan fossils (at UALP loc. 7691) in the De-na-zin section. *Periptychus* occurs slightly higher, about 240 ft. (73 m) (at UALP loc. 7782) and 250 ft. (76 m) (at UALP loc. 77114) above diagnostic Puercan fossils in the Betonnie-Tsosie and Kimbetoh sections, respectively (Lindsay et al. 1981). The highest stratigraphic records of all Puercan mammals known from the San Juan Basin occur in sediments with normal polarity, interpreted as magnetic polarity chron 29N. The lowest records of *Periptychus* in the San Juan Basin all occur in the next higher normal polarity magnetozone, interpreted as magnetic polarity chron 28N. Therefore, a stratigraphic interval of 150 to 250 ft. (46–76 m) with both normal and reversed polarity separates Puercan and Torrejonian assemblages in the San Juan Basin.

Definition and Characterization

As pointed out earlier, the greatest departure from the Wood committee (1941) is the inclusion here of the Dragonian Mammal Age within the Torrejonian Mammal Age (Tomida and Butler 1980, Tomida 1981). According to this, we define the Torrejonian Mammal Age to include faunas that occur during the time between the first appearance of the periptychid condylarth, *Periptychus*, and the first appearance of the plesiadapid primate, *Plesiadapis*. As discussed above, the appearance of *Periptychus* is probably an evolutionary first appearance, best recorded in sediments of the San Juan Basin, from a species of *Carsioptychus*.

Tomida and Butler (1980) convincingly demonstrated that the sediments of the North Horn Formation, Utah, which yield the Dragon Local Fauna (the type fauna for the Dragonian Mammal Age), correlate best to the portion of the section in San Juan Basin that lies between the classical Puercan and Torrejonian faunas. Tomida (1981) further showed that the time representing the "Dragonian" Mammal Age in the San Juan Basin is also faunally distinct and shares greater affinity with the Torrejonian Mammal Age than with the Puercan Mammal Age. This "Dragonian," or earliest Torrejonian interval-zone, was designated the *Periptychus-Loxolophus* Chronozone by Tomida (1981) because the range of these mammals overlap during this interval and because the interval can be identified by its distinctive polarity sequences in the absence of fossils. As discussed below, our *Periptychus/Tetraclaenodon* Interval-Zone is equivalent to both the "Dragonian" Mammal Age and Tomida's *Periptychus-Loxolophus* Chronozone.

In addition to the inclusion of the "Dragonian" Mammal Age within an expanded Torrejonian Mammal Age, there have been changes in the taxonomic characterization of both these mammal ages. Of the five taxa listed by the Wood committee (1941) as first appearances for the "Dragonian" Mammal Age, only one, *Periptychus*, remains in this category. The others, *Catopsalis*, *Haploconus*, mixodectids, and *Ptilodus*, occur, or probably occur, in Puercan faunas. For the Torrejonian Mammal Age, only one of the seven genera (*Chriacus*) recognized as first appearances by the Wood committee has been reported from Puercan or older faunas. The other taxonomic characterizations (last appearances and index and characteristic fossils) for the "Dragonian" and the Torrejonian mammal ages have remained relatively unchanged except for some additions given below.

Based especially on the Kutz Canyon section, Torrejonian faunas appear in sediments of normal polarity (interpreted as magnetic polarity chron 28N), continue upward in sediments of reversed polarity, and are last known in superjacent sediments of normal polarity (interpreted as magnetic polarity chron 27N). As noted in the discussion of the Puercan/Torrejonian boundary ("Pu3"/To1), however, as much as 250 ft. (76 m) of unfossiliferous strata, including all of magnetic polarity chron 28R and part of the super- and subjacent normal magnetic polarity chrons, could separate Puercan from overlying Torrejonian faunas in the Betonnie-Tsosie and Kimbetoh arroyos. The faunal data permit a more accurate placement of the To1/To2 and To2/To3 boundaries relative to stratigraphy and magnetostratigraphy. For the latter, these boundaries occur, respectively, just above the base and slightly above the middle of magnetic polarity chron 27R (Butler and Lindsay 1985).

The following is an updated version of the Wood committee's (1941) faunal characterization of the Torrejonian (including their "Dragonian") Mammal Age. Occurrences for these taxa are given in table 3.2.

First appearances: *Acmeodon, Anconodon, Aphronorus, Arctocyon, Dissacus, Elphidotarsius, Elpidophorus, Gelastops, Ignacius, Mckennatherium, Mimetodon, Myrmecoboides, Palaechthon, Palaeoryctes, Palenochtha, Paleotomus, Pantolambda, Paromomys, Periptychus, Picrodus, Plesiolestes, Prolimnocyon, Pronothodectes, Propalaeosinopa, Protictis, Psittacotherium, Simpsonictis.*

Last appearances: *Ellipsodon, Goniacodon, Haploconus, Ictidopappus, Loxolophus, Oxyclaenus, Stygimys, Xyronomys.*

Index fossils: *Ankalagon, Avunculus, Bryanictis, Caenolambda, Conoryctella, Conoryctes, Coriphagus, Deltatherium, Deuterogonodon, Draconodus, Dracon-*

tolestes, Eudaemonema, Huerfanodon, Intyrictis, Jepsenella, Leptonysson, Litaletes, Microclaenodon, Mioclaenus, Mixodectes, Pantomimus, Pentacodon, Prothryptacodon, Stelocyon, Stilpnodon, Talpohenach, Tetraclaenodon, Torrejonia, Triisodon, Xanoclomys.

Characteristic fossils: *Anisonchus, Catopsalis, Chriacus, Desmatoclaenus, Ectypodus, Eucosmodon, Hapaletes, Leptacodon, Litomylus, Mesodma, Mimotricentes, Neoplagiaulax, Parectypodus, Peradectes, Prodiacodon, Promioclaenus, Protoselene, Ptilodus.*

Taxa absent but known before and after the Torrejonian: *Microcosmodon.*

Zonation

Tomida (1981) designated three faunally distinct and apparently superposed subdivisions of the expanded Torrejonian Mammal Age as follows: *Periptychus-Loxolophus* Chronozone, *Deltatherium* Chronozone, and *Pantolambda* Chronozone. Although Tomida's chronozones are acceptable, we apply the terminology of interval-zones to be consistent with terminology used in other parts of this chapter.

The recommended Torrejonian interval-zones are the *Periptychus/Tetraclaenodon* Interval-Zone (To1), the *Tetraclaenodon/Pantolambda* Interval-Zone (To2), and the *Pantolambda/Plesiadapis praecursor* Interval-Zone (To3). The *Periptychus/Tetraclaenodon* Interval-Zone (To1) is equivalent to the *Periptychus-Loxolophus* Chronozone of Tomida (1981) which is also equivalent to the Dragonian Mammal Age of Wood et al. (1941). The *Tetraclaenodon/Pantolambda* Interval-Zone (To2) is approximately equivalent to the *Deltatherium* Zone of Osborn (1929) and the *Deltatherium* Chronozone of Tomida (1981). The *Pantolambda/Plesiadapis praecursor* Interval-Zone (To3) is approximately equivalent to the *Pantolambda* Zone of Osborn (1929), as recognized by Sinclair and Granger (1914) and the *Pantolambda* Chronozone of Tomida (1981). These three interval-zones are best represented in Kutz Canyon, New Mexico, although the type fauna for the *Periptychus/Tetraclaenodon* Interval-Zone (the "Dragonian" Mammal Age) is from the North Horn Formation, Utah, and the type faunas for the *Tetraclaenodon/Pantolambda* (actually Osborn's *Deltatherium* Zone) and the *Pantolamba/Plesiadapis praecursor* Interval-Zones [the traditional Torrejonian Mammal Age]) are from the Nacimiento Formation, Arroyo Torreon (Ojo Encino), New Mexico.

The equivalent of a fourth Torrejonian interval-zone (To4) has been proposed (e.g., Gingerich 1975a, 1976; Gingerich, Houde, and Krause 1983) based primarily on faunal differences between the Gidley Quarry Local Fauna, Crazy Mountain Field, Montana (with *Pronothodectes matthewi*), and the Rock Bench Quarry Local Fauna, Bighorn Basin, Wyoming (with *Pronothodectes jepi*). Following this interpretation, the Gidley Quarry Local Fauna would represent the To3 interval-zone, and the Rock Bench Local Fauna would represent the To4 interval-zone. Other suggested correlatives of the *Pronothodectes jepi* (To4) "interval-zone" are the Cub Creek Local Fauna, Wyoming (with *Pronothodectes jepi?*), and possibly the Calgary 2E Local Fauna.

We reject a fourth Torrejonian interval-zone (To4) at this time, primarily because an unpublished magnetostratigraphic section indicates that the Cub Creek Local Fauna comes from sediments with normal magnetization (Butler, pers. comm. to EHL 1984) and is overlain by an early Tiffanian fauna (Ti1) from sediments having reversed magnetization. The *Pantolambda/Plesiadapis praecursor* Interval-Zone (To3) is correlated in the San Juan Basin (where *Pronothodectes* has never been recorded) with magnetic polarity chron 27N and the upper part of magnetic polarity chron 27R, which suggests that the Cub Creek Local Fauna from sediments with normal polarity should probably be correlated with the *Pantolambda/Plesiadapis praecursor* Interval-Zone (To3). The Rock Bench Quarry in Wyoming appears, however, to be bracketed by reversed polarity (Butler, pers. com. to EHL 1984), which, if correlated with magnetic polarity chron 26R rather than 27R, would support the interpretation of a short To4 interval-zone between the To3 and Ti1 interval-zones.

The appearance of *Plesiadapis praecursor* establishes the upper limit of the *Pantolambda/Plesiadapis praecursor* Interval-Zone and the beginning of the Tiffanian Mammal Age. Gingerich, Houde, and Krause (1983) note the appearance of *Microcosmodon, Carpodaptes, Nannodectes, Ectocion,* and *Phenacodus* as well as *Plesiadapis* at the beginning of the Tiffanian. A species of *Microcosmodon* has since been described from the Puercan Mammal Age (Johnston and Fox 1984).

It is important to point out that *Pantolambda* was apparently never common in North America and thus it is hazardous to base a biostratigraphic interval-zone on it. Subsequent collecting from the *Tetraclaenodon/Pantolambda* Interval-Zone (To2) may provide additional specimens of *Pantolambda,* which would shift downward the biostratigraphic position of the To2/To3 boundary. However, we believe the To2/To3 division is justified on the basis of the existing fossil record and the biostratigraphic framework for that record. We retain the appearance of *Pantolambda* as the basis for the To3 interval-zone for historical reasons and because we have not found a more suitable taxon to replace it. We have changed the criterion for the To1/To2 boundary to the appearance of *Tetraclaenodon* rather than that of *Deltatherium* because, like *Pantolambda, Deltatherium* is poorly represented in the existing record, whereas *Tetraclaenodon* is one of the most common taxa in the To2 and To3 faunal intervals (except at Gidley Quarry, Crazy Mountain Basin, Montana).

Periptychus/Tetraclaenodon Interval-Zone (To1)

We define this interval-zone to include faunas that occur during the time between the first appearance of *Periptychus* and the first appearance of *Tetraclaenodon*. The Dragon Local Fauna of Utah has the best faunal representation of the *Periptychus/Tetraclaenodon* Interval-Zone. It was described by Gazin (1938, 1939, 1941*b*), with notable additions and revisions by Wilson (1956*b*), MacIntyre (1966), Szalay (1969), West (1976), and Tomida and Butler (1980). In the last contribution, a revised faunal list and discussion were presented.

The faunal characterization provided by Wood et al. (1941) for what we term the *Periptychus/Tetraclaenodon* Interval-Zone is in need of considerable revision. The single index fossil recognized by these authors as *Dracoclaenus* has been synonymized with *Protoselene* by Van Valen (1978). *Protoselene* ranges from the Puercan Mammal Age (as *P. bombadili* of Van Valen [1978]) through the Torrejonian Mammal Age (as *P. opisthacus*), but the species *P.* (= *Dracoclaenus*) *griphus* appears to be restricted to the *Periptychus/Tetraclaenodon* Interval-Zone (Tomida and Butler 1980).

The Wood committee (1941) recognized the first appearance of the following genera in the Dragonian Mammal Age (i.e., the *Periptychus/Tetraclaenodon* Interval-Zone): *Catopsalis, Haploconus,* mixodectids, *Periptychus,* and *Ptilodus. Catopsalis* was subsequently revised to include Late Cretaceous species from Asia which were formerly placed in the genus *Djadochtatherium* (Kielan-Jaworowska and Sloan 1979), and species referable to this genus also have been reported from Lancian and Puercan sites (D. E. Russell 1967; Sloan 1981; Middleton 1982; Archibald 1982). *Ptilodus* is now represented by a species (*P. tsosiensis*) in the Puercan faunas of San Juan Basin (Sloan 1981). Both *Haploconus*(?) *elichistus* and an unnamed mixodectid (Gazin 1941*b*, Szalay 1969) are questionably present in the late Puercan ("Pu3") Wagonroad Local Fauna, North Horn Formation, Utah. *Dracontolestes* of the Dragon Local Fauna is the oldest definite mixodectid (Szalay 1969).

Oxyclaenus was the only genus whose last appear-

ance was noted in the Wood committee's Dragonian Mammal Age (= To1 interval-zone), and both *Anisonchus* and *Ellipsodon* were noted as characteristic fossils. These assignments remain valid, but additional taxa are given below.

In addition to the Dragon Local Fauna, the *Periptychus/Tetraclaenodon* Interval-Zone is documented in strata of the Nacimiento Formation of the San Juan Basin (Tomida 1981) and possibly in the Tullock Formation of Montana (Archibald 1982; Clemens, pers. observ. 1984).

As noted in the discussion of the Puercan/Torrejonian boundary, mammals assigned to the *Periptychus/Tetraclaenodon* Interval-Zone have been found at sites superposed over localities yielding Puercan faunas in De-na-zin Wash and Kimbetoh and Betonnie-Tsosie arroyos (Lindsay et al. 1981), although a considerable stratigraphic interval separates these sites. In the Kutz Canyon section of the San Juan Basin, faunas of the *Periptychus/Tetraclaenodon* Interval-Zone are also present; here they are not underlain by known Puercan sites (although unfossiliferous strata are present, probably representing Puercan time) but are overlain by faunas referable to the *Tetraclaenodon/Pantolambda* Interval-Zone (Taylor and Butler 1980; Taylor 1981). In Kutz Canyon, the lowest stratigraphic occurrence of *Tetraclaenodon* is UALP locality 75139 (Bob's Jaw). *Periptychus* does not occur at this locality, but it does occur approximately 33 ft. (10 m) lower at UALP locality 7899. Both UALP localities 75139 and 7899 occur in strata with reversed polarity, interpreted as the lower portion of magnetic polarity chron 27R by Butler and Lindsay (1985). The lowest stratigraphic occurrence of the *Periptychus/Tetraclaenodon* Interval-Zone in Kutz Canyon (UALP loc. 7896, located 138 ft. [42 m] below UALP loc. 75139) is in strata with normal polarity, correlated with the upper part of magnetic polarity chron 28N (see Puercan/Torrejonian boundary discussion). Thus, the *Periptychus/Tetraclaenodon* Interval-Zone is interpreted to correlate with the upper part of magnetic polarity chron 28N and the lower part of magnetic polarity chron 27R (Butler and Lindsay 1985).

A tabulation of taxa in the *Periptychus/Tetraclaenodon* Interval-Zone is as follows. Occurrences for the taxa listed below are given in table 3.2.

First appearances: *Acmeodon, Aphronorus, Conoryctella, Litaletes, Mioclaenus, Palaechthon, Paromomys, Periptychus, Protictis, Triisodon.*

Last appearances: *Oxyclaenus.*

Index fossils: *Draconodus, Dracontolestes.*

Characteristic fossils: *Anisonchus, Catopsalis, Chriacus, Desmatoclaenus, Goniacodon, Haploconus,*

Litomylus, Loxolophus, Mimotricentes, Parectypodus, Protictis, Protoselene, Ptilodus.

Taxa absent but known before and after To1: *Ectypodus, Haploconus, Ictidopappus*(?), *Mesodma, Neoplagiaulax, Peradectes, Prodiacodon, Promioclaenus, Stygimys.*

Tetraclaenodon/Pantolambda Interval-Zone (To2)

We define this interval-zone to include faunas that occur during the time between the first appearance of *Tetraclaenodon* and the first appearance of *Pantolambda*. This interval-zone is best represented in Kutz Canyon, San Juan Basin, New Mexico (Taylor and Butler 1980, Taylor 1981), and includes the Angel Peak Local Fauna of Wilson (1951). In Kutz Canyon this interval-zone is recorded between the 436 ft. and 663 ft. (133 m and 202 m) level of the Kutz Canyon magnetostratigraphic section (Taylor 1981, fig. 11.2), superposed over the *Periptychus/Tetraclaenodon* Interval-Zone and subjacent to the *Pantolambda/Plesiadapis praecursor* Interval-Zone. This interval-zone is also subjacent to the *Pantolambda/Plesiadapis praecursor* Interval-Zone in the area of Arroyo Torreon (= Ojo Encino), San Juan Basin. The *Tetraclaenodon/Pantolambda* Interval-Zone correlates with the lower half, more or less, of magnetic polarity chron 27R.

The Laudate Local Fauna (McKenna 1960, West 1976) from the poorly fossiliferous Goler Formation in southern California is also tentatively assigned to the *Tetraclaenodon/Pantolambda* Interval-Zone. Another fauna that might belong in the *Tetraclaenodon/Pantolambda* Interval-Zone is the Calgary 2E Local Fauna (L.S. Russell 1958, Krause 1978) from the Porcupine Hills Formation of Alberta. Only seven mammal taxa, including *Tetraclaenodon* and a primate near *Palaechthon* or *Torrejonia* (Krause 1978), are known from the Calgary 2E Local Fauna (D. E. Russell 1967).

The following is a taxonomic tabulation of the *Tetraclaenodon/Pantolambda* Interval-Zone. Occurrences for the taxa are given in table 3.2.

First appearances: *Anconodon, Conoryctes, Coriphagus, Deltatherium, Deuterogonodon, Dissacus, Microclaenodon, Mixodectes, Palaeoryctes, Pentacodon, Prothryptacodon*(?) *Psittacotherium, Tetraclaenodon, Torrejonia.*

Last appearances: *Conoryctella, Ellipsodon, Goniacodon, Triisodon.*

Index fossils: *Talpohenach.*

Characteristic fossils: *Acmeodon, Anisonchus, Catopsalis, Chriacus, Ectypodus, Eucosmodon, Haplo-*

conus, Mimotricentes, Mioclaenus, Palaechthon, Parectypodus, Periptychus, Prodiacodon, Promioclaenus, Protoselene, Protictis, Ptilodus, Triisodon.

Taxa absent but known before and after To2: *Aphronorus, Desmatoclaenus, Ictidopappus*(?), *Litaletes, Litomylus, Loxolophus, Mesodma, Neoplagiaulax, Peradectes, Stygimys.*

Pantolambda/Plesiadapis praecursor Interval-Zone (To3)

We define this interval-zone to include faunas that occur during the time between the first appearance of *Pantolambda* and the first appearance of *Plesiadapis praecursor*. This interval-zone (To3) is much better represented than the *Tetraclaenodon/Pantolambda* Interval-Zone (To2), both paleontologically and geographically. The best representation of faunas of the *Pantolambda/Plesiadapis praecursor* Interval-Zone in the San Juan Basin is from the "type" Torrejonian on the east side of the Continental Divide at the head of Arroyo Torreon near Ojo Encino. This area was collected during the 1890s by J. L. Wortman and W. Granger for the American Museum of Natural History (designated loc. 10 by Sinclair and Granger [1914]). Many institutions have collected from these strata over a period of almost ninety years, and new discoveries are still found in the well-exposed and richly fossiliferous deposits. Tsentas (1981) reported a productive new screen-washing site (BUNM-77-184) from the *Pantolambda/Plesiadapis praecursor* Interval-Zone in the type area that promises to yield small mammals not previously recorded from these strata.

Other diverse and well-known local faunas in the *Pantolambda/Plesiadapis praecursor* Interval-Zone are those from Gidley Quarry and Siberling Quarry (Simpson 1937a, Rose 1981b) of the Crazy Mountain Basin, Montana; Rock Bench Quarry (Jepsen 1930b, 1940; Rose 1981a) in the Bighorn Basin, Wyoming; and Swain Quarry (Rigby 1980) in the Washakie Basin, Wyoming. Less diverse local faunas that are tentatively assigned to this interval-zone include O'Neill, Coprolite Point, and Little Pocket (KU loc. 9), in or near Kutz Canyon, San Juan Basin; Cub Creek, Bighorn Basin; Medicine Rocks, southeastern Montana; Donnybrook, Lloyd, and Hares, western North Dakota; the Calgary faunas, Alberta; and faunas from Fossil Basin, Wyoming.

In the San Juan Basin, the *Pantolambda/Plesiadapis praecursor* Interval-Zone is superposed above the *Tetraclaenodon/Pantolambda* Interval-Zone in Kutz Canyon as well as in Arroyo Torreon (= Ojo Encino). The lowest (and only) occurrence of *Pantolambda* in the

Kutz Canyon section is at UNM locality 113, reported by Lucas and O'Neill (1981). Lucas and O'Neill considered this locality to be about 33 feet (10 m) above the Big Pocket Locality (KU loc. 13) of Wilson (1951). In 1982, O'Neill, Butler, and Lindsay visited UNM locality 113. In tracing this site, a correlation with the 664 foot (202 m) level in Butler and Lindsay's Kutz Canyon section was found. This is about 128 feet (39 m) above Big Pocket, at the 534 foot (163 m) level. Thus, one can cautiously suggest that faunas of the *Pantolambda/Plesiadapis praecursor* Interval-Zone occur above the 664 foot (202 m) level in the Kutz Canyon section. This interpretation places the Coprolite Point (UALP loc. 7650) and other sites above the 656 foot (200 m) level (Taylor 1981, fig. 11.2) of the Kutz Canyon section in the *Pantolambda/Plesiadapis praecursor* Interval-Zone. Bab's Basin (UALP loc. 7671) occurs near the top of the *Tetraclaenodon/Pantolambda* Interval-Zone according to this interpretation. Fossil mammals are very rare above the Coprolite Point site, at the 842 foot (256 m) level in the Kutz Canyon magnetostratigraphic section.

Pantolambda also occurs at UALP locality 7595, which is near (if not identical to) KU locality 9 between Kutz Canyon and type Torrejonian at Ojo Encino (= Arroyo Torreon). The strata containing UALP locality 7595 occurs up section, although it is separated by a broad covered interval from the Kimbetoh Arroyo magnetostratigraphic section of Lindsay et al. (1981). The short stratigraphic interval in the upper drainage of Kimbetoh Arroyo which yields *Pantolambda* has reversed polarity and is correlated with magnetic polarity chron 27R. Puercan sites lower in the section are from strata with normal polarity, correlated with magnetic polarity chron 29N, and the lowest stratigraphic record of *Periptychus* in the Kimbetoh section (at UALP loc. 77114) is recorded from the next higher normal magnetozone, correlated with magnetic polarity chron 28N. The occurrence of *Pantolambda* in the Ojo Encino section of the San Juan Basin is from normally magnetized strata, correlated with magnetic polarity chron 27N according to the revised magnetostratigraphic correlation of the San Juan Basin (Butler and Lindsay 1985). Polarity determinations have not been established in exposures of the Nacimiento Formation north of Aztec, New Mexico, where Granger (1917) collected the type of *Pantolambda*. Nor have paleomagnetic determinations been established for KU locality 15, Sandoval County, New Mexico, where Wilson (1956a) reported *Pantolambda*.

A summary of the magnetostratigraphic data for the *Pantolambda/Plesiadapis praecursor* Interval-Zone (To3) based largely on work done in the San Juan Basin shows that the To2/To3 boundary occurs in reversely magnetized strata and that the To3 interval-zone continues up section well into normally magnetized strata correlated with magnetic polarity chron 27N. It is not possible to identify a magnetostratigraphic limit for the Torrejonian/Tiffanian boundary in this area as definitive Tiffanian taxa such as *Plesiadapis* have not been collected from the Nacimiento Formation of the San Juan Basin. As mentioned previously in the general discussion of the zonation of the Torrejonian, superposition of a Tiffanian (Ti1) fauna over the Torrejonian Cub Creek Local Fauna occurs in the Cub Creek magnetostratigraphic section (Butler, pers. com. to EHL 1984), Clark's Fork Basin, Wyoming. Other faunas close to the boundary but considered Tiffanian are the Black Peaks faunal sequence in Texas (Schiebout 1974) and the Cochrane faunas in Alberta. These faunas and their biochronologic placement will be discussed below (section on Torrejonian/Tiffanian boundary).

The *Pantolambda/Plesiadapis praecursor* Interval-Zone is dominated by *Tetraclaenodon* and *Mimotricentes* in the San Juan Basin, New Mexico; by *Ptilodus*, *Paromomys*, and *Promioclaenus* in the Crazy Mountain Basin, Montana; by *Ptilodus* and *Palaechthon* in the Big Horn Basin, Wyoming; and by *Paromomys* and *Mimotricentes* in Swain Quarry near the Colorado-Wyoming border. In general, the *Pantolambda/Plesiadapis praecursor* Interval-Zone is dominated by *Ptilodus*, *Mimotricentes*, and *Promioclaenus;* primates, especially *Palaechthon* or *Paromomys*, may be as dominant in northern faunas, whereas *Tetraclaenodon*, *Periptychus*, and *Mixodectes* may be as dominant in southern faunas. Plesiadapid and carpolestid primates show a strong affinity for northern latitudes, in contrast to mixodectids, which occur more frequently in southern latitudes during the time represented by the *Pantolambda/Plesiadapis praecursor* Interval-Zone.

A taxonomic listing for the *Pantolambda/Plesiadapis praecursor* Interval-Zone follows. Occurrences for the taxa are given in table 3.2.

First appearances: *Aphronorus, Arctocyon, Elphidotarsius, Elpidophorus, Gelastops, Ignacius, Mckennatherium, Mimetodon, Myrmecoboides, Palenochtha, Paleotomus, Pantolambda, Picrodus, Plesiolestes, Prolimnocyon, Pronothodectes, Propalaeosinopa, Simpsonictis.*

Last appearances: *Conoryctes, Coriphagus, Deltatherium, Deuterogonodon, Goniacodon, Haploconus, Ictidopappus, Litaletes, Loxolophus, Microclaenodon, Mioclaenus, Mixodectes, Pentacodon, Prothryptacodon, Stygimys, Tetraclaenodon, Torrejonia, Xyronomys.*

Index fossils: *Ankalagon, Avunculus, Bryanictis, Eudaemonema, Huerfanodon, Intyrictis, Jepsenella,*

Leptonysson, Pantomimus(?), *Prolimnocyon*(?), *Stelocyon, Stilpnodon, Xanoclomys.*

Characteristic fossils: *Acmeodon, Anconodon, Anisonchus, Catopsalis, Chriacus, Dissacus, Ectypodus, Eucosmodon, Haplaletes, Leptacodon, Litomylus, Mesodma, Mimotricentes, Neoplagiaulax, Palaechthon, Palaeoryctes, Parectypodus, Paromomys, Peradectes, Periptychus, Prodiacodon, Promioclaenus, Protictis, Protoselene, Psittacotherium, Ptilodus.*

Taxa absent but known before and after To3: *Desmatoclaenus, Microcosmodon.*

TIFFANIAN MAMMAL AGE

Introduction

Walter Granger (1917) first used the term *Tiffany* to refer to strata and their contained faunas in the northern San Juan Basin, southern Colorado. The "Tiffany beds" are now assigned to a distal facies of the Animas Formation, which intertongues with the Nacimiento and San Jose formations to the south. Stratigraphically, the Tiffany beds are probably equivalent to part of the Cuba Mesa Sandstone member, the unfossiliferous basal unit of the San Jose Formation. Definite placement of these beds between the underlying Nacimiento Formation and the overlying San Jose Formation has never been demonstrated because they are separated from distinctive exposures of these formations by thick and discontinuous sandstones.

"Tiffany" refers to a small settlement in southern Colorado, not far from the New Mexico state line. The first collection of fossil mammals from Tiffany beds was made by J. W. Gidley (Gidley, in Wegemann 1917), but Granger's collection was the first of significance to be studied in detail. The principal locality found by Granger, Mason Pocket, yielded a rich microfauna intermediate in evolutionary grade between "Torrejon" and "Wasatch" faunas. For this reason, Granger (1917) suggested that the Tiffany fauna of Colorado might be correlative with the Clark's Fork fauna of Wyoming. He tentatively regarded both of these as early Eocene in age, while noting that Matthew was inclined to place both in the late Paleocene. The Tiffany Local Fauna from Mason Pocket (and fossils from slightly higher stratigraphic levels in the vicinity) was fully described by Simpson (1935a, 1935b, 1935c), and only minor additions and modifications have been published since then.

During the 1920s and 1930s, a number of additional new mammalian faunas were discovered which resemble the Tiffany fauna in general aspect. These were all in northern basins. Simpson (1927) described a small faunal sample from Erickson's Landing in the Paskapoo Formation of Alberta which he regarded as equivalent to the Tiffany-Clark's Fork faunas, and Russell (1929) added a number of new localities and taxa from Alberta. Jepsen (1930b, 1940) described a remarkable sequence of Puerco, Torrejon, Tiffany, and Clark's Fork faunas from Polecat Bench in the Clark's Fork Basin, Wyoming, and Simpson (1936b, 1937a, 1937b) detailed a similar but less extensive sequence from the Crazy Mountain Field in Montana. These demonstrated clearly that Tiffany faunas represented the upper Paleocene and differed from those of the Torrejon faunas from beds below as well as from the Clark's Fork faunas from beds above (Simpson 1933).

In 1941, the Wood committee named the Tiffanian Land Mammal Age based on the fauna from the Tiffany beds of Colorado. At the time, two principal correlatives were named, Bear Creek and Silver Coulee. These referred, respectively, to the Bear Creek Local Fauna, Fort Union Formation, Montana (Simpson 1928, 1929a, 1929b; Jepsen 1937), and to the Silver Coulee Local Fauna and beds, Fort Union Formation (= Polecat Bench Formation), Wyoming (Jepsen 1930b, 1940). Although the many quarries and localities discovered in the Silver Coulee beds confirm the Tiffanian Mammal Age assigned to them by the Wood committee (1941), the Bear Creek Local Fauna has since been determined to be of Clarkforkian age (Rose 1981a). (See Clarkforkian Mammal Age and introduction and methodology for further comments.)

In recent years, many new Tiffanian faunas have been discovered and described which add considerably to our understanding and characterization of the Tiffanian Mammal Age. These faunas have come from strata ranging geographically from northern Alberta to southern Texas, including the Paskapoo (Swan Hills) and the Ravenscrag (Police Point) formations, Alberta (D. E. Russell 1967, Krishtalka 1973); the Ravenscrag Formation, southern Saskatchewan (Roche Percée—Krause 1977, 1978); the Fort Union Formation, central Montana (Bangtail—Gingerich et al. 1983); the Tongue River Formation, eastern Montana (Circle and Olive—Wolberg 1979); the Tongue River and possibly the Sentinel Butte formations, western North Dakota (Brisbane, Judson, and other localities—Holtzman 1978); the Fort Union Formation, Clark's Fork and Bighorn basins, northern Wyoming (Cedar Point, Witter, Schaff, and Long Draw quarries—Gingerich 1976, Rose 1981a); the Hoback Formation, Hoback Basin, Wyoming (Battle Mountain and Dell Creek—Dorr 1952, 1958, 1978); the "sandstone and shale sequence," Togwotee Pass area, Wyoming (Love Quarry—McKenna 1980); the Shotgun member, Fort Union Formation, Wind River Basin, Wyoming (Keefer Hill and Malcolm's locality—Patterson and McGrew 1962; Gazin 1971; Krishtalka et al. 1975); the Fort Union Group, Bison Basin, Wyoming (Saddle, Ledge, and the *Titanoides* localities—Gazin 1956a); the Chappo Member, Wasatch Formation, Wyoming (Chappo Type Locality—Dorr and Gingerich 1980); the Evanston Formation, Fossil Basin, Wyoming (Twin Creek and Little Muddy Creek—Gazin 1956b, 1969); and the Black Peaks Formation, Big Bend area, Texas (Ray's Bone Bed and Joe's Bone Bed—Schiebout 1974). The relative ages of these faunas as well as other largely undescribed Tiffanian faunas are discussed in the section on zonation of the Tiffanian Mammal Age.

Torrejonian/Tiffanian Boundary

The only known clear superposition of Tiffanian over Torrejonian faunal assemblages is on the divide between Hunt Creek and Cub Creek near the Wyoming/Montana state line in the Clark's Fork Basin. In this area, 144 feet (44 m) of continuous section separates strata yielding the Cub Creek Local Fauna (To3) from strata that yield the "Eagle Nest" Local Fauna (Ti1) (Lindsay, pers. observ. 1984). In the Crazy Mountain Basin, earliest Tiffanian faunas (specifically, Locality 68 and Douglass Quarry) overlie Torrejonian faunas (Gidley and Silberling quarries), but there is a covered interval of approximately 984 to 1,640 feet (300–500 m) between these faunas which has yielded only sporadic fossils. To the south on Polecat Bench in the Bighorn Basin, an early Tiffanian assemblage (from UM loc. 263) is known from strata about 492 feet (150 m) above, and separated by, a fault from the Torrejonian Rock Bench Quarry.

The Schiebout-Reeves Quarry (UT loc. 41274), located about 75 ft. (23 m) above the base of the Black Peaks Formation on Tornillo Flats, Big Bend area of Texas, has yielded a fauna with *Promioclaenus acolytus* (a species known only from Torrejonian faunas), plus the condylarth *Phenacodus* and the pantodont *Caenolambda* (Schiebout 1974, Rapp et al. 1983). Approximately 66 ft. (20 m) stratigraphically above the Schiebout-Reeves Quarry, the Black Peaks strata have yielded a fauna that includes the primate *Navajovius* and the pantodont *Titanoides,* both genera known only from Tiffanian deposits. Fossils from this level are considered equivalent to the *Plesiadapis rex/P. churchilli* Lineage-Zone (Ti3) in Wyoming. Slightly higher in the Black Peaks Formation, the fauna from Joe's Bone Bed is considered correlative with the *Plesiadapis simonsi/P. gingerichi* Lineage-Zone (Ti5) (Rapp et al. 1983). Thus, the Black Peaks Formation appears to show superposition

of a Tiffanian faunal sequence, with the possibility of a subjacent Torrejonian fauna (UT loc. 41274). We consider the lower Black Peaks fauna (e.g., UT loc. 41274) to be early Tiffanian in age. Although it lacks primates that distinguish Tiffanian lineage-zones, it includes *Phenacodus* and *Caenolambda*, genera not otherwise known from the Torrejonian Mammal Age. The rationale for this interpretation is based, in part, on the Black Peaks magnetostratigraphic sequence.

The Cochrane I and II faunas from central Alberta have been considered either Torrejonian (Krause 1978) or Tiffanian (Russell 1929, 1958; Gingerich 1982a) based on faunal similarity. The most recent interpretation for biochronologic assignment of these faunas (Gingerich 1982a) is that they should be considered Tiffanian in age. This is based, in part, on reidentification of "*Pronothodectes* sp." from Cochrane II as *Nannodectes* cf. *N. intermedius* and "*Meniscotherium semicingulatum*" from Cochrane II as *Ectocion collinus*, which also occurs in the Cochrane I Fauna. According to this interpretation, the Cochrane faunas include some of the earliest records of *Nannodectes* and *Ectocion* in addition to several genera characteristic of Torrejonian faunas (e.g., *Elphidotarsius*). On the basis of these records, it is possible to characterize the Torrejonian/Tiffanian boundary using first appearances of a number of mammalian genera.

In the Crazy Mountain Basin, earliest Tiffanian faunas include the oldest known records of *Plesiadapis*, *Nannodectes*, *Ectocion*, *Phenacodus*, and several less common genera (Krause and Gingerich 1983). These genera are also present at another earliest Tiffanian locality, Keefer Hill in the Wind River Basin (Gingerich 1976, West 1976), where their appearance coincides with the first appearance of *Carpodaptes* (Rose 1975). Patterson and McGrew (1962) assigned Keefer Hill an early Tiffanian age, as did MacIntyre (1966) and Gingerich (1975). However, Gazin (1971) and Rose (1975, 1977) regarded Keefer Hill as latest Torrejonian in age because of the large number of typically Torrejonian primate genera ("*Pronothodectes*," which is now, in part, placed in *Nannodectes*; *Palenochtha, Palaechthon, Plesiolestes, Torrejonia, Paromomys,* and *Elphidotarsius*) that occur here. Placement of Douglass Quarry and Keefer Hill in either the latest Torrejonian or the earliest Tiffanian mammal ages requires a decision that is, to some extent, arbitrary. These faunas are clearly intermediate between those of the Torrejonian and the Tiffanian mammal ages, and there is no clear faunal precedent deciding the question one way or the other. However, it is customary to use the first appearance datum (FAD of Van Couvering and Berggren [1977]) of a taxon, rather than the last appearance datum (LAD), to set boundaries of successive biostratigraphic units (George et al. 1969; Murphy 1977; Woodburne 1977). Following this procedure, we emphasize the first appearance of *Plesiadapis, Nannodectes, Ectocion,* and *Phenacodus* at Keefer Hill and Douglass Quarry—rather than the last appearances of the various primates noted above—in placing these localities and their contained faunas at the base of the Tiffanian Mammal Age and not in the Torrejonian Mammal Age. If the first appearance of a single genus is to be taken as defining the Tiffanian Mammal Age (Woodburne 1977), *Plesiadapis* is the most appropriate for this purpose. *Plesiadapis* has traditionally served as a taxon marking the beginning of the Tiffanian Mammal Age (Wood et al. 1941), and it has been thoroughly studied biostratigraphically (Gingerich 1976).

It should be noted that all of the genera first appearing at the beginning of the Tiffanian Mammal Age are plausibly derived from genera present in the Torrejonian Mammal Age of North America. The boundary between the Torrejonian and the Tiffanian mammal ages is thus probably a product of intracontinental evolution and dispersal. This is in contrast to the boundary between the Tiffanian and the Clarkforkian mammal ages, which is apparently marked by a major immigration of new genera, families, and even orders of mammals from Asia.

Definition and Characterization

We define the Tiffanian Mammal Age to include faunas that occur during the time between the first appearance of the plesiadapid primate, *Plesiadapis,* and the first appearance of the Rodentia.

The Wood committee (1941) listed the following taxa as making their first appearance in the Tiffanian Mammal Age: *Palaeosinopa, Phenacodus, Plesiadapis, Probathyopsis,* Rodentia, and *Thryptacodon.* This list remains almost unchanged except for the Rodentia, which do not appear until the Clarkforkian Mammal Age. Two of the five genera noted as last appearances for the Tiffanian Mammal Age, *Anisonchus* and *Arctocyon,* retain this distinction. However, of the other three, *Leptacodon* is questionably reported from the Clarkforkian Mammal Age whereas well-documented records of *Tetraclaenodon* and *Pantolambda* are not known beyond the Torrejonian Mammal Age. Wood et al. (1941) listed the following as index fossils for the Tiffanian Mammal Age: *Barylambda, Bathyopsoides, Labidolemur, Phenacodus grangeri, Sparactolambda,* and *Titanoides. Sparactolambda* is now considered a synonym of *Titanoides* and *Bathyopsoides* a synonym of

Probathyopsis. Of the index fossils listed by Wood et al., only *Titanoides* is still restricted to the Tiffanian. The genus *Ectypodus* was given as the single characteristic fossil for the Tiffanian. This remains valid although the list has been greatly augmented, now including eleven genera.

Paleomagnetic sections have been developed in Clark's Fork and Bighorn basins, northern Wyoming (Butler et al. 1980, 1981), in conjunction with major fossil localities. The signature of these paleomagnetic sections is one of the more distinctive for any in Paleocene terrestrial sediments in the Western Interior. Although not all of the fossiliferous portion of this section has been amenable to magnetostratigraphic analysis, the available portion extends from within magnetic polarity chron 26R through 24R (27R through 24R, Butler, unpublished data and written communication to EHL 1984) and includes the Paleocene/Eocene boundary. In these basins Tiffanian faunas extend from magnetic polarity chron 26R into 25N.

Rapp et al. (1983) published the Black Peaks paleomagnetic sequence, correlating the Schiebout-Reeves Quarry (UT loc. 41274) with the Torrejonian/Tiffanian boundary. The lower part of the Black Peaks Formation, including UT locality 41274 and the sites (UT locs. 40147 and 41217) correlated with the Ti3 lineage-zone, has reversed polarity. Joe's Bone Bed, correlated with the Ti5 lineage-zone, occurs in the overlying and shorter reversed magnetozone. Rapp et al. (ibid.) correlated these magnetozones (and faunas) with magnetic polarity chrons 25R (includes the Ti5 fauna) and 26R (includes the Ti1 and Ti3 faunas), which is consistent with the paleomagnetic correlation of Tiffanian lineage-zones in the Clark's Fork Basin (Butler et al. 1981) and is compatible with reinterpretation of the San Juan Basin magnetostratigraphic sequence by Butler and Lindsay (1985).

To summarize, we place the Torrejonian/Tiffanian boundary at or near the boundary of magnetic polarity chrons 27N and 26R. The *Pantolambda/Plesiadapis praecursor* Interval-Zone (To3) is correlated with magnetic polarity chron 27N (e.g., the type section for the Torrejonian Mammal Age in Arroyo Torreon, New Mexico, and Cub Creek, Wyoming) and the upper part of magnetic polarity chron 27R (e.g., Kutz Canyon sites, New Mexico). The *Plesiadapis praecursor/P. anceps* (Ti1) and *P. anceps/P. rex* (Ti2) lineage-zones (including the lower Black Peaks fauna, UT loc. 41274) are correlated with the lower part of magnetic polarity chron 26R. The *P. rex/P. churchilli* Lineage-Zone (Ti3) is correlated with the top of magnetic polarity chron 26R and most of 26N. The *P. churchilli/P. simonsi* Lineage-Zone (Ti4) is correlated with the top of magnetic polarity chron 26N and the base of chron 25R. The *P. simonsi/P. gingerichi* Lineage-Zone (Ti5) is correlated with most of magnetic polarity chron 25R and about the lower one-third of chron 25N. The *P. gingerichi/Rodentia* Interval-Subzone (Ti6) of the *P. gingerichi/P. cookei* Lineage-Zone (Ti6-Cf1) is correlated with about the middle one-third of magnetic polarity chron 25N.

These data suggest that the Tiffanian commences early in magnetic polarity chron 26R (also see discussion of zonation in the Torrejonian section). Paleomagnetic samples were also analyzed from the area for the type Tiffanian Mammal Age in southern Colorado, including the important Mason Pocket Quarry (Butler et al. 1981). The entire section was magnetically reversed and, based on faunal correlation to the Clark's Fork-Bighorn basins, was assigned to magnetic polarity chron 25R.

The following taxonomic characterization of the Tiffanian Mammal Age is updated from Wood et al. (1941). Occurrences for the taxa are provided in table 3.2.

First appearances: *Aletodon, Arctostylops, Barylambda, Carpolestes, Chiromyoides, Cyriacotherium, Diacocherus, Didymictis, Dipsalodon, Ectocion, Ectoganus, Esthonyx(?), Haplolambda, Labidolemur, Lambertocyon, Micromomys, Neoliotomus, Oxyaena, Palaeosinopa, Phenacodaptes, Phenacodus, Phenacolemur, Plesiadapis, Probathyopsis, Prochetodon, Thryptacodon, Titanoides, Viverravus.*

Last appearances: *Acmeodon, Anconodon, Anisonchus, Aphronorus, Arctocyon, Catopsalis, Desmatoclaenus, Elphidotarsius, Elpidophorus, Eucosmodon(?), Gelastops, Haplaletes, Litomylus, Mckennatherium, Mesodma, Mimetodon, Mimotricentes, Myrmecoboides, Neoplagiaulax, Palaechthon, Palenochtha, Paleotomus, Pantolambda, Paromomys, Periptychus, Picrodus, Plesiolestes, Promioclaenus, Pronothodectes(?), Propalaeosinopa, Protictis, Protoselene, Psittacotherium, Ptilodus, Simpsonictis(?).*

Index fossils: *Aaptoryctes, Amelotabes, Bisonalveus, Caenolambda, Carpodaptes, Cedrocherus, Colpoclaenus, Diacodon(?), Dorraletes, Litolestes, Litocherus, Melaniella, Nannodectes, Navajovius, Pararyctes, Pentacosmodon, Propalaeanodon, Protoselene, Raphictis, Saxonella, Tytthaena, Unuchinia, Utemylus, Xenacodon, Zanycteris.*

Characteristic fossils: *Chriacus, Dissacus, Ectypodus, Ignacius, Leptacodon, Microcosmodon, Palaeoryctes, Parectypodus, Peradectes, Prodiacodon, Prolimnocyon.*

Taxa absent but known before and after the Tiffanian: *Prolimnocyon.*

Zonation

The large number of mammalian faunas belonging to the Tiffanian Mammal Age in the Western Interior and the fact that many of these are isolated geographically in separate depositional basins has led to some difficulty in determining the relative ages of localities and their contained faunas. In recent years, considerable progress has been made toward placing Tiffanian localities into successive biostratigraphic zones. These biostratigraphic zones are faunally equivalent to the biochronologic zones used here. This progress can be measured to some degree by comparing the temporal distribution of localities outlined here with views current ten to fifteen years ago (e.g., Sloan and Van Valen 1965; D. E. Russell 1967; Sloan 1970). This has been achieved almost entirely by application of the stratigraphic principle of faunal succession and correlation wherever two or more faunas are preserved in stratigraphic sequence.

As recognized by the authors of this chapter, the Tiffanian Mammal Age is subdivided into five lineage-zones (Ti1–Ti5) and one interval-subzone (Ti6) (part of a sixth lineage-zone, Ti6-Cf1) based on five apparently nonoverlapping species of the primate *Plesiadapis* that have been argued to form successive evolutionary stages. *Plesiadapis* is one of the most abundant and most widely distributed genera of late Paleocene mammals and is a suitable taxon for lineage-zonation, although as noted in the introduction and methodology section, interval-zones are preferable because they are less arbitrary. The five lineage-zones and one interval-subzone of the Tiffanian that we recognize are the *Plesiadapis praecursor/P. anceps* Lineage-Zone (Ti1), the *P. anceps/P. rex* Lineage-Zone (Ti2), the *P. rex/P. churchilli* Lineage-Zone (Ti3), the *P. churchilli/P. simonsi* Lineage-Zone (Ti4), the *P. simonsi/P. gingerichi* Lineage-Zone (Ti5), and the *P. gingerichi/Rodentia* Interval-Subzone (Ti6) of the *P. gingerichi/P. cookei* Lineage-Zone (Ti6-Cf1). The first three lineage-zones are represented by faunas from the Crazy Mountain Basin, Montana (Simpson 1937b, Gingerich 1976), and the second through fifth lineage-zones and the sixth interval-subzone are represented by faunas from the Clark's Fork-Bighorn basins, Wyoming (Gingerich 1976, Gingerich et al. 1980).

Plesiadapis praecursor/P. anceps Lineage-Zone (Ti1)

We define the *Plesiadapis praecursor/P. anceps* Lineage-Zone to include faunas that occur during the time between the first appearance of *P. praecursor* and the first appearance of *P. anceps*.

Earliest Tiffanian faunas are currently known from central Alberta to southern Wyoming (and probably southern Texas), but this zone remains one of the least well known for the Tiffanian Mammal Age. The samples recovered from Ti1 localities are either small or as yet only partially described. Small samples are known from Cochrane I and II in central Alberta (L. S. Russell 1929, 1932, 1958), the Little Muddy Creek Locality in the Fossil Basin of southwestern Wyoming (Gazin 1969), and the Bangtail Locality in the western Crazy Mountain Basin of south-central Montana (Gingerich et al. 1983). The Schiebout-Reeves Quarry in the Big Bend area of Texas (Schiebout 1974, Rapp et al. 1983) can probably also be included.

One of the largest and potentially most important collections from the Ti1 lineage-zone, that from Keefer Hill in the northern Wind River Basin, is still largely undescribed; among higher taxa only primates have received thorough attention (Gazin 1971). Preliminary faunal lists have been published for the Keefer Hill Local Fauna (Keefer 1961, D. E. Russell 1967). Many of the taxa cited in these preliminary lists would be new records for the Ti1 lineage-zone; however, until these temporal range extensions are substantiated through detailed description and analysis, we feel it is premature to record them as definite occurrences.

A second major locality, Douglass Quarry in the eastern Crazy Mountain Basin, was worked in 1940 by a field party from Princeton University. That collection was recently described by Krause and Gingerich (1983), but a much larger collection obtained since 1982 by field parties from the State University of New York at Stony Brook remains to be studied. Douglass Quarry is especially important because it has been placed in stratigraphic sequence between Gidley and Silberling quarries (To3) below and Scarritt Quarry above (Ti2) (Simpson 1937a, Krause and Gingerich 1983). Very near Douglass Quarry, and at stratigraphically similar levels, are a number of mammal-bearing fossil localities, one of which (loc. 68) yielded the type specimen of *Ectocion montanensis*, now considered a junior synonym of *E. collinus* (Gingerich 1982a).

New localities, such as Bangtail in the Crazy Mountain Basin (Gingerich et al. 1983), and new collections from previously known localities such as Cochrane Site II in Alberta (R. C. Fox, pers. com. to DWK 1984) promise to add considerably to our knowledge of mammals during the Ti1 lineage-zone. The Cochrane localities, like Keefer Hill, have only recently been assigned an earliest Tiffanian age (Gingerich 1982a). Un-

fortunately, earliest Tiffanian mammals have not been found in the Polecat Bench section; this interval is therefore the only one of the five Tiffanian lineage-zones not yet represented in that stratigraphic sequence. It is still not possible to provide reliable estimates of mammalian diversity for the Ti1 lineage-zone, nor is it possible to make an adequate comparison of northern faunas with their southern counterparts. Preliminary data suggest that *Ectocion* and *Ptilodus* were dominant forms during the earliest portion of the Tiffanian Mammal Age.

In addition to the appearance of the defining taxon, *Plesiadapis praecursor*, other taxa such as *Nannodectes intermedius* and *Aphronorus orieli* are important in recognizing the Ti1 lineage-zone. A notable genus restricted to this zone is *Colpoclaenus*.

Occurrences for the taxa given below are presented in table 3.2.

First appearances: *Bisonalveus, Caenolambda, Carpodaptes, Diacodon*(?), *Ectocion, Nannodectes, Pararyctes*(?), *Phenacodus, Plesiadapis, Thryptacodon, Titanoides.*

Last appearances: *Anisonchus, Aphronorus, Catopsalis, Eucosmodon*(?), *Gelastops, Palaechthon, Palenochtha, Pantolambda, Paromomys, Pronothodectes*(?).

Index fossils: *Aphronorus orieli, Colpoclaenus, Plesiadapis praecursor, Nannodectes intermedius.*

Characteristic fossils: *Anconodon, Arctocyon, Chriacus, Elphidotarsius, Ectypodus, Leptacodon, Litomylus, Mckennatherium, Microcosmodon, Mimetodon, Mimotricentes, Myrmecoboides, Neoplagiaulax, Paleotomus, Peradectes, Periptychus, Picrodus, Plesiolestes, Prodiacodon*(?), *Promioclaenus, Propalaeosinopa, Protictis, Psittacotherium, Ptilodus.*

Taxa absent but known before and after Ti1: *Acmeodon, Desmatoclaenus, Dissacus, Elpidophorus, Hapaletes, Ignacius, Mesodma, Palaeoryctes, Parectypodus, Prolimnocyon*(?), *Protoselene, Simpsonictis.*

Plesiadapis anceps/P. rex Lineage-Zone (Ti2)

We define the *Plesiadapis anceps/P. rex* Lineage-Zone to include faunas that occur during the time between the first appearance of *P. anceps* and the first appearance of *P. rex*.

Late early Tiffanian (Ti2) localities are currently known only from Montana and Wyoming. Like the Ti1 lineage-zone, the Ti2 lineage-zone is poorly known paleontologically and is poorly represented geographically. Papers on the Crazy Mountain Basin Scarritt Quarry of south-central Montana (Simpson 1936b,

1937*b*) and the Bison Basin Saddle Locality of south-central Wyoming (Gazin 1956*b*) are the only faunal studies completed to date for the Ti2 lineage-zone. Both local faunas are small, however, and at least the Scarritt Quarry sample appears to be biased in favor of small mammals (Rose 1981*a*, 1981*b*). An updated faunal list for Scarritt Quarry appears in Rose (1981*a*), but since this time the sample from Scarritt Quarry has been approximately quadrupled by field parties from the State University of New York at Stony Brook. The small mammals *Litocherus*, *Neoplagiaulax*, and *Propalaeosinopa* are dominant forms at Scarritt Quarry (Rose 1981*a*), whereas the large condylarth *Phenacodus* is overwhelmingly dominant at the Saddle Locality, Bison Basin, Wyoming (Gazin 1956*b*). Much smaller collections of Ti2 lineage-zone mammals are known from UM locality 263 in the Polecat Bench section, Bighorn Basin, Wyoming, and several localities (White Site, 7-Up Butte, Highway Blowout) in the Medicine Rocks area of southeastern Montana.

First appearances: *Litocherus*, *Pararyctes*, *Unuchinia*.

Last appearances: *Anconodon*, *Desmatoclaenus*, *Plesiolestes*, *Simpsonictis*(?).

Index fossils: *Plesiadapis anceps*, *Nannodectes gazini*.

Characteristic fossils: *Arctocyon*, *Bisonalveus*, *Carpodaptes*, *Caenolambda*, *Chriacus*, *Dissacus*, *Ectocion*, *Ectypodus*, *Elpidophorus*, *Haplaletes*, *Ignacius*, *Leptacodon*, *Litomylus*, *Mimotricentes*, *Nannodectes*, *Neoplagiaulax*, *Paleotomus*, *Peradectes*, *Phenacodus*, *Picrodus*, *Plesiadapis*, *Prodiacodon*, *Promioclaenus*, *Propaleosinopa*, *Protictis*, *Protoselene*, *Ptilodus*, *Thryptacodon*, *Titanoides*.

Taxa absent but known before and after Ti2: *Acmeodon*, *Aphronorus*, *Diacodon*(?), *Elphidotarsius*, *Gelastops*, *Mckennatherium*, *Mesodma*, *Microcosmodon*, *Mimetodon*, *Myrmecoboides*, *Palaeoryctes*, *Parectypodus*, *Periptychus*, *Prolimnocyon*(?), *Psittacotherium*.

Plesiadapis rex/P. churchilli Lineage-Zone (Ti3)

We define the *Plesiadapis rex/P. churchilli* Lineage-Zone to include faunas that occur during the time between the first appearance of *P. rex* and the first appearance of *P. churchilli*.

The middle part of the Tiffanian Mammal Age is much better represented, both paleontologically and geographically, than the previous two lineage-zones. Approximately 50 percent more genera are represented in the Ti3 lineage-zone than in either the Ti1 or Ti2 lineage-zones. Furthermore, more than double the number of localities are represented for faunas in the Ti3 lineage-zone than either of the previous Tiffanian lineage-zones, and these localities range from southern Texas to central Alberta, a distance of almost 1,900 miles (3,000 km). Cedar Point Quarry, in the Bighorn Basin of northwestern Wyoming, contains the largest known sample (almost 2,000 specimens) and lies stratigraphically beneath Witter (= Croc. Tooth) and Divide quarries (both in the Ti4 lineage-zone). Several mammalian taxa from Cedar Point Quarry have been described (e.g., adapisoricids—Krishtalka 1976*a*, Gingerich 1983; nyctitheriids—Krishtalka 1976*b*; apatemyids—West 1973; plesiadapids—Gingerich 1976; carpolestids—Rose 1975; arctocyonids—Van Valen 1978; phenacodontids—West 1971, 1976; carnivores—Gingerich and Winkler 1985; creodonts—Gingerich 1980*a*; pantodonts—Simons 1960), and Rose (1981*a*) has presented a preliminary list of the entire fauna. The Cedar Point Local Fauna is dominated by *Plesiadapis* and *Ptilodus*. Smaller samples that have received more detailed descriptive treatment are known from the Big Bend area of Texas (Ray's Bone Bed and Annex—Schiebout 1974), the Bison Basin of Wyoming (Ledge, Saddle Annex, and West End localities—Gazin 1956*b*), the Williston Basin of North Dakota (Judson and Brisbane localities—Holtzman 1978), the Chappo Type Locality (Dorr and Gingerich 1980), the Hoback Basin of Wyoming (Battle Mountain Locality—Dorr 1958), and southeastern Alberta (Police Point Local Fauna—Krishtalka 1973). Wolberg (1979) has presented a preliminary faunal list for the Circle Local Fauna of eastern Montana. Several mammalian taxa from two recently discovered localities (UADW-1 and UADW-2) in central Alberta have recently been described by Fox (1983*b*, 1984*a*, 1984*b*, 1984*c*, 1984*d*; preliminary faunal list in 1984*a*). Specimens from these localities are particularly noteworthy because of their relative completeness.

First appearances: *Aletodon*, *Barylambda*, *Chiromyoides*, *Cyriacotherium*, *Diacocherus*, *Dorraletes*, *Labidolemur*, *Lambertocyon*, *Litolestes*, *Micromomys*, *Navajovius*, *Prochetodon*, *Zanycteris*.

Last appearances: *Acmeodon*, *Aphronorus*(?), *Bisonalveus*, *Caenolambda*, *Elphidotarsius*, *Elpidophorus*, *Gelastops*, *Promioclaenus*, *Protoselene*.

Index fossils: *Cedrocherus*, *Chiromyoides minor*, *Melaniella*, *Nannodectes simpsoni*, *Plesiadapis rex*, *Raphictis*, *Saxonella*, *Tytthaena*.

Characteristic fossils: *Acmeodon*, *Arctocyon*, *Carpodaptes*, *Chriacus*, *Dissacus*, *Ectocion*, *Ectypodus*, *Haplaletes*, *Ignacius*, *Labidolemur*, *Leptacodon*, *Lito-*

cherus, Litomylus, Mckennatherium, Mesodma, Microcosmodon, Mimetodon, Mimotricentes, Myrmecoboides, Nannodectes, Neoplagiaulax, Paleotomus, Palaeoryctes, Pararyctes, Parectypodus, Peradectes, Periptychus, Phenacodus, Picrodus, Plesiadapis, Prodiacodon(?), Propalaeosinopa, Protictis, Psittacotherium, Ptilodus, Thryptacodon, Titanoides, Unuchinia.

Taxa absent but known before and after Ti3: *Diacodon*(?), *Prolimnocyon*(?).

Plesiadapis churchilli/P. simonsi Lineage-Zone (Ti4)

We define the *Plesiadapis churchilli/P. simonsi* Lineage-Zone to include faunas that occur during the time between the first appearance of *P. churchilli* and the first appearance of *P. simonsi*.

The type Tiffanian fauna from the Mason Pocket Locality of southwestern Colorado lies within the Ti4 lineage-zone and was described in detail by Simpson (1935*a*, 1935*b*, 1935*c*). Samples of very few other Ti4 lineage-zone localities have been treated in full, those from the Rock Springs Uplift of southwestern Wyoming (Winterfeld 1982), Malcolm's Locality in the Wind River Basin of central Wyoming (Krishtalka et al. 1975), the Riverdale Locality in the Williston Basin of central North Dakota (Holtzman 1978), and Swan Hills Site 1 in central Alberta (L. S. Russell 1967) being the exceptions. Probably the largest sample (more than 5,000 specimens) of Ti4 lineage-zone mammals comes from the Roche Percée localities in southeastern Saskatchewan. Only the multituberculates (Krause 1977), primates (Krause 1978), and a pantodont (Rose and Krause 1982) have been described from the Roché Percée Local Fauna. Wolberg (1979) has presented a preliminary faunal list for the Olive Locality of eastern Montana. Included in Wolberg's list are several taxa that are otherwise unknown from the Ti4 lineage-zone (e.g., *Nyctitherium, Protentomodon*, cf.? *Purgatorius, Phenacolemur*); they have not been included in the lists below pending publication of full descriptions and analyses. Swan Hills Site 1 is the most northerly Tiffanian (and Paleocene) fossil mammal locality known (L. S. Russell 1967). Several localities (e.g., Airport, Witter Quarry, Divide Quarry) in the Bighorn Basin are especially significant because they have been placed in stratigraphic relationship to localities that have yielded mammals from either the earlier Ti3 or the later Ti5 lineage-zones or both.

Although the faunal composition of none of the Ti4 lineage-zone localities has been analyzed, it appears that, as in the Ti3 lineage-zone, *Ptilodus* and *Plesiadapis* are dominant.

First appearances: *Haplolambda, Palaeosinopa, Phenacodaptes.*

Last appearances: *Labidolemur, Litomylus, Mesodma, Pararyctes, Periptychus, Zanycteris.*

Index fossils: *Amelotabes, Chiromyoides caesor, Nannodectes gidleyi, Plesiadapis churchilli, Utemylus, Xenacodon.*

Characteristic fossils: *Aletodon, Arctocyon, Barylambda, Carpodaptes, Chiromyoides, Chriacus, Diacocherus, Dissacus, Ectocion, Ectypodus, Hapalodectes, Ignacius, Lambertocyon, Leptacodon, Litolestes, Litocherus, Microcosmodon, Micromomys, Mimetodon, Mimotricentes, Nannodectes, Navajovius, Neoplagiaulax, Peradectes, Phenacodus, Picrodus, Plesiadapis, Prochetodon, Propalaeosinopa, Protictis, Ptilodus, Thryptacodon, Titanoides.*

Taxa absent but known before and after Ti4: *Diacodon*(?), *Dorraletes, Mckennatherium, Myrmecoboides, Palaeoryctes, Paleotomus, Parectypodus, Prodiacodon, Prolimnocyon*(?), *Psittacotherium, Unuchinia.*

Plesiadapis simonsi/P. gingerichi Lineage-Zone (Ti5)

We define the *Plesiadapis simonsi/P. gingerichi* Lineage-Zone to include faunas that occur during the time between the first appearance of *P. simonsi* and the first appearance of *P. gingerichi*.

The vast majority of Ti5 lineage-zone localities are from the Clark's Fork and Bighorn basins. The mammalian fauna from the best known of these, Princeton Quarry, was recently reexamined by Rose (1981*a*, 1981*b*). The Princeton Quarry sample is dominated by *Phenacodaptes* and *Plesiadapis*, but like Scarritt Quarry in the Ti2 lineage-zone, it probably contains an overrepresentation of small forms owing to size sorting. Much smaller collections of Ti5 lineage-zone mammals have been described from the following localities: Bayfield (northern San Juan Basin, Colorado—Simpson 1935*a*, 1935*b*, 1935*c*), Joe's Bone Bed (Big Bend area, Texas—Schiebout 1974), several UW localities (eastern Rock Springs Uplift, Wyoming—Winterfeld 1982), the *Titanoides* Locality (Bison Basin, Wyoming—Gazin 1956*b*), and Dell Creek Quarry (Hoback Basin, Wyoming—Dorr 1952, 1958, 1978).

First appearances: *Arctostylops, Carpolestes, Didymictis, Dipsalodon, Ectoganus, Neoliotomus, Oxyaena, Phenacolemur, Probathyopsis, Viverravus.*

Last appearances: *Arctocyon, Carpodaptes, Diacodon*(?), *Dorraletes, Hapalodectes, Litolestes, Litocherus, Mckennatherium, Mimetodon, Myrmecoboides, Nannodectes, Navajovius, Neoplagiaulax, Paleotomus, Picro-*

dus, Propalaeosinopa, Protictis, Psittacotherium(?), *Ptilodus, Unuchinia.*

Index fossils: *Aaptoryctes, Chiromyoides potior, Pentacosmodon, Plesiadapis fodinatus, Plesiadapis simonsi, Propalaeanodon.*

Characteristic fossils: *Aletodon, Barylambda, Chiromyoides, Cyriacotherium, Diacocherus, Dissacus, Ectocion, Ectypodus, Haplolambda, Ignacius, Lambertocyon, Leptacodon, Microcosmodon, Micromomys, Mimotricentes, Palaeoryctes, Palaeosinopa, Parectypodus, Peradectes, Phenacodaptes, Phenacodus, Plesiadapis, Prochetodon, Thryptacodon, Titanoides.*

Taxa absent but known before and after Ti5: *Chriacus, Labidolemur, Prodiacodon, Prolimnocyon.*

Plesiadapis gingerichi/Rodentia Interval-Subzone (Ti6) of the *P. gingerichi*/*P. cookei* Lineage-Zone (Ti6-Cf1)

Plesiadapis gingerichi was recently described by Rose (1981), who interpreted it to be phylogenetically and temporally intermediate between *P. simonsi* (latest Tiffanian, Ti5) and *P. cookei* (middle Clarkforkian, Cf2). Following Rose, we define the *Plesiadapis gingerichi*/ *P. cookei* Lineage-Zone to include faunas that occur during the time between the first appearance of *P. gingerichi* and the first appearance of *P. cookei.*

In working out the relationships of the *Plesiadapis gingerichi*/*P. cookei* Lineage-Zone (Ti6-Cf1) as first defined by Rose (1980, 1981), it became apparent that this lineage-zone straddles the Tiffanian/Clarkforkian boundary. To specify this relationship clearly, we further subdivide this lineage-zone into two interval-subzones. The end of the first interval-subzone (Ti6) and the commencement of the second interval-subzone (Cf1) equals the Tiffanian/Clarkforkian boundary, which corresponds to the first appearance of rodents (and other taxa). Thus, we define the first interval-subzone, the *Plesiadapis gingerichi*/Rodentia Interval-Subzone, to include faunas that occur during the time between the first appearance of *P. gingerichi* and the first appearance of the Rodentia.

Within the Clark's Fork Basin, local faunas referable to the *P. gingerichi*/*P. cookei* Lineage-Zone occur in the lowest 328 ft. (100 m) of strata containing Clarkforkian faunas and in strata extending approximately 328 ft. (100 m) below the first occurrence of Clarkforkian faunas. Thus, the lower 328 ft. (100 m) of this section yield mammals that are referable to the *P. gingerichi*/ Rodentia Interval-Subzone.

At present, the *Plesiadapis gingerichi*/*P. cookei* Lineage-Zone (Ti6-Cf1) can only be recognized with certainty within the Clark's Fork Basin, probably because there are few other localities of early Clarkforkian age. Several other faunas that will be discussed under the Rodentia/*P. cookei* Interval-Subzone (Cf1) portion of the Ti6-Cf1 lineage-zone may, however, be referable to this second subzone. For now, local faunas belonging to the Ti6 interval-subzone appear to be restricted to the Clark's Fork Basin and are very poorly known. Thus, the sole purpose in recognizing two interval-subzones within the *P. gingerichi*/*P. cookei* Lineage-Zone is to highlight the fact that this lineage-zone straddles the Tiffanian/Clarkforkian boundary.

Occurrences for the taxa listed below are given in table 3.2.

First appearances: *Esthonyx*(?), *Plesiadapis gingerichi, P. dubius.*

Last appearances: *Mimotricentes.*

Index fossils: none.

Characteristic fossils: *Carpolestes, Chiromyoides, Cyriacotherium, Diacocherus, Didymictis, Dipsalodon, Ectocion, Ectoganus, Leptacodon, Neoliotomus, Oxyaena, Palaeosinopa, Phenacodus, Phenacolemur, Probathyopsis, Prochetodon, Prolimnocyon*(?).

Taxa absent but known before and after Ti6: *Aletodon, Arctostylops, Barylambda, Chriacus, Dissacus, Ectypodus, Haplolambda, Ignacius, Labidolemur, Lambertocyon, Microcosmodon, Micromomys, Palaeoryctes, Parectypodus, Peradectes, Phenacodaptes, Prodiacodon, Thryptacodon, Titanoides, Viverravus.*

CLARKFORKIAN MAMMAL AGE

Introduction

Granger (1914) applied the term *Clark Fork* to a stratigraphic interval in the Clark's Fork Basin of northwestern Wyoming (specifically, at the southeastern end of Polecat Bench) where he had found fossils he recognized to be older than what we refer to as the Wasatchian Mammal Age (see also Sinclair and Granger 1912). This "Clark Fork fauna" was described by Matthew (1915*a*, 1915*b*, 1915*c*), Granger (1915), Jepsen (1930*b*, 1940), and Simpson (1929*c*, 1937*c*). The fauna proved to be so distinctive that, in 1941, Wood et al. formally proposed the Clarkforkian as a North American provincial age, "based on the Clark Fork member (and faunal zone) of the Polecat Bench Formation." They selected Granger's locality on Polecat Bench as the type locality. Wood et al. (1941), like most workers before and after, considered the Clarkforkian the last of the Paleocene provincial ages, what we call the Clarkforkian Mammal Age.

Several factors—relatively small collections, inadequate stratigraphic documentation, and confusion of lithologic, temporal, and biochronologic units—led to skepticism about the legitimacy of the Clarkforkian Mammal Age. This culminated in R. C. Wood's (1967) detailed reappraisal and ultimate rejection of the Clarkforkian as a valid land mammal "age." Intensive collecting in the Clark's Fork Basin during the past several years, however, has yielded thousands of new specimens that clearly reaffirm the existence of a distinctive Clarkforkian fauna (Gingerich and Rose 1977; Rose 1978, 1980, 1981a; D. Parris, unpublished data and written communication to KDR, 1984). In addition, these collections indicate that, contrary to earlier belief, Clarkforkian assemblages in the type area are not restricted to the Fort Union Formation (= Polecat Bench Formation) but occur primarily in the lower part of the variegated Willwood Formation. Approximately the upper 328 ft. (100 m) of the Fort Union Formation along Polecat Bench contain mammals of early Clarkforkian age, but there is no lithologic basis at present to justify separating this unit as the "Clark Fork member."

The Wood committee (1941) did not recognize any faunal correlatives of the Clarkforkian Mammal Age. Correlatives of this age are now recognized and have been discussed by Rose (1981a). These faunas occur in the following formations: the Fort Union and Willwood formations, Clark's Fork and Bighorn basins, northern Wyoming and southern Montana (Rough Gulch, Foster Gulch, Ries Locality, Bear Creek, and others—Sinclair and Granger 1912; Simpson 1928, 1929a; 1929b; Jepsen 1937; Van Houten 1944; Van Valen and Sloan 1966; Gingerich and Rose 1979); the "lower variegated sequence," Togwotee Pass area, northwestern Wyoming (probably the "Low" and "Rohrer" localities and definitely other localities—McKenna 1972, 1980); the Chappo Member, Wasatch Formation, Hoback Basin, western Wyoming (several localities—Dorr 1952, 1958, 1978; Dorr and Steidtmann 1970; Dorr et al. 1977), and Green River Basin, southwestern Wyoming (Buckman Hollow Locality of La Barge Creek—Gazin 1942, 1956a; Dorr and Gingerich 1980); the Fort Union Formation, Washakie Basin, southwestern Wyoming (Big Multi Locality, unpublished data, see Rose 1981a); the Atwell Gulch Member, Wasatch Formation, Piceance Creek Basin, northwestern Colorado (Plateau Valley— Patterson 1933, 1936, 1937, 1939, 1949; Patterson and Simons 1958; Patterson and West 1973); possibly localities in the Black Peaks Formation, Big Bend area, southwestern Texas (Schiebout 1974).

Rose (1981a) provided stratigraphic sections and descriptions and ranges of Clarkforkian mammals from the type area as well as a discussion of the Clarkforkian assemblages from elsewhere (listed above).

Tiffanian/Clarkforkian Boundary

In the Clark's Fork Basin, the beginning of the Clarkforkian Mammal Age can be recognized by the first occurrence of the orders Rodentia and Tillodontia (*Esthonyx*) and the genera *Haplomylus* (Condylarthra) and *Coryphodon* (Pantodonta). As discussed below, it is the appearance of the Rodentia that we use to define the beginning of this mammal age (Gingerich and Gunnell 1979; Rose 1980, 1981a). These first appearances were apparently all immigrants. There is no evidence at present that any of them appeared significantly earlier than the others; rather, their first occurrence seems to have been synchronous. This suggests that these mammals arrived in a single wave of immigration (see also Repenning 1967). Nonetheless, their geographic source is uncertain. A Central American center of origin has been suggested (Sloan 1970; Gingerich 1976; Gingerich and Rose 1977), but recent discoveries in the Paleocene of China suggest that rodents and tillodonts may have originated in Asia (Wang 1975; Zhou et al. 1977; Gingerich 1980c; Zhang 1980; Dawson et al. 1984).

The first occurrence of any of these four immigrants is, in practice, a good indication of the beginning of the Clarkforkian Mammal Age. None is very common, however, in the early part of the Clarkforkian Mammal Age; all four constitute only 6 to 7 percent of the individuals presently known for this time. By the middle of the Clarkforkian Mammal Age and during the remainder of this period, these groups were well established and accounted for 15 to 25 percent of the known individuals (Rose 1981a).

As we have already indicated, the beginning of a (land) mammal age is defined by the initial occurrence of a single taxon (as advocated by Woodburne [1977] and Murphy [1977]). We have selected the appearance of the Rodentia as the herald of Clarkforkian time (Rose 1981a). Identification of fragmentary rodent remains to lower taxonomic levels is difficult; however, ordinal characteristics of rodents are distinctive, and, in practice, the presence of any rodent is an indication that the Tiffanian/Clarkforkian boundary has been crossed. Wood et al. (1941) listed the Tiffanian as the oldest record of Rodentia. This was based on the occurrence of rodents at Bear Creek, Montana (Jepsen 1937), a locality that is now argued to be of Clarkforkian age (Van Valen and Sloan 1966; Sloan 1970; Rose 1975, 1977, 1981a; Gingerich 1976). More recently, Korth (1984) has suggested that the original Tiffanian age assignment for the Bear Creek Local Fauna is correct and thus that the appearance of rodents in North America occurred during the Tiffanian Mammal Age. (It should be noted that Korth incorrectly stated that Rose [1981a] indicated an Eocene age for Bear Creek; in fact, Rose's correlations clearly indicate a Paleocene age.) We argue that a Clarkforkian age assignment for the Bear Creek Local Fauna is more in keeping with the evidence based on the co-occurrence of taxa (including rodents) in Clarkforkian faunas, Clark's Fork Basin, Wyoming, and in the Bear Creek Local Fauna (Rose 1981a). Further, simply by definition, the Bear Creek Local Fauna is Clarkforkian in age (even if it could be shown to be older than the type Clarkforkian faunas), because it yields rodents (but not taxa indicating a post-Clarkforkian age).

The only Clarkforkian faunas known outside of the Clark's Fork Basin which may overlie Tiffanian faunas and thus include the Tiffanian/Clarkforkian boundary are from strata preserved in the Togwotee Pass area, the Hoback Basin (both in western Wyoming), and the Plateau Valley area (Colorado). Collections from these strata do not yet permit precise location of the Tiffanian/Clarkforkian boundary.

Definition and Characterization

Rose's (1980, 1981a) recent study of the mammalian fauna from the area of the type Clarkforkian Mammal Age permits a definition and characterization that is modified and much expanded from that of Wood et al. (1941). Accordingly, we define the Clarkforkian Mammal Age to include faunas that occur during the time between the first appearance of the Rodentia and the first appearance of the Artiodactyla. Rose reported seventy species of mammals from the Clarkforkian Mammal Age of the Clark's Fork Basin. These species are primarily of Paleocene aspect; several taxa typical of the Wasatchian Mammal Age also are present, however, whereas many standard Wasatchian forms are absent. Thus, the Clarkforkian fauna is truly intermediate, combining elements of both the Paleocene and Eocene. Exposures yielding the type Clarkforkian fauna in the Polecat Bench-Clark's Fork Basin area occur in an interval about 1,542 ft. (470 m) thick in the upper Fort Union and lower Willwood formations. The earliest Clarkforkian faunas are found about 1,148 ft. (350 m) above the level of the late Tiffanian Princeton Quarry.

The Wood committee (1941) recognized four genera that appear in the Clarkforkian Mammal Age: cf. *Coryphodon*, *Ectocion*, *Esthonyx*, and *Oxyaena*. Of these taxa, only *Coryphodon* and *Esthonyx* are now known to appear for the first time in this mammal age; *Ectocion* and *Oxyaena* have been recorded from Tiffanian faunas. The last appearances recorded by Wood et al. for the Clarkforkian Mammal Age were *Carpolestes* and *Plesiadapis*. Except for a single specimen of *Plesiadapis dubius* from an early Wasatchian fauna (Rose and Bown 1982), these last appearances remain valid. The single index fossil listed for the Clarkforkian Mammal Age by the Wood committee was *Plesiadapis cookei*. This remains a valid assignment, but now additional taxa also can be recorded as index fossils for the Clarkforkian Mammal Age. Finally, the characteristic fossils originally recognized for this mammal age—*Didymictis*, *Ectypodus*, *Phenacodus*, *Probathyopsis*, *Thryptacodon*—remain valid but can be supplemented.

In addition to the updated faunal listings provided below, several aspects of Clarkforkian faunas merit further comment. Relatively common index fossils of the Clarkforkian include *Plesiadapis cookei*, *Carpolestes nigridens*, *Aletodon gunnelli*, *Apheliscus nitidus*, *Haplomylus simpsoni*, *Dissacus praenuntius*, *Esthonyx xenicus*, *E. ancylion*, and *Acritoparamys atavus*. Some of these species, such as *Plesiadapis cookei* (see below), are restricted to only part of the Clarkforkian Mammal Age. All occur in at least one Clarkforkian fauna outside of the Clark's Fork Basin in addition to the type Clarkforkian fauna. The other index fossils noted below are too rare or too limited in distribution to be useful as index fossils. Five genera that were thought to appear first in the Clarkforkian Mammal Age by Rose (1977) and Gingerich and Rose (1977) are now recorded from Tiffanian faunas. These genera are *Ectoganus* (*Lampadophorus*), Dipsalodon, Arctostylops, Probathyopsis, and *Oxyaena*. The most characteristic and most common mammals of the Clarkforkian Mammal Age are phenacodontid condylarths (*Ectocion osbornianus*, *Phenacodus primaevus*, and *P. vortmani*), which together constitute about 50 percent of the individuals at most levels in the Clark's Fork Basin (Rose 1981a, 1981b). *Ectocion* is ubiquitous and the most common mammal at most localities. Phenacodontids persist into Wasatchian time but exhibit a dramatic decline in abundance at the Clarkforkian/Wasatchian boundary.

As discussed in the characterization of the Tiffanian Mammal Age, magnetostratigraphic sections have been developed in the Clark's Fork and Bighorn basins, northern Wyoming (Butler et al. 1980, 1981). These sections encompass all three of the zones recognized by Rose (1981a) for the type Clarkforkian Fauna as well as most of the older Tiffanian faunas and a portion of the next younger Wasatchian faunas. In the Clark's Fork and

Bighorn basins, Clarkforkian faunas extend from magnetic polarity chron 25N into 24R.

The following list of taxa characterizing the Clarkforkian Mammal Age is an update of Wood et al. (1941) based in large measure on the work of Rose (1981*a*). Occurrences are given in table 3.2.

First appearances: *Acritoparamys, Apatemys, Apatosciuravus, Apheliscus, Coryphodon, Franimys, Haplomylus, Hyopsodus, Leipsanolestes, Microsyops, Mimoperadectes*(?), *Niptomomys, Palaeanodon, Paramys, Plagioctenodon*(?), *Plagiomene, Pontifactor*(?), *Tinimomys, Uintacyon, Worlandia.*

Last appearances: *Aletodon, Arctostylops, Carpolestes, Chiromyoides, Cyriacotherium, Diacocherus, Dipsalodon, Haplolambda, Lambertocyon, Microcosmodon, Palaeoryctes, Phenacodaptes, Plesiadapis, Prochetodon, Titanoides*(?).

Index fossils: *Acritoparamys atavus, A. atwateri* (= *Paramys annectens*), *Aletodon gunnelli, Apheliscus nitidus, Carpolestes nigridens, Chiromyoides major, Cyriacotherium psamminum, Dissacus praenuntius, Esthonyx ancylion, E. xenicus, Haplomylus simpsoni, Palaeonictis, Plagiomene accola, Planetetherium, Plesiadapis cookei, Prosthecion, Protentomodon.*

Characteristic fossils: *Barylambda, Bisonalveus, Chriacus, Didymictis, Dissacus, Ectocion, Ectoganus, Ectypodus, Esthonyx, Ignacius, Labidolemur, Leptacodon*(?), *Neoliotomus, Oxyaena, Palaeosinopa, Parectypodus, Peradectes, Phenacodus, Phenacolemur, Probathyopsis, Prodiacodon*(?), *Prolimnocyon*(?), *Thryptacodon, Viverravus.*

Taxa absent but known before and after the Clarkforkian: *Micromomys.*

Zonation

In the Clark's Fork Basin, the Clarkforkian Mammal Age can be subdivided into one subzone and two zones (Rose 1980, 1981*a*). The first subzone in the Clarkforkian Mammal Age, the Rodentia/*Plesiadapis cookei* Interval-Subzone (Cf1), is the second of two interval-subzones within the *Plesiadapis gingerichi/P. cookei* Lineage-Zone (Ti6-Cf1). The second zone in the Clarkforkian Mammal Age is the *Plesiadapis cookei* Lineage-Zone (Cf2). As was the case for the first five zones of the Tiffanian Mammal Age, the above two zones are lineage-zones because it is argued that they represent the duration of successive species within a single evolving lineage of *Plesiadapis.*

The *Plesiadapis gingerichi/P. cookei* Lineage-Zone (Ti6-Cf1), as defined by Rose (1980, 1981*a*), straddles the Tiffanian/Clarkforkian boundary. We have therefore

recognized two interval-subzones within this lineage-zone. The first of these, the *Plesiadapis gingerichi/*Rodentia Interval-Subzone (Ti6), corresponds to the Tiffanian portion of the Ti6-Cf1 lineage-zone, and the second, the Rodentia/*P. cookei* Interval-Subzone (Cf1), corresponds to the Clarkforkian portion of this lineage-zone (see zonation of the Tiffanian Mammal Age).

The second Clarkforkian zone mentioned above, the *Plesiadapis cookei* Lineage-Zone, only bears the name of the taxon defining the beginning of the zone. This is because the third and final Clarkforkian zone recognized by Rose is not based on the first appearance of a single (name-bearing) taxon and thus is neither a lineage-zone nor an interval-zone. This third zone, the *Phenacodus-Ectocion* Acme-Zone (Cf3), is, as the name suggests, based on the simultaneous abundance of the two named condylarths.

Recognition of the above zonation within the Clark's Fork section has been augmented by the use of species of *Phenacolemur* and *Esthonyx* (Rose 1981*a*). *Esthonyx xenicus* occurs within the *Plesiadapis gingerichi/P. cookei* Lineage-Zone and through the lowest 98 ft. (30 m) of strata bearing faunas referable to the *Plesiadapis cookei* Lineage-Zone. *Esthonyx ancylion* continues above the 98 ft. (30 m) level in strata bearing faunas of the *Plesiadapis cookei* Lineage-Zone into about the lowest 66 ft. (20 m) of strata with faunas assigned to the *Phenacodus-Ectocion* Acme-Zone. *Esthonyx grangeri* continues through the remainder of the *Phenacodus-Ectocion* Acme-Zone (and the Clarkforkian Mammal Age) and into the Wasatchian Mammal Age. *Phenacolemur pagei* first appears in the later part of the Tiffanian Mammal Age and continues into the Clarkforkian Mammal Age, coexisting with *Esthonyx xenicus* and *E. ancylion. Phenacolemur praecox* follows *P. pagei* and, as does *Esthonyx grangeri,* continues into the Wasatchian Mammal Age. Although these additional taxa may prove to be helpful in further delimiting Clarkforkian zones, it must be kept in mind that each of the two genera involved is argued to constitute an evolving lineage that is somewhat arbitrarily divided into species.

Rodentia/*Plesiadapis cookei* Interval-Subzone (Cf1) of the *P. gingerichi/ P. cookei* Lineage-Zone (Ti6-Cf1)

The rationale and basis for the subdivision of the Ti6-Cf1 lineage-zone are discussed under the *Plesiadapis gingerichi/*Rodentia Interval-Subzone (Ti6) within the Tiffanian Mammal Age. The definition of the Ti6-Cf1 lineage-zone can be found in the same discussion. We define the Rodentia/*Plesiadapis cookei* Interval-Subzone to include faunas that occur during the time between the first appearance of the Rodentia and the first appearance of *P. cookei*. It can be further noted that "the Clark-forkian part of the *P. gingerichi* zone [= Cf1 interval-subzone] is recognized by the mutual occurrence of *P. gingerichi* and any of the taxa characterizing the beginning of the Clarkforkian: *Paramys, Coryphodon, Esthonyx,* or *Haplomylus*" (Rose 1981*a*, p. 27).

At present, the *Plesiadapis gingerichi/P. cookei* Lineage-Zone can be recognized with certainty only within the Clark's Fork Basin, probably because there are few other localities of early Clarkforkian age. The only other local fauna (in addition to those from the type area in the Clark's Fork Basin) that can tentatively be referred to the Ti6-Cf1 lineage-zone is that of Bear Creek. This local fauna occurs at the northern end of Clark's Fork Basin in southern Montana. Although this local fauna lacks *P. gingerichi*, the joint occurrence of *Chiromyoides potior, Carpolestes nigridens, Phenaco-daptes sabulosus,* and *Haplomylus simpsoni* and the absence of *Plesiadapis cookei* argues for reference to the *Plesiadapis gingerichi/P. cookei* Lineage-Zone (Rose 1981*a*). Further, the presence of *Acritoparamys atavus* (Korth 1984) supports the argument that this local fauna is referable to the Clarkforkian portion of this lineage-zone (Rose 1981) (= Cf1 interval-subzone). As noted in the discussion of the Tiffanian/Clarkforkian boundary, there are three areas where this boundary may be preserved (the Togwotee Pass area and Hoback Basin, western Wyoming, and Plateau Valley, Colorado); thus, there is some possibility of recovering additional fossils referable to the *P. gingerichi/P. cookei* Lineage-Zone in the future.

As is the case for the fauna of the Ti6 interval-subzone of the *Plesiadapis gingerichi/P. cookei* Lineage-Zone, the fauna of the Cf1 interval-subzone is poorly known. This probably accounts for the absence of some characteristic Clarkforkian forms from this interval-sub-zone (e.g., *Plagiomene accola, Worlandia inusitata, Ignacius graybullianus, Aletodon gunnelli, Dissacus praenuntius, Oxyaena aeguidens,* and *Uintacyon rudis*).

Occurrences for the taxa listed below are given in table 3.2.

First appearances: *Acritoparamys, Apatemys, Apatosciuravus, Apheliscus, Coryphodon, Haplomylus, Leipsanolestes, Paramys, Planetetherium.*

Last appearances: *Haplolambda, Lambertocyon, Phenacodaptes, Plesiadapis gingerichi.*

Index fossils: *Prosthecion, Protentomodon.*

Characteristic fossils: *Aletodon, Barylambda, Carpolestes, Chiromyoides, Cyriacotherium*(?), *Diacocherus, Didymictis, Dipsalodon*(?), *Dissacus, Ectocion,*

Ectoganus, Esthonyx, Microcosmodon, Neoliotomus, Oxyaena, Palaeosinopa, Peradectes(?), *Phenacodus, Phenacolemur, Plesiadapis dubius, Probathyopsis, Prochetodon, Prolimnocyon*(?), *Thryptacodon, Viverravus.*

Taxa absent but known before and after Cf1: *Arctostylops, Chriacus, Dipsalodon, Ectypodus, Ignacius, Labidolemur,* cf. *Leptacodon packi, Micromomys, Palaeoryctes, Parectypodus, Prodiacodon.*

Plesiadapis cookei Lineage-Zone (Cf2)

Plesiadapis cookei is restricted to the middle of the Clarkforkian Mammal Age, and its appearance marks the beginning of the lineage-zone bearing its name. It is relatively common in this interval, accounting for up to 11 percent of the individuals in subintervals (Rose 1981*a*). It disappears abruptly and without issue in the Clark's Fork Basin section and apparently elsewhere, and its conspicuous absence is characteristic of the succeeding *Phenacodus-Ectocion* Acme-Zone. Based on these data, we define this lineage-zone to include faunas that occur between the first and last appearances of *Plesiadapis cookei*.

In the Clark's Fork Basin section, the *Plesiadapis cookei* Lineage-Zone can also be recognized by the overlapping ranges of *Aletodon gunnelli* and *Microcosmodon rosei,* the former species appearing at the beginning of the interval zone and the latter disappearing at about the end. Several other species first or last appear during this lineage-zone (see list below). Within the Clark's Fork Basin, local faunas referable to the lineage-zone occur in the middle 656 ft. (200 m) of strata containing Clarkforkian faunas.

Of the three Clarkforkian zones, the *Plesiadapis cookei* Lineage-Zone (Cf2) can be recognized over the widest geographic area. The first series of sites to be noted is to the south and east of Clark's Fork Basin in the Bighorn Basin. The major sites are Rough Gulch, Foster Gulch, and Ries localities. The first two localities have produced *Plesiadapis cookei,* suggesting assignment to Cf2. Rose (1981*a*) reported that one of the largest and most diverse Clarkforkian assemblages outside of the Bighorn Basin occurs in the Togwotee Pass area in northwestern Wyoming. As noted earlier, there is the possibility that the Tiffanian/Clarkforkian boundary is preserved in this section, but the Clarkforkian assemblages so far discovered appear to be referable definitely only to Cf2, in part because *P. cookei* occurs. Lower localities that are less well known and lack *P. cookei* may belong to the Ti6-Cf1 lineage-zone and thus preserve the Tiffanian/Clarkforkian boundary. The local fauna from the La Barge area (= Buckman Hollow) of the Green River Basin, Wyoming, is one of the few mammalian assemblages originally assigned to the Clarkforkian Mammal Age (Gazin 1942, 1956c). Among other occurrences, the presence of *P. cookei* in this local fauna suggests referral to Cf2. The final area that has yielded mammals definitely belonging to the *Plesiadapis cookei* Lineage-Zone (including the namesake) is in Bitter Creek, the Washakie Basin, Wyoming. The single site of Clarkforkian age from this area, the Big Multi Locality, has produced a large and diverse assemblage (Rose 1981a). All but one of the mammals from the site, a *Navajovius*-like microsyopid, have been recovered from the type area for the Clarkforkian Mammal Age. However, two genera common in the type Clarkforkian assemblage, *Coryphodon* and *Haplomylus*, are absent from Big Multi. As noted above, both the Hoback Basin, Wyoming, and Plateau Valley, Colorado, have also produced Clarkforkian assemblages, but assignment to Cf2 or another zone is uncertain at present.

Occurrences for the taxa listed below are given in table 3.2.

First appearances: *Aletodon gunnelli, Esthonyx ancylion, Franimys, Ignacius graybullensis, Microsyops, Niptomomys, Palaeanodon, Phenacolemur simonsi,* cf. *Plagioctenodon krausae, Plagiomene,* cf. *Pontifactor bestiola, Tinimomys, Uintacyon, Worlandia.*

Last appearances: *Chiromyoides, Esthonyx xenicus, Microcosmodon, Prochetodon.*

Index fossils: *Chiromyoides major, Plesiadapis cookei.*

Characteristic fossils: *Acritoparamys*(?), *Aletodon, Apatemys, Apatosciuravus, Apheliscus, Arctostylops, Barylambda, Carpolestes, Chriacus*(?), *Coryphodon, Cyriacotherium, Diacocherus, Didymictis, Dipsalodon, Dissacus, Ectocion, Ectoganus, Ectypodus, Esthonyx, Haplomylus, Ignacius, Labidolemur, Leipsanolestes,* cf. *Leptacodon packi, Neoliotomus, Oxyaena, Palaeoryctes, Palaeosinopa, Paramys, Parectypodus, Peradectes, Phenacodus, Phenacolemur, Planetetherium*(?), *Plesiadapis dubius, Probathyopsis, Prodiacodon*(?), *Prolimnocyon*(?), *Thryptacodon, Viverravus.*

Taxa absent but known before and after Cf2: *Micromomys.*

Phenacodus-Ectocion Acme-Zone (Cf3)

According to Rose (1981a), the beginning of the *Phenacodus-Ectocion* Acme-Zone occurs immediately following the last appearance of *Plesiadapis cookei.* This acme-zone can be "further recognized by the evolutionary first occurrence of *Esthonyx grangeri* and *Phenacolemur praecox* (which make their appearance during but not at

the beginning of the zone)" (ibid., p. 28). For the present, we do not offer a formal definition of this zone. The above comments, with the additional note that the end of this zone is marked by the appearance of the Artiodactyla, can be used to recognize the zone. Common taxa during this zone are *Ectocion, Phenacodus, Probathyopsis,* and *Didymictis.*

Outside of the Clark's Fork and Bighorn basins, no assemblages can be referred with certainty to the *Phenacodus-Ectocion* Acme-Zone. In addition to the sites of uncertain age noted in the discussions of the other two Clarkforkian zones, two sites from the Big Bend area of Texas may be referable to the Clarkforkian Mammal Age, with one possibly belonging to the Cf3 acme-zone. This site, Southwall, produced only two taxa, *Hyracotherium angustidens* and *Barylambda* sp. (Schiebout 1974). As Rose (1981a) indicates, the presence of *Hyracotherium* elsewhere suggests a Wasatchian age because this genus is not known from any definitely identified Clarkforkian site. In contrast, *Barylambda* is known from Tiffanian sites in the Bighorn and Clark's Fork basins in Wyoming, the Clarkforkian site of Buckman Hollow in Wyoming, and the latest Tiffanian or earliest Clarkforkian sites from Plateau Valley in Colorado (Gingerich and Childress 1983). It is also known from a Wasatchian site in Baja California (Flynn and Novacek 1984). Coupling these data with the observation that the first appearance of *Hyracotherium* is a better indicator of age than the last appearance of *Barylambda,* Southwall is likely to be Wasatchian in age.

Occurrences for the taxa listed below are given in table 3.2.

First appearances: *Esthonyx grangeri, Hyopsodus, Mimoperadectes*(?), *Phenacolemur praecox.*

Last appearances: *Arctostylops, Aletodon, Apheliscus nitidus, Carpolestes, Cyriacotherium, Diacocherus, Dipsalodon*(?), *Dissacus praenuntius, Esthonyx ancylion, Haplomylus simpsoni, Palaeoryctes, Plesiadapis.*

Index fossils: *Palaeonictis peloria*(?) (but rare).

Characteristic fossils: *Acritoparamys*(?), *Apatemys, Apatosciuravus, Apheliscus, Barylambda*(?), *Chriacus, Coryphodon, Didymictis, Dissacus, Ectocion, Ectoganus, Ectypodus, Esthonyx, Ignacius, Leipsanolestes,* cf. *Leptacodon packi, Microsyops, Niptomomys, Oxyaena, Palaeanodon, Palaeosinopa, Paramys, Peradectes, Phenacodus, Phenacolemur, Plagiomene, Probathyopsis, Prodiacodon*(?), *Thryptacodon, Uintacyon, Viverravus, Worlandia.*

Taxa absent but known before and after Cf3: *Franimys, Labidolemur, Micromomys, Parectypodus,* cf. *Plagioctenodon krausae,* cf. *Pontifactor bestiola, Prolimnocyon, Neoliotomus, Tinimomys.*

INTERCONTINENTAL CORRELATIONS AND CONCLUSIONS

The North American mammalian succession of Puercan through Clarkforkian mammal ages is the best known such succession in the world. Other successions are either less complete or only now being fully examined. Here, we will briefly discuss and correlate the other age-equivalent faunas. A fuller global treatment and more complete comparison of mammalian paleofaunas is provided by Savage and Russell (1983).

Europe

Correlation of North American faunas to European faunas not only involves the more specific comparisons of fossil mammals but also the more general determination of the Paleocene/Eocene boundary. This would also be the case for the Late Cretaceous/Paleocene boundary, but no earliest Paleocene mammalian faunas have been reported from Europe or elsewhere in the world. As discussed under the section dealing with the Lancian/ Puercan boundary, the lack of any detailed correlations between continental and marine sections makes determination of the Upper Cretaceous/Paleocene boundary in continental sections speculative at best. The situation is improved for the Paleocene/Eocene boundary, but even this boundary has long been controversial. This is due, in part, to a paucity of detailed, well-correlated marine and continental biostratigraphic sections spanning the boundary and, in part, to ambiguity in the original definition of "Paleocene."

"Paleocene" was originally used chronostratigraphically by Schimper (1874), a paleobotanist, for floras from the *Sables de Bracheux* (Thanetian), *Travertins Anciens de Sézanne* (Thanetian), and *Lignites et Grès du Soissonais* (Sparnacian and Cuisian, respectively) in the Paris Basin (France). At the same time, he included the London Clay (Sparnacian/Cuisian) and its fossil floras in the Eocene Series. In other words, French Sparnacian and Cuisian beds were included in the Paleocene, whereas their English equivalents were included in the Eocene Series. This contradiction in usage is the source of much ambiguity in placement of the Paleocene/Eocene boundary, making a redefinition desirable (Pomerol 1969; Schorn 1971; Gingerich 1975b).

Paleobotanists sometimes place the Paleocene/ Eocene boundary at the top of the Paris Basin Cuisian Stage or Substage (top of Planktonic Foraminiferal Zone P9) or between the Sparnacian and Cuisian (top of Zone P7). Invertebrate paleontologists sometimes place the boundary between the Sparnacian and Cuisian stages (top of Zone P7), at the base of the Ypresian Stage (base of Zone P6b; Berggren 1972), or at the base of the London Clay (base of Zone P6a; Curry et al. 1978). Vertebrate paleontologists generally place the Paleocene/ Eocene boundary at the base of the Sparnacian Stage in the Paris Basin (base of Planktonic Foramimiferal Zone P5; D. E. Russell 1967, 1968), reflecting the profound change from a mammalian fauna dominated by archaic multituberculates, plesiadapiform primates, and condylarths to one dominated by modern orders (e.g., Rodentia, Perissodactyla, Artiodactyla).

Added to this complexity of definitions of the Paleocene/Eocene boundary in Europe is the problem of correlating North American mammal ages to the type areas in Europe. Some authors have argued that the Paleocene/Eocene boundary falls at the base of what we call the *Plesiadapis cookei* Lineage-Zone (Cf2) (Gingerich 1976; Gingerich and Rose 1977; Rose 1981a). This is based largely on what are thought to be parallel lineages of *Plesiadapis* in the Bighorn and Paris basins. Rose (1981a) noted "that the early Clarkforkian (*P. gingerichi* Zone) correlates most closely with the upper *P. tricuspidens* Zone (latest Thanetian, late Paleocene), whereas the middle Clarkforkian (*P. cookei* Zone) correlates most closely with the *P. russelli* Zone (early Sparnacian = early Ypresian, early Eocene)." He also indicated that this correlation suggests that rodents, *Esthonyx,* and *Coryphodon* reached Europe after their first appearance in North America (which occurs at the beginning of the Clarkforkian Mammal Age). Similarly, *Hyracotherium* may occur slightly earlier in Europe than in the Western Interior of North America. He argued that earlier reports (Jepsen and Woodburne 1969) of pre-Wasatchian *Hyracotherium* in the Clark's Fork Basin are very doubtful; a fauna from Baja California containing *Hyracotherium* that was first thought to be Paleocene in age now seems to be Wasatchian (Flynn and Novacek 1984) in age. This leaves the Southwall Locality from Texas (Schiebout 1974) as the only possible pre-Wasatchian locality bearing *Hyracotherium,* although a Wasatchian age seems likeliest.

More recently, Wing (1984) has argued that the Paleocene/Eocene boundary falls within the lower part of the Wasatchian Mammal Age rather than within the Clarkforkian Mammal Age as advocated by Rose and Gingerich. This is based on the presumed first appearance of the Eocene index pollen species, *Platycarya platycaryoides,* in sediments bearing Wasatchian mammals. *P. platycaryoides* first occurs at or near the boundary of the standard nannofossil zones 9 and 10 in marine sections from Alabama, California, South Carolina, and Virginia (Wing 1984). This same boundary is also the generally accepted Paleocene/Eocene boundary in marine sections. Based on his work on pantodonts, Lucas drew similar conclusions to those of Wing and argued that the Paleocene/Eocene boundary falls within the Wasatchian Mammal Age (S. Lucas, unpublished data and pers. comm. to JDA 1984).

Although redefinition and correlation of the Paleocene/Eocene boundary is certainly important, it is beyond the scope and intent of this chapter. Briefly, the position taken by Wing is defensible based on our greater ability to correlate pollen and marine nannofossils on an intercontinental scale. For now, however, we have questionably retained the Paleocene/Eocene boundary at the boundary of the Cf1 and Cf2 lineage-zones (indicated in fig. 3.2 by a dotted line). Of more concern here is the intercontinental correlation of mammalian faunas at the level of the mammal age, or, if possible, even zonal level, and the way in which our discussions of the Paleocene/Eocene boundary affect such correlations. There are, however, two older Paleocene local faunas in Europe which are not affected by the controversies surrounding the placement of the Paleocene/Eocene boundary.

The oldest European Paleocene mammalian fauna is the Hainin Local Fauna from the type area of the Montian Stage (or substage of the Danian Stage) in Belgium (Russell et al. 1982). This local fauna includes endemic taxa mixed with North American forms which suggest affinity with the Torrejonian Mammal Age (Vianey-Liaud 1979, Savage and Russell 1983). The second-oldest assemblage appears to be the Walbeck Local Fauna of central Germany. Based solely on stage of evolution, this fissure-fill assemblage appears to be late middle Paleocene (Russell et al. 1982). It could be the temporal equivalent of the early Tiffanian Mammal Age and correlate with the earliest Thanetian marine deposits (Savage and Russell 1983).

Disagreements over age assignments and correlation become evident with the next group of local faunas. These are grouped as the Cernaysian localities by Russell et al. (1982) and include about ten localities, mostly in the Paris Basin of northern France (Savage and Russell 1983). They have not yielded any of the larger herbivores such as pantodonts or uintatheres known from presumably comparable faunas in North America or Asia. As discussed above, Rose (1981a; Gingerich 1976; Gingerich and Rose 1977) uses lineages of plesiadapids in North America and Europe to argue that the Ti6-Cf1 lineage-zone is a temporal equivalent of at least the younger Cernaysian faunas, which thus, according to these arguments, correlate with the Tiffanian/Clarkfork-

ian boundary. The Cernaysian faunas correlate to the later part of the Thanetian Age; accordingly, they, and at least the Ti6-Cf1 lineage-zone, would represent the latest Paleocene faunas in Europe and North America, respectively. Wing's (1984) correlation (following Costa et al. 1978) would suggest that the Cernaysian faunas are somewhat older and would correlate with later Tiffanian, rather than earlier Clarkforkian, faunas. As noted above, his correlation places the Paleocene/Eocene boundary within the Wasatchian Mammal Age, considerably later than the above faunas. As was also noted above, Lucas similarly places the epochal boundary within the Wasatchian Mammal Age. However, he considers the Cernaysian faunas to be younger than Wing, Rose, or Gingerich do, suggesting they correlate with the Cf2 lineage-zone.

Asia

Paleocene mammals have been discovered in both China and Mongolia. Because of the quickened pace of recovery of Paleocene mammals from China, suggested correlations are tentative. Faunal equivalents of the Puercan Mammal Age have not been documented at this time.

The multituberculate *Buginbaatar transaltaiensis* from the Buginstav Basin of Mongolia is believed to be earlier Paleocene in age (Trofimov 1975, Savage and Russell 1983). Considerably more material has been recovered from China. Li and Ting (1983) record nine different major collecting areas for the Paleocene Epoch. Of these, three basins (Nan-xiong, Chi-jiang, and Qian-shan) have produced early to late Paleocene faunas that Li and Ting correlate to the "Dragonian" (= To1 interval-zone) through Tiffanian mammal ages of North America. Another basin (Tan-tou) is noted as having early to late Paleocene faunas, but reference to North American mammal ages are not given. The Cha-ling Basin is said to have produced early through middle Paleocene faunas and is correlated to the Torrejonian Mammal Age by Li and Ting. Localities from the Xuan-cheng and Turpan basins and the Nao-mu-gen area have yielded faunas of late Paleocene age which they correlate with the Tiffanian Mammal Age. Finally, the Shi-men Basin has produced a few mammals that they simply refer to the Paleocene. Except for those faunas from the Turpan Basin, which is in northwestern China, all of the faunas come from eastern China.

Clearly, China has already proven to have faunal sequences that may soon rival those in North America. Some interesting faunal patterns are already appearing between North America and China, such as the greater abundance of pantodonts and anagalidans in China compared to North America. This suggests a considerable degree of endemism, or at least faunal separation of the two areas. At the same time, there are supposed notoungulates and edentates in China, suggesting a faunal tie to South America, presumably via North America (see Savage and Russell 1983).

A last fauna to note is the Gashato Fauna from Mongolia. Savage and Russell indicate that similarities of the Gashato Fauna to the early Eocene fauna from the Naran Bulak Formation, also in Mongolia, have been used to suggest that these two are contemporaneous (Dashzeveg and McKenna 1977, Rose 1980). They imply that a later Paleocene age for the Gashato Fauna is also possible because, unlike the fauna from the Naran Bulak Formation, it lacks *Hyopsodus,* a tapiroid, *Altanius* (an omomyid primate), *Pachyaena, Coryphodon,* and a hyaenodontid. More recently, D. E. Russell (pers. comm. to JDA 1985) has further clarified the situation for Naran Bulak. He reports that there are two faunal levels at Naran Bulak: one "is essentially the same as that of Gashato, and overlying it is a Holarctic early Eocene fauna." Thus, both Gashato and a lower fauna of Naran Bulak could be late Paleocene.

Africa

A fauna from the Ouarzazte Basin, Morocco, constitutes the only suggested Paleocene fauna from Africa (Cappetta et al. 1978). It includes palaeoryctids, creodonts, and possible carnivores and is associated with chondrichthyean and osteichthyean fishes and reptiles. On the basis of some of the chondrichthyeans and invertebrates, the fauna appears to be Montian or earlier Paleocene in age (Savage and Russell 1983).

South America

Within the Cenozoic Era, the earliest known faunas from South America are not earlier than late Paleocene in age. This is determined primarily by the superposition of the mammal-bearing Rio Chico Formation on the marine Salamanca Formation; the latter unit has been correlated with the Dano-Montian Stage of Europe based on foraminiferans (Loeblich and Tappan 1957, Savage and Russell 1983). The five or so faunas from the Rio Chico Formation occur in the southern part of Argentina near the Atlantic coast. The Itaboraí Fauna of Brazil, inland from Rio de Janeiro, can be approximately correlated with the Rio Chico faunas. Together, the Itaboraí and Rio Chico faunas include what is known of the Riochican Mammal Age, which is late Paleocene in age (Simpson 1940; Marshall et al. 1977; Savage and Russell 1983).

These fauna are notably endemic, with a variety of marsupials, edentates, native South American ungulates, and condylarths. One group of the native ungulates, the Notoungulata, has been reported from the Paleocene of China and North America, whereas the edentates have been reported from China. Only some of the condylarths suggest definite faunal ties to areas outside of South America.

CONCLUSIONS

Since the publication of Wood et al. (1941) some forty years ago, our knowledge of North American land mammal ages has been greatly enhanced. This is particularly true for the Puercan through Clarkforkian mammal ages, which have helped to firmly entrench the concept of a Paleocene Series/Epoch in the paleontological and geologic literature. This does not mean we have anything approaching a firm biochronostratigraphic framework for the continental rocks deposited in western North America during this interval of time. The definitions and characterizations of the mammal ages and zones included in this chapter still rest heavily on faunal data, but the increased emphasis on tighter stratigraphic controls for these faunas suggests that a truly chronostratigraphic framework (stages) is not unrealistically far ahead. Such a suggestion for one of the mammal ages included in this chapter, the Clarkforkian Mammal Age, has already appeared (Rose 1981).

Clearly, if one is to suggest an agenda for future progress in further refining the Puercan through Clarkforkian mammal ages, the development of a chronostratigraphic framework would head this list. This will require even more detailed biostratigraphic and stratigraphic fieldwork coupled with continued emphasis on systematic work and faunal correlation. More specifically and more immediately, there are a number of aspects of these particular mammal ages and zones that require attention. Rather than list all of them, we note only a few in approximate geochronologic order, oldest to youngest.

First, there is the need for a thorough, systematic review of many Puercan taxa, especially among the condylarths, such as arctocyonids. A more thorough, more detailed review of most families of condylarths will be of benefit for the later mammal ages discussed in this chapter. Other Puercan mammals, for example, the taeniolabidids, are now being reexamined in the light of new discoveries so that the systematics of such biostratigraphically important groups will be more fully understood.

Second, the Puercan/Torrejonian boundary represents a gap in our knowledge of the mammalian faunas.

Sediments yielding mammals of Torrejonian age definitely overlie (or can be closely correlated to) sediments yielding mammals of Puercan age both in the San Juan Basin and on the Wasatch Plateau. The sediments between those yielding Puercan and Torrejonian faunas in both areas, however, are largely unfossiliferous. Another area with possible superposition of Torrejonian over Puercan faunas in the type area of the Hell Creek Formation, Montana, warrants further study.

Third, neither the Torrejonian/Tiffanian boundary nor the Ti1/Ti2 boundary are well understood at the present time. As discussed earlier, a probable superpositional relationship of Tiffanian over Torrejonian faunas exists in the Clark's Fork-Bighorn Basin, Wyoming. A similar but stratigraphically less tightly controlled situation occurs in the Crazy Mountain Basin, Montana. One difficulty in placing the Torrejonian/Tiffanian boundary is attributable to the differences between northern and southern Torrejonian faunas (e.g., the lack of plesiadapids in southern Torrejonian faunas).

Fourth, although faunas are now known bracketing the Tiffanian/Clarkforkian boundary, particularly in the Clark's Fork Basin, the latest Tiffanian faunas remain to be more fully documented. This may lead to a fuller characterization of the *Plesiadapis gingerichi*/Rodentia Interval-Subzone (Ti6), which for the present can only be definitely recognized by the appearance of the name-bearing taxon. Similarly, within the Clarkforkian Mammal Age, it would be desirable to modify or recast the *Phenacodus-Ectocion* Acme-Zone (Cf3) as a lineage-zone or, preferably, as an interval-zone to enhance its utility in faunal correlation, provided that taxa appropriate for this purpose can be found.

Fifth, and finally, there is the need to expand the magnetostratigraphic framework so as to encompass more of the mammal-producing sections, which, in turn, will provide additional checks on faunal correlation throughout the Western Interior of North America. Where possible, radiometric dates should also be obtained in association with mammal-bearing sediments to provide better calibration points outside of the Western Interior.

REFERENCES

Archibald, J. D. 1981. The earliest known Palaeocene mammal fauna and its implications for the Cretaceous-Tertiary transition. Nature 291: 650–652.

————. 1982. A study of Mammalia and geology across the Cretaceous-Tertiary boundary in Garfield County, Montana. Univ. Calif. Publ. Geol. Sci. 122:1–286.

————. 1984. Bug Creek Anthills (BCA), Montana: Faunal evidence for Cretaceous age and non-catastrophic extinctions. Abstr. with Programs, 97th Ann. Mtg. Geol. Soc. Amer. 16:432.

————. In press. Stepwise and non-catastrophic late Cretaceous terrestrial extinctions in the Western Interior of North America: Testing observations in the context of a historical science. Mém. Soc. Géol. France.

Archibald, J. D., R. F. Butler, E. H. Lindsay, W. A. Clemens, and L. Dingus 1982. Upper Cretaceous-Paleocene biostratigraphy and magnetostratigraphy, Hell Creek and Tullock formations, northeastern Montana. Geology 10:153–159.

Archibald, J. D., and W. A. Clemens. 1982. Late Cretaceous extinctions. Amer. Sci. 70:377–385.

————. 1984. Mammal evolution near the Cretaceous-Tertiary boundary. In Catastrophes in earth history: The New Uniformitarianism, eds. W. A. Berggren and J. A. Van Couvering. Princeton: Princeton Univ. Press. Pp. 339–371.

Archibald, J. D., J. K. Rigby, Jr., and S. F. Robison. 1983a. Systematic revision of *Oxyacodon* (Condylarthra, Periptychidae) and a description of *O. ferronensis* n. sp. J. Paleont. 57:53–72.

Archibald, J. D., R. M. Schoch, and J. K. Rigby, Jr. 1983b. A new subfamily, Conacodontinae, and new species, *Conacodon kohlbergeri*, of the Periptychidae (Condylarthra, Mammalia). Postilla 191:1–24.

Berggren, W. A. 1972. A Cenozoic time-scale: Some implications for regional geology and paleobiogeography. Lethaia 5:195–215.

Berggren, W. A., D. V. Kent, J. J. Flynn, and J. A. Van Couvering. 1985. Cenozoic geochronology. Bull. Geol. Soc. Amer. 96:1407–1418.

Bown, T. M., and P. D. Gingerich. 1973. The Paleocene primate *Plesiolestes* and the origin of the Microsyopidae. Folia Primatol. 19:1–8.

Brown, R. W. 1943. Cretaceous-Tertiary boundary in the Denver Basin, Colorado. Bull. Geol. Soc. Amer. 54:65–86.

————. 1952. Tertiary strata in eastern Montana and western North and South Dakota. Billings Geol. Field Guidebk. 3:89–92.

Butler, R. F., E. H. Lindsay, and P. D. Gingerich. 1980. Magnetic polarity stratigraphy and Paleocene-Eocene biostratigraphy of Polecat Bench, northwestern Wyoming. In Early Cenozoic paleontology and stratigraphy of the Bighorn Basin, Wyoming, 1880–1980, ed. P. D. Gingerich. Univ. Mich. Papers Paleont. 24:95–98.

Butler, R. F., P. D. Gingerich, and E. H. Lindsay. 1981. Magnetic polarity stratigraphy and biostratigraphy of Paleocene and lower Eocene continental deposits, Clark's Fork Basin, Wyoming. J. Geol. 89:299–316.

Butler, R. F., and E. H. Lindsay. 1985. Mineralogy of magnetic minerals and revised magnetic polarity stratigraphy of continental sediments, San Juan Basin, New Mexico. J. Geol. 94:535–554.

Butler, R. F., E. H. Lindsay, L. L. Jacobs, and N. M. Johnson. 1977. Magnetostratigraphy of the Cretaceous-Tertiary boundary in the San Juan Basin, New Mexico. Nature 267:318–323.

Cappetta, H., J.-J. Jaeger, M. Sabatier, J. Sudre, and M. Vianey-Liaud. 1978. Decouverte dans le Paléocène du Maroc des plus anciens mammifères eutheriens d'Afrique. Gèobios 11:257–263.

Clemens, W. A. 1964. Fossil mammals of the type Lance Formation, Wyoming. Pt. I: Introduction and Multituberculata. Univ. Calif. Publ. Geol. Sci. 48:1–105.

———. 1966. Fossil mammals of the type Lance Formation, Wyoming. Pt. II: Marsupialia. Univ. Calif. Publ. Geol. Sci. 62:1–122.

———. 1973. Fossil mammals of the type Lance Formation, Wyoming. Pt. III: Eutheria and Summary. Univ. Calif. Publ. Geol. Sci. 94:1–102.

———. 1974. *Purgatorius,* an early paromomyid primate (Mammalia). Science 184:903–905.

Clemens, W. A., J. A. Lillegraven, E. H. Lindsay, and G. G. Simpson. 1979. Where, When, and What—A survey of known Mesozoic mammal distribution. In Mesozoic mammals: The first two-thirds of mammalian history, eds. J. A. Lillegraven, Z. Kielan-Jaworowska, and W. A. Clemens, 7–58. Berkeley, Los Angeles, London: Univ. Calif. Press.

Conroy, G. C. 1981. A review of the Torrejonian (middle Paleocene) primates from the San Juan Basin, New Mexico. In Advances in San Juan Basin paleontology, eds. S. G. Lucas, J. K. Rigby, Jr., and B. S. Kues. Albuquerque: Univ. New Mexico Press. Pp. 161–176.

Cope, E. D. 1875. Report on the geology of that part of northwestern New Mexico examined during the field season of 1874. In Ann. Geog. Explor. West of the 100th Mer. and Appendix LL, Ann. Rept. Chief of Engineers for 1875. Pp. 61–97 of separate issue; pp. 981–1017 of full report.

———. 1877. Report upon the extinct Vertebrata obtained in New Mexico by parties of the expedition of 1874. Geog. Surveys West of the 100th Mer., pt. 2:1–370.

———. 1885. The Vertebrata of the Tertiary formations of the West. Book I. Rept. U.S. Geol. Survey Territories, F. V. Hayden in charge, 3:1–1009.

———. 1888. Synopsis of the vertebrate fauna of the Puerco series. Trans. Amer. Phil. Soc., n.s., 16:298–361.

Costa, L., C. Denison, and C. Downie. 1978. The Paleocene/ Eocene boundary in the Anglo-Paris Basin. J. Geol. Soc. 135:261–264.

Curry, D., C. G. Adams, M. C. Boulter, F. C. Dillay, F. E. Eames, B. M. Funnell, and M. K. Wells. 1978. A correlation of Tertiary rocks in the British Isles. Geol. Soc. London, Spec. Report no. 12.

Dashzeveg, D., and M. C. McKenna. 1977. Tarsoid primate from the early Tertiary of the Mongolian People's Republic. Acta Palaeont. Pol. 22:119–137.

Dawson, M. R., C.-K. Li, and T. Qi. 1984. Eocene ctenodactyloid rodents (Mammalia) of eastern and central Asia. Carnegie Mus. Nat. Hist. Spec. Publ. 9:138–150.

Dingus, L. 1984. Effects of stratigraphic completeness on interpretations of extinction rates across the Cretaceous-Tertiary boundary. Paleobiology 10:420–438.

Dorr, J. A., Jr. 1952. Early Cenozoic stratigraphy and vertebrate paleontology of the Hoback Basin, Wyoming. Bull. Geol. Soc. Amer. 63:59–94.

———. 1958. Early Cenozoic vertebrate paleontology, sedimentation and orogeny in central western Wyoming. Bull. Geol. Soc. Amer. 69:1217–1244.

———. 1978. Revised and amended fossil vertebrate faunal lists, early Tertiary, Hoback Basin, Wyoming. Contrib. Geol. Univ. Wyoming 16:79–84.

Dorr, J. A., Jr., and P. D. Gingerich. 1980. Early Cenozoic mammalian paleontology, geologic structure, and tectonic history in the overthrust belt near LaBarge, western Wyoming. Contrib. Geol. Univ. Wyo. 18:101–115.

Dorr, J. A., Jr., D. R. Spearing, and J. R. Steidtmann. 1977. Deformation and deposition between a foreland uplift and an impinging thrust belt, Hoback Basin, Wyoming, Geol. Soc. Amer. Spec. Paper 177:1–82.

Dorr, J. A., Jr., and J. R. Steidtmann. 1970. Stratigraphic-tectonic implications of a new, earliest Eocene, mammalian faunule from central western Wyoming. Mich. Academician 3:25–41.

Douglass, E. 1908. Vertebrate fossils from the Fort Union beds. Ann. Carnegie Mus. 5:11–26.

Flynn, J. J., and M. J. Novacek. 1984. Early Eocene vertebrates from Baja California: Evidence of intracontinental age correlations. Science 224:151–153.

Fox, R. C. 1968. A new paleocene mammal (Condylarthra: Arctocyonidae) from a well in Alberta, Canada. J. Mammal. 49:661–664.

———. 1983. Notes on the North American Tertiary marsupials *Herpetotherium* and *Peradectes.* Can. J. Earth Sci. 20:1565–1578.

———. 1984*a.* First North American record of the Paleocene primate *Saxonella.* J. Paleont. 58:892–894.

———. 1984*b.* The definition and relationships of the Paleocene primate *Micromomys* Szalay, with description of a new species. Can. J. Earth Sci. 21:1262–1267.

———. 1984*c.* A new species of the Paleocene primate *Elphidotarsius* Gidley: Its stratigraphic position and evolutionary relationships. Can. J. Earth Sci. 21:1268–1277.

———. 1984*d. Melaniella timosa* n. gen. and n. sp.: An unusual mammal from the Paleocene of Alberta, Canada. Can. J. Earth Sci. 21:1335–1338.

Gardner, J. H. 1910. The Puerco and Torrejon formations of the Nacimiento Group. J. Geology 18:702–741.

Gazin, C. L. 1938. A Paleocene mammalian fauna from central Utah. J. Wash. Acad. Sci. 28:271–277.

———. 1939. A further contribution to the Dragon Paleocene fauna of central Utah. J. Wash. Acad. Sci. 29:273–286.

———. 1941*a.* Paleocene mammals from the Denver Basin, Colorado. J. Wash. Acad. Sci. 31:289–295.

———. 1941*b.* The mammalian faunas of the Paleocene of central Utah, with notes on the geology. Proc. U.S. Natl. Mus. 91:1–53.

———. 1942. Fossil Mammalia from the Almy Formation in western Wyoming. J. Wash. Acad. Sci. 32:217–220.

———. 1956*a.* The occurrence of fossil mammalian remains

in the Fossil Basin of southwestern Wyoming. J. Paleont. 30:707–711.

———. 1956b. Paleocene mammalian faunas of the Bison Basin in south-central Wyoming. Smithsonian Misc. Coll. 131 (6):1–57.

———. 1956c. The upper Paleocene Mammalia from the Almy Formation in western Wyoming. Smithsonian Misc. Coll. 131 (7):1–18.

———. 1963. Paleocene mammals from the Denver Basin, Colorado. In Guidebook to the geology of the northern Denver Basin and adjacent uplifts. Rocky Mt. Assoc. Geologists, 14th Field Conference. Pp. 167–169.

———. 1968. A new primate from the Torrejon middle Paleocene of the San Juan Basin, New Mexico. Proc. Biol. Soc. Wash. 81:629–634.

———. 1969. A new occurrence of Paleocene mammals in the Evanston Formation of southwest Wyoming. Smithsonian Contrib. Paleobiol. 2:1–17.

———. 1971. Paleocene primates from the Shotgun member of the Fort Union Formation in Wind River Basin, Wyoming. Proc. Biol. Soc. Wash. 84:13–38.

George, T. N., W. D. Harland, D. V. Ager, H. W. Ball, W. H. Blow, R. Casey, C. H. Holland, N. S. Hughes, G. A. Kellaway, P. E. Kent, W. H. C. Ramsbottom, James Stufflefield, and A. W. Woodland. 1969. Recommendations on stratigraphic usage. Proc. Geol. Soc. London 1656:139–166.

Gidley, J. W. 1915. An extinct marsupial from the Fort Union with notes on the Myrmecobidae and other families of this group. Proc. U.S. Natl. Mus. 48:395–402.

———. 1917. Report on Wasatch fossils. (In C. H. Wegemann 1917.) U.S. Geol. Surv. Prof. Papers 108:59.

———. 1923. Paleocene primates of the Fort Union, with discussion of relationships of Eocene primates. Proc. U.S. Natl. Mus. 63:1–38.

Gingerich, P. D. 1975a. New North American Plesiadapidae (Mammalia, Primates) and a biostratigraphic zonation of the middle and upper Paleocene. Contrib. Mus. Paleont. Univ. Mich. 24:135–148.

———. 1975b. Discussion "What is Type Paleocene?" Amer. J. Sci. 275:984–985.

———. 1976. Cranial anatomy and evolution of early Tertiary Plesiadapidae (Mammalia, primates). Univ. Mich. Papers Paleont. 15:1–141.

———. 1977. Aletodon gunnelli, a new Clarkforkian hyopsodontid (Mammalia, Condylarthra) from the early Eocene of Wyoming. Contrib. Mus. Paleont. Univ. Mich. 24:237–244.

———. 1978. New Condylarthra (Mammalia) from the Paleocene and early Eocene of North America. Contrib. Mus. Paleont. Univ. Mich. 25:1–9.

———. 1980a. Tytthaena parrisi, oldest known oxyaenid (Mammalia, Creodenta) from the later Paleocene of western North America. J. Paleont. 54:570–576.

———. 1980b. A new species of Paleosinopa (Insectivora, Pantolestidae) from the late Paleocene of western North America. J. Mammal. 61:449–454.

———. 1980c. Evolutionary patterns in early Cenozoic mammals. Ann. Rev. Earth Planet. Sci. 8:407–424.

———. 1982a. Paleocene "Meniscotherium semicingulatum" and the first appearance of the Meniscotheriidae (Condylarthra) in North America. J. Mammal. 63:488–491.

———. 1982b. Aaptoryctes (Palaeoryctidae) and Thelysia (Palaeoryctidae?): New insectivorous mammals from the late Paleocene and early Eocene of western North America. Contrib. Mus. Paleont. Univ. Mich. 26:37–47.

———. 1983. New Adapisoricidae, Pentacodontidae, and Hyopsodontidae (Mammalia, Insectivora, and Condylarthra) from the late Paleocene of Wyoming and Colorado. Contrib. Mus. Paleont. Univ. Mich. 26:227–255.

Gingerich, P. D., and C. G. Childress 1983. Barylambda churchilli, a new species of Pantolambdidae (Mammalia, Pantodonta) from the late Paleocene of western North America. Contrib. Mus. Paleont. Univ. Mich. 26:141–155.

Gingerich, P. D., and G. F. Gunnell. 1979. Systematics and evolution of the genus Esthonyx (Mammalia, Tillodontia) in the early Eocene of North America. Contrib. Mus. Paleont. Univ. Mich. 25:125–153.

Gingerich, P. D., P. Houde, and D. W. Krause. 1983. A new earliest Tiffanian (late Paleocene) mammalian fauna from Bangtail Plateau, western Crazy Mountain Basin, Montana. J. Paleont. 57:957–970.

Gingerich, P. D., and K. D. Rose. 1977. Preliminary report on the American Clark Fork mammal fauna, and its correlation with similar faunas in Europe and Asia. Geobios Mem. Spec. 1:39–45.

———. 1979. Anterior dentition of the Eocene condylarth Thryptacodon: Convergence with the tooth comb of lemurs. J. Mammal. 50:16–22.

Gingerich, P. D., K. D. Rose, and D. W. Krause. 1980. Early Cenozoic mammalian faunas of the Clark's Fork Basin-Polecat Bench area, northwestern Wyoming. In Early Cenozoic paleontology and stratigraphy of the Bighorn Basin, Wyoming, ed. P. D. Gingerich. Univ. Mich. Papers Paleont. Pp. 51–64.

Gingerich, P. D., and D. A. Winkler. 1985. Systematics of Paleocene Viverravidae (Mammalia, Carnivora) in the Bighorn Basin and Clark's Fork Basin, Wyoming. Contrib. Mus. Paleont. Univ. Mich. 27:87–128.

Granger, W. 1914. On the names of lower Eocene faunal horizons of Wyoming and New Mexico. Bull. Amer. Mus. Nat. Hist. 33:201–207.

———. 1915. A revision of the lower Wasatch and Wind River faunas. Pt. III. Order Condylarthra, families Phenacodontidae and Meniscotheriidae. Bull. Amer. Mus. Nat. Hist. 34:329–361.

———. 1917. Notes on Paleocene and lower Eocene mammal horizons of northern New Mexico and southern Colorado. Bull. Amer. Mus. Nat. Hist. 37:821–830.

Granger, W., and G. G. Simpson. 1929. A revision of the Tertiary Multituberculata. Bull. Amer. Mus. Nat. Hist. 41:601–676.

Hedberg, H. D., ed. 1976. International stratigraphic guide. New York: John Wiley and Sons.

Holtzman, R. C. 1978. Late Paleocene mammals of the Tongue River Formation, western North Dakota. N. Dak. Geol. Surv. Rept. Investig. 65:1–88.

Holtzman, R. C., and D. L. Wolberg. 1977. The Microcosmodontidae and *Microcosmodon woodi*, new multituberculate taxa (Mammalia) from the late Paleocene of North America. Sci. Mus. Minn. Sci. Publ. 4:1–13.

Jepsen, G. L. 1930*a*. New vertebrate fossils from the lower Eocene of the Bighorn Basin, Wyoming. Proc. Amer. Phil. Soc. 69:117–131.

―――. 1930*b*. Stratigraphy and paleontology of the Paleocene of northeastern Park County, Wyoming. Proc. Amer. Phil. Soc. 69:463–528.

―――. 1937. A Paleocene rodent, *Paramys atavus*. Proc. Amer. Phil. Soc. 78:291–301.

―――. 1940. Paleocene faunas of the Polecat Bench Formation, Park County, Wyoming. Pt. I. Proc. Amer. Phil. Soc. 83:217–341.

Jepsen, G. L., and M. O. Woodburne. 1969. Paleocene hyracothere from Polecat Bench Formation, Wyoming. Science 164:543–547.

Johnston, P. A. 1980. First record of Mesozoic mammals from Saskatchewan. Can. J. Earth Sci. 17:512–519.

Johnston, P. A., and R. C. Fox. 1984. Paleocene and late Cretaceous mammals from Saskatchewan, Canada. Palaeontographica A 186:166–222.

Keefer, W. R. 1961. Waltman Shale and Shotgun members of Fort Union Formation (Paleocene) in Wind River Basin, Wyoming. Amer. Assoc. Petrol. Geol. Bull. 45:1310–1323.

Kielan-Jaworowska, Z., and R. E. Sloan. 1979. *Catopsalis* (Multituberculata) from Asia and North America and the problem of taeniolabidoid dispersal in the Late Cretaceous. Acta Palaeont. Pol. 24:187–197.

Korth, W. W. 1984. Earliest Tertiary evolution and radiation of rodents in North America. Bull. Carnegie Mus. Nat. Hist. 24:1–71.

Krause, D. W. 1977. Paleocene multituberculates (Mammalia) of the Roche Percée Local Fauna, Ravenscrag Formation, Saskatchewan, Canada. Palaeontographica A 159:1–36.

―――. 1978. Paleocene primates from western Canada. Can. J. Earth Sci. 15:1250–1271.

―――. 1980. Multituberculates from the Clarkforkian land mammal age, late Paleocene-early Eocene, of western North America. J. Paleont. 54:1163–1183.

Krause, D. W., and P. D. Gingerich. 1983. Mammalian fauna from Douglass Quarry, earliest Tiffanian (late Paleocene) of the eastern Crazy Mountain Basin, Montana. Contrib. Mus. Paleont. Univ. Mich. 26:157–196.

Krishtalka, L. 1973. Late Paleocene mammals from the Cypress Hills, Alberta. Spec. Publ. Mus. Texas Tech. Univ., 2:1–77.

―――. 1976*a*. Early Tertiary Adapisoricidae and Erinaceidae (Mammalia, Insectivora) of North America. Bull. Carnegie Mus. Nat. Hist. 1:1–40.

―――. 1976*b*. North American Nyctitheriidae (Mammalia, Insectivora) Ann. Carnegie Mus. 46:7–28.

Krishtalka, L., C. C. Black, and D. W. Riedel. 1975. Paleontology and geology of the Badwater Creek area, central Wyoming. Ann. Carnegie Mus. 45:179–212.

Krishtalka, L., and R. K. Stucky. 1983. Revision of the Wind River faunas, early Eocene of central Wyoming. Pt. 3: Marsupialia. Ann. Carnegie Mus. 52:205–227.

Li, C.-K., and S.-Y. Ting. 1983. The Paleocene mammals of China. Bull. Carnegie Mus. Nat. Hist. 21:1–93.

Lillegraven, J. A. 1969. Latest Cretaceous mammals of upper part of Edmonton Formation of Alberta, Canada, and review of marsupial-placental dichotomy in mammalian evolution. Univ. Kans. Paleont. Contrib., Art. 50 (Vert. 12):1–122.

Lindsay, E. H., L. L. Jacobs, and R. F. Butler. 1978. Biostratigraphy and magnetostratigraphy of Paleocene terrestrial deposits, San Juan Basin, New Mexico. Geology 6:425–429.

Lindsay, E. H., R. F. Butler, and N. M. Johnson. 1981. Magnetic polarity zonation and biostratigraphy of late Cretaceous and Paleocene continental deposits, San Juan Basin, New Mexico. Amer. J. Sci. 281:390–435.

Loeblich, A. R., and H. Tappan. 1957. Correlation of the Gulf and Atlantic coastal plain Paleocene and lower Eocene formations by means of planktonic Foraminifera. J. Paleont. 31:1109–1137.

Lucas, S. G. 1984*a*. Early Paleocene vertebrates, stratigraphy, and biostratigraphy, West Fork of Gallegos Canyon, San Juan Basin, New Mexico. New Mexico Geology 6:56–60.

―――. 1984*b*. Systematics, biostratigraphy, and evolution of early Cenozoic *Coryphodon* (Mammalia, Pantodonta). Ph.D. diss., Yale Univ.

Lucas, S. G., and F. M. O'Neill. 1981. Occurrence of *Pantolambda* (Mammalia, Pantodonta) in the Torrejonian *Deltatherium* "Zone," San Juan Basin, New Mexico. Amer. J. Sci. 2:187–191.

McGrew, P. O., and B. Patterson. 1962. A picrodontid insectivore(?) from the Paleocene of Wyoming. Breviora, no. 175, pp. 1–9.

MacIntyre, G. T. 1966. The Miacidae (Mammalia, Carnivora) Pt. 1: The Systematics of *Ictidopappus* and *Protictis*. Bull. Amer. Mus. Nat. Hist. 131:115–210.

McKenna, M. C. 1960. A continental Paleocene vertebrate fauna from California. Amer. Mus. Novitates 2024:1–20.

―――. 1961. A note on the origin of rodents. Amer. Mus. Novitates 2037:1–5.

―――. 1972. Vertebrate paleontology of the Togwotee Pass area, northwestern Wyoming. In Guidebook, Field Conference on Tertiary biostratigraphy of southern and western Wyoming, ed. R. M. West. Privately printed. Pp. 80–101.

―――. 1975. Towards a phylogenetic classification of the Mammalia. In Phylogeny of the Primates. eds. W. P. Luckett and F. S. Szalay. New York and London: Plenum Press. Pp. 21–46.

―――. 1980. Late Cretaceous and early Tertiary vertebrate paleontological reconnaissance, Togwotee Pass area, northwestern Wyoming. In Aspects of vertebrate history: Essays in honor of Edwin Harris Colbert, ed. L. L. Jacobs. Flagstaff: Museum Northern Arizona Press. Pp. 321–343.

Marshall, L. G., R. Pascual, G. H. Curtis, and R. E. Drake. 1977. South American geochronology: Radiometric time scale for middle to late Tertiary mammal-bearing horizons in Patagonia. Science 195:1325–1328.

Matthew, W. D. 1897. A revision of the Puerco fauna. Bull. Amer. Mus. Nat. Hist. 9:259–323.

———. 1914. Evidence of the Paleocene vertebrate fauna on the Cretaceous-Tertiary problem. Bull. Geol. Soc. Amer. 25:381–402.

———. 1915a. A revision of the lower Eocene Wasatch and Wind River faunas. Pt. I: Order Ferae (Carnivora), suborder Creodonta. Bull. Amer. Mus. Nat. Hist. 34:4–103.

———. 1915b. A revision of the lower Eocene Wasatch and Wind River faunas. Pt. II: Order Condylarthra, family Hyopsodontidae. Bull. Amer. Mus. Nat. Hist. 34:311–328.

———. 1915c. A revision of the lower Eocene Wasatch and Wind River faunas. Pt. IV: Entelonychia, Primates, Insectivora (part). Bull. Amer. Mus. Nat. Hist. 34:429–483.

———. 1937. Paleocene faunas of the San Juan Basin, New Mexico. Trans. Amer. Phil. Soc., n.s., 30:1–510.

Matthew, W. D., and W. Granger. 1921. New genera of Paleocene mammals. Amer. Mus. Novitates 13:1–7.

Middleton, M. D. 1982. A new species and additional material of *Catopsalis* (Mammalia, Multituberculata) from the Western Interior of North America. J. Paleont. 56:1197–1206.

———. 1983. Early Paleocene vertebrates of the Denver Basin, Colorado. Ph.D. diss., Univ. Colo., Boulder.

Murphy, M. A. 1977. On time-stratigraphic units. J. Paleont. 51:213–219.

North American stratigraphic code. 1983. Amer. Assoc. Petrol. Geol. Bull. 67:841–875.

Novacek, M. J. 1977. A review of Paleocene and Eocene Leptictidae (Eutheria: Mammalia) from North America. Paleobios 24:1–42.

Novacek, M. J., T. M. Bown, and D. Schankler. 1985. On the classification of the early Tertiary Erinaceomorpha (Insectivora, Mammalia). Amer. Mus. Novitates 2813:1–22.

Novacek, M. J., and W. A. Clemens. 1977. Aspects of intrageneric variation and evolution of *Mesodma* (Multituberculata, Mammalia). J. Paleont. 51:701–717.

Osborn, H. F. 1929. The titanotheres of ancient Wyoming, Dakota, and Nebraska. U.S. Geol. Surv. Monogr. 55:1–701.

Osborn, H. F., and C. Earle. 1895. Fossil mammals of the Puerco beds: Collection of 1892. Bull. Amer. Mus. Nat. Hist. 7:1–70.

Osborn, H. F., and W. D. Matthew. 1909. Cenozoic mammal horizons of western North America. Bull. U.S. Geol. Surv. 361:1–138.

Patterson, B. 1933. A new species of the ambylopod *Titanoides* from western Colorado. Amer. J. Sci. 25:415–425.

———. 1936. Mounted skeleton of *Titanoides* with notes on the associated fauna. Proc. Geol. Soc. Amer. 1935:397–398.

———. 1937. A new genus, *Barylambda,* for *Titanoides faberi,* Paleocene ambylopod. Field Mus. Nat. Hist. Geol. Ser. 6:229–231.

———. 1939. New Pantodonta and Dinocerata from the upper Paleocene of western Colorado. Field Mus. Nat. Hist. Geol. Ser. 6:351–384.

———. 1949. A new genus of taeniodonts from the late Paleocene Fieldiana: Geology 10:41–42.

Patterson, B., and P. O. McGrew. 1962. A new arctocyonid from the Paleocene of Wyoming. Breviora 174:1–10.

Patterson, B., and E. L. Simons, 1958. A new barylambdid pantodont from the late Paleocene. Breviora 93:1–8.

Patterson, B., and R. M. West. 1973. A new late Paleocene phenacodont (Mammalia, Condylarthra) from western Colorado. Breviora 403:1–7.

Pomerol, C. 1969. Rapport sur les discussions au sujet de la limite Palèocène-Eocène. Colloque sur l'Eocène. Fr. Bur. Rech. Géol. Minières Mém. 69:447–450.

Rapp, S. D., B. J. MacFadden, and J. A. Schiebout. 1983. Magnetic polarity stratigraphy of the early Tertiary Black Peaks Formation: Big Bend National Park, Texas. J. Geol. 91:555–572.

Repenning, C. A. 1967. Palearctic-Nearctic mammalian dispersal in the late Cenozoic. In The Bering land bridge, ed. D. M. Hopkins. Stanford: Stanford Univ. Press. Pp. 288–311.

Reynolds, T. E. 1936. Two new insectivores from the lower Paleocene of New Mexico. J. Paleont. 10:202–209.

Rigby, J. K., Jr. 1980. Swain Quarry of the Fort Union Formation, middle Paleocene (Torrejonian), Carbon County, Wyoming: Geologic setting and mammalian fauna. Evol. Monogr. 3:1–179.

———. 1981. A skeleton of *Gillisonchus gillianus* (Mammalia, Condylarthra) from the early Paleocene (Puercan) Ojo Alamo Sandstone, San Juan Basin, New Mexico, with comments on the local stratigraphy of Betonnie-Tsosie Wash. In Advances in San Juan Basin paleontology, eds. S. G. Lucas, J. K. Rigby, Jr., and B. S. Kues. Albuquerque: Univ. New Mexico Press. Pp. 89–126.

Rigby, J. K., Jr., and S. G. Lucas. 1977. Fossil mammals from the Ojo Alamo Sandstone. New Mexico Geol. Soc. Guidebook, 28th Field Conf., supplement. Pp. 55–56.

Robison, S. F. 1980. Paleocene (Puercan-Torrejonian) mammalian faunas of the North Horn Formation, central Utah. M.S. thesis, Brigham Young Univ., Provo.

Romer, A. S. 1966. Vertebrate paleontology. Chicago: Univ. Chicago Press.

Rose, K. D. 1975. The Carpolestidae—Early Tertiary primates from North America. Bull. Mus. Comp. Zool. 147:1–74.

———. 1977. Evolution of carpolestid primates and chronology of the North American middle and late Paleocene. J. Paleont. 51:536–542.

———. 1978. A new Paleocene epoicotheriid (Mammalia), with comments on the Palaeanodonta. J. Paleont. 52:658–674.

———. 1979. A new Paleocene palaeanodont and the origin of the Metacheiromyidae (Mammalia). Breviora 455:1–14.

———. 1980. Clarkforkian land-mammal age: Revised definition, zonation, and tentative intercontinental correlation. Science 208:744–746.

———. 1981a. The Clarkforkian land-mammal age and mammalian faunal composition across the Paleocene-Eocene boundary. Univ. Mich. Papers Paleont. 26:1–197.

———. 1981b. Composition and species diversity in

Paleocene and Eocene mammal assemblages: An empirical study. J. Vert. Paleont. 1:367–388.

Rose, K. D., and T. M. Bown. 1982. New plesiadapiform primates from the Eocene of Wyoming and Montana. J. Vert. Paleont. 2:63–69.

Rose, K. D., and D. W. Krause. 1982. Cyriacotheriidae: A new family of early Tertiary pantodonts from western North America. Proc. Amer. Phil. Soc. 126:26–50.

Russell, D. E. 1967. Le Paléocène continental d'Amerique du Nord. Mém. Mus. Nat. d'Hist. Natur., Série C, vol. 16:1–99.

———. 1968. Succession, en Europe, des faunes mammaliennes au debut du Tertiaire. Fr. Bur. Rech. Geol. Minieres Mem. 58:291–296.

———. 1980. Sur les condylarthres Cernaysiens Tricuspiodon et Landenodon (Paléocène supérieur de France). Palaeovert. Mem. Jubil. R. Lavocat, pp. 127–166.

Russell, D. E., J.-L. Hartenberger, C. Pomerol, S. Sen, N. Schmidt-Kittler, and M. Vianey-Liaud. 1982. Mammals and stratigraphy: The Paleocene of Europe. Palaeovert. Mem. Extraord.: 1–77.

Russell, L. S. 1926. A new species of the genus Catopsalis Cope from the Paskapoo Formation of Alberta. Amer. J. Sci. 212:230–234.

———. 1929. Paleocene vertebrates from Alberta. Amer. J. Sci. 217:162–178.

———. 1932. New data on the Paleocene mammals of Alberta, Canada. J. Mammal. 13:48–54.

———. 1948. A middle Paleocene mammal tooth from the foothills of Alberta. Amer. J. Sci. 246:152–156.

———. 1958. Paleocene mammal teeth from Alberta. Bull. Nat. Mus. Canada 147:96–103.

———. 1964. Cretaceous non-marine faunas of north-western America. Royal Ont. Mus. Life Sci. Contrib. 64:1–24.

———. 1967. Palaeontology of the Swan Hills area, north-central Alberta. Royal Ont. Mus. Life Sci. Contrib. 71:1–31.

———. 1974. Fauna and correlation of the Ravenscrag Formation (Paleocene) of southwestern Saskatchewan. Royal Ont. Mus. Life Sci. Contrib. 102:1–53.

———. 1975. Mammalian faunal succession in the Cretaceous System of western North America. In The Cretaceous System in the Western Interior of North America, ed. W. G. E. Caldwell. Geol. Assoc. Can. Spec. Pap. 13:137–161.

Rutherford, R. L. 1927. Geology along the Bow River between Cochrane and Kananaskis, Alberta. Sci. Indust. Res. Council Alberta, Rept. no. 17, pp. 1–46.

Savage, D. E., and D. E. Russell. 1983. Mammalian paleofaunas of the world. Reading, Mass.:Addison-Wesley Publishing Co.

Schiebout, J. A. 1974. Vertebrate paleontology and paleoecology of Paleocene Black Peaks Formation, Big Bend National Park, Texas. Texas Mem. Mus. Bull. 24:1–88.

Schimper, W. P. 1874. Traité de Paléontologie Vegétale. Vol. 3. Paris: J. B. Bailliere.

Schoch, R. M. 1981. Revision of the middle Paleocene (Torrejonian) taeniodont (Mammalia) Psittacotherium Cope, 1882. In Advances in San Juan Basin paleontology, eds.

S. G. Lucas, J. K. Rigby, Jr., and B. S. Kues. Albuquerque: Univ. New Mexico Press. Pp. 177–185.

———. 1986. Systematics, functional morphology, and macroevolution of the extinct mammalian order Taeniodonta. Peabody Mus. Nat. Hist. Bull. 42.

Schoch, R. M., and S. G. Lucas. 1981a. A new species of Conoryctella (Mammalia: Taeniodonta) from the Paleocene of the San Juan Basin, New Mexico, and a revision of the genus. Postilla 185:1–23.

———. 1981b. New conoryctines (Mammalia, Taeniodonta) from the middle Paleocene (Torrejonian) of western North America. J. Mammal. 62:683–691.

Schorn, H. E. 1971. What is type Paleocene? Amer. J. Sci. 271:402–409.

Simons, E. L. 1960. The Paleocene Pantodonta. Trans. Amer. Phil. Soc. 50:1–99.

Simpson, G. G. 1927. Mammalian fauna and correlation of the Paskapoo Formation of Alberta. Amer. Mus. Novitates 268:1–10.

———. 1928. A new mammalian fauna from the Fort Union Formation of southern Montana. Amer. Mus. Novitates 297:1–15.

———. 1929a. A collection of Paleocene mammals from Bear Creek, Montana. Ann. Carnegie Mus. 19:115–122.

———. 1929b. Third contribution to the Fort Union fauna at Bear Creek, Montana. Amer. Mus. Novitates 345:1–12.

———. 1929c. A new Paleocene uintathere and molar evolution in the Amblypoda. Amer. Mus. Novitates 387:1–9.

———. 1932. A new Paleocene mammal from a deep well in Louisiana. Proc. U.S. Natl. Mus. 82:1–4.

———. 1933. Glossary and correlation charts of North American Tertiary mammal-bearing formations. Bull. Amer. Mus. Nat. Hist. 67:79–121.

———. 1935a. The Tiffany fauna, upper Paleocene. I. Multituberculata, Marsupialia, Insectivora, and ?Chiroptera. Amer. Mus. Novitates 795:1–19.

———. 1935b. The Tiffany fauna, upper Paleocene. II. Structure and relationships of Plesiadapis. Amer. Mus. Novitates 816:1–30.

———. 1935c. The Tiffany fauna, upper Paleocene. III. Primates, Carnivora, Condylarthra, and Amblypoda. Amer. Mus. Novitates 817:1–28.

———. 1935d. New mammals from the Fort Union of Montana. Proc. U.S. Natl. Mus. 83:221–244.

———. 1936a. Additions to the Puerco fauna, lower Paleocene. Amer. Mus. Novitates 849:1–11.

———. 1936b. A new fauna from the Fort Union of Montana. Amer. Mus. Novitates 873:1–27.

———. 1937a. The Fort Union of the Crazy Mountain Field, Montana, and its mammalian faunas. U.S. Natl. Mus. Bull. 169:1–287.

———. 1937b. Additions to the upper Paleocene fauna of the Crazy Mountain Field. Amer. Mus. Novitates 940:1–15.

———. 1937c. Notes on the Clark Fork, upper Paleocene, fauna. Amer. Mus. Novitates 954:1–24.

———. 1940. Review of the mammal-bearing Tertiary of South America. Proc. Amer. Phil. Soc. 83:649–709.

————. 1959. Fossil mammals from the type area of the Puerco and Nacimiento strata, Paleocene of New Mexico. Amer. Mus. Novitates 1957:1–22.

Sinclair, W. J., and W. Granger. 1912. Notes on the Tertiary deposits of the Bighorn Basin. Bull. Amer. Mus. Nat. Hist. 31:57–67.

————. 1914. Paleocene deposits of the San Juan Basin, New Mexico. Bull. Amer. Mus. Nat. Hist. 33:297–316.

Sloan, R. E. 1970. Cretaceous and Paleocene terrestrial communities of western North America. In Proc. No. Amer. Paleont. Conv. (1969), ed. E. L. Yochelson. Pp. 427–453.

————. 1981. Systematics of Paleocene multituberculates from the San Juan Basin, New Mexico. In Advances in San Juan Basin paleontology, eds. S. G. Lucas, J. K. Rigby, Jr., and B. S. Kues. Albuquerque: Univ. of New Mexico Press. Pp. 127–160.

————. 1985. Gradual extinction of latest Cretaceous dinosaurs in the Hell Creek Formation, McCone County, Montana. Abstr. with Programs, 38th Ann. Mtng. Rocky Mt. Sect. Geol. Soc. Amer. 17:265.

Sloan, R. E., and L. Van Valen. 1965. Late Cretaceous mammals from Montana. Science 148:220–227.

Smit, J., and S. van der Kaars. 1984. Terminal Cretaceous extinctions in the Hell Creek area, Montana, compatible with catastrophic extinction. Science 223:1177–1179.

Spieker, E. M. 1960. The Cretaceous-Tertiary boundary in Utah. Proc. 21st Intern. Geol. Congr. Pt. 5, sect. 5, pp. 14–24.

Szalay, F. S. 1969. Mixodectidae, Microsyopidae, and the insectivore-primate transition. Bull. Amer. Mus. Nat. Hist. 140:195–330.

————. 1977. Phylogenetic relationships and a classification of the eutherian Mammalia. NATO Advanced Study Institute, Series A, Vol. 14, pp. 315–374.

Taylor, L. H. 1981. The Kutz Canyon local fauna, Torrejonian (middle Paleocene) of the San Juan Basin, New Mexico. In Advances in San Juan Basin paleontology, eds. S. G. Lucas, J. K. Rigby, Jr., and B. S. Kues. Albuquerque: Univ. of New Mexico Press: Pp. 242–263.

Taylor, L. H., and R. F. Butler. 1980. Magnetic-polarity stratigraphy of Torrejonian sediments, Nacimiento Formation, San Juan Basin, New Mexico. Amer. J. Sci. 280:97–115.

Tomida, Y. 1981. "Dragonian" fossils from the San Juan Basin and status of the "Dragonian" land mammal "age." In Advances in San Juan Basin paleontology, eds. S. G. Lucas, J. K. Rigby, Jr., and B. S. Kues. Albuquerque: Univ. of New Mexico Press. Pp. 222–241.

————. 1982. A new genus of picrodontid primate from the Paleocene of Utah. Folia Primatol. 37:37–43.

Tomida, Y., and R. F. Butler. 1980. Dragonian mammals and Paleocene magnetic polarity stratigraphy, North Horn Formation, central Utah. Amer. J. Sci. 280:787–811.

Trofimov, B. A. 1975. [New data on *Buginbaatar* (Mammalia, Multituberculata) from Mongolia.] Kramarenko, N. N. et al. (eds.) Sovmestnaya Soveto-Mongol'skaya paleontolo-

gicheskaya ekspeditsiya, Trudy; Vypusk 2, Iskopayemaya fauna i flora Mongolii. Moscow: Nauka. Pp. 7–13. (incl. English sum.)

Tschudy, R. H. 1970. Palynology of the Cretaceous-Tertiary boundary in the northern Rocky Mountain and Mississippi embayment regions. Geol. Soc. Amer. Spec. Pap. 127:65–111.

Tsentas, C. 1981. Mammalian biostratigraphy of the middle Paleocene (Torrejonian) strata of the San Juan Basin: Notes on Torreon Wash and the status of the *Pantolambda* and *Deltatherium* faunal "zones." In Advances in San Juan Basin paleontology, eds. S. G. Lucas, J. K. Rigby, Jr., and B. S. Kues. Albuquerque: Univ. of New Mexico Press. Pp. 262–292.

Van Couvering, J. A., and Berggren, W. A. 1977. Biostratigraphical basis of the Neogene time scale. In Kauffman, E. G. and Hazel, J. E., eds. Concepts and methods of biostratigraphy. Dowden, Hutchinson, and Ross, Inc., Stroudsburg, PA. Pp. 283–306.

Van Houten, F. B. 1944. Stratigraphy of the Willwood and Tatman Formations in northwestern Wyoming. Bull Geol. Soc. Amer., 55:165–210.

Van Valen, L. 1966. Deltatheridia, a new order of mammals. Bull. Amer. Mus. Nat. Hist., 132:1–126.

————. 1978. The beginning of the age of mammals. Evol. Theory, 4:45–80.

Van Valen, L., and R. E. Sloan. 1965. The earliest primates. Science, 150:743–745.

————. 1966. The extinction of the multituberculates. Syst. Zool., 15:261–278.

Vianey-Liaud, M. 1979. Les mammifères montiens de Hainin (Paléocène moyen de Belgique); part I; multituberculés. Palaeovert., 9:117–139.

Voigt. E. 1981. Critical remarks on the discussion concerning the Cretaceous-Tertiary boundary. Newsletters on Strat., 10:92–114.

Wang, B. 1975. Paleocene mammals of Chaling Basin, Hunan. Vert. Pal. Asiat., 13:154–162. (incl. English sum.).

Ward, P. 1984. The extinction of the ammonites. Sci. Amer. 249:136–147.

Wegemann, C. H. 1917. Wasatch fossils in so-called Fort Union beds of the Powder River Basin, Wyoming. U.S. Geol. Surv. Prof. Paper 108-D:57–60.

West, R. M. 1971. Deciduous dentition of the early Tertiary Phenacodontidae (Condylarthra, Mammalia). Amer. Mus. Novitates 2461:1–37.

————. 1973. Antemolar dentitions of the Paleocene apatemyid insectivorans *Jepsenella* and *Labidolemur*. J. Mammal. 54:33–40.

————. 1976. The North American Phenacodontidae (Mammalia, Condylarthra). Contrib. Biol. Geol., Milwaukee Publ. Mus. 6:1–78.

Wilson, J. A. 1965. Cenozoic history of the Big Bend area, west Texas. In Geology of the Big Bend area, Texas. West Texas Geol. Soc. Publ., 65–51. Pp. 34–36.

————. 1967. Early Tertiary mammals. In R. A. Maxwell,

J. T. Lonsdale, R. T. Hazzard, and J. A. Wilson. Geology of Big Bend National Park, Brewster County, Texas. Univ. Texas Bur. Econ. Geol. Publ. 671. Pp. 157–169.

Wilson, R. W. 1951. Preliminary survey of a Paleocene faunule from the Angels Peak area, New Mexico. Univ. Kans. Publ. Mus. Nat. Hist. 5:1–11.

———. 1956a. A new multituberculate from the Paleocene Torrejon fauna of New Mexico. Trans. Kans. Acad. Sci. 59:76–84.

———. 1956b. The condylarth genus *Ellipsodon*. Univ. Kans. Publ. Mus. Nat. Hist. 9:105–116.

———. 1956c. Additional remains of the multituberculate genus *Eucosmodon*. Univ. Kans. Publ. Mus. Nat. Hist. 9:117–123.

Wing, S. L. 1984. A new basis for recognizing the Paleocene/Eocene boundary in the Western Interior North America. Science 226:439–441.

Winterfeld, G. F. 1982. Mammalian paleontology of the Fort Union Formation (Paleocene), eastern Rock Springs Uplift, Sweetwater County, Wyoming. Contrib. Geol. Univ. Wyo. 21:73–112.

Wolberg, D. L. 1978. The mammalian paleontology of the late Paleocene (Tiffanian) Circle and Olive localities, McCone and Powder River counties, Montana. Ph.D diss., Univ. Minnesota, Minneapolis.

———. 1979. Late Paleocene (Tiffanian) mammalian fauna of two localities in eastern Montana. Northwest Geol. 8:83–93.

Wood, A. E. 1962. The early Tertiary rodents of the family Paramyidae. Trans. Amer. Phil. Soc. 52:1–261.

Wood, H. E., II, R. W. Chaney, J. Clark, E. H. Colbert, G. L. Jepsen, J. B. Reeside, Jr., and C. Stock. 1941. Nomenclature and correlation of the North American continental Tertiary. Bull. Geol. Soc. Amer., 52:1–48.

Wood, R. C. 1967. A review of the Clark Fork vertebrate fauna. Breviora 257:1–30.

Woodburne, M. O. 1977. Definition and characterization in mammalian chronostratigraphy. J. Paleont. 51:220–234.

Zhang Y.-P. 1980. A new tillodontlike mammal from the Paleocene of Nanxiong Basin, Guangdong. Vert. PalAsiat. 18:126–130. (incl. English sum.)

Zhou, M., Y. Zhang, B. Wang, and S. Ding. 1977. Mammalian fauna from the Paleocene of Nanxiong Basin, Guangdong. Pal. Sin., n.s., C, 20:1–100. (incl. English sum.)

4

EOCENE (WASATCHIAN THROUGH DUCHESNEAN) BIOCHRONOLOGY OF NORTH AMERICA

Leonard Krishtalka

Robert M. West

Craig C. Black

Mary R. Dawson

John J. Flynn

William D. Turnbull

Richard K. Stucky

Malcolm C. McKenna

Thomas M. Bown

David J. Golz

Jason A. Lillegraven

INTRODUCTION

The history of attempts by vertebrate paleontologists over the past century to construct an effective chronology of the North American late Mesozoic and Cenozoic based on both physical stratigraphy and fossil mammal distributions was reported by Tedford (1970). He pointed out, as had R. W. Wilson (1967) and Savage (1955), the fundamental inconsistencies in the definitions and usages of the terms proposed by the Wood committee (Wood et al. 1941). A primary problem was the lack of a clear distinction between intervals based on temporal durations of recognizable assemblages of fossils, on the one hand, and intervals based on the depositional history of specific rock units, on the other. Although Wood et al. intended to avoid using formation names for time units, fourteen of their eighteen North American provincial ages are based on lithostratigraphic units. All of the provincial

time terms considered in this chapter are so founded. The essay by J. A. Wilson (1975) considers the intent of Wood et al. which has been altered in usage over the past third of a century.

The Wasatchian, Bridgerian, Uintan, and Duchesnean land mammal ages are based on mammalian fossils from sedimentary rock units in geographically distinct areas with different depositional histories. For example, the Uintan is based on fossil assemblages from the Uinta Basin whereas the Wasatchian is defined on the Wasatch Formation and its faunas in the southwestern Green River Basin. Another problem is that disconformities occur in some continental basins, resulting in apparent gaps in the Eocene terrestrial depositional record.

Numerous local assemblages have received intensive study since the compilation of the Wood committee report. The faunal sequences in several of these show that the age boundaries are not, and need not be, necessarily synchronous with lithostratigraphic boundaries. For example, in both the Washakie and Green River basins (fig. 4.1), Bridgerian mammals have been recovered from rocks referred to the upper part of the Cathedral Bluffs Tongue of the Wasatch Formation. Most of the lower part of the Duchesne River Formation, containing

1. Fort Union and Willwood formations, Clark's Fork Basin
2. Lower variegated beds, Togwotee Pass
3. Wasatch Formation, Four Mile area, Washakie Basin
4. "Wasatch" Formation, Powder River Basin
5. "Gray Bull beds," Willwood Formation, Big Horn Basin
6. Debeque Formation, Rifle area, Piceance Basin
7. Colton Formation, Book Cliffs area, Uinta Basin
8. Indian Meadows Formation, northwest Wind River Basin
9. Hannold Hill Formation, Big Bend National Park, Texas
10. Wasatch Formation, Bitter Creek area, Washakie Basin
11. Wasatch Formation, Fossil Basin
12. Golden Valley Formation, North Dakota
13. "Wind River" Formation, Cooper Creek area, Laramie Basin
14. Wasatch Formation and Pass Peak formations, Hoback Basin
15. Lysite Member, Wind River Formation, Wind River Basin
16. "Lysite beds," Willwood Formation, Big Horn Basin
17. Wasatch Formation, Evanston area, Green River Basin
18. Wasatch Formation, LaBarge area, Green River Basin
19. San Jose Formation, San Juan Basin
20. Lost Cabin Member, Wind River Formation, Wind River Basin
21. Lower Huerfano Formation, Huerfano Basin
22. "Lost Cabin beds," Willwood Formation, Big Horn Basin
23. Wind River Formation, Boysen Reservoir area, Wind River Basin
24. Cuchara Formation, Huerfano Basin
25. L-41, Aycross Formation, Togwotee Pass
26. Upper Huerfano Formation, Huerfano Basin
27. Cathedral Bluffs Tongue, Wasatch Formation, Washakie Basin
28. Cathedral Bluffs Tongue, Wasatch Formation, Green River Basin
29. Tatman Formation, western Big Horn Basin
30. Lower Blacks Fork Member, Bridger Formation, Green River Basin
31. Upper Blacks Fork Member, Bridger Formation, Green River Basin
32. Aycross Formation, Big Horn Basin
33. Princeton locality, British Columbia
34. Lower Bridger Formation, New Fork-Big Sandy area, Green River Basin
35. Powder Wash, Green River Formation, Uinta Basin
36. Localities 17 and 18, Wagonbed Formation, Badwater area, Wind River Basin
37. Aycross Formation, northwest Wind River Basin
38. Aycross Formation, Togwotee Summit, Togwotee Pass
39. Kinney Rim Member, Washakie Formation, Washakie Basin
40. Twin Buttes Member, Bridger Formation, Green River Basin
41. Upper Bridger Formation, Tabernacle Butte, Green River Basin
42. Fowkes Formation, Utah
43. Nut bed, Clarno Formation, Oregon
44. Lower Adobe Town Member, Washakie Formation, Washakie Basin
45. Washakie Formation, Sand Wash Basin
46. Pruett Formation, Texas
47. Bone Bed A, Tepee Trail Formation, East Fork River, Wind River Basin
48. Wagon Bed localities, Wagonbed Formation, Beaver Divide area, Wind River Basin
49. Wiggins Formation, Owl Creek area, Absaroka Mountains
50. Wagonhound Member, Uinta Formation, Uinta Basin
51. Friars Formation, southern California
52. Mission Valley Formation, southern California
53. Locality 1, Wagonbed Formation, Badwater area, Wind River Basin
54. Upper Adobe Town Member, Washakie Formation, Washakie Basin
55. Tapo Canyon and Brea Canyon localities, Sespe Formation, southern California
56. Swift Current Creek beds, Cypress Hills, Saskatchewan
57. Myton Member, Uinta Formation, Uinta Basin
58. Laguna Riviera, Santiago Formation, southern California
59. Camp San Onofre, Santiago Formation, southern California
60. Randlett fauna, Duchesne River Formation, Uinta Basin
61. Localities 5, 6, and 7, Hendry Ranch Member, Badwater area, Wind River Basin
62. Climbing Arrow Formation, Shoddy Springs area, Montana
63. Halfway fauna, Duchesne River Formation, Uinta Basin
64. Colmena and Chambers tuffs, Candelaria and Porvenir faunas, west Texas
65. Green River Formation, central Utah
66. LaPoint Member, Duchesne River Formation, Uinta Basin
67. Pearson Ranch, Sespe Formation, southern California
68. Localities Rodent, Wood, and 20, Hendry Ranch Member, Badwater area, Wind River Basin
69. Slim Buttes Formation, South Dakota
70. Hancock Quarry, Clarno Formation, Oregon
71. Galisteo Formation, New Mexico
72. Baca and Cub Mountain formations, New Mexico
73. Carthage Coal Field, Baca Formation, New Mexico
74. Windmill Hill locality, New Mexico

Fig. 4.1. Significant Eocene fossil mammal localities in western North America and southwestern Canada arranged chronologically; some contain faunas of several land mammal ages (see pocket for figure).

the Randlett and Halfway local faunas, is Uintan in age, whereas some of the lower part as well as the upper part, which produces the LaPoint Local Fauna, is Duchesnean (Gazin 1955; Clark et al. 1967; Tedford 1970).

Part of the Eocene sequence may now be correlated to a radiometric time scale (as shown in figs. 4.2–4.4). The K-Ar dates used in this paper include the original date followed by the recalibrated date (marked with an *), which has been calculated using the constants suggested by the International Union of Geological Sciences Subcommission on Geochronology (Steiger and Jager 1977, Dalrymple 1979). This correlation is especially effective in the region immediately south and southeast of the Yellowstone Plateau, where extensive igneous and volcaniclastic units were deposited between about forty and fifty million years ago. These permit reasonably precise radiometric dating of late Wasatchian through early Uintan time in that area. It is to be expected that radiometric chronologies will become progressively

more useful as volcaniclastic rocks and tuffs are studied elsewhere in the Rocky Mountain region.

Most Eocene mammalian fossil assemblages, however, are at present related to the radiometric scale only by the traditional method of faunal similarity. A magnetostratigraphy is currently being developed (e.g., Butler et al. 1980, 1981; Flynn, 1986) that may soon allow accurate correlation of Eocene mammal-bearing strata to a standard magnetic polarity time scale.

Chronology based on sequential mammalian faunas depends on the successful correlation of biostratigraphic units in widely separated areas as well as on detailed and accurate stratigraphic and taxonomic work. Until recently, mammal collections usually were assigned to relatively thick lithostratigraphic units, frequently of the magnitude of member or tongue. Notable early exceptions to this crude paleontological stratigraphy are Matthew's (1909) study of Bridger Formation faunas in the Green River Basin and Peterson's (1919) work in the

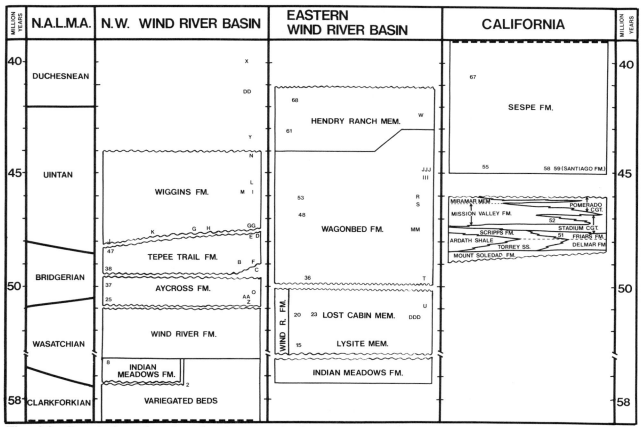

Fig. 4.2. Correlation of rock units that contain fossil mammals of Wasatchian through Duchesnean age, northwestern Wind River Basin, eastern Wind River Basin, and California. Million years refers to the radioisotopic time scale. N.A.L.M.A. refers to the North American mammal ages listed here. Arabic numerals refer to: localities listed in fig. 4.1. Letters refer to: radiometric age listed in table 4.1. Refer to text for lithostratigraphic names used here.

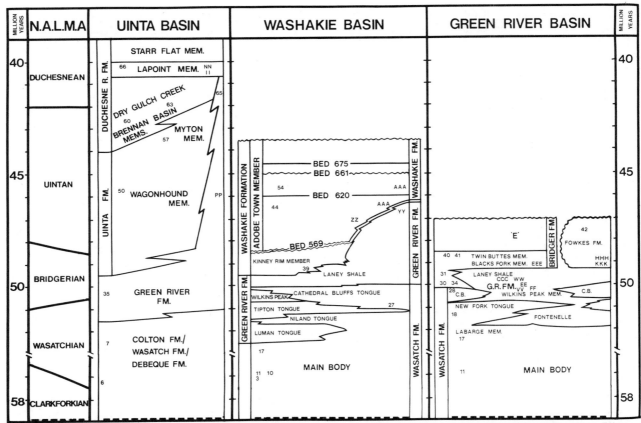

Fig. 4.3. Correlation of rock units that contain fossil mammals of Wasatchian through Duchesnean age, Uinta, Washakie, and Green River basins. Numerals and letters as in figure 4.2.

Uinta Basin. Ongoing studies, particularly in the Bighorn, Wind River, Huerfano, and Green River basins, are developing more refined zonations. Ultimately, we expect that the ranges of many Eocene mammalian taxa will be calibrated accurately enough for a comprehensive biostratigraphic zonation to be implemented.

OCCURRENCE AND DISTRIBUTION OF EOCENE MAMMALIAN FOSSILS

Fossil mammals are common in intermontane basin deposits of the western half of North America. Important here are recent screen-washing efforts that have yielded large assemblages of many taxa of smaller mammals. The productivity is generally poorer in areas marginal to the large basins and in marine and volcaniclastic rocks. Figure 4.1 shows the areas from which significant North American Eocene mammal fossils have been collected.

HISTORY OF TERMINOLOGY OF EOCENE NORTH AMERICAN LAND MAMMAL AGES

The major regions of Eocene basin deposits were known by the 1880s through the pioneering work of Hayden, Leidy, Cope, Marsh, Wortman, and Scott. From the very beginning of systematic exploration and collecting, it was realized that the sedimentary rocks in the various basins of New Mexico, Colorado, Utah, and Wyoming were of different faunal ages, and, by the early twentieth century, the general sequence was understood. As there is no controversy over either the validity or placement of the Wasatchian, Bridgerian, and Uintan, their histories will be considered first; the Duchesnean, subject of some dispute, will be considered later in the discussion.

Wasatchian

The name Wasatch Group was given by Hayden (1869) to a reddish fluvial sequence and was derived from

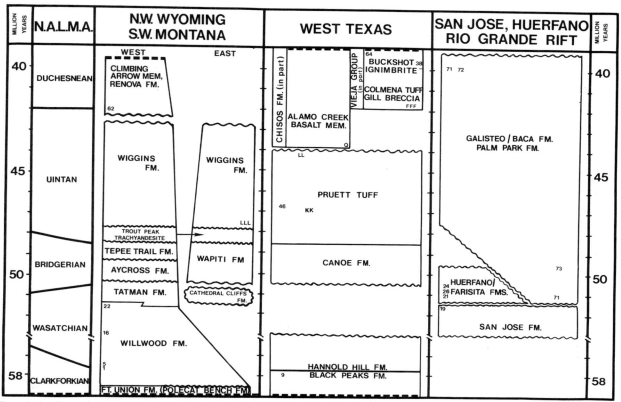

Fig. 4.4. Correlation of rock units that contain fossil mammals of Wasatchian through Duchesnean age, northwestern Wyoming, southwestern Montana, west Texas, San Jose and Huerfano formations, and Rio Grande Rift. Numerals and letters as in figure 4.2.

Wasatch Station in Weber Canyon, Summit County, Utah. "The type locality of the Wasatch Group of Hayden thus extends from Carter, Wyoming, to the Narrows on Weber River, 7 miles below Echo City, Utah, and some 10 to 15 miles east of the crest of the Wasatch Mountains" (Veatch 1907, p. 88). Marsh and Cope both collected in the eastern part of this type area in the 1870s and, from the finer grained rocks, recovered a small fauna that included *Hyracotherium, Coryphodon,* and *Phenacodus.* The presence of these genera in the San Juan Basin of northern New Mexico and the Bighorn Basin of northern Wyoming was evidence enough for Cope (1877, 1882) to extend the Wasatch "beds" to those areas, identifying the rocks as the *Coryphodon* zone. There obviously was no formalized use of the term "formation" to imply a mappable unit; rather, the "beds" were defined faunally and, quite incidentally, were usually reddish. Hayden (1878) similarly referred sedimentary rocks in the Wind River Basin of central Wyoming to the Wasatch Formation on the basis of lithology.

Veatch (1907) subdivided Hayden's Wasatch into three formations, Almy at the base, Fowkes disconformably overlying it, and Knight at the top, supposedly

disconformably overlying the Fowkes. At that time only the Knight was known to be fossiliferous, yielding the assemblages mentioned above. Sinclair and Granger (1912) then modified the Bighorn "Wasatch" to Knight Formation. Dissatisfaction quickly set in about this extension of the Knight Formation, and the informal name "Gray Bull beds" was proposed (Granger 1914, p. 203) for the lower part of the Bighorn Basin sequence. Granger realized that *Coryphodon* was not a definitive characterizing genus, so he changed the characterization to the *Systemodon* (= *Homogalax*) beds. Loomis (1907) had found *Lambdotherium,* already known from the Wind River Basin to the south, high in the Bighorn Basin sequence, so Granger (1914) extended the Lost Cabin beds (or *Lambdotherium* level) into the Bighorn Basin. He then referred 500 feet (152 m) of rock between the *Lambdotherium*-bearing deposits and the Gray Bull beds to the Lysite beds (another name adopted from the Wind River Basin sequence), characterized by *Heptodon.* The Lysite and Lost Cabin beds had initially been recognized as distinct units by Granger (1910), and the two names were proposed as formations by Sinclair and Granger (1911). A geologically older stratum was recognized in the Bighorn Basin by Granger (1914): the Sand Coulee beds presumably lacked *Systemodon* (= *Homogalax*) but did have *Eohippus* (= *Hyracotherium*), thus leading Granger to place the sequence within the Eocene Epoch. Jepsen (1930, p. 119), having found *Homogalax* in the Sand Coulee beds, disputed their faunal distinctiveness despite Granger's other criteria for the definition of Sand Coulee.

Lithostratigraphic terminology has slowly been standardized in the Wyoming basins. The Wasatchian rocks of the Wind River Basin were called the Wind River Formation as early as 1883 (St. John 1883, pp. 228–269), but, as was usual, no type section was designated. Sinclair and Granger (1911) defined the Lysite and Lost Cabin formations and designated a type section for the former. Granger (1910) had essentially done the same for the Lost Cabin beds a year earlier. Later workers (Wood et al. 1941, p. 24; Tourtelot 1948, p. 114) reduced them to members of the Wind River Formation and recognized them only in the northern and northeastern parts of the basin. Tourtelot (1948) finally clarified and confirmed the geographic location of the type areas of both members. Temporally, the Wind River Formation appears to span medial Wasatchian to early Bridgerian time, and three faunal levels are now recognized: Lysitean, Lostcabinian, and Gardnerbuttean. The mammals from the classic collecting areas of the Wind River Formation were last discussed by Guthrie (1967, 1971); a comprehensive review of the Wind River faunas was recently begun (Stucky and Krishtalka 1982, 1983; Krishtalka and Stucky 1983, 1985; Korth 1982; Stucky 1982, 1984a).

The "Big Horn Wasatch" finally was formalized by Van Houten (1944, p. 176) as the Willwood Formation. This includes about 2,300 feet (770 m) of rocks laid down through most of Wasatchian time. The Willwood Formation is conformable in most places on rocks variously referred to the Fort Union Formation or the Polecat Bench Formation and is subdivided lithologically into the Elk Creek and Sand Creek facies (Bown 1979a). The three faunal levels recognized by the early workers are still retained: Graybullian, Lysitean, and Lostcabinian. Now, however, the names connote only faunal composition rather than faunal and rock units. The physical geology of the Willwood Formation was recently studied by Neasham and Vondra (1972); ongoing detailed biostratigraphic work is producing a local zonation (Bown 1979a, 1982; Schankler 1980; Bown and Schankler 1982; Gingerich 1980a, 1980b, 1983).

As study of the faunas of the Wyoming basins progressed, it became apparent that the fauna of the Knight Formation in southwestern Wyoming represented only a part of later Wasatchian time and that the "Gray Bull" assemblage was older. It was not until 1961 (Oriel et al. 1962) that early Wasatchian mammals were found in the type area of Veatch's Almy Formation in the Fossil Basin, thus confirming the preservation of at least most of Wasatchian time in the type region of the Wasatch Formation. Veatch's Fowkes Formation is now known to be Bridgerian in age (Nelson 1973, 1979).

The Knight Formation of Veatch was used irregularly through the first sixty years of the twentieth century to designate the usually red-banded fluvial rocks underlying the Bridger and Washakie formations (see Gazin 1952, 1962). Nightingale (1930, p. 1023) suggested separation of that part of the Wasatch Formation overlain by the Tipton Tongue of the Green River Formation as the Hiawatha Member; McKenna (1960) followed this usage in his discussion of early Wasatchian assemblages from northwestern Colorado. In 1960, the U.S. Geological Survey standardized usage of Wasatch Formation across the entire Green River Basin, Washakie Basin, and Great Divide Basin (*sensu* Love 1961). Oriel (1962) advocated elimination of Veatch's formations altogether in favor of a Wasatch Formation with a lower "main body" (which included Nightingale's Hiawatha) and a series of tongues in the upper part, each of which has an interdigitating relationship with tongues of the lacustrine Green River Formation. This system generally has been accepted by recent workers.

Granger (1914) pointed out that Cope's (1877) use of "Wahsatch" in the San Juan Basin of New Mexico was overly general and suggested that the lower part of the New Mexico early Eocene sequence be called the Almagre beds and the upper part the Largo beds. They were differentiated primarily by the abundance of *Meniscotherium* in the Largo and its absence from the Almagre (it has since been collected in small numbers from the Almagre; Lucas 1977). Simpson (1948) concluded that although there is a superpositional relationship between the Almagre and the Largo, they are not distinct mappable units but should be regarded as facies of a single formation, for which he suggested the name San Jose Formation. Study of the fossils from the San Jose suggested to Simpson (1948, pp. 382–383) that the Almagre is early Wasatchian and the Largo medial to late Wasatchian. Gingerich and Simons (1977) and Gingerich and Gunnell (1979), on the basis of adapid primates and tillodonts, respectively, concluded that there is a close correlation of the Almagre-Largo with the Lost Cabin beds (late Wasatchian) of the Bighorn Basin. Recent work by Lucas (1977, Lucas et al. 1981) and Stucky and

Krishtalka (1983), however, suggests that there is little temporal difference between these facies and that both local faunas are early to middle Wasatchian.

The four major basins with consequential sequences of Wasatchian mammalian fossil assemblages are now recognized as lithostratigraphically distinct and representative of essentially the same period of time. Other areas in which Wasatchian time is represented include the Hoback Basin of central western Wyoming, the Togwotee Pass area southeast of Yellowstone National Park, the Powder River Basin of northeastern Wyoming, south-central North Dakota, the Laramie Basin of southeastern Wyoming, central Utah, the Rifle area of western Colorado, the Huerfano Basin of southeastern Colorado, west Texas, and Ellesmere Island, Canada.

Bridgerian

The Bridger Formation was named by Hayden (1869, p. 191) as the "Bridger Group," composed of "more or less fine sands and sandstones . . . usually weathering into those castellated and dome-like forms," with the type area at Church Buttes Station, Wyoming. Marsh designated the "Bridger series" as the *Dinoceras* beds (1885, p. 6), even though uintatheres were then unknown from the lower part of the sequence (and still, as of 1986, have not been recovered from the Bridger B). The American Museum of Natural History conducted several expeditions into the southern Green River Basin at the turn of the century and, in 1909, Matthew published a comprehensive Bridger stratigraphy. The Bridger Formation was divided into five alphabetically designated zones (A-E) demarcated by laterally extensive white marker beds and further subdivided (B_1, B_2, etc.) on the basis of persistent benches held up by resistant marl beds. All collections made during Matthew's study contain this subzone data, and other institutions (especially the U.S. National Museum) also used this system. H. E. Wood (1934) recognized the apparent faunal similarity between Bridger A and B and between Bridger C and D. He combined these zones into two members, the lower Blacks Fork Member and the higher Twin Buttes Member. This was essentially a return to the bipartite Bridger Formation advocated by Wortman (1901) and was most recently followed by Gazin (1976). West and Hutchison (1981) designated the uppermost part of the Bridger Formation (Matthew's Bridger E) as the Cedar Mountain Member. McGrew and Sullivan (1970) examined the exposures of Matthew's Bridger A near Opal, Wyoming, and argued for the basic faunal similarity of Bridger A and B. Gingerich (1979), however, recognized

different species of adapid primates in Bridger A and Bridger B.

The term *Bridger Formation* has been extended inappropriately to several nearby basins; until recently, the U.S. Geological Survey regarded the lower part of the medial to late Eocene sequence in the Uinta Basin as Bridger Formation and also used that term for medial and late Eocene fluvial rocks of the Washakie Basin. Roehler (1973, p. 8) formally reactivated the name Washakie Formation (initially applied by Hayden [1869, p. 190]) for those rocks. The surficial exposures of the central part of the Piceance Basin of northwestern Colorado were mapped as Bridger Formation on the 1935 edition of the Geologic Map of Colorado (Burbank et al. 1935) but those rocks are lacustrine, referable to the Green River Formation (Cashion and Donnell 1974, Tweto 1979).

The Bridgerian age of Wood et al. (1941) is based on the time of deposition and the faunas of Bridger A-D, inclusive; Matthew's Bridger E is now known to be fossiliferous (West and Hutchison 1981) and should be included in the definition. The Bridger Formation has never been called by any other name, and there are only the lithological subdivisions mentioned above (West 1976*b*). With this calm history, there has been little opportunity for confusion about the unit. Other areas where Bridgerian time is represented include Wyoming (Green River Basin, Washakie Basin, Wind River Basin, Bighorn Basin), northeastern Utah, Colorado, west Texas, Oregon, New Jersey, and perhaps Ellesmere Island, Canada.

Uintan

Comstock (1875) first formally recognized the Uinta Formation of northeastern Utah, although Marsh (1870) had already reported vertebrate fossils from that region. The early work, including the faunal study by Scott and Osborn (1890), considered only the upper part of the sequence. American Museum fieldwork in the mid-1890s (Peterson, in Osborn 1895) showed the presence of lower fossiliferous beds referred to as Uinta A and B, with the upper fossiliferous beds being Uinta C. Osborn (1929, pp. 91–97) revised Uinta Formation terminology, calling the lower unfossiliferous beds Uinta A and the two rich middle segments, Uinta B_1 and B_2. Study of the faunas allowed the following characterization of Uinta B and Uinta C (Osborn 1929): Uinta B_1, *Metarhinus* zone; Uinta B_2, *Eobasileus-Dolichorhinus* zone; Uinta C, *Diplacodon-Epihippus* zone. H. E. Wood (1934) proposed the names Wagonhound Member for the lower part of the Uinta Formation (A and B) and Myton Member for the upper part (C). The U.S. Geological Survey originally used Bridger Formation to denote the lower Uinta, based on presumed correlations to the Washakie Basin, but the most recent geologic map of Utah (Stokes and Madsen 1961) limited use of Bridger Formation to regions north of the Uinta Mountains. Bradley (1964, p. 54) referred the upper fossiliferous levels of the Washakie Basin to "Bridger and Uinta formations," but Roehler (1973) reinstituted use of Washakie Formation for the Bridgerian-Uintan sequence there. The final alteration in Uinta Formation usage was the separation of the beds above Uinta C as the Duchesne Formation (Peterson 1932, p. 61), modified to Duchesne River Formation (Kay 1934). The Uintan Land Mammal Age is based on the fauna and time of deposition of the Uinta Formation plus the lower part of the Duchesne River Formation. Areas containing Uintan rocks and faunas include southwestern Saskatchewan, southwestern Montana, northwestern South Dakota, central Wyoming, south-southeast of Yellowstone National Park, west Texas, northern New Mexico, northwestern Colorado, southern California, and Mississippi.

Duchesnean

The youngest North American continental Eocene land mammal age is the Duchesnean, "based on the Duchesne River Formation of northeastern Utah" (Wood et al. 1941, p. 10). Wood et al. regarded faunal characterization of the Duchesnean as premature, although the relative abundance of *Teleodus* was noted; instead, the complete faunas of both the Duchesne River Formation and California Institute of Technology locality 150 (Pearson Ranch) in the Sespe Formation of California were listed.

The Duchesne River Formation overlies and intertongues with the Uinta Formation, although there is a substantial change in lithofacies (Scott 1945, p. 209; Andersen and Picard 1972, p. 9). There are three faunal levels within the Duchesne River Formation which were not originally recognized by Wood et al. (1941): the lowest original member, the Randlett, has been abandoned, but rocks and faunas once contained in it are now included within the time transgressive (Uintan-Duchesnean) Brennan Basin Member of the Duchesne River Formation (Andersen and Picard 1972); the middle, the Halfway fauna, occurs in the Dry Gulch Creek Member; and the upper, the LaPoint fauna, is in the LaPoint Member. A fourth unit, the Starr Flat Member, overlies the LaPoint but is, as yet, unfossiliferous. This entire thickness was the original basis for the Duches-

nean. Gazin (1955, chart 1) limited the Duchesnean geochron to the Halfway and LaPoint members of the Duchesne River Formation, whereas Clark and Beerbower (in Clark et al. 1967, p. 59) and Tedford (1970, pp. 690–692) suggested a redefinition of the Duchesnean to include only the LaPoint Member of the Duchesne River Formation as the geochron for the Duchesnean Land Mammal Age, with the Randlett and Halfway faunas included in the late Uintan. Emry (1981) advocated that the Duchesnean, based on the Halfway and LaPoint faunas, be considered the earliest part (possibly a subage) of the Chadronian; Wilson (1978) also proposed synonymy of the Duchesnean (based on the LaPoint fauna only) into the Chadronian but recently (1984) has included it as the earliest subage of the Chadronian.

Scott (1945) and Clark and Beerbower (in Clark et al. 1967, p. 57) regarded the fauna of the Duchesne River Formation as early Oligocene in age. Simpson (1946) and Black and Dawson (1966) retained it in the Eocene. The validity of the Duchesnean is still a subject of debate. If valid, its assignment to the Eocene and/or Oligocene cannot be adequately determined without correlation to the type epochs of Europe. In addition to the Uinta Basin and Sespe localities, Duchesnean faunas have been collected in the Wind River Basin, southwestern Texas, Oregon, and New Mexico.

THE EOCENE LAND MAMMAL AGES

Wasatchian

The Wasatchian of Wood et al. (1941) had *Anaptomorphus, Eotitanops, Hyopsodus, Miacis, Sinopa, Viverravus,* and *Vulpavus* as first appearances. Van Houten (1945, p. 437) added the following: *Entomolestes nitens* (*Macrocranion* of Krishtalka [1976a]), *Hyrachyus, Notharctus, Nyctitherium celatum* (*Pontifactor* of Krishtalka [1976b]), *Peratherium* (*Herpetotherium* of Crochet [1977]), *Stylindodon, Tritemnodon,* and *Uintacyon*.

Last occurrences, according to Wood et al. (1941), include *Chriacus, Coryphodon, Didymictis, Dissacus, Ectocion, Ectypodus, Esthonyx,* Multituberculata, *Oxyaena, Probathyopsis, Palaeosinopa, Phenacodus,* and *Psittacotherium*. Van Houten added several other genera: *Apheliscus, Carpolestes, Diacodon, Phenacolemur, Haplomylus, Meniscotherium, Neoliotomus, Palaeanodon, Phenacodaptes, Prochetodon, Plesiadapis,* and *Thryptacodon*.

Since then, a great deal of paleontological and

geologic research has substantially modified these first and last occurrences of the Wasatchian. Concerning first appearances, *Anaptomorphus* (*s.s.*), *Hyrachyus*, and *Eotitanops* (= *Palaeosyops;* see Wallace 1980) are now restricted to the Bridgerian (Szalay 1976, Stucky 1984*b*); the *Anaptomorphus* of Wood et al. (1941) and Van Houten (1945) (*A. homunculus*) has since been referred to *Tetonius* (Szalay 1976), which first appears in the Wasatchian. *Hyopsodus, Peratherium, Viverravus,* and *Uintacyon* have since been recorded from the Clarkforkian (Rose 1981). Last appearances no longer valid are *Ectypodus* and Multituberculata, which occur from the Bridgerian into the Chadronian of the Western Interior (Krishtalka and Black 1975; Krishtalka et al. 1982; Ostrander et al. 1979; Sutton and Black 1972), and *Coryphodon, Didymictis,* and *Esthonyx,* which have been reported from recently recognized (see below) earliest Bridgerian deposits of the Wind River and Huerfano formations (Robinson 1966; Stucky 1984*b*; Stucky and Krishtalka 1983).

The abundant Wasatchian condylarth *Phenacodus* is now known from a number of Bridgerian sites including locality 5 at Tabernacle Butte, Badwater Locality 17 (West and Atkins 1970), the Aycross Formation (Bown, unpublished data), Carter Mountain (Eaton 1980), and localities in the Wind River Formation, Wind River Basin (Stucky 1984*b*). One of the latter also preserves Bridgerian *Ectocion*.

Phenacolemur (including species now referred to *Ignacius;* Bown and Rose 1976) are now known from Bridgerian (West and Dawson 1973) as well as Uintan and Duchesnean deposits (Robinson 1968, Krishtalka 1978). *Phenacodaptes, Psittacotherium* and *Prochetodon* are now restricted to the Paleocene.

The occurrence of *Palaeosinopa* in a small sample from the Cathedral Bluffs Tongue of the Wasatch Formation in the Washakie Basin (Gazin 1965) is either late Wasatchian or early Bridgerian (Morris 1954; McGrew and Roehler 1960; West 1969; West and Dawson 1973). The genus has been recovered from a Bridgerian locality in the Wind River Formation (Stucky 1984*a*).

Paleontological and geologic work accomplished since the syntheses of Wood et al. (1941) and Van Houten (1945) allows the following list of important taxa and genera that first appear in the Wasatchian: Perissodactyla, Artiodactyla, Adapidae, Omomyidae, Hyaenodontidae, Sciuravidae, *Palaeictops, Didelphodus, Macrocranion, Pachyaena, Miacis, Vulpavus,* and *Megalesthonyx* (Schankler 1980, Rose 1981). Of these, the simultaneous appearance of Perissodactyla (*Hyracotherium*), Artiodactyla (*Diacodexis*), Adapidae (*Pelycodus*), and Hyaenodontidae mark the onset of the Wasatchian and the end of the Clarkforkian (see chap. 3).

Important last occurrences in the Wasatchian (a criterion of minor biostratigraphic utility) now include Pantodonta, *Meniscotherium, Homogalax, Xenicohippus, Lambdotherium, Anacodon, Niptomomys, Tetonius, Pelycodus,* and *Pachyaena* (Schankler 1980; Stucky 1984*b*; Bown and Kihm 1981).

Of the genera listed by Wood et al. (1941) and Van Houten (1945) as Wasatchian index fossils (those restricted to the Wasatchian), the following are still valid: *Ambloctonus, Diacodon, Homogalax, Lambdotherium, Meniscotherium, Pachyaena, Tetonius, Pelycodus, Ectoganus, Wasatchia* (*s.s.*) (Krishtalka and Stucky, 1986), and *Prolimnocyon.* To these we add *Xenicohippus, Cantius, Copelemur, Anemorhysis, Loveina,* and *Notoparamys* (Korth 1982). *Anacodon* is reported from several late Tiffanian or Clarkforkian localities, but the generic reference is questionable (Gazin 1956, Rose 1981). *Diacodexis* and *Didelphodus* are now known from Bridgerian deposits in the Wind River Basin and the northern Green River Basin (West 1973*a*; Krishtalka and Stucky, 1985). *Didelphodus* is also known from the late Uintan of Saskatchewan (Storer 1984).

Hyracotherium marks the onset of the Wasatchian and is now known to range into the Bridgerian in the Huerfano Basin (Robinson 1966), the Washakie Basin (Gazin 1965), the Green River Basin (Stucky 1984*b*), the Uinta Basin (Krishtalka and Stucky 1983), and the Wind River Basin (Stucky 1984*a*).

Paramys is now known from the Clarkforkian through the Uintan. *Teilhardella* was synonymized with *Apatemys* by Guthrie (1971) and West (1973*b*); the genus ranges from late Tiffanian to Uintan. *Palaeonictis* and *Plagiomene* have been recorded from the Clarkforkian (Rose 1981) and *Absarokius, Hapalodectes, Heptodon, Bathyopsis, Bunophorus,* and *Vassacyon* from the Bridgerian (Szalay 1976; McGrew and Sullivan 1970; Bown 1982; Stucky 1984*b*). Species of *Pelycodus* (except for *P. jarrovii*) have recently been referred to *Cantius* and *Copelemur* (Gingerich and Simons 1977, Gingerich and Haskin 1981). *Microsyops,* now considered congeneric with *Cynodontomys* (Szalay 1969), ranges from the Clarkforkian into the Uintan.

The Wasatchian may now be typified by the occurrence of the following genera (not all of which are restricted to Wasatchian time): *Hyracotherium, Coryphodon, Phenacodus, Ectocion, Hyopsodus, Paramys, Microsyops, Cantius, Absarokius, Prolimnocyon, Prototomus, Arfia, Oxyaena, Didymictis, Viverravus, Diacodexis, Lambdotherium, Homogalax, Esthonyx,* and *Ectoganus.* The presence of abundant *Hyopsodus, Cantius, Hyracotherium,* and *Diacodexis* differentiates the Wasatchian from the earlier Clarkforkian. The end of the Wasatchian (= the beginning of the Bridgerian) can now be defined by the penecontemporaneous appearance of *Hyrachyus, Palaeosyops, Trogosus, Omomys, Washakius, Anaptomorphus, Smilodectes, Pantolestes, Homacodon, Microsus,* and *Helohyus.*

The traditional tripartite division of the Wasatchian into the Graybullian, Lysitean, and Lostcabinian has been considerably emended and refined in the last decade as a result of detailed stratigraphic collecting and analysis in the "type" areas of the three Wasatchian subages: the Bighorn Basin (Graybullian) (Gingerich 1980*a;* Schankler 1980; Rose 1981; Bown 1979*a*) and the Wind River Basin (Lysitean and Lostcabinian) (Krishtalka and Stucky 1983; Stucky and Krishtalka 1983; Stucky 1984 *a*). The earliest subage of the Wasatchian, as now defined by Gingerich (1983), is the Sandcouleean, a biostratigraphic interval previously recognized by Granger (1914). Its onset coincides with that of the Wasatchian and is defined likewise. It is distinguished from the Graybullian by the presence in the Sand Coulee fauna of more primitive species of *Hyracotherium, Cantius, Homogalax,* and other genera. The beginning of the Graybullian (= end of the Sandcouleean) is marked by Schankler's (1980) Biohorizon A—a faunal turnover event characterized, in part, by the first appearance of *Homogalax protapirinus.*

The *Homogalax* beds provided the original faunal definition of the early Wasatchian; *Homogalax* is indeed abundant in many early Wasatchian assemblages but has recently been reported from the Lysite (Guthrie 1967) and some Lostcabinian (Radinsky 1963, Gazin 1962) faunas as well. Phenacodont condylarths are present in great abundance in the early Wasatchian (West 1976*a*, Schankler 1981). *Plesiadapis* makes its last appearance, as do *Haplomylus, Carpolestes,* and *Neoliotomus.* The early Wasatchian (Sandcouleean and Graybullian) is characterized (common occurrence) by multituberculates, *Homogalax, Phenacodus, Coryphodon, Hyracotherium, Hyopsodus, Haplomylus, Ectocion, Pelycodus,* and *Diacodexis.* The combination of these taxa, in an assemblage zone, will now serve to identify the early Wasatchian.

The Lysitean (medial Wasatchian) was defined originally as the *Heptodon* beds, with both *Homogalax* and *Lambdotherium* thought to be absent. *Homogalax* is common in the Bighorn Basin (Bown, unpublished data) but rare in the Wind River Basin (Guthrie 1967), and *Lambdotherium* remains absent. Forms that appear first in the Lysitean are *Heptodon, Absarokius, Loveina,* and *Hexacodus* (Guthrie 1967, Krishtalka and Stucky 1985). Since Guthrie's (1967) review, Krishtalka, Stucky, and Dawson (Carnegie Museum of Natural History) have recovered a more diverse and abundant Lysitean fauna

from the Lysite Member, Wind River Formation, which will help refine Lysitean biostratigraphy. The Bighorn Basin Lysite fauna is becoming better known through the work of Schankler (1980), Bown (1980), and the ongoing work of Bown (U.S. Geological Survey, Denver) and Rose (Johns Hopkins University).

The Lostcabinian (late Wasatchian) was originally based on the fauna of the Lost Cabin Member of the Wind River Formation and typified by the presence of the primitive paleothere *Lambdotherium* (Guthrie 1971). The onset of the Lostcabinian (= end of the Lysitean) is marked by the first appearance of *Lambdotherium;* the subage as a whole is characterized by the first occurrence of *Shoshonius, Antiacodon, Orohippus, Megalesthonyx, Pauromys, Sciuravus,* and *Armintodelphys* as well as derived species of *Esthonyx, Diacodexis, Absarokius, Hyopsodus, Cantius/Notharctus,* and *Hyracotherium.* Detailed stratigraphic collecting from the upper part of the Wind River Formation and the local biostratigraphic zonation (Stucky 1984*a;* see also Stucky and Krishtalka 1983, Krishtalka and Stucky 1983) have shown that the Lost Cabin Member (and equivalent units) preserves two distinct faunas and biostratigraphic zones. One, restricted to the lower part of the Lost Cabin Member (and equivalent lithostratigraphic units), is the *Lambdotherium* Range-Zone fauna, the "type" fauna of the Lostcabinian. The other, restricted to the upper part, is the *Palaeosyops borealis* Assemblage-Zone fauna, which is equivalent to the Gardnerbuttean fauna, as defined by Robinson (1966). Robinson originally assigned that fauna (from the Huerfano Basin) and the "Gardnerbuttean substage" to the Wasatchian. Stucky and Krishtalka, however, now consider the *Palaeosyops borealis* Assemblage-Zone and the Gardnerbuttean as earliest Bridgerian, an action presently endorsed by Robinson and other workers. The distinction between the two zones is a major faunal turnover event that is recognizable in many of the basins of the Western Interior (see below). Corollaries of this conclusion are (1) the end of the Lostcabinian (and the *Lambdotherium* Range-Zone) is the end of the Wasatchian, and (2) the Lost Cabin Member straddles the Wasatchian-Bridgerian boundary, which is synonymous with the Lostcabinian-Gardnerbuttean boundary.

Wasatchian/Bridgerian Boundary

The demarcation between the Wasatchian and the Bridgerian has not been made as yet in the "type" areas of the two ages. Elsewhere, particularly in the Washakie, the eastern Wind River, the northeastern Green River, and the Huerfano and Bighorn basins, Bridgerian rocks conformably overlie Wasatchian rocks. In the Wind River and Huerfano basins, the faunas derived from these sequences are as extensive as those from the typical late Wasatchian or classic early Bridgerian (Blacks Fork Member of the Bridger Formation) deposits and are dated primarily by biochronologic methods. They provide an opportunity to document the Wasatchian-Bridgerian faunal boundary in presumably unbroken stratigraphic sequences.

One critical set of rocks that spans the boundary belongs to the Cathedral Bluffs Tongue of the Wasatch Formation. This is the uppermost of several tongues of the Wasatch Formation that interdigitate with the Green River Formation. The lower part of the unit produces a few fossils that apparently are late Wasatchian in age (Morris 1954, Gazin 1962). Higher in the local section, along the eastern side of the Washakie Basin, are several assemblages that are post-Lostcabinian in aspect and probably best regarded as Bridgerian (McKenna and Manning, unpublished data).

Farther northwest, north of Tabernacle Butte, a referred section of the Cathedral Bluffs Tongue overlies the New Fork Tongue of the Wasatch Formation. The latter unit has produced a mixed late Wasatchian/ early Bridgerian fauna from over 250 feet of strata (*Hyracotherium, Meniscotherium, Coryphodon, Palaeosyops, Lambdotherium, Phenacodus,* and *Oxyaena*) (West 1973a). The overlying Cathedral Bluffs Tongue (West and Dawson 1973) lacks typical Wasatchian mammals and has, instead, characteristic Bridgerian species of *Orohippus, Helaletes, Antiacodon, Pauromys, Tillomys,* and *Mysops.* Although there is a lithologic difference between the New Fork Tongue and the Cathedral Bluffs Tongue in the northern Green River Basin, there is no indication of a significant temporal or depositional hiatus. Given the nature of the New Fork fauna, the Wasatchian-Bridgerian boundary is probably preserved in this unit. Stratigraphically controlled collections will provide a test of conclusions concerning the Wasatchian-Bridgerian faunal turnover from studies of the Wind River and Huerfano formations.

Recent work in upper Wind River Formation rocks in the northeastern part of the Wind River Basin (Stucky and Krishtalka 1982, 1983; Krishtalka and Stucky 1983; Stucky 1984a) indicates the presence of a post-*Lambdotherium* fauna there, which Stucky characterizes as the *Palaeosyops borealis* Assemblage-Zone. The onset of this zone is marked by the first appearance of *Palaeosyops, Pantolestes, Hyrachyus, Homacodon, Trogosus, Washakius,* and *Helohyus.* It lacks *Lambdotherium* in the Wind River Basin, and its assemblage is a correlative of the Huerfano B fauna (see below).

As suggested by Wood et al. (1941, p. 22), another place the Wasatchian-Bridgerian boundary is preserved is in the Huerfano Basin of southern Colorado. Robinson (1966) and earlier workers concluded that the upper beds of the Huerfano Formation (Huerfano B) contain a mixed Wasatchian-Bridgerian fauna and represent a time interval between that of the Lost Cabin Member and the early Bridgerian. Robinson called this the Gardnerbuttean Substage of the Wasatchian, a term that until recently has not been generally accepted. Elements of this assemblage (*Mesonyx, Eotitanops* [= *Palaeosyops*], *Trogosus,* and *Antiacodon pygmaeus*) are indicative of early Bridgerian time; other taxa are holdovers from the Wasatchian. McKenna (1976), Gingerich (1979), and Stucky (1984b) have since added *Esthonyx acutidens, Smilodectes mcgrewi,* and *Omomys carteri* to the upper Huerfano fauna. The latter two are also indicators of the earliest Bridgerian. It now seems that the Huerfano B assemblage should be considered earliest Bridgerian (Stucky 1984b; Stucky and Krishtalka 1983; but see McKenna 1976 and Dorr, in press).

The onset of the Bridgerian (Wasatchian-Bridgerian boundary) is best defined by the first, penecontemporaneous, and abrupt appearance of a number of exotic and new taxa: *Palaeosyops, Trogosus, Hyrachyus, Homacodon, Helohyus, Smilodectes, Omomys, Washakius,* and *Pantolestes.* This also defines the beginning of the Gardnerbuttean. The first three taxa are widespread and especially common at their first occurrence. Rocks of the upper Huerfano and upper Wind River formations best preserve this event, although it is apparently also recorded in the New Fork and Cathedral Bluffs tongues of the Wasatch Formation, the Green River Formation (Utah), and the Willwood and Aycross formations (Bighorn Basin). Thus, the Wasatchian-Bridgerian boundary is the same as the Lostcabinian-Gardnerbuttean boundary. The earliest Bridgerian (= Gardnerbuttean) is characterized by the first appearance of the above as well as the occurrence of holdover Wasatchian taxa: *Esthonyx, Coryphodon, Bunophorus, Diacodexis, Didymictis, Prolimnocyon, Hyracotherium, Shoshonius, Absarokius, Thryptacodon, Palaeosinopa,* and *Knightomys.* Savage (1977) arrived at a similar conclusion when he defined the Wasatchian Stage, except for the use of *Hemiacodon* and *Uintatherium* for the top of the Wasatchian and *Eotitanops* (= *Palaeosyops*) and *Hyrachyus* for the lower limit of the "*Lambdotherium* concurrent Range-Zone."

Bridgerian

Detailed paleontological and stratigraphic work in the Huerfano, Green River, Wind River, and Washakie basins has produced a clear demarcation between the latest Wasatchian (= Lostcabinian) and earliest Bridgerian (= Gardnerbuttean). The Bridger Formation of the southern Green River Basin apparently represents continuous deposition and therefore includes most of Bridgerian time in accordance with the Wood et al. definition of "time of deposition of Bridger A-D, inclusive." Earlier Bridgerian rocks and faunas are now recognized elsewhere (see above). In addition, 500 feet (150 m) of rock termed Bridger E by Matthew (1909) have been regarded as poorly fossiliferous. Wood et al. (1941, p. 15) suggested that these might be equivalent to "some portion of the Uinta." West and Hutchison (1981) collected eight vertebrate species from the Bridger E, which they named the Cedar Mountain Member of the Bridger Formation, and affirmed its Bridgerian biochronologic affinities.

Wood et al. listed thirteen genera as index fossils for the Bridgerian. Of these, *Homacodon, Hyrachyus, Patriofelis, Palaeosyops, Mysops, Thinocyon,* and *Trogosus* (*Tillotherium* of Wood et al.) are still valid as index fossils for the Bridgerian. *Orohippus* (and probably *Helaletes*) are now known to occur in the late Wasatchian of the Wind River Basin (Korth and Evander 1982, Stucky 1984a). *Apatemys* has undergone taxonomic modifications (West 1973b) that give it a Tiffanian to Duchesnean range. *Helohyus* and *Tillomys* are known from Uintan localities in the Sand Wash Basin (West and Dawson 1975; see below) and elsewhere. Several specimens best referred to *Uintatherium* were collected from the Uinta B by American Museum of Natural History expeditions in 1894–95 (Wheeler 1961, pp. 45–46). To the Wood et al. (1941) list of Bridgerian index fossils, we add *Pantolestes, Anaptomorphus, Smilodectes, Microsus, Taxymys,* and *Mesatirhinus.*

Harpagolestes, Limnocyon, Mesonyx, and *Telmatherium,* listed by Wood et al. as having their first occurrences in the Bridgerian, are still valid as such; two other genera, *Paramys* and *Sciuravus,* are now known from Wasatchian and Uintan deposits as well. In addition to the index fossils, *Omomys, Hemiacodon, Washakius, Helohyus, Proviverra, Pantolestes, Dilophodon, Tillomys, Telmatherium, Manteoceras, Parisectolophus, Uintatherium,* and leptochoerids (Huerfano Basin; Krishtalka and Stucky, pers. observ.) are added to the list of first occurrences.

Only *Vulpavus* was given as a last occurrence in the Bridgerian. We add *Entomolestes, Patriofelis, Phenacodus, Hyracotherium, Antiacodon, Diacodexis, Bunophorus, Coryphodon, Bathyopsis, Absarokius, Shoshonius, Hapalodectes, Knightomys, Palaeosinopa, Thryptacodon, Esthonyx, Heptodon, Helaletes, Ectocion, Prolimnocyon,* and *Didymictis.*

The roster of characteristic Bridgerian taxa has been considerably expanded since 1941, largely as a result of the field collecting of Gazin (1976), West (1973a), Bown (1982), and Eaton (1982). Screen washing and quarrying have combined to add many smaller specimens. In addition to the characteristic (common) genera *Hyopsodus, Hyrachyus,* and *Miacis* listed by Wood et al., we add *Sciuravus, Paramys, Pauromys, Peratherium, Antiacodon, Helohyus, Microsus, Omomys, Pantolestes, Microsyops, Notharctus, Hemiacodon, Orohippus, Helaletes, Apatemys, Scenopagus, Pontifactor, Nyctitherium, Centetodon, Entomolestes,* and *Uintasorex.*

Wood's (1934) subdivision of the Bridger Formation into two members was predicated on the close similarity of the Bridger A and B faunas and the Bridger C and D faunas. When this subdivision was made, few mammals were known from the Bridger A beds. McGrew and Sullivan (1970) carefully measured and collected the lowermost exposures of the Bridger Formation in the vicinity of Opal, Wyoming. The fauna they recovered "for the most part is identical to the fauna of the Bridger B" (p. 66), thus confirming the lower of Wood's faunal units. As they and Gingerich (1979) have shown, Bridger A and B faunas, although similar, may contain different species of the same genus. Now it is evident that the Gardnerbuttean precedes Bridger A and is the earliest subage of the Bridgerian; it is followed by the Blacksforkian (Bridger A and B) and the Twinbuttean (Bridger C and D) (see Wood 1934; Matthew 1909; Robinson 1966; Gazin 1976).

The fauna from the Blacksforkian is characterized by the almost total lack of uintatheres (*Bathyopsis* is known only from Bridger A) and the presence of *Trogosus, Tillodon, Vulpavus, Tritemnodon, Notharctus tenebrosus, Smilodectes gracilis, Orohippus pumilus, Hyopsodus minisculus,* and *Microsyops elegans.* The smallest mammals are too poorly known to be included in such a characterization.

The late Bridgerian fauna (Twinbuttean) contains abundant uintatheres (*Uintatherium*), and titanothere diversity (*Telmatherium, Manteoceras, Mesatirhinus*) is increased over that of earlier faunas. *Hemiacodon gracilis, Notharctus robustior, Homacodon vagans, Orohippus sylvaticus, Hyopsodus lepidus,* and *Microsyops annectens* are also unique to the late Bridgerian.

Bridgerian-Uintan Boundary

Comparatively little work has been done on the Bridgerian-Uintan boundary since the Wood et al. (1941) report. There are no published instances where the deposits are continuously fossiliferous across the boundary, although sediments in the East Fork Basin, Wyoming (McKenna 1980b), the Washakie Basin, Wyoming (Roehler 1973), the Uinta Basin, Utah (Kay 1957), Beaver Divide, Wyoming (Emry 1975), the Baca Formation in New Mexico (Lucas et al. 1981), the Badwater Creek area, Wyoming (Black 1969), the Sand Wash Basin, Colorado (West and Dawson 1975), the Pruett Formation in Trans-Pecos, Texas (West 1982), and the Friars and Mission Valley formations, southern California (Golz and Lillegraven 1977), may preserve all or part of this interval.

Another problem surrounding the definition of this boundary concerns the faunal composition of Uinta A. Some authors have claimed that the Uinta A sequence of the Uinta Formation is unfossiliferous (see Osborn 1929; Simpson 1933; Roehler 1973) and therefore impossible to correlate with other rock units. However, the work of Riggs (1912), Peterson (1919, 1934) and Kay (1957) as well as the collections in the Carnegie Museum of Natural History indicate that the Uinta A sediments have yielded a few perissodactyls, five of which are unique to the Uintan and valuable biostratigraphically: *Amynodon, Triplopus, Metarhinus, Dolichorhinus,* and *Forstercooperia* (= *Hyrachyus grandis;* see Radinsky 1967a, 1967b). Contrary to the claim of Wood et al., there are no known artiodactyls from the Uinta A sequence (Kay 1957).

An equivalent fauna from unit 24 (Bone Bed A) of the type Tepee Trail Formation (McKenna 1980b) is intermediate between known late Bridgerian and Uinta B assemblages. It contains, among other taxa, the first appearance of *Protoreodon* (and other primitive species of low-crowned selenodont artiodactyls), *Epihippus, Amynodon, Forstercooperia,* and *Achaenodon* (McKenna 1980b, pers. com. 1984) as well as holdover Bridgerian taxa. Similarly, the Sand Wash fauna (West and Dawson 1975), with *Eobasileus, Dolichorhinus* (= *Tanyorhinus*), *Metarhinus, Triplopus* (= *Hyrachyus* sp. of West and Dawson), and *Protoreodon* (Univ. of Colorado collections; R. Stucky, pers. com. 1984), represents a Uinta A assemblage. In sum, the Bridgerian-Uintan boundary may be defined by the first appearance of some or all of the following: agriochoerids (*Protoreodon*), hyracodontids (*Triplopus, Forstercooperia*), amynodonts (*Amynodon*), and *Metarhinus, Dolichorhinus, Epihippus,* and *Achaenodon.*

Uintan

Substantial faunal differences are noted between Bridgerian and Uintan time. Most prominent is the appearance in the Uintan of several mammal groups that have no apparent North American ancestors. These include the lagomorphs and several important selenodont artiodactyl families (agriochoerids, protoceratids, oromerycids), which form a substantial part of Uintan faunas.

The Uintan of Wood et al. included sixteen genera of index fossils. *Achaenodon, Amynodon, Diplacodon, Dolichorhinus, Eobasileus, Leptotragulus, Oxyaenodon, Prodaphoenus, Prothyracodon* (= *Triplopus, fide* Radinsky 1967b), *Protitanotherium,* and *Protoptychus* are all still valid. *Mytonolagus* and *Protylopus* range into the Duchesnean, and *Protoreodon* (= *Protagriochoerus, fide* Golz 1976) ranges into the Chadronian.

Uintan first appearances listed by Wood et al.— agriochoerids, *Amynodon,* and lagomorphs—are all still valid. Apart from the index taxa, we add soricids, *Ankylodon, Thylacaelurus,* and *Oligoryctes* (Krishtalka and Setoguchi 1977), proscalopids (Storer 1984), and *Ourayia* and *Macrotarsius* (Krishtalka 1978) as well as protoceratids, camelids, oromerycids, hyracodonts, *Epihippus,* eomyids, aplodontids, and possibly canids (Black and Dawson 1966).

Last occurrences in the Uintan listed by Wood et al. which are still valid include *Hyrachyus, Ischyrotomus, Limnocyon,* oxyaenids, *Notharctus, Paramys, Sciuravus, Telmatherium,* and Dinocerata. We add taeniodonts, *Helohyus, Scenopagus, Macrocranion, Talpavus, Trogolemur, Ourayia, Pantolestes, Washakius, Omomys, Palaeictops, Didelphodus, Hemiacodon, Mesonyx, Microsyops,* and uintasoricines.

Characteristic Uintan fossils are *Epihippus, Protoreodon, Amynodon, Eobasileus, Metarhinus, Dolichorhinus, Triplopus, Protylopus, Mytonolagus,* and *Ischyrotomus.*

The Uintan is subdivisible faunally into early and late segments; the early segment is based on the fauna of Uinta A and B, from the Wagonhound Member; the late segment is based on the fauna of Uinta C, from the Myton Member of the Uinta Formation, and now also includes faunas from the lower part of the Brennan Basin Member of the Duchesne River Formation. The early Uintan (A and B) is marked by the first occurrence of *Epihippus,* hyracodonts, some brontotheres (*Metarhinus, Dolichorhinus*), some homacodontines (*Mytonomeryx, Bunomeryx, Hylomeryx, Mesomeryx*), *Achaenodon,* protoptychids, amynodonts, agriochoerids, and oromerycids. Taxa that disappeared at the end of Uinta B include *Protoptychus, Metarhinus, Telmatherium,* taeniodonts, and uintatheres. The first camelids, eomyids, and, possibly, canids appeared in North America at the beginning of Uinta C, and limnocyonids decreased in diversity. Late Uintan first appearances also include *Domnina, Thylacaelurus, Colodon, Poebro-*

don, *Prodaphoenus*, *Simidectes*, *Procynodictis*, and *Epitriplopus*.

Duchesnean

The Duchesnean was originally based on the fauna from the entire Duchesne River Formation of northeastern Utah but is now based solely on the fauna of the LaPoint Member and its correlatives. The Duchesne River Formation directly overlies the Uinta Formation in much of the Uinta Basin, with intertonguing occurring through a thickness of at least 1,064 feet (325 m) (Andersen and Picard 1972, p. 9). There apparently is no significant depositional hiatus between the members of the Duchesne River Formation.

Evaluation of the two lower faunas of the Duchesne River Formation (Randlett and Halfway) suggests they are extremely similar to those of the Myton Member of the Uinta Formation. Genera in common are *Epihippus*, *Protitanotherium*, *Leptotomus*, *Mytonomys*, *Pentacemylus*, *Diplobunops*, *Epitriplopus*, *Dilophodon*, *Amynodon*, *Mytonolagus*, and *Teleodus*. The Randlett fauna (from the Brennan Basin Member) and the Halfway fauna (from the Brennan Basin and lower Dry Gulch Creek Member) are Uintan (see Gazin 1955; Tedford 1970; Emry 1981). This would restrict the Duchesnean to the faunas from the LaPoint Member and upper Dry Gulch Creek Member; recognition of the Duchesnean as a valid biostratigraphic interval depends on the uniqueness of these faunas. According to Emry (1981), the LaPoint assemblage has the earliest North American records of *Duchesneodus* (Lucas and Schoch 1982; = *Teleodus uintensis* of Emry 1981), *Brachyhyops*, *Hyaenodon*, *Simimeryx*, *Poabromylus*, *Hyracodon*, and *Agriochoerus*. These taxa, with the exception of *Duchesneodus*, are also known from Chadronian rocks, and some are known from younger deposits. This post-Uintan faunal turnover may represent, in part, an immigration event from Asia. It is equivalent in magnitude to faunal events used to define the biostratigraphic boundaries between the other Eocene land mammal ages. As such, the lower boundary of the Duchesnean can be defined by the first appearance of the aforementioned taxa. Whether the Duchesnean deserves recognition as a distinct land mammal age or as a subage of the Chadronian depends on the definition of the onset of the Chadronian. According to Emry (1981: see also chap. 5) and Wilson (1984), the latter interpretation may be warranted, in which case the Uintan-Duchesnean boundary would be synonymous with the Uintan-Chadronian boundary. Clearly, to resolve this issue additional faunas from this period as well as detailed stratigraphic collections are needed.

Other Duchesnean localities include Badwater Locality 20, Wyoming (Wagon Bed Formation; *Poabromylus*, *Apternodus*, daphoenine amphicyonids; Krishtalka and Setoguchi 1977; Black 1978; Dawson 1980); Pearson Ranch, California (Sespe Formation; *Hyaenodon*, *Simimeryx*, *Duchesneodus;* Savage and Russell 1983); Tonque Local Fauna, New Mexico (Galisteo Formation; *Duchesneodus*, *Poabromylus;* Lucas and Kues 1979); Mariano Mesa, New Mexico (Baca Formation; *Brachyhyops*, ?*Hyaenodon;* Lucas et al. 1981). Reported Duchesnean faunas that require further study are those from Shoddy Springs, Montana (Krishtalka and Black 1975); Kishenehn Formation, British Columbia and Montana (Russell 1954, Savage and Russell 1983); and Antelope Creek, South Dakota (Savage and Russell 1983). Badwater Locality 20, with an overlying radiometric date of 41.2 Ma (Black 1969; 42.3 Ma as emended below), is considered to be at the base of the Duchesnean.

CORRELATION AND CALIBRATION

The Wasatchian, Bridgerian, and Uintan-Duchesnean ages described and characterized above generally have been understood to represent early, medial, and late Eocene time. These Eocene time periods are defined in Europe on quite different bases from those used to define land mammal ages in North America (Berggren et al. 1978). There is no logical reason for the boundaries of European epochs and their subdivisions and North American land mammal ages to coincide.

Recent developments in radiometric and magnetostratigraphic dating techniques have produced numerous dates calibrating Clarkforkian, Wasatchian, Bridgerian, Uintan, and Duchesnean rocks and faunas. This allows construction of the correlation calibration charts (figs. 4.2–4.4) with radiometric and magnetostratigraphic dates to provide a temporal framework. Biostratigraphy is used to correlate those formations and faunas that have no radiometric controls. Table 4.1 lists the radiometric dates used in the construction of our composite chronology. Not all of these dates have been given equal weight and included on figures 4.2, 4.3, and 4.4; important here is their repeatability and corroboration from biostratigraphy. Only in southern California are there interfingerings with marine rocks that allow some correlation of prominent terrestrial mammal sequences with macroinvertebrate and foraminiferal assemblages.

We take the Wasatchian through Duchesnean interval (approximately the Eocene epoch) to have lasted from approximately 57.5–56.5 to approximately 39–38

TABLE 4.1
Radiometric Ages on Which Calibration is Based

Original Date _Recalibrated Date (*)_	_Rock Unit_	_Relations_	_Mineral_	_Significance_	_Reference_
A 49.2 ± 1.5 m.y. 50.5 ± 1.5*	Lost Creek Tuff	Overlies Willwood Formation	Sanidine	Latest Wasatchian or younger	Smedes and Prostka 1972
B 48.0 ± 1.3 49.2 ± 1.3*	Pacific Creek Tuff Member of Trout Peak Trachyandesite	Correlates with Aycross Formation (Bridgerian) and overlies Willwood Formation	Biotite	Indirectly dates part of Bridgerian	Smedes and Prostka 1972
C 47.9 ± 1.3 49.1 ± 1.3*	"Two Ocean Formation"—Formation actually Langford ?	Underlies correlated ?Tepee Trail Formation of Bridgerian—early Uintan age; overlies latest Wasatchian or earliest Bridgerian	Biotite, sanidine	Older than ?Tepee Trail Formation; younger than Wasatchian	Smedes and Prostka 1972
D 46.1 ± 1.2 47.3 ± 1.2*	Correlated Tepee Trail Formation	Ash 10 ft. below top of Tepee Trail Formation of Bridgerian—early Uintan age; overlies a Bridgerian fauna	Sanidine	Bridgerian or early Uintan; postdates Bridgerian fauna	Smedes and Prostka 1972
E 49.3 ± 1.4 50.6 ± 1.4	Correlated Tepee Trail Formation	Ash 100 ft. below top of Tepee Trail Formation	Biotite (altered)	Bridgerian or early Uintan; postdates Bridgerian fauna	Smedes and Prostka 1972
F 47.8 ± 1.3 49.0 ± 1.3* 47.9 ± 1.3 49.1 ± 1.3*	Tepee Trail Formation (?)	400 ft. below top of referred Tepee Trail Formation; 230 ft. below Bridgerian fauna	Sanidine, biotite	Dates a Bridgerian fauna in the ?Tepee Trail Formation	Smedes and Prostka 1972
G 46.2 ± 1.8 47.4 ± 1.8*	Base of Wiggins Formation (same loc. as H), lava flow, Pinnacle Buttes area		Hornblende	Bridgerian or younger	Rohrer and Obradovich 1969; Smedes and Prostka 1972
H 46.5 ± 2.3 47.7 ± 2.3*	Base of Wiggins Formation (same loc. as G), lava flow, Pinnacle Buttes area		Hornblende	Bridgerian or younger	Rohrer and Obradovich 1969; Smedes and Prostka 1972
I 44.4 ± 1.4 45.6 ± 1.4* 45.5 ± 1.3 46.7 ± 1.3*	Wiggins Formation, about 800 ft. above base		Hornblende, biotite	?Uintan or younger	Smedes and Prostka 1972; Love and Keefer 1975
J 47.1 ± 1.3 48.3 ± 1.3*	Wiggins Formation	500–600 ft. above base of formation, Wiggins Fork area	Biotite	Early Uintan or younger	Smedes and Prostka 1972
K 46.7 ± 1.5 47.9 ± 1.5*	Wiggins Formation	500–600 ft. above base of formation, Wiggins Fork area	Biotite	Early Uintan or younger	Smedes and Prostka 1972
L 44.6 ± 1.2 45.8 ± 1.2*	Wiggins Formation	650–750 ft. above base of formation, Wiggins Fork area	Biotite	Early Uintan or younger	Smedes and Prostka 1972
M 45.0	High in Wiggins Formation	Same as G		Early Uintan or younger	Love et al. 1978
N 43.1 ± 1.1	High in Wiggins Formation	Same as G; highest Wiggins sample		Early Uintan or younger	Love and Keefer 1975

TABLE 4.1
Radiometric Ages on Which Calibration is Based—*Continued*

Original Date / Recalibrated Date (*)		Rock Unit	Relations	Mineral	Significance	Reference
O	49.2 ± 0.5 / 50.3 ± 0.5*	Aycross Formation, type area	Low in type section of Aycross; 70.7 m above flora, near Bridgerian mammals	Biotite	Overlies Wasatchian fauna; dates Bridgerian fauna and underlies early Uintan faunas	Love et al. 1976
P	49.4 ± 1	Basalt at summit of Pinyon Peak	Volcanic rocks that lie unconformably on principal reference section of Pinyon Conglomerate	Whole-rock date by Isotopes, Inc.	May date Langford or Trout Peak Formation	McKenna and Love 1970
Q	42.7 / 43.9* / (42.4) / (43.6)*	Alamo Creek Basalt, Texas	Underlies Chisos Formation, whose Ash Spring Basalt Member yields dates of 32–34 m.y.		Predates possible Uintan fauna in Texas, but paleontological control poor; not useful at present	Evernden et al. 1964; KA1274
R	45.0 / 46.2*	Wagon Bed Formation, Badwater, Wyoming	Associated with early Uintan fossils		Dates early Uintan fossils, but fauna poor	Evernden et al. 1964; KA1024
S	45.4 / 46.6*	Unit 3, Wagon Bed Formation	Laterally equivalent to either Wiggins or Tepee Trail Formation		Listed as late Bridgerian/early Uintan by Evernden on basis of three poorly known specimens	Evernden et al. 1964; KA1018
T	49.0 / 50.3*	Unit 1, Wagon Bed Formation	Overlies KA1012 (U)	Bentonitic tuff	Probably early Bridgerian, but no fossil control nearby	Evernden et al. 1964; KA1021
U	49.2 / 50.5*	Halfway Draw Tuff, Wind River Formation	Underlies KA1021 (T)	Biotite	Calibrates late Wasatchian fossils	Evernden et al. 1964; KA1012
V	"33.9 ± 3.4"	Blue Point Conglomerate Member, Wiggins Formation Irish Rock	Wiggins Formation of Carter Mountain area associated with Eocene fauna	"Slightly chloritized biotite"	Unreliable (supplanted by a date (GG) of 46.7 for rock above yellow tuffs with bones)	J. D. Love 1970
W	41.2 ± 1.4 / 42.3 ± 1.4*	Correlated "Tepee Trail Formation," Badwater, Wyoming	Hendry Ranch Member, Wagon Bed Formation, loc. 20	Biotite	Dates Duchesnean fossils	Black 1969
X	38.8 ± 1.6 / 39.9 ± 1.6*	Washakie Needles Dacite	Intrudes Wiggins Formation		Younger than part or all of Wiggins	L. L. Love et al. 1976
Y	42.5 ± 2.6 / 43.7 ± 2.6*	Birch Hills Dacite intrusion	Intrudes Wiggins Formation		Younger than Bridgerian	L. L. Love et al. 1976
Z	"about 50"	Lapilli tuff	Correlated Aycross Formation		Latest Wasatchian	Rohrer, in MacGinitie et al. 1974; McKenna, unpubl. data

TABLE 4.1
Radiometric Ages on Which Calibration is Based—*Continued*

Original Date / *Recalibrated Date (*)*		*Rock Unit*	*Relations*	*Mineral*	*Significance*	*Reference*
AA	49.3 50.6*	?Aycross Formation White Pass Bentonite	Below Kissinger Lakes flora; correlates with L-41 (McKenna 1980)	Biotite	Correlates with an earliest Bridgerian fauna at L-41	MacGinitie et al. 1974
BB	48.6 49.9*	Basaltic intrusives and extrusives on Pilgrim Creek	Cuts pre-Eocene but underlies 45.9 (47.1*) m.y. volcaniclastics (CC)		Predates a 45.9 (47.1*) m.y. unit (CC)	J. D. Love and J. D. Obradovich, pers. com. to McKenna, 1976
CC	45.9 47.1*	Volcaniclastics on Pilgrim Creek	Overlies BB 48.6 (49.9*) m.y. intrusives and extrusives; underlies a unit with earliest Chadronian mammals		Predates an earliest Chadronian fauna	J. D. Love and J. D. Obradovich, pers. com. to McKenna, 1976
DD	40.2 ± 1.4 41.3 ± 1.4*	Dike intruding Wiggins Formation	Quartz monzonite dike intruding Wiggins Formation		Postdates Wiggins at this location	Schassberger 1972
EE	48.9 50.1*	Main tuff in Wilkins Peak Member, Green River Formation	In volcanic-rich environment; defines Wasatchian-Bridgerian boundary		Dates Wasatchian-Bridgerian boundary	Mauger 1977
FF	49 50.2*	Little Mountain Tuff, Wilkins Peak Member, Green River	Top 1/3 of Wilkins Peak Member; same as above	Biotite	Dates Wasatchian-Bridgerian boundary	Mauger 1977
GG	46.7 47.9*	Above yellow tuffs that bear fossil vertebrates on Carter Mountain	Eocene on top of Carter Mountain	Biotite	Corrects 33.9 date (V)	L. L. Love et al. 1976
HH	38.6 ± 1.2 39.7 ± 1.2*	Buckshot Ignimbrite	Overlies Candelaria local fauna	Sanidine	Dates Uintan-Duchesnean fauna	Wilson et al. 1968
II	39.5 40.6*	Duchesne River Formation	Contact of Dry Gulch and LaPoint members	Biotite	Dates Duchesnean	Unpublished rerun of 39.3 date (NN) by J. A. Wilson
JJ	34.4 ± 1.4 35.5 ± 1.4*	Oligocene at Badwater			Younger than Wood locality	Black 1969
KK	45.8 46.9*	Pruett Tuff	Whistler Squat #2 Quarry		Dates early Uintan fauna	McDowell 1979
LL	42.9 ± 0.9 44.0 ± 0.9* 48.6 ± 1.3 49.8 ± 1.3*	Pruett Tuff	Channel above Whistler Squat #2 Quarry	Biotite Alkali feldspar	Postdates the early Uintan faunas at Whistler Squat #2 Quarry	McDowell 1979
MM	46.2 ± ? 47.4 ± ?*	"Tepee Trail equivalent" (?Wiggins) Hawks Butte near Lysite Mountain		Biotite		J. D. Love 1970
NN	39.3 ± 0.8 40.4 ± 0.8*	Duchesne River Formation	Contact of Halfway and LaPoint members	Biotite	Dates Duchesnean (see II)	McDowell et al. 1973

TABLE 4.1
Radiometric Ages on Which Calibration is Based—*Continued*

Original Date / Recalibrated Date (*)		Rock Unit	Relations	Mineral	Significance	Reference
OO	43.6 ± 1.0 44.7 ± 1.0*	Wavy Tuff Member, Green River Formation, Gate Canyon, Utah, 320 ft. below Horsebench sandstone	50–100 ft. above Mahogany Tuff, 20 ft. above Mahogany Oil Shale	Biotite	Predates basal Uinta Formation sandstone in eastern Utah	Mauger 1977
PP	44.8 ± 0.9 46.0 ± 0.9*	Wavy Tuff Member, Green River Formation, Indian Canyon, Utah	50–100 ft. above Mahogany Tuff, 20 ft. above Mahogany Oil Shale; 98 in. below Horsebench SS marker, Green River Formation	Biotite	Predates basal Uinta Formation sandstone in eastern Utah	Mauger 1977
QQ	44.7 ± 0.9 45.9 ± 0.9*	Unit IC–6–105 Green River Formation, Indian Canyon, Utah	50–100 ft. above Mahogany Tuff, 20 ft. above Mahogany Oil Shale; 91 in. below Horsebench SS marker, Green River Formation	Biotite	Predates basal Uinta Formation sandstone in eastern Utah	Mauger 1977
RR	41.9 ± 1.3 43.1 ± 1.3*	Gray Tuff below contact between Green River Formation and saline facies of Uinta Formation—Indian Canyon		Biotite		Mauger 1977
SS	41.7 ± 1.0 m.y. 42.8 ± 1.0*	Tuff in saline facies of Uinta Formation, Indian Canyon, Utah, 63 ft. below contact		Biotite	?Uintan	Mauger 1977
TT	37.1 ± 1.1 38.2 ± 1.1* 34.8 ± 0.9 35.9 ± 0.9*	Duchesne River Formation 50–100 ft. below boundary between LaPoint and Halfway members		Biotite	Unreliable?	Mauger 1977
UU	45.8 ± 0.7 47.0 ± 0.7* 46.0 ± 0.7 47.2 ± 0.7*	Tawny Tuff Member, Green River Formation, Sanpeteol, Utah		Biotite		Mauger 1977
VV	49.1 ± 1.1 50.4 ± 1.1*	Big Island Tuff (#3) in Wilkins Peak Member, Green River Formation	Lateral correlative of Bridger B	Biotite	Early Bridgerian	Mauger 1977
WW	48.8 ± 1.2 50.1 ± 1.2*	Tuff #3, Wilkins Peak Member, Green River Formation	Lateral correlative of Bridger B	Biotite	Early Bridgerian	Mauger 1977
XX	47.2 ± 1.2 48.4 ± 1.2*	Tuff #6, 2.4 m below top of Wilkins Peak Member, Green River Formation	Lateral correlative of Bridger B	Biotite	Unreliable?, ?early Bridgerian	Mauger 1977
YY	45.5 ± 0.7 46.7 ± 0.7*	Tuff in Laney Shale Member Green River Formation, Kinney Rim	Bed 452 in Washakie Basin Section, near early Bridgerian mammals	Biotite	early Bridgerian	Mauger 1977

TABLE 4.1
Radiometric Ages on Which Calibration is Based—*Continued*

Original Date		Rock Unit	Relations	Mineral	Significance	Reference
Recalibrated Date (*)						
ZZ	48.4 ± 1.0 49.6 ± 1.0*	Robin's Egg Blue Tuff in Washakie Formation	Bed 579 of Roehler	Biotite	Bridgerian (Uintan as modified by Turnbull)	Mauger 1977
AAA	44.5 ± 0.9 45.7 ± 0.9* 45.5 ± 0.9 46.7 ± 0.9*	Washakie Formation	Bed 664 of Roehler	Biotite	Uintan	Mauger 1977
BBB	45 46.2*	Green River Formation (no. Colo.); several hundred feet above Mahogany marker			Uintan	MacGinitie et al. 1974
CCC	49 50.3*	Laney Shale Member, Green River Formation, T8N R106W southeastern Green River Basin	Dates Little Mountain flora = Kissinger Lake flora		Early Bridgerian	MacGinitie et al. 1974
DDD	50.2–52.0 51.5–53.3*	Lost Cabin Member, Wind River Formation			Dates late Wasatchian	MacGinitie et al. 1974
EEE	48.5 ± 0.5 49.75 ± 0.5*	Bridger Formation Tabernacle Butte, Wyo.	Tuff overlies a late Bridgerian site		Dates late Bridgerian	Berggren et al. 1978
FFF	40.0 ± 2.0 41.2 ± 2.0*	Gill Breccia	Underlies Candelaria Local Fauna	Whole rock	Dates Uintan/ Duchesnean fauna	Wilson et al. 1968
GGG	39.8 ± 2.8 41.0 ± 2.8*	Chambers Tuff	Dates Candelaria local fauna	Sanidine	Dates Uintan/ Duchesnean fauna	Wilson et al. 1968
HHH	47.7 ± 1.5 48.9 ± 1.5*	Fowkes Formation, 7 m above Bulldog Hollow Member	State Line Quarry		Bridgerian	Oriel and Tracey 1970
III	44.0 ± 2.6 45.1 ± 2.6*	Intrusive cutting Wagon Bed Formation, Rattlesnake Hills area		Rhyodacite	Uintan or younger	Pekarek et al. 1974
JJJ	43.6 ± 1.0 44.7 ± 1.0*	Intrusive cutting Wagon Bed Formation, Rattlesnake Hills area		Phonolite	Uintan or younger	Pekarek et al. 1974
KKK	47.9 ± 1.9 49.1 ± 1.9*	Fowkes Formation, 7 m above Bulldog Hollow Member	State Line Quarry		Bridgerian	Nelson 1979
LLL	47.9 ± 0.5*	"Blue Point Conglomerate Member," Wiggins Formation, Carter Mountain	Overlies Bridgerian mammals and Trout Peak Trachyandesite		Bridgerian or younger	Bown 1982
MMM	48.5 ± 0.6*	"Blue Point Conglomerate Member," Wiggins Formation, Carter Mountain	Overlies Bridgerian mammals and Trout Peak Trachyandesite		Bridgerian or younger	Bown 1982
NNN	49.2 ± 0.6*	Wiggins Formation near Sylvan Pass				Bown 1982

Ma (Berggren et al. 1985). The Wasatchian age (ca. 57.5–51 Ma) is equated with the early Eocene of Europe but may begin in the late Thanetian, depending on how the base of the European Ypresian is defined (Berggren et al. 1978; Rose 1980, 1981). The Bridgerian age (51–48 Ma) is equivalent to only part of the European medial Eocene, the Uintan (48–42 Ma) is equivalent to late medial Eocene, and the Duchesnean (42–38 Ma) is equated with late medial Eocene and late Eocene (Berggren et al. 1985). The dates for the late Wasatchian, the Bridgerian, and most of the Uintan are reasonably secure, but the time lines for the beginning of the Wasatchian and the end of the Duchesnean are not radiometrically documented. Intercontinental faunal correlations are good for the early and medial Eocene (Savage 1977), but later Eocene correlations between Europe and North America suffer from a decline in the shared taxa and rely almost exclusively on radiometric and magnetostratigraphic evidence (Berggren et al. 1985).

A difficulty with paleontological chronology is the likelihood of substantial differences existing between synchronous faunas because of evolutionary, geographic, and ecologic factors. This can be particularly confusing when either great distances (e.g., Wyoming to Texas or California) or altitudinal differences of several thousand feet (basins to surrounding highlands) are involved. The accompanying correlation/calibration charts represent the present consensus of the authors. The various number and letter symbols on the charts refer to local faunas mentioned in the text and figure 4.1 and to radiometric dates listed in table 4.1. As mentioned above, recalibrated dates (see Dalrymple 1979, Steiger and Jager 1977) are marked with an asterisk (*).

Wind River Basin

Northwestern Wind River Basin (fig. 4.2)

Although most of the vertebrate fossil localities in the northwestern Wind River Basin are poorly productive in comparison with the more extensive, well-known northeastern basin sites, they have assumed an important correlative role because of their close association with K-Ar dated volcanic and volcaniclastic rocks. Recent publications (Rohrer and Obradovich 1969; Smedes and Prostka 1972; MacGinitie et al. 1974; Love and Keefer 1975; J. D. Love et al. 1976; McKenna 1980b) have outlined the Tertiary geology of the Yellowstone Plateau and the area bordering it to the south and east and have provided many of the dates recorded in table 4.1.

The oldest "Eocene" fauna in the northwestern Wind River Basin is derived from the "lower variegated sequence" of Love (1947) through a thickness of about 900 feet (275 m) of variable clastic, mostly nontuffaceous sediments. There are as yet no radiometric dates for this assemblage (McKenna 1972, p. 86). The vertebrate fossils (McKenna 1980b, Rose 1981) show a change in faunal composition from the Clarkforkian to Wasatchian as higher levels within the unit are sampled. Species of common genera such as *Pelycodus, Hyopsodus,* and *Diacodexis* firmly place the upper part of the "lower variegated sequence" in the very early Wasatchian, but the lower part is clearly Clarkforkian, with *Coryphodon, Plesiadapis dubius, P. cookei, Esthonyx ancylion,* and *Arctostylops steini.* These fossils are known from the Purdy Basin in the Sheridan Pass Quadrangle and along Hardscrabble Creek and Red Creek at the boundary between the Tripod Peak and Lava Mountain quadrangles. The lower part of the Indian Meadows Formation (Love 1939), as redefined by Keefer (1965, p. 36), about 40 miles (65 km) east-southeast of the two sites discussed above and physically discontinuous, produced an early—but apparently not earliest—Wasatchian fauna (Denison 1937; McKenna, unpublished data).

Stratigraphically above the lower variegated sequence, separated from it by a 300-foot (91.5 m) coal-bearing unit, is Love's (1947) "upper variegated unit." Its fauna, although not well known, is clearly Wasatchian in age (McKenna 1980b). Overlying the upper variegated sequence is a volcaniclastic sequence (Aycross Formation) that contains datable volcanic debris about 500 feet (150 m) above the base, the Coyote Creek flora (MacGinitie et al. 1974, pp. 14–15), fossil land mollusks, and a few mammalian and other vertebrate remains. The vertebrate fossils are late Wasatchian or early Bridgerian (McKenna 1980b), but one locality is associated with a K-Ar date of "about 50 my" (Rohrer, in MacGinitie et al. 1974).

After a period of uplift, folding, and erosion, a highly tuffaceous third variegated unit was deposited in the northwestern Wind River Basin. This unit and the volcaniclastic sequence beneath it are perhaps best referred to the Aycross Formation (Love 1939) and are possibly correlative with the uppermost "Wind River Formation" of Keefer (1956) north of Dubois and the Cathedral Bluffs/Wilkins Peak complex of the Green River Basin. Fossil vertebrate locality L-41 is in these Aycross rocks southwest of the summit of Togwotee Pass. Its small fauna suggests latest Wasatchian or early Bridgerian age (McKenna 1980b), as does a date of 49.3 (50.6*) Ma (Rohrer, in MacGinitie et al. 1974, p. 16) on the White Pass Bentonite of the Aycross Formation (J. D. Love et al. 1976).

Overlying the unit that contains locality L-41 is a mafic lahar that has been dated at 47.9 ± 1.3 (49.1 ± 1.3*) Ma (sanidine) and 48.5 ± 1.3 (49.7 ± 1.3*) Ma (biotite) (Smedes and Prostka 1972). This is overlapped, in turn, by a greenish volcaniclastic unit, exposed in a small badlands area at the summit of Togwotee Pass, that Love (1939) traced into the Tepee Trail Formation but now (Love et al. 1978) prefers to refer to the Aycross Formation. This unit has been dated 400 feet (122 m) below its top at 47.8 ± 1.3 (49.0 ± 1.3*) Ma (sanidine) and 47.9 ± 1.3 (49.1 ± 1.3*) Ma (biotite) (Smedes and Prostka 1972). The fauna from Togwotee Summit (including *Hyrachyus, Palaeosyops*, cf. *Trogosus, Microsyops, Washakius, Tillomys, Sciuravus, Hyopsodus*, and cf. *Orohippus*) is early Bridgerian and is similar to the early Bridgerian fauna from the south central Green River Basin and the type Aycross Formation. The Togwotee Summit fauna and its associated dates serve to calibrate part of the Bridgerian in a way that has not yet been done in the Green River Basin.

Approximately 40 miles (64 km) east of Togwotee Pass, a vertebrate assemblage has been quarried from unit 24 (Bone Bed A) of the type section of the Tepee Trail Formation (Love 1939) in the East Fork Basin. *Epihippus, Dilophodon, Amynodon*, a *Tapocyon*-like miacid, *Achaenodon, Forstercooperia*, and primitive selenodont and bunodont artiodactyls are included in the fauna (McKenna 1980b, MacFadden 1980). This assemblage is younger in age than any known Bridgerian assemblage, although it is more primitive than the Uinta B fauna from northern Utah. The fauna from Bone Bed A correlates well with that from Uinta A; both mark the onset of the Uintan. The Tepee Trail Formation below that locality is considered late Bridgerian or early Uintan in age. Available dates place the Tepee Trail Formation in the interval from about 49.5 Ma to about 48 Ma, which therefore includes the Bridgerian/Uintan boundary (as discussed above).

At the southeastern end of the Absaroka Mountains, in the drainage of Owl Creek, Eaton (1980, 1982) and Bown (1982) have collected definitive Bridgerian faunas from the Aycross Formation and other horizons. The occurrence of *Scenopagus, Microsyops, Uintasorex, Omomys, Anaptomorphus, Washakius, Viverravus, Mesonyx, Hyopsodus paulus, Trogosus, Orohippus, Helohyus, Helaletes*, and *Hyrachyus* confirm the biochronologic placement in the Bridgerian (see Bown 1982 and Eaton 1982 for the age of the different faunas).

Middle and upper Tepee Trail Formation rocks in the Owl Creek drainage have yielded the Uintan taxa *Amynodon, Forstercooperia, Epihippus, Achaenodon*, and *Hylomeryx* (Eaton 1980). Numerous K-Ar dates

(Smedes and Prostka 1972) give a temporal range of about 48* to 44* Ma. The spectacular, cliff-forming Wiggins Formation overlies the Tepee Trail Formation; long thought to be Oligocene, vertebrate fossils from referred Wiggins exposures at the southern margin of the Wind River Basin are Uintan in age (Emry 1975). Finally, Eaton (1980) reported a small Uintan fauna from the Wiggins Formation near Cottonwood Creek on the North Fork of Owl Creek. It includes *Ourayia, Prodaphoenus, Hyopsodus uintensis, Epihippus, Amynodon*, and *Protoreodon*.

Central and Eastern Wind River Basin (fig. 4.2)

The Indian Meadows Formation, as redefined by Keefer (1965), is exposed in few places east of its type section. An early Wasatchian fauna has been collected from it at Shotgun Butte and includes *Hyracotherium, Hyopsodus, Haplomylus, Coryphodon, Diacodexis*, and *Pelycodus* (Keefer 1965, table 2). In the Badwater area, isolated unfossiliferous outliers of Indian Meadows lie unconformably on Fort Union Formation rocks and are overlain unconformably by the Wind River Formation (Krishtalka et al. 1975). There are difficulties in separating the type section of the Indian Meadows Formation from the Wind River Formation in the northwestern part of the basin. Until additional study of the Indian Meadows Formation is completed, we tentatively follow Keefer, who used both composition (the Indian Meadows Formation has a substantial number of clasts of both Paleozoic and Precambrian origin, whereas Wind River Formation clasts are primarily Precambrian) and apparent age (the Indian Meadows Formation is early Wasatchian, whereas the Wind River Formation is middle Wasatchian to early Bridgerian) to differentiate the units.

The several thousand feet of the Wind River Formation produce at least three discrete faunas: a Lysitean (medial Wasatchian) from the Lysite Member, a Lostcabinian (late Wasatchian) from the lower part of the Lost Cabin Member, and a Gardnerbuttean (earliest Bridgerian) from the upper part of the Lost Cabin Member (Stucky and Krishtalka 1983; Stucky 1984a; Krishtalka and Stucky 1983). The first two are the faunal standards against which other presumed Lysitean and Lostcabinian assemblages are compared. The Lostcabinian is based on the *Lambdotherium* Range-Zone; the Gardnerbuttean, originally defined by the Huerfano B fauna, is now also characterized by the *Palaeosyops* Assemblage-Zone. Both zones are defined by Stucky (1984a). Given ages for the Lysitean and Lostcabinian are determined by correlation with dated rocks to the northwest, near Yellowstone National Park, which contain similar faunas and to a late Wasatchian date of 50.5 Ma from the upper part of the Wind River Formation (Lostcabinian part) associated with a specimen of *Lambdotherium* (Evernden et al. 1964, KA 1012).

Overlying the early Bridgerian part of the Wind River Formation in the northeastern Wind River Basin is a nearly unfossiliferous middle (?) Eocene volcaniclastic paraconglomerate (Stucky 1984*a*) and a thick long-ranging sequence originally referred to the Tepee Trail Formation (Tourtelot 1957) but now allocated to the Wagon Bed Formation (Love et al. 1978). The latter sequence is located in a graben between exposures of the Wind River Formation to the south and the Owl Creek/ Bighorn mountains to the north. It contacts the Wind River Formation along the Cedar Ridge normal fault system in the Badwater Creek area. The Wagon Bed Formation here contains the lower Green and Brown Member and the conformably overlying Hendry Ranch Member (Tourtelot 1957; Krishtalka et al. 1975; Love 1978).

Faunas from the Badwater series of localities suggest that *Phenacodus*-bearing locality 17 (West and Atkins 1970) is early Bridgerian in age, as is the nearby locality 18 (see also Wood et al. 1936). Localities 5, 5A, 6, and 7 and associated sites are late Uintan equivalents. Still higher are the Wood and Rodent localities and locality 20. The last of these is associated with a K-Ar date of 41.2 (42.3*) Ma (Black 1969) and contains a fauna similar to that from the LaPoint Member of the Duchesne River Formation. For this reason, the Duchesnean has its base fixed at about 42 Ma.

The nomenclatural treatment of rocks of Bridgerian, Uintan, and Duchesnean ages in the central and eastern Wind River Basin is at this time unclear. We have used the name Wagon Bed Formation for these units, which contain Bridgerian to Duchesnean faunas, but the upper unit, the Hendry Ranch Member, may be a distinct mappable unit, thus deserving formation rank, or it may be a distal (and later) fine-grained expression of the Wiggins Formation (Emry 1975). The entire Badwater area needs sedimentological analysis, with close comparisons to both the northwestern Wind River Basin and the Beaver Divide area.

Southern California (fig. 4.2)

Radiometric dates are not yet available from the Uintan-Duchesnean deposits of southern California. Thus, such age terms as "early," "medial," or "late" are relative and defined by paleontological correlations with Wyoming and Texas, where radiometric dates are available. Inter-

digitation with fossiliferous marine units, however, permits the southern California sites to be related to the European sequence with far greater precision than obtains for the inland areas. A summary of known occurrences of land-vertebrate taxa on a locality-by-locality basis in Eocene deposits of southern California can be found in Golz and Lillegraven (1977).

Significant collecting efforts for land vertebrates in the greater San Diego area have been confined to the dominantly nonmarine Friars Formation and the mixed marine and nonmarine Mission Valley Formation (of Kennedy and Moore [1971]). These formations are everywhere separated by the highly variable deltaic Stadium Conglomerate. The Friars Formation is a time-transgressive unit, partly contemporaneous with two principally marine formations farther to the west: the Ardath Shale and the Scripps Formation. In addition to earlier megafossil work, micropaleontological studies have been done in recent years on the Ardath Shale and Stadium Conglomerate. For example, Bukry and Kennedy (1969, p. 43) suggest that the Ardath Shale (old Rose Canyon Shale Member of the La Jolla Formation of Hanna [1926]) allows correlation, on the basis of calcereous nanoplankton, with "the upper part of the lower middle Eocene *Discoaster sublodoensis* Concurrent-range Zone," which correlates with Lutetian (medial Eocene) strata of France. Gibson (1971) and Steineck and Gibson (1971) have recognized that the Ardath Shale contains classic "Ulatisian" and the Stadium Conglomerate contains "Narizian" West Coast benthonic foraminiferal assemblages. According to Givens (1974, pp. 28–29), on the basis of fossil molluscan faunas, the Ardath Shale and basal Scripps Formation are considered parts of the "Domengine Stage" (of Clark and Vokes [1936]), whereas the upper part of the Scripps Formation shows elements characteristic of the "Transition Stage" (of Clark and Vokes [ibid.]).

Virtually all terrestrial vertebrate-bearing localities in the Friars Formation are found high in the section, not far below the contact with the Stadium Conglomerate. Similarly, the fauna from the Mission Valley Formation is derived from localities low in the section, not far above the Stadium Conglomerate. The mammalian assemblages from the two formations seem to represent a single fauna with variations in relative abundances of taxa resulting mainly from environmental differences. Golz (1976), however, recognizes some differences that he interprets as evolution within artiodactyl taxa between the two formations.

The mammalian fossils from the upper parts of the Friars Formation and Mission Valley Formation have traditionally been considered to occur earlier in the Uintan than the Uintan fossils from the Laguna Riviera localities, from Camp San Onofre, Ventura County (Stock 1948), and from most of the Rocky Mountain Uintan sites. The fossils have not been considered to be so primitive as to be referred to the Bridgerian.

The Friars-Mission Valley complex fauna is likely temporally correlative to the Uinta A assemblage from Bone Bed A in the type section of the Tepee Trail Formation (Love 1939; Smedes and Prostka 1972, p. 41; Berggren et al. 1978). Comparisons of specific taxa await detailed study of the Tepee Trail material by McKenna. The age of the Tepee Trail section is discussed by Leopold (in MacGinitie et al. 1974, p. 64) and McKenna (1980b).

The Camp San Onofre locality is in a sandstone lens near the northern extreme of Camp Pendleton Marine Corps Base. It is tentatively placed in the Santiago Formation (of Woodring and Popenoe [1945]) as no published maps or descriptions of the Camp San Onofre area exist. On the basis of fossil mammals, the age seems to be significantly younger than the Friars-Mission Valley fauna, and the taxa seem nearly equivalent to those from older parts (e.g., the Tapo Canyon and Brea Canyon Local Fauna sites) of the Sespe Formation in Ventura County, California (Golz 1976).

The Laguna Riviera localities are distributed along a north-south line on the eastern borders of the towns of Oceanside and Carlsbad in northern San Diego County in a section of lagoonal, fluviatile, and near-shore marine sandstone and mudstone. The rocks are probably of the Santiago Formation. The most productive localities are in and around the Laguna Riviera housing subdivision at the southeast edge of Carlsbad. The fossil mammals indicate a correlation with the Camp San Onofre locality, with the Brea Canyon and Tapo Canyon local faunas of the Sespe Formation, and with the fauna from the Myton Member of the Uinta Formation of Utah.

Fossil mollusks of the medial Eocene "Domengine Stage" have been collected from the Santiago Formation in the type areas in the Santa Ana Mountains north of Santiago Creek (Woodring and Popenoe 1945) and from rocks possibly referable to the Santiago in the Vista area northeast of Carlsbad (Givens and Kennedy 1976). The fossil vertebrates from Laguna Riviera are much younger than those from stratigraphic levels correlated with the "Transition Stage" (of Clark and Vokes [1936]) in San Diego. We will not be able to improve Santiago correlations until the stratigraphic and structural relationships of the invertebrate and vertebrate fossil localities are established by means of detailed stratigraphic mapping in the Carlsbad-Oceanside area.

Truex (1976, p. 68) shows a correlation between the

Santiago Formation as seen in the Santa Ana Mountains and the lower part (Eocene) of the Sespe Formation in the Santa Monica Mountains. According to him, the two areas were nearly contiguous at the time of sedimentary deposition but have been separated by almost 60 kilometers of post-early Miocene left-lateral motion along the Malibu Coast-Santa Monica-Raymond Hill-Sierra Madre fault system.

The Sespe Formation (see Kew 1924, pp. 30–39, and Dibblee 1966, pp. 36–40, for general features) is a continental clastic unit of great stratigraphic range, extending from ?Uintan at its base to Arikareean near its top. The formation represents a gradual, prolonged, and major westward regression of the sea from the southern California landscape. Thus, it is a large clastic wedge that is thickest to the east and laterally correlative with several marine formations to the west. Interpretations of facies relationships in the coastal area are clearly shown by Van de Kamp et al. (1974).

The Eocene mammal-bearing localities are mainly in the Simi Anticline area north of Simi Valley, Ventura County. Stock (1932, p. 521) shows the Sespe Formation at Brea Canyon to be more than 7,000 feet (2,135 m) thick with all Eocene mammal localities being within the lower 3,000 feet (915 m) (see also Durham et al. 1954, p. 60). Correlating these nonmarine mammal localities with specific parts of the local marine section is difficult for the following reasons. First, the Sespe rocks north of Simi Valley rest unconformably on the marine Llajas Formation (Weaver et al. 1944, chart 11). The Llajas is laterally equivalent to the Juncal Formation and part of the Matilija Sandstone (names formalized by Vedder [1972]) farther to the northwest. Mega- and microfossil assemblages from various localities in the Matilija summarized by Vedder (ibid. p. D9) suggest a medial to late Eocene age ("Tejon Stage" of Clark and Vokes [1936]), but the time represented by the unconformity between the Llajas and Sespe cannot be directly determined. Second, as yet, the precise levels of the Sespe at which the Eocene mammal localities occur has nowhere been recognized to coincide laterally with a specific fossiliferous marine sequence.

Overlying the Matilija Sandstone is the Cozy Dell Shale, and above that is the Coldwater Sandstone. Foraminifera from the latter two bathyal rock units at the Tecolote Tunnel northwest of the city of Santa Barbara were studied by Bandy and Kolpack (1963). They found that, on the basis of planktonic foraminiferans, the Cozy Dell Shale is medial Eocene in age and that "there is not one Priabonian (upper Eocene) index planktonic species in the Cozy Dell Shale of Tecolote Tunnel, but there are indices of the Ypresian-Lutetian, primarily lower Lutetian" (ibid., p. 120). Such an interpretation is compatible with megafossil evidence from the Cozy Dell Shale farther to the east in the Pine Mountain area (Givens 1974, pp. 22–23). Thus, the Cozy Dell would approximately correlate with the medial Eocene mammal-bearing localities of the greater San Diego area.

The Coldwater Sandstone in the Tecolote Tunnel lacks planktonic foraminifera, is about 2,000 feet (610 m) thick, and is thought to be late medial Eocene in age on the basis of its conformable relations with the underlying Cozy Dell Shale (Bandy and Kolpack 1963, p. 126). Either a sharp environmental break or a fault (ibid.) is present between the top of the bathyal Coldwater and the bottom of the directly overlying oxidized continental Sespe Formation. The Sespe is thus clearly conformable with the medial Eocene Cozy Dell and Coldwater formations at Tecolote Tunnel, and, again, the length of time represented by the hiatus is unknown; it could have been quite long. According to Bandy and Kolpack (p. 132), "the Sespe can be traced laterally to where it contains . . . various land mammals of upper Eocene to lower Miocene age." It is unclear, however, how much confidence one can actually have in the lateral equivalence of the Simi Anticline mammal localities and the Sespe section at Tecolote Tunnel.

Stock (1938) described a titanothere from Sespe Creek (locality CIT 292) in the Sespe Formation far to the northwest of the Simi Anticline vertebrate localities. The specimen shows similarities to Uintan and Chadronian titanotheres from the Rocky Mountain region and the stratigraphically highest Eocene vertebrate localities at the Simi Anticline. Locality CIT 292 is 400 to 700 feet (122–213 m) above the Coldwater Sandstone, with relations that are presumably conformable (Stock 1938, p. 508). The Coldwater Sandstone at Sespe Creek apparently represented near-shore marginal marine environments (Givens 1974, p. 36) in contrast to its bathyal nature at Tecolote Tunnel. Invertebrate fossils from the Coldwater were studied by Dreyer (1935), who regarded their affinities as late Eocene. According to Stock (1938, p. 510), Woodring (1931) considered the fauna to represent "the youngest Eocene faunal zone in California." However, in reevaluating the molluscan fauna from the same area, Givens (1974, p. 29) provided strong evidence of a Transition Stage (roughly medial Eocene age) correlating with the upper part of the Scripps Formation in the greater San Diego area.

It is perplexing to see the presence of a mid-Eocene Coldwater unit apparently conformably overlain by the latest Eocene mammal-bearing Sespe Formation, with the two units being separated by only 400 to 700 feet (122–213 m) of rock at Sespe Creek. Either the rates of deposition were unusually slow or the nature of the intervening rocks is more complex than was at first realized. Stock (1938, p. 508) pointed out that "deformational and structural complications in the immediate vicinity of the fossil locality make it difficult to determine the exact position of the titanothere remains in the Sespe above the contact with the Coldwater." Thus, it seems that some sort of unconformity representing a major amount of time could easily be hidden in the Sespe Creek area. Mason (pers. com. to West, 1981) suggests a fault below locality CIT 292 which accounts for the difficulties in determining local stratigraphic relationships.

Dibblee (1950, pp. 30–31) showed that the 1,200-foot-thick (366 m) marine Alegria Formation north of Point Conception is the lateral marine equivalent of at least part of the continental Sespe Formation. The top of "Member C" of the Alegria carries a molluscan assemblage characteristic of the "Refugian" Stage. The question remains whether the Alegria is the marine time equivalent of the Eocene mammal-bearing part of the Sespe farther to the east or whether the Alegria could be significantly younger.

The stages of evolution of the mammals from the Sespe Formation are far advanced compared to those of the animals recovered from the early Uintan San Diego section. The Tapo Ranch Local Fauna (= Tapo Canyon and Brea Canyon local faunas of Golz [1976]) is stratigraphically the lowest in the Sespe Formation. The presence of *Ischyrotomus* and *Leptoreodon* permit correlation with the Myton Member (Uinta C level) of the Uinta Formation of northeastern Utah (Stock 1948, p. 329; Black and Dawson 1966, p. 345). The Pearson Ranch Fauna is found stratigraphically higher in the Sespe Formation, and the fauna, which includes *Chumashius*, *Presbymys*, *Hyaenodon*, *Teleodus* (now = *Duchesneodus*; Savage and Russell 1983, *fide* Lucas and Schoch 1982), *?Triplopus*, *Simimeryx*, *Amynodontopsis*, and *Eotylopus*, is more advanced than the Tapo Ranch assemblage. The Pearson Ranch fossils suggest correlation with the LaPoint Member of the Duchesne River Formation of northeastern Utah and are considered Duchesnean in age (Stock 1948, p. 329).

Thus, interpretations of the Sespe mammal assemblages as being markedly younger than the Coldwater Sandstone at Tecolote Tunnel (Lutetian = medial Eocene) and roughly correlative with the Alegria Formation north of Point Conception (Refugian = late Eocene) are consistent with all available evidence but cannot yet be proven on lithostratigraphic information alone. Assuming a Refugian age for the mammal-bearing parts of the Sespe Formation, a correlation with the Bartonian-Priabonian-Auversian-Ludian medial to late Eocene sequence of Europe seems likely.

Uinta Basin and Western Colorado (fig. 4.3)

The Wasatchian in these areas is best represented on the southeastern side of the Piceance Basin of Colorado and in the Book Cliffs region on the southwest rim of the Uinta Basin of Utah. Extensive collections were made for the Field Museum of Natural History in the 1930s and 1940s from the Colorado River Valley by Patterson and for the University of Colorado in the 1970s and 1980s by Robinson and Kihm. Patterson thought that Tiffanian through Wasatchian rocks are present, and he reported many of the "Tiffanian" taxa (Patterson 1934, 1935, 1937, 1939a, 1939b, 1949; Patterson and Simons 1958; Patterson and West 1973). Wood et al. (1941) regarded the fossiliferous areas as two levels within the Debeque Formation. Donnell (1969) called all this the Wasatch Formation, following U.S. Geological Survey practice, with a Tiffanian Atwell Gulch Member and Wasatchian Moliner and Shire members. Until 1984, fossils recorded from the Wasatchian rocks included *Hyracotherium* (Kitts 1956), ischyromyid rodents (Wood 1962), and phenacodont condylarths (West 1976a). Gingerich (1978) described an arctocyonid from Clarkforkian rocks within the Debeque Formation; this age assignment is based on the occurrence of *Plesiadapis dubius* at the same locality.

Kihm (1984), in a recent review of the geology and mammalian paleontology of the Debeque Formation in the Piceance Basin, has recorded 124 mammalian species. They compose faunas of middle Clarkforkian through late Wasatchian age and possibly of Bridgerian age. The Plateau Valley Local Fauna, previously assigned to the Tiffanian, is regarded by Kihm as mid-Clarkforkian. J. Honey (pers. com., in Kihm 1984) also reports a Tiffanian fauna from the Debeque Formation. Apparently, much—if not all—of the Wasatchian is represented in the Piceance Basin. Kihm's work corroborates the Wasatchian faunal sequences established in the Bighorn and Wind River basins, although there are some differences in faunal composition.

Two fossiliferous early Eocene units are present on the southwest side of the Uinta Basin. The Colton Formation, a clastic fluvial floodplain deposit, is considered to be Wasatchian in age because of its intertonguing relationship with the Wasatchian Flagstaff Limestone (Marcantel and Weiss 1968). Fragments of mammals have been recovered by McKenna from the Colton,

but no identifiable material is yet available. The Flagstaff Limestone has produced one dentary of *Vulpavus australis* (Rich and Collinson 1973).

A series of localities in the Wasatch and Green River formations in the eastern Uinta Basin, collectively known as the Powder Wash sites (Burke 1935, Kay 1957), have produced two poor Wasatchian assemblages and one rich Bridgerian fauna. The Bridgerian locality is located 270 feet (82 m) below the Mahogany Oil Shale bed, in the Douglas Creek Member of the Green River Formation (Cashion, written com. 1967, in Dawson 1968, p. 327), and places the Powder Wash site low in that formation locally. Detailed faunal studies for most groups have not been completed; only the marsupials (Krishtalka and Stucky 1984), primates (Gazin 1958, Szalay 1976), rodents (Dawson 1968), an artiodactyl (Burke 1969), and adapisoricid, nyctitheriid, and geolabidid insectivores (Krishtalka 1975, 1976a, 1976b; Lillegraven et al. 1981) have been described. Krishtalka and Stucky (1984) have presented a revised faunal list and concluded that this fauna is early Bridgerian and post-Gardnerbuttean in age.

Lacustrine conditions persisted until the end of the Eocene in the Uinta Basin, as a recent recovery of the Duchesnean titanothere *Teleodus uintensis* from the Green River Formation in Sanpete County, Utah, indicates (Nelson et al. 1980). This species has since been referred to *Duchesneodus* (Lucas and Schoch 1982).

The younger fluvial formations of the Uinta Basin, the Uinta Formation, and the Duchesne River Formation are the type areas for the two youngest ages (Uintan and Duchesnean) considered in this chapter. Recent lithostratigraphic work by Andersen and Picard (1972) suggests an intertonguing relationship for the Uinta and Duchesne River formations through a thickness of at least 1,064 feet (325 m).

The consensus here is that the faunas from the Wagonhound Member are Uinta A and B (= early Uintan) and those from the Myton Member are Uinta C (= late Uintan). Much more fieldwork and collecting is necessary, especially in the areas of intertonguing of the Green River and Uinta formations (Cashion 1957, Dane 1954), the region of the Uinta A deposits.

The Brennan Basin Member of the Duchesne River Formation contains the Randlett Fauna; the Halfway Fauna comes from the lower two-thirds of the Dry Gulch Creek Member of the Duchesne River Formation. These two are considered Uinta C in age. The fauna from the LaPoint Member is Duchesnean. A date of 39.5 (40.4*) Ma (McDowell et al. 1973) at the contact of the Dry Gulch Creek and LaPoint members of the Duchesne River Formation serves to approximate the beginning of

Duchesnean time as restricted by Clark and Beerbower (in Clark et al. 1967) and by Tedford (1970), although the date just above Badwater locality 20 (41.2 ± 1.4; now 42.3 ± 1.4* Ma), with its post-Uintan assemblage, suggests that the Duchesnean began somewhat earlier (Berggren et al. 1978, 1985).

Washakie Basin (including Sand Wash and Great Divide Basins) (fig. 4.3)

The Wasatch Formation, exposed around the flanks of the Washakie Basin and rather extensively in the Great Divide Basin (see Bradley 1964, pl. 1), has yielded numerous local faunas. These demonstrate the apparent presence of all of Clarkforkian and Wasatchian time as the oldest assemblages appear to be roughly equivalent in age to those from the lowest part of the Willwood Formation, while the youngest are transitional into the Bridgerian. Two major assemblages come from the lower part of the Wasatch Formation. At the southeastern edge of the basin, in Moffat County, Colorado, are the numerous localities that produce the Four Mile Fauna (McKenna 1960). This fauna is equivalent to those from the lower Willwood Formation, and McKenna (1960, p. 26) cites several examples of specific identity.

In the vicinity of Bitter Creek, along the northern edge of the Washakie Basin, Savage and associates have made collections from a series of localities scattered through a continuous sedimentary section from the upper part of the Fort Union Formation to the Cathedral Bluffs Tongue of the Wasatch Formation. Although analysis of this collection is still in an early stage (Savage and Waters 1978, Savage and Russell 1983), it is clear that the faunas represent the entire Clarkforkian and Wasatchian interval. Other Washakie Basin and Great Divide Basin Wasatchian localities were enumerated by Gazin (1962). Although these are generally small assemblages with little stratigraphic control, they further confirm the age of the Wasatch Formation in the Washakie Basin.

The Niland Tongue of the Wasatch Formation along the west side of the Washakie Basin has produced the Dad Local Fauna, which is late Wasatchian in age. It contains the typical Lostcabinian paleothere, *Lambdotherium,* as well as other characteristic late Wasatchian mammals. The Niland Tongue is overlain by the Tipton Tongue and Wilkins Peak members of the lacustrine Green River Formation, and they are overlain by the uppermost Wasatch Formation subunit, the Cathedral Bluffs Tongue. As discussed above, it appears that the Cathedral Bluffs Tongue transgresses the Wasatchian-Bridgerian boundary.

The Laney Shale Member of the Green River Formation represents the last expansion of Gosiute Lake in southwestern Wyoming (Bradley 1964). This lacustrine sequence gave way to the fluvial deposits of the Washakie Formation, which contain the youngest record of early Tertiary fossil mammals in the Washakie Basin. Recent biostratigraphic work by Turnbull (1972, 1978) and Roehler (1973) has established the presence of considerable geologic time in the Washakie Formation. Roehler presented detailed sections for the Washakie Formation covering 3,213.4 feet (979.9 m), including his beds 515 to 708. He designated two members: the 893.9-foot (272.5 m) Kinney Rim Member (beds 515–568) and the 2,319-foot (707.2 m) Adobe Town Member, which is, in turn, divided into a lower part, beds 569–621 (Granger's [1909] Lower Washakie plus about 110 ft. [33.5 m] of his Upper Washakie), a middle part, beds 622–675 (most of Granger's Upper Washakie), and an upper part, beds 676–708 (a possible Uinta C equivalent not previously recognized) (Turnbull 1978, p. 577).

The Kinney Rim Member of the Washakie Formation contains Bridgerian taxa present in both Bridger B and Bridger C-D in the Green River Basin (Turnbull 1972, 1978). This particular level had not been recognized or sampled prior to Roehler's and Turnbull's work. The lowest part of the Adobe Town Member is Granger's (1909) Washakie A and is equivalent to the late Bridgerian. Such taxa as *Notharctus robustior, Hemiacodon, Stylinodon, Tetheopsis, Uintatherium, Mesatirhinus,* and (?)*Diplobunops* secure this age assignment. The middle Adobe Town, Washakie B, of Granger (1909) is early Uintan given the occurrence of *Protoptychus, Eobasileus, Dolichorhinus, Eomoropus, Triplopus, Amynodon, Achaenodon,* and *Protylopus.* The highest part of the Washakie Formation, beds 676–708 (upper Adobe Town), may represent another zone not recognized by Granger, who assumed that the summit of Haystack Mountain was the uppermost part of the Washakie Basin section. Roehler's work has shown that the top of Haystack Mountain is bed 661, and over 500 feet (153 m) of higher beds extend to the southwest of that prominent elevation. The upper 341 feet (104 m) are more carbonaceous than are the lower rocks and appear to represent a different depositional regime. The small vertebrate assemblage from this unit is inadequate for age assignment but may be Uinta C (Turnbull 1978) on the basis of superposition.

A recent attempt by Mauger (1977) to provide radiometric dates for the Washakie Basin has had mixed results. He reports seventeen K-Ar dates for tuffaceous ash falls throughout the Green River, Washakie, and Uinta basins. Many of his dates are at variance with our calibration. Mauger is aware of the inconsistencies in his results and has attempted to devise a means of assessing the reliability of each date. Like Mauger, we are reluctant to accept these dates until some repeatability has been established. Nonetheless, two dates have been carefully examined by Turnbull and seem to him to be reasonably accurate. One is a modification of Mauger's original 45.5 ± 0.9 (46.7 ± 0.9*) Ma to 43–44 (44–45*) Ma resulting from removal of extraneous "Cretaceous" biotite from a sample from marker bed 664. This, then, equates the middle Adobe Town Member with the medial or late Uintan as dated in the Wind River Basin. The other date accepted by Turnbull is Mauger's 45.5 ± 0.7 (46.7 ± 0.7*) Ma on Roehler's bed 452 at the top of the lower Laney Shale Member of the Green River Formation. This provides an adequate time framework for the 1,500-foot (457.5 m) thickness of Laney on the northwest side of the basin and extends Laney deposition well into the late Eocene. A third date (ZZ on fig. 4.3) from bed 579 (Robin's Egg Blue Tuff marker) was originally given a date of 48.4 ± 1.0 (49.6 ± 1.0*) Ma (represented by a bimodal [MgO/FeO] sample) and has been modified by Mauger to about 44 Ma. On stratigraphic and paleontological grounds, Turnbull agrees that the unadjusted date was too old, but he believes that the adjusted estimate is too young and that a more likely approximation is 46 Ma.

The Sand Wash Basin, a small depositional basin south of the Washakie Basin, contains Bridger Formation rocks (Tweto 1979) equivalent to, and initially continuous with, the lower part of the Adobe Town Member of the Washakie Formation. The small fauna (West and Dawson 1975) is earliest Uintan (*Triplopus, Protoreodon*) and includes Bridgerian holdover taxa.

Green River Basin (including Hoback and Fossil Basins) (fig. 4.3)

The Wasatch Formation is exposed along the western and northern margins of the Green River Basin (see Bradley 1964, Pl. I). In the type area, near Evanston in southwestern Wyoming, is a small medial Wasatchian mammalian assemblage that includes *Heptodon*. Clarkforkian and early Wasatchian mammals have recently been reported from near LaBarge, on the western side of the basin (Dorr and Gingerich 1980). Younger assemblages, Lostcabinian equivalents, have been found at several localities along the western and northern margins of the basin (Gazin 1952, 1962; West 1970, 1973a). The age is confirmed by the presence of *Lambdotherium* in the LaBarge and New Fork faunas and by the positions

of the fossiliferous fluvial rocks relative to the tongues of the Green River Formation.

The only attempt to provide radiometric dates for the Green River Basin Wasatchian has been by Mauger (1977), who dated tuffs in the upper part of the Wilkins Peak Member of the Green River Formation. Tuff 3 (Culbertson 1961) gave ages of 48.8 ± 1.2 (50.1 ± 1.2*) Ma and 49.1 ± 1.1 (50.4 ± 1.1*) Ma; tuff 6, 100 feet (30 m) higher in the section and only a few feet below the top of the Wilkins Peak Member, gave dates of 47.2 ± 1.1 (48.4 ± 1.1*) Ma and 45.1 ± 2.0 (46.3 ± 2.0*) Ma on two runs of the same sample. The latter dates are a bit younger than those we have used in compiling the calibration/correlation charts. They do, however, lend credence to placement of the beginning of the Bridgerian Land Mammal Age at about 51 or 50.5 million years ago.

On the basis of the various referred areas in the Yellowstone Plateau region (discussed above), we regard the Bridgerian as lasting 2 to 3 million years, from about 51–50.5 Ma to about 48.5–48 Ma.

Isolated areas of Bridgerian rocks crop out in the northeastern Green River Basin, in down-dropped blocks related to the western end of the Continental Fault system (McKenna et al. 1962; West and Atkins 1970; West 1973a; West and Dawson 1973). The oldest Bridgerian assemblage in this region comes from arkosic rocks of the Cathedral Bluffs Tongue of the Wasatch Formation and seems best placed in the early Bridgerian. It is overlain by more typical Bridger Formation rocks that produce a Bridger B fauna. Conformably overlying this early Bridgerian sequence are the tuffaceous rocks of Tabernacle Butte with a late Bridgerian assemblage (McGrew 1959). This particular assemblage is of interest as it contains a late Bridgerian *Phenacodus* and the only multituberculate known from the Bridgerian.

Fossil Basin is a separate depositional basin a few miles to the west of the western edge of the Green River Basin proper near Kemmerer, Wyoming. It is the site of the world-famous Green River fish beds that have produced so many exceptionally well-preserved teleosts. It also has the type sections of the Knight and Almy formations of Veatch's Wasatch Group (1907). Mammalian assemblages of both early and medial Wasatchian ages have been found at several localities (Gazin 1962, Oriel et al. 1962), and the upper assemblages are physically coincident with the fish-bearing beds. The fish beds are thus middle Wasatchian in age (Jepsen 1966).

Nelson (1973, 1974, 1977) collected a suite of Bridgerian mammals from the Fowkes Formation northwest of Evanston, Wyoming. This unit was initially recognized by Veatch (1907) as the middle part of the

Wasatch Group; recent U.S. Geological Survey work (summarized by Oriel and Tracey 1970) has shown that the Fowkes Formation is younger than the Wasatch Formation (Almy and Knight formations of Veatch). Nelson's fauna from the Fowkes Formation includes *Notharctus, Hemiacodon, Omomys, Uintasorex, Hyopsodus lepidus, Orohippus,* and several late Bridgerian ischyromyid rodents. The Bridgerian assignment is supported by a K-Ar age of 47.9 ± 1.9 (49.1 ± 1.9*) Ma on a biotite sample (Nelson 1979).

North of the present Green River Basin is a small physiographic depression, the Hoback Basin. J. A. Dorr and students from the University of Michigan have demonstrated virtually continuous sedimentation from Paleocene into medial Wasatchian time (Dorr 1952, 1958, 1969; Dorr and Steidtmann 1971; Dorr et al 1977). Although the paleontological record from the Wasatch and Pass Peak formations is not particularly good, specimens on hand (Dorr 1978) are adequate to demonstate the presence of three Clarkforkian sites (UM locs. 10, 20, and 7), four early Wasatchian sites (UM locs. 2, 16, 28, and 29), and two medial Wasatchian localities (UM locs. 23 and 27) (see also Dorr and Gingerich 1980). Sullivan (1980) has recently reviewed the Eocene stratigraphy of southwestern Wyoming.

West Texas (fig. 4.4)

Rocks producing fossils of Wasatchian, Bridgerian, and Uintan ages are present in three areas of West Texas: Big Bend National Park, the Vieja area of Presidio County, and the Agua Fria area of Brewster County. The oldest Eocene faunas have been collected from the uppermost part of the Black Peaks Formation and overlying Hannold Hill Formation in Big Bend National Park (Schiebout 1974; Rapp et al. 1983; Rose 1981). These faunas include *Phenacodus, Coryphodon,* and *Hyracotherium,* genera typical of the Wasatchian (see Flynn and Novacek 1984). Unconformably overlying the Hannold Hill Formation is the Canoe Formation, which contains a scanty fauna (indeterminate brontothere, *Hyrachyus,* and *Helohyus*) that is most likely late Bridgerian in age (Wilson 1967, 1977).

North of Big Bend National Park, the Whistler Squat and Serendipity local faunas are found in a restricted zone in the Devil's Graveyard Formation (which includes what was formerly called the Pruett Formation; see Stevens et al. 1984) at the base of the Buck Hill Group. The Whistler Squat Local Fauna was collected from rocks below a micaceous tuff dated at 42.9 ± 0.9 (44.0 ± 0.9*) Ma and above a calcareous tuff dated at 45.8 ± 1.1 (46.9 ± 1.1*) and 48.6 ± 1.3 (49.8 ± 1.3*) Ma

(McDowell 1979). The Serendipity Local Fauna comes from rocks above the 42.9 ± 0.9 (44.0 ± 0.9*) Ma tuff. The dates and the faunas indicate that the Whistler Squat Local Fauna is early Uintan and the Serendipity Local Fauna late Uintan in age (West 1982). Although the rodents from Whistler Squat suggest a late Bridgerian age to Wood (1973, 1974), the presence of *Amynodon, Sthenodectes, Protoreodon, Malaquiferus,* and *Leptoreodon* are indicative of the Uintan (Wilson 1971, 1977). West (1982) reviewed the Whistler Squat marsupials, primates, condylarths, taeniodonts, and bunodont artiodactyls, none of which preclude an early Uintan age.

Well to the northwest of the park is another fossiliferous sequence in datable volcanic rocks. The lower part of the Vieja Group, which unconformably overlies Cretaceous rocks, includes the fossiliferous Colmena Tuff. The Colmena produces the Candelaria Local Fauna (*Manitsha, Ischyrotomus, Epihippus, Sthenodectes, Protoreodon, Leptoreodon,* and *Toromeryx*), which correlates well with the latest Randlett and Halfway faunas of Utah. A date from the Gill Breccia (which directly underlies the Colmena Tuff) is 40.0 ± 2.0 (41.2 ± 2.0*) Ma, and a date of 38.6 ± 1.2 (39.7 ± 1.2*) Ma has been derived from the overlying Buckshot Ignimbrite (Wilson et al. 1968). Wilson (1977, 1984) regards the Candelaria Local Fauna as Uintan, rather than Duchesnean (which he does not recognize), because of the presence of *Epihippus.* Also, this fauna lacks any of the first appearances that mark the beginning of the Duchesnean (see above).

The Porvenir Local Fauna comes from the Chambers Tuff, above the Buckshot Ignimbrite (38.6 ± 1.2; now 39.7 ± 1.2* Ma) and below the Bracks Rhyolite (36.5 ± 1.2; now 37.7 ± 1.2* Ma) (McDowell 1979). It correlates biostratigraphically with the lower beds at Flagstaff Rim (Emry 1973) and is here considered Duchesnean; Wilson (1977), however, regards it as early Chadronian. Both conclusions are consistent with the suggestion that the Duchesnean may be the earliest subage of the Chadronian (Wilson 1984; Emry 1981; chap. 5).

The Alamo Creek Basalt Member of the Chisos Formation has an average date of 41.55 (42.75*) Ma (Maxwell et al. 1967, p. 137) but it may actually be a little older (Wilson, pers. com. to West, 1976); it is beneath the occurrence of a miacid referred to *Uintacyon.*

San Jose, Huerfano, Rio Grande Rift (fig. 4.4)

Several separate occurrences of Eocene mammals are noted in southern Colorado and New Mexico. None has radiometric control, so correlation of these to other areas is strictly biochronologic. The oldest assemblage occurs in the San Jose Formation of the northern San Juan Basin of northwestern New Mexico. Granger (1914) and Simpson (1948) recognized two main fossiliferous units of the San Jose Formation—the lower Almagre and upper Largo "beds" or "facies." Simpson also distinguished an unnamed basal sandstone facies. Baltz (1967) divided the San Jose into four members; the Regina Member includes the Almagre and lower Largo beds, and the Tapicitos, the upper Largo beds. The Llaves Member either overlies or intertongues with the Regina Member and, in turn, underlies or grades laterally into the Tapicitos Member. The Cuba Mesa Member includes Simpson's (1948) basal sandstone facies and underlies the Regina Member. The two faunas, one from the Almagre facies and the other from the Largo facies, are Wasatchian. Van Houten (1945) and Simpson (1948) regarded them as spanning the Graybullian to early Lysitean, a conclusion recently corroborated by Lucas et al. (1981) and Stucky and Krishtalka (1983). These two faunas are not as different as previously thought, and Lucas et al. (1981) suggest abandonment of the Largo-Almagre faunal distinction.

Well to the north, in the Huerfano Valley of southern Colorado, four superposed assemblages have been collected from the Huerfano Formation (Robinson 1966, Stucky 1984b). They correspond to four faunal zones: a Lysitean (Huerfano Locs. VIII, IX, XII; lower part of Robinson's Huerfano A); a Lostcabinian (Locs. IV, VI, XI; upper part of Robinson's Huerfano A); and two Gardnerbuttean (Loc. VII, Univ. of Michigan loc., Locs. I, II, III, V; uppermost part of Huerfano A, Huerfano B). As in the Wind River Basin, the Lostcabinian zone is defined by the first appearance of *Lambdotherium*. The Gardnerbuttean, first defined by Robinson (1966) on the basis of the fauna from Huerfano B, is now also recognized in the northeastern Wind River Basin (Stucky 1984a, 1984b; Stucky and Krishtalka 1983), and in the Cathedral Bluffs Tongue of the Wasatch Formation, by the first appearance of *Palaeosyops, Hyrachyus,* and *Trogosus,* among other taxa, and the absence of *Lambdotherium*. Robinson (1966) originally included the Gardnerbuttean in the latest Wasatchian (post-Lostcabinian and pre-Bridgerian), a position followed by McKenna (1976; see Dorr, in press); recent work (Stucky 1984a, 1984b) indicates that the Gardnerbuttean is the earliest subage of the Bridgerian, a view now endorsed by Robinson and other workers.

The upper part of the Galisteo Formation of north-central New Mexico (Stearns 1943) has produced a limited mammalian fauna, including *Teleodus* sp. (=

Duchesneodus; Lucas and Schoch 1982) and *Hyaenodon* (Mellett 1977), which suggests a Duchesnean age. Other scattered fossils from the Galisteo (Galusha 1966, Galusha and Blick 1971) are Eocene in aspect but not definitive. Robinson (1957), however, reported a *Coryphodon* tooth from 700 feet (213.5 m) above the base of the formation, indicating a probable Wasatchian age for the lower part of the formation. Lucas and Kues (1979) and Lucas et al. (1981) amplified the faunas from the Galisteo and recognized two local faunas. The lower, Cerrillos Local Fauna, now has *Coryphodon, Ectoganus, Microsyops, Hyopsodus,* cf. *Homogalax,* and *Hyracotherium* and is clearly Wasatchian, and probably Lysitean, whereas the upper, the Tonque Local Fauna, has *Forstercooperia, Pterodon, Amynodon, Teleodus (= Duchesneodus), Protoreodon,* and *Poabromylus* and is Duchesnean.

The Baca Formation, well exposed in western New Mexico, has produced small suites of fossil mammals from localities west of the Rio Grande which indicate an age span of Bridgerian to Chadronian (Schiebout and Schrodt 1981, Lucas et al. 1981). Gardner (1910) mentioned a titanothere, referred to ?*Palaeosyops* by Gidley, from variegated shale and sandstone above the coal in the Carthage Coal Field of central New Mexico. Lucas et al. (1981) reported cf. *Manteoceras* from essentially the same locality (east of the Rio Grande) which is Bridgerian in age. West of the Rio Grande, in the areas of White Mesa and Mariano Mesa, Snyder (1970), Schiebout and Schrodt (1981), and Lucas et al. (1981) reported assemblages of late Eocene mammals, including ?*Hyaenodon, Brachyhyops, Protoreodon, Leptomeryx,* and *Eotylopus.* These indicate a Duchesnean age for the western part of the Baca Formation.

Bighorn Basin and Southwestern Montana (fig. 4.4)

The 2,300-foot-thick (770 m) Willwood Formation of north-central Wyoming has produced a splendid series of fossil mammals, apparently continuous through Clarkforkian and Wasatchian time. Clarkforkian time is defined on the fauna that appears in both the upper Polecat Bench Formation and, in places, in the lowermost Willwood Formation. Early Wasatchian time (Sandcouleean and Graybullian) is based on assemblages from low in the Willwood Formation (Van Houten 1945; Gingerich 1980b; see discussion, above, of the term *Wasatchian*). Higher beds in the Willwood Formation produce assemblages that correlate with the faunas of the Lysite and Lost Cabin members of the Wind River Formation. At about 1,475 to 1,610 feet (475–520 m) above the base of the Willwood Formation is the lowest known occurrence of *Heptodon* (? = lowest boundary of Lysitean). *Heptodon* and *Homogalax protapirinus* occur together at two localities. *Lambdotherium* first occurs at about 2,015 feet (650 m) above the base of the Willwood Formation (? = base of Lostcabinian) and is found up to within 25 feet (7.6 m) of the Willwood-Tatman contact. The Willwood sequence traditionally has been divided into "Gray Bull," "Lysite," and "Lost Cabin" units; however, these terms are difficult to apply at this time. Current research indicates there is no lithologic basis for these divisions. *Homogalax*, Granger's (1914) index to the "Gray Bull," probably occurs in post-early Wasatchian rocks of the Washakie Basin and does not occur at all in 590 feet (180 m) of rocks at the base of the Willwood Formation east of the Bighorn River (Bown 1975). Moreover, the genus is extremely rare in the lower Willwood samples of the Clark's Fork Basin (the Sand Coulee of Granger [1914]). Local biozonations using species of *Pelycodus* and *Hyracotherium* (Gingerich 1980a, 1983) and *Haplomylus, Ectocion,* and *Bunophorus* (Schankler 1980) now serve to define the early and middle Wasatchian in the Bighorn Basin. The "Lysite" part of the Willwood sequence now is based informally on association of *Pelycodus jarrovii* and *Heptodon calciculus* in the absence of both *Homogalax* and *Lambdotherium* (Gingerich 1980a, Schankler 1980). This middle part of the Bighorn Basin Wasatchian is also under intensive study by T. M. Bown and K. D. Rose. The later Wasatchian is traditionally defined by the occurrence of *Lambdotherium*, although the genus is not present in all presumed late Wasatchian areas. In the central Bighorn Basin, the Willwood Formation is usually conformable on the older Polecat Bench Formation, and in the Clark's Fork Basin, Clarkforkian fossil occurrences are continuous across the lithologic boundary (Gingerich et al. 1980, Rose 1981).

The Tatman Formation, which conformably overlies and intertongues with the Willwood Formation in the southwestern part of the Bighorn Basin, was presumed to be Bridgerian in age by Van Houten (1944). D. Parris (Bown 1982) has found late Wasatchian mammals from low in the formation. So-called Tatman equivalents are overlain by, and intertongue with, the Aycross Formation to the south of Carter Mountain in the southeastern Absarokas (Bown 1982); the Aycross is also of early Bridgerian age, as indicated by the work of Jepsen (1939) and, more recently, Bown (1979b, 1982).

North of Carter Mountain, the Willwood is overlain unconformably by the Wapiti Formation, a lateral equivalent of the Aycross and Tepee Trail formations (Bown 1982, Eaton 1982). The Wapiti contains a middle Eocene fauna (Bown 1979b) and is overlain unconformably by the Trout Peak Trachyandesite (dated at 48.0 ± 1.2 (49.2 ± 1.2*) Ma; J. Obradovich, unpublished data) and the Wiggins Formation. At Carter Mountain, Eaton (1980, 1982) collected a characteristic Bridgerian fauna (including *Stylinodon, Notharctus, Washakius, Palaeictops, Hyopsodus, Phenacodus, Orohippus,* cf. *Palaeosyops, Hyrachyus,* and *Helohyus*) from rocks referred to the Wiggins Formation. In the Owl Creek area, the upper part of the Tepee Trail Formation and the Wiggins Formation have yielded a Uintan fauna (Eaton 1980; *Forstercooperia, Metarhinus, Epihippus, Achaenodon, Protoreodon*).

Quite removed from the Bighorn Basin is the Climbing Arrow Member of the Renova Formation, which crops out extensively near Three Forks, Montana. It ranges from "middle or late Eocene to early Oligocene" (Robinson 1963, p. 75; also see Wallace 1980). Recent screen washing at Shoddy Springs (Black 1967) has expanded the initial fauna (Robinson et al. 1957; Krishtalka 1979; Krishtalka and Black 1975). It is tentatively considered a close correlative of the extensive assemblage of Duchesnean mammals from Badwater Locality 20.

Miscellaneous Localities

A number of miscellaneous North American sites produce suites of fossil mammals that are Wasatchian to Duchesnean in age. These are geologically and geographically isolated from the areas discussed above and usually are single fossiliferous levels correlative with major productive areas only biochronologically. They are not included on the correlation/calibration charts.

Baja California. A small collection from the Tepetate Formation, 15 miles (25 km) south of the village of Punta Prieta, Baja California del Norte, includes a species of *Hyracotherium*, didelphid, *Esthonyx*, barylambdid, *Meniscotherium, Hyopsodus,* and creodont (Morris 1966, Flynn and Novacek 1984). The age of the fauna, originally suggested as Clarkforkian (Morris 1966, Rose 1981), is now thought to be Wasatchian (Flynn and Novacek 1984).

Note: J. J. Flynn (1986, Correlation and Geochronology of Middle Eocene strata from the western United States. Palaeogeography, Paleoclimatology, Palaeoecology, 55: 335–406) has recently published a revised paleomagnetic and biostratigraphic analysis of rocks which preserve faunas that cross the Bridgerian-Uintan boundary in Wyoming and California. Flynn names and characterizes a new land mammal subage, the Shoshonian, which he considers to be earliest Uintan. Recognition of the Shoshonian Land Mammal Subage clarifies the Bridgerian-Uintan boundary. Earliest Uintan faunas from the Sand Wash Basin, Colorado, and Whistler Squat, Texas, may also be referable to the Shoshonian, as discussed in the text.

Golden Valley. The fluvial Golden Valley Formation conformably overlies the Sentinel Butte Shale Member of the Fort Union Formation in southwestern North Dakota. A collection made by Jepsen (1963) and supplemented by West (1973c) is early Wasatchian in age. The Golden Valley Formation extends well below the mammal-producing level and, if fossiliferous, could yield a series of faunas spanning Tiffanian-Clarkforkian-Wasatchian time in southwestern North Dakota.

Powder River Basin: Delson (1971) reported on collections made by H. E. Wood II and others in the Powder River Basin of northeastern Wyoming. The rocks there, although at the opposite corner of Wyoming and separated by several structural highs from the type area, are regarded by the U.S. Geological Survey as belonging to the Wasatch Formation. The assemblage discussed by Delson is early Wasatchian in age, perhaps most directly correlative with the Four Mile Local Fauna of northern Colorado (McKenna 1960).

Also in the Powder River Basin, Whitmore (in Soister 1968, p. 42) reported the presence of mammals (including a deciduous premolar of *Lambdotherium, Hyracotherium,* and *Coryphodon*) representing the Lostcabinian at Pumpkin Buttes. Robinson and associates (University of Colorado; pers. com.) have recently made more extensive collections from early Wasatchian deposits.

Laramie and Shirley basins. A small mammalian fauna from rocks called Wind River Formation 25 miles (40 km) northwest of Laramie, Wyoming, was studied by Prichinello (1971). The fauna includes *Pelycodus, Haplomylus, Hyopsodus, Phenacodus, Coryphodon,* and *Hyracotherium* and is early Wasatchian in age. The likelihood of the rocks being deposited in a basin quite separate from the Wind River Basin, as well as lithologic differences, provokes suspicion that the Laramie Basin rocks belong in a formation distinct from the Wind River Formation. Prichinello (1971 p. 76) and Eaton (pers. com. 1981) report successful washing efforts in the Cooper Creek Basin north of Laramie. The fauna now contains fifteen species, including *Tetonius, Homogalax, Oxyaena, Esthonyx,* and *Diacodexis.*

In the Shirley Basin, north of the Laramie Basin,

Harshman (1972) mapped both the Wind River and Wagon Bed formations. Fossils found in the Wind River Formation are characteristic of the Wasatchian (Harshman 1972, p. 23) but cannot be assigned more precisely. The Wagon Bed conformably overlies the Wind River in the Shirley Basin; a specimen of *Notharctus tenebrosus* (Harshman 1972) suggests an early Bridgerian age.

New Jersey. An isolated lower molar of the tillodont *Anchippodus* was collected from the marine Shark River Marls of northeastern New Jersey. The tooth is at the same stage of evolutionary development as those of western Bridgerian genera (Gazin 1953, p. 34).

British Columbia: Two teeth, referable to the Bridgerian tillodont *Trogosus,* have been collected at a coal mine near the town of Princeton (Russell 1935, Gazin 1953).

Oregon: The Clarno Formation has two mammal-producing levels. The lower level, in a very hard matrix and called the Nut Bed for its abundant plant fossils, has produced a small assemblage (*Patriofelis, Orohippus, Telmatherium,* and *Hyrachyus*) indicative of the Bridgerian (B. Hanson, pers. com. 1981). A stratigraphically higher locality, the Hancock Quarry, has produced *Epihippus* and *Diplobunops,* generally regarded as Uintan, but other taxa (*Hemipsalodon, Haplohippus, Protapirus,* cf. *Procadurcodon,* and *Caenopus*) are more usually considered Duchesnean or Chadronian.

South Dakota: The Slim Buttes Formation of northwestern South Dakota contains *Epihippus, Teleodus,* (= *Duchesneodus*), *Colodon, Amynodontopsis,* an indeterminate agriochoerid, and an indeterminate leptotraguline (Bjork 1967). The closest correlative of this small assemblage is the fauna from the upper part of the Duchesne River Formation of Utah.

Saskatchewan: At the northern edge of the Cypress Hills of southwestern Saskatchewan a diverse mammalian fauna, the Swift Current Creek Fauna, has been collected by the Royal Ontario Museum (Russell 1965), the National Museum of Canada, and the Saskatchewan Museum of Natural History (Storer 1978, 1984; see also Krishtalka 1979). The presence of eomyids, *Procaprolagus, Auxontodon, Colodon, Epihippus, Protoreodon,* and *Leptoreodon* confirms a late Uintan age.

Mississippi: A single titanothere skull, the holotype of *Notiotitanops* (= *?Protitanops*) *mississippiensis,* was found in the Lutetian Lisbon Formation of Clark County,

Mississippi (Gazin and Sullivan 1942). The skull is morphologically closest to several Uintan titanotheres of the Utah-Wyoming region, and the Lisbon Formation is probably best considered Uintan or Duchesnean in age.

Mexico: Paleogene vertebrates from Guanajuato, Mexico, have been described by Fries et al. (1955), Black and Stephens (1973), and most recently, by Ferrusquia-Villafranca (1984). The mammals—a sciuravid rodent *Floresomys*, fragments of tapiroid forelimb, a soricoid, and a rodent of indeterminate family (*Guanajuatomys*)—do not permit an accurate assessment of age. The most similar animals from northern localities are Bridgerian and Uintan.

Ellesmere Island: A suite of vertebrates from several localities at about 7° north latitude on Ellesmere Island, Northwest Territories, Canada, is suggestive of a late Wasatchian and early Bridgerian age for the upper part of the Eureka Sound Formation (Dawson et al. 1976; West and Dawson 1978; McKenna 1980*a*). As presently known, the assemblage does not correlate readily with any particular southern fauna and, partly on the basis of paleomagnetic data, has provoked discussions concerning heterochroneity (Hickey et al. 1983, 1984; Kent et al. 1984; Norris and Miall 1984; Flynn and Novacek 1984).

Paleomagnetic Stratigraphy

Several studies currently in progress (e.g., Butler et al. 1980, 1981; Flynn 1981; Shive et al. 1980) integrate biostratigraphic, magnetostratigraphic, and radiometric data to refine the correlation of Wasatchian to Duchesnean age strata in North America. An important goal of such studies is intracontinental correlation of mammal-bearing strata and coordination of the North American Land Mammal Ages with other biostratigraphic chronologies and standard geochronologic time scales.

Butler et al. (1981) have constructed a magnetic polarity zonation for early Tiffanian to early middle Wasatchian strata in the Bighorn Basin. The Clarkforkian extends from the lower or middle part of a normal polarity interval that Butler et al. (1981) correlate with anomaly 25 to approximately the middle of a reversed polarity interval correlated with the reversed zone below anomaly 24. The Clarkforkian/Wasatchian boundary in the Bighorn Basin (Butler et al. 1981) therefore lies within the reversed interval between anomalies 24 and 25, and early to early middle Wasatchian correlates with the

latter part of this reversed interval. Rapp et al. (1983) also allocated the Wasatchian (= "?Clarkforkian" in Rapp et al. 1983, fig. 8) part of the Black Peaks Formation, west Texas area, to the interval between anomalies 24 and 25.

Late middle Wasatchian to early Bridgerian strata have not been paleomagnetically sampled. Correlation of the Wasatchian/Bridgerian boundary to the magnetic polarity time scale thus can be determined only by inference.

Magnetostratigraphic studies of Bridgerian to Uintan strata are currently under way in the Absaroka Range of the northwestern Wind River Basin, the Washakie Basin, and southern California (Flynn 1981, 1986; Berggren et al. 1985) as well as in the southeastern Absaroka Range of the Bighorn Basin (Shive et al. 1980). Results from all four areas indicate that the Bridgerian extends at least from within a normal polarity zone correlative with anomaly 21 to approximately the middle of the reversed polarity interval between anomalies 20 and 21. The Bridgerian/Uintan boundary is clearly defined faunally in the Aycross and Tepee Trail formations of the northwestern Wind River Basin and Bighorn Basin and in the Washakie Formation of the Washakie Basin; the boundary lies within the reversed interval between anomalies 20 and 21 in all three areas. The base of the Bridgerian is not well defined in any of these sections, and the Wasatchian/Bridgerian boundary may lie within the normal interval correlated with anomaly 21, the reversed interval between anomalies 21 and 22, or the normal polarity zone correlated with anomaly 22. Radiometric data on Bridgerian strata cited earlier indicate a short temporal duration (approximately 2–3 million years) for this interval, which suggests that the base of the Bridgerian probably lies within the normal polarity zone correlative with anomaly 21 or slightly below it in the reversed interval between anomalies 21 and 22 (Berggren et al. 1985).

The magnetostratigraphic sequences in both Absaroka Range areas only extend into the reversed interval above anomaly 21, and in both cases, early Uintan faunas are associated with this reversed interval. The southern California and Washakie Basin sequences extend at least through a normal polarity zone correlative with anomaly 20 (Flynn, 1986). Both of these sections contain early Uintan faunas (possibly Uinta B correlatives) within this normal zone as well as within the underlying reversed interval. There are no published magnetic polarity sequences on late Uintan strata; therefore, the Uintan/Duchesnean boundary cannot be directly correlated to the magnetic polarity time scale.

Testarmata and Gose (1979, 1980) presented a magnetostratigraphy for part of a sequence in west Texas that extends from Uintan to Chadronian. Their magnetostratigraphic section included strata containing the Porvenir, Little Egypt, and Airstrip local faunas. Wilson (1977, 1980) assigned all of these local faunas to the early Chadronian, but Wilson et al. (1968) considered the Porvenir Local Fauna, and probably the Little Egypt Local Fauna, as Duchesnean. Testarmata and Gose (1979, 1980) correlated the interval containing the Porvenir and Little Egypt local faunas with anomaly 13 and the base of the overlying reversed interval. However, the correlation of their paleomagnetic data is ambiguous and equivocal: the section contains numerous short polarity events not recorded in the seafloor magnetic anomaly pattern; their "simplified" magnetostratigraphy cannot be uniquely correlated because it contains only two predominantly normal polarity intervals and one predominantly reversed polarity interval; and associated radiometric dates do not preclude correlation of the two normal polarity intervals with anomalies 13 and 15 or 15 and 16 (instead of 12 and 13, as suggested by Testarmata and Gose).

Work in progress (Prothero and Denham 1981) on Chadronian to Whitneyan strata in Wyoming, Nebraska, and Texas provides a better constraint on the minimum magnetochronologic age of Duchesnean strata. Magnetic polarity intervals correlated with anomalies 13 to 9 are present in this sequence. Based on these data and on biostratigraphic and radiometric correlation of the Chadronian part of the Prothero and Denham section to the Texas sequence, the top of the Duchesnean *must* be older than anomaly 13 and probably lies within the reversed interval below anomaly 13 or anomaly 15. The base and the major part of the Duchesnean have not yet been sampled paleomagnetically.

ACKNOWLEDGMENTS

We are grateful for the assistance given to us by G. Curtis, J. A. Dorr, Jr., J. Eaton, P. Gingerich, B. Hanson, J. H. Hutchison, A. Kihm, J. D. Love, S. Lucas, E. Manning, M. Mason, R. Mauger, J. Obradovich, P. Robinson, W. Rohrer, K. Rose, D. E. Savage, J. Schiebout, J. Wahlert, and J. A. Wilson.

Among the authors of this chapter, West, McKenna, Black, Bown, Dawson, Golz, Flynn, Lillegraven, D. E. Savage (originally), and Turnbull compiled the data and wrote various drafts. Most recently (1985–86), Krishtalka and Stucky revised and updated the chapter.

The illustrations were prepared by Christine Costello, Nancy Perkins, and Susan Speerbrecher. Cheryl Castelli, Carol A. Knox, and Elizabeth A. Hill cheerfully typed the numerous versions of the manuscript.

REFERENCES

Andersen, D. W., and M. D. Picard 1972. Stratigraphy of the Duchesne River Formation (Eocene-Oligocene), northern Uinta Basin, northeastern Utah. Bull. Utah Geol. Min. Surv. 97:1–29.

Baltz, E. H. 1967. Stratigraphy and regional tectonic implications of part of Upper Cretaceous and Tertiary rocks, east-central San Juan Basin, New Mexico. U.S. Geol. Surv. Prof. Paper 552.

Bandy, O. L., and R. L. Kolpack. 1963. Foraminiferal and sedimentological trends in the Tertiary section of Tecolote Tunnel, California. Micropaleontology 9:117–170.

Berggren, W. A., M. C. McKenna, J. Hardenbol, and W. Obradovich. 1978. Revised Paleogene polarity time scale. J. Geol. 86:67–81.

Berggren, W. A., D. V. Kent, J. J. Flynn, and J. A. Van Couvering. 1985. Cenozoic geochronology. Bull. Geol. Soc. Amer. 96:1407–1418.

Bjork, P. R. 1967. Latest Eocene vertebrates from northwestern South Dakota. J. Paleont. 41:227–236.

Black, C. C. 1967. Middle and late Eocene mammal communities: A major discrepancy. Science 156:62–64.

———. 1969. Fossil vertebrates from the late Eocene and Oligocene Badwater Creek area, Wyoming, and some regional correlations. Wyo. Geol. Assoc. Guidebook, 21st Ann. Field Conf., pp. 43–48.

———. 1978. Geology and paleontology of the Badwater Creek area, central Wyoming. Pt. 14: The artiodactyls. Ann. Carnegie Mus. 47:223–259.

Black, C. C., and M. R. Dawson. 1966. A review of late Eocene mammalian faunas from North America. Amer J. Sci. 264:321–349.

Black, C. C., and J. J. Stephens III. 1973. Rodents from the Paleogene of Guanajuato, Mexico. Occas. Papers Mus. Texas Tech Univ., no. 14.

Bown, T. M. 1975. Paleocene and lower Eocene rocks in the Sand Creek—No Water Creek area, Washakie County, Wyoming. Wyo. Geol. Assoc. Guidebook, 27th Ann. Field Conf., pp. 55–61.

———. 1979a. Geology and mammalian paleontology of the Sand Creek facies, lower Willwood Formation (lower Eocene), Washakie County, Wyoming. Geol. Surv. Wyo. Mem, no. 2.

———. 1979b. Correlation of Eocene volcaniclastic rocks, southeastern Absaroka Range in northwestern Wyoming. U.S. Geol. Surv. Prof. Paper 1150, pp. 68–69.

———. 1980. The Willwood Formation (lower Eocene) of the southern Bighorn Basin, Wyoming, and its mammalian fauna. In Early Cenozoic paleontology and stratigraphy of the Bighorn Basin, Wyoming, 1880–1980, ed. P. D. Gingerich, pp. 127–138. Univ. Mich. Papers Paleont., no. 24.

―――. 1982. Geology, paleontology, and correlation of Eocene volcanistic rocks, southeast Absaroka Range, Hot Springs County, Wyoming. U.S. Geol. Surv. Prof. Paper 1201-A.

Bown, T. M., and A. J. Kihm. 1981. *Xenicohippus,* an unusual new hyracotheriine (Mammalia, Perissodactyla) from lower Eocene rocks of Wyoming, Colorado, and New Mexico. J. Paleont. 55 (1):257–270.

Bown, T. M., and K. D. Rose. 1976. New early Tertiary primates and a reappraisal of some Plesiadapiformes. Folia Primat. 26:109–138.

Bown, T. M., and D. M. Schankler. 1982. A review of the Proteutheria and Insectivora of the Willwood Formation (lower Eocene), Bighorn Basin, Wyoming. U.S. Geol. Surv. Prof. Paper 1201.

Bradley, W. H. 1964. Geology of Green River Formation and associated Eocene rocks in southwestern Wyoming and adjacent parts of Colorado and Utah. U.S. Geol. Surv. Prof. Paper 496-A.

Bukry, D., and M. P. Kennedy. 1969. Cretaceous and Eocene coccoliths at San Diego, California. Calif. Div. Mines Geol. Spec. Rept. 100, pp. 33–43.

Burbank, W. S., T. S. Lovering, E. N. Goddard, and E. B. Eckel. 1935. Reprinted 1967. Geologic map of Colorado. U.S. Geol. Surv.

Burke, J. J. 1935. Preliminary report of fossil mammals from the Green River Formation in Utah. Ann. Carnegie Mus. 25:13–14.

―――. 1969. An antiacodont from the Green River Eocene of Utah. Kirtlandia 5:1–7.

Butler, R. F., E. H. Lindsay, and P. D. Gingerich. 1980. Magnetic polarity stratigraphy and Paleocene-Eocene biostratigraphy of Polecat Bench, northwestern Wyoming. In Early Cenozoic paleontology and stratigraphy of the Bighorn Basin, Wyoming, ed. P. D. Gingerich, pp. 95–98. Univ. Mich. Papers Paleont., no. 24.

Butler, R. F., P. D. Gingerich, and E. H. Lindsay. 1981. Magnetic polarity stratigraphy and biostratigraphy of Paleocene and lower Eocene continental deposits, Clark's Fork Basin, Wyoming. J. Geol. 89:299–316.

Cashion, W. B. 1957. Stratigraphic relations and oil shale of the Green River Formation in the eastern Uinta Basin. Intermt. Assoc. Petrol. Geol. Guidebook, 8th Ann. Field Conf., pp. 131–135.

Cashion, W. B., and J. R. Donnell. 1974. Revision of nomenclature of the upper part of the Green River Formation, Piceance Creek Basin, Colorado, and eastern Uinta Basin, Utah. Bull. U. S. Geol. Surv. no. 1394–G.

Clark, B. L., and H. E. Vokes. 1936. Summary of marine Eocene sequence of western North America. Bull. Geol. Soc. Amer. 47:851–877.

Clark, J., J. R. Beerbower, and K. E. Kietzke. 1967. Oligocene sedimentation, stratigraphy, paleoecology and paleoclimatology in the Big Badlands of South Dakota. Fieldiana: Geol. Mem., vol. 5.

Comstock, T. B. 1875. Report upon the reconnaissance of northwestern Wyoming including Yellowstone National Park, for 1873, by Wm. A. Jones. House Rep. Exec. Doc. no. 285, 43d Congr., 1st ses., Jan. 1875.

Cope, E. D. 1877. Report upon the extinct Vertebrata obtained in New Mexico by parties of the expedition of 1874. Geogr. Surv. West of the 100th Meridian, pt. 2.

―――. 1882. Contributions to the history of the Vertebrata of the lower Eocene of Wyoming and New Mexico made during 1881. Proc. Amer. Philos. Soc. 20:139–197.

Crochet, J.-Y. 1977. Les Didelphidae (Marsupicarnivora, Marsupialia) holarctiques tertiaires. C. R. Acad. Sci. Paris, t. 284, Ser. D, pp. 357–360.

Culbertson, W. C. 1961. Stratigraphy of the Wilkins Peak Member of the Green River Formation, Firehole Basin Quadrangle, Wyoming. U.S. Geol. Surv. Prof. Paper 424-D, pp. 170–173.

Dalrymple, G. B. 1979. Critical tables for conversion of K-Ar ages from old to new constants. Geology 7:558–559.

Dane, C. H. 1954. Stratigraphic and facies relationships of upper part of Green River Formation and lower part of Uinta Formation in Duchesne, Uintah, and Wasatch counties, Utah. Amer. Assoc. Petrol. Geol. Bull. 38:405–425.

Dawson, M. R. 1968. Middle Eocene rodents (Mammalia) from northeastern Utah. Ann. Carnegie Mus. 39:327–370.

―――. 1980. Geology and paleontology of the Badwater Creek area, central Wyoming. Pt. 20: The late Eocene Creodonta and Carnivora. Ann. Carnegie Mus. 49:79–91.

Dawson, M. R., R. M. West, W. Langston, Jr., and J. H. Hutchison. 1976. Paleogene terrestrial vertebrates: Northernmost occurrence, Ellesmere Island, Canada. Science 192:781–782.

Delson, E. 1971. Fossil mammals of the early Wasatchian Powder River local fauna, Eocene of northeast Wyoming. Bull. Amer. Mus. Nat. Hist. 146:305–364.

Denison, R. H. 1937. Early lower Eocene mammals from the Wind River Basin, Wyoming. Proc. New Eng. Zool. Club 16:11–14.

Dibblee, T. W., Jr. 1950. Geology of southwestern Santa Barbara County, California. Calif. Div. Mines Bull., no. 150.

―――. 1966. Geology of the central Santa Ynez Mountains, Santa Barbara County, California. Calif. Div. Mines Geol. Bull., no. 186.

Donnell, J. R. 1969. Paleocene and lower Eocene units in the southern part of the Piceance Creek Basin, Colorado. Bull. U.S. Geol. Surv. no. 1274-M.

Dorr, J. A., Jr. 1952. Early Cenozoic stratigraphy and vertebrate paleontology of the Hoback Basin, Wyoming. Bull. Geol. Soc. Amer. 63:59–94.

―――. 1958. Early Cenozoic vertebrate paleontology, sedimentation, and orogeny in central western Wyoming. Bull. Geol. Soc. Amer. 69:1217–1244.

―――. 1969. Mammalian and other fossils, early Eocene Pass Peak Formation, central western Wyoming. Contrib. Mus. Paleont. Univ. Mich. 22:207–219.

―――. 1978. Revised and amended fossil vertebrate faunal lists, early Tertiary, Hoback Basin, Wyoming. Univ. Wyo. Contrib. Geol. 16:79–84.

————. In press. Early Tertiary fossil vertebrate assemblages and paleoenvironments, Huerfano Park, Colorado. Geol. Soc. Amer. Spec. Paper.

Dorr, J. A., Jr., and P. D. Gingerich. 1980. Early Cenozoic mammalian paleontology, geologic structure and tectonic history in the overthrust belt near LaBarge, western Wyoming. Univ. Wyo. Contrib. Geol. 18 (2):101–115.

Dorr, J. A., Jr., and J. R. Steidtmann. 1971. Stratigraphic-tectonic implications of a new, earliest Eocene, mammalian faunule from central western Wyoming. Mich. Academician 3:25–41.

Dorr, J. A., Jr., D. R. Spearing, and J. R. Steidtmann. 1977. Deformation and deposition between a foreland uplift and an impinging thrust belt: Hoback Basin, Wyoming. Geol. Soc. Amer. Spec. Paper 177.

Dreyer, E. E. 1935. Geology of a portion of Mt. Pinos Quadrangle, Ventura County, California. M.A. thesis, Dept. Geol., Univ. Calif., Los Angeles.

Durham, J. W., R. H. Johns, and D. E. Savage. 1954. Marine-nonmarine relationships in the Cenozoic section of California. Calif. Div. Mines Bull. 170:59–71.

Eaton, J. G. 1980. Preliminary report on paleontological exploration of the southeastern Absaroka Range, Wyoming. In Early Cenozoic paleontology and stratigraphy of the Bighorn Basin, Wyoming, ed. P. D. Gingerich, pp. 139–142. Univ. Mich. Papers Paleont., no. 24.

————. 1982. Paleontology and correlation of Eocene volcanic rocks in the Carter Mountain area, Park County, southeastern Absaroka Range, Wyoming. Univ. Wyo. Contrib. Geol. 21 (2):153–194.

Emry, R. J. 1973. Stratigraphy and preliminary biostratigraphy of the Flagstaff Rim area, Natrona County, Wyoming. Smithsonian Contrib. Paleobiol., no. 18, pp. 1–43.

————. 1975. Revised Tertiary stratigraphy of the western Beaver Divide, Fremont County, Wyoming. Smithsonian Contrib. Paleobiol., no. 25.

————. 1981. Additions to the mammalian fauna of the type Duchesnean, with comments on the status of the Duchesnean "Age." J. Paleont. 55:563–570.

Evernden, J. R., D. E. Savage, G. H. Curtis, and G. T. James. 1964. Potassium-argon dates and the Cenozoic mammalian chronology of North America. Amer. J. Sci. 262:145–198.

Ferrusquia-Villafranca, I. 1984. Review of the early and middle Tertiary mammal faunas of Mexico. J. Vert. Paleont. 4:187–198.

Flynn, J. J. 1981. Magnetic polarity stratigraphy and correlation of Eocene strata from Wyoming and southern California (abstr.). EOS, Trans. Amer. Geophys. Union 62:264.

Flynn, J.J., and M. J. Novacek. 1984. Early Eocene vertebrates from Baja California: Evidence for intracontinental age correlations. Science 224:151–153.

Fries, C., Jr., C. W. Hibbard, and D. H. Dunkle. 1955. Early Cenozoic vertebrates in the red conglomerate at Guanajuato, Mexico. Smithsonian Misc. Coll., vol. 123, no. 7.

Galusha, T. 1966. The Zia Sand Formation, new early to medial Miocene beds in New Mexico. Amer. Mus. Novitates, no. 2271.

Galusha, T., and J. C. Blick. 1971. Stratigraphy of the Santa Fe group, New Mexico. Bull. Amer. Mus. Nat. Hist. 144:1–128.

Gardner, J. H. 1910. The Carthage Coal Field, New Mexico. Bull. U.S. Geol. Surv., no. 381, pp. 452–460.

Gazin, C. L. 1952. The lower Eocene Knight Formation of western Wyoming and its mammalian faunas. Smithsonian Misc. Coll., vol. 117, no. 8.

————. 1953. The Tillodontia: An early Tertiary order of mammals. Smithsonian Misc. Coll., vol. 121, no. 10.

————. 1955. A review of the upper Eocene Artiodactyla of North America. Smithsonian Misc. Coll., vol. 128, no. 8.

————. 1956. The upper Paleocene Mammalia from the Almy Formation in western Wyoming. Smithsonian Misc. Coll., vol. 131, no. 7.

————. 1958. A review of the middle and upper Eocene primates of North America. Smithsonian Misc. Coll., vol. 136, no. 1.

————. 1962. A further study of the lower Eocene mammalian faunas of southwestern Wyoming. Smithsonian Misc. Coll., vol. 141, no. 1.

————. 1965. Early Eocene mammalian faunas and their environment in the vicinity of the Rock Springs Uplift, Wyoming. Wyo. Geol. Assoc. Guidebook, 19th Ann. Field Conf., pp. 171–180.

————. 1976. Mammalian faunal zones of the Bridger middle Eocene. Smithsonian Contrib. Paleobiol., no. 26.

Gazin, C. L., and J. M. Sullivan. 1942. A new titanothere from the Eocene of Mississippi, with notes on the correlation between the marine Eocene of the Gulf coastal plain and continental Eocene of the Rocky Mountain region. Smithsonian Misc. Coll., vol. 101, no. 13.

Gibson, J. M. 1971. Benthonic foraminifera of the Ardath Shale and Stadium Conglomerate (Eocene), San Diego Basin, California. Bull. So. Calif. Acad. Sci. 70:125–130.

Gingerich, P. D. 1978. New Condylarthra (Mammalia) from the Paleocene and early Eocene of North America. Contrib. Mus. Paleont. Univ. Mich. 25:1–9.

————. 1979. Phylogeny of middle Eocene Adapidae (Mammalia, Primates) in North America: *Smilodectes* and *Notharctus*. J. Paleont. 53:153–163.

————. 1980a. Evolutionary patterns in early Cenozoic mammals. Ann. Rev. Earth Planet. Sci. 8:407–424.

————., ed. 1980b. Early Cenozoic paleontology and stratigraphy of the Bighorn Basin, Wyoming. Univ. Mich. Papers Paleont., no. 24.

————. 1983. Paleocene-Eocene faunal zones and a preliminary analysis of Laramide structural deformation in the Clark's Fork Basin, Wyoming. Wyo. Geol. Assoc. Guidebook, 34th Ann. Field Conf., pp. 185–195.

Gingerich, P. D., and G. F. Gunnell. 1979. Systematics and evolution of the genus *Esthonyx* (Mammalia, Tillodontia) in the early Eocene of North America. Contrib. Mus. Paleont. Univ. Mich. 25:125–153.

Gingerich, P. D., and R. A. Haskin. 1981. Dentition of early Eocene *Pelycodus jarrovii* (Mammalia, Primates) and the generic attribution of species formerly referred to *Pelycodus*.

Contrib. Mus. Paleont. Univ. Mich. 25:327–337.

Gingerich, P. D., and E. L. Simons. 1977. Systematics, phylogeny and evolution of early Eocene Adapidae (Mammalia, Primates) in North America. Contrib. Mus. Paleont. Univ. Mich. 24:245–279.

Gingerich, P. D., K. D. Rose, and D. W. Krause. 1980. Early Cenozoic mammalian faunas of the Clark's Fork Basin—Polecat Bench area, northwestern Wyoming. In Early Cenozoic paleontology and stratigraphy of the Bighorn Basin, Wyoming, ed. P. D. Gingerich, pp. 51–68. Univ. Mich. Papers Paleont., no. 24.

Givens, C. R. 1974. Eocene molluscan biostratigraphy of the Pine Mountain area, Ventura County, California. Univ. Calif. Publ. Geol. Sci., vol. 109.

Givens, C. R., and M. P. Kennedy. 1976. Middle Eocene mollusks from northern San Diego County, California. J. Paleont. 50:954–975.

Golz, D. J. 1976. Eocene Artiodactyla of southern California. Nat. Hist. Mus. Los Angeles Co. Sci. Bull., no. 26.

Golz, D. J., and J. A. Lillegraven. 1977. Summary of known occurrences of terrestrial vertebrates from Eocene strata of southern California. Univ. Wyo. Contrib. Geol. 15:43–65.

Granger, W. 1909. Faunal horizons of the Washakie Formation of southern Wyoming. Bull. Amer. Mus. Nat. Hist. 26:13–23.

———. 1910. Tertiary faunal horizons in the Wind River Basin, Wyoming, with descriptions of new Eocene mammals. Bull. Amer. Mus. Nat. Hist. 28:235–251.

———. 1914. On the names of lower Eocene faunal horizons of Wyoming and New Mexico. Bull. Amer. Mus. Nat. Hist. 33:201–207.

Guthrie, D. A. 1967. The mammalian fauna of the Lysite Member, Wind River Formation (early Eocene) of Wyoming. Mem. So. Calif. Acad. Sci., vol. 5.

———. 1971. The mammalian fauna of the Lost Cabin Member, Wind River Formation (lower Eocene) of Wyoming. Ann. Carnegie Mus. 43:47–113.

Hanna, M. A. 1926. Geology of the La Jolla Quadrangle, California. Univ. Calif. Publ. Geol. Sci. 16:187–246.

Harshman, E. N. 1972. Geology and uranium deposits, Shirley Basin area, Wyoming. U.S. Geol. Surv. Prof. Paper 745.

Hayden, F. V. 1869. First, second, and third annual reports of the United States Geological Survey of the Territories for the years 1867, 1868, and 1869. U.S. Geol. Surv. Terr., 3d Ann. Rept., pp. 109–199.

———. 1878. Wasatch Group. In General notes, geology, and paleontology. Amer. Nat. 12:831.

Hickey, L. J., R. M. West, M. R. Dawson, and D. K. Choi. 1983. Arctic terrestrial biota: Paleomagnetic evidence of age disparity with mid-northern latitudes during the late Cretaceous and early Tertiary. Science 221:1153–1156.

Hickey, L. J., R. M. West, and M. R. Dawson. 1984. Arctic biostratigraphic heterochroneity. Science 224:175–176.

Jepsen, G. L. 1930. New vertebrate fossils from the lower Eocene of the Big Horn Basin, Wyoming. Proc. Amer. Philos. Soc. 69:117–131.

———. 1939. Dating Absaroka rocks by vertebrate fossils (abstr.). Bull. Geol. Soc. Amer. 50:1914.

———. 1940. Paleocene faunas of the Polecat Bench Formation, Park County, Wyoming. Proc. Amer. Philos. Soc. 83:217–341.

———. 1963. Eocene vertebrates, coprolites, and plants in the Golden Valley Formation, western North Dakota. Bull. Geol. Soc. Amer. 74:673–684.

———. 1966. Early Eocene bat from Wyoming. Science 154:1333–1339.

Kay, J. L. 1934. The Tertiary formations of the Uinta Basin, Utah. Ann. Carnegie Mus. 23:357–371.

———. 1957. The Eocene vertebrates of the Uinta Basin, Utah. Intermt. Assoc. Petrol. Geol. Guidebook, 8th Ann. Field Conf., pp. 110–114.

Keefer, W. R. 1956. Tertiary rocks in the northwestern part of the Wind River Basin, Wyoming. Wyo. Geol. Assoc. Field Conf. Guidebook, pp. 109–116.

———. 1965. Stratigraphy and geologic history of the uppermost Cretaceous, Paleocene, and lower Eocene rocks in the Wind River Basin, Wyoming. U.S. Geol. Surv. Prof. Paper 495-A.

Kennedy, M. P., and G. W. Moore. 1971. Stratigraphic relations of Upper Cretaceous and Eocene formations, San Diego coastal area, California. Amer. Assoc. Petrol. Geol. Bull. 55:709–722.

Kent, D. V., M. C. McKenna, N. D. Opdyke, J. J. Flynn, and B. J. MacFadden. 1984. Arctic biostratigraphic heterochroneity. Science 224:173–174.

Kew, W. S. W. 1924. Geology and oil resources as a part of Los Angeles and Ventura counties, California. Bull. U.S. Geol. Surv. no. 753.

Kihm, A. J. 1984. Early Eocene mammalian faunas of the Piceance Creek Basin, northwestern Colorado. Ph.D. diss., Univ. Colo., Boulder.

Kitts, D. B. 1956. American *Hyracotherium* (Perissodactyla, Equidae). Bull. Amer. Mus. Nat. Hist. 110:1–60.

Korth, W. W. 1982. Revision of the Wind River faunas, early Eocene of central Wyoming. Pt. 2: Geologic setting. Ann. Carnegie Mus. 51:57–78.

Korth, W. W., and R. L. Evander. 1982. A new species of *Orohippus* (Perissodactyla, Equidae) from the early Eocene of Wyoming. J. Vert. Paleont. 2:167–171.

Krishtalka, L. 1975. Systematics and relationships of early Tertiary Lipotyphla (Mammalia, Insectivora) of North America. Ph.D. diss., Texas Tech Univ., Lubbock.

———. 1976a. Early Tertiary Adapisoricidae and Erinaceidae (Mammalia, Insectivora) of North America. Bull. Carnegie Mus. Nat. Hist. 1:1–40.

———. 1976b. North American Nyctitheriidae (Mammalia, Insectivora). Ann. Carnegie Mus. 46:7–28.

———. 1978. Paleontology and geology of the Badwater Creek area, central Wyoming. Pt. 15: A review of the late Eocene primates of Wyoming and Utah, and the Plesitarsiiformes. Ann. Carnegie Mus. 47:335–360.

———. 1979. Paleontology and geology of the Badwater

Creek area, central Wyoming. Pt. 18: Revision of late Eocene *Hyopsodus*. Ann. Carnegie Mus. 48:377–389.

Krishtalka, L., and C. C. Black. 1975. Paleontology and geology of the Badwater Creek area, central Wyoming. Pt. 12: Description and review of late Eocene Multituberculata from Wyoming and Montana. Ann. Carnegie Mus. 45:287–297.

Krishtalka, L., C. C. Black, and D. W. Riedel. 1975. Paleontology and geology of the Badwater Creek area, central Wyoming. Pt. 10: A late Paleocene mammal fauna from the Shotgun Member of the Fort Union Formation. Ann. Carnegie Mus. 45:179–212.

Krishtalka, L., R. J. Emny, J. E. Storer, and J. F. Sutton. 1982. Oligocene Multituberculates (Mammalia, Allotheria): Youngest known records. J. Paleont. 56: 791–794.

Krishtalka, L., and T. Setoguchi. 1977. Paleontology and geology of the Badwater Creek area, central Wyoming. Pt. 13: The late Eocene Insectivora and Dermoptera. Ann. Carnegie Mus. 46:71–99.

Krishtalka, L., and R. K. Stucky. 1983. Revision of the Wind River faunas, early Eocene of central Wyoming. Pt. 3: Marsupialia. Ann. Carnegie Mus. 52:205–227.

———. 1984. Middle Eocene marsupials (Mammalia) from northeastern Utah, and the mammalian fauna from Powder Wash. Ann. Carnegie Mus. 53:31–45.

———. 1985. Revision of the Wind River faunas, early Eocene of central Wyoming. Pt. 7: Revision of *Diacodexis* (Mammalia, Artiodactyla). Ann. Carnegie Mus. 54:413–486.

———. 1986. Early Eocene artiodactyls from the San Juan Basin, New Mexico, and the Piceance Basin, Colorado. Univ. Wyo. Contrib. Geol. Spec. Paper no. 3.

Lillegraven, J. A., M. C. McKenna, and L. Krishtalka. 1981. Evolutionary relationships of middle Eocene and younger species of *Centetodon* (Mammalia, Insectivora, Geolabididae) with a description of the dentition of *Ankylodon* (Adapisoricidae). Univ. Wyo. Publ. 45:1–115.

Loomis, F. R. 1907. Origin of the Wasatch deposits. Amer. J. Sci. 4th ser. 23:356–364.

Love, J. D. 1939. Geology along the southern margin of the Absaroka Range, Wyoming. Geol. Soc. Amer. Spec. Paper 20.

———. 1947. Tertiary stratigraphy of the Jackson Hole area, northwestern Wyoming. U.S. Geol. Surv. Oil Gas Invest. Prelim. Chart 27.

———. 1961. Definition of Green River, Great Divide, and Washakie basins, southwestern Wyoming. Amer. Assoc. Petrol. Geol. Bull. 45:1749–1755.

———. 1970. Cenozoic geology of the Granite Mountains area, central Wyoming. U.S. Geol. Surv. Prof. Paper 495-C.

———. 1978. Cenozoic thrust and normal faulting, and tectonic history of the Badwater area, northeastern margin of Wind River Basin, Wyoming. Wyo. Geol. Assoc. Guidebook, 30th Ann. Field Conf., pp. 235–238.

Love, J. D., and W. R. Keefer. 1975. Geology of sedimentary rocks in southern Yellowstone National Park, Wyoming. U.S. Geol. Surv. Prof. Paper 729-D.

Love, J. D., A. C. Christiansen, J. L. Earle, and R. W. Jones.

1978. Preliminary geologic map of the Arminto 1′ × 2′ Quadrangle, central Wyoming. U.S. Geol. Surv. Open-File Rept. 78–1089.

Love, J. D., M. C. McKenna, and M. R. Dawson. 1976. Eocene, Oligocene, and Miocene rocks and vertebrate fossils at the Emerald Lake locality, three miles south of Yellowstone National Park, Wyoming. U.S. Geol. Surv. Prof. Paper 932-A.

Love, L. L., A. M. Kudo, and D. W. Love. 1976. Dacites of Bunsen Peak, the Birch Hills, and the Washakie Needles, northwest Wyoming, and the relationship to the Absaroka volcanic fields, Wyoming-Montana. Bull. Geol. Soc. Amer. 87:1455–1462.

Lucas, S. G. 1977. Vertebrate paleontology of the San Jose Formation, east-central San Juan Basin, New Mexico. New Mex. Geol. Soc. Guidebook, 28th Field Conf., pp. 221–225.

Lucas, S. G., and B. S. Kues. 1979. Vertebrate biostratigraphy of the Eocene Galisteo Formation, north-central New Mexico. New Mex. Geol. Soc. Guidebook, 30th Field Conf., pp. 225–229.

Lucas, S. G., and R. M. Schoch. 1982. *Duchesneodus*, a new name for some titanotheres (Perissodactyla, Brontotheriidae) from the late Eocene of western North America. J. Paleont. 56:1018–1023.

Lucas, S. G., R. M. Schoch, E. Manning, and C. Tsentas. 1981. The Eocene biostratigraphy of New Mexico. Bull. Geol. Soc. Amer., pt. 1, 92:951–967.

McDowell, F. W. 1979. Potassium-argon dating in the Trans-Pecos Texas volcanic field. Bur. Econ. Geol. Univ. Texas Guidebook, no. 19, pp. 10–18.

McDowell, F. W., J. A. Wilson, and J. Clark. 1973. K-Ar dates for biotite from two paleontologically significant localities: Duchesne River Formation, Utah, and Chadron Formation, South Dakota. Isochron/West, no. 7, pp. 11–12.

MacFadden, B. J. 1980. Eocene perissodactyls from the type section of the Tepee Trail Formation of northwestern Wyoming. Univ. Wyo. Contrib. Geol. 18:135–143.

MacGinitie, H. D., E. B. Leopold, and W. L. Rohrer. 1974. An early middle Eocene flora from the Yellowstone-Absaroka volcanic province, northwestern Wind River Basin, Wyoming. Univ. Calif. Publ. Geol. Sci., vol. 108.

McGrew, P. O., ed. 1959. The geology and paleontology of the Elk Mountain and Tabernacle Butte area, Wyoming. Bull. Amer. Mus. Nat. Hist. 117:117–176.

McGrew, P. O., and H. W. Roehler. 1960. Correlations of Tertiary units in southwestern Wyoming. Wyo. Geol. Assoc. Guidebook, 15th Ann. Field Conf., pp. 156–158.

McGrew, P. O., and R. Sullivan. 1970. The stratigraphy and paleontology of Bridger A. Univ. Wyo. Contrib. Geol. 9:66–85.

McKenna, M. C. 1960. Fossil Mammalia from the early Wasatchian Four Mile fauna, Eocene of northwest Colorado. Univ. Calif. Publ. Geol. Sci. 37:1–130.

———. 1972. Vertebrate paleontology of the Togwotee Pass area, northwest Wyoming. In Guidebook, Field Conf. Tert. Biostrat. Southern and Western Wyoming, pp. 80–101.

———. 1976. *Esthonyx* in the upper faunal assemblage, Huerfano Formation, Eocene of Colorado. J. Paleont. 50:354–355.

———. 1980*a*. Eocene paleolatitude, climate, and mammals of Ellesmere Island. Palaeogr., Palaeoclimatol., Palaeoecol. 30:349–362.

———. 1980*b*. Late Cretaceous and early Tertiary vertebrate paleontological reconnaissance, Togwotee Pass area, northwestern Wyoming. In Aspects of vertebrate history, ed. L. L. Jacobs, pp. 321–343. Flagstaff: Museum of Northern Arizona Press.

McKenna, M. C., and J. D. Love. 1970. Local stratigraphic and tectonic significance of *Leptoceratops,* a Cretaceous dinosaur in the Pinyon Conglomerate, northwestern Wyoming. U.S. Geol. Surv. Prof. Paper 700-D, pp. D55–D61.

McKenna, M. C., P. Robinson, and D. W. Taylor. 1962. Notes on Eocene Mammalia and Mollusca from Tabernacle Butte, Wyoming. Amer. Mus. Novitates, no. 2102.

Marcantel, E. L., and M. P. Weiss. 1968. Colton Formation (Eocene) fluviatile and associated lacustrine beds, Gunnison Plateau, central Utah. Ohio J. Sci. 68:40–49.

Marsh, O. C. 1870. Professor Marsh's Rocky Mountain expedition: Discovery of the Mauvaises Terres Formation in Colorado. Amer. J. Sci. 2d ser. 50:292.

———. 1885. Dinocerata. U.S. Geol. Surv. Monogr., no. 10.

Matthew, W. D. 1909. The Carnivora and Insectivora of the Bridger Basin, middle Eocene. Mem. Amer. Mus. Nat. Hist. 9:291–567.

Mauger, R. L. 1977. K-Ar ages of biotites from tuffs in Eocene rocks of the Green River, Washakie, and Uinta basins, Utah, Wyoming, and Colorado. Univ. Wyo. Contrib. Geol. 15:17–41.

Maxwell, R. A., J. T. Lonsdale, R. T. Hazzard, and J. A. Wilson. 1967. Geology of Big Bend National Park. Univ. Texas Publ., no. 6711.

Mellet, J. S. 1977. Paleobiology of North American *Hyaenodon* (Mammalia, Creodonta). Contrib. to Vert. Evol., no. 1. Basel: S. Karger.

Morris, W. J. 1954. An Eocene fauna from the Cathedral Bluffs Tongue of the Washakie Basin, Wyoming. J. Paleont. 28:195–203.

———. 1966. Fossil mammals from Baja California: New evidence on early Tertiary migrations. Science 153:1376–1378.

Neasham, J. W., and C. F. Vondra. 1972. Stratigraphy and petrology of the lower Eocene Willwood Formation, Big Horn Basin, Wyoming. Bull. Geol. Soc. Amer. 83:2167–2180.

Nelson, M. E. 1973. Age and stratigraphic relations of the Fowkes Formation, Eocene, of southwestern Wyoming and northeastern Utah. Univ. Wyo. Contrib. Geol. 12:27–31.

———. 1974. Middle Eocene rodents from southwestern Wyoming. Univ. Wyo. Contrib. Geol. 15:1–10.

———. 1977. Middle Eocene primates (Mammalia) from southwestern Wyoming. Southwestern Nat. 22:487–493.

———. 1979. K-Ar age for the Fowkes Formation (middle Eocene) of southwestern Wyoming. Univ. Wyo. Contrib. Geol. 17:51–52.

Nelson, M. E., J. H. Madsen, Jr., and W. L. Stokes. 1980. A titanothere from the Green River Formation, central Utah: *Teleodus uintensis* (Perissodactyla: Brontotheriidae). Univ. Wyo. Contrib. Geol. 18:127–134.

Nightingale, W. T. 1930. Geology of Vermilion Creek gas area in southwest Wyoming and northwest Colorado. Amer. Assoc. Petrol. Geol. Bull. 14:1013–1040.

Norris, G., and A. D. Miall. 1984. Arctic biostratigraphic heterochroneity. Science 224:174–175.

Oriel, S. S. 1962. Main body of Wasatch Formation near LaBarge, Wyoming. Amer. Assoc. Petrol. Geol. Bull. 46:2161–2173.

Oriel, S. S., C. L. Gazin, and J. I. Tracey, Jr. 1962. Eocene age of Almy Formation, Wyoming, in its type area. Amer. Assoc. Petrol. Geol. Bull. 48:1936–1943.

Oriel, S. S., and J. I. Tracey, Jr. 1970. Uppermost Cretaceous and Tertiary stratigraphy of Fossil Basin, southwestern Wyoming. U.S. Geol. Surv. Prof. Paper 635.

Osborn, H. F. 1895. Fossil mammals of the Uinta Basin: Expedition of 1894. Bull. Amer. Mus. Nat. Hist. 7:71–105.

———. 1929. The titanotheres of ancient Wyoming, Dakota, and Nebraska. U.S. Geol. Surv. Monogr., no. 55.

Ostrander, G., C. A. Jones, and R. Cape. 1979. The occurrence of a multituberculate in the lower Oligocene Chadron Formation of northwest Nebraska. Geol. Soc. Amer. Abstr. with Programs 11:299.

Patterson, B. 1934. A contribution to the osteology of *Titanoides* and the relationships of the Amblypoda. Proc. Amer. Philos. Soc. 73:71–101.

———. 1935. Second contribution to the osteology and affinities of the Paleocene amblypod *Titanoides.* Proc. Amer. Philos. Soc. 75:143–162.

———. 1937. A new genus, *Barylambda,* for *Titanoides faberi,* Paleocene amblypod. Field Mus. Nat. Hist. Geol. Ser. 6:229–231.

———. 1939*a*. New Pantodonta and Dinocerata from the upper Paleocene of western Colorado. Field Mus. Nat. Hist. Geol. Ser. 6:351–383.

———. 1939*b*. A skeleton of *Coryphodon.* Proc. New Eng. Zool. Club 17:97–110.

———. 1949. A new genus of taeniodonts from the late Paleocene. Fieldiana: Geol. 10:41–42.

Patterson, B., and E. L. Simons. 1958. A new barylambdid pantodont from the late Paleocene Breviora, no. 93.

Patterson, B., and R. M. West. 1973. A new late Paleocene phenacodont (Mammalia, Condylarthra) from western Colorado. Breviora, no. 403.

Pekarek, A., R. F. Maruin, and H. H. Mehnert. 1974. K-Ar ages of the volcanics in the Rattlesnake Hills, central Wyoming. Geology 2:282–285.

Peterson, O. A. 1919. Report upon the material discovered in the upper Eocene of the Uinta Basin by Earl Douglas in the years 1908–1909, and by O. A. Peterson in 1912. Ann. Carnegie Mus. 12:40–169.

Eocene Biochronology of North America   115

————. 1932. New species from the Oligocene of the Uinta. Ann. Carnegie Mus. 21:61–78.

————. 1934. List of species and description of new material from the Duchesne River Oligocene, Uinta Basin, Utah. Ann. Carnegie Mus. 23:373–389.

Prichinello, K. A. 1971. Earliest Eocene mammalian fossils from the Laramie Basin of southeast Wyoming. Univ. Wyo. Contrib. Geol. 10:73–88.

Prothero, D. R., and C. R. Denham. 1981. Magnetostratigraphy of the White River Group and its implications for Oligocene geochronology (abstr.) Geol. Soc. Amer. Abstr. with Programs 13:534.

Radinsky, L. 1963. Origin and early evolution of North American Tapiroidea. Peabody Mus. Nat. Hist. Yale Univ. Bull. 17:1–106.

————. 1967a. *Hyrachyus, Chasmotherium,* and the early evolution of helaletid tapiroids. Amer. Mus. Novitates, no. 2313.

————. 1967b. Review of the rhinoceratoid Family Hyracodontidae (Perissodactyla). Bull. Amer. Mus. Nat. Hist. 136:1–45.

Rapp, S. D., B. J. MacFadden, and J. A. Schiebout. 1983. Magnetic polarity stratigraphy of the early Tertiary Black Peaks Formation, Big Bend National Park, Texas. J. Geol. 91:555–572.

Rich, T. H. V., and J. W. Collinson. 1973. First mammalian fossil from the Flagstaff limestone, central Utah: *Vulpavus australis* (Carnivora: Miacidae). J. Paleont. 47:854–860.

Riggs, E. S. 1912. New or little-known titanotheres from the lower Uintah formations. Field Mus. Nat. Hist. Geol. Ser. 4 (2):17–41.

Robinson, G. E. 1963. Geology of the Three Forks Quadrangle, Montana. U.S. Geol. Surv. Prof. Paper 370.

Robinson, G. E., E. Lewis, and D. W. Taylor. 1957. Eocene continental deposits in Three Forks Basin, Montana (abstr.). Bull. Geol. Soc. Amer. 68:1786.

Robinson, P. 1957. Age of Galisteo Formation, Santa Fe County, New Mexico. Amer. Assoc. Petrol. Geol. Bull. 41:757.

————. 1966. Fossil mammals of the Huerfano Formation, Eocene, of Colorado. Peabody Mus. Nat. Hist. Yale Univ. Bull., vol. 21.

————. 1968. The paleontology and geology of the Badwater Creek area, central Wyoming. Pt. 4: Late Eocene Primates from Badwater, Wyoming, with a discussion of material from Utah. Ann. Carnegie Mus. 39:307–326.

Roehler, H. W. 1973. Stratigraphy of the Washakie Formation in the Washakie Basin, Wyoming. U.S. Geol. Surv. Bull., no. 1369.

Rohrer, W. L., and J. D. Obradovich. 1969. Age and stratigraphic relations of the Tepee Trail and Wiggins formations, northwestern Wyoming. U.S. Geol. Surv. Prof. Paper 650-B, pp. 57–62.

Rose, K. D. 1981. The Clarkforkian Land Mammal Age and mammalian faunal composition across the Paleocene-Eocene boundary. Univ. Mich. Papers Paleont., no. 26.

Russell, L.S. 1935. A middle Eocene mammal fauna from British Columbia. Amer. J. Sci. 29:54–55.

————. 1954. Mammalian fauna of the Kishenehn Formation, southeastern British Columbia. Ann. Rept. Natl. Mus., Fiscal Year 1952–53, Bull. no. 132, pp. 92–111.

————. 1965. Tertiary mammals of Saskatchewan. Pt. I: The Eocene fauna. Royal Ont. Mus. Life Sci. Contrib., no. 67.

St. John, O. H. 1883. Report on the geology of the Wind River district. U.S. Geol. Surv. Terr. 12th Ann. Rept., pt. 1, pp. 173–269.

Savage, D. E. 1955. Nonmarine lower Pliocene sediments in California. Univ. Calif. Publ. Geol. Sci. 31:1–26.

————. 1977. Aspects of vertebrate paleontological stratigraphy and geochronology. In Concepts and methods of biostratigraphy, eds. E. G. Kauffmann and J. E. Hazel, pp. 427–442. Stroudsburg, Pa.: Dowden, Hutchison, and Ross.

Savage, D. E., and D. E. Russell. 1983. Mammalian paleofaunas of the world. Reading, Mass.: Addison-Wesley.

Savage, D. E., and B. T. Waters. 1978. A new omomyid primate from the Wasatch Formation of southern Wyoming. Folia Primat. 30:1–29.

Schankler, D. M. 1980. Faunal zonations of the Willwood Formation in the central Bighorn Basin, Wyoming. In Early Cenozoic paleontology and stratigraphy of the Bighorn Basin, Wyoming, ed. P. D. Gingerich, pp. 99–114. Univ. Mich. Papers Paleont., no. 24.

————. 1981. Local extinction and ecological re-entry of early Eocene mammals. Nature 293:135–138.

Schassberger, H. T. 1972. A K-Ar age of a quartz monzanite dike in the Kerwin [sic] mining district, Park County, Wyoming. Isochron/West, no. 4, p. 31.

Schiebout, J. A. 1974. Vertebrate paleontology and paleoecology of Paleocene Black Peaks Formation, Big Bend National Park, Texas. Texas Mem. Mus. Bull., vol. 24.

Schiebout, J. A., and A. K. Schrodt. 1981. Vertebrate paleontology of the lower Tertiary Baca Formation of western New Mexico. Amer. Assoc. Petrol. Geol. Bull. 65:568.

Scott, W. B. 1945. The Mammalia of the Duchesne River Oligocene. Trans. Amer. Philos. Soc., n.s. 34:209–233.

Scott, W. B., and H. F. Osborn. 1890. The Mammalia of the Uinta Formation. Trans. Amer. Philos. Soc., n.s. 16:461–572.

Shive, P. N., K. A. Sundell, and J. Rutledge. 1980. Magnetic polarity stratigraphy of Eocene volcaniclastic rocks from the Absaroka Mountains of Wyoming (abstr.). EOS, Trans. Amer. Geophys. Union 61:945.

Simpson, G. G. 1933. Glossary and correlation charts of North American Tertiary mammal-bearing formations. Bull. Amer. Mus. Nat. Hist. 67:79–121.

————. 1946. Discussion of the Duchesnean fauna and the Eocene-Oligocene boundary. Amer. J. Sci. 244:52–57.

————. 1948. The Eocene of the San Juan Basin, New Mexico. Amer. J. Sci. 246:257–282, 363–385.

Sinclair, W. J., and W. Granger. 1911. Eocene and Oligocene of the Wind River and Bighorn basins. Bull. Amer. Mus. Nat. Hist. 30:83–117.

————. 1912. Note on the Tertiary deposits of the Big Horn Basin. Bull. Amer. Mus. Nat. Hist. 31:57–67.

Smedes, H. W., and H. J. Prostka. 1972. Stratigraphic framework of the Absaroka volcanic supergroup in the Yellowstone National Park region. U.S. Geol. Surv. Prof. Paper 729–C.

Snyder, D. O. 1970. Fossil evidence of Eocene age of Baca Formation, New Mexico. New Mex. Geol. Soc. Guidebook 21:65–67.

Soister, P. E. 1968. Stratigraphy of the Wind River Formation in south-central Wind River Basin, Wyoming. U.S. Geol. Surv. Prof. Paper 594–A.

Stearns, C. E. 1943. The Galisteo Formation of north-central New Mexico. J. Geol. 51:301–319.

Steiger, R. H., and E. Jager. 1977. Subcommission on geochronology: Conventions on use of decay constants in geo- and cosmochronology. Earth Planet. Sci. Letters 36:359–362.

Steineck, P. L., and J. M. Gibson. 1971. Age and correlation of the Eocene Ulatisian and Narizian stages, California. Bull. Geol. Soc. Amer. 82:447–480.

Stevens, J. B., M. S. Stevens, and J. A. Wilson. 1984. Devil's Graveyard Formation (new), Eocene and Oligocene age, Trans-Pecos Texas. Texas Mem. Mus. Bull., no. 32, pp. 1–21.

Stock, C. 1932. Eocene land mammals on the Pacific Coast. Proc. Natl. Acad. Sci. 18:518–523.

———. 1938. A titanothere from the type Sespe of California. Proc. Natl. Acad. Sci. 24:507–512.

———. 1948. Pushing back the history of land mammals in western North America. Bull. Geol. Soc. Amer. 59:327–332.

Stokes, W. L., and J. H. Madsen, Jr. 1961. Geologic maps of Utah (northeast quarter). Salt Lake City: College of Mines and Mining Industry Univ. Utah.

Storer, J. E. 1978. Rodents of the Swift Current Creek local fauna (Eocene: Uintan) of Saskatchewan. Can. J. Earth Sci. 15:1673–1674.

———. 1984. Mammals of the Swift Current Creek local fauna (Eocene: Uintan, Saskatchewan). Contrib. Saskatchewan Mus. Nat. Hist., no. 7, pp. 1–158.

Stucky, R. K. 1982. Mammalian fauna and biostratigraphy of the upper part of the Wind River Formation (early to middle Eocene), Natrona County, Wyoming, and the Wasatchian-Bridgerian boundary. Ph.D. diss., Univ. Colo., Boulder.

———. 1984a. Revision of the Wind River faunas, early Eocene of central Wyoming. Pt. 5: Geology and mammalian biostratigraphy of the upper part of the Wind River Formation. Ann. Carengie Mus. 53:231–294.

———. 1984b. The Wasatchian-Bridgerian Land Mammal Age boundary (early to middle Eocene) in western North America. Ann. Carnegie Mus. 53:347–382.

Stucky, R. K., and L. Krishtalka. 1982. Revision of the Wind River faunas, early Eocene of central Wyoming. Pt. 1: Introduction and Multituberculata. Ann. Carnegie Mus. 51:39–56.

———. 1983. Revision of the Wind River faunas, early Eocene of central Wyoming. Pt. 4: The Tillodontia. Ann. Carnegie Mus. 52:375–391.

Sullivan, R. 1980. A stratigraphic evaluation of Eocene rocks of southwestern Wyoming. Geol. Surv. Wyo. Rept. Invest., no. 20, pp. 1–50.

Sutton, J. F., and C. C. Black. 1972. Oligocene and Miocene deposits of Jackson Hole, Wyoming. Guidebook, Field Conf. on Tert. Biostrat. Southern and Western Wyoming, pp. 73–79.

Szalay, F. S. 1969. Mixodectidae, Microsyopidae, and the insectivore-primate transition. Bull. Amer. Mus. Nat. Hist. 140:193–330.

———. 1976. Systematics of the Omomyidae (Tarsiiformes, Primates): taxonomy, phylogeny, and systematics. Bull. Amer. Mus. Nat. Hist. 156:157–450.

Tedford, R. H. 1970. Principles and practices of mammalian geochronology in North America. Proc. No. Amer. Paleont. Conv., Pt. F, pp. 666–703.

Testarmata, M. M., and W. A. Gose. 1979. Magnetostratigraphy of the Eocene-Oligocene Vieja Group, Trans-Pecos Texas. In Cenozoic geology of the Trans-Pecos volcanic field of Texas, eds. A. W. Walton and C. D. Henry, pp. 55–66. Bur. Econ. Geol. Univ. Texas Guidebook, no. 19.

———. 1980. Magnetostratigraphy in the Trans-Pecos volcanic field: Preliminary results from the Eocene-Oligocene Vieja Group. New Mex. Geol. Soc. Guidebook, 31st Ann. Field Conf., pp. 101–103.

Tourtelot, H. A. 1948. Tertiary rocks in the northeastern part of the Wind River Basin, Wyoming. Guidebook, 3d Ann. Field Conf. Soc. Vert. Paleont. In Southeastern Wyoming, pp. 53–67.

———. 1957. The geology and vertebrate paleontology of upper Eocene strata in the northeastern part of the Wind River Basin, Wyoming. Pt. 1: Geology. Smithsonian Misc. Coll., vol. 134, no. 4.

Truex, J. N. 1976. Santa Monica and Santa Ana mountains—relation to Oligocene Santa Barbara Basin. Amer. Assoc. Petrol. Geol. Bull. 60:65–86.

Turnbull, W. D. 1972. The Washakie Formation of Bridgerian-Uintan ages, and the related fauna. Guidebook, Field Conf. Tertiary Biostrat. of Southern and Western Wyoming, pp. 20–31.

———. 1978. The mammalian faunas of the Washakie Formation, Eocene age, of southern Wyoming. Pt. 1: Introduction: The geology, history, and setting. Fieldiana: Geol. 33:569–601.

Tweto, O. 1979. Geologic map of Colorado. U.S. Geol. Surv.

Van de Kamp, P. C., J. D. Harper, J. J. Conniff, and D. A. Morris. 1974. Facies relations in the Eocene-Oligocene Santa Ynez Mountains, California. J. Geol. Soc. Lond. 130:545–565.

Van Houten, F. B. 1944. Stratigraphy of the Willwood and Tatman formations in northwestern Wyoming. Bull. Geol. Soc. Amer. 65:165–210.

———. 1945. Review of latest Paleocene and early Eocene mammalian faunas. J. Paleont. 19:421–461.

Veatch, A. C. 1907. Geography and geology of a portion of southwestern Wyoming. U.S. Geol. Surv. Prof. Paper 56.

Vedder, J. G. 1972. Revision of stratigraphic names for some

Eocene formations in Santa Barbara and Ventura counties, California. Bull. U.S. Geol. Surv., no. 1354-C.

Wallace, S. M. 1980. A revision of North American early Eocene Brontotheriidae (Mammalia, Perissodactyla). M.S. thesis, Univ. Colo., Boulder.

Weaver, C. E., Stanley Beck, M. N. Bramlette, Stanley Carlson, B. L. Clark, T. W. Dibblee, Jr., Wyatt Durham, G. C. Ferguson, L. C. Forest, U. S. Grant, IV, Mason Hill, F. R. Kelley, R. M. Kleinpell, W. D. Kleinpell, J. Marks, W. C. Putnam, H. G. Schenck, N. T. Taliaferro, R. R. Thorup, Elizabeth Watson, and R. T. White. 1944. Correlation of the marine Cenozoic formations of western North America. Bull. Geol. Soc. Amer. 55:569–598.

West, R. M. 1969. Biostratigraphy of fluvial sediments of the upper Wasatch Formation in the northern Green River Basin, Wyoming. Univ. Wyo. Contrib. Geol. 8:184–196.

———. 1970. Sequence of mammalian faunas of Eocene age in the northern Green River Basin, Wyoming. J. Paleont. 14:142–147.

———. 1973a. Geology and mammalian paleontology of the New Fork-Big Sandy area, Sublette County, Wyoming. Fieldiana: Geol., vol. 29.

———. 1973b. Review of the North American Eocene and Oligocene Apatemyidae (Mammalia: Insectivora). Spec. Publ. Mus. Texas Tech Univ., no. 3.

———. 1973c. New records of fossil mammals from the early Eocene Golden Valley Formation, North Dakota. J. Mammal. 54:749–750.

———. 1976a. The North American Phenacodontidae (Mammalia, Condylarthra). Milwaukee Pub. Mus. Contrib. Biol. Geol., no. 6.

———. 1976b. Paleontology and geology of the Bridger Formation, southern Green River Basin, southwestern Wyoming. Pt. 1: History of fieldwork and geological setting. Milwaukee Pub. Mus. Contrib. Biol. Geol., no. 7.

———. 1982. Fossil mammals from the lower Buck Hill Group, Eocene of southwest Texas: Marsupicarnivora, Primates, Taeniodonta, Condylarthra, bunodont Artiodactyla, and Dinocerata. Pearce-Sellards Series, n. 35, pp. 1–20.

West, R. M., and E. G. Atkins. 1970. Additional middle Eocene (Bridgerian) mammals from Tabernacle Butte, Sublette County, Wyoming. Amer. Mus. Novitates, no. 2404.

West, R. M., and M. R. Dawson. 1973. Fossil mammals from the upper part of the Cathedral Bluffs Tongue of the Wasatch Formation (early Bridgerian), northern Green River Basin, Wyoming. Univ. Wyo. Contrib. Geol. 12:33–41.

———. 1975. Eocene fossil Mammalia from the Sand Wash Basin, northwestern Moffat County, Colorado. Ann. Carnegie Mus. 45:231–253.

———. 1978. Vertebrate paleontology and the Cenozoic history of the North Atlantic region. Polarforschung 48:103–119.

West, R. M., and J. H. Hutchison. 1981. Geology and paleontology of the Bridger Formation, southern Green River Basin, southwestern Wyoming. Pt. 6: The fauna and correlation of Bridger E. Milwaukee Pub. Mus. Contrib. Biol. Geol., no. 46.

Wheeler, W. H. 1961. Revision of the uintatheres. Peabody Mus. Nat. Hist. Yale Univ. Bull. vol. 14.

Wilson, J. A. 1967. Early Tertiary mammals. In Geology of Big Bend National Park, eds. R. A. Maxwell, J. T. Lonsdale, R. T. Hazzard, and J. A. Wilson, pp. 157–169. Univ. Texas Publ., no. 6711.

———. 1971. Early Tertiary vertebrate fauna, Vieja Group, Trans-Pecos Texas: Agriochoeridae and Merycoidodontidae. Texas Mem. Mus. Bull., no. 18.

———. 1975. Geochronology, stratigraphy, and typology. Fieldiana: Geol. 33:193–204.

———. 1977. Early Tertiary faunas, Big Bend area, Trans-Pecos Texas: Brontotheriidae. Pearce-Sellards Series, no. 25.

———. 1978. Stratigraphic occurrence and correlation of early Tertiary vertebrate faunas, Trans-Pecos Texas. Pt. 1: Vieja area. Texas Mem. Mus. Bull., no. 25.

———. 1980. Geochronology of the Trans-Pecos Texas volcanic field. New Mex. Geol. Soc. Guidebook, 31st Ann. Field Conf., pp. 205–211.

———. 1984. Vertebrate faunas forty-nine to thirty-six million years ago and additions to the species of *Leptoreodon* (Mammalia: Artiodactyla) found in Texas. J. Vert. Paleont. 4:199–207.

Wilson, J. A., P. C. Twiss, R. K. DeFord, and S. E. Clabaugh. 1968. Stratigraphic succession, potassium-argon dates, and vertebrate faunas, Vieja Group, Rim Rock County, Trans-Pecos Texas. Amer. J. Sci. 266:590–604.

Wilson, R. W. 1967. Fossil mammals in Tertiary correlations. In Essays in paleontology and stratigraphy, eds. C. Teichert and E. L. Yochelson, pp. 590–606. Univ. Kan. Dept. Geol. Spec. Publ. no. 2.

Wood, A. E. 1962. The early Tertiary rodents of the Family Paramyidae: Trans. Amer. Philos. Soc., n.s., vol. 52.

———. 1973. Eocene rodents, Pruett Formation, southwest Texas; their pertinence to the origin of the South American Caviomorpha. Pearce-Sellards Series, no. 20.

———. 1974. Early Tertiary vertebrate faunas, Vieja Group, Trans-Pecos Texas: Rodentia. Texas Mem. Mus. Bull., no. 21.

Wood, H. E. 1934. Revision of the Hyrachyidae. Bull. Amer. Mus. Nat. Hist. 67:182–295.

Wood, H. E., R. W. Chaney, J. Clark, E. H. Colbert, G. L. Jepsen, J. B. Reeside, Jr., and C. Stock. 1941. Nomenclature and correlation of the North American continental Tertiary. Bull. Geol. Soc. Amer. 52:1–48.

Wood, H. E., H. Seton, and C. J. Hares. 1936. New data on the Eocene of the Wind River Basin, Wyoming. Proc. Geol. Soc. Amer., 1935, pp. 394–395.

Woodring, W. P. 1931. Age of the orbitoid-bearing limestone and *Turritella varinta* zone of the western Santa Ynez Range, California. Trans. San Diego Nat. Hist. Soc. 6:371–388.

Woodring, W. P., and W. P. Popenoe. 1945. U.S. Geol. Surv. Oil Gas Invest. Prelim. Chart 12.

Wortman, J. L. 1901. Studies of Eocene Mammalia in the Marsh Collection, Peabody Museum. Pt. 1: Carnivora. Amer. J. Sci., 4th ser. 11:333–348.

5

THE CHADRONIAN, ORELLAN, AND WHITNEYAN NORTH AMERICAN LAND MAMMAL AGES

Robert J. Emry

Philip R. Bjork

Loris S. Russell

INTRODUCTION

The history of the development of the North American mammalian geochronology, including the principles on which it is based, the practices (not always compatible with the principles), and the problems that remain, were so thoroughly and clearly discussed by Tedford (1970) that any lengthy discussion here would be largely reiteration. We will therefore limit the following discussion to a very brief analysis of the status of the "North American Land Mammal Ages," with emphasis on the considerations relevant to the Chadronian, Orellan, and Whitneyan ages.

A committee, led by H. E. Wood, was appointed by the Vertebrate Section of the Paleontological Society (later to become the Society of Vertebrate Paleontology) to prepare a time scale for the North American continental Tertiary, which was completed and published in 1941 (Wood et al. 1941). The units defined and characterized in that report were intended to be "of purely temporal significance," were to be "defined in terms of precisely analyzed faunas and the related stratigraphy," were to "cover all of Tertiary time," and were "emphatically not defined in relation to either the epochs or the European standard" (ibid., pp. 1, 6). Part of the justification for the new time scale, with its new nomenclature, was to

make it possible to convey exact information "without facing the continual dilemma between trying to conform to the European standard time scale or using American formation names as time units" and "to discuss problems of relative age relationship and stratigraphic correlation without the distraction of endless controversies over epoch boundaries."

But these objectives were largely compromised when the committee based fourteen of the eighteen "North American Provincial Ages" on lithostratigraphic units, and of these fourteen, the names of ten were derived from the corresponding lithostratigraphic terms. The time units are therefore technically geochrons (i.e., the time values of rock units), and because the rock units on which they were based may be separated by disconformities or unconformities, the time scale does not "cover all of Tertiary time." Fortunately, the North American Provincial Ages, as developed by Wood et al. (1941) were also faunally characterized by "index fossils," "first appearance," "last appearance," and "characteristic fossils." This faunal information has made the units useful because it allows the recognition of the "Ages" beyond the geographic limits of the lithostratigraphic units on which they were based. The ages were based, therefore, on two sets of criteria that did not necessarily correspond. Additional statements by Wood et al. (1941, p. 6) made the definitions even more ambiguous while at the same time introducing the flexibility needed to escape, where necessary, from the lithostratigraphic basis. They stated that "the type of each age necessarily belongs to it, and the sequence and approximate scope of the ages are thus intended to be definitely fixed (barring new discoveries which should lead to radically different interpretation). However, the ages are not necessarily coextensive with their types, and the precise limits between successive ages are intended to be somewhat flexible and may presumably be modified in the light of later discoveries." We recommend that, in any improved definitions, full advantage be taken of this permission and that attention be focused on biostratigraphic rather than lithostratigraphic criteria.

In spite of the shortcomings of the definitions, the Wood committee's time units have been operational, as demonstrated by their wide usage. They correspond to major phases of mammalian history and allow correlation of units of about Stage/Age magnitude.

Even though the Chadronian, Orellan, and Whitneyan ages were based on lithostratigraphic units (Wood et al. 1941, p. 11) the Chadronian-Orellan and Orellan-Whitneyan boundaries were quite precisely fixed because the units on which they were based are lithostratigraphic subdivisions of one essentially continuous sequence. A potential problem exists, however, in recognizing these boundaries beyond the geographic limits of the lithostratigraphic units. The Orella and Whitney members of the Brule, on which the Orellan and Whitneyan ages were based, cannot be recognized even in southwestern South Dakota, which is part of the type area of these ages. The lithologic boundaries of the Scenic and Poleslide members of the Brule in South Dakota are probably not precisely temporally coincident with those of the Orella and Whitney members, respectively, in Nebraska. An additional potential problem is introduced by the fact that lithostratigraphic boundaries, even where they can be traced, may be time transgressive. The limits of the ages should be based on biostratigraphic criteria and should be set at the most widely recognizable and most convenient faunal breaks, which may or may not coincide with lithostratigraphic boundaries.

A more precise biochronology for the Chadronian through Whitneyan interval will require a great amount of effort. But at present the mammals seem to provide greater potential for temporal resolution than do other geochronologic techniques. Radiometric dates on rocks associated with Chadronian faunas allow a general calibration of the Chadronian age, although the number of reliable dates is still insufficient for very precise correlation. Orellan and Whitneyan faunas are not yet dated

radiometrically. Magnetic polarity stratigraphy will undoubtedly be useful at some degree of resolution, particularly as it might be applied to correlating the mammalian chronology with other chronologies, including the epochs (see Prothero et al. 1982; 1983). But it appears unlikely that the magnetic polarity sequence will be useful in improving the resolution of the mammalian chronology. An example is the attempt by Prothero (1982) to test the isochroneity of mammalian biostratigraphic events by comparing them to paleomagnetic events. In his study, it appears that the isochronous marker beds (e.g., tuffs) to which the fossils were zoned when collected, enabling the recognition of biostratigraphic events over his study area, occur with greater frequency than do the paleomagnetic events. The result is analogous to calibrating a scale marked in centimeters by using a yardstick marked in inches. For those interested in studying the relative temporal relationships of biological units, the mammalian biochronology will not become obsolete, even if it should be supplanted by other means of measuring time with greater resolution.

A biochronology based on the succession of fossil mammals depends on establishing the sequential relationship of the faunas, and this ultimately depends on demonstrating their superpositional relationships. This poses no serious problem with the Chadronian, Orellan, and Whitneyan ages, which are based on lithologic divisions of one essentially continuous sequence in a common type area, and the superpositional relationships of the faunas contained in the units are therefore also easily demonstrated. But the temporal fidelity of a biochronology based on these faunas can be no better than the precision in stratigraphic documentations and the detail in taxonomy. The stratigraphic documentation of specimens from the White River Group has traditionally consisted of recording the lithostratigraphic unit, usually of formation or member magnitude, from which they came. Consequently, the biochronology has consisted of a series of bulk units, which can be recognized by the presence of certain taxa that existed together long enough so that their mutual occurrence is common. For most of the mammalian taxa occurring in the White River Group, we still have very little information as to the actual vertical distribution of species within the lithostratigraphic units, and thus we lack the information needed to develop a chronology based on range-zone, and concurrent range-zone, biostratigraphy.

A biochronology for the Chadronian through Whitneyan interval, if it is to be applicable at a regional or continental scale, must include information from correlated faunal sequences. This is particularly true of the Chadronian, in which faunas are less completely known in the type area than they are in correlated sequences. When correlated faunas are incorporated into the biochronologic scheme, care must be taken to minimize any ecological or zoogeographic bias. These considerations do not pose any serious problems for the Chadronian through Whitneyan interval as the faunal provincialism that became so pronounced later in the Tertiary is not apparent there. The apparent lack of provincialism is thought to reflect reality, although it may also be partly due to the fact that deposits and faunas representing this time interval are not nearly so widespread geographically in North America as are the later Tertiary deposits and faunas. Although there are undoubtedly some ecological controls on the distribution of some taxa, particularly in the Chadronian, the effects of ecological bias can be minimized if correlations are based on a relatively large proportion of faunal taxa rather than on just a few taxa. Because larger animals have, in general, wider geographic ranges and greater environmental tolerance, they are likely to be more valuable in correlation than small ones. Close homotaxial relationship between the larger elements of two faunas should outweigh the dissimilarity that may be seen in the micromammals. Many of the smaller mammals are so widespread, however, that they are also often useful. In the Chadronian, for example, the rodents *Adjidaumo minimus, Paradjidaumo minor,* and species of *Ischyromys* and the insectivores *"Icotops" acutidens* and species of *Apternodus* are so widespread that we must either conclude that uniformly favorable environments were widespread or that the species were tolerant of a variety of environments (the fossil morphospecies may include more than one biological species, each with its own specific ecological preference). A. E. Wood (1974) noted the considerable similarity between the rodents of the Vieja sequence of Trans-Pecos Texas and those from Montana and the northern Great Plains and commented that the extensive north-south distributions suggest less climatic zonation than at present. He also pointed out, however, that a distinct southern element is suggested by some of the Vieja and southern California rodents that are not known to occur farther north, but some of these are Uintan and/or Duchesnean species. That the few remaining Chadronian species are not known to occur farther north may not be significant zoogeographically; they may represent a segment of time not represented farther north, and we have no way of knowing how closely the known occurrences approximate the total geographic ranges. At any rate, it does not alter the fact that the Chadronian faunas of the Vieja are in large part homotaxial with faunas of the White River Group and its equivalents as far north as Montana and Saskatchewan.

Refinement of the mammalian biochronology can be accomplished only through detailed analysis of the relationships between mammalian taxa and the rock bodies in which they occur. In some parts of the North American continental Tertiary, particularly in rocks of Arikareean and later ages, mammal remains often occur as local concentrations, at what amount to single horizons, in thick sequences of strata that may be otherwise unfossiliferous. These conditions make it impractical to attempt to apply range-zone biostratigraphy. We believe, however, that the most promising way to refine the biochronology for the Chadronian through Whitneyan interval is through development of a detailed range-zone biostratigraphy. Factors favoring the development of a range-zone biostratigraphy for this interval are (1) the three ages are based on three superposed lithostratigraphic subdivisions of a single, essentially continuous sequence, (2) there is apparent environmental stability, resulting in a relatively stable chronofauna that retains much of its identity throughout the interval, and (3) the mode of occurrence of most fossil specimens representing these ages is suitable to such an appraisal.

Continuity of the Stratigraphic Record

As previously mentioned, Wood et al. (1941) based most of the "North American Provincial Ages" on lithostratigraphic units. In many instances, the rock unit bases for any two consecutive ages are isolated either by depositional hiatuses or by wide geographic separation; these make it exceedingly difficult, or impossible, to establish a single boundary between two consecutive ages on the basis of the lithostratigraphic criteria. This problem is largely nonexistent in the Chadronian, Orellan, and Whitneyan interval. The first was based on the Chadron Formation of northwestern Nebraska and southwestern South Dakota. The Orellan and Whitneyan were based on the Orella and Whitney members, respectively, of the Brule Formation in northwest Nebraska, southwest South Dakota, and eastern Wyoming. The type areas of these three consecutive ages are therefore virtually coextensive, the only exception being that the Chadron Formation in eastern Wyoming was excluded, for some reason, perhaps oversight, from the type area of the Chadronian age.

Over most of this common type area, the Brule Formation overlies the Chadron in what appears to be a continuous, conformable sequence. At many localities the Chadron and Brule formations can be studied in single continuous outcrops. Particularly in the Chadron Formation and Orella Member of the Brule, there are innumerable channel deposits showing cut and fill relationships. Lateral to the channel deposits, however, depositional sequences seem to be continuous, with no apparent physical stratigraphic or faunal evidence to indicate hiatuses. The erosion cycles were apparently short-lived and are not unconformities or disconformities as those terms are usually understood and applied.

Chronofaunal Stability

Virtually all known North American mammalian faunas of Chadronian through Whitneyan age appear to be part of a single chronofauna according to the definition given by Olson (1952), that is, "a geographically restricted, natural assemblage of interacting animal populations that has maintained its basic structure over a geologically significant period of time." The term "chronofauna," as used by Olson in his Permian vertebrate example, is basically defined as the fauna of the whole ecosystem and may include the assemblages occupying a number of different ecological subzones. The various habitats may be successively occupied by a series of phyletically related species, which may shift from one to another of the ecological subzones within the ecosystem while remaining part of the same chronofauna. The chronofauna may change in taxonomic content through time, and the proportions of the fauna occupying different ecological subzones may change through time, but overall stability is maintained. Clark et al. (1967), in reconstructing the environment of the Chadron Formation and the Scenic Member of the Brule Formation, used the term "chronofauna" in a sense different from Olson's. The chronofaunas of Clark et al. approximate the different subzonal assemblages of Olson. What they interpret as the destruction of the Chadronian wet-forest chronofauna and the commencement of the Orellan savanna chronofauna would be equivalent, in Olson's example, to a shift of phyla (of a single chronofauna) from one ecological subzone to another.

What may be termed the White River chronofauna first became a recognizable entity early in Chadronian time. Some of its elements, or at least its ancestral elements, can be discerned in the fauna of the Uinta Formation and its correlatives, but by Chadronian time many new elements had appeared, some apparent immigrants from Eurasia and many others whose ancestry is not yet clearly established. Once the chronofauna was established, it maintained its basic structure throughout the Chadronian, Orellan, and Whitneyan, and only after the early part of the Arikareean is there a marked reorganization suggesting important changes in the ecosystem. Even the archaic forms, such as *Hyaenodon,*

the marsupial *Peratherium,* and the primitive leptochoerid and enthelodontid artiodactyls, that managed to survive into Chadronian time were able to exist into the early Arikareean before becoming extinct. There are, of course, important events that modified the chronofauna, such as the extinction of the titanotheres at the end of Chadronian time and the occasional appearance of new forms. Among the various lineages that existed simultaneously, the predominance of one group at one time may shift to predominance of another group at a later time. An example of this is the shift in smaller rodents from predominantly eomyids to predominantly eumyine cricetids to predominantly heteromyids from the Chadronian to Orellan to Whitneyan, respectively. But as a whole, the basic structure of the fauna is maintained, with the various phyletic lineages of mammals showing species-level, and even generic-level, evolution through the interval. The long-term mutual association of many lineages indicates a relatively stable ecosystem spanning more than ten million years.

Mode of Occurrence

The White River Group, which has provided most of the fossil mammal specimens of Chadronian, Orellan, and Whitneyan age, is exceptionally well exposed. Often the entire thickness of strata is exposed and can be followed for miles or tens of miles. A great majority of the fossil mammal remains occur as individual specimens, widely distributed, with few local concentrations through the strata, although at any given locality there are usually some levels at which fossil bones are very abundant and other levels that are relatively unfossiliferous. The record for this interval nevertheless appears to be less episodic in nature than that of the later Tertiary, where fossil bones often occur in concentrations, limited both vertically and laterally, in sequences that may be otherwise unfossiliferous. The more or less continuous vertical distribution of abundant fossil specimens in an essentially complete sequence of strata that is well exposed over hundreds of square miles provides the conditions necessary for detailed biostratigraphic analysis. In the common taxonomic groups for which the record is substantially complete, the potential emerges for determining range-zones of species and ultimately establishing a biochronology based on concurrent range-zones.

HISTORY OF WHITE RIVER ROCK AND FAUNAL SUBDIVISION

Fossil mammals were first discovered in the White River deposits and made known to science before the middle of the nineteenth century (e.g., Prout 1846, 1847; Leidy 1847), and many species were described by Leidy during the following decade. Almost from the beginning, attempts were made to subdivide the fossiliferous deposits on faunal, as well as lithologic, grounds.

Meek and Hayden are often credited with defining the White River Formation in 1857. But in their 1857 paper, the term "White River Formation" was not used. They did use the term "White River formations," but it was used interchangeably with "White River deposits," "White River beds," "Tertiary deposits on White River," and "Bad Lands of White River." It is clear that at that time the term was not used as a name for a discrete set of rocks but simply to refer to all of the "formations" outcropping in the "White River Basin," as opposed to the "Great Lignite Basin," "Judith River," and so forth.

Later in the same year, Hayden published the first lithologic subdivisions of the White River deposits. He simply listed and gave general descriptions of eight units (Beds A through H), which he considered "different beds of the Bad Lands of White River" (1857, p. 153). Included was the complete sequence from the base of the Tertiary along White River to the top of the divide between White River and the Running Water (Niobrara) to the south. Bed A, which he also called the "Titanotherium Bed," is clearly the Chadron Formation of present usage. Bed H is equally clearly what is now some part of the Ogallala Group. There has been disagreement as to which of the intervening "Beds" belong to the White River Group as it is now recognized. Hayden's Bed B, which he also called the "Turtle and Oreodon Bed," is clearly at least part of the Brule Formation. Bed C was described as being on "both sides of White River" and is presumably also part of the Brule, although in his 1857 list of fossils, Hayden listed none from this unit. At that time, he reported *Leptomeryx evansi* as the only mammal from Bed D, whereas *Leptauchenia decora* was reported from Beds B and E and *Leptauchenia major* from Bed B. A year later, Hayden (1858, pp. 157–158) listed these two species of *Leptauchenia* only in Bed D, along with a number of other Brule species and several later species, including *Anchitherium (Hypohippus) affinus, Anchitherium (Parahippus) cognatus,* and *Merycochoerus proprius.* In 1858, he included Beds A, B, and C in a section "of the different beds, as shown on White River" (p. 156). And in the same paper, he described Bed D as occurring beneath the Pliocene deposits along the Niobrara River, composing most of the divide between the White and Niobrara rivers, between the Niobrara and Fort Laramie on the North Platte, well developed in the region of Fort Laramie, and westward to the foot of the mountains. It

is apparent that, by 1858, the lithologic units on which Hayden based his concept of Bed D were predominantly those now included in the Arikaree Group, although the fossils he reported from that bed pertain to a much wider stratigraphic range. Essentially this same conclusion was reached by Matthew (1899, p. 22). Hayden's units are now of interest only historically. Except for Bed A, which corresponds to the Chadron Formation, it is virtually impossible to equate his units with any of the presently recognized subdivisions of the White River Group.

Meek and Hayden (1861) were the first to use the White River terminology in reference to a discrete set of rocks. They recognized the "White River Group" as one of the three or four groups of Nebraska Tertiary rocks that they believed belonged to at least three, and probably four, distinct epochs (p. 432). But their "White River Group" was much more inclusive than the same term in modern usage. It included all the beds ("1000 feet or more") beneath the "Loup Fork Beds." This presumably included Beds A through E, which Hayden classified as Miocene (1858, p. 149), while assigning Bed F to "Pliocene Tertiary," covering "a very large area on Loup Fork," along the Niobrara River, on Bijou Hills, and so forth. The White River Group of Meek and Hayden apparently corresponds approximately to the present-day White River Group plus Arikaree Group, whereas their "Loup Fork Beds" correspond approximately to the present Ogallala Group and younger rocks.

Hayden's stratigraphy served as the basis for collection and generalization until the late 1800s, although the White River Group became restricted to approximately its present scope, and the terminology evolved into an essentially two-part division: the "*Titanotherium* Beds," overlain by the "*Oreodon,*" or "Turtle-*Oreodon,*" Beds (Wortman 1893, p. 96). Hatcher (1893) recognized three divisions of the *Titanotherium* Beds, and later in the same year Wortman elaborated on subdivisions of the *Oreodon* Beds. Wortman noted lithologic changes in the section and separated the "*Protoceras* Beds," with an upper "*Leptauchenia* layer," from the upper part of the *Oreodon* Beds, basing the separation largely on faunal characters (ibid.). He recorded 135 to 170 feet of *Oreodon* Beds, 100 feet of Barren Clay, and 150 to 225 feet of *Protoceras* Beds.

Unfortunately, Wortman was somewhat ambiguous about the limits of the units. He reported that at about 75 to 100 feet above the "Oreodon layer" (lower nodules) is another distinct nodule-bearing layer (upper nodules) that appears to be the uppermost limit of the fossil-bearing Oreodon Beds, and he stated, "it is at this point, therefore, that I draw the line between the middle primary division [Oreodon Beds] and the uppermost division, Protoceras Beds" (p. 101). This implies that everything above the upper nodules was assigned to the *Protoceras* beds (fig. 5.1). On the same page, however, Wortman wrote that "between what I have taken to represent the uppermost limit of the Oreodon Beds and the Protoceras Beds there is a very considerable thickness of light-colored clay in which few fossils occur. These strata reach a thickness of 100 feet or more, and on this account it is easy to distinguish, in this region at least, between the Oreodon and Protoceras Beds." This implies that he considered the 100 feet of barren clay neither part of the *Oreodon* Beds nor part of the *Protoceras* Beds. In his chart, in fact, Wortman shows the 100 feet of "Barren Clays" as a separate unit occurring between the *Oreodon* and the *Protoceras* beds (pp. 98–99). He did not further subdivide the *Oreodon* Beds; he simply stated, "if it is desirable to subdivide the Oreodon Beds I would suggest that all those strata between the top of the Titanotherium Beds and the typical Oreodon layer [lower nodules] would constitute the first division, the Oreodon layer itself would form the second division, and

all those strata above the Oreodon layer, between it and the Protoceras Beds, would constitute the third division" (p. 101). Again, it is not clear whether Wortman intended that this third division include the 100 feet of Barren Clays, but his chart indicates that he did not; the third unit shown on his chart stops at the top of the upper nodules. His chart was shown again, unchanged, by Osborn and Wortman (1894, 1895).

Matthew (1899), in his provisional classification of the Tertiary, included in his correlation chart a column that he attributed to "Wortman 1895." But instead of using Wortman's suggested divisions of the *Oreodon* Beds, he simply indicated Lower and Upper *Oreodon*, overlain by *Protoceras* Beds. Matthew thus introduced the new terms "Lower *Oreodon*" and "Upper *Oreodon*" without indicating how they related to the three divisions suggested by Wortman or to the 100 feet of Barren Clay.

The lithostratigraphic terminology of the White River Group was formalized by Darton (1899a, 1899b), who recognized the White River Group in western Nebraska and applied formation names, primarily on the basis of observations in northwestern Nebraska. It is

Wortman, 1893 Wortman and Osborn, 1894 Wortman and Osborn, 1895		Matthew, 1899 (Credited to Wortman, 1895)	Osborn, 1907 Osborn and Matthew, 1909		Wanless, 1923		Bump, 1956	
PROTOCERAS BEDS	Leptauchenia layer 100'	Leptauchenia (sub-zone)	Upper Brule'	Leptauchenia 100'	LEPTAUCHENIA - PROTOCERAS BEDS	White Ash Layer 15 - 25'	Basal Arikaree White Ash	BRULE FORMATION
	Coarse sandstones not continuous, etc. 50 - 75 '	Protoceras		Protoceras 50 - 75'		Division 3 72'	Poleslide Member Standard Section = 299'	
						Division 2 65'		
						Division 1 45 - 55'		
BARREN CLAYS	Light-colored clays 100'	Upper Oreodon		Oreodon (upper) 100'	OREODON BEDS	Upper Oreodon Red Clays 60'		
						Middle Oreodon Green Sandstones 24 - 55'		
OREODON BEDS	Nodulous clay stratum	3rd Suggested Divisions	Lower Brule'	Upper Nodular Layer		Upper Nodular Layer 1'	Upper Nodular Zone	
	Sandstones and clays 75 - 100'			Oreodon (Middle) 75 - 100'		Lower Oreodon Banded Silts 55 - 58'	Scenic Member Standard Section = 159'	
	Oreodon layer 10- 20'	2nd		Lower Nodular Layer 10 - 20'				
	Metamynodon Layer 50'	1st	Lower Oreodon	Oreodon (Lower) 70'		Lower Nodular or Caliche Zone 40 46'		
TITANOTHERIUM BEDS --- CHADRON FORMATION								

Fig. 5.1. Correlation of various differing classifications of the Brule Formation in South Dakota, showing particularly the different uses of the same terms for different parts of the "*Oreodon* Beds." Except for Matthew's divisions (1899), the upper and lower nodular layers are distinctly described in all sections and the columns are justified at these two marker levels.

quite evident that he applied the name Chadron Formation to deposits previously known as *Titanotherium* Beds (1899*b*, p. 759). It is less clear whether Darton's Brule Clay (ibid., p. 736) was meant to apply as well to deposits in South Dakota. He stated, "the White River beds in their extension from South Dakota into Nebraska present some differences in stratigraphic range and relations. They expand considerably and include, at their top, beds which appear not to be represented in the typical regions. Accordingly, to afford distinct definitions for the members in Nebraska I have introduced the designation *Brule clay* and separated the underlying Titanotherium beds as the *Chadron formation*" (ibid.). This suggests that he was proposing the names for deposits in Nebraska which he thought were distinct from those in South Dakota, but on the same page, he states that the Brule clay "extends far to the northeast in South Dakota." And, later, he reports that the section at Adelia, Nebraska, "closely resembles the typical section in the Big Bad Lands in South Dakota, but appear to include some higher beds" and that "the deposits lying on the Chadron sands is similar to the Oreodon series and yields many of the same mammalian remains" (p. 758). Two years later, Darton (1901) used the terms "Chadron" and "Brule" in reference to deposits southeast of the Black Hills in South Dakota. It seems evident that his original intent was for these terms to apply to deposits in South Dakota as well as Nebraska. Darton did not designate type localities for the Chadron and Brule formations. Wilmarth (1938) reported, however, that "Mr. Darton stated (pers. com. April 8, 1931) that he named this fm. for exposures at Chadron, Nebr." and that the name was "for the Brule Indians, who once roamed over Pine Ridge Ind. Res. in southern S. Dak., where the fm. covers large areas, and that it is not present in the Brule Ind. Res., which occurs farther N. in S. Dak."

Osborn (1907) was the first to clearly extend Darton's lithologic terms into the typical region for the White River Group in the Big Badlands of South Dakota. In his classification (fig. 2), which was used again, essentially unchanged, by Osborn and Matthew (1909), the "*Oreodon* (Lower)" is the equivalent of Wortman's suggested first division (i.e., the strata between the *Titanotherium* Beds and the lower nodules). "Lower Nodular Layer" is shown as a distinct unit and is equivalent to Wortman's suggested second division, and "*Oreodon* (Middle)" is equivalent to Wortman's suggested third division (i.e., up to and including the upper nodules). But at this time, the 100 feet of Barren Clays, which Wortman apparently did not include in either the *Oreodon* or *Protoceras* Beds, was shown as "*Oreodon* (Upper)."

The next major contribution to White River stratigraphy was that of Wanless (1923), who further confused the nomenclature. His lowest unit of the Brule included everything above the *Titanotherium* Beds, up to and including the lower nodules. What he termed the "Lower *Oreodon* Banded Silts" was equal to Osborn's Middle *Oreodon* minus the upper nodular layer, or Wortman's suggested third division minus the upper nodules. Wanless treated the "Upper Nodular Layer" as a separate unit, and his Middle *Oreodon* and Upper *Oreodon* were divisions of Osborn's Upper *Oreodon,* or Wortman's Barren Clays.

Bump (1956) formalized the lithostratigraphic subdivision of the Brule in South Dakota by defining two members. He designated as the Scenic Member "the unit formerly known as the Oreodon beds (Wortman), minus the upper Oreodon bed" (p. 430). This leaves some ambiguity because Wortman had no Upper *Oreodon*. It is clear from his description of the standard sections that Bump excluded the Upper *Oreodon* of Osborn (1907), which equals the Middle and Upper *Oreodon* of Wanless (1923). Bump's Poleslide Member included all the strata from the top of the upper nodular layer to the base of the "basal Arikaree white ash" (Rockyford Ash).

Schultz and Stout (1938) applied the formal lithologic terms "Orella Member" and "Whitney Member" to subdivisions of the Brule Formation in northwestern Nebraska. It is problematical whether these two members can ever be shown to be coextensive with, respectively, the Scenic and Poleslide members of the Big Badlands of South Dakota, but faunal evidence indicates they are approximate equivalents. The Wood committee (1941) made the Chadron Formation and the Orella and Whitney members of the Brule Formation the lithostratigraphic basis for, respectively, the Chadronian, Orellan, and Whitneyan North American Provincial Ages. Additional suggestions, correlations, and refinements of the stratigraphy of these deposits have occurred over the last thirty years. These topics will be explored in further detail in the sections that follow.

GEOGRAPHIC DISTRIBUTION OF CHADRONIAN, ORELLAN, AND WHITNEYAN ROCKS AND FAUNAS

The Chadronian, Orellan, and Whitneyan ages were based on lithostratigraphic divisions of the White River Group and the faunas contained in them (Wood et al. 1941). The faunal characterizations of the time units also depend, however, on faunas from other rock units in other areas which can be correlated with the White River faunas. Even though the White River faunas, particularly those of the Chadron Formation, are not so completely known as contemporary faunas in other areas, they nevertheless provide sufficient faunal information to allow the correlated faunas to be used in the faunal characterization and, therefore, play a preeminent role in the development of a biochronology for this interval. Because these ages are based on (and derive their names from) lithostratigraphic divisions of the White River Group and the faunas found in them, it seems worthwhile to generalize briefly about the geographic distribution of the White River and the lateral and vertical distribution of lithofacies within it.

The White River Group is exposed widely in southwestern South Dakota and northwestern Nebraska and can be traced almost continuously westward, north of the Pine Ridge escarpment, to the vicinity of Douglas, Wyoming, and from there southward, east of the Laramie Range, nearly to the Colorado border. It crops out extensively in the valley of the North Platte River and in the valleys of its tributaries in western Nebraska and eastern Wyoming. In northeastern Colorado, the White River crops out extensively along the south-facing escarpment where the High Plains break off into the Colorado Piedmont. Figure 5.2 shows the approximate areal extent of the White River Group.

In northwestern South Dakota, southwestern North Dakota, southeastern Montana, and in the higher Black Hills are smaller isolated outcrops of White River. In central Wyoming, in the Bates Hole, Flagstaff Rim, and Beaver Divide areas, deposits have the general lithologic characteristics that allow them to be called White River but are generally so uniform that they are not subdivided lithologically and are locally treated as a formation rather than as a group.

Deposits that can justifiably be called White River occur as far southwest as the northwestern edge of the Great Divide Basin in Wyoming, from where they can be traced northward across the divide at the western end of the Granite Mountains into the Beaver Divide area of the Wind River Basin. The areas of White River Formation along Beaver Divide, Flagstaff Rim, and Bates Hole are undoubtedly remnants of deposits that once extended northward across much of the Wind River Basin and continued northeastward across the divide into the Powder River Basin, where remnants remain on the Pumpkin Buttes. From the Powder River Basin, they were apparently continuous with the White River deposits that now crop out nearly continuously from the vicinity of Douglas, Wyoming, eastward into northwestern Nebraska and southwestern South Dakota.

If the White River terminology is applied to rocks extending from South Dakota into Wyoming as far as the Great Divide Basin, then rocks with the same lithostratigraphic terminology occur in what are several different depositional basins, at least with respect to the fluviatile components. Separate lithologic nomenclatures are normally employed for rock sequences of similar age in separate basins of deposition when the sediments in the two basins are transported to, and deposited in, them primarily by streams, particularly when the sediments are derived from different source areas and differ lithologically. But the bulk of the White River, predominantly so toward the west, is aeolian and was transported and deposited across this broad area irrespective of stream drainage boundaries. This preponderance of aeolian material not only gives the White River deposits lateral continuity across drainage divides but its lithologic and lithogenetic uniformity masks the minor differences in the fluviatile components from place to place, giving the deposits the general lithologic characteristics that allow the valid application of the White River terminology over such a broad area.

That the White River nomenclature can be used over such a broad area does not mean the lithology is identical everywhere. There are lateral and vertical facies changes of several kinds (see Wood 1949). Laterally, sediments become finer away from the source as well as away from the main stream channel sandstones, through floodplain deposits, to aeolian deposits. These facies are partly masked by a less orthodox facies based on the presence, relative amount, and condition of volcanic ash. The presence and amount of volcanic ash is related in a general way to the distance and direction from the source (upwind-downwind facies), whereas its condition is more dependent on where it occurs within the coeval channel-floodplain-aeolian facies.

Although there are many local variations within the White River deposits, it could be said, generally, that the facies changes seen in contemporaneous deposits from northeast to southwest are paralleled by the changes seen at any one place from older to younger deposits. If one takes as a starting point the Chadron Formation in South Dakota, the change is from predominantly fluviatile, floodplain deposits to predominantly aeolian deposits as one moves southwestward, in contemporary deposits, into central Wyoming. A similar change is seen vertically from the Chadron Formation upward through the Poleslide Member of the Brule in South Dakota. The volcanic facies follow the same pattern, particularly with respect to the amount and condition of the ash: progressively more ash in less weathered condition from northeast to southwest and a similar change upward from Chadronian through Whitneyan deposits. This may simply be another way of saying that there is

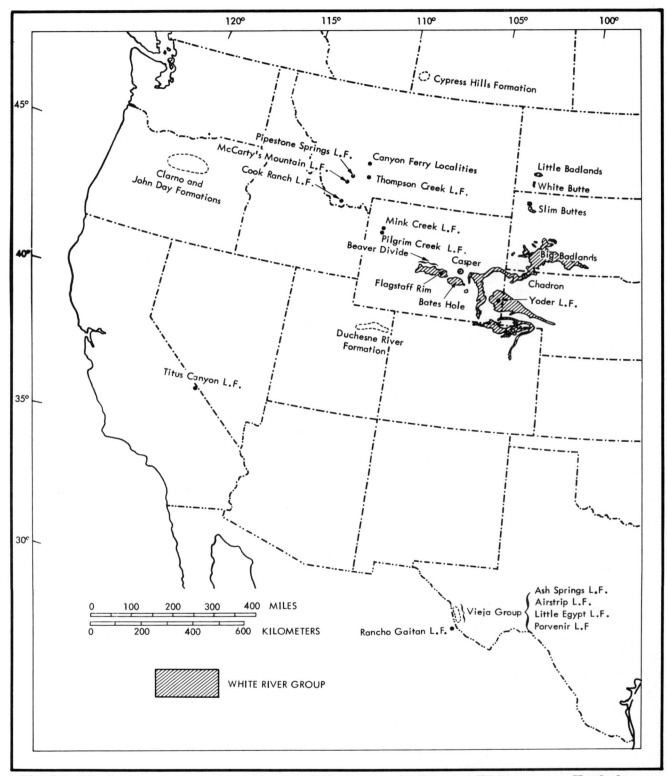

Fig. 5.2. Distribution of rock and faunal units of Chadronian, Orellan, and Whitneyan age. Hatched area represents approximate outcrop area of White River Group ("Formation" in central Wyoming).

a positive correlation between the amount and condition of volcanic ash and the relative amount of aeolian deposits. In the floodplain deposits, the aeolian material, including the volcanic ash, may simply be so thoroughly reworked and altered that it is not so apparent.

In South Dakota, the Chadron Formation can be characterized briefly as predominantly claystone and silty claystone, with innumerable sandstone and conglomerate stream channel fillings. From a distance, the approximate level of the contact with the Brule is usually easily recognized, although its precise position may be more difficult to determine on close inspection. In northwestern Nebraska, the lower part of the Chadron is similar in appearance to that in South Dakota, but the upper part looks more like the overlying Brule and is, in fact, separated from the Brule more or less arbitrarily at the "upper purplish white layer" (see Schultz and Stout 1955). In both northwestern Nebraska and southwestern South Dakota, most of the volcanic ash present is reworked and redeposited by water and, for the most part, is weathered and altered to clays. Farther west, in Niobrara County, Wyoming, the Chadron and overlying Brule appear to be predominantly aeolian, although some parts of the Chadron still have numerous channel sandstones and greenish and brownish clay lenses, which are reminiscent of the Chadron in South Dakota. In this area, the upper part of the Chadron is a smooth-weathering, uniformly textured silty clay, with no evidence of bedding. It is so similar to the overlying Brule that separation must rely on the arbitrary division at the upper purplish white layer. The volcanic ash content is apparently greater than in contemporary deposits in South Dakota or is at least less weathered and altered. Farther west, in central Wyoming, in the Bates Hole, Flagstaff Rim, and Beaver Divide areas, the Chadronian White River Formation is predominantly an aeolian, volcanic ash facies. Numerous small-scale channel fills of sandstone and conglomerate occur in sequences that are otherwise massive, unbedded, tuffaceous, aeolian siltstones, with numerous distinct beds of volcanic ash, apparently not reworked and redeposited by water.

The Scenic Member of the Brule Formation in South Dakota has numerous small-scale stream channel sandstones, but the bulk of the member is made up of silty mudstones, laminated mudstones, and laminated siltstones deposited on confluent floodplain surfaces (see Clark, in Clark et al. 1967). The sediments have minor amounts of volcanic ash, but this, and any other aeolian component, is apparently thoroughly reworked and redeposited by surface water. The horizontal bedding and other evidence of deposition by water becomes less evident upward, so that in the Poleslide Member the aeolian

(including volcanic ash) components are more apparent, and toward the top of the Poleslide Member some units almost qualify as a tuff.

In northwestern Nebraska, the Orella Member is a composite of channel sandstones, floodplain fluviatile silty clays, and aeolian deposits. Much of the Orella Member is similar in appearance to the Scenic Member, with horizontally bedded siltstones and mudstones that undoubtedly include some reworked aeolian material, but there are also distinct units of uniformly textured, unbedded aeolian deposits. Farther west, north of Harrison in Sioux County, Nebraska, the aeolian units become thicker and make up a greater proportion of the deposits. Even farther west, in Niobrara County, Wyoming, the aeolian deposits predominate, although there are still thin units of horizontally bedded sediments with sedimentary structures indicating reworking and deposition by water. In this area, rocks with Orellan faunas are, in general, more like the Whitney Member in color, lithology, and weathering characteristics. The Whitney Member in western Nebraska and eastern Wyoming and the equivalent Vista Member in northeastern Colorado are almost entirely aeolian. The volcanic ash content is higher than in the underlying Orella Member and Chadron Formation, and the ash is relatively unweathered.

Faunal differences are correlated with some of the lithologic facies of the White River. Some taxa (e.g., *Protoceras, Metamynodon*) occur almost exclusively in the stream channel sandstones and are found only rarely in the floodplain and aeolian facies. One gets the impression, from collecting in contemporary floodplain and aeolian facies, that there is no faunal distinction between them, although detailed studies may show there are differences in relative abundance of some taxa. The presence and amount of volcanic ash has no apparent influence on the faunas.

Deposits with mammalian faunas of Chadronian, Orellan, and Whitneyan age occur beyond the geographic limits of the White River Group. Among the more important are the Cypress Hills Formation in southwestern Saskatchewan; the Climbing Arrow and Dunbar Creek formations of the South Townsend, Clarkston, and Three Forks basins and the Renova Formation of the Jefferson Basin (which contains the important Pipestone Springs Local Fauna), all in southwestern Montana; the Clarno Formation and part of the John Day Formation in Oregon; and the Chambers Tuff and Capote Mountain Tuff of the Vieja Group in Trans-Pecos Texas. The mammalian assemblages from these units can be correlated, with varying degrees of precision, with the White River faunal sequence. Some of them provide much faunal information not known from contemporary White River faunas and are therefore important in developing a mammalian biochronology. There are numerous other occurrences of mammalian fossils of Chadronian, Orellan, or Whitneyan age which are not mentioned here. We have not attempted to be comprehensive but have chosen to discuss those with faunas important to the development of a biochronology and/or those that can be related to radiometric dates.

Through the Chadronian-Whitneyan interval the known mammalian faunas become increasingly restricted geographically (i.e., the geographic distribution of Chadronian faunas is much greater than that of Orellan faunas, which is, in turn, greater than that of Whitneyan faunas). The maximum geographic distribution of faunas representing any part of this interval is essentially the same as the distribution of Chadronian faunas, which occur as far north as southwestern Saskatchewan and as far south as Trans-Pecos Texas and adjacent Chihuahua and from the Clarno and John Day areas of Oregon and Titus Canyon of California on the west to southwestern South Dakota, northwestern Nebraska, and northeastern Colorado on the east. The Chadronian faunas of the Clarno, John Day, and Titus Canyon areas are so poorly known, however, that they contribute little to the development of a biochronology. Nelson (1976) reports "early Oligocene" vertebrate fossils from tuffaceous sandstones and lacustrine limestone near Peoa, Utah, but does not otherwise elaborate. If these are excluded, virtually all known Chadronian faunas occur east of the present continental divide. (Figure 5.2 indicates the approximate locations of many of the local faunas.)

Orellan faunas occur in southwestern Montana in the Dunbar Creek Formation in the Three Forks, Clarkston, and South Townsend basins, the Dunbar Creek Member of the Renova Formation in the Jefferson Basin, and the Cook Ranch Local Fauna east of Lima. Other than these, Orellan faunas are virtually all from the Orellan part of the Brule Formation: isolated localities in southwestern North Dakota and northwestern South Dakota, the Scenic Member in southwestern South Dakota, the Orella Member in western Nebraska and eastern Wyoming, and the equivalent Cedar Creek Member in northeastern Colorado.

Whitneyan faunas are essentially restricted to the Whitneyan part of the Brule Formation: the Poleslide Member in southwestern South Dakota, the Whitney Member in western Nebraska and eastern Wyoming, the equivalent Vista Member in northeastern Colorado, and Units F to H of Lillegraven (1970) in northwestern South Dakota. Whitneyan deposits are indicated in southwestern North Dakota by some authors (e.g., Schultz and Falkenbach 1968), while others (e.g., Stone 1972) report

they do not occur in this area. The Cedar Ridge Local Fauna from the Badwater Creek area in the northeast part of the Wind River Basin of Wyoming (Black 1968b, Setoguchi 1978) is a probable Whitneyan fauna beyond the geographic limits of the Whitney Member, although the Whitneyan age of this fauna is by no means certain. Another is the possible Whitneyan fauna reported by Patton (1969) in northern Florida.

To the best of our knowledge, there are no occurrences of Chadronian, Orellan, or Whitneyan land mammals in deposits that can be related directly to any marine sequence. Correlation with any other biochronology can be accomplished at present only indirectly through radiometric dates. Paleomagnetic stratigraphy may prove to be valuable in correlating these North American Land Mammal Ages with other chronologies. Figure 5.3 shows suggested correlations of the North American rock and faunal units with the epoch and radiometric chronologies.

BIOCHRONOLOGY

Although we advocate the development of a mammalian biochronology based on biostratigraphic units for the Chadronian through Whitneyan interval, such a biochronology cannot yet be realized. A number of studies now in progress will provide detailed biostratigraphic information on some of the more common taxa, but much additional work is needed before detailed information on most of the taxa will be available. In any new definitions, the limits of the ages should be based on the most important and most widely recognizable faunal breaks, and these cannot be recognized until we have detailed biostratigraphic information, at least, on all of the commonly occurring taxa. The development of such a chronology will necessarily include the efforts of many workers and should be a consensus of all those with firsthand knowledge of the problems and of the information that can be brought to bear on them.

The following discussions of the ages and their boundaries can be viewed, in a sense, as a report of progress made since the appearance of the Wood committee report in 1941. We discuss the problems that need attention and present additional faunal information that may be useful.

Duchesnean-Chadronian Boundary

The Duchesnean and Chadronian present one instance, of which there are several (Wood et al. 1941), in which two consecutive North American land mammal "ages" were based on lithostratigraphic units that are neither stratigraphically nor geographically continuous. The Duchesnean was based on the Duchesne River Formation of northeastern Utah, which is separated by about 350 miles from the Chadron Formation of southwestern South Dakota and northwestern Nebraska, the type locality of the Chadronian.

At the time these units were defined, there was apparently considerable uncertainty about the relative temporal positions of some of the faunas within the Duchesnean-Chadronian interval. Wood et al. (1941) believed that a time interval existed between the Duchesne River Fauna, on the one hand, and the Pipestone Springs and Thompson Creek faunas, on the other, and furthermore that the latter were slightly older than the Chadron Formation. It is now clear that a time interval does exist between these faunas, because the Pipestone Springs and Thompson Creek faunas are not earlier than the Chadron Formation but are at least as young as medial Chadronian. Thus, the interval that Wood et al. thought existed between these faunas is at least partly occupied by the earlier part of the Chadronian. Some authors (e.g., Gazin 1955; Clark et al. 1967; Wilson 1971*a*) have pointed out that the lower part of the Duchesne River Formation (Randlett horizon of previous usage) is homotaxial with the upper part of the Uinta Formation and should, therefore, be considered Uintan. This means the Duchesnean is based on the upper part of the Duchesne River Formation (Halfway and LaPoint horizons of previous usage), which is relatively unfossiliferous (see Andersen and Picard 1972 for current lithostratigraphic terminology).

Black (1970) mentioned that the fauna of the LaPoint Member has few genera in common with the Randlett but also emphasized that it shows little resemblance to the faunas of the Chadron Formation. This picture is changing, however, as the Chadronian, particularly the early Chadronian, faunas become better known. Emry (1981) has reported taxa (*Agriochoerus maximus, ?*daphoenine) not previously known from the LaPoint and has shown that the LaPoint fauna has more taxa in common with White River faunas than previously believed. In addition, several taxa (*Brachyhyops, Simimeryx, Hyaenodon,* and probably several others) from the LaPoint are apparently the earliest North American records of migrants from Asia. It is becoming increasingly evident that an important faunal discontinuity occurs within the Duchesne River Formation, with some of the earliest elements of the White River chronofauna first appearing then. If it becomes desirable to base the beginning of a land mammal age on these first occurrences, as advocated by Repenning (1967), then it may be most useful to recognize this major discontinuity as

the beginning of Chadronian time and to consider the Duchesnean the earliest part, perhaps a subage, of the Chadronian.

Chadronian Age

This age was originally "based on the Chadron formation, type locality near Chadron, Nebraska; type area, northwestern Nebraska and southwestern South Dakota; includes the old term '*Titanotherium* beds,' used in its most extended sense. It may also be defined, faunally, as the time during which *Mesohippus* and titanotheres co-existed" (Wood et al. 1941, p. 11).

Within the type area of the Chadronian, the Chadron Formation seems to be naturally divisible into three parts, which are based on a combination of lithologic and faunal characteristics. Three divisions were apparently first used by Hatcher (1893), who referred to them as the lower, middle, and upper beds. Hatcher's subdivisions were arbitrary units, seemingly not related to lithology but determined by dividing the formation into three equal parts by measuring footage above the base. Clark (1937) demonstrated the invalidity of these divisions, even as faunal zones, and described three members based on lithologic criteria. Clark later (1954) named these members the Ahearn, Crazy Johnson, and Peanut Peak, in ascending order. The upper two are not everywhere separable on lithologic criteria but do appear to have faunal differences, although the faunal evidence is quite incomplete (Clark et al. 1967). His three South Dakota members are not recognizable as lithologic units in northwestern Nebraska, where the Chadron Formation has not been divided into formally named members.

Schultz and Stout (1955) proposed a "classification of the Oligocene sediments in Nebraska," which they intended to be a regional classification, applicable as well to sediments in eastern Wyoming and southwestern South Dakota. In their scheme, the Chadron Formation was again divided, based principally on lithologic characteristics, into three parts: Chadron A (Lower Chadron), Chadron B (Middle Chadron), and Chadron C (Upper Chadron). Schultz and Stout (1955, p. 31) regarded their Chadron A as essentially temporally equivalent to the "Yoder Formation" of Schlaijker (1935) and to the "Lower" or "Ahearn Member" of Clark (1937, 1954). Chadron B was regarded as only partly equivalent to Clark's "Middle" or "Crazy Johnson Member," whereas Chadron C was thought to correspond closely to his "Upper" or "Peanut Peak Member." Just as Clark's upper two members are not everywhere separable on lithologic criteria, the Chadron A and Chadron B of Schultz and Stout are similar lithologically and were

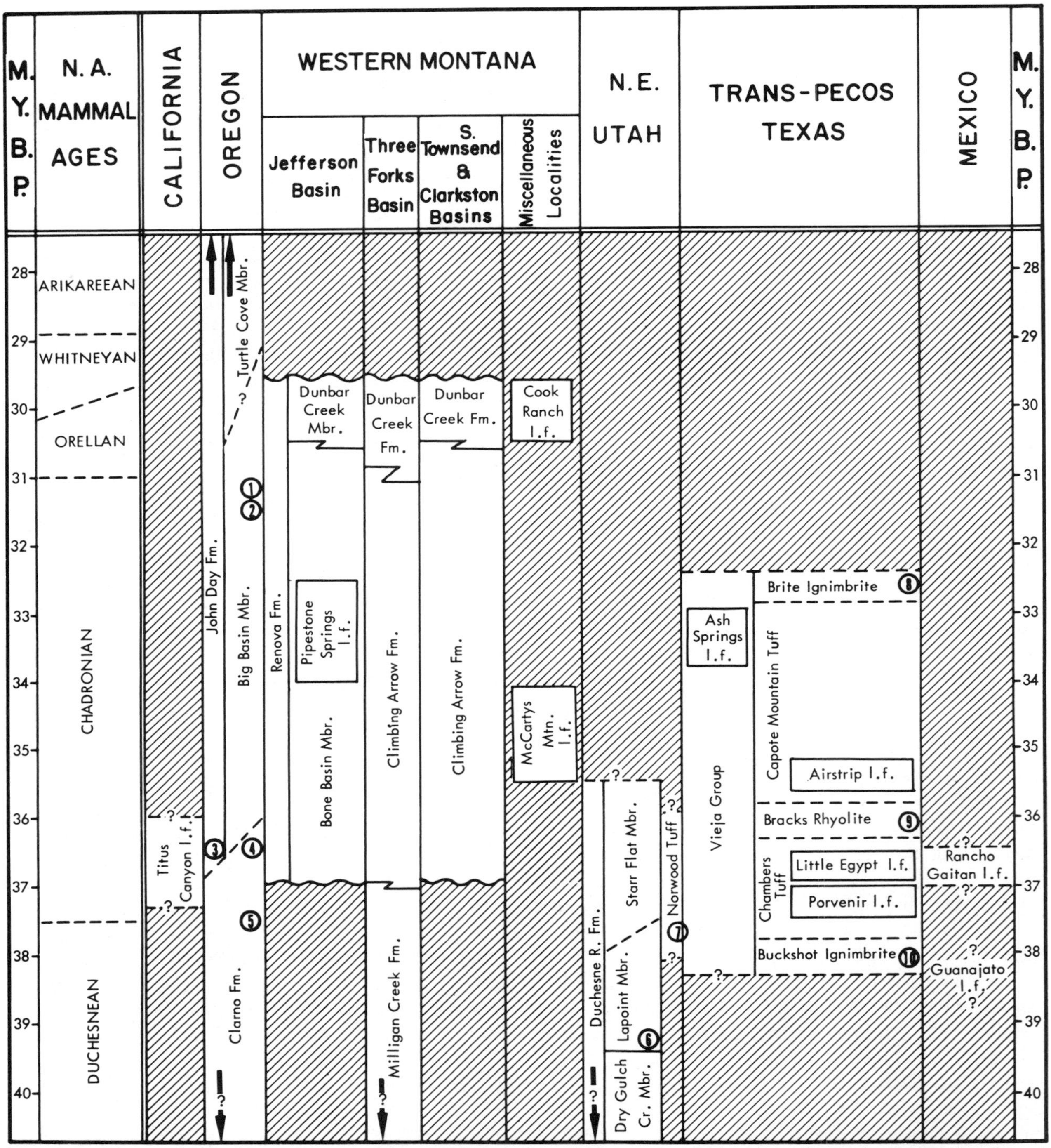

Fig. 5.3. Time relationships and correlation of North American continental rock units and mammalian faunal units of Chadronian, Orellan, and Whitneyan age. Circled numbers indicate radiometric age determinations, listed by their respective numbers in the last section of the text. The epochs are shown as calibrated by Berggren et al. (1978), and they correlate with the North American units only through the m.y.b.p. column. Arrows indicate that units on which they are placed continue beyond the border of the chart.

M.Y.B.P.	SASKATCHEWAN	BRITISH COLUMBIA	N.E. COLORADO	WYOMING					W. NEBRASKA	SOUTH DAKOTA		EPOCH-SERIES	M.Y.B.P.
				N.W.	Beaver Divide	Flagstaff Rim	Goshen Hole	Niobrara County		N.W. (SLIM BUTTES)	BIG BAD-LANDS		

Chart columns and labeled units:

- **SASKATCHEWAN:** Cypress Hills Formation
- **BRITISH COLUMBIA:** Kishenehn Formation; Alexandria l.f. (?)
- **N.E. COLORADO:** White River Formation; Cedar Cr. / Vista Mbr.; Horsetail Creek Mbr.
- **WYOMING N.W.:** Mink Cr. l.f.; Pilgrim Cr. l.f. — ⑰
- **WYOMING Beaver Divide:** White River Fm. UNDIVIDED; Cameron Springs l.f.; Beaver Divide Cgl.; Big Sand Draw Ss. Lentil — ⑯
- **WYOMING Flagstaff Rim:** White River Fm.; Ash J ⑪; Ash G ⑫; Ash F ⑬; Ash B ⑭
- **WYOMING Goshen Hole:** Arikaree Gp.; Brule Fm.; Chadron Formation; Yoder l.f.
- **WYOMING Niobrara County:** Arikaree Gp.; Brule Fm.; Chadron Formation
- **W. NEBRASKA:** Arikaree Gp. — ⑩; Brule Fm.; Orella/Whitney Mbr.; Chadron Formation
- **SOUTH DAKOTA N.W. (SLIM BUTTES):** Arikaree (?); A–E F–H Brule Fm.; Chadron Formation
- **SOUTH DAKOTA BIG BADLANDS:** Sharps Fm.; Poleslide Mbr.; Scenic Mbr.; Peanut Peak Mbr.; Crazy Johnson Mbr.; Ahearn Mbr. — ⑮
- **EPOCH-SERIES:** OLIGOCENE; EOCENE

Time scale (left and right M.Y.B.P.): 28, 29, 30, 31, 32, 33, 34, 35, 36, 37, 38, 39, 40

separated arbitrarily at the base of the "Second" or "Lower Purplish White Layer." The various purplish white layers recognized by Schultz and Stout were regarded by them as partly remnant soil profiles, although others (e.g., Clark, in Clark et al. 1967, p. 106) recognize them as altered volcanic ash beds.

Within the type area of the Chadronian, the Chadron Formation is relatively thin. In the Big Badlands of South Dakota, the three members are not all present everywhere, and each varies in thickness. The maximum thickness of the formation at any one place is about 130 feet, although the combined maximum thicknesses of the three members is about 150 feet (Clark et al. 1967, p. 21). In northwestern Nebraska, the maximum thickness of the Chadron Formation is about 200 feet (see Schultz and Stout 1955, fig. 3 and table 1). As mentioned elsewhere, the Chadronian may span as much as six million years. Deposition in the type area must have been extremely slow, or, more realistically, intermittent, throughout Chadronian time. In the Flagstaff Rim area of central Wyoming, the Chadronian White River Formation is approximately 750 feet thick (Emry 1973), and although it cannot be determined how much of Chadronian time is represented, the sequence does appear to span nearly all of Chadronian time. In the Flagstaff Rim sequence, fossil mammal remains are much more abundant, much more taxonomically diverse, and more evenly distributed throughout the strata than in the Chadron Formation in South Dakota, Nebraska, and eastern Wyoming. As mentioned below, in the Flagstaff Rim sequence, the right conditions are met for eventually developing a biochronology based on range-zones, or at least to begin such a chronology, which could then be supplemented and further refined by adding information from other areas. Much work remains to be done, however, before this kind of biochronology can be realized. For our purposes here, the least that can be done is to review the faunal characterization given by Wood et al. (1941, p. 11), point out the taxa whose designated roles are now obsolete because of range extensions and taxonomic changes, and include additional information that may be useful.

The Chadronian "index fossils" listed by Wood et al. are "*Allops, Brontotherium,* Cylindrodontidae, *Hyracodon priscidens, Megalagus brachyodon, Menodus, Palaeolagus temnodon, Titanotheriomys, Trigonias.*" With the exception of Cylindrodontidae, these remain valid, although some require qualification. While the genus *Cylindrodon* is restricted to the Chadronian, cylindrodonts are now known to occur earlier. *Hyracodon priscidens* was synonymized with *H. nebraskensis* by Radinsky (1967); however, we believe it is a valid species (see discussion under Orellan Age, below). Black (1968a) considers *Titanotheriomys* a synonym of *Ischyromys;* if this is accepted, the taxon is not valid as a Chadronian index fossil although some of the species of *Ischyromys* (e.g., *I. douglassi,* Black 1968a) are restricted to the Chadronian.

Additional taxa that appear to be restricted to the Chadronian—and are common enough to potentially be useful—are "*Icotops*" *acutidens, Ardynomys, Yoderimys, Adjidaumo minimus, Paradjidaumo minor, Hesperocyon paterculus, Merycoidodon forsythae, Leptomeryx* cf. *L. mammifer, Leptomeryx yoderi,* and *Lep-*

tomeryx esulcatus. Some of the species of *Mesohippus* (e.g., *M. celer, M. hypostylus, M. latidens*) are probably restricted to the Chadronian, unless one accepts the synonymies proposed by Forsten (1970). The diminutive merycoidodont *Bathygenys* is quite common and widespread in early to medial Chadronian faunas and could be considered an index, except that J. A. Wilson (1971a, p. 35) mentioned a single jaw from the Brule of northwest Nebraska, and Clark and Kietzke (in Clark et al. 1967, p. 127) mentioned another from the Scenic Member in South Dakota. These two occurrences need further substantiation. If the field data and identifications are correct, these two specimens are the only *Bathygenys* known from deposits younger than medial Chadronian.

Taxa first appearing in the Chadronian were listed by Wood et al. as *Agriochoerus, Archaeotherium, Daphoenus, Dinictis, Hoplophoneus, Ictops, Metamynodon, Oreodon, Palaeolagus,* (?)*Poëbrotherium,* and *Pseudocynodictis.* These are generally still valid, except that taxonomic manipulations have rendered some of the names invalid. The Chadronian species referred to *Ictops* (= *Leptictis*) probably belong to an undescribed genus, *Oreodon* = *Merycoidodon,* and *Pseudocynodictis* = *Hesperocyon. Poëbrotherium* is now definitely known in the Chadronian so the question mark can be removed. To these first occurrences might be added *Megalagus, Palaeogale, Leptomeryx,* and *Hyaenodon horridus.*

Repenning's (1967) suggestion that the lower boundaries of the ages could be based on the first appearance of immigrant taxa may be a particularly appropriate consideration for the Chadronian inasmuch as this was one of the more important times of faunal interchange between Eurasia and North America. This episode of interchange, however, involved only a small and peculiarly assorted part of the fauna. And many of the taxa common to Eurasia and North America at that time have no known ancestry in either area, so the direction of migration cannot be determined confidently. A noticeable feature of this interchange is the great expansion of the fissiped Carnivora. The amphicynodontine *Parictis* and the mustelid *Palaeogale* first appeared in North America, apparently as immigrants from Eurasia. The daphoenids may also have arrived in North America from Eurasia at that time, although their ancestry is not definitely known in either hemisphere. The felids are apparently of Palaearctic ancestry, with the first definite appearance in North America in the Chadronian, but the evidence is equivocal; the genus *Eusmilus* occurs in both the Old and New worlds, although Morea (1975) reassigned the pre-Arikareean "*Eusmilus*" to *Hoplophoneus.* Anthracotheres are definitely of Old World origin and first appear in North America in the early Chadronian.

Scott (1940) referred North American species to the European genus *Bothriodon*, although Macdonald (1956) believed these species were generically distinct and should be retained in the North American genus *Aepinacodon*. In any event, the species *A. americanus* and *A. rostratus* are closely related to *Bothriodon*.

According to A. E. Wood (1970), the direction of migration for the cylindrodont rodent *Ardynomys* was from North America to Asia, rather than the reverse as was previously thought (e.g., see Simpson 1947, p. 636).

Leptomeryx first appears very early in the Chadronian (at many localities as one of the most common taxa) but has no known ancestor in the earlier Tertiary of North America. *Archaeomeryx*, from the Upper Eocene Shara Murun Formation of Mongolia, is separated from *Leptomeryx* by a considerable morphological gap but meets all the requirements for an ancestor, suggesting a Palaearctic origin for *Leptomeryx*. Because of its abundance and sudden appearance, *Leptomeryx* may be useful in a revised definition of the Chadronian age; at least it, and all the other immigrant taxa, should be fully considered.

Wood et al. (1941) listed as taxa last appearing in the Chadronian the "Brontotheriidae (largest forms with largest horns), *Brontops*." This is generally valid; the joint occurrence of titanotheres and *Mesohippus* has been an operational faunal definition of Chadronian (see our discussion under the following section, Chadronian-Orellan Boundary, where we suggest that titanotheres may occur in the Orellan age if it is defined as the geochron of the Orella Member). Last occurrences, of course, include those taxa mentioned above as index fossils. To this can be added Cylindrodontidae, *Apternodus*, and *Oligoryctes*.

Characteristic fossils listed by Wood et al. are "*Hyaenodon, Leptomeryx, Mesohippus, Subhyracodon*." If characteristic fossils are meant to be the most common taxa found in Chadronian deposits, the following should be added: *Cylindrodon, Ischyromys, Adjidaumo minimus, Paradjidaumo minor, Agriochoerus, Bathygenys, Trigonias*, and, of course, the titanotheres or brontotheres. The common Chadronian species of *Leptomeryx* are *L. yoderi, L. esulcatus*, and *L.* cf. *L. mammifer*.

Recognition of intervals of time of much lesser magnitude within Chadronian time will eventually be possible, but pending the development of a biostratigraphically based biochronology, we will discuss the Chadronian only in terms of three very informal divisions, loosely referred to as early, medial, and late

Chadronian. Below we attempt to characterize each faunally and discuss the various rock and faunal units that fall loosely into each category.

Early Chadronian

Within the type area of the Chadronian age, the early Chadronian is represented by the Ahearn Member of the Chadron Formation and its fauna in South Dakota and by "Chadron A" and its fauna in northwestern Nebraska. The faunas from these units are still very poorly known. The Yoder Local Fauna from the Goshen Hole area of southeastern Wyoming provides more faunal information that allows correlation in a general way with the Ahearn and with other areas that have even more faunal information, such as the Flagstaff Rim area of central Wyoming (Emry 1973) and part of the Vieja sequence of Trans-Pecos Texas.

The fauna of the lower part of the White River Formation in the Flagstaff Rim area (Unit 2 of the Little Lone Tree Gulch sections, Emry 1973, p. 26; or "lower banded zone" of the generalized zonation section, ibid., p. 29) includes *Leptomeryx yoderi, Caenopus yoderensis, Yoderimys* cf. *Y. bumpi*, and *Hemipsalodon*. These taxa, as most of the names indicate, are also elements of the Yoder Local Fauna. *Hemipsalodon* occurs elsewhere in the Clarno Formation of Oregon, the Cypress Hills Formation of Saskatchewan, and in the Porvenir Local Fauna of the Vieja Group of Texas (pers. com. from Eric Gustafson, who is now studying the Vieja material, to RJE indicates that the Vieja specimen is a new species, smaller than *H. grandis* but closer to it than to *Pterodon*). *Yoderimys lustrorum* A. E. Wood, 1974, which is slightly more primitive than *Y. bumpi*, occurs in the Porvenir Local Fauna. The fauna of the lower part of the Flagstaff Rim White River also includes the entelodontid *Brachyhyops*, which occurs elsewhere in the Big Sand Draw Sandstone Lentil of the White River Formation in the Beaver Divide area of central Wyoming (the type locality for *B. wyomingensis*), in the Porvenir Local Fauna, and in the LaPoint "Member" of the Duchesne River Formation of Utah. The Big Sand Draw Sandstone Lentil contains *Hyracodon, Leptomeryx, Caenopus yoderensis*, and other typically Chadronian taxa (Van Houten 1964, Emry 1975). Clark and Beerbower (in Clark et al. 1967, pp. 57, 59) correlated the Big Sand Draw Sandstone Lentil with the Crazy Johnson Member, or middle Chadron, while noting that it "may be earlier Chadronian, but the known fauna does not definitely suggest such a dating." However, *Brachyhyops* is known elsewhere only from deposits regarded as early Chadronian or older, and *Caenopus yoderensis* (see Van Houten 1964, p. 67) suggests a correlation with the Yoder Local Fauna, which Clark (1937) and Clark et al. (1967) agree is early Chadronian. Van Houten (1964, p. 67) also notes the presence in the Big Sand Draw Sandstone Lentil of "cf. *Epihippus intermedius* Peterson or small species of *Mesohippus* (USGS specimen)." This specimen, now USNM 19108, is a left M₃, measuring 12.3 mm anteroposteriorly and 6.8 mm transversely, slightly larger than the measurements given by McGrew (1971, p. 9) for *Mesohippus texanus* from the Porvenir and Little Egypt local faunas and within the range of measurements of *Mesohippus* from the Ahearn Member given by Clark and Beerbower (in Clark et al. 1967, p. 37). Schlaijker (1935, p. 82) also described a small M₂ from Yoder that he referred to ?*Mesohippus,* although he noted its similarity in size to *Epihippus,* particularly *E. intermedius.* Measurements given by Schlaijker indicate the tooth is within the size range of *Mesohippus texanus* from the Vieja and the Ahearn Member *Mesohippus.*

Although *Mesohippus* is apparently fairly common, relative to other taxa, in the Ahearn Member in South Dakota (Clark et al. 1967) and a number of specimens were reported by McGrew (1971) from the Porvenir and Little Egypt local faunas, other early Chadronian deposits show a notable scarcity of *Mesohippus.* We have previously mentioned the single teeth from the Yoder Local Fauna and from the Big Sand Draw Sandstone Lentil. In the Flagstaff Rim sequence, Emry has collected hundreds of specimens of a variety of mammalian taxa from the early Chadronian part of the section but as yet has not recognized a single specimen as *Mesohippus.* As the genus certainly lived during this time, its scarcity or absence in these deposits must be regarded as an effect of local environmental conditions.

Clark and Beerbower's assignment (in Clark et al. 1967, pp. 56–57, 59) of the "Vieja" to the Duchesnean and their proposal that the fauna of the "Vieja Formation of Texas" be considered the type for late Duchesnean time was based on only a part of the Porvenir Local Fauna (Wilson 1971a, p. 6). Their proposal has been rendered obsolete by later work showing that the Vieja faunas span a considerable amount of time, that at least some of the Vieja local faunas are definitely not Duchesnean, and that there is substantial justification for assigning even the Porvenir Local Fauna to the Chadronian. Wilson et al. (1968, pp. 602–603) regarded the Porvenir and Little Egypt local faunas as Duchesnean. Later, Wilson (1971b) suggested that the Duchesnean straddles the Eocene-Oligocene boundary and proposed that only the

terms "Uintan" and "Chadronian" be used, with the "Eocene" Duchesnean (i.e., the Duchesne River) being assigned to the Uintan and the "Oligocene" Duchesnean (i.e., the Porvenir and Little Egypt) to the Chadronian. Still later, Wilson (1974) assigned an "early Chadronian age" to taxa from the Porvenir and Little Egypt local faunas.

Radiometric dates figured prominently in the original assignment of the Porvenir and Little Egypt local faunas to the Duchesnean by Wilson et al. (1968, p. 602). Part of their reasoning for this age assignment was that these two local faunas occur in the Chambers Tuff, which is overlain by the Bracks Rhyolite that was dated at 36.5 and 36.8 Ma. This, they noted, was somewhat older than Ash B of the White River Formation of the Flagstaff Rim area of Wyoming, which was dated at 35.2 and 33.3 Ma and was labeled "early Chadronian" by Evernden et al. (1964, p. 165). This "early Chadronian" label for Ash B was unfortunate. Although Ash B was the oldest ash in the Flagstaff Rim White River which could be dated by Evernden et al., much of the White River Formation there, including other ash beds that were not dated, underlies Ash B. And in this sequence, some of the taxa, *Leptomeryx* in particular, show more evolutionary change in the part of the section below Ash B (Emry 1973, p. 34) than in the dated part of the section above Ash B. If we assume that change was relatively constant through time, this suggests more time may be represented by the part of the section below Ash B than by the part above it. Ash B may be more accurately called medial Chadronian. The part of the Flagstaff Rim White River containing Yoder and Ahearn equivalent faunas is certainly considerably older than Ash B and may be no younger than the Porvenir and Little Egypt local faunas.

Among the taxa of the Porvenir Local Fauna are the rodents *Ischyromys, Ardynomys, Pseudocylindrodon, Adjidaumo, Aulolithomys, Yoderimys,* and *Eutypomys* (Wood 1974), which occur elsewhere only in deposits regarded as Chadronian and younger. Also included are *Mesohippus, Colodon, Hyracodon, Archaeotherium, Protoreodon, Agriochoerus, Hyaenodon, Merycoidodon,* "*Leptotragulus*" (cf. *L. profectus*), *Pseudoprotoceras, Heteromeryx, Eotylopus,* and *Leptomeryx* (Wilson et al. 1968; Wilson 1971a, 1971b, 1974), all of which are typical of the Chadronian and most of which occur elsewhere in deposits no older than Chadronian. The Porvenir and Little Egypt local faunas could be most confidently assigned to the Chadronian in view of their strong homotaxial relationship to the Chadron faunas. Wood et al. (1941, p. 11) defined the Chadron faunally as the time during which *Mesohippus* and titanotheres coexisted; the Porvenir and Little Egypt local faunas are Chadronian if this critierion is applied.

Early Chadronian Faunal Characterization

Faunal characterization is made difficult because the early Chadronian is simply discussed here as the early part of Chadronian time instead of being defined and also because most of the faunas have not been studied in sufficient detail to allow species ranges to be established. A list of genera occurring in early Chadronian rocks would be of little help as most range through Chadronian time and many continue into the Orellan and even later. There are, nevertheless, a number of taxa that do seem to be uniquely early Chadronian and can be said to characterize this time: *Yoderimys bumpi, Y. lustrorum, Hemipsalodon, Caenopus yoderensis, Mesohippus texanus* and/or other small *Mesohippus* of the size range of *M. texanus, Mesohippus celer, Brachyhyops,* and *Leptomeryx yoderi.* (We believe that at least some of the *Mesohippus* species reduced to synonymy by Forsten [1970] should be retained as valid species.)

The small merycoidodont *Bathygenys* is not restricted to early Chadronian but does seem to be the most common merycoidodont during this time. It is abundant in the Little Egypt Local Fauna and in the early Chadronian part of the Flagstaff Rim White River and occurs in the Yoder Local Fauna, among others. In the early Chadronian, in contrast to later Chadronian and Orellan times, *Agriochoerus* is abundant relative to large merycoidodonts (i.e., excluding *Bathygenys*).

As Chadronian faunas become more completely known, particularly at the species level, there will surely be many other taxa restricted to the early Chadronian which will help in characterizing it faunally. The units that will be most important in providing faunas representative of early Chadronian time are the Ahearn Member of the Chadron Formation in South Dakota, Chadron "A" of western Nebraska and eastern Wyoming, including the Yoder, the lower part of the White River Formation in the Flagstaff Rim area of central Wyoming, and the Chambers Tuff of the Vieja Group of Trans-Pecos Texas.

Medial Chadronian

We are not defining medial Chadronian here as a distinct unit; we use it loosely as a category that includes the rock and faunal units that are demonstrably younger than the early Chadronian faunas (discussed above) and yet

appear to be older than the late Chadronian. Usage is strictly in the relative sense. We are not implying that medial Chadronian is the middle third of Chadronian time on an absolute chronological scale.

Within the type area of the Chadronian age, medial Chadronian is represented by the Crazy Johnson Member of the Chadron Formation and its fauna in South Dakota and by Chadron "B" and its fauna in western Nebraska and eastern Wyoming. Although these two units probably correlate in part, they are not necessarily coextensive in time, but each occupies some part of medial Chadronian time.

Clark (1937) remarked that the Middle Member (Crazy Johnson) is the most fossiliferous of the three members of the formation in South Dakota and that most of the fossils are of titanotheres (including the famous "titanothere graveyards"), rhinoceroses, *Mesohippus,* and *Archaeotherium.* A more recent review by Clark et al. (1967) shows that most of the known fauna is of larger mammals; the only rodent listed, for example, is *Adjidaumo.* Clark et al. listed fewer taxa from the Crazy Johnson than from the Ahearn or Peanut Peak. Schultz and Stout (1955, p. 34) believed that their "Chadron B (Middle Chadron)" of Nebraska was only partly equivalent to the Crazy Johnson Member of Clark but noted that Chadron B is also the most fossiliferous part of the Chadron in Nebraska. They gave no faunal list, however, and it is virtually impossible to compile a list from the literature because stratigraphic documentation of specimens is not sufficiently detailed.

Wood et al. (1941, p. 11) named the Pipestone Springs Local Fauna of Montana as one of the "principal correlatives" of the Chadronian but remarked in their discussion of the Duchesnean-Chadronian boundary (ibid.) that Pipestone Springs is "probably slightly older than the Chadron Formation." For reasons given below, we regard the Pipestone Springs Local Fauna as no older than medial Chadronian. More than one level is probably represented by the various collecting localities in the Pipestone Springs area, but they all apparently represent a relatively short period of time.

Clark (1937) believed that the Upper Member (Peanut Peak) of the Chadron in South Dakota is somewhat younger than the "*Titanotherium* beds" of Montana, although he did not specifically correlate the latter with the Middle Member (Crazy Johnson). Later, Clark and Beerbower (in Clark et al. 1967, pp. 56–59) favored a correlation of the Pipestone Springs with the Peanut Peak Member; however, the evidence they gave for the correlation seems to be largely contradicted by other evidence (Emry 1973, pp. 37–38).

The taxonomically diverse fauna occurring from

about 250 feet to about 400 feet above the base of the generalized zonation section of the White River Formation in the Flagstaff Rim area of Wyoming (ibid., p. 29) essentially duplicates the Pipestone Springs Local Fauna, predominantly at the species level, and is therefore presumably contemporaneous with it. Radiometric dates (Evernden et al. 1964; Emry 1973, p. 29) indicate that this part of the Flagstaff Rim sequence may span the interval from about 35 Ma to about 33 Ma. The Capote Mountain Tuff of the Vieja Group of Trans-Pecos Texas, which contains the Airstrip Local Fauna, is underlain by the Bracks Rhyolite with dates of 37.8 and 37.4 Ma and overlain by the Brite Ignimbrite with dates of 33.9 and 30.5 Ma (Wilson et al. 1968, p. 598). Assuming that the dates are reliable, the Airstrip Local Fauna could be equivalent to the Pipestone Springs Local Fauna and its equivalent in the Flagstaff Rim White River, although it may be slightly older.

The Airstrip Local Fauna includes so few taxa that correlation on a faunal basis can only be suggested. It does, however, have *Limnenetes, Pseudocylindrodon,* and *Ardynomys,* which occur together elsewhere only in the McCartys Mountain Local Fauna of western Montana. It also has *Parvitragulus priscus,* which occurs only below Ash B in the Flagstaff Rim, Wyoming, sequence (Emry 1978). A. E. Wood (1974, p. 105) believed the age of the Airstrip Local Fauna is "not far from that of Pipestone Springs." We believe it is slightly older.

The Ash Springs Local Fauna, thought to be the highest stratigraphically (it occurs in undifferentiated Vieja Group, but the meager fauna suggests it is younger) of the Vieja faunas, is also very limited in the number of taxa represented and difficult to correlate confidently. It includes the diminutive rhinocerotoid *Toxotherium* (Harris 1967), which occurs also in the Cypress Hills Formation of Saskatchewan (Wood 1961), in the White River Formation at Ledge Creek in central Wyoming (Skinner and Gooris 1966), in the Yoder Local Fauna (Kihm 1975), and only from levels below Ash B (Emry 1979) in the Flagstaff Rim White River of Wyoming. Emry (1979) also showed that *Schizotheroides jackwilsoni* (Schiebout 1977), from the Porvenir and Little Egypt local faunas of the Vieja sequence, is a synonym of *Toxotherium.* Although this genus is quite rare, its occurrence seem to be limited to the interval from early Chadronian into medial Chadronian but probably still not quite as late as Pipestone Springs time.

The rodent *Meliakrouniomys wilsoni* from the Ash Springs Local Fauna is, according to Wood (1974, p. 80), more primitive than *Meliakrouniomys skinneri,* which occurs at about 405 feet above the base of the

Flagstaff Rim White River (Emry 1972b). This also suggests that the Ash Springs Local Fauna is slightly older than the Pipestone Springs Local Fauna and its Flagstaff Rim equivalent.

Medial Chadronian Faunal Characterization

The fauna of the Crazy Johnson Member of the Chadron Formation of South Dakota was most recently reviewed by Clark and Beerbower (in Clark et al. 1967). Except for the rodent *Adjidaumo,* the taxa listed are all of larger species. *Mesohippus hypostylus* is the common horse in the Crazy Johnson Member (the synonymies of Forsten 1970 notwithstanding), and although it also occurs in the Ahearn Member, according to Clark and Beerbower (in Clark et al. 1967, pp. 48–49), the average size is larger in the Crazy Johnson. *Mesohippus latidens* occurs in the Crazy Johnson, and while it also occurs in the later Peanut Peak, it could be said to have its first occurrence in the medial Chadronian. Clark and Beerbower (in Clark et al. 1967) did not identify the species of *Leptomeryx* in the South Dakota Chadron because, they noted, the taxonomy is so confused they were reluctant to assign them to known taxa. However, they did comment (p. 55) that the Ahearn and Crazy Johnson were characterized by an abundance of medium to large hypertraguloids. The Pipestone Springs Local Fauna of Montana and its faunal equivalent in the Flagstaff Rim White River of Wyoming also have abundant large *Leptomeryx.* In fact, the large species from Pipestone Springs, referred to *L. mammifer* by Matthew (1903), is the largest described *Leptomeryx* and seems to be unique to medial Chadronian faunas. It occurs abundantly in the Flagstaff Rim White River from about 250 to 400 feet above the base of the zonation section and is apparently descended from *L. yoderi.* In the Flagstaff Rim sequence, there is a gradual increase in size in a rather complete graded sequence from *L. yoderi* to *L.* cf. *mammifer.* The medial Chadronian is characterized by *Leptomeryx* cf. *L. mammifer,* having a lower cheek tooth series (P_2-M_3) with a length of about 50 mm or longer. Those in the Flagstaff Rim sequence have a mean of about 54 mm for this measurement. Where this species occurs, it is usually abundant and is usually associated with an abundantly represented smaller leptomerycid (cf. *Leptomeryx speciosus* or *Hendryomeryx esulcatus*) (Storer 1981) and abundant *Cylindrodon fontis.* The Pipestone Springs Local Fauna and its equivalent in the Flagstaff Rim White River have an unusually diverse fauna, including many kinds of small rodents and insectivores, but as yet we know so little about the geologic ranges of most of these taxa that they are not particularly useful for characterizing a limited time interval. They may eventually be most profitably used in a formal biostratigraphic chronology once they have been studied in a biostratigraphic context.

Rock and faunal units that will be important in developing the chronology for the middle part of Chadronian time are the Crazy Johnson Member of the Chadron Formation in South Dakota, Chadron "B" of western Nebraska and eastern Wyoming, probably part of the Horsetail Creek Member in northeastern Colorado, the Pipestone Springs Local Fauna of western Montana, the 250- to 400-foot interval of the White River Formation in the Flagstaff Rim area of central Wyoming, and the Airstrip and Ash Springs local faunas of the Vieja Group in Trans-Pecos Texas.

Late Chadronian

We use late Chadronian not in a formal sense but simply to refer to the rock and faunal units representative of the later part of Chadronian time. These reduce primarily to the upper part of the Chadron Formation in the type area of the Chadronian and probably also in northeastern Colorado and eastern Wyoming. In these areas, the Chadron Formation immediately underlies the Brule, often with no apparent discontinuity separating them (see discussion of Chadronian-Orellan boundary, below).

In the type area of the Chadronian age, late Chadronian is represented by the Peanut Peak Member of the Chadron Formation and its fauna in South Dakota (see Clark et al. 1967) and by "Chadron C (Upper Chadron)" in northwestern Nebraska (Schultz and Stout 1955). The fauna of the Peanut Peak Member is somewhat better known than that of the lower two members of the South Dakota Chadron (Clark and Beerbower, in Clark et al. 1967), primarily because a microfaunal locality in the Peanut Peak has produced a variety of micromammals not known from the other members. Clark and Beerbower (pp. 56–59) favored a correlation of the Peanut Peak with the Pipestone Springs Local Fauna of Montana. Part of their evidence was the presence of the insectivores *Apternodus mediaevus,* "*A.*" *altitalonidus,* and "*Metacodon*" *magnus* in the Peanut Peak Member and Pipestone Springs Local Fauna but not in the pre-Peanut Peak members of the Chadron. As mentioned previously, other evidence indicates that Pipestone Springs is older, as Clark (1937) had previously suggested, and some additional new evidence also has a bearing on this correlation. A small collection made in 1975 by the Museum of Geology, South Dakota School of Mines and Technology, from the middle Chadron,

between 15 and 18 meters below the Chadron-Brule contact and not more than 10 meters above typical Ahearn deposits, includes the following taxa: *Domnina* cf. *D. thompsoni,* "*Metacodon*" *magnus,* "*Apternodus*" *altitalonidus, Heliscomys* cf. *H. vetus, Paradjidaumo minor,* and two other eomyid rodents. The stratigraphic position of this new collection argues for an extension of these taxa into the middle Chadron of South Dakota. Such an association is similar to that of Pipestone Springs and contains two of the three insectivores not known to Clark and Beerbower from Peanut Peak members. This does not necessarily disprove Clark and Beerbower's correlation of the Peanut Peak with Pipestone Springs but does invalidate part of their evidence for the correlation. This, along with other information, previously mentioned, suggests that Pipestone Springs is medial Chadronian and correlates with the Crazy Johnson Member.

Clark (1937) mentioned similarities between the Peanut Peak fauna and that of the overlying Brule. For example, "*Ictops*" *dakotensis* from the microfauna locality is close to typical "*I.*" *dakotensis* from the Brule rather than to "*I.*" *acutidens* from Pipestone Springs. *Hyaenodon cruentus* from the Peanut Peak is typical of the Brule as well. *Hesperocyon gregarius* of the Peanut Peak is close to typical Brule *H. gregarius* rather than to *H. paterculus* of the Montana Chadronian. *Hoplophoneus robustus* of the Peanut Peak is a characteristic Brule taxon (although this may be *H. mentalis,* according to Morea 1975). *Adjidaumo minutus* occurs also in the Brule, as do *Perchoerus nanus, Eutypomys* near *E. thompsoni,* and oreodonts of the "*Oreodon-Eporoedon* type" (Clark 1937, p. 326). Clark also noted, however, that some of the forms in the Peanut Peak are more reminiscent of older Chadronian, rather than Brule, among these being titanotheres, *Clinopternodus,* "*Metacodon,*" and *Sinclairella, Leptomeryx esulcatus* rather than *L. evansi,* and *Mesohippus latidens* rather than one of the Brule species. In short, the fauna of the Peanut Peak Member seems to be intermediate between the Pipestone Springs Local Fauna and its equivalents, on the one hand, and the Brule fauna, on the other. *Mesohippus grandis* Clark and Beerbower, 1967, if it is valid (see Forsten 1970), from the Peanut Peak Member has not, to the best of our knowledge, been recognized in older or younger deposits and can provisionally be regarded as characteristic of the late Chadronian.

The fauna of "Chadron C (Upper Chadron)" (Schultz and Stout 1955) in Nebraska and eastern Wyoming is not as well known, or at least not as well described, as that of the Peanut Peak, but the information available suggests it also has faunal similarities with the lower

Brule. *Merycoidodon culbertsoni*, for example, occurs both in "Chadron C" and lower Brule (Schultz and Falkenbach 1968) and *Sthenopsochoerus* (*Pseudosthenopsochoerus*) *chadronensis* and *S.* (*P.*) *douglasensis* both occur in "Chadron C" and "Brule A" (Schultz and Falkenbach 1956). Schultz and Falkenbach (1968) note that the oreodonts show less change between Chadron C and Brule A than they do between Chadron B and C or between Brule A and B.

Wood (1969) remarked that the rodents from "*Chadronia* Pocket," a Chadronian locality north of Crawford, Nebraska, suggest a very short time interval before Brule time, whereas the rodents from Pipestone Springs seem to be separated by a considerable interval from those of the Brule. The *Chadronia* pocket rodents, for example, include *Adjidaumo* close to *A. minutus*, *Paradjidaumo* cf. *P. trilophus*, *Palaeolagus haydeni*, and *Eumys elegans*, all species common in the Brule. *Eumys* was also reported from the Chadron Formation in northwest Nebraska by Hough and Alf (1956), but the material was all from anthills, and they emphasized that it might have been concentrated by the ants from a wider vertical range. The possibility that these, as well as those from *Chadronia* Pocket, are a lag concentrate reworked from the Brule cannot be ruled out (see R. W. Wilson 1971). Russell (1972) described a new species, *Eumys pristinus*, from the Cypress Hills Formation of Saskatchewan. A skull of a *Eumys*-like cricetid has been reported from apparent late Chadronian deposits southeast of Douglas, Wyoming (Wahlert, pers. com., 1975). It is becoming increasingly apparent that *Eumys*, or closely related cricetids, may not be limited to Orellan and later deposits, as long believed, but may also occur in at least the late Chadronian.

In the Flagstaff Rim area of Wyoming, the upper part of the White River Formation (i.e., above 450 ft. on the zonation section) may represent late Chadronian time, but so few fossils occur in this part of the section that it cannot be so assigned on a faunal basis. Titanothere bones occur to within five feet of the upper contact, above Ash J, allowing the conclusion that it is no younger than Chadronian, and the radiometric date of 32.4 Ma (Evernden et al. 1964) suggests that the top of the formation, as exposed there, may be a million years younger than Ash G, which overlies the medial Chadronian, Pipestone Springs equivalent, faunas.

None of the local faunas of the Vieja sequence of Trans-Pecos Texas are indicative of late Chadronian time. Representation of this interval is essentially restricted to the upper part of the Chadron Formation: the Peanut Peak Member in southwestern South Dakota (Clark 1954), Chadron B (Middle Chadron) in northwestern Nebraska and eastern Wyoming (Schultz and Stout 1955), and probably the upper part of the Horsetail Creek Member in northeastern Colorado (Galbreath 1953). These are the areas that must provide the faunal basis for late Chadronian biochronology.

Late Chadronian Faunal Characterization

Although many mammal species are now known from upper Chadron deposits, the exact geologic ranges of most are so incompletely known that we hesitate to say which, if any, are restricted to late Chadronian time. The generalization can be made that late Chadronian faunas include a significant number of species that are known also from the lower Brule (early Orellan) deposits or are more closely related to early Orellan than to medial Chadronian species. Among these are *Adjidaumo* closer to *A. minutus* than to *A. minimus*; *Paradjidaumo* closer to *P. trilophus* than to *P. minor*; *Eutypomys* near *E. thompsoni*; ?*Eumys*; leptictid insectivore closer to "*Ictops*" *dakotensis* than to "*I*". *acutidens*; *Palaeolagus* closer to *P. haydeni* than to *P. temnodon*; *Hyaenodon cruentus*; *Hesperocyon* closer to *H. gregarius* than to *H. paterculus*; and *Merydoidodon culbertsoni*. *Mesohippus grandis*, if valid, may be unique to late Chadronian. *Leptomeryx* cf. *L. mammifer*, which is so abundant in the medial Chadronian, is apparently absent in late Chadronian faunas, although *L. esulcatus*, which occurs with cf. *L. mammifer* in the medial Chadronian, continues into late Chadronian time. Titanotheres are comparatively rare in the late Chadronian but do continue at least through this interval and may occur in lower Brule deposits (see following discussion of Chadronian-Orellan boundary).

Chadronian-Orellan Boundary

The type areas of the Chadronian and Orellan ages, as defined by Wood et al. (1941, p. 11), are essentially coextensive. Both included southwestern South Dakota and northwestern Nebraska, although the type area of the Orellan also included eastern Wyoming. Throughout the common type area, the Brule Formation is directly superposed on the Chadron Formation. In many areas, particularly in northwestern Nebraska and eastern Wyoming, deposition was apparently continuous, or nearly so, from the Chadron into the Brule. At most localities there is no significant lithologic change across the boundary, no evidence of a significant break in the stratigraphic record, and very little change in fauna, except that in the Brule fossil mammal remains are much more abundant and the titanotheres that were a prominent part of the Chadronian fauna are missing.

In the Toadstool Park area of northwestern Nebraska (the type localities for the Orella and Whitney members of the Brule Formation, Schultz and Stout 1938), the uppermost of several "purplish white layers" (volcanic ash beds) was defined as marking the top of the Chadron Formation (see also Schultz and Stout 1955, fig. 3). What is apparently the same purplish white ash occurs widely in the Seaman Hills area to the west in Niobrara County, Wyoming, and can be traced from there eastward into Sioux County, Nebraska, where it occurs in a sequence very similar to that at the Orella type locality. In the Seaman Hills area, the lithology is the same above and below the ash, and titanothere bones have been found in situ as much as 25 feet above the ash. The same is true in the area six to eight miles southeast of Douglas, Wyoming, where titanothere bones occur up to 25 feet above what is apparently the same ash bed. Schultz and Stout (1955, p. 27, fn. 4) comment that "all parts of the Chadron and the lowest part of the Brule (basal Orella or Orella A) should be expected to yield titanothere remains", but they provide no further explanation.

In most of the Seaman Hills area, a sequence of channel sandstones fills a valley that was cut down from approximately 100 feet stratigraphically above the purplish white ash. At some places the valley containing this channel sandstone sequence was cut through the ash, indicating at least 100 feet of relief at the time the valley was eroded. The sandstones in the lower part of this valley fill have the unusual weathering characteristics of the Toadstool Park channel at the Orella type locality. The trend of the valley fill deposit in Wyoming is generally east-west. It can be traced for many miles in Wyoming and eastward beyond the state line into Sioux County, Nebraska. Physical stratigraphic, lithologic, and faunal evidence suggests that this channel sequence in Wyoming represents the same cut-and-fill cycle as the Toadstool Park channel at Orella.

Several questions remain to be resolved in this area. Does the approximately 100 feet of strata above the purplish white ash and below the channel sequence in the Seaman Hills area correlate with the approximately 80 feet occupying what is apparently the same interval at Toadstool Park? Oreodont faunal evidence (Schultz and Falkenbach 1968) indicates that they do correlate; both are oreodont faunal zone Brule A. If so, titanothere bones occur in Wyoming in rocks temporally equivalent to the lower part of the Orella Member of the Brule, although none are known to occur above the upper purplish white ash at the Orella type locality. Wood et al. (1941) defined the Chadronian faunally as the time

during which *Mesohippus* and titanotheres coexisted and based the Orellan on the Orella Member. Is there, then, some overlap of Chadronian and Orellan time if this combination of criteria is used? Fortunately, Wood et al. (1941) were explicit in stating that the ages were not necessarily coextensive with their types. Inasmuch as the biological characterizations of the ages are the most useful criteria for recognizing them outside the type areas, the biological criteria should be used as the basis for definitions. If the coexistence of *Mesohippus* and titanotheres is strictly applied as an indicator of Chadronian time, then the upper limit of the Chadronian age may not coincide with the upper limit of the Chadron Formation but may occur somewhere in the lower part of the Brule. Such a conclusion would also effectively remove part of the Orella Member from the Orellan age.

It is premature to attempt to redefine the boundary here, but we can state our opinion that the age boundary ought to be based on biostratigraphic rather than lithostratigraphic criteria and that it should be placed at the most prominent and most widely recognizable faunal break, which may or may not coincide with lithostratigraphic boundaries. The single criterion of presence or absence of titanotheres is insufficient—the absence of titanotheres at any particular locality does not necessarily mean non-Chadronian. Studies now in progress will eventually provide a better biostratigraphic basis for the limits of the ages.

Orellan Age

Wood et al. (1941) based the Orellan age on "the Orella member of the Brule formation, type locality, Orella, northwestern Nebraska; type area, northwestern Nebraska, southwestern South Dakota and eastern Wyoming; includes the old term, 'Oreodon beds,' used in the most extended sense."

We should perhaps begin by pointing out that the use of the old term "*Oreodon* beds," in the most extended sense, is inappropriate here. As pointed out in the preceding historical section, this designation once included all of the Brule, until Wortman (1893) separated the *Protoceras* from the *Oreodon* Beds. The "Upper *Oreodon*" of Osborn (1907) and Osborn and Matthew (1909) and the "Upper and Middle *Oreodon*" of Wanless (1923) are now part of the Poleslide Member of Bump (1956), which is presumed to be approximately equivalent to the Whitney Member and therefore Whitneyan. The Orellan age includes only the "*Oreodon*" Beds of Wortman (1893).

To the best of our knowledge, there are no published radiometric dates of rocks containing Orellan faunas. If the late Chadronian and early Arikareenan dates are considered reliable, however, then the Orellan and Whitneyan ages together span no more than about three million years, from about 31 to about 28 Ma, whereas the Chadronian apparently represents six to seven million years. Thus, the Orellan age is very short relative to the Chadronian.

Very few taxonomic groups of fossil mammals have been studied from the standpoint of where they occur stratigraphically *within* Orellan deposits. Studies of the oreodonts, among the most common of Orellan mammals, by Schultz and Falkenbach (1954, 1956, 1968) are exceptions. The Orella Member was divided into four lithostratigraphic units, "Orella A, B, C, and D," by University of Nebraska collectors, who then zoned the fossil specimens with respect to these four "stratigraphic collecting horizons." The oreodonts, when studied in this framework, led Schultz and Falkenbach to the recognition of two "oreodont faunal zones" within the Orella Member and its equivalents. According to Schultz and Falkenbach (1968, pp. 412–413), collecting horizons Orella A, B, and C correlate with oreodont faunal zone A of the Brule, and Orella D correlates with oreodont faunal zone B of the Brule (the potentially confusing use of letter symbols for both stratigraphic units and noncorresponding oreodont faunal zones is unfortunate). Schultz and Falkenbach (1968, p. 412) also stated that oreodont faunal zone A of the Brule equals the "Lower *Oreodon*" faunal zone of Wortman (1893) and oreodont faunal zone B of the Brule equals Wortman's "Middle *Oreodon*." Wortman (1893), however, did not divide the *Oreodon* Beds into Lower and Middle *Oreodon*. As mentioned previously, Matthew (1899) was the first to introduce the terms "Lower *Oreodon*" and "Upper *Oreodon*" and he did not relate them to Wortman's proposed three divisions of the *Oreodon* Beds. Osborn (1907) was the first to use the terms "Lower," "Middle," and "Upper *Oreodon*." Schultz and Falkenbach (1968, p. 412) surely mean that oreodont faunal zone A of the Brule equals the Lower *Oreodon* of Osborn (1907), and oreodont faunal zone B of the Brule equals the Middle *Oreodon* of Osborn (1907).

The biostratigraphic utility of the oreodonts is somewhat diminished by the extremely fine taxonomic splitting by Schultz and Falkenbach. In addition, stratigraphic information associated with specimens was sometimes equated to taxonomic characters in recognition of lineages. They state, for example, that without precise stratigraphic data associated with each specimen, the six phylogenetic lines of Leptaucheniinae would have to be reduced to perhaps two or three because of the close morphological resemblance in parallel lines (1968, p.

412). Schultz and Falkenbach again comment (1968, p. 199) that "due to the lack of adequate geologic data associated with John Day oreodonts, the writers consider their identifications of the referred specimens to various species as tentative. It is extremely difficult to identify a particular skull based on measurements only, without information concerning its geologic occurrence. If geologic data are not available, the research worker is not certain whether he is dealing with individual variation of forms that lived at essentially the same time, geologically speaking, or with variation due to differences in stratigraphic levels."

The fact that precise stratigraphic data may be necessary for recognition of oreodont lineages does not necessarily mean that the lineages are not real. But it does reduce the level of resolution with which oreodonts can be used as biostratigraphic indicators. Because the oreodonts are so finely divided taxonomically, it is sometimes impossible to place a specimen in a species, or genus, without knowing where it occurred in a stratigraphic sequence in which the oreodont faunal sequence is already known. But there is certainly some level of resolution at which oreodonts will be useful biostratigraphically.

A study by Howe (1966) of stratigraphically controlled specimens of the rodent *Ischyromys* from the Orella Member shows that statistically significant changes occur with time through this interval. According to Howe, *Ischyromys parvidens* occurs in the lower part of the Orella, *I. typus* in the middle part, and *I. pliacus* in the upper part. Changes are primarily in size, and although the differences among the means for the three samples is significant, there is so much overlap in size ranges of the samples that it may not be possible to place a single specimen more confidently in one group than in another. The importance of Howe's study is that it demonstrates that at least one genus, *Ischyromys*, does increase in size, in a statistical sense, through Orellan time.

Galbreath (1953) demonstrated the replacement of *Palaeolagus haydeni* by *P. burkei* within the Orellan Cedar Creek Member in northeastern Colorado. If collections from the Orella and Scenic members show that this replacement occurs over a broader area, it will be a useful biostratigraphic indicator, particularly so because rabbits are such a common element in Orellan faunas. The evidence from oreodonts *Ischyromys* and *Palaeolagus* suggests that faunal change occurs within Orellan time. Similarly oriented studies of other mammalian groups may provide sufficient information to allow construction of a biochronology that can resolve intervals of time within the Orellan age.

Clark (in Clark et al. 1967) believed that the entire

Scenic Member of the Brule Formation in South Dakota was deposited in a minimum of 1,100 years and a maximum of 11,000 years. This range was estimated on the basis of a combination of assumptions about depositional rates, degree of perthotaxis of fossil assemblages, lack of evidence of fossil soils, and apparent lack of evolution of mammalian taxa between the lowest and highest faunal horizons within the Scenic Member. Clark's calculations derive from so many assumptions, some built on other assumptions, that very little confidence can be placed in them. Some of his assumptions are even contradicted in other parts of the same monograph. For example, Clark (in Clark et al. 1967, p. 99), in promoting his hypothesis of very rapid deposition of the Scenic Member, stated that there is no evidence of weathered zones or soils within the Scenic because no surface was exposed long enough for them to develop. Yet, Clark and Kietzke (in Clark et al. 1967, p. 128) discussed such adjacent life habitats existing through the Lower Nodular Zone of the Scenic as "near-stream zone presumably occupied by gallery forests; an open-plains area, far from any stream, which might have borne plains, prairie or savanna vegetation; and a swamp area within the plains." These habitats, with the presumed vegetation, require soil development. The same conclusion is apparent without analyzing specific habitats, for the vast numbers of vertebrate fossils preserved over thousands of square miles indicate that the area was well populated with animals, and, at least during the times that these mammals occupied the area, substantial soil development would have been necessary to support the vegetation required by the large animal populations. Numerous fossil soil horizons have recently been identified and studied by Retallack (1981, 1983a, 1983b) in the Scenic Member.

Clark (in Clark et al. 1967, p. 99) also cited as evidence of very rapid deposition of the Scenic Member his observation that six species, representing five mammalian orders, show no apparent evolutionary change from the bottom to the top of the member, which he suggested would indicate a probable maximum of five hundred thousand years for the interval. Clark indicates that his observations were based on a few specimens. Statistically significant samples may show, however, that there is evolutionary change in these taxa and others as well. Much more study is needed before we can confidently accept or reject Clark's hypotheses.

In an attempt to further promote his hypothesis of very rapid deposition of the Scenic Member in South Dakota, Clark (in Clark et al. 1967) also questioned the evolutionary advance shown in oreodonts by Schultz and

Falkenbach, because he thought it was "based upon stratigraphy which overlooks a 75-foot fault in a 270-foot section, and uses as marker beds zones of sheet-flood sediments interpreted as paleosols, plus zones of volcanic ash [the "purple white" layers] which can be demonstrated to be local in South Dakota." But these concerns of Clark can be largely ruled out as factors affecting the stratigraphy on which the oreodont faunal zones are based.

Clark declared (in Clark et al. 1967, p. 107) that there is no evidence of significant channel-cutting or erosional episodes during Orellan time, that those shown by Schultz and Stout (1955) were simply misinterpretations of a faulted sequence. In fact, the faults in the Orella type area were recognized and accounted for in the stratigraphy. Furthermore, there is abundant evidence of channel-cutting episodes, with relief of at least 100 feet developed, at the Orella type locality and many other localities from there westward into Niobrara County, Wyoming. Moreover, Schultz and Falkenbach recognized the oreodont faunal zones in areas not affected by faulting, including South Dakota. Slickensides on channel sandstones, such as those shown by Clark (in Clark et al 1967, p. 107, fig. 50), do not necessarily indicate faulting of any significance but are often the result of differential compaction between the channel sandstones and the claystone channel "banks," which results in sufficient relative movement to produce slickensides.

As previously mentioned, the apparent lack of paleosols in the Scenic Member does not mean that no soils were developed in the Scenic depositional sequence and certainly does not necessarily mean that paleosols do not exist in the Orella Member. Even if the marker beds in the Orella can be demonstrated to be something other than paleosols, their utility as marker beds is not necessarily invalidated. A unit of sheet-flood sediments, if it can be traced or correlated throughout the collecting area, may be as valid a marker as a fossil soil horizon.

And finally, the fact that volcanic ashes have local distribution in the Scenic Member in South Dakota does not suggest that the purplish white layers of the Nebraska sections are also local. The upper purplish white layer can in fact be traced visually for tens of miles in the northwestern Nebraska and Niobrara County, Wyoming, areas.

The point to be made here is that the stratigraphy of the Orella Member, and Schultz and Falkenbach's oreodont faunal zonation based on it, are probably valid. Even though it may be difficult to recognize all of Schultz and Falkenbach's oreodont lineages at any one time interval, the changes that occur through time are readily apparent. In any event, they are not rendered invalid for the reasons given by Clark.

We cannot yet conclusively resolve the conflicts between, on the one hand, Clark et al. (1967), who conclude that the Orellan is such a short time interval that biostratigraphic subdivision is impossible, and, on the other hand, Schultz and Falkenbach (1968) and Howe (1966), who present evidence that evolutionary change can be detected within Orellan time. Additional work toward the resolution of this problem is clearly needed.

Orellan Faunal Characterization

The Orellan age as a whole is a relatively short time interval that does have a characteristic fauna. As might be expected, some species range from Chadronian into Orellan time, many species first appearing in the Orellan are but new species of genera that also occur in the preceding Chadronian, and a number of taxa first appear as new genera in the Orellan.

The faunal characterization of the Orellan as given by Wood et al. (1941, p. 11) is now largely obsolete, not so much as a result of new discoveries as of taxonomic manipulations. The taxa listed as Orellan "index fossils" were *Hoplophoneus primaevus, Hyracodon arcidens, Poëbrotherium*(?), *Metamynodon planifrons*, and *Subhyracodon occidentalis*. The last two may still be valid as Orellan index fossils. *Metamynodon planifrons* is, however, so rare and was apparently so ecologically restricted that its utility is limited, and the taxonomy of the rhinocerotoids is so much in need of revision that we hesitate to assign so important a role as index fossil to *S. occidentalis. Poëbrotherium* is now definitely known far back into the Chadronian (e.g., Wilson 1974). Hough (1949) synonymized all of the Orellan species of *Hoplophoneus*, including *H. robustus*, with *H. primaevus*. The specimen that Clark (1937) identified as *H. robustus* from the Peanut Peak Member of the Chadron Formation is, according to Morea (1975), *H. mentalis*, which leaves *H. robustus* apparently still restricted to the Orellan. All of the species of *Hyracodon* were placed in the synonymy of *H. nebraskensis* by Radinsky (1967). If these synonymies are accepted, the range of the species becomes very long, from the early Chadronian to the early Arikareean, a period of ten to twelve million years. Although there may be more names than there are distinct species, Radinsky's synonymies are probably too sweeping. *H. priscidens*, at least, appears to be distinct, but much additional work is needed to stabilize the taxonomy of the genus.

The Orellan "first appearances" (Wood et al. 1941,

p. 11) are also now largely obsolete, due both to subsequent discoveries in older deposits and to taxonomic changes. *Eumys* and *Palaeolagus haydeni* may be present in the upper Chadron Formation (see discussion, above, under late Chadronian), although some doubt remains as to whether or not the reported material was lag concentrate from higher levels. *Ischyromys* is now known from many Chadronian localities. *Hyracodon nebraskensis*, as discussed in the preceding paragraph, occurs in the Chadronian if Radinsky's synonymies are accepted. Schultz and Falkenbach (1968) restricted *Eporeodon* to the species occurring in the middle and upper John Day Arikareean of Oregon. Some of the Orellan and Whitneyan species previously included in *Eporeodon* were assigned by Schultz and Falkenbach (1968) to their new genus *Otionohyus* (a member of Merycoidodontinae rather than Eporeodontinae), which occurs as early as Chadron "C" and can therefore not be used at the generic level as an Orellan first occurrence. The species *Otionohyus (Otarohyus) bullatus* (= *Eporeodon bullatus*) can, however, be considered an Orellan first occurrence.

Of the Orellan "last appearances" listed by Wood et al. (1941) *Metamynodon* and *Poëbrotherium* are apparently still valid, although "*Oreodon*" (*Merycoidodon*) ranges into the late Whitneyan according to Schultz and Falkenbach (1968).

The Orellan "characteristic fossils" listed by Wood et al. (1941)—*Archaeotherium, Hyracodon, Leptomeryx, Megalagus, Subhyracodon,* and *Stylemys*—are still largely valid. These forms are not restricted to, but are common elements of, Orellan faunas. There are a number of genera, however, that are even more common and more characteristic. *Palaeolagus*, for example, is much more common than *Megalagus. Merycoidodon* is one of the most prominent taxa in Orellan deposits; hence the term "*Oreodon* beds." Other taxa characteristic of the Orellan are *Leptictis* (= *Ictops*); *Hyaenodon horridus* and *H. crucians;* the rodents *Ischyromys, Eumys, Paradjidaumo trilophus,* and *Adjidaumo minutus;* the carnivores *Hesperocyon, Daphoenus, Dinictis,* and *Hoplophoneus;* the horse *Mesohippus:* and the artiodactyls *Poëbrotherium* and *Hypertragulus.*

Many mammalian genera occurring in the Orellan also occur in Chadronian and/or Whitneyan faunas. And because the Orellan species are generally better known, specimens from earlier and later deposits are sometimes referred to the Orellan species, not so much because it can be determined that they are in fact the Orellan species but rather because they cannot be assigned confidently to any others. There are, for example, undoubtedly many Chadronian specimens identified as *Leptomeryx evansi* and *Archaeotherium mortoni* which do not belong in these species but were identified as such because the Chadronian species of these genera are generally so poorly defined that specimens cannot be confidently assigned to any of them.

A number of species that are characteristic of the Orellan are probably also restricted to the Orellan, although they are recorded in the literature from younger and older deposits. Once the taxonomy of these groups is better understood, the following species will probably be recognized only from the Orellan: *Leptictis haydeni, Ischyromys typus, Eumys elegans, Mesohippus bairdi* (with due deference to the synonymies of Forsten 1970), *Archaeotherium mortoni, Poëbrotherium wilsoni, Hypertragulus calcaratus,* and *Leptomeryx evansi.*

Modern approaches to and concerns with the microvertebrates indicate that they may prove to be exceedingly important biostratigraphically. Modern collecting techniques, such as wet screening, have not sampled enough of the column to allow any confidence in determining stratigraphic ranges, but for the present, the following can be regarded as characteristic of the Orellan but not necessarily restricted to it: *Nanodelphys hunti, Oligoscalops galbreathi, Domnina gradata, Trimylus compressus, Scottimus? exiguus, Leidymys vetus,* and *Hypisodus minimus.*

Within the White River Group, *Hypertragulus* first appears in the Orellan, but Ferrusquia-Villafranca (1969) described a species, *Hypertralgulus heikeni,* from the early Chadronian Rancho Gaitan Local Fauna of northeastern Chihuahua. If this species is correctly referred to *Hypertragulus,* it is the first definite record of the genus in pre-Orellan deposits.

The faunas that will be important in improving the definition and faunal characterization of the Orellan age, and possibly in developing a biostratigraphically based chronology within Orellan time, are essentially those of the Orellan part of the Brule Formation (i.e., the Scenic Member in southwestern South Dakota, Units A to E at Slim Buttes in northwestern South Dakota, the Orella Member in western Nebraska and eastern Wyoming, and the Cedar Creek Member in northeastern Colorado). Other scattered localities in southwestern Montana (e.g., Cook Ranch Local Fauna and some of the Canyon Ferry sites), southwestern North Dakota, southeastern Montana, and central Wyoming, will be less useful biochronologically but may provide important zoogeographic information.

Orellan-Whitneyan Boundary

Recognition of a boundary between the Orellan and Whitneyan has not received much attention in the litera-

ture. Because these two ages are based on the Orella and Whitney members, the boundary is easily resolved lithostratigraphically as far as these members can be recognized, and fossils are determined to be Whitneyan or Orellan according to the member in which they occur instead of the age of the rocks being determined by the fossil content. Unfortunately, the Orella and Whitney members are not even continuous throughout the designated typical area of the two ages. The Scenic and Poleslide members in South Dakota are correlated with, respectively, the Orella and Whitney members. The Orellan-Whitneyan boundary is therefore usually drawn at the Scenic-Poleslide boundary in South Dakota, although it is doubtful whether this lithostratigraphic boundary coincides exactly with the Orella-Whitney boundary.

Outside the typical region for these two ages, the boundary must be recognized on a faunal basis. Galbreath (1953), in a thorough taxonomic and stratigraphic treatment of the Tertiary of northeastern Colorado, records the distribution of taxa in the White River Formation to a degree far surpassing previous workers. In the lower and middle Cedar Creek Member a typical Orellan assemblage is present. The upper Cedar Creek Member is less typically Orellan, although this may be due, at least in part, to the scarcity of fossils from this unit. The overlying Vista Member is clearly Whitneyan, although the fauna is sparse. Surely the boundary here is at, or close to, the lithologic boundary; however, it is important that we recognize it is drawn there on the basis of paleontological rather than lithostratigraphic criteria.

Lillegraven (1970) presented another sequence of superposed faunas from the Brule Formation of northwestern South Dakota. The faunas are found in units that are lithically defined. A pattern similar to that established by Galbreath emerged. Except for Lillegraven's lowest unit, A, which may be transitional Chadronian-Orellan, the preserved faunas in the lower units (B-E) are typically Orellan. Unit F has elements of both Orellan and Whitneyan, and Units G-H have produced sparse Whitneyan faunas. Lillegraven (1970) chose to place the boundary at the bottom of Unit F but noted that such a correspondence between lithic and temporal boundaries is improbable. (It should be pointed out that whether or not lithic boundaries correspond, or should be expected to correspond, with time boundaries depends on how the time units are defined.) In the case of the Orellan and Whitneyan, they were based on lithic units, and, therefore, the time boundaries correspond to the lithic boundaries by definition. These are not the same lithic units that Lillegraven was dealing with at the Slim Buttes, but his faunal units were stratigraphically zoned with respect to, and therefore coincide with, his stratigraphic Units A–H. Therefore, an age boundary drawn between any of these faunas will also be drawn at a lithologic boundary. The basis for Lillegraven's division between Units E and F was both lithologic and paleontological. In the typical area, Whitneyan deposits have a greater amount of volcanic ash than the underlying Orellan; Lillegraven's Unit F has a greater amount of ash than Unit E. The presence of *Leptauchenia* and *Scottimus lophatus* in Unit F is a positive indicator of Whitneyan age, while the absence or rarity of *Adjidaumo, Paradjidaumo, Pelycomys,* and *Leptictis* suggests non-Orellan.

Both Galbreath's (1953) and Lillegraven's (1970) work represent reasonable attempts at recognizing the Orellan-Whitneyan boundary outside the typical area, primarily on faunal criteria. This kind of problem would be greatly facilitated if the two ages were defined on biostratigraphic rather than lithostratigraphic grounds. More detailed work in the typical area, particularly with small vertebrates, is required before the boundary can be defined and recognized biostratigraphically. A boundary based on biostratigraphic criteria may or may not coincide with lithostratigraphic boundaries, but if it does, it should not be by definition.

Whitneyan Age

The Whitneyan age was "based on the Whitney member of the Brule formation, type locality, Whitney, northwestern Nebraska; type area, northwestern Nebraska, southwestern South Dakota and eastern Wyoming; includes the old term, '*Protoceras-Leptauchenia* beds' used in the most extended sense." As previously mentioned, and shown in figure 5.1, the Poleslide Member, which is regarded as an approximate correlative of the Whitney Member, includes deposits that were never classified as part of the *Protoceras-Leptauchenia* beds.

Within the typical area, Whitneyan deposits differ from the underlying Orellan deposits in the increased volcanic ash content, in their generally more massive nature, and in their tendency to weather into very steep, to vertical, slopes. The bulk of the sediments appear to be wind-borne volcanic ash and dust, some of which is altered to clay. In western Nebraska, two widespread volcanic ash beds provide convenient markers for dividing the Whitney Member into three units (see Schultz and Stout 1955) and also facilitate correlation of exposures north of the Pine Ridge in northwestern Nebraska with those of the North Platte River valley to the south. These two ash beds have not been recognized in the Poleslide Member in southwestern South Dakota. Local channel sandstones that carry the well-known *Protoceras*

fauna are characteristic of the Poleslide Member but do not occur in the Whitney Member in Nebraska. Little attention has been given to the Whitney and Poleslide members in terms of sedimentologic features. Clark et al. (1967) mention the Poleslide only in passing, which diminishes their monograph's scope as implied in the title.

Very little information of biostratigraphic significance has been published since the definition of the Whitneyan by Wood et al. (1941). Several factors may be responsible for the lack of progress. The White River monographs of Scott and Jepsen (1936–1941) brought together much information on the fauna, but such treatment tends to indicate to many students that the subject matter has been completely studied. Whitneyan faunas are limited geographically and thus do not invite the comparisons that Chadronian faunas do. Outcrops of Whitneyan rocks are typically steep, which makes prospecting and collecting difficult except in the resistant channel sandstones. Little emphasis was placed on detailed stratigraphic documentation by most earlier collectors. The Frick Collection (American Museum of Natural History) is an exception. It does contain abundant material with sufficient stratigraphic information to provide insight into Whitneyan biostratigraphy as the collections are studied. Some studies are completed on important Whitneyan taxa, including the oreodonts (Schultz and Falkenbach 1949, 1954, 1956, 1968), leptochoerids (Macdonald 1955), anthracotheres (Macdonald 1956), and protoceratids (Patton and Taylor 1973).

Whitneyan Faunal Characterization

The Whitneyan "index fossils" given by Wood et al. (1941, p. 11) were *Protoceras* and *Subhyracodon tridactylus.* In their recent review of the Protoceratidae, Patton and Taylor (1973) record *Protoceras* from Arikareean deposits of Nebraska, South Dakota, and Wyoming, eliminating it as an index. Patton and Taylor restrict the species *Protoceras celer* to the Whitneyan and synonymize all other known Whitneyan protoceratids with it. *P. celer* could thus be regarded as a Whitneyan index fossil, although its utility as a biostratigraphic indicator is diminished by its apparent environmental restriction. It is known only from the "*Protoceras* channels" of the Poleslide Member in South Dakota. Protoceratids are known in the Chadronian and Whitneyan but not from the intervening Orellan, which underscores the environmental control on the distribution of the group. *Subhyracodon tridactylus* has not been the subject of recent taxonomic revision and thus appears to retain its restriction to the Whitneyan. The range of this species within the Whitneyan has not been documented, however. It is part of a lineage that gives rise to *Diceratherium*, a common Arikareean rhinocerotid.

As Whitneyan first appearances, Wood et al. (1941) listed "Castoridae, *Leptauchenia*, *Miohippus*." Castorids are now well known in Orellan deposits of northeastern Colorado (R. W. Wilson 1949) and from the Chadronian of Wyoming (Emry 1972a). *Leptauchenia* was reported by Clark et al. (1967) from Orellan deposits, and another Orellan specimen was questionably referred by Lillegraven (1970). Schultz and Falkenbach (1968) restrict *Leptauchenia* to Whitneyan and later times but recognize closely related genera, *Hadroleptauchenia* and *Pseudocyclopidius*, from the Orellan. The specimens indicated by Clark et al. and Lillegraven may be referable to one of these genera rather than to *Leptauchenia*. *Miohippus* does appear in the Whitneyan, if this genus can be adequately differentiated from *Mesohippus*. Stirton (1952) expressed an opinion favoring the synonymy of the two genera. A comprehensive study of the large collections now available should make it possible to define the species more rigorously and to prove or disprove the validity of *Mesohippus*.

Taxa last appearing in the Whitneyan were listed by Wood et al. (1941) as "*Agriochoerus, Archaeotherium, Hyracodon, Mesohippus, Palaeolagus, Pseudocynodictis, Subhyracodon*." Of these, *Agriochoerus, Hyracodon, Palaeolagus*, and *Hesperocyon* (= *Pseudocynodictis*) have since been recognized by Macdonald (1963, 1970) in the Wounded Knee-Sharps Fauna, which directly overlies Whitneyan faunas in South Dakota. *Archaeotherium* occurs in the Turtle Buttes Formation (Arikareean) of south-central South Dakota (Skinner et al. 1968). Of the last occurrences cited by Wood et al., only *Mesohippus* and *Subhyracodon* have not since been documented in the Arikareean.

Leptomeryx and *Eporeodon* were cited as Whitneyan "characteristic fossils" by Wood et al. *Leptomeryx* is a common element of Whitneyan faunas but also is characteristic of Chadronian and Orellan. *Eporeodon* has been restricted in concept and content by Schultz and Falkenbach (1968) so that it is confined to the middle and upper John Day (Arikareean) of Oregon. *Paramerycoidodon major* and *P. wanlessi* are characteristic Whitneyan species that would have been called *Eporeodon* by earlier workers.

Certain taxa other than those used by Wood et al. (1941) may prove useful in a biostratigraphically based redefinition of the Whitneyan age. Among the more promising are *Agnotocastor praetereadens, Eumys brachyodus, Hyaenodon brevirostrus, Leptauchenia decora, Leptomeryx, Nimravus brachyops, Oxetocyon cuspidatus, Paramerycoidodon major, Proheteromys nebraskensis, Proteryx loomisi, Proteryx bicuspis, Protoceras celer, Proscalops miocaenus, Proscalops tertius, Pseudolabis dakotensis, Scottimus lophatus*, and *Sunkahetanka sheffleri*. A number of taxa with presently recorded last occurrences in the Whitneyan, which may make them useful biostratigraphically, are *Elomeryx, Eumys, Heptacodon, Ischyromys, Leptictis, Merycoidodon, Nanochoerus, Palaeolagus burkei, Paradjidaumo, Perchoerus, Stibarus*, and *Subhyracodon*. When detailed range-zones for these and other taxa are documented, a more precise biostratigraphic definition of the Whitneyan will be possible. Such studies must be carried out in the typical region before peripheral areas and localities can be accurately correlated with the Whitneyan.

Whitneyan-Arikareean Boundary

The type areas of the Whitneyan and Arikareean ages, as defined by Wood et al. (1941, p. 11), overlap in northwestern Nebraska. Here the Arikaree Group, the lithostratigraphic basis for the Arikareean age, is directly superposed on the Whitney Member of the Brule Formation, the lithostratigraphic basis of the Whitneyan age. The two lithologic units are, however, separated by a disconformity. In this area the age boundary is therefore easily recognized on lithostratigraphic criteria, while at the same time, if the ages are regarded as coextensive with the lithostratigraphic units, a certain amount of time is not represented by rocks. If the ages are to "cover all of Tertiary time" (as Wood et al. 1941 intended), a single boundary must be recognized. Should it be drawn at the top of the Whitney Member, at the base of the Arikaree Group, or somewhere in between? Wherever it is drawn, it should be based on faunal criteria, which will also facilitate its recognition beyond the geographic limits of the Whitney Member and the Arikaree Group.

In South Dakota, the Brule Formation is overlain by the Sharps Formation without apparent hiatus. The Whitneyan-Arikareean boundary cannot be recognized here on lithostratigraphic grounds, and the lack of a significant break in the stratigraphic and faunal sequences make it necessary to consider alternatives in the placement of the age boundary. Macdonald (1963, 1970) placed the age boundary at the contact of the Poleslide Member of the Brule Formation with the Rockyford Ash Member of the Sharps Formation. The progression of early Arikareean faunas over those of the Whitneyan is gradational, as evidenced by the continuance of many Whitneyan taxa into the Arikareean documented by Macdonald (1963, 1970). We have previously noted that the White River chronofauna retains much of its identity into Arikareean time, and only after the early part of the Arikareean is there a marked reorganization of the faunas suggesting a major change in the ecosystem. Among the genera that occur as early as Chadronian, the following have been recorded in early Arikareean deposits: *Agriochoerus, Hesperocyon, Hyaenodon, Leptochoerus, Leptomeryx,* and *Palaeogale* (Macdonald 1970); *Archaeotherium* (Skinner et al. 1968); and *Eutypomys, Geolabis, Heliscomys, Palaeolagus,* and *Peratherium* (various authors). Many of these genera range into the middle Sharps Formation or higher. Macdonald (1963, 1970) recorded *Eumys* in the Arikareean, but these references stretch the concept of the genus far beyond that usual for cricetid taxonomy.

The lower part of the Sharps Formation is not nearly so fossiliferous as the middle and upper parts, which is not particularly helpful in our attempt to recognize the Whitneyan-Arikareean boundary. Such typically Arikareean forms as *Nanotragulus intermedius, Palaeocastor nebrascensis, Palaeolagus hypsodus,* and *Sanctimus* (collected in 1971 by PRB) occur low in the Sharps Formation. It seems most reasonable, therefore, to include the lower part of the Sharps Formation in the Arikareean. Persistence of Whitneyan forms into the Arikareean might argue for placing the boundary higher, probably within the Sharps Formation, but this would imply correlation of the upper Whitney of Nebraska with the lower Sharps Formation of South Dakota. The continuity of the South Dakota sequence makes it more difficult to recognize the exact position of the Whitneyan-Arikareean boundary as it is now defined. But at the same time it provides the necessary faunal information that may allow a definition based on biostratigraphic units. For additional information pertaining to this problem, refer to the section on the Arikareean in chapter 6 of this volume.

CORRELATION WITH OTHER CHRONOLOGIES

Chadronian, Orellan, and Whitneyan land mammal occurrences are peculiarly lacking in any sequence that can be related to a marine invertebrate chronology. To the best of our knowledge, there is not a single land mammal occurrence representing this interval in any marine rocks or in any continental rocks that can be directly related to a marine sequence. This contrasts with some parts of both earlier and later North American Tertiary. In California, for example, the predominantly continental Sespe Formation, which intertongues with a marine sequence, has Uintan, possibly Duchesnean, and Arikareean land mammal faunas, but none representing the

intervening ages. The Chadronian through Whitneyan interval can therefore be correlated with the marine sequence only indirectly, and we can say little more than that it probably correlates with the uppermost Refugian through lower Zemorrian benthonic foraminiferal stages.

As previously mentioned, with the exception of a few poorly known faunas (e.g., Titus Canyon Local Fauna of the Death Valley area of California; Clarno-John Day sequence of Oregon, which apparently spans the Chadronian to Whitneyan interval but has very few mammalian fossils pertaining to these ages), virtually all known mammalian faunas of the Chadronian through Whitneyan interval are east of the present-day continental divide but no further east than the western Great Plains. Correlation of these with any other chronologies, including the epoch and European Stage-Age chronologies, cannot be accomplished paleontologically. Except for indirect correlation, by their relative age compared to faunas that can be correlated, we are limited to correlation by radiometric age determinations or other geophysical means.

The White River Group and its faunas have long been regarded as North American continental Oligocene. On the basis of radiometric dates, it appears that the epoch assignment is correct; they are probably Oligocene but do not represent all of Oligocene time. But the Oligocene terminology for the White River faunas has become so ingrained that many workers apparently consider them synonymous, even to that point of using early Oligocene, middle Oligocene, and late Oligocene as synonyms for, respectively, Chadronian, Orellan, and Whitneyan. Other North American mammal faunas are assigned to the Oligocene Epoch, not because they can be correlated with the European standard but because they correlate with the White River "Oligocene." Some authors attempt to be more precise by using the term "North American Oligocene," with the unstated implication that the Oligocene in North America differs in some way from the Oligocene elsewhere. But Oligocene, as a unit of time, is the same everywhere; that it cannot be recognized everywhere does not justify its independent and arbitrary usage in North America.

There has been considerable discussion (Peterson and Kay 1931; Peterson 1931; Kay 1934; Simpson 1933; Scott 1945; Simpson 1946) as to whether the Duchesnean is Eocene or Oligocene, and it has been alternately argued from one to the other, with the implication that it must be all one or the other. Later, Wilson (1971*a*) suggested that because the LaPoint Local Fauna of the Duchesne River Formation is "Duchesnean and Eocene" (i.e., more like the Uinta "Eocene" faunas) and the Porvenir Local Fauna of the Vieja Group is "Duchesnean and Oligocene" (i.e., more like the White River "Oligocene" faunas), the Duchesnean straddles the Eocene-Oligocene boundary. Wilson therefore proposed, as a solution, that the term "Duchesnean" be dropped from usage and the "Eocene" part assigned to the Unitan and the "Oligocene" part assigned to the Chadronian. But the fact that faunas may have greater affinities with Uinta faunas, or with White River faunas, is not relevant to the question of whether they are Eocene or Oligocene. Even if it can be demonstrated that the Duchesnean straddles the Eocene-Oligocene boundary, an adjustment of the North American Land Mammal Age boundaries to coincide is not necessary or even desirable.

As an illustration of how the Wood committee's report (1941) has been misinterpreted, it is important to mention that the controversy over the Duchesnean-Chadronian boundary and its relationship to the Eocene-Oligocene boundary continued even after the appearance of the committee's report, one of the stated purposes of which was to make it possible to avoid just this kind of controversy regarding epoch boundaries in the North American continental Tertiary. What the principals in the controversy have apparently failed to consider is that no amount of comparison and correlation of the North American faunas with each other can determine whether the Duchesnean is Eocene or Oligocene. Simpson (1946, p. 53) argued that whether the Eocene-Oligocene boundary is drawn above or below the Duchesnean is "a matter of convenience rather than right or wrong" and that "the most important thing is that all students follow the same usage, whatever it is." But it is, of course, improbable that both American and European students could follow the same usage if the boundary is drawn independently and arbitrarily in North America, simply for the sake of convenience. As long as one is considering only the mutual temporal relationships of North American units, where the Eocene-Oligocene boundary is drawn is irrelevant. This is a completely separate problem and becomes relevant only when one wants to know how the North American units relate to the epochs, and this is a matter of correlation, by whatever means available, rather than an arbitrary decision for the sake of convenience.

Some workers have apparently gained their concept of the North American land mammal ages by reading the correlation chart but not the text of the Wood committee report (1941). Simpson (1946, p. 53), for example, wrote that Wood et al. had "proposed Duchesnean as a provincial time term for the latest Eocene," in spite of the fact that the term Eocene was not mentioned in the definition of the Duchesnean age, and Wood et al. (1941, p. 6) stressed the point that "although the supposed equivalence of the proposed terms to the epochs and

European ages and stages is indicated on the correlation chart and sometimes by reference in the text, the new terms are emphatically not defined in relation to the epochs or the European standard, but only as indicated below in the Definitions of Age Terms."

We must get away from the practice of using the North American land mammal ages as if they are simply subdivisions of the epochs. The former were not defined in relation to the latter. They are independent chronologies, based on independent criteria. It is unlikely that any of the North American land mammal age boundaries would coincide with any of the epoch boundaries. The mutual temporal relationships of the boundaries must be determined by correlation. The independent nature of the North American land mammal age chronology is one of its greatest merits and the main reason for its existence. There would be no real advantage in having a separate chronology with its own terminology if it were possible to use the epoch or European stage-age chronologies.

Although the Duchesnean-Chadronian boundary is not precisely defined, either in lithostratigraphic or faunal terms, radiometric dates indicate that faunas that could best be considered Chadronian may be as old as, or older than, 38 Ma. Recent calibration of the Paleogene (Hardenbol and Berggren 1978; Berggren et al. 1978; LaBrecque et al. 1979; Prothero et al. 1982; but also see Tarling and Mitchell 1976 and Berggren 1972) places the Eocene-Oligocene boundary at about 37 Ma. If this is correct, then the Eocene-Oligocene boundary may be slightly younger than the Duchesnean-Chadronian boundary, although possibly by a lesser amount than can be confidently resolved radiometrically. It is important to keep in mind that the two boundaries are not related by definition. Radiometric determination of the Eocene-Oligocene boundary has no influence on recognition or definition of the Duchesnean-Chadronian boundary, which must be based on North American mammalian biostratigraphic criteria that will make North American time units more widely recognizable, and therefore more useful, in classifying North American mammalian faunas.

Berggren (1972) indicated that the beginning of the Miocene, if defined as the base of the Aquitanian, may be as young as 22–23 Ma, whereas Tarling and Mitchell (1976) show it at slightly less than 22 Ma. Both these calculations are considerably younger than the base of the Arikareean, which is now thought to be between 28 and 29 Ma (Obradovich et al. 1973) and which was long thought to be the base of the Miocene in the North American continental Tertiary. If all these dates are substantiated, it is clear that the Chadronian through Whitneyan interval is not coincident with the Oligocene Epoch. Those who find it necessary, or desirable, to apply epoch terminology to North American land mammal faunas and want to use it correctly will have to include most of the Arikareean in the Oligocene. To continue to call the Arikareean early Miocene implies that the epoch began in North America long before it did in Europe.

CORRELATION CHART

The included correlation chart (Fig. 5.3) may be viewed as a report of progress made since the appearance of the Wood committee report in 1941, but it should also be taken as a graphic presentation of hypotheses, many of which need further testing. The units of correlation are both lithic and faunal. While some of the indicated correlations are reasonably certain, others are of the most tentative nature. The greatest uncertainties are with regard to the limits of units, particularly when the units of correlation are lithostratigraphic. Known mammalian faunas may have very limited vertical distribution within rock units, so it is possible to correlate certain parts of the rock units paleontologically, but we have no way of knowing the total temporal span of the rock unit. Considerable uncertainty exists, therefore, as to where the boundaries should be drawn with respect to those of other units or with respect to the m.y.b.p. (million years before present) scale. Accordingly, many of the units shown are bounded by dashed lines and question marks.

This chart is not intended to include all known North American mammal occurrences within the time interval represented but rather the sequences in which radiometric dates are associated in some way with mammalian faunas, along with the more important rock and faunal units that can be correlated with them.

The epochs are shown as calibrated by Berggren et al. (1978) and relate directly only to the m.y.b.p. scale (i.e., the epochs correlate with the North American units only as they all relate to the m.y.b.p. column).

There are still too few radiometric or fission-track dates to allow a very precise calibration of the Chadronian-Orellan-Whitneyan interval, but there are enough to allow the following generalizations. The three ages together span about eight to nine million years, from about 37 or 38 Ma to about 29 Ma. As the dates accumulate, the conclusion is becoming inescapable that the Chadronian is by far the longest of the three, spanning about six to seven million years, whereas the Orellan and Whitneyan combined may represent no more than two to three million years (see also Prothero et al. 1982).

On the accompanying chart, radiometric dates are indicated in their approximate positions by circled numbers, which refer to the respective numbers in the following compilation. The dates are cited here as they were given in the original publications, but each is followed here by the date, in parentheses, corrected for new constants, according to Dalrymple (1979).

1. Bridge Creek Flora, John Day Formation. 31.1 Ma (31.9), KA 489 (Evernden et al. 1964).
2. Bridge Creek Flora, John Day Formation, 50 feet below KA 489. 31.5 Ma (32.3), KA 845 (Evernden et al. 1964).
3. Base of John Day Formation in Horse Heaven Mining District. 36.4 ± 1.1 Ma (37.3), (Swanson and Robinson 1968; see also Fisher and Rensberger 1972).
4. Uppermost part of Clarno Formation. 36.5 ± 0.9 Ma (37.4), KA 824A (Evernden et al. 1964).
5. Uppermost part of Clarno Formation, overlying KA 824A. 37.5 Ma (38.5), KA 818 (Evernden et al. 1964).
6. Red ashy siltstone at contact of Dry Gulch Creek and LaPoint members of Duchesne River Formation. 39.3 ± 0.8 Ma (40.3), (McDowell et al. 1973).
7. Norwood Tuff. 37.4 Ma (38.4) on sanidine; 37.5 Ma (38.5) on biotite; 36.0 Ma (36.9) on glass. KA 825, 826, 827, respectively (Evernden et al. 1964).
8. Brite Ignimbrite. 29.7 Ma (30.5), KA 1000 (Evernden et al. 1964). 33.0 ± 1.1 Ma (33.9), (Wilson et al. 1968).
9. Bracks Rhyolite. 36.8 Ma (37.8), KA 1010 (Evernden et al. 1964); 36.5 ± 1.2 Ma (37.4) (Wilson et al. 1968).
10. Buckshot Ignimbrite. Sample 1, 35.2 ± 2.3 Ma (36.1); Sample 2, 34.7 ± 2.0 Ma (35.6) and 38.6 ± 1.2 Ma (39.6) (Wilson et al. 1968).
11. Volcanic ash in White River Formation. 31.6 Ma (32.4) on biotite, KA 1032 (Evernden et al. 1964; see also Emry 1973).
12. Volcanic ash in White River Formation. 32.6 Ma (33.4) on biotite, KA 898 (Evernden et al. 1964; see also Emry 1973).
13. Volcanic ash in White River Formation. 33.7 Ma (34.6) on biotite; 35.7 Ma (36.6) on sanidine; KA 899 and 900, respectively (Evernden et al. 1964, see also Emry 1973).
14. Volcanic ash in White River Formation. 35.2 Ma (36.1) on sanidine; 33.3 Ma (34.2) on biotite; KA 895 and 897, respectively (Evernden et al. 1964, see also Emry 1973).
15. Volcanic ash 3 feet below top of Ahearn Member

of Chadron Formation. 36.3 ± 0.7 Ma (37.2), (McDowell et al. 1973). Independent analysis on volcanic ash 3 feet below top of Ahearn Member of Chadron Formation (probably same unit as above). 35.1 Ma (36.0) and 36.2 Ma (37.1) (M. Skinner and R. Tedford, pers. com.).

16. White biotitic tuff 300 feet above base of White River Formation, Beaver Divide area, section 4, T29N, R96W, Fremont County, Wyoming. 32.2 ± 2.0 Ma (33.0) (Love 1970, p. 53, table 5).

17. White biotite tuff, White River Formation, Emerald Lake locality, 16,000 feet (4,900 m) due south of milepost 29 along south boundary of Yellowstone National Park. 35.8 ± 0.8 Ma (36.7), (Love et al. 1976, p. 17, table 2). This date is associated with mammalian fossils that Hunt (1974, p. 1043, fig. 9) called the Mink Creek Local Fauna, and which Love et al. (1976, p. 14) refer to as the "Emerald Lake assemblage." Pilgrim Creek Local Fauna occurs nearby (Sutton and Black 1975) but is not associated with date.

18. Volcanic ash and pumice beds in the Gering Formation, southwestern Nebraska. K-Ar age of 27.0 ± 0.7 Ma (27.7) on biotite; fission-track age of 27.8 ± 3.1 Ma on zircons; both from Carter Canyon Ash Bed as Helvas Canyon. Biotite from same ash at Roundhouse Roch has K-Ar age of 28.0 ± 0.7 Ma (28.7). Twin Sisters Pumice Conglomerate Bed has K-Ar age of 27.7 ± 0.6 Ma (27.7) on sanidine and fission-track age of 26.8 ± 2.5 Ma on zircons (Obradovich et al. 1973).

The compilation of a correlation chart such as this is, of course, dependent on the work of so many authors that it would be impractical to cite all of them. Citations for the more important sections will serve the dual purpose of acknowledging those authors' contributions and facilitating entry into the original literature. The Oregon column is abstracted from Fisher and Rensberger (1972). The first three columns under western Montana are adapted from Kuenzi and Fields (1971). The northeastern Utah column follows the latest revision of the stratigraphy by Anderson and Picard (1972). Wilson et al. (1968) worked out the sequence from which the Trans-Pecos Texas column is adapted. Galbreath (1953) described the northeastern Colorado section. Under Wyoming, the Beaver Divide section follows Van Houten (1964) and Emry (1975), and the Flagstaff Rim sequence is shown in more detail by Emry (1973). The northwestern Nebraska sequence has been presented by a number of authors, most of which follow Schultz and Stout (1955). The northwestern South Dakota (Slim Buttes)

sequence is that of Lillegraven (1970), whereas the remainder of the South Dakota column follows, with minor modifications, Clark (1954), Clark et al. (1967), and Bump (1956). Many of the indicated correlations and relationships shown on the chart, as well as much of the information in the text of this report, cannot be found in the literature. Much of it is directly attributable to many of our colleagues through personal communications and conversations. We want to take this opportunity to thank all of those who have contributed in this way to this chapter.

REFERENCES

Andersen, D. W., and M. D. Picard. 1972. Stratigraphy of the Duchesne River Formation (Eocene-Oligocene?), northern Uinta Basin, northeastern Utah: Bull. Utah Geol. and Min. Surv., no. 97.

Berggren, W. A. 1972. A Cenozoic time scale—Some implications for regional geology and paleobiogeography. Lethaia 5:195–215.

Berggren, W. A., M. C. McKenna, J. Hardenbol, and J. D. Obradovich, 1978. Revised Paleogene polarity time scale. J. Geol. 86:67–81.

Black, C. C. 1968a. The Oligocene rodent *Ischyromys* and discussion of the family Ischyromyidae. Ann. Carnegie Mus. 39:273–305.

———. 1968b. Late Oligocene vertebrates from the northeastern Wind River Basin. Univ. Colo. Mus., Field Conf. Guidebook for the high altitude and mountain basin deposits of Miocene age in Wyoming and Colorado, pp. 50–54.

———. 1970. A new *Pareumys* (Rodentia: Cylindrodontidae) from the Duchesne River Formation, Utah. Fieldiana: Geol. 16:453–459.

Bump, J. D. 1956. Geographic names for members of the Brule Formation of the Big Badlands of South Dakota. Amer. J. Sci. 254:429–432.

Clark, J. 1937. The stratigraphy and paleontology of the Chadron Formation in the Big Badlands of South Dakota. Ann. Carnegie Mus. 25:261–350.

———. 1954. Geographic designation of the members of the Chadron Formation in South Dakota. Ann. Carnegie Mus. 33:197–198.

Clark, J., J. R. Beerbower, and K. K. Kietzke. 1967. Oligocene sedimentation, stratigraphy, paleoecology, and paleoclimatology in the Big Badlands of South Dakota. Fieldiana: Geol. Mem. no. 5.

Dalrymple, G. B. 1979. Critical tables for conversion of K-Ar ages from old to new constants. Geology 7:558–560.

Darton, N. H. 1899a. Relations of Tertiary formations in the western Nebraska region. Amer. Geologist 23:94.

———. 1899b. Preliminary report on the geology and water resources of Nebraska west of the one hundred and third meridian. U.S. Geol. Surv., Ann. Rep. 19 (for 1897–98), pt. 4, pp. 719–785. (Reprinted with minor changes as U.S. Geol. Surv. Prof. Paper 17 [1903].)

———. 1901. Preliminary description of the geology and water resources of the southern half of the Black Hills and adjoining regions in South Dakota and Wyoming. U.S. Geol. Surv., Ann. Rept. 21, pt. 4, pp. 489–599.

Emry, R. J. 1972a. A new species of *Agnotocastor* (Rodentia, Castoridae) from the early Oligocene of Wyoming. Amer. Mus. Novitates, no. 2485.

———. 1972b. A new heteromyid rodent from the early Oligocene of Natrona County, Wyoming. Proc. Biol. Soc. Washington 85:179–180.

———. 1973. Stratigraphy and preliminary biostratigraphy of the Flagstaff Rim area, Natrona County, Wyoming. Smithsonian Contr. Paleobiol., no. 18.

———. 1975. Revised Tertiary stratigraphy and paleontology of the western Beaver Divide, Fremont County, Wyoming. Smithsonian Contr. Paleobiol., no. 25.

———. 1978. A new hypertragulid (Mammalia, Ruminantia) from the early Chadronian of Wyoming and Texas. J. Paleont. 52:1004–1014.

———. 1979. Review of *Toxotherium* (Perissodactyla: Rhinocerotoidea) with new material from the early Oligocene of Wyoming. Proc. Biol. Soc. Washington 92:28–41.

———. 1981. Additions to the mammalian fauna of the type Duchesnean, with comments on the status of the Duchesnean "age." J. Paleont. 55:563–570.

Evernden, J. F., D. E. Savage, G. H. Curtis, and G. T. James. 1964. Potassium-argon dates and the Cenozoic mammalian chronology of North America. Amer. J. Sci. 262:145–198.

Ferrusquia-Villafranca, I. 1969. Rancho Gaitan local fauna, early Chadronian, northeastern Chihuahua. Bol. Soc. Geol. Mexicana 30:99–138.

Fisher, R. V., and J. M. Rensberger. 1972. Physical stratigraphy of the John Day Formation, central Oregon. Univ. Calif. Publ. Geol. Sci. 101:1–33.

Forsten, A. 1970. *Mesohippus* from the Chadron of South Dakota, and a comparison with Brulean *Mesohippus bairdii* Leidy. Commentationes Biologicae Societas Scientiarum Fennica 31:1–22.

Galbreath, E. C. 1953. A contribution to the Tertiary geology and paleontology of northeastern Colorado. Univ. Kan. Paleont. Contrib., art. 4, Vertebrata.

Gazin, C. L. 1955. A review of the upper Eocene Artiodactyla of North America. Smithsonian Misc. Coll., vol. 128.

Hardenbol, J., and W. A. Berggren. 1978. A new Paleogene numerical time scale. Amer. Assoc. Petrol. Geol. Studies in Geology 6:213–234.

Harris, J. M. 1967. *Toxotherium* (Mammalia: Rhinocerotoidea) from western Jeff Davis County, Texas. Pearce-Sellards Series, no. 9.

Hatcher, J. B. 1893. The *Titanotherium* beds. Amer. Natur. 27:204–221.

Hayden, F. V. 1857. Notes on the geology of the Mauvaises Terres of White River, Nebraska. Acad. Nat. Sci. Philadelphia Proc. 9:151–158.

———. 1858. Explorations under the War Department— Explanations of a second edition of a geological map of Nebraska and Kansas, based upon information obtained in an expedition to the Black Hills, under the command of Lieut. G. K. Warren, Top. Engr. U.S.A. Acad. Nat. Sci. Philadelphia Proc. 10:139–158.

Hough, J. 1949. The subspecies of *Hoplophoneus:* A statistical study. J. Paleont. 23:536–555.

Hough, J., and R. Alf. 1956. A Chadron mammalian fauna from Nebraska. J. Paleont. 30:132–140.

Howe, J. A. 1966. The Oligocene rodent *Ischyromys* in Nebraska. J. Paleont. 40:1200–1210.

Hunt, R. M., Jr. 1974. *Daphoenictis,* a cat-like carnivore (Mammalia, Amphicyonidae) from the Oligocene of North America. J. Paleont. 48:1030–1047.

Kay, J. L. 1934. The Tertiary formations of the Uinta Basin, Utah. Ann. Carnegie Mus. 23:357–371.

Kihm, A. J. 1975. Mammalian paleontology of the Yoder local fauna. M.S. thesis, South Dakota School of Mines and Technology.

Kuenzi, W. D., and R. W. Fields. 1971. Tertiary stratigraphy, structure, and geologic history, Jefferson Basin, Montana. Bull. Geol. Soc. Amer. 82:3373–3394.

LaBrecque, J. L., D. V. Kent, and S. C. Cande. 1979. Revised magnetic polarity time scale for late Cretaceous and Cenozoic time. Geology 5:330–335.

Leidy, J. 1847. On a new genus and species of fossil *Ruminantia: Poëbrotherium wilsoni.* Acad. Nat. Sci. Philadelphia Proc. 3:322–326.

Lillegraven, J. A. 1970. Stratigraphy, structure, and vertebrate fossils of the Oligocene Brule Formation, Slim Buttes, northwestern South Dakota. Bull. Geol. Soc. Amer. 81:831–850.

Love, J. D. 1970. Cenozoic geology of the Granite Mountains area, central Wyoming. U.S. Geol. Surv. Prof. Paper 495-C.

Love, J. D., M. C. McKenna, and M. R. Dawson. 1976. Eocene, Oligocene, and Miocene rocks and vertebrate fossils at the Emerald Lake locality, 3 miles south of Yellowstone National Park, Wyoming. U.S. Geol. Surv. Prof. Paper 932-A.

Macdonald, J. R. 1955. The Leptochoeridae. J. Paleont. 29:439–459.

———. 1956. The North American anthracotheres. J. Paleont. 30:615–645.

———. 1963. The Miocene faunas from the Wounded Knee area of western South Dakota. Bull. Amer. Mus. Nat. Hist. 125:139–238.

———. 1970. Review of the Miocene Wounded Knee faunas of southwestern South Dakota. Los Angeles Co. Mus. Nat. Hist. Bull. Sci. no. 8.

McDowell, F. W., J. A. Wilson, and J. Clark 1973. K-Ar dates for biotite from two paleontologically significant localities: Duchesne River Formation, Utah, and Chadron Formation, South Dakota. Isochron/West, no. 7, pp. 11–12.

McGrew, P. O. 1971. Early Tertiary vertebrate faunas, Vieja Group, Trans-Pecos Texas. Equidae. Pt. 2: *Mesohippus* from the Vieja Group, Trans-Pecos Texas. Pearce-Sellards Series, no. 18, pp. 6–11.

Matthew, W. D. 1899. A provisional classification of the fresh-water Tertiary of the west. Bull. Amer. Mus. Nat. Hist. 12:19–75.

———. 1903. The fauna of the *Titanotherium* beds at Pipe-stone Springs, Montana. Bull. Amer. Mus. Nat. Hist. 19:197–226.

Meek, F. B., and F. V. Hayden. 1857. Descriptions of new species and genera of fossils, collected by Dr. F. V. Hayden in Nebraska Territory, under the direction of Lieut. G. K. Warren, U.S. Topographical Engineer, with some remarks on the Tertiary and Cretaceous formations of the north-west, and the parallelism of the latter with those portions of the United States and Territories. Acad. Nat. Sci. Philadelphia Proc. 9:117–148.

———. 1861. Descriptions of new Lower Silurian, (Primordial), Jurassic, Cretaceous, and Tertiary fossils, collected in Nebraska, by the exploring expedition under the command of Capt. Wm. F. Reynolds, U.S. Top. Engrs.; with some remarks on the rocks from which they were obtained. Acad. Nat. Sci. Philadelphia Proc. 13:415–447.

Morea, M. F. 1975. On the species of *Hoplophoneus* and *Eusmilus* (Carnivora, Felidae) Master's thesis, South Dakota School of Mines and Technology.

Nelson, M. E. 1976. Early Cenozoic stratigraphy of northeastern Utah and southwestern Wyoming (abstr.). Geol. Soc. Amer., Abstracts with programs 8:614–615.

Obradovich, J. S., G. A. Izett, and C. W. Naeser. 1973. Radiometric ages of volcanic ash and pumice beds in the Gering Sandstone (earliest Miocene) of the Arikaree Group, southwestern Nebraska. Geol. Soc. Amer., Abstracts with programs. 5:499–500.

Olson, E. C. 1952. The evolution of a Permian vertebrate chronofauna. Evolution 6:181–196.

Osborn, H. F. 1907. Tertiary mammal horizons of North America. Bull. Amer. Mus. Nat. Hist. 23:237–254.

Osborn, H. F., and W. D. Matthew. 1909. Cenozoic mammal horizons of western North America, with faunal lists of the Tertiary Mammalia of the west. Bull. U.S. Geol. Survey no. 361.

Osborn, H. F., and J. L. Wortman. 1894. Fossil mammals of the lower Miocene White River beds, collection 1892. Bull. Amer. Mus. Nat. Hist. 6:199–228.

———. 1895. Perissodactyls of the lower Miocene White River Beds. Bull. Amer. Mus. Nat. Hist. 7:343–375.

Patton, T. H. 1969. An Oligocene land vertebrate fauna from Florida. J. Paleont. 43:543–546.

Patton, T. H., and B. E. Taylor. 1973. The Protoceratinae (Mammalia, Tylopoda, Protoceratidae) and the systematics of the Protoceratidae. Bull. Amer. Mus. Nat. Hist. 150:349–413.

Peterson, O. A. 1931. New species from the Oligocene of the Uinta. Ann. Carnegie Mus. 21:61–78.

Peterson, O. A., and J. L. Kay. 1931. The upper Uinta Formation of northeastern Utah. Ann. Carnegie Mus. 20:293–306.

Prothero, D. R. 1982. How isochronous are mammalian biostratigraphic events? Proc. Third No. Amer. Paleont. Conv. 2:405–409.

Prothero, D. R., C. R. Denham, and H. G. Farmer. 1982. Oligocene calibration of the magnetic polarity time scale. Geology 10:650–653.

———. 1983. Magnetostratigraphy of the White River Group and its implications for Oligocene geochronology. Palaeogeogr., Palaeoclimatol., Palaeocecol. 42:151–166.

Prout, H. A. 1846. Gigantic *Palaeotherium*. Amer. J. Sci., 2d ser., vol. 2, pp. 288–289.

———. 1847. Description of a fossil maxillary bone of *Palaeotherium,* from near White River. Amer. J. Sci, 2d ser., vol. 3, pp. 248–250.

Radinsky, L. B. 1967. A review of the rhinocerotoid family Hyracodontidae (Perissodactyla). Bull. Amer. Mus. Nat. Hist. 136:1–45.

Repenning, C. A. 1967. Palearctic-Nearctic mammalian dispersal in the late Cenozoic. In The Bering Land Bridge, ed. D. M. Hopkins. Stanford: Stanford University Press. Pp. 288–311.

Retallack, G. 1981. Fossil soils: Indicators of ancient terrestrial environments: In Paleobotany, Paleoecology, and Evolution. Ed. K. J. Niklas. Vol. 1. New York: Praeger. Pp. 55–102.

———. 1983*a*. A paleopedological approach to the interpretation of terrestrial sedimentary rocks: The mid-Tertiary fossil soils of Badlands National Park, South Dakota. Bull. Geol. Soc. Amer. 94:823–840.

———. 1983*b*. Late Eocene and Oligocene Paleosols from Badlands National Park, South Dakota. Geol. Soc. Amer. Spec. Paper 193.

Russell, L. S. 1972. Tertiary mammals of Saskatchewan. Pt. II: The Oligocene fauna, non-ungulate orders. Life Sci. Contr. Royal Ont. Mus., no. 84.

Schiebout, J. A. 1977. *Schizotheroides* (Mammalia: Perissodactyla) from the Oligocene of Trans-Pecos Texas. J. Paleont. 51:455–458.

Schlaijker, E. M. 1935. Contributions to the stratigraphy and paleontology of the Goshen Hole area, Wyoming. III: A new basal Oligocene formation. Bull. Mus. Comp. Zool. 76:69–93.

Schultz, C. B., and C. H. Falkenbach. 1949. Promerycochoerinae, a new subfamily of oreodonts. Bull. Amer. Mus. Nat. Hist. 93:69–198.

———. 1954. Desmatochoerinae, a new subfamily of oreodonts. Bull. Amer. Mus. Nat. Hist. 105:147–256.

———. 1956. Miniochoerinae and Oreonetinae, two new subfamilies of oreodonts Bull. Amer. Mus. Nat. Hist. 109:377–482.

———. 1968. The phylogeny of the oreodonts, parts 1 and 2. Bull. Amer. Mus. Nat. Hist. 139:1–498.

Schultz, C. B., and T. M. Stout. 1938. Preliminary remarks on the Oligocene of Nebraska (abstr.). Bull. Geol. Soc. Amer. 49:1921.

———. 1955. Classification of Oligocene sediments in Nebraska. Bull. Univ. Nebr. State Mus. 4:17–52.

Scott, W. B. 1940. The mammalian fauna of the White River Oligocene, part IV, Artiodactyla. Amer. Phil. Soc. Trans., n.s., vol. 28, pp. 363–746.

———. 1945. The Mammalia of the Duchesne River

Oligocene. Amer. Phil. Soc. Trans., n.s., vol. 34, pp. 209–253.

Scott, W. B., and G. L. Jepsen, eds. 1936–1941. The mammalian fauna of the White River Oligocene, parts I-V. Amer. Phil. Soc. Trans. 28:1–980.

Setoguchi, T. 1978. Paleontology and geology of the Badwater Creek area, central Wyoming. Pt. 16: The Cedar Ridge local fauna (late Oligocene). Carnegie Mus. Nat. Hist. Bull., no. 9.

Simpson, G. G. 1933. Glossary and correlation charts of North American Tertiary mammal-bearing formations. Bull. Amer. Mus. Nat. Hist. 67:79–121.

———. 1946. Discussion: The Duchesnean fauna and the Eocene-Oligocene boundary. Amer. J. Sci. 244:52–57.

———. 1947. Holarctic mammalian faunas and continental relationships during the Cenozoic. Bull. Geol. Soc. Amer. 58:613–688.

Skinner, M. F., S. M. Skinner, and R. J. Gooris. 1968. Cenozoic rocks and faunas of Turtle Butte, south-central South Dakota. Bull. Amer. Mus. Nat. Hist. 138:381–436.

Skinner, S. M., and R. J. Gooris. 1966. A note on *Toxotherium* (Mammalia, Rhinocerotoidea) from Natrona County, Wyoming. Amer. Mus. Novitates, no. 2261.

Stirton, R. A. 1952. Are Petaluma horse teeth reliable in correlation? Amer. Assoc. Petrol. Geol. Bull. 36:2011–2025.

Stone, W. J. 1972. Middle Cenozoic stratigraphy of North Dakota. In Depositional environments of the lignite bearing strata in western North Dakota, ed. F.T.C. Ting. North Dakota Geol. Surv. Misc. Ser., no. 50, Pp. 123–132.

Storer, J. E. 1981. Leptomerycid Artiodactyla of the Calf Creek local fauna (Cypress Hills Formation, Oligocene, Chadronian) Saskatchewan. Saskatchewan Mus. Nat. Hist. Contr., no. 9, pp. 1–32.

Sutton, J. F., and C. C. Black. 1975. Paleontology of the earliest Oligocene deposits in Jackson Hole, Wyoming. Pt. 1: Rodents exclusive of the Family Eomyidae. Ann. Carnegie Mus. 45:299–315.

Swanson, D. A., and P. T. Robinson. 1968. Base of the John Day Formation in the Horse Heaven mining district, north central Oregon. U.S. Geol. Surv. Prof. Paper 600 D, pp. D154–D161.

Tarling, D. H., and J. G. Mitchell. 1976. Revised Cenozoic polarity time scale. Geology 4:133–136.

Tedford, R. H. 1970. Principles and practices of mammalian geochronology in North America. Proc. No. Amer. Paleont. Conv. Pt. F, pp. 666–703.

Van Houten, F. B. 1964. Tertiary geology of the Beaver Rim area, Fremont and Natrona counties, Wyoming. Bull. U.S. Geol. Surv., no. 1164.

Wanless, H. R. 1923. The stratigraphy of the White River beds of South Dakota. Amer. Phil. Soc. Proc. 62:190–269.

Wilmarth, M. G. 1938. Lexicon of geologic names of the United States (including Alaska). Bull. U.S. Geol. Surv. no. 896.

Wilson, J. A. 1971a. Early Tertiary vertebrate faunas, Vieja Group, Trans-Pecos Texas: Agriochoeridae and Merycoidontidae. Texas Mem. Mus. Bull., no. 18.

———. 1971b. Early Tertiary vertebrate faunas, Vieja Group, Trans-Pecos Texas: Entelodontidae. Pearce-Sellards Series, no. 17.

———. 1974. Early Tertiary vertebrate faunas, Vieja Group and Buck Hill Group, Trans-Pecos Texas: Protoceratidae, Camelidae, Hypertragulidae. Texas Mem. Mus. Bull., no. 23.

Wilson, J. A., P. C. Twiss, R. K. Deford, and S. E. Clabaugh. 1968. Stratigraphic succession, potassium-argon dates, and vertebrate faunas, Vieja Group, rim rock country, Trans-Pecos Texas. Amer. J. Sci. 266:590–604.

Wilson, R. W. 1949. On some White River fossil rodents. Carnegie Inst. Wash. Publ., no. 584, pp. 27–50.

———. 1971. Recovery of small mammals from the Oligocene of western South Dakota. Nat. Geog. Soc. Research Repts., 1965, pp. 279–287.

Wood, A. E. 1969. Rodents and lagomorphs from the "*Chadronia* pocket," early Oligocene of Nebraska. Amer. Mus. Novitates, no. 2366.

———. 1970. The early Oligocene rodent *Ardynomys* (family Cylindrodontidae) from Mongolia and Montana. Amer. Mus. Novitates, no. 2418.

———. 1974. Early Tertiary vertebrate faunas, Vieja Group, Trans-Pecos Texas: Rodentia. Texas Mem. Mus. Bull., no. 21.

Wood, H. E. 1949. Oligocene faunas, facies, and formations. Geol. Soc. Amer. Mem. 39, pp. 83–90.

———. 1961. *Toxotherium hunteri*, a peculiar new Oligocene mammal from Saskatchewan. Natl. Mus. Canada Nat. Hist. Papers, no. 13.

Wood, H. E., R. W. Chaney, J. Clark, E. H. Colbert, G. L. Jepsen, J. B. Reeside, Jr., and C. Stock. 1941. Nomenclature and correlation of the North American continental Tertiary. Bull. Geol. Soc. Amer. 52:1–48.

Wortman, J. L. 1893. On the divisions of the White River or lower Miocene of Dakota. Bull. Amer. Mus. Nat. Hist. 5:95–105.

6

FAUNAL SUCCESSION AND BIOCHRONOLOGY OF THE ARIKAREEAN THROUGH HEMPHILLIAN INTERVAL (LATE OLIGOCENE THROUGH EARLIEST PLIOCENE EPOCHS) IN NORTH AMERICA

Richard H. Tedford

Morris F. Skinner

Robert W. Fields

John M. Rensberger

David P. Whistler

Theodore Galusha

Beryl E. Taylor

J. Reid Macdonald

S. David Webb

THE FAUNAL SUCCESSION

Biochronology as developed from the succession of mammal faunas is ultimately based on the demonstrable superpositional sequence of these assemblages and is only as useful as the relevant stratigraphy and taxonomy are detailed and as correlations between faunal sequences are refined to eliminate ecological or zoogeographic bias. We propose to discuss certain aspects of the mammal faunal succession and correlation in North America during the span formerly (Wood et al. 1941) thought to encompass most of the Miocene and Pliocene epochs but now attributed to the late Oligocene through earliest Pliocene time. We wish to explore how completely mammal faunas account for the total time represented and thus how useful they will be in characterizing intervals

of a biochronologic scale. In the concluding section of this chapter, the data gathered in the section that follows will be used to review the biochronology presently available for the interval under discussion.

The faunal sequences in carefully selected areas (fig. 6.1) are graphically summarized in the accompanying correlation chart (fig. 6.2, in pocket). These areas have been specifically chosen for one or more of the following reasons: (1) they include an unusually complete and directly superposed succession, (2) they contain faunas that can be related to other geochronologic systems, or (3) they include assemblages important in the historical development of mammalian biochronology. It must be emphasized that this study is not intended to be a comprehensive summary of all the faunas of the subject interval despite the fact that all such faunas would be

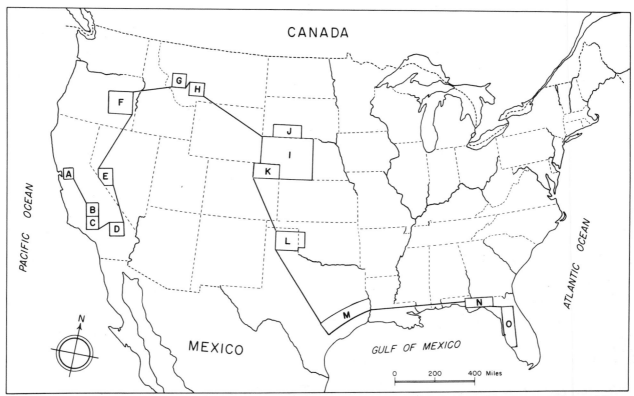

Fig. 6.1. Map of the United States showing the regions (lettered boxes) from which the faunal sequences of figure 6.2 were compiled. The lettered boxes are linked by lines that trace out the correlation traverse depicted in figure 6.2.

potentially useful and necessary for full exploration of the bases for a continentwide biochronology. We have ignored many well-known faunas and potentially important areas such as those of the Santa Fe Group, New Mexico (although this has recently been reviewed by Tedford [1981]), because they do not meet the above criteria or were too poorly known to be useful at the time this review was compiled. In making our selection, we have emphasized those successions that we believe to have had the greatest historical influence on the biochronology of the interval under discussion. In addition, the correlation chart brings out the points of relationship to the marine record and hence the evidence for interrelationships with marine biostratigraphic data in both the Gulf and West coasts of North America. Correlation with the Neogene planktonic zonation is suggested for part of the Gulf Coast succession (explored more fully in Tedford and Hunter [1984]), and interrelationships with Pacific Coast benthonic foraminiferal stages is available for the mammal faunal sequence in the California coast ranges.

The faunal sequence in the West Coast, Great Basin, and Columbia Plateau has been calibrated with many radiometrically dated tuffs and lava flows. All the volcanic units shown on the chart are in direct stratigraphic sequence with the rocks containing the mammal faunas listed, and in a few cases the fossil remains were taken directly from dated tuffs. Appendix A gives further data and references for these important calibration points, all of which were recalculated with respect to the 1976 International Union of Geological Sciences constants following the method of Dalrymple (1979). The Great Plains and Gulf Coast sequences are poorly calibrated at present, although an increasing number of the many known vitric tuffs in the Great Plains are being dated by fission-track and radiometric means. We have incorporated such new data regarding the age of some of these tuffs where they occur in fossiliferous rocks in demonstrable succession with the mammalian faunas mentioned herein. Independent calibration of correlative marine biostratigraphies provides further sources of geochronologic data that can be compared with the mammalian scale. More recently, the magnetostratigraphy of some important late Oligocene and Miocene mammal-bearing sections has been accomplished (Lindsay et al. 1976; MacFadden 1977; MacFadden et al. 1979; Barghoorn

1982; Prothero et al. 1983) and this promises to be a very important geochronologic tool for the future. It is important to remember that radiometry and paleomagnetics only provide calibration for the biochronology and offer another geochronologic technique to check correlations. They cannot substitute as a means of defining and characterizing biochrons.

The following paragraphs constitute a series of explanatory notes for the correlation chart and are intended to bring out details of particular biochronologic importance, to review accepted concepts, and to discuss interpretations that depart from those in the literature. We also give the salient features of new or little-known mammal faunas deemed important enough to deserve mention. Appendix B is an index of all the faunas mentioned in the text. Together with the text, it will serve the same purpose as the useful "glossary" of Wood et al. (1941). We are quite aware that some readers will object to our presenting faunal lists for undescribed assemblages. We do so in the hope that our identifications will not be unduly misleading (we made special efforts to closely check biochronologically significant taxa). We believe that the knowledge that these assemblages exist and deserve further study will outweigh the obvious disadvantages of this procedure. The bibliographic citations include only the most modern summary or most useful papers rather than a complete accounting of the vast literature involved.

Faunal terminology follows the summary of Tedford (1970) with the important exception that the term "Fauna" is used for stratigraphically as well as geographically diverse samples and the term "Local Fauna" is correspondingly restricted, bringing it into conformity with the definition of most authors (i.e., "Local Fauna" refers to an essentially contemporaneous assemblage derived from a limited geographic area). In both cases, close taxonomic affinities of the samples composing these faunas is an essential feature and one that recalls the use of the word "fauna" in the neontological literature. The taxonomy reflects the results of the most recent revisions, although we have not given the authorities for all the names cited. The large collections at our disposal (especially the Frick Collection at the American Museum of Natural History) clearly render some of the older taxonomy impractical. In these cases, we register dissent from the existing taxonomy by placing the currently used generic or specific name in quotation marks. Our purpose is to indicate more precisely the taxonomic identities necessary in correlation and to flag the problems in taxonomy of late Tertiary mammals that are badly in need of further work.

California Coast Ranges

A. San Francisco Bay Area. The mammal faunal succession in this area was initially discussed by Stirton (1939*a*) and important additions were made by Ritchie (1948) and Macdonald (1948). Savage (1955) reviewed the biostratigraphy in the Mount Diablo area. Local faunas correlative with those from the stratotype of the Cerrotejonian Stage occur in continental deposits interfingering with the San Pablo Formation of Mohnian age in the Berkeley Hills (Orinda Formation sites, Ritchie 1943) and on the flanks of Mount Diablo (Sycamore Creek Fauna ["Older Black Hawk Ranch faunule" of Ritchie 1948]) beneath the Black Hawk Ranch Local Fauna. Both of these Cerrotejonian assemblages contain the horses *Hipparion tehonense* (conspecific with "*N. lenticularis*" of the Clarendon beds of the Texas Panhandle; see MacFadden 1980*b*) and *Neohipparion trampasense* (Edwards 1982) characteristic of faunas of that stage. In direct superposition above the dated volcanics of the Moraga Formation in the Berkeley Hills are the Siesta Formation sites (Stirton 1939*a*). The correlative Black Hawk Ranch Local Fauna (Ritchie 1948; Macdonald 1948) occurs near the base of the thick Green Valley Formation in the Mount Diablo area. The Montediablan Stage (Savage 1955) is based biologically on these assemblages and is characterized by the horses *Hipparion forcei* and "*Pliohippus*" *leardi*, the canids "*Osteoborus*" *diabloensis* and *Aelurodon* cf. *taxoides* (referred to "*A.*" *aphobus* by Macdonald 1948), the large felid *Nimravides thinobates,* and the beaver *Eucastor lecontei.*

Above the dated Bald Peak volcanics, but in fault contact with them in the Berkeley Hills, are rocks now formalized (Creely et al. 1982) as the Mulholland Formation. These deposits contain the Hemphillian Mulholland Fauna, including the only known North American record of a cricetodontine rodent, *Pliotomodon* (see May 1981 for review), as well as megalonychid sloths, "*Pliohippus*" cf. *spectans, Indarctos,* and *Dipoides,* found at various sites along the outcrop of the unit. Megalonychid sloth remains also occur in the Hemme Hills Local Fauna at the base of the Tassajara Formation and just above the tuff taken as the upper limit of the underlying Green Valley Formation. This tuff has been correlated with the Pinole Tuff, which crops out on the eastern shore of San Francisco Bay in the Rodeo syncline (Sarna-Wojcicki 1976). At the latter site, fossil mammals (Pinole Local Fauna, Stirton 1939*a*) occur in the Pinole Tuff just beneath the dated unit. They include *Machairodus, Plesiogulo, Osteoborus,* "*Pliohippus*" *coalingensis* (probably conspecific with *Dinohippus interpolatus*; see discussion in James 1963, pp. 15–18), *Neohipparion eurystyle,* "*Sphenophalos,*" and *Megalonyx* (Hirschfeld and Webb 1968). This is one of the youngest radiometrically dated (5.2 Ma, KA 1005; Evernden et al. 1964) Hemphillian fossil mammal occurrences.[1] Thus, the Pinole Local Fauna is of critical interest in calibration of the upper limit of the Hemphillian age. Farther north, near Danville, at the western foot of Mount Diablo, Repenning (this volume) reports early Blancan microtines (*Cosomys sawrockensis*) in the Maxum Local Fauna within the Tassajara Formation and below the Lawlor Tuff (ash bed 7 of Appendix A, this chapter). The faunal succession contained in the thick continental and near-shore marine deposits of the eastern San Francisco Bay region deserves further attention because of its relative completeness, stratigraphic documentation, and the presence of interfingering datable volcanics and marine deposits.

B. Southern San Joaquin Valley. East of the San Andreas fault, thick sequences of marine and nonmarine Tertiary rocks are exposed around the margins of the southern San Joaquin or Great Valley of California. These preserve an important fossil mammal succession that deserves more study than it has received in view of the opportunity for establishing a direct relationship with marine biostratigraphic disciplines.

In the San Emigdio Range at the southwestern end of the Valley, the nonmarine Tecuya Formation contains mammals of Arikareean age, including *Protosciurus tecuyensis* (Black 1963), *Dapheonus ruber* (Stock 1932), *Hypsiops erythroceps* (Schultz and Falkenbach 1950), *Hypertragulus* (Stock 1920), and *Nanotragulus*. This assemblage of genera suggests that the deposits possibly range in age from early to late Arikareean, but without relevant biostratigraphy, the number and the limits of the assemblages present cannot be determined except to note that the fossil mammals all occur beneath the dated dacites and andesites that cap the formation.

Richly fossiliferous shallow-water marine strata assigned to the Temblor Formation crop out along the western flank of the Sierra Nevada east of Bakersfield. These rocks and their molluscan faunas have long served as an informal biostratigraphic standard for the Pacific Coast. The Temblor has been broken into many local rock units for mapping purposes, and land mammal re-

mains occur in some of these units along with marine invertebrates and locally rich concentrations of marine vertebrates. The Pyramid Hill[2] and Woody local faunas (Mitchell and Tedford 1973), the Barker's Ranch Local Fauna[3] (Savage and Barnes 1972), and the Sharktooth Hill Local Fauna[4] (Mitchell 1965, Savage and Barnes 1972) are principally marine mammal assemblages, but they contain fragmentary land mammal remains of late Arikareean, late Hemingfordian, and late Barstovian ages, respectively.

On the western side of the San Joaquin Valley flanking the Diablo Range north of Coalinga, shallow-water marine deposits at the top of the Temblor Formation and just beneath the Big Blue Formation carry conglomerate lenses packed with isolated teeth and bones of mammals representing the North Coalinga Local Fauna (Bode 1935). This assemblage generally resembles other Barstovian faunas of the California Coast Ranges, especially in the presence of cranioceratine dromomerycids that otherwise are not known in the Great Basin. The North Coalinga Local Fauna has been regarded as early Barstovian based on the stage of evolution of some of its horses (Downs 1961). It can be directly related, however, to the molluscan and foraminiferal biostratigraphies and on this basis is placed at or just above the Relizian-Luisian boundary. The radiometric calibration of this boundary (13.7–14.5 Ma, Turner 1970) and the presence of Proboscidea in turn suggests that the North Coalinga Local Fauna should be correlated with the Barstow Fauna (as restricted here, p. 187) of late Barstovian age.

Disconformably overlying the Temblor strata are the coarser grained clastics of the near-shore marine "Santa Margarita" Formation. Savage (1955) summarized the biostratigraphy of these rocks in the Tejon Hills on the southeastern side of the San Joaquin Valley. The lowest fossil mammals (Comanche Point Local Fauna) in this succession include a species of *Cormohipparion* comparable to those from the Valentine Formation of Nebraska. *Cormohipparion* of this type are poorly represented west of the Rocky Mountains; the only other described occurrence is associated with the Two Mile

---

[1] A younger date has been cited (4.1 Ma, KA 1027, Evernden et al. 1964, p. 190) for the Hemphillian White Cone Local Fauna, northeastern Arizona, but this was only claimed to be a minimum figure. Later K-Ar dating of the middle member of the Bidahochi Formation, just beneath the White Cone Local Fauna, yielded a 6.7 Ma maximum date for the fauna (Scarborough et al. 1974). May and Repenning (1982) have commented on the age of other faunas from California and Mexico which lie near the younger limit of the Hemphillian.

[2] In addition to the *Anchitherium* and *Hesperhyus* previously reported (Mitchell and Tedford 1973, p. 272), *Menoceras* is also present.

[3] Reexamination of the Barker's Ranch terrestrial mammals indicates the presence of *Tomarctus* cf. *optatus,* "*Merychippus,*" and *Bouromeryx* cf. *submilleri* ("cf. *Aletomeryx*" in Savage and Barnes 1972, p. 133).

[4] Examination of the Los Angeles County Museum collection of terrestrial mammals from this site indicates the presence of *Miomastodon, Merychippus brevidontus, Anchitherium* sp., tapir, ?*Prosynthetoceras,* and *Bouromeryx milleri.*

Bar Local Fauna (Stirton and Goeriz 1942, not shown on fig. 6.2) from the lower part of the Mehrten Formation of the western slope of the Sierra Nevada in central California (Tuolumne County).

The South Tejon Hills Fauna occurs in nonmarine beds assigned to the "Santa Margarita" Formation overlying the near-shore marine facies of the same unit. Savage (1955) used the South Tejon Hills Fauna as the type assemblage of his Cerrotejonian Stage, a time-rock unit characterized by the limited stratigraphic occurrence of *Hipparion tehonense* (see MacFadden 1980*b*) and "*Pliohippus*" *tehonensis* in association with "*Osteoborus*" cf. *litoralis* (close to *Epicyon saevus*), *Cosoryx* cf. *cerroensis,* and *Cranioceras* cf. *clarendonensis,* which indicate affinity with early Clarendonian faunas of the Great Plains. In the gradationally overlying nonmarine Chanac Formation, the presence of the Montediablan Stage is indicated by the composition of the North Tejon Hills Fauna: *Hipparion forcei* and "*Pliohippus*" *leardi* associated with *Ustatochoerus* cf. *californicus*, "*Paracosoryx*" cf. *furlongi*, and *Cranioceras* cf. *unicornis*. These taxa support correlation with late Clarendonian assemblages elsewhere.

Deeper in the San Joaquin Basin, the Chanac Formation grades upward into the nonmarine Kern River Formation, but in outcrops along the flanks of the Sierra Nevada a disconformity breaks the sequence. The lower part of the Kern River Formation contains local concentrations of fossil mammal remains whose exact stratigraphic relationship and faunal composition need comprehensive study. Some elements of these assemblages have been described: *Bassariscus antiquus* (Hall 1930*c*), *Eomellivora* cf. *winmani* (Stock and Hall 1933), *Prosthennops kernensis* (Colbert 1938), *Peromyscus pliocenicus* (Wilson 1937), *Hypolagus* cf. *limnetus* (Wilson 1937), and *Spermophilus* (*Otospermophilus*) *argonatus* (Black 1963). Other undescribed taxa include *Cranioceras* (*Yumaceras*), *Pliohippus,* and *Neohipparion* of the *N. eurystyle* group. Many of these taxa have equivalents elsewhere in the early Hemphillian of the Pacific Coast and Great Basin, and for some there is a wider distribution into the midcontinent.

To the west, in subsurface, the Kern River Formation grades laterally into the marine Etchegoin Formation that is exposed in folds on the western side of the San Joaquin Valley. Scattered fossil mammal remains (Merriam 1915, Nomland 1916) have been collected from those near-shore deposits, including the otter "*Enhydriodon*" (an immigrant, Repenning 1976) and the type specimens of "*Pliohippus*" *coalingensis* and *Neohipparion molle* (a member of the *N. eurystyle* group), suggesting equivalence with other late Hemphillian faunas of

the West Coast. The Etchegoin Formation grades upward into the San Joaquin Formation, which contains Blancan mammals (Repenning 1976; this volume).

C. Transverse Ranges. West of the San Andreas fault, in the structurally complex Transverse Ranges of southern California, thick interfingering marine and nonmarine deposits in the Ventura Basin and the Cuyama Valley-Caliente Range area preserve locally abundant fossil mammal remains. The sequence in the Cuyama Valley and adjacent Caliente Range contains one of the most important faunal successions in North America from the standpoint of its completeness and its relationship to radiometric and marine geochronologies. Study of this region is still in the preliminary stages of investigation despite the early recognition of its significance in the 1930s.

Early Arikareean faunas are not yet recognized in the Simmler Formation of the Cuyama Valley region, but they have long been known from the upper part of the correlative Sespe Formation of the Ventura Basin. Scattered fossils in the South Mountain area near Ventura and eastward into the Simi Valley yield the oreodonts *Sespia californica, Desmatochoerus*? *thurstoni,* and *Mesoreodon hesperus* (nomenclature follows Schultz and Falkenbach 1949, 1954, 1968) and geomyoid rodents (Wilson 1949), which resemble forms from the Gering and Monroe Creek formations of Nebraska. The Kew Quarry (Stock 1933*a*, 1933*b*, 1935; Wilson 1934), developed in Sespe strata in the nearby Las Posas Hills, contains a mixture of taxa of varying biochronologic significance. If the principle of biasing correlation toward the more "advanced" elements in the fauna (e.g., *Temnocyon, Ekgmoiteptecela* ["*Hoplophoneus*"] *belli, Miohippus, Dyseotylopus migrans* [an early stenomyline camel], and *Nanotragulus* ["*Hypertragulus*"] *fontanus*) is followed, then equivalence with assemblages from the Gering or Sharps formations of the northern Great Plains is indicated.

The oldest known fossil vertebrate sites in the Caliente Range occur near the top of near-shore marine deposits equated with the Vaqueros Formation. Similar assemblages extend upward into the base of the thick nonmarine Caliente Formation. These sites were designated with the letter "A" in Repenning and Vedder's (1961) summary of their biostratigraphic work in the Caliente Range. The composite fauna from the "A" sites was thought to be Arikareean by Repenning, but his listing of *Tanymykter brachyodontus* and *Pseudoblastomeryx* cf. *falkenbachi* suggests a late Arikareean or early Hemingfordian age based on the geochrons of these taxa as established in the northern Great Plains (Honey and Taylor 1978). An important micromammal fauna has been obtained from the Vedder site (Hutchison and Lindsay 1974; Lindsay 1974; Munthe 1979) in the marine Branch Canyon Formation. This assemblage shares some elements with late Hemingfordian assemblages of the Great Plains and with late Hemingfordian sites as represented by California Institute of Technology locality 315 (Dougherty 1940) in the Caliente Formation of the Caliente Range and its Cuyama badlands equivalent, the Hidden Treasure Spring Local Fauna of James (1963). In addition, the Vedder site contains the earliest North American occurrence of the European eomyid rodent *Eomys* and the petauristine squirrel *Blackia*. These assemblages, like their equivalents to the east in the Tehachapi Mountains (Phillips Ranch Local Fauna [Buwalda 1916, Buwalda and Lewis 1955; not shown in fig. 6.2]) and Mojave Desert region (see below), usually include the horse *"Merychippus" carrizoensis* (probably conspecific with *"M." tehachapiensis*), a taxon so far unknown east of the Great Basin. Such faunas contain carnivores and artiodactyls that agree best with those from late Hemingfordian assemblages of the Great Plains. Higher in the Caliente Formation, Barstovian faunas occur at California Institute of Technology localities 322 and 323 in the Caliente Range and in the Cuyama badlands (Upper Dry Canyon and the younger Dome Spring faunas, James 1963). These Barstovian assemblages are homotaxial with the Green Hills and Barstow faunas in the Barstow Formation, and radiometric determinations confirm this correlation.

Cerrotejonian and Montediablan equivalents (Mathews Ranch and Nettle Spring faunas, respectively) occur in succession within the Cuyama badlands outcrops of the Caliente Formation (James 1963). Poorly represented Hemphillian local faunas occur at the top of the Caliente Formation in both the Cuyama badlands (Sequence Canyon Fauna, James 1963) and Caliente Range ("Hh" sites of Repenning and Vedder 1961). These contain late *Dinohippus* species and megalonychid sloths (including *Pliometanastes*, Hirschfeld and Webb 1968), similar to other late Hemphillian faunas in California.

Great Basin

D. Mojave Desert. In recent years paleontological exploration of the scattered outcrops of late Tertiary sediments in the Mojave Desert of California has resulted in the discovery of assemblages older than the classic "Barstow fauna." Continuing study of the latter and the well-known "Ricardo fauna" has progressed to the extent that it is now possible to recognize some of the details of the faunal successions that are contained within these thick bodies of rock. For the present, it is possible to

recognize a superposed sequence of faunas, but eventually chronostratigraphic units useful in correlation might be based on the large, stratigraphically controlled collections from these areas. Lindsay (1972) has proposed a zonation based on the succession of rodents in the Barstow Formation. Radiometric calibration of parts of these sequences is already available, and the opportunity for further dating is excellent in this volcanic province. Dibblee (1967) ably reviewed the physical stratigraphy of the area that includes these classic sites.

The earliest known fossil mammals from the Mojave Desert were described (Woodburne et al. 1974) from the Hector Formation of the southern Cady Mountains in the central part of the desert. The Black Butte Mine[5] and Logan Mine faunas were found to be closely comparable with assemblages from the Marsland Formation of western Nebraska. Recent revision (Hunt 1978, 1981) of the biostratigraphy of the Marsland Formation indicates that the Hector assemblages are late Arikareean in age (see discussion, pp. 166–167). Toward the western border of the Mojave Desert in the Kramer beds of the upper part of the Tropico Group in the U.S. Borax and Chemical Company's open cut at Boron, giant earth movers "recovered" a concentration of fossil mammal remains, the Boron Local Fauna (Whistler 1965, 1984). This assemblage includes species of *Merychyus* and *Aletomeryx* comparable to those from the Runningwater Formation of Nebraska. The Boron Local Fauna also includes the earliest appearance of the heteromyid *Cupidinimus*.

In the northern Cady Mountains, fragmentary remains (Lower Cady Mountains Local Fauna, fig. 6.2; Miller 1980; Woodburne et al. 1982) indicate the presence of aletomerycine dromomerycids and *Merychyus* cf. *calaminthus* at the base of a succession that extends into later Hemingfordian time. The Upper Cady Mountains Local Fauna (Miller 1980, Woodburne et al. 1982) includes *Tomarctus* cf. *hippophagus*, *"Merychippus" tehachapiensis*, *"Miolabis" tenius*, *Aepycamelus*, and cf. *Anchitheriomys* indicating correlation with the Sheep Creek Fauna of Nebraska and with other faunas of similar character in the Great Basin and Pacific Coast. An equivalent of the Upper Cady Mountain Local Fauna occurs in the Red Division Quarry at the base of the faunal sequence within the Barstow Formation in the Mud Hills, north of Barstow. Above the level of this quarry many local concentrations of fossils discovered and worked by the Frick Laboratory establish a framework for the faunal succession which typifies the Barstovian Mammal Age.

---

[5] Note that preoccupation of the term "Black Butte Local Fauna" (Shotwell et al. 1963) has necessitated changing the Cady Mountain synonym to "Black Butte Mine Fauna."

As detailed by Woodburne and Tedford (1982), the sequence in the Mud Hills has been broken into two assemblages that maintain their faunal composition through several hundred feet of strata. The lower assemblage, the Green Hills Fauna, includes *Copemys*, *Peridiomys*, *Euoplocyon*, *Amphicyon* cf. *ingens*, *Hemicyon* (*Plithocyon*) sp., "*Merychippus*" *stylodontus*, *Hesperhyus*, *Merriamoceros*, protolabine camels, and *Aepycamelus*. Most of these taxa are similar to those from the Lower Snake Creek Fauna of Nebraska.

The term Barstow Fauna will be restricted to the upper assemblage of this succession because material from these levels dominated the collections available to Merriam (1919) and were thus the principal faunal basis for the Barstovian Mammal Age as defined by Wood et al. (1941). Stratigraphically controlled collections now available establish the following taxa as characteristic of the restricted Barstow Fauna, the youngest assemblage within the Barstow Formation of the Mud Hills: *Hemicyon* (*Plithocyon*) *barstowensis* (incl. *H. californicus*), "*Merychippus*" *intermontanus*, "*M.*" *sumani*, *Archaeohippus mourningi*, *Megahippus mckennai*, *Paramoceros*, *Meryceros*, *Mediochoerus*,[6] and the first appearance of *Parapliosaccomys*, *Epicyon*, and *Gomphotherium*. Faunas of this character may extend upward in an adjacent basin into deposits of nearly 12.5 Ma in age if the technically credible date for the Cronese Local Fauna is accurate. Detailed comparative studies are still lacking, but the Barstow Fauna seems to find its closest equivalents in the Great Plains with assemblages from the upper part of the Pawnee Creek Formation (as revised here, pp. 172–173) and lower part of the Valentine Formation. Such biological correlations must rely heavily on taxa other than the abundant equine horses, which seem peculiarly restricted geographically.

Younger faunas are restricted to the borders of the Mojave structural province; the best sequence is contained within the Ricardo Formation exposed on the flanks of the El Paso Range just north of the Garlock fault and adjacent to the Sierra Nevada. Biostratigraphic work by two of us (DPW and RHT) allows the tentative recognition of three superposed faunas: the lowest is the Iron Canyon Fauna with *Cormohipparion* cf. *occidentale*, *Megahippus*, *Epicyon* cf. *saevus*, *Hadrocyon mohavensis*, *Ustatochoerus* cf. *profectus*, and *Paracosoryx furlongi*, an association of forms most similar to those that occur in the Burge Fauna of Nebraska. We restrict the term Ricardo Fauna to collections obtained from above the prominent basalts. The fauna of this part of the Ricardo Formation is represented by the taxa that were best known to Merriam (1919): *Cormohipparion occidentale* (formerly *Hipparion mohavense* following MacFadden 1984), *Pliohippus tantalus*, "*Tomarctus*" *robustus*, *Barbourofelis osborni*, *Ustatochoerus californicus*, and *Cosoryx*. These taxa suggest correlation with the Minnechaduza Fauna of Nebraska. The highest Ricardo assemblage, the Dove Springs Fauna, is of Montediablan age, with *Hipparion forcei*, "*Pliohippus*" *leardi*, *Epicyon aphobus* (close to *E. haydeni*), and *Plioceros*, all of which equate with the late Clarendonian faunas of the upper part of the Ash Hollow Formation of north-central Nebraska. The Ricardo sequence seems to overlap the Cerrotejonian and Montediablan faunas of the Pacific border and fill the gap between those assemblages (Whistler 1969).

An important, but undescribed, early Hemphillian fauna has been collected from the Bedrock Springs Formation exposed in the Lava Mountains just south of the Garlock fault and northeast of the Randsburg mining district (Smith 1964; Dibblee 1967). The fauna, herein termed the Lava Mountains Fauna, is known from twenty-four sites most concentrated in the lower third of the formation whose thickness exceeds 500 feet (152 m). Tentative identifications (Lewis, in Smith 1964; slightly modified by RHT) of the taxa include *Hypolagus*, cf. *Neotomodon*, *Vulpes*, *Osteoborus*, "*Pliohippus*" cf. *leardi*, cf. *Aphelops*, *Megatylopus*, *Hemiauchenia*, and cf. *Sphenophalos*, indicating an early Hemphillian age.

A late Hemphillian fauna from the western Mojave Desert region, the Warren Local Fauna, is known from outcrops of the Horned Toad Formation exposed adjacent to the Garlock fault on the flanks of the Tehachapi Mountains near the town of Mojave. A faunal list of the assemblage was recently published by May (1981) and includes *Repomys gustelyi*, cf. *Agriotherium*, *Osteoborus* cf. *cyonoides*, *Machairodus* cf. *coloradensis*, *Dinohippus* cf. *edensis*, *Teleoceras* cf. *fossiger*, *Pliomastodon vexillarius*, and "*Cuvieronius*" aff. *edensis*, suggesting correlation with such late Hemphillian West Coast assemblages as the Pinole and Mount Eden (not shown on fig. 6.2), although May and Repenning (1982) adduce evidence that the Warren Local Fauna is significantly older than the latter. A late Hemphillian age, closely similar to the Coffee Ranch Local Fauna of Texas, is supported by the large mammal fauna.

E. Western Nevada. The record of fossil mammals

---

[6] "*Ustatochoerus medius mohavensis*" of Schultz and Falkenbach (1941) is now recognized as a species of *Mediochoerus*, a rare taxon also recorded from the Hemingfordian and early Barstovian of western Nebraska. Schultz and Falkenbach (1941, p. 32) state that the type of "*U. m. mohavensis*" was obtained from the "'*Hemicyon* Stratum' of the First Division" (i.e., within the stratigraphic range of the Barstow Fauna of this report), but the field records give no data to substantiate this.

in the Great Basin essentially begins in the Barstovian after the initiation of the major phase of Basin and Range faulting. Fragmentary remains representing pre-Barstovian faunas are known within the state,[7] but these are not geochronologically important at this time.

The best-known sequence of late Tertiary mammal faunas in Nevada are those of the west-central part of the state (Esmeralda and Mineral counties) where a number of radiometric dates help to calibrate the faunal sequence established by physical stratigraphy. In the San Antonio Range north of the Tonopah Mining District, the Tonopah Local Fauna from the Siebert Tuff (Henshaw 1942) represents a Barstovian assemblage including *"Merychippus calamarius," Hypohippus* cf. *affinus,* *"Tomarctus" kelloggi, Aelurodon asthenostylus, Paracosoryx loxocerus,* and *Meryceros hookwayi.* This assemblage lacks Proboscidea and oreodonts, but it otherwise equates best with younger Barstovian faunas.

Northwest of Tonopah on the northern flanks of Cedar Mountain, thick sediments usually equated with the Esmeralda Formation preserve both Barstovian and Clarendonian faunas in stratigraphic superposition. The Barstovian Stewart Spring Fauna (Stirton 1939b) is generalized in this review to include a number of sites (University of California localities 2027, V5570, V5915, and V6020) of close stratigraphic relationship but disparate composition so that the total assemblage is not so biased by the ecology at a single site (e.g., the "Stewart Spring fauna" of Stirton [1939b] mainly represents the small mammals of pond and streambank). This composite includes *Tardontia nevadanus, Anchitheriomys,* *"Monosaulax"* cf. *pansus, "Tomarctus"* cf. *kelloggi, Aelurodon, "Merychippus"* cf. *californicus* or *sumani, Merychippus brevidontus,* Proboscidea, and *Paracosoryx loxocerus.* The presence of Proboscidea and the stage of evolution of the horses suggest equivalence with the Barstow Fauna; the merycodonts and carnivores suggest correlation with the Tonopah Local Fauna.

Sites producing Clarendonian mammals at Cedar Mountain occur in the Esmeralda Formation stratigraphically above the Stewart Spring Fauna. These are grouped as the Cedar Mountain Local Fauna, which, together with a correlative local fauna from Fish Lake Valley to the south, have been combined under the term Fish Lake Valley Fauna following Mawby (1965, 1968a, 1968b). The composite assemblage includes the following larger mammals: *"Eucastor" dividerus, Epicyon* cf. *saevus* (identified as *"Aelurodon mortifer"* by Kitts 1957), *Aelurodon taxoides, Leptarctus, Barbourofelis, Megabelodon minor, Hypohippus nevadanus, Megahippus* cf. *matthewi, Cormohipparion* cf. *occidentale, Cosoryx* cf. *cerroensis, Paracosoryx* cf. *loxocerus,* and *Merycodus.* The abundant micromammals from these sites, dominated by cricetid and heteromyid rodents, have been studied by Mawby (1965) for the Cedar Mountain Local Fauna and by Hall (1930a, 1930b), Clark et al. (1964), and Suthard (1966) for the Fish Lake Valley Local Fauna. These rich assemblages differ somewhat in composition from Clarendonian faunas elsewhere, but the horses and carnivores seem to correlate best with early Clarendonian faunas of the Great Plains.

Radiometric dating indicates correlation of the Fish Lake Valley Fauna with the undescribed Coal Valley Fauna from the Aldrich Station and lower part of the Coal Valley formations exposed along the East Walker River northwest of Cedar Mountain. This assemblage (Stirton 1939b; Axelrod 1956; Macdonald and Pelletier 1958) includes *Epicyon* cf. *saevus,* cf. *Rhynchotherium, Hipparion tehonense, "Pliohippus,"* and *Cormohipparion,* which suggests a Cerrotejonian or early Clarendonian age.

Higher in the Coal Valley Formation (*sensu* Gilbert and Reynolds 1973), in rocks formerly designated the "Smiths Valley beds," scattered sites exposed along the West Walker River on the north slope of the Pine Grove Hills and in Wilson Canyon have yielded the Smiths Valley Fauna (Wilson 1936, Macdonald 1959). The composite fauna includes *Dipoides* cf. *stirtoni, Pliosaccomys dubius, Pliozapus solus, "Osteoborus," Indarctos nevadanus, Machairodus, Barbourofelis fricki* (Macdonald and Macdonald 1976), *Eomellivora, "Pliohippus"* cf. *spectans,* and *Pliomastodon nevadanus.* A Hemphillian age is indicated by this suite of taxa whose relationships with early and medial Hemphillian faunas of the Great Plains is suggested by the horses and carnivores.

F. Columbia Plateau, Oregon. The richly fossiliferous sediments of that portion of the Columbia Plateau traversed by the John Day River and tributaries have been known since the last century, but biostratigraphic investigation of these rocks has only begun in recent years. Merriam and Sinclair's (1907) pioneer study of the John Day Formation is now superseded by the work of Fisher and Rensberger (1972).

Radiometric and faunal evidence indicates that the John Day Formation extends from the Chadronian through Arikareean and into early Hemingfordian time. The John Day "Fauna" of previous authors probably is

---

[7] The best represented is the Rizzi Ranch Local Fauna (Repenning 1966) of north-central Nevada (not shown on fig. 6.2) with *Meniscomys, Capacikala,* and ?*Paciculus,* which can be correlated with the *Meniscomys* Concurrent Range-Zone within the John Day Formation, Oregon.

confined to the rocks above the Big Basin Member.[8] The *Diceratherium* and *Promerycochoerus* zones are partly sequential as stated in the early literature, but they overlap broadly just as the zeolitic green Turtle Cove Member overlaps the nonzeolitic buff Kimberly Member from which these faunal units were typified. Merriam and Sinclair (1909, pp. 184, 191) also recognized a third faunal horizon in the "gravels and tuffs at the top of the Upper John Day" (equivalent to Fisher and Rensberger's [1972] Haystack Valley Member), which contains *Mylagaulodon angulatus*, *Protapirus*, and "*Paratylopus*" *cameloides*.

In a series of contributions, Rensberger (1971, 1973, 1983) has detailed the systematics and biostratigraphy of certain geomyoid and aplodontid rodents in the John Day Formation. His studies have led to the definition (see especially Fisher and Rensberger 1972) and characterization of a suite of concurrent range-zones based on these rodents and some other taxa within the John Day Formation. The lowest chronostratigraphic unit, the *Meniscomys* Concurrent Range-Zone, begins somewhat beneath the Picture Gorge Ignimbrite (ash bed 30 in fig. 6.2, approx. 26.0 Ma) and extends above the Deep Creek Tuff to incorporate the *Pleurolicus* Partial Range-Zone in which no *Meniscomys* are known to occur in the John Day. This zone is also characterized by the earliest North American occurrence of the aplodontid *Allomys*, the first appearance (in the upper part of the zone) of *Palaeocastor* in the Oregon record (a derived species relative to those from the lower Arikaree Group of the Great Plains), and the first appearance (at the base of the zone) of *Promerycochoerus* (an older record for the genus than in the Great Plains). The last North American primate, *Ekgmowechasala*, occurs in the lower part of the *Meniscomys* Concurrent Range-Zone in Oregon. The base of the *Entoptychus-Gregorymys* Concurrent Range-Zone lies just above the highest stratigraphic occurrence of *Pleurolicus* in the John Day Formation and extends into the base of the Haystack Valley Member of the John Day. The geographic restriction of *Entoptychus* to strata west of the continental divide necessitated joint typification with *Gregorymys* known only to the east of the divide in a comparable stratigraphic position. In Oregon, this zone contains *Promerycochoerus*, and the upper limit of the zone records the last local appearance of *Entoptychus*, *Allomys*, and *Paleocastor*. *Promerycochoerus* ranges through the highest John Day zone, the *Mylagaulodon* Concurrent Range-Zone, which contains

the limited Oregon occurrence of *Schizodontomys*, blastomerycine moschid artiodactyls, and perhaps the advanced meniscomyine *Sewellelodon*.

The correlation chart (fig. 6.2) attempts to diagram the revised physical stratigraphy and to indicate the limits of the concurrent range-zones proposed by Rensberger (see legend for fig. 6.2). These biostratigraphic units are proving to be of considerable value in correlating the John Day with other sequences in the northern Rocky Mountains (Montana, Rasmussen 1973; Rich and Rasmussen 1973; Rensberger 1981; Idaho, Nichols 1976) and, to a more limited extent, with the northern Great Plains (South Dakota, Fisher and Rensberger 1972). Resolution of some vexing correlation problems (e.g., Schultz and Falkenbach 1968, pp. 194 ff.) appears to be at hand.

West of the John Day Valley on the eastern flank of the Cascade Range near Warm Springs, Jefferson County, Oregon, higher horizons in the John Day Formation are exposed yielding the Warm Springs Local Fauna (Woodburne and Robinson 1977; revised identifications by L. Dingus, pers. com., 1978), including *Archaeohippus*, *Parahippus*, *Cynorca*, *Michenia*, *Merycochoerus*, *Merychyus*, and *Bouromeryx*, taxa that agree best with faunas from the Runningwater Formation of Nebraska.

The Picture Gorge Basalt of the Columbia Basalt Group unconformably overlies the John Day Formation and disconformably underlies and intertongues with the Mascall Formation in its type area. The fauna of the Mascall Formation, long confused with that from the John Day, and especially with the overlying Rattlesnake Formation, has been completely revised by Downs (1956). Downs grouped the material from the type area in Picture Gorge with assemblages from distant sites on the Crooked River and near Gateway as his Mascall Fauna, and this is the sense in which we use the term here. This fauna is characterized by *Tomarctus rurestris* (close to *T. hippophagus* of the Lower Snake Creek Fauna, Nebraska), *Amphicyon* cf. *sinapius*, *Leptarctus oregonensis*, *Desmatippus avus*, *Archaeohippus ultimus*, "*Merychippus*" *isonesus* (= "*M. seversus*," *sensu* Downs 1956), *Ticholeptus obliquidens*, *Miolabis transmontanus*, and *Dromomeryx borealis* (all species listed have their holotypes from Mascall). Notably absent are any remains of the Proboscidea from any of the twenty-five sites that produced the Mascall Fauna.

In southeastern Oregon, the Owyhee Basalt, also a member of the Columbia Basalt Group, and its associated rhyolites disconformably underlie and intertongue with volcaniclastic sediments of the Sucker Creek Formation (equivalent to the Deer Butte Formation of Kittleman et al. [1965], *fide* Geldsetzer [1966]) which contain the

---

[8] The Big Basin Member is approximately equivalent to the "lower John Day" of Merriam and Sinclair (1907) in which only fragmentary entelodont remains have been found.

essentially synchronous Sucker Creek (Scharf 1935) and Skull Springs (Gazin 1932, Shotwell 1968) faunas. These large assemblages are compositionally similar to the Mascall Fauna and are characterized by the horse *"Merychippus" isonesus* in association with *Merychippus brevidontus, Desmatippus avus, Hypohippus* cf. *osborni, Euoplocyon, "Tomarctus" kelloggi, Tomarctus rurestris, Hemicyon, Amphicyon* cf. *frendens, Dromomeryz borealis, Rakomeryx, Ticholeptus obliquidens,* and *Paracosoryx*. Proboscidean remains are recorded from the Sucker Creek Fauna and the Red Basin Local Fauna. The latter assemblage and the correlative Quartz Basin Local Fauna compose the Skull Springs Fauna following Shotwell (1968). The Mascall, Sucker Creek, and Skull Springs faunas agree best with the Lower Snake Creek Fauna of Nebraska and the Flint Creek and McKanna Spring faunas of Montana. The presence of Proboscidea in the Sucker Creek and Skull Springs faunas may represent an earlier appearance of the group in the northwest or more likely may indicate that more precise correlation of these assemblages may be with faunas slightly younger than the Lower Snake Creek. Support for the latter interpretation is provided by recent radiometric (Bottomley and York 1976) and paleomagnetic (Watkins and Baksi 1974) studies of the Owyhee Basalt which suggest that its age may be significantly younger than the Picture Gorge Basalt (approximately 14 Ma vs. 15 Ma, respectively), and we have indicated this alternative on figure 6.2 (see data in Appendix A). Critical comparison of these faunas is needed.

In the Juntura Basin, Shotwell et al. (1963) have described a Clarendonian through Hemphillian succession that can be calibrated radiometrically. The Black Butte Local Fauna from the top of the Juntura Formation agrees best with late Clarendonian faunas of the Ash Hollow Formation of Nebraska (*Hystricops, Leptarctus* ["*Pliotaxidea,*" Shotwell 1963], *Platybelodon, Ustatochoerus* and *Megatylopus*), with Montediablan faunas of coastal California, and with certain western Great Basin assemblages (Brady Pocket and Nightingale Road local faunas [Macdonald 1956a], Truckee Formation, Nevada; not shown on fig. 6.2). Within the overlying Drewsey Formation, the Bartlett Mountain Local Fauna, along with the Otis Basin and Drinkwater local faunas in succession beneath it, resembles other early Hemphillian sites in the Great Basin (e.g., Smiths Valley and Thousand Creek faunas) and the Great Plains (e.g., Kimball fauna), particularly those containing *Dipoides stirtoni, Paramicrotoscoptes, Pliosaccomys, Amebelodon,* and *Sphenophalos*.

Lying unconformably above the Mascall Formation, the Rattlesnake Formation of the John Day Basin has been the source of Hemphillian faunas since the early days of collecting in Oregon. Earlier collectors often mixed the Rattlesnake and Mascall fossils or failed to note that the younger material sometimes occurred as float on the older beds directly below. Merriam and Sinclair (1907) formalized the name for these rocks, and later Merriam et al. (1925) gave a comprehensive description of the rocks and their fauna. The Rattlesnake Fauna equates with early to medial Hemphillian faunas of the Great Basin and Great Plains in containing Megalonychidae, *Dipoides* cf. *stirtoni, Indarctos oregonensis, "Pliohippus" spectans, Hipparion, Neohipparion* cf. *leptode* (a member of the *eurystyle* group), and *Sphenophalos*.

Northern Rocky Mountains

G-H. Montana. Fossil mammal remains were discovered in the intermontane basins of central and western Montana during the last century and were first described by Cope and Scott. In the last decade of the nineteenth century, Earl Douglass (University of Montana and later the Carnegie Museum) began a systematic program of exploration of these basins. In later years Douglass's work was carried forward by J. Leroy Kay (Carnegie Museum) and parties from other institutions, notably the University of Michigan and the Frick Laboratory. Recently, one of us (RWF) and students at the University of Montana have been engaged in a detailed study of the stratigraphy, sedimentology, biostratigraphy, and paleoecology of these basin deposits.

At first consideration, the scattered exposures of Tertiary rocks in the intermontane basins of the northern Rockies would seem to be of limited potential for developing a useful biochronology for any geologically significant span of time. The record as developed in the literature of the area supports the idea of the occurrence of isolated local faunas whose temporal placement depends on comparison with standard sequences outside Montana. However, recent studies (many of which are still in progress) show great promise for the development of a local biostratigraphy and hence a local biochronology supported by stratigraphic evidence within the intermontane deposits themselves.

The importance of the Montana Tertiary faunas has been recognized from the beginning of work on them. Their zoogeographic and temporal relationships with the John Day region to the west and Great Plains to the east placed these faunas in a critical position for resolution of the correlation problems arising from provincialism in western North America.

Regional geologic study and comparison of intermontane basin fills have led to the recognition that most of these basin deposits can be divided into two groups of strata separated by a regional unconformity (Kuenzi and Richard 1969, Rasmussen 1973). This unconformity is centered in Hemingfordian time, resulting in the loss of most of the rock and faunal records of that age. In some areas, the hiatus represented by the unconformity is enlarged to eliminate strata of Arikareean age as well. In only a few areas have Whitneyan faunas been recognized, although, in some areas, deposits with Orellan faunas grade conformably up into those with Arikareean assemblages. Across the regional unconformity the oldest deposits are of early Barstovian age, and in a few areas these are succeeded by Clarendonian and Hemphillian faunas within a single body of rocks. In the paragraphs that follow, we shall emphasize those areas with the most continuous records rather than those with well-known fossil deposits.

Arikareen faunas have been known from the intermontane basins from the earliest collections, although in the early work of Cope and Scott these were usually mixed with remains representing younger assemblages (e.g., the "fauna of the Deep River beds"). One of the achievements of Douglass and later authors was the recognition of the stratigraphic separation of these faunas (e.g., the separation of the Fort Logan from the Deep River faunas by Douglass [1903]). It is only in recent years (Rasmussen 1969, 1977; Rensberger 1981), however, that a local biostratigraphy has been developed for a portion of the Arikareean of Montana.

Tertiary rocks exposed in the interconnected Flint Creek, Clark Fork, and Deer Lodge valleys just west of the continental divide in Granite and Powell counties contain one of the more useful faunal sequences. Douglass (1903) discovered several of these sites, including one containing the Arikareean fauna from three miles east of Drummond, later exploited by other workers (Hibbard and Keenmon 1950; Macdonald 1956b; Riel 1964) and used by Konizeski and Donohoe (1958) and Rasmussen (1977) as the type section of the Cabbage Patch beds. Detailed study of these rocks by Rasmussen (1969, 1977) has produced a biostratigraphy that can be compared with those being developed in the John Day and northern Great Plains regions. Early Arikareean mammals from the base of the Cabbage Patch succession include *Agnotocastor, Mesocyon, Desmatochoerus, Megoreodon,* the anthracothere *Kukusepasutanka,* and the leptomerycid *Pronodens. Diceratherium* cf. *armatum, Meniscomys, Pleurolicus,* and *Capatanka* occur in the middle of the section. Locally abundant rodents in the middle part of the Cabbage Patch section indicate correlation with the upper part of the *Meniscomys* Con-

current Range-Zone (that bearing *Pleurolicus;* Rensberger 1973, Rich and Rasmussen 1973) of medial Arikareean age. Higher horizons within rocks correlated with the Cabbage Patch beds in outcrops in the Deer Lodge Valley on the Tavenner Ranch (Konizeski 1957, Wood and Konizeski 1965) contain *Gregorymys douglassi.* These levels are correlative with the *Gregorymys-Entoptychus* Concurrent Range-Zone (Rich and Rasmussen 1973). At this locality, the range of meniscomyine rodents overlaps that of *Gregorymys; Eutypomys* also is present, as in comparable levels in South Dakota (Monroe Creek, Macdonald 1972). Thus, the Cabbage Patch succession equates with that within the *Meniscomys* and *Entoptychus-Gregorymys* concurrent range-zones of the "Middle John Day" and the Gering or Sharps through Monroe Creek sequences of Nebraska and South Dakota. It may extend into the hiatus between the Monroe Creek and Harrison formations. It is also interesting to note the absence of leptauchenine oreodonts in these Montana faunas west of the present divide. In that sense, they show faunal similarity with the John Day, but the lack of *Entoptychus* and presence of *Gregorymys* relates the microfauna to the Great Plains.

Apparently equivalent early and later Arikareean faunas are known to the east of the continental divide in the Missouri River Valley (Canyon Ferry) and along the Smith (= Deep) River. The larger mammals of these faunas (most recently reviewed by Koerner [1940]; not shown on fig. 6.2) include *Mesocyon* (= *Cynodesmus*), *Agnotocastor, Desmatochoerus, Promerycochoerus* (*Pseudopromerycochoerus*), *Mesoreodon,* and *Pronodens.* They also include the leptauchinines *Cyclopidius, Pseudocyclopidius, Sespia,* and *Pithecistes* (Schultz and Falkenbach 1968), genera common in the Gering and Monroe Creek faunas in the Great Plains.

Recent studies by Rensberger (1979, 1981) in the Deep River Formation have further elucidated the succession of aplodontoid rodents of that basin. Only local stratigraphic associations could be observed, so the composite biochronology for species of the meniscomyine aplodontid *Niglarodon* was determined by stage-of-evolution means. This was compared with the actual biostratigraphic arrangement of a *Niglarodon* species succession in the Lemhi Valley of eastern Idaho (Nichols 1976) and with phyletic trends in the biostratigraphic sequence of the related *Meniscomys* species in the John Day Formation of Oregon. The base of the Deep River succession contains a primitive *Niglarodon* comparable with primitive *Meniscomys* (the sister taxon) and thus can be correlated with the lower *Meniscomys* Concurrent Range-Zone of Oregon, whereas the top of the Montana sequence is represented by an advanced *Niglarodon* in association with *Gregorymys* and *Promylagaulus,* indicating a position within the lower part of the *Entophychus-Gregorymys* Concurrent Range-Zone. These correlations lead to an early to later Arikareean age for the Deep River Formation in part similar to the Cabbage Patch local faunas of Montana west of the continental divide. This conclusion is in agreement with the relationships of the large mammal taxa of the Deep River Formation. This fauna is important historically as noted, but these recent detailed studies indicate that its significance as a biochronologic reference sequence that is located geographically between the Columbia Plateau and Great Plains is capable of considerable further development.

The hiatus characteristic of the Tertiary record in Montana may be narrowed by a few assemblages. Faunas equivalent to those from the Harrison Formation of Nebraska are indicated by part of the sequence in the North Boulder Valley (Douglass 1903, 1907) and outcrops north of Divide (Douglass 1907) which contain *Hypsiops* (Schultz and Falkenbach 1950, pp. 116, 120), possibly the Blacktail Deer Creek Local Fauna (Hibbard and Keenmon 1950; not shown in fig. 6.2) containing *Promerycochoerus barbouri, Arretotherium arcidens,* "*Monosaulax*" *hesperus,* and the unique occurrence of *Entoptychus* (Rensberger 1971) east of the continental divide.

Faunas from the east side of the valley of the North Boulder River were discovered by Douglass (1903, near the now-abandoned Cold Spring Post Office), and collections were made there by Matthew and Thomson in 1902 (Douglass 1907) and Falkenbach in 1936, 1942, 1950–51, and 1954. Only the oreodonts have been described, including the type specimens of the phenacocoelines *Hypsiops brachymelis* (Douglass 1907), *Pseudomesoreodon rolli* (Schultz and Falkenbach 1950), ?*P. boulderensis* (Schultz and Falkenbach 1950), and the desmatochoerine *Pseudodesmatochoerus longiceps* (Douglass 1907). Collections in the American Museum of Natural History show that the North Boulder Valley Fauna also includes *Stenomylus* cf. *hitchcocki, Oxydactylus* cf. *lacota,* and *Nanotragulus,* indicating equivalence with the Harrison and possibly earliest Marsland faunas of the Great Plains. Kuenzi and Richard (1969) have indicated that the Tertiary rocks in the North Boulder Valley are continuous with those to the south and west in the Jefferson River Valley. For this reason, the rocks containing the North Boulder Valley Fauna are referred to the Renova Formation (typified in the Jefferson Valley; Kuenzi and Fields 1971).

Above the regional unconformity in the Flint Creek, Clark Fork, and Deer Lodge valleys, a sequence of disconformity-bounded rock units yields faunas representing the Barstovian, Clarendonian, and Hemphillian mammal ages. The Barstovian Flint Creek beds and fauna were discovered by Douglass (1903; Black 1961*b*) and extensions of these rocks have been recognized resting on the Cabbage Patch beds in the Clark Fork Valley (Rasmussen 1969, 1977). The local faunas from these two areas share *Ticholeptus zygomaticus,* but other taxa are dissimilar. However, an early Barstovian age is indicated for these assemblages, and they are grouped as the Flint Creek Fauna in this summary. Affinity with the Mascall Fauna is indicated by *T. zygomaticus,* "*Merychippus*" *relictus, Archaeohippus ultimus, Desmatippus, Tomarctus* cf. *rurestris,* and *Dromomeryx borealis. Brachycrus laticeps* also occurs in the Flint Creek Fauna; a genus is not presently known from the Columbia Plateau.

Gravels overlapping the Flint Creek equivalent in the northern Clark Fork Valley (Rasmussen 1969, 1973) have yielded the Bert Creek Local Fauna, including *Pliohippus, Megahippus,* and *Hypohippus* in association with *Merycodus* and Proboscidea. This fauna equates with the Burge or Minnechaduza faunas of north central Nebraska.

To the southeast, in the Deer Lodge Valley, Konizeski (1957) has described the Deer Lodge Fauna from scattered sites within gravels overlying correlatives of the Flint Creek and Cabbage Patch beds. The Deer Lodge Fauna is the youngest Tertiary assemblage recorded from Montana and includes *Dipoides stirtoni, Amebelodon* cf. *hicksi,* "*Nannippus,*" *Procamelus,* and *Plioceros* cf. *blicki,* which are also found in Great Plains faunas of early Hemphillian age.

Comparable later Miocene faunal successions are present elsewhere in Montana. East of the continental divide in the Jefferson River Valley, the strata referred to the Six Mile Creek Formation contains a promising Barstovian-Clarendonian-Hemphillian sequence (Kuenzi and Fields 1971). The superposed local faunas shown in figure 6.2 record the changing horse taxa from "*Merychippus*" *isonesus* ("*Merychippus serversus,*" *sensu* Downs 1951), in the Sant Ranch and Frank Ranch local faunas of early Barstovian age, through "*M. (Protohippus)*" in the Antelope Hills Local Fauna to assemblages with *Hipparion,* "*Nannippus lenticularis,*" *Dinohippus,* and *Merycodus* in the Old Windmill, Old Wagonroad, and Mayflower Mine local faunas. The latter assemblages indicate homotaxis with Valentine through early Ash Hollow faunas of the Great Plains (Clarendonian at the youngest). A comparable sequence may be present in the classic Madison Valley beds southeast of the Jefferson Valley (Douglass 1899, 1903; Dorr 1956). Younger faunas, probably of early Hemphillian age, occur in the adjacent North Silver Star Triangle in pediment remnants between the Jefferson River and local tributaries. Geological mapping (Kuenzi and Fields 1971) has established these outcrops as the youngest part of the Six Mile Creek Formation preserved in this basin.

Matthew's party (Douglass 1907) discovered early Barstovian mammals in the Six Mile Creek Formation exposed in the North Boulder Valley disconformably overlying the Renova Formation with its late Arikareean North Boulder Valley Fauna (see above). This younger fauna, here termed the McKanna Spring Fauna, closely resembles Barstovian assemblages from the Columbia Plateau and Great Basin in containing *Leptarctus* cf. *bozemanensis,* "*Merychippus*" *isonesus,* "*M.*" cf. *intermontanus,* Proboscidea, *Dromomeryx borealis, Rakomeryx kinseyi, Paracosoryx,* and *Merriamoceros.* Close correspondence is also indicated with part of the Madison Valley succession particularly the Anceney Local Fauna (Dorr 1956; not shown on fig. 6.2).

Northern Great Plains

I. Nebraska. Diligent stratigraphic collecting and long study of the Cenozoic deposits so magnificently exposed in Nebraska and adjacent states has made the faunal succession in that area of prime importance in the development of mammalian biochronology. Unfortunately, the results of much of the ongoing work in Nebraska have yet to be published, especially the careful biostratigraphic studies that are needed to refine our present knowledge of the chronological ranges of the various taxa that occur there. At present, a listing of taxa by formational unit is the best that can be done for much of the Nebraska stratigraphic column. Thus the "faunas" bearing the names of certain stratigraphic units must be a composite of all taxa recorded from those units.

Recent study of the Gering Formation of western Nebraska and its fauna has resulted in a revision of the physical stratigraphy (Vondra 1963; Vondra et al. 1969; Swisher 1982), geochronology of the contained volcanic ashes (Evernden et al. 1964, Obradovich et al. 1973), and vertebrate paleontology (Martin 1973, 1974, 1975a; Swisher 1982). The typical exposures of the Gering Formation occur in the Wildcat Ridge near Scottsbluff where parts of several Gering paleovalleys are exposed in superposition. Distinctive volcanic ash and volcaniclastic sediments led Vondra (1963) to the definition of the members shown on figure 6.2. Fission-track and radiometric dating of these ashes suggest that the unit spans at least three million years. Recently, Swisher (1982) has revised the physical stratigraphy of the Gering Formation in the

eastern Wildcat Ridge, allowing a more detailed biostratigraphic treatment of the unit there.

It should be noted that the concept of the Gering Formation followed by Martin (1973, 1974) is that of Vondra (1963), which includes strata in the base of a revised Gering which lie below the Gering-Brule contact most consistently traced by Darton (1899) when he described the unit. The revised boundary does bracket the lowest occurrence of some of the larger mammals that characterize the higher parts of the Gering Formation (especially the leptauchinines). This stratigraphic extension is particularly critical in the vicinity of Redington Gap where the type specimens of *Mesocyon geringensis* and *Sespia marianae* were obtained from the interval in question. At Redington Gap, the rocks included by Vondra (1963) and Vondra et al. (1969) in the base of the revised Gering are stratigraphically continuous with the underlying Brule. They record a gradual upward shift in texture from massive siltstone to massive fine to very fine silty sandstone before they are disconformably truncated by the coarser and more poorly sorted sandstones that represent the Gering of Darton. We have chosen to represent the rocks in question as a part of the Brule Formation on figure 6.2 and to show that the Gering Fauna as presently conceived extends downward into these deposits. An analogous problem is discussed in the case of the Sharps Formation and its faunas (pp. 171–172).

Martin (1973, 1974, 1975a) considered the fauna of the Gering Formation as a unit and correlated it with the assemblage from the upper part of the Sharps Formation of South Dakota (i.e., the "Wounded Knee-Sharps Fauna" of Macdonald [1963, 1970]). Only a few elements of the fauna of the Gering Formation have been described (see Martin 1974 for references). Among them are the cricetid *Paciculus* (possibly from post-Gering strata; Swisher, pers. com., 1982), the geomyid *Tenudomys,* the zapodid *Plesiosminthus,* the enigmatic rodent *Zetamys,* the canid *Mesocyon geringensis,* the nimravid *Nimravus,* and the oreodonts, of which a diverse leptauchinine fauna including hypsodont genera (*Sespia, Megasespia*) are characteristic along with *Desmatochoerus, Mesoreodon,* and *Megoreodon.* Martin (1973) believed that the occurrence of *Meniscomys,* with *Tenudomys,* indicates that the *Meniscomys* Concurrent Range-Zone may extend to older levels in the Great Plains than presently documented in the Columbia Plateau (see Rensberger 1973, 1983), but Swisher (1982) has shown that another aplodontid is represented by this material. *Allomys* does occur higher in the Gering (Swisher 1982), suggesting that the base of the *Meniscomys* Concurrent Range-Zone lies in the younger part of the Gering. The occurrence of *Promylaugaulus* in these upper levels

(Swisher 1982) provides another point of correlation with the *Meniscomys* Concurrent Range-Zone (see Rensberger 1979). Immigrants[9] that first appear within, but not necessarily at the base of, the Gering Formation include the talpine moles, the hedgehog *Ocajila,* the zapodid rodent *Plesiosminthus* (Martin 1973), and, from higher in the unit, *Allomys* (see remarks on the phyletic relationships of allomyines in Rensberger 1983).

The fauna of the Monroe Creek Formation in western Nebraska has not been critically reviewed. Assemblages from the type area of the unit in Monroe Creek Canyon north of Harrison have been described by Peterson (1907). In a recent study of the type area, Hunt (1985) has confirmed Peterson's assignment of the type specimens of the oreodonts *Promerycochoerus carrikeri* and *Phenacocoelus typus* and the beaver *Euhapsis platyceps* to the upper part of the Monroe Creek Formation (*contra* Schultz and Falkenbach [1949, 1950], who attribute the oreodonts to the Harrison Formation). Knowledge of the Monroe Creek Fauna has depended to a large extent on assemblages from correlated rocks in South Dakota ("Lower Rosebud" [in part], Matthew 1907; Wounded Knee-Monroe Creek Fauna of J. R. Macdonald [1963, 1970] and L. Macdonald [1972]; and the Wewela Local Fauna of the Turtle Buttes, Skinner et al. [1968]; not shown on fig. 6.2), and in Wyoming west of the Hartville uplift (Muddy Creek [Niobrara County] of Schultz and Falkenbach's oreodont revisions). The fauna so far identified from the Monroe Creek Formation seems closely allied at the generic level with that from the Gering or Sharps Formation. A few immigrants make their appearance in the Monroe Creek Formation of western Nebraska and adjacent Wyoming and South Dakota, including the hedgehog *Parvericius,* the eomyid rodent *Pseudotheridiomys,* and possibly the mustelid *Promartes* and the chalicothere *Moropus* (see Coombs 1978). The leptauchinine oreodonts have their last occurrence in the Monroe Creek Formation. The appearance of *Stenomylus* camels in the Monroe Creek Formation provides faunal continuity with the succeeding Harrison Fauna.

Recent studies of the Arikaree Group stratigraphy in Sioux County, western Nebraska, by R. M. Hunt, Jr. (1978, 1981, 1985), and associates have served to define the lower limit of the Upper Harrison Formation of Peterson (1907; equivalent to the lower part of the Marsland Formation, *sensu* Schultz 1938) and to establish an objective regional lithostratigraphic characterization of the

Marsland and Harrison formations. As discussed below, the principal biostratigraphic result has been the allocation of the Agate Springs Local Fauna and correlative local faunas (Hunt 1972, 1978, 1985) to the Marsland Formation rather than to the Harrison to which they were traditionally attributed. This significantly alters the concept of the fauna of the Harrison Formation, which had been based chiefly on the local faunas from the Agate Spring quarries. The only significant concentrations of fossils in the Harrison Formation in Sioux County, Nebraska, are those from the *Syndyoceras* Quarry near Agate Spring Ranch and the *Stenomylus* Quarry and Peterson's Quarry A (see Hunt 1972, p. 3), both within the boundaries of the Agate Fossil Beds National Monument.

Along the Pine Ridge escarpment in western Nebraska and the Hat Creek breaks, its western extension into Wyoming, the Harrison Formation presents a virtually unbroken line of exposures. The composite fauna from this outcrop belt is characterized by diversity of flat-incisored beavers (*Palaeocastor, Euhapsis, Capacikala,* and *Capatanka*). *Paleocastor* burrows are preserved as the "*Daimonelix*" typical of the Harrison Formation (Martin and Bennett 1977). The carnivore fauna is generically similar to that of the Monroe Creek: the canid *Phlaocyon* is added to the suite of small borophagines ("*Nothocyon*") and canines (*Leptocyon*); the immigrant procyonid *Zodiolestes,* the mustelid *Oligobunis,* and probably the mustelid *Promartes* appear in the Harrison Formation; and the daphoenine amphicyonid *Temnocyon* is joined by an immigrant amphicyonine, *Daphoenodon,* as the largest carnivores. Nimravids are exceedingly rare at this time in the Great Plains and apparently do not persist into the Marsland. Most of the ungulate genera continue from representatives in the Monroe Creek. Oreodonts reach their maximum diversity; representatives of six subfamilies (*sensu* Schultz and Falkenbach 1968) are recognized and *Phenacocoelus* and *Merychyus* appear. *Syndyoceras,* the earliest synthetocerine protoceratid, appears (Patton and Taylor 1971). *Anchitherium, Parahippus, Moropus, Menoceras, Diceratherium, Dinohyus, Oxydactylus,* and *Stenomylus* are the common larger ungulates.

Peterson (1909, p. 75) designated the exposures along the Niobrara River just east of the state line, in Sioux County, Nebraska, the type section for his Upper Harrison Formation, and in 1907 he listed the fauna from this area. Correlative rocks are widely exposed in adjacent Wyoming south of Lusk in Goshen and Niobrara counties east of the Hartville uplift. In 1938, Schultz applied the name Marsland Formation to these rocks as a replacement term for Peterson's "Upper Harrison,"

[9] The record of the rhinoceratid *Menoceras* mentioned by Martin (1974, 1975) cannot be substantiated. It seems that the genus first appears within the Harrison Formation (Hunt 1985).

believing that these deposits were the direct equivalent of those exposed along the northern edge of the Box Butte Table south of Marsland in adjacent Box Butte County. Some subsequent revisors (McKenna 1965) have therefore maintained that the name Marsland must be equated with the Upper Harrison of Peterson. We follow this recommendation here. Yatkola (1978, pp. 20–23) discusses an alternative interpretation in which the Upper Harrison (the informal Lower Member of Yatkola) and the Runningwater Formation of Cook (1965) are considered members of the Marsland Formation in agreement with the usage of Schultz (1938).

Detailed stratigraphic and petrologic study of the Marsland Formation now under way by Hunt (1978, 1981, 1985; he continues to use the term "Upper Harrison Formation," *sensu* Peterson 1907) has defined the lower contact of the Marsland as a regionally traceable disconformity marked by paleosol development or the incision of stream channels at the top of the Harrison Formation. The Agate Springs and Harper quarries represent local accumulations of bones in gray to white, tuffaceous, calcareous, sandy ephemeral stream channel deposits just above the disconformity (Hunt 1978, 1985). Upward in the Marsland Formation, massive-appearing, pinkish buff, silty sandstones characterize the unit most typically in the concept of Peterson and many later authors. Fossils are more common in this part of the section, although few concentrations have been found. The composition of the fauna shows little change through the unit as far as now known, and it will be treated as a unit pending more detailed biostratigraphic study.

For the oreodonts (Schultz and Falkenbach 1968, chart 16, pp. 420–421), the hiatus between the Harrison and Marsland formations marks a profound drop in diversity, whereas other forms (e.g., rodents, Robinson 1970, p. 89; stenomyline camels, Frick and Taylor 1968) maintain continuity between these units. The Marsland Fauna thus shows a clear biological relationship to the Harrison Fauna. Some taxa of North American origin which are characteristic and abundant in these and later strata appear for the first time in the Marsland, for example, *Cynarctoides, Merycochoerus,* and the protolabine camels (*Michenia*). Important immigrants appearing in the Marsland Formation include a representative of the ursid subfamily Hemicyoninae (*Cephalogale*), the amphicyonids *Cynelos* and *Ysengrinia* (Hunt 1972), and among the artiodactyls, the blastomerycine moschid *Blastomeryx,* the dromomerycid *Barbouromeryx,* the antilocaprid *Paracosoryx* (the latter three taxa revised from Cook 1934).

The increasing appearance of immigrants representing a broad ecological spectrum foreshadows the larger invasion recorded in the succeeding Runningwater Formation. Changes in the endemic groups also foreshadow the fauna of the Runningwater, and for this reason, the Marsland Fauna seems to connect the assemblages of later Arikareean time with those characteristic of the Hemingfordian.

Included in Schultz's (1938) concept of the Marsland Formation were coarse stream channel fills carrying plutonic and metamorphic debris and associated deposits that rest with strong disconformity on the Harrison and Monroe Creek formations in exposures along the edge of the Box Butte Table, which forms the southern wall of the Niobrara River Valley south of Marsland in Box Butte County, Nebraska. Later, Schultz (1941) selected these rocks as the type section of his Marsland Formation, ignoring the type section already proposed (Peterson 1909, p. 75) for the supposedly equivalent Upper Harrison. The basal channel fill of the Marsland succession southwest of Marsland was later used as the type section of the Runningwater Formation by Cook (1965), and that name became available for these post-Upper Harrison (i.e., post-Marsland) rocks. We use the term Runningwater Formation in the latter sense (see McKenna 1965 and Yatkola 1978 for opposing conclusions).

Fossil mammals have been collected from the type section of the Runningwater Formation and from many concentrations of fossils discovered in correlative rocks in Box Butte and Dawes counties, Nebraska, by the University of Nebraska and Frick Laboratory parties. Outlying occurrences of the same faunas occur at the Bridgeport quarries (Morrill County, Nebraska, Stecher et al. 1962), *Aletomeryx* Quarry (Antelope Creek, Sheridan County, discovered by Lull [1920]), the Flint Hill Quarry, Bennett County, South Dakota (Harksen and Macdonald 1967), and at Quarry A within the upper part of the Martin Canyon beds of Logan County, northeastern Colorado (Wilson 1960).

The composite Runningwater Fauna has a chronofaunal relationship with the fauna of the underlying Marsland; *Merychyus, Merycochoerus,* and *Michenia* continue to be the most abundant artiodactyls and *Parahippus, Moropus,* and *Menoceras* the most characteristic perissodactyls. A number of immigrant groups appear in these rocks, including ochotonids (*Oreolagus*), the carnivores *Amphicyon,* Mustelinae ("*Miomustela*"), Leptarctinae (*Leptarctus* and *Craterogale*), and Procyoninae (*Edaphocyon, Amphictis*), the phocid *Potamotherium,* and the dromomerycine artiodactyl *Aletomeryx.*

For many years, the stratigraphic position of the "Box Butte Member of the Sheep Creek Formation" of Cady (1940) in Box Butte County, Nebraska, has been controversial (see McKenna 1965). Galusha (1975) has clarified its status as a distinct lithostratigraphic unit. Its demonstrable stratigraphic relationships are shown by arrows on the correlation chart (fig. 6.2). The mammal fauna obtained from the Box Butte, although clearly related to that of the Sheep Creek, represents an earlier stage in the evolution of the latest Hemingfordian faunas that succeed it. The Box Butte Formation was deposited after an important hiatus in which the Marsland-Runningwater chronofauna was modified by evolution, extinction, and the appearance of new elements, including abundant hypsodont horses (*Merychippus s.l.*) and rhinos, *Mylagaulus* rodents, *Brachycrus* oreodonts, cranioceratine dromomerycids, and large camelids (*Aepycamelus*). Members of the earlier chronofauna do continue, particularly among the Carnivora (*Amphicyon, Tomarctus, Cynarctoides, Leptocyon, Leptarctus,* and *Brachypsalis*), but some older groups make their last appearance in the Box Butte (the dromomerycid *Barbouromeryx* and the camelid *Oxydactylus*). The rhino *Aphelops* represents the only immigrant known to occur in the Box Butte Formation.[10]

In western Sioux County, on the divide between the North Platte and Niobrara drainages, a small area at the confluence of the Sheep and Snake creeks has contributed very large collections of fossil remains that have been of great importance to our knowledge of the late Tertiary faunas of the northern Great Plains. A detailed historical and stratigraphic review of this classic area has been completed by Skinner et al. (1977). At the base of the succession, lying in a paleovalley cut into the Harrison and Marsland formations, is the Sheep Creek Formation and Fauna of Matthew and Cook (1909). Matthew (1924), Cook and Cook (1933), and Skinner et al. (1977) list the large fauna from these rocks which has become a standard for comparison and the definitive assemblage characterizing the close of Hemingfordian time (Wood et al. 1941). A few immigrants make their appearance in the Sheep Creek Formation, including the Felidae (*Pseudaelurus*), musteline mustelids (*Miomustela, Plionictis,* and *Sthenictis*), and lutrine mustelids (*Mionictis*). No direct superpositional evidence is available for the stratigraphic relationship of the Sheep Creek and the Box Butte formations. The faunas of the Sheep Creek and Box Butte formations are closely related but that from

the Sheep Creek is represented by more advanced taxa in most groups.

Significant faunal change occurs between the Sheep Creek and directly overlying Olcott Formation (Skinner et al. 1977, new name for the Lower Snake Creek beds of Matthew 1924), but many groups continue and thus preserve the essential chronofaunal relationship of the Sheep Creek and Lower Snake Creek faunas. But most of the Lower Snake Creek species show perceivable change over their Sheep Creek representatives. No immigrant groups occur in the collections from the Olcott Formation, but correlative horizons elsewhere produce *Hemicyon* (*Plithocyon*) (Green Hills Fauna, California, Skull Springs Fauna, Oregon, undescribed fauna of the Skull Ridge Member, Tesuque Formation, New Mexico; Galusha and Blick 1971, Tedford 1982). Despite intensive large-scale collecting in the many Olcott Formation channel fills, no remains of Proboscidea have been found. Correlatives of the Lower Snake Creek Fauna (e.g., at Survey Quarry) occur in the Sand Canyon beds ("Sand Canyon Member, of the Sheep Creek Formation," Dawes County, as described by Elias 1942) that directly overlie the Box Butte Formation. The *Merychippus* and *Brachycrus* from this unit have been mentioned by Elias (1942, p. 129). The undescribed fauna from Observation Quarry in the Sand Canyon beds may fill the gap between the faunas of the Sheep Creek and Olcott formations.

A long hiatus separates the Olcott Formation from the overlying Snake Creek Formation with its Clarendonian and Hemphillian faunas. This hiatus is partially filled by the Valentine Formation exposed along the Niobrara River in north-central Nebraska. Recently, Skinner and Johnson (1984) have been able to demonstrate that the Norden Bridge Fauna occurs in a previously unrecognized member of the Valentine Formation. This unit, the Cornell Dam Member, consists of sands and tuffaceous silts that disconformably rest on the Rosebud Formation and older rock units and are, in turn, conformably overlain by the nonvolcanic Crookston Bridge Member of the Valentine Formation. Of the mammals, only the rodents (Klingener 1968) and erinaceids (Rich 1981) have so far been described from the Norden Bridge Local Fauna, and these include the latest record of the erinaceine *Parvericius* and a late Tertiary occurrence in the Great Plains of the aplodontid *Allomys,* a genus whose youngest occurrence is late Arikareean in the Columbia Plateau. Skinner and Voorhies (1977) have listed the larger mammals and note that the Proboscidea are represented. The horse fauna includes *Megahippus* cf. *mckennai* and is otherwise similar in composition to

---

[10] A form similar to *Brachypotherium americanum* (Yatkola and Tanner 1979) from the early Hemingfordian of northeastern Colorado is suggested by Galusha's description (1975, p. 60) of F:AM 95544 from Dry Creek Prospect A in the Red Valley Member of the Box Butte Formation.

the Niobrara River Fauna of the Crookston Bridge Member of the overlying Valentine Formation. The amphicyonid *Pseudocyon* has its first North American record in this fauna. *Leptarctus, Ramoceros, Cranioceras,* and teleoceratine rhinos also occur in the Norden Bridge Quarry.

The lithostratigraphy and rock and faunal nomenclature of the Valentine Formation have had a complex history most usefully and recently reviewed by Skinner et al. (1968) and Skinner and Johnson (1984). Rich fossil collections have been made from all the members of this unit, and these show an overall chronofaunal unity despite perceivable change in most of the groups as the Valentine Formation is ascended. The largest discontinuity occurs between the Devils Gulch and Burge members where a disconformity breaks the stratigraphic section. Published details useful in faunal analysis of this sequence are essentially limited to the lowermost and uppermost units of the succession: the Niobrara River Fauna from the Railway and Crookston Bridge quarries in the Crookston Bridge Member and the Burge Fauna from the Gordon Creek and Burge quarries in the Burge Member (see Skinner et al. 1968; Webb 1969a; Skinner and Johnson 1984). The faunas of the intervening Devils Gulch Member help fill the gap and establish taxonomic continuity. The characteristic elements of this chronofauna include conspicuous gomphotheriid mastodonts; *Eucastor* beavers; the canids *Aelurodon, Strobodon, Tomarctus,* and *Cynarctus*; and horses that reach their maximum generic diversity by Burge time. *Pseudhipparion retrusum* is common as are early species of *Calippus, Pliohippus, Cormohipparion, Protohippus,* and *Dinohippus,* associated with late species of genera presently grouped under "*Merychippus*" and the large anchitheriines *Hypohipus* and *Megahippus*. The oreodonts include only *Ustatochoerus*. Camels are diverse, including *Protolabis, Aepycamelus,* and the earliest record of *Procamelus,* cranioceratine dromomerycids; *Longirostromeryx* (Blastomerycidae); and a variety of late merycodontine antilocaprids occur (*Paracosoryx* and *Merycodus* continue and *Ramoceros* and *Cosoryx* first appear). Immigrant groups that enter the record at this time are few. The gelocid *Pseudoceras* is first recorded in the Burge and the amphicyonid *Pseudocyon* makes its first appearance in the Norden Bridge Local Fauna in the Cornell Dam Member at the base of the Valentine Formation. The Valentine faunas help fill the gap between the fauna of the highest part of the Barstow Formation and correlated successions and those of the earlier part of the Clarendon beds. Equivalent assemblages in the Great Basin and Pacific Coast are rare and perhaps difficult to recognize because of biogeographic differences.

The disconformably overlying Ash Hollow Formation of north-central Nebraska has also yielded large collections from various stratigraphic horizons. Those from the lower or Cap Rock Member (Skinner et al. 1968, Skinner and Johnson 1984) have been collectively termed the Minnechaduza Fauna (see Webb 1969a for review). Higher parts of the Ash Hollow Formation (the Merritt Dam Member of Skinner and Johnson [1984]) above the Cap Rock Member have yielded rich local faunas from specific quarries (e.g., Xmas Quarry, Kat Quarry and extensions, and *Leptarctus* Quarry). As a whole, Ash Hollow faunas retain an essential chronofaunal affinity with the Valentine Formation faunas, as Webb (1969a) has pointed out. The hiatus between these faunas seems to be bridged by some assemblages from the Ogallala Group in nearby South Dakota such as the Big Spring Canyon Local Fauna (Gregory 1942; not shown on fig. 6.2). Most of the faunal change involves species level change, but some new elements appear in the Great Plains by Ash Hollow time, including the *Epicyon saevus* group of canids; the horses *Neohipparion* (both the *eurystyle* and *whitneyi-affine* groups), *Griphippus,* and *Hipparion tehonense*; the moschid *Parablastomeryx*; the camels *Megatylopus* and *Hemiauchenia*; and the first antilocaprines (*Proantilocapra, Plioceros*). Immigrant groups appearing at this time are *Barbourofelis* (Nimravidae) at the base of the Ash Hollow Formation and *Beckia* (probably *Ischyrictis* [*Hoplictis*], Mustelidae) and platybelodont mastodonts in the upper part of the unit.

The Bear Tooth Local Fauna from high stream channel deposits that cut through the Ash Hollow Formation in Brown County, north-central Nebraska (Skinner and Hibbard 1972, fig. 4), contain megalonychid sloths remains (Hirschfeld and Webb 1968), *Epigaulus, Dipoides,* and *Plionarctos,* indicating a late Hemphillian assemblage similar to those recently discovered in northeastern Nebraska (Martin 1975b; Voorhies 1977, pers. com. 1976).

Elias (in Stirton 1936a, p. 184) chose an outcrop on the Feltz Ranch, near Ogallala, western Nebraska, as the "lectotype section" for the Ogallala Formation of Darton. These rocks yielded the Feltz Ranch Local Fauna ("Feldt Ranch" of Hesse [1935]). Schultz and Stout (1941, p. 14) traced these beds into the upper part of the Ash Hollow Formation at Cedar Point and westward to Englemann's type section in Ash Hollow Canyon. The Ogallala Formation, *sensu* Elias, thus equates with the Ash Hollow Formation of Englemann. Recent usage, however, favors a broader interpretation at group rank for the Ogallala of Darton (as indicated on the correlation chart, fig. 6.2). The fragmentary Feltz Ranch Local

Fauna is clearly of early Hemphillian age with *Dipoides, Ambelodon, Neohipparion* (*eurystyle* group), *Calippus,* and *Pseudoceras* (the "?*Blastomeryx*" in Hesse 1935, p. 95).

Certain stream channel deposits contained within the upper part of the Ash Hollow Formation in western Nebraska have been described as the Sidney Gravel and the Kimball Formation (Lugn 1939). Breyer (1975) showed that these are local units within the Ash Hollow Formation rather than regionally traceable formations. Fission-track dating (Boellstorff 1976) has revealed that the Ash Hollow Formation in its type area includes deposits laid down over a span of one to two million years. Some local faunas (Oshkosh and Dalton local faunas), regarded as part of the composite Kimball Fauna, represent the earlier phases of deposition, probably seven to eight million years in age, whereas others (Uptegrove Local Fauna, Voorhies 1984) may be younger than six million years in age. These Ash Hollow local faunas are similar at the generic level (Schultz and Stout 1948), and this fact was used to correlate and group them with the large Cambridge Local Fauna of south-central Nebraska as the Kimball Fauna.

Recent review of the Oshkosh Local Fauna and materials from the Greenwood Canyon (near Dalton Quarry) by Breyer (1981) has confirmed the generic level similarity of these assemblages with the Feltz Ranch Local Fauna. Critical in this comparison are *Epicyon* (*E.* cf. *validus*), *Nimravides* (*N.* cf. *catocopis*), *Calippus, Pseudoceras,* and *Cranioceras* (*Yumaceras*), which continue from the Clarendonian, associated with "*Megalonyx*" (at Oshkosh, Schultz and Stout 1948), *Vulpes, Osteoborus, Machairodus* (at Greenwood Canyon), and *Texoceras* (at Oshkosh), which appear in later early Hemphillian faunas elsewhere in the Great Plains. The occurrence of sloth remains at Oshkosh has been cited (Tedford, in Marshall et al. 1979) as the earliest known in North America, but Breyer's analysis reveals that the Oshkosh Local Fauna is approximately coeval with those from Greenwood Canyon and other later early Hemphillian sites calibrated between 7 and 8 Ma.[11]

The Ash Hollow Formation (including the "Kimball Formation") has been recognized eastward into the Republican River drainage in south central Nebraska where outcrops in Frontier County, near Cambridge, have yielded a large fauna (Cambridge Local Fauna). This is the principal local fauna used to characterize the Kimball Fauna (Schultz et al. 1970). The Cambridge Local Fauna contains megalonychid sloth, *Dipoides stirtoni, D. williamsi, Indarctos, Barbourofelis fricki, Amebelodon fricki,* ?*Tapirus simpsoni, Calippus, Neohipparion* (*eurystyle* group), *Nannippus* cf. *ingenuus,* "*Protohippus,*" *Dinohippus leidyanus, Teleoceras, Aphelops kimballensis, Prosthennops, Cranioceras* (*Yumaceras*), *Texoceras,* and *Sphenophalos middleswarti.*

The diversity of the Kimball horse fauna and the persistence of *Barbourofelis, Pseudoceras,* and *Cranioceras* indicate chronofaunal affinity (but not synchroneity) with the assemblages from the correlated Ash Hollow Formation exposed along the Niobrara River in northern Nebraska. New elements, typical of Hemphillian faunas, that appear in the Kimball Fauna are *Dipoides, Amebelodon, Texoceras,* and *Sphenophalos* accompanied by such immigrant groups as the sloths, arvicoline rodents (*Paramicrotoscoptes,* Martin 1975*b*), the sabre-cat *Machairodus,* and the bear *Indarctos.*

The youngest faunas of the Sheep Creek-Snake Creek area of westernmost Nebraska form a succession closely similar to that discussed above from the Ash Hollow Formation. As revised by Skinner et al. (1977), the Snake Creek Formation includes the deposits of at least four crosscutting deep stream channels. The oldest of these (the Murphy Member of Snake Creek Formation of Skinner et al. 1977) disconformably overlies the Olcott Formation at Olcott Hill and also occurs as slump blocks reworked into the youngest channels of the Snake Creek Formation (Johnson Member of Skinner et al. 1977) at the head of Pliohippus Draw. These rocks have produced a few fossils (unnamed fauna, fig. 6.2), including *Prosthennops, Ustatochoerus,* and *Longirostromeryx,* whose affinities lie with comparable species from the Minnechaduza Fauna. Resting disconformably on these rocks is the channel fill capping Olcott Hill which has provided the rock and faunal typification of the Snake Creek Formation (i.e., the Laucomer Member of Skinner et al. 1977). The restricted Snake Creek Fauna is from this site ("*Hesperopithecus*" site) and others in the same channel to the west (American Museum of Natural History Quarry 7). Fossil mammals from these sites include a suite of forms closely resembling those from the higher parts of the Ash Hollow Formation of north-central Nebraska.

Matthew (1924, p. 73) provisionally recognized the distinctive character of the fauna of the channels capping the section at the head of Pliohippus Draw and now referred to as the ZXBar Local Fauna (Skinner et al. 1977). The ZXBar Local Fauna is of late Hemphillian age, containing *Dinohippus leidyanus, Osteoborus di-*

---

[11] The oldest radiometrically dated sloth, the megalonychid *Pliometanastes protistus,* is from the base of the Disaster Peak Member of the Mehrten Formation, in the foothills of the Sierra Nevada, Stanislaus County, California. A tuff 4 m above the sloth is 8.19 ± 0.16 Ma (Hirschfeld 1981), early Hemphillian as calibrated here.

reptor, and *Pediomeryx*, which are comparable with forms from the Optima and Coffee Ranch local faunas of the southern Great Plains. Older Hemphillian faunas occur in the channel fills at the head of Aphelops Draw where *Ustatochoerus major* (Schultz and Falkenbach 1941, p. 21), *Cranioceras (Yumaceras)*, *Hystricops*, *Leptarctus*, and *Epicyon validus* are present along with such typical Hemphillian forms as *Dipoides*, *Pliotaxidea*, *Osteoborus secundus*, and *Megatylopus gigas* and the immigrants *Machairodus*, *Megalonyx curvidens*, and *Neotragocerus*. This assemblage (the Aphelops Draw Fauna of Skinner et al. 1977) is comparable in composition to those from the upper part of the Ash Hollow Formation of southwestern Nebraska and northeastern Colorado.

J. South Dakota. In a series of expeditions early in this century, Matthew and Gidley (1904) and Matthew (1907) and Thomson attempted to work out the stratigraphy and paleontology of the rocks that overlie the White River Group in the Pine Ridge and Rosebud reservations of south-central South Dakota. This work resulted in the recognition of the "Rosebud Beds" in the Rosebud Reservation. To the west in the Pine Ridge Reservation, rocks correlated with the Rosebud Beds were further subdivided into a "Lower" and an "Upper" member. The faunas from these members (Matthew 1907) became a standard for comparison in subsequent literature. Macdonald (1963) and Skinner et al. (1968) reviewed the history of this early work. The revised stratigraphy presented on the correlation chart (fig. 6.2) is based on their detailed studies. The principal stratigraphic result of these studies has been the recognition of the Sharps Formation (Harksen et al. 1961) with its basal Rockyford Ash Member (Nicknish and Macdonald 1963). The Sharps Formation had been equated with the "White River Formation" by Matthew (1907) and Osborn (1907). Wanless (1923), in his pioneering study of the stratigraphy of the "White River beds," recognized the "White ash layer" (Rockyford Ash) as the base of the "Rosebud beds," pointing out the close resemblance of the rocks above and below this marker. Rocks now correlated with the Monroe Creek and Harrison formations of adjacent Nebraska overlie the Sharps Formation without perceivable erosional hiatuses. These younger units produced the Lower Rosebud Fauna of Matthew (1907) and the Wounded Knee-Monroe Creek and Wounded Knee-Harrison faunas of Macdonald (1963, 1970; for small mammals of the Wounded Knee-Monroe Creek Fauna, see L. Macdonald 1972). In 1963, Macdonald restricted the term "Rosebud Formation" to rocks above the Harrison Formation in the Pine Ridge Reservation. This decision was objected to by Skinner et al. (1968)

whose studies of the type Rosebud Formation indicated only the presence of early Arikareean mammals and hence pre-Harrison rocks there. Later, Macdonald and Harksen (1968) and Macdonald (1970) correlated the pink siltstones and fine-grained sandstone of the type Rosebud Formation with the Harrison, Monroe Creek, and Sharps formations of the Pine Ridge Reservation. On the correlation chart (fig. 6.2), this view is expressed by showing the Rosebud Formation as an eastern facies of the Sharps through Harrison formations.

Recently, Harksen (in Harksen and Macdonald 1969) and Martin (1973, 1974) have suggested that the Sharps Formation may be divisible lithically into a lower unit (we estimate approximately the lower 100 feet of the type section) of Brule Formation (White River Group) lithology and an upper unit (all of the second part of the composite Sharps type section) of Arikaree lithology. This latter allocation is supported by the work of Denson (1969, table 1, sec. 8, and fig. 3). The prominent stream channel deposits resting with marked disconformity on the lower unit at the top of Cedar Pass in the Big Badlands (Harksen 1974) and cutting deeply through it into the Poleslide Member in the Castle Butte area south of the White River possibly mark the contact of these units. As the upper unit provided the bulk of the Sharps fossils, the term Wounded Knee-Sharps Fauna is tentatively restricted to that unit. The lower unit is here retained as part of the Sharps Formation using the Rockyford Ash as the base. As here restricted, the lower part of the Sharps Formation has yielded *Hyracodon apertus* associated with the beavers *Capacikala* and *Paleocastor nebrascensis* (Parris and Green 1969), the canid *Mesocyon geringensis*, *Desmatochoerus*, *Mesoreodon*, and a suite of Whitneyan leptauchenine oreodonts (Schultz and Falkenbach 1968). The hypsodont leptauchenine *Sespia* appears in the upper part of this lower Sharps unit, as recently detailed by Tedford et al. (1985). The Wounded-Knee-Sharps Fauna, however, is closely comparable with the fauna of the Gering Formation of Nebraska (Macdonald 1963, 1970; Martin 1973) and with most of the limited material secured from the Rosebud Formation in its type area near the town of Rosebud.

In the Pine Ridge Reservation in South Dakota, equivalents of the Monroe Creek Formation conformably overlie the Sharps Formation without evidence of a hiatus, but to the east, the equivalent Rosebud Formation is overlain disconformably by the Turtle Butte Formation containing the Wewela Local Fauna (Skinner et al. 1968; not shown on fig 6.2) of Monroe Creek age. Rodents from the Wounded Knee-Monroe Creek Fauna enabled Rensberger (1973; Fisher and Rensberger 1972) to correlate this assemblage with the uppermost part of the *Meniscomys* and lower *Entoptychus-Gregorymys* Concurrent Range-Zone as indicated on the correlation chart. Subsequent taxonomic revisions by Rensberger (1979, 1981, 1983) have relegated Macdonald's (1963, 1970) *Meniscomys* species to other genera, although *Allomys* (or a closely related allomyine) is present in the Wounded Knee-Monroe Creek anthill samples. The occurrence of *Pleurolicus* in these samples gives evidence of the *Meniscomys* Concurrent Range-Zone, as does the allomyine, although there is insufficient testing of the range-zones of these taxa in the Great Plains to be sure of the temporal significance of the joint assemblage.

A disconformity occurs beneath the Marsland equivalent Rosebud Formation (Harksen, in Harksen and Macdonald 1969) in the Pine Ridge Reservation. This disconformity marks the approximate point of separation of Matthew's Upper and Lower Rosebud beds. Macdonald (1963, 1970) refers to the Marsland equivalent faunas of the Rosebud as the Wounded Knee-Rosebud Fauna. Disconformably overlying the Rosebud Formation in Bennett County between the Pine Ridge and Rosebud reservations is the Batesland Formation (Harksen and Macdonald 1967) containing the partly described Flint Hill Local Fauna (faunal list in Harksen and Macdonald 1967, p. 8–9; small mammals in J. Martin 1976). This assemblage equates with that from the Runningwater Formation of Nebraska especially in the presence of "*Cynodesmus*" (= *Tomarctus*), *Amphicyon,* the species of *Parahippus, Anchitherium,* and *Archaeohippus, Arretotherium fricki, Merychyus arenarum,* "?*Parablastomeryx*" (= *Barbouromeryx*), *Pseudoblastomeryx,* and *Problastomeryx.* J. Martin (1976) showed that the small mammals of the Flint Hill Local Fauna compared closely with those from the Martin Canyon beds at Quarry A of the University of Kansas (Wilson 1960). This assemblage has yielded the earliest North American occurrence of the little bear, *Ursavus.*

K. Northeastern Colorado. Matthew and Brown's expeditions of the turn of the century into Weld and Logan counties of northeastern Colorado provided a stratigraphic framework for Cope's earlier investigation of the same region. In 1901, Matthew designated the buff nodular siltstones resting on the Cedar Creek beds (White River Group) in Martin Canyon, Logan County, Colorado (Galbreath 1953, Sec. XVI, units 2 and 3), as the "Martin Canyon beds." These rocks contained *Merycochoerus proprius magnus* and *Phlaocyon leucosteus* (unnamed local fauna, see fig. 6.2), and Matthew correlated them with the *Leptauchenia* beds of the "White River Formation." The caption of his published photograph of the site (1907, fig. 17) clearly shows that he

recognized the thick conglomerate of sedimentary rock clasts (Galbreath 1953, Sec. XVI, units 4–6) that cuts into the "Martin Canyon beds" as the base of his "Pawnee Creek beds" (then assigned to the "Loup Fork Formation"). Subsequent study of this section and those nearby by University of Kansas field parties (Galbreath 1953, Wilson 1960) resulted in the discovery of a concentration of fossils (Quarry A) in the nodular tan silty sandstone equivalent to the unit conformably above the conglomerate marking the base of Matthew's Pawnee Creek beds (Galbreath 1953, Sec. XV, unit 4 and Sec. XVI, unit 7). Galbreath (1953, p. 32) has combined the fauna from the "Martin Canyon beds" of Matthew and that from University of Kansas Quarry A as the Martin Canyon Fauna (Wilson 1960 deals specifically with the local fauna of Quarry A). The Quarry A Local Fauna is important as it represents one of the few described faunas of Runningwater age.

Matthew did not specify a type section for his Pawnee Creek beds, but Galbreath (1953, p. 18) designated a section near the Pawnee Buttes in Weld County, Colorado as the type. Study of this area by three of us (RHT, MFS, BET) has led to a modification of Galbreath's (1953, Sec. I) subdivision and correlation of this section. At its type section, the Pawnee Creek Formation does not include Hemingfordian deposits at its base. Rocks equivalent to the Martin Canyon beds are exposed beneath the Pawnee Creek Formation in this area, but they are separated by a strong disconformity and important lithologic distinction from the Pawnee Creek.[12] In the deep axial parts of its paleovalley, the Pawnee Creek Formation rests directly on the Cedar Creek Member of the White River Formation. The Pawnee Creek Formation consists of tuffaceous silty sandstones showing complex cut-and-fill structure containing conglomerate lenses (principally of sedimentary rock clasts with rarer and smaller igneous and metamorphic clasts) and abundant lenticular vitric tuffs. These valley fills contain scattered fossils and local concentrations that have been exploited by all the parties that collected in the area but intensively so by the Frick Laboratory in the 1930s and 1950s. Our recent (and still incomplete) biostratigraphic study has shown that agradation in these valleys was slow enough to witness important faunal change as exemplified by the two local faunas shown on the correlation chart which occur near the stratigraphic limits of the revised Pawnee Creek Formation.

The nature of the fauna of the lower part of the

---

[12] An equivalent disconformity is also present in Martin Canyon, but the rocks that overlie this surface are younger than the Pawnee Creek as defined here.

Pawnee Creek Formation is indicated by the Eubanks Local Fauna of Galbreath (1953) from the base of the type section. The Eubanks Fauna (here generalized from the type locality and correlated sites) is similar in composition to assemblages from the Olcott Formation (Lower Snake Creek Fauna), including *Amphicyon ingens, Merychippus* cf. *insignis*, "*Merychippus*" *sejunctus*, "*M.*" *eohipparion, Calippus, Hypohippus osborni, Desmatippus*, a variety of camelid genera, including *Miolabis, Protolabis, Homocamelus*, and *Aepycamelus*, and the dromomerycids *Dromomeryx* and *Bouromeryx*. *Ticholeptis* and an early member of the genus *Ustatochoerus* occur, but *Brachycrus*, so common in the Lower Snake Creek Fauna, has not been recorded. The presence of *Calippus* and *Ustatochoerus* in Colorado is a point of difference between the Eubanks and Lower Snake Creek faunas.

The fauna of the upper part of the Pawnee Creek Formation is well indicated by that obtained from the Frick Laboratory Horse and Mastodon Quarry. This younger fauna retains the character of the underlying parts of the formation, but *Ustatochoerus* cf. *medius, Dromomeryx, Paracosoryx, Merycodus, Meryceros*, and *Teleoceras* become well represented as does the canid *Aelurodon* and mammutid (*Miomastodon*, Frick 1933), and gomphotheriid mastodonts (referred to *Serridentinus* and *Rhynchotherium* by Osborn 1936) make their first appearance. The fauna of the Horse and Mastodon Quarry is transitional in temporal position and character between faunas from the Olcott and Valentine formations of Nebraska as demonstrated by the occurrence of assemblages similar to those from the Valentine Formation in the unnamed rocks directly overlying the Pawnee Creek Formation. Northeastern Colorado is one of the few areas in North America where such a faunal transition is recorded, and for this reason alone it deserves more intensive study than it has received.

At its type section, the Pawnee Creek Formation is overlain with strong disconformity by tan arkosic sands and gravels and micaceous shales (part of unit 6 and units 7–7, Sec. I of Galbreath 1953). These upper beds crop out widely in the vicinity of the Pawnee Buttes. In the axial parts of their paleovalleys, the streams that deposited these younger rocks have cut completely through the Pawnee Creek Formation and deeply into the White River Formation. The sediments filling these channels include sands and pebble conglomerates containing mainly igneous and metamorphic clasts. In the Pawnee Buttes area, these rocks contain *Mylagaulus, Ursavus pawniensis, Pliohippus, Neohipparion, Pseudhipparion, Teleoceras*, and *Merycodus*. Traced eastward into Logan County, these rocks appear to equate with those referred

to the Pawnee Creek Formation by Matthew (1907) and Galbreath (1953, Secs. II–XVII). In that area they rest on the White River Formation or on the Martin Canyon beds, and they are, in turn, disconformably overlain by younger units of the Ogallala Group (probably including equivalents of the Ash Hollow Formation). In Logan County, these post-Pawnee Creek rocks yield the Kennesaw and Vim-Peetz local faunas described by Galbreath (1953), superposed assemblages but of very similar character which can be equated with the Valentine Formation faunas, especially through the presence of *Cynarctus, Calippus, Pliohippus campestris, Ustatochoerus medius, Cosoryx*, and *Ramoceros osborni*. Osborn (1918, p. 19) distinguished certain taxa from the Sand Canyon outcrops as a younger fauna (Sand Canyon Fauna, in Galbreath 1953, pp. 35–36), but the taxa designated, for example, *Cormohipparion sphenodus, Calippus proplacidus, Pliohippus*, and large *Aepycamelus* (*A. leptocolon, A. giraffinus*), are known to be members of the Valentine Fauna elsewhere (Webb 1969a, Woodburne et al. 1981). They represent advanced elements of the Kennesaw and Vim-Peetz assemblages that mark an early phase in the development of the chronofauna ultimately characteristic of the Clarendonian of the Great Plains.

The Ogallala (Ash Hollow) rocks that cap the sequence in Logan County can be traced eastward, and they appear in outcrops along the Republican River near Wray, Colorado, where Cook (1922) reported the presence of an early Hemphillian fauna closely comparable to that from Feltz Ranch and Kimball in nearby Nebraska. Important elements in this correlation are *Epicyon validus, Osteoborus pugnator, Machairodus coloradensis, Amebelodon hicksi* (including *A. paladentatus*, these forms seem very close to *A. fricki*), *Dinohippus* cf. *interpolatus, Neohipparion, Teleoceras hicksi, Aphelops* (*Paraphelops*) *yumensis* (including ?*Peraceras ponderis*, and close to *A. kimballensis*), *Cranioceras* (*Yumaceras*) *figginsi, Texoceros*, and *Megatylopus* cf. *gigas*.

Southern Great Plains

L. Panhandle of Texas and Adjacent Oklahoma. The dissected eastern edge of the Llano Estacado from the Red River in the Texas Panhandle northward to the Cimmaron River at the southern border of the Oklahoma Panhandle has been an important source of late Tertiary fossil mammals since the last century. The large collections from the vicinity of Clarendon, Donley County, Texas, and on the Coffee Ranch near Miami in Hemphill County, Texas, have figured importantly in the development of a biochronology for the late Tertiary. Except for the early work of Cummins (1893), Gidley (1903), Reed and Longnecker (1932), and, later, that of Johnston and Savage (1955), little biostratigraphic work has been published on this important area, and thus its full potential to provide a detailed faunal succession documented by physical stratigraphy remains largely unappreciated. The faunal succession presented here is primarily based on the unpublished stratigraphic studies of M. F. Skinner. An excellent summary incorporating some of these new data has been compiled by Schultz (1977).

North of Clarendon in Donley County, at the head of the northern tributaries of the Salt Fork of the Red River, are many localities in the Clarendon beds of Cummins (1893) which have been worked through the years by a large number of institutions. The fauna from these sites has been collectively treated as the Clarendon Fauna (see Webb 1969a for a composite list of the published records). Stratigraphic and faunal studies based on the Frick collections have established that the Clarendon Fauna actually includes a faunal succession of which the MacAdams and Gidley Horse quarries represent the temporal extremes. This succession is equivalent to the Minnechaduza through Xmas-Kat Quarry sequence within the Ash Hollow Formation of north-central Nebraska (Skinner and Johnson 1984). The major part of the reported fauna, however, was taken from the more fossiliferous lower levels equivalent to the Cap Rock Member of the Ash Hollow Formation of Nebraska. Some of the minor faunal differences between north-central Nebraska and the Texas Panhandle in Clarendonian time seem best explained by ecological factors: protoceratids (*Synthetoceras* and *Paratoceras*) and abundant *Hipparion tejonense* (MacFadden 1980b; the "*Hipparion lenticularis*" of Osborn 1918) occur at Clarendon; antilocaprids and abundant beavers occur in the Ash Hollow sites.

West of the Clarendon sites near Goodnight in Armstrong County, on the upper part of Mulberry Creek which drains southeast to the Prairie Dog Town Fork of the Red River, Cummins (1893) discovered fossil mammals (Cope 1893) representing a younger fauna. He designated these rocks the Goodnight beds and maintained on stratigraphic grounds that they overlie the Clarendon beds. Gidley (1903) took issue with this evidence and equated the Goodnight and Clarendon beds, but our data definitely support Cummins's conclusion. The fauna of the Goodnight beds includes the type specimens of *Nannippus lenticularis* (= *N. ingenuus*, MacFadden 1984), *Neohipparion eurystyle*, and *Dinohippus interpolatus*. Subsequent collecting has established that the fauna is specifically identical with that obtained from

the better-known Coffee Ranch site. Southwest of the Goodnight sites, on a branch of the Palo Duro Canyon, deposits containing equivalents of the Goodnight Fauna (from Frick Laboratory Christian Ranch Pit 2) are overlain by rocks containing the Christian Ranch Local Fauna (Johnston and Savage 1955) of latest Hemphillian age. This locality is one of several places in the Texas Panhandle and adjacent Oklahoma where the stratigraphic relationships of such assemblages can be demonstrated. The Christian Ranch Local Fauna (Frick Laboratory Christian Place Quarry) includes the characteristic horse taxa *Neohipparion* cf. *eurystyle, Dinohippus mexicanus,* and *Astrohippus stocki*.

North of Clarendon on tributaries of the Canadian River in Hemphill and Lipscomb counties, Texas, and adjacent Ellis County, Oklahoma, an important stratigraphically controlled succession serves to bridge the gap between the Clarendon and Goodnight faunas. At the base of the succession, the Frick Laboratory Cole Highway Pit, south of Higgins in Lipscomb County, Texas, yielded a limited fauna comparable to that from the Clarendon beds (possibly the upper part of that sequence). Superposed on these rocks northeast and east of Higgins and into adjacent Ellis County, Oklahoma, a series of sites occur in a stratigraphic succession, the more important of which are those producing the Capps Pit Local Fauna (Ellis County), the Arnett Local Fauna (Adair Ranch Quarry of the University of Oklahoma; Kitts 1957; and its nearby equivalent, the Frick Laboratory Port of Entry Pit, Ellis County), and the younger Higgins Local Fauna (Sebits Ranch, Lipscomb County; Hesse 1940). These local faunas are compositionally similar and contain large *Epicyon* species, *Nimravides* ("*Machairodus catocopis*" of Hesse 1940; see Martin and Schultz 1975), *Barbourofelis* cf. *fricki* ("*Albanosmilus*? sp." of Kitts 1957), *Amebelodon, Pliohippus, Cormohipparion, Hipparion, Calippus, Cranioceras (Yumaceras), Procamelus,* and *Aepycamelus.* These taxa show species level progression when compared with their Clarendonian counterparts. In addition, the following forms characteristic of the Hemphillian appear: megalonychid sloth (Sebits Ranch, Schultz 1977) *Osteoborus, Neohipparion* cf. *leptode* (*eurystyle* group), and antilocaprines (first appearance in the local sequence). Outcrops north of Higgins in Lipscomb County show that a disconformity appears above the beds producing the Higgins and Arnett faunas. The disconformity is marked by the appearance of pebbly sands bearing basalt scoria clasts. The Frick Laboratory Box T Quarry occurs in such a stream channel deposit just above the disconformity. The large fauna from Box T Quarry is similar in composition to the Higgins faunas, indicating continued persistence of the "Clarendonian chronofauna" (Webb 1969a). New elements appear, however, including the immigrant carnivore genera (*Indarctos, Eomellivora* and *Machairodus*) and the sloths *Pliometanastes* and *Thinobadistes*.

Basalt scoria clasts are characteristic of the stream channel deposits within the Hemphill beds of Reed and Longnecker (1932). They appear at levels 100 feet or more beneath the Coffee Ranch Quarry (Reed and Longnecker locality 20, Frick Laboratory Miami Quarry) southwest of Higgins and south of the Canadian River, Hemphill County, Texas. This is used to relate the Box T and Coffee Ranch sites to the same depositional cycle (Hemphill beds); they represent the early and late phases, respectively, of this cycle. The Box T represents the last appearance of elements of the chronofauna that characterized the preceding deposits. It contains the last local occurrence of *Leptarctus, Nimravides, Pliohippus, Calippus, Cormohipparion, Hipparion, Cranioceras (Yumaceras), Pseudoceras,* and *Amebelodon*. Other chronofaunally related taxa such as *Barbourofelis, Epicyon, Procamelus,* and *Aepycamelus* made their last local appearance in the Higgins and Arnett local faunas.

The Coffee Ranch Quarry (Matthew 1932; Matthew and Stirton 1930b; Stirton 1936; Burt 1931; Dalquest 1969, 1983) and its equivalent in the Oklahoma Panhandle, the Optima or Guymon quarries (Texas County; Hesse 1936, Savage 1941; not shown on fig. 6.2), contain a less diverse fauna than in older rocks but include *Mylagaulus, Osteoborus cyonoides, Machairodus* cf. *coloradensis, Dinohippus interpolatus, Astrohippus ansae, Neohipparion eurystyle, Nannippus ingenuus* (MacFadden 1984), abundant *Aphelops* and rarer *Teleoceras* rhinos, *Pediomeryx, Texoceras,* and the rhynchorostrine gomphothere *Rhynchotherium*. The immigrant carnivores *Plesiogulo* and *Agriotherium* make their first appearance at this time.

A younger fauna has been collected from the gravels deposited in deep channels cutting into the older Hemphillian rocks east of Higgins in Ellis County, Oklahoma. Several gravel pits, including the Virgil Clark, Campbell, Miller, and Nation pits, have yielded teeth of *Astrohippus stocki* and *Neohipparion* cf. *eurystyle*. The stratigraphic relationships of these gravels demonstrate again the superposition of this characteristic latest Hemphillian fauna.

The Panhandle sequence is very important not only because of its potential for better biostratigraphic characterization of the Clarendonian and Hemphillian mammal ages that have been typified there but also because the sequence depicts the nature of a major chronofaunal change marked by extinction, immigration, and evolution.

Gulf Coast

M. Texas Coastal Plain. Fossil mammal remains of Tertiary age have been collected from scattered outcrops on the Texas coastal plain since the last century (see Hesse 1943 for history). Early in this century, such remains figured importantly in the development of a lithostratigraphy for the outcropping strata (see Wilson 1956 for review). The considerable confusion that resulted from use of fragmentary fossils from imprecisely located sites and a complex lithostratigraphic nomenclature has been largely dispelled by the work of Hesse (1943) and, particularly, that of Wilson and his students. Hesse's important review began the modern collation of data on the stratigraphy and faunal composition of the Gulf Coast sites, especially those discovered and worked by Mark Francis (Texas A&M College Collection) and the WPA project supervised by the University of Texas (the Bureau of Economic Geology Collection, hereafter UTBEG, is now under the care of the Texas Memorial Museum). Hesse died before he was able to publish the data he used to construct his faunal lists, but subsequently Wilson studied the entelodonts (1957) and carnivores (1960), Quinn (1955) and Forsten (1975) the horses, Prothero and Sereno (1982) and Prothero and Manning (in press) the rhinos, and Patton (1969) the artiodactyls from these faunas.

Wilson (1956) and Quinn (1955) generalized the biostratigraphy into a system applicable to the entire fossiliferous outcrop belt in coastal Texas and advocated the use of the term "fauna" as essentially synonymous with assemblage-zone (Wilson 1959, 1975). Patton (1969) and Forsten (1975) have discussed the age of the faunal units recognized by Wilson and Quinn. In the present review of the data, including that accompanying the large Frick collection from this area, we emphasize those areas in which stratigraphic superposition can be observed and indicate some details of the faunal succession in each area. We have used some of Hesse's (1943) faunal terms to denote segments of the local sequences. These, in turn, are equated with the faunas of Wilson and others. Despite the scattering of fossil mammal sites, there are three areas that are of prime importance in establishing a faunal sequence: (1) the Garvin Farm and associated sites within the Oakville Formation near Navasota in Grimes and Washington counties, (2) the important sequence north of Cold Spring in San Jacinto County, where Garvin Farm equivalents and older assemblages are succeeded by the Burkeville equivalent Point Blank and younger Cold Spring faunas all within the Fleming Formation, and (3) the Lapara Creek and Labahia Mission faunas within the Goliad Formation in Bee and adjacent Goliad counties.

At the base of the Oakville Formation in Washington County, Wood and Wood (1937) discovered the Cedar Run Local Fauna, which together with other scattered sites low in the Oakville and the approximately equivalent lower part of the Fleming Formation to the northeast in Walker and San Jacinto counties (Aiken Hill Local Fauna and *Dinohyus* site, UTBEG locality 40224) contain an assemblage including *Paleocastor, Daphoenodon, Dinohyus,* early *Prosynthetoceras* ("*Blastomeryx texanus*" of Wood and Wood 1937), *Blastomeryx, Archaeohippus,* and possibly *Anchippus texanus,* suggesting equivalence with late Arikareean assemblages of the northern Great Plains. These sites were considered part of the Garvin Gully Fauna of Wilson (1956).

Higher in the Oakville Formation (including the Moulton Sandstone Member at the top), the Garvin Farm and correlative local faunas in Grimes and Washington counties typify the Garvin Gully Fauna of Wilson (1956). The horses and rhinos from these local faunas, especially species of *Anchitherium, Parahippus, Archaeohippus,* and *Menoceras,* agree best with forms from the Runningwater Formation of Nebraska, as does the occurrence of *Amphicyon* and the advanced species of *Oxydactylus* (including *Australocamelus,* Patton 1969). A diverse tylopod element, including an endemic group of camelids (*Nothokemas* and *Floridatragulus*) and protoceratids (*Prosynthetoceras*), typifies the Garvin Gully as part of the Miocene Gulf Coast chronofauna that included Florida and probably Central America (Whitmore and Stewart 1965, Patton and Taylor 1973) as well. Conspicuously rare are the diverse moschid and dromomerycid artiodactyls that characterize the contemporaneous chronofauna in the Great Plains.

To the northeast, in Walker and adjacent San Jacinto counties, the Aiken Hill and associated sites near the base of the Fleming Formation are succeeded in the higher parts of the same unit by a group of sites (including UTBEG localities 31190, 31242, and 31243) that Hesse collectively regarded as representing his Point Blank Fauna. The continued presence of *Prosynthetoceras* and *Floridatragulus* (to the exclusion of other tylopods) indicates chronofaunal continuity, although mylagaulid rodents appear and the horse fauna is sharply distinct with the appearance of hypsodont, cement-bearing forms. These were assigned by Quinn (1955) to species of *Merychippus, Hippodon,* and *Protohippus* comparable to those from early Barstovian assemblages

elsewhere. Three genera of rhinos are present, as in contemporary deposits of the Great Plains, but dwarf species of *Peraceras* and *Teleoceras* occur with *Aphelops* of "normal" size (Prothero and Sereno 1982). The Holarctic beaver *Anchitheriomys* is present at the Point Blank sites and is an important mammal at the Burkeville site in Newton County near the state line to the east.

The Burkeville site (Stenzel et al. 1944) is especially noteworthy as fossil vertebrate remains (including *Aphelops, Merychippus, Prosynthetoceras,* and possibly Proboscidea)[13] occur there in close stratigraphic association with brackish and freshwater mollusca characteristic of the *Potamides matsoni* Zone of Ellisor (1936). This biostratigraphic unit has been traced downdip in the subsurface of adjacent Louisiana into relationship with marine benthonic foraminiferal assemblages ranging from the top of the *Operculinoides* to the *Textularia* (W) zones (summarized by Tipsword 1962). Correlation of these benthonic foraminiferal zones with the Neogene planktonic scale by Echols and Curtis (1973) indicates that the Burkeville mammal fauna lies within Zones N9 through early N13 calibrated at 15.5–12.5 Ma (Berggren et al. 1984) and thus within the temporal range for Barstovian faunas as recognized in this review. The possible joint occurrence of Proboscidea and *Anchitheriomys* at Burkeville indicates an early phase of the late Barstovian, possibly between 14.5 and 13.0 Ma, and further suggests that the Burkeville Local Fauna is younger than the Point Blank, Trinity River, and Moscow local faunas.

A large and varied mammal fauna was obtained by the Frick Laboratory from Fleming rocks stratigraphically between the Point Blank and Cold Springs faunas of Hesse (1943). Stratigraphic studies by one of us (MFS) shows that this new site, the Trinity River Quarry, is also approximately equivalent to Hesse's Moscow faunal site (UTBEG locality 31057) in nearby Polk County. A curious feature of the Trinity River Local Fauna (commented on by Patton and Taylor 1973, p. 400) is the surprisingly close similarity of its artiodactyls to those of the Lower Snake Creek Fauna of Nebraska. A diverse group of cranioceratine and dromomerycine dromomerycids occur, as do blastomerycine moschids and the camel *Aepycamelus* as well as protolabine and miolabine forms common in the High Plains Barstovian. Even the protoceratids show the presence of the High Plains *Lambdoceras,* whereas the Gulf Coast *Prosynthetoceras* and *Floridatragulus* are absent at this site. *Paratoceras* makes its first Gulf Coast appearance, and

---

[13] Reported as "?*Desmostylus*?" (Stenzel et al. 1944, pp. 1005–1006). These enamel fragments are not desmostylian, but they may be proboscidean (see discussion in Reinhart 1976, pp. 286–287).

Anchitheriomys is present. The curious geomyoid *Texomys* that occurs at both the Trinity River and Moscow sites (Slaughter 1981) is very closely related to *Jimomys* (Wahlert 1976) from Observation Quarry of western Nebraskan early Barstovian. The horse fauna is more diverse than in previous assemblages, comparable in that respect to the equivalent Lower Snake Creek Fauna of Nebraska, but with a different frequency of species than to the north; *Hypohippus, Desmatippus,* "*Merychippus*" *sejunctus,* and *Merychippus* cf. *insignis* are common. In addition, the Trinity River Local Fauna contains the earliest known member of the genus *Cormohipparion* (Skinner and MacFadden 1977) later to become a common element in the "Clarendonian chronofauna" (MacFadden and Skinner 1981). The rhinos include the same *Aphelops* and *Teleoceras* species as in the Great Plains, but they coexist with dwarf species of *Teleoceras* and *Peraceras* in the Moscow and Trinity River local faunas (Prothero and Sereno 1982). The occurrence of such an assemblage suggests a complex environmental patterning of the Gulf Coast Barstovian and the trend toward midcontinent faunal uniformity reinforced in succeeding ages.

Still higher in the Fleming Formation near the town of Cold Spring, San Jacinto County, Hesse (1943) defined the Cold Spring Local Fauna (UTBEG locality 31219) and succeeding Sam Houston Local Fauna (UTBEG locality 31191). These local assemblages and the higher Goodrich Local Fauna (UTBEG localities 31183 and 31200) of nearby Polk County constitute the principal characterization of the Cold Spring Fauna of Wilson (1956). The Proboscidea are present in the Cold Spring Local Fauna of Hesse; the horses (including the earliest *Hipparion*; MacFadden 1984) are even more diverse, resembling those of the early part of the Valentine Formation or its equivalent in the lower Ogallala Group in northeastern Colorado. The sympatry of four rhino species as found at Trinity River continues. Advanced camels (*Aepycamelus*) and moschids (*Longirostromeryx*), cranioceratine dromomerycids (*Cranioceras*), and canids (*Aelurodon francisi*) appear. These new elements indicate a continuing introduction of northern forms strengthened in the succeeding Lapara Creek Fauna. The Gulf Coast tylopods *Prosynthetoceras* and *Floridatragulus* continue.

Younger Tertiary faunas are not present in the Cold Spring vicinity; instead, the succeeding vertebrate faunas are derived from the Goliad Formation that disconformably overlies the Fleming in the southwestern part of the Tertiary outcrop in Bee and adjacent Goliad counties. The Lapara Creek Fauna of Wilson (1956) from the lower or Lapara Member of the Goliad Formation includes several fossil sites that can be divided into two local faunas. The older local fauna, here termed the Bridge Ranch Local Fauna (UTBEG locality 31132), contains horses that appear to differ considerably at the specific level from succeeding assemblages (Quinn 1955). Although it is difficult to equate Quinn's taxonomy with that in use elsewhere, the horses, the canid *Aelurodon,* and the presence of merycodonts seem to agree best with those of the Burge of Nebraska. Near the top of the Lapara Member, a more diverse assemblage occurs, here termed the Farish Ranch Local Fauna (UTBEG localities 30896 and 31081), which appears to be comparable to that from the lower part of the Clarendon beds (e.g., MacAdams Quarry) and the Minnechaduza Fauna of the Ash Hollow Formation. The presence of advanced species of *Procamelus,* a late miolabine camel (*Nothotylopus*), and early *Megatylopus,* plus *Cranioceras clarendonensis, Ustatochoerus profectus,* and *Teleoceras major,* supports this correlation more clearly than the equids principally because of Quinn's unusual taxonomy for the latter. Nevertheless, the composition of the equid fauna seems closely similar to that from the earlier part of the Clarendon succession in agreement with the artiodactyls. Thus, the Lapara Creek Fauna of Wilson includes a succession of local faunas that would usually be assigned an early Clarendonian age. It is interesting that *Synthetoceras* represents the sole element surviving into the Lapara Creek of the diverse tylopods characteristic of the Gulf Coast Miocene chronofauna. By Clarendonian time, except for differences at the specific level and relative abundance of taxa, a north-south uniformity had spread over the midcontinent macromammal assemblages from the Gulf to the Canadian border, justifying the term "Clarendonian Chronofauna" as proposed by Webb (1969*a*).

The youngest Tertiary fauna known from the Texas coastal plain is represented by a few specimens from the Labahia Member of the Goliad Formation, the uppermost member of that unit (Wilson 1956). These have not been listed or described but are said to support a Hemphillian age for the Labahia Mission Local Fauna (UTBEG locality 30895).

N-O. Florida. The stratigraphy of the late Tertiary rocks of Florida has been studied for three-quarters of a century, yet major problems remain to be solved, particularly with regard to the fossil mammal-bearing units. Physical stratigraphy is of limited use at present in ordering the locally rich mammal faunas obtained from this state. Nevertheless, Florida is important geochronologically because of the number of occurrences, especially in northern Florida, of land mammals in near-shore marine strata. We emphasize these occurrences here and discuss their relationship to marine biostratigraphies following the recent summary of these data by Tedford and Hunter (1984). In addition, geochronological ordering of the Hemphillian faunas provides a basis for dating Tertiary sea level changes (Webb and Tessman 1968) recorded by low-level estuarine deposits and high-level shorelines developed on the stable landmass of central Florida during late Neogene time.

Two of the oldest Miocene faunas known from northern Florida occur in the vicinity of Newberry in Alachua County. The Franklin Phosphate Company Pit No. 2 discussed by Simpson (1930) yielded *Daphoenodon* sp. ("*Mesocyon iamonensis*"; Simpson 1930, pp. 160–161, Hunt 1971), *Dinohyus, Parahippus,* and *Blastomeryx.* The presence of *Blastomeryx* in this local fauna suggests a late Arikareean age as moschids appear in North America in the Marsland Fauna. An older Newberry assemblage is the Buda Local Fauna (Frailey 1979). The latter contains a small chalicothere (*Moropus*) and other mammals, along with various reptiles, amphibians, and fish. The presence of *Nanotragulus loomisi, Cynarctoides, Daphoenodon,* and an early phenacocoeline oreodont all indicate a late Arikareean age for the Buda Local Fauna and suggest correlation with the fauna of the Harrison Formation of Nebraska. The same age is indicated for the SB-1A Local Fauna (Frailey 1978) from Suwanee County northwest of Alachua County. Other early Miocene faunas have been recovered in central Florida. Patton (1967, p. 5) described a collection from a quarry near Brooksville, in Hernando County, and concluded that the stage of evolution of the various mammals in that local fauna indicated a late Arikareean assignment. Frailey (1979, p. 133–134), in his study of *Daphoenodon* in Florida, considers the Brooksville species to be more primitive than that from the Buda and Franklin sites, suggesting a slightly older assignment for the Brooksville assemblage. Farther south, MacFadden (1980a) has recently reported the occurrence in Marion County of *Phenacocoelus* ("Oreodont Site" of fig. 6.2) and other mammals (Martin-Anthony Local Fauna) in near-shore marine deposits referred to the Hawthorn Formation (see discussion in Tedford and Hunter 1984).

In northern Florida, several occurrences of fragmentary fossil mammal remains have been found within the "lower Hawthorn" (mostly equivalent to the Torreya Formation of Banks and Hunter 1973). Of particular importance are the Seaboard Air Line Railway Company site (Seaboard Local Fauna, Olsen 1964a), the City Waterworks site (Colbert 1932; not shown on fig. 6.2) at Tallahassee in Leon County, and the Jim Woodruff Dam site (Olsen 1964b; not shown on fig. 6.2) at Chattachootchee in Gadsden County. The Seaboard Local Fauna is the largest of these assemblages and contains taxa apparently identical to those of the better known Thomas Farm Local Fauna (see Patton 1967 for a recent faunal list) from Gilchrist County on the northern flank of the Ocala Arch. Characteristic of all of these faunas are the horses *Archaeohippus blackbergi, Anchitherium clarencei,* and *Parahippus leonensis*; a typical Gulf Coast tylopod fauna with advanced *Oxydactylus*-like forms (*Nothokemas*), the monotypic Floridatragulinae, and the protoceratid *Prosynthetoceras*; and the wider ranging moschid *Blastomeryx,* a leptomerycid ("*Machaeromeryx*"), and canids (*Tomarctus* and *Euoplocyon*). The Thomas Farm Local Fauna contains the earliest North American record of the ursid *Hemicyon* (*Phoberocyon*) ("*Aelurodon*") *johnhenryi,* Tedford and Frailey 1976, and the first aceratherine rhino, the giant *Floridaceras,* found only at Thomas Farm associated with *Menoceras,* itself an Arikareen immigrant. This fauna is compositionally similar to the Garvin Farm Local Fauna of the Texas coastal plain, although it is generally thought to be slightly younger in age. Both assemblages seem to be intermediate in age between the faunas of the Runningwater and Box Butte formations of Nebraska.

Slightly younger faunas than the Thomas Farm are known in northern Florida from fuller's earth pits near Midway (Simpson 1930, 1932) and Quincy (Simpson 1930) in Gadsden County. Simpson (1932, p. 11) concluded that these assemblages were approximately equivalent stratigraphically, and we have grouped them as the Midway Fauna. Banks and Hunter (1973, p. 361) suggested that the fuller's earth deposits represent a distinct pre-Chipola unit of formational rank or perhaps an upper member of their Torreya Formation. These rocks now constitute the Dogtown Member of the Torreya Formation (Hunter and Huddlestun 1982). These local faunas are small assemblages but ones in which the horse *Merychippus gunteri* replaces *Parahippus leonensis; Archaeohippus* and *Anchitherium* continue, and mylagaulids, dromomerycids, and larger camelids appear. When compared with the Texas coastal plain, the fauna seems to be pre-Burkeville; it may equate with late Hemingfordian assemblages from the Box Butte Formation of Nebraska.

Thus, in northern Florida we have faunas ranging from late Arikareean to late Hemingfordian in age. The Thomas Farm equivalent Seaboard Local Fauna and local correlatives occur in strata assigned to the Torreya Formation (equivalent to part of the "Hawthorn" of older usage), a shallow-water marine and estuarine unit stratigraphically beneath the marine Chipola Formation. The younger Midway-Quincy assemblages from the fuller's earth deposits occur in the upper part of the Torreya. Discovery of *Miogypsina globulina* within the Torreya (Banks and Hunter 1973) indicates that part of that unit equates with planktonic foraminiferal zones N5 and N6. The overlying Chipola Formation contains planktonic foraminifera equivalent to the upper part of N7 and N8 (Zone N7 was tentatively preferred by Akers 1972, p. 10). A helium-uranium age of 16.1 Ma (Bender 1973) has also been obtained from corals from the Chipola. In terms of the radiometric calibration of the planktonic Neogene zones advanced by Berggren et al. (1984), the Torreya Formation ranges in age from 17.0–21.0 Ma, a span of time clearly including the Hemingfordian as recognized by the data used in this chapter. Many uncertainties naturally remain, but the agreement indicated by these correlations offers hope that more intensive study of the relationships of marine and nonmarine biostratigraphies in Florida and the Gulf Coast will provide mutual critiques of the various biostratigraphic disciplines (Tedford and Hunter 1984).

Younger Miocene local faunas were discovered in northern Florida (Ashville, Jefferson County; Olsen 1963) and adjacent Georgia (Statenville, Echols County; Voorhies 1974) in correlative nonmarine strata representing the later phase of deposition of the Alum Bluff Group. Horse teeth were the only biochronologically useful material from these sites. These were assigned to "*Merychippus*" by Olsen, but they represent *Calippus* and *Cormohipparion*-like forms comparable to those from early Valentine assemblages of Nebraska and correlates in the Gulf Coast of Texas (Cold Springs).

Younger Tertiary faunas have long been known from central and southern Florida where they occur in mottled montmorillinitic clay (the "Alachua Clays") filling the karst surface developed on the older Tertiary limestones of the Ocala Arch or in gray phosphatic sands (the Bone Valley Formation) resting disconformably on the Hawthorn Formation on the western flank of the arch and on the karst surface developed on older rocks to the north (see Webb and Tessman 1968 for review). Early collections described by Leidy and Hay were often a mixture of Tertiary and Quaternary forms. Simpson (1930) reviewed the older work and, on the basis of Florida Geological Survey collections, did much to clarify the provenance of the faunas. In recent years, Webb and co-workers have concentrated on the problems of composition and sequence of the latest Tertiary faunas, and some of their results have now been published (Webb 1964, 1966, 1967, 1969*b*, 1973; Webb and Tessman 1968; Hirschfeld and Webb 1968; MacFadden and Webb

1982; Webb and Crissinger 1983). For the most part, the taxa present in these younger Florida assemblages are similar to those of the midcontinent, and for this reason it is possible to correlate the various Florida local faunas with equivalents in the Great Plains. Most of the Florida assemblages can be divided into four groups representing the late Barstovian (equivalent to Valentine Formation faunas), Clarendonian (equivalent to Ash Hollow faunas), early Hemphillian (equivalent to the Southern Plains Arnett, Higgins, and Box T local faunas), and late Hemphillian (equivalent to the Coffee Ranch, Optima, and Christian Ranch local faunas).

It appears that most of the described fossil mammals found in situ in the Alachua Formation sediments are of Hemphillian age. An important recently discovered exception is the latest Clarendonian local fauna from the Love Bone Bed attributed to the Alachua Formation near Archer, Alachua County (Webb et al. 1981). Mammals from the Love Bone Bed show clear affinity to those from late Clarendonian faunas of the midcontinent, particularly the diverse horses *Pliohippus, Neohipparion, Hipparion, Nannippus* cf. *minor, Griphippus* cf. *gratus, Astrohippus martini, Calippus* cf. *regulus,* carnivores *Epicyon, Leptarctus, Barbourofelis,* and *Nimravides,* and the artiodactyls *Aepycamelus, Procamelus, Hemiauchenia, Pseudoceras,* and *Yumaceras.* The mastodont *Amebelodon* and mustelid *Ischyrictis* ("*Beckia*") are late Clarendonian immigrants that also occur in the northern Great Plains. The tiny *Nannippus* cf. *minor* and the early abundance of *Neohipparion* of the *eurystyle* group are taxa that suggest the distinctive composition of the Florida horse fauna of the Hemphillian, otherwise the Love Bone Bed Local Fauna shares most of its taxa with the "Clarendonian Chronofauna" of the Great Plains (Webb et al. 1981).

Representing the early Hemphillian are the fauna of the Mixson's Bone Bed of Leidy (Leidy and Lucas 1896), the type locality of the Alachua Clays of Sellards near Williston in Levy County, and the McGehee Local Fauna (Webb 1964, 1969; Hirschfeld and Webb 1968) in Alachua County in red clays and phosphatic sands. These assemblages both contain taxa representative of the early Hemphillian of the southern plains such as *Cranioceras* (*Yumaceras*), *Aepycamelus,* early species of *Osteoborus* (*O. galushai*), and large *Epicyon validus* (Webb 1969). In addition, the McGehee site contains *Synthetoceras* cf. *tricornatus* (Patton and Taylor 1971) and a primitive *Mylagaulus* (Webb 1966*a*), regarded as relictual forms. The horse fauna from these sites is largely made up of "hipparion" types, including *Nannippus ingenuus, N.* cf. *minor, Neohipparion* (*eurystyle* group), and "*Hipparion*" *plicatile,* which together with

Calippus and "*Pliohippus*" cf. *hondurensis* suggest the diverse equid faunas of the Great Plains early Hemphillian. No Eurasiatic immigrant forms are known, but a primitive megalonycid sloth, *Pliometanastes,* occurs at McGehee, whereas at Mixson's, a mylodontid, *Thinobadistes,* occurs, representing an early phase of exchange with tropical America. Both sloths have been identified outside Florida associated with early Hemphillian faunas (they occur together in the Box T Local Fauna).

Recent work by Webb and Crissinger (1983) on the regional stratigraphy of the central and southern phosphate districts of southern Florida (Polk County south to De Soto County) has demonstrated the existence of a superposed suite of disconformity-bounded fluviatile to near-shore marine deposits that contain vertebrate fossils, including terrestrial mammals. The lithostratigraphic term "Bone Valley Formation" has historically been applied to the entire commercial phosphate-bearing, post-Hawthorn sequence, although the type section for the formation apparently represents only the uppermost two Tertiary units in the stratigraphic column (units 6 and 7 of Webb and Crissinger 1983). These are the rocks that produced nearly all of the classic Bone Valley Fauna of late Hemphillian age discussed below. The Lower Bone Valley Formation (units 1 through 5 of Webb and Crissinger 1983) are distinctly older, that is, of late Barstovian and early Clarendonian age. A large hiatus extending from late Clarendonian through early Hemphillian time thus separates the lower and upper parts of the Bone Valley Formation. This hiatus corresponds to the time of accumulation of the Alachua Formation in sinkholes on the Ocala Arch in central Florida and in estuarine deposits near present sea level on the western flank of the arch.

Waldrop (pers. com. 1977) reports an assemblage of early Barstovian age obtained in place in the central district at the base of the Bone Valley Formation of unknown correlation with the scheme of Webb and Crissinger (1983) but presumably with unit 1 or an older post-Hawthorn unit. The fauna consists mainly of isolated teeth of *Merychippus* and remains of beavers, both of which resemble early Barstovian taxa. Units 2 and 3 of Webb and Crissinger (1983) have produced a mutually similar fauna, containing both gomphotheriid and mammutid mastodonts (including a form near the primitive *G. calvertense*) and a suite of horses that includes *Merychippus insignis,* "*M.*" cf. *republicanus, Calippus, Protohippus, Cormohipparion* cf. *sphenodus* (*sensu* Woodburne et al. 1981), and *Hipparion* closely resembling taxa from the lower part of the Valentine Formation or the Cold Springs Fauna of the Texas Gulf Coast and

also the material mentioned above from northern Florida (Ashville) and adjacent Georgia (Stattenville).

A disconformity separates these early late Barstovian strata from unit 5 of the Lower Bone Valley Formation which contains an early Clarendonian fauna whose horses (*Calippus* cf. *regulus, Cormohipparion* cf. *occidentale,* and *Pliohippus* cf. *supremus*) resemble counterparts from the Clarendon and Minnechaduza faunas of the Great Plains.

These new assemblages bridge a long gap formerly present in the Florida faunal record. These faunas, like their Texas counterparts, show that the peninsula had become a part of the midcontinent biome characterized by the major elements of the Clarendonian chronofauna. Endemic Gulf Coast taxa have not yet appeared in the small collections from these sites, but they should be expected in view of their persistence in Florida in the Hemphillian faunas of the same region.

For the most part, the Lower Bone Valley Formation is a marine unit, the members of which are separated by disconformities that correspond to marine regressions. The Lower Bone Valley as a whole seems correlative with the Alum Bluff Group of north Florida; the Upper Bone Valley and intertonguing Tamiami Formation are comparable to the Choctawhatchee and Jackson Bluff formations of north Florida. The relative sea level changes recorded by these regionally traceable discontinuities have been studied by Webb and Tessman (1968) and Peck et al. (1979) and recently summarized by MacFadden and Webb (1982). During transgressive phases, represented by the deposits of the Lower Bone Valley, sea level stood at about 25 meters above present levels. Similar levels are recorded on the western flank of the Ocala Arch by the rich shark and ray fauna in the late Clarendonian Love Bone Bed (Webb et al. 1981) and at the early Hemphillian McGehee deposit (see faunal list in Hirschfeld and Webb 1969).

The vertebrates give evidence of only a single drop in sea level in late Hemphillian time (contra Webb and Tessman 1968; see MacFadden and Webb 1982) which is manifested in the Bone Valley deposits by the strong disconformity between the lower and upper parts of the Bone Valley Formation (Webb and Tessman 1968, p. 790; MacFadden and Webb 1982, p. 197) and by lithologic, faunal, and floral changes in the correlative marine Tamiami Formation discussed by Peck et al. (1979). During the regressive phase, when the sea stood at approximately its present elevation, Upper Bone Valley deposition is recorded by vertebrate-bearing estuarine deposits in Manatee County and in the lower reaches of the Withlacoochee River in Marion County. The Manatee County Dam Site (Webb and Tessman 1968) has yielded a fragmentary mammal fauna, including *Rhynchotherium, Griphippus,* and a suite of "hipparion" horses similar to that which occurs at the Withlacoochee River Site 4A of the University of Florida. The latter site yielded a richer fauna, including *Pliometanastes, Thinobadistes, Platybelodon, Pseudoceras,* and *Indarctos* associated with *Osteoborus orc, Machairodus, Megatylopus, Hemiauchenia,* and horse lineages continuing from older deposits ("*Hipparion*" *plicatile, Nannippus ingenuus, N.* cf. *minor, Neohipparion* cf. *phosphorum, Astrohippus*). These local faunas are comparable to those from Box T Quarry north of Higgins in the Texas Panhandle as indicated by the continued presence of earlier taxa associated with the first appearance of the immigrants *Enhydritherium, Machairodus* (Berta and Morgan 1985), and *Indarctos* characteristic of the medial and later parts of the Hemphillian.

Some taxa characteristic of the early part of the Hemphillian continue to be present in the upper part of the Bone Valley Formation (unit 6 and 7 of Webb and Crissinger 1983) as exposed by open-cut phosphate mining in Polk County. These deposits contain estuarine vertebrates and indicate a latest Hemphillian (earliest Pliocene) restoration of sea level to at least 50 meters above that of the present (MacFadden and Webb 1982). Relictual forms such as the protoceratid *Kyptoceras* (Webb 1981) and late forms of *Griphippus, Carpocyon* (Webb 1969), and several *Gomphotherium* ("*Serridentinus*") species have been recorded that represent survivors of earlier lineages. Later elements in the Upper Bone Valley Fauna include *Dinohippus* cf. *mexicanus* and *Astrohippus, Neohipparion phosphorum, Nannippus minor, N.* cf. *ingenuus,* "*Hipparion*" cf. *plicatile, Rhynchotherium,* and "*Pliomastodon.*" The antilocaprids are well represented for the first time in Florida (*Subantilocapra* and *Hexameryx,* Webb 1973). Several taxa recently described from the upper Bone Valley deposits (*Felis rexroadensis,* MacFadden and Galiano 1981; *Megantereon hesperus,* Berta and Galiano 1983; *Mylohyus elmorei,* Wright and Webb 1984; odocoileine deer, Webb n.d.; and probably *Borophagus* ["*Osteoborus*" *dudleyi*]) are representatives of Blancan taxa. *Enhydritherium* and *Agriotherium schneideri* represent immigrants from the Old World in this fauna.

The refugium of subtropical peninsular Florida is evident in the late occurrence of certain groups as indicated, but some of the advanced elements and the presence of *Agriotherium* suggest that the Upper Bone Valley is essentially similar to late Hemphillian assemblages of the southern Great Plains. Other taxa are either species known previously only in the Blancan or Bone Valley

species belonging to Blancan genera, and these forms give a very late Hemphillian aspect to the Upper Bone Valley Fauna. As the Upper Bone Valley Fauna is contained in strata that postdate the basal Pliocene rise in sea level, it is younger than 5.0 Ma. Evidence from the Atlantic coastal plain (summarized in Tedford and Hunter 1984) indicates that the Yorktown Formation, containing a correlative of the Upper Bone Valley Fauna, was also deposited during the early Pliocene transgression. The Yorktown is a marine unit that contains plantonic foraminifers and glauconite, permitting correlation with the Neogene planktonic geochronology and radiometry, both of which agree in indicating a 4.5 Ma date for such vertebrate faunas and, hence, a maximum date for the Hemphillian-Blancan boundary.

BIOCHRONOLOGY

In 1941, the Vertebrate Section of the Paleontological Society (Wood et al. 1941) reviewed the stratigraphic succession of North American fossil mammals with the intention of developing an independent time scale based on these data. They sought to generalize from "precisely analyzed faunas and the related stratigraphy" a sequence of units of "purely temporal significance" which would "cover all of Tertiary time." These were to be biochronologic units characterized by demonstrable sequential changes in the Tertiary mammal fauna of North America. For the most part, these spans of time lacked formal biostratigraphic typification but were characterized biologically by listing the genera thought to be restricted to, or characteristic of, each temporal unit and those making their first and last appearance during a given interval.

Unfortunately, ambiguity was introduced when the "North American Provincial Ages" were formally established by this committee. Instead of following the principles they so ably stated, most of the ages were equated with the geochron of the rock unit containing the best-known faunas. This shifted the emphasis from biological to stratigraphic criteria in formal definition. Nevertheless, the committee's intent was clearly not to set the limit of the ages at formational contacts, for they stated that "the ages are not necessarily coextensive with their types and the precise limits between successive ages are intended to be somewhat flexible and may presumably be modified in the light of later discoveries" (Wood et al. 1941, p. 6).

In subsequent usage, the biological criteria have been the only means by which the ages could be recognized from region to region. Despite the way in which they were established, the ages have been construed as biochronologic units. As the record has become more completely developed, the problem of the spatial and temporal limits as well as the biological definition of these ages becomes important.

Our review of the faunal sequence in various areas across North America serves to emphasize that the record is episodic and strongly controlled by hiatuses in the stratigraphic column. Changes in the composition of mammal faunas often closely follows change in depositional regime with its implication of changing local environment. The episodic nature of the record is particularly noticeable in the tectonically active region west of the Rocky Mountains. In the central and southeastern part of the continent, however, we can discern the development and persistence, often across depositional hiatuses, of chronofaunas whose generic composition changes very little with time. The component genera do show change, usually recorded at the species level, but mutual occurrence of genera and their long coexistence are maintained through a significant interval of time implying the establishment of a stable ecosystem. An outstanding example of such phenomena is the faunal sequence through the Valentine and Ash Hollow (including the "Kimball") formations in Nebraska (see pp. 169–170). The origin of this chronofauna can be discerned in the succession within the Pawnee Creek Formation. It becomes a recognizable entity with the Norden Bridge Local Fauna of the basal Valentine Formation and, with some modifications through immigration of Eurasian and Neotropical forms, persists into medial Hemphillian time despite the occurrence of several hiatuses in deposition during the course of the seven million years involved. Chronofaunas of like persistence are indicated within the Gulf Coast region (see pp. 175–177), but the details of composition and succession are not so clearly worked out. The Great Plains and the related late Miocene Gulf Coast chronofaunas seem to largely represent the response of ungulates to developing savannas across midlatitude North America. This point is explored in more detail in a recent review by Webb (1977) based partly on the data provided here.

The occurrence of chronofaunas also implies the persistence of certain zoogeographic configurations over significant periods of time. A comparison of faunas across North America during the Miocene clearly indicates the presence of mammal faunal provinces, perhaps more broadly drawn in the earlier Miocene than in the later Miocene but nonetheless discernable. Such spatial discontinuities present special problems for correlation and especially for the definition of units of a biochronology applicable to the continent as a whole. Widely ranging taxa with well-known biochrons will have a preeminent place in the development of a continentwide system

if it can be shown that these forms extend across ecological boundaries to enable interprovincial correlation.

The question of the definition[14] of the boundaries of the North American mammal ages has received little specific attention in the literature. Vertebrate paleontologists have been content to regard these ages as somewhat loosely defined sequential units with diffuse boundaries. Repenning (1967), however, suggested that the lower boundary of each age could best be defined with reference to the appearance of immigrant (i.e., allochthonous) taxa. It should be noted that "first appearances" (including both allochthonous and autochthonous taxa) were an important part of the biological characterization of the "North American Provincial Ages" by Wood et al. (1941). Focusing attention on exotic taxa does provide an unambiguous point of recognition, but other factors such as the distribution and rate of dispersal (see Wilson 1967 for discussion) as well as the phyletic affinities of the supposed immigrant taxa (see Engesser 1979 for discussion) become important limits on the usefulness of such criteria. Intercontinental dispersal usually involves more than one taxon and may be accompanied by dispersal in both directions so that these episodes are often of prime importance to correlation. Hence, the importance of such phenomena in definition of a biochronology of potentially intercontinental applicability might outweigh other objections. For the ages under discussion, intercontinental dispersal, especially across Holarctica, was an important factor in faunal change, and so it seems particularly appropriate to include these phenomena in the eventual biochronologic definition of the North American mammal ages. In figure 6.3, we list the immigrant taxa discussed in this chapter and show their temporal first occurrences as now understood.

It was acknowledged in the introductory section of this work that biostratigraphic analysis represents the only means of significantly refining the present biochronologic system used for fossil mammals in North America. As much of the necessary field and laboratory research has yet to be published, or even begun, however, we believe that it is worthwhile to evaluate the biochronologic system currently in use in light of the knowledge gained in the many years since its inception. This review will employ the same principles and the same kind of data (temporal and spacial ranges of generic taxa) as used by Wood et al. (1941) to suggest refinement

---

[14] The terms "definition" and "characterization" have been given formal meaning in chronostratigraphy by Murphy (1977) and Woodburne (1977). We have adopted these terms in the same sense in the context of biochronology.

DEFINITION AND CALIBRATION OF SOME NORTH AMERICAN MAMMAL AGES

EPOCHS	Million Years	North American Mammal Ages	DEFINING TAXA (Listed are genera and higher taxa exotic to North America that are used to define the beginning of indicated age or subage)	K/Ar and Fission Track Dates

PLIOCENE

BLANCAN

5

Late — *Bretzia, Chasmaporthetes, Lynx, Mimomys, Nebraskomys, Parailurus, Trigonictis, Ursus*

HEMPHILLIAN — *Agriotherium, Felis, Megantereon, Ochotona, Odocoileini, Plesiogulo, Promimomys*

L — *Enhydritherium, Eomellivora, Indarctos, Lutravus, Machairodus, Neotragoceros, Plionarctos, Simocyon*

Early / E

Late — *Megalonyx, Microtoscoptes, Paramicrotoscoptes, Pliometanastes, Pliotomodon, Thinobadistes*

10

CLARENDONIAN — *Amebelodon, Ischyrictis, Platybelodon*

Early

L — *Barbourofelis*

Late — *Pseudoceras*

E

BARSTOVIAN

15 — *Gomphotherium, Miomastodon, Pseudocyon*

Early

Late — *Copemys, Plithocyon*

HEMINGFORDIAN — *Aphelops, Blackia, Eomys, Miomustela, Mionictis, Plionictis, Petauristodon, Pseudaelurus, Sthenictis, Teleoceras*

Early

Aletomeryx, Amphictis, Amphicyon, Angustidens, Antesorex, Brachypotherium, Craterogale, Edaphocyon, Leptarctus, Oreolagus, Phoberocyon, Plesiosorex, Potamotherium, Ursavus

20

L — *Barbouromeryx, Blastomeryx, Cephalogale, Cynelos, Paracosoryx, Ysengrinia*

Late

E — *Daphoenodon, Menoceras, Oligobunis, Zodiolestes*

L

ARIKAREEAN

25 — *Moropus, Parvericius, Promartes, Pseudotheridiomys*

Early

E

OLIGOCENE

WHITNEYAN — *Allomys, Ocajila, Plesiosminthus, Talpinae*

Fig. 6.3. Summary of the calibration and defining taxa (immigrants) used to delineate the North American mammal ages discussed in this chapter. The distribution of relevant K-Ar and fission-track dates (see Appendix A) indicates the precision of the boundary calibrations. Note that this chart supersedes a similar version published in Tedford and Hunter (1984, fig. 1).

of the biochronology in accordance with modern data. It will suffer in the same way as previous work in that the biostratigraphy for most taxa is known only at the level of formational occurrence. Thus, we have been forced to consider defining taxa occurring within a unit as being present at the base. We hope this expedient will not be unduly misleading.

In the pages that follow, the "Provincial Ages" of Wood et al. (1941) and subsequently published subdivisions or modifications of these ages are examined in the light of data reviewed in the previous section of this chapter. We introduce an informal subdivision of the mammal ages where it seems warranted by the evidence and useful in establishing greater precision in correlation and in so doing provide revised definitions and characterizations of the units proposed by Wood et al. (1941). Our intent is to initiate discussion directed toward revision of this useful biochronology.

Arikareean

This age was "based on the Arikaree group of western Nebraska, Agate being most typical locality, with the limits as redefined by Schultz (1938), but including the Rosebud" (Wood et al. 1941, p. 11). As originally conceived, the age includes the faunas of the Gering through Harrison formations. The Rosebud Formation was equated with the Arikaree Group. Typological overlap with the Hemingfordian was demonstrated by Macdonald's (1963) correlation of the upper part of the Rosebud of Matthew (1907) with the Upper Harrison (= Marsland of this chapter). However, Hunt (1977, 1978, 1981, 1985) has recently allocated the Upper Harrison to the Arikaree Group and shown that the Agate Springs Local Fauna occurs at the base of the Upper Harrison (= Marsland) rather than in the Harrison as traditionally believed. This fauna provided most of the taxa in the biological characterization of the Arikareean and was regarded by Wood et al. (1941) as the typical Arikareean assemblage even though it occurs late in the age.

It has long been recognized that the faunas of the early Arikareean are more closely allied to the preceding Whitneyan (Macdonald 1963, Martin 1973) than to the younger part of the Arikareean. The nature and magnitude of the faunal change within the Arikareean are comparable in scope to those characterizing other ages. A useful division into two subunits would seem desirable at least for the Great Plains and seems to have utility elsewhere. In this work we propose an informal subdivision of the Arikareean into an earlier and later phase. Each phase is defined and characterized biologically.

The definition of the early Arikareean serves at the same time to define the age of which it is part; the combined characterization of both phases typifies the Arikareean as a whole. Proposals by Wilson (1960, fig. 7) and Martin (1975) to subdivide or revise the Arikareean are not followed because their subdivisions are denoted by lithostratigraphic terms and, furthermore, the same terms are employed for different concepts (e.g., the "Harrisonian" of Wilson 1960 seems to include the same geochron as the "Geringian" plus "Harrisonian" of Martin 1975). Some of their proposals lack stated biological typification (e.g., "Harrisonian" of both Wilson 1960 and Martin 1978) and thus their use here would have to be in conformation with our data in a manner that would probably not correspond to the concepts intended by their authors. It is hoped that more formal subdivision will be based on a greater array of biostratigraphic data than is presently available.

The early Arikareean (and hence the Arikareean Mammal Age) is defined by the earliest appearance of the following immigrants: the hedgehog (Erinaceidae), *Ocajila* (Galericinae), the talpine moles (Talpinae), the zapodid rodent *Plesiosminthus* (Sicistinae), and the aplodontid rodent *Allomys* (Allomyinae). The early Arikareean is characterized by the earliest appearance of *Archaeolagus*, Entoptychinae, Mylagaulidae, *Diceratherium*, *Dinohyus*, *Promerycochoerus* (*Pseudopromerycochoerus*), *Desmatochoerus*, Stenomylinae (*Dyseotylopus*), *Miotylopus*, and *Nanotragulus*; the limited occurrence of hypsodont leptauchenine oreodonts and *Mesoreodon*; and the latest occurrence of Primates, *Eumys*, *Paleolagus*, *Hyaenodon*, *Eusmilus*, *Nimravus*, *Hyracodon*, *Subhyracodon*, *Miohippus*, *Archaeotherium*, *Elomeryx*, *Hypisodus*, and leptauchenine oreodonts. All of these are also characteristic of Whitneyan faunas. The principal faunas contributing the above biochronologic data are the assemblages from the Gering and Monroe Creek formations of Nebraska and southeastern Wyoming, the Wounded Knee-Sharps and Wounded Knee-Monroe Creek faunas of South Dakota, and the fauna of the Kew Quarry, California (see the correlation chart, fig. 6.2).

Subdivision of the early Arikareean in the Great Plains may be effected in the future when the fauna of the Monroe Creek Formation becomes better known. Information presently at hand shows that these strata record no Whitneyan genera, that they contain the last appearance of leptauchinine oreodonts and *Promylagaulus*, and that they include the earliest record of such immigrants as the hedgehog *Parvericius*, the eomyid *Pseudotheridiomys* and possibly the mustelid *Promartes*, and the chalicothere *Moropus*. Such autochthones as *Stenomylus*, and probably the cricetid *Paciculus*, first occur in the Monroe Creek Formation in the northern Great Plains. We indicate this tentative subdivision of the early Arikareean in figures 6.2 and 6.3, but like the criteria used to define some other units in this revision, we are working at the limit of our present biochronologic resolving power.

A younger phase of Arikareean time can be clearly distinguished which begins with the fauna of the Harrison Formation and closes with the fauna of the Upper Harrison or Marsland Formation. The "typical locality" (Wood et al. 1941, p. 11) of the Arikareean, the Agate Springs quarries, belongs to this later phase. The late Arikareean spans an interval of accelerated immigration from Eurasia. The occurrence of the more widespread exotic taxa can be used to recognize two phases within the span of late Arikareean time corresponding essentially to the faunas of the Harrison and succeeding Marsland formations. In the definition that follows, this subdivision is indicated.

The late Arikareean is defined by the earliest appearance of the following immigrants: the early phase (Harrison Fauna) contains the mustelid carnivore *Oligobunis*, the procyonid carnivore *Zodiolestes*, the amphicyonid carnivore *Daphoenodon*, and the rhinoceratid *Menoceras*; the later phase (Marsland Fauna) contains the ursid *Cephalogale* (Hemicyoninae), the amphicyonids *Cynelos* and *Ysengrinia*, the rhinoceratid *Menoceras*, the blastomerycine *Blastomeryx* (Moschidae), the dromomerycid *Barbouromeryx* ("*Blastomeryx*" *cursor*, Cook 1934), and antilocaprid *Paracosoryx* ("*Merycodus*" *prodromus*, Cook 1934). The late Arikareean as a unit is characterized by the earliest appearance of *Cynarctoides*, *Archaeohippus*, *Parahippus*, *Merycochoerus*, *Merychyus*, synthetocerine protoceratids (*Syndyoceras* and *Prosynthetoceras*), protolabidine camels (*Michenia* and *Tanymykter*), and *Oxydactylus*; the limited occurrence of *Oligobunis*, *Zodiolestes*, *Aelurocyon*, *Syndyoceras*, *P.* (*Promerycochoerus*), and *Hypsiops*; the maximum diversity of oreodonts and flat-incisor beavers (including the burrower *Palaeocastor*, "*Daimonelix*"); and the latest occurrence of the Entoptychinae, *Temnocyon*, *Promartes*, *Diceratherium*, the oreodont subfamilies (*sensu* Schultz and Falkenbach) Merycoidodontinae, Eporeodontinae, Promerycochoerinae, and Desmatochoerinae, the Hypertragulidae (*Nanotragulus*), and the protoceratid *Protoceras*. Sufficient biostratigraphic knowledge is now available (Hunt 1981; data gathered for this chapter) to indicate that the later phase of the late Arikareean (Marsland and Wounded Knee-Rosebud faunas) includes the earliest appearance of *Mylagaulodon*, *Aelurocyon* (including *Megalictis*), *Cynarctoides*, *Archaeohippus*, *Anchitherium* (including *Kalobatippus*),

protolabidine camels (*Michenia* and *Tanymykter*), and *Merycochoerus* (a brief overlap in range of *M.* and *Promerycochoerus* occurs at the base of the Marsland Formation) among North American autochthones.

Besides the principal faunas of the late Arikareean noted, the Wounded Knee-Rosebud Fauna (the upper Rosebud Fauna of Matthew 1907) of South Dakota, assemblages in Montana, and especially those within the upper part of the John Day Formation of Oregon are of particular importance in characterization of this phase of the Arikareean. Biogeographic provinces are discernible in the Arikareean, especially between the Columbia Plateau and northern Great Plains as evidenced by the distribution of entoptychine rodents and leptauchenine oreodonts. This provinciality presents problems in defining and characterizing chronostratigraphic units such as Rensberger's concurrent range-zones typified by the biostratigraphy of certain rodents in the John Day Formation (Fisher and Rensberger 1972). This zonation has been extended stepwise into the northern Rocky Mountain basins in Idaho and Montana and finally to South Dakota and Nebraska. The typical aplodontid of the lower zone, *Meniscomys*, apparently cannot be recognized east of Idaho. Its sister taxon, *Niglarodon*, is absent at John Day but present in the Rockies eastward to the Great Plains. The latter genus, along with the wider ranging emigrant *Allomys* and the geomyoid *Pleurolicus*, serves to identify at least part of the *Meniscomys* Concurrent Range-Zone east of the continental divide. Rensberger (1971) noted early the restriction of *Entoptychus* west of the divide and elected to use the allied *Gregorymys* of approximately similar stratigraphic position east of the divide to characterize an *Entoptychus-Gregorymys* Concurrent Range-Zone even though the ranges of these taxa cannot be directly compared at any locality. Thus continentwide recognition of the Arikareean, and its admittedly provincial subdivisions proposed herein, depend largely on wide-ranging taxa that link faunal provinces and on faunal sequences that bridge Great Plains stratigraphic hiatuses to provide a more continuous and detailed record of the faunal succession within this span of time.

Hemingfordian

This age was originally (Wood et al. 1941, p. 12) "based on the Hemingford group including the Marsland and, especially, the limited or lower Sheep Creek fauna (Cook and Cook 1933, pp. 38–40), and not on the formation limits as extended upward (Lugn 1939b)." It is clear from the glossary entries under "Marsland formation" and "Upper Harrison" in Wood el al. (1941) that they accepted the equivalence of these units and their faunas. Thus, typological overlap ostensibly exists between the Hemingfordian as originally proposed and the Arikareean as defined here. Examination of the biological definition provided by Wood et al. (1941) for the Hemingfordian reveals that the genera making their "first appearance" in the Hemingfordian are all forms whose biozones are not known to extend beneath the Runningwater Formation (i.e., the upper part of the Marsland Formation, *sensu* Schultz 1938; see McKenna 1965). We propose here to use the fauna of the upper part of the Marsland Formation of Schultz (1938) (= Runningwater Formation of Cook 1965) as the earliest assemblage of the temporal unit Hemingfordian. In doing so, we follow the principles enunciated by Wood et al. (1941) in the text of their report rather than their inadvertent designation of the Hemingfordian as the geochron of a lithostratigraphic unit (i.e., "new provincial time term, based on the Hemingford Group" [p. 12]).

It is important to note that an important faunal discontinuity exists within the Hemingfordian, signaling an abrupt shift in the Great Plains from the chronofauna characteristic of the late Arikareean and early Hemingfordian to one typifying the late Hemingfordian and early Barstovian. A regional disconformity in the stratigraphic column of the northern Great Plains accentuates the faunal change, and a corresponding lack of record or poor sampling of this interval across the United States leads to a natural twofold subdivision of the Hemingfordian.

Wilson (1960) recognized the importance of the faunal discontinuity within the Hemingfordian and proposed, but did not define or characterize (shown only in his fig. 7), the "Marslandian" and "Sheepcreekian" ages. He relegated the "Marslandian" to the Arikareean on the grounds of faunal similarity with his "Harrisonian." The "Sheepcreekian" was placed in a revised Hemingfordian that also included a "Mascallian" age for younger assemblages usually referred to the Barstovian. Departure from typology and established usage of the Wood et al. (1941) mammal ages should be avoided whenever possible to reduce confusion. Modifications of boundaries may be necessary, as we advocate in some instances in this review, but if major departure from original usage is required, new units should be proposed whose names are not based on lithostratigraphic terms.

The typification of the early Hemingfordian is based mainly on the rich fauna of the Runningwater Formation of Nebraska and correlatives in South Dakota (Flint Hill Local Fauna) and Colorado (Quarry A Local Fauna). In the Gulf Coast, the Thomas Farm Local Fauna of Florida and the Garvin Farm Local Fauna of Texas can be recognized as correlates, using taxa whose geographic ranges extend from the Great Plains into the Gulf Coast faunal province (principally carnivores and perissodactyls). In the West, faunas of early Hemingfordian age are rare and mostly undescribed (e.g., the Boron and Warm Springs local faunas) but can be recognized as early Hemingfordian in age primarily on the identity of their artiodactyls (oreodonts and dromomerycids) with those of the Great Plains.

The early Hemingfordian (and hence the Hemingfordian as a whole) can be defined by the earliest appearance of the following immigrants: the soricine (*Antesorex*) and limnoecine (*Angustidens*) shrews, the plesiosoricid *Plesiosorex*, the ochtonid lagomorph *Oreolagus*, the carnivores *Amphicyon*, *Hemicyon* (*Phoberocyon*), *Ursavus* (Ursinae), and *Edaphocyon* (Procyoninae), the leptarctine mustelids (*Craterogale* and *Leptarctus*), the Mustelinae (unnamed taxon, see Tedford and Frailey 1976), the phocid *Potamotherium* (Semantorinae) and the procyonid *Amphictis* (Simocyoninae), the rhino *Brachypotherium* (Yatkola and Tanner 1979), and the dromomerycid *Aletomeryx*. The early Hemingfordian is characterized by the earliest appearance of *Mesogaulus*, *Cupidinimus*, *Tomarctus*, *Brachypsalis*, Floridatragulinae, and *Protolabis*; the limited occurrence of *Aletomeryx* and *Machaeromeryx*; and the latest occurrence of *Trogomys*, *Ysengrinia*, *Cynelos*, *Menoceras*, Entelodontidae, *Stenomylus*, *Phenacocoelus*, and *Merycochoerus*.

The late Hemingfordian is based principally on the classic Sheep Creek Fauna (equivalent to the "lower Sheep Creek fauna" of Cook and Cook 1933; see Skinner et al. 1977 for review) as recommended by Wood et al. (1941, p. 12). They specifically excluded extension of the Hemingfordian to the Lower Snake Creek Fauna of the Olcott Formation (former "Lower Snake Creek beds") thought by Lugn (1939) to represent the upper part of the "Sheep Creek Formation" and hence to belong to the Hemingford Group. Galusha (1975) has shown that the fauna of the Box Butte Formation is clearly related taxonomically to that of the Sheep Creek and furthermore that the Box Butte is not a phase of Sheep Creek deposition. Superposition with the Sheep Creek is lacking, but the faunal similarities and the presence of some early Hemingfordian forms in the Box Butte (e.g., *Parahippus*, *Barbouromeryx*, and *Oxydactylus*) suggest a pre-Sheep Creek age. It seems reasonable in view of these similarities to regard the Box Butte Fauna as representative of an early phase of the late Hemingfordian and to use it along with the Sheep Creek Fauna in definition and characterization of this phase of Hemingfordian time.

The differences between the faunas of the Box Butte through Sheep Creek interval and the chronofaunally related younger faunas here referred to the Barstovian (Observation Quarry through Lower Snake Creek) can be ascribed mainly to anagenetic change in persistent lineages, making it necessary to distinguish these ages at the specific rather than the generic level. Immigrant taxa are used to define these ages. Thus, the complex of stream channel deposits of late Hemingfordian age in Sioux, Dawes, and Box Butte counties, Nebraska, has provided the principal faunal and stratigraphic evidence characterizing the close of Hemingfordian time. Outside the Great Plains, late Hemingfordian faunas, many showing provincial character, can be recognized by the criteria outlined below. It is significant that the succession in the Barstow Formation includes faunas of late Hemingfordian age beneath the younger assemblages that were used to establish the succeeding Barstovian age.

The late Hemingfordian is defined by the earliest appearance of the following immigrants: the petauristine squirrels (*Petauristodon*, Engesser 1979, and *Blackia*), the eomyid rodent *Eomys*, the musteline mustelids *Miomustela*, *Plionictis* and *Sthenictis*, the lutrine mustelid *Mionictis*, the earliest Felidae (*Pseudaelurus*), and the rhinos *Teleoceras* and *Aphelops*. It is characterized by the earliest appearance of *Hypolagus*, *Anchitheriomys*, *Mylagaulus*, *Merychippus* s.l., *Hypohippus*, *Brachycrus*, *Ticholeptus*, the Cranioceratinae (*Bouromeryx*), the Dromomerycinae (*Dromomeryx*) *Aepycamelus*, *Merycodus*, and *Merriamoceros*, and the last appearance of *Parahippus*, *Barbouromeryx*, and *Oxydactylus*.

Barstovian

This mammal age was "based on the Barstow Formation, San Bernardino County, California, and specifically on the fossiliferous tuff member in the Barstow syncline and its fauna" (Wood et al. 1941, p. 12). In a typological sense, only the Barstow Fauna, as restricted in this chapter (see p. 159), can be considered as representing the age within the Barstow Formation, for it is the assemblage from the beds informally designated the "fossiliferous tuff member" by Baker (1911). This fauna is the youngest recognized assemblage in the formation as exposed in the Barstow Syncline (Woodburne and Tedford 1982). At the base of the fossiliferous portion of the Barstow Formation, the Red Division Quarry contains a Sheep Creek-equivalent fauna that represents the upper limit of the Hemingfordian in the Barstow succession. The Green Hills Fauna occurs in rocks between the level of the Red Division Quarry and the lowest part of the "fossiliferous tuff member" and thus, in a typological sense, is not contained within either age. The Wood committee (1941, p. 6) was aware of the consequences

of their definition for they stated that "The Barstovian age includes units . . . which are certainly older than any of the faunules now known from the Barstow." This qualification is borne out in their proposal as "principal correlates" of the Barstovian the "Pawnee Creek," "Deep River," "Virgin Valley," and "Mascall" faunas. The latter three are correlates of the Green Hills Fauna rather than of the Barstow Fauna. Moreover, the "Pawnee Creek" is a composite (Wood et al. 1941, p. 28, and discussion above). In addition, the "index fossils" recognized for the Barstovian age include forms also known in the Green Hills Fauna, such as *Hemicyon* (*Plithocyon*), *Dyseohyus fricki*, and *Peridiomys*. Furthermore, "*Amblycastor*" (= *Anchitheriomys*) and "*Monosaulax*" occur in the equivalent Lower Snake Creek Fauna. Thus, it seems logical to regard the Green Hills Fauna as representing an early phase of the Barstovian despite the rather marked faunal change that occurs between it and the Barstow Fauna in the conformably overlying beds (see p. 159) and between these assemblages and those outside the southern Great Basin.

The Barstovian represents an early phase in the increasingly provincial geographic distribution of mammals that appears to be a feature of later Miocene time in North America. Development of a biochronology of continentwide applicability will be particularly difficult under these circumstances. Several concurrent biochronologies based on local faunal provinces may prove to be more useful and appropriate ways to segment the faunal sequence. This may be particularly useful in areas such as the northern Great Plains in which chronofaunal continuity persisted with little influence from outside. A case in point is the sequence within the Pawnee Creek Formation as here restricted (see pp. 172–173). This apparently covers about the same temporal span as that of the Green Hills through Barstow succession, but there is much greater continuity of genera through the succession. The California and Colorado faunal sequences have few genera in common but can be correlated stepwise through adjacent areas to the southwest and northwest. In each case, gomphotheriid Proboscidea appear in the later phases. The Pawnee Creek succession is an important one for it lies directly beneath Ogallala rocks containing Valentine equivalent faunas and hence provides the stratigraphic evidence for the relationship of the Barstovian to younger mammal ages.

Wilson has suggested (1960, in chart form only, fig. 7) the recognition of a "Mascallian age" between his "Sheepcreekian" (= late Hemingfordian) and the Barstovian. The "Mascallian" apparently includes the diverse faunas grouped here as an early phase of the Barstovian. The term would be particularly appropriate as a provincial age for the faunas of the Columbia Plateau and adjacent Great Basin. So far, however, no superpositional evidence is available to establish the temporal relationship of the "Mascallian" to adjacent ages. Moreover, to be of continentwide applicability, as apparently intended by Wilson, the criteria for its recognition would necessarily be the same as for the recognition of the Barstovian age. It seems useful nevertheless to recognize the distinctive characteristics of the faunas of the early part of the Barstovian from those of the later part, especially in view of the important taxonomic relationship of the later Barstovian assemblages of the Great Plains with succeeding Clarendonian and Hemphillian faunas. The nearly synchronous appearance of gomphotheriid Proboscidea (accompanied by mammutids in some cases) across the United States provides a convenient means of defining the boundary between these subdivisions of the Barstovian.

The beginning of Barstovian time, and hence the early Barstovian, can be defined by the earliest appearance of the ursid *Hemicyon* (*Plithocyon*) and the cricetid rodent *Copemys*. No other immigrants are known during this interval, but some longer ranging autochthonous genera have their earliest records at this time: *Perognathus*, *Cormohipparion*, *Dyseohyus*, and *Meryceros*. The early Barstovian contains the limited occurrence of *Desmatippus* and *Rakomeryx* and the last appearance of *Lambdoceras*, *Ticholeptus*, *Brachycrus*, and *Merriamoceras*. The characteristic taxa are a composite of forms from the many early Barstovian correlates from the California Coast Ranges to the Gulf Coast of Texas as indicated on the correlation chart (fig. 6.2) and in the discussions of the various assemblages in the preceding section of this chapter.

As mentioned above, the Barstow Fauna, as biostratigraphically restricted here, corresponds in most respects with the assemblage known to Merriam (1919) by the same name from the "fossiliferous tuff member" of the Barstow Formation (Baker 1911). This assemblage then assumes the status of the typical fauna of the Barstovian Mammal Age as designated by Wood et al. (1941). The Barstow Fauna contains the first appearance (although rare) of Proboscidea in the Barstow sequence, and a number of autochthonous taxa also appear in this fauna (as detailed on p. 159). Assemblages of the same taxonomic composition (Cronese Local Fauna) occur in rocks as young as 12.5 Ma in the Mojave Desert area, indicating a possible span of at least 2 m.y. for faunas of that character in the southern Great Basin (fig. 6.2 and Appendix A).

Correlation of the Barstow Fauna with assemblages in coastal California, the Great Basin, Columbia Plateau,

and eastward into the Rocky Mountains can be effected with reasonable confidence on the basis of taxonomic similarity. Differences in composition increase with distance from the Barstow site, but the effect is accentuated for many groups of mammals when the Great Plains and Gulf Coast faunas are compared with their presumed western equivalents. This is especially true of the equine horses, long a favorite geochronologic subject, but much less so in the case of the Anchitheriinae. Nevertheless, there is a biological basis for correlating the Barstow and Niobrara River faunas, as Wood et al. (1941) indicate on their correlation chart. This is particularly supported by the occurrence of Proboscidea and certain genera of Carnivora, Camelidae, and Antilocapridae, despite the lack of correspondence in the Equinae. The extent of the faunal overlap is difficult to judge without detailed comparison of the assemblages involved, but if the occurrence of gomphotheriid Proboscidea is used as a datum, it seems very likely that the Barstow Fauna is to be correlated with faunas from the lower part of the Valentine Formation (Norden Bridge and Niobrara River) of Nebraska and equivalents in Colorado within the upper part of the Pawnee Creek Formation (Horse and Mastodon Quarry) and overlying rocks.

Faunas from the upper members of the Valentine Formation (Devil's Gulch and Burge) in north-central Nebraska are closely related taxonomically to those from the lower part of the Valentine (Cornell Dam and Crookston Bridge members) as discussed on pp. 168–169. These faunas probably extend beyond the geochron of the Barstow Fauna and related assemblages as suggested by the more advanced nature of the species of shared genera. Faunal continuity within the Valentine Formation is maintained across the hiatuses that bound the constituent members of that unit. The first noteworthy faunal change occurs at the base of the Ash Hollow Formation, and for this reason we have included the entire Valentine faunal succession within the later part of the Barstovian.

Schultz and Stout (1961, fig. 3), implicitly, and Schultz et al. (1970), explicitly, define a "Valentinian Provincial Age" for the fauna of the Valentine Formation and included the Norden Bridge Local Fauna in their concept. They gave no biological definition or characterization of this provincial age but merely listed all the taxa so far reported from the Valentine Formation. Schultz et al. (1970) apparently intended that the "Valentinian" should be a local biochronologic unit applicable to the geographic and temporal limits of the Valentine Formation. The important question of the relationship with the ostensibly continentwide Barstovian Mammal Age was not discussed. In addition, the Wood committee's explicit (1941, pl. 1, p. 26) reference of the Niobrara River Fauna from the Crookston Bridge Member of the Valentine to the Barstovian was not commented on beyond the general statement that "the usage of the Barstovian is greatly misunderstood" (Schultz et al. 1970, p. 25). For these reasons, we see no particular value in the term "Valentinian" as it is essentially synonomous with the younger part of the Barstovian. Its authors based the unit on the geochron of the Valentine Formation and gave no faunal definition or characterization of the corresponding biochron. Thus, its application must be set aside for the same reasons we have rejected previous subdivisions of the Arikareean and Hemingfordian as discussed above. There are, nevertheless, fundamental chronofaunal relationships of the faunal succession within the Valentine Formation. It represents the early phase of High Plains late Miocene chronofauna whose separation from later phases is partly an artifact of the stratigraphic record.

The definition and characterization of the late Barstovian interval is thus based primarily on the Barstow Fauna and western equivalents, on correlative faunas from the Valentine Formation of Nebraska, on the Pawnee Creek Formation and overlying Ogallala rocks in northeastern Colorado, and on the Cold Spring Fauna of the Texas Gulf Coast. We include the Burge Fauna in this interval on the grounds of generic compositional similarity with earlier Valentine assemblages.

The late Barstovian is defined by the earliest appearance of the following immigrants (genera denoted by asterisk are limited to the Great Plains and Gulf Coast faunal provinces): Proboscidea (Gomphotheriidae), the amphicyonid carnivore *Pseudocyon**, and later in the interval, the gelocid *Pseudoceras**. The latter two taxa are presently known only in the Great Plains and Gulf Coast. This interval is characterized by the earliest appearance of *Megasminthus**, *Eucastor* (= *Monosaulax* (Stirton 1935; *fide* T. M. Stout, pers. com., 1978), *Ischyrocyon*, *Aelurodon*, *Carpocyon*, *Cynarctus**, *Megahippus*, *Calippus**, *Neohipparion**, *Pliohippus*, *Protohippus*, *Dinohippus* (late in interval)*, *Hipparion*, *Prosthennops*, *Ustatochoerus*, *Procamelus*, *Cranioceras*, and *Longirostromeryx**; the limited occurrence of *Strobodon* and *Pseudhipparion**; and the last appearance of *Anchitheriomys*, *Parvericius*, *Ursavus*, *Amphicyon*, *Archaeohippus*, *Anchitherium**, chalicotheres*, Leptomerycidae (*Pseudoparablastomeryx**), *Blastomeryx*, and *Dromomeryx*.

Clarendonian

This age is the only one we discuss that was proposed as a faunal rather than a lithostratigraphic unit, "based on the Clarendon local fauna (and member?), near Clarendon, Donley County, Panhandle of Texas" (Wood et al. 1941, p. 12). Some idea of the limits of the age as originally conceived are contained in the list of "principal correlatives" ("Burge, Big Spring Canyon, Fish Lake Valley, Ricardo," ibid.) and on the correlation chart of Wood et al. (1941, pl. 1). The "Clarendon local fauna" is shown as occurring only in the later half of the Clarendonian, mostly equivalent to the Minnechaduza Fauna of the Cap Rock Member of the Ash Hollow Formation, north-central Nebraska. The age was extended to include the fauna of the Burge Member of the Valentine Formation, disconformably beneath the Ash Hollow Formation, but not to earlier faunas in the Valentine Formation which were referred to the Barstovian.

In his review of the fauna of the Burge Member of the Valentine Formation, Webb (1969a) considered it of Clarendonian age citing the precedence of Wood et al. (1941). Webb's (1969a, p. 16) characterization of the Burge Fauna was an implicit revision of the criteria for recognition of early Clarendonian time in the Great Plains. Unfortunately, he was not aware that most of the genera and even some of the species he listed also occur in the underlying Devil's Gulch and older members of the Valentine Formation. As discussed above, we now know that many of the genera held diagnostic of the Clarendonian both by Wood et al. (1941) and Webb (1969a) also occur in the earlier Niobrara River Fauna from the Crookston Bridge Member (assigned to the late Barstovian by Wood et al. 1941). This overall faunal continuity is an expression of the chronofaunal relationships of the Valentine and Ash Hollow faunas. However, we believe that the beginning of Clarendonian time is more readily defined, and its fauna more easily characterized, by placing the faunas from the base of the Ash Hollow Formation of north-central Nebraska in the earliest part of the age. In the sequence exposed there the important superposition of the Clarendonian and late Barstovian ("Valentinian") faunas can be seen. Webb (1969a) has furthermore demonstrated the close similarity of the fauna of the Clarendon beds with that of the Ash Hollow. The hiatus between the Valentine and Ash Hollow formations is accompanied by perceivable faunal change, and this provides the basis for an objective characterization of the Clarendonian. With this slight modification, necessitated by our intention to suggest boundary criteria, the Clarendonian is revised to include in its earliest phase faunas synchronous with those of the Clarendon beds of Texas and Cap Rock Member of the Ash Hollow Formation, north-central Nebraska. The Burge Fauna is thus the latest Great Plains Barstovian assemblage by this criterion.

The time span covered by the Clarendonian was an interval during which limited interchange took place with Eurasia. Nevertheless, this appears to be the interval during which the horse *Hipparion* reached the Old World from North America. The oldest Eurasian species of *Hipparion* compare best with indigenous forms of Clarendonian age (MacFadden 1980*b*, 1984). Old World immigrants entering North America which might be used to define the boundaries of the Clarendonian Mammal Age are few. Among the larger mammals appearing during this interval are the nimravid carnivore *Barbourofelis*, the gomphotheriid mastodonts *Platybelodon* and *Amebelodon*, and the mustelid *Ischyrictis* (*Hoplictis*) (= *Beckia*). Of these forms *Barbourofelis* appears to be the most widespread. It occurs in the early Clarendonian of Texas, Nebraska, South Dakota, and California. *Amebelodon*, *Platybelodon*, and *Ischyrictis* are rare in collections but appear in younger Clarendonian deposits from the Columbia Plateau to Florida. Their first occurrence seems to be associated with later Clarendonian faunas, and they could serve to define a younger phase of the age along with perceivable change in the autochthonous fauna as sometimes noted in the literature and suggested in figure 6.2.

The Clarendonian Mammal Age can be characterized by the first appearance of the felid *Nimravides*, the *Epicyon saevus* group of canids in the Great Plains and their joint occurrence there with *Aelurodon*, the first appearance of the horses *Griphippus*, *Nannippus* (restricted to Florida, MacFadden 1984), and *Astrohippus*, the peccary *Macrogenis*, the protoceratid *Synthetoceras*, the camels *Hemiauchenia* and *Megatylopus*, and the antilocaprine antilocaprids (*Plioceros* and *Proantilocapra*). The age is also marked by the last occurrence of several genera that survived from early Barstovian time, such as *Brachypsalis*, *Tomarctus*, *Merychippus*, *Hypohippus*, *Paratoceras*, *Miolabis*, *Protolabis*, the Blastomerycinae, and the merycodontine antilocaprids. A few forms that appeared as members of the Great Plains late Miocene chronofauna in late Barstovian time also do not survive the Clarendonian, such as *Eucastor*, *Cynarctus*, *Aelurodon*, *Tomarctus*, *Ischyrocyon*, *Megahippus*, and possibly *Ustatochoerus* (the early Hemphillian occurrences seem equivocal).

The Clarendonian, in this restricted sense, is clearly recognizable in the western United States, although as noted (pp. 156–157), a provincial character is still present which justifies the proposal of a local biochronology for the Pacific Coast region. Savage's (1955) Cerrotejonian Stage (for definition, see p. 157) probably includes a Barstovian equivalent (Comanche Point Local Fauna) at the base of his stratotype, but the major part of it is Clarendonian, as in his Montediablan Stage (p. 155). It should be noted that Savage intended to define a sequence of chronostratigraphic units of provincial usage, a procedure fundamentally different in principle from the biochronologic units of regional significance which cover part of the same span of time.

Hemphillian

This age was defined by Wood el al. (1941, p. 12) "on the Hemphill member of the Ogallala, which includes both the Hemphill local fauna from the Coffee Ranch Quarry and the Higgins Local Fauna, Hemphill County, Panhandle of Texas." In the Great Plains a major faunal discontinuity occurs within this age, and the two assemblages mentioned in the definition fall on opposite sides of that discontinuity. In this chapter (pp. 173–175), we have shown that a faunal sequence overlapping the Clarendon and extending beyond the Coffee Ranch can be constructed from stratigraphic data from the type area in the Panhandle of Texas and adjacent Oklahoma. These data, and those from correlated sites throughout North America, help to revise the temporal ranges and associations of some of the critical taxa used in the definition and characterization of the age.

On their correlation chart, Wood et al. (1941, pl. 1) show the Higgins Local Fauna as occupying the early half of Hemphillian time. In our compilation, the Higgins Local Fauna is temporally preceded by the Arnett and Capps Pit local faunas, which, in turn, are younger than the Clarendonian fauna of the Cole Highway Pit. These assemblages occur superposed in an unnamed formation of the Ogallala Group in Texas and adjacent Oklahoma (contra Wood et al. [1941] who regarded the Higgins Local Fauna as from the "Hemphill member of the Ogallala"). The Higgins, Arnett, and Capps Pit local faunas represent a continuation of the chronofauna established by Clarendonian time. They are characterized by *Leptarctus*, *Barbourofelis*, *Nimravides*, *Epicyon*, *Osteoborus*, *Amebelodon*, and diverse equine horses including *Pliohippus*, *Protohippus*, *Calippus*, *Astrohippus*, *Griphippus*, *Nannippus*, *Cormohipparion*, *Hipparion*, and *Neohipparion* (but lacking the anchitherine horses and *Merychippus*). The artiodactyls *Prosthennops*, *Cranioceras* (*Yumaceras*), *Pseudoceras*, antilocaprines, *Procamelus*, *Aepycamelus*, *Hemiauchenia*, and *Megatylopus* also occur. Most of these taxa are represented by different species than their Clarendonian counterparts. In addition, new autochthonous taxa characterize the beginning of Hemphillian time, such as *Dipoides*, *Pliosaccomys*, *Pliotaxidea*, *Vulpes*, "*Canis*," *Osteoborus*, and *Cranioceras* (*Yumaceras*). Immigrants appearing at the beginning of this interval are few and include a single occurrence of the cricetodontine rodent *Pliotomodon* from the Mullholland Formation, California, the arvicoline rodents *Microtoscoptes* and *Paramicrotoscoptes* that occur in the northern Great Plains, Rocky Mountains, Great Basin, and northern Columbia Plateau (see Repenning, this volume), and the megalonychid sloth *Pliometanastes* (see n. 11). The occurrence of *Thinobadistes* in the Mixon Local Fauna (its type locality) of Florida may predate its first occurrence in the Great Plains. Such a definition would thus exclude certain assemblages (e.g., Xmas, Kat, and *Leptarctus* Quarry local faunas from the upper part of the Ash Hollow Formation of north-central Nebraska) correlated by Wood et al (1941, pl. 1) with the Hemphillian but here retained in the late Clarendonian.

The late early or medial Hemphillian faunas contain the immigrant carnivores *Simocyon*, *Plionarctos* (both from the Rattlesnake Fauna, Oregon), *Lutravus* (Thousand Creek Fauna, Nevada; not shown on fig. 6.2), and *Enhydritherium* (Withlacoochee 4A, Local Fauna, Florida). The rare bovid *Neotragocerus* also appears in the medial Hemphillian Aphelops Draw Fauna (Skinner et al. 1977) of Nebraska. At the base of the Hemphill beds of the Texas Panhandle, the fauna of the Box T Quarry still carries the "Clarendonian chronofauna" but with the important addition of such Eurasiatic immigrant carnivores as *Indarctos*, *Eomellivora*, and *Machairodus* and the sloth *Thinobadistes*, the earliest mylodontid from the neotropics. *Indarctos* is also present in Oregon (Rattlesnake Fauna), Nevada (Smiths Valley Fauna), and Nebraska (Cambridge Local Fauna).

Stratigraphic evidence calibrated radiometrically suggests that most of the Eurasian immigrants first appear about 6 to 7 Ma, at the close of that portion of Hemphillian time dominated by elements of the "Clarendonian chronofauna." Evidence now available (Hirschfeld 1981) reinforces an earliest Hemphillian first occurrence of at least the megalonycid sloths in agreement with the analysis recently contributed by Tedford to the paper by Marshall et al. (1979) on the interchange of mammals with the neotropics in late Cenozoic time.

We believe that the Hemphillian can be objectively and usefully subdivided into two phases separated by an event during which rather striking faunal turnover eliminated most of the prominent elements of the "Clarendonian chronofauna," including Amphicyonidae, *Leptarctus*, *Sthenictis*, *Nimravides*, *Barbourofelis*, *Epicyon*, *Pliohippus*, *Protohippus*, *Hipparion*, *Cormohipparion*, *Prosthennops*, *Aepycamelus*, *Procamelus*, *Pseudoceras*, and *Plioceras*. Most of the immigrants also do not survive; the exceptions are *Machairodus*, *Neotragocerus*,

and the sloths. The resulting fauna characteristic of the late Hemphillian was thus reduced in the diversity of its autochthonous forms, yet at the same time it was significantly augmented by immigrants.

It now seems clear from the stratigraphic relationships of correlative assemblages and faunal composition that the Kimball Fauna of Nebraska, type assemblage of the "Kimballian Provincial Age" of Schultz and Stout (1961, fig. 3) and Schultz et al. (1970), represents part of this early Hemphillian interval. The "Kimballian" was based on faunal assemblages from the type area of the Kimball Formation in Kimball and Cheyenne counties, Nebraska, and from other localities in southwestern Nebraska (Schultz et al. 1970), but the faunal list provided was drawn mostly from the Cambridge Local Fauna, from deposits in southern Nebraska far removed from the type area of the Kimball Formation. In terms of the Texas-Oklahoma faunal sequence, the closest match of the Cambridge Local Fauna is the Box T Quarry Local Fauna. However, the evidence from stratigraphy (Breyer 1975) and radiometry (Boellstorff 1976) indicates that the "Kimball Formation" ranges through a significant interval, extending from about 8 to 7 Ma and perhaps beyond if the rocks bearing the Uptegrove Local Fauna are assigned to that unit (Martin 1975, but see comments in Voorhies 1984). Recently Stout and Tanner (1983) have termed the Ogallala deposits at Santee, northeastern Nebraska, "Kimball equivalent" and thus extended the geochron of this unit into late Hemphillian time (Voorhies 1977, 1984). Breyer's review (1981) of the composition and age relationships of the local faunas assigned to the "Kimball Fauna" from western Nebraska indicates that these assemblages are mostly correlative with Hemphillian faunas from the southern Great Plains (including the Higgins Local Fauna assigned to the early Hemphillian by Wood et al. 1941) which preceded the mid-Hemphillian extinction event. The term "Kimballian" thus joins "Valentinian" as a stratigraphic geochron without faunal definition or characterization. Through the years it has been extended to younger deposits until it has virtually become synonomous with the Hemphillian. We reject its use on these grounds.

The superposition of late Hemphillian on early Hemphillian faunas is present within the Hemphill beds: the Coffee Ranch Local Fauna (we prefer this term to "Hemphill local fauna" [Wood et al. 1941] to avoid confusion of rocks, time, and faunas) occurs in the upper part of the unit and is faunally distinct from that of the Box T Quarry in the lower part of the unit. The Coffee Ranch Local Fauna and its equivalent in Oklahoma (Optima) show a marked drop in ungulate diversity when compared with early Hemphillian faunas. The horses are represented by four genera (*Dinohippus, Astrohippus, Neohipparion,* and *Nannippus*); the camels by *Hemiauchenia* and *Megatylopus*; the cranioceratine *Pediomeryx* is restricted to the late Hemphillian; and of the gomphotheres, only rhynchorostrine *Rhynchotherium* is widespread. The sloth *Megalonyx* appears, indicating further opportunities for interchange with the neotropics. The immigrant carnivores *Agriotherium* and *Plesiogulo* and true cats of the genus *Felis* appear. *Machairodus* is the only sabre-cat present until latest Hemphillian time when the earliest smilodontine *Megantereon* appears in Florida (Berta and Galiano 1983). In the Columbia Plateau and northern Great Plains, other immigrant taxa appear in equivalent faunas, such as the pika *Ochotona* and the arvicoline rodent *Promimomys* (both from the McKay Reservoir Local Fauna, Oregon, Shotwell 1956, and the Mailbox Local Fauna, Antelope County, Nebraska, Repenning, chap. 8; neither shown on fig. 6.2). Martin (1975) reports another arvicoline "*Propliophenacomys*" from the Santee Local Fauna (Voorhies 1977, 1984) of northeastern Nebraska regarded as an autochthonous form by Repenning (chap. 8).

Younger faunas of similar character, showing mainly species level change, can be found in rocks superposed on those containing Coffee Ranch equivalents in the Panhandle of Texas and Oklahoma (e.g., Christian Ranch Local Fauna, Texas, and assemblages from the high gravels of Oklahoma; see p. 175). These faunas characteristically contain advanced species of the horses *Astrohippus, Dinohippus, Nannippus,* and *Neohipparion* associated with other taxa typical of the Coffee Ranch, indicating the persistence of the derived Great Plains chronofauna representing late Hemphillian time. This fauna can be traced with little change into northern Mexico (Yepomera Fauna, Lance 1950; not shown on fig. 6.2), but in the Gulf Coast (Upper Bone Valley Fauna, see pp. 180–181) a number of taxa (Protoceratids, *Griphippus, Gomphotherium*) suggest the survival there of elements of the Clarendonian chronofauna. In the southwestern United States, latest Hemphillian faunas (undescribed Redington and Wikieup faunas, Arizona, and Mt. Eden Fauna, southern California, Frick 1921; May and Repenning 1982; not shown on fig. 6.2) have *Dinohippus* and *Onohippidium* (MacFadden and Skinner 1971) but lack hipparion horses and rhinos. Rhinos, but not hipparion horses, occur in the southern Great Basin (Warren Local Fauna, Mojave Desert, California; May 1981). To the north in central California (Pinole Local Fauna, Modesto Reservoir Local Fauna [Wagner 1976, 1981]; not shown on fig. 6.2) and the Columbia Plateau (McKay Reservoir Local Fauna; not shown on fig. 6.2), *Hipparion* and *Neohipparion* (*eurystyle* group) horses

occur with *Dinohippus* and rhinos, including *Teleoceras*. These differences in geographic range suggest the presence of new environmental factors that were fragmenting older patterns.

The end of Hemphillian time is marked by the extinction of most of the characteristic elements of the late Hemphillian, including forms with long Miocene histories such as the Mylagaulidae, Rhinoceratidae, and Protoceratidae. The late Hemphillian faunal provincialism noted above suggests that the process of change was taking place at different rates in different geographic areas. The result was a further loss of diversity among the large mammals only partly augmented by continued immigration from Eurasia and tropical America. Eurasiatic immigrants such as *Nebraskomys, Mimomys, Trigonictis, Lutra, Chasmaporthetes, Lynx, Ursus, Parailurus,* and diverse true cervids (*Bretzia, Odocoileus*), in addition to the glyptodonts, chlamytheres, and sloths from the neotropics, distinguish Blancan faunas as does the appearance of the indigenous genera *Borophagus, Equus, Titanotylopus,* and *Camelops.* The Upper Bone Valley Fauna of peninsular Florida appears to be one of the latest Hemphillian assemblages known (see pp. 180–181) and contains the earliest representatives of such common Blancan and younger taxa as *Megantereon, Borophagus, Mylohyus,* and odocoileine deer. The accelerating pace of immigration from Hemphillian into Pleistocene time reflects the availability of dispersal routes to North America and increasing environmental instability, particularly at high latitudes, that provided the goad for the movement of mammals.

SUMMARY

We have reviewed much of the evidence used in 1941 by Wood et al. to establish the Arikareean through Hemphillian North American mammal ages as independent biochronologic units. Since 1941, knowledge of the faunal succession has gradually improved so that a meaningful discussion of the adequacy of that scale is possible. In the text, we review the present state of knowledge of the faunal sequence covering this interval. Attention is focused on those areas across the United States where the faunal sequence is unusually comprehensive and where stratigraphic superposition provides an independent means of establishing the temporal succession of faunas. We believe that the successions thus chosen represent the best controlled and hence the most influential data bearing on the development of the biochronologic scale. Sequences in coastal California, the Great Basin of California and Nevada, the Columbia Plateau of Oregon, the northern Rocky Mountains in Montana, the northern Great Plains of South Dakota, Wyoming, and Nebraska, the southern Great Plains of Texas and Oklahoma, and the Gulf Coast of Texas and Florida include most of the historic localities (fig. 6.1) important in the establishment of the biochronology. Continued study of these faunal successions, and others not discussed herein, will provide data for the refinement of the biochronologic scale and the establishment of the detailed biostratigraphies necessary for more precise geochronologic subdivision.

A correlation chart (fig. 6.2) summarizes our analysis of the temporal relationships of the faunas used in this work. Comparative study of these successions leads to the following generalities about the nature of the faunal change in midlatitude North America during late Oligocene through Miocene time. Geographic provincialism is evident throughout this interval, especially between the western and central parts of the United States, and becomes more clearly manifested in the Miocene Epoch, particularly in its latter half. Provincialism involves the development of regional faunas or chronofaunas whose overall generic composition changes little through geologically significant spans of time suggesting ecosystem stability marked by briefer intervals of faunal turnover when new chronofaunas were formed from surviving autochthonous taxa, augmented by immigrants.

Immigration is shown to have taken place throughout the interval (fig. 6.3), with the Hemingfordian and Hemphillian being times of particularly active flow of Eurasiatic forms into North America. The direct effect of immigration on chronofaunal evolution is hard to demonstrate with the data on hand, but it seems rarely to have involved faunal replacement. Apparently most of the immigrants found suitable habitats that often allowed them to persist beyond the range of the chronofauna with which they first became associated. Chronofaunal evolution on the Great Plains of the United States can be reconstructed with some confidence because the record is more continuous there than elsewhere. At the level of data presented in this review, it is possible to recognize five Great Plains chronofaunas (Whitneyan through early Arikareean; late Arikareean through early Hemingfordian; late Hemingfordian through early Barstovian; late Barstovian through early Hemphillian; and late Hemphillian) with major faunal change taking place between these intervals. The intervals themselves range from 1.5 to 7.0 m.y. in duration and are separated by short spans of 0.5 to 1.0 m.y. during which faunal turnover took place. The Gulf Coast seems to have been a separate province for most of the interval discussed, although by Clarendonian time, the Texas portion of this

province contained a southern phase of the Great Plains chronofauna. Florida remained a haven for a distinctive assemblage whose long development is indicated by the persistence there of many "relict" forms. In the West, the Rocky Mountains and Great Basin constitute a distinct faunal province but one that provides little evidence for the persistence of distinctive chronofaunas. Perhaps the lack of environmental stability in this tectonically active region inhibited the development of regional chronofaunas and encouraged the formation of greater provincialism whose complex history can barely be discerned with the data at hand.

For the above reasons, the faunal succession in the Great Plains has assumed a prominent place in the development of a biochronology for the Arikareean through Hemphillian interval. With the exception of the Barstovian, all the mammal ages were primarily typified in this area. More recently, subdivisions have been suggested to segment the original scale into fragments reflecting details of the local succession. We review all these proposals as well as the established biochronology with the intention of suggesting boundary definitions and revised characterizations for the mammal ages. We propose an informal subdivision of these ages where it seems clearly indicated by the faunal succession and where subdivision would seem to lead to greater precision in correlation. We utilize the first appearance of certain immigrant taxa to delimit the earliest part of each mammal age (fig. 6.3); a characterizing fauna of immigrants and widely ranging endemic taxa permit recognition of these biochrons over as wide a geographic range as possible within the limitations of the data. These principles lead to the following proposals.

Arikareean (Wood et al. 1941, pp. 11–12). Definition follows that of the early Arikareean; the characterization is a composite of that for the early and late phases of the age.

Early Arikareean. Definition: earliest appearance of *Ocajila*, Talpinae, *Plesiosminthus*, and *Allomys*. A late phase may be defined by *Parvericius*, *Pseudotheridiomys*, *Promartes*, and *Moropus*. Characterization: earliest appearance of *Archaeolagus*, Entoptychinae, Mylagaulidae, *Diceratherium*, *Dinohyus*, *Promerycochoerus* (*Pseudopromerycochoerus*), *Desmatochoerus*, Stenomylinae (*Dyseotylopus*, but *Stenomylus* in the later phase), *Miotylopus*, and *Nanotragulus*; the limited occurrence of hypsodont leptauchenine oreodonts and *Mesoreodon*; and the latest occurrence of Primates, *Eumys*, *Paleolagus*, *Hyaenodon*, *Eusmilus*, *Nimravus*, *Hyracodon*, *Subhyracodon*, *Miohippus*, *Archaeotherium*, *Elomeryx*, *Hypisodus*, and leptauchenine oreodonts.

Late Arikareean. Definition: Early phase—earliest

appearance of *Oligobunis, Zodiolestes, Daphoenodon,* and *Menoceras.* Late phase—earliest appearance of *Cephalogale, Cynelos, Ysengrinia, Blastomeryx, Barbouromeryx,* and *Paracosoryx.* Characterization: Early phase—earliest appearance of *Parahippus, Anchitherium, Merychyus,* Synthetoceratinae (*Syndyoceras, Lambdoceras,* and *Prosynthetoceras*), *Oxydactylus.* Late phase—earliest appearance of *Mylagaulodon, Aleurocyon, Cynarctoides, Archaeohippus, Michenia, Tanymykter,* and *Merycochoerus;* the limited occurrence of *Oligobunis, Aelurocyon, Zodiolestes, Syndyoceras, P. (Promerycochoerus),* and *Hypsiops;* the maximum diversity of oreodonts and flat-incisor beavers (including the burrows, "*Daimonelix,*" of *Palaeocastor*); the latest occurrence of Entoptychinae, *Temnocyon, Promartes, Diceratherium,* Merycoidodontinae, Eporeodontinae, Promerycochoerinae, Desmatochoerinae, Hypertragulidae, and *Protoceras.*

Hemingfordian (Wood et al. 1941, p. 12). Definition follows that for the early Hemingfordian; the characterization is a composite of that for the early and late phases of the age.

Early Hemingfordian. Definition: earliest appearance of Soricinae (*Antesorex*) and Limnoecinae (*Angustidens*) shrews, *Plesiosorex, Oreolagus, Amphicyon, Hemicyon (Phoberocyon), Ursavus,* Leptarctinae (*Craterogale* and *Leptarctus*), Mustelinae, *Potamotherium, Amphictis, Brachypotherium,* and *Aletomeryx.* Characterization: earliest appearance of *Mesogaulus, Cupidinimus, Tomarctus, Brachypsalis,* Floridatragulinae, and *Protolabis;* the limited occurrence of *Brachypotherium, Aletomeryx,* and *Machaeromeryx;* the latest occurrence of *Trogomys, Ysengrinia, Cynelos, Menoceras,* Entelodontidae, *Stenomylus, Phenacocoelus,* and *Merycochoerus.*

Late Hemingfordian. Definition: earliest appearance of Petauristinae (*Petauristodon* and *Blackia*), *Eomys, Miomustela, Plionictis, Sthenictis,* Lutrinae (*Mionictis*), Felidae (*Pseudaelurus*), *Teleoceras,* and *Aphelops.* Characterization: earliest appearance of *Hypolagus, Anchitheriomys, Mylagaulus, Merychippus* s.l., *Hypohippus, Brachycrus, Ticholeptus,* Cranioceratinae (*Bouromeryx*), *Dromomeryx, Aepycamelus, Merycodus,* and *Merriamoceras;* latest appearance of *Parahippus, Barbouromeryx,* and *Oxydactylus.*

Barstovian (Wood el al. 1941, p. 12). Definition follows that for the early Barstovian; the characterization is a composite of that for the early and late phases of the age.

Early Barstovian. Definition: earliest appearance of *Hemicyon (Plithocyon)* and *Copemys.* Characterization: earliest appearance of *Perognathus, Cormohipparion,*

Dyseohyus, and *Meryceros;* limited occurrence of *Desmatippus* and *Rakomeryx;* latest appearance of *Lambdoceras, Ticholeptus, Brachycrus,* and *Merriamoceros.*

Late Barstovian (taxa bearing asterisk restricted to the Great Plains and Gulf Coast regions). Definition: earliest appearance of Proboscidea (Gomphotheriidae), *Pseudocyon,** and *Pseudoceras** (late in interval). Characterization: earliest appearance of *Megasminthus*, Eucastor, Ischyrocyon, Aelurodon, Epicyon* (in Great Basin of California and New Mexico), *Carpocyon, Cynarctus*, Megahippus, Calippus*, Neohipparion, Hipparion, Pliohippus, Protohippus, Dinohippus** (late in interval), *Prosthennops, Ustatochoerus, Procamelus, Cranioceras, Longirostromeryx*;* limited occurrence of *Strobodon* and *Pseudhipparion*;* latest appearance of *Anchitheriomys, Parvericius, Ursavus, Amphicyon, Archaeohippus, Anchitherium** (both horses early in interval), Chalicotheriidae, Leptomerycidae (*Pseudoparablastomeryx**), *Blastomeryx,* and *Dromomeryx.*

Clarendonian (Wood et al. 1941, p. 12). Definition: earliest appearance of *Barbourofelis* and, later in the interval, *Platybelodon, Amebelodon,* and *Ischyrictis (Hoplictis).* Characterization: earliest appearance of *Nimravides, Epicyon* (in the Great Plains and Gulf Coast), *Griphippus, Astrohippus, Nannippus* (Gulf coast), *Macrogenis, Synthetoceras, Hemiauchenia, Megatylopus,* Antilocaprinae (*Plioceros* and *Proantilocapra*); latest occurrence of *Eucastor, Brachypsalis, Ischyrocyon, Cynarctus, Aelurodon, Tomarctus, Hypohippus, Megahippus, Merychippus, Paratoceras, Miolabis, Protolabis,* and probably *Ustatochoerus.*

Hemphillian (Wood et al. 1941, p. 12). Definition follows that for the early Hemphillian; the characterization is a composite of that for the early and late phases of the age.

Early Hemphillian. Definition: earliest appearance of Arvicolinae (limited occurrence of *Microtoscoptes* and *Paramicrotoscoptes*), *Pliotomodon,* Mylodontidae (*Thinobadistes*), and Megalonychidae (*Pliometanastes*); limited occurrence late in interval of *Simocyon, Indarctos, Lutravus,* and *Eomellivora;* earliest appearance, late in interval, of *Megalonyx, Enhydritherium, Machairodus, Plionarctos,* and the Bovidae (*Neotragocerus*). Characterization: earliest appearance of *Dipoides, Pliosaccomys, Pliotaxidea, Vulpes,* "*Canis,*" *Osteoborus,* and *Cranioceras (Yumaceras);* latest occurrence of Amphicyonidae, *Leptarctus, Sthenictis, Nimravides, Barbourofelis, Epicyon, Pliohippus, Protohippus, Cormohipparion, Prosthennops, Aepycamelus, Pseudoceras,* and *Plioceros.*

Late Hemphillian. Definition: limited occurrence of *Promimomys,* "*Propliophenacomys,*" *Plesiogulo,* and

Agriotherium; earliest appearance of *Ochotona, Megantereon, Felis,* and odocoiline Cervinae. Characterization: earliest appearance of *Taxidea, Borophagus, Rhynchotherium, Platygonus,* and *Mylohyus*; limited occurrence of *Pediomeryx*; latest occurrence of Mylagaulidae, *Osteoborus, Astrohippus, Neohipparion, Dinohippus,* Rhinocerotidae, and Protoceratidae.

ACKNOWLEDGMENTS

This chapter is an outgrowth of material gathered at the invitation of D. E. Savage to be presented at a symposium entitled "Vertebrate Paleontology as a Discipline in Geochronology: Examples and Problems" organized by the Geological Society of America and the Society of Vertebrate Paleontology in 1973. An abstract (Tedford et al. 1973) and an oral presentation of some of our results were contributed at the societies' annual joint meeting, in Dallas, Texas, November 14, 1973. We wish to thank Don Savage for his invitation and his counsel in the preparation of that material. In addition, we are grateful to have had the use of his unpublished summaries of California mammal faunas.

The senior author assumed the task of compiling the data from the literature, records, and collections, principally at the American Museum, and from the data supplied by the junior authors. A great deal of unpublished material has been used in this report, including that contained in the junior authors' files and in unpublished theses. Additional data were developed in examining the relevant collections discussed herein. Besides contributing factual information, the junior authors exercised editorial supervision over this work, but in all fairness we must add that no group of nine people can ever agree completely on so complex a subject, and thus all of us hold reservations with regard to some aspects of the completed work. Nevertheless, we have tried to present a consensus and believe we have done so for the most part.

Many others have helped us directly by criticizing parts of this work or by contributing data. In particular, we are grateful for the advice of L. Dingus, R. J. Emry, R. M. Hunt, Jr., M. E. Hunter, F. W. Johnson, E. B. Lander, E. L. Lundelius, S. Mallory, E. J. Manning, L. D. Martin, T. H. Patton, D. L. Rasmussen, C. A. Repenning, T. M. Stout, C. C. Swisher III, M. Voorhies, J. Waldrop, J. A. Wilson, and M. O. Woodburne.

Important unpublished radiometric and fission-track dates have been generously donated by J. D. Boellstorff, Conservation and Survey Division, State of Nebraska; G. A. Izett and C. W. Naeser, U.S. Geological Survey, Denver; and A. M. Sarna-Wojcicki, U.S. Geological Survey, Menlo Park, California. We are indebted to these men and their institutions for permitting us to use these data to calibrate the correlation chart (fig. 6.2).

Raymond Gooris has skillfully rendered the figures. The text was patiently typed by Janice Quinter and Alejandra Lora.

A compilation of data such as this is based on the published and unpublished work of many people, some of whom are cited in the bibliography while others are listed above. In addition, we believe it is appropriate to acknowledge the indefatigable labors in the field of the unsung heroes of the Frick Laboratory whose combined efforts over the past forty years have produced the collection and data that lie behind many of the statements made herein. To them go our profound thanks.

APPENDIX A

Selected radiometric and fission-track dates used to calibrate correlation chart (K-Ar dates recalculated using IUGS constants following method of Dalrymple [1979] ± one standard deviation if given).

No.	Date (Ma)	Reference	Unit Dated	Remarks
1	10.3	(1)	Moraga Fm.	Revised date of basal andesitic basalt flow (see KA 993, 1001 refr. [2]).
2	10.2	(2)	Siesta Fm.	Plagioclase from tuff, base of unit, KA 829.
3	7.9	(2)	Bald Peak Vol.	Basalt, minimum date, KA 1003.
4	5.3 ± 0.1	(22)	Pinole Tuff	Feldspar from tuff a few feet above fauna, KA 1005.

No.	Date (Ma)	Reference	Unit Dated	Remarks
5	5.9 ± 0.6; 6.3 ± 0.1	(22, 23)	Green Valley Fm.	Tuff near top of unit.
6	5.5 ± 0.2	(22)	Pinole Tuff	Tuff at top of Green Valley Fm., immediately beneath Hemme Hills Local Fauna.
7	4.1 ± 1.0; 4.6 ± 0.5	(22)	Lawlor Tuff	Tuff within Tassajara Fm.
8	22.1–22.9	(3)	Dacite, dacite agglomerate	Intertongues with top of Tecuya Fm., minimum date for fauna(s), KA 2114–5, 2166, 2175.
9	16.5 ± 1.3	(3)	Caliente Fm.	Lowest Triple Basalt, KA 2127.
10	15.6	(2)	Caliente Fm.	Biotite from tuff, contains Dome Spring Fauna, KA 161.
11	14.6 ± 0.6; 14.8 ± 0.8	(3)	Caliente Fm.	Uppermost Triple Basalt, KA 2116, 2125.
12	21.6	(4)	Hector Fm.	Tuff near top of stratigraphic occurrence of Black Butte Mine Local Fauna, KA 2223.
13	20.3 ± 0.7	(5)	Saddleback Basalt	Boron L. F. 146 m above top of basalt, B-4.
14	18.6 ± 0.2	(26)	Unnamed basalt	Lower Cady Mtn. Local Fauna 30 m above and below dated basalt.
15	17.9	(6)	Unnamed tuff	Tuff stratigraphically between local faunas, northeastern Cady Mtns.
16	16.3 ± 0.3	(7)	Barstow Fm.	Biotite from tuff just below Oreodon Quarry, Mud Hills, San Bernardino Co., Calif.
17	14.8 ± 0.3; 15.5	(2, 8)	Barstow Fm.	Biotite from tuff just below New Year Quarry, Mud Hills, San Bernardino Co., Calif., KA 449.
18	13.4 ± 0.7	(9)	Barstow Fm.	Biotite from tuff just above Hemicyon Quarry, Mud Hills, San Bernardino Co., Calif.
19	12.6	(2)	Unnamed tuff	Biotite from tuff just below (contra refr. 2) local fauna, KA 1368.
20	10.8	(6)	Ricardo Fm.	Fission-track from sanidine in tuff, 61 m above base of uppermost basalt.
21	17.4 ± 0.3; 17.6 ± 0.3	(10)	Fraction Tuff	Sanidine and biotite, respectively, USGS (M) 11549–1.
22	16.6 ± 0.4	(11)	Brougher Dacite	Sanidine and biotite, 659–66, see also refr. 10.

No.	Date (Ma)	Reference	Unit Dated	Remarks
23	11.8	(2)	Esmeralda Fm.	Sanidine from tuff near middle of fossiliferous section (Mawby 1965, pl. 3), KA 577.
24	11.4; 11.7	(2)	Esmeralda Fm.	Biotite from correlative (*contra* refr. 2) tuff, just beneath micromammals, KA 480, 499.
25	11.5	(2)	Coal Valley Fm. (see refr. 19)	Biotite from tuff, near base of fossiliferous section, KA 414.
26	11.1	(2)	Coal Valley Fm.	Biotite from tuff near middle of fossiliferous section, KA 551.
27	9.6	(2)	Coal Valley Fm., (see refr. 19)	Biotite from tuff low in unit containing Smiths Valley Fauna, KA 485.
28	6.8 – 7.6	(19)	Unnamed basalt	Whole rock dates from basalts unconformably overlying Wassuk Group; minimum date for Smiths Valley Fauna, KA 2341, 2365–9, 2496–7, and 2582.
29	31.9	(2)	John Day Fm.	Sanidine from tuff within Big Basin Mbr.; containing Bridge Crk. Flora, KA 489.
30	26.0	(2)	John Day Fm.	Obsidian from Picture Gorge Ignimbrite, KA 648.
31	15.6 ± 0.6	(12)	Picture Gorge Basalt	Whole rock dates, average of 7 flows.
32	14.7 ± 0.3	(14)	Owyhee Basalt	Whole rock dates, average of 7 flows.
33	12.4	(15)	Juntura Fm.	Basalt at top of lower member, above Stinking Water flora, KA 1240.
34	9.4 ± 0.6	(16)	Drewsey Fm.	Sanidine from Welded Tuff of Devine Cyn., lowest unit in Drewsey Fm., beneath local faunas.
35	7.1 ± 1.09	(17)	Drinkwater Basalt	Whole rock date; minimum age for Bartlett Mtn., etc., local faunas.
36	6.6 ± 0.1; 6.8 ± 0.2	(13)	Rattlesnake Fm.	Sanidine from ignimbrite member of Rattlesnake Formation, above fauna.
37	29.5 ± 2.8	(21)	Unnamed ignimbrite	Fission-track from zircons in welded tuff unconformably beneath Cabbage Patch Fm.
38	27.7 ± 0.7; 27.6 ± 0.6; 28.8 ± 0.6	(18, 27)	Helvas Cyn. Mbr., Gering Fm.	Biotite from Carter Cyn. Ash; fission-track from zircon of the same ash.
39	27.7 ± 0.6	(18)	Mitchell Pass Mbr., Gering Fm.	Sanidine from pumice in Twin Sisters Pumice Conglomerate.

No.	Date (Ma)	Reference	Unit Dated	Remarks
40	26.3; 23.4 ± 0.4	(2, 21)	Gering Fm.	Glass shards from correlated Mitchel Pass Mbr. at Scotts Bluff, KA 985. Fission-track from glass of the same ash.
41	21.9; 20.7 ± 5.1	(2, 21)	Harrison Fm.	Biotite from tuff about 9 m below Agate Spring Quarry. Fission-track from glass of the same ash.
42	17.5 ± 0.5; 16.5 ± 0.6	(27)	Sheep Creek Fm.	Zircon fission-track from black vitric tuff, head of Merychippus Draw, same ash as KA 891, refr. (2); above fauna.
43	14.2 ± 1.4	(21)	Sand Canyon beds	Fission-track from glass, tuff near top of unit, Shimek BM (Galusha 1975, fig. 13F).
44	10.3 ± 0.3; 10.6 ± 0.6	(24, 27)	Cap Rock Mbr., Ash Hollow Fm.	Fission-track from zircon and glass, vitric tuff (Swallow Ash) at base of Fm., Snake Riv., Cherry Co., Nebr.
45	10.2 ± 0.7; 9.7 ± 1.2	(21, 28)	Ash Hollow Fm.	Fission-track from glass, vitric tuff (Davis Ash) above top of Cap Rock Mbr., Snake Riv., Cherry Co., Nebr.
46	8.0 ± 0.3	(24)	Ash Hollow Fm.	Fission-track from glass, vitric tuff about 37 m above base of type section, Garden Co., Nebr.
47	8.0 ± 0.7	(24)	"Ogallala Fm."	Fission-track from glass, vitric tuff in lectotype section of Elias (in Stirton, 1936a) beneath Feltz Ranch Local Fauna.
48	7.7 ± 0.7	(21)	Ash Hollow Fm.	Fission-track from glass, vitric tuff above ash 46 near middle of type section, Garden Co., Nebr.
49	6.6 ± 0.3	(24)	Ash Hollow Fm.	Fission-track from glass, vitric tuff above ash 48 very near top of type section, Garden Co., Nebr.
50	5.3 ± 0.2	(24)	Unnamed	Fission-track from glass, vitric tuff overlying fauna, Knox Co., Nebr.
51	19.2 ± 0.5	(29)	Marsland (= Upr. Harrison beds)	Fission-track from zircon, Eagle Crags Ash, near base of unit in type area.
52	4.9 ± 0.33 (glass, Izett); 5.5 ± 0.4 (glass, Boellstorff); 6.8 ± 0.2 (zircon, Izett)	(24, 27)	Hemphill Beds	Three fission-track dates, from vitric tuff immediately above Coffee Ranch Quarry.
53	16.1 ± 1.0	(25)	Chipola Fm.	Helium-uranium date on coral.

References

(1) Savage, pers. com., 1973
(2) Evernden et al. 1964
(3) Turner 1970
(4) Woodburne et al. 1974
(5) Armstrong and Higgins 1973
(6) Woodburne, pers. com., 1973
(7) Isotopes KA 70–11, avg. of two determinations (15.6, 16.2), full data in senior author's file.
(8) Isotopes KA 70–12, avg. of two determinations (14.2, 14.5), full data in senior author's file.
(9) Isotopes KA 70–13, avg. of two determinations (13.6, 12.3), full data in senior author's file.
(10) Silberman and McKee 1972
(11) Albers and Stewart 1972
(12) Baksi 1974
(13) Parker and Armstrong 1972
(14) Bottomley and York 1976
(15) Evernden and James 1964
(16) Greene 1973
(17) Greene et al. 1972
(18) Obradovich et al. 1973
(19) Gilbert and Reynolds 1973
(20) Naeser, pers. com. to D. Rasmussen, 1973
(21) Boellstroff, pers. com., 28 Sept. 1973, 1977, 1980 (all dates are considered preliminary, full data on file, Conservation and Survey Division, University of Nebraska)
(22) Sarna-Wojcicki 1976
(23) Bartow et al. 1973
(24) Boellstorff 1976
(25) Bender 1973
(26) Miller 1980
(27) Naeser et al. 1980
(28) Izett 1975, p. 202
(29) Hunt et al., 1983, p. 366

APPENDIX B

Index of Faunas and Sites and Their Ages

(*Names not shown on correlation chart, fig. 6.2. North American Mammal Ages of Wood et al. (1941) with provincial equivalents in parentheses where identified; "E." denotes the early and "L." the late phases of ages as designated herein.)

"A" sites, Vaqueros and Caliente formations, Calif., L. Arikareean or E. Hemingfordian
*Adair Ranch Quarry, Okla., E. Hemphillian
Agate Springs Local Fauna, Nebr., L. Arikareean
Aiken Hill Local Fauna, Tex., L. Arikareean
*Aletomeryx Quarry, Nebr., E. Hemingfordian

*Amer. Mus. Nat. Hist. Quarry 7, Nebr., L. Clarendonian
*Anceney Local Fauna, Mont., L. Barstovian
Antelope Hills Local Fauna, Mont., L. Barstovian
Aphelops Draw Fauna, Nebr., E. Hemphillian
Arnett Local Fauna, Okla., E. Hemphillian
Ashville Local Fauna, Fla., L. Barstovian
Barker's Ranch Local Fauna, Calif., L. Hemingfordian
Barstow Fauna (restricted), Calif., L. Barstovian
Bartlett Mountain Local Fauna, Ore., E. Hemphillian
Bear Tooth Local Fauna, Nebr., L. Hemphillian
Bert Creek Local Fauna, Mont., L. Barstovian or E. Clarendonian
*Big Spring Canyon Local Fauna, S. Dak., E. Clarendonian
Black Butte Local Fauna, Ore., L. Clarendonian
Black Butte Mine Fauna, Calif., L. Arikareean
Black Hawk Ranch Local Fauna, Calif., L. Clarendonian (Montediablan, type fauna)
*Blacktail Deer Creek Local Fauna, Mont., L. Arikareean
Boron Local Fauna, Calif., E. Hemingfordian
Box T Quarry, Local Fauna, Tex., E. Hemphillian
*Brady Pocket Local Fauna, Nev., L. Clarendonian
Bridge Ranch Local Fauna, Tex., L. Barstovian
*Bridgeport quarries, Nebr., E. Hemingfordian
Brooksville Local Fauna, Fla., L. Arikareean
Buda Local Fauna, Fla., L. Arikareean
Burge Fauna, Nebr., L. Barstovian
Burkeville Fauna, Tex., E.-L. Barstovian
Burkeville Local Fauna, Tex., L. Barstovian
Cabbage Patch local faunas, Mont., E. Arikareean
California Institute of Technology Site 315, Calif., L. Hemingfordian
California Institute of Technology Sites 322–323, Calif., E. Barstovian
Cambridge Local Fauna, Nebr., E. Hemphillian
Campbell gravel pit, Okla., Latest Hemphillian
Capps Pit Local Fauna, Okla., E. Hemphillian
*Cedar Mountain Local Fauna, Nev., E. Clarendonian
Cedar Run Local Fauna, Tex., L. Arikareean
Christian Ranch Local Fauna, Tex., latest Hemphillian
City Waterworks Site, Fla., E. Hemingfordian
Clarendon Fauna, Tex., Clarendonian
Coal Valley Fauna, Nev., E. Clarendonian
Coffee Ranch Local Fauna, Tex., L. Hemphillian
Cold Spring Fauna, Tex., L. Barstovian
Cold Spring Local Fauna, Tex., L. Barstovian
Cole Highway Pit Local Fauna, Tex., Clarendonian
Comanche Point Local Fauna, Calif., E. Clarendonian (Cerrotejonian)
Cronese Local Fauna, Calif., L. Barstovian

*Crookston Bridge Quarry, Nebr., L. Barstovian
*Dalton Local Fauna, Nebr., E. Hemphillian
*Deep River Fauna, Mont., E. Hemingfordian-E. Barstovian
Deer Lodge Fauna, Mont., E. Hemphillian
Devils Gulch Mbr., fauna of, Nebr., L. Barstovian
*Dinohyus Site, Tex., L. Arikareean
Dome Spring Fauna, Calif., E. Barstovian
Dove Springs Fauna, Calif., L. Clarendonian
Drinkwater Local Fauna, Ore., E. Hemphillian
Etchegoin Formation sites, Calif., Hemphillian
Eubanks Fauna, Colo., E. Barstovian
*Eubanks Local Fauna, Colo., E. Barstovian
Farish Ranch Local Fauna, Tex., E. Clarendonian
Feltz Ranch Local Fauna, Nebr., E. Hemphillian
Fish Lake Valley Fauna, Nev., E. Clarendonian
*Fish Lake Valley Local Fauna, Nev., E. Clarendonian
Flint Creek Fauna, Mont., E. Barstovian
Flint Hill Local Fauna, S. Dak., E. Hemingfordian
*Fort Logan Fauna, Mont., E. Arikareean
Frank Ranch Local Fauna, Mont., E. Barstovian
Franklin Phosphate Pit No. 2, Fla., L. Arikareean
Garvin Farm Local Fauna, Tex., E. Hemingfordian
Garvin Gully Fauna, Tex., L. Arik.-E. Heming.
Gering Formation, fauna of, Nebr., E. Arikareean
Gidley Horse Quarry, Tex., L. Clarendonian
Goodnight Fauna, Tex., L. Hemphillian
Goodrich Local Fauna, Tex., L. Barstovian
*Gordon Creek Quarry, Nebr., L. Barstovian
Green Hills Fauna, Calif., E. Barstovian
*Guymon quarries (= Optima quarries), Tex., L. Hemphillian
Harrison Formation, fauna of, Nebr., L. Arikareean
Hemme Hills Local Fauna, Calif., L. Hemphillian
*"Hesperopithecus" site, Nebr., L. Clarendonian
"Hh" sites, Caliente Formation, Calif., L. Hemphillian
Hidden Treasure Spring Local Fauna, Calif., L. Hemingfordian
Higgins Local Fauna, Okla., E. Hemphillian
Horse and Mastodon Quarry, Colo., L. Barstovian
Iron Canyon Fauna, Calif., E. Clarendonian
*Jim Woodruff Dam Site, Fla., E. Hemingfordian
John Day Fauna, Ore., Arikareean-E. Hemingfordian
Kat Quarry Local Fauna, Nebr., L. Clarendonian
Kennesaw Local Fauna, Colo., L. Barstovian
Kern River Formation sites, Calif., E. Hemphillian
Kew Quarry Local Fauna, Calif., E. Arikareean
Kimball Fauna, Nebr., E. Hemphillian
Labahia Mission Local Fauna, Tex., Hemphillian
Lapara Creek Fauna, Tex., L. Barstovian-E. Clarendonian
Lava Mountains Fauna, Calif., E. Hemphillian

*Leptarctus Quarry Local Fauna, Nebr., L. Clarendonian
Logan Mine Fauna, Calif., L. Arikareean
Love Bone Bed Local Fauna, Fla., L. Clarendonian
Lower Bone Valley Fauna, Fla., E. Hemphillian
Lower Cady Mountain Local Fauna, Calif., E. Hemingfordian
*Lower Rosebud Fauna, S. Dak., E.-L. Arikareean
Lower Snake Creek Fauna, Nebr., E. Barstovian
MacAdams Quarry Local Fauna, Tex., E. Clarendonian
Manatee Local Fauna, Fla., L. Hemphillian
Marsland Formation, fauna of, Nebr., L. Arikareean
Martin-Anthony Local Fauna, Fla., L. Arikareean
*Martin Canyon Fauna, Colo., E. Hemingfordian
Mascall Fauna, Ore., E. Barstovian
Matthews Ranch Fauna, Calif., E. Clarendonian
Maxum Local Fauna, Calif., E. Blancan
Mayflower Mine Local Fauna, Mont., Clarendonian
McGehee Local Fauna, Fla., E. Hemphillian
McKanna Spring Fauna, Mont., E. Barstovian
*McKay Reservoir Local Fauna, Ore., L. Hemphillian
*Miami Quarry (= Coffee Ranch Q.), Tex., L. Hemphillian
Midway Fauna, Fla., L. Hemingfordian
Miller gravel pit, Okla., Latest Hemphillian
Minnechaduza Fauna, Nebr., E. Clarendonian
Mixon Local Fauna, Fla., E. Hemphillian
*Modesto Reservoir Local Fauna, Calif., L. Hemphillian
Monroe Creek Formation, fauna of, Nebr., E. Arikareean
Moscow Local Fauna, Tex., E. Barstovian
*Mt. Eden Fauna, Calif., L. Hemphillian
Mulholland Fauna, Calif., E. Hemphillian
Nation gravel pit, Okla., Latest Hemphillian
Nettle Spring Fauna, Calif., L. Clarendonian
*Nightingale Road Local Fauna, Nev., L. Clarendonian
*Niobrara River Fauna, Nebr., L. Barstovian
Norden Bridge Quarry Local Fauna, Nebr., L. Barstovian
North Boulder Valley Fauna, Mont., L. Arikareean
North Coalinga Local Fauna, Calif., L. Barstovian
North Silver Star Triangle Local Faunas, Mont., E. Hemphillian
North Tejon Hills Fauna, Calif., L. Clarendonian (Montediablan)
Observation Quarry Local Fauna, Nebr., E. Barstovian
Old Wagon Road Local Fauna, Mont., E. Clarendonian
Old Windmill Local Fauna, Mont., L. Barstovian
*Optima quarries, Local Fauna, Okla., L. Hemphillian
Oreodont Site, Fla., L. Arikareean
Oshkosh Local Fauna, Nebr., E. Hemphillian
Otis Basin Local Fauna, Ore., E. Hemphillian

*Pawnee Creek Fauna, Colo., E. Hemingfordian-L. Barstovian

*Philips Ranch Local Fauna, Calif., L. Hemingfordian

Pinole Local Fauna, Calif., L. Hemphillian

Point Blank Fauna, Tex., E. Barstovian

*Port of Entry Pit, Okla., E. Hemphillian

Pyramid Hill Local Fauna, Calif., L. Arikareean

Quarry A Local Fauna, Colo., E. Hemingfordian

*Quartz Basin Local Fauna, Ore., L. Barstovian

*Railway Quarry, Nebr., L. Barstovian

Rattlesnake Fauna, Ore., E. Hemphillian

*Red Basin Local Fauna, Ore., L. Barstovian

Red Division Quarry, Calif., L. Hemingfordian

*Redington Fauna, Ariz., L. Hemphillian

Ricardo Fauna (restricted), Calif., E. Clarendonian

*Rizzi Ranch Local Fauna, Nev., E. Arikareean

*Rome Fauna, Ore., E. Hemphillian

Runningwater Formation, and Fauna of, Nebr., E. Hemingfordian

Sam Houston Local Fauna, Tex., L. Barstovian

Sand Canyon Fauna, Colo., L. Barstovian

Sant Ranch Local Fauna, Mont., E. Barstovian

Santee Local Fauna, Nebr., L. Hemphillian

Seaboard Local Fauna, Fla., E. Hemingfordian

Sequence Canyon Fauna, Calif., L. Hemphillian

Sespe Formation sites, Calif., E. Arikareean

Sharktooth Hill Local Fauna, Calif., L. Barstovian

Sheep Creek Fauna, Nebr., L. Hemingfordian

Siesta Formation sites, Calif., L. Clarendonian

Skull Springs Fauna, Ore., L. Barstovian

Smiths Valley Fauna, Nev., E. Hemphillian

Snake Creek Fauna, Nebr., L. Clarendonian

South Tejon Hills Fauna, Calif., E. Clarendonian (Cerrotejonian)

Stewart Spring Fauna, Nev., L. Barstovian

Sucker Creek Fauna, Ore., L. Barstovian

Survey Quarry Local Fauna, Nebr., E. Barstovian

Sycamore Creek Fauna, Calif., E. Clarendonian (Cerrotejonian)

Tavenner Ranch Local Faunas, Mont., E.-L. Arikareean

Tecuya Formation sites, Calif., Arikareean

Thomas Farm Local Fauna, Fla., E. Hemingfordian

*Thousand Creek Fauna, Nev., E. Hemphillian

Tonopah Local Fauna, Nev., L. Barstovian

Trinity River Local Fauna, Tex., E. Barstovian

*Two Mile Bar Local Fauna, Calif., L. Barstovian

Unnamed fauna, lower Sharps Formation, S. Dak., E. Arikareean

Unnamed fauna, Murphy Member, Snake Creek Formation, Nebr., E. Clarendonian

Unnamed local fauna, Martin Canyon beds, Colo., E. Hemingfordian

Upper Bone Valley Fauna, Fla., L. Hemphillian

Upper Cady Mountain Local Fauna, Calif., L. Hemingfordian

Upper Dry Canyon Fauna, Calif., E. Barstovian

Upper Rosebud Fauna (= Wounded Knee-Rosebud Fauna), S. Dak., L. Arikareean

Uptegrove Local Fauna, Nebr., L. Hemphillian

Vedder site, Calif., L. Hemingfordian

Vim-Peetz Local Fauna, Colo., L. Barstovian

Virgil Clark gravel pit, Okla., Latest Hemphillian

*Virgin Valley Fauna, Nev., ?L. Hemingfordian-E. Barstovian

Warm Springs Local Fauna, Ore., E. Hemingfordian

Warren Fauna, Calif., L. Hemphillian

*Wewela Local Fauna, S. Dak., E. Arikareean

*White Cone Local Fauna, Ariz., L. Hemphillian

*Wikieup Fauna, Ariz., L. Hemphillian

Withlacootchee 4A Local Fauna, Fla., E. Hemphillian

Woody Local Fauna, Calif., L. Arikareean

Wounded Knee-Harrison Fauna, S. Dak., L. Arikareean

Wounded Knee-Monroe Creek Fauna, S. Dak., E. Arikareean

Wounded Knee-Rosebud Fauna (= Upper Rosebud Fauna), S. Dak., L. Arikareean

Wounded Knee-Sharps Fauna, S. Dak., E. Arikareean

Wray Fauna, Colo., E. Hemphillian

Xmas Quarry Local Fauna, Nebr., L. Clarendonian

*Yepomera Fauna, Chihuahua, Mex., Latest Hemphillian

ZXBar Local Fauna, Nebr., L. Hemphillian

REFERENCES

Akers, W. H. 1972. Planktonic foraminifera and biostratigraphy of some Neogene formations, northern Florida and Atlantic Coastal Plain. Tulane Studies in Geol. and Paleont. 9:1–137.

Albers, J. P., and J. H. Stewart. 1972. Geology and mineral resources of Esmeralda County, Nevada. Nev. Bur. Mines and Geol. Bull. 78:1–80.

Armstrong, R. L., and R. E. Higgins. 1973. K-Ar dating of the beginning of Tertiary volcanism in the Mojave Desert, California. Bull. Geol. Soc. Amer. 84:1095–1100.

Axelrod, D. I. 1956. Mio-Pliocene floras from west-central Nevada. Univ. Calif. Publ. Geol. Sci. 33:1–322.

Baker, C. L. 1911. Notes on the later Cenozoic history of the Mojave Desert region in southeastern California. Univ. Calif. Publ. Bull. Dept. Geol. 6:333–383.

Baksi, A. K. 1974. Isotopic fractionation of a loosely held atmospheric argon component in the Picture Gorge basalts. Earth Planet. Sci. Letters 21:431–438.

Banks, J. E., and M. E. Hunter. 1973. Post-Tampa, pre-Chipola sediments exposed in Liberty, Gadsden, Leon, and

Wakulla counties, Florida. Gulf Assoc. Geol. Soc. Trans. 33:355–363.

Barghoorn, S. 1981. Magnetic-polarity stratigraphy of the Miocene type Tesuque Formation, Santa Fe Group, in the Espanola Valley, New Mexico. Bull. Geol. Soc. Amer. 92:1027–1041.

Bartow, J. A., A. Sarna-Wojcicki, W. O. Addicott, and K. R. Lajoie. 1973. Correlation of marine and continental Pliocene deposits in northern California by tephrochronology. Amer. Assoc. Pet. Geol. Bull. (Abstr.), Vol. 57.

Bender, M. 1973. Helium-uranium dating of corals. Acta Geochemica et Cosmochimica: 37:1229–1247.

Berggren, W. A., D. V. Kent, J. J. Flynn, and J. A. Van Couvering. 1984. Cenozoic geochronology. Bull. Geol Soc. Amer. Vol. 96:1407–1418.

Berta, A., and H. Galiano. 1983. *Megantereon hesperus* from the late Hemphillian of Florida with remarks on the phylogenetic relationship of machairodonts (Mammalia, Felidae, Machairodontinae). J. Paleont. 57:892–899.

Berta, A., and G. S. Morgan. 1985. A new sea otter (Carnivora: Mustelidae) from the late Miocene and early Pliocene (Hemphillian) of North America. J. Paleont. 59:809–819.

Black, C. C. 1961a. Fossil mammals from Montana. Pt. 1: Additions to the late Miocene Flint Creek Local Fauna. Ann. Carnegie Mus. 36:69–76.

———. 1963. A review of the North American Tertiary Sciuridae. Mus. Comp. Zool. Bull. 130:109–248.

Bode, F. C. 1935. The fauna of the Merychippus Zone, North Coalinga district, California. Carnegie Inst. Wash. Publ., no. 453, pp. 66–96.

Boellstorff, J. D. 1976. The succession of late Cenozoic volcanic ashes in the Great Plains: A progress report. 24th Ann. Mtg. Midwest Friends of the Pleistocene, Kan. Geol. Surv. Guidebook Ser. 1:37–71.

Boellstorff, J. D., and P. L. Steinneck. 1975. The stratigraphic significance of fission-track ages on volcanic ashes in the marine late Cenozoic of southern Califonria. Earth Planet. Sci. Letters 27:143–154.

Bottomley, R. J., and D. York. 1976. ^{40}A–^{39}Ar age determinations on the Owyhee Basalt of the Columbia Plateau. Earth Plan. Sci. Letters 31:75–84.

Breyer, J. 1975. The classification of Ogallala sediments in western Nebraska. Univ. Michigan Mus. Paleont. Papers on Paleont., no. 12, pp. 1–8.

———. 1981. The Kimballian Land Mammal Age: Mene, Mene, Tekel, Upharsin (Dan. 5:25). J. Paleont. 55:1207–1216.

Burt, W. H. 1931. *Machaerodus catocopis* Cope from the Pliocene of Texas. Univ. Calif. Publ. Bull. Dept. Geol. Sci. 20:261–292.

Buwalda, J. P. 1916. New mammalian faunas from Miocene sediments near Tehachapi Pass in the southern Sierra Nevada. Univ. Calif. Publ. Dept. Geol. 10:75–85.

Buwalda, J. P., and G. E. Lewis. 1955. A new species of Merychippus. U.S. Geol. Surv. Prof. Paper 264-G, pp. 147–152.

Cady, R. C. 1940. The Box Butte Member of the Sheep Creek Formation, Nebraska. Amer. J. Sci. 238:663–667.

Clark, J. B., M. R. Dawson, and A. E. Wood. 1964. Fossil mammals from the Lower Pliocene of Fish Lake Valley, Nevada. Mus. Comp. Zool. Bull. 131:27–63.

Colbert, E. H. 1932. *Aphelops* from the Hawthorn Formation of Florida. Fla. State Geol. Surv. Bull., no. 10, pp. 55–58.

———. 1938. Pliocene peccaries from the Pacific Coast region of North America. Carnegie Inst. Wash. Publ. 487:241–269.

Cook, H. J. 1922. A Pliocene fauna from Yuma County, Colorado, with notes on the closely related Snake Creek beds from Nebraska. Colo. Mus. Nat. Hist. Proc. 4:3–30.

———. 1934. New artiodactyls from the Oligocene and lower Miocene of Nebraska. Amer. Midland Nat. 15:148–165.

———. 1965. Runningwater Formation, middle Miocene of Nebraska. Amer. Mus. Novitates, no. 2227.

Cook, H. J., and M. C. Cook. 1933. Faunal lists of the Tertiary Vertebrata of Nebraska and adjacent areas. Nebraska Geol. Surv. Paper, no. 5.

Coombs, M. C. 1978. A reevaluation of Early Miocene North American *Moropus* (Perissodactyla, Chalicotheriidae, Schizotheriinae). Bull. Carnegie Mus. Nat. Hist., no. 4, pp. 1–62.

Cope, E. D. 1893. A preliminary report on the vertebrate paleont. of the Llano Estacado. 4th Ann. Rept. Geol. Surv. Texas, pp. 1–136.

Creely, S., D. E. Savage, and B. A. Ogle. 1982. Stratigraphy of upper Tertiary nonmarine rocks of central Contra Costa Basin, California. In Cenozoic nonmarine deposits of California and Arizona, The Pacific Section, eds. R. Ingersoll and M. Woodburne. Society of Economic Paleontologists and Mineralogists, Los Angeles, Calif., pp. 11–22.

Cummins, W. F. 1893. Notes on the geology of northwest Texas. 4th Ann. Rept. (1892), Geol. Surv. Texas, pp. 179–238.

Dalquest, W. W. 1969. Pliocene carnivores of the Coffee Ranch. Texas Mem. Mus. Bull., no. 15.

———. 1983. Mammals of the Coffee Ranch Local Fauna Hemphillian of Texas. Pearce-Sellards Series, no. 38, pp. 1–41.

Dalrymple, G. B. 1979. Critical tables for conversion of K-Ar ages from old to new constants. Geology 7:558–560.

Darton, N. H. 1899. Preliminary report on the geology and water resources of Nebraska west of the one hundred and third meridian. U.S. Geol. Surv. 19th Ann. Rept., pt. 4 (for 1897–1898), pp. 719–814.

Denson, N. M. 1969. Distribution of nonopaque heavy minerals in Miocene and Pliocene rocks of central Wyoming and parts of adjacent states. U.S. Geol. Surv. Prof. Paper 650-C, pp. C25-C32.

Dibblee, T. W., Jr. 1967. Areal geology of the western Mojave Desert, California. U.S. Geol. Surv. Prof. Paper 522.

Dorr, J. A., Jr. 1956. Anceney local mammalian fauna, latest Miocene, Madison Valley Formation, Montana. J. Paleont. 30:62–74.

Dougherty, J. F. 1940. A new Miocene mammalian fauna

from Caliente Mountain, California. Carnegie Inst. Wash. Publ. 514, pp. 111–143.

Douglass, E. 1899. The Neocene lake beds of western Montana. M.S. thesis, Univ. Montana, Missoula.

———. 1903. New vertebrates from the Montana Tertiary. Ann. Carnegie Mus. 2:145–200.

———. 1907. New merycoidodonts from the Miocene of Montana. Bull. Amer. Mus. Nat. Hist. 23:809–822.

Downs, T. 1956. The Mascall fauna from the Miocene of Oregon. Univ. Calif. Publ. Geol. Sci. 31:199–354.

———. 1961. A study of variation and evolution in Miocene *Merychippus*. Los Angeles Co. Mus. Contrib. Sci., no. 45, pp. 1–75.

Echols, D. J., and D. M. Curtis. 1973. Paleontologic evidence for mid-Miocene refrigeration, from subsurface marine shales, Louisiana Gulf Coast. Gulf Coast. Assoc. Geol. Soc. Trans. 23:422–426.

Edwards, S. W. 1982. A new species of *Hipparion* (Mammalia: Equidae) from the Clarendonian (Miocene) of California. J. Vert. Paleont. 2:173–183.

Elias, M. K. 1942. Tertiary prairie grasses and other herbs from the High Plains. Geol. Soc. Amer. Spec. Paper 41.

Ellisor, A. C. 1936. "Potamides matsoni" zone of Texas (Burkeville beds). Amer. Assoc. Petrol. Geol. Bull. 20:494–495.

Engesser, B. 1979. Relationships of some insectivores and rodents from the Miocene of North America and Europe. Bull. Carnegie Mus. Nat. Hist., no. 14, pp. 1–68.

Evernden, J. F., D. E. Savage, G. H. Curtis, and G. T. James. 1964. Potassium-argon dates and the Cenozoic mammalian chronology of North America. Amer. J. Sci. 262:145–198.

Fisher, R. V., and J. M. Rensberger. 1972. Physical stratigraphy of the John Day Formation, central Oregon. Univ. Calif. Publ. Geol. Sci. 101:1–33.

Forstén, A. 1975. The fossil horses of the Texas Gulf Coastal Plain: A revision. Pearce-Sellard Series, no. 22, pp. 1–86.

Frailey, D. 1978. An early Miocene (Arikareean) fauna from north-central Florida (the 5B-1A Local Fauna). Univ. Kansas Mus. Nat. Hist. Occ. Papers, no. 75, pp. 1–20.

———. 1979. The large mammals of the Buda Local Fauna (Arikareean: Alachua County, Florida). Fla. State Mus. Bull. 24:123–173.

Frick, C. 1921. Extinct vertebrate faunas of the badlands of Bautista Creek and San Timoteo Canon, southern California. Univ. Calif. Publ. Bull. Dept. Geol. 12:277–424.

———. 1933. New remains of Trilophodont-Tetrabelodon mastodons. Bull. Amer. Mus. Nat. Hist. 59:505–652.

Frick, C., and B. E. Taylor. 1968. A generic review of the Stenomyline camels. Amer. Mus. Novitates, no. 2353.

Galbreath, E. C. 1953. A contribution to the Tertiary geology and paleontology of northeastern Colorado. Univ. Kan. Paleont. Contrib., Vertebrata, art. 4, pp. 1–120.

Galusha, T. 1975. Stratigraphy of the Box Butte Formation, Nebraska. Bull. Amer. Mus. Nat. Hist. 156:1–68.

Galusha, T., and J. C. Blick. 1971. Stratigraphy of the Santa Fe Group, New Mexico. Bull. Amer. Mus. Nat. Hist. 144:1–128.

Gazin, C. L. 1932. A Miocene mammalian fauna from southeastern Oregon. Carnegie Inst. Wash. Publ. 418, pp. 37–86.

Geldsetzer, H. 1966. Cenozoic stratigraphy and structure, Owyhee Reservoir, Sucker Creek region, east-central Oregon. Ph.D. diss. Univ. Wash.

Gidley, J. W. 1903. The freshwater Tertiary of northwestern Texas, American Museum expeditions of 1899–1901. Bull. Amer. Mus. Nat. Hist. 19:617–635.

Gilbert, D. M., and M. W. Reynolds. 1973. Character and chronology of basin development, western margin of the Basin and Range Province. Bull. Geol. Soc. Amer. 84:2489–2510.

Greene, R. C. 1973. Petrology of the Welded Tuff of Devine Canyon, southeastern Oregon. U.S. Geol. Surv. Prof. Paper 797.

Greene, R. C., G. W. Walker, and R. E. Corcoran. 1972. Geologic map of the Burns Quadrangle, Oregon. U.S. Geol. Surv. Misc. Geol. Invest. Map I-680.

Gregory, J. T. 1942. Pliocene vertebrates from Big Spring Canyon, South Dakota. Univ. Calif. Publ. Bull. Dept. Geol. Sci. 26:307–446.

Hall, E. R. 1930a. Rodents and lagomorphs from the later Tertiary of Fish Lake Valley, Nevada. Univ. Calif. Publ. Bull. Dept. Geol. Sci. 19:295–312.

———. 1930b. A new genus of bat from the later Tertiary of Nevada. Univ. Calif. Publ. Bull. Dept. Geol. Sci. 19:319–320.

———. 1930c. A bassarisk and a new mustelid from the later Tertiary of California. Mammal. 11:23–26.

Harksen, J. C. 1974. Miocene channels in the Cedar Pass area, Jackson County, South Dakota. S. Dak. Geol. Surv. Rept. Invest., no. 111.

Harksen, J. C., and J. R. Macdonald. 1967. Miocene Batesland Formation named in southwestern South Dakota. S. Dak. Geol. Surv. Rept. Invest., no. 96.

———. 1969. Guidebook to the major Cenozoic deposits of southwestern South Dakota. S. Dak. Geol. Surv., Guidebook 2.

Harksen, J. C., J. R. Macdonald, and W. D. Sevon. 1961. New Miocene Formations in South Dakota. S. Dak. Geol. Surv. Misc. Invest., no. 3.

Henshaw, P. C. 1942. A Tertiary mammalian fauna from the San Antonio Mountains near Tonopah, Nevada. Carnegie Inst. Wash. Publ. 530, pp. 79–168.

Hesse, C. J. 1935. A vertebrate fauna from the type locality of the Ogallala Formation. Univ. Kansas Sci. Bull. 22:79–101.

———. 1936. A Pliocene vertebrate fauna from Optima, Oklahoma. Univ. Calif. Publ. Bull. Dept. Geol. Sci. 24:57–70.

———. 1940. A Pliocene vertebrate fauna from Higgins, Lipscomb County, Texas. Univ. Texas Publ., no. 3945, pp. 671–698.

———. 1943. A preliminary report on the Miocene vertebrate faunas of southeast Texas. Trans. Texas Acad. Sci. Proc. 26:157–179.

Hibbard, C. W., and K. A. Keenmon. 1950. New evidence of the lower Miocene age of the Blacktail Deer Creek Formation in Montana. Contrib. Univ. Michigan Mus. Paleont. 8:193–204.

Hirschfeld, S. E. 1981. *Pliometanastes protistus* (Edentata, Megalonychidae) from Knight's Ferry, California, with discussion of early Hemphillian megalonychids. PaleoBios, no. 36.

Hirschfeld, S. E., and S. D. Webb. 1968. Plio-Pleistocene megalonychid sloths of North America. Fla. State Mus. (Biol. Sci.) Bull. 12:213–296.

Honey, J. G., and B. E. Taylor. 1978. A generic revision of the Protolabidini (Mammalia, Camelidae), with a description of two new Protolabidines. Bull. Amer. Mus. Nat. Hist. 161:367–426.

Hunt, R. M., Jr. 1971. North American amphicyonids (Mammalia: Carnivora). Ph.D. diss., Columbia University.

———. 1972. Miocene amphicyonids (Mammalia, Carnivora) from the Agate Spring Quarries, Sioux County, Nebraska. Amer. Mus. Novitates, no. 2506, pp. 1–39.

———. 1977. Stratigraphy and vertebrate paleontology of Miocene rocks, Arikaree Group, central Sioux County, Nebraska. Geol. Soc. Amer. Abstr. Prog. 9 (6):734.

———. 1978. Depositional setting of a Miocene mammal assemblage, Sioux County, Nebraska. Palaeogeogr., Palaeoclimat., Palaeoecol. 24:1–52.

———. 1981. Geology and vertebrate paleontology of the Agate Fossil Beds National Monument and surrounding region, Sioux County, Nebraska (1972–1978). Nat. Geogr. Soc. Research Reports 13:263–285.

———. 1985. Faunal succession, lithofacies, and depositional environments in Arikaree rocks (Lower Miocene) of the Hartville Table, Nebraska and Wyoming. In Fossiliferous Cenozoic deposits of western South Dakota and northwestern Nebraska, ed. J. E. Martin. Dakoterra 2:155–204.

Hunt, R. M., Jr., X. X. Xue, and J. Kaufmann. 1983. Miocene burrows of extinct beardogs; indication of early denning behavior of large mammalian carnivores. Science 221:364–366.

Hunter, M. E., and P. F. Huddlestun. 1982. The biostratigraphy of the Torreya Formation of Florida. In Miocene of the Southeastern United States, eds. T. Scott and S. Church. Florida Bur. Geol. Spec. Publ., no. 25, pp. 211–223.

Hutchinson, J. H., and E. H. Lindsay. 1974. The Hemingfordian mammal fauna of the Vedder Locality, Branch Canyon Formation, Santa Barbara County, California. Pt. 1: Insectivora, Chiroptera, Lagomorpha, and Rodentia (Sciuridae). PaleoBios, no. 15, pp. 1–19.

Izett, G. L. 1975. Late Cenozoic sedimentation and deformation in northern Colorado and adjoining areas. In Cenozoic history of the southern Rocky Mountains, ed. B. F. Curtis. Geol. Soc. Amer. Mem. 144. pp. 179–209.

James, G. T. 1963. Paleontology and nonmarine stratigraphy of the Cuyama Valley bandlands, California. Pt. 1: Geology, faunal interpretation, and systematic descriptions of Chiroptera, Insectivora, and Rodentia. Univ. Calif. Publ. Geol. Sci., vol. 45.

Johnston, C. S., and D. E. Savage. 1955. A survey of various late Cenozoic vertebrate faunas of the Panhandle of Texas.

Pt. 1: Introduction, description of localities, preliminary faunal lists. Univ. Calif. Publ. Geol. Sci. 31:27–50.

Kittleman, L. R., A. R. Green, A. R. Hagood, A. M. Johnson, J. M. McMurray, R. G. Russell, and D. A. Weeden. 1965. Cenozoic stratigraphy of the Owyhee Region, southeastern Oregon. Bull. Mus. Nat. Hist. Univ. Ore., no. 1.

Kitts, D. B. 1957. A Pliocene vertebrate fauna from Ellis County, Oklahoma. Okla. Geol. Surv. Circ. 45.

Klingener, D. 1968. Rodents of the Mio-Pliocene Norden Bridge Local Fauna, Nebraska. Amer. Midland Nat. 80:65–74.

Koerner, H. E. 1940. The geology and vertebrate paleontology of the Fort Logan and Deep River formations of Montana. Pt. 1: New vertebrates. Amer. J. Sci. 238:837–862.

Konizeski, R. L. 1957. Paleoecology of the middle Pliocene Deer Lodge Local Fauna, western Montana. Bull. Geol. Soc. Amer. 68:131–150.

Konizeski, R. L., and J. C. Donohoe. 1958. Faunal and stratigraphy relationships of the Cabbage Patch beds, Granite County, Montana. Soc. Vert. Paleont. Guidebook, 8th Field Conf. western Montana (R. W. Fields, ed.). Missoula: Montana State University Press. Pp. 45–49.

Kuenzi, W. D., and R. W. Fields. 1971. Tertiary stratigraphy, structure, and geological history, Jefferson Basin, Montana. Bull. Geol. Soc. Amer. 82:3373–3394.

Kuenzi, W. D., and B. H. Richard. 1969. Middle Tertiary unconformity, North Boulder and Jefferson basins, southwestern Montana. Bull. Geol. Soc. Amer. 80:315–320.

Lance, J. F. 1950. Paleontologia y estratigraphia del Plioceno de Yepomera, estado de Chihuahua 1ª parte: Equidos, excepto *Neohipparion*. Univ. Nac. Aut. Mexico Bull., no. 54.

Leidy, J., and F. A. Lucas. 1896. Fossil vertebrates from Alachua clays. Wagner Free Inst. Sci. Trans. 4:1–61.

Lindsay, E. H. 1972. Small mammal fossils from the Barstow Formation, California. Univ. Calif. Publ. Geol. Sci. 93:1–104.

———. 1974. The Hemingfordian mammal fauna of the Vedder locality, Branch Canyon Formation, Santa Barbara County, California. Pt. II: Rodentia (Eomyidae and Heteromyidae). PaleoBios, no. 16, pp. 1–19.

Lindsay, E. H., N. M. Johnson, and N. D. Opdyke. 1976. Preliminary correlation of North American Land Mammal Ages and geomagnetic chronology. Univ. Michigan Papers Paleont., no. 12, pp. 111–119.

Lugn, A. L. 1939. Classification of the Tertiary System in Nebraska. Bull. Geol. Soc. Amer. 50:1245–1276.

Lull, R. S. 1920. New Tertiary artiodactyls. Amer. J. Sci. 50:83–130.

Macdonald, J. R. 1948. The Pliocene carnivores of the Black Hawk Ranch fauna. Univ. Calif. Publ. Bull. Dept. Geol. Sci. 28:53–80.

———. 1956a. A new Clarendonian fauna from the Truckee Formation of Western Nevada. J. Paleont. 30:186–202.

———. 1956b. The North American anthracotheres. J. Paleont. 30:615–645.

———. 1959. The middle Pliocene mammalian fauna from Smiths Valley, Nevada. J. Paleont. 33:872–887.

————. 1963. The Miocene faunas from the Wounded Knee area of western South Dakota. Bull. Amer. Mus. Nat. Hist. 125:141–238.

————. 1970. Review of the Miocene Wounded Knee faunas of southwestern South Dakota. Los Angeles Co. Mus. Nat. Hist. Bull., no. 8, pp. 1–82.

Macdonald, J. R., and J. C. Harksen. 1968. Rosebud Formation in South Dakota. S. Dak. Geol. Surv. Rept. Invest., no. 97.

Macdonald, J. R., and L. J. Macdonald. 1976. *Barbourofelis fricki* from the Early Hemphillian of Nevada. J. Paleont. 50:792–794.

Macdonald, J. R., and W. J. Pelletier. 1958. The Pliocene mammalian faunas of Nevada, U.S.A. Internat. Geol. Congr., 20th session, Sec. VII, pp. 365–388.

Macdonald, L. J. 1972. Monroe Creek (early Miocene) microfossils from the Wounded Knee area, South Dakota. S. Dak. Geol. Surv. Rept. Invest., no. 105.

MacFadden, B. J. 1977. Magnetic polarity stratigraphy of the Chamita Formation stratotype (Mio-Pliocene) of north-central New Mexico. Amer. J. Sci. 277:769–800.

————. 1980a. An early Miocene land mammal (Oreodonta) from a marine limestone in northern Florida. J. Paleont. 54:93–101.

————. 1980b. The Miocene horse *Hipparion* from North America and from the type locality in southern France. Palaeontology 23:617–635.

————. 1984. Systematics and phylogeny of *Hipparion Neohipparion, Nannippus,* and *Cormohipparion* (Mammalia, Equidae) from the Miocene and Pliocene of the New World. Bull. Amer. Mus. Nat. Hist. 179:1–196.

MacFadden, B. J., and H. Galiano. 1981. Late Hemphillian cat (Mammalia, Felidae) from the Bone Valley Formation of central Florida. J. Paleont. 55:218–226.

MacFadden, B. J., and M. F. Skinner. 1979. Diversification and biogeography of the one-toed horses, *Onohippidium* and *Hippidion*. Postilla 175:1–10.

————. 1981. Earliest Holarctic hipparion, *Cormohipparion goorisi* n. sp. (Mammalia, Equidae) from the Barstovian (medial Miocene) Texas Gulf Coastal Plain. J. Paleont. 55:619–627.

MacFadden, B. J., and S. D. Webb. 1982. The succession of Miocene (Arikareean through Hemphillian) terrestrial mammal localities and faunas in Florida. In Miocene of the southern United States, eds. T. Scott and S. Church. Fla. Bur. Geol. Spec. Publ., no. 25, pp. 186–199.

MacFadden, B. J., N. M. Johnson, and N. D. Opdyke. 1979. Magnetic polarity stratigraphy of the Mio-Pliocene mammal-bearing Big Sandy Formation of western Arizona. Earth Planet. Sci. Letters 44:349–364.

McKenna, M. C. 1965. Stratigraphic nomenclature of the Miocene Hemingford Group, Nebraska. Amer. Mus. Novitates, no. 2228.

Marshall, L. G., R. F. Butler, R. E. Drake, G. H. Curtis, and R. H. Tedford. 1979. Calibration of the Great American interchange. Science 204:272–279.

Martin, J. E. 1976. Small mammals from the Miocene Batesland Formation of South Dakota. Univ. Wyo. Contrib. Geol. 14:69–98.

Martin, L. D. 1973. The mammalian fauna of the Lower Miocene Gering Formation of western Nebraska and the early evolution of the North American Cricetidae. Ph.D. diss. Univ. Kansas, Lawrence.

————. 1974. New rodents from the Lower Miocene Gering Formation of western Nebraska. Mus. Nat. Hist. Univ. Kan. Occ. Paper, no. 32, pp. 1–12.

————. 1975a. Biostratigraphy relationships of the early Miocene Gering fauna. Nebr. Acad. Sci. Proc. (Abstr.) 85:41.

————. 1975b. Microtine rodents for the Ogallala Pliocene of Nebraska and the early evolution of the Microtinae in North America. Univ. Mich. Mus. Paleont. Papers Paleont., no. 12, pp. 101–110.

Martin, L. D., and D. K. Bennett. 1977. The burrows of the Miocene beaver *Paleocastor,* western Nebraska, U.S.A. Palaeogeogr., Palaeoclimat., Palaeoecol. 22:173–193.

Martin, L. D., and C. B. Schultz. 1975. Cenozoic mammals of the central Great Plains. Pt. 5: Scimitar-toothed cats, *Machairodus* and *Nimravides* from the Pliocene of Kansas and Nebraska. Univ. Nebr. St. Mus. Bull. 10:55–63.

Matthew, W. D. 1907. A Lower Miocene fauna from South Dakota. Bull. Amer. Mus. Nat. Hist. 23:169–219.

————. 1924. Third contribution to the Snake Creek fauna. Bull. Amer. Mus. Nat. Hist. 50:59–210.

————. 1932. A review of the rhinoceroses with a description of *Aphelops* material from the Pliocene of Texas. Univ. Calif. Publ. Bull. Dept. Geol. Sci. 20:411–480.

Matthew, W. D., and H. J. Cook. 1909. A Pliocene fauna from western Nebraska. Bull. Amer. Mus. Nat. Hist. 26:361–414.

Matthew, W. D., and J. W. Gidley. 1904. New or little-known mammals from the Miocene of South Dakota: American Museum Expedition of 1903. Bull. Amer. Mus. Nat. Hist. 20:241–268.

Matthew, W. D., and R. A. Stirton. 1930. Equidae from the Pliocene of Texas. Univ. Calif. Publ. Bull. Dept. Geol. Sci. 19:349–396.

Mawby, J. E. 1965. Pliocene vertebrates and stratigraphy in Stewart and Ione valleys, Nevada. Ph.D. diss., Dept. Paleont., Univ. Calif., Berkeley.

————. 1968a. *Megabelodon minor* (Mammalia, Proboscidea), a new species of mastodon from the Esmeralda Formation of Nevada. PaleoBios, no. 4.

————. 1968b. *Megahippus* and *Hypohippus* (Perissodactyla, Mammalia) from the Esmeralda Formation of Nevada. PaleoBios, no. 7.

May, S. R. 1981. *Repomys* (Mammalia: Rodentia gen. nov.) from the late Neogene of California and Nevada. J. Vert. Paleont. 1:219–230.

May, S. R., and C. A. Repenning. 1982. New evidence for the age of the Mount Eden fauna, southern California. J. Vert. Paleont. 2:109–113.

Merriam, J. C. 1915. Tertiary vertebrate faunas of the North Coalinga region of California. Amer. Phil. Soc. Trans. 22:191–234.

———. 1919. Tertiary mammalian faunas of the Mojave Desert. Univ. Calif. Publ. Bull. Dept. Geol. 11:437a-e–585.

Merriam, J. C., and W. J. Sinclair. 1907. Tertiary faunas of the John Day region. Univ. Calif. Publ. Bull. Dept. Geol. 5:171–205.

Merriam, J. C., C. Stock, and C. L. Moody. 1925. The Pliocene Rattlesnake Formation and fauna of eastern Oregon, with notes on the geology of the Rattlesnake and Mascall deposits. Carnegie Inst. Wash. Publ. 347, pp. 43–92.

Miller, S. T. 1980. Geology and mammalian biostratigraphy of a part of the northern Cady Mountains, Mohave Desert, California. U.S. Geological Surv. Open File Rept. 80–878.

Mitchell, E. D. 1965. History of research at Sharktooth Hill. Kern Co. Hist. Soc. Spec. Publ.

Mitchell, E. D., and R. H. Tedford. 1973. The Enaliarctinae, a new group of extinct aquatic Carnivora and a consideration of the origin of the Otariidae. Bull. Amer. Mus. Nat. Hist. 151:201–284.

Munthe, J. 1979. The Hemingfordian mammal fauna of the Vedder locality, Branch Canyon Sandstone, Santa Barbara County, California. Pt. III: Carnivora, Perissodactyla, Artiodactyla, and summary. PaleoBios, no. 29.

Murphy, M. A. 1977. On time-stratigraphic units. J. Paleont. 51:213–219.

Naeser, C. W., G. A. Izett, and J. D. Obradovich. 1980. Fission-track and K-Ar ages of natural glasses. U.S. Geol. Surv. Bull. 1489, pp. 1–31.

Nichols, R. 1976. Early miocene mammals from the Lemhi Valley of Idaho. Tebiwa 18:9–33.

Nicknish, J. M., and J. R. Macdonald. 1963. Basal Miocene ash in White River Badlands, South Dakota. S.D. Geol. Surv. Misc. Invest., no. 7.

Nomland, J. O. 1916. Relationship of the invertebrate to the vertebrate faunal zones of the Jacalitos and Etchegoin formations in the North Coalinga region, California. Univ. Calif. Publ. Bull. Dept. Geol. 9:77–88.

Obradovich, J. D., G. A. Izett, and C. W. Naeser. 1973. Radiometric ages of volcanic ash and pumice beds in the Gering Sandstone (Earliest Miocene) of the Arikaree Group, southwestern Nebraska. Geol. Soc. Amer. Abstr. with Programs 5:499–500.

Olsen, S. J. 1963. An Upper Miocene fossil locality in north Florida. Fla. Acad. Sci. Quart. J. 26:308–314.

———. 1964a. The stratigraphic importance of a lower Miocene vertebrate fauna from north Florida. J. Paleont. 38:477–482.

———. 1964b. Vertebrate correlation and Miocene stratigraphy of north Florida fossil localities. J. Paleont. 38:600–604.

Osborn, H. F. 1907. Tertiary mammal horizons of North America. Bull. Amer. Mus. Nat. Hist. 23:237–253.

———. 1918. Equidae of the Oligocene, Miocene and Pliocene of North America, inconographic type revision. Amer. Mus. Nat. Hist. Mem. 2:1–217.

———. 1936. Proboscidea. Vol. I: Moeritherioidea, Deinotherioidea and Mastodontoidea. New York: American Museum of Natural History.

Parker, D., and R. L. Armstrong. 1972. K-Ar dates and Sr isotope initial ratios for volcanic rocks in the Harney Basin, Oregon. Isochron/West, no. 5, pp. 7–12.

Parris, D. C., and M. Green. 1969. *Dinohyus* (Mammalia: *Entelodontidae*) in the Sharps Formation, South Dakota. J. Paleont. 43:1277–1229.

Patton, T. H. 1967. Oligocene and Miocene vertebrates from central Florida. Southeastern Geol. Soc., 13th Field Trip Guidebook, pp. 3–10.

———. 1969. Miocene and Pliocene artiodactyls, Texas Gulf coastal plain. Fla. State Mus. Bull. Biol. Sci. 14:115–226.

Patton, T. H., and B. E. Taylor. 1971. The Synthetoceratinae (Mammalia, Tylopoda, Protoceratidae). Bull. Amer. Mus. Nat. Hist. 145:119–218.

———. 1973. The Protoceratinae (Mammalia, Tylopoda, Protoceratidae) and the systematics of the Protoceratidae. Bull. Amer. Mus. Nat. Hist. 150:347–414.

Peck, D. M., T. M. Missimer, D. H. Slater, S. W. Wise, Jr., and T. H. O'Donnel. 1979. Late Miocene glacial-eustatic lowering of sea level: Evidence from the Tamiami Formation of south Florida. Geology 7:285–288.

Peterson, O. A. 1907. The Miocene beds of western Nebraska and eastern Wyoming and their vertebrate faunae. Ann. Carnegie Mus. 4:21–72.

———. 1909. A revision of the Entelodontidae. Carnegie Mus. Mem. 4:41–158.

Prothero, D. R., and E. Manning. In press. Miocene rhinoceroses from the Texas Gulf Coastal Plain.

Prothero, D. R., and P. C. Sereno. 1982. Allometry and paleoecology and the medial Miocene dwarf rhinoceroses from the Texas Gulf Coastal Plain. Paleobiol. 8:16–30.

Prothero, D. R., C. R. Denham, and H. G. Farmer. 1983. Magnetostratigraphy of the White River Group and its implications for Oligocene geochronology. Palaeogeogr., Palaeoclimat., Palaeoecol. 42:151–166.

Quinn, J. H. 1955. Miocene Equidae of the Texas Gulf coastal plain. Univ. Texas Publ., no. 5516.

Rasmussen, D. L. 1969. Late Cenozoic geology of the Cabbage Patch area, Granite and Powell counties, Montana. M.A. thesis, Univ. Montana, Missoula.

———. 1973. Extension of the middle Tertiary unconformity into western Montana. Northwest Geol. 2:27–34.

———. 1977. Geology and mammalian paleontology of the Oligocene-Miocene Cabbage Patch Formation, central-western Montana. Ph.D. diss., Univ. Kansas.

Reed, L. C., and O. M. Longnecker, Jr. 1932. The geology of Hemphill County, Texas. Univ. Texas Bull., no. 3231.

Reinhart, R. H. 1976. Fossil sirenians and desmostylians from Florida and elsewhere. Fla. St. Mus. Bull. Biol. Sci. 20:187–300.

Rensberger, J. M. 1971. Entoptychine pocket gophers (Mammalia, Geomyoidea) of the early Miocene John Day Formation, Oregon. Univ. Calif. Publ. Geol. Sci. 90:1–163.

———. 1973. Pleurolicine rodents (Geomyoidea) of the John

Day Formation, Oregon, and their relationships to taxa from the early and middle Miocene South Dakota. Univ. Calif. Publ. Geol. Sci. 102:1–95.

———. 1979. Promylagaulus, progressive aplodontoid rodents of the early Miocene. Los Angeles Co. Nat. Hist. Mus. Contrib. Sci., no. 312.

———. 1981. Evolution in a late Oligocene-early Miocene succession of meniscomyine rodents in the Deep River Formation, Montana. J. Vert. Paleont. 1:185–209.

———. 1983. Successions of meniscomyine and allomyine rodents (Aplodontidae) in the Oligo-Miocene John Day Formation, Oregon. Univ. Calif. Publ. Geol. Sci., vol. 124.

Repenning, C. A. 1966. Early Miocene mammals in Nevada. U.S. Geol. Surv. Prof. Paper 550A, pp. 7–8.

———. 1976. Enhydra and Enhydriodon from the Pacific Coast of North America. U.S. Geol. Surv. J. Res. 4:305–315.

Repenning, C. A., and J. G. Vedder. 1961. Continental vertebrates and their stratigraphic correlation with marine mollusks, eastern Caliente Range, California. U.S. Geol. Surv. Prof. Paper 424C, pp. C235–C239.

Rich, T. H. V. 1981. Origin and history of the Erinaceinae and Brachyericinae (Mammalia, Insectivora) in North America. Bull. Amer. Mus. Nat. Hist. 171:1–116.

Rich, T. H., and D. L. Rasmussen. 1973. New North American erinaceine hedgehogs (Mammalia: Insectivora). Univ. Kan. Mus. Nat. Hist. Occ. Paper, no. 21, pp. 1–54.

Riel, S. J. 1964. A new oreodont from the Cabbage Patch local fauna, western Montana. Postilla, no. 85.

Ritchie, K. A. 1943. A marine invertebrate fauna from the Orinda, California, Formation. Univ. Calif. Publ. Bull. Dept. Geol. Sci. 27:25–36.

———. 1948. Lower Pliocene horses from Black Hawk Ranch, Mount Diablo, California. Univ. Calif. Publ. Bull. Geol. Sci. 28:1–44.

Robinson, P. 1970. The Tertiary deposits of the Rocky Mountains—A summary and discussion of unsolved problems. Univ. Wyo. Contrib. Geol. 9:86–96.

Sarna-Wojcicki, A. M. 1976. Correlation of late Cenozoic tuffs in the central coast ranges of California by means of trace and minor-element chemistry. U.S. Geol. Surv. Prof. Paper 972.

Savage, D. E. 1941. Two new middle Pliocene carnivores from Oklahoma with notes on the optima fauna. Amer. Midland Naturalist 25:692–710.

———. 1955. Nonmarine Lower Pliocene sediments in California: A geochronologic-stratigraphic classification. Univ. Calif. Publ. Geol. Sci. 31:1–26.

———. 1977. Aspects of vertebrate paleontological stratigraphy and geochronology. In Concepts and methods of biostratigraphy, eds. E. Kaufman and J. Hazel. Stroudsburg, Pa.: Dowden, Hutchinson and Ross.

Savage, D. E., and L. G. Barnes. 1972. Miocene vertebrate geochronology of the west coast of North America. In Proceedings of the Pacific Coast Miocene Biostratigraphic Symposium: Soc. Econ. Paleont., Min., Pacific Sec., Bakersfield, pp. 124–145.

Scarborough, R. B., P. E. Damon, and M. Shafiqullah. 1974. K-Ar Age for a basalt from the Volcanic Member (unit 5) of the Bidahochi Formation. Geol. Soc. Amer. Abstr. with Programs, vol. 6.

Scharf, D. W. 1935. A Miocene mammalian fauna from Sucker Creek, southeastern Oregon. Carnegie Inst. Wash. Publ. 453, pp. 97–118.

Schultz, C. B. 1938. The Miocene of western Nebraska. Amer. J. Sci. 35:441–444.

———. 1941. Marsland Formation. Bull. Geol. Soc. Amer. 52:1990–1991.

Schultz, C. B., and C. H. Falkenbach. 1941. Ticholeptinae, a new subfamily of oreodonts. Bull. Amer. Mus. Nat. Hist. 79:1–105.

———. 1949. Promerycochoerinae, a new subfamily of oreodonts. Bull. Amer. Mus. Nat. Hist. 93:69–198.

———. 1950. Phenacocoelinae, a new subfamily of oreodonts. Bull. Amer. Mus. Nat. Hist. 95:87–150.

———. 1954. Desmatochoerinae, a new subfamily of oreodonts. Bull. Amer. Mus. Nat. Hist. 105:143–256.

———. 1968. The phylogeny of the oreodonts, parts 1 and 2. Bull. Amer. Mus. Nat. Hist. 139:1–498.

Schultz, C. B., and T. M. Stout. 1941. Guide for a field conference on the Tertiary and Pleistocene of Nebraska. Univ. Nebraska State Mus. Spec. Publ. 1.

———. 1948. Pleistocene mammals and terraces in the Great Plains. Bull. Geol. Soc. Amer. 59:553–588.

———. 1961. Field conference on the Tertiary and Pleistocene of western Nebraska. Univ. Nebr. Spec. Publ., no. 2.

Schultz, C. B., M. R. Schultz, and L. D. Martin. 1970. A new tribe of saber-toothed cats (Barbourofelini) from the Pliocene of North America. Univ. Nebr. State Mus. Bull. 9:1–31.

Schultz, G. E. 1977. Guidebook field conference on late Cenozoic biostratigraphy of the Texas panhandle and adjacent Oklahoma, August 4–6, 1977. West Texas State University (Canyon), Kilgore Res. Ctr., Dept. Geol. and Anthro., Spec. Publ., no. 1.

Shotwell, J. A. 1956. Hemphillian mammalian assemblage from northeastern Oregon. Bull. Geol. Soc. Amer. 67:717–738.

———. 1968. Miocene mammals of southeast Oregon. Univ. Ore. Mus. Nat. Hist. Bull., no. 14.

Shotwell, J. A., R. G. Bowen, W. L. Gray, D. C. Gregory, D. E. Russell, and D. W. Taylor. 1963. The Juntura Basin: Studies in early history and paleoecology. Amer. Phil. Soc. Trans., n.s., vol. 53, pp. 5–77.

Silberman, M. L., and E. H. McKee. 1972. A summary of radiometric determinations on Tertiary volcanic rocks from Nevada and eastern California. Pt. II: western Nevada. Isochron/West., no. 4, pp. 7–28.

Simpson, G. G. 1930. Tertiary land mammals of Florida. Bull. Amer. Mus. Nat. Hist. 59:149–211.

———. 1932. Miocene land mammals from Florida. Fla. State Geol. Surv. Bull., no. 10, p. 11–41.

Skinner, M. F., and C. W. Hibbard. 1972. Early Pleistocene pre-glacial and glacial rocks and faunas of north-central

Nebraska. Bull. Amer. Mus. Nat. Hist., vol. 148.

Skinner, M. F., and F. W. Johnson. 1984. Tertiary stratigraphy and the Frick Collection of fossil vertebrates from north-central Nebraska. Bull. Amer. Mus. Nat. Hist. 178:215–368.

Skinner, M. F., and B. J. MacFadden. 1977. *Cormohipparion* n. gen. (Mammalia: Equidae) from the North American Miocene (Barstovian-Clarendonian). J. Paleont. 51:912–926.

Skinner, M. F., S. M. Skinner, and R. J. Gooris. 1968. Cenozoic rocks and faunas of Turtle Butte, south-central South Dakota. Bull. Amer. Mus. Nat. Hist. 138:379–436.

———. 1977. Stratigraphy and biostratigraphy of late Cenozoic deposits in central Sioux County, western Nebraska. Bull. Amer. Mus. Nat. Hist. 158:263–370.

Skinner, M. F., and M. R. Voorhies. 1977. Vertebrate fossils from lowermost Valentine Formation, proposed Norden Dam and Reservoir area. Nebr. Acad. Sci. Proc. (1977), p. 40.

Slaughter, B. H. 1981. A new genus of geomyoid rodent from the Miocene of Texas and Panama. J. Vert. Paleont. 1:111–115.

Smith, G. I. 1964. Geology and volcanic petrology of the Lava Mountains, San Bernardino County, California. U.S. Geol. Surv. Prof. Paper 457.

Stecher, R. M., C. B. Schultz, and L. G. Tanner. 1962. A middle Miocene rhinoceros quarry in Morril County, Nebraska (with notes on hip disease in *Diceratherium*). Univ. Nebr. State Mus. Bull. 4:101–111.

Stenzel, H. B., F. E. Turner, and C. J. Hesse. 1944. Brackish and non-marine Miocene in southeastern Texas. Amer. Assoc. Petrol. Geol. Bull. 28:977–1011.

Stirton, R. A. 1936a. Succession of North American continental Pliocene mammalian faunas. Amer. J. Sci. 32: 161–206.

———. 1936b. A new ruminant from the Hemphill middle Pliocene of Texas. J. Paleont. 10:644–647.

———. 1939a. Cenozoic mammal remains from the San Francisco Bay region. Univ. Calif. Publ. Bull. Dept. Geol. Sci. 24:339–410.

———. 1939b. The Nevada Miocene and Pliocene mammalian faunas as faunal units. Sixth Pacific Sci. Congr. Proc., pp. 627–638.

Stirton, R. A., and H. F. Goeriz. 1942. Fossil vertebrates from the superjacent deposits near Knight's Ferry, California. Univ. Calif. Publ. Bull. Dept. Geol. Sci. 26:447–472.

Stock, C. 1920. An early Tertiary vertebrate fauna from the southern Coast Ranges of California. Univ. Calif. Publ. Bull. Dept. Geol. Sci. 12:267–276.

———. 1932. Additions to the mammalian fauna of the Tecuya beds, California. Carnegie Inst. Wash., Publ. 418, pp. 89–92.

———. 1933a. Perissodactyla from Sespe of the Las Posas Hills, California. Carnegie Inst. Wash. Publ. 440, pp. 16–27.

———. 1933b. Carnivora from the Sespe of the Las Posas Hills, California. Carnegie Inst. Wash. Publ. 440, pp. 30–41.

———. 1935. Artiodactyla from the Sespe of the Las Posas Hills, California. Carnegie Inst. Wash. Publ. 453, pp. 121–125.

Stock, C., and E. R. Hall. 1933. The Asiatic genus *Eomellivora* in the Pliocene of California. J. Mammal. 14:63–65.

Stout, T. M., and L. G. Tanner. 1983. The Tertiary-Quaternary boundary in eastern Nebraska and surrounding region: A symposium. Late Cenozoic Continental Glacial, Periglacial, and Marine Correlations in the Great Plains-Gulf Coast., Inst. for Tert.-Quat. Studies, Nebr. Acad. Sci., Lincoln, Program with Abstracts.

Suthard, J. A. 1966. Stratigraphy and paleontology in Fish Lake Valley, Esmeralda County, Nevada. M.S. thesis, Dept. Geol. Sci., Univ. Calif., Riverside.

Swisher, C. J. 1982. Stratigraphy and Biostratigraphy of the Eastern portion of Wildcat Ridge, Western Nebraska. M.S. thesis. Univ. Nebraska, Lincoln. 126 pp.

Tedford, R. H. 1970. Principles and practices of mammalian geochronology in North America. No. Amer. Paleont. Conv., Chicago, 1969, Proc. F, pp. 666–703.

———. 1981. Mammalian biochronology of the late Cenozoic basins of New Mexico. Bull. Geol. Soc. Amer. 92:1008–1022.

Tedford, R. H., and D. Frailey. 1976. Review of some Carnivora (Mammalia) from the Thomas Farm local fauna (Hemingfordian, Gilchrist County, Florida). Amer. Mus. Novitates, no. 2610.

Tedford, R. H., and M. E. Hunter. 1984. Miocene Marine-nonmarine correlations, Atlantic and Gulf coastal plains, North America. Palaeogeogr., Palaeoclimat., Palaeoecol., 47(½):129–151.

Tedford, R. H., T. Galusha, M. F. Skinner, F. E. Taylor, R. Fields, J. R. Macdonald, R. H. Patton, J. M. Rensberger, and D. P. Whistler. 1973. Faunal succession and biochronology of the Arikareean through Clarendonian interval (Miocene epoch), North America. Geol. Soc. Amer. Abstr. with Programs, vol. 5, pp. 837–838.

Tedford, R. H., J. B. Swinehart, R. M. Hunt, and M. R. Voorhies. 1985. Uppermost White River and lowermost Arikaree rocks and faunas, White River Valley, northwestern Nebraska, and their correlation with South Dakota. In Fossiliferous Cenozoic deposits of western South Dakota and northwestern Nebraska, ed. J. E. Martin. Dakoterra 2:335–352.

Tipsword, H. L. 1962. Tertiary foraminifera in Gulf Coast petroleum exploration and development. In Geology of the Gulf Coast and central Texas and guidebook of excursions, eds. E. H. Rainwater and P. R. Zengula. Houston: Houston Geological Society, pp. 16–57.

Turner, D. L. 1970. Potassium-argon dating of Pacific Coast Miocene foraminiferal stages. Geol. Soc. Amer. Spec. Paper 124, pp. 91–129.

Van Couvering, J. A. 1978. Status of late Cenozoic boundaries. Geology 6:169.

Vondra, C. F. 1963. The stratigraphy of the Gering Formation in the Wildcat Ridge in western Nebraska. Ph.D. diss., Univ. Nebraska, Lincoln.

Vondra, D. F., C. B. Schultz, and T. M. Stout. 1969. New members of the Gering Formation (Miocene) in western Nebraska, including a geological map of Wildcat Ridge and related outliers. Nebr. Geol. Surv. Paper 18.

Voorhies, M. R. 1974. Late Miocene terrestrial mammals, Echols County, Georgia. Southeast Geol. 15:223–235.

———. 1977. Fossil moles of late Hemphillian age from northeastern Nebraska. Nebr. Acad. Sci. Trans. 4:129–138.

———. 1984. "*Citellus kimballensis*" Kent and "*Propliophenacomys uptegrovensis*" Martin, supposed Miocene rodents are Recent intrusives. J. Paleont. 58:254–258.

Wagner, H. M. 1976. A new species of *Pliotaxidea* (Mustelidae: Carnivora) from California. J. Paleont. 50:107–127.

———. 1981. Geochronology of the Mehrten Formation in Stanislaus County, California. Ph.D. diss., Univ. of Calif., Riverside.

Wahlert, J. H. 1976. *Jimomys labaughi,* a new geomyoid rodent from the early Barstovian of North America. Amer. Mus. Novitates, no. 2591.

Wanless, H. R. 1923. The stratigraphy of the White River beds of South Dakota. Amer. Phil. Soc. Proc. 62:190–269.

Watkins, N. D., and A. K. Baksi. 1974. Magnetostratigraphy and oroclinal folding of the Columbia River, Steens and Owyhee basalts in Oregon, Washington, and Idaho. Amer. J. Sci. 274:148–189.

Webb, S. D. 1964. The Alachua Formation. Soc. Vert. Paleont. 1964 Field Trip Guidebook, pp. 22–29.

———. 1966. A relict species of the burrowing rodent, *Mylagaulus,* from the Pliocene of Florida. J. Mammalogy 47:401–412.

———. 1967. Pliocene terrestrial deposits of peninsular Florida. Southeastern Geol. Soc., 13th Field Trip Guidebook, pp. 11–15.

———. 1969*a*. The Burge and Minnechaduza Clarendonian mammalian faunas of north-central Nebraska. Univ. Calif. Publ. Geol. Sci. 78:1–191.

———. 1969*b*. The Pliocene Canidae of Florida. Fla. State Mus. Bull. 14:273–308.

———. 1973. Pliocene pronghorns of Florida. J. Mammalogy 54:203–221.

———. 1977. A history of savanna vertebrates in the New World. Pt. I: North America. Ann. Rev. Ecol. System. 8:355–380.

———. 1981. *Kyptoceras amatorum,* new genus and species from the Pliocene of Florida, the last protoceratid artiodactyl. J. Vert. Paleont. 1:357–365.

Webb, S. D., and N. Tessman. 1968. A Pliocene vertebrate fauna from low elevation in Manatee County, Florida. Amer. J. Sci. 266:777–811.

Webb, S. D. and D. B. Crissinger. 1983. Stratigraphy and vertebrate paleontology of the central and southern phosphate districts of Florida. Geol. Soc. Amer., Southeastern Section, Field Trip Guidebook, Central Florida Phosphate District, pp. 28–72.

Webb, S. D., B. J. MacFadden, and J. A. Baskin. 1981. Geology and paleontology of the Love Bone Bed from the late Miocene of Florida. Amer. J. Sci. 281:513–544.

Whistler, D. P. 1965. A new Hemingfordian (middle Miocene) mammalian fauna from Boron, California, and its stratigraphic implication within the western Mojave Desert. M.A. thesis, Dept. Geol. Sci., Univ. Calif., Riverside.

———. 1969. Stratigraphy and small fossil vertebrates of the Ricardo Formation, Kern County, California. Ph.D. diss., Dept. Paleont., Univ. Calif., Berkeley.

———. 1984. An early Hemingfordian (early Miocene) fossil vertebrate fauna from Boron, western Mojave Desert, California. Los Angeles Co. Mus. Nat. Hist. Contrib. Sci., no. 355.

Whitmore, F. C., Jr., and R. H. Stewart. 1965. Miocene mammals and Central American seaways. Science 148:180–185.

Wilson, J. A. 1956. Miocene formations and vertebrate biostratigraphic units, Texas coastal plain. Amer. Assoc. Petrol. Geol. Bull. 40:2233–2246.

———. 1957. Early Miocene enteledonts, Texas coastal plain. Amer. J. Sci. 255:641–649.

———. 1959. Stratigraphic concepts in vertebrate paleontology. Amer. J. Sci. 257:770–778.

———. 1960. Miocene carnivores, Texas coastal plain. J. Paleont. 34:983–1000.

———. 1975. Geochronology, stratigraphy and typology. Fieldiana: Geology 33:193–204.

Wilson, R. W. 1934. Two rodents and a lagomorph from the Sespe of the Las Posas Hills, California. Carnegie Inst. Wash. Publ. 453, pp. 12–17.

———. 1936. A Pliocene rodent fauna from Smiths Valley, Nevada. Carnegie Inst. Wash. Publ. 473, pp. 16–34.

———. 1937. New Middle Pliocene rodent and lagomorph faunas from Oregon and California. Carnegie Inst. Wash. Publ. 487, pp. 1–19.

———. 1949. Rodents and lagomorphs of the Upper Sespe. Carnegie Inst. Wash. Publ. 584, pp. 53–65.

———. 1960. Early Miocene rodents and insectivores from northeastern Colorado. Univ. Kansas Paleont. Contrib., Vertebrata, art. 7, pp. 1–92.

———. 1967. Fossil mammals in Tertiary correlations. Univ. Kan. Dept. Geol. Spec. Publ. 2, pp. 590–606.

Wood, A. E., and R. L. Konizeski. 1965. A new eutypomyid rodent from the Arikareean (Miocene) of Montana. J. Paleont. 39:492–496.

Wood, H. E., II, and A. E. Wood. 1937. Mid-Tertiary vertebrates from the Texas coastal plain: Fact and fable. Amer. Midland Nat. 18:129–146.

Wood, H. E., R. W. Chaney, J. Clark, E. H. Colbert, G. L. Jepsen, J. B. Reeside, Jr., and C. Stock. 1941. Nomenclature and correlation of the North American continental Tertiary. Bull. Geol. Soc. Amer. 52:1–48.

Woodburne, M. O. 1977. Definition and characterization in mammalian chronostratigraphy. J. Paleont., 51:220–234.

Woodburne, M. O., and P. T. Robinson. 1977. A new Late Hemingfordian mammal fauna from the John Day Formation, Oregon, and its stratigraphic implications. J. Paleont. 51:750–757.

Woodburne, M. O., and R. H. Tedford. 1982. Litho- and

biostratigraphy of the Barstow Formation, Mojave Desert, California. Guidebook, Late Cenozoic tectonic and magnetic evolution of the central Mojave Desert, California. Geol. Soc. of Amer. (Cordilleran Section), pp. 65–76.

Woodburne, M. O., S. T. Miller, and R. H. Tedford. 1982. Stratigraphy and geochronology of Miocene strata in the central Mojave Desert, California. Guidebook, Late Cenozoic tectonic and magnetic evolution of the central Mojave Desert, California. Geol. Soc. of Amer. (Cordilleran Section), pp. 47–64.

Woodburne, M. O., B. J. MacFadden, and M. F. Skinner. 1981. The North American "Hipparion" datum and implications for the Neogene of the Old World. Geobios, no. 14, pp. 493–524.

Woodburne, M. O., R. H. Tedford, M. S. Stevens, and B. E. Taylor. 1974. Early Miocene mammalian faunas, Mojave Desert, California. J. Paleont. 48:6–26.

Wright, D. E., and S. D. Webb. 1984. Primitive *Mylohyus* (Artiodactyla: Tayassuidae) from the late Hemphillian Bone Valley of Florida. J. Vert. Paleont., 3:152–159.

Yatkola, D. A. 1978. Tertiary stratigraphy of the Niobrara River Valley, Marsland Quadrangle, western Nebraska. Nebr. Geol. Surv. Paper II.

Yatkola, D. A., and L. G. Tanner. 1979. *Brachypotherium* from the Tertiary of North America. Univ. Kan. Mus. Nat. Hist. Occ. Paper, no. 77, pp. 1–11.

7

THE NORTH AMERICAN QUATERNARY SEQUENCE

Ernest L. Lundelius, Jr.

Theodore Downs

Everett H. Lindsay

Holmes A. Semken

R. J. Zakrzewski

C. S. Churcher

C. R. Harington

Gerald E. Schultz

S. David Webb

INTRODUCTION

Quaternary vertebrate local faunas of North America are known from more than three hundred localities distributed over a wider geographic area than those of any other epoch (fig. 7.1). Superpositional control of the North American faunal succession for the Pliocene and Pleistocene epochs is limited, however, to Meade County, Kansas, northern Nebraska, the Snake River Plain of Idaho, the San Pedro Valley of Arizona, Medicine Hat, Alberta, the Anza-Borrego Desert of California, and shorter sequences in several other areas. The problems involved in the use of vertebrate fossils for Quaternary geochronology are similar to those of older time periods, with the added complicating factor of strong environmental zonation that shifted over short time intervals with glacial advance and retreat.

This chapter examines the last three land mammal ages of the Cenozoic. The oldest of these, the Blancan, is largely pre-Pleistocene (Pliocene) in the strict sense but is included in this section because the faunal break between the Blancan and the succeeding Irvingtonian is less pronounced than that between the Blancan and the preceding Hemphillian (latest Miocene-early Pliocene). The Blancan mammalian faunas are therefore more closely related to those of the Pleistocene than to those of preceding land mammal ages (Kurtén and Anderson 1980).

BEGINNING OF THE PLEISTOCENE AND LAND MAMMAL AGES

The term "Pleistocene" was proposed by Lyell (1839) for his concept of Newer Pliocene (Lyell 1833, chap. 5), based on the preponderance of Recent species of marine Mollusca collected primarily from Ischia and the Val di Noto in southern Italy. The Newer Pliocene (Pleistocene) was characterized by more than 70 percent Recent species, whereas the Older Pliocene, from northern Italy, was characterized by 40 to 70 percent Recent species. Subsequently, Forbes (1846, p. 386) equated the Pleistocene Epoch with the glacial formations of Europe, and

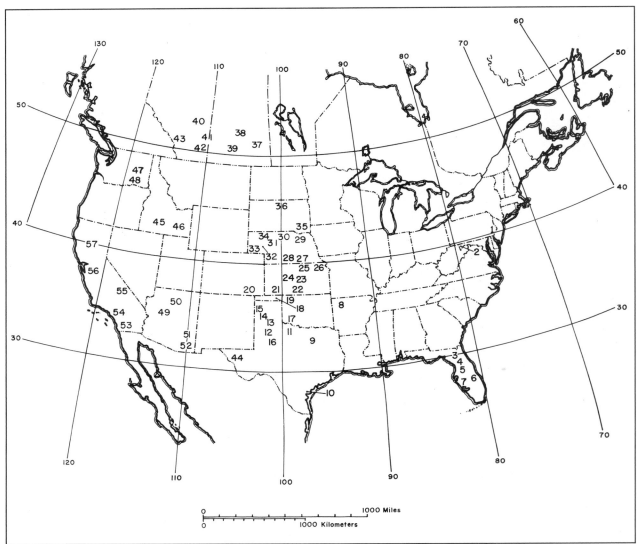

Fig. 7.1. Map showing location of faunas mentioned in figure 7.3. 1. Port Kennedy Cave; 2. Cumberland Cave; 3. Haile XVA, Haile XIVA, Haile XVIA, Arredondo, Santa Fe River IB; 4. Williston IIIA; 5. Coleman IIA, Inglis IA, Reddick; 6. Melbourne, Vero; 7. Bradenton; 8. Conard Fissure; 9. Hill-Shuler, Moore Pit; 10. Ingleside; 11. Howard Ranch, Easley Ranch, Vera, Gilliland; 12. Slaton, Blanco; 13. Rock Creek, unnamed l.f., Cudahy l.f. equivalent; 14. Cita Canyon; 15. Red Corral; 16. Beck Ranch; 17. Holloman; 18. Berends, Buis Ranch; 19. Doby Springs; 20. Donnelly Ranch, Mesa de Maya; 21. Deer Park, Sanders, Fox Canyon, Keefe Canyon, Rexroad, Seger, Borchers, Adams, Cudahy, Butler Spring, Cragin Quarry equivalent, Robert, Jinglebob, Jones, Mt. Scott, Cragin Quarry, Nash, Saw Rock Canyon, Bender; 22. Dixon; 23. Rezabek, Kanopolis, Sandahl, Kentuck; 24. Duck Creek; 25. White Rock, Courtland Canal, Hall Ash; 26. Aries, Wathena; 27. Angus; 28. Sappa; 29. Santee, Devil's Nest, Big Springs; 30. Sand Draw, Seneca; 31. Mullen I, Mullen II; 32. Lisco; 33. Broadwater; 34. Hay Springs, Rushville, Gordon; 35. Delmont; 36. Java; 37. Ft. Qu'Appelle; 38. Saskatoon; 39. Wellsch Valley; 40. Camrose; 41. Empress; 42. Medicine Hat Sequence; 43. Cochrane; 44. Red Light, Hudspeth; 45. Hagerman, Horse Quarry, Flat Iron Butte, Sand Point, Jackass Butte, Grande View, Wildhorse Butte; 46. American Falls, Rainbow Beach; 47. Taunton; 48. White Bluffs; 49. Verde; 50. Anita; 51. Flat Tire, Tusker, III Ranch; 52. Curtis Ranch, California Wash, Wolf Ranch, McCrae Wash, Mendevil Ranch, Benson; 53. Layer Cake, Arroyo Seco, Vallecito Creek; 54. Rancho La Brea; 55. Coso Mountains; 56. Pinole, Irvington; 57. Tehama.

the concept of worldwide Pleistocene glaciation followed rapidly thereafter. A more precise definition for the base of the Pleistocene was given in 1948 by the 18th International Geological Congress. By their edict, the Lower Pleistocene Series included the Calabrian Stage of Gignoux (1910, 1916) with its recognized terrestrial equivalent, the Villafranchian Stage, as its basal member. The Pliocene-Pleistocene Commission of that congress noted that this boundary coincided with evidence of climatic deterioration in the Italian Neogene succession. The commission retained the concept of worldwide glaciation, but climatic deterioration in Italy, not appearance of continental glaciation, characterized the base of the Pleistocene. Thus, it is reasonable to suppose that there was pre-Pleistocene glaciation in high latitudes and high elevations. Glacial activity in the Sierra Nevada, Iceland, or New Zealand and ice rafting in the Antarctic probably predated the Pleistocene. Major late Miocene and Pliocene sea level changes in Florida provide evidence for pre-Pleistocene continental glaciation. Webb et al. (1978) attribute the changes to glacioeustatic response to southern hemisphere glaciation. This may indicate that continental glaciation predated the onset of Pleistocene time in North America as well.

The earliest midlatitude continental glaciation in North America may approximate the beginning of the Pleistocene. Fission-track dates of volcanic ash deposits associated with the type Aftonian and Nebraskan sections of North America demonstrate that New World continental glaciation predates 2.2 Ma. Especially significant in this respect is core 5-A-75, drilled by the Nebraska Geological Survey near Afton, Iowa, in the type area of the Aftonian. This core revealed at least two tills underlying the classic Nebraskan till exposed in the region. The lowermost till in this core is overlain by a "Pearlette-type" ash now dated at 2.2 Ma (Hallberg and Boellstorff 1978). This date places the earliest known North American continental glaciation near the interval of climatic change recorded in Italy (Boellstorff 1978a).

Ashes dated at approximately 0.6 Ma (Type 0 or Lava Creek B of Izett; Pearlette restricted of Boellstorff) and 0.7 Ma (Hartford Ash) lie stratigraphically above classic Nebraskan till and below classic Kansan till (Hallberg 1980). The Cudahy Local Fauna, commonly designated as late Kansan, also lies immediately below the 0.6 Ma ash and thus is approximately the age of classic Aftonian sediments. As noted above, the Nebraskan till certainly does not represent the earliest North American continental glaciation, and the differentiation of at least seven tills (Boellstorff 1978a) within the type Nebraskan-Kansan sequence demonstrates that these terms are meaningless in the classic area. It is clear that

glacial age designations of High Plains local faunas are misaligned with respect to the till sequences and that the terms "Nebraskan," "Aftonian," and "Kansan" have lost meaning as chronological units. It is doubtful that climatic criteria are a sound basis for any chronostratigraphic or geochronologic unit. Thus, utilization of this nomenclature with Pleistocene faunas is not appropriate and is not followed here.

Correlations for the base of the Pleistocene Epoch outside Italy must be established on evidence independent of local climate and correlated with the defined base in Italy. Land mammal faunas can contribute to those correlations. Villafranchian and Villanyian faunas of Europe correlate approximately with Blancan faunas of North America, whereas Biharian faunas of Europe correlate approximately with North American Irvingtonian faunas. Savage and Curtis (1970) compared the mammalian faunas and potassium-argon dates of Villafranchian and Blancan land mammal ages and confirmed that the durations of the Villafranchian and the Blancan were approximately equal and that both may have extended from 4.0 to 1.7 Ma. Work at Villafranca d'Asti (Hurzeler 1967, Savage and Curtis 1970) suggests that part or all of the Villafranchian is older than the Calabrian. Azzaroli and Berzi (1970) reviewed the Villafranchian mammals from Imola, northern Italy, where Gignoux (1916) established the correlation between Villafranchian and Calabrian. They concluded that the correlation of Gignoux is correct. Azzaroli and Ambrosetti (1970) noted that the late Villafranchian vertebrate fauna at Imola occurs more than 1,000 meters stratigraphically above a cold-adapted Calabrian marine fauna. Therefore, late Villafranchian may correlate with Calabrian (or younger) deposits, and early Villafranchian faunas probably are pre-Calabrian, that is, pre-Pleistocene. Climatic deterioration is not presently evident in Villafranchian faunas of Europe; however, Kurtén (1963, 1968) noted an alternation between forest and steppe faunas during this interval, with a progressive decrease in woodland forms and an increase in steppe forms between faunas of early Villafranchian and late Villafranchian age.

Controversy over the Pliocene-Pleistocene boundary outside Italy is now being resolved. The Pliocene-Pleistocene boundary was discussed at length by Berggren and Van Couvering (1974). They noted significant changes in the planktonic record (e.g., the *Globorotalia menardii* complex) near this interval. Changes in planktonic foraminifers are caused, in part, by temperature differences of surface waters. Banner and Blow (1965) noted the appearance of the foraminifer *Globorotalia truncatulinoides* in the lower part of the type Calabrian section at Santa Maria di Catanzaro, Italy. The *G. trun-*

catulinoides datum marks the beginning of planktonic foraminiferal zone N22. This zone occurs in deep-sea cores at the base of the Olduvai magnetic subchron, at about 1.85 Ma (Berggren et al. 1967, Glass et al. 1967). In a later study of ocean cores, Berggren et al. (1980) placed the base of the Quaternary at the top of the Olduvai magnetic subchron (1.7 Ma) where significant changes (4 first appearance datums [FAD], 12 last appearance datums [LAD], 2 acme datums, and 1 ratio reversal datum) occur over a wide geographic and latitudinal area. Recent reevaluation of the Calabrian biostratigraphy, primarily of the calcareous nannoplankton, by Haq et al. (1977) indicates that the Pliocene-Pleistocene "boundary stratotype" at Le Castella should be correlated to the top of the Olduvai magnetic subchron at about 1.6 Ma. The base of Calabrian-like lithology and fauna at another important section in Calabria, Santa Maria di Catanzaro, is approximately the same age, but the Calabrian faunal stage is 75 meters higher in that section. Recently, a new stratotype for the Calabrian Stage at Vrica has been proposed by R. Selli and others (1977 INQUA Congress, oral pres.). Work is presently under way to accurately document the biostratigraphy, magnetostratigraphy, and radiometric dates of the Vrica section which promises to clarify anomalous results from other Calabrian sections.

In the San Pedro Valley of Arizona, a rabbit previously identified as *Lepus* (which may be *Sylvilagus;* J. White, pers. com. 1985) appears at about 1.9 Ma at the Olduvai magnetic subchron. In the Anza-Borrego Desert of California, *Lepus* appears at about 2.0 Ma (White, pers. com., 1985). *Lepus* has also been identified from the Borchers Local Fauna, Kansas, which lies stratigraphically above the Type B Pearlette (or Huckleberry Ridge) Ash dated at about 2.0 Ma (Izett and Wilcox 1982), and from the slightly earlier Big Springs Local Fauna, Antelope County, Nebraska (White, pers. com., 1985). *Sylvilagus* appears earlier in the Blancan in Florida and Nebraska (ca. 2.4 Ma), in southern Arizona (ca. 2.4 Ma), and in the Anza-Borrego Desert, California (ca. 2.5 Ma), and it appears that some of the records of *Lepus* prior to about 2.0 Ma might have to be reevaluated and possibly referred to *Sylvilagus. Lepus* has been regarded as being of Irvingtonian or later age in North America, although it occurs in faunas such as the Borchers Local Fauna which may be regarded as latest Blancan or transitional between Blancan and Irvingtonian. The North American appearance of *Lepus* may therefore prove to be a useful criterion for approximating the base of the Pleistocene on this continent. We are approaching a much more objective basis for recognizing the base of the Pleistocene in terms of North American land mammal ages than was available under previous practices, when considerations of climate played an important role. As elsewhere, however, more work is needed to verify our conclusions. The dates of these appearances of *Lepus* agree closely with the age of the late Villafranchian Mount Coupet Local Fauna near Le Puy, France, which underlies a basalt dated by K-Ar at 1.9 Ma (Savage and Curtis 1970). It appears that the base of the Pleistocene is near the end of the Blancan and Villafranchian land mammal ages or just above the Blancan-Irvingtonian transition.

NORTH AMERICAN LATE CENOZOIC MAMMALIAN SEQUENCE

Three land mammal ages recording successive changes in the Pliocene-Pleistocene mammalian fauna of North America have been established, the Blancan, the Irvingtonian, and the Rancholabrean, each based on the first appearance of certain immigrant and endemic taxa. The Blancan appears to be pre-Pleistocene by the correlations reviewed above. It is characterized by *Nannippus phlegon, Equus (Dolichohippus) simplicidens, Stegomastodon, Borophagus diversidens, Trigonictis, Nekrolagus, Procastoroides,* the cotton rat lineage *Sigmodon medius-S. minor,* and numerous arvicoline rodents with rooted teeth (fig. 7.2, in pocket). It differs from the preceding Hemphillian Land Mammal Age by the absence of *Machairodus, Agriotherium, Plesiogulo, Osteoborus, Osbornoceros, Prosthennops, Pliohippus, Astrohippus, Dinohippus, Neohipparion, Teleoceras, Aphelops, Microtoscoptes,* and mylagaulids and from the succeeding Irvingtonian and Rancholabrean ages by the absence of *Mammuthus* and *Bison.* As noted above, the rabbit *Sylvilagus* appears in the late Blancan, and *Lepus* in the latest Blancan. The Irvingtonian is characterized by the first appearance of *Equus sensu stricto, Mammuthus, Euceratherium, Smilodon,* and *Microtus,* the disappearance of *Hypolagus, Prodipodomys,* and most of the Blancan forms listed above, and the absence of *Bison.* The Rancholabrean is characterized by the appearance of *Bison* and many mammalian species virtually indistinguishable from Recent forms.

The relative ages of these faunal changes may be confirmed by superpositional or other geologic criteria such as the relatively much greater deformation of strata bearing Irvingtonian faunas as compared to strata bearing Rancholabrean faunas in California (Savage 1951). Nevertheless, the definition of these mammal ages ultimately must rest on biostratigraphic criteria. It will be of great interest to develop further local first and last appearance data and to determine how rapidly these species replacements took place. The usefulness of land mammals in geochronology will depend to a great extent on how rapid the dispersal of key species was. The large number of apparently sudden transberingian dispersals, especially among steppe-adapted mammals, promises to provide further useful refinements.

The problem of contemporaneity and duration of transitions can best be checked by some independent dating methods. Figure 7.3 places the major Blancan, Irvingtonian, and Rancholabrean mammal faunas of North America in a chronological framework based on faunal correlations, volcanic ash beds, and magnetic polarity reversals. It is recognized that many excellent faunas have been recovered from elsewhere in the continent (e.g., Alaska, the Yukon, Mexico) but because most of these lack reliable stratigraphic, radiometric, or magnetic data on which to base their ages and because of the probability of dischroneity in faunal events across wide geographic areas of ecological boundaries, they have been omitted from consideration here as their inclusion would add little to the discussion. Some of the faunas shown in figure 7.3 are tentatively placed because of inadequate dating or faunal correlation but are included because they are significant for other reasons.

Blancan

The term "Blancan" was first proposed as a provincial time term (Wood et al. 1941) based on the local fauna at "Mt. Blanco" and the adjoining draws, near the "old rock house" north of Crawfish Draw, Crosby County, Panhandle of Texas. The Blanco Local Fauna has at different times been regarded as Pliocene (Osborn and Matthew 1909; Osborn 1910; Matthew 1924; Simpson 1933) and early Pleistocene (Meade 1945, Hibbard 1958).

Blancan faunas occur primarily in the part of the United States west of the Mississippi River, but they are also found in Florida and Mexico. The most nearly complete known sequences of Blancan faunas are in the Snake River Plain in Idaho, the Anza-Borrego Desert in southern California, the San Pedro Valley in southern Arizona, and in the Great Plains, especially Meade County, Kansas. The dates of most of these sequences have been established by a combination of radiometric and paleomagnetic methods (Johnson et al. 1975; Lindsay et al. 1975; Opdyke et al. 1977; Neville et al. 1979; Lindsay et al. 1984; Lindsay et al., chap. 9, herein). First and last appearances of many key taxa (lowest and highest stratigraphic datum) have been noted for the more complete sequences, and these sequences

serve as standards for the dating of other Blancan magnetic subchrons and faunas.

In Idaho, a series of faunas ranging from early Blancan (Hagerman Local Fauna) to late Blancan (Grand View Local Fauna) occur within the Glenns Ferry Formation along the Snake River over a distance of more than 100 miles (160 km). The Hagerman Local Fauna (Hibbard 1969; Zakrzewski 1969; Bjork 1970) spans a vertical stratigraphic interval of over 400 feet (122 m). Lava flows and ash units within the section yielded K-Ar dates ranging from 3.2 to 3.57 Ma and a zircon fission-track date of 3.75 ± 0.36 Ma (Evernden et al. 1964, Izett 1981). Paleomagnetic studies by Neville et al. (1979) indicate that the Hagerman Local Fauna corresponds to the upper part of the Gilbert Reversed Chron and the lower part of the Gauss Normal Chron. The somewhat younger Sand Point Local Fauna (Hibbard 1959), 30 miles west of Hagerman, straddles the base of the Kaena subchron and underlies normally magnetized sediments within the Gauss Normal Chron (White, pers. com., 1981; Conrad, pers. com., 1981). The Grand View Local Fauna (Hibbard 1959, Shotwell 1970) from localities 75 to 100 miles (120 to 160 km) west of Hagerman spans the upper part of the Gauss Normal Chron and the lower part of the Matuyama Reversed Chron (White, pers. com., 1981; Conrad, pers. com., 1981). Newly discovered faunas from the region (e.g., Flat Iron Butte, Nine Foot Rapids) will fill critical gaps in the biostratigraphic and paleomagnetic sequence and will better document evolutionary trends within mammal lineages (Conrad, pers. com., 1981).

At Anza-Borrego State Park, California, in the Imperial and Palm Springs formations, the fossiliferous section is over 12,000 feet (3,600 m) thick and extends from the base of the Cochiti subchron in the Gilbert Chron to the Jaramillo subchron in the Matuyama Chron and includes three successive faunas—Layer Cake (very early Blancan), Arroyo Seco (early to middle Blancan), and Vallecito Creek (late Blancan to early Irvingtonian)—that correspond approximately to the upper part of the Gilbert, the Gauss, and the lower Matuyama chrons, respectively (Downs and White 1968, Opdyke et al. 1977). Recent fission-track analysis by N. Johnson and co-workers of ash sampled in 1982 at the Arroyo Seco-Vallecito faunal transition or at the Gauss-Matuyama boundary (specifically, normal polarity) is dated 2.3 ± 0.2 Ma (N. Johnson, pers. com. to T. Downs, July 9, 1982). Only preliminary studies of these faunas are presently available, but further work will provide a better understanding of the faunal changes through time and aid in correlation with Blancan faunas elsewhere in the United States and Mexico.

In the San Pedro Valley in southern Arizona, the St. David Formation is nearly 400 feet (120 m) thick and extends from the upper part of the Gilbert Reversed Chron to the lower part of the Brunhes Normal Chron (Johnson et al. 1975, Lindsay et al. 1975). Within these sediments a series of faunas range in age from the early Blancan Benson Local Fauna (Gidley 1922, 1926; Gazin 1942) within the Gauss Normal Chron to the earliest Irvingtonian Curtis Ranch Local Fauna (ibid.) at the Olduvai normal subchron in the Matuyama Reversed Chron. Radiometric control within the paleomagnetic sequence is provided by a zircon fission-track date of 3.1 ± 0.7 Ma on an ash bed immediately below the Post Ranch (type Benson) faunal horizon and by K-Ar dated reversely magnetized ash beds higher in the section just above and below the California Wash faunal site (Scarborough, pers. com., 1981).

In the Great Plains, especially southwest Kansas and the Texas Panhandle, the faunal sequence must be compiled from shorter local sections using mainly paleomagnetic and biostratigraphic criteria because few radiometric dates are available. Low sedimentation rates and short stratigraphic sequences, together with weaker remanent magnetism, low magnetic stability of samples, and the lack of adequate radiometric control, have made the paleomagnetic data more difficult to interpret. It is more likely, for example, that short magnetic subchrons are missed. However, careful biostratigraphic studies have enabled the late C. W. Hibbard and his co-workers to compile an impressive succession of Blancan faunas in Meade County, Kansas.

The Hemphillian-Blancan boundary is not well dated, although it falls within the Gilbert Chron, probably between 4.0 and 4.4 Ma. The youngest radiometrically dated Hemphillian faunas comprise the Pinole Local Fauna in California, which is in tuff dated by K-Ar methods at 5.2 ± 0.1 Ma (Evernden et al. 1964, Sarna-Wojcicki 1976), and the Santee Local Fauna in northeastern Nebraska, which is overlain by a volcanic ash dated at 5.0 ± 0.2 Ma by fission-track methods on glass shards (Voorhies 1977). The Pinole Local Fauna contains *Machairodus, Plesiogulo, Osteoborus, Dinohippus, Sphenophalos,* and *Megalonyx* (Tedford et al., chap. 6, herein), whereas the Santee Local Fauna contains *Hesperoscalops mcgrewi, Dipoides,* mylagaulids, megalonychids, rhinoceros, and a primitive arvicoline, "*Propliophenacomys*" *parkeri* (Voorhies 1977, L. D. Martin 1975).

The Concha, Verde, Saw Rock Canyon, and Buis Ranch local faunas appear to most closely mark the Hemphillian-Blancan boundary. The Concha Local Fauna from Chihuahua, Mexico, occurs well upsection

from the late Hemphillian Yepomera Local Fauna in reversely magnetized sediments just below a normal magnetic polarity subchron here interpreted to be the Nunivak subchron of the Gilbert Reversed Chron and hence dated at about 4.26 Ma. The fauna contains the type of a new arvicoline rodent, *Pliophenacomys wilsoni* (Lindsay and Jacobs, in press), which is intermediate in morphology between "*Propliophenacomys*" *parkeri* Martin from the Santee and Devil's Nest Airport local faunas (L. D. Martin 1975) and *Pliophenacomys finneyi* from the Fox Canyon Local Fauna of Kansas (Hibbard and Zakrzewski 1972). The Concha Local Fauna also contains a horse that may be regarded either as an advanced *Dinohippus* close to *D. mexicanus* or as a primitive dolichohippine. The late Hemphillian Yepomera Local Fauna lower in the section occurs above and below a normal magnetic polarity subchron here interpreted to be the Sidufjall (C^1) subchron in the Gilbert Reversed Chron, thus dating between 4.5 and 4.3 Ma by extrapolation from the magnetic polarity time scale. The Yepomera Local Fauna contains *Machairodus, Megantereon, Pseudaelurus, Agriotherium, Taxidea,* canids, *Paenemarmota, Spermophilus, Notolagus, Prosthennops, Hexabelomeryx, Megatylopus, Astrohippus stocki, Dinohippus mexicanus, Nannippus, Neohipparion, Teleoceras,* and a proboscidean (Ferrusquia-Villafranca 1978, Lindsay et al. 1984). The Verde Local Fauna, a new discovery from Yavapai County in central Arizona, is largely unstudied, but the arvicoline rodents *Pliophenacomys wilsoni* and *Nebraskomys rexroadensis* have been identified. The Verde Local Fauna is placed at the base of the Nunivak subchron of the Gilbert Chron at about 4.24 Ma. The Saw Rock Canyon Local Fauna from Kansas, generally regarded as terminal Hemphillian, is primarily a microfauna with several rodent species that are more primitive than, and possibly ancestral to, species in the early Blancan Fox Canyon and Rexroad local faunas (Hibbard 1949, 1953, 1964, 1967; Zakrzewski 1967). It contains a beaver (*Dipoides wilsoni*) a gopher with rooted teeth (*Pliogeomys*), a primitive arvicoline (*Ogmodontomys sawrockensis*), and an advanced species of the canid *Osteoborus* but no horses. The Buis Ranch Local Fauna of Oklahoma (Hibbard 1954a, 1963c) contains *Pliogeomys* and a late Hemphillian camel, *Hemiauchenia vera,* and may be nearly the same age as the Saw Rock Canyon Local Fauna, but both faunas lack radiometric and paleomagnetic control.

The earliest faunas containing characteristic Blancan genera are the Layer Cake (California), Fox Canyon (Kansas), and White Bluffs (Washington) local faunas. A record of cf. *Dinohippus* (Downs, pers. com., 1981) (ca. 4.0 Ma) marks the inception of the Layer Cake

Local Fauna at the base of the Cochiti subchron in the Gilbert Chron. This datum may lie close to the Hemphillian-Blancan boundary. The Layer Cake Local Fauna, which contains *Sigmodon,* a genus characteristic of Blancan and later mammal ages, and a large species of *Hypolagus* (*H. vetus*), correlates approximately with the Fox Canyon Local Fauna of Kansas based on its magnetic polarity and fauna (Lindsay et al. 1975). The Fox Canyon Local Fauna (Hibbard 1950, Hibbard and Zakrzewski 1972) occurs in reversely magnetized sediments that probably represent the upper part of the Gilbert Chron and is the oldest Blancan fauna recognized from the Great Plains. Small mammals are abundant, but large mammals are rare. Taxa that occur in Blancan or later mammal ages include *Hypolagus vetus* (White, pers. com., 1981), the arvicoline *Pliophenacomys finneyi, Geomys,* and *Odocoileus. Paenemarmota,* known from the late Hemphillian as well, is also present.

The White Bluffs Local Fauna from the Ringold Formation in south-central Washington (Gustafson 1978) contains a number of characteristic Blancan genera, including *Borophagus, Trigonictis, Equus* (*Dolichohippus*), *Ophiomys,* and *Nekrolagus* as well as a few forms with late Hemphillian aspects or affinities, such as *Canis davisi* and *Hypolagus ringoldensis.* Most of the reported fossils come from an interval extending from 45 feet (13 m) above to 40 feet (12 m) below an undated tuff that lies near the middle of a 200- to 300-foot (60 to 90 m) section of sediments showing predominantly reversed magnetism and thought to represent the upper part of the Gilbert Chron. The arvicoline rodent *Ophiomys mcknighti* is more primitive than *O. taylori* from the Hagerman Local Fauna and occurs about 30 feet (9 m) stratigraphically below the tuff and about 30 feet (9 m) above a thin, normally magnetized zone that probably represents the Cochiti subchron. Above the reversed section that contains the White Bluffs Local Fauna, a more advanced *Ophiomys* that closely resembles *O. taylori* occurs in the undescribed Haymaker's Orchard Local Fauna. Gustafson (1978; pers. com., 1981) therefore considers the White Bluffs Local Fauna to be older than the Hagerman Local Fauna. In a footnote (1978, p. 51) he mentions that "Specimens of *Ophiomys mcknighti* from Alturas, California, underlie a basalt dated at 4.7 ± 0.5 million years" (Repenning, pers. com., 1977). If the date is correct, then either *O. mcknighti* occurs much earlier at Alturas than at White Bluffs or the White Bluffs Local Fauna is older than the Verde, Concha, and Yepomera local faunas and considerably older than any other Blancan fauna. The presence of Hemphillian fossils in the Alturas Formation was noted by Evernden et al. (1964, p. 193). Further biostratigraphic and paleomagne-

tic studies are needed to define the Hemphillian-Blancan boundary in the Pacific Northwest.

The Blancan-Irvingtonian boundary is better defined than the Hemphillian-Blancan boundary. Faunas of late Blancan age (such as early Vallecito Creek, Grand View, and Blanco) occur in reversely magnetized sediments of the early Matuyama Chron. The transitional Blancan-Irvingtonian Borchers Local Fauna of Kansas (Hibbard 1941*a,* 1942, 1943*a;* Zakrzewski 1981) occurs in and just above a reversely magnetized type B Pearlette or Huckleberry Ridge Ash dated at 1.96 ± 0.20 Ma by fission-track methods on glass shards (Boellstorff 1976), 1.9 ± 0.1 Ma by fission-track methods on zircons (Naeser et al. 1973), and 2.01 Ma by K-Ar methods on source rocks in Yellowstone Park (Izett 1981, Izett and Wilcox 1982), whereas the Curtis Ranch Local Fauna in Arizona, which is of earliest Irvingtonian age, straddles the base of the Olduvai subchron at about 1.88 Ma. The Blancan Land Mammal Age thus extends from the upper part of the Gilbert Chron (4.0–4.4 Ma) to the Olduvai subchron (1.88 Ma) and has a duration of at least 2 Ma.

Genera that survived the end of Hemphillian time in North America include *Paenemarmota, Prodipodomys, Dipoides, Ogmodontomys, Hypolagus, Rhynchotherium,* and *Nannippus.* Many new genera made their appearance during early Blancan time, between about 4.0 and 3.4 Ma (late Gilbert Chron). Endemic forms such as *Equus* (*Dolichohippus*), which evolved from *Dinohippus* (Dalquest 1978*b*), and *Borophagus,* which evolved from *Osteoborus* (Vanderhoof and Gregory 1940), occur in the White Bluffs and Hagerman local faunas as do the Eurasian immigrants, *Trigonictis* and *Ursus* as well as *Ophiomys* (origin disputed). *Ophiomys* may have appeared earlier at Alturas, California, as noted above. *Chasmaporthetes,* another Eurasian immigrant, appears in the Fox Canyon Local Fauna (Bjork 1974) along with *Pliophenacomys finneyi, Geomys,* and *Odocoileus. Sigmodon* appears below the Cochiti subchron at about 4.0 or 4.1 Ma in the Layer Cake Local Fauna in the Anza-Borrego sequence, whereas *Geomys* appears just above the base of the Gauss Chron at about 3.3 Ma in the Arroyo Seco Local Fauna (Opdyke et al. 1977, Becker and White 1981). Both genera occur in the Benson Local Fauna in Arizona, in the lower part of the Gauss Chron at about 3.1 Ma and in the Beck Ranch Local Fauna of Texas (Dalquest 1978*a*). The latter is tentatively correlated with the Rexroad Local Fauna of Kansas, but no radiometric or paleomagnetic data are available. *Pratilepus,* a Eurasian immigrant, and the muskrat *Pliopotamys* occur in the Hagerman Local Fauna (Hibbard 1969, Zakrzewski 1969). Taxa that first appeared in the early part of the Gauss Chron include *Procas-*

toroides, Stegomastodon, and *Nannippus phlegon* in the Rexroad Local Fauna (Hibbard 1938, 1941*b*, 1941*c*, 1941*d*, 1972; Woodburne 1961) and *Pliolemmus* in the Bender Local Fauna (Hibbard 1972). *Nannippus phlegon* and *Stegomastodon* also appear early in the San Pedro sequence.

A second wave of first occurrences in the late Gauss Chron at about 2.5 to 2.7 Ma marks the beginning of the late Blancan. The Panamanian land bridge was established by 3.0 Ma and a number of South American mammals reached North America during Chapadmalalan (late Blancan) time (Marshall et al. 1979). These immigrants and their earliest North American records include *Glossotherium* in the Lower Cita Canyon (Schultz 1977) and Blanco (Dalquest 1975) local faunas of Texas, the Donnelly Ranch Local Fauna of Colorado (Hager 1975), and the Haile XVA and Santa Fe River IB local faunas of Florida (Webb 1974, Robertson 1976); *Glyptotherium* in Upper Cita Canyon, Blanco, Hudspeth (Strain 1966), and Red Light (Akersten 1972) local faunas of Texas and the Tusker Local Fauna of Arizona (Gillette and Ray 1981); *Kraglievichia* and *Dasypus* in Haile XVA and Santa Fe River IB (Webb 1974, Robertson 1976); *Neochoerus* in the Flat Tire and Tusker local faunas, 111 Ranch, Arizona (Lindsay and Tessman 1974, Ahearn and Lance 1980); and *Erethizon* in the Grand View Local Fauna, Idaho, and the Wolf Ranch Local Fauna, Arizona (Harrison 1978, Frazier 1982). *Synaptomys* (*Plioctomys*), a Eurasian immigrant, appears in the Great Plains in the Dixon (Hibbard 1956, Koenigswald and Martin 1984) and White Rock (Eshelman 1975, Koenigswald and Martin 1984) local faunas of Kansas and the Upper Cita Canyon Local Fauna of Texas (Schultz 1977), and *Tremarctos* is recorded at the top of the Arroyo Seco Local Fauna at about 2.5 Ma and may be present in the Hagerman Local Fauna (Bjork 1970). *Ondatra idahoensis* evolved from *Pliopotamys* at about the Gauss-Matuyama boundary, and *Mictomys* (*Metaxyomys*) also appeared at about this time; both taxa occur in the Grand View (Wilson 1933) and Borchers (Hibbard 1954*b*) local faunas.

The Blancan Land Mammal Age is characterized by many genera that did not survive into the Irvingtonian. Those that became extinct at or before the end of the Gauss Chron include *Dipoides, Ogmodontomys, Nebraskomys, Pliolemmus, Pliopotamys,* and *Pratilepus.* Those that disappeared during the early Matuyama Chron at or before the Olduvai magnetic subchron include *Paenemarmota, Procastoroides, Prodipodomys, Pliophenacomys, Ophiomys, Mictomys* (*Metaxyomys*), *Hypolagus, Borophagus, Rhynchotherium, Equus* (*Dolichohippus*), and *Nannippus.* Most of the

latter group make their last appearance in the Grand View, Blanco, or Borchers local faunas. *Borophagus* and *Pliophenacomys* last occur in the Wellsch Valley Local Fauna of Saskatchewan at the Olduvai subchron, where they are associated with *Mammuthus, Allophaiomys* n. sp., and *Microtus paroperarius* (Churcher and Stalker, in press). *Chasmoporthetes* last occurs in the late Blancan or early Irvingtonian Anita Local Fauna of Arizona (Hay 1921) and the early Irvingtonian Inglis IA Local Fauna of Florida (Berta 1981). *Trigonicitis* disappeared at the end of Blancan time in the western United States, but a derived species evidently survived into the early Irvingtonian in the Haile XVIA and Inglis IA faunas in Florida (Ray et al. 1981). *Stegomastodon* survived well into the Irvingtonian where it occurs with *Mammuthus* in the Gilliland Local Fauna of Texas (Hibbard and Dalquest 1966) and at the base of the Tule Formation in an unnamed local fauna below the Rock Creek Local Fauna at the same stratigraphic level as a volcanic ash dated at 1.2 to 1.3 Ma (Izett 1977, 1981; Izett et al. 1981).

Several efforts have been made to subdivide the Blancan into lower and upper parts using first and last appearances of key mammalian taxa that reflect immigration and extinction events as well as progressive species evolution within particular lineages. Such efforts are hampered by the fact that mammalian taxa may not appear or disappear simultaneously in all regions or in all faunas of the same age. Latitudinal, regional, and ecological factors lead to faunal provincialism that together with lack of radiometric and paleomagnetic control makes correlation of faunas difficult. Gustafson (1978) noted, for example, that the White Bluffs Local Fauna of Washington lacks such common southern and plains forms as *Nannippus*, glyptodonts, *Geomys, Ogmodontomys,* and *Sigmodon,* making it impossible to use the major faunal datum planes set up by Johnson et al. (1975) for the Blancan deposits of the San Pedro Valley, Arizona, which were based on *Nannippus* and *Sigmodon.* He noted further that *Scapanus, Ammospermophilus, Thomomys,* and *Castor* (known from Blancan deposits of the Santa Fe River locality in Florida [Webb 1974]) are all western forms in the Blancan and that microtine (arvicoline) rodents are scarce or absent in southern faunas, thus making the northwestern faunas such as Grand View, Hagerman, and White Bluffs appear similar despite probable age differences.

In spite of such difficulties, some progress has been made in subdividing the Blancan Mammal Age, although to date no single method or proposal has been universally adopted or considered universally applicable. In the Great Plains, Hibbard demonstrated that the faunas of the Rexroad Formation, such as Fox Canyon, Keefe Canyon, Rexroad, and Bender, were older than the Deer Park, Sanders, Sand Draw, and Dixon local faunas. The Borchers Local Fauna has been considered latest Blancan (Zakrzewski 1975, 1981). Biostratigraphic ranges of individual taxa have been plotted for the longer faunal sequences, such as Anza-Borrego (Downs and White 1968, Opdyke et al. 1977), San Pedro Valley (Johnson et al. 1975), and Snake River Plain (Neville et al. 1979, Conrad 1980) although no formal subages have been proposed. Kurtén and Anderson (1980) considered the appearance of certain South American immigrants at around 2.5 to 2.7 Ma to mark the boundary between early and late Blancan faunas. Schultz et al. (1977, 1978) proposed a twofold division of Blancan faunas in the Great Plains. The lower unit, the Rexroadian of Kurtén (1971), was expanded to include the Sand Draw, Broadwater, Lisco, Blanco, Hagerman, and Rexroad local faunas; the Rexroadian was characterized by the first appearance in North America of the dirk-tooth cat *Megantereon,* which now is also known from the Late Hemphillian of Florida (Berta and Galiano 1983), *Chasmaporthetes, Ursus, Trigonictis,* the extinct otter *Satherium, Stegomastodon, Mammut, Glyptotherium* (actually a late Blancan arrival), true cervids, and, in part, by certain microtine (arvicoline) rodents lacking cement in their reentrant angles (e.g., *Nebraskomys, Pliopotamys, Ophiomys,* and *Pliolemmus*), and giant beavers that lack distinct ridges on their incisor enamel (*Procastoroides sweeti*).

The upper part of the Blancan, for which Schultz et al. (1978) proposed the name Senecan, includes the Grand View, White Rock, Dixon, and Seneca local faunas as well as part of the Mullen assemblage (Martin 1972). Senecan faunas are characterized by the first appearance of *Synaptomys* (*Plioctomys*) and *Mictomys* (*Metaxyomys*), *Ondatra* and "*Mimomys*" *monohani,* and *Procastoroides idahoensis,* which has ridged incisors. The Rexroadian-Senecan boundary appears to fall at or just below the Gauss-Matuyama boundary. The Blanco Local Fauna, included by Schultz et al. (1978) within the Rexroadian, lies within reversely magnetized sediments interpreted by Lindsay et al. (1975) as representing the early Matuyama Chron, which indicates a late Blancan age for the fauna. No microtine rodents are present, but the presence of *Glyptotherium* and *Glossotherium* supports this age assignment. The Guaje ash bed, which overlies the Blanco Formation and Local Fauna, has a glass fission-track date of 1.4 ± 0.2 Ma (Izett et al. 1972).

Arvicoline rodents have proven very useful in biostratigraphic correlations of late Cenozoic faunas. They are abundant, they show a diversity of types, and their teeth demonstrate a number of signficant evolutionary trends, including increase in hypsodonty and height of dentine tracts, the reduction, fusion, or loss of roots, the addition of cement in the reentrant angles, and an increase in crown complexity and length of M_1 (see section, Chronoclines and Evolution, below). L. D. Martin (1979) established a series of arvicoline rodent zones for the late Cenozoic faunas of the United States, whereas Repenning (chap. 8) subdivided these ages based on first appearances of immigrants and evolutionary trends within endemic groups.

Although the Blancan Mammal Age is now considered to predate the Pleistocene, there is evidence for both alpine and early continental glaciation in North America during this time. Following the reappraisal of the Pearlette-like ash beds by Izett et al. (1971), which suggested that the Kansan glaciation was bracketed between 0.6 and 1.2 Ma, Hibbard (1972) acknowledged the probable existence of pre-Nebraskan cold-climate cycles and concluded that the later Blancan "interglacial," which included the Broadwater, Sand Draw, and Sanders local faunas, was not Aftonian in age but represented a pre-Nebraskan warm-climate period. Very early cold-climate indicators are known from Alaska (e.g., a till dated at 3.6 Ma [Denton and Armstrong 1969]), but no evidence for cold climate has been found in the early Blancan faunas of the United States. There is evidence for at least two alpine glacial events in California within the Blancan (Dalrymple 1972). The oldest is represented by the Deadman Pass Till in the Sierra Nevada (Curry 1966), bracketed by radiometric dates of 2.7 and 3.0 Ma; the second, the Sierran, is represented by the McGee Till (Cox et al. 1963), underlain by a basalt flow dated at 2.6 Ma.

From a study of oxygen isotope data obtained from a deep Pacific core, Shackleton and Opdyke (1977) concluded that between about 3.5 and 3.2 Ma no large ice sheets accumulated in the Northern Hemisphere and that the ocean was in an interglacial state with more or less constant isotopic composition. After 3.2 Ma, the ocean began a cooling trend and "glaciations of a magnitude of at least two-thirds that of the late Pleistocene glacial maxima were occurring in the time interval from 2.5 to 1.8 m.y. ago" (Shackleton and Opdyke 1977, p. 219). Boellstorff (1978a, 1978b) demonstrated the presence of a "pre-Nebraskan" glacial till beneath a volcanic ash dated at 2.2 Ma in a test hole in Iowa and concluded that an early continental glaciation reached its maximum about 2.5 Ma. On the basis of stones derived from the Canadian Shield, Stalker (Churcher and Stalker, in press) concluded that a continental ice sheet had at least covered the Canadian prairies before the existence of the Wellsch Valley Local Fauna, that is, before the Olduvai subchron of earlier than 1.8 Ma. It seems likely that the McGee Till, Boellstorff's Iowa Till, and Stalker's evidence of early glaciation in Saskatchewan represent part of the same climatic cycle—one that is reflected in the moist, cool, but mild pre-Nebraskan late Blancan Dixon, White Rock, and Upper Cita Canyon local faunas of the Great Plains and the low sea level Santa Fe River IB Local Fauna of Florida.

Irvingtonian

The Irvingtonian Land Mammal Age was originally defined by Savage (1951) as a Provincial Age based on the fauna from gravel pits southeast of Irvington, Alameda County, California (Stirton 1939, Savage 1951). These gravel pits are now abandoned and are partly overlain by Interstate Highway 680. Strata adjacent to the pits and at the level where the fossils occurred are reversely magnetized, and the fauna has been referred to the upper part of the Matuyama Chron below the Jaramillo subchron (Lindsay et al. 1975). The fauna contains *Mammuthus, Equus* s.s., *Tetrameryx, Euceratherium,* and *Smilodon* but lacks *Bison.* The absence of *Bison* and the presence of mammalian species less advanced than related forms from the Rancholabrean Mammal Age and the Recent led Savage to assign the Irvingtonian Mammal Age to an earlier Pleistocene phase.

The faunal transition from Blancan to Irvingtonian is gradual. Blancan genera such as *Paenemarmota, Procastoroides, Prodipodomys, Pliophenacomys, Ophiomys, Mictomys (Metaxyomys), Hypolagus, Borophagus, Equus (Dolichohippus),* and *Nannippus* disappeared during the early Matuyama Chron at or before the Olduvai subchron while characteristic Irvingtonian genera such as *Mammuthus, Euceratherium, Soergelia, Tetrameryx, Smilodon,* and *Lepus* began to appear in North American faunas.

This raises the question of where a boundary should be placed: at the last appearance of a Blancan form, at the first appearance of an Irvingtonian form, or at some arbitrary point in between? The appearance of a new immigrant from another region is a more reliable time indicator than the last appearance of an old form. This avoids the problems of absence of a taxon not being proof of absence and of relict populations in locally favorable areas, although both extinction and the spread of immigrants over wide areas are time transgressive to varying degrees. R. A. Martin (1979, p. 27) has noted that the vast majority of small mammal speciation events that he could recognize from the Pliocene and Pleistocene

fossil record coincide with ecological or geological shifts of some magnitude which end a period of relatively prolonged stasis. This supports the concept that immigration and evolutionary events can be useful in defining and subdividing land mammal ages.

In certain stratigraphic sequences, such as the Anza-Borrego Desert, California, and the San Pedro Valley, Arizona, the change from one fauna to the other is transitional and deposition is continuous across the transition, with gradual replacement of Blancan genera by Irvingtonian genera. The Blancan-Irvingtonian boundary may then be arbitrarily drawn at the point at which the fauna is more characteristically Irvingtonian than Blancan. In the Vallecito Creek Local Fauna in the Anza-Borrego sequence, the boundary is arbitrarily drawn at the level above the Olduvai subchron at about 1.6 Ma with the first appearance of the saber-toothed cat *Smilodon* (Opdyke et al., 1977). The Eurasian immigrant *?Euceratherium* occurs slightly higher stratigraphically, as do *Stegomastodon* and *Microtus. Lepus* cf. *callotis* occurs at the base of the Olduvai subchron at about 1.9 Ma (White, pers. com., 1985). This rabbit is identified in White (1984) as *Lepus* or *Sylvilagus.* According to White (pers. com., 1981), distinguishing between *Lepus* and *Sylvilagus* on the basis of dental material is difficult, and size alone is not conclusive unless the diastemal portion of the lower jaw is present as some Mexican *Sylvilagus* may exceed *Lepus* in size. In view of this, early forms referred to *Lepus* should be carefully restudied, particularly those associated with *Hypolagus* from late Blancan or earliest Irvingtonian faunas (e.g., Anita and Tusker, Arizona; Borchers, Kansas).

In the San Pedro Valley, paleomagnetic data show that the transition from the Blancan to the Irvingtonian Mammal Age occurs in the early Matuyama Chron. The boundary is arbitrarily drawn at about 1.9 Ma at the first local appearance of Lowest Stratigraphic Datum (LSD) of *Lepus* (or *Sylvilagus*), in the Curtis Ranch Local Fauna (Lindsay et al. 1975). The Curtis Ranch Local Fauna occurs in sediments that straddle the base of the Olduvai subchron at about 1.88 Ma and includes *Ondatra idahoensis, Lepus* (or *Sylvilagus*), the earliest local record of *Dipodomys,* and a late record of *Stegomastodon.* Extrapolating from paleomagnetic data, *Ondatra idahoensis* appears in the local sequence (California Wash Local Fauna) at about 2.3 Ma, whereas *Nannippus* disappears at about 2.4 or 2.5 Ma.

The Blancan-Irvingtonian transition is not as well documented in the central Great Plains. In Meade County, Kansas, the Borchers Local Fauna immediately overlies the Huckleberry Ridge or type B Pearlette Ash, which has been dated at 1.9 to 2.0 Ma (Naeser et al.

1973; Boellstorff 1976; Izett 1981). Zakrzewski (1975, 1981) considered the fauna to be late Blancan in age on the basis of its warm climatic nature and the stage of evolution of the taxa present. The fauna, which consists primarily of microvertebrates, is unusual in that it lacks many diagnostic Blancan forms, although *Prodipodomys* is still present. *Dipodomys* and *Lepus,* characteristic of Irvingtonian and later faunas, are also present. The only arvicoline rodents are *Ondatra* cf. *idahoensis* and *Mictomys* (*Metaxyomys*), suggesting that the fauna may postdate the extinction of most of the characteristic Blancan genera (Schultz and Martin 1977). Recently, Izett (pers. com., 1982) identified *Stegomastodon* and *Dolichohippus* in the Borchers Local Fauna. This fauna and ash occur in reversely magnetized sediments of the early Matuyama Chron (Lindsay et al. 1975). The Borchers Local Fauna is therefore the same age as, or slightly older than, the Curtis Ranch Local Fauna.

The Wellsch Valley Local Fauna, near Swift Current, Saskatchewan, occurs in a deposit underlying at least four unfossiliferous glacial tills (Stalker and Churcher 1972; Churcher and Stalker, in press). The fauna contains the Blancan survivor *Borophagus* and one of the earliest records of *Mammuthus meridionalis* in North America. *Equus, Microtus,* and *Allophaiomys* are also present. Recent paleomagnetic evidence (Foster and Stalker 1976; Stalker, pers. com., 1981) indicates that the fossiliferous unit was deposited during the Olduvai subchron.

Based on the evidence from the faunas just discussed, the Blancan-Irvingtonian transition falls within a time span between about 1.6 and 2.0 Ma and appears to coincide closely with the Olduvai subchron dated at 1.88 to 1.72 Ma (Lindsay et al., chap. 9). The Blancan-Irvingtonian boundary thus approximates the Pliocene-Pleistocene boundary, which, as noted earlier, has been drawn either at the base or at the top of the Olduvai subchron.

It is reasonable to assume that the Bering land bridge was open to migration during the time of the early Matuyama Chron, allowing faunal exchange to occur at that time. The beginning of the Irvingtonian is marked by an influx of Eurasian immigrants into North America starting about 1.8 Ma. These include *Mammuthus, Euceratherium, Soergelia,* and jaguars (Kurtén and Anderson 1980). The place of origin of *Lepus* is uncertain.

In addition to the Wellsch Valley site, other early records of *Mammuthus* come from the Bruneau Formation of Idaho, in which the youngest basalt has been dated by the K-Ar method at 1.36 Ma (Malde and Powers 1962, Evernden et al. 1964); the Holloman Local Fauna from Frederick, Oklahoma (Meade 1953, Dal-

quest 1977); the Gilliland Local Fauna from Baylor and Knox counties, Texas (Hibbard and Dalquest 1966); the Rock Creek Local Fauna (Troxell 1915a); and from an unnamed fauna at the base of the Tule Formation below the Rock Creek Local Fauna. In the Gilliland Local Fauna and the unnamed fauna, *Mammuthus* occurs with an advanced species of *Stegomastodon* (Madden, pers. com., 1980). At the level of the unnamed fauna in the Tule Formation, an ash bed, Cerro Toledo X, showing reversed magnetic polarity, has been dated at 1.2 to 1.3 Ma on the basis of correlation with source area tephra from the Cerro Toledo Rhyolite, Jemez Mountains, New Mexico (Izett 1977, 1981; Izett et al. 1981). *Mammuthus* is not known from the St. David Formation in the San Pedro Valley or from the stratigraphically continuous part of the Anza-Borrego section, but it does occur 25 miles (40 km) north of the Anza-Borrego Desert in reversely magnetized, steeply dipping, faulted sediments that cannot be precisely correlated with the main section (Opdyke et al. 1977). *Mammuthus* also occurs in the type Irvington Local Fauna (Savage 1951).

As noted above, *Euceratherium* is known from the Vallecito Creek and Irvington faunas. It is also known from the younger Cumberland Cave Local Fauna from Maryland (Gidley and Gazin 1938) and possibly from Wellsch Valley. *Soergelia* probably arrived in North America slightly later than *Euceratherium*. *Soergelia* occupies an intermediate position between *Euceratherium* and advanced Ovibovini, being less high-horned than the former. It occurs in Germany, Czechoslovakia, Romania, and Siberia but is known from only a few sites in North America, presumably all of Irvingtonian age. These include Old Crow River locality 11A, Yukon Territory (Harington 1978), Rock Creek, Texas (as *Preptoceras,* Troxell 1915b), and Courtland Canal, Jewell County, Kansas (Nelson and Neas 1980, Eshelman and Hager 1984). The Rock Creek Local Fauna occurs about 100 feet (30 m) stratigraphically above the Cerro Toledo X Ash dated at 1.2 to 1.3 Ma (Izett 1977, 1981; Izett et al. 1981; Schultz 1984) and 15 feet (4.5 m) below the Lava Creek B or type O Pearlette Ash dated at 0.61 Ma (Naeser et al. 1971, Izett 1981). The Kansas specimen was recovered from sediments that apparently lie below the Hartford Ash, dated at 0.74 Ma (Eshelman and Hager 1984). Zoogeographic and stratigraphic evidence suggests a rapid Holarctic dispersal of *Soergelia,* making it a useful guide for correlation of Irvingtonian-aged deposits in Kansas and Texas in North America with deposits of the Olyor Suite and its equivalents in the U.S.S.R. and with Mindel and Elster sediments in Europe (Harington 1977, 1980).

Panthera onca occurs in faunas of early Irvingtonian

age (Curtis Ranch, Irvington, and Port Kennedy Cave) and later Irvingtonian age (e.g., Coleman IIA, Conard Fissure, and Cumberland Cave) as well as in many faunas of Rancholabrean age. *P. onca* underwent a progressive size reduction during this time (Kurtén and Anderson 1980).

Other Irvingtonian immigrants include species of *Clethrionomys, Canis lupus, Mustela erminea,* and *Lutra,* all of which probably migrated from the Palaearctic to the Nearctic; *Microtus,* whose area of origin is debated; and *Rangifer, Lemmus,* and the *Dicrostonyx*-like lemmings, arctic forms that may have originated in Beringia (Kurtén and Anderson 1980). The earliest known North American occurrences of *Lemmus, Rangifer,* and *Cervus* are recorded from the Cape Deceit Local Fauna from western Alaska. *Microtus, Ochotona whartoni,* and *Predicrostonyx* are also present (Guthrie and Matthews 1971). The fauna shows closer affinities to Siberian faunas than to North American assemblages. The paleoenvironment was probably a treeless lowland tundra.

Sometime during latest Blancan or earliest Irvingtonian time several South American immigrants reached North America. These include *Eremotherium, Nothrotheriops,* and *Holmesina.* The earliest record of *Eremotherium* is in the Inglis IA Local Fauna of Florida (Webb 1974). *Nothrotheriops* occurs in the Vallecito Creek Local Fauna at Anza-Borrego, California, at about 2.1 Ma, the Gilliland Local Fauna of Texas, and Medicine Hat, Alberta. *Holmesina* is known from numerous localities in Texas, Oklahoma, Kansas, and Florida.

The Irvingtonian Mammal Age, which began about 1.9 Ma and ended with the arrival of *Bison* in North America about 0.3 Ma, spans most of the Pleistocene. Unfortunately, long continuous sequences of superimposed faunas like those discussed for the Blancan are not available for the Irvingtonian Mammal Age. However, a few shorter sequences exist, the best of which are found in conjunction with the Vallecito Creek and Medicine Hat faunas and several others in Kansas and Texas. Paleomagnetic data are available for some faunas, and in the Great Plains where the greatest number of faunas occur, a series of volcanic ash beds datable by fission-track methods have helped to provide a chronological framework. Earlier studies by Hibbard and others attempted to assign these Great Plains local faunas to the glacial and interglacial stages of the midcontinent region (Hibbard 1958, 1970; Hibbard et al. 1965). There are only a few areas where such a relationship can be established at present. The recent reevaluation of the classic tills in Iowa and Nebraska by Boellstorff (1978*a*, 1978*b*) has made correlations of this kind dubious at best.

Schultz et al. (1977, 1978) proposed a division of the Irvingtonian Mammal Age into at least two smaller units, the Sappan (older) and the Sheridanian (younger), based primarily on faunas from the Great Plains. Sappan faunas include the type Sappa Local Fauna, Harlan County, Nebraska, which directly underlies the Mesa Falls or type S Pearlette Ash dated at 1.27 Ma (Schultz and Martin 1970; Naeser et al. 1971; Izett 1981; Izett and Wilcox 1982); the Nash Local Fauna, Meade County, Kansas (Bayne 1976), from a channel in the Crooked Creek Formation (R. Eshelman, pers. com., 1981; Eshelman and Hibbard 1981), which is younger than the Borchers Local Fauna and the Huckleberry Ridge or type B Pearlette Ash and which is overlain by the Cerro Toledo B Ash dated at 1.2 to 1.5 Ma (Boellstorf 1976; Izett 1977, 1981; Izett et al. 1981); the Aries Local Fauna from just below the Cerro Toledo B Ash (Izett, pers. com., 1982); the Wathena Local Fauna, which lies beneath a glacial till in Doniphan County, Kansas (Einsohn 1971); the Kentuck Local Fauna, McPherson County, Kansas (Hibbard 1952; Semken 1966; R. A. Martin 1975) from a channel fill cut into a type B ash (Izett 1981); the Java Local Fauna, Walworth County, South Dakota (R. A. Martin 1973, 1975); and probably the Gilliland Local Fauna of Knox and Baylor counties, Texas (Hibbard and Dalquest 1966). Like the slightly older Borchers Local Fauna, these faunas are dominated by heteromyid and cricetine rodents and have a low diversity of microtine or arvicoline rodents. With the exception of the Gilliland Local Fauna, the Sappan faunas generally are characterized by *Ondatra* cf. *annectens, Microtus (Allophaiomys)* (R. A. Martin 1975), and *Mictomys (Kentuckomys) kansasensis* (Zone IV of L. D. Martin 1979; Koenigswald and Martin 1984). The Gilliland Local Fauna contains only one microtine, a primitive water rat, *Proneofiber guildayi* (Hibbard and Dalquest 1973). During Sappan time, *Mammuthus meridionalis* also appeared, whereas *Stegomastodon* made its last appearance. *Microtus (Allophaiomys)* may be an immigrant from Eurasia which entered North America during the early Pleistocene; if so, it could be of value in correlation with the European sequence because microtines of this grade (*Allophaiomys pliocaenicus*) occur near the base of the Biharian in Europe (Martin 1977, Van der Meulen 1978). The Villanyian, which precedes the Biharian, has been radiometrically dated at 1.8 Ma in its upper part. Thus, the Villanyian-Biharian boundary appears to correlate closely with the Blancan-Irvingtonian boundary.

The next youngest faunas include the Cudahy Local Fauna, Meade County, Kansas (Hibbard 1944, Paulson 1961), and its Texas equivalents, the Vera Local Fauna (Hibbard and Dalquest 1966) and several Panhandle sites, all of which immediately underlie the Lava Creek B or type 0 Pearlette Ash dated at 0.61 Ma (Naeser et al. 1971; Izett 1981; Izett and Wilcox 1982). These faunas have a much greater diversity of microtines than the Sappan faunas and include *Microtus paroperarius, Pitymys meadensis, Pedomys llanensis, Mictomys (Mictomys) meltoni, Ondatra annectens,* and *Phenacomys* (Zone V of L. D. Martin 1979, Koenigswald and Martin 1984). Schultz et al. (1978) did not propose a subage name for these faunas, but if one is desirable, the term "Cudahyan" would be appropriate. Other faunas that belong to this phase are Conard Fissure, Arkansas (Graham 1972), Cumberland Cave, Maryland (Van der Meulen 1978), and possibly Port Kennedy Cave, Pennsylvania (Hibbard 1955*b*). These localities contain microtines at the same stage of evolution as those in the Cudahy Local Fauna, but they are assigned to different species. The Port Kennedy microtine material is very fragmentary and most of it is indeterminate. This fauna also contains *Smilodon gracilis,* a more primitive cat than *S. fatalis* from the later "Sheridanian" faunas. The Cape Deceit Local Fauna may fall within this age range because of the advanced dental pattern of *Microtus deceitensis,* but it may be slightly older (L. D. Martin 1979).

The Sheridanian subage (Schultz et al. 1977, 1978) is based primarily on the Hay Springs, Rushville, and Gordon local faunas, all from Sheridan County, and the Angus Local Fauna (Martin 1971) from Nuckolls County, Nebraska. These faunas differ from the earlier Irvingtonian faunas, including the Cudahy, in the presence of *Ondatra nebrascensis* rather than *O. annectens, Microtus pennsylvanicus* rather than *M. paroperarius, Microtus (Pedomys) ochrogaster* rather than *M. (P.) llanensis,* and *Smilodon fatalis* rather than *S. gracilis* (Schultz et al. 1977). The microtines are those of Zone VI of L. D. Martin (1979). The Irvington Local fauna was also included in this "sub-age," but this fauna is certainly older as it comes from reversely magnetized sediments of the upper Matuyama Chron (Lindsay et al. 1975), whereas the "Sheridanian" faunas are more advanced than the Cudahy Local Fauna and hence younger than 0.6 Ma. This places them in the early part of the Brunhes Normal Chron. Other faunas of Sheridanian age include Kanopolis (Hibbard et al. 1978), Rezabek (Hibbard 1943*b*), Sandahl (Semken 1966), and Adams (Schultz 1969) from Kansas, Berends (Starrett 1956) from Oklahoma, and Slaton (Dalquest 1967) from Texas. The Kanopolis, Rezabek, and Slaton local faunas contain *Neofiber leonardi* and are presumably the same age (Hibbard and Dalquest 1973, Hibbard et al. 1978).

Rancholabrean

The Rancholabrean Mammal Age was established as a Provincial Age by Savage (1951) and is named for the Rancho La Brea Local Fauna of California. Rancholabrean faunas are characterized by the presence of *Bison,* an Eurasian immigrant, many recently extinct genera and/or species of larger mammals (e.g., *Smilodon fatalis, Panthera leo atrox, Canis dirus, Mammuthus*), and many extant species of smaller mammals, especially carnivores and rodents. Important Eurasian immigrants to North America during this age include *Oreamnos, Ovis, Ovibos, Alces,* and *Homo.*

Because many characteristic Rancholabrean species are now known from late Irvingtonian faunas and because not all Rancholabrean faunas contain *Bison,* the distinction between the Irvingtonian and the Rancholabrean is not as sharp as that between the Blancan and the Irvingtonian mammal ages. Moreover, the beginning of the Rancholabrean Mammal Age is poorly dated, with estimates ranging from 0.2 to 0.55 Ma. Establishment of a reliable date depends to a large extent on the successful recognition and dating of those faunas previously assigned to the Illinoian glacial stage because many workers regarded *Bison* as having made its earliest appearance in North American faunas of presumed late Illinoian age. Schultz and Hillerud (1977) have argued, however, that *Bison* first appeared in the Great Plains in "post-Kansan to early Illinoian times," although faunas of this age are generally considered to be late Irvingtonian. It may be significant that no bison remains are known from the rich "Sheridanian" faunas of the Hay Springs area of Nebraska.

No good basis presently exists for an absolute chronology within the Rancholabrean Mammal Age except for its terminal phase, which falls within the range of radiocarbon techniques. The age lies completely within the Brunhes Chron, which has no positively demonstrated events of reversed magnetic polarity. Thus, for most of the Rancholabrean, it is necessary to rely on faunal relationships and attempts to fit faunas into a glacial-interglacial framework tentatively correlated with that of Europe.

Although it now seems likely that the Eemian (= Devensian) interglacial of Europe correlates with the North American Sangamonian, which presumably peaked at about 100,000 years ago (Kurtén and Anderson 1980), and that the Wisconsinan glaciation *sensu stricto* began about 70,000 years B.P. (Flint 1971; Hays et al. 1976; Woldstedt 1969), correlation of the Illinoian glacial with the European sequence is still controversial.

Cooke (1973) suggested a correlation of the Illinoian with the European Elster-Mindel glaciation centered at about 0.5 Ma. In contrast, Boellstorff (1978a, 1978b) and Hallberg and Boellstorf (1978) demonstrated that the classic Kansan till of the midcontinent area is younger than the 600,000-year-old type O Pearlette Ash on the basis of test hole data from Iowa. Hallberg (1980) placed the classic Kansan till as pre-Illinoian with respect to the glacial sequence.

Difficulty in referring faunas to either a glacial or interglacial stage stems in part from a suggestion made by Graham and Semken (1976) that the climate in the Great Plains may have been more equable during certain glacial phases than during a typical interglacial, which would have resulted in local faunas that do not seem "arctic" in nature because of apparently incompatible or disharmonious elements (see discussion below). In addition, short-term climatic fluctuations related to a stadial-interstadial transition may go unrecognized in the faunal record or, if recognized, may be difficult to date.

Of the 185 Rancholabrean faunas listed by Kurtén and Anderson (1980), only a few show a superpositional relationship. Near Medicine Hat, Alberta, in bluffs along the South Saskatchewan River, a sequence of faunas ranging in age from middle Irvingtonian ("mid-Kansan") to early Holocene occur in a series of river and floodplain deposits interbedded with several glacial tills. This is the richest known Pleistocene vertebrate assemblage from the northern Great Plains (Stalker 1969; Stalker and Churcher 1970, 1972). On the Big Springs Ranch in Meade County, Kansas, the Mt. Scott Local Fauna, regarded as late Illinoian, is overlain by the Cragin Quarry Local Fauna, considered to be a "warm" Sangamonian interglacial fauna (Hibbard and Taylor 1960, Hibbard 1963a). *Bison* is present in the Mt. Scott Local Fauna. In the Butler Springs area of the same county, the Adams (early Illinoian) and Butler Spring (late Illinoian) local faunas are overlain by an equivalent of the Cragin Quarry Local Fauna, and this, in turn, is overlain by the late Wisconsinan Robert Local Fauna, dated at 11,000 ± 300 years ago (Schultz 1965, 1967, 1969). Floral evidence indicates a progressive warming of the climate during the "late Illinoian" and "early Sangamonian." There is no evidence of *Bison* in the Butler Spring sequence.

Attempts at subdividing the Rancholabrean on the basis of the species of *Bison* have produced varying results (Schultz and Frankforter 1946; Schultz et al. 1972; Hibbard 1955a; Schultz and Hillerud 1977), and no one system has been generally accepted. The differences result both from different correlations of the glacial-interglacial sequence in the midcontinent area with the nonglacial faunal sequence and from differences in the interpretation of *Bison* phylogeny and taxonomy (Wilson 1974a, 1974b; McDonald 1981). The taxonomy of the genus is still controversial; variation is considerable, sexual dimorphism is pronounced, and the picture is greatly complicated by the presence of shifting geographic and temporal clines. Furthermore, in the Great Plains, there evidently was a trend toward gradual reduction in size over time.

Parts of Alaska and the Yukon evidently were populated continuously or intermittently since Illinoian time and perhaps earlier by bison conspecific with the Eurasian form, *Bison priscus* (= *B. crassicornis*) (Guthrie 1970, Kurtén and Anderson 1980). This northern population appears to have been the source of bison immigrations to North America south of the ice. Guthrie (1970) believes that an earlier immigration gave rise to *B. latifrons* through increase in body and horn size, whereas *B. bison,* the small-horned species of late Wisconsinan and Holocene time, may represent a second invasion that replaced *B. antiquus* following the opening of the Cordilleran Corridor. *B. antiquus,* in turn, may represent a smaller-horned end member of a *B. latifrons-B. alleni* lineage.

Reeves (1973) showed, however, that coalescence of the continental and Cordilleran ice sheets was a minor event, brief in duration and local in extent. Both he and Wilson (1974b) believe that the northern and southern populations could have maintained or easily reestablished gene flow through the Wisconsinan, resulting in a subspecific relationship between *B. b. occidentalis* and *B. b. antiquus,* and that *B. b. antiquus* underwent a reduction in size through time, which ultimately led to *B. b. bison.* Whatever view is correct, data indicate that *B. latifrons* and *B. alleni* are, in general, older than either *B. b. antiquus* or *B. b. occidentalis* (Skinner and Kaisen 1947; Guthrie 1970; Schultz et al. 1972; Schultz and Hillerud 1977) and that these, in turn, are older than *B. b. bison.* However, *B. latifrons* evidently survived into Wisconsinan time, at least in California, and was contemporaneous with *B. b. antiquus* (Miller 1968, 1971; Miller and Brotherson 1979; Wyman 1926). If the relative ages of the various species of *Bison* outlined above can be confirmed, even for part of North America, then it might be possible to subdivide the Rancholabrean Mammal Age on this basis.

The temporal duration of many mammalian species is greater than the relatively short span of the Rancholabrean Mammal Age, thus making faunal correlation difficult. However, studies of microevolutionary changes at the intraspecific level (such as for *Ursus americanus, Bison latifrons, Ondatra zibethicus,* and *Microtus penn-*

sylvanicus) may be useful. Determination of the first appearance of selected immigrants from Beringia, such as *Ursus arctos* and *Alces alces,* may provide useful datum lines (Kurtén and Anderson 1980).

The later part of the Rancholabrean is known in greater detail than the earlier part because of the applicability of the carbon-14 dating method and the greater frequency of specimen recovery. Kurtén and Anderson (1980) list 150 faunas from the Wisconsinan alone. Many of these are cave faunas or, as in Florida, spring and sinkhole faunas.

During the last decade much has been learned about the large mammal fauna of eastern Beringia (unglaciated parts of Alaska and the Yukon Territory) during the peak of the Wisconsinan glaciation, which is usually considered to cover the period from 25,000 to 15,000 years ago (Mickelson et al. 1983). Radiocarbon dates on bone indicate that *Bison crassicornis, Equus* sp., *Mammuthus primigenius, M. columbi* and/or *M. armeniacus, Camelops hesternus, Symbos cavifrons,* and *Bootherium sargenti* (probably the latter taxon is the female of the former), *Ovis dalli,* and *Panthera leo atrox* lived in eastern Beringia during the peak of the Wisconsinan glaciation (Pewe 1975; Harington 1977, 1978, in press; Matthews 1979). Yet questions remain concerning the overall geochronologic ranges of these and other species. As yet there are no pre-late Wisconsinan dates on Alaskan specimens of *Taxidea taxus, Mammut americanum, Castoroides ohioensis,* or *Megalonyx jeffersonii.* It is not known when they first reached eastern Beringia from the more southerly parts of North America and whether the extinction of *Mammut, Castoroides,* and *Megalonyx* in this region was contemporaneous with their extinction to the south. Available data show that there were extensive geographic differences in the North American fauna during Wisconsinan time. A number of species were restricted to various parts of the continent—glyptodonts and large armadillos to the southeast; *Castoroides, Ovibos,* and lemmings to the north and east; *Nothrotheriops* and *Euceratherium* to the west and southwest. *Bison, Mammuthus,* and certain camels and horses were less restricted geographically. Both Graham (1979) and Martin and Neuner (1978) have defined biogeographic provinces based on these differences.

The end of Rancholabrean time is marked by the mass extinction of most of the megafauna. Many possible causes have been proposed, including overkill by early man, seasonally out-of-step mating periods, epidemics, climatic stress, loss of habitat, vegetation changes, and food shortages (P. S. Martin 1967, 1973; Axelrod 1967; Guilday 1967; Slaughter 1967; Dreimanis 1968; Wilson 1973; Alford 1974; Mosimann and Martin 1975; Martin

and Neuner 1978). The only recent comprehensive treatment of these causes is that of Van Valen (1969), which arrived at no conclusions. The phenomenon remains a puzzle.

Carbon-14 dates can be used to determine the approximate date of the last occurrence of some species (Hester 1960, 1967; Kurtén and Anderson 1980) in the late Wisconsinan. Most sites and many species have not been critically dated, however. Caution must be exercised in the use of radiocarbon dates because of the possibility of contamination or of ambiguous stratigraphic association of the sample and the fauna and because some species may have survived longer in some areas than in others. Most of the terminal dates fall between 9,400 and 12,700 years ago. (Kurtén and Anderson 1980). A number of new dates in the 9,000-year range appear to be valid. If the dates of 7,000 and 8,000 years old for Devil's Den (Martin and Webb 1974) are reliable, Florida may have been an early Holocene refugium where some species survived after becoming extinct elsewhere.

The commonly used criterion for the end of the Pleistocene is deglaciation. Like the disappearance of the large mammals, this event is time transgressive in the glaciated areas (Bryson et al. 1969). The time ranges for the two events coincide closely in North America and provide distinctive boundaries for both a land mammal age and a geological epoch. It is the most precisely dated of all the land mammal age boundaries.

CHRONOCLINES AND EVOLUTION

A number of studies on evolutionary trends in certain mammal lineages have appeared recently and some of these lineages may offer the possibility of subdividing the mammal ages faunally or correlating portions of the faunal sequence with the glacial-interglacial sequences. The rates of evolution and dispersal will place ultimate limits on the resolution of faunal divisions and correlations. Evolutionary changes at the specific and subspecific levels may provide faunal subdivisions for local geographic areas.

At present, arvicoline or microtine rodents offer the best opportunities for finer subdivision (L. D. Martin 1979; Repenning, chap. 8). They are abundant in most local faunas and occur in all three Pleistocene mammal ages. Their teeth show a number of important evolutionary trends, including increases in hypsodonty and the height of dentine tracts; the reduction, fusion, or loss of roots; the addition of cement in the reentrant angles; and an increase in crown complexity and length of M_1. Excellent recent studies of these rodents are those of Zakrzewski (1967) on *Ogmodontomys*, Hibbard and Zakrzewski (1967) on *Ophiomys*, Hibbard and Zakrzewski (1972) on *Pliophenacomys*, Zakrzewski (1984) on *Hibbardomys* and *Pliophenacomys*, Nelson and Semken (1970) and Martin and Tedesco (1976) on *Ondatra*, Semken (1966) on *Microtus pennsylvanicus*, and Van der Meulen (1978) on *Microtus* and *Pitymys*. The study of *Ondatra* by Nelson and Semken (1970) shows a nearly continuous increase through time in size and height of dentine tracts in M_1 which permits fine subdivision where large samples are available. Semken (1966) demonstrated that a high percentage of M_1's of *Microtus pennsylvanicus* from early Illinoian faunas had only five closed triangles, whereas specimens from younger faunas showed a progressively higher frequency of six and seven triangled teeth.

Evolutionary trends in several genera of cricetine rodents have also been demonstrated. Hibbard (1972) emphasized the taxonomic utility of dental root morphology, particularly within the genus *Sigmodon*. R. A. Martin (1979) later referred extinct and extant species of *Sigmodon* to three species groups. He observed that *Sigmodon* evolution is characterized by an increase in the number of roots on M_1 from two to four and concluded that this is directly coupled with the evolution of hypsodonty and a successful transition from browsing to grazing. Martin noted than an evolutionary trend toward small size is apparent within the *Sigmodon medius* species group beginning with *S. medius* from the early Blancan Rexroad Local Fauna and ending with *S. minor* in the terminal Blancan or earliest Irvingtonian Borchers and Curtis Ranch local faunas. He interpreted this trend as a character displacement response to the invasion of *Sigmodon* habitats by the larger, more advanced *S. hudspethensis* and its relative *S. curtisi*.

Carleton and Eshelman (1979) performed univariate and multivariate analyses on species of the grasshopper mouse, *Onychomys*, and concluded that two lineages, each consisting of three successive species, spanned the time from the Blancan to the present. These two lineages closely paralleled one another in dental modifications, including increase in height of the primary cusps and reduction in relative length of the third molar with corresponding increases in the relative lengths of the first and second molars. The evolutionary increase in tubercular hypsodonty apparently marks a shift in the diet of *Onychomys* from a more omnivorous or granivorous feeding niche toward more exclusive insectivory. Increase in length of the first and second molars occurred at the expense of the third molar either to equip newly weaned young individuals with a larger surface area for triturat-

ing their insect prey or because it was advantageous for chewing insects to increase the area of those teeth possessing high cusps.

Another evolutionary lineage among the rodents is the *Zapus sandersi-Zapus hudsonius* lineage that extends from the late Blancan to the Recent (Klingener 1963). Unfortunately, jumping mice are rare in Pleistocene faunas and therefore are of limited use in subdivision or correlation of these faunas.

Evolutionary trends in Pleistocene insectivores have not been established to the extent that they have been in the rodents. Jammot's (1972) study of *Sorex cinereus* shows a morphological progression from the Cudahy Local Fauna (middle Irvingtonian) to the Recent which is potentially useful for fine subdivision where large samples of shrews are available. This study also shows the presence of a similar but distinct form in the Mt. Scott Local Fauna of Kansas (early Rancholabrean) which Jammot interprets as a member of a diverging phyletic line. The phylogeny and paleobiogeography of *Blarina* have been studied recently by Jones et al. (1984).

Large mammals offer some possibilities for the establishment of evolutionary lineages or at least successional species. Many recent studies have focused on the trend toward less massive horns in fossil bison as well as the problem of recognizing species and subspecies. In the molars of *Mammuthus*, width decreased, the number of enamel plates increased, the enamel became thinner, and crown height increased as evolution progressed (Schultz et al. 1972). Four or five species or stages representing more or less successional populations are now recognized. Unfortunately, identification of isolated and fragmentary teeth is difficult, as pointed out by Churcher (1972). In the cat family, Schultz et al. (1978) proposed an increase in canine length leading from the dirk-tooth *Megantereon hesperus* of the middle Blancan through *Megantereon* or *Smilodon gracilis* of the middle Irvingtonian to *S. fatalis* and *S. californicus*, saber-tooth cats of the late Irvingtonian and Rancholabrean, respectively. Evolutionary trends within the genus *Canis* have also been described (Nowak 1979).

Two other mammal groups appear to be potentially useful as biostratigraphic tools for the Blancan and Pleistocene—the rabbits and the packrats. The significance of the evolutionary change in the P_3 of rabbits was emphasized by Hibbard (1963b) for the *Nekrolagus-Sylvilagus* line and by Downey (1968, 1970) for *Pratilepus-Aluralagus*. Studies in progress by White (see also White 1984) will add much to our knowledge of rabbit evolution. Except for work done by Hibbard (1967), the packrats (*Neotoma*) have received little attention to date.

Present studies by Zakrzewski on *Neotoma* will provide much useful information about evolution within these rodents.

GLACIAL CLIMATES: HARMONIOUS VERSUS DISHARMONIOUS FAUNAS

Climatic changes associated with alternating glacial-interglacial environments provide a means for subdividing the Pleistocene sequence. Because each of the three established land mammal ages spans at least one cool-warm climatic alternation associated with either mountain or continental glacial stages, it is expected that the environmental changes associated with the shifting of the ice sheets are reflected in the faunas. Early and middle Pleistocene changes in southwestern Kansas are related to such environmental changes (Hibbard et al. 1965). Similar changes in faunal composition from the later part of the Rancholabrean and the post-Pleistocene confirm the methodology because they have been correlated with glacial changes by radiocarbon dates (Guilday et al. 1964; Dalquest 1965; Dalquest et al. 1969; Lundelius 1967; Kurtén and Anderson 1972). Such an approach in the absence of independent dating methods runs the risk, however, of circular reasoning as it involves assumptions about climates for nonglaciated areas distant from the ice front and the assumption that all glacial and interglacial climates were alike and equally severe.

This potential problem is illustrated by the occurrence of many ecologically disharmonious faunas, that is, assemblages that contain species that no longer coexist in the same region. This is clearly shown by a number of late Wisconsinan faunas (Hibbard 1960; Hibbard et al. 1965; Dalquest 1965; Dalquest et al. 1969; Gilday et al. 1964; Graham and Semken 1976; Lundelius 1974). Pruitt (1959) has noted that plant and animal ranges are frequently limited by seasonal extremes. The reduction of seasonal extremes of temperature and/or precipitation results in a more equable climate, which, according to Connell and Orias (1964) and Benninghoff (1968), allows organisms to spend less energy on physical maintenance and more on biological stresses such as competition. Graham and Semken (1976) postulate that this could lead to a community reorganization that would support increased species diversity. The widespread co-occurrence in Wisconsinan local faunas of taxa that now inhabit areas of different climates suggests the existence of more equable climates during that time and shows that glacial age climatic zones were not simply displaced analogues of modern climates. Palynological evidence

also suggests that plant assemblages in glacial periods were parkland communities quite different from those of Recent forest communities (Wright 1970, Webb and Bryson 1972). In the Ozark Mountains and on some parts of the plains, there is evidence of mixed spruce and deciduous forest parkland (Wright 1970; Mehringer et al. 1970; King 1973). These more diverse plant communities support the interpretation of more equable Wisconsinan climates south of the ice front. It is likely that the climates of the earlier glaciations were similar, but the difference between them and the earlier interglacials is not well known. Correlations based on the assumptions of specific kinds of glacial or interglacial climates could hinder the reconstruction of Pleistocene climatic regimes on a regional scale.

In Florida, an additional approach to glacial-interglacial correlation of mammalian faunas utilizes glacioeustatic cycles. Many sites in the Florida peninsula, especially those at low elevations, reveal that the sea stood either lower or higher than at present and thus indicate whether or not deposition occurred during a given glacial or interglacial interval. Sedimentological evidence is often supplemented by paleoecological evidence; for example, predominance of semiarid terrestrial taxa suggests a low stand of sea level (Webb 1974). When this eustatic approach is combined with the biostratigraphic approach, it may yield secure glacial age correlations for many Florida fossil mammal sites. The total number of both the faunal and glacial-interglacial alternations must be known, at least for the time interval under consideration, before any climatically based correlation can be considered secure. The recognition in deep-sea deposits of as many as twenty glacial-interglacial alternations during the Brunhes Chron alone (Shackleton and Opdyke 1976) complicates the task of correlating them with terrestrial events.

Another problem concerns areas located at the extremities of the continent. Mexico and Florida presumably were subjected to less extreme climatic conditions than the continental interior and were refugia into which some warm-adapted species retreated during glacial stages (Deevey 1949). The unglaciated parts of Alaska and the Yukon provided a refuge for at least one tundra species, *Ovibos moschatus* (Harington 1970), along with a variety of other animals.

Alaska is likely to differ faunally from the continental interior not only because of climatic differences but also because Alaska is on the dispersal route between Asia and North America. New immigrants from Asia will inhabit Alaska before they move farther south. An error in correlation between Alaska and southern North America depends on the degree to which the southward dispersion of these immigrants is time-transgressive. Environmental barriers between Alaska and central North America may have blocked dispersal, as indicated by the lack of wide distribution in North America of *Saiga, Praeovibos,* and *Bos (Poephagus). Bison crassicornis* appears to have moved into central North America well after its arrival in Beringia (Harington, pers. com., 1981). This kind of delay in dispersal may explain the association of *Mammuthus* with *Borophagus* in the Wellsch Valley Local Fauna and of *Mammuthus* with *Stegomastodon* in the Gilliland Local Fauna along with the absence of these associations in either the San Pedro Valley or the Anza-Borrego local faunas.

SUMMARY

The Pleistocene has been divided into slightly more than two land mammal ages that cover a total of 1.5 to 2.0 Ma. Pre-Pleistocene mammal ages average 3.5 Ma each, with some variation. There is no reason that all Cenozoic land mammal ages should be of the same duration, but they should be based on easily recognizable faunal changes (Cooke 1948, p. 44) resulting from evolution, extinction, or dispersal. Substantially shorter Quaternary mammal ages indicate that faunal change accelerated following the Tertiary.

New information bearing on contemporaneity of widely separated faunas has come from the fossil vertebrate sequence and from various independent dating methods that promise to give better dating resolution to the faunas. Isotopic dating methods (potassium-argon and radiocarbon) have made important contributions but have limitations (Evernden et al. 1964, Savage and Curtis 1970). More recently, petrographic studies show the Pearlette Ash actually consists of at least three separate tephra units, which provide multiple widespread datable markers for the Pleistocene (Izett et al. 1971; Naeser et al. 1973; Izett 1981; Izett and Wilcox 1982). Paleomagnetic studies have already contributed in the San Pedro Valley sequence (Johnson et al. 1975) and have limited the uncertainty in other areas. Fission-track dating (Boellstorff 1972; Naeser et al. 1971, 1973) has provided data relating vertebrate biostratigraphy to the glacial section. More recently, a new method of dating using the racemization of proteins in fossil bones has been suggested (Turekian and Bada 1972). If this method proves generally applicable, we can look forward to solutions to many geochronologic problems in the near future.

Despite a number of inherent problems, the Pleistocene vertebrate record offers the possibility of greater chronological resolution than the earlier epochs because of its greater frequency of occurrence, independent age-dating controls, and presence of many extant taxa. It is the ideal case for the use of vertebrate paleontology in geochronology.

REFERENCES

Ahearn, M. E., and J. F. Lance. 1980. A new species of *Neochoerus* (Rodentia: Hydrochoeridae) from the Blancan (Late Pliocene) of North America. Proc. Biol. Soc. Washington 93:435–442.

Akersten, W. A. 1972. Red Light local fauna (Blancan) of the Love Formation, southeastern Hudspeth County, Texas. Tex. Mem. Mus. Bull. 20:1–53.

Alford, J. J. 1974. The geography of mastodon extinction. Prof. Geog. 26:425–429.

Axelrod, D. 1967. Quaternary extinctions of large mammals. Univ. Calif. Publ. Geol. Sci. 74:1–42.

Azzaroli, A., and P. Ambrosetti. 1970. Late Villafranchian and early Mid-Pleistocene faunas in Italy. Palaeogeogr., Palaeoclimatol., Palaeoecol. 8:107–111.

Azzaroli, A., and A. Berzi. 1970. On an upper Villafranchian fauna at Imola, northern Italy, and its correlation with the marine Pleistocene sequence of the Po plain. Paleontogr. Ital. 66:1–12.

Banner, F. T., and W. H. Blow. 1965. Progress in the planktonic foraminiferal biostratigraphy of the Neogene. Nature 208:1164–1166.

Bayne, C. K. 1976. Early and medial Pleistocene faunas of Meade County, Kansas. In Guidebook, 24th Ann. Mtg., Midwestern Friends of the Pleistocene: Stratigraphy and Faunal Sequence—Meade County, Kansas, May 22–23, 1976. Kans. Geol. Surv. Guidebook, ser. 1:1–25.

Becker, J. J., and J. A. White. 1981. Late Cenozoic geomyids (Mammalia: Rodentia) from the Anza-Borrego Desert, Southern California. J. Vert. Paleont. 1:211–218.

Benninghoff, W. S. 1968. Biological consequences of Quaternary glaciations in the Illinois region. In The Quaternary of Illinois ed. R. E. Bergstrom, pp. 70–77. Urbana: Univ. Ill. Press.

Berggren, W. A., L. H. Burckle, M. B. Cita, H. B. S. Cooke, B. M. Funnell, S. Gartner, J. D. Hays, J. P. Kennett, N. D. Opdyke, L. Pastouret, N. J. Shackleton, and Y. Takayanagi. 1980. Towards a Quaternary time scale. Quat. Res. 13:277–302.

Berggren, W. A., J. D. Phillips, A. Bertels, and D. Wall. 1967. Late Pliocene-Pleistocene stratigraphy in deep sea cores from the south-central north Atlantic. Nature 216:253–255.

Berggren, W. A., and J. A. Van Couvering. 1974. The Late Neogene: Biostratigraphy, geochronology and paleoclimatology of the last fifteen million years in marine and continental sequences. Palaeogeogr., Palaeoclimatol., Palaeoecol. 16:1–216.

Berta, A. 1981. The Plio-Pleistocene hyaena *Chasmaporthetes ossifragus* from Florida. J. Vert. Paleont. 1:341–356.

Berta, A., and H. Galiano. 1983. *Megantereon hesperus* from the Late Hemphillian of Florida with remarks on the phylogenetic relationships of machairodonts (Mammalia, Felidae, Machairodontinae). J. Paleont. 57:892–899.

Bjork, P. R. 1970. The Carnivora of the Hagerman local fauna (Late Pliocene) of southwestern Idaho. Trans. Amer. Phil. Soc., n.s. 60 (7):1–54.

———. 1974. Additional carnivores from the Rexroad Formation (Upper Pliocene) of southwestern Kansas. Trans. Kans. Acad. Sci. 76:24–38.

Boellstorff, J. D. 1972. Fission track ages of shards from some mid-continent Pleistocene volcanic ash deposits. Geol. Soc. Amer. Abstr. Prog., South-Central Sect. 4:274.

———. 1976. The succession of Late Cenozoic volcanic ashes in the Great Plains: A progress report. In Guidebook, 24th Ann. Mtg., Midwestern Friends of the Pleistocene: Stratigraphy and Faunal Sequence—Meade County, Kansas, May 22–23, 1976. Kans. Geol. Surv. Guidebook, ser. 1:37–71.

———. 1978a. North American Pleistocene stages reconsidered in light of probable Pliocene-Pleistocene continental glaciation. Science 202:305–307.

———. 1978b. Chronology of some Late Cenozoic deposits from the central United States and the Ice Ages. Trans. Nebr. Acad. Sci. 6:35–49.

Bryson, R. A., W. M. Wendland, J. D. Ives, and J. T. Andrews. 1969. Radiocarbon isochrones on the disintegration of the Laurentide ice sheet. Arctic Alpine Res. 1 (1):1–14.

Carleton, M. D., and R. E. Eshelman. 1979. A synopsis of fossil grasshopper mice, genus *Onychomys,* and their relationships to recent species. Claude W. Hibbard Mem. vol. 7, Univ. Mich. Papers Paleont. 21:1–63.

Churcher, C. S. 1972. Imperial mammoth and Mexican half-ass from near Bindloss, Alberta. Can. J. Earth Sci. 9 (11):1562–1567.

Churcher, C. S., and A. Stalker. In press. Geology and vertebrate paleontology of the Wellsch Valley Site, Saskatchewan. Bull. Geol. Surv. Canada.

Connell, J. H., and E. Orias. 1964. The ecological regulation of species diversity. Amer. Nat. 98:399–414.

Conrad, G. 1980. The biostratigraphy and mammalian paleontology of the Glenns Ferry Formation from Hammett to Oreana, Idaho. Ph.D. diss., Idaho State Univ., Pocatello.

Cooke, H. B. S. 1948. The Plio-Pleistocene boundary and mammalian correlation. Geol. Mag. (London) 85:41–47.

———. 1973. Pleistocene chronology: Long or short? Quat. Res. 3:206–220.

Cox, A., R. R. Doell, and G. B. Dalrymple. 1963. Geomagnetic polarity epochs and Pleistocene geochronology. Nature 198:1049–1051.

Curry, R. P. 1966. Glaciations about 3,000,000 years ago in the Sierra Nevada. Science 154:770–771.

Dalquest, W. W. 1965. New Pleistocene formation and local fauna from Hardeman County, Texas. J. Paleont. 39 (1):63–79.

———. 1967. Mammals of the Pleistocene Slaton local fauna of Texas. Southwestern Nat. 12 (1):1–30.

———. 1975. Vertebrate fossils from the Blanco local fauna of Texas. Occas. Papers Mus. Texas Tech. Univ. 30:1–52.

———. 1977. Mammals of the Holloman local fauna, Pleistocene of Oklahoma. Southwestern Nat. 22 (2):255–268.

———. 1978a. Early Blancan mammals of the Beck Ranch local fauna of Texas. J. Mammal. 59:269–298.

———. 1978b. Phylogeny of American horses of Blancan and Pleistocene age. Ann. Zool. Fennici 15:191–199.

Dalquest, W. W., E. Roth, and F. Judd. 1969. The mammal fauna of Schulze Cave, Edwards County, Texas. Fla. State Mus. Bull. Biol. Sci. 13 (4):205–276.

Dalrymple G. B. 1972. Potassium-argon dating of geomagnetic reversals and North American glaciations. In Calibration of Hominoid evolution, recent advances in isotopic and other dating methods applicable to the origin of man, eds. W. W. Bishop and J. A. Miller, pp. 107–134. New York: Wenner-Gren Found. Anthropol. Res.

Deevey, E. S., Jr. 1949. Biogeography of the Pleistocene. Bull. Geol. Soc. Amer. 60:1315–1416.

Denton, G. H., and R. L. Armstrong. 1969. Miocene-Pliocene glaciations in southern Alaska. Amer. J. Sci. 267:1121–1142.

Downey, J. S. 1968. Late Pliocene lagomorphs of the San Pedro Valley, Arizona. U.S. Geol. Surv. Prof. Paper 600-D, pp. 169–173.

———. 1970. Middle Pleistocene Leporidae from the San Pedro Valley, Arizona. U.S. Geol. Surv. Prof. Paper 700-B, pp. 131–136.

Downs, T., and J. A. White. 1968. A vertebrate faunal succession in superposed sediments from late Pliocene to middle Pleistocene in California. Proc. 23d Int. Geol. Cong., Prague 10:41–47.

Dreimanis, A. 1968. Extinction of mastodons in eastern North America: Testing new climatic environmental hypothesis. Ohio J. Sci. 68 (6):257–272.

Einsohn, S. D. 1971. The stratigraphy and fauna of a Pleistocene outcrop in Doniphan County, northeastern Kansas. M.S. thesis, Univ. Kansas, Lawrence.

Eshelman, R. E. 1975. Geology and paleontology of the early Pleistocene (late Blancan) White Rock fauna from north-central Kansas. In Studies on Cenozoic Paleontology and Stratigraphy. Claude W. Hibbard Mem. vol. 4, Univ. Mich. Papers Paleont. 13:1–60.

Eshelman, R. E., and M. Hager. 1984. Two Irvingtonian (Medial Pleistocene) vertebrate faunas from north-central Kansas. In Contributions in Quaternary Vertebrate Paleontology: A volume in memorial to John E. Guilday, eds. H. H. Genoways and M. R. Dawson, Carnegie Mus. Nat. Hist. Spec. Publ. 8:384–404.

Eshelman, R. E., and C. W. Hibbard, 1981. Nash local fauna (Pleistocene: Aftonian) of Meade County, Kansas. Contrib. Mus. Paleontol. Univ. Mich. 25 (16):317–326.

Evernden, J. F., D. E. Savage, G. Curtis, and G. T. James. 1964. Potassium-argon dates and the Cenozoic mammalian chronology of North America. Amer. J. Sci. 262 (2):145–198.

Ferrusquia-Villafranca, I. 1978. Distribution of Cenozoic vertebrate faunas in Middle America and problems of migration between North and South America. In Conexiones Terrestres Entre Norte Y Sudamerica. Bol. Inst. Geol. Univ. Nat. Auton. Mexico 101:193–329.

Flint, R. F. 1971. Glacial and Quaternary geology. New York: John Wiley and Sons.

Forbes, E. 1846. On the connection between the distribution of the existing fauna and flora of the British Isles, and the geological changes which have affected their area, especially during the epoch of the Northern Drift. Mem. Great Britain Geol. Surv. 1:336–432.

Foster, J. H., and A. M. Stalker. 1976. Paleomagnetic stratigraphy of the Wellsch Valley site, Saskatchewan. In Report of activities, Pt. C. Geol. Surv. Canada Paper 76–1c, pp. 191–193.

Frazier, M. 1982. A revision of the fossil Erethizontidae of North America. Bull. Fla. State Mus. Biol. Sci. 27 (1):1–76.

Gazin, C. L. 1942. The late Cenozoic vertebrate faunas from the San Pedro Valley, Arizona. Proc. U.S. Natl. Mus. 92:475–518.

Gidley, J. W. 1922. Preliminary report on fossil vertebrates of the San Pedro Valley, Arizona, with descriptions of new species of rodents and lagomorphs. U.S. Geol. Sur. Prof. Paper 131–E pp. 119–131.

———. 1926. Fossil Proboscidea and Edentata of the San Pedro Valley, Arizona. U.S. Geol. Surv. Prof. Paper 140-B, pp. 83–95.

Gidley, J. W., and C. L. Gazin. 1938. The Pleistocene vertebrate fauna from Cumberland Cave, Maryland. Bull. U.S. Natl. Mus. 171:1–99.

Gignoux, M. 1910. Sur la classification du Pliocene et du Quaternaire de l'Italie du Sud. Acad. Sci. Paris Comptes Rendus 150:841–844.

———. 1916. L'Etage Calabrien (Pliocene superieur marin) sur le versant nord-est de l'Apennine, entre le Monte Gargano et Plaisance. Bull. Soc. Geol. France. ser. 4, 14:324–348.

Gillette, D. D., and C. E. Ray. 1981. Glyptodonts of North America. Smithsonian Contrib. Paleobiol., no. 40.

Glass, B., D. B. Ericson, B. C. Heezen, N. D. Opdyke, and J. A. Glass. 1967. Geomagnetic reversals and Pleistocene chronology. Nature 216:437–442.

Graham, R. W. 1972. Biostratigraphy and paleoecological significance of the Conard Fissure local fauna with emphasis on the genus Blarina. M.S. thesis, Univ. Iowa, Iowa City.

———. 1979. Paleoclimates and late Pleistocene faunal provinces in North America. In Pre-Llano cultures of the Americas: Paradoxes and possibilities, eds. R. L. Humphrey and D. Stanford. Anthropol. Soc. Washington.

Graham, R. W., and H. A. Semken. 1976. Paleoecological significance of the short-tailed shrew (Blarina), with a systematic description of Blarina ozarkensis. J. Mammal. 57 (3):433–449.

Guilday, J. E. 1967. Differential extinction during late-Pleistocene and Recent times. In Pleistocene extinctions: the search for a cause, eds. P. S. Martin and H. E. Wright, Jr., pp. 121–140. New Haven and London: Yale Univ. Press.

Guilday, J. E., P. S. Martin, and A. D. McCrady. 1964. New Paris No. 4: A Pleistocene cave deposit in Bedford County, Pennsylvania. Bull. Natl. Speleol. Soc. 26 (4):121–194.

Gustafson, E. P. 1978. The vertebrate faunas of the Pliocene Ringold Formation, south-central Washington. Bull. Mus. Nat. Hist. Univ. Oreg. (Eugene) 23:1–62.

Guthrie, R. D. 1970. Bison evolution and zoogeography in North America during the Pleistocene. Qtly. Rev. Biol. 45 (1):1–15.

Guthrie, R. D., and J. V. Matthews. 1971. The Cape Deceit Fauna-Early Pleistocene mammalian assemblage from the Alaskan Arctic. Quat. Res. 1 (4):474–510.

Hager, M. W. 1975. Late Pliocene and Pleistocene history of the Donnelly Ranch vertebrate site, southwestern Colorado. Contrib. Geol. Univ. Wyoming Spec. Paper 2.

Hallberg, G. R. 1980. Status of Pre-Wisconsinan Pleistocene stratigraphy in Iowa. Geol. Soc. Amer. Abstr. Prog. North-Central Sect. 12:228.

Hallberg, G. R., and J. D. Boellstorff, 1978. Stratigraphic "confusion" in the region of the type areas of Kansan and Nebraskan deposits. Geol. Soc. Amer. Abstr. Prog. North-Central Sect. 10:255–256.

Haq, B. U., W. A. Berggren, and J. A. Van Couvering. 1977. Corrected age of the Pliocene/Pleistocene boundary. Nature 269:483–488.

Harington, C. R. 1970. A postglacial muskox (Ovibos moschatus) from Grandview, Manitoba, and comments on the zoogeography of Ovibos. Can. Natl. Mus. Publ. Paleont. 2:1–13.

———. 1977. Pleistocene mammals of the Yukon Territory. Ph.D. diss., Univ. Alberta, Edmonton.

———. 1978. Quaternary vertebrate faunas of Canada and Alaska and their suggested chronological sequence. Syllogeus 15:1–105.

———. 1980. Faunal exchanges between Siberia and North America: Evidence from Quaternary land mammal remains in Siberia, Alaska, and the Yukon Territory. Can. J. Anthropol. 1 (1):45–49.

———. In press. Radiocarbon dates on some Quaternary mammals and artifacts from northern North America, Arctic.

Harrison, J. A. 1978. Mammals of the Wolf Ranch local fauna, Pliocene of the San Pedro Valley, Arizona. Occas. Papers. Mus. Nat. Hist. Univ. Kans. 73:1–18.

Hay, O. P. 1921. Descriptions of species of Pleistocene Vertebrata, types or specimens most of which are preserved in the United States National Museum. Proc. U.S. Natl. Mus. 59:599–642.

Hays, J. D., J. Imbrie, and N. J. Shackleton. 1976. Variations in the earth's orbit: Pacemaker of the Ice Ages. Science 194:1121–1132.

Hester, J. J. 1960. Late Pleistocene extinction and radiocarbon dating. Amer. Antiquity 26 (1):58–77.

———. 1967. The agency of man in animal extinctions. In Pleistocene extinctions: The search for a cause, eds. P. S. Martin and H. E. Wright, Jr., pp. 169–192. New Haven and London: Yale Univ. Press.

Hibbard, C. W. 1938. An Upper Pliocene fauna from Meade

County, Kansas. Trans. Kans. Acad. Sci. 40:239–265.

———. 1941*a*. The Borchers fauna, a new Pleistocene interglacial fauna from Meade County, Kansas. Bull. Kans. Geol. Surv. 38 (7):197–220.

———. 1941*b*. Mammals of the Rexroad fauna from the Upper Pliocene of southwestern Kansas. Trans. Kans. Acad. Sci. 44:265–313.

———. 1941*c*. New mammals from the Rexroad fauna, Upper Pliocene of Kansas. Amer. Midl. Nat. 26 (2):337–368.

———. 1941*d*. Paleoecology and correlation of the Rexroad fauna from the Upper Pliocene of southwestern Kansas, as indicated by the mammals. Bull. Univ. Kans. Sci. 27:79–104.

———. 1942. Pleistocene mammals from Kansas. Kans. Geol. Surv. Bull. 41 (6):261–269.

———. 1943*a*. *Etadonomys*, a new Pleistocene heteromyid rodent, and notes on other Kansas mammals. Trans. Kans. Acad. Sci. 46:185–191.

———. 1943*b*. The Rezabek fauna, a new Pleistocene fauna from Lincoln County, Kansas. Bull. Univ. Kans. Sci. 29 (2):235–247.

———. 1944. Stratigraphy and vertebrate paleontology of Pleistocene deposits of southwestern Kansas. Bull. Geol. Soc. Amer. 55:707–754.

———. 1949. Pliocene Saw Rock Canyon fauna in Kansas. Contrib. Mus. Paleont. Univ. Mich. 7 (5):91–105.

———. 1950. Mammals of the Rexroad Formation from Fox Canyon, Meade County, Kansas. Contrib. Mus. Paleont. Univ. Mich. 8 (6):113–192.

———. 1952. Vertebrate fossils from late Cenozoic deposits of central Kansas. Univ. Kans. Paleontol. Contr. Vertebrata 2:1–14.

———. 1953. The Saw Rock Canyon fauna and its stratigraphic significance. Papers Mich. Acad. Sci. Arts Letters 38:387–411.

———. 1954*a*. A new Pliocene vertebrate fauna from Oklahoma. Papers Mich. Acad. Sci. Arts Letters 39:339–359.

———. 1954*b*. A new *Synaptomys*, an addition to the Borchers interglacial (Yarmouth?) fauna. J. Mammal. 35 (2):249–252.

———. 1955*a*. The Jinglebob interglacial (Sangamon?) fauna from Kansas and its climatic significance. Contrib. Mus. Paleontol. Univ. Mich. 12 (10):179–228.

———. 1955*b*. Notes on the microtine rodents from Port Kennedy Cave deposit. Proc. Acad. Natl. Sci. Phila. 107:87–97.

———. 1956. Vertebrate fossils from the Meade Formation of southwestern Kansas. Papers Mich. Acad. Sci. Arts Letters 41:145–203.

———. 1958. Summary of North American Pleistocene mammalian local faunas. Papers Mich. Acad. Sci. Arts Letters 43:3–32.

———. 1959. Late Cenozoic microtine rodents from Wyoming and Idaho. Papers Mich. Acad. Sci. Arts Letters 44:3–40.

———. 1960. An interpretation of Pliocene and Pleistocene climates in North America. Rept. Mich. Acad. Sci. Arts

Letters (for 1959–60), President's address, pp. 5–30.

———. 1963*a*. A late Illinoian fauna from Kansas and its climatic significance. Papers Mich. Acad. Sci. Arts Letters 68:187–221.

———. 1963*b*. The origin of the P_3 pattern of *Sylvilagus, Caprolagus, Oryctolagus,* and *Lepus*. J. Mammal. 44 (1):1–15.

———. 1963*c*. *Tanupolama vera* (Matthew) from the Late Hemphillian of Beaver County, Oklahoma. Trans. Kans. Acad. Sci. 66 (2):267–269.

———. 1964. A contribution to the Saw Rock Canyon local fauna of Kansas. Papers Mich. Acad. Sci. Arts Letters 49:115–127.

———. 1967. New rodents from the late Cenozoic of Kansas. Papers Mich. Acad. Sci. Arts and Letters 52:115–131.

———. 1969. The rabbits (*Hypolagus* and *Pratilepus*) from the Upper Pliocene, Hagerman local fauna of Idaho. Mich. Academician 1:81–97.

———. 1970. Pleistocene mammalian local faunas from the Great Plains and central lowland provinces of the United States. In Pleistocene and Recent environments of the central Great Plains, eds. W. Dort, Jr., and J. K. Jones, Jr. Dept. Geol. Kans. Univ. Spec. Publ. 3, pp. 395–433.

———. 1972. Class Mammalia (excluding horses) and Sand Draw local fauna: Correlation, age, and paleoecology. In M. F. Skinner and C. W. Hibbard. (with the collaboration of others). Early Pleistocene preglacial and glacial rocks and faunas of north-central Nebraska, Bull. Amer. Mus. Nat. Hist. 148 (1):77–116, 131–134.

Hibbard, C. W., and W. W. Dalquest. 1966. Fossils from the Seymour Formation of Knox and Baylor counties, Texas, and their bearing on the late Kansan climate of that region. Contrib. Mus. Paleont. Univ. Mich. 21 (1):1–66.

———. 1973. *Proneofiber*, a new genus of vole (Cricetidae, Rodentia) from the Pleistocene Seymour Formation of Texas, and its evolutionary and stratigraphic signficance. Quat. Res. 3 (2):269–274.

Hibbard, C. W., C. E. Ray, D. E. Savage, D. W. Taylor, and J. E. Guilday. 1965. Quaternary Mammals of North America. In The Quaternary of the United States, eds. H. E. Wright, Jr., and D. G. Frey, pp. 509–525. Princeton: Princeton Univ. Press.

Hibbard, C. W., and D. W. Taylor. 1960. Two late Pleistocene faunas from southwestern Kansas. Contrib. Mus. Paleont. Univ. Mich. 16 (1):1–223.

Hibbard, C. W., and R. J. Zakrzewski. 1967. Phyletic trends in the late Cenozoic microtine *Ophiomys* gen. nov. from Idaho. Contrib. Mus. Paleont. Univ. Mich. 21 (12):255–271.

———. 1972. A new species of microtine from the late Pliocene of Kansas. J. Mammal. 53 (4):834–839.

Hibbard, C. W., R. J. Zakrzewski, and R. E. Eshelman, G. Edmund, C. D. Griggs, and Caroline Griggs. 1978. Mammals from the Kanopolis local fauna, Pleistocene (Yarmouth) of Ellsworth County, Kansas. Contrib. Mus. Paleont. Univ. Mich. 25 (2):11–44.

Hurzeler, J. 1967. Nouvelles decouvertes de mammiferes dans

les sediments fluviolacustres de Villafranca d'Asti. Colloq. Cent. Nation. Recherch. Sci. 163:633–636.

Izett, G. A. 1977. Volcanic ash beds in continental deposits of the southern High Plains: Their bearing on the time of the Blancan-Irvingtonian faunal transition. Geol. Soc. Amer. Abstr. Prog. Ann. Mtg., 1034.

———. 1981. Volcanic ash beds: Recorders of Upper Cenozoic silicic pyroclastic volcanism in the western United States. J. Geophys. Res. 86:10200–10222.

Izett, G. A., J. D. Obradovich, C. W. Naeser, and G. T. Cebula. 1981. Potassium-Argon and fission track zircon ages of Cerro Toledo rhyolite tephra in the Jemez Mountains, New Mexico. U.S. Geol. Surv. Prof. Paper 1199–D, pp. 37–43.

Izett, G. A., and R. E. Wilcox. 1982. Map showing localities and inferred distributions of the Huckleberry Ridge, Mesa Falls, and Lava Creek ash beds (Pearlette family ash beds) of Pliocene and Pleistocene age in the western United States and southern Canada. U.S. Geol. Surv. Misc. Invest., Map I-1325 (scale 1:4,000,000).

Izett, G. A., R. E. Wilcox, and G. A. Borchardt. 1972. Correlation of a volcanic ash bed in Pleistocene deposits near Mount Blanco, Texas, with the Guaje pumice bed of the Jemez Mountains, New Mexico. Quat. Res. 2 (4):554–578.

Izett, G. A., R. E. Wilcox, J. D. Obradovich, and R. L. Reynolds. 1971. Evidence for two Pearlette-like ash beds in Nebraska and adjoining areas. Geol. Soc. Amer. Abstr. Prog. North-Central Sect. 3 (4):265–266.

Jammot, D. 1972. Relationships between the new species *Sorex scottensis* and the fossil shrews *Sorex cinereus* Kerr. Mammalia 36 (3):449–458.

Johnson, N. M., N. D. Opdyke, and E. H. Lindsay. 1975. Magnetic polarity stratigraphy of Pliocene-Pleistocene terrestrial deposits and vertebrate faunas, San Pedro Valley, Arizona. Bull. Geol. Soc. Amer. 86:5–12.

Jones, C. A., J. R. Choate, and H. H. Genoways. 1984. Phylogeny and paleobiogeography of short-tailed shrews (genus *Blarina*). Contributions in Quaternary vertebrate paleontology: A volume in memorial to John E. Guilday, eds. H. H. Genoway and M. R. Dawson. Carnegie Mus. Nat. Hist. Spec. Publ. 8:56–148.

King, J. E. 1973. Late Pleistocene palynology and biogeography of the western Missouri Ozarks. Ecol. Monogr. 43:539–565.

Klingener, D. 1963. Dental evolution of *Zapus*. J. Mammal. 44 (2):248–260.

Koenigswald, W. V., and L. D. Martin. 1984. Revision of the fossil and recent Lemminae (Rodentia, Mammalia). In Papers in vertebrate paleontology honoring Robert Warren Wilson, ed. R. M. Mengel. Carnegie Mus. Nat. Hist. Spec. Publ. 9:122–137.

Kurtén, B. 1963. Villafranchian faunal evolution. Comment. Biol. Soc. Sci. Fennica 26 (3):1–18.

———. 1968. Pleistocene mammals of Europe. Chicago: Aldine.

———. 1971. The Age of mammals. New York: Columbia Univ. Press.

Kurtén, B., and E. Anderson. 1972. The sediments and fauna of Jaguar Cave. II: The fauna. Tebiwa 15 (1):21–45.

———. 1980. Pleistocene mammals of North America. New York: Columbia Univ. Press.

Lindsay, E. H., and L. L. Jacobs. 1985. Pliocene small mammal fossils from Chihuahua, Mexico. Paleontologia Mexicana. Universidad Autonoma de Mexico. Instituto de Geologia 51:1–59.

Lindsay, E. H., N. M. Johnson, and N. D. Opdyke. 1975. Preliminary correlation of North American land mammal ages and geomagnetic chronology. In Studies on Cenozoic paleontology and stratigraphy. Claude W. Hibbard Mem. vol. 3, Univ. Mich. Papers Paleont. 12:111–119.

Lindsay, E. H., N. D. Opdyke, and N. M. Johnson. 1984. Blancan-Hemphillian land mammal ages and late Cenozoic mammal dispersal events. Ann. Rev. Earth Planet. Sci. 12:445–488.

Lindsay, E. H., and N. T. Tessman. 1974. Cenozoic vertebrate localities and faunas in Arizona. J. Ariz. Acad. Sci. 9:3–24.

Lundelius, E. L., Jr. 1967. Late Pleistocene and Holocene faunal history of Central Texas. In Pleistocene extinctions: The search for a cause, eds. P. S. Martin and H. E. Wright, Jr., pp. 287–319. New Haven and London: Yale Univ. Press.

———. 1974. The last fifteen thousand years of faunal change in North America. In History and prehistory of the Lubbock Lake site, ed. C. C. Block, pp. 141-160. Mus. Tex. Tech. Univ. Lubbock.

Lyell, C. 1833. Principles of geology, 1st ed., vol. 3. London: J. Murray.

———. 1839. Nouveaux elements de geologie. Paris: Pitois-Levrault and Cie.

McDonald, J. 1981. North American Bison—Their classification and evolution. Berkeley, Los Angeles, London: Univ. Calif. Press.

Malde, H. E., and H. A. Powers. 1962. Upper Cenozoic stratigraphy of western Snake River Plain, Idaho. Bull. Geol. Soc. Amer. 73:1197–1220.

Marshall, L. G., R. F. Butler, R. E. Drake, G. H. Curtis, and R. H. Tedford. 1979. Calibration of the great American interchange. Science 204:272–279.

Martin, L. D. 1971. Stratigraphic position and paleoecology of the Angus local fauna. Geol. Soc. Amer. Abstr. Prog. North-Central Sect. 3 (4):270–271.

———. 1972. The microtine rodents of the Mullen assemblage from the Pleistocene of north central Nebraska. Bull. Univ. Nebr. State Mus. 9 (5):173–182.

———. 1975. Microtine rodents from the Ogallala Pliocene of Nebraska and the early evolution of the Microtinae in North America. In Studies on Cenozoic Paleontology and Stratigraphy. Claude W. Hibbard Mem. vol. 3, Univ. Mich. Papers Paleont. 12:101–110.

———. 1977. The relationship of the sequence of microtine rodents in North America to the Neogene/Quaternary boundary. Abstr. 10th INQUA Cong., Birmingham, August, p. 289.

———. 1979. The biostratigraphy of arvicoline rodents in North America. Trans. Nebr. Acad. Sci. 7:91–100.

Martin, L. D., and A. M. Neuner. 1978. The end of the Pleistocene in North America. Trans. Nebr. Acad. Sci. 6:117–126.

Martin, P. S. 1967. Prehistoric overkill. In Pleistocene extinctions: The search for a cause, eds. P. S. Martin and H. E. Wright, Jr., pp. 75–120. New Haven and London: Yale Univ. Press.

―――. 1973. The discovery of America. Science 179:969–974.

Martin, R. A. 1973. The Java local fauna, Pleistocene of South Dakota: A preliminary report. Bull. N. J. Acad. Sci. 18 (2):48–56.

―――. 1975. *Allophaiomys* Kormos from the Pleistocene of North America. In Studies on Cenozoic Paleontology and Stratigraphy. Claude W. Hibbard Mem. vol. 3, Univ. Mich Papers Paleont. 12:97–100.

―――. 1979. Fossil history of the rodent genus *Sigmodon*. Evol. Monogr. 2:1–36.

Martin, R. A., and R. Tedesco. 1976. *Ondatra annectens* (Mammalia: Rodentia) from the Pleistocene Java local fauna of South Dakota. J. Paleon. 50 (5):846–850.

Martin, R. A., and S. D. Webb. 1974. Late Pleistocene mammals from the Devil's Den fauna, Levy County. In Pleistocene Mammals of Florida, ed. S. D. Webb, pp. 114–145. Gainesville: Univ. Press Fla.

Matthew, W. D. 1924. Correlation of the Tertiary formations of the Great Plains. Bull. Geol. Soc. Amer. 35:743–754.

Matthews, J. V., Jr. 1979. Beringia during the late Pleistocene: Arctic steppe or discontinuous herb-tundra? A review of the paleontological evidence. Burg. Wartenstein Symposium, vol. 81.

Meade, G. E. 1945. The Blanco fauna. Univ. Tex. Publ. 4401:509–556.

―――. 1953. An early Pleistocene vertebrate fauna from Frederick, Oklahoma. J. Geol. 61 (5):452–460.

Mehringer, P. J., Jr., J. E. King, and E. H. Lindsay. 1970. A record of Wisconsin-age vegetation and fauna from the Ozarks of western Missouri. In Pleistocene and Recent Environments of the central Great Plains, eds. W. Dort, Jr., and J. K. Jones, Jr. Univ. Kans. Dept. Geol. Spec. Pub. 3, pp. 173–183.

Mickelson, D. M., L. Clayton, D. S. Fullerton, and H. W. Borns, Jr. 1983. The late Wisconsin glacial record of the Laurentide ice sheet in the United States. In H. E. Wright, Jr., Late Quaternary environments of the United States, ed. S. C. Porter, pp. 3–52. Vol 1: The Late Pleistocene. Minneapolis: University of Minnesota Press.

Miller, W. E. 1968. Occurrence of a giant bison, *Bison latifrons,* and a slender-limbed camel, *Tanupolama,* at Rancho La Brea. Mus. Nat. Hist. Los Angeles Co. Contrib. Sci. 147:1–9.

―――. 1971. Pleistocene vertebrates of the Los Angeles Basin and vicinity (exclusive of Rancho La Brea). Mus. Nat. Hist. Los Angeles Co. Contrib. Sci. 10:1–124.

Miler, W. E., and J. D. Brotherson. 1979. Size variation in foot elements of *Bison* from Rancho La Brea. Mus. Nat. Hist. Los Angeles Co. Contrib. Sci. 323:1–19.

Mosimann, J. E., and P. S. Martin. 1975. Simulating overkill by Paleoindians. Amer. Sci. 63:304–313.

Naeser, C. W., G. A. Izett, and R. E. Wilcox. 1971. Zircon fission track ages of Pearlette-like volcanic ash beds in the Great Plains. Geol. Soc. Amer. Abstr. Prog. Ann. Mtg. 3 (7):657.

―――. 1973. Zircon fission-track ages of Pearlette family ash beds in Meade County, Kansas. Geology 1 (4):187–189.

Nelson, M. E., and J. Neas. 1980. Pleistocene muskoxen from Kansas. Trans. Kans. Acad. Sci. 83 (4):215–229.

Nelson, R. S., and H. A. Semken, Jr. 1970. Paleoecological and stratigraphic signficance of the muskrat in Pleistocene deposits. Bull. Geol. Soc. Amer. 81:3733–3737.

Neville, C., N. D. Opdyke, E. H. Lindsay, and N. M. Johnson. 1979. Magnetic stratigraphy of Pliocene deposits of the Glenns Ferry Formation, Idaho, and its implications for North American mammalian biostratigraphy. Amer. J. Sci. 279:503–526.

Nowak, R. M. 1979. North American Quaternary *Canis.* Monogr. Mus. Nat. Hist. Univ. Kans. 6:1–154.

Opdyke, N. D., E. H. Lindsay, N. M. Johnson, and T. Downs. 1977. The paleomagnetism and magnetic polarity stratigraphy of the mammal-bearing section of Anza-Borrego State Park, California. Quat. Res. 7 (3):316–329.

Osborn, H. F. 1910. The Age of mammals. New York: Macmillan.

Osborn, H. F., and W. D. Matthew. 1909. Cenozoic mammal horizons of western North America with faunal lists of the Tertiary mammalia of the West. Bull. U.S. Geol. Surv. 361:1–138.

Paulson, G. R. 1961. The mammals of the Cudahy fauna. Papers Mich. Acad. Sci. Arts Letters 46:127–153.

Pewe, T. L. 1975. Quaternary geology of Alaska. U.S. Geol. Surv. Prof. Paper 835, pp. 1–145.

Pruitt, W. O., Jr. 1959. Microclimates and local distribution of small mammals on the George Reserve, Michigan. Misc. Pub. Mus. Zool. Univ. Mich. 109:1–27.

Ray, C. E., E. Anderson, and S. D. Webb. 1981. The Blancan carnivore *Trigonictis* (Mammalia: Mustelidae) in the eastern United States. Brimleyana 5:1–36.

Reeves, B. O. K. 1973. The nature and age of the contact between the Laurentide and Cordilleran ice sheets in the western interior of North America. Arctic Alpine Res. 5:1–16.

Robertson, J. S., Jr. 1976. Latest Pliocene mammals from Haile XVA, Alachua County, Florida. Bull. Fla. State Mus. Biol. Sci. 20 (3):111–186.

Sarna-Wojcicki, A. M. 1976. Correlation of Late Cenozoic tuffs in the central Coast Ranges of California by means of trace and minor element chemistry. U.S. Geol. Surv. Prof. Paper 972, pp. 1–30.

Savage, D. E. 1951. Late Cenozoic vertebrates of the San Francisco Bay region. Calif. Univ. Publ. Dept. Geol. Sci. 28 (10):215–314.

Savage, D. E., and G. H. Curtis. 1970. The Villafranchian Stage-Age and its radiometric dating. Spec. Papers Geol. Soc. Amer. 124:207–231.

Schultz, C. B., and W. D. Frankforter. 1946. The geologic history of the bison in the Great Plains (a preliminary report). Bull. Univ. Nebr. State Mus. 3 (1):1–10.

Schultz, C. B., and J. M. Hillerud. 1977. The antiquity of *Bison latifrons* in the Great Plains of North America. Trans. Nebr. Acad. Sci. 4:103–116.

Schultz, C. B., and L. D. Martin. 1970. Quaternary mammalian sequence in the central Great Plains. In Pleistocene and Recent environments of the central Great Plains, eds. W. Dort, Jr., and J. K. Jones, Jr. Univ. Kans. Dept. Geol. Spec. Publ. 3:341–353.

————. 1977. Biostratigraphy of the Neogene-Quaternary Boundary in North America. Proc. 2d Symposium on the Neogene-Quaternary Boundary, Bologna-Crotone, October, 1975. G. Geol., Ann. Mus. Geol. Bologna, ser. 2, 41:285–295.

Schultz, C. B., L. G. Tanner, and L. D. Martin. 1972. Phyletic trends in certain lineages of Quaternary mammals. Bull. Univ. Nebr. State Mus. 9:183–195.

Schultz, C. B., L. D. Martin, L. G. Tanner, and R. G. Corner. 1977. Provincial land mammal ages for the North American Quaternary. Abstr. 10th INQUA Cong., Birmingham, England.

————. 1978. Provincial land mammal ages for the North American Quaternary. Trans. Nebr. Acad. Sci. 5:59–64.

Schultz, G. E. 1965. Pleistocene vertebrates from the Butler Spring local fauna, Meade County, Kansas. Papers Mich. Acad. Sci. Arts Letters 50:235–265.

————. 1967. Four superimposed late Pleistocene vertebrate faunas from southwest Kansas. In Pleistocene extinctions: The search for a cause, eds. P. S. Martin and H. E. Wright, Jr., pp. 321–326. New Haven and London: Yale Univ. Press.

————. 1969. Geology and paleontology of a late Pleistocene basin in southwest Kansas. Spec. Papers Geol. Soc. Amer. 105:1–85.

————. 1977. Blancan and post-Blancan faunas in the Texas Panhandle. In Guidebook, Field Conference on Late Cenozoic Biostratigraphy of the Texas Panhandle and Adjacent Oklahoma, August 4–6, 1977, ed. G. E. Schultz, pp. 105–145. Spec. Publ. 1, Killgore Res. Center, Dept. Geol. Anthropol., West Tex. State Univ., Canyon.

————. 1984. Biostratigraphy and volcanic ash deposits of the Tule Formation along the East Fork of Rock Creek, Briscoe County, Texas. In Elements of the geomorphology and Quaternary stratigraphy of the Rolling Plains of the Texas Panhandle, ed. T. C. Gustavson, pp. 126—132. Guidebook, Friends of the Pleistocene Field Trip, April 6–8, 1984.

Semken, H. A., Jr. 1966. Stratigraphy and paleontology of the McPherson *Equus* beds (Sandahl local fauna), McPherson County, Kansas. Contrib. Mus. Paleontol. Univ. Mich., 20:121–178.

Shackelton, N. J., and N. D. Opdyke. 1976. Oxygen-isotope and paleomagnetic stratigraphy of Pacific core V28–239: Late Pliocene to latest Pleistocene. In Investigation of Late Quaternary paleoceanography and paleoclimatology, eds.

R. M. Cline and J. D. Hays, pp. 449–464. Geol. Soc. Amer. Mem. 145.

————. 1977. Oxygen-isotope and paleomagnetic evidence for early northern hemisphere glaciation. Nature 170:216–219.

Shotwell, J. A. 1970. Pliocene mammals of southeast Oregon and adjacent Idaho. Bull. Univ. Oreg. Mus. Nat. Hist. 17:1–103.

Simpson, G. G. 1933. Glossary and correlation charts of North American Tertiary mammal-bearing formations. Bull. Amer. Mus. Nat. Hist. 67 (3):79–121.

Skinner, M. F., C. W. Hibbard, with the collaboration of E. D. Gutentag, G. R. Smith, J. G. Lundeberg, J. Alan Holman, J. Alan Feduccia, and P. V. Rich. 1972. Early Pleistocene pre-glacial rocks and faunas of north-central Nebraska. Bull. Amer. Mus. Nat. Hist. 148 (1):1–148.

Skinner, M. F., and O. C. Kaisen. 1947. The fossil *Bison* of Alaska and preliminary revision of the genus. Bull. Amer. Mus. Nat. Hist. 89 (3):123–256.

Slaughter, B. H. 1967. Animal ranges as a clue to late Pleistocene extinctions. In Pleistocene extinctions: The search for a cause, eds. P. S. Martin and H. E. Wright, Jr., pp. 155–167. New Haven and London: Yale Univ. Press.

Stalker, A. M. 1969. Quaternary stratigraphy in southern Alberta. II: Sections near Medicine Hat. Geol. Surv. Can. Paper 69–26:1–28.

Stalker, A. M., and C. S. Churcher. 1970. Deposits near Medicine Hat, Alberta, Canada. (Display chart with marginal notes.) Ottawa: Geol. Surv. Canada.

————. 1972. Glacial stratigraphy of the southwestern Canadian prairies: The Laurentide record. Proc. 24th Int. Geol. Cong., Montreal, Quebec, Quat. Geol. Sect. 12:110–119.

Starrettt, A. 1956. Pleistocene mammals of the Berends fauna of Oklahoma. J. Paleont. 30 (5):1187–1192.

Stirton, R. A. 1939. Cenozoic mammal remains from the San Francisco Bay region. Univ. Calif. Publ. Bull. Dept. Geol. Sci. 24 (13):339–410.

Strain, W. S. 1966. Blancan mammalian fauna and Pleistocene formation of Hudspeth County, Texas. Tex. Mem. Mus. Bull. 10:1–55.

Troxell, E. L. 1915a. The vertebrate fossils of Rock Creek, Texas. Amer. J. Sci., ser. 4, 39:613–638.

————. 1915b. A fossil ruminant from Rock Creek, Texas, *Preptoceras mayfieldi* sp. nov. Amer. J. Sci., ser. 4, 40:479–482.

Turekian, K. K., and J. L. Bada. 1972. The dating of fossil bones. In Calibration of hominoid evolution, eds. W. W. Bishop and J. A. Miller, pp. 171–185. Edinburgh: Scottish Academic Press.

Vanderhoof, V. L., and J. T. Gregory. 1940. A review of the genus *Aelurodon*. Univ. Calif. Publ. Bull. Dep. Geol. Sci. 25 (3):143–164.

Van der Meulen, A. J. 1978. *Microtus* and *Pitymys* (Arvicolidae) from Cumberland Cave, Maryland, with a comparison of some New and Old World species. Carnegie Mus. Ann. 47 (6):101–145.

Van Valen, L. 1969. Evolution of communities and late Pleistocene extinctions. Proc. No. Amer. Paleont. Conv., Pt. E, pp. 469–485.

Voorhies, M. R. 1977. Fossil moles of Late Hemphillian age from northeastern Nebraska. Trans. Nebr. Acad. Sci. 4:129–138.

Webb, S. D. 1974. Chronology of Florida Pleistocene mammals. In Pleistocene mammals of Florida, ed. S. D. Webb, pp. 5–31. Gainesville: Univ. Fla. Press.

Webb, S. D., S. W. Wise, Jr., and R. Wright. 1978. Late Miocene glacio-eustatic cycles in Florida: Marine and fluvio-estuarine sequences. Geol. Soc. Amer. Abstr. Prog. Ann. Mtg. 10:513.

Webb, T., III, and R. A. Bryson. 1972. Late and postglacial climatic change in the northern midwest U.S.A.: Quantitative estimates derived from fossil pollen spectra by multivariate statistical analysis. Quat. Res. 2:70–115.

White, J. 1984. Late Cenozoic Leporidae (Mammalia, Lagomorpha) from the Anza-Borrego Desert, Southern California. In Papers in vertebrate paleontology honoring Robert Warren Wilson, ed. R. M. Mengel, pp. 41–57. Carnegie Mus. Nat. Hist. Spec. Publ. 9.

Wilson, J. W. 1973. Photosynthetic pathways and spatial heterogeneity on the North American plains: Suggestion for the cause of the Pleistocene extinction. Soc. Vert. Paleont., 33d Ann. Mtg., 1973. Abstr.

Wilson, M. 1974a. History of the bison in Wyoming, with particular reference to early Holocene forms. In Applied geology and archaeology: The Holocene history of Wyoming, ed. M. Wilson. Geol. Surv. Wyo.. Rept. of Inv. 10:91–99.

———. 1974b. The Casper local fauna and its fossil bison. In The Casper site, a Hell Gap Bison kill on the High Plains, ed. G. C. Frison, pp. 125–171. New York: Academic Press.

Wilson, R. W. 1933. A rodent fauna from later Cenozoic beds of southwestern Idaho. Carnegie Inst. Wash. Pub. 440:117–135.

Woldstedt, P. 1969. Quartar: Handbuch der straitigraphischen Geologie. Enke, Stuttgart, 2:1–263.

Wood, H. E., II, R. W. Chaney, J. Clark, E. H. Colbert, G. L. Jepsen, J. B. Reeside, Jr., and C. Stock. 1941. Nomenclature and correlation of the North American continental Tertiary. Bull. Geol. Soc. Amer. 52:1–48.

Woodburne, M. O. 1961. Upper Pliocene geology and vertebrate paleontology of part of the Meade Basin, Kansas. Papers. Mich. Acad. Sci. Arts Letters 66:61–101.

Wright, H. E., Jr. 1970. Vegetational history of the central plains. In Pleistocene and Recent environments of the central Great Plains, eds. W. Dort, Jr., and J. K. Jones, Jr., pp. 157–172. Univ. Kans. Dept. Geol. Spec. Publ. 3.

Wyman, L. E. 1926. Notes on the Pleistocene fossils obtained from Rancho La Brea asphalt pits. Los Angeles Co. Mus. Nat. Hist. Misc. Publ. 2 (rev. ed.), pp. 1–39.

Zakrzewski, R. J. 1967. The primitive vole, *Ogmodontomys,* from the late Cenozoic of Kansas and Nebraska. Papers Mich. Acad. Sci. Arts Letters 52:133–150.

———. 1969. The rodents from the Hagerman local fauna, upper Pliocene of Idaho. Contrib. Mus. Paleont. Univ. Mich. 23 (1):1–36.

———. 1975. Pleistocene stratigraphy and paleontology in western Kansas: The state of the art, 1974. In Studies on Cenozoic paleontology and stratigraphy. Claude W. Hibbard Mem. vol. 3, Univ. Mich. Papers Paleont. 12:121–128.

———. 1981. Kangaroo rats from the Borchers local fauna, Blancan, Meade County, Kansas. Trans. Kans. Acad. Sci. 84 (2):78–88.

———. 1984. New arvicolines (Mammalia: Rodentia) from the Blancan of Kansas and Nebraska. In Contributions in Quaternary vertebrate paleontology: A volume in memorial to John E. Guilday, eds. H. H. Genoways and M. R. Dawson, pp. 200–217. Carnegie Mus. Nat. Hist. Spec. Publ. 8.

Note: Von Koenigswald (1980) indicates that *Mimomys* does not occur in North America and that *Cosomys, Ogmodontomys,* and *Ophiomys* should be accorded generic status.

8

BIOCHRONOLOGY OF THE MICROTINE RODENTS OF THE UNITED STATES

Charles A. Repenning

INTRODUCTION

Following upon the practicability of K-Ar age determinations, there developed a network of correlation between several disciplines with the common factor of K-Ar years which can be employed to establish other correlations. The network includes data of geomagnetic stratigraphy, tephrochronology, uniform rates of deposition in the deep sea, measurement of the isotopic or other variations in deep-sea deposits that correlate with climatic change, and K-Ar dated rocks. In terms of this network, it is possible to reconstruct historically the evolution and biogeography of climatically sensitive mammalian groups whose development has been too rapid and too complex for comprehension within the temporal resolution previously available. The microtine rodents are animals adapted to temperate to arctic grasslands and are of Holarctic distribution. In the last eight million years, they have diversified from four known genera to possibly twenty-five living genera. Their correlation to the K-Ar network produces a biochronology for the last 5 million years which has a maximum possible error of 0.27 million years. This is less than that of many of the K-Ar dates used to construct this biochronology, because correlation of many radiometric dates with relatively instantaneous events, such as ash falls, polarity reversals, and immigration waves, often results in a refined age interpretation more precise than the estimated analytical precision of an individual K-Ar age determination.

The study of microtine rodents is no more recent than the study of any other mammalian group. Its distinguishing feature has been that the group is so large and evolved so rapidly that its study has led only to confusion. Although earlier monographs had considered the living microtine fauna, the first comprehensive investigation of both fossil and living microtines was by Martin A. C. Hinton (1926). This work remains today the most valuable single contribution to the understanding of microtine rodents, despite the fact that Hinton completed only Part I of his work and covered in detail only fourteen of as many as twenty-five living genera.

None of the living genera are over 3 Ma old, with the exception of *Synaptomys* and *Lemmus,* and it has been extremely difficult to establish ancestor-descendant relationships in the fossil record before K-Ar age determinations were available. Now that such age determinations are available, or can be inferred through such other lines of evidence as geomagnetic polarity stratigraphy and tephrochronology, it is possible to recognize and document relationships between the microtine rodents that Hinton had inferred in 1926 on the basis of his unexcelled understanding of the group.

By the late 1930s two men assumed the major burden of trying to unravel the history of the microtine rodents, Claude Hibbard in the United States and Miklos Kretzoi in Hungary. They, and their students, built most of the history of the microtine rodents. By 1965, Kretzoi could see enough of this history to realize that there were major gaps in the European record. These were marked by the abrupt appearance in the fossil faunas of new, more advanced microtines. He concluded that the major evolution of the microtine rodents was outside of Europe, probably in Asia, and that from there Europe was repeatedly invaded by more advanced forms. By 1976, the statement of Fejfar (1976, p. 351) that "there was a strong tendency for steppe types [microtines] to migrate from Asia to central Europe, especially in the climax of cold oscillations" was well documented throughout Europe.

Kretzoi has always seen a strong similarity between European and North American fossil microtines. Although Hibbard had earlier agreed, at least to some extent, he became increasingly convinced that the microtine fauna of North America was a product of endemic evolution and that there were no repeated invasions from Asia. This hypothesis was held by Hibbard despite ample evidence of repeated invasions of North America by other types of mammals. This opinion has been carried on by several of his students and was most recently voiced by Larry D. Martin (1979), who, however, conceded that the lemmings must have immigrated from Asia.

The concept that North American microtines evolved endemically has completely frustrated attempts to reconstruct phylogenies except in those cases where the lineage actually did evolve in North America. Even with respect to these North American lineages, the lack of understanding of the evolution of other lineages caused many uncertainties with resulting errors in interpretation. Thus, there exist in the nomenclature such names as *Pliophenacomys* and *Pliolemmus,* genera of completely North American distribution but named in a way that suggests relationship to forms known also in the Old World.

The microtines are not the only group of mammals that can be developed into a new, more detailed biochronology. Any group that has evolved into a very diverse living fauna in the relatively short time since the late Miocene must have a similarly useful history awaiting reconstruction by means of the now-existing intercorrelated matrix of stratigraphies and chronologies. This matrix now includes the outline of the biochronology of the microtine rodents.

Age assignments of the geomagnetic polarity time scale used here follow Mankinen and Dalrymple (1979). Other dates in K-Ar years have been corrected to the new decay and abundance constants (Steiger and Jager 1977). The interpretation of the identity of the geomagnetic polarity events and epochs here presented are those of the author and in many cases do not agree with the authority cited for the polarity determinations. The use of European mammal ages follows that of Fejfar (1976) with subsequent modifications as indicated by personal

communication from him. These are more recently amended by Fejfar and Heinrich (1981, 1983). In this chapter, the use of generic and subgeneric terms represents discrete evolutionary lineages, and species or subspecies terms indicate evolutionary stages within single lineages. A recognized diphyly, although commonly acknowledged by species distinction in the living fauna, is accredited at least subgeneric rank in the fossil record. Where diphyly is not clear in the fossil record, two species of the same genus or subgenus may be recognized as coeval. Hyphenated double species indicate intermediate forms that are unnamed. This work is a byproduct of collaboration by the author and Oldrich Fejfar of the Czechoslovakian Geological Survey, Prague; our final report on the Holarctic history of microtine rodents, which defends changes in nomenclature, is in compilation.

Abbreviations used are:

Ma   million years ago in the radioisotopic time scale

m.y.   million years

ya   years ago

loc.   locality

US   U.S. Geological Survey, Paleontology and Stratigraphy Branch. Localities are kept in several registers. "Cenozoic" localities refer to a register of invertebrate megafossil localities. "Vertebrate" refers to a register of vertebrate fossil localities. "D" before the locality number refers to a register in the Denver office, "M" to the Menlo Park office, and no letter refers to a register in the Washington, D.C., office.

AM   American Museum of Natural History, New York.

F:AM   Frick collection of the AM.

CAS   California Academy of Sciences, San Francisco

CM   Carnegie Museum of Natural History, Pittsburgh.

ISU   Idaho State University Museum of Natural History, Pocatello.

LA   Los Angeles County Natural History Museum.

LA:CIT   California Institute of Technology collection in LA.

UA   University of Arizona Laboratory of Paleontology, Tucson.

UC University of California Museum of Paleontology, Berkeley.

UK University of Kansas, Lawrence.

UM University of Michigan Museum of Paleontology, Ann Arbor.

UN University of Nebraska State Museum, Lincoln.

UO University of Oregon Museum of Natural History, Eugene.

USNM National Museum of Natural History, Washington, D.C.

UW University of Washington, Burke Memorial Museum, Seattle.

M upper molar.
m lower molar.

CLASSIFICATION

It is the purpose of this chapter to outline the microtine biochronology of the United States and not to document the classification of these rodents, a work still in progress by the author and O. Fejfar. No new species are introduced, and generic reassignments have been done in such a way that their previous usage is apparent, usually in the form of a subgenus. One exception is *Mimomys (Cosomys) sawrockensis* (Hibbard) (removed from the subgenus *Ogmodontomys* because it is not sufficiently derived to always show the pronounced anterolabial flattening of the anteroconid complex that characterizes that subgenus).

The microtine rodents are primarily grass eaters and are specialized lineages of the cricetid rodents (deer mice, wood rats, hamsters, and many more), which are basically seed eaters. As with many larger herbivorous mammals that have adapted to grass feeding, their major skeletal modification has been an increase in tooth complexity and height, resulting in prismatic cusps that provide greater resistance to wear and more tooth to be worn by abrasive food.

From the fossil record as now known, it is evident that the microtine rodents do not constitute a discrete phylogenetic group. Instead, the adaptation to grass eating, with consequent evolution of a microtine grade of prismatic cusps of the teeth, appears to have evolved at least five different times in the cricetid rodents. Each of these five lineages with the microtine dental specialization survives today in some parts of Holarctica, but their earliest records vary from possibly 9 to as little as 2.0 Ma. As used here, therefore, the word "microtine" is an adjective and refers to a member of one of the five lineages of cricetid rodents that have evolved triangularly prismatic cusps on their molar teeth, similar to the cusps on the molar teeth of the genus *Microtus*; the word microtine has no taxonomic status.

The oldest lineage to evolve the microtine grade of prismatic tooth cusps derives from a low-crowned cricetid with opposing cusps on its teeth. These oldest microtine cricetids are *Goniodontomys* from Wyoming and Oregon and *Microtoscoptes,* known from deposits that may be as much as 8.5 Ma old as far west as Kazakh S.S.R. (Zazhigin 1980) and as far east as Nebraska (Martin 1975). This group, here assigned to the subfamily Prometheomyinae, survived until earliest Pleistocene time in North America and still lives in Eurasia.

Probably as old as *Microtoscoptes* are two species of the genus *Ischymomys* from Petropavlosk, Siberia, and Formosovka 2 in southern Russia (Topachevski et al. 1978). These species have extremely low-crowned teeth with five, rather than three, alternating triangles on m1 that are so broadly confluent that in some individuals they almost appear opposing. They appear to be ancestral to the Ondatrinae, a subfamily known from Europe in faunas younger than 4.8 Ma and from North America in faunas younger than 3.7 Ma.

The next oldest microtine lineage of the cricetid rodents clearly derives from a low-crowned cricetid with alternating cusps on its teeth that form three alternating triangles. A variety of possible nonmicrotine ancestors are known from Eurasian deposits between 7 and 5 Ma; many of these possible ancestors are contemporaries of the oldest genus of this microtine lineage, *Promimomys* (or *Prosomys,* an irresolvable nomenclatorial conflict of opinion). This Holarctic genus is widely recognized as the most primitive member of the microtine subfamily Arvicolinae of the cricetid rodents. The great majority of living microtine cricetid rodents belong in this subfamily.

Primitive forms (with rooted cheek teeth) of the youngest two cricetid lineages having microtine tooth specialization are not yet certainly known and the nature of their nonmicrotine cricetid ancestors cannot be inferred. However, both lineages are characterized by a distinctive orientation of their lower incisors. These two subfamilies, Lemminae and Dicrostonychinae, are first known from deposits more than 4 Ma in Bashkir (Suchov 1976) and 2.5 Ma in eastern Siberia and Alaska (Repenning 1984), respectively. The little-known species *Aratomys multifidus* Zazhigin from Chono-Chariach 2, Mongolia, may represent a primitive, low-crowned, and rooted member of the Lemminae. It is comparable in crown development to *Promimomys* but is Pontian in age, approximately as old as *Microtoscoptes* from Ertemte, Mongolia.

These five recognized lineages are here grouped within the Family Cricetidae as subfamilies. The Family Arvicolidae Gray, 1921 (or Microtidae Cope, 1891) is considered a polyphyletic grouping and is abandoned. The subfamilies Prometheomyinae (Kretzoi 1955), Arvicolinae (as used and defended by Kretzoi 1955, 1962), Ondatrinae (Kretzoi 1955, as a Tribe), Lemminae (Gray 1825), and Dicrostonychinae (Kretzoi 1955, as a Tribe) are here treated as separate lineages of the cricetid rodents, all of which have evolved the microtine grade of tooth specializations.

BIOCHRONOLOGY

The history of Holarctic microtine rodents is one of great diversification, culminating in the varied fauna of today. Only part of this history can be explained by evolution in North America and Europe. Although both areas have a fossil record indicating endemic evolution, the microtine fauna of both Europe and North America is repeatedly altered in composition by invasions of more advanced forms from Asia. These invasions resulted in the partial extinction of the then endemic microtine fauna and its replacement by a more modern type. Insofar as available evidence indicates, these invasions occurred at the same times in Europe and in North America (Repenning 1980, 1984).

The following dates and events in the United States appear to be reasonable conclusions on the basis of evidence available at present. The figures following the plus and minus symbol ($\pm$) do not represent an estimate of analytical precision of some K-Ar age determination but are the author's estimate of possible error in age assignment of the event based on all available evidence of the K-Ar network of correlations.

Event 1. 6.7 $\pm$ 0.5 Ma—the primitive microtine *Promimomys* immigrated to the United States. *Promimomys* appears at a slightly later date in Europe.

Event 2. 4.8 $\pm$ 0.2 Ma—two subgenera of *Mimomys*, *M.* (*Ophiomys*) and *M.* (*Cosomys*), immigrated to the United States. These are hardly distinguishable from the contemporaneous European immigrants *M.* (*Cseria*) and *M.* (*Hintonia*). *Nebraskomys* appears to also have immigrated at this time.

Event 3. 4.25 $\pm$ 0.3 Ma—the endemic microtine fauna of the United States evolved into a recognizably distinct fauna.

Event 4. 3.7 $\pm$ 0.1 Ma—the primitive muskrat *Pliopotamys* immigrated to the United States. At this same time, *Lemmus, Synaptomys,* and *Villanyia* appear in Europe.

Event 5. 3.2 $\pm$ 0.2 Ma—the endemic microtine fauna of the United States again evolved into a recognizably distinct fauna.

Event 6. 2.6 $\pm$ 0.1 Ma—two subgenera of the lemming *Synaptomys, S.* (*Synaptomys*) and *S.* (*Mictomys*), immigrated to the United States. In Europe, *Clethrionomys, Lagurodon,* and *Pliomys* appear as immigrants or reimmigrants.

Event 7. 1.9 $\pm$ 0.0 Ma—the microtine genera *Phenacomys, Proneofiber, Microtus,* and *Allophaiomys* immigrated to the United States. *Microtus, Allophaiomys, Dicrostonyx,* and *Pitymys* (and *Neodon,* although the definition of this genus remains obscure) appear in Europe at this time.

Event 8. 0.85 Ma—the microtine genera *Clethrionomys,* and *Pitymys* immigrated to the United States. This immigration introduced no recognized microtines to western Europe (*Eolagurus* and *Lagurus* to eastern Europe) but was marked throughout Holarctica by the extreme southward dispersal of *Microtus* (Repenning 1984).

Event 9. 400,000 $\pm$ 25,000 years ago—three new species of *Microtus* and *Lagurus* immigrated to the United States. New species of *Microtus* also appeared in Europe along with *Lagurus* (western Europe) and the first *Arvicola* (possibly by endemic evolution).

Event 10. Probably 150,000 $\pm$ 25,000 years ago—the microtine genera *Dicrostonyx, Lemmus,* and several new species of *Microtus* immigrated to the United States. In Europe, immigration was only of a new species.

Of these ten microtine events, eight were invasions of the United States. Each of these microtine invasions was in the company of other types of immigrating mammals and coincided with some global event, as detected by other criteria, that can be presumed to have accompanied, or induced, cooling, changes in atmospheric storm patterns, or lowering of sea level. Each of these eight invasions is recognizable in Europe and thus they are Holarctic dispersal events of the microtine rodents, although the composition of the immigrants usually differed provincially. Their correlation with European immigrations is based on similarity of immigrating forms and on independent dating in Europe and in North America. The two longest periods without invasion of new forms into the United States resulted in recognizable endemic evolution and consequent faunal difference (events 3 and 5) and were also experienced in Europe as a result of endemic evolution in the microtines into recognizably distinct faunas. The invasions into Europe and North America should not be thought of as dispersal to the east and west out of Asia but, instead, as southward dispersals during cooler periods occurring with the expansion of the arctic steppe from a single Siberian-Beringian arctic fauna that encircled more than half of the Holarctic world (Repenning 1984).

In comparison with other mammals, the rapid rate of evolutionary change in the microtine rodents seems astounding. A comment about cause might be appropriate. The following approximate statements are conservative and based on the history of the California meadow mouse, *Microtus californicus*. A female may have her first litter seven weeks after her birth. She will have a gestation period of only twenty-one days and at least five litters in the year she was born, which is usually the year of her life. The average litter will have 6.5 mice, about half of which will be female and have their first litter seven weeks after their birth. If this is projected into the first litter of the third year and if the great effects of natural predation and disease are ignored, it will be seen that after the first litter of the third year following her birth, one female could have over 6,000,000 descendants.

A female horse may have ten colts in thirty years and a female elephant may have five calves in sixty years. The availability of genetic variation in microtine rodents is astronomical in comparison with most larger animals.

On the correlation chart that accompanies this report (fig. 8.1, in pocket), these ten microtine events are marked by horizontal lines that indicate, on the time scales, the best current (1984) approximation of when these events took place. In all cases, except the event marking the beginning of late Hemphillian, these are rather closely dated by correlation with the K-Ar chronologic network. Two dashed events (numbers 3 and 5) mark arbitrary selections of times that subdivide the two prolonged periods (about 1 Ma each) when no invasion of Europe or of the United States is recognized. These two arbitrary microtine age boundaries are characterized by endemic evolutionary changes in the microtine fauna of the United States and are thus based upon gradational criteria.

These ten microtine events separate microtine faunas of the United States which are distinctly characteristic of that period of time. Any species whose temporal range includes only part of a specific period of time is counted as a member of the microtine fauna of the United States during that entire period. These are the listings in the column "Microtine Faunas." Species capitalized are new immigrants. The species listed are those for the entire

conterminous United States, but, because of provinciality, all species listed do not occur in all parts of the nation. Mexico, Canada, and Alaska are excluded from the chart for the most part; provincial differences are too great to include here. Within the boundaries of the United States, there are both latitudinal and longitudinal range limits known for most species. Provinciality becomes more distinctive and restrictive with decreasing geologic age, especially longitudinally, and is discussed in the text below.

Throughout the history of the microtine rodents in the United States, latitudinal range restrictions are prominent, and it is evident, at this stage of study, that the ancient faunas of Canada and Mexico had marked differences in composition. The limited record from Alaska strongly indicates much greater similarity to the microtine history of Asia than to that of the conterminous United States. Hence this chapter, and the species listed on the correlation chart, applies only to the contiguous forty-eight states.

Those periods of time defined by the ten microtine events and characterized by the species listed may reasonably be referred to as microtine ages. They are numbered in Roman numerals on the correlation chart in an older-to-younger sequence within the conventional North American land mammal age that they represent. Their assignment to specific land mammal ages is reasonably defended by the original definitions of these ages.

Wood et al. (1941, p. 13) list *Mimomys* as first appearing in Blancan faunas, and this characterization is retained herein. Savage (1951, p. 289), less specifically, defines Irvingtonian faunas as those containing "some mammalian species which appear to be unadvanced as compared to the most nearly related forms of the Rancholabrean and Recent" and Rancholabrean faunas as those containing mammals "which are inseparable from Recent inhabitants of the same area." These definitions apply reasonably well to those microtine faunas here assigned to these mammal ages, given our present greater understanding of fossil mammals and of faunal displacement during cold spells. Other mammalian fossils associated with microtines provide additional support for the assignment of microtine ages to North American land mammal ages.

It should not be construed in any way that the inclusion of North American land mammal ages on the correlation chart is an attempt to refine their definition. They are shown only to provide familiar chronologic terminology and so shown and positioned according to the author's interpretation of their most conventional usage. On the chart, the mammal ages are shown once, the geomagnetic polarity scale is shown twice, and the time scale three times. These proportions reflect the usefulness of microtine rodents. Larry Martin (1979) recently suggested a system of microtine ages (his "N.A. Arvicoline Zones") of similar nature as here defined and numbered them consecutively from the late Miocene to the late Pleistocene; possibly this would be a better procedure. Here, however, the microtine ages are referred to by both Roman numerals and assigned North American mammal ages, as "Blancan II," "Irvingtonian II," or Rancholabrean II," as was done by Repenning (1978, 1980, 1983c, 1984).

Following Fejfar (1976) and Fejfar and Heinrich (1981, 1983), this chapter uses a European mammal age classification that recognizes more subdivisions than that used by the Commission on Mediterranean Neogene (Mein 1975). The comparison between the two age classifications is shown on the right side of the correlation chart. For the most part, the terminology used here is based on a subdivision according to microtine events in Europe; the exception is the base of the Ruscinian for which the definition of the Commission on Mediterranean Neogene is followed. These ages are shown here only for orientation, and no further discussion is presented.

Faunal localities listed on the correlation chart have been separated into two groups, west and east of Denver. At least by Blancan II time, east-west (longitudinal) provinciality became prominent in the microtine faunas of the United States, separated by the Rocky Mountains. The differing characterizations of the provincial microtine faunas are discussed in the text to follow. In addition, all faunas shown on the chart are summarized in the Appendix.

All faunal localities marked with a # symbol are positioned on the chart relative to time and other faunas so marked by both faunal and external control consisting of K-Ar dates, tephrochronologic association, paleomagnetic control, or stratigraphic superposition. Those marked with an "x" are positioned on the chart only by faunal interpretation. And those not marked by any symbol are assigned to a microtine age on the basis of their contained fauna but with no implication of what part of that age they represent. These criteria are discussed in the Appendix.

With the possible exception of the primitive *Pliopotamys* (see discussion under locality 22 in the Appendix), dispersal of the microtine rodents appears to be instantaneous in the United States in terms of available time discrimination. Anomalies exist, however, that indicate significant periods of interruption in dispersal or relict survival in a refuge. Thus, *Microtus paroperarius* is listed on the chart as an immigrant during Event 7,

marking Irvingtonian I faunas. It is, however, only known from southern Canada at this time (Wellsch Valley Local Fauna, locality 54 in the Appendix) and does not appear in a flood across the Great Plains of the United States until Irvingtonian II time. Similarly, *Pitymys meadensis* is an immigrant of Event 8 and characterizes Irvingtonian II and Rancholabrean I faunas from the Pacific Coast to the Great Plains; it is not known from younger faunas of the United States but is known from Rancholabrean deposits in the Valley of Mexico (El Tajo de Tequixquiac Local Fauna) and appears to still live near there under the name *Pitymys quasiater* (Repenning 1983b). It is hoped that these irregularities are satisfactorily explained in the following text and Appendix.

The discussion of individual microtine ages must begin with the Clarendonian mammal age because microtines have been reported in faunas believed to be this old.

Clarendonian

There are no known microtine rodents in faunas of Clarendonian age, that is, greater than 9.0 Ma (Tedford, chap. 6). Shotwell (1970) mentions one tooth fragment from the Clarendonian Black Butte Local Fauna of Oregon identified as *Microtoscoptes* sp. On further examination, the specimen does not belong in this genus; it may be a heteromyid.

Evernden et al. (1964) published two K-Ar dates related to early microtines: Stroud Claim, Idaho, cited by them as 10 Ma, and Teewinot Formation, Wyoming, cited as being based on a 9.2 Ma tuff 106 feet below the microtine fauna. According to these authors, both faunas contain the Hemphillian genus *Dipoides* in association with *Microtoscoptes*. The Teewinot Local Fauna (Kelley Road Local Fauna) specimens actually belong to *Goniodontomys,* a genus named by Wilson (1937). In both cases, the associated fauna is clearly of Hemphillian age, and the strata separating the fauna and data in Wyoming could easily account for the discrepancy in the age determination for such a fauna. The Stroud Claim date is more likely to be in error than the several dates that otherwise indicate an approximately 9.0 Ma Hemphillian-Clarendonian faunal change.

Early Hemphillian (9.0 to 6.7 ± 0.5 Ma)

Microtoscoptes and *Goniodontomys* (subfamily Prometheomyinae) occur in early Hemphillian faunas in Oregon, Idaho, Nevada, Wyoming, and Nebraska (localities 1–6 in the Appendix). *Microtoscoptes* was first described from Ertemte, China, and has also been reported from Central Asia (see Gromov and Polyakov 1977 for a summary). These are the only microtines from the early Hemphillian, and their temporal relationships are uncertain. *Microtoscoptes* appears to be more advanced than *Goniodontomys,* which has not been recognized outside of the United States. Endemic descendants are known, but there is no external evidence that *Microtoscoptes* is younger than *Goniodontomys.* Their ancestry is unknown.

Late Hemphillian (Event 1 to Event 2; 6.7 ± 0.5 to 4.8 ± 0.0 Ma)

In the United States, late Hemphillian faunas are marked by the immigration of the very primitive microtine *Promimomys* (subfamily Arvicolinae). The genus is known from three North American localities, two in Oregon and one in Nebraska (localities 7, 8, and 12 in the Appendix). Only one of these three (locality 12) has any basis for external control of its age, that is, evidence of age other than that provided by the fauna itself, and this is weak but suggests an age somewhat older than 5 Ma.

Promimomys occurs with characteristic late Hemphillian mammalian faunas that have been dated as old as 6.69 Ma (Baskin 1979). Mammals that appear to have immigrated into the United States with *Promimomys* that further characterize the late Hemphillian faunas include *Castor, Agriotherium, Enhydriodon, Plesiogulo,* and *Ochotona.*

The appearance of the genus *Promimomys* in southeastern Europe is recorded in many faunas of Ruscinian type from the central Russian plain to southern France (Agadjanian and Kowalski 1978, as *Prosomys*). The Ruscinian Stage has been defined by the Committee on Mediterranean Neogene (Mein 1975) as beginning with the end of the Messinian Stage (marine), or at about 5.27 Ma. It is not possible to correlate known "Ruscinian" faunas to marine stages but several of them that contain *Promimomys,* including Podlesice in Poland and Vendargues in France, appear to be "pre-Ruscinian" (late Turolian marine stage) from the total composition of their fauna (Fejfar and Heinrich 1981).

Although not dated in either Europe or the United States, the immigration of *Promimomys* seems likely to have taken place during magnetic polarity Epoch 6 on the basis of the earliest appearance of other late Hemphillian immigrants. On figure 8.1 it is placed below the base of that epoch, at 6.69 Ma, but is given a wide margin of possible error.

In the United States, *Promimomys* was not the only microtine of the late Hemphillian. Martin (1975) named the genus *Propliophenacomys* (subfamily Prometheomyinae) from three localities in Nebraska (two, localities 10 and 11, are discussed in the Appendix). These records also are older than 5 Ma, but *Propliophenacomys* has not been found with *Promimomys. Propliophenacomys* is an endemic product of North American evolution; it has also been found in the Ringold Formation of southeastern Washington along Lind Coulee (locality 9 in Appendix) in a normally magnetized section just below reversely magnetized beds (Packer and Johnston 1979). Generalized history of deposition in the Ringold Basin of south-central Washington suggests that the Lind Coulee Local Fauna is most likely of latest Hemphillian age, and, accordingly, the normal event of the Lind Coulee Local Fauna is here considered to represent the Thvera (C_2) normal subchron of the Gilbert Reversed Chron, between 5.0 and 4.85 Ma. If so, it may be the youngest recognized Hemphillian fauna in the United States. The Ringold Formation includes both late Hemphillian and Blancan mammals and will be discussed further with respect to Blancan microtines. Elsewhere Gustafson (1977) has reported *Teloceras,* presumably of Hemphillian age, from the Ringold Formation but the locality cannot be correlated with Lind Coulee.

Blancan I (Event 2 to Event 3; 4.8 ± 0.2 to 4.25 ± 0.0 Ma)

The beginning of the Blancan mammal age is marked by the immigration of *Nebraskomys* and two subgenera of *Mimomys,* M. (*Ophiomys*) and M. (*Cosomys*). These subgenera of *Mimomys* are of small and large size, respectively, and the synchronous invasion of Europe also introduced small- and large-size subgenera, there called M. (*Cseria*) and M. (*Hintonia*), into Csarnotan faunas. In addition, such forms as the bear *Ursus,* possibly cervids, the leporid *Nekrolagus,* and the grison *Trigonictis* also entered the United States at this time (Repenning 1967).

The oldest species of *Mimomys* in the United States are *Mimomys* (*Cosomys*) *sawrockensis* Hibbard and *Mimomys* (*Ophiomys*) *mcknighti* Gustafson. Both occur 21 meters below a basalt flow near Alturas, California, in the Upper Alturas Local Fauna (CAS locality 3685; UO locality 2424; locality 13 in Appendix). The basalt has been dated three times with an average age of 4.7 ± 0.5 Ma (M. Silberman, pers. com., 1978, FY78–85). Although the fauna is well downsection from the dated basalt, its maximum age is restricted by the age of *Propliophenacomys* from the Ringold Formation and by several other late Hemphillian dates of about 5.0 Ma (Evernden et al. 1964; Boellstorff 1976; Tedford, chap. 6).

The type locality of *Mimomys* (*Ophiomys*) *mcknighti*

is in the Ringold Formation of southeastern Washington; it is called the White Bluffs Local Fauna (Gustafson 1978; locality 17 in Appendix). The fauna is in strata a short distance above the top of a normal event of the Gilbert Reversed Chron (Packer and Johnston 1979, Packer 1979). Overlying deposits are nearly all reversely magnetized, but there is a 15-meter unsampled interval midway up the bluff below which magnetic polarity tends to move toward normal upsection and above which magnetic polarity begins at about 15°N latitude (weakly normal) and rapidly changes upsection to strong south (reversed) polarity; this distribution suggests that the unsampled interval might have included a normal polarity event. The remainder of the section is strongly reversed up to and slightly beyond a second local fauna in the Ringold Formation, Haymaker's Orchard (locality 19 in Appendix). The highest sample in the Ringold Formation (Packer's sample 22) is about 3 meters above the Haymaker's Orchard Local Fauna and is normal, so a normal event may begin at this point (Packer 1979). These magnetic polarities are shown by Packer (1979, fig. 8, on which White Bluffs Local Fauna would be at about 32 m and Haymaker's Orchard Local Fauna would be at about 97 m).

Blancan II (Event 3 to Event 4; 4.25 ± 0.3 to 3.7 ± 0.1 Ma)

The microtine from Haymaker's Orchard locality is intermediate between *M. (O.) mcknight* found in the lower part of the section and *M. (O.) taylori* found above the Cochiti normal subchron of the Gilbert Reversed Chron near Hagerman, Idaho (Neville et al. 1979). Because of its recognizable advancement beyond *M. (O.) mcknighti,* the microtine from Haymaker's Orchard Local Fauna is here referred to informally as *M. (O.) mcknighti-taylori.* It is believed to indicate a Blancan II fauna. Thus the magnetics at White Bluffs, Washington, are here interpreted to record the Sidufjall (C_1) normal subchron of the Gilbert Chron near the horizon of *M. (O.) mcknighti,* to have missed the Nunivak normal subchron in the sampling upsection, and possibly to include the very base of the Cochiti normal subchron at its top above the Haymaker's Orchard Local Fauna.

Zakrzewski (1967) has recognized evolutionary change between *Mimomys (Cosomys) sawrockensis* from the Saw Rock Canyon Local Fauna in Seward County, Kansas, (locality 18 in Appendix), *M. (Ogmodontomys) poaphagus transitionalis* from the Fox Canyon Local Fauna (locality 21 in Appendix), and *M. (O.) poaphagus poaphagus* from the Rexroad 3 Local Fauna (locality 22 in Appendix), both in Meade County, Kansas. In addi-

tion, Hibbard and Zakrzewski (1972) have recognized evolutionary differences between *Pliophenacomys finneyi* of the Fox Canyon Local Fauna and *Pliophenacomys primaevus* from the Sand Draw Local Fauna of Nebraska (locality 29 in Appendix). There is no *Pliophenacomys* from the Rexroad 3 Local Fauna or from the Saw Rock Canyon Local Fauna, but Martin (1975) has suggested the derivation of *Pliophenacomys* from *Propliophenacomys* of late Hemphillian faunas. Lindsay and Jacobs (1985) described a new species, *Pliophenacomys wilsoni,* from the Concha Local Fauna (locality 16 in Appendix) overlying the Yepomera late Hemphillian fauna of Chihuahua, Mexico; this species is intermediate in derived characters between *Pliophenacomys finneyi* from Fox Canyon and *Propliophenacomys* from Santee, Nebraska (locality 11 in Appendix). This new species of *Pliophenacomys* occurs with a horse that may be a very primitive species of *Dolichohippus* or a very advanced form of *Pliohippus mexicanus* (G. Simpson, pers. com. through E. Lindsay, 1980). Lindsay, Opdyke, and Johnson have made paleomagnetic studies that are here interpreted as showing the Yepomera Local Fauna lying both below and above the Thvera (C_2) subchron and the Concha Local Fauna to be just below the Sidufjall (C_1) subchron of the Gilbert Chron (May and Repenning 1982). Lindsay et al. interpret this paleomagnetic section to represent the Cochiti and Nunivak subchrons (3.80 = 4.20 Ma), approximately 0.6 to 0.8 Ma younger than the interpretation here preferred (E. Lindsay, pers. com., 1980).

In that *Pliophenacomys wilsoni* of Lindsay and Jacobs is intermediate in morphology between *Propliophenacomys parkeri* Martin from late Hemphillian faunas and *Pliophenacomys finneyi* from the Blancan II Fox Canyon Local Fauna, the Concha Local Fauna is here considered roughly equivalent in age to Blancan I Saw Rock Canyon Local Fauna, Kansas, and to the Maxum (locality 15 in Appendix) and Upper Alturas (locality 13 in Appendix) faunas of California, all containing *M. (C.) sawrockensis*. On the basis of the interpretation of its paleomagnetic pattern used here, the Yepomera Local Fauna, underlying the Concha Local Fauna, is considered equivalent in approximate age to the Santee, Nebraska, and Lind Coulee, Washington, faunas.

A recent discovery (Verde locality; number 14 in Appendix) in the Verde Formation of central Arizona is of latest Blancan I age, as Blancan I and II are hereby arbitrarily subdivided, and includes *Pliophenacomys* sp. of Lindsay and Jacobs and *Nebraskomys rexroadensis*. The locality is about 56 meters above a basalt dated 5.6 Ma (Doell and Cox 1965). Paleomagnetic correlations by Bressler and Butler (1978) place the fossiliferous section just below the Nunivak subchron of the Gilbert Chron (about 2 m below, and somewhat more than 4.20 Ma).

Both Fox Canyon and Rexroad 3 faunas of Kansas show evolution beyond the condition seen in *M. (C.) sawrockensis* and are placed in Blancan II. Because of the evolution also seen between Fox Canyon and Rexroad 3 faunas, however, the Fox Canyon Local Fauna is considered older. Lindsay et al. (1975) have indicated that the geomagnetic polarity of these two localities differs (Fox Canyon is reversely magnetized and Rexroad 3 is normally magnetized). Because of limited exposures, however, it is not possible to obtain a significant polarity section.

The selection of a temporal boundary in a sequence of evolving lineages must be arbitrary, and, where more than one lineage is involved, it is based on the unlikely premise that recognizable evolutionary change occurs at the same time in two or more lineages. The uncertainty of boundary position probably increases in direct proportion to the number of lineages used to define the evolutionary transition. Woodburne (1977) has suggested that such a boundary be based on one evolutionary lineage to avoid this conflict in differing rates of, or in recognizability of, evolution in different lineages. Nevertheless, provinciality in an area as large as the United States may require that different lineages be used in different provinces. Such a temporal boundary can only be defended by external age control in each province where a different lineage is used for definition.

The arbitrary boundary between Blancan I and Blancan II is here placed at 4.25 ± 0.3 Ma. In the Pacific Northwest, this is based on evolution of *Mimomys (Ophiomys)* and placed upsection from the White Bluffs Local Fauna of Washington; to the south and east, from California to Kansas, it is based on the evolution of *Pliophenacomys* or of large *Mimomys*, whichever is present, and is placed at the Verde Local Fauna of Arizona. The two systems overlap only in one fauna, at Alturas, California, a Blancan I fauna that underlies a dated basalt (locality 13 in Appendix). *Mimomys (Cosomys)* is not known in the Pacific Northwest until late Blancan II time, and although *Propliophenacomys* is known from the state of Washington, *Pliophenacomys* is not known in the Pacific Northwest until Blancan V time (G. Conrad, pers. com., 1980). *Mimomys (Ophiomys)* does not appear in the Great Plains until Blancan III time, as will be discussed below.

In the Pacific Northwest, the evolution of the small *Mimomys* is well documented and closely related to paleomagnetic stratigraphy with a few K-Ar dates for cross-correlation; the 4.25 Ma age of the arbitrary Blancan II base can be supported. In the Great Plains, the evolution of large *Mimomys* and of *Pliophenacomys* is well documented, but there is no paleomagnetic stratigraphy, nor are there K-Ar age determinations for external control between the immigration marking event 2 and that marking event 4. The arbitrary faunal definition of the base of Blancan II in this area could easily be much younger than 4.25 Ma.

The evolution of large *Mimomys,* as subgenus *Ogmodontomys,* is well documented (subgenus *Cosomys* evolved west of Denver into *Mimomys (Cosomys) primus* and then became extinct). The oldest possible age of *M. (C.) sawrockensis* is rather well established at Alturas, California, but there is no way to estimate its youngest possible age or to infer the age range of *M. (Ogmodontomys) poaphagus transitionalis,* known from Fox Canyon, Kansas. We do not regain temporal control of its history until Blancan III faunas.

The evolution of *Pliophenacomys* is well documented. The oldest possible age of *P. wilsoni* of Lindsay and Jacobs is rather well established as younger than *Propliophenacomys* at Lind Coulee, Washington, and older than Concha, Chihuahua; the species can be at least as young as Verde, Arizona, but there is no way to infer its youngest possible age or to infer the age of *Pliophenacomys finneyi* from Fox Canyon, Kansas. By Blancan III time, the lineage had evolved into a new species.

The placement of the Fox Canyon Local Fauna (locality 21 in Appendix) in the middle of Blancan II is defensible only on the basis of an assumed constant rate of evolution (an assumption not contradicted by the history of microtine rodents). Species of *Hesperoscalops* from Santee, Saw Rock Canyon, and Fox Canyon faunas appear to show the same rate of evolution and support equal temporal spacing (Voorhies 1977).

In Europe, nearly identical forms of *Mimomys* appear to mark the beginning of Csarnotan faunas, along with forms resembling *Propliophenacomys* and early muskrats. As in the United States, there are small and large subgenera of *Mimomys*. *M. (C.) gracilis* Kretzoi is the small form, and its m_1s could be placed in a collection of *M. (O.) mcknighti* and be lost. *Mimomys (Hintonia) davakosi* van de Weerd and the somewhat more advanced *Mimomys (Hintonia) occitanus* Thaler are the large forms and are almost as similar to *M. (C.) sawrockensis*. As noted by Hibbard and Zakrzewski (1967), however, there is a strong tendency in European species of *Mimomys* to retain a closed basin on the posterior loop of M^3, much as does North American *Promimomys* (Repenning 1968), but in the North American species of *Mimomys*, the basin of M^3 is breached on the lingual side to form a second alternating triangle and a lingually hooked posterior loop, a breaching that is more common in later species of *Mimomys* in Europe.

This invasion by *Mimomys* and other microtines is not dated in Europe. It is considerably older than the Vialette Local Fauna, which underlies a lava dated at 3.9 Ma (Savage and Curtis 1970) and younger than Ruscinian faunas, which begin, by definition, with the end of the Messinian Stage at 5.27 Ma. Similar stages of evolution of these immigrants and presumed Holarctic synchroneity of microtine dispersal events suggest that the European immigration of *Mimomys* is the same age as the Blancan I microtine dispersal, about 4.8 Ma. It should be noted that by 4 Ma, the small *Mimomys* lineage had evolved into a recognizably different species in North America, *M. (O.) mcknighti-taylori,* and the large species of *Mimomys* had evolved into *M. (Ogmodontomys) poaphagus.* Both were distinctly derived in character and could not be confused with European species. The short duration of *Mimomys* species thus emphasizes the synchroneity of dispersal events based on similar species.

As in North America, about a million years separate the invasion marking the beginning of Csarnotan faunas and the next microtine dispersal event. During this time, endemic faunal evolution also produced a noticeably different microtine fauna that is typified by the Arondelli-Triversa Fauna of the early Villafranchian Mammal Age. The transition from Csarnotan faunas to Villafranchian faunas was before the Vialette Local Fauna beneath a 3.9 Ma lava.

Blancan III (Event 4 to Event 5; 3.7 ± 0.1 to 3.2 ± 0.2 Ma)

The Blancan III mammalian age is completely included in the highly fossiliferous exposures at Hagerman, in the Snake River drainage basin of Idaho. Here it is underlain by youngest Blancan II faunas and is closely correlated to K-Ar dates and paleomagnetic correlations (Neville et al. 1979). In the Hagerman area and in the Pasco area of Washington, also part of the Snake River drainage basin, the immigration of the first North American muskrat, *Pliopotamys* (subfamily Ondatrinae), marks the beginning of Blancan III faunas. In both areas, the lowest occurrence is upsection from the Cochiti subchron of the Gilbert Chron. The panda *Parailurus* (Tedford and Gustafson 1977) appears to have immigrated with this first North American muskrat; the onager *Equus (Hemionus)* sp. and the first North American caprines may have also.

Once the muskrats entered North America, they became an abundant and widespread part of the fauna. The most primitive form, *Pliopotamys minor,* appears to have entered the United States by way of the Pacific Northwest and there encountered the Snake River drainage basin. It stayed in this major basin with little detectable evolution well into Blancan IV time. It was a very successful species there, but elsewhere it is unknown. Instead, more advanced forms called *Pliopotamys meadensis* are clearly in evidence in Blancan III deposits of southern Nevada and the Great Plains. There are not enough age data available in the plains area to determine whether *Pliopotamys meadensis* was a second microtine immigrant at 3.7 Ma, along with *P. minor,* possibly entering the United States by a different route east of the Cordillera, or derived from a population of *P. minor* that continued its dispersal southward and eastward beyond the Snake River drainage and evolved rather rapidly into a larger form with more derived dental characters. By early Blancan V time, *P. meadensis,* very nearly evolved into *Ondatra idahoensis,* spread westward (through Wyoming) with advanced *Pliophenacomys primaevus* or *P. osborni,* and both entered the Snake River drainage.

The morphological transition from *Pliopotamys meadensis* to *Ondatra idahoensis,* characteristic of Blancan V faunas, is very minor and seems to take place both in the plains area and in the Snake River basin. In comparison, the change from *Pliopotamys minor* to *Pliopotamys meadensis* in the Snake River basin seems to represent a major change in morphology that took place abruptly (between Sand Point and Flatiron Butte localities; numbers 33 and 36 in Appendix) in comparison with the long history of *P. meadensis* evolution in the plains (from Deer Park to Dixon localities; numbers 28 and 47 in Appendix). This situation suggests that *P. meadensis* immigrated into the Snake River area from the plains and displaced the native *P. minor.*

Within the endemic fauna of the United States, the small species *Mimomys (Ophiomys) mcknighti-taylori* of Blancan II time evolved into *M. (O.) taylori,* characteristic of Blancan III faunas of the Snake River basin, as has been mentioned. *M. (O.) mcknighti* is also known from northern California, and farther south it appears to have evolved into a different species, *M. (O.) magilli,* by Blancan III times, although there are no known Blancan II faunas showing an intermediate form. Although described from the Sand Draw Local Fauna of Nebraska (Hibbard 1972; locality 29 in Appendix), *M. (O.) magilli* is widespread in the southern United States and is known from the Panaca Local Fauna of southern Nevada (locality 26 in Appendix), in the Duncan Local Fauna of Arizona (UA7937), from Buttonwillow (locality 27 in Appendix) and Kettleman Hills (UC locality V3520), California, and from Beck Ranch, Texas (locality 31 in

Appendix). At Sand Draw and at Panaca, it is associated with *Pliopotamys meadensis.*

M. (Cosomys) sawrockensis, known from Blancan I deposits of northern and central California, appears to have evolved into *M. (Cosomys) primus* in the west, first known in late Blancan II faunas in Idaho and Washington. In the plains area, Zakrzewski (1967) has traced its development into the subgenus *Ogmodontomys* and through *M. (Ogmodontomys) poaphagus transitionalis* of the Blancan II Fox Canyon Local Fauna, to *M. (O.) poaphagus poaphagus* of the late Blancan II Rexroad 3 Local Fauna and the early Blancan III Sand Draw Local Fauna where it is associated with the oldest plains records of *Mimomys (Ophiomys)* and *Pliopotamys. M. (Ogmodontomys)* continued the evolutionary trends Zakrzewski has identified and by Blancan V had evolved high dentine tracts that break the enamel pattern at an early stage of wear. By this time, the lineage *M. (Cosomys)* had become extinct west of the Rocky Mountains.

The evolutionary pattern of the genus *Pliophenacomys* was documented by Hibbard and Zakrzewski (1972). They described the primitive characters of the species from the Blancan II Fox Canyon Local Fauna, *P. finneyi,* in comparison with *P. primaevus* from the undated type locality (UK-2) of Kansas and the early Blancan III Sand Draw Local Fauna of Nebraska. This evolutionary pattern consists primarily of increasing the height of dentine tracts, and the trend continued throughout the Blancan. A conspicuous increase in dentine tract height is evident in early Blancan IV faunas. The trend continues in Blancan V faunas where a new species, *Pliophenacomys osborni* Martin, is recognized.

The remarkably advanced genus *Pliolemmus* appears in Blancan II time (if the age assignment for the Bender Local Fauna, Kansas, is correct), derived from some stage of the *Pliophenacomys* lineage. It continues without change throughout the rest of the Blancan time in the Great Plains; *Pliolemmus* is the first North American microtine with rootless teeth.

Blancan IV (Event 5 to Event 6; 3.2 ± 0.2 to 2.6 ± 0.1 Ma)

As with the Blancan I dispersal event, about one million years followed the dispersal event marking the beginning of Blancan III faunas during which there was no introduction of exotic microtines. During this time, a variety of endemic trends in the microtine fauna of the United States permit recognition of a distinct Blancan IV fauna. The faunal changes, however, seem very provincial.

They were as follows:

1. In the Snake River basin, *Mimomys (Ophiomys) taylori* evolved into *M. (O.) taylori-parvus.* This change is first recognized in the Sand Point Local Fauna (locality 33 in Appendix) and is used to characterize the arbitrary faunal boundary. It is between 2.9 and 3.2 Ma on the basis of geomagnetic correlations (C. Neville, pers. com., 1979). *Pliopotamys minor* is present in this and other earlier Blancan IV faunas, *Pliopotamys meadensis* in later faunas; the change appears to be abrupt and to suggest dispersal of *P. meadensis* into the area rather than evolution within the Snake River basin. *Mimomys (Cosomys) primus* appears to have been extirpated before Blancan IV time in the Snake River basin (Neville et al. 1979), although it survived until about 3.0 Ma in southern California (C. Bacon, pers. com., 1980; locality 35 in Appendix).

2. An advanced form of *Pliophenacomys primaevus* with dentine tracts much more developed than that in the Sand Draw Local Fauna of Nebraska is present in the Benson and Mendevil Ranch faunas of Arizona which have been dated as 3.0 to 3.2 Ma by paleomagnetic correlation (Johnson et al. 1975). These are the oldest microtines in the San Pedro Valley of Arizona, and it is unknown whether they represent a new entry into the area. As has been mentioned, the Blancan I *Pliophenacomys* n. sp. of Lindsay and Jacobs is known from the Verde Local Fauna of a different part of Arizona.

3. In the Great Plains, *Mimomys (Ophiomys) magilli* appears to have disappeared by Blancan IV time, but a new species, *Mimomys (Ophiomys) meadensis* appeared. This species had an occlusal enamel pattern very similar to *Mimomys (Ophiomys) parvus* from Blancan V faunas of the Snake River basin but was much lower crowned and had less developed dentine tracts. In Blancan V time, contemporaneous with *M. (O.) parvus, M. (O.) meadensis* is known as far west as western Wyoming (locality 44 in Appendix) and southwestern Utah (Beaver, Utah, US Vertebrate loc. M1468). Its origin could have been out of *M. (O.) magilli,* but a record of the transition is lacking. The oldest record of *M. (O.) meadensis* in the Great Plains appears to be from its type locality in the latest Blancan IV Sanders Local Fauna of Kansas (locality 38 in Appendix).

In all, the species of *Mimomys (Ophiomys)* and dentine tract development in both *Pliophenacomys primaevus* and in *M. (Ogmodontomys) poaphagus* appear, at present, to be the most widespread guide for separation of Blancan III and IV faunas in the area east of Denver, but only *Pliophenacomys* appears in the Pacific Northwest and then not until earliest Blancan V time (G. Conrad, pers. com., 1980). There is, however, correlation of time with evolution of *Pliophenacomys* in Arizona, with *Mimomys* (*O.*) *magilli* in Arizona, Nevada, and California, and with *Pliopotamys meadensis* at different times in Idaho, Nevada, and Arizona. Projection of the time of the arbitrary boundary between Blancan III and IV into the Great Plains is not as uncertain as is that of the boundary between Blancan I and II.

In Europe, the microtine dispersal event correlative with the immigration of *Pliopotamys* into the United States introduced *Synaptomys* and *Lemmus*, genera that appeared later in North America, as well as *Villanyia*, a relative of *Lagurus* but not known in North America. This immigration into Europe is rather closely dated between the Vialette Local Fauna, France (3.9+ Ma) and the Etouaires Local Fauna, France (3.6 to 3.5 Ma) (Savage and Curtis 1970). There appears to be little possibility of confusion of correlative events in that a full million years separate this dispersal event from others.

This immigration of microtines separates the early Villafranchian (Arondelli-Triversa) faunas from the late Villafranchian (Rebielice) faunas. Again, about one million years follow before another dispersal event brought new microtines to Europe to introduce Villanyian faunas, dated by the Roca Neyra Local Fauna, France, as being 2.6 Ma (Savage and Curtis, 1970). In Europe there seems to be no evidence for subdivision of this time span on the basis of endemic evolution in the microtine fauna.

Blancan V (Event 6 to Event 7; 2.6 ± 0.1 to 1.9 ± 0.0 Ma)

There has been some discussion of faunal provincialism in the United States to this point. Mention has been made of differences in distribution-related northern or southern faunas, to apparent endemism of some forms in the Snake River drainage basin of the northwest, and to provincial criteria for recognition of Blancan II and IV microtine faunas. It was suggested that *Pliopotamys meadensis* might represent an immigrant to the United States at the same time as, but by a different route than, *Pliopotamys minor*; a route east of the Rocky Mountain Cordillera to the plains was suggested. But the microtine invasion of the United States which marks the beginning of Blancan V faunas was the first to clearly demonstrate two routes of dispersal from Beringia: one to the west of the Cordillera into the Pacific Northwest and another to the east into the Great Plains.

The presence of two subgenera of the lemming *Synaptomys* characterize Blancan V faunas. They represent the second microtine genus of North America with rootless teeth. Although primitive species, they represent the living subgenera *S.* (*Synaptomys*) and *S.* (*Mictomys*). The earliest records appear to be essentially simultaneous in the Grandview Local Fauna of Idaho, Tusker Local Fauna of Arizona, and Cita Canyon Local Fauna of Texas. The Tusker Local Fauna (locality 40 in Appendix) occurs about 3 meters below the Matuyama-Gauss polarity boundary (E. Lindsay, pers. com., 1978), and the Cita Canyon record (locality 46 in Appendix) is less than 4.5 meters below the same polarity epoch boundary (Lindsay et al. 1975). At Grandview (locality 41 in Appendix), the lowest discovered *Synaptomys* occurs a short distance above the top of the Gauss Chron (G. Conrad and C. Neville, pers. com., 1979). A distance of perhaps 10 meters in the magnetic polarity section crossing the Gauss-Matuyama boundary encompasses the first records of *Synaptomys* from Idaho to Texas.

In and west of the Rockies, the species *Synaptomys* (*Mictomys*) *vetus* Wilson is present in many faunas, but its range does not extend to the plains area until latest Blancan V where it is first found in the Borchers Local Fauna, Kansas (locality 50 in Appendix), in a slightly different form known as *Synaptomys* (*Mictomys*) *landesi* Hibbard. *Synaptomys* (*Synaptomys*) *rinkeri*, however, is the immigrant of the Plains Blancan V faunas. This subgenus persists to the modern fauna but is never found west of the Rockies. Its route of dispersal was likely east of the Canadian Rockies. Subsequent dispersal events increasingly show these two avenues of dispersal from Beringia to the United States.

Although not common in Blancan V faunas, *Lepus* or *Lepus*-like advanced leporids immigrated into the United States with *Synaptomys* and are associated with microtines in the Tusker Local Fauna, Arizona (Downey 1962); Thayne Local Fauna, Wyoming (US Cenozoic locality 22613); California Wash, Arizona (Lindsay and Tessman 1974); and Borchers, Kansas (Hibbard 1941*b*). Large species of *Hypolagus* (cf. *regalis* in the plains and cf. *vetus* in the west) are known only from very early Blancan V faunas, although smaller species persist to the beginning of the Irvingtonian.

In the endemic fauna of the United States, Blancan V is characterized by *Ondatra idahoensis* (although its difference from *Pliopotamys meadensis* is slight), *Mimomys* (*Ophiomys*) *parvus* out of *M.* (*O.*) *taylori-parvus* in the Snake River drainage, *M.* (*O.*) *meadensis* carries on from latest Blancan IV faunas, *Pliophenacomys osborni* with very extended dentine tracts, and *Mimomys*

(*Ogmodontomys*) *monohani* with very extended dentine tracts.

In Europe, the correlative microtine dispersal event introduced *Kislangia, Lagurodon,* and *Clethrionomys* to characterize Villanyian faunas, the earliest of which may be the Roca Neyra Local Fauna, France, dated at 2.6 Ma. One of the youngest of these is the Le Coupet Local Fauna, France, dated as 1.95 Ma (Savage and Curtis 1970).

About 3 Ma, near the beginning of Blancan IV faunas, a marked cooling in ocean temperatures began (Shackleton and Opdyke 1977), the Bering Strait first opened up, as indicated by K-Ar dates in the area (Hopkins 1967), North Pacific mollusks first arrived in Iceland (Gladenkov 1978) and, roughly, North Atlantic-Arctic seals first appeared in the North Pacific (Repenning et al. 1979). By 2.4 Ma, this cooling trend, as indicated in deep-sea records (Shackleton and Opdyke 1977), climaxed in the first significant accumulation of continental ice. Boellstorff (1978) reports a pre-Nebraskan till in western Iowa of about this age, shortly after the Blancan V dispersal event, and evidence of permafrost is first reported in eastern Siberia (Sher et al. 1979) and northwestern Germany (Brunnacker et al. 1982).

According to European correlations, toward the end of the following Villanyian mammalian age, temperatures again rose, marking the Tegelen warm period (O. Fejfar, pers. com., 1979), and, in the correlative Blancan V mammal age, the second Beringian transgression occurred (Hopkins 1967). In Europe, the Villanyian age, and in North America, the Blancan age, terminated with the most marked change in microtine faunas known. In North America there was evidence of two pronounced microtine dispersal routes from Beringia, possibly indicating the growth of Cordilleran ice field, but there is no clear-cut evidence of continental glaciation: the Nebraskan glacial stage was yet to come.

Deep-sea records of changes in isotope and/or carbonate composition are inconclusive at the time of the Blancan-Irvingtonian boundary but do not seem to show a major cold period. In both Europe and North America, the faunal change from Villanyian to Biharian faunas and from Blancan V to Irvingtonian faunas is closely tied to the beginning of the Olduvai normal subchron of the Matuyama Chron and, as mentioned, is characterized by the most dramatic Holarctic microtine dispersal known. For the first time in the history of microtine rodents, fossil faunas of both Europe and North America are primarily composed of genera with rootless teeth. This change was earlier and more gradual in northern Asia (Repenning 1984).

Irvingtonian I (Event 7 to Event 8; 1.9 ± 0.0 to about 0.9 Ma)

The stratigraphic thicknesses (usually projected) between the Type "B" and Type "S" ashes (Naeser et al. 1973) are not great in the plains states. Boellstorff (1976) mentions 21.5 feet at the Borchers, Kansas (locality 50 in Appendix), fauna. These ashes essentially limit the age of known Irvingtonian I faunas. The position of the late Blancan V Borchers Local Fauna in the top of and immediately above the Type "B" ash, which is 1.9 to 2.0 Ma, indicates that closely overlying Irvingtonian I faunas, as the nearby Aries Local Fauna of Meade County, Kansas (J. Honey, pers. com., 1979; not in Appendix), are not as old as 2 Ma. The Sappa Local Fauna, Harlan County, Nebraska, (locality 58 in Appendix), underlies the 1.2 Ma Type "S" ash (G. Izett, pers. com., 1978) and is the youngest Irvingtonian I fauna here recognized, although the oldest Irvingtonian II faunas recognized here are not as old as 900,000 years: no faunas are known to be of an age within the 300,000 year span between the Type "S" ash and 900,000 years ago. The very early Irvingtonian I Wellsch Valley Local Fauna of Saskatchewan (locality 54 in Appendix) was deposited during the Olduvai subchron of the Matuyama Chron (Churcher and Stalker, in press). In Arizona, the oldest Irvingtonian Curtis Ranch Local Fauna (locality 51 in Appendix) immediately underlies and extends upward into rocks of normal polarity identified as the Olduvai subchron (Johnson et al. 1975). And in California (locality 53 in Appendix), the earliest microtine indicating an Irvingtonian age is upsection from a normal event in the Palm Springs Formation, which must be the Olduvai subchron (Opdyke et al. 1977).

The immigration of *Microtus* (in a restricted sense excluding *Lasiopodomys, Allophaiomys, Phaiomys, Pitymys, Alticola, Neodon, Pedomys,* and other less prominent genera sometimes included in *Microtus*), *Allophaiomys, Phenacomys,* and, apparently, *Proneofiber* characterizes Irvingtonian I microtine faunas. A good number of other mammals also arrived in North America with this dispersal event. *Microtus californicus* characterizes faunas west of the Rockies and, although known from a wider area than its modern distribution, is never known east of, or in, the Rockies. To the east, *Allophaiomys* is present in many faunas of the Great Plains and has been discussed in some detail (as a subgenus of *Microtus*) by van der Meulen (1978). Hibbard and Dalquest (1973) point out that the shortness of the incisor in *Pronefiber* (and living *Neofiber*) make it awkward to derive this genus from *Pliopotamys*. Although its ancestry is uncertain, it does not seem to be in North America and *Proneofiber* is here counted as an Irvingtonian I immigrant. *Allophaiomys* and *Proneofiber,* as well as their descendants, are not known west of the Rockies.

Within the endemic fauna of the United States, most older forms with rooted teeth become extinct by Irvingtonian I time, and microtine faunas of this age are characterized by forms with rootless teeth. *Mimomys (Ophiomys)*, *Mimomys (Ogmodontomys)*, *Pliolemmus*, and, except for the earliest Irvingtonian Wellsch Valley Local Fauna of Saskatchewan, *Pliophenacomys,* all vanished from the microtine fauna of the United States. *Ondatra idahoensis* evolved into *Ondatra annectens* largely by increasing in size and developing more cementum on the teeth. *Synaptomys (Mictomys) landesi* evolved into *S. (M.) kansasensis* more or less following a straight-line change in characters leading to the living *S. (M.) borealis*; in California, *S. (M.) kansasensis* is known from the El Casco Local Fauna (locality 52 in Appendix). This change into species predominantly characterized by rootless teeth was the most distinctive change in the microtine history of North America.

The primitive species *Microtus paroperarius* Hibbard is an Irvingtonian I immigrant to North America and is well represented in the Wellsch Valley Local Fauna of Saskatchewan (Churcher and Stalker, in press). It is not known in the Great Plains of the United States, however, until Irvingtonian II faunas. There seems to be little reason for this delay in dispersal unless it relates to former temperatures and their decline. Boellstorff (1978), on the basis of interbedded ashes in western Iowa, estimates the age of the Nebraskan glacial till to be about 1.0 Ma, so that Irvingtonian I faunas may have experienced increasing cold and possibly *M. paroperarius* moved southward ahead of the glacial advance.

In Europe, *Allophaiomys*, *Dicrostonyx*, *Prolagurus*, *Microtus*, *Neodon*, and the immigrant species *Mimomys (Hintonia) savini* and *Pliomys lenki* first appear as new immigrants in the early Biharian faunas and are correlated with the Olduvai paleomagnetic event in one locality (Repenning 1983*a*). The end of the Biharian Mammal Age correlates well with the end of Irvingtonian faunas in the United States, and there appears to have been a late Biharian southward dispersal of microtines in Europe that correlates with that which subdivides the Irvingtonian in the United States (Repenning 1984). In addition, two of the new genera immigrants to Europe at the beginning of Biharian time are immigrants to the Great Plains in Irvingtonian II time: *Microtus*, as just mentioned, and *Pitymys* (Repenning 1983*b*). The other Irvingtonian II immigrants is *Clethrionomys*. The delay in dispersal

southward by *M. paroperarius* to the United States and the similarity of some of the Irvingtonian II immigrants to early Biharian immigrants point to an environmental cause for the mid-Irvingtonian dispersal, possibly the Nebraskan glaciation as just mentioned.

The dispersal of *Microtus* to California and Nevada but not to the Great Plains, the dispersal of *Allophaiomys* and presumably *Proneofiber* to the Great Plains but not to the West Coast area, and the apparent delay of some genera to move southward from the Canadian plains all indicate some barrier between two major dispersal routes from the Beringian arctic to the United States. This barrier was suggested by earlier immigrations, particularly that of the two subgenera of *Synaptomys*, but from Irvingtonian I time to the present, the microtine faunal provinciality on either side of the Rockies is marked and reflected in the immigrants to each province. It is inferred that the barrier was the development of the Cordilleran ice field before the Nebraskan glacial episode. Toward the end of Irvingtonian I time, about the time of the Type "S" ash in the Great Plains, Kent et al. (1971) note a pronounced increase in ice-rafted detritus in the northern part of the North Pacific basin.

Irvingtonian II (Event 8 to Event 9; 900,000 to 400,000 ± 25,000 years ago)

As has been just mentioned, east of the Rockies in the United States, the abrupt appearance of *Microtus paroperarius* in most faunas younger than the Jaramillo normal subchron from Colorado to Maryland is a prominent biochronologic event that makes the presence of *M. paroperarius* in Saskatchewan during the Olduvai normal subchron very surprising. In addition, most of these same faunas have the first United States records of *Pitymys meadensis*, which is known from the Mississippi River to southern Colorado and from three California localities. One of these, Centerville Beach Local Fauna (locality 61 in Appendix), is from strata above the Jaramillo subchron of the Matuyama Chron that ends 900,000 years ago. In southern Colorado, the Alamosa faunal succession (locality 62 in the Appendix) begins in the reversely magnetized deposits of the Matuyama Chron younger than Jaramillo subchron and persists in the section well into the Brunhes Chron of normal polarity, nearly to 600,000 years ago. Two faunas in Kansas are associated with the 600,000-year-old Type "O" ash. The other localities have no external basis for age control. However, at one California locality, North Livermore Avenue (locality 64 in Appendix), the association with five living rodent species suggests a much younger age than the 600,000-year-old Cudahy Local Fauna of Kansas (locality 72 in Appendix) which has a high percentage of extinct rodent species. Whether *Pitymys meadensis* came to areas west of the Rockies from Beringia or from the Great Plains seems unanswerable at present, but the weight of suggestion is on the side of its westward dispersal from the Great Plains (see Repenning 1983*b*). Its occurrence with *Microtus paroperarius* in the Irvingtonian II Alamosa Local Fauna of Colorado (locality 62 in Appendix; Rogers 1985) near the south end of the Rockies suggests this latter dispersal route.

In the plains area, the endemic microtine fauna continued to evolve. *Allophaiomys* of Irvingtonian I age evolved into *Allophaiomys guildayi* and possibly into *Pedomys llanensis* by mid-Irvingtonian II time (van der Meulen 1978). Other Irvingtonian evolutionary changes include *Neofiber* from *Proneofiber*, *S.* (*Mictomys*) *meltoni* from *S.* (*M.*) *kansasensis*, and *S.* (*Synaptomys*) *cooperi* from Blancan V *Synaptomys* (*S.*) *rinkeri*.

West of the Rockies the record of Irvingtonian microtines is very weak; only an advanced *Ondatra idahoensis* and its derivative *Ondatra annectens*, the poorly understood *Synaptomys* ("*Metaxyomys*") *anzaensis* and *S.* (*Mictomys*) *kansasensis*, *Microtus californicus*, and *Pitymys meadensis* have been recognized in western Irvingtonian faunas, and, of these, only *Pitymys* is restricted to the Irvingtonian II faunas. There are no known Irvingtonian microtine faunas from the Pacific Northwest or from Nevada or Utah. This absence is believed to represent a deficiency in sampling.

As mentioned, on the basis of tuff correlations in southwestern Iowa, Boellstorff (1978) suggested that the Nebraskan glacial till of that area was about 1 Ma old. Holarctic correlation of microtine faunas and terrestrial events with ocean records indicate that the Nebraskan glaciers extended to Iowa more like 850,000 years ago (Repenning 1984), a timing that is supported by the sequence containing the Alamosa Local Fauna of Colorado (Rogers 1985). This would be in the early part of Irvingtonian II. Boellstorff also indicated that the classic Kansan glacial till of Iowa was younger than the Type "O" ash (600,000 years) or younger than mid-Irvingtonian II time.

Kukla (1977), in a very thorough synthesis of oxygen isotope stages, European loess sections and terraces, and Alpine and North European Pleistocene subdivisions, has correlated the boundary between the European Steinheimian and Biharian mammal ages with oxygen isotope Stage 12. As approximated by Emiliani's (1978) averaged composite Caribbean core, this would center on 400,000 years ago and, as the first maximum glaciation younger than 600,000 years ago in the deep-sea

record, would most probably be the time of the major surge of the Kansan glacial advance. The microtine invasion of Europe characterizing the early Steinheimian Mammal Age correlates well in composition with that which introduced the first Rancholabrean microtines into the United States (Repenning 1984). The microtine invasion of the United States which marks the beginning of the Rancholabrean Mammal Age is thus dated as being about 400,000 years old and is believed to correlate with the major advance of the multiple-staged Kansan glaciation.

Rancholabrean I (Event 9 and Event 10; 400,000 ± 25,000 to 150,000 ± 25,000 years ago)

The beginning of the Rancholabrean Mammal Age in the United States is characterized by the introduction of *Lagurus* and several new species of the genus *Microtus*. East of the Rockies the species *M. pennsylvanicus* is abruptly and widely distributed, replacing *Microtus paroperarius*. The two species seem similar enough so that a strong case of ancestor-descendant relationship could be made, but the abundance of each in many fossil faunas, in the absence of transitional forms, would seem to indicate that if such a relationship existed, its transitional evidence is in Asia and the record in the United States shows only abrupt replacement. West of the Rockies the monopoly of the territory held by *Microtus californicus* since the beginning of Irvingtonian time was broken by the first appearance of *Microtus montanus* and *Microtus mexicanus* in several faunas along the western flank of the Cordillera. These faunas are in Mexico, Arizona, Utah, possibly Colorado, and Idaho; much farther west, *Microtus californicus* remained dominant and is so today.

In the endemic Rancholabrean I faunas, *Pedomys illanensis* survived east of the Rockies but was replaced in time by the living *Pedomys ochrogaster*; *Pitymys meadensis* persists and is known also only from Mexico (Repenning 1983*b*), where it lives today in an obvious refuge situation as *Pitymys quasiater*. *Pitymys nemoralis* of the eastern plains and prairie states is quite similar but has some differences that make a close relationship with *P. meadensis* doubtful (Repenning 1983*b*). *Ondatra nebrascensis* is present and is intermediate between *Ondatra annectens* and living *O. zibethicus* but with considerable overlap of characters (Nelson and Semken 1970). *Synaptomys* (*Synaptomys*) *australis* appeared as a size variant, and *Synaptomys* (*Mictomys*) was restricted to its modern distribution and is not known from the Great Plains but is known from the Appalachian mountains and northern Utah as a form intermediate between *S.* (*M.*) *meltoni* and living *S.* (*M.*) *borealis* in what must have been a cold fauna (locality 73 in Appendix).

The general character of Rancholabrean I microtine faunas is the absence of several late Irvingtonian forms and of several late Rancholabrean forms in combination with *Microtus pennsylvanicus* to the east of the Rockies or *M. montanus* or *mexicanus* to the west. In addition, those larger mammals that characterize Rancholabrean faunas were present except, apparently, *Bison.*

In Europe, the beginning of Steinheimian faunas is marked by the appearance of *Lagurus, Arvicola,* and several species of *Microtus,* including the Eurasian equivalent of *M. pennsylvanicus, M. agrestris.* Other immigrants are recognized later in the Steinheimian, which does not include the Holocene but is subdivided into three faunal stages—Mauer, Swanscombe, and Taubach. Fejfar and Heinrich (1981, 1983) have introduced the Toringian age to include all faunas from the beginning of the Steinheimian to the present. The forms that first immigrate to characterize Swanscombe faunas are living species of *Dicrostonyx, Lemmus,* and *Lagurus* as well as species of *Microtus* including *oeconomus* and *gregalis* (Fejfar and Heinrich 1981); these also first appear together in North America and characterize Rancholabrean II faunas. Most of the characteristic microtines of Rancholabrean II are northern and appear in the fossil record of non-Alaskan United States only in cold faunas.

Tornewton Cave in Devonshire contains a succession of rodent faunas that begin with the Swanscombe invasion and extend into early Holocene (Kowalski 1967). British workers are currently trying to date these deposits, but the work is not complete. It is their opinion, on the basis of counting cold spells, that the oldest fauna, "Glutton Stratum," correlates with oxygen isotope Stage 6 (D. Bowen, pers. com., 1978). In Emiliani's (1978) composite Caribbean core, Stage 6 is the first cold stage younger than 12 to show equal or greater accumulation of continental ice and would thus seem most likely to have stimulated a Holarctic dispersal event out of Siberia. Tentatively, therefore, it is selected as the most likely time of introduction of Rancholabrean II microtines into North America (Repenning 1984).

There is no record of *Bison* in association with Rancholabrean I microtines.

Rancholabrean II (Event 10 to the present; 150,000 ± 25,000 years ago to today)

Rancholabrean II faunas are marked by the presence of *Dicrostonyx,* and *Lemmus,* as well as several living spe-

cies of *Microtus,* including *oeconomus, gregalis, xanthognathus, longicaudus,* and probably others. There is reason to suspect that some living species are endemic North American products; an example of such an endemic species could be *Microtus richardsoni,* which may have evolved out of *M. xanthognathus* in the late Wisconsinan or in the Holocene, but as yet the fossil record is far too incomplete to identify such derivations certainly. The microtine fauna of the United States is entirely modern in Rancholabrean II time, although distribution beyond modern ranges is characteristic of colder periods, of which there would appear to have been two since Stage 6, the dual advances of the Wisconsin glaciation.

The complex subdivision and apparent multiple invasions of the Steinheimian and post-Steinheimian microtine faunas of Europe appear to represent several cold periods; Fejfar and Heinrich (1981) recognize five invasions or reinvasions in Europe from the beginning of Steinheimian faunas 400,000 years ago. These appear to correlate with oxygen isotope Stages 12, 8, 6, 4, and 2. The present ability to recognize only two Rancholabrean invasions possibly results from less attention paid to late microtine faunas in the United States but may instead reflect the effect of extensive continental ice that would certainly have inhibited dispersal over long periods of time. In addition, what appears as changes in ranges with climatic changes in the United States may appear as invasions in Europe. If the frequency of invasions into the United States were less, the history should be easier to reconstruct.

DISCUSSION

Presented here is an outline of the history of the microtine rodents in the United States over the last 6 Ma. During this time, there were eight microtine dispersal events and two evolutionary gradations that enable the recognition of ten faunal subdivisions. The dispersal events consist of the invasion of new microtines from the north that changed the aspect of the microtine fauna of the United States. Between 6 and 2.6 Ma, these invasions were very nearly 1.10 Ma apart, between 2.6 Ma and 400,000 years ago, they reoccurred very nearly every 700,000 years. The last invasion followed the preceding one by only 300,000 years and took place only 150,000 years ago.

Seven of these eight microtine dispersal events have been correlated with similar invasions of Europe by independent dating and similarity of immigrants. On both sides of the Northern Hemisphere, most of these invasions can be correlated with cold spells. All of these invasions are rather precisely dated by cross-correlations between K-Ar dates, geomagnetic polarity scales, tephrochronology, and climatic interpretations.

On the basis of intercorrelation of other events with the tephrochronology of tills in southwestern Iowa reported by Boellstorff (1978), the first major pre-Nebraskan glaciation occurred about 2.4 Ma in the earliest part of the Blancan V mammal age and in agreement with the oxygen isotope record as reported by Shackleton and Opdyke (1977).

The major surge of the Nebraskan glacial advances (that which extended as far southward as southwestern Iowa) occurred 850,000 years ago at the beginning of the Irvingtonian II mammal age and following the initiation of marked increase in ice-transported debris in the North Pacific as reported by Kent et al. (1971). The major southward surge of the Kansan glacial stage must have taken place during oxygen isotope Stage 12 with the immigration of Rancholabrean I microtines and other mammals. Boellstorff (1978) does not offer evidence from southwest Iowa regarding later glacial advances; however, there are few choices left (Repenning 1984).

The next major accumulation of continental ice is marked by oxygen isotope Stage 6 and the Rancholabrean II microtine invasion into the United States, which may have been accompanied by *Bison*; this must mark the end of Illinoian ice advances as there are only oxygen stages 4 and 2 left for the two Wisconsin glacial advances.

During the period between 3.7 and 2.6 Ma, the last of the two-million-year-long periods between immigrations of exotic microtines, there was sufficient time for the endemic microtine fauna of the United States to evolve recognizably different faunas. Although vaguer in definition and more provincial in character than were the faunal changes brought about by invasions of the United States, this evolutionary change is here used to subdivide this period in microtine history. Blancan III and IV are thus separated by recognition of changes resulting from evolution in North America. Similarly, the long period of no invasion between about 4.8 and 3.7 Ma is also subdivided on the basis of endemic evolution.

With these two evolutionary subdivisions, the total of ten mammal ages defined on the basis of microtine rodent history are clearly established during the last 6 Ma. The faunas change markedly with latitude and the criteria change with longitude, but within the United States the temporal resolution is remarkably more precise than before possible. With a diagnostic fossil microtine fauna it is possible to tell time at any point in the last 5 Ma with a minimum precision of 270,000 years. This,

coupled with a minimal paleomagnetic determination, can easily reduce the uncertainty to 150,000 years. In late Irvingtonian or younger deposits, the microtine evidence in combination with climatic suggestion from the entire fauna and flora, when correlated with the deep-sea oxygen isotope stages, may reduce the margin of error to 25,000 years as, for example, the North Livermore Avenue fauna of California (locality 64 in Appendix).

Possibly of greatest future use would be the development of biochronologies for other rapidly and complexly evolving lineages. Some of these have become obvious in the study of faunas containing microtines. Leporids and hypsodont cricetids have seemed to be the most common associates that changed rapidly with time. Thanks to the great familiarity of John White with leporids, these lagomorphs already have been quite helpful, but the great and varied assortment of rapidly evolving "pack rats" will take considerable study before their detailed biochronology can be understood.

As it stands, the biochronology of the microtine rodents of the United States may be poorly documented in some geographic areas and weak in some periods of time, but it is functional and functioning. Many modern geologic interests are concerned with relatively recent geologic time. To these interests, a biochronology that has a minimum temporal resolution of 250,000 years beyond the range of C_{14} is the answer to many a prayer.

APPENDIX

Listed below by mammal age are brief descriptions of the microtine localities shown on the correlation chart. The author would be most grateful for any information about any microtine fauna not included or for corrections and additions for those that are. Locality numbers are not given if previously published in the cited reference.

Early Hemphillian

Native?: *Microtoscoptes* and *Goniodontomys*

(1) Jackson, Wyoming: Teton County, US Cenozoic loc. and UM loc.
  Microtine: *Goniodontomys disjunctus*.
  External Age Control: K-A 929 of Evernden et al. (1964), 9.2-Ma tuff 106 ft. stratigraphically below fossils.
  Reference: Hibbard (1959, 1970).
  Remarks: Associated with *Dipoides stirtoni*. Hibbard (1970) has called this locality the Kelley Road Local Fauna.

(2) Rome, Oregon: Malheur County, LA:CIT locs., US Vertebrate M locs.
    Microtine: *Goniodontomys disjunctus* (type loc.).
    External Age Control: None.
    Reference: Wilson (1937), Repenning (1968).
    Remarks: Associated with *Dipoides stirtoni*.

(3) Stroud Claim, Idaho: Gooding County, US Cenozoic loc.
    Microtine: *Microtoscoptes hibbardi*.
    External Age Control: K-Ar 830 of Evernden et al. (1964), 10.0-Ma ash bed in fossiliferous diatomite.
    Reference: Hibbard (1970).
    Remarks: Associated with *Dipoides stirtoni*.

(4) Bartlett Mtn., Oregon: Harney County, UO loc.
    Microtine: *Microtoscoptes hibbardi*.
    External Age Control: K-A 1225 of Evernden et al. (1964), 8.9-Ma basalt ± 600 ft. below fauna.
    References: Shotwell (1970).
    Remarks: Associated with *Dipoides stirtoni*.

(5) Rabbit Hole, Nevada: Pershing County, US Vertebrate loc. M1254, UC loc. V73117.
    Microtine: *Microtoscoptes hibbardi*.
    External Age Control: Stratigraphy is essentially continuous from Clarendonian faunas into early Hemphillian faunas.
    Reference: This chapter.
    Remarks: Associated with *Dipoides stirtoni*.

(6) Lemoyne, Nebraska: Keith County, UN loc.
    Microtine: *Microtoscoptes hibbardi* (type loc.).
    External Age Control: None.
    Reference: Martin (1975).
    Remarks: Associated with *Dipoides stirtoni*.

Late Hemphillian

Immigrant: *Promimomys*

Native: *Propliophenacomys*

(7) Christmas Valley, Oregon: Lake County, US Vertebrate loc.
    Microtine: *Promimomys mimus*.
    External Age Control: None.
    Reference: Repenning (1968).
    Remarks: This fauna is essentially identical to McKay, Oregon. Associated with *Dipoides smithi* and *Parapliosaccomys oregonensis*.

(8) McKay, Oregon: Umatilla County, UO loc.
    Microtine: *Promimomys mimus* (type loc.).

External Age Control: None.
Reference: Shotwell (1956).
Remarks: Associated with *Dipoides smithi* and *Parapliosaccomys oregonensis*.

(9) Lind Coulee, Washington: Grant County, US Vertebrate loc. M1438.
    Microtine: *Propliophenacomys parkeri*.
    External Age Control: Thvera (C₂) polarity event of Gilbert Chron with overlying reversed beds (Packer and Johnston 1979).
    Reference: This chapter.
    Remarks: Small fauna subsequently covered by St. Helens ash, preventing further collection to date.

(10) Devil's Nest, Nebraska: Knox County, UN loc.
     Microtine: *Propliophenacomys parkeri* (type loc.).
     External Age Control: Presumably same horizon as Santee, Nebraska.
     Reference: Martin (1975).
     Remarks: This collection was not examined.

(11) Santee, Nebraska: Knox County, UN loc.
     Microtine: *Propliophenacomys parkeri*.
     External Age Control: 1.6 miles south overlying beds contain 5.0 ± 0.2 Ma tuff (Boellstorff 1976).
     Reference: Voorhies (1977).
     Remarks: Associated with *Dipoides* sp. and *Hesperoscalops mcgrewi*.

(12) Mailbox, Nebraska: Antelope County, UN loc. AP-125.
     Microtine: *Promimomys mimus*.
     External Age Control: None. Although farther removed geographically from dated tuff at Santee, the fauna is clearly above the Cap Rock Member of Skinner et al. (1968) of the Ash Hollow Formation of Lugn (1938) and seems to be at about the same stratigraphic position as Santee and Devil's Nest cited above.
     Reference: Unpublished. Barbara Ruff (pers. com. 1978).
     Remarks: Associated with *Dipoides* sp. and *Parapliosaccomys* sp. This collection was not examined.

Blancan I

Immigrants: *Mimomys (Cosomys) sawrockensis*, *Mimomys (Ophiomys) mcknighti*, and *Nebraskomys* sp.

Native: *Pliophenacomys wilsoni* of Lindsay and Jacobs (1985).

(13) Upper Alturas, California: Modoc County, UO loc. 2424, CAS loc. 36805.

Microtines: *Mimomys (Ophiomys) mcknighti, Mimomys (Cosomys) sawrockensis.*

External Age Control: 70 ft. downsection from a basalt dated 4.7 ± 0.5 Ma: average of three measurements (M. Silberman, pers. com., 1978, FY78–75). About 10 ft. downsection from an ash bed whose chemical composition, on the basis of preliminary study, is identical to one in Deep Sea Drilling Project (DSDP) Core 34 judged to be 4.8 Ma on the basis of marine microfauna (A. Sarna-Wojcicki, pers. com. 1985).

Reference: This chapter.

Remarks: This locality is upsection from the Alturas Local Fauna dated by Everden et al. (1964). Associated with ?*Copemys vasquezi.*

(14) Verde, Arizona: Yavapai County, US Vertebrate loc. M1454: UA loc. 113–80.

Microtines: *Pliophenacomys* n. sp., *Nebraskomys rexroadensis.*

External Age Control: About 185 ft. upsection from a basalt dated 5.6 ± 0.2 Ma (Doell and Cox 1965). According to paleomagnetic correlations by Bressler and Butler (1978), fossils are about 6 ft. below the base of the Nunivak subchron of the Gilbert Chron.

Reference: This chapter.

Remarks: Fauna is under study by Nick Czaplewski; only the microtines and pack rats have been examined.

(15) Maxum, California: Contra Costa County, UC loc. V6869.

Microtine: *Mimomys (Cosomys) sawrockensis.*

External Age Control: None.

Reference: This chapter; May 1981.

Remarks: Associated with the hypsodont cricetid *Repomys maxumi,* known also from the Hemphillian (May 1981; May and Repenning 1982).

(16) Concha, Chihuahua: near Yepomera, UA loc. Y35.

Microtine: *Pliophenacomys wilsoni.*

External Age Control: From reversed beds just below normal event and well upsection from the late Hemphillian Yepomera Local Fauna (E. Lindsay and N. Johnson, pers. com., 1980). Here interpreted to underlie the Sidufjall (C₁) normal polarity subchron of the Gilbert Chron.

Reference: Jacobs and Lindsay (1981).

Remarks: Associated with a primitive species of horse, possibly transitional between *Pliohippus mexicanus* and *Dolichohippus simplicidens*; also *Prosigmodon* (Jacobs and Lindsay 1981).

(17) White Bluffs, Washington: Franklin County, UW loc.

Microtine: *Mimomys (Ophiomys) mcknighti* (type loc.).

External Age Control: Just above normal event in Ringold Formation paleomagnetic section (Packer 1979) here interpreted to represent the Sidufjall (C₁) normal polarity subchron of the Gilbert Chron. Paleomagnetic section continues upward to the base of a normal event above the Haymaker's Orchard loc. of Blancan II age which is interpreted here as recording the base of the Cochiti subchron, if not younger deposits.

Reference: Gustafson (1978, 1985).

Remarks: Associated with the White Bluffs Local Fauna of Gustafson, including a primitive species of the horse *Dolichohippus, Dipoides rexroadensis,* and *Thomomys* sp.

(18) Saw Rock Canyon, Kansas: Seward County, UK and UM locs.

Microtine: *Mimomys (Cosomys) sawrockensis* (type loc.).

External Age Control: None.

References: Hibbard (1949, 1957, 1964, 1967), Zakrzewski (1967).

Remarks: Associated with *Hesperoscalops sewardensis.*

Blancan II

Immigrants: None.

Natives: *Mimomys (Ophiomys) mcknighti-taylori, Mimomys (Cosomys) primus, Mimomys (Ogmodontomys) poaphagus transitionalis, Mimomys (Ogmodontomys) poaphagus poaphagus, Pliophenacomys finneyi, Nebraskomys rexroadensis,* and *Pliolemmus antiquus.*

(19) Haymaker's Orchard, Washington: Franklin County, US Vertebrate loc. M1439.

Microtine: *Mimomys (Ophiomys) mcknighti-taylori.*

External Age Control: Near top of reversed polarity section just below normal event possibly in the Ringold Formation paleomagnetic section of Packer (1979). Here interpreted as probably just below Cochiti normal subchron of Gilbert Reversed Chron. Same exposures as White Bluff.

Reference: This chapter, Gustafson (1985).

Remarks: Interpretation of Cochiti subchron depends on an interpretation that the Nunivak subchron was missed in a part of the underlying section with no paleomagnetic control (Packer 1979). This is the only known occurrence of this transitional form between *M. (O.) mcknighti* and the younger *M. (O.) taylori*. The associated fauna is not significant as far as has been discovered except that in an abundance of *Mimomys* specimens there was no sign of *Pliopotamys*.

(20) Lowest Hagerman, Idaho: Twin Falls County, UM locs. below 2,950-ft. elevation.

Microtine: *Mimomys (Cosomys) primus.*

External Age Control: 38 to 88 ft. above the Cochiti subchron of the Gilbert Chron; below the lowest occurrence of *Pliopotamys minor* (Neville et al. 1979).

Reference: Zakrzewski (1969).

Remarks: The occurrence of *Pliopotamys minor,* marking Blancan III faunas, occurs at about the same distance above the Cochiti subchron at Taunton, Washington.

(21) Fox Canyon, Kansas: Meade County, UM loc.

Microtines: *Pliophenacomys finneyi* (type loc.), *Mimomys (Ogmodontomys) poaphagus transitionalis* (type loc.).

External Age Control: None. Lindsay et al. (1975) indicate that the deposits are reversely magnetized.

References: Hibbard (1950), Hibbard and Zakrzewski (1972), Zakrzewski (1967).

Remarks: Associated with *Hesperoscalops rexroadi.*

(22) Rexroad 3, Kansas: Meade County, UK and UM locs.

Microtines: *Mimomys (Ogmodontomys) poaphagus poaphagus* (type loc.), *Nebraskomys rexroadensis* (type loc.).

External Age Control: None. Lindsay et al. (1975) indicate that the deposits are normally magnetized.

References: Hibbard (1941a, 1952, 1972).

Remarks: Associated with *Dipoides rexroadensis.* At least since Hibbard (1958), the Hagerman Local Fauna has been considered somewhat younger than the Rexroad Local Fauna. In consideration of the entire rodent fauna, Zakrzewski (1969) concurred. In consideration of the carnivores, Bjork (1970) concluded that they were of different age but could not demonstrate which was older. The microtines are of little help in this concern except that both faunas are clearly younger than *Mimomys sawrockensis;* a provincialism in the evolution in the Great Plains and in the western microtines is as evident as in the carnivores and is more expectable. If the lack of *Pliopotamys* in the Rexroad is of age significance, this fauna would seem older than most of the Hagerman faunal succession; but the *Pliopotamys* in the somewhat younger (on the basis of the slight evolution of *Mimomys [Ogmodontomys] poaphagus*) Deer Park and Sand Draw faunas may not mark the earliest time that this genus and lineage appeared in the United States. It seems possible that *Pliopotamys* arrived through the Pacific Northwest and did not reach the Great Plains until some later time after evolving into *P. meadensis* and that, therefore, Rexroad may be pre-*Pliopotamys* of the Plains but the same age as the Hagerman. The Hart Draw Local Fauna (30) seems to indicate that Rexroad, Bender, Deer Park, and Sand Draw cannot be younger than Hagerman.

(23) Bender, Kansas: Meade County, UM locs.

Microtines: *Mimomys (Ogmodontomys) poaphagus poaphagus, Pliolemmus antiquus.*

External Age Control: None. Lindsay et al. indicate that the deposits are normally magnetized.

References: Zakrzewski (1967), Hibbard (1972).

Remarks: Zakrzewski (1967) mentions a second locality that he assigns to the Bender Local Fauna and that contains a very advanced *Mimomys (Ogmodontomys) poaphagus,* more so than from Deer Park and Sand Draw. This referred fauna, UM loc. K2–57, is in Hart Draw and is downsection from the Sanders Local Fauna (see section in Hart Draw, Stop 5 in Bayne, 1976, pp. 33–34, labeled "Rexroad fauna"). The advanced nature of the *M. (O.) poaphagus* from this locality is here taken to indicate a much younger age than the Bender form, an age comparable to Beck Ranch, Texas. In terms of development of dentine tracts, *M. (O.) poaphagus poaphagus* from Rexroad 3, Bender, Deer Park, and Sand Draw and *Pliophenacomys primaevus* from Sand Draw are much more primitive than comparable specimens from Hart Draw, Beck Ranch, and White Rock (assignable to *M. [O.] monohani* and *Pliophenacomys osborni*). Although in the Great Plains pediplane, overlying the surface cut on

Late Cretaceous or older rocks, it is difficult to assume any significant continuity between overlapping channels, Lindsay et al. (1975) report that both the Hart Draw Local Fauna and the overlying Sanders Local Fauna are in normally magnetized deposits overlain by a short reversed section. This paleomagnetic pattern, in combination with the advanced nature of *M. (O.) poaphagus* described by Zakrzewski, seems to best fit the Gauss/Matuyama Chron boundary. This collection was not examined.

Blancan III

Immigrant: *Pliopotamys minor,* possibly *Pliopotamys meadensis* by a route east of the Cordillera.

Natives: Possibly *Pliopotamys meadensis* by evolution out of *Pliopotamys minor, Mimomys (Cosomys) primus, Mimomys (Ogmodontomys) poaphagus, Mimomys (Ophiomys) taylori, Mimomys (Ophiomys) magilli, Mimomys (Ophiomys) fricki, Pliophenacomys primaevus, Pliolemmus antiquus, Nebraskomys mcgrewi.*

(24) Taunton, Washington: Adams County, LA loc.
   Microtine: *Pliopotamys minor.*
   External Age Control: Reversed section overlying normal event (Packer and Johnston 1979) here interpreted to represent the Cochiti subchron of the Gilbert Chron.
   References: Tedford and Gustafson (1977), Gustafson (1985).
   Remarks: Associated with the *Parailurus* sp. and *Hypolagus* "vetus."

(25) Hagerman, Idaho: Twin Falls County, many localities above 2,950 ft. elevation recorded by USNM, UM, UC, ISU, UO, US, and others.
   Microtines: *Pliopotamys minor* (type loc.), *Mimomys (Ophiomys) taylori* (type loc.), *Mimomys (Cosomys) primus.*
   External Age Control: From 88 ft. above the Cochiti subchron of the Gilbert Chron to well into the Gauss Chron (Neville et al. 1979). K-A dates cited in same reference.
   References: Zakrzewski (1969), Bjork (1970).
   Remarks: All of Blancan III is recorded in the many localities at Hagerman, but the fauna is provincial and confined to the ancient Snake River drainage of the Pacific Northwest.

(26) Panaca, Nevada: Lincoln County, F:AM locs. "Limestone Corner," "Rodent Quarry."

Microtines: *Mimomys (Ophiomys) magilli, Pliopotamys meadensis?*
   External Age Control: None.
   References: This chapter, May (1981).
   Remarks: Stock (1921) originally described fossils from this area which indicate that the deposits also contain Hemphillian fossils in their older parts. The Blancan fauna is similar to Sand Draw.

(27) Buttonwillow, California: Kern County, UC loc.
   Microtine: *Mimomys (Ophiomys) magilli.*
   External Age Control: Barbat and Galloway (1934) describe the containing rocks as being from the upper part of the San Joaquin Formation, which is of Blancan age and contains a mammal fauna that has been compared with the Hagerman Local Fauna. See Repenning (1976).
   References: Hesse (1934), Wilson (1937).
   Remarks: The specimens are from a well core. Similar material was collected in the upper part of the San Joaquin Formation of the Kettleman Hills, California, by A. C. Hall in about 1936 (UC loc. V3520), but his locality information is confused.

(28) Deer Park, Kansas: Meade County, UK loc.
   Microtines: *Mimomys (Ogmodontomys) poaphagus poaphagus, Pliopotamys meadensis* (type loc.), *Pliolemmus antiquus* (type loc.).
   External Age Control: None.
   References: Hibbard (1956), Zakrzewski (1969).
   Remarks: As indicated under Rexroad 3 (22) and Bender (23), age assignment of Blancan III faunas from the Great Plains is here based upon the evolutionary stage of *M. (O.) poaphagus* and *Pliophenacomys primaevus,* or both. Zakrzewski (1967) notes that the teeth of *M. (O.) poaphagus* from this locality are the same as those from Rexroad 3; Hibbard (in Skinner and Hibbard, 1972) states that the fusion of the anterior roots of M^3 from Sand Draw distinguishes these specimens from those from Rexroad 3. In addition, the presence in Sand Draw of *M. (Ophiomys) magilli,* which appears to be derived from *M. (O.) mcknighti-taylori* of the Pacific Northwest, suggests that its arrival in the plains area separates the Deer Park from Sand Draw. For these reasons, Deer Park is considered slightly older than Sand Draw. This collection was not examined.

(29) Sand Draw, Nebraska: Brown County, UM locs.
   Microtines: *Mimomys (Ogmodontomys) poaphagus*

poaphagus, Mimomys (Ophiomys) magilli (type loc.), "*Mimomys (Ophiomys)*" *fricki* (type loc.), *Nebraskomys mcgrewi* (type loc.), *Pliophenacomys primaevus, Pliopotamys meadensis, Pliolemmus antiquus.*

External Age Control: Essentially none; unconformably overlain by the "first evidence" of continental glaciation.

Reference: Skinner and Hibbard (1972).

Remarks: According to Hibbard (1972), *M. (O.) poaphagus poaphagus* differs from the type from Rexroad 3 only in that three out of four M³ had the two anterior roots fused. The two teeth that are the type of *M. (O.) fricki* resemble unworn specimens of *Nebraskomys mcgrewi,* but this collection was not examined.

(30) Hart Draw, Kansas: Meade County, UM loc.

Microtine: *Mimomys (Ogmodontomys) poaphagus.*

External Age Control: From deposits with normal polarity here interpreted to represent the Gauss Chron; see discussion under Bender Local Fauna (23).

Reference: Zakrzewski (1967).

Remarks: This is locality UM– K2–57. I have been unable to determine from the literature what other mammals were found. The collection was not examined.

(31) Beck Ranch, Texas: Scurry County, Midwestern University loc.

Microtines: *Mimomys (Ophiomys) magilli, Mimomys (Ogmodontomys) poaphagus, Pliophenacomys primaevus.*

External Age Control: None.

Reference: Dalquest (1978).

Remarks: *M. (O.) poaphagus* is advanced with quite high dentine tracts on M_1 and a single large anterior root on M³. *Pliophenacomys primaevus* is represented only by an M³ that has dentine tracts high enough to break the enamel pattern on the occlusal surface.

Blancan IV

Immigrant: None.

Natives: *Mimomys (Ophiomys) taylori-parvus, Mimomys (Ophiomys) meadensis, Mimomys (Cosomys) primus, Mimomys (Ogmodontomys) poaphagus, Pliophenacomys primaevus-osborni, Pliopotamys minor, Pliopotamys meadensis, Pliolemmus antiquus.*

(32) Benson, Arizona: Cochise County, UA locs.

Microtine: *Pliophenacomys* sp.

External Age Control: Just below Mammoth reversed subchron of Gauss Chron (Johnson et al. 1975).

Reference: Lindsay and Tessman (1974).

Remarks: This collection was not examined.

(33) Sand Point, Idaho: Owyhee County, US Cenozoic locs.

Microtines: *Mimomys (Ophiomys) taylori-parvus, Pliopotamys minor.*

External Age Control: In reversed beds above normal beds (C. Neville, pers. com., 1979), here interpreted to be in the Mammoth subchron of the Gauss although the Kaena reversed subchron cannot be ruled out.

References: Hibbard (1959), Hibbard and Zakrzewski (1967).

Remarks: Many researchers have carefully prospected this locality, and no indication of *Mimomys (Cosomys) primus* has been found. In fact, it is not found in the youngest localities at Hagerman (Zakrzewski 1969). It seems to have become extinct in the Snake River drainage by this time although it lived longer in southern California.

There is no demonstrable evolution in *Pliopotamys minor,* and this is its youngest occurrence. The microtines are associated with *Paracryptotis gidleyi, Hypolagus* sp. cf. *H. vetus, Castor californicus?, Thomomys* sp., mastodont, and *Dolichohippus* cf. *simplicidens. Hypolagus vetus* became extinct at the end of Blancan IV time and is not known from the younger Grand View Local Fauna.

(34) Mendevil Ranch, Arizona: Cochise County, UA loc.

Microtine: *Pliophenacomys primaevus-osborni.*

External Age Control: Normal polarity deposits between Mammoth and Kaena reversed subchron of the Gauss Chron (Johnson et al. 1975).

Reference: Lindsay and Tessman (1974).

Remarks: Very well-developed dentine tracts on the specimens.

(35) Coso Mountains, California: Inyo County, LA:CIT loc.

Microtine: *Mimomys (Cosomys) primus* (type loc.).

External Age Control: 3 Ma by dates on tuffs and flows above and below loc. (Bacon et al. 1979; C. Bacon, pers. com., 1980).

References: Wilson (1932), Schultz (1937).

Remarks: Associated with *Paraneotoma fossilis,* known also from localities 32, 31, and Duncan, Ariz. (UA 7937, Y. Tomida, pers. com.).

(36) Flatiron Butte, Idaho: Owyhee County, ISU loc.

Microtines: *Mimomys (Ophiomys) taylori-parvus, Pliopotamys meadensis.*

External Age Control: Deposits all normal polarity, upper Gauss Chron (C. Neville, pers. com., 1979).

Reference: This chapter.

Remarks: This is one of several localities discovered by Greg Conrad, ISU, between Sand Point and Grand View. They support and strengthen Hibbard and Zakrzewski's (1967) interpretation of the evolution of *Ophiomys taylori* into *Ophiomys parvus* of the Grand View Local Fauna, the extinction of the large species *Hypolagus vetus,* and the time of immigration of the first lemming in the United States, *Synaptomys.* This fauna is the oldest known record of *Pliopotamys meadensis* in the Snake River drainage basin.

(37) Sanders, Kansas: Meade County, UM and UK loc.

Microtines: *Mimomys (Ophiomys) meadensis* (type loc.), *Pliolemmus antiquus.*

External Age Control: Possibly just below Matuyama Chron (Lindsay et al. 1975). See discussion of Bender and Hart Draw localities (nos. [23] and [30]).

References: Hibbard (1956), Skinner and Hibbard (1972).

Remarks: This the oldest record of *M. (O.) meadensis,* which is more primitive than *M. (O.) parvus* in having much less development of dentine tracts and a shorter incisor. However, the two have a very similar dental pattern. Possibly the difference can again be attributed to provincialism, and *M. (O.) meadensis* was derived from *M. (O.) magilli,* whereas *M. (O.) parvus* was derived from *M. (O.) taylori* in the Snake River drainage. This collection was not examined.

(38) Broadwater, Nebraska: Morrill County, UN loc.

Microtines: *Pliopotamys meadensis, Pliophenacomys primaevus, ?Ogmodontomys poaphagus.*

External Age Control: None.

References: Schultz and Stout (1948), Skinner and Hibbard (1972).

Remarks: As far as I am aware, only parts of this fauna have been described, and, except for Martin (1972) and Schultz et al. (1972), who give

some description of the Broadwater *Pliopotamys,* the microtines are not included in these parts. Faunal lists abound, however, and show considerable difference in the included microtines. This collection was not examined. Its age assignment is problematical.

Blancan V

Immigrants: *Synaptomys (Mictomys) vetus, Synaptomys (Synaptomys) rinkeri.*

Natives: *Mimomys (Ophiomys) parvus, Mimomys (Ophiomys) meadensis, Mimomys (Ogmodontomys) monohani, Pliophenacomys osborni, Pliopotamys meadensis, Ondatra idahoensis, Pliolemmus antiquus, Synaptomys (Mictomys) landesi, Nebraskomys mcgrewi.*

(39) Boyle Ditch, Wyoming: Teton County, US Cenozoic loc.

Microtine: *Pliophenacomys osborni, Synaptomys, Ondatra.*

External Age Control: None.

Reference: Taylor (1966, his locality 38).

Remarks: Very well-developed dentine tracts on *Pliophenacomys.* C. W. Hibbard (pers. com. to J. D. Love 1967) first examined this material and A. D. Barnosky has recollected this fauna (pers. com. 1982).

(40) Tusker, Arizona: Graham County, UA loc.

Microtines: *Pliopotamys meadensis, Pliophenacomys osborni, Synaptomys (Mictomys) vetus.*

External Age Control: Deposits with normal polarity and 10 ft. downsection from the Matuyama-Gauss boundary according to E. Lindsay (pers. com. 1978).

References: Lindsay and Tessman (1974), Downey (1962), Cantwell (1969).

Remarks: Associated with "*Lepus*" and small *Hypolagus. Synaptomys* is the second rootless microtine in North America.

(41) Wild Horse Butte, Idaho: Owyhee County, UO and ISU locs.

Microtines: *Mimomys (Ophiomys) parvus, Synaptomys (Mictomys) vetus, Ondatra idahoenis.*

External Age Control: Several localities on either side of the Matuyama-Gauss boundary according to G. Conrad and C. Neville (pers. com., 1979).

Reference: Shotwell (1970).

Remarks: G. Conrad reports only the small *Hypolagus furlongi.*

(42) Ninefoot Rapids, Idaho: Owyhee County, ISU locs.
Microtines: *Mimomys (Ophiomys) taylori-parvus, Synaptomys (Mictomys) vetus, Pliophenacomys osborni.*
External Age Control: None.
Reference: This chapter.
Remarks: G. Conrad has collected *Hypolagus limnetus* (a small Hagerman form), *Hypolagus furlongi* (a small Grand View form), and the large *Hypolagus vetus*. These, in addition to the intermediate nature of *M. (O.) taylori-parvus,* suggest that this fauna may be the oldest known Blancan V fauna.

(43) Grand View, Idaho: (Jackass Butte), Owyhee County, LA:CIT, UO, ISU, US, and other locs.
Microtines: *Synaptomys (Mictomys) vetus* (type loc.), *Mimomys (Ophiomys) parvus* (type loc.), *Ondatra idahoensis* (type loc.).
External Age Control: Lower reversed part of the Matuyama Chron (Neville et al. 1979). Paleomagnetic samples from two sections on the east and on the west sides of Jackass Butte record one short normal event upsection from the principal rodent faunas which, because it was found on both sides of the Butte at the same approximate elevation, may represent one of the Reunion subchrons rather than secondary polarization of reversed sediments.

(44) Thayne, Wyoming: Lincoln County, US Cenozoic loc. 22613.
Microtines: *Synaptomys (Mictomys) vetus, Mimomys (Ophiomys) meadensis, Ondatra idahoenis?*
External Age Control: None.
Reference: Taylor (1966, his loc. 39)
Remarks: The small amount of ondatrine material is insufficient for specific identification, and, hence, the genus *Pliopotamys* might equally be applicable.

(45) California Wash, Arizona: Cochise County, UA loc.
Microtines: *Synaptomys (Mictomys) vetus, Ondatra idahoensis.*
External Age Control: Reversed bed in the early Matuyama Chron (Johnson et al. 1975).
Reference: Lindsay and Tessman (1974).
Remarks: None.

(46) Cita Canyon, Texas: Randall County, UC loc.
Microtines: *Synaptomys* sp., *Pliopotamys* sp., *Pliophenacomys* sp., *Pliolemmus* sp.

External Age Control: Fifteen ft. and less downsection from the Gauss-Matuyama Chron boundary (Lindsay et al. 1975).
Reference: G. Schultz (1977).
Remarks: Schultz reports a large *Hypolagus* cf. *regalis*. The presence of a large species of *Hypolagus* suggests that this fauna may be as old as Ninefoot Rapids, Idaho (42). This collection was not examined.

(47) Dixon, Kansas: Kingman County, UM and UK locs.
Microtines: *Mimomys (Ophiomys) meadensis, Synaptomys (Synaptomys) rinkeri* (type loc.), *Pliopotamys meadensis, Pliophenacomys osborni, Pliolemmus antiquus.*
External Age Control: None.
References: Hibbard (1956); Skinner and Hibbard (1972); Eshelman (1975).
Remarks: This collection was not examined.

(48) White Rock, Kansas: Republic County, UM and UK locs.
Microtines: *Mimomys (Ophiomys) meadensis, Mimomys (Ogmodontomys) monohani, Ondatra idahoensis, Synaptomys (Synaptomys) rinkeri, Pliophenacomys osborni, ?Nebraskomys mcgrewi.*
External Age Control: None.
Reference: Eshelman (1975).
Remarks: Eshelman reports only small species of *Hypolagus*. This collection was not examined.

(49) Mullen, Nebraska (part): Cherry and Hooker counties, UN locs.
Microtines: *Pliophenacomys osborni* (UN loc. Ho–102 type loc.), *Mimomys (Ogmodontomys) monohani* (UN loc. Cr–10 type loc.), *Ondatra idahoensis* (UN loc. Cr–10).
External Age Control: None.
Reference: Martin (1972).
Remarks: As noted by Martin, several (possibly four) different ages may be represented in the six localities grouped under this name. All three microtines were recovered from UN loc. Cr–10, Pit 3, but so were obviously younger microtines (Martin 1972).

(50) Borchers, Kansas: Meade County, UK loc.
Microtines: *Synaptomys (Mictomys) landesi* (type loc.), *Ondatra idahoensis.*
External Age Control: In the top of and just above the Type B ash dated as 1.9 to 2.0 Ma (Naeser et al. 1973).

References: Hibbard (1941b, 1954, 1967).

Remarks: *S. (M.) landesi* is not greatly advanced over *S. (M.) vetus* toward the living species. *Ondatra idahoensis* is not well represented; the differences between *Pliopotamys meadensis* and this species are slight and qualitative: *O. idahoensis* averages somewhat larger and has some cement in the reentrant angles of many, but not all, individuals, and *P. meadensis* averages somewhat smaller and has no cement in the reentrants of many, but not all, individuals. *Lepus* is reported from this locality, apparently the oldest record from the plains. See remarks under Curtis Ranch Local Fauna (no. 51).

Irvingtonian I

Immigrants: *Phenacomys* sp., *Microtus californicus, Microtus paroperarius, Allophaiomys* sp., *Proneofiber guildayi.*

?Native: *Synaptomys ("Metaxyomys") anzaensis.*

Natives: *Synaptomys (Mictomys) kansasensis, Ondatra annectens, Pliophenacomys osborni* (early).

(51) Curtis Ranch, Arizona: Cochise County, UA locs.
   Microtine: *Ondatra idahoensis.*
   External Age Control: Microtine loc. ("Gidley," UA loc. 25–3) is just below the Olduvai subchron of the Matuyama Chron (Johnson et al. 1975).
   References: Gazin (1942), Lindsay and Tessman (1974).
   Remarks: Although this fauna is considered early Irvingtonian on the basis of *Equus (Equus)* sp. that presumably immigrated with the Irvingtonian microtines, the single microtine is not diagnostic of this age. External age control indicates that this fauna may be separated from the Borchers Local Fauna by less than 100,000 years. However, unlike Curtis Ranch, beds shortly overlying the Borchers fauna contain immigrant Irvingtonian microtines (G. Izett and J. Honey, pers. com., 1979) so that their absence in the Borchers Local Fauna is considered significant; in addition, Borchers has not produced a horse.

(52) El Casco, California: Riverside County, F:AM loc.
   Microtines: *Ondatra annectens, Synaptomys (Mictomys) kansasensis.*
   External Age Control: None.
   References: Frick (1937), White (1970).
   Remarks: This fauna, collected in the early 1920s,

contains *Equus (Equus)* sp. (H. Galiano, pers. com. to M. Frazier 1978), an Irvingtonian immigrant. The *Ondatra* material is being described by M. K. Frazier. Associated pack rats are more derived than Blancan V species and less so than Irvingtonian II forms and are also present in the nearby Shutt Ranch locality which contains *Microtus californicus* (R. E. Reynolds, pers. com., 1984).

(53) Vallecito Creek, California: San Diego County, LA locs.
   Microtines: *Synaptomys ("Metaxyomys") anzaensis, Microtus californicus.*
   External Age Control: Above the Olduvai subchron of the Matuyama Chron (Opdyke et al. 1977), see "Remarks."
   Reference: Zakrzewski (1972).
   Remarks: Opdyke et al. (1977) were uncertain of the identity of the normal event close to the top of their polarity section, but the presence of *Microtus californicus* in reversed beds shortly above it indicates that the event cannot be one of the Reunion subchrons and must be the Olduvai; these were the two possible choices of Opdyke et al. (1977). The lemming from the same approximate horizon, described by Zakrzewski (1972), has recently been found to have a very unusual M_3. One M_3 is known, but, if not aberrant, the species is unique for the genus and certainly merits subgeneric separation. The subgenus *Metaxyomys* (or *Metaxomys*) could be applied except that Zakrzewski selected *S. vetus* as the type species and this species is, in all respects, a primitive member of the subgenus *Mictomys.*

(54) Wellsch Valley, Saskatchewan: National Museums of Canada loc.
   Microtines: *Synaptomys (Mictomys) kansasensis, Microtus paroperarius, Allophaiomys* sp., *Pliophenacomys osborni.*
   External Age Control: Normal deposits of the Olduvai subchron of the Matuyama Chron (Churcher and Stalker, in press).
   Reference: Churcher and Stalker, in press.
   Remarks: This rather remarkable fauna contains several Blancan holdovers including the youngest known *Pliophenacomys.* It also contains the only Irvingtonian I record of *Microtus paroperarius,* which does not appear farther south in the Plains until Irvingtonian II faunas.

(55) Kentuk, Kansas: McPherson County, UK and UM locs.

Microtines: *Ondatra annectens, Synaptomys (Mictomys) kansasensis* (type loc.), *Allophaiomys* sp.

External Age Control: None.

References: Hibbard (1952), Semken (1966).

Remarks: Hibbard and Semken both indicate that this fauna is mixed both environmentally (*Sigmodon* with *Synaptomys* [*Mictomys*]) and temporally (two species of *Ondatra* and a modern species of *Sigmodon*). Some of the reasons are debatable (*Sigmodon* occurs with *Synaptomys* [*Mictomys*] elsewhere), but the geologic setting and the modern appearance of *Sigmodon* certainly suggests mixing. According to Zakrzewski (1975*b*), Semken now believes that it is not mixed. This collection was not examined.

(56) Wathena, Kansas: Doniphan County, UK and UM locs.

Microtines: *Ondatra annectens, Synaptomys (Mictomys) kansasensis, Allophaiomys* sp.

External Age Control: Essentially none. Underlies Kansan glacial till (Zakrzewski 1975*b*).

Reference: van der Meulen (1978).

Remarks: According to published statements, this fauna was described in 1971 in an unpublished thesis by S. O. Einsohn, which I have not seen. The microtines listed are from van der Meulen (1978). This collection was not examined.

(57) Gilliland, Texas: Knox County, UM loc.

Microtine: *Proneofiber guildayi.*

External Age Control: Unconformably below Vera Local Fauna, which is below Type "O" ash.

Reference: Hibbard and Dalquest (1966, 1973).

Remarks: This collection was not examined.

(58) Sappa, Nebraska: Harlan County, UN loc.

Microtines: *Ondatra* sp., *Synaptomys meltoni, Allophaiomys* sp.

External Age Control: Below Type "S" ash.

Reference: Schultz and Martin (1970).

Remarks: Undescribed. The collection was not examined.

Irvingtonian II

Immigrants: *Pitymys meadensis, Pitymys mcnowni, Clethrionomys* cf. *gapperi.*

Natives: *Microtus californicus, Microtus paroperarius, Synaptomys (Synaptomys) cooperi, Synaptomys (Mictomys) meltoni, Synaptomys (Mictomys) kansasensis,* *Neofiber leonardi, Ondatra annectens, Pedomys llanensis, Pitymys cumberlandensis, Allophaiomys guildayi, Allophaiomys* sp., *Atopomys texensis, Atopomys salvelinus, Phenacomys* sp.

Note: Several faunas are not listed.

(59) Olive Dell Ranch, California: San Bernardino County, US Vertebrate loc. M1449.

Microtines: *Microtus californicus*

External Age Control: None.

Reference: This chapter.

Remarks: Association with four other rodents, all of which are relatively primitive extinct species, suggests earlier Irvingtonian II.

(60) Irvington, California: Alameda County, UC loc.

Microtine: *Microtus californicus.*

External Age Control: Lindsay et al. (1975) indicate that the deposits are reversely magnetized.

Reference: Savage (1951).

Remarks: The microtine is not diagnostic of Irvingtonian II age; the fauna is assigned this young an age on the basis of *Euceratherium,* but both reversed magnetic polarity and high percentage of extinct rodents indicate that the fauna must be in the earlier part of Irvingtonian II.

(61) Centerville Beach, California: Humboldt County, UC loc. V76178.

Microtine: *Pitymys mcnowni.*

External Age Control: Locality is in reversed beds above the Jaramillo subchron of the Matuyama Chron according to the magnetic section of Dodd et al. (1977).

Reference: Repenning (1983*b*).

Remarks: There was no associated mammalian fauna.

(62) Alamosa, Colorado: Alamosa County, Adams State College locs.

Microtines: *Microtus paroperarius, Pitymys meadensis, Ondatra annectens, Synaptomys (Mictomys) kansasensis, Clethrionomys* sp.

External Age Control: The fauna is distributed through a section of sediments with the Matuyama/Brunhes boundary and the Bishop Ash in the center. Age range is interpreted to be from 840,000 to 700,000 years ago.

References: Repenning (1983*b*), Rogers et al. (1985).

Remarks: *Microtus paroperarius* and *Pitymys meadensis* are present throughout the section. *M. paroperarius* from the oldest horizons is considerably larger than reported in any other fossil fauna and is from a time of hot and dry summers before or during the Nebraskan glaciation. *M. paroperarius* from the youngest horizons is the size of this species in the 600,000-year-old Cudahy Local Fauna and also from a climatically interglacial time. Boellstorff (1978) has located the Cudahy ash (type O) in the type Aftonian deposits of Iowa. A section of lacustrine and fluvial deposits with few vertebrate remains, deposited during warm winters and moist summers, marks the center of the section (Rogers et al. 1985).

(63) Upper Tecopa, California: Inyo County, US Vertebrate loc. M1089.

Microtine: *Ondatra annectens*.

External Age Control: Slightly upsection from the 600,000-year-old Type "O" tuff (Sheppard and Gude 1968, Izett et al. 1970).

Remarks: No associated fauna; mentioned for temporal and geographic control. There are faunas in the lower part of the Tecopa Lake Beds underlying Type "B" ash, both UC Riverside and LA localities; these contain no microtines.

(64) North Livermore Ave., California: Alameda County, US Vertebrate loc. M1441.

Microtine: *Pitymys meadensis*.

External Age Control: None.

Reference: Repenning (1983*b*).

Remarks: Associated with five living species of rodents and hence considered very young. Most associated rodent species are now confined to Nevada, southernmost California and Arizona, and Mexico and are not native to the area of the locality. In the San Francisco Bay area, this would indicate an interglacial period.

The Cudahy Local Fauna is 600,000 years old and contains a high percentage of extinct rodents; it is thus believed to be considerably older than the North Livermore Ave. Fauna. Immigration of microtines during event 9 is believed responsible for local extinction of *Pitymys meadensis* in the United States; event 9 is correlated with oxygen isotope Stage 12, about 400,000 years old. The Cudahy Local Fauna correlates approximately with oxygen Stage 16 on the basis of its age or with the transition between Stage 15 and 16. Therefore, the North Livermore Ave. Fauna most likely lived during the interglacial indicated by oxygen isotope Stage 13 and is between 450,000 and 500,000 years old on the basis of

data in Emiliani (1978). Because it lacks extinct rodent species, the fauna is not likely to have lived during the interglacial just following the Cudahy Local Fauna.

(65) Java, South Dakota: Walworth County, South Dakota School of Mines and Technology loc.

Microtines: *Ondatra annectens, Synaptomys (Mictomys) kansasensis, Allophaiomys* sp.*, Phenacomys sp., Nebraskomys* or *Atopomys*.

External Age Control: None. Underlies a late Wisconsin glacial till.

References: R. Martin (1973), Martin and Tedesco (1976).

Remarks: This fauna has not been completely described and has not been examined for this chapter. It is placed in Irvingtonian II, but early in this age because it contains *Allophaiomys*. The absence of the nearly ubiquitous *Microtus paroperarius* and *Pitymys meadensis* seems difficult to explain; it may be Irvingtonian I. Recent evidence provided by W. W. Dalquest (pers. com., 1985) indirectly suggests that *Phenacomys* may be an Irvingtonian I immigrant. The genus is known from Blancan V of Alaska and N. E. Siberia (Repenning et al. 1987).

(66) Fyllan Cave, Texas: Travis County, University of Texas at Austin loc.

Microtines: *Atopomys texensis, Allophaiomys guildayi*.

External Age Control: None.

References: Patton (1965); Zakrzewski (1975*a*); van der Meulen (1978).

Remarks: I am somewhat hesitant to accept the close relationship between *Allophaiomys* and *Pedomys* expressed by van der Meulen (1978), and I believe that *Allophaiomys guildayi* (van der Meulen) is more appropriate. Van der Meulen himself says that his new species, *Pedomys guildayi* from Cumberland Cave, "fit the definition of the subgenus *Allophaiomys* Kormos" (p. 113) but that "those attempting a natural grouping of species cannot accept the uniting in a single subgenus of *Phaiomys* and *Pedomys,* which seem to have evolved independently in Asia and North America" (p. 114). For further discussion, see Repenning (1983*b*).

(67) Cumberland Cave, Maryland: Allegany County, CM loc.

Microtines: *Ondatra annectens, Synaptomys (Mic-*

tomys) sp., *Synaptomys (Synaptomys) cooperi*, *Allophaiomys guildayi* (type loc.), *Microtus paroperarius*, *Pitymys cumberlandensis* (type loc.), *Phenacomys* sp., *Clethrionomys* cf. *gapperi*, *Atopomys salvelinus*.
External Age Control: None.
References: Gidley and Gazin (1938); Guilday (1971); van der Meulen (1978).
Remarks: Associated with *Euceratherium*. This collection was not examined.

(68) Conard Fissure, Arkansas: Newton County, AM and State University of Iowa locs.
Microtines: *Ondatra annectens* (type loc.), *Pedomys llanensis*, *Microtus paroperarius*, *Pitymys cumberlandensis*.
External Age Control: None.
References: Brown (1908); van der Meulen (1978).
Remarks: R. Graham has described this fauna in an unpublished thesis that I have not seen. This material was not examined.

(69) Wilson Valley, Kansas: Lincoln County, UK loc.
Microtines: *Synaptomys (Mictomys) meltoni*, *Microtus paroperarius*, *?Phenacomys* sp.
External Age Control: Unknown, underlies ash bed.
Reference: Hibbard (1944).
Remarks: This collection was not examined.

(70) County Line, Iowa: Harrison County, UM loc.
Microtine: *Phenacomys* sp.
External Age Control: Underlies Hartford Ash of Boellstorff (1976) dated at 770,000 years old (Boellstorff 1976).
Reference: Guilday and Parmalee (1972).
Remarks: This fauna has not been published, and I have not examined it.

(71) Vera, Texas: Baylor and Knox counties, UM locs.
Microtines: *Ondatra annectens*, *Microtus paroperarius*, *Pedomys llanensis*.
External Age Control: Below Type "O" ash.
Reference: Hibbard and Dalquest (1966).
Remarks: This collection was not examined.

(72) Cudahy, Kansas: (Sunbrite ash mine) Meade County, UK and UM locs.
Microtines: *Ondatra annectens*, *Pedomys llanensis* (type loc.), *Microtus paroperarius* (type loc.), *Pitymys meadensis* (type loc.), *Synaptomys (Mictomys) meltoni* (type loc.).
External Age Control: In base of the Type "O" ash.
References: Hibbard (1944), Paulson (1961).

Rancholabrean I

Immigrants: *Microtus pennsylvanicus*, *Microtus montanus*, *Microtus mexicanus*, *Lagurus* sp.

Natives: *Microtus californicus*, *Ondatra nebrascensis*, *Pedomys ochrogaster*, *Pedomys llanensis*, *Synaptomys (Mictomys) meltoni-borealis*, *Synaptomys (Synaptomys) australis*, *Neofiber leonardi*, *Clethrionomys* sp., *Phenacomys* sp., and *Pitymys* spp.

Note: Many faunas are not listed. No *Bison* reported.

(73) Snowville, Utah: Box Elder County, US Vertebrate loc. M1456.
Microtines: *Microtus montanus*, *Synaptomys (Mictomys) meltoni-borealis*.
External Age Control: None.
Reference: This chapter.
Remarks: This fauna is under study by P. McClellan, US.

(74) Downey Dump, Idaho: Bannock County, US Vertebrate loc. M1455.
Microtines: *Microtus montanus*, *Ondatra nebrascensis*.
External Age Control: None.
Reference: This chapter.
Remarks: This fauna is under study by P. McClellan, USGS.

(75) Hay Springs, Nebraska: Sheridan County, UN locs.
Microtines: *Microtus pennsylvanicus*, *Ondatra nebrascensis*, *Ondatra annectens*.
Extenal Age Control: None. Below Loveland loess.
Reference: Schultz and Martin (1970).
Remarks: This collection was not examined.

(76) Kanopolis, Kansas: Ellsworth County, UM and UK locs.
Microtines: *Neofiber leonardi*, *Ondatra nebrascensis*, *Pedomys llanensis*, *Microtus pennsylvanicus*.
External Age Control: None.
Reference: Hibbard et al. (1978).
Remarks: This collection was not examined.

(77) Angus, Nebraska: Nuckolls County, UN loc.
Microtines: *Ondatra nebrascensis*, *Microtus pennsylvanicus*, *Pedomys ochrogaster*, *Synaptomys* sp.
External Age Control: None.
Reference: Schultz and Martin (1970).
Remarks: This collection was not examined.

(78) Sandahl, Kansas: McPherson County, UM locs.

Microtines: *Ondatra nebrascensis, Pedomys ochro-gaster, Microtus pennsylvanicus.*
External Age Control: None.
Reference: Semken (1966).
Remarks: This collection was not examined.

(79) Rezabek, Kansas: Lincoln County, UK loc.
Microtines: *Microtus pennsylvanicus, Pedomys ochrogaster, Neofiber leonardi* (type loc.), *On-datra nebrascensis.*
External Age Control: None.
Reference: Semken (1966).
Remarks: This collection was not examined.

Rancholabrean II

Immigrants: *Microtus miurus, Microtus xanthognathus, Microtus oeconomus, Dicrostynyx, Lemmus,* and *Bison.*

Native: Living species of native microtine genera. Associated with *Bison.*

Addendum

The following localities have come to light since this chapter was prepared.

1. Beaver, Utah: Beaver County, US Vertebrate locality M1468.
   Microtines: *Ondatra idahoensis, Mimomys (Ophiomys) meadensis.*
   External Age Control: 50 m below Type B ash (G. Izett, pers. com., 1980).
   Remarks: Blancan V; apparently the first Blancan mammal fauna from Utah.

2. Duncan, Arizona: Greenlee County, UA7937.
   Microtine: *Mimomys (Ophiomys) magilli.*
   External Age Control: None.
   Remarks: Associated with *Paenemarmota fossilis* (described from Benson, Arizona) and probably late Blancan III. This fauna is under study by Yukimitsu Tomida.

3. Murietta, California: Riverside County, US M1476.
   Microtines: *Microtus californicus, Clethrionomys* sp.
   External Age Control: Bishop ash (740,000 years old) is in the section but not stratigraphically correlated to the locality.
   Remarks: Remarkable for the presence of *Clethri-*

onomys at a modern position of 33° N. latitude and 1200 ft. above sea level.

Recent work on the Java Local Fauna (65) by R. A. Martin indicates that it is an early Irvingtonian I fauna and is assigned an incorrect age in this chapter.

REFERENCES

Agadjanian, A. K., and K. Kowalski. 1978. *Prosomys insuliferus* (Kowalski, 1958) (*Rodentia, Mammalia*) from the Pliocene of Poland and of the European part of the U.S.S.R. Acta Zool. Cracoviensia 23:29–53.

Bacon, C. R., D. M. Giovannetti, W. A. Duffield, and G. B. Dalrymple. 1979. New constraints on the age of the Coso Formation, Inyo County, California. Geol. Soc. America Cordilleran Section, 75th Ann. Mtg., San Jose, Calif., Abstracts with Programs 11 (3):67.

Barbat, W. F., and J. Galloway. 1934. San Joaquin Clay, California. Am. Assoc. Petrol. Geol. Bull. 18:476–499.

Baskin, J. A. 1979. Small mammals of the Hemphillian age White Cone local fauna, northeastern Arizona. J. Paleont. 53:695–708.

Bayne, C. F. 1976. Early and medial Pleistocene faunas of Meade County, Kansas. In Guidebook, 24th Ann. Mtg., Midwestern Friends of the Pleistocene, ed. C. K. Bayne, pp. 1–25. Kansas Geol. Survey Univ. Kansas, Guidebook Series 1.

Bjork, P. R. 1970. The Carnivora of the Hagerman local fauna (late Pliocene) of southwestern Idaho. Am. Philos. Soc. Trans., vol. 60.

Boellstorff, J. 1976. The succession of late Cenozoic volcanic ashes in the Great Plains: A progress report. In Guidebook 24th Ann. Mtg., Midwestern Friends of the Pleistocene, ed. C. K. Bayne, pp. 37–71. Kansas Geol. Survey, Univ. Kansas, Guidebook Series 1.

———. 1978. North American Pleistocene stages reconsidered in the light of probable Pliocene-Pleistocene continental glaciation. Science 202:305–307.

Bressler, S. L., and R. F. Butler. 1978. Magnetostratigraphy of the late Tertiary Verde Formation, central Arizona. Earth Planet. Sci. Letters 38:319–330.

Brown, B. 1908. The Conard Fissure, a Pleistocene bone deposit in northern Arkansas: With descriptions of two new genera and twenty new species of mammals. Am. Mus. Nat. History Mem. 9:155–208.

Brunnacker, K., M. Loscher, W. Tillmanns, and B. Urban. 1982. Correlation of the Quaternary terrace sequence in the Lower Rhine Valley and northern Alpine foothills of central Europe. Quat. Res. 18:152–173.

Cantwell, R. J. 1969. Fossil *Sigmodon* from the Tusker locality, 111 Ranch, Arizona. J. Mammal. 50:375–378.

Churcher, C. S., and A. M. Stalker. In press. Geology and vertebrate paleontology of the Wellsch Valley Site, Saskatchewan. Geol. Survey Can. Bull.

Dalquest, W. W. 1978. Early Blancan mammals of the Beck Ranch local fauna of Texas. J. Mammal. 59:269–298.

Dodd, J. R., J. Mead, and R. J. Stanton, Jr. 1977. Paleomagnetic stratigraphy of Pliocene Centerville Beach section, northern California. Earth Planet. Sci. Letters 34:381–386.

Doell, R. R., and A. Cox. 1965. Measurement of remnant magnetization of igneous rocks. U.S. Geol. Surv. Bull. 1203–A.

Downey, J. S. 1962. Leporidae of the Tusker local fauna from southeastern Arizona. J. Paleont. 36:1112–1115.

Emiliani, C. 1978. The cause of the ice ages. Earth Planet. Sci. Letters 37:349–352.

Eshelman, R. E. 1975. Geology and paleontology of the early Pleistocene (late Blancan) White Rock fauna from north-central Kansas. Univ. Mich. Mus. Paleont. Papers Paleont. 13.

Evernden, J. F., D. E. Savage, G. H. Curtis, and G. T. James. 1964. Potassium-argon dates and the Cenozoic mammalian chronology of North America. Am. J. Sci. 264:146–198.

Fejfar, O. 1976. Plio-Pleistocene mammal sequences. In Project 73–1–24, Quaternary Glaciations in the Northern Hemisphere, eds. D. J. Easterbrook and V. Sibrava. Report No. 3, Prague, pp. 351–366.

Fejfar, O., and W. D. Heinrich.. 1981. Zur biostratigraphischen Untergliederung des Kontinentalen Quartars in Europa anhand von Arvicolidae (Rodentia: Mammalia). Eclogae geologicae Helvetiae 74:997–1006.

———. 1983. Arvicoliden-Sukzession and Biostratigraphie des Oberpliozans and Quartars in Europa. Schriftenr. geol. Wiss. Berlin 19/20:61–109.

Frick, C. 1937. Horned ruminants of North America. Am. Mus. Nat. Hist. Bull. vol. 69.

Gazin, C. L. 1942. The late Cenozoic vertebrate faunas from San Pedro Valley, Arizona. Proc. U.S. Natl. Mus. 92:475–518.

Gidley, J. W., and C. L. Gazin. 1938. The Pleistocene vertebrate fauna from Cumberland Cave, Maryland. Bull. U.S. Natl. Mus., vol. 171.

Gladenkov, Yu. B. 1978. Correlation of upper Cenozoic marine deposits in boreal regions (based on mollusks). Int. Geol. Rev. 20:59–72.

Gray, J. E. 1825. Outline of an attempt at the deposition of the Mammalia into tribes and families with a list of genera apparently appertaining to each tribe. Ann. Philos., n.s. 10:337–344.

Gromov, I. M., and I. Ya. Polyakov. 1977. Voles (Microtinae). Academy of Sciences of the USSR, Zoological Institute, n.s., vol. 3 (8). (In Russian).

Guilday, J. E. 1971. The Pleistocene history of the Appalachian mammal fauna. In The Distributional history of the biota of the southern Appalachians. Pt. III: Vertebrates, ed. P. C. Holt, R. A. Peterson, and J. P. Hubbard, pp. 233–262. Virginia Polytechnic Inst. and State Univ., Res. Div. Monogr. 4.

Guilday, J. E., and P. W. Parmalee. 1972. Quaternary periglacial records of voles of the genus *Phenacomys* Merriam (Cricetidae, Rodentia). Quat. Res. 2:170–175.

Gustafson, E. P. 1977. First record of *Teleoceras* (Rhinocerotidae) from the Ringold Formation, Pliocene of Washington. PaleoBios, vol. 27.

———. 1978. The vertebrate faunas of the Pliocene Ringold Formation, south-central Washington. Univ. Ore. Mus. Nat. History Bull., vol. 23.

———. 1985. Soricidae (Mammalia, Insectivora) from the Blufftop local fauna, Blancan Ringold Formation of central Washington, and the correlation of Ringold Formation faunas. J. Vert. Paleont. 5:88–92.

Hesse, C. J. 1934. Another record of the fossil vole *Mimomys primus* (Wilson) from California. J. Mammal. 15:246.

Hibbard, C. W. 1941a. Mammals of the Rexroad fauna from the upper Pliocene of southwestern Kansas. Kans. Acad. Sci. Trans. 44:265–313.

———. 1941b. The Borchers fauna, a new Pleistocene interglacial fauna from Meade County, Kansas. Geol. Surv. Kans. Bull. 38:197–220.

———. 1944. Stratigraphy and vertebrate paleontology of Pleistocene deposits of southwestern Kansas. Bull. Geol. Soc. Amer. 55:707–754.

———. 1949. Pliocene Saw Rock Canyon fauna in Kansas. Univ. Mich. Mus. Contrib. Paleont. 7:91–105.

———. 1950. Mammals of the Rexroad Formation of Fox Canyon, Meade County, Kansas. Univ. Mich. Mus. Contrib. Paleont. 8:113–192.

———. 1952. Vertebrate fossils from late Cenozoic deposits of central Kansas. Univ. Kans. Paleont. Contrib. Vertebrata 2:1–14.

———. 1954. A new *Synaptomys,* an addition to the Borchers interglacial (Yarmouth?) fauna. J. Mammal. 35:249–252.

———. 1956. Vertebrate fossils from the Meade Formation of southwestern Kansas. Mich. Acad. Sci. Arts Letters Papers 41:145–203.

———. 1957. Two new Cenozoic microtine rodents. J. Mammal. 38:39–44.

———. 1958. Summary of North American Pleistocene mammalian local faunas. Mich. Acad. Sci. Arts Letters papers 43:3–32.

———. 1959. Late Cenozoic microtine rodents from Wyoming and Idaho. Mich. Acad. Sci. Arts Letters Papers 44:3–40.

———. 1964. A contribution of the Saw Rock Canyon local fauna of Kansas. Mich. Acad. Sci. Arts Letters Papers 49:115–127.

———. 1967. New rodents from the late Cenozoic of Kansas. Mich. Acad. Sci. Arts Letters Papers 52:115–131.

———. 1970. The Pliocene rodent *Microtoscoptes disjunctus* (Wilson) from Idaho and Wyoming. Univ. Mich. Mus. Paleont. Contrib. 23:95–98.

———. 1972. Class Mammalia [excluding horses]. In M. F. Skinner and C. W. Hibbard, with the collaboration of others, Early Pleistocene preglacial and glacial rocks and faunas of north-central Nebraska. Am. Mus. Nat. Hist. Bull. 148:77–116.

Hibbard, C. W., and W. W. Dalquest. 1966. Fossils from the Seymour Formation of Knox and Baylor Counties, Texas, and their bearing on the late Kansas climate of that region. Univ. Mich. Mus. Paleont. Contrib. 21:1–66.

————. 1973. *Proneofiber,* a new genus of vole (Cricetidae, Rodentia) from the Pleistocene Seymour Formation of Texas, and its evolutionary and stratigraphic significance. Quat. Res. 3:269–274.

Hibbard, C. W., and R. J. Zakrzewski. 1967. Phyletic trends in the late Cenozoic microtine *Ophiomys* gen. nov., from Idaho. Univ. Mich. Mus. Paleont. Contrib. 21:255–271.

————. 1972. A new species of microtine from the late Pliocene of Kansas. J. Mammal. 53:834–839.

Hibbard, C. W., R. J. Zakrzewski, R. E. Eshelman, G. Edmund, C. D. Griggs, and C. Griggs. 1978. Mammals from the Kanopolis fauna, Pleistocene (Yarmouth) of Ellsworth County, Kansas. Univ. Mich. Mus. Paleont. Contrib. 25:11–44.

Hinton, M. A. C. 1926. Monograph of the voles and lemmings (Microtinae) living and extinct. British Mus. (Nat. Hist.), London, vol. 1.

Hopkins, D. M. 1967. Quaternary marine transgressions in Alaska. In The Bering land bridge. ed. D. M. Hopkins, pp. 47–90. Stanford: Stanford Univ. Press.

Izett, G. A., H. A. Wilcox, H. A. Powers, and G. A. Desborough. 1970. The Bishop ash bed: A Pleistocene marker bed in the western United States. Quat. Res. 1:121–132.

Jacobs, L. L., and E. H. Lindsay. 1981. *Prosigmodon oroscoi,* a new sigmodont rodent from the late Tertiary of Mexico. J. Paleont. 55:425–430.

Johnson, N. M., N. D. Opdyke, and E. H. Lindsay. 1975. Magnetic polarity stratigraphy of Pliocene-Pleistocene terrestrial deposits and vertebrate faunas, San Pedro Valley, Arizona. Geol. Soc. Amer. Bull. 86:5–12.

Kent, D., N. D. Opdyke, and M. Ewing. 1971. Climatic change in the North Pacific using ice-rafted detritus as a climatic indicator. Geol. Soc. Amer. Bull. 82:2741–2758.

Kowalski, K. 1967. *Lagurus lagurus* (Pallas, 1773) and *Cricetus cricetus* (Linnaeus, 1758) (Rodentia, Mammalia) in the Pleistocene of England. Acta Zool. Cracoviensia 12:111–122.

Kretzoi, M. 1955. *Promimomys cor* n. g. n. sp., ein altertumlicher arvicolide aus dem ungarischen Unterpleistozan. Acta Geologica 3:89–94.

————. 1962. Arvicolidae oder Microtidae. Vertebrata Hungarica 4:171–175.

Kukla, G. J. 1977. Pleistocene land-sea correlations. I: Europe. Earth-Sci. Rev. 13:307–374.

Lindsay, E. H., and L. L. Jacobs. 1985. Pliocene small mammal fossils from Chihuahua, Mexico. Paleont. Mex., Univ. Auto. Mex. Inst. Geol. 51:1–59.

Lindsay, E. H., N. M. Johnson, and N. D. Opdyke. 1975. Preliminary correlation of North American land mammal ages and geomagnetic chronology. Univ. Mich. Papers Paleont. no. 12, Studies on Cenozoic paleontology and stratigraphy in honor of Claude W. Hibbard, pp. 111–119.

Lindsay, E. H., and N. T. Tessman. 1974. Cenozoic vertebrate localities and faunas in Arizona. Ariz. Acad. Sci. J. 9:3–24.

Lugn, A. L. 1938. The Nebraska State Geological Survey and the "Valentine" problem. Am. J. Sci., 5th ser. 36:220–227.

Mankinen, E. A., and G. B. Dalrymple. 1979. Revised geomagnetic polarity time scale for the interval 0 to 5 m.y.b.p. J. Geophys. Res. 84:615–626.

Martin, L. D. 1972. The microtine rodents of the Mullen assemblage from the Pleistocene of north central Nebraska. Univ. Nebr. St. Mus. Bull. 9:173–182.

————. 1975. Microtine rodents from the Ogallala Pliocene of Nebraska and the early evolution of the Microtinae in North America: Univ. Mich. Papers Paleont. no. 12, Studies on Cenozoic paleontology and stratigraphy in honor of Claude W. Hibbard, pp. 101–110.

————. 1979. The biostratigraphy of arvicoline rodents in North America. Nebr. Acad. Sci. Trans. 7:91–100.

Martin, R. A. 1973. The Java local fauna, Pleistocene of South Dakota: A preliminary report. N.J. Acad. Sci. Bull. 18:48–56.

Martin, R. A., and R. Tedesco. 1976. *Ondatra annectens* (Mammalia: Rodentia) from the Pleistocene Java local fauna of South Dakota. J. Paleont. 50:846–850.

May, S. R. 1981. *Repomys* (Mammalia: Rodentia gen. nov.) from the late Neogene of California and Nevada. J. Vert. Paleont. 1 (2):219–230.

May, S. R., and C. A. Repenning. 1982. New evidence for the age of the Mount Eden fauna, southern California. J. Vert. Paleont. 2 (1):109–113.

Mein, P. 1975. Resultats du groupe de travail des vertebres. In Report on activity of the RCMNS working group (1971–1975), ed. J. Senes, pp. 78–81. Bratislava.

Naeser, C. W., G. A. Izett, and R. E. Wilcox. 1973. Zircon fission-track ages of Pearlette Family ash beds in Meade County, Kansas. Geology 1:187–189.

Nelson, R. S., and H. S. Semken. 1970. Paleoecological and stratigraphic significance of the muskrat in Pleistocene deposits. Bull. Geol. Soc. Amer. 81:3733–3738.

Neville, C., N. D. Opdyke, E. H. Lindsay, and N. M. Johnson. 1979. Magnetic stratigraphy of Pliocene deposits of the Glenns Ferry Formation, Idaho, and its implications for North American mammalian biostratigraphy. Am. J. Sci. 279:503–526.

Opdyke, N. D., E. H. Lindsay, N. M. Johnson, and T. Downs. 1977. The paleomagnetism and magnetic polarity stratigraphy of the mammal-bearing section of Anza-Borrego State Park, California. Quat. Res. 7:316–329.

Packer, D. R. 1979. Paleomagnetism and age dating of the Ringold Formation and loess deposits in the State of Washington. Ore. Geology 41:119–132.

Packer, D. R., and J. M. Johnston. 1979. A preliminary investigation of the magnetostratigraphy of the Ringold Formation. San Francisco: Woodward-Clyde Consultants Report RHO–BW1–C–42.

Patton, T. H. 1965. A new genus of fossil microtine from Texas. J. Mammal. 46:466–471.

Paulson, G. R. 1961. The mammals of the Cudahy fauna. Mich. Acad. Arts Sci. Letters Papers 46:127–153.

Repenning, C. A. 1967. Palearctic-Nearctic mammalian dispersal in the late Cenozoic. In The Bering land bridge, ed. D. M. Hopkins, pp. 288–311. Stanford: Stanford Univ. Press.

———. 1968. Mandibular musculature and the origin of the Subfamily Arvicolinae (Rodentia). Acta Zool. Cracoviensia 13:29–72.

———. 1976. *Enhydra* and *Enhydroidon* from the Pacific coast of North America. J. Res. U.S. Geol. Surv. 4:305–315.

———. 1978. Faunal exchanges between Siberia and North America. American Quaternary Assoc. Abstracts. 5th Biennial Meeting, Sept. 2–4, Edmonton, Alberta, pp. 40–55.

———. 1980. Faunal exchanges between Siberia and North America. Can. J. Anthropol. 1:37–44.

———. 1983*a*. Matters arising: Evidence for earlier date of Ubeidiya, Israel hominid site: Repenning replies. Nature 304:375–376.

———. 1983*b*. *Pitymys meadensis* Hibbard from the Valley of Mexico and the classification of North American species of *Pitymys* (Rodentia: Cricetidae). J. Vert. Paleont. 2:471–482.

———. 1983*c*. Faunal exchanges between Siberia and North America. Schriftenr. geol. Wiss. Berlin 19/20:333–346.

———. 1984. Quaternary rodent biochronology and its correlation with climatic and magnetic stratigraphies. In Quaternary Chronologies, ed. W. C. Mahaney Norwich: Geoabstracts Ltd.

Repenning, C. A., C. E. Ray, and D. Grigorescu. 1979. Pinniped Biogeography. In Historical biogeography, plate tectonics, and the changing environment, eds. J. Gray and A. J. Boucot, pp. 357–369. Corvallis: Oregon State Univ. Press.

Repenning, C. A., E. M. Brouwers, L. D. Carter, L. Marincovich, Jr., and T. A. Ager. 1987. The Beringian ancestry of *Phenaeomys* (Rodentia: Cricetidae) and the beginning of the modern Arctic Ocean Borderland Biota. U.S. Geol. Survey Bull. 1687.

Rogers, K. L., C. A. Repenning, R. M. Forester, E. E. Larson, S. A. Hall, G. R. Smith, E. Anderson, and T. J. Brown. 1985. Middle Pleistocene (Late Irvingtonian: Nebraskan) climatic changes in south-central Colorado. Nat. Geogr. Res. 1:535–563.

Savage, D. E. 1951. Late Cenozoic vertebrates of the San Francisco Bay region. Univ. California Publ. Dept. Geol. Sci. Bull. 28:215–314.

Savage, D. E., and G. H. Curtis. 1970. The Villafranchian Stage-Age and its radiometric dating. Geol. Soc. Amer. Spec. Paper 124, pp. 207–231.

Schultz, C. B., and L. D. Martin. 1970. Quaternary mammalian sequence in the central Great Plains. Univ. Kans. Dept. Geol. Spec. Publ. 3, pp. 341–353.

Schultz, C. B., and T. M. Stout. 1948. Pleistocene mammals and terraces in the Great Plains. Bull. Geol. Soc. Amer. 59:553–588.

Schultz. C. B., L. G. Tanner, and L. D. Martin. 1972. Phyletic trends in certain lineages of Quaternary mammals. Univ. Nebr. St. Mus. Bull. 9:183–195.

Schultz, G. E. 1977. Blancan and post-Blancan faunas in the Texas Panhandle. West Texas State Univ., Canyon, Killgore Res. Center, Dept. Geol. Anthropol. Spec. Publ. 1, pp. 105–145.

Schultz, J. R. 1937. A late Cenozoic vertebrate fauna from the Coso Mountains, Inyo County, California. Carnegie Inst. Wash. Publ. 487, pp. 75–109.

Semken, H. A., Jr. 1966. Stratigraphy and paleontology of the McPherson Equus Beds (Sandahl local fauna), McPherson County, Kansas. Univ. Mich. Mus. Paleont. Contrib. 20:121–178.

Shackleton, N. J., and N. D. Opdyke. 1977. Oxygen isotope and paleomagnetic evidence for early northern hemisphere glaciation. Nature 170:216–219.

Sheppard, R. A., and A. J. Gude, III. 1968. Distribution and genesis of authigenic silicate minerals in tuffs of Pleistocene Lake Tecopa, Inyo County, California. U.S. Geol. Surv. Prof. Paper 597.

Sher, A. V., and others. 1979. Late Cenozoic of the Kolyma Lowland. 14th Pacific Science Congress, Tour Guide XI, Acad. Sci. U.S.S.R., Moscow, pp. 1–115.

Shotwell, J. A. 1956. Hemphillian mammalian assemblage from northeastern Oregon. Bull. Geol. Soc. Amer. 67:717–738.

———. 1970. Pliocene mammals of southeastern Oregon and adjacent Idaho. Univ. Ore. Mus. Nat. Hist. Bull. 17.

Skinner, M. F., and C. W. Hibbard. 1972. Early Pleistocene pre-glacial and glacial rocks and faunas of north-central Nebraska. Bull. Am. Mus. Nat. Hist., vol. 148.

Skinner, M. F., S. M. Skinner, and R. J. Gooris. 1968. Cenozoic rocks and faunas of Turtle Butte, south-central South Dakota. Bull. Am. Mus. Nat. Hist. 138:379–436.

Steiger, R. H., and E. Jager. 1977. Subcommission on Geochronology: Convention on the use of decay constants in geo- and cosmochronology. Earth Plant. Sci. Letters 36:359–362.

Stock. C. 1921. Later Cenozoic mammalian remains from Meadow Valley region, southeastern Nevada. Am. J. Sci., ser. 2, 5:250–264.

Suchov, V. P. 1976. Remains of lemmings in the Bashkirian Pliocene deposits. In Rodents evolution and history of their recent fauna, ed. I. M. Gromov, pp. 117–121. Zool. Inst. Leningrad, Proc. (in Russian).

Taylor, D. W. 1966. Summary of North American Blancan nonmarine mollusks. Malacologia 4:1–172.

Tedford, R. H., and E. P. Gustafson. 1977. First North American record of the extinct panda *Parailurus*. Nature 165:621–623.

Topachevski, V. A., A. F. Skorik, and L. I. Rekovets. 1978. The most ancient voles of the Microtini Tribe (Rodentia, Microtidae) from the south of the Ukrainian SSR. Zoologic Record. Academy of Sciences, Ukrainian SSR, pp. 35–41 (in Russian with English summary).

van der Meulen, A. J. 1978. *Microtus* and *Pitymys* (Arvicolidae) from Cumberland Cave, Maryland, with a comparison of some New and Old World species. Annals Carnegie Museum, 47:101–145.

Voorhies, M. R. 1977. Fossil moles of late Hemphillian age from northeastern Nebraska. Nebr. Acad. Sci. Trans. 4:139–138.

White, J. A. 1970. Late Cenozoic porcupines (Mammalia, Erethizontidae) of North America. Am. Mus. Novitates, no. 2421.

Wilson, R. W. 1932. *Cosomys,* a new genus of vole from the Pliocene of California. J. Mammal. 13:150–154.

———. 1937. Pliocene rodents of western North America. Carnegie Inst. Wash. Publ. no. 487, pp. 21–73.

Wood, H. E., II, and six others. 1941. Nomenclature and correlation of the North American continental Tertiary. Bull. Geol. Soc. Amer. 52:1–48.

Woodburne, M. O. 1977. Definition and characterization in mammalian chronostratigraphy. J. Paleont. 51:220–234.

Zakrzewski, R. J. 1967. The primitive vole *Ogmodontomys* from the late Cenozoic of Kansas and Nebraska. Mich. Acad. Sci. Arts Letters Papers 52:133–150.

———. 1969. The rodents from the Hagerman local fauna, upper Pliocene of Idaho. Univ. Mich. Mus. Paleont. Contrib. 23:1–36.

———. 1972. Fossil microtines from late Cenozoic deposits in the Anza-Borrego Desert, California, with a description of a new subgenus of *Synaptomys.* Los Angeles Co. Nat. History Mus. Contrib. Sci., vol. 221.

———. 1975a. The late Pleistocene arvicoline rodent *Atopomys.* Ann. Carnegie Mus. 45:255–261.

———. 1975b. Pleistocene stratigraphy and paleontology in western Kansas: The state of the art, 1974. Univ. Mich. Mus. Paleont. Papers Paleont. 12:121–128.

Zazhigin, V. S. 1980. Late Pliocene and Anthropogene rodents of the south of western Siberia. Academy of Sciences of the USSR Trans., vol. 339 (in Russian).

9

MAMMALIAN CHRONOLOGY AND THE MAGNETIC POLARITY TIME SCALE

Everett H. Lindsay

Noye M. Johnson

Neil D. Opdyke

Robert F. Butler

INTRODUCTION

The primary chronological reference in Tertiary terrestrial deposits has been and continues to be mammalian fossils. This biochronologic frame of reference is founded on the orderly succession of fossils whose time relations are known principally by evolutionary changes and, secondarily, by superposition. Ordering of terrestrial deposits by mammalian biochronology has proven reliable and is internally consistent within the limits imposed by morphological evolution and dispersal of mammals. An independent check of mammalian biochronology is provided by a rather thin network of radiometric dates. The scarcity of radiometrically datable rocks directly associated with terrestrial faunas and the uneven quality of these dates are limits to the exact age correlation of terrestrial deposits and faunas.

An inherent problem of any biochronologic time frame is that boundaries between adjacent biochronologic units become less distinct as that boundary is approached. Calibration of these boundaries by radiometric methods is never exact, and generally an interpretation of several radiometric dates and several faunas is required. Nevertheless, radiometric dates in combination with fossil data provide the most reliable chronological framework for terrestrial deposits from the Cenozoic to the present time.

Magnetic polarity stratigraphy is a new stratigraphic tool well suited for the recognition and correlation of biochronologic units. A unique attribute of magnetic polarity stratigraphy is that magnetic reversals are global in extent and geologically instantaneous. If a terrestrial fossil or fossil fauna can be associated with an identifiable reversal event, the potential for age correlation on a worldwide basis is obvious. Like any correlation or dating method, however, magnetic polarity stratigraphy has limitations and can be misused.

The purpose of this chapter is to discuss the theory, practice, and limitations of magnetic polarity stratigraphy as applied to terrestrial rocks and mammalian fossils.

Development of the Magnetic Polarity Time Scale

Reversal of the earth's magnetic field had been suspected since early in this century. Brunhes (1906) observed that certain lavas from the south of France were magnetized in a direction opposite to the present geomagnetic field. This observation was confirmed by Mercanton (1926) and Matuyama (1929) who suggested that reversals were time synchronous and could thus be used for stratigraphic-chronological purposes. In the early 1950s rocks with self-reversing properties were discovered by Nagata and his co-workers in Japan (Nagata et al. 1952). This discovery led to a debate as to the reality of field reversals which was finally resolved by the felicitous combination of K-Ar dating and paleomagnetic measurements (Cox et al. 1963, McDougall and Tarling 1963). These studies showed clearly that magnetic reversals in igneous rocks are time dependent. This led to the construction of a radiometrically calibrated history of the earth's magnetic field for the last 4 Ma. Within this time span, long intervals of normal and reversed polarity were designated as magnetic polarity epochs, whereas short intervals of constant polarity were designated as magnetic polarity events (Cox et al. 1963).

Following the model developed by Vine and Matthews (1963) in which periodic reversals of the earth's magnetic field and slow spreading of the ocean floor along linear ridges combine to produce seafloor anomaly patterns, Heirtzler et al. (1968) established a composite sequence of the seafloor anomalies from the North and South Pacific, the South Indian, and the South Atlantic oceans. This resulting reversal sequence became the first magnetic anomaly time scale for the entire Cenozoic period. It is important to note the initial magnetic anomaly time scale of Heirtzler et al. (1968) was calibrated using the Gauss/Gilbert magnetic boundary at 3.35 Ma for the upper 10 percent of the scale and extrapolation for the rest of the scale based on the assumption of relatively uniform but unequal spreading rates in the separate ocean basins. During the last ten years, a number of revisions of the magnetic anomaly time scale have been added, the most notable being Sclater et al. (1974), Tarling and Mitchell (1976), McDougall et al. (1977), LaBrecque et al. (1977), Ness et al. (1980), and Lowrie and Alvarez (1981). The magnetic polarity time scale (= magnetic anomaly time scale) was recalibrated by Mankinen and Dalrymple (1979) using revised decay constants for K-Ar. A formal and uniform terminology for the magnetic time scale was proposed by the IUGS (Hedberg et al. 1979) and will be used here (fig. 9.1). The most important aspect of this change is the dropping of the terms "epoch" and "event" and their replacement by chron and subchron, respectively.

We emphasize that the generalized pattern of reversals established and enumerated by Heirtzler et al. (1968) is still in general use. Revisions of that polarity time scale involve new correlations of radiometric or paleontologic data with some part of the reversal sequence, such as correlation of anomaly 29 with the Cretaceous/ Tertiary boundary by Alvarez et al. (1977). It should also be noted that the seafloor anomaly sequence at present is incomplete as it does not include many short reversal events that are present in the history of the earth's magnetic field.

The directly dated upper part of the magnetic polar

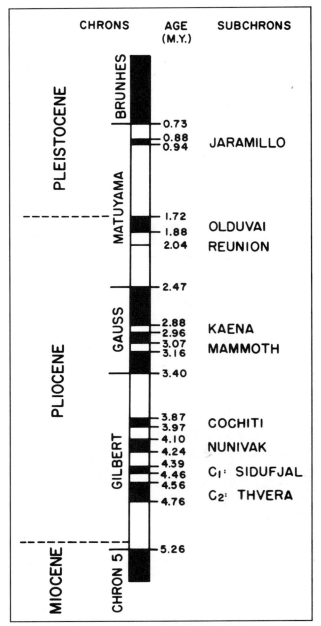

Fig. 9.1. Geomagnetic time scale.

ity time scale has been used with great success in stratigraphic studies of upper Cenozoic marine sediments (Harrison and Funnell 1964; Opdyke et al. 1966; Opkyke 1972). Similarly, the long magnetostratigraphic record in Siwalik deposits of Pakistan (e.g., Johnson et al. 1982) coupled with more but shorter duration magnetostratigraphic records in North America (e.g., Lindsay et al. 1984) demonstrate the potential resolution of mammalian biochronology by incorporating magneto stratigraphic and biostratigraphic studies in terrestrial sequences. We anticipate that a more precisely age-calibrated magnetic polarity time scale for the entire Cenozoic and the Late Cretaceous is a realistic goal and cite the results of Prothero et al. (1982) and Butler and Lindsay (1985) as significant steps toward achieving that goal. Perhaps ten years from now the magnetic polarity time scale will be broadly utilized to constrain rates of morphological evolution in mammalian lineages and the timing of intercontinental dispersal of land mammals.

An important requirement for correlation of terrestrial deposits with the magnetic polarity time scale is a thick continuous stratigraphic section of relatively fine-grained and well-exposed rocks. Numerous suitable sections, which are also fossiliferous, have produced reliable magnetic polarity sequences and serve as guides to correlation of mammalian biochronology with the magnetic polarity time scale (fig. 9.2). An early magnetostratigraphic study in terrestrial deposits of North America was developed in the San Pedro Valley of Arizona (Johnson et al. 1975). In that study a 130-meter-thick section in the Saint David Formation yielded samples with strong remanent magnetization that have permitted unambiguous polarity zonation from the upper Gilbert, through the Gauss, and part of the lower Matuyama polarity chrons. This approximately two-million-year time span, coupled with biostratigraphic zonation of mammalian fossils, has served as a model for later studies that combine magnetostratigraphic and biostratigraphic data.

METHODOLOGY

Clastic sediments acquire a magnetization during the process of sedimentation, called depositional remanent magnetization (DRM). When small magnetic particles, say magnetic grains, settle out of suspension, they will orient themselves parallel to the ambient magnetic field. Ideally, a clastic sediment will "remember" the orientation of the earth's magnetic field at the time of deposition. It is of paramount importance to note that it is the small-sized magnetic grains (silt and smaller) that carry the desired DRM, not large-sized grains. Generally speaking, sandstone and conglomerates are not suitable for a DRM determination. The starting point for any magnetic polarity stratigraphy study, then, is to ascertain the DRM contained in the stratigraphic section under examination. In practice, this involves laboratory measurements with sensitive instruments; oriented pieces of sedimentary rock must be brought back to the laboratory for analysis.

A standard technique for obtaining oriented cores

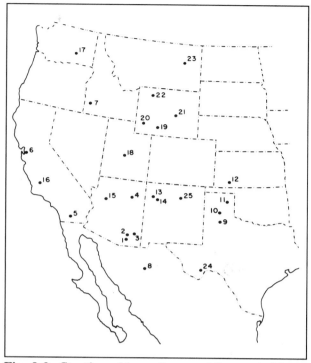

Fig. 9.2. Stratigraphic sections and faunas in North America where magnetostratigraphic studies have been undertaken prior to 1980. (1) Upper San Pedro Valley, Arizona (Benson, Curtis Ranch, Wolf Ranch, and California Wash faunas); (2) Lower San Pedro Valley, Arizona (Redington and Camel Canyon faunas); (3) III Ranch, San Simon Valley, Arizona; (4) White Cone, Arizona; (5) Anza-Borrego Desert, California (Layer Cake, Arroyo Seco, and Vallecito Creek faunas); (6) Irvington, California; (7) Grand View, Idaho; (8) Yepómera, Chihuahua; (9) Mount Blanco, Texas; (10) Cita Canyon and Axtel, Texas; (11) Coffee Ranch, Texas; (12) Meade County, Kansas (Fox Canyon, Rexroad, Bender, Borcher, Cudahy, Butler Spring, Cragin, Mount Scott, and Adam faunas); (13) Hunter Wash and Alamo Wash, San Juan Basin, New Mexico; (14) Torrejon Arroyo, San Juan Basin, New Mexico; (15) Wikieup, Arizona; (16) Cuyama Badlands, California; (17) Ringold, Washington; (18) Dragon Canyon, Utah; (19) Washakie Basin, Wyoming; (20) Bridger Basin, Wyoming; (21) Flagstaff Rim, Wyoming; (22) Big Horn Basin, Wyoming; (23) Hell Creek and Fort Peck, Montana; (24) Big Bend, Texas; (25) Chamita Formation, New Mexico.

for paleomagnetic study is to use a water-cooled diamond drilling apparatus, constructed from a commercially available hand-held chain saw. This method is not commonly suitable for the collection of Cenozoic terrestrial claystones and siltstones as they would dissolve in the coolant. In some instances, coring techniques using forced air as a coolant have been successful in Cenozoic rocks, but the equipment required is bulky and difficult to handle in rough terrain. Thus, we have developed a different method for collecting oriented blocks from poorly indurated Cenozoic sediments.

The following list includes equipment needed for our specimen collection method. Other variations are possible, but we strongly recommend use of a compass with a 360° scale: (1) a small pick and shovel; (2) a pocket plane (Stanley 399 Surform) and replacement blades (allow 2/day); (3) Brunton compass (360° scale); (4) newspaper or toilet paper and masking tape; and (5) a felt marking pen.

The number of sampling sites will usually be determined by the available exposed lithologies and the stratigraphic sampling interval desired. It is important, however, to select a site that will yield good paleomagnetic results rather than to adhere rigidly to a fixed sampling interval. Our experience indicates superior results for claystones and fine-grained siltstones, in comparison to sandstones or coarser rocks. It is always best to favor finer-grained lithologies when selecting a sampling site. Altering the sample interval by a meter or less so as to collect a better lithology is not likely to negate the resulting sampling interval. But sampling a fine sandstone or coarser lithology so as to adhere to a desired sampling interval could result in ambiguous paleomagnetic results for that site. This would, of course, lead to uncertain polarity stratigraphy.

Sampling sites can be easily marked by placing a large rock or other distinctive object adjacent to the site. The site number should be written on the rock with a felt marking pen and the marked side should be placed down, away from the sun, rain, and so forth, that might bleach or erase the marking. We have tried marking sites by placing stakes, placing large nails, painting rocks, and building rock cairns at the site and have found the procedure above adequate and most suitable for relocating the site.

Samples should be collected only from hard, dry (even in arid regions unweathered sediments are usually damp), and unweathered sediments below the weathered zone. This may require digging a hole a meter or more into a bank to get below the weathered zone.

At each site, three or more oriented samples are collected. These samples should be on the same stratigraphic level and within a lateral distance of about 0.5 meter. Homogeneous samples approximately the size of a cigarette pack are ideal. Orientation is accomplished by cutting a horizontal surface on the top, or a vertical

surface on the side of the in situ sample with a pocket plane. Our tolerance for this surface is ±3° and can be readily checked using the Brunton compass. Azimuthal orientation is scribed on the level surface by marking a pencil line with arrow at one end and measuring the strike of this line with the Brunton compass. A cross-hatch is drawn through the arrow if the planed surface is horizontal, or a vertical dip line is drawn downward from the arrow if the planed surface is vertical. The sample number and orientation are written directly on the planed surface as well as in the field book. A stratigraphic profile should be measured giving the location of each sample and variable lithologies in the section.

Following orientation and marking, the sample is broken from the outcrop and trimmed with a small pick. Care must be taken not to disturb the orientation marking. To prevent breakage during transport, samples are wrapped in paper and secured with masking tape. Sample number and orientation should be written on the masking tape.

Frequently, the best exposures for sampling are in canyons or steep exposures where weathered material is rapidly removed. Avoiding sections with deeply weathered sediments will surely lead to a higher success ratio in the laboratory. Another cautionary note is to avoid high prominences that might be subject to lightning strikes. Lightning strikes will induce an isothermal remanent magnetization that may be difficult or impossible to remove. The magnetizing effect of lightning strikes is usually limited to less than 3 meters from the lightning contact, although the lightning is liable to follow (or seek) cracks in the rock and be transmitted farther along those cracks. Therefore, promontories that tend to have a high frequency of lightning strikes should be avoided during sampling.

The next step is to cut the collected samples to a size and shape to fit into the magnetometer. Water-cooled saws cannot be used. We have found that dry-cutting carborundum masonry blades are most suitable for cutting the samples. These blades can be mounted on a disc sander or bench grinder. A sanding disc (of very coarse texture) may be useful for final trimming of the sample. Care must be taken to prevent heating of the sample during the cutting operation as a heated sample may alter the remanent magnetization or induce an additional magnetic overprint. The use of ferromagnetic tools to collect and cut the sample poses no problem relative to the sample's remanent magnetization as long as the sample is not heated above a temperature that would prevent it being handheld.

We have used two sizing techniques. One method is to cut the sample to the shape of a cylinder of 25 mm length and diameter, or to a cube of 25 mm side dimension. A second method is to reduce the sample to a polyhedron small enough to fit inside a clear plastic micromount box with an outside dimension of 25 mm. In each case, the sample is cut so that one edge of the cube or polyhedron is parallel to the orientation arrow. If placed in a plastic box, the sample can be glued (with Elmer's glue), placing the orientation surface against the box, and a label with the sample number and orientation can be affixed to the box. Placing samples in plastic boxes has the advantage of securing friable samples that might crumble during handling. However, this prevents the use of thermal demagnetization procedures, as the micromount boxes melt at temperatures below 300°C.

In summary, problems may be introduced by insufficient care regarding the selection of samples. If the sampled lithology is too coarse, the energy of the transporting medium may not permit individual grains to align themselves relative to the earth's magnetic field. If the sampled lithology has been weathered or otherwise chemically altered, the detrital remanent magnetization may be weakened or destroyed and a new chemical remanent magnetization may be produced if a ferromagnetic mineral is precipitated as a result of weathering. These problems can be addressed only at the time samples are collected. The collector must be aware of these problems and be alert to weathering, postdepositional deformation, proximity of cracks and rootlets to the sample, and excessive moisture that may have affected the chemistry of the sample. Collection of samples is one of the most critical aspects of terrestrial magnetostratigraphy. Blunders made in the field will be propagated through the entire study. Sophisticated machinery, computer analyses, or statistics cannot correct mistakes made during the collection of samples.

Laboratory Measurement Methods

After the samples have been sized, the directions of magnetization must be determined. Fortunately, magnetometers capable of accurately measuring the weak magnetic moments found in terrestrial sediments are now commercially available. The magnetometers most widely used are either cryogenic instruments capable of measuring weak moments down to about 1×10^{-8} gauss-cm^3 or low-speed spinner magnetometers utilizing fluxgates as the detecting unit (Foster 1966) and capable of detecting moments of about 5×10^{-8} gauss-cm^3.

The technological problems involved with measuring the samples are, therefore, solvable. A major problem in paleomagnetic research of all types is that the direction of magnetization of the natural remanent magnetization (NRM) is a composite of the original DRM acquired at the time of deposition of the sediment plus a secondary remanence acquired at a later time, often during the Bruhnes polarity chron.

The most serious of these secondary magnetizations is called chemical remanent magnetizations, or CRM, and is the result of chemical changes involving the ferromagnetic minerals. CRM is often acquired during weathering of the sediment at the outcrop when the magnetites and titanomagnetities, which often carry the original DRM, may be oxidized to hematite. If this reaction proceeds to completion, the original remanent magnetization is lost and the sediment becomes remagnetized, effectively resetting the magnetic clock. If the process has not gone to completion, it is sometimes possible to remove this secondary magnetization (McElhinny 1973).

In the presence of any external field, magnetite above ≈ 0.01 mm grain size tends to acquire a secondary component of magnetization due to the movement of domain walls within the magnetic mineral. This magnetization is called viscous remanent magnetization (VRM) and is both time and temperature dependent. Figure 9.3 shows the increase in magnetization with time of a sample from Anza Borrego. Fortunately, however, if the sediments have escaped being elevated to high temperatures, then relatively moderate alternating field (AF) demagnetization, say, 150 oersteds peak field, is adequate to remove these unwanted soft components. Figure 9.4 shows the result of AF demagnetization on sediments from the San Pedro Valley containing a VRM. It can be seen that AF demagnetization is successful in revealing a group of normal vectors and a group of nearly antiparallel reversed vectors. Unfortunately, however, in some cases it is not possible to completely remove the secondary component of magnetization. Figure 9.5 shows the behavior of four reversely magnetized samples, three of which move to stable reversed direction upon partial demagnetization by alternating fields. The fourth sample (101B) moves toward a reversed direction but never achieves a stable direction opposed to the present dipole field. In each case, the sample is interpreted as reversely magnetized.

In our studies we have found that three samples are the minimum number to unambiguously determine polarity in the overwhelming majority of cases. In a study by Opdyke et al. (1977), a ranking system for the sites with respect to reliability was used. In class one sites, the results are all of one polarity and statistically significant (Watson 1956). In class two sites, two of the samples are concordant (i.e., reversed). The third sample may be missing, or if present, forms a wide angle relative to the

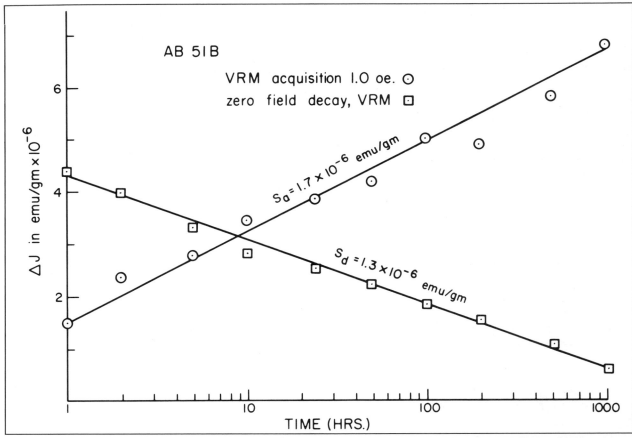

Fig. 9.3. **Demagnetization of a sample AB51B from sediments at the Anza-Borrego Desert, California.**

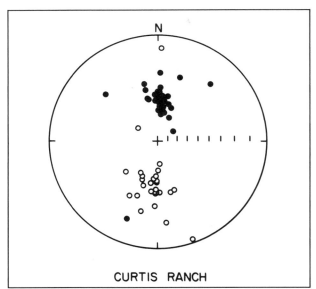

Fig. 9.4. **Polar projection for mean direction of magnetization for fifty-seven sites from Curtis Ranch in the San Pedro Valley, Arizona, after AF demagnetization.**

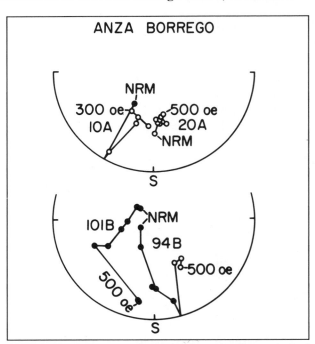

Fig. 9.5. **Polar projection plots showing incremental AF demagnetization of four reversely magnetized samples from the Anza-Borrego Desert, California.**

other two samples. The polarity of class two sites is usually clear but not statistically significant. In class three sites, sample directions are strung between a reversed direction of the field and the present direction of the earth's field. This type of pattern results from the inability of the cleaning method to adequately remove hard secondary components of magnetization. Polarity of class three sites may in many instances be interpreted from the change in direction during demagnetization; however, little confidence can be placed in these determinations. In the class four sites, the directions of magnetization are randomly directed and no useful results can be obtained. The results of this analysis are shown in figure 9.6 for the paleomagnetic section from the Anza-Borrego Desert in California.

The mean direction of magnetization of a terrestrial stratum represents in geologic terms the direction of the earth's magnetic field over a very short time, on the order of thousands of years. Given the latitude and the mean declination and inclination obtained from the site, a pole position corresponding to a geocentric dipole can be calculated. This can be done because the observed declination gives the direction corresponding to a great circle on the earth's surface along which the pole will lie, whereas the inclination determines the distance along this great circle from the site of the pole. The formulas for calculating this pole position are given by McElhinny (1973, pp. 23–25). By convention, virtual geomagnetic pole latitudes are positive for the northern hemisphere and negative for the southern hemisphere; longitudes are measured eastward from the Greenwich meridian and lie between 0° and 360°. The latitude of a Virtual Geomagnetic Pole (VGP) position is simply the latitude of the pole in the present coordinate system of the earth. For Cenozoic deposits, the VGP positions of normally magnetized sites are expected to yield poles near the present geographic north pole, whereas reversed magnetized sites can be expected to yield VGPs near the present geographic south pole. Kent et al. (1984) pointed out that VGP latitude determinations within 45° of the paleoequator may be records of excursions or polarity transitions of the magnetic field, but more often they represent poor or unreliable magnetic polarity data such as the incomplete removal of magnetic overprint. Inclination, declination, and VGP latitude for early Paleocene deposits of the Nacimiento Formation in the San Juan Basin, New Mexico, are shown in figure 9.7. The use of VGP latitude plots in magnetostratigraphy is generally preferable to the use of plots of declination or inclination as a more complete use of the data is made.

In magnetic stratigraphy, two basic collecting patterns are in use at the present time. The first pattern is

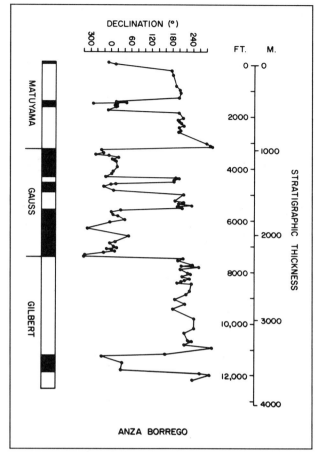

Fig. 9.6. Magnetic polarity of sequence in the Anza-Borrego Desert, California.

to take a single sample at intervals of 10 to 100 cm throughout the section being studied, which may be a sedimentary core or drilled outcrop. This is the common and preferred sampling pattern in deep-sea marine sediments where sedimentation rate is slow. The second pattern, preferred in terrestrial sediments that are deposited at faster rates, is to collect three or more samples per site (all three samples within a distance of 0.5 m). The sites are spaced sequentially, at intervals of approximately 3 to 20 meters, throughout the section. This second type of sampling pattern allows the application of Fisherian statistics at each sampled site. In general, obtaining more than one sample per site guards against the occasional misoriented sample and gives the investigator more confidence in the results. In other types of paleomagnetic investigations where higher precision is required (e.g., in the determination of paleomagnetic pole positions), five or more samples are usually taken per site to ensure greater precision.

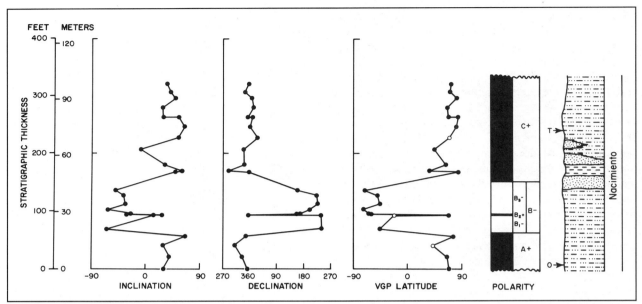

Fig. 9.7. Magnetic polarity sequence, including plot of inclination, declination, and Virtual Geomagnetic Pole latitude for the early Paleocene Nacimiento Formation in Kimbetoh Arroyo, San Juan Basin, New Mexico.

Magnetic Polarity Zonation

Single site magnetic polarity data may on occasion yield instructive results. Because of physical limitations inherent to some outcrops, one site may be all that can be obtained. In most outcrops, however, it is usually possible and desirable to obtain a superposed set of magnetic samples, that is, a local magnetic stratigraphy. Under perfect conditions, the local magnetic polarity stratigraphy should faithfully record every magnetic field reversal in the time interval under study. Intrinsic factors that may compromise or confuse the local magnetic polarity stratigraphy are (1) an abbreviated stratigraphic section, (2) unconformities involving relatively large gaps of time, (3) systematically distorted sedimentation rates, or (4) an absence of suitable lithologies.

Another factor, apart from the sediments themselves, is also crucial when a local magnetic polarity stratigraphy is established. This factor involves the number and frequency of paleomagnetic sites that are actually used in a given case. When using a finite set of paleomagnetic data as described above, the means of finding a magnetic reversal within a given stratigraphic section is strictly a statistical process (Johnson and McGee 1983). The number of reversals that are found in a given section, as opposed to the number actually contained in the section, is a function of the number of paleomagnetic sites used and their distribution (Johnson and McGee 1983). In a stratigraphic section that spans

a significant amount of time, say, $>10^5$ years, placing more and more paleomagnetic sites will theoretically find more and more reversals, if the present concept of the earth's magnetic field is valid (Cox 1968). The ideal sampling program is one that would account for each instant of time represented in the stratigraphic section. This is obviously impossible as a practical matter. Just what then is a reasonable sampling strategy when approaching a new stratigraphic section? Although there are no "rules" in this regard, we can suggest some guidelines on the basis of our experience.

We know that magnetic reversals are generally at least twice as frequent in the Neogene as in the Paleogene. This implies that Neogene strata generally require a higher sampling density than Paleogene strata. Ideally, a site placed at intervals of 50,000 years in Neogene strata, or at intervals of 100,000 years in Paleogene strata, should prove adequate. For most terrestrial environments, we have found that a sample spacing of 3 to 5 meters for Neogene strata and 20 to 30 meters for Paleogene strata is usually sufficient. These limits should not be taken too rigidly, however. In one instance we collected 200 sites over more than 1,000 meters of early Eocene terrestrial strata in the Clark's Fork Basin of Wyoming without detecting any polarity reversals. This illustrates the point that adding more paleomagnetic data in a given section will not necessarily mean that more reversals will be found. The crux of the sampling problem is then: How much is enough? It can be shown theoretically that when the ratio of reversals found (R) to number of paleomagnetic sites (N) is eight or more, that is, (R/N≥8), diminishing returns have been reached (Johnson and McGee 1983).

When we started collecting Cretaceous and Paleocene terrestrial strata from the San Juan Basin of New Mexico, we had no information on the expected polarity sequence, so we attempted to collect at a sample interval of about 3 to 4 meters. We later found that a 10 to 15 meter sample interval would have been sufficient. In contrast, in our initial studies of the Siwalik Group in Pakistan, we employed a sampling interval of 15 to 30 meters (Keller et al. 1977; Opdyke et al. 1979; Barndt et al. 1978). However, we subsequently found that this sampling frequency was not sufficient to resolve the top of Chron 9, and a sampling interval of 6 to 10 meters was needed (Tauxe 1979).

In summary, a reliable polarity zonation is achieved as a result of careful field and laboratory measurement procedures. Polarity interpretation can only be made after the successful isolation of a primary or characteristic direction of magnetization using either thermal or AF partial demagnetization. Some of the most significant indications of reliable polarity zonation are the internal consistency and redundancy of the data both within and between the sampling sites and relatively high paleomagnetic VGP latitudes. Magnetic polarity zonation is most reliable when a large number of paleomagnetic sites are placed sequentially in a thick stratigraphic section and resulting VGP latitudes approach 90°. A number of tests for internal consistency and reliability of paleomagnetic data are well known (e.g., fold tests and conglomerate tests discussed by Graham 1949). New tests (e.g., IRM acquisition discussed by Butler 1982 and Butler and Lindsay, 1985) are being developed and additional tests are likely to be developed in future studies. Perhaps the best test for reliability will prove to be consistency within an ever-growing data base.

Application of Magnetic Polarity Data

Although the bulk of terrestrial rocks do not contain mammalian fossils, they probably contain a remanent magnetization. As described above, this magnetization can often be interpreted in terms of the polarity of the magnetic field at the time of deposition. How, then, can these magnetic data be used as a stratigraphic tool?

By itself, a single magnetic polarity determination can impart no time information. Nevertheless, by comparing polarity of a single site with that from strata in other areas, relative time evaluations can sometimes be made. For example, if the magnetic polarities are of opposite sign, normal versus reversed, then the two sites being compared can*not* be synchronous. By way of illustration, we had established on the basis of one magnetic polarity site from the Fox Canyon local faunas of Kansas that this faunal interval was contained in reversely magnetized sediments. We had established previously that the Benson Local Fauna of Arizona was contained in normally magnetized sediments. We concluded, therefore, that the Fox Canyon and Benson faunas were not exact correlatives (Lindsay et al. 1975). If our confidence in the reality of worldwide magnetic intervals is justified, then this conclusion must necessarily follow.

For another illustration we also attempted to correlate the Rexroad Fauna of Kansas with the Benson Fauna. Our characterization of the Rexroad Fauna was based on one paleomagnetic site. In this case, however, we found that both faunas were associated with normally magnetized rocks. We knew also, by independent means, that the strata that yielded the Benson Fauna was deposited during the Gauss Chron. We knew from other independent criteria that the Rexroad Fauna was not likely to be as young as the Brunhes Chron or as old as Chron V (see fig. 9.1). We concluded, therefore, that the Rexroad Fauna might most likely be correlated with the Gauss Chron. In this latter instance, we specify "most likely" advisedly, because normal polarity of the earth's field is not exclusive to the Brunhes, Gauss, and Chron V. Also, short normal polarity subchrons are also present within the intervening Matuyama Chron (e.g., the Olduvai subchron) and Gilbert (e.g., the Cochiti subchron). The constraint on a precise correlation when comparing limited data from strata with like magnetic polarities is negligible, requiring independent data. The independent data may take the form of additional paleomagnetic data from elsewhere in the same strata, fossil criteria, or radiometric data from the same strata.

The real power of paleomagnetic data, however, emerges when a local magnetic stratigraphy is reliably correlated with the magnetic polarity time scale (MPTS). When such a correlation is made, all the age information contained in the MPTS can be brought to bear on the local stratigraphic problems.

Correlation with the Magnetic Polarity Time Scale

In some terrestrial sections it is possible to order magnetozones by starting at the top of the section in the Brunhes polarity chron and working back in time through each succeeding polarity chron. This was true in the San Pedro Valley of Arizona and to some extent in the Siwaliks of Pakistan. In these instances, placement of magnetozones relative to the MPTS is straightforward. In most other instances, however, it is not.

The MPTS for the last 10 Ma is now known well enough so that in most cases a single radiometric date will allow the correct placement of magnetozones relative to the MPTS. In Cenozoic rocks greater than 10 Ma, it is more difficult, but not impossible, to tie terrestrial magnetozones to the MPTS even when radiometric data are absent. In those instances, the correlation is dependent on the relative length as well as the pattern of magnetozones in long stratigraphic sequences. When a local magnetic sequence is to be correlated with the magnetic polarity time scale by pattern alone, seven or more reversals should be present in the sequence (Johnson and McGee 1983). With less than seven reversals in the sequence, there will not be enough character for comparison, and correlation will be unacceptably tenuous. An important exception to this guideline would involve those parts of the magnetic polarity time scale where a unique feature (i.e., a "fingerprint") is present. In the Late Cretaceous, the length and closeness of polarity chrons 30N and 31N are a unique fingerprint for that part of the magnetic polarity time scale. In the late Paleocene, the couplet of two normal and short magnetozones placed close together and separated from other normal magnetozones by long reversed intervals is another unique fingerprint for chrons 25N and 26N. Similarly, polarity chron 9N, which is a 1.5 Ma normal polarity interval, is a useful fingerprint in the late Miocene. Reversal sequences with other characteristic fingerprint patterns will likely be identified in the future.

Even if it is not possible to affect an immediate tie to the magnetic polarity time scale, it may be possible in one sedimentary basin to correlate between fossil sites using similar sequences of magnetozones. Eventually, it should be possible to correlate the entire magnetic polarity time scale to dated (paleontological and radiometric) terrestrial sequences. The union of radiometric data in terrestrial sediments and magnetic anomalies on the seafloor will provide a well-calibrated time scale for the Cenozoic and Late Cretaceous. Such a unified and calibrated time scale is likely to supersede all other time scales. Vertebrate faunas in terrestrial sediments will contribute to the development, and enhance the utility, of that time scale.

Faunal Datum Events and the Magnetic Polarity Time Scale

During the last twenty years, correlations of Tertiary marine deposits have been aided by the application of radiometric and paleomagnetic data. The resulting chronology, summarized by Berggren and Van Couvering (1974) for the Neogene, permits recognition of several faunal "datum" events. Berggren and Van Couvering (1974, p. IX) define datum events, termed "First Appearance Datum" (FAD) and "Last Appearance Datum" (LAD), as "changes in the fossil record with extraordinary geographical limits." Berggren has applied these datum events primarily to planktonic foraminiferal zones, with calibration of the zones based on faunal change, magnetic polarity reversals, and radiometric dating. In practice, these FAD and LAD events usually (but not always) mark the limits of individual biostratigraphic zones. For the most part, they are equivalent to the boundary of temporally significant biozones. As with all methods of geochronology, some of these datum events have better foundations than others.

In our studies of various terrestrial faunas, we have found it convenient to use a somewhat different "datum" concept. Our use of stratigraphic faunal datum events, termed "Highest Stratigraphic Datum" (HSD) and "Lowest Stratigraphic Datum" (LSD), differ from the use of LAD and FAD by Berggren and Van Couvering (and others). Our indication of *highest stratigraphic datum* rather than *last appearance datum* (and *lowest stratigraphic datum* rather than *first appearance datum*) indicates a local stratigraphic event rather than a widespread temporal event. The HSD and LSD events are restricted to a local section and geographic region; they are explicitly biostratigraphic events. Other faunas with the same taxon may be younger or older than the HSD or LSD taxon, where so designated.

An LAD and FAD event is recognized as a significant biological and biochronologic event prior to evaluating its chronological limits. All records of that taxon are then evaluated biostratigraphically and/or radiometrically to limit the taxon in a precise time frame (Van Couvering and Berggren 1977, p. 284). All faunas containing the designated taxon (e.g., *Hipparion*) are implicitly interpreted younger than the assigned FAD (or older in the case of an LAD). In contrast, HSD and LSD events evaluate dispersals and evolution of an individual taxon (e.g., dispersal of *Equus* from the Glenns Ferry Formation, Idaho; the Palm Springs Formation, California; the Saint David Formation, Arizona; and to the Siwalks and Europe) but say little about the relative age of other faunas that contain that taxon.

Our San Pedro Valley faunal datum events were the first precise stratigraphic calibration of sequential mammalian faunal events in North America (Johnson et al. 1975). Subsequent work (Lindsay et al. 1975; Opdyke et al. 1977; MacFadden 1977; MacFadden et al. 1979;

Neville et al. 1979; Lindsay et al. 1984) has extended the geographic range of some of those faunal changes and added new faunal datum events. In each of these studies, the datum events were based primarily on correlation by magnetic polarity in the stratigraphic sections.

Figure 9.8 is a revision of faunal datum events for the late Cenozoic, based on data presented in 1975 and subsequently elaborated. LSD and HSD faunal events in figure 9.8 are based on references mentioned above and on work undertaken before 1980 but published later (Lindsay et al. 1984). We have revised our correlation of the Hemphillian faunas given in Lindsay et al. (1975) and the correlation of the Chamita Local Fauna by Mac-Fadden (1977) and MacFadden et al. (1979). Those faunas had previously been correlated with polarity chron 5N, but we now correlate the Chamita Local Fauna with polarity chron 6N. We continue to correlate the Coffee Ranch faunas of Texas and the Wikieup Local Fauna of Arizona (MacFadden et al. 1979), along with the Camel Canyon and Redington local faunas (Jacobs 1977) in polarity chron 5N. Following these new interpretations,

we recognize eleven magnetostratigraphically restricted intervals of faunal change in late Cenozoic deposits of North America related to (and limiting) late Hemphillian, Blancan, and Irvingtonian land mammal ages. Note particularly that these faunal datum events do not include all the known records of these taxa in North America. The intervals might be extended or shortened by later work or by records that have not been correlated with the magnetic polarity time scale.

The rationale for restricting faunal datum events to biostratigraphic units is the realization that mammalian biochronology (e.g., land mammal ages) becomes less precise and more difficult to apply as one approaches the boundary between two units. We believe the most accurate means to define the boundary between land mammal ages, and to resolve these units into smaller divisions, is to apply independent chronological methods, that is, paleomagnetic and radiometric data, to biostratigraphic studies. Such studies are especially useful in type sections and in stratigraphically superposed reference sections.

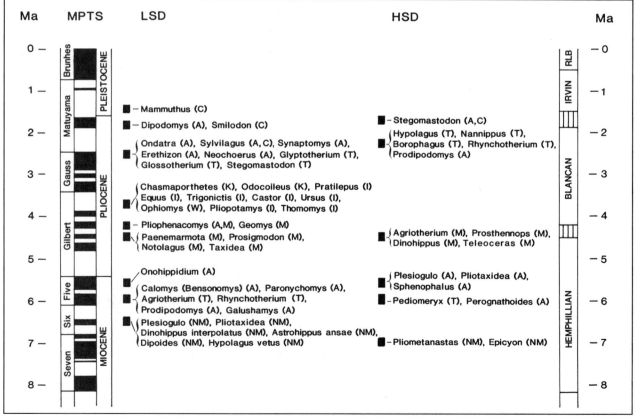

Fig. 9.8. North American late Cenozoic faunal datum events, based on first and last occurrences in faunas and sections with magnetic polarity sequences. (From Lindsay et al. 1984)

Two benefits of defining biostratigraphic faunal datum events are (1) rates of phyletic evolution can be evaluated independently. Previous studies of phyletic evolution were comparisons of morphological evolution between different organisms. Eventually, we should be able to compare rates of faunal turnover and phyletic evolution between continents and at different intervals of time. This type of documentation will bring new insight to evolutionary processes. (2) Dispersal of immigrants between continents and within continents can be calibrated. Approximately one million years elapsed between the appearance of *Equus* in North America and its dispersal to Asia and Europe (Lindsay et al. 1980). The timing of *Equus* dispersal was comparatively short (about 100,000 years or less). Similar studies of the dispersal history of other land mammals, such as *Hipparion,* await documentation of biostratigraphic faunal events in North America and in other continents. As a first step in this direction, figure 9.9 summarizes our current interpretation of the magnetic polarity sequence through approximately 2,000 meters of terrestrial strata in the Potwar Plateau of Pakistan, representing deposition for a period of about twelve million years (Johnson et al. 1982), and figure 9.10 summarizes our current interpretation of almost 2,000 meters of middle and lower Siwalik terrestrial strata in a prime reference section near Chinji village (Barry et al. unpub. data). New Siwalik HSD and LSD events are being defined for the Chinji-Kamlial section. Another illustration of the application of magnetostratigraphy to geochronology is figure 9.11, which summarizes paleomagnetic correlation of Paleocene land mammal ages in deposits from the San Juan Basin, New Mexico, and the Clark's Fork Basin, Wyoming. Full details of the revision to previous results from the San Juan Basin are given in Butler and Lindsay (1985). The combined results from the San Juan Basin and the Clark's Fork Basin have yielded consistent and sequential placements within the magnetic polarity time scale for all North American land mammal ages in the Paleocene through early Eocene.

SUMMARY AND CONCLUSION

It is noteworthy that the Age of Mammals happens to correspond to a period of frequent reversals of the earth's magnetic field. This happy coincidence affords a rare opportunity for independent age-calibration of mammalian evolution.

As with any new chronology, the magnetic polarity time scale must be thoroughly tested. Its acceptance depends, in part, on replication of similar data and its application toward the solution of significant scientific problems. We recognize that the resolution of vertebrate biochronology is an important application of magnetostratigraphy. This resolution is approaching completion for the late Neogene and early Paleogene and is well under way for the Oligocene and Miocene. More long stratigraphic sequences with good faunal records are needed for the completion of this task.

We urge critical evaluation of paleomagnetic data before its acceptance and emphasize (1) internal consistency of paleomagnetic results, analysis of demagnetization cleaning methods, plus various mineralogic and geologic tests are aids to evaluating paleomagnetic data; (2) multiple paleomagnetic sites and multiple samples per site strengthen the confidence of paleomagnetic correlations; and (3) fossil records must be placed precisely relative to magnetic polarity zonation in order for magnetic-chronologic resolution to contribute to understanding of vertebrate evolution.

Finally, the collection of paleomagnetic data in the field is a very critical part of terrestrial magnetostratigraphy because all later interpretations rest on the quality of samples and other data collected in the field.

ACKNOWLEDGMENTS

This work has been supported by NSF research grants EAR-7413860 and EAR-7803326 and the Smithsonian Foreign Currency Program (SFCP 80254100). We gratefully acknowledge this support. Text figures 9.1, 9.2, and 9.8 were drawn by Francine Bonnello.

REFERENCES

Alvarez, W., M. A. Arthur, A. G. Fischer, W. Lowrie, G. Napoleon, I. Premoli Silva, and W. M. Roggenthen. 1977. Upper Cretaceous-Paleocene magnetic stratigraphy at Gubbio, Italy—V. Type section for the late Cretaceous-Paleocene geomagnetic reversal time scale. Bull. Geol. Soc. Amer. 88:383–389.

Barndt, S., X. M. Johnson, N. D. Opdyke, E. H. Lindsay, D. Pilbeam, and R. A. K. Tahirkaheh. 1978. The magnetic polarity stratigraphy and age of the Siwalik group near Dhok Pathan village, Potwar Plateau, Pakistan. Earth Planet. Sci. Letters 41:355–364.

Berggren, W. A., and J. A. Van Couvering. 1974. The late Neogene. Amsterdam: Elsevier.

Brunhes, B. 1906. Recherches sur la direction d'aimentation des roches volcaniques (1) J. Physique, ser. 4, 5:705–724.

Butler, R. F. 1982. Magnetic mineralogy of continental deposits, San Juan Basin, New Mexico, and Clark's Fork Basin, Wyoming. J. Geophys. Res. 87:7843–7852.

Butler, R. F., and E. H. Lindsay. 1985. Mineralogy of magnetic minerals and revised magnetic polarity stratigraphy of

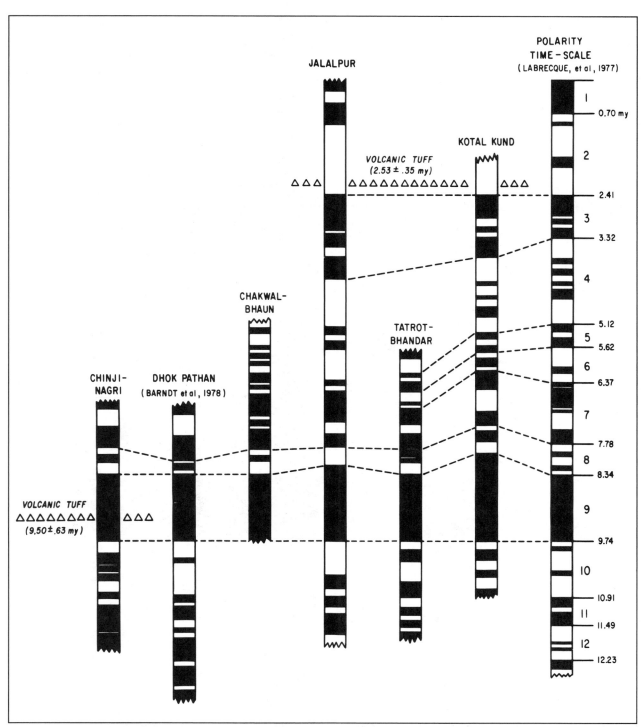

Fig. 9.9. Magnetic polarity sequence of Siwalik deposits in the Potwar Plateau of Pakistan correlated with the magnetic polarity time scale of LaBrecque et al. (1977). (From Johnson et al. 1982)

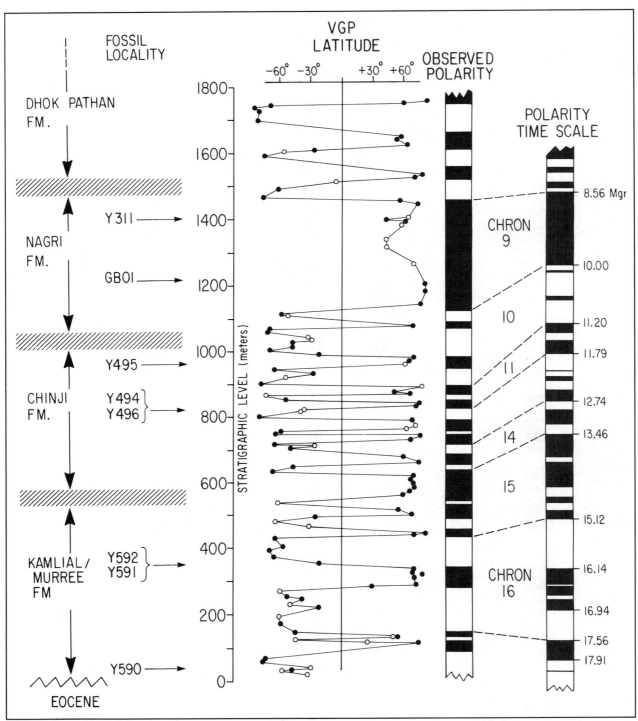

Fig. 9.10. Chinji-Kamlial magnetic polarity sequence near Chinji village, Potwar Plateau, Pakistan. (From Barry et al., unpub. data)

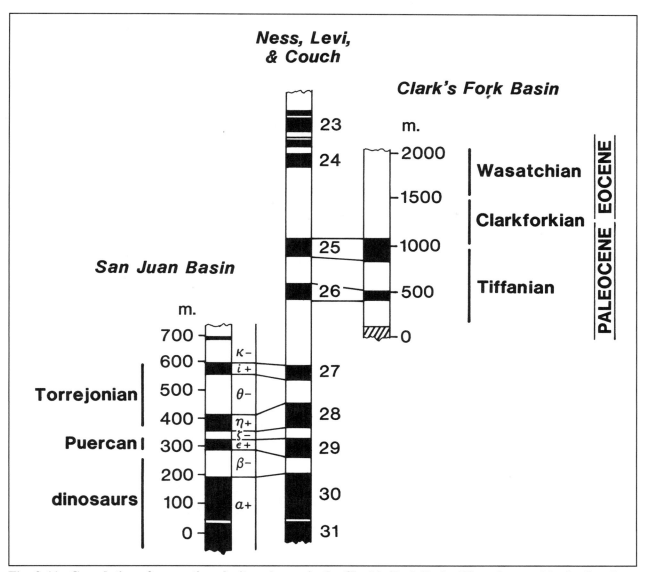

Fig. 9.11. Correlation of magnetic polarity columns in the Clark's Fork Basin, Wyoming, and in the San Juan Basin, New Mexico, with the magnetic polarity time scale of Ness et al. (1980). Stratigraphic intervals of fossil mammals and dinosaurs are shown adjacent to the polarity columns. (From Butler and Lindsay, 1985)

continental sediments, San Juan Basin, New Mexico. J. Geol. 535–554.

Cox, A. 1968. Geomagnetic reversals. Science 163:237–245.

Cox, A., R. R. Doell, and G. B. Dalrymple. 1963. Geomagnetic polarity epochs and Pleistocene geochronometry. Nature 198:1049–1051.

Foster, J. H. 1966. A paleomagnetic spinner magnetometer using a fluxgate gradiometer. Earth Planet. Sci. Letters 1:463–466.

Graham, J. W. 1949. The stability and significance of magnetism in sedimentary rocks. J. Geophys. Res. 54:131–167.

Harrison, C. G. A., and B. M. Funnell. 1964. Relationship of paleomagnetic reversals and micropaleontology in two late Cenozoic cores from the Pacific Ocean. Nature 204:566.

Hedberg, H. D., A. Salvador, and N. D. Opdyke. 1979. Magnetostratigraphic polarity units—A supplementary chapter of ISSC international stratigraphic guide. Geology 7:578–583.

Heirtzler, J. R., G. O. Dickson, E. M. Herron, W. C. Pitman, III, and X. Le Pichon, 1968. Marine magnetic anomalies, geomagnetic field reversals, and motions of the ocean floor and continents. J. Geophys. Res. 73:2119–2136.

Jacobs, L. L. 1977. Rodents of the Hemphillian age Redington local fauna, San Pedro Valley, Arizona. J. Paleont. 51:505–519.

Johnson, N. M., N. D. Opdyke, and E. H. Lindsay. 1975. Magnetic polarity stratigraphy of Pliocene-Pleistocene terrestrial deposits and vertebrate fauna, San Pedro Valley, Arizona. Bull. Geol. Soc. Amer. 86:5–11.

Johnson, N. M., N. D. Opdyke, G. D. Johnson, E. H. Lindsay, and P. A. K. Tahirkheli. 1982. Magnetic polarity stratigraphy and ages of Siwalik Group rocks of the Potwar Plateau, Pakistan. Palaeogeog., Palaeoclimatol., Palaeoecol. 37:17–42.

Johnson, N. M., and V. E. McGee, 1983. Magnetic polarity stratigraphy: Stochastic properties of data, sampling problems, and the evaluation of interpretations. J. Geophys. Res. 88:1213–1221.

Keller, H. M., R. A. K. Tahirkheli, M. A. Mirza, J. D. Johnson, N. M. Johnson, and N. D. Opdyke. 1977. Magnetic polarity stratigraphy of the upper Siwalik deposits, Pabbi Hills, Pakistan. Earth Planet Sci. Letters 36:187–201.

Kent, D. V., M. C. McKenna, N. D. Opdyke, L. J. Flynn, and B. J. MacFadden. 1984. Arctic biostratigraphic heterochroneity. Science 224:173–174.

LaBrecque, J. L., D. V. Kent, and S. C. Cande. 1977. Revised magnetic polarity time scale for the late Cretaceous and Cenozoic time. Geology 5:330–335.

Lindsay, E. H., N. M. Johnson, and N. D. Opdyke, 1975. Preliminary correlation of North American land mammal ages and geomagnetic chronology. In Studies on Cenozoic paleontology and stratigraphy, eds. G. R. Smith and N. E. Friedland, pp. 111–119. Claude W. Hibbard Mem., vol. 3., Univ. Mich. Papers Paleont. 12.

Lindsay, E. H., N. D. Opdyke, and N. M. Johnson. 1980. Pliocene dispersal of *Equus* and late Cenozoic mammalian dispersal events. Nature 287:135–138.

Lindsay, E. H., N. M. Opdyke, and N. M. Johnson. 1984. Blancan-Hemphillian land mammal ages and late Cenozoic mammal dispersal events. Ann. Rev. Earth Planet. Sci. 12:445–488.

Lowrie, W., and W. Alvarez. 1981. One hundred million years of geomagnetic polarity history. Geology 9:392–397.

McDougall, I., and D. H. Tarling. 1963. Dating of polarity zones in the Hawaiian Islands. Nature 200:54–56.

McDougall, I., K. Saemundson, H. Johanneson, N. D. Watkins, and L. Kristjansson. 1977. Extension of the geomagnetic polarity time scale to 6.5 m.y. Bull. Geol. Soc. Amer. 88:1–15.

McElhinny, M. W. 1973. Paleomagnetism and plate tectonics. London: Cambridge University Press.

MacFadden, B. J. 1977. Magnetic polarity stratigraphy of the Chamita Formation stratotype (Mio-Pliocene) of north-central New Mexico. Amer. J. Sci. 277:769–800.

MacFadden, B. J., N. M. Johnson, and N. D. Opdyke. 1979. Magnetic polarity stratigraphy of the Mio-Pliocene mammal-bearing Big Sandy Formation of western Arizona. Earth Planet. Sci. Letters 44:349–364.

Mankinen, E. A., and G. B. Dalrymple. 1979. Revised geomagnetic polarity time scale for the interval 0–5 m.y.b.p. J. Geophys. Res. 84:615–626.

Matuyama, J. 1929. On the direction of magnetization of basalt in Japan, Tyosen, and Manchuria. Japan Acad. Proc. 5:203–205.

Mercanton, P. L. 1926. Inversion de l'inclinaison magnetique terrestre aux ages geologiques. J. Geophys. Res. 31:187–190.

Nagata, T., S. Uyeda, and S. Akimoto. 1952. Self-reversal of thermoremanent magnetism in igneous rocks. J. Geomag. Geoelect. 4:22–32.

Ness, G., S. Levi, and R. Couch. 1980. Marine magnetic anomaly timescales for the Cenozoic and late Cretaceous: A precis, critique, and synthesis. Rev. Geophys. and Space Phys. 18:753–770.

Neville, C., N. D. Opdyke, E. H. Lindsay, and N. M. Johnson. 1979. Magnetic stratigraphy of Pliocene deposits of the Glenns Ferry Formations, Idaho, and its implications for North American mammalian biostratigraphy. Amer. J. Sci. 279:503–526.

Opdyke, N. D. 1972. Paleomagnetism of deep-sea cores. Rev. Geophys. and Space Phys. 10:213–249.

Opdyke, N. D., B. P. Glass, J. D. Hays, and J. H. Foster. 1966. Paleomagnetic study of Antarctic deep-sea cores. Science 154:349–357.

Opdyke, N. D., E. H. Lindsay, N. M. Johnson, and T. Downs. 1977. The paleomagnetism and magnetic polarity stratigraphy of the mammal-bearing section of Anza-Borrego State Park, California. J. Quat. Res. 7:316–329.

Opdyke, N. D., E. H. Lindsay, G. D. Johnson, N. M. Johnson, R. A. K. Tahirkheli, and M. A. Mirza. 1979. Magnetic polarity stratigraphy and vertebrate paleontology of the upper Siwalik Subgroup of northern Pakistan. Palaeogeogr., Palaeoclimatol., Palaeoecol. 27:1–34.

Prothero, D. R., C. R. Denham, and H. G. Farmer. 1982. Oligocene calibration of the magnetic polarity time scale. Geology 10:650–653.

Sclater, J. G., R. D. Jarrard, B. McGowran, and S. Gardner, Jr. 1974. Comparison of the magnetic and biostratigraphic time scales since the late Cretaceous. In Initial Reports of the Deep-Sea Drilling Project, vol. 22. Washington, D.C.: U. S. Govt. Printing Office. Pp. 381–386.

Tarling, D. H., and J. G. Mitchell. 1976. Revised Cenozoic polarity time scale. Geology 4:133–136.

Tauxe, L. 1979. A new date for *Ramapithecus*. Nature 282:399–401.

Vine, F. J., and D. H. Matthews. 1963. Magnetic anomalies over oceanic ridges. Nature 199:947–949.

Watson, G. S. 1956. A test for randomness of directions. Monthly Notices of the Royal Astronom. Soc. Geophys. Suppl. 7:160–161.

10

A PROSPECTUS OF THE NORTH AMERICAN MAMMAL AGES

Michael O. Woodburne

INTRODUCTION

At the time work on this volume began, it was hoped that its development would allow mammalian paleontologists in North America to appraise much more accurately than previously the extent to which the system of mammal ages comprises a succession of temporal intervals that neither overlap in time nor are separated from one another by significant hiatuses. In short, the mammal ages should be able to accurately "cover all of Tertiary time" (Wood et al. 1941). In essence, it now seems that the system of mammal ages does do what Wood et al. (1941) intended. There are few temporal overlaps of the mammal ages, and there are on average few major temporal discontinuities within and between the mammal ages.

It is possible to make these statements for a number of reasons. The first is normal progress of the discipline in gathering more stratigraphic data (and becoming more dedicated to doing that) and upgrading the taxonomy of many groups of mammals. The second is maintaining a distinction between the geochron of a rock unit and the biochron of a faunal unit (one of the common criticisms of the practices employed by Wood et al. 1941). The third is the result of utilizing the growing number of radioisotopic analyses of strata interbedded with mammal-bearing sequences and the more recent application of magnetostratigraphic techniques to those same sequences.

All of these advances, however, would not yield their potential power were it not for the contributors to this volume having accepted the challenge to define as well as characterize the units being developed, whether they are mammal ages, stages, or various kinds of zones.

In this chapter, I have taken the results found in other sections of the book and have put together a master correlation chart of mammal ages, stages, subages, and zones specifically designed to evaluate whether these units actually "cover all of Tertiary time" (fig. 10.1a and b, in pocket). The units are arrayed with respect to their radioisotopic calibration. General correlation also is shown relative to the Cenozoic epochs. Portions of the magnetic polarity time scale also are included (but not for those units still lacking their own magnetic analysis; magnetic signatures have not been extrapolated from oceanic to continental contexts). Except for being the basis of the above-mentioned relationships between mammal ages and other data systems, the stratigraphic details illustrated in other chapters are not repeated here.

Figure 10.1b (in pocket) shows that the Puercan through Clarkforkian mammal ages are of nominally Paleocene age, range in radioisotopic years from about 66.4 to about 58 Ma, and span the interval of time during which magnetic chrons C29 through C24 (part) were developed. There appears to be an unresolved faunal hiatus (the rock succession is essentially continuous, but there is a faunal hiatus) between the Puercan and Torrejonian mammal ages. There also is a faunal as well as a typological stratigraphic hiatus between the Torrejonian and Tiffanian mammal ages and probably a minor faunal as well as a major typological hiatus between the Tiffanian and Clarkforkian mammal ages in the sequence exposed in the Clark's Fork region of Wyoming (see fig. 10.1b, notes 38 to 45).

In greater detail, the reference sections of the lowermost zone of the Puercan (Pu1; including mammal-bearing strata formerly included in the "Mantuan Mammal Age"; Van Valen 1978) is essentially restricted in occurrence to sites in Wyoming, Montana, and Colorado; the type Puercan succession is found in New Mexico. The other Puercan zones (Pu2 and Pu3) are only tentatively recognized in places other than the type sequences in New Mexico. T symbols indicate the probable age-range for stratotype Puercan of Wood et al. (1941).

The faunal hiatus between the Puercan and Torrejonian mammal ages is due to there being at least 150 feet of section in the San Juan Basin between highest Puercan taxa and the first stratigraphic occurrence of *Periptychus carinidens,* the defining criterion for the Torrejonian. Faunas of earliest Torrejonian age (To1) are effectively based on the type fauna of the former Dragonian Mammal Age, Utah. Some sections in the San Juan Basin (with what are type Torrejonian forms) occur stratigraphically above those that yield taxa that are correlative with "Dragonian" taxa, however, so it is possible to bridge the geographic gap by the use of reference sections. Note that the correlation of the "Dragonian Mammal Age" to the Torrejonian type section has been assisted by magnetostratigraphic information (chap. 3). The T symbol indicates the age of the Torrejonian stratotype of Wood et al. (1941).

Sediments containing *Plesiadapis praecursor,* which heralds the beginning of the Tiffanian Mammal Age (Ti1), are not found in the Clark's Fork Basin sequences, Wyoming (Fort Union Formation), which yield the rest of the main fossil record for developing a zonation of Tiffanian strata. Typologically, the Mason Pocket of Colorado, which is the original basis of the Tiffanian Mammal Age, is shown to be correlated to a position (Ti4) stratigraphically well above those that are referred by Archibald et al. (chap. 3) to the base of the Tiffanian. Thus, the gap in typology and apparent age between type Torrejonian and Tiffanian mammal ages must be filled in with fossiliferous strata from Wyoming and Montana deemed to be referable to the Tiffanian Mammal Age (chap. 3).

The lineage-zones of *Plesiadapis* species, with which most of the zones of the Tiffanian and Clarkforkian mammal ages are partitioned, are found in rocks of the Fort Union Formation, Clark's Fork Basin, Wyoming. There appears to be little, if any, faunal hiatus within the terminal Tiffanian-earliest Clarkforkian zone (Ti6/Cf1) based on the stratigraphic disposition of the faunal sites in Polecat Bench (Archibald et al., chap. 3; fig. 3.2, in pocket). The Clarkforkian Stage-Age begins within this zone, as recognized by the abrupt co-occurrence of Rodentia, Tillodontia, *Haplomylus,* and *Coryphodon.* See also fig. 10.1b, notes 39, 41.

In spite of the problems cited above, the data presented in chapter 3 seem to hold promise of further tightening of relationships between the Puercan, Torrejonian, Tiffanian, and Clarkforkian mammal ages and the zonal subdivisions with which they may be partitioned.

A comparable situation is reported for fossiliferous sediments attributed to the Wasatchian, Bridgerian, Uintan, and Duchesnean mammal ages (chap. 4). These mammal ages appear to range in age from about 57 to 39 Ma and to correlate with most of the Eocene Epoch (fig. 10.1b).

Magnetic polarity data are not fully developed for rocks of these ages, and the contributors to chapter 4 have not proposed as full a range of zones as those discussed in chapter 3. Nevertheless, it appears that as defined in chapter 4, the Wasatchian, Bridgerian, Uintan, and Duchesnean mammal ages do not overlap in time but are effectively sequential. At the same time, finely detailed internal subdivisions still are needed (and, once found, to be geographically replicated) for many of these intervals (see notes 29 to 37).

The Wasatchian Stage-Age (Savage 1977) provides a strong means of correlation with early (if not earliest) Eocene mammal faunas of Europe, and taxa that form the basis of the definition of the Duchesnean Mammal Age appear to be immigrants from Asia. In addition to this, mammal-bearing units in California attributable to the Uintan Mammal Age interdigitate with marine rocks capable of correlation to type marine Eocene epochal sequences. For these reasons, the Wasatchian-Duchesnean interval appears to be potentially, if not completely actually, relatable to chronologies in other areas without recourse to radioisoptopic or magnetic polarity information.

Both in chapter 3 and chapter 4, districts are noted where mammals of Clarkforkian age occur stratigraphically below those of Wasatchian age. Important sequences are the variegated beds of the Wind River Basin (fig. 4.2) and the Willwood Formation of the Polecat Bench, Wyoming. See also figure 10.1b, note 37.

Beds with mammals of Wasatchian age do not underlie those with mammals of Bridgerian age in the type areas of either unit. Nevertheless, detailed work in the Huerfano Basin, Colorado, and in the Wind River and Washakie basins, Wyoming, is noted as providing good opportunities to develop reference sections spanning the boundary between the Wasatchian and Bridgerian mammal ages (chap. 4). See figure 10.1b, note 34.

Similarly, work needs to be accomplished in rocks that contain mammals that span the boundary between the Bridgerian and Uintan mammal ages, although this task should be lightened by the fact that the earliest unit of the Uintan (Uinta A, formerly considered to be unfossiliferous) has now been shown to contain taxa by which the beginning of the Uintan Mammal Age may be defined (chap. 4). See also figure 10.1b, note 31.

The Duchesnean Mammal Age begins stratigraphically well up in the Duchesne River Formation, which contains mammals of Uintan age in subjacent strata. Detailed stratigraphic sections apparently could be developed to tightly describe the boundary between the Uintan and Duchesnean mammal ages. See figure 10.1b, note 30.

With respect to internal subdivisions, the Wasatchian has traditionally been divided into three subages, originally based on lithic members (Wood et al. 1941) but now on faunal content. Another, earliest Wasatchian subage (Sandcoulean; fig. 4.1; also chap. 4) has been added, and it and the superjacent Graybullian subage appear to be equivalent to the *Haplomylus-Ectocion* Range-Zone and the *Bunophorus* Interval-Zone developed by Schankler (1980) in strata of the Clark's Fork Basin, Wyoming (fig. 10.1b). The remaining subages of the Wasatchian, the Lysitean and Lostcabinian, appear to equate with the *Heptodon* Range-Zone of the Clark's Fork Basin. The upper part of the *Heptodon* Range-Zone and the Lostcabinian subage appear to be equivalent in age to the *Lambdotherium* Zone proposed by Savage (1977; but see Stucky 1984 for clarification of the temporal extent of this zone). Thus, rocks of Wasatchian age are treated by a hierarchy of mammal subages as well as local (Clark's Fork Basin) and regionally more widespread (*Lambdotherium* Zone) zonations. See figure 10.1b, notes 35, 36.

Subdivisions of the Bridgerian Mammal Age are the Gardnerbuttean, Blacksforkian, and Twinbuttean. The Gardnerbuttean was first coined for mammal-bearing sequences in Colorado (and considered to be Wasatchian in age; chap. 4). This has now been revised to early Bridgerian and in Colorado strata with mammals of Gardnerbuttean age occur stratigraphically above those of Lostcabinian age (and taxa representative of the *Lambdotherium* Zone). Mammals that define the beginning of the Gardnerbuttean subage are also those that define the beginning of the Bridgerian Mammal Age in other locations. These are followed stratigraphically upward in various locations by faunas attributed to "Bridger

A" of the base of the Blacksforkian subage. The Blacksforkian contains faunal elements formerly attributed to "Bridger A and B" in previous terminology. Rocks with Blacksforkian mammals underlie those with mammals of Twinbuttean age (comprised of forms formerly attributed to "Bridger C and D" units). As noted in chapter 4, the Bridger Formation was deposited without obvious hiatuses so the above mammal-bearing succession should be able to account for all of Bridgerian time. See figure 10.1b, notes 31, 32, 33, and 34.

Zonations have not been proposed for rocks of Uintan age; the Uintan Mammal Age has been subdivided into an "early" and a "late" portion (chap. 4), but little detailed biostratigraphic work has been accomplished in that the faunal subdivisions are at the scale of lithic members of the Uinta and Duchesne River formations (chap. 4). No faunal or zonal subdivisions have been proposed for the Duchesnean Mammal Age, which is now restricted to faunas from the upper Dry Gulch Creek and LaPoint members of the Duchesne River Formation (fig. 10.1b, n. 30). In chapter 5, it is noted that the chronofaunal stability seen in faunas of Chadronian, Orellan, and Whitneyan age begins in the Duchesnean and that the most significant faunal change (also see below) in this interval occurs at the base of the Duchesnean, with the immigration of the taxa listed in chapter 5 and on figure 10.1b. Workers concerned with this problem emphasize it by suggesting that the Duchesnean could become a subage of the Chadronian. Alternatively, one could suggest (but this is not formally proposed here) that a new mammal age name be devised to encompass as subages the Duchesnean, Chadronian, Orellan, and Whitneyan mammal ages. This would preserve the original sequential relationships of these units, and the faunal characteristics by which they may be recognized, and at the same time recognize that they occur within an interval of Tertiary time characterized by "chronofaunal creep" (R. J. Emry, pers. com., 1986), so that the boundaries between the "subages" would be subtle (see below), reflecting extinctions and species-level innovations when such could be documented.

Fossiliferous strata attributable to the Chadronian, Orellan, and Whitneyan mammal ages apparently range in age from about 39 to 29 Ma and probably correlate with about the early two-thirds of the Oligocene Epoch (figs. 5.1, 10.1 b). In spite of the fact that fossils are very abundant in rocks of the White River Group in South Dakota, Nebraska, Colorado, and other places in North America, rigorous definition and characterization of even mammal ages in this sequence was hampered by the fact that little close attention was given to stratigraphic detail by those workers who accumulated the outstandingly preserved specimens from these rocks during the past century. Because of this it is virtually impossible for present-day workers to reconstruct many of the stratigraphic details needed for the establishment of closely controlled biostratigraphies and biochronologies. From the data presented in chapter 5, a number of conclusions can be reached, however.

One of these is that the Duchesnean Mammal Age (as currently restricted; chap. 4) can be defined by the co-occurrence of a number of newly appearing taxa, many of which appear to have been immigrants from Asia. Many of these same taxa appear to be characteristic of faunas attributed to the Chadronian Mammal Age so that even though the Duchesne River Formation of Utah (that contains the type Duchesnean faunas) is not stratigraphically continuous with the Chadron Formation of Nebraska and South Dakota (with type Chadronian faunas), it has been suggested (chap. 5) that the Duchesnean might become a subage of the Chadronian Mammal Age (e.g., fig. 10.1b, n. 29). In that case, some of the taxa listed in chapter 5 and on figure 10.1b (note 29) as characteristic of the early Chadronian could distinguish a Duchesnean from a Chadronian portion of this age. These data, and others mentioned below, point to the fact that a major chronofaunal structure developed subsequent to the appearance of the immigrant taxa at the beginning of the Duschesnean and persisted without major reorganization (except at the species level, and with some groups becoming extinct) until the Arikareean, when another suite of immigrants appear in the record (below; chap. 6; fig. 10.1b, notes 25–30). This relatively stable structure promotes continuity rather than change, so that adjustments are likely to be of small scale and made even more difficult to recognize in the absence of a well-controlled biostratigraphy.

Thus, until detailed biostratigraphies, radioisotopic calibrations, and magnetic polarity stratigraphies are developed, the Duchesnean-Whitneyan record is characterized by "chronofaunal creep," obviating a facile definition of mammal age or subage boundaries.

The work of D. R. Prothero and colleagues (see Prothero 1986 and references therein) is filling this need, but a great deal of alpha-level taxonomy and biostratigraphy still needs to be accomplished for the strata involved. The sequence exposed in the Trans-Pecos district of Texas is a good candidate for a place at which to attempt to determine a boundary between the Duchesnean and Chadronian ages or subages, and many of the basic data already have been accumulated there (see chap. 5). At the same time, lack of detailed biostratigraphies for essentially all parts of the White River Group obviate this possibility for the present.

Even at the present state of information, however, it appears that the Chadronian Mammal Age may be divisible into three parts. The first is chiefly recognized on having taxa that are related to those involved with the Duchesnean immigration mentioned above (with certain additional differences; chap. 5; fig. 10.1b). The medial interval can be said to contain taxa that are not of that stamp, and neither are like those found in the late interval which appear to have affinities to species of the Orellan Mammal Age. See also figure 10.1a, note 27.

Whereas it appears that mammalian faunas of Orellan age can be distinguished from those of the Chadronian, the problem is more acute with respect to distinguishing taxa of Whitneyan age from Orellan forms (fig. 10.1a, note 26). More biostratigraphic work is needed to securely delineate the stratigraphic position of the boundary between these mammal ages as based on paleontological criteria.

Prothero (1982, 1985) and Prothero et al. (1982, 1983) proposed certain biostratigraphic zonations for strata of the White River Group and developed the correlation of these rocks to the magnetic polarity time scale, replicated in figure 10.1a and b. The slanted dashed lines between the Chadronian, Orellan, and Whitneyan mammal ages point up the lack of a regionally secure biostratigraphic definition for these units and the lack of a detailed radioisotopic calibration and magnetic polarity characterization of that regional boundary.

Fossiliferous sequences attributed to the Arikareean through Hemphillian mammal ages range in age from about 29 to 5 Ma, are largely correlative with the Miocene Epoch, and record a continuing, but intermittently reorganized, chronofaunal structure with increasing regional endemism through time. Many radioisotopic data are available, but an integrated magnetic polarity sequence is yet to be developed. The base of the Arikareean is defined on the immigrant taxa discussed in chapter 6 and shown in figures 6.3 and 10.1a.

The style of sedimentation that gave rise to what appears to have been a largely continuously deposited succession of rocks attributed to earlier mammal ages changed in the "Miocene" to a succession of local sequences in which the individual parts are separated from one another by unconformities, especially in the midcontinent region of the United States. Partly for this reason, few zonal hierarchies have been proposed. It is instructive that the *Meniscomys, Entoptychus-Gregorymys,* and *Mylagaulodon* concurrent range-zones were developed in the John Day Formation, Oregon, and that two or more of these zones can be correlated to strata in Idaho, Montana, South Dakota, and Nebraska which reflect relatively continuous sedimentation. (See fig. 10.1a, note 23). Other zonal constructs (the *Cupidinimus ne-braskensis, Pseudadjidaumo stirtoni, Copemys longidens,* and *Copemys russelli* assemblage-zones of the Barstow Formation, California) have not been recorded in other sites as yet.

As seen in chapter 6, subdivisions of the "Miocene" mammal ages are informal and take the form of "early" and "late," with some of these being partitioned into further "early" and "late" intervals. All of the units have defined boundaries, and most of those are based on taxa that appear to have been Eurasian immigrants. Beginning about 8 Ma, however (*Pliometanastes,* etc.), immigrant taxa from South America also are important and define the beginning of the Hemphillian Mammal Age (figs. 6.3, 10.1a; the age of the Clarendonian-Hemphillian boundary follows Lindsay et al. 1984; see also chap. 9).

From the above and as detailed in chapter 6, typological hiatuses are not a problem from a geographic point of view; only the Barstovian Mammal Age was typified in a succession (California) not part of the Great Plains region (fig. 10.1a, note 22). At the same time, revision or extension of the concept of what rocks and faunas are attributed to a given mammal age has suffered greater development in those of the "Miocene" than for any other Cenozoic epoch (fig. 10.1a, notes 11, 15, 19, 21, 22, 24, 25). At the same time, the stage has been set for the development of local biostratigraphies with the potential for regional biochronologic correlation at the zonal level, but detailed sampling and taxonomic analysis at the specific level will be required before this can be realized. As presently correlated, no serious overlaps in the "Miocene" mammal ages are known, but that may be due to the fact that taxonomic analysis largely is at the generic level (or that, as named, species are not widely ranging geographically). Rather than overlaps, however, there appear to be definite, if relatively short, hiatuses within and between the Arikareean and Hemingfordian and Hemingfordian and Barstovian mammal ages (fig. 10.1a, notes 22, 24), and a distinct hiatus has been reported within the Arikareean, Hemingfordian, and Hemphillian mammal ages (e.g., fig. 10.1a, n. 15; chap. 6).

Whether or not the "Miocene" mammal ages can be said to cover all of Arikareean through Hemphillian time remains to be determined, but future advances should—based on discussions in chapter 6—constitute relatively minor innovations. Stratigraphically "long" sequences do exist, the most notable of which are the Caliente Formation of southern California, the John Day Formation of Oregon, the Arikaree Group of Nebraska and Colorado, and the units of the Texas coastal plain (chap. 6). Work in progress (MacFadden and Woodburne) may

result in the development of a magnetic polarity stratigraphy in the Hector and Barstow formations of the Mojave Desert, California, spanning the late Arikareean through late Barstovian interval to aid in the biochronologic ranking of faunas of those ages in other parts of North America.

The fossiliferous successions attributed to the Blancan, Irvingtonian, and Rancholabrean mammal ages range in age from about 5 Ma to the present and are essentially correlative with the Pliocene and Pleistocene epochs (fig. 10.1a). As discussed in chapter 7, the local stratigraphic sequences are generally of short duration and bounded by unconformities. At the same time, and especially for faunas of Blancan age, a few stratigraphically "long" sequences are known. These, chiefly in the Anza-Borrego district of southern California, the Saint David Formation in the San Pedro Valley of Arizona, and the Glenns Ferry Formation of the Snake River Plain of Idaho, not only have allowed the collection of a stratigraphic array of fossil mammals but also are interbedded with volcanic materials amenable to radioisotopic analysis and additionally have been sampled for magnetic polarity data. These reference sections have enabled the more precise biochronologic and geochronologic correlation of others in North America, so that the problem of typology is largely circumvented (see fig. 10.1a, notes 10, 11, 15).

Inspection of figure 7.3 invites the interpretation that, if all of the correlations portrayed there are correct, the combination of faunal sequences accounts for most, if not all, of the time span represented by the Blancan, Irvingtonian, and Rancholabrean mammal ages. Although there may be some debate as to the beginning of the Irvingtonian Mammal Age, depending on criteria chosen (chap. 7), the potential for overlap with faunas of Blancan age appears to be small (fig. 10.1a, n. 11).

Like those of the "Miocene," the "Pliocene" and "Pleistocene" mammal ages are divided into a number of subages; two for the Blancan Mammal Age, three for the Irvingtonian. The Rancholabrean remains undivided in this context (fig. 10.1a, notes 8, 9).

At the same time, C. A. Repenning (chap. 8) has proposed a number of zonations of the same span of time (actually beginning in the Hemphillian Mammal Age) which (see fig. 8.1 and discussion in chap. 2) are more refined than the subages proposed in chapter 7. Where the two systems meet in the stratigraphic column, they are relatively congruent, and one is left with the impression that any contradictions (based on different interpretations of where a particular taxon first occurs in the record) can be resolved (see fig. 10.1a, notes 7, 8, 9).

In summary, those mammal ages that appear to be

potentially close to the original intent of Wood et al. (1941), that is, that the units account for all of the geologic time they represent, are Tiffanian, Clarkforkian, Wasatchian, Blancan, and Irvingtonian. Those for which a geologically essentially continuous stratigraphy is known but which need more biostratigraphic work include Puercan, Torrejonian, Bridgerian, Uintan, Duchesnean, Chadronian, Orellan, Whitneyan, Arikareean, Hemingfordian (Caliente Formation, Hector and Barstow formations, California), Barstovian, Clarendonian, and Rancholabrean (Medicine Hat sequence, Alberta). The Hemphillian Mammal Age could be part of the latter list (Caliente Formation, California). It is hoped that one result of this volume will be to stimulate research in accomplishing the goal of developing a temporal sequence based on fossil mammals which "covers all of Tertiary time."

A final note is offered on the extent to which the fossil mammal record is capable of finely subdividing and discriminating intervals of time. Inspection of figure 10.1a and b suggests that zonal schemes based on endemic evolution of taxa (e.g., Puercan through Clarkforkian mammal ages) can discriminate temporal intervals distinctly less than one million years in duration. Some sequences of immigration coupled with endemic evolution (Blancan through Rancholabrean microtine events; chap. 8) discriminate comparably brief intervals. For other parts of the time scale (e.g., Arikareean through Hemphillian), temporal intervals recognized by successive immigrations are generally of longer duration. At the moment, one of the best examples of the potential resolving power of mammalian biostratigraphy is seen in figure 7.2, where the closely sequential stratigraphic array—in various sections—of first occurrences of taxa generated from whatever source (immigration, endemic evolution) suggests that at least local zonal sequences could be established wherein the intervals of time contained between boundaries defined on those first occurrences would be considerably shorter than 0.5 Ma. This is comparable to estimates suggested by Woodburne (1977) for temporal intervals based on cricetid and geomyoid rodents, taken from examples in Lindsay (1972) and Rensberger (1971). Claims made or alluded to in this book regarding the strong potential for zonations based on the evolution of mammals to finely sub-divide the rock and temporal record of which they are a part appear to be justified by the evidence presented herein.

REFERENCES

Berggren, W. A., D. V. Kent, J. J. Flynn, and J. A. Van Couvering. 1985. Cenozoic geochronology. Bull. Geol. Soc. Amer. 96:1407–1418.

Lindsay, E. H. 1972. Small mammal fossils from the Barstow Formation, California. Univ. Calif. Publ. Geol. Sci., vol. 93.

Lindsay, E. H., N. D. Opdyke, and N. M. Johnson. 1984. Blancan-Hemphillian land mammal ages and late Cenozoic mammal dispersal events. Ann. Rev. Earth Planet. Sci. 12:445–448.

Prothero, D. R. 1982. How isochronous are mammalian biostratigraphic events? 3d No. Amer. Paleont. Conv. Proc. 2:405–409.

———. 1985. North American mammalian diversity and Eocene-Oligocene extinctions. Paleobiol. 11:389–405.

Prothero, D. R., C. R. Denham, and H. G. Farmer. 1982. Oligocene calibration of the magnetic polarity time scale. Geology 10:650–653.

Prothero, D. R., C. R. Denham, and H. G. Farmer. 1983. Magnetostratigraphy of the White River Group and its implications for Oligocene geochronology. Palaeogeogr., Palaeoclimat., Palaeoecol. 42:151–166.

Rensberger, J. M. 1971. Entoptychine pocket gophers (Mammalia, Geomyoidea) of the early Miocene John Day Formation, Oregon. Univ. Calif. Publ. Geol. Sci., vol. 90.

Savage, D. E., 1977. Aspects of vertebrate paleontological stratigraphy and geochronology. In Concepts and methods of biostratigraphy, eds. E. G. Kauffman and J. E. Hazel, pp. 427–442. Stroudsburg, Pa.: Dowden, Hutchinson, and Ross.

Stucky, R. K. 1984. The Wasatchian-Bridgerian Land Mammal Age boundary (early to middle Eocene) in western North America. Ann. Carnegie Mus. 53:347–382.

Van Valen, L. 1978. The beginning of the age of mammals. Evol Theory 4: 45–80.

Wood, H. E., II, R. W. Chaney, J. Clark, E. H. Colbert, G. L. Jepsen, J. B. Reeside, Jr., and C. Stock. 1941. Nomenclature and correlation of the North American continental Tertiary. Bull. Geol. Soc. Amer. 52:1–48.

Woodburne, M. O. 1977. Definition and characterization in mammalian chronostratigraphy. J. Paleont. 51:220–234.

INDEXES

SYSTEMATIC INDEX

In an attempt to make the age ranges of generic and specific level taxa as unambiguous (and hopefully as accurate) as possible, the following conventions have been used.

All generic taxa are listed in unmodified form.

The age range of a genus may be: age entry—age entry, with no modification, e.g., Wa3-Br3 as for *Absarokius*. In this instance there appear to be no ambiguous aspects as to the age range of the taxon.

In such cases where the earliest or latest age for the genus is taken from species questionably referred to that genus, usually indicated by " " around the generic name associated with the species, that portion of the age range is preceded by a ?, e.g., ?He2, Ba1-Cl2, for *Merychippus*. Thus it is possible to differentiate the portion of the age range of the genus based on secure identifications versus that based on questionable entries.

Species under the genus that are uncontroversially allocated (specific name preceded in the case of *Merychippus* by *M.*) are distinguished from those of questionable allocation (specific name preceded in this case by "*M.*"). If different from the ages of securely allocated species, generic age-ranges preceded by ? derive from the ages of those questionably allocated species.

Comparably, the age range for species based on taxa designated by modifiers such as "cf." or "aff." before the species name is qualified by the age being preceded by a ?. An example is the earliest age of *Dipoides* cf. *stirtoni,* ?Hh1, versus Hh2 for unequivocal identifications of *D. stirtoni*. In rare cases, the page number for an entry is queried (?). This indicates that whereas the overall age range of the taxon is not in doubt, its presence is queried at a particular locality (signified at the page in question). Finally, in some relatively small number of instances where the complete age range of a taxon is not derivable from the text, that has been supplied by the pertinent chapter chairman. This support is gratefully acknowledged.

It is hoped that these conventions will result in two aims: (1) an accurate as possible current estimate of the age range of a taxon; (2) the age and taxonomic assignment of ambiguously allocated species (unambiguous as to either referral of a species to a genus, or referral of a taxon to a species). In a departure from certain conventions, this approach suggests that species are viable taxonomic and stratigraphic entities; they are not solely geographic or stratigraphic varieties; their generic affinities (or lack of them) are important to determining the stratigraphic ranges of genera; that a deliberate scientific decision is required to include or exclude such species from a genus when summarizing age range information of taxa from any source, including this book. Whether or not these distinctions are important for those who construct notions of, e.g., origination/extinction/faunal turnover from these types of data, the distinctions certainly must be important for those who attempt to generalize age-ranges of taxa for biostratigraphic or biochronologic appraisals.

As for the subject index, L = left-hand column; R = right-hand column; no letter means that the page is not divided into columns. First and last occurrences are indicated by numerical subdivision of the mammal ages. For instance, Pu1, Wa1, and Br1 correspond to the earliest subdivision of the Puercan, Wasatchian, and Bridgerian mammal ages, respectively. If the original authors show no subdivision of a mammal age, none are used here (e.g., Orellan, Whitneyan). Arabic numerals for the Blancan, Irvingtonian, and Rancholabrean mammal ages follows useage in chap. 7; Roman numerals for the same mammal age follows subdivisions used in chap. 8. Irvingtonian 1, 2, 3 correspond respectively to Sappan, Cudahyan, and Sheridan sub-ages, as in chap. 7. Ir3 in chap. 7 is the approximately same interval as RlbI of chap. 8. Rct. = Recent.

ALGAE

Discoaster sublodoensis, 98R

POLLEN

Aquillpollenites, 41L
Platycarya, 66R
  P. platycaryoides, 66R

FORMINIFERANS

benthic (benthonic) foraminiferans, 146R, 154L, 176R
foraminiferans, 68L, 99R, 156R, 213R
Globoratalia, 213R
  G. menardi, 213R
  G. truncatulinoides, 213R, 124L
Operculinoides, 176R
planktonic foraminiferans, 99R, 100L, 154L, 176R, 213R
Textularia, 176R

MOLLUSCS

mollusca(n), mollusks, 96R, 100L, 100R, 156L, 156R, 176R
Potamides, 176R
  P. matsoni, 176R

FISHES

chondrichthyean, 68L
fish, 178L
osteichthyean, 68L

AMPHIBIANS

amphibians, 178L

REPTILES

reptiles, 68L, 178L
Stylemys, 142R

MAMMALS

Aaptoryctes, Ti5, 34, 56L, 60L
Absarokius, Wa3-Br2, 85R, 86L, 86R, 87R, 88L
aceratherine rhino (artiodactyl), 178R
Achaenodon, Ui1-Du, 89L, 89R, 97L, 102R, 106R
Acheronodon, Pu1, 33, 40R, 43L, 44L
  A. garbani, Pu1, 40R
Acmeodon, To1-Ti3, 34, 48R, 50R, 51L, 53L, 56L, 57R, 58L, 58R
Acritoparamys, Cf1-Br1, 39, 63L, 64L, 65L, 65R
  A. atavus, Cf, 63L, 64L
  A. atwateri (=*Paramys annectens*), Cf, 63L
Adapidae, 85L
adapid (primate), 82R, 83R
adapisoricid(s) (primate), 58R, 101R
Adjidaumo, Ch-Or, 120L, 133L, 134R, 135R, 138L, 138R, 142R, 144L
  A. minimus, Ch1-2, 120L, 138R
  A. minutus, Ch3-Or, 138L, 138R, 142R
Aelurocyon, Ar4, 185L, 194L
Aelurodon, Ba2-Cl2, 155R, 160L, 160R, 169L, 173L, 177L, 177R, 189L, 190L, 194R
  A. asthenostylus, Ba2, 160L
  A. francisi, Ba3, 177L
  A. mortifer (= *Epicyon* cf. *saevus*), Cl1, 160R
  A. taxoides (= *A. aphobus*), Cl1-2, 155R, 160R
Aepinacodon, Ch1, 133L
  A. americanus, Ch1, 133L

A. rostratus, Ch1, 133L
Aepycamelus, He2-Hh1, 158R, 159L, 168L, 169L, 173L, 173R, 174R, 175L, 176R, 177L, 179R, 187L, 190R, 191L, 194L, 194R
  A. leptocolon, Ba3, 173R
  A. giraffinus, Ba3, 173R
Agnotocastor, Wh-Ar1, 145L, 163L, 163R
  A. praetereadens, Wh, 145L
agriochoerids (artiodactyl), 89L, 89R, 107R
Agriochoerus, Du-Ar1, 90L, 129L, 132R, 133L, 134R, 135L, 145L, 146L
  A. maximus, Du-Ch, 129L
Agriotherium, Hh3, 159, 175L, 181L, 183, 192L, 194R, 214R, 216R, 242L, 279L, 279R
  A. schneideri, Hh3, 181L
"*Albanosmilus*" (= *Barbourofelis*), Hh1, 174R
Alces, Rlb-Rct., 223R, 225L
  A. alces, Rlb-Rct., 225L
Aletodon, Ti3-Cf3, 37, 56L, 58L, 59L, 60L, 60R, 62L, 63L, 64L, 64R, 65L, 65R
  A. gunnelli, Cf2-?3, 62R, 63L, 64L, 64R, 65L
aletomerycine dromomerydids (artiodactyl), 158R
Aletomeryx, He1, 56R, 158R, 167R, 183, 186R, 194L
Allomyinae, allomyine (rodent), 166L, 172L, 184R
Allomys, Ar1-Ba3, 161L, 165R, 166L, 168R, 172L, 183, 184R, 185L, 193R
Allophaiomys, subgenus of *Microtus* of authors
Allophaiomys, Ir1-2, IrI-II, 21R, 22L, 218R, 221L, 222R, 238R, 239R, 248R, 249L, 249R, 250L, 260L, 260R, 261L, 261R, 262R
  A. guildayi, Ir2, IrII, 22L, 261R, 262R
  A. pliocaenicus, Biharian, Europe, 222R
Allops, Ch1-3, 132L
Altanius, early Eocene, Asia, 68L
Alticola, Rct., Asia, 248R
Aluralagus, Bl2-Ir1, 226R
Ambloctonus, Wa2-Wa4, 85R
"*Amblycastor*" (= *Anchitheriomys*), Ba1, 187R
Amebelodon, Cl2, Hh1-2, 162L, 164R, 170L, 170R, 173R, 174R, 175L, 179R, 183, 190L, 190R, 194R
  A. fricki, Hh2, 170R, 173R
  A. hicksi (incl. *A. paladentatus*), Hh1, 164R, 173R
Amelotabes, Ti4, 39, 56L, 59
Ammospermophilus, Ba2-Rct., 13R, 218R
  A. fossilis, Cl1, 13R
Amphictis, He1, 167R, 183, 186R, 194L
amphicynodontine (carnivore), 132R
Amphicyon, He1-Ba1, 159L, 161R, 162L, 167R, 168L, 172L, 173L, 176L, 183, 186R, 189L, 194L, 194R
  A. frendens, Ba1, 162L
  A. ingens, Ba1, 159L, 173L
  A. sinapius, Ba1, 161R
Amphicyonidae, amphicyonid (carnivore), 90R, 129L, 166R, 167L, 169L, 185L, 189L, 191L, 194R
Amphicyoninae, amphicyonine (carnivore), 166R
Amynodon, Ui1-Du, 89L, 89R, 90L, 97L, 97R, 102R, 104R, 105R
Amynodontopsis, Ui1-Du, 100R, 107R
amynodonts (perissodactyl), 89L, 89R
Anacodon, Ti-Wa3, 85R
anagalidans, 67R
Anaptomorphus, Br2, 18R, 84R, 85L, 86L, 88L, 97L
  A. homunculus (= *Tetonius*), Wa, 85L
Anchippodus, Br, 107R
Anchippus, Ar4, 176L
  A. texanus, Ar4, 176L
Anchitheriomys, He2-Ba2, 158R, 160L, 176R, 177L, 187L, 187R, 189L, 194L, 194R
Anchitheriinae, anchitheriine equid (perissodactyl), 169L, 188R, 190R
Anchitherium, Ar3-Ba2, 156R, 166R, 172L, 176L, 178R, 185L, 194L, 194R
  A. clarencei, He1, 178R

Anchitherium (Hypohippus), 122L
Anchitherium (Parahippus), 122L
Anconodon, To3-Ti2, 33, 48R, 51L, 53L, 56L, 57R, 58L
    A. pygmaeus, Br1, 87R
Anemorhysis, Wa3-Wa4, 85R
Angustidens, He1, 183, 186R, 194L
Anisonchus, Pu2-Ti1, 37, 42L, 43L, 46L, 46R, 49L, 50R, 51L, 53L, 55L, 56L, 57R
Ankalagon, To3, 37, 48R, 52R
Ankylodon, Ui2-Ch2, 89R
anthracothere(s), 132R, 163L
Antesorex, He1, 183, 186R, 194L
Antiacodon, Wa3-Br3, 86R, 87L, 88L, 88R
Antilocapridae, antilocaprid (artiodactyl), 167L, 174R, 181L, 185L, 188R, 190L, 194R
antilocaprine (artiodactyl), 169R, 174R, 190L, 190R
Apatemys, Cf1-Du, 18R, 34, 63L, 64L, 65R, 85R, 88L, 88R
Apatemyidae, apatemyids (proteutherian), 34, 58R
Apatosciuravus, Cf1-Wa, 39, 63L, 64L, 65L, 65R
Apheliscus, Cf1-Wa3, 37, 62R, 63L, 64L, 65L, 65R, 84R
    A. nitidus, Cf1-3, 62R, 63L, 65R
Aphelops, He2-Hh3, 159R, 170R, 173R, 175L, 176R, 177L, 183, 187L, 194L, 214R
    A. kimballensis, Hh1-2, 170R, 173R
    A. (Paraphelops) yumensis (incl. ?*Paraceras ponderis*), Hh2, 173R
Aphronorus, To1-?Ti3, 34, 48R, 50R, 51R, 52R, 56R, 57R, 58R
    P. orieli, Ti1, 57R
aplodontid(s), aplodontoid (rodents), 89R, 161L, 163R, 165R, 168R, 184R, 185R
Apternodus, Du-Ch2, 90R, 120L, 133L, 137L
    "*A*". *altitalonidus*, Ch2, 137L, 137R
    A. mediaevus, Ch2, 137L
Aratomys multifidus, ca 6 Ma, Mongolia, 328R
Archaeohippus, Ar4-Ba2, 159L, 161R, 164R, 172L, 176R, 178R, 185L, 189L, 194L, 194R
    A. blackbergi, He1, 178R
    A. mourningi, Ba1-2, 159L
    A. ultimus, Ba1, 161R, 164R
Archaeolagus, Ar1-4, 184R, 193R
Archaeomeryx, 133L
Archaeotherium, Ch1-Ar1, 132R, 134R, 135R, 142R, 145L, 146L, 184R
    A. mortoni, Ch3-Or, 143L
Arctocyon, To3-Ti5, 37, 42R, 48R, 52R, 55L, 56L, 57R, 58L, 58R, 59R
Arctocyonidae, arctocyonid(s) (condylarth), 36, 42L, 42R, 58R, 68R, 101L
Arctocyonoides, 42R
Arctostylopidae (notoungulate), 38
Arctostylops, Ti5-Cf3, 38, 56L, 59R, 60R, 62R, 63L, 64L, 65L, 65R, 96R
    A. steini, Cf2, 96R
Ardynomys, Ch1, 132L, 133L, 134R, 136L
Arfia, Wa1-Br1, 85R
armadillo (edentate), 225L
Armintodelphys, Wa4-Br2, 86R
Arretotherium, Ar3-He1, 164L
    A. arcidens, Ar3, 164L
    A. fricki, He1, 172L
Artiodactyla, artiodactyl, 62L, 66R, 85L, 89L, 142R, 158L, 161R, 167L, 167R, 175R, 176L, 177R, 179R, 190R
Arvicola, Steinheimian-Rct., 239R
Arvicolidae, Arvicolinae, arvicoline (rodent), 21L, 191L, 192L, 214R, 216L, 216R, 217L, 218R, 219L, 219R, 221L, 225R, 238R, 242L
Astrohippus, Cl2-Hh3, 174R, 175L, 179R, 181L, 190L, 190R, 192L, 194R, 195L, 214R, 216R, 279L
    A. ansae, Hh3, 175L
    A. martini, Cl2, 179R
    A. stocki, Hh3, 174R, 175L, 216R

Atopomys, IrII, 22L, 261R, 262R
    A. salvelinus, IrII, 22L, 261R, 263L
    A. texensis, IrII, 22L, 261R, 262R
Australocamelus, He1, 176L
Aulolithomys, Ch1-2, 134R
Auxontodon, Ui1-Ui2, 107R
Avunculus, To3, 34, 48R, 52R
Baioconodon, Pu1-Pu3, 36, 43L, 44L, 46R
Barbourofelis, Cl1-Hh2, 159R, 160R, 169R, 170R, 174R, 175L, 179R, 183, 190L, 190R, 191L, 194R
    B. fricki, Hh1-2, 160R, 170R, 174R
    B. osborni, Cl1, 159R
Barbouromeryx, Ar4-He2, 167L, 168L, 172L, 183, 185L, 186R, 187L, 194L
Barylambda, Ti3-Wa3, 38, 55L, 56L, 58R, 59R, 60L, 60R, 63L, 64L, 65L, 65R
Barylambdidae (pantodont), 38, 106R
Bassariscus, Hh1-Rct., 157L
    B. antiquus, Hh1, 157L
Bathygenys, Ch1-Or?, 132R, 133L, 135L
Bathyopsis, ?Wa1-Br2, 85R, 88L, 88R
Bathyopsoides, 55L
bear (carnivore), 170R
beaver(s) (rodent), 155R, 166R, 169L, 171R, 174L, 180L, 185L, 216R
Beckia, Cl2, 169R, 179R, 190L
Bensonomys, subgenus of *Calomys*
Bison, Rlb; RlbII-Rct., 21R, 214R, 220L, 244L, 244R, 225L, 228L, 251L, 252L, 264L
    B. alleni, Rlb, 244R
    B. antiquus, Rlb, 244R
    B. bison, Rlb-Rct., 244R
    B. bison bison, Rlb-Rct., 244R
    B. bison antiquus, Rlb, 244R
    B. crassicornis, Rlb, 225L, 228L
    B. bison occidentalis, Rlb, 244R
    B. latifrons, Rlb, 244R
    B. priscus (= *B. crassicornis*), Rlb, 244R
Bisonalveus, Ti1-Ti3, 34, 56L, 57R, 58L, 58R, 63L
Blackia, He2, 158L, 183, 187L, 194L
Blarina, BlV-Rct., 226R
Blastomerycidae, Blastomerycinae, blastomerycine moschid (artiodactyl), 161R, 167L, 169L, 176R, 185L, 190L
Blastomeryx, Ar4-Ba2, 167L, 176L, 178L, 178R, 183, 185L, 189L, 194L, 194R
    "*B*." *cursor* (= *Barbouromeryx*), Ar4, 185L
    "*B*." *texanus*," Ar4, 176L
bog lemmings (rodent), 21L
Bomburia, Pu2-Pu3, 38, 43L, 46L, 46R
Bootherium, Rlb, 225L
    B. sargenti, Rlb, 225L
borophagine (carnivore), 166R
Borophagus, Hh3-Ir1, BlI-Ir1, 181L, 192R, 195L, 214R, 217L, 217R, 218L, 218R, 220L, 221L, 228L, 279R
    B. diversidens, BlI, 214R
    B. ("*Osteoborus*") *dudleyi*, Hh3-BlI, 181L
Bos (Poephagus), Rlb-Rct., 228L
Bothriodon, 133L
Bouromeryx, He1-Ba1, 156R, 161R, 187L, 194L
    B. milleri, Ba2, 156R
    B. submilleri, He2, 156R
Bovidae, bovid (artiodactyl), 191L, 194R
Brachycrus, He2-Ba1, 164R, 168L, 168R, 173L, 187L, 188L, 194L, 194R
    B. laticeps, Ba1, 164R
Brachyhyops, Du-Ch1, 90L, 90R, 105R, 129L, 133R, 135L
    B. wyomingensis, Ch1, 133R
Brachypotherium, He1, 183, 186R, 194L
Brachypsalis, He1-Cl2, 186R, 190L, 194L, 194R

Bretzia, Bl1, 183, 192R
Brontops, Ch1, 133L
brontothere(s), 89R, 104L, 133L
Brontotheriidae (perissodactyl), 133L
Brontotherium, Ch, 132L
Bryanictis, To3, 39, 48R, 52R
Bubogonia, Pu2, 38, 46R
Buginbaatar transaltaiensis, 67R
bunodont artiodactyls, 97L, 104R
Bunomeryx, Ui1-Ui2, 89R
Bunophorus, Wa1-Br1, 19R, 20L, 85R, 87R, 88L, 106L, 287L
Caenolambda, Ti2-Ti3, 38, 54L, 54R, 56L, 57R, 58L, 58R
Caenopus, Du-Ch, 107R, 133R, 135L
　C. yoderensis, Ch1, 133R, 134L, 135L
Calippus, Ba2-Hh2, 169L, 170L, 170R, 173L, 173R, 174R, 175L, 179L, 179R, 180L, 180R, 189L, 190R, 194R
　C. regulus, Cl1, 179R
　C. proplacidus, Ba2, 173R
Calomys, Hh3-Rct., 279L
　C. (*Bensonomys*), Hh3-Bl2, 279L
Camelidae, camelid(s), camel (artiodactyl), 89R, 157R, 159L, 167L, 168L, 169L, 169R, 173L, 176L, 176R, 177L, 177R, 178R, 185L, 185R, 188R, 190L, 192L, 216R, 225L
Camelops, Bl1-Rlb, 192R, 225L
　C. hesternus, Rlb, 225L
Canidae, canid(s) (carnivore), 89R, 155R, 166R, 169L, 169R, 171R, 173R, 177L, 177R, 178R, 190L, 216R
"*Canis*," Hh1-3, 190R, 194R
Canis, Hh3, Bl1-Rct., 217L, 226R
　C. davisi, Hh3-Bl1, Bl1, 217L
　C. dirus, Rlb, 223R
　C. lupus, Ir1-Rct., 222L
Cantius, Wa1-4, 85R, 86L, 86R
Capacikala, Ar1-Ar3, 166R, 171R
Capatanka, Ar1-3, 163L, 166R
caprine (artiodactyl), 245L
Carcinodon, Pu2, 36, 43L, 46R
Carnivora, carnivore, 39, 58R, 68L, 132R, 142R, 158L, 166R, 167R, 168L, 175L, 175R, 179R, 185L, 186R, 188R, 189L, 190L, 191L, 192L, 223R, 255L, 255R
Carpocyon, Ba2-Hh3, 181L, 189L, 194R
Carpodaptes, Ti1-Ti5, 36, 49R, 56L, 57L, 58L, 58R, 59R
Carpolestes, Ti5-Wa1, 26, 56L, 59R, 60R, 62R, 63L, 64L, 65L, 65R, 84R, 86L
　C. nigridens, Cf1, 62R, 63L, 64L
Carpolestidae, carpolestid(s), 36, 52R, 58R
Carsioptychus, Pu2-Pu3, 25L, 37, 42R, 43L, 46L, 46R, 47R
　C. coarctatus, ?Pu2, 47R
　C. matthewi, ?Pu3, 47R
Castor, ?Bl2, Hh3-Rct., 218R, 242L, 257R, 279L
　C. californicus, ?BlIV, 257R
Castorid(ae)(ids) (rodent), 145L
Castoroides, IrI-Rlb, 225L
　C. ohioensis, IrI-Rlb, 225L
cat (carnivore), 192L
Catopsalis, L-Ti1, 33, 40R, 43L, 44L, 46R, 48R, 49L, 50L, 50R, 51L, 53L, 56L, 57R
　C. alexanderi, Pu1, 40R, 44L
Cedrocherus, Ti3, 35, 56L, 58R
Centetodon, Wa1-Ar1, 88R
Cephalogale, Ar4-He1, 167R, 183, 185L, 194L
Cervidae, cervid (artiodactyl), 192R
Cervinae (artiodactyl), 195L
Cervus, Ir1-Rct., 222L
Chadronia, Ch3, 138L
Chalicotheriidae, chalicothere (perissodactyl), 166L, 178L, 189L, 194R
Chasmoporthetes, Bl1-Ir1, 183, 192R, 217R, 219L, 279L
chlaymthere (edentate), 192R

Choeroclaenus, Pu2-Pu3, 37, 43L, 46L, 46R
Chriacus, Pu3-Wa4, 36, 42R, 43L, 46R, 48R, 49L, 50R, 51L, 53L, 56L, 57R, 58L, 58R, 59R, 60L, 60R, 63L, 64R, 65L, 65R, 84R
Chiromyoides, Ti3-Cf2, 36, 56L, 58R, 59R, 60L, 60R, 63L, 64L, 65L
　C. caesor, Ti4, 59R
　C. major, Ti3-Cf2, 63L, 65L
　C. minor, Ti3, 58R
　C. potior, Ti5, 60L, 64L
Chumashius, Ui2-Du, 100R
Cimexomys, L-Pu3, 33, 43L, 43R, 44L, 46R
　C. minor, L-Pu1, 43R
　C. hausoi, Pu1, 44L
Cimolestes, L-Pu3, 34, 43L, 44R, 46R
Cimolodon, L-Pu3?, 33, 43L, 44R, 46R
Cimolodontidae, 33
Clethrionomys, Ir1, IrI-Rct., 22L, 222L, 239R, 248L, 249L, 261L, 261R, 263L, 263R, 264L
　C. gapperi, ?IrII, 261L, 263L
Claenodon (= *Arctocyon*), 42R
Clinopternodus, Ch1-3, 137R
Colodon, Ui2-Ch, 89R, 107R, 134R
Colpoclaenus, Ti1, 36, 56L, 57R
Conacodon, Pu2-Pu3, 37, 42R, 43L, 46L, 46R
Condylarthra, condylarth(s), 36, 42L, 42R, 43L, 44L, 45L, 45R, 46L, 54L, 58L, 61R, 66R, 68L, 104R
Conoryctella, To1-To2, 39, 48R, 50R, 51L
Conoryctes, To2-To3, 39, 48R, 51L, 52R
Conoryctidae (taeniodont), 39
Copemys, Ba1-Hh3, 19L, 159L, 183, 188L, 194L, 289
　C. longidens, Ba2, 19L, 289L
　C. russelli, Ba2, 19L, 289L
Copelemur, Wa2-B41, 85R
Coriphagus, To2-To3, 34, 48R, 50L, 52R
Cormohipparion, Ba1-Hh2, 156R, 159L, 159R, 160R, 169L, 173R, 174R, 175L, 177L, 179L, 180L, 180R, 188L, 190R, 191L, 194L, 194R
　C. occidentale, Cl1-2, 159L, 159R, 160R, 180R
　C. sphenodus, Ba3, 173R, 180L
Coryphodon, Cf1-Br1, 18R, 19L, 38, 61R, 62L, 62R, 63L, 64L, 65L, 65R, 66R, 68L, 81L, 81R, 84R, 85L, 85R, 86L, 87L, 87R, 88L, 96R, 97R, 104L, 105R, 107L, 286R
Coryphodontidae (pantodont), 38
Cosomys, subgenus of *Mimomys*
Cosoryx, Ba3-Cl1, 157L, 159R, 160R, 169L, 173R
　C. cerroensis, ?Cl1, 157L, 160R
cotton rat (rodent), 214R
Cranioceras, Ba3-Hh2, 157L, 169L, 170L, 170R, 171L, 173R, 174R, 175L, 177L, 177R, 179R, 190R, 194R
　C. clarendonensis, Cl1, 157L, 177R
　C. unicornis, ?Cl2, 157L
　C. (Yumaceras), Hh1-2, 157L, 170L, 173R, 174R, 175L, 194R
　C. (Yumaceras) figginsi, Hh2, 173R
Cranioceratinae, cranioceratine dromomerycid (artiodactyl), 156R, 168L, 169L, 176R, 177L, 192R, 194L
Craterogale, He1, 167R, 183, 186R, 194L
Creodonta, creodont(s), 39, 42L, 58R, 68L, 106R
Cricetidae, cricetid, cricetine (rodent), 160R, 165R, 188L, 222R, 226L, 238L, 238R, 239L
cricetodontine rodent, 155R, 191L
Cseria, subgenus of *Mimomys*
Cupidinimus, He1-Hh2, 19L, 186R, 194L, 289L
　C. nebraskensis, Ba1, 19L, 289L
Cuvieronius, ?Hh3-Rlb, 159R
　"*C*". *edensis*, ?Hh3, 159R
Cyclopidius, Ar1-2, 163R
Cylindrodon, Ch1-Or, 132L, 136R
　C. fontis, Ch2, 136R
Cylindrodontidae, cylindrodontid (rodent), 132L, 133L
Cynarctoides, Ar4-Ba1, 167L, 168L, 185L, 194L

Cynarctus, Ba2-Cl2, 169L, 173R, 189L, 194R
Cynelos, Ar4-He1, 167L, 183, 185L, 194L
Cynodesmus, ?He1, 172L
Cynodontomys, (= *Microsyops*), 85R
Cynorca, He1-Ba2, 161R
Cyriacotheriidae (pantodont), 38
Cyriacotherium, Ti3-Cf3, 38, 56L, 58R, 60L, 60R, 63L, 64L, 65L, 65R
  C. psammimum, 63L
"*Daimonelix*,", Ar3, 166R, 185L, 194L
daphoenine amphicyonid (carnivore), 90R, 129L, 166R
Daphoenodon, Ar3-4, 166R, 176L, 178L, 183, 185L, 194L
  D. ("*Mesocyon iamonensis*") *iamonensis*, Ar4, 178L
Daphoenus, Ch1-Ar1 or 2, 132R, 142R, 156L
  D. ruber, Ar1 or 2, 156L
Dasypus, Bl2-Rct., 218L
deer (artiodactyl), 181L
deer mice (rodent), 238L
Deltatherium, To2-To3, 28, 36, 46R, 48R, 49L, 50L, 51L, 52R
Dermoptera, 35
Desmatippus, Ba1, 161R, 162L, 164R, 173L, 177L, 188L, 194R
  D. avus, Ba1, 161R, 162L
Desmatochoerinae, desmatochoerine oreodont, 164L, 185L, 194L
Desmatochoerus, Ar1-2, 157R, 163L, 163R, 165R, 172R, 184R, 193R
  D? thurstoni, Ar1, 157R
Desmatoclaenus, Pu2-Ti2, 36, 43L, 46L, 46R, 49L, 50R, 51R, 53L, 56L, 57R, 58L
Deuterogonodon, To2-To3, 36, 48R, 51L, 52R
Diacocherus, Ti3-Cf3, 35, 56L, 58R, 59R, 60L, 60R, 63L, 64L, 65L, 65R
Diacodexis, Wa1-Br3, 18R, 85L, 85R, 86L, 86R, 87R, 88L, 96R, 97R, 107L
Diacodon, To3-Wa3, ?Ui2, 35, 56L, 57R, 58L, 59L, 59R, 84R, 85R
Diceratherium, Ar1-4, 145L, 161L, 163L, 184R, 185L, 193R
  D. armatum, ?Ar1, 163L
Dicrostonychinae, 238R, 239L
Dicrostonyx, Rlb, RlbII-Rct., 22R, 222L, 239R, 249L, 251L, 264L
Didelphidae, 34, 106R
Didelphodus, Wa1-Ui2, 18R, 85L, 85R, 89R
Didymictidae (carnivore), 39
Didymictis, Ti5-Br1, 39, 56L, 59L, 60R, 62R, 63L, 64L, 65L, 65R, 84R, 85L, 85R, 87R, 88L
Dilophodon, Br3-Du, 88L, 90L, 97L
Dinictis, Ch1-Or, 132R, 142R
Dinocerata, 38, 89R
Dinohippus, Ba3-Bl1; Bll-II, 155R, 158L, 159R, 164R, 169L, 170R, 173R, 174L, 174R, 175L, 181L, 189L, 192L, 192R, 194R, 195L, 214R, 216L, 216R, 217R, 279L, 279R
  D. edensis, Hh3, 159R
  D. interpolatus, ?Hh2, Hh3, 155R, 173R, 174L, 175L, 279L
  D. leidyanus, Hh3, 170R
  D. mexicanus, Hh3, ?Bll; Bll, 174R, 181L, 216R
Dinohyus, Ar1-He1, 166R, 176L, 178L, 184R, 193R
Diplacodon, Ui2, 89R
Diplobunops, Ui1-Du, 90L, 102R
Dipodomys, BlV, ?Bl2, Ir1-Rct., 220R, 221L, 279L
Dipoides, Hh1-?Bl1; Bll, 155R, 160R, 162L, 164R, 169R, 170L, 170R, 171L, 190R, 194R, 216L, 216R, 217R, 252R, 253L, 253R, 254R, 255L, 279L
  D. rexroadensis, Bll-II, 254R, 255L
  D. stirtoni, Hh1, 160R, 162L, 164R, 170R, 252R, 253L
  D. smithi, Hh3, 253L, 253R
  D. williamsi, Hh2, 170L
  D. wilsoni, Hh3 or ?Bl1; Bll, 216R
Dipsalodon, Ti5-Cf3?, 39, 56L, 59L, 60R, 62R, 63L, 64L, 64R, 65L, 65R
Dissacus, To2-Wa1, 37, 48R, 51L, 53L, 56L, 57R, 58L, 58R, 59R, 60L, 60R, 62R, 63L, 64L, 65L, 65R, 84R

D. praenuntius, 62R, 63L, 64L, 65R
Djadochtatherium, 50L
dolichohippine (perissodactyl), 216R
Dolichohippus, subgenus of *Equus*
Dolichorhinus (= *Tanyorhinus*), Ui1, 89L, 89R, 102R, 220L
Domnina, Ui2-Ch2, 89R, 137L, 143L
  D. gradata, Or, 143L
  D. thompsoni, Ch2, 137R
Dorraletes, Ti3-Ti5, 37, 56L, 58R, 59R
Dracoclaenus (= ?*Protoselene*), 50L
Draconodus, To1, 36, 48R, 50R
Dracontolestes, To1, 34, 48R, 50L, 50R
Dromomerycinae, dromomerycine (artiodactyl), 176R
Dromomerycidae, dromomerycid (artiodactyl), 156R, 158R, 167L, 167R, 168L, 173R, 176L, 176R, 177L, 178L, 186R
Dromomeryx, He2-Ba2, 161R, 162L, 164R, 165L, 173L, 194L, 194R
  D. borealis, Ba1, 161R, 162L, 164R, 165L
Duchesneodus, Du, 90L, 90R, 100R, 101R, 105R, 107R
Dyseohyus, Ba1-2, 187R, 188L, 194R
  D. fricki, Ba1, 187R
Dyseotylopus, Ar1, 157R, 184R, 193R
  D. migrans, Ar1, 157R
Earendil, Pu1, 37, 43L, 44L
  E. undomiel, Pu1, 44L
Ectoconus, Pu2-Pu3, 25R, 28, 37, 40R, 42R, 43L, 43R, 44L, 45L, 45R, 46L, 46R
Ectocion, Ti1-Br1, 19R, 20L, 25R, 38, 49L, 54L, 54R, 55L, 56L, 57L, 57R, 58L, 58R, 59R, 60L, 60R, 62L, 62R, 63L, 63R, 64L, 64R, 65L, 65R, 84L, 85L, 85R, 86L, 88L, 106L, 287L
  E. collinus, Ti1, 54R
  E. montanensis, Ti1, 57L
  E. osbornianus, 62R, Cf
Ectoganus, Ti5-Wa4, 39, 56L, 59R, 60R, 63L, 64L, 65L, 65R, 85L, 85R, 105R
Ectypodus, Pu2-Ch2, 33, 43L, 46L, 46R, 49L, 51L, 53L, 55L, 56L, 57L, 58L, 58R, 59R, 60L, 60R, 62R, 63L, 64L, 65L, 65R, 84R, 85L
Edaphocyon, He1, 167R, 183, 186R
edentates, 21L, 68L, 68R
Ekgmoiteptecela, Ar1, 157R
  E. belli, Ar1, 157R
Ekgmowechasala, Ar1, 161L
Ellipsodon, Pu3-To2, 38, 46R, 48R, 50R, 51L
Elphidotarsius, To3-Ti3, 36, 48R, 52R, 54R, 56L, 57R, 58L, 58R
Elpidophorus, To3-Ti3, 35, 48R, 52R, 56L, 57R, 58L, 58R
Elomeryx, Wh-Ar1, 145R, 184R, 193R
Enhydriodon, ?Hh3-BlIII, 157L, 242L
Enhydritherium, Hh2-3, 181L, 183, 191L, 194R
Entelodontidae, entelodontid(s) (artiodactyl), 121R, 133R, 161L, 175R, 186R, 194L
Entomolestes, Br2-Ui1, 84R, 88L, 88R
  "*E.*" (= *Macrocranion*) *nitens*, Wa1, 84R
Entoptychinae, entoptychine (rodent), 184R, 185L, 185R, 193R, 194L
Entoptychus, Ar2-3, 19L, 161L, 163R, 164L, 172L, 185R, 288R
Eobasileus, Ui1, 89L, 89R, 102R
Eoconodon, Pu1-Pu3, 36, 42R, 43L, 44L, 46R
  E. copanus, Pu1, 44L
Eohippus (= *Hyracotherium*), 82L
Eolagurus, Biharian-Rct., Europe, 239R
Eomellivora, Hh2, 157L, 160R, 175L, 183, 191L, 194R
  E. winmani, ?Hh2, 157L
Eomoropus, Ui1, 102R
eomyid(s) (rodents), 89R, 107R, 121R, 158L, 166L, 187L
Eomys, He2, 158L, 183, 187L, 194L
Eotitanops (= *Palaeosyops*), Br1, 84R, 85L, 87L
Eotylopus, Du-Ch1, 100R, 105R, 134R
Epicyon, Ba1-Hh2, 157L, 159L, 159R, 160R, 169R, 170L, 171R, 173R, 174R, 175L, 179R, 190L, 190R, 191L, 194R, 279R
  E. aphobus (near *E. haydeni*), Cl2, 159

E. saevus, Cl1, 157L, 159L, 160R, 169R, 190L
E. validus, Hh2, 170L, 171L, 173R, 179R
Epigaulus, Hh3, 169R
Epihippus, Ui1-Du, 89L, 89R, 90L, 97L, 97R, 104R, 106R, 107R, 134L
   E. intermedius, Ui2, 134L
Epitriplopus, Ui2, 90L
Epoicotheriidae (palaeanodont), 39
Eporeodon, Or-Ar2, 142R
   "*E.*" *bullatus* (= *Otionohyus bullatus*), Or, 142R, 145L
Eporeodontinae (artiodactyl), 142R, 185L, 194L
Equidae, equid(s) (perissodactyl), 177R
Equinae, equine (perissodactyl), 188R, 190R
Equus, Bl1, BlI-Holocene, reintroduced; Rct., 192R, 214R, 217L, 220L, 221L, 225L, 245L, 278R, 279L, 280L
   E. (Dolichohippus), Bl1-2, BlII-V, ?Ir1, IrI, 216R, 217L, 217R, 218L, 220L, 221L, 243R, 257R
   E. (D.) simplicidens, BLIII-V, 214R, ?257R
   E. (Equus), Ir1, Ir1-Holocene, reintroduced; Rct., 214R, 220L, 221L, 225L, 260L, 260R
   E. (Hemionus), Bl1, BlIII-Rct., 245L
Eremotherium, Ir1-Rlb, 222L
Erethizon, Bl2, BlV, 21L, 279L
Erinaceidae, erinaceid (insectivore), 35, 168R
erinaceomorph (insectivore), 42R
Escatepos, Pu1, 37, 43L, 46R
Esthonychidae, 38
Esthonyx, ?Ti6-Br1, 19L, 38, 56L, 60R, 61R, 62L, 62R, 63L, 63R, 64L, 64R, 65L, 65R, 66R, 84R, 85L, 85R, 86R, 88L, 106R, 107L
   E. acutidens, Wa4-Br1, 87R
   E. ancylion, Cf2-Cf3, 62R, 63L, 63R, 65L, 65R, 96R
   E. grangeri, ?Cf2-?Wa1, 63R, 65L, 65R
   E. xenicus, Cf2, 62R, 63L, 63R, 65L
Eucastor, Ba2-Cl2, 155R, 169L, 189L, 190L, 194R
   "*E.*" *dividerus,* Cl1, 160R
   E. lecontei, Cl2, 155R
Euceratherium, Ir1-Rlb, 214R, 220L, 220R, 221L, 221R, 225L, 261R, 263L
Eucosmodon, Pu2-?Ti1, 33, 42L, 43L, 46L, 46R, 49L, 51L, 53L, 56L, 57R
Eucosmodontidae, 33
Eudaemonema, To3, 34, 49L, 52R
Euhapsis, Ar2-3, 166L, 166R
   E. platyceps, Ar2, 166L
eumyine(s) (cricetid[s] rodent[s]), 121R
Eumys, Ch3-Ar1, 138L, 138R, 142R, 143L, 145L, 145R, 184R
   E. brachyodus, Wh, 145L
   E. elegans, Ch3-Or, 138L, 143L
   E. pristinus, Ch3-Or, 138L
Euoplocyon, He1-Ba1, 159L, 162L, 178R
Eusmilus, ?Ch1-Ar1, 132R, 184R, 193R
Eutypomys, Ch1-Ar2, 134R, 137R, 138R, 146L, 163R
   E. thompsoni, Ch3-Or, 137R, 138R
Felidae, felid(s), 155R, 168L, 187L, 190L, 194L
Felis, Hh3-Rct., 181L, 183, 192L, 195L
   F. rexroadensis, Bl1, BlII, 181L
Floresomys, Br-Or, 108L
Floridaceras, He1, 178R
Floridatragulinae (artiodactyl), 178R, 186R, 194L
Floridatragulus, He1-Ba3, 176L, 176R, 177L
Forstercooperia (= *Hyrachyus grandis*), Ui1-Du, 89L, 97L, 105R, 106R
Franimys, Cf2-Wa3, 30, 39, 63L, 65L, 65R
Galericinae (insectivores), 184R
Galushamys, Hh3, 279L
Gelastops, To3-Ti3, 34, 48R, 52R, 56L, 57R, 58L, 58R
Gelocidae, gelocid (artiodactyl), 169L, 189L

geolabidid insectivore, 101R
Geolabis, Ch1-Ar1 (= *Centetodon,* in part), 146L
Geomys, Bl1, II-Rct., 217L, 217R, 218R, 279L
geomyoid rodents, 157R, 161L, 165R, 177L, 185R
giant beaver (rodent), 219L
Gillisonchus, Pu2-Pu3, 37, 43L, 46R
Glossotherium, Bl2, 21L, 218L, 219L, 279L
glyptodont (edentate), 192L, 218R, 225L, 279L
Glyptotherium, Bl2, BlV, 21L, 218L, 219L
Gomphotheriidae, gomphotheriid (gomphothere) mastodont (proboscidean), 169L, 173L, 175L, 180L, 187R, 188L, 188R, 189L, 190L, 192L, 194R
Gomphotherium, Ba2-Hh3, 159L, 180L, 181L, 183, 192L
   G. calvertense, Ba2, 180L
Goniacodon, Pu3-To3, 36, 43L, 46R, 48R, 50R, 51L, 52R
Goniodontomys, Hh1, ?Hh2, 238R, 241R, 242L, 252R, 253L
   G. disjunctus, Hh1, 252R, 253L
gopher (rodent), 216R
grasshopper mouse (rodent), 226L
Gregorymys, Ar2-3, 19L, 161L, 163R, 164L, 172L, 185R, 288R
   G. douglassi, Ar2, 163R
Griphippus, Cl1-Hh3, 169R, 179R, 181L, 190L, 190R, 192L, 194R
   G. gratus, ?Cl2, 179R
Guanajuatomys, Br or Ui, 108L
Hadrocyon, Cl1, 159L
   H. mohavensis, Cl1, 159L
Hadroleptauchenia, Or-Ar1, 145L
hamster (rodent), 238L
Hapaletes, Pu3-Ti5, 37, 43L, 46R, 49L, 53L, 56L, 57R, 58L, 58R, 59R
Hapalodectes, Wa3-Br1, 85R, 88L
Haploconus, Pu2-To3, 37, 43L, 46R, 48R, 50L, 50R, 51L, 52R
   H.(?) elichistus, Pu3, 50L
Haplohippus, Du-Ch?, 107R
Haplomylus, Ti4-Wa2, 18R, 19L, 19R, 20L, 37, 61R, 62R, 63L, 64L, 65L, 65R, 84R, 86L, 97L, 106L, 107L, 286R
   H. simpsoni, Cf1-3, 62R, 63L, 64L, 65R
Haplolambda, Ti4-Cf1, 38, 56L, 59R, 60L, 60R, 63L, 64L
Harpagolestes, Br2-Du, 88L
hedgehog (insectivore), 166L, 184R
Helaletes, Wa4-Br3, 18R, 87L, 88L, 88R, 97L
Heliscomys, Ch2-Ar1, 137L, 146L
   H. vetus, ?Ch2, 137R
Helohyus, Br1-Ui1, 86L, 87L, 87R, 88L, 88R, 89R, 97L, 104L, 106R
Hemiacodon, Br1-Ui1, 18R, 87R, 88L, 88R, 89R, 102R
   H. gracilis, Br3, 88R
Hemiauchenia, Cl1-Rlb, 159R, 169R, 179R, 181L, 190L, 190R, 192L, 194R, 216R
   H. vera, Hh3; Bl1, 216R
Hemicyon, He1-Cl2, 159L, 162L, 168R, 186R, 187R, 188L, 194L
   H. (Phoberocyon) ("*Aelurodon*") *johnhenryi,* He1, 178R
   H. (Plithocyon), Ba1, 159L, 168R, 183, 187R
   H. (Plithocyon), barstowensis, Ba2, 159L
   H. (Plithocyon), californicus, Ba2, 159L
Hemicyoninae (carnivore), 167L, 185L
Hemipsalodon, Du-Ch, 107R, 133R, 135L
   H. grandis, Ch1, 133R
Hemithlaeus, Pu2-Pu3, 37, 43L, 44R, 45R, 46R
Hendryomeryx, Ch2, 136R
   H. esulcatus (= *Leptomeryx esulcatus*), Ch2, 136R
Heptacodon, Wh, 145R
Heptodon, Wa3-Br2, 20L, 81R, 85R, 86L, 88L, 103L, 106R, 287L
   H. calciculus, Wa3, 106L
Herpetotherium (= *Peratherium*), 84R
Hesperhys, Ar3-Ba1, 156R, 159L
Hesperocyon, Ch1-Ar1, 132L, 132R, 138R, 142R, 145L, 146L
   H. gregarius, Ch3-Or, 138R
   H. paterculus, Ch?1-2, 132L, 138R
"*Hesperopithecus,*" Cl2, 170R

Hesperoscalops, Hh3-Bl1, BlI-II, 216L, 242R, 253R, 254R, 255L
  H. mcgrewi, Hh3, 216L, 253R
  H. rexroadi, BlII, 255L
  H. sewardensis, BlI, 254R
Heteromeryx, Ch1–3, 134R
heteromyid(s) (rodents), 121R, 158R, 160R, 222R, 241R
Hexabelomeryx, Hh3, 216R
Hexacodus, Wa3-Br1, 86L
Hexameryx, Hh3, 181L
Hibbardomys, Bl2; BlIII-BlV, 226L
Hipparion, Ba2-Hh3, 155R, 157L, 159R, 164R, 169R, 174L, 174R,
  175L, 179R, 180L, 181L, 189L, 190L, 190R, 191L, 192L, 194R,
  278R, 280L
  H. forcei, Cl2-Hh1, 155R, 157L, 159R
  H. mohavense (= *Cormohipparion occidentale*; Cl1), 159R
  "*H.*" *plicatile*, Hh1–2, ?Hh3, 179R, 181L
  H. shirleyi, Ba2 (B. J. MacFadden, 1984; AMNH Bull. 179:58)
  H. tehonense ("*N.*" *lenticularis*), Cl1–2, 155R, 157L, 160R, 164R,
    169R, 174L
Hippodon, Ba1, 176L
Holmesina, Ir1-Rlb, 222L
Homacodon, Br1–3, 18R, 86L, 87L, 87R, 88L, 88R
  H. vagans, Br3, 88R
homacodontines (artiodactyl), 89R
Homo, Rlb-Rct., 223R
Homocamelus, Ba1, 173R
Homogalax, Wa1-Wa4, 18R, 81R, 85L, 85R, 86L, 105R, 106L, 107L
  H. protapirinus, Wa2-Wa3, 86L, 106L
Hoplictis (= *Ischyrictis*), Cl2, 169R, 190L, 194R
Hoplophoneus, Ch1-Or, 132R, 137R, 142L, 142R, 157R
  H. mentalis, Ch3, 137R, 142L
  H. primaevus, Or, 142L
  H. robustus, Or, 137R, 142L
horse(s) (perissodactyl), 142R, 155R, 168L, 168R, 169L, 169R, 170R,
  175R, 176L, 177L, 177R, 178R, 179L, 179R, 180L, 181L,
  190L, 190R, 194R, 216L, 225L
Huerfanodon, To3, 39, 49L, 52R
Hyaenodon, Du-Ar1, 90L, 90R, 100R, 105R, 121L, 129L, 132R,
  133L, 134R, 137R, 138R, 142L, 145L, 146L, 184R, 193R
  H. brevirostris, Wh, 145L
  H. crucians, Or, 142R
  H. cruentus, Ch3-Or, 137R, 138R
  H. gregarius, Ch3-Or, 137R
  H. horridus, Ch1-Or, 132R, 142R
  H. paterculus, Ch2, 137R
Hyaenodontidae, hyaenodontid (carnivore), 39, 68L, 85L
Hylomeryx, Ui1–2, 89R, 97L
Hypertragulidae (artiodactyl), 185L, 194L
Hypertragulus, Ch1-Ar1 or 2, 142R, 143L, 156L, 157R
  H. calcaratus, Or, 143L
  H. heikeni, Ch1, 143L
Hypisodus, Or-Ar1, 143L, 184R, 193R
  H. minimus, Or, 143L
Hypohippus, He2-Cl2, 160L, 162L, 164R, 169L, 173L, 177L, 190L,
  194R
  H. affinus, Ba3-Cl2, 122L, 160L
  H. osborni, Ba1, 162L, 173L
  H. nevadanus, Cl1, 160L
Hypolagus, He2-Bl2, He2-BlV, 157L, 159R, 187L, 194L, 214R,
  217L, 217R, 218L, 220L, 220R, 247R, 257R, 258R, 259L,
  259R, 279L, 279R
  H. furlongi, BlV, 258R, 259L
  H. limnetus, ?Hh1, BlIII-V, 157L, 259L
  H. regalis, ?BlV, 247R, 259R
  H. ringoldensis, Hh3-Bl2, BlI-III, 217L
  H. vetus, Hh1, Bl1, ?BlIII, BlIV, 217L, 247L, 257L, 259L, 279L
Hyopsodontidae, 37, 42L, 42R
Hyopsodus, Cf3-Du, 18R, 37, 65R, 68L, 85R, 86L, 86R, 88R, 96R,
  97L, 97R, 105R, 106L, 107L

  H. lepidus, Br3, 88R
  H. minisculus, Br2, 88R
  H. paulus, Wa2-Ui2, 97L
  H. uintensis, Ui2, 97R
Hypsiops, ?Ar1 or 2, Ar3–4, 156L, 164L, 185L, 194L
  H. brachymelis, Ar3, 164L
  H. erythroceps, ?Ar1 or 2, 156L
hyracodont(ids) (perissodactyl), 89L, 89R
Hyracodon, Du-Ar1, 90L, 132L, 133R, 134R, 142L, 142R, 145L,
  171R, 184R, 193R
  H. apertus, Ar1, 171R
  H. arcidens (= *H. nebraskensis*), Or, 142L
  H. nebraskensis, Ch1-Ar1, 132L, 142L, 142R
  H. priscidens, Ch, 132L, 142L
Hyracotherium, ?Cf3, Wa1-Br2, 18R, 65R, 66R, 81L, 82L, 85L,
  85R, 86L, 86R, 87L, 87R, 88L, 97L, 101L, 104L, 105R, 106L,
  106R, 107L
  H. angustidens, 65R
Hyrachyus, Br1-Ui2, 84R, 85L, 86L, 87L, 87R, 88L, 88R, 89L, 97L,
  104L, 105L, 106R, 107R
Hystricops, Cl2-Hh1, 162L, 171L
Ictidopappus, ?Pu2-To3, 39, 43L, 46R, 48R, 51L, 51R, 52R
"*Ictops*," Ch1-Or, 120L, 132L, 132R, 137R, 138R, 142R
  "*I.*" *acutidens*, Ch2, 120L, 132L, 137R, 138R
  "*I.*" *dakotensis*, Ch3-Or, 137R, 138R
Ignacius, To3-Ui2, 35, 48R, 52R, 56R, 57R, 58L, 58R, 59R, 60L,
  60R, 63L, 64L, 64R, 65L, 65R
  I. graybullianus, Cf3, 64L, 65L
Indarctos, Hh2, 155R, 160R, 170R, 175L, 181L, 183, 191L, 194R
  I. nevadanus, Hh2, 160R
Insectivora, insectivore(s), 35, 120L, 136R, 137L, 137R, 138R, 226R
Intyrictis, To3, 39, 49L, 52R
Ischymomys, ca 6 Ma, Asia, 238R
Ischyrictis (= *Hoplictis*; "*Beckia*"), Cl2, 169R, 179R, 183, 190L,
  194R
Ischyrocyon, Ba3-Cl1, 189L, 194R
Ischyromyidae, ischyromyid (rodent), 39, 101L
Ischyromys, Du-Wh, 120L, 132L, 133L, 134R, 140R, 142R, 143L,
  145R
  I. douglassi, Ch, 132L
  I. parvidens, Or, 140R
  I. pliacus, Or, 140R
  I. typus, Or, 140R, 143L
Ischyrotomus, Br2-Du, 89R, 100R, 104R
jaguar (carnivore), 221L
Jepsenella, To3, 34, 49L, 52R
Jimomys, Ba1, 177L
Kalobatippus (= *Anchitherium*), Ar3–4, 185L
Kimbetohia, Pu2-Pu3, 33, 43L, 44R, 46R
Kislangia, Triversa-Villanyian, Europe, 248L
Knightomys, Wa1-Br1, 87R, 88L
Kraglievichia, Bl2, 21L, 218L
Kukusepasutanka, Ar1, 163L
Kyptoceras, Hh3, 181L
Labidolemur, Ti3-Cf1, 34, 55L, 56L, 58R, 59R, 60L, 60R, 63L, 64R,
  65L, 65R
lagomorph(s), 89R, 186R, 252R
Lagurodon, Villanyian-Biharian, Europe, 239R, 248L
Lagurus, Biharian-Rct., Europe; Rlb, RlbI-Rct., N. Amer., 22R,
  239R, 247L, 241L, 250R, 263R
Lambdoceras, He1-Ba1, 176L, 188L, 194R
Lambdotherium, Wa4-Br1, 19L, 20L, 81R, 85L, 86L, 86R, 87L,
  87R, 97L, 98L, 102L, 103L, 105L, 106L, 107L, 287L
Lambertocyon, Ti3-Cf1, 37, 56L, 58R, 59R, 60L, 60R, 63L, 64L
Lasiopodomys, BlV-equiv. - Rct., Asia, 248R
Leidymys, Or-Ar1, 143L
  L. vetus, Or, 143L
Leipsanolestes, Cf1-Wa1, 35, 63L, 64L, 65L, 65R
Lemminae (rodent), 238R, 239L

lemming (rodent), 225L, 237L
Lemmus, BlV, Ir1-Rct., 22R, 222L, 236R, 239R, 247L, 251L, 264L
leporid (lagomorph), 247R, 252R
Leptacodon, ?Pu3-Wa2, 35, 43L, 46R, 49L, 53L, 55L, 56L, 57R, 58L, 58R, 59R, 60L, 60R, 63L, 64R, 65L, 65R
   L. packi, 64R, 65L, 65R
Leptarctinae, leptarctine (carnivore), 167R, 186R, 194L
Leptarctus, He1-Hh2, 161R, 162L, 164R, 167R, 168L, 169L, 171L, 175L, 179R, 186R, 190R, 191L, 194L, 194R
   L. cf. *bosemanensis*, ?Ba1, 165L
   L. oregonensis, Ba1, 161R
Leptauchenia, Wh-Ar2, 122L, 122R, 144L, 145L, 172L
   L. decora, Wh, 122L, 145L
   L. major, 122L
Leptaucheniinae, leptauchenine oreodont(s) (artiodactyl), 140L, 163R, 165R, 166L, 171R, 184R, 185R, 193R
Leptictidae, leptictid, 34, 138R
Leptictis, Ch1-Wh, 132R, 142R, 143L, 144L, 145R
   L. haydeni, Or, 143L
leptochoerids (artiodactyls), 88L, 121R
Leptochoerus, Ch1-Ar1, 146L
Leptocyon, Ar1-Cl2, 166R, 168L
Leptomerycidae, leptomerycid(s) (artiodactyl), 163L, 178R, 194R
leptotraguline (artiodactyl), 107R
Leptomeryx, ?Du, Ch1-Ar1, 105R, 122L, 132L, 132R, 133L, 134R, 135L, 136R, 138R, 142R, 143L, 145L, 146L
   L. esulcatus, Ch2-3, 132L, 133L, 136R, 137R, 138R
   L. evansi, ?Ch, Or-Ar1, 122L, 142R, 143L
   L. mammifer, Ch2, 132L, 133L, 136R, 138R
   L. speciosus, Ch2 (= *Hendryomeryx esulcatus*, according to Storer, 1981; Chap. 5), 136R, 186R
   L. yoderi, Ch1, 132L, 133L, 133R, 135L, 136R
Leptonysson, To3, 34, 49L, 53L
Leptoreodon, Ui1-Du, 100R, 104R, 107R
Leptotomus, Br1-Ch1, 18R, 90L
Leptotragulus, 134R
   L. profectus, ?Ch1, 134R
Lepus, ?Bl2, Ir1-Rct., 21R, 214L, 214R, 220L, 220R, 221L, 247R, ?258R, 260L
   L. callotis, ?Ir1, 220R
Limnenetes, Ch1, 136L
Limnocyon, Br1-Ui2, 88L, 89R
limnocyonids (carnivore), 89R
Limnoecinae, limnoecine (soricid) (insectivore), 186R, 194L
Litaletes, To1-To3, 38, 49L, 50R, 51R, 52R
Litocherus, ?Ti1-Ti5, 35, 56L, 58L, 59R
Litolestes, Ti3-Ti5, 35, 56L, 58L, 59R
Litomylus, Pu2-Ti4, 37, 43L, 46R, 49L, 51L, 51R, 53L, 56L, 57R, 58L, 59L, 59R
Longirostromeryx, Ba2-Cl1, 169L, 170R, 177L, 189L, 194R
Loveina, Wa3-4, 85R, 86L
Loxolophus, Pu2-To3, 36, 42R, 43L, 46R, 48L, 48R, 49L, 51L, 51R, 52R
   L. spiekeri, To1, 42R
Lutra, Bl1-Rct., 192R
Lutravus, Hh2, 183, 191L, 194R
Lutrinae, lutrine (carnivore), 168L, 187L
Lynx, Bl1-Rct., 183, 192R
"*Machaeromeryx*," He1, 178R, 186R, 194L
Machairodus, Hh2-3, 155R, 159R, 160R, 170L, 170R, 171L, 173R, 174R, 175L, 181L, 183, 191L, 192L, 194R, 214R, 216L, 216R
   "*M.*" *catocopis* (= *Nimravides*), Hh2, 174R
   M. coloradensis, Hh2, ?Hh3, 159R, 173R, 175L
Macrocranion, Wa1-Ui2, 84R, 85L, 89R
Macrogenis, Cl1-Hh2, 190L, 194R
Macrotarsius, Ui1-?Ch1, 89R
Maiorana, Pu1, 37, 43L, 44L
   M. noctiluca, Pu1, 44L
Malaquiferus, Ui1-2, 104R

Mammut, Bl1-Rlb, 219L, 225L
   M. americanum, Rlb, 225L
Mammuthus, Ir1-Rlb, Irl-RlbII, 214R, 218R, 220L, 221L, 221R, 222R, 223R, 225L, 226R, 228L, 279L
   M. armenaicus, Rlb, 225L
   M. columbi, Rlb, 225L
   M. meridionalis, Ir1, IrI, 221L, 222R
   M. primigenius, Rlb, 225L
Mammutidae, mammutid mastodont (proboscidean), 173L, 180L, 188L
Manitsha, Ui2-Ch1, 104R
Manteoceras, Br3-Ui2, 88L, 88R, 105R
marsupial(s), 44L, 68R, 101R, 104R, 121R
Marsupialia, 34
mastodont (proboscidean), 179R, 180L, 190L
Mckennatherium, To3-Ti5, 35, 48R, 52R, 56L, 57R, 58L, 59L, 59R
Megabelodon, Cl1, 160R
   M. minor, Cl1, 160R
Megahippus, Ba2-Cl1, 159L, 160R, 164R, 168R, 169L, 189L, 190L, 194R
   M. matthewi, Ba3-Cl1, 160R
   M. mckennai, Ba2, ?Ba3, 159L, 168R
Megalagus, Ch1-Or, 132L, 132R, 142R
   M. brachyodon, Ch, 132L
Megalesthonyx, Wa4, 85L, 86R
Megalictis, (= *Aelurocyon*), Ar4, 185L
Megalonychidae, megalonychid sloth (edentate), 155R, 158L, 169R, 170L, 170R, 174R, 180L, 191L, 216L
Megalonyx, Hh2-Rlb, 156L, 183, 192L, 195L, 196L, 225L
   M. curvidens, Hh2, 171L
   M. jeffersoni, Rlb, 225L
Megantereon, Hh3-?Ir2, 181L, 183, 192L, 192R, 195L, 216R, 219L, 226L
   M. hesperus, Hh3-Bl2, 181L, 226R
Megasespia, Ar1-2, 165R
Megasminthus, Ba2, 189L, 194R
Megatylopus, Cl1-Hh3, 159R, 162L, 169R, 171L, 173R, 177R, 181L, 190L, 190R, 194R
   M. gigas, Hh1 or 2, 171L, 173R
Megoreodon, Ar1-2, 163L, 165R
Melaniella, Ti3, 39, 56L, 58L
Meliakrouniomys, Ch2, 136L
   M. wilsoni, Ch2, 136L
   M. skinneri, Ch2, 136L
Meniscotherium, Cf3-Wa4, 19L, 54R, 82R, 84R, 85R, 87L, 106R
   "*M.*" "*semicingulatum*" (= *Ectocion collinus*), Ti1, 54R
meniscomyine rodent, 161R, 163R
Meniscomys, Ar1-2, 19L, 161L, 163R, 165R, 166L, 172L, 185R, 288R
Menoceras, Ar3-He1, 156R, 166L, 166R, 167R, 176L, 178R, 183, 185L, 186R, 194L
Menodus, Ch, 132L
Merriamoceros, He2-Ba1, 159L, 165L, 187L, 188L, 194L, 194R
Meryceros, Ba1-2, 159L, 160L, 173L, 188L, 194R
   M. hookwayi, Ba2, 160L
Merychippus, He2-Cl2, 156R, 158L, 158R, 159L, 160L, 161R, 162L, 164R, 168L, 168R, 169L, 173R, 176L, 176R, 179L, 180L, 187L, 190L, 190R, 194L
   M. brevidontus, Ba1-Ba2, 156R, 160L, 162L
   "*M.*" *calamarius*, Ba2, 160L
   "*M.*" *californicus*, Ba2, 160L
   "*M.*" *carrizoensis*, He2, 158L
   "*M.*" *eohipparion*, Ba1, 173L
   M. gunteri, He2, 178R
   M. insignis, ?Ba1, Ba2, 173R, 177L, 180L
   "*M.*" *intermontanus*, ?Ba1, Ba2-3, 159L, 165L
   "*M.*" *isonesus*, Ba1, 161R, 162L, 164R, 165L
   "*M.*" *relictus*, Ba1, 164R
   "*M.*" *republicanus*, ?Ba2, 180L

"*M.*" *sejunctus,* Ba1, 173L, 177L
"*M.*" *seversus,* Ba1, 161R, 164R
"*M.*" *stylodontus,* Ba1–2, 159L
"*M.*" *sumani,* Ba2, 159L, 160L
"*M.*" *tehachapiensis,* He2-Ba1, 158L, 158R
"*M.*" (*Protohippus*), Ba2–3, 164R, 169L, 170R, 189L
Merychyus, Ar3-He1, 158R, 161R, 166R, 167R, 172L, 185L, 194L
   M. arenarum, He1, 172L
   M. calaminthus, ?Ar3-?He1, 158R
Merycochoerus, Ar4-He1, 122L, 161R, 167L, 167R, 172L, 185L, 185R, 186R, 194L
   M. proprius, 122L
   M. proprius magnus, Ar4, 172L
merycodontine antilocaprid (artiodactyl), 169L, 190L
merycodont(s) (artiodactyl), 160L, 177R
Merycodus, He2-Cl2, 160R, 164R, 169L, 173L, 194L
   "*M.*" *prodromus* (= *Paracosoryx*), Ar4, 185L
Merycoidodon, Ch1-Wh, 132L, 132R, 134R, 138L, 138R, 142R, 145R
   M. culbertsoni, Ch3-Or, 138L, 138R
   M. forsythae, Ch, 132L
merycoidodont, 132R
Merydoidodontinae, 142R, 185L, 194L
Mesatirhinus, Br3, 88L, 88R, 102R
Mesocyon, (= *Cynodesmus*), Or-Ar2, 163L, 163R, 165R, 171R
   M. geringensis, Ar1, 165R, 171R
Mesodma, L-Ti4, 33, 40R, 43L, 44L, 46R, 49L, 51L, 51R, 53L, 56L, 57R, 58L, 59L, 59R
   M. ambigua, Pu1, 44L
   M. garfieldensis, Pu1, 40R
Mesogaulus, He1-Ba1, 186R, 194L
Mesohippus, Ch-Or, 132R, 133L, 134L, 134R, 135L, 135R, 136R, 138R, 139R, 143L, 145L
   M. bairdi, Or, 143L
   M. celer, Ch, 132R, 135L
   M. grandis, Ch3, 137R, 138R
   M. hypostylus, Ch1–2, 132R, 136R
   M. latidens, Ch2–3, 132R, 136R, 137R
   M. texanus, Ch, 134L, 135L
Mesomeryx, Ui1–2, 89R
Mesonyx, Br1-Ui2, 18R, 87R, 88L, 89R, 97L
Mesonychidae, 37
Mesoreodon, Ar1, 157R, 163R, 165R, 171R, 184R, 193R
   M. hesperus, Ar1, 157R
Metacheiromyidae (palaeanodont), 39
Metachriacus, 42R
Metacodon, Ch1–3, 137L
   "*M.*" *magnus,* Ch2-Ar (= *Centetodon,* in part), 137L, 137R
Metamynodon, Ch1-Or, 127R, 132R, 142R
   M. planifrons, Or, 142L
Metarhinus, Ui1–2, 89L, 89R, 106R
Metaxomys, subgenus of *Mictomys* or *Synaptomys* according to author, Bl2, BlV, ?Ir1, 21L, 218L, 219L, 220L, 221L
Miacis, Wa1-Ch1, 18R, 84R, 85L, 88R
miacid (carnivore), 104R
Michenia, Ar4-Cl2, 161R, 167R, 185L, 185R, 194L
Microclaenodon, To2-To3, 37, 49L, 51L, 52R
Microcosmodon, Pu2-Cf2, 33, 43L, 46R, 49L, 49R, 53L, 56L, 57R, 58L, 59L, 59R, 60R, 63L, 64R, 65L
   M. rosei, 64R
Micromomys, Ti3-WA1, 35, 56L, 58R, 59L, 60L, 60R, 63L, 64R, 65L, 65R
Microsus, ?Wa4, Br2–3, 86L, 88L, 88R
microsyopid, 65L
Microsyopidae, 36
Microsyops, Cf2-Ui1, 36, 63L, 65L, 65R, 85R, 88R, 89R, 97L, 105R
   M. elegans, Br2, 88R
   M. annectens, Br3, 88R
Microtidae (polyphyletic), 239L

microtine (rodent), 21L, 156L, 218R, 219L, 222R, 223L, 225R, 236L, 236R, 237L, 237R, 238L, 238R, 240L, 240R, 241L, 241R, 242L, 242R, 243L, 246L, 246R, 247L, 247R, 248L, 249L, 249R, 250L, 250R, 251L, 251R, 252L, 252R, 253L, 253R, 254L, 254R, 255L, 255R, 256L, 256R, 257L, 257R, 258L, 258R, 259L, 259R, 260L, 260R, 261L, 261R, 262L, 262R, 263L, 263R, 264L
Microtoscoptes, Hh1-?Hh3, 183, 191L, 194R, 214R, 238R, 239L, 241R, 242L, 252R, 253L
   M. hibbardi, Hh1, 253L
Microtus, Ir1, IrI-Rct., 22L, 214R, 218R, 220R, 221L, 222L, 222R, 223L, 226L, 238R, 240L, 248L, 251L, 251R, 260L, 260R, 262L, 264L
Microtus (*Allophaiomys*); see *Allophaiomys* 222R
Microtus (*Pedomys*), Ir2, IrII-Rct., 21R, 223L, 238R [= subgenus of *Pitymys* of authors]
   M. (*Pedomys*) *llanensis,* Ir2, IrII, 223L
   M. (*Pedomys*) *ochrogaster,* Ir3, RlbI-Rct., 223L
Microtus (*Microtus*), Ir1, IrI-Rct., 21R, 22L, 218R, 222L, 222R, 226L, 238R, 239R, 241L, 249L, 249R, 260L, 260R, 261L, 261R, 262L, 263L, 263R, 264L
   M. (*M.*) *agrestis,* Steinheimian, Europe, 251L
   M. (*M.*) *californicus,* Ir1, IrI-Rct., 240L, 248R, 250L, 250R, 260L, 260R, 261L, 261R, 263R
   M. (*M.*) *deceitensis,* ?Ir1; BlV, 223L, (= *Lasiopodomys* of authors)
   M. (*M.*) *longicaudus,* RlbII-Rct., 251L
   M. (*M.*) *mexicanus,* RlbI-Rct., 22L, 250R, 251L, 263R
   M. (*M.*) *montanus,* RlbI-Rct., 21R, 250R, 215L, 263R
   M. (*M.*) *oeconomus,* RlbII-Rct., 251L, 251R, 264L
   M. (*M.*) *paroperarius,* Ir1–2, IrI-II, 21R, 218R, 223L, 241L, 249L, 249R, 250L, 250R, 260L, 260R, 261L, 261R, 262L, 263L
   M. (*M.*) *pennsylvanicus,* Ir3, RlbI-Rct., 21L, 22L, 223L, 224R, 226L, 250R, 251L, 263R, 264L
   M. (*M.*) *richardsoni,* RlbII-Rct., 251R
   M. (*M.*) *xanthognathus,* RlbII-Rct., 251R, 264L
Microtus (*Stenocranius*), Toringian, RlbII-Rct., 251L, 251R, 264L
   M. (*S.*) *gregalis,* Steinheimian-Rct., Europe, 251L, 251R
   M. (*M.*) *miurus,* RlbII-Rct., 264L
Mictomys (= *Synaptomys* subgenus of some authors), Bl2, BlV, ?Ir1-Rct., 218L, 219L, 220L, 221L, 223L
Mictomys (*Kentuckyomys*), Ir1, IrI, 21R, 222R, 238R
   M. (*Kentuckyomys*) *kansasensis,* Ir1, 222R
   M. (*Mictomys*) *meltoni,* Ir2, IrII, 223L
Mimatuta, L-Pu1, 37, 40R, 43L, 43R, 44L
   M. minuial, Pu1, 40R, 44L
   M. morgoth, L-Pu1, 43R
Mimetodon, To3-Ti5, 33, 48R, 52R, 56L, 57R, 58L, 59L, 59R
"*Mimomys*" *monohani,* Bl2, BlV, 21L, 219L
Mimomys, ?Hh3, Bl1; BlI-IrI, 22L, 183, 192R, 239L, 240R, 244L, 244R, 245L, 245R, 249L, 253R, 254L, 254R, 255L, 255R, 256L, 256R, 257L, 257R, 258L, 258R, 259L, 259R, 264L
Mimomys (*Cosomys*), ?Hh3, Bl1; BlI-III, 22L, 238L, 239R, 242R, 244L, 244R, 254L, 254R, 256L, 257L, 257R
   M. (*C.*) *sawrockensis,* ?Hh3, Bl1; BlI, 156L, 216R, 238L, 242R, 243L, 243R, 244L, 244R, 246L, 253R, 254L, 254R, 255R
   M. (*C.*) *primus,* Bl1, BlII, 22L, 244R, 246L, 254R, 255L, 256L, 257L, 257R
Mimomys (*Cseria*), "Pontian"-Biharian, Europe, 239L, 242R, 244R
   M. (*C.*) *gracilis,* Csarnotan, Europe, 244R
Mimomys (*Hintonia*), Ruscinian-Biharian, Europe, 242R, 244R, 249L
   M. (*C.*) *davakosi,* Csarnotan, Europe, 244R
   M. (*H.*) *occitanus,* Csarnotan, Europe, 244R
   M. (*H.*) *savini,* Biharian, Eurasia, 249L
Mimomys (*Ogmodontomys*), ?Hh3 or Bl1; BlI-Bl2, 22L, 216R, 218L, 218R, 226L, 238L, 244L, 245L, 246L, 256R, 247R, 248L, 249L, 254R, 255L, 255R, 257L, ?258L, 258R, 259R
   M. (*O.*) *monohani,* Bl2, BlV, 22L, 248L, 255R, 258R, 259R
   M. (*O.*) *poaphagus,* Bl1, BlII-IV, 22L, 243L, 245L, 246L, 246R, 254R, 255L, 255R, 256L, 256R, 257L

M. (O.) poaphagus poaphagus, Bl1, BlII-III, 243L, 246L, 254R, 255L, 255R, 256R, 257L

M. (O.) poaphagus transitionalis, Bl1, BlII, 243L, 244R, 246L, 254R, 255L

Mimomys (Ophiomys), Hh3, Bl1-2, ?Ir1, BlI-V, 22L, 226L, 239L, 242R, 244L, 245L, 245R, 246L, 246R, 247L, 247R, 249L, 253R, 254L, 254R, 255L, 256L, 256R, 258L, 258R, 259L, 259R, 264L, 279L

M. (O.) fricki, BlIII, 256L, ?257L

M. (O.) magilli, BlIII, 245R, 246R, 247L, 256L, 256R, 257L, 258L, 264L

M. (O.) mcknighti, Bl1, BlI, 217L, 242R, 243L, 244R, 245R, 253R, 254L, 254R, 255L

M. (O.) mcknighti-taylori, Bl1, BlII, 22L, 243L, 245L, 245R, 254R, 256R

M. (O.) meadensis, Bl2, BlIV-V, 22L, 246R, 247R, 257L, 258L, 258R, 259R, 264L

M. (O.) parvus, Bl2, BlV, 22L, 246R, 247R, 258L, 258R

M. (O.) taylori, Bl1, BlIII, 217L, 243L, 246R, 255L, 256L, 257L, 257R, 258L

M. (O.) taylori-parvus, Bl2, BlIV, 22L, 246R, 247R, 258L, 259L

Mimoperadectes, ?Cf3-Wa2, 34, 63L, 65R

Mimotricentes, Pu2-Ti6, 36, 42R, 43L, 46R, 49L, 51L, 51R, 52R, 53L, 56L, 57R, 58L, 59L, 59R, 60L, 60R

Mioclaenidae, 38

Mioclaenus, To1-To3, 38, 49L, 50R, 51R, 52R

Miohippus, Wh-Ar1, 145L, 157R, 184R, 193R

miolabine camel (artiodactyl), 176R, 177R

Miolabis, ?He2-Cl1, 158R, 161R, 173L, 190L, 194R

"*M.*" *tenuis*, He2, 158R

M. transmontanus, Ba1, 161R

Miomastodon, Ba2, 173L, 183

Miomusela, ?He1, He2-Ba1, 167R, 168L, 183, 187L, 194L

Mionictis, He2-Cl1, 168L, 187L, 194L

Miotylopus, Ar1-2, 184R, 193R

Mixodectes, To2-To3, 34, 42R, 49L, 51L, 52L

Mixodectidae, 34

mixodectids, 48R, 50L, 52R

mole(s), 166L

"*Monosaulax*," Ar3, Ba1-2, 160L, 164L, 187R, 189L

"*M.*" *hesperus*, Ar3, 164L

"*M.*" *pansus*, ?Ba2, 160L

Moropus, ?Ar2, Ar3-He1, 166L, 167R, 183, 184R, 193R

Moschidae, moschid (artiodactyl), 161R, 169R, 176L, 177L, 178L, 178R, 185L

Multituberculata (Jurassic; ?Kimmeridgian, to Oligocene; Chadronian), 33, 84L, 85L

multituberculate(s), 43R, 44L, 59L, 66R, 67R

muskrat (rodent), 239L, 245L

Mustela, Bl1-Rct., 222L

M. erminea, Ir1-Rct., 222L

Mustelidae, mustelid (carnivore), 132R, 166L, 166R, 168L, 169R, 179R, 186R, 187L, 190L

Mustelinae, musteline (carnivore), 167R, 168L, 186R, 187L, 194L

Mylagaulodon, Ar4, 19L, 161L, 194L, 288R

M. angulatus, Ar4, 161L

Mylagaulidae, mylagaulid (rodent), 176L, 178R, 184R, 192L, 193R, 195L, 214L, 216L

Mylagaulus, He2-Hh3, 168L, 173L, 175L, 179R, 187L, 194L

Mylodontidae, mylodontid sloth (edentate), 180L, 194R

Mylohyus, Hh3, 181L, 192R, 195L

M. elmorei, Hh3, 181L

Mysops, Br1-Ui2, 87L, 88L

Myrmecoboides, To3-Ti5, 34, 48L, 52L, 56L, 57R, 58L, 59L, 59R

Mytonolagus, Ui2-Du, 89R, 90L

Mytonomeryx, Ui1-2, 89R

Mytonomys, Wa3-Du, 90L

Nannippus, ?Cl1, Cl2-Bl2, 155R, 164R, 170R, 174L, 175L, 179R, 181L, 190L, 190R, 192L, 194R, 214R, 216R, 217R, 218L,

218R, 220L, 279R

N. ingenuus, Hh1-Hh3, 170R, 175L, 179R, 181L

"*N.*" *lenticularis* (= *Hipparion tehonense*), Cl1-2, 155R, 164R

N. lenticularis (= *N. ingenuus*), Hh3, 174L

N. minor, ?Cl2, ?Hh2, Hh3, 179R, 181L

N. phlegon, Bl1-2, BlII, 214R, 218L

Nannodectes, Ti1-Ti5, 35, 49R, 54R, 55L, 56L, 57R, 58L, 58R, 59L, 59R

N. gazini, Ti2, 58L

N. gidleyi, Ti4, 59R

N. intermedius, ?Ti1, 54R, 57R

N. simpsoni, Ti3, 58R

Nanochoerus, Ch1-Wh, 145R

Nanodelphys, Or, 143L

N. hunti, Or, 143L

Nanotragulus, Ar1-4, 146L, 156L, 157R, 164L, 178L, 184R, 185L, 193R

N. fontanus, Ar1, 157R

N. intermedius, Ar1, 146L

N. loomisi, Ar3, 178L

Navajovius, Ti3-Wa2, 35, 54L, 56L, 58L, 59L, 65L

Nebraskomys, Bl1-2; BlI-IV, 21L, 22L, 183, 192R, 218L, 219L, 242R, 253R, 254L, 254R, 255L, 256L, 257L, 258R, 259R, 262R

N. mcgrewi, Bl1-2, BlIII-V, 256L, 257L, 258R, ?259R

N. rexroadensis, Bl1; BlI, BlII, 216R, 243R, 254L, 254R, 255L

Nekrolagus, Bl1, BlI-II?, 214R, 217L, 226R, 242R

Neochoerus, Bl2, BlV, 21L, 279L

Neodon, Biharian-Rct., Eurasia, 239R, 248R, 249L

Neohipparion, Ba1-Hh3, 155R, 157L, 169R, 170L, 170R, 173L, 173R, 174L, 174R, 175L, 179R, 181L, 189L, 190R, 192L, 194R, 195L, 214R, 216R

N. coloradense, Ba1-2, ?Cl1 (B. J. MacFadden, 1984; AMNH Bull. 179:85)

N. eurystyle, ?Cl1, Hh1-Hh3, 156L, 157L, 169R, 174L, 174R, 175L

N. leptode, ?Hh1-2, 174R

N. molle, Hh3, 157L

N. phosphorum, ?Hh2, Hh3, 181L

N. trampasense, Cl1, 155R

N. whitneyi-affine, Cl1, 169R

Neofiber, Ir3, IrII-Rct., 22L, 223L, 248R, 250L, 261R, 263R, 264L

N. leonardi, Ir3, IrII-RlbI, 22L, 223L, 261R, 263R, 264L

Neoliotomus, Ti5-Wa3, 33, 56L, 59R, 60R, 63L, 64R, 65L, 65R, 84R, 86L

Neoplagiaulacidae, 33

Neoplagiaulax, L?-Wa1, 33, 43L, 44R, 46R, 49L, 51L, 51R, 53L, 56L, 57R, 58L, 59L, 59R

Neotomodon, Hh1 or 2, 159R

Neotoma, Hh2-Rct., 226R, 227L, 264L

Neotragocerus, Hh2-3, 171L, 183, 191L, 194R

Niglarodon, Ar1-Ar2, 163R, 185R

Nimravidae, nimravid (carnivore), 165R, 169R, 190L

Nimravides, Cl2-Hh2, 155R, 170L, 174R, 175L, 179R, 190L, 190R, 191L, 194R

N. catocopis, Hh1-2, 170L, 174R

N. thinobates, Cl2, 155R

Nimravus, Wh-Ar1, 145L, 184R, 193R

N. brachyops, Wh, 145L

Niptomomys, Cf2-Wa4?, 36, 63L, 65L, 65R, 85R

Notharctus, Br1-Ui1, 84R, 86L, 88R, 89R, 102R, 107R

N. tenebrosus, Br1-2, 88R, 107R

N. robustior, Br3, 88R, 102R

"*Nothocyon*," Ar3, 166R

Nothokemas, He1, 176L, 178R

Nothotylopus, Cl1, 177R

Nothrotheriops, Ir1-Rlb, 222L

Notolagus, Hh3-BlIV, 216R, 279L

Notoparamys, Wa3, 85R

Nototitanops (= ?*Protitanops*), Ui or Du, 107R

N. mississippiensis, 107R
Notoungulata, 38, 68R
notoungulates, 68L
Nyctitheriidae, 35
nyctitheriid(s), 38R, 101R
Nyctitherium, ?Ti3, Wa3-Du, 59L, 84R, 88R
"*N.*" *celatum* (= *Pontifactor*), Wa1 or 2, 84R
Ocajila, Ar1, 166L, 183, 184R, 193R
Ochotona, Hh3-Rct., 183, 192L, 195L, 222L, 242L
   O. whartoni, ?BlV, Ir1-IrII, 222L
ochotonid (lagomorph), 167R, 186R
odocoileine deer (artiodactyl), 181L, 192R, 195L
Odocoileini, Hh3-Rct., 183
Odocoileus, Bl1, BlII-Rct., 192R, 217L, 279L
Ogmodontomys, subgenus of *Mimomys*
Oligobunis, Ar3–4, 166R, 183, 185L, 194L
Oligoryctes, Ui1-Ch3, 89R, 133L
Omomyidae, 85L
omomyid primate, 68L
Omomys, Br1-Ui2, 86L, 87R, 88L, 88R, 89R, 97L
   O. carteri, Br1–3, 87R
onager, 245L
Ondatra, Bl2, BlV-Rct., 21L, 218L, 219L, 220R, 221L, 222R, 223L,
   226L, 245R, 247L, 249L, 250L, 250R, 258R, 259L, 259R,
   260L, 260R, 261L, 261R, 262L, 262R, 263L, 263R, 264L, 279L
   O. annectens, ?Ir1, Ir1–II, 21R, 22L, 222R, 223L, 249L, 250L,
   250R, 260L, 261L, 261R, 262L, 262R, 263L, 263R
   O. idahoensis, Bl2, BlV-Ir1, 22L, 218L, 220R, 221L, 245R, 247R,
   250L, 258R, 259L, 259R, 260L, 264L
   O. nebraskensis, Ir3, RlbI, 21R, 22R, 223L, 250L, 264L
   O. zibethicus, Rlb, RlbI-Rct., 224R
Ondatrinae (rodent), 238R, 239L, 245L
Onohippidium, Hh3, 192L, 279L
Onychodectes, Pu2-Pu3, 39, 42R, 43L, 46R
Onychomys, ?Hh3, Bl2-Rct., 226L
Oligoscalops, Or, 143L
   O. galbreathi, Or, 143L
Ophiomys, subgenus of *Mimomys*
Oreamnos, Rlb-Rct., 223R
"*Oreodon,*" 122R, 123L, 123R, 124L, 124R, 132R, 139R, 140L,
   142R
Oreodon-Eporeodon type, 137R
oreodont(s) (artiodactyl), 138L, 139L, 140L, 140R, 141R, 157R,
   160L, 163R, 164L, 165R, 166L, 166R, 167L, 168L, 169L, 171R,
   178L, 185L, 185R, 186R
Oreolagus, He1–2, 167R, 183, 186R, 194L
Orohippus, Wa4-Ui1, 18R, 86R, 87L, 88L, 88R, 97L, 106R, 107R
   O. pumilus, Br1–2, 88R
   O. sylvaticus, Br3, 88R
oromerycids, 89R
Osbornoceros, Hh3, 214R
Osteoborus, Hh1–3; BlI, 155R, 157L, 159R, 160R, 170L, 170R,
   171L, 173R, 174R, 175L, 179R, 181L, 190R, 194R, 195L,
   214R, 216L, 217R
   O. cyonoides, Hh3, 159R, 175L
   "*O.*" *diabloensis* (= *Epicyon saevus*), Cl2, 155R
   O. direptor, Hh3, 170R
   O. galushai, Hh1, 179R
   "*O.*" *littoralis,* (= *Epicyon saevus*), Cl1, 157L
   O. pugnator, Hh1, 173R
   O. orc, Hh2, 181L
   O. secundus, Hh1, 171L
Otionohyus, Ch3-Or, 142R
   O. (Otarohyus) bullatus, Or, 142R
Ourayia, Ui1-Ui2, 89R, 97R
Ovibos, Rlb-Rct., 223R, 225L, 227R
Ovibovini (artiodactyl), 221R
Ovis, Rlb-Rct., 223R, 225L
   O. dalli, Rlb-Rct., 225L

Oxetocyon, Wh, 145L
   O. cuspidatus, Wh, 145L
Oxyacodon, Pu2-Pu3, 37, 42R, 43L, 44L, 46R
   "*O.*" *josephi,* Pu1, 44L
Oxyaena, Ti5-Wa4, 39, 56L, 59R, 60R, 61L, 62R, 63L, 64L, 64R,
   65L, 65R, 84R, 85R, 87L, 107L
   O. aequidens, 64L
Oxyaenidae, oxyaenids (creodont), 39, 44L, 89R
Oxyaenodon, Ui1, 89R
Oxyclaenus, Pu2-To1, 36, 42L, 43L, 46R, 48R, 50L, 50R
Oxydactylus, Ar3-He2, 164L, 166R, 168L, 176L, 178R, 185L, 186R,
   187L, 194L
   O. lacota, ?Ar3, 164L
Oxyprimus, L-Pu1, 37, 42R, 43L, 44L
   O. galadrielae, Pu1, 44L
   O. erikseni, L-Pu1, 43R
   O. putorius, Pu1, 44L
Pachyaena, Wa1-Wa4?, 18R, 68L, 85R
Paciculus, ?Ar1–2, 160L, 165R, 184R
packrat (rodent), 226R, 252R
Paenemarmota, Hh3-Bl2, 216R, 217L, 217R, 218L, 220L, 264L,
   279L
   P. fossilis, BlIII, 264L
Palaeanodon, Cf2-Wa3, 39, 63L, 65L, 65R, 84R
Palaeanodonta, 39
Palaechthon, To1-Ti1, 35, 48R, 50R, 51L, 51R, 52R, 53L, 54R, 56L,
   57R
Palaeocastor, Ar1–4, 146L, 166R, 171R, 176L, 185L
   P. nebrascensis, Ar1, 146L, 171R
Palaeogale, Ch1-He1, 132R, 146L
Palaeictops, Wa3-Ui2, 85L, 89R, 106R
Palaeocastor, Ar2–3, 161L, 194L
Palaeolagus, Ch1-Ar1, 132L, 138L, 138R, 142R, 145L, 145R, 146L,
   184R, 193R
   P. burkei, Or-Wh, 140R
   P. haydeni, Ch3-Or, 138L, 138R, 142R
   P. hypsodus, Ar1, 146L
   P. temnodon, Ch2–3, 132L, 138R
   P. primus, Ch1 (R. Emry, pers. commun., 1987)
Palaeonictis, Cf3-Wa2, 39, 63L, 65R, 85R
   P. peloria, Cf3, 65R
Palaeoryctes, To2-Wa1, 34, 51L, 53L, 56L, 57R, 58L, 59L, 60L,
   60R, 63L, 64R, 65L, 65R
palaeorcytids, 68L
Palaeoryctidae (proteutherian), 34
Palaeosinopa, Ti4-Br1, 18R, 19L, 34, 55L, 56L, 59L, 60L, 60R,
   63L, 64R, 65L, 65R, 84R, 88L
Palaeosyops, Br1–3, 18R, 85L, 86L, 86R, 87L, 87R, 88L, 97L, 97R,
   105L, 105R, 106R
   P. borealis, Br1, 86R, 87L
Palenochtha, To3-Ti1, 35, 48L, 52R, 54L, 56L, 57R
paleothere (perissodactyl), 86L, 102L
Paleotomus, To3-Ti5, 34, 48R, 52R, 56L, 57R, 58L, 59L, 59R
panda (carnivore), 245L
Panthera, Ir1-Rct., 221R, 222L, 223R, 225R
   P. leo atrox, Rlb-Rct., 223R, 225L
   P. onca, Ir1-Rct., 221R, 222L
pantodont(s), 54L, 58R, 59L, 67L, 67R
Pantodonta, 38, 61R, 85R
Pantolambda, To3-Ti1?, 28, 38, 46R, 48R, 49L, 49R, 50L, 50R,
   51L, 51R, 52L, 52R, 55R, 56L, 57R
Pantolambdidae (pantodont), 38
Pantolestidae (proteutherian), 34
Pantolestes, Br1-Ui1, 86L, 87L, 87R, 88L, 88R, 89R
Pantomimus, ?To3, 34, 49L, 53L
Paraphelops, Hh2, 173R
   P. yumensis, Hh2, 173R
Parablastomeryx, ?He1, Cl1–2, 169R, 172L
Paracosoryx, Ar4, Ba1-?Cl2, 157L, 159R, 160L, 160R, 162L, 165L,

167L, 169L, 173L, 183, 185L, 194L
"*P.*" *furlongi,* Cl1–2, 157L, 159R
P. loxocerus, Ba2–?Cl1, 160L, 160R
Paracryptotis, BlIII–IV, 257R
  P. gidleyi, BlIII–IV, 257R
Paradjidaumo, Ch2–Wh, 132L, 133L, 137R, 138L, 138R, 142R, 144L, 145R
  P. minor, Ch2, 132L, 133L, 137R, 138R
  P. trilophus, Ch3–Or, 138L, 138R, 142R
Parahippus, Ar3–He2, 161R, 166R, 167R, 172L, 176L, 178L, 178R, 185L, 186R, 187L, 194L
  P. cognatus, He1, 122L
  P. leonensis, He1, 178R
Parailurus, Bl1, BlIII, 183, 192R, 245L
Paramerycoidodon, Wh, 145L, 145R, 191L
  P. major, Wh, 145L, 145R
  P. wanlessi, Wh, 145L
Paramicrotoscoptes, Hh1–2, 162L, 170R, 183, 194R
Paramoceros, Ba2, 159L
Paramys, Cf1–Ui1, 19L, 39, 63L, 64L, 65L, 65R, 85R, 88L, 88R, 89R
  P. atavus (= *Acritoparamys*), 62R
Paraneotoma, BlIII–IV, 258L
  P. fossilis, BlIII–IV, 258L
Parapliosaccomys, Ba2–Hh3, 159L, 253L
  P. oregonensis, Hh3, 253L, 253R
Pararyctes, ?Ti1–Ti3, 34, 56L, 57R, 58L, 59L, 59R
Paratoceras, Ba1–Cl1, 174L, 190L, 194R
Paratylopus, Ar4, 161L
  P. cameloides, Ar4, 161L
Parectypodus, Pu2–W, 33, 43L, 46R, 49L, 51L, 51R, 53L, 57R, 58L, 59L, 59R, 60L, 60R, 63L, 65L, 65R
Parictis, Ch1–Ar1 or 2, 132R
Parisectolophus, Br2–3, 88L
Paromomys, To1–Ti1, 35, 48R, 50L, 52R, 53L, 54R, 56L, 57R
Paromomyidae, 35
Paronychomys, Hh3, 279L
Parvericius, Ar2–Ba3, 168R, 183, 184R, 193R, 194R
Parvitragulus, Ch1, 136L
  P. priscus, Ch1, 136L
Patriofelis, Wa4–Br3, 88L, 107R,
Pauromys, Wa3–Br3, 86R, 87L, 88R
peccary (artiodactyl), 190L
Pediomeryx, Hh3, 171L, 175L, 192L, 195L, 279R
Pedomys, Ir2, IrII–Rct., 22L, 223L, 248R, 250L, 250R, 261R, 262R, 263L, 263R, 264L
  P. guildayi (= *Allophaiomys*), IrII, 262R
  P. llanensis, Ir2, IrII–RlbI, 22L, 223L, 250L, 250R, 261R, 263L, 263R
  P. ochrogaster, Ir3, RlbI–Rct., 22R, 223L, 250R, 263R, 264L
Pelycodus, Wa2–Wa4, 18R, 19R, 85L, 85R, 86L, 96R, 97L, 106L, 107L
  "*P.*" (= *Cantius*) *abditus,* 19R
  P. jarrovii, Wa2–4, 19R, 85R, 106L
Pelycomys, Or, 144L
Pentacodon, To2–To3, 34, 49L, 51L, 52R
Pentacodontidae (proteutherian), 34
Pentacemylus, Ui1–Du, 90L
Pentacosmodon, Ti5, 33, 56L, 60L
Peraceras, Ba1–Cl1, 176R, 177L
Peradectes, Pu1–Or (L. Marshall, pers. commun., 1987), 25R, 34, 40R, 42L, 43L, 43R, 44L, 46R, 49L, 51L, 51R, 53L, 56L, 57R, 58L, 59L, 59R, 60L, 60R, 63L, 64R, 65L, 65R
  P. pusillus, Pu1, 44L
Peratherium, Wa1–Ar1, 44R, 85L, 88R, 121R, 146L
Perchoerus, Ch1–Wh, 137L, 145R
  P. nanus, Ch3–Or, 137R
Peridiomys, Ba1, 187R
Periptychidae, periptychid, 37, 42L, 42R, 47R, 48L

Periptychus, To1–Ti4, 25L, 28, 37, 42L, 42R, 43L, 44R, 45L, 45R, 46L, 47R, 48L, 48R, 50L, 50R, 51L, 51R, 52L, 52R, 53L, 56L, 57R, 58L, 59L, 59R, 286L
  P. carinidens, To1, 47R, 286L
Perissodactyla, perissodactyl, 66R, 85L, 89L, 167R, 186R
Perognathoides (= *Cupidinimus*), Ba1–Hh3, 279R
Perognathus, Ba1–Rct., 188L, 194L
Peromyscus, Hh1–Rct., 157L
  P. pliocenicus, Hh1, 157L
Petauristinae, petauristine (rodent), 158L, 187L
Petauristodon, He2, 183, 187L, 194L
Phaiomys, Rct., Asia, 262R
phenacocoeline oreodont (artiodactyl), 164L, 178L
Phenacocoelus, Ar2–He1, 166L, 166R, 178L, 186R, 194L
  P. typus, Ar2, 166L
Phenacodaptes, Ti3–Cf1, 37, 56L, 59R, 60L, 60R, 63L, 64L, 84R, 85L
  P. sabulosus, Cf1, 64L
Phenacodontidae, 38
phenacodontid(s); phenacodont condylarths, 58R, 86L, 101L
Phenacodus, Ti1–Br3, 25R, 38, 49R, 54L, 54R, 55L, 56L, 57R, 58L, 59L, 59R, 60L, 60R, 62R, 63L, 63R, 64R, 65L, 65R, 81L, 84R, 85R, 86L, 87L, 88L, 98L, 103R, 104L, 106R, 107L
  P. grangeri, Ti, 55L
  P. primaevus, Cf., 62R
  P. vortmani, Cf., 62R
Phenacolemur, Ti5–Du, 35, 56L, 59L, 59R, 60R, 63L, 63R, 64R, 65L, 65R, 84R, 85L
  P. pagei, T–5–?Cf2, 63R
  P. praecox, Cf1–Wa1, 63R, 65L, 65R
  P. simonsi, Cf2, 65L, 65R
Phenacomys, Ir2, IrI–Rct., 22L, 223L, 239R, 248L, 260L, 263L, 263R
Phoberocyon, He1, 178R, 183, 186R, 194L
  P. ("*Aelurodon*") *johnhenryi,* He1, 178R
Phlaocyon, Ar3–He1, 166R, 172L
  P. leucosteus, He1, 172L
phocid (carnivore), 167R, 186R
pika (lagomorph), 192L
Picrodontidae, 36
Picrodus, To3–Ti5, 36, 48R, 52R, 56L, 57R, 58L, 59L, 59R
Pithecistes, Ar1–2, 163R
Pitymys, Ir2, IrII–Rct., 21R, 22L, 223L, 226L, 239R, 241R, 248R, 249L, 249R, 250L, 250R, 261L, 261R, 262L, 262R, 263L, 263R
  P. cumberlandensis, IrII, 263L
  P. mcnowni, IrII, 261L, 261R
  P. meadensis, Ir2, IrII, 21R, 223L, 241R, 249R, 250L, 250R, 261L, 261R, 262L, 262R, 263L
  P. nemoralis, Rct., 250R
  P. quasiater, Rct., 241R, 250R
Plagioctenodon, ?Cf2–Wa4, 35, 63L, 65L, 65R
  P. krausae, ?Cf2–Cf3, 65L, 65R
Plagiomene, Cf2–Wa2, 35, 63L, 64L, 65L, 65R, 85R
  P. accola, Cf., 63L, 64L
Plagiomenidae, 35
Planetetherium, Cf1–?Cf3, 35, 63L, 64L, 65L
Platybelodon, Cl2–Hh2, 162L, 181L, 183, 190L, 194R
platybelodont mastodont (proboscidean), 169R
Platygonus, Hh3–Rlb, 195L
Platymastus, Pu2, 36, 43L, 46R
plesiadapid(s), 48L, 52R, 58R, 67L
plesiadapiform primates, 66R
Plesiadapis, Ti1–Wa1, 19R, 36, 48L, 49L, 49R, 51L, 51R, 52L, 52R, 54L, 54R, 55L, 55R, 56L, 57R, 58L, 58R, 59L, 59R, 60L, 62R, 63L, 64L, 64R, 65L, 65R, 66R, 84R, 86L, 96L, 101L, 286L
  P. anceps, Ti2, 25R, 55R, 56R, 57R, 58L
  P. churchilli, Ti4, 54L, 55R, 56R, 58L, 59L, 59R
  P. cookei, Cf2, 56L, 56R, 60L, 60R, 62R, 63L, 63R, 64L, 64R, 65L, 66L, 96R

P. dubius, Ti6–Wa1?, 60R, 62R, 64R, 65L, 96R, 101L
P. fodinatus, Ti5, 60L
P. gingerichi, Ti6, 54L, 56L, 56R, 59R, 60L, 60R, 63L, 63R, 64L, 66R
P. praecursor, Ti1, 25R, 49L, 49R, 51L, 51R, 52L, 52R, 55R, 56R, 57R, 286L
P. rex, Ti3, 54L, 55R, 56R, 57R, 58L, 58R
P. russelli, Sparnacian, Europe, 66R
P. simonsi, Ti5, 54L, 55R, 56R, 59L, 59R, 60L
P. tricuspidens, Thanetian, Europe, 66R
Plesiadapidae, 35
Plesiogulo, Hh3, 155R, 175L, 183, 192L, 194R, 214R, 216L, 242L, 279L, 279R
Plesiolestes, To3–Ti2, 35, 48R, 52R, 54R, 56L, 57L, 58L
Plesiosminthus, Ar1, 165R, 166L, 183, 184L, 193R
Plesiosorex, He1, 183, 186R, 194L
plesiosoricid (insectivore), 186R
Pleurolicus, Ar2, 161L, 163L, 163R, 172L, 185R
Plioceros, Cl1–Hh1, ?2, 159R, 164R, 169R, 190L, 194R
    P. blicki, ?Hh1, 164R
Pliogeomys, Hh3 or ?Bl1; Bl1, 216R
Plioctomys, subgenus of *Synaptomys*, Bl2, BlV, 21L, 218L, 219L
Pliohippus, Ba3–Hh2, ?Hh3, Bl1, 155R, 157L, 159R, 160R, 164R, 169L, 173L, 173R, 175L, 179R, 180L, 180R, 189L, 190R, 191L, 194R, 214R, 243R, 254R
    P. campestris, Ba3, 173R
    "*P.*" *coalingensis* (= ?*Dinohippus interpolatus*) Hh3, 155R, 157L
    "*P.*" *hondurensis*, ?Hh1, 180L
    "*P.*" *leardi*, Cl2, 155R, 157L, 159R
    P. mexicanus, Bl1, 243R, 254R
    "*P.*" *spectans*, ?Hh1–2, 155R, 160R
    P. supremus, ?Cl1, 180R
    P. tantalus, Cl1, 159R
    "*P.*" *tehonensis*, Cl1, 157L
Pliolemmus, Bl1–2, BlII–V, 21L, 218L, 219L, 237L, 246L, 249L, 254R, 255R, 256L, 256R, 257L, 258L, 258R, 259L, 259R
    P. antiquus, BlII–V, 22L, 254R, 255R, 256L, 256R, 257L, 258L, 258R, 259R
Pliomastodon, Hh1–3, 159R, 160R, 181L
    P. nevadanus, Hh1, 160R
    P. vexillarius, Hh3, 159R
Pliometanastes, Hh1–?3, 158L, 170L, 175L, 180L, 181L, 183, 191L, 194R, 279R, 289L
    P. protistus, Hh1, 170L
Pliomys, Csarnotan–Steinheimian, Europe, 239R, 249L
    P. lenki, Villanyian–Steinheimian, Europe, 249L
Plionarctos, Hh2–3, 169R, 183, 191L, 194R
Plionictis, He2–Ba2, 168L, 183, 194L
Pliophenacomys, Bl1–Ir1; Bl1–Ir1, 22L, 216R, 217R, 218R, 226L, 237L, 243R, 244L, 244R, 246L, 246R, 247L, 247R, 249L, 253R, 254L, 254R, 255L, 255R, 256L, 256R, 257L, 257R, 258L, 258R, 259L, 259R, 260L, 260R, 279L
    P. finneyi, Bl1–2; BlII, 22L, 216R, 243R, 244R, 246L, 254R, 255L
    P. osborni, BlV–Ir1, 22L, 246L, 247L, 255R, 258R, 259L, 259R, 260L, 260R
    P. primaevus, Bl1, BlIII, 243R, 246L, 246R, 255R, 256L, 257L, 258L
    P. primaevus-osborni, BlIV, 22L, 257L, 257R
    P. wilsoni, Bl1; Bl1, 216R, 244R, 253R, 254L
Pliopotamys, Bl1–2, BlIII–V, 21L, 22L, 217L, 218L, 219L, 239L, 241L, 245L, 245R, 246L, 246R, 247L, 247R, 249L, 255L, 255R, 256L, 256R, 257L, 257R, 258L, 258R, 259L, 259R, 260L, 279L
    P. meadensis, BlIII–V, 245R, 246L, 246R, 247L, 247R, 255R, 256L, 256R, 257L, 258L, 258R, 259R, 260L
    P. minor, BlIII–IV, 22L, 245R, 246L, 255L, 256L, 257L, 257R
Pliosaccomys, Hh1 or 2, 160R, 162L, 190R, 194R
    P. dubius, Hh1 or 2, 160R
Pliotaxidea, Hh1–3, 171L, 190R, 194R, 279L, 279R
Pliotomodon, Hh1 or 2, 155R, 183, 191L, 194R

Pliozapus, Hh1 or 2, 160R
    P. solus, Hh1, 160R
Plithocyon, Ba1–Cl2, 159L, 168R, 183, 187R, 188L, 194L
    P. barstowensis, Ba2, 159L
    P. californicus, Ba2, 159L
Poabromylus, Du–Ch, 90L, 90R, 105R
Poëbrotherium, Ch1–Or, 132R, 142L, 142R, 143L
    P. wilsoni, Or, 143L
Poebrodon, Ui2, 89R
Pontifactor, Cf2–Br3, 35, 63L, 65L, 65R, 84R, 88R
    P. bestiola, Cf2–Br3, 65L, 65R
    P. celatum, Wa1 or 2, 84L
Potamotherium, He1–Ba3, 167R, 183, 186R, 194L
Praeovibos, Rlb, 228L
Pratilepus, Bl1–?2, BlIII–?V, 217R, 218L, 226R, 279L
Predicrostonyx, ?Ir1, 222L
Preptoceras (= *Soergelia*), Ir1, 211R
Presbymys, Du, 100R
Primates, primate(s), 35, 48L, 51L, 52R, 54L, 54R, 59L, 68L, 101R, 104R, 161L, 184R, 193R
Proantilocapra, Cl1–Or 2, 169R, 190L, 194R
Probathyopsis, Ti5–Wa4, 38, 55L, 55R, 56L, 59R, 60R, 62R, 63L, 64R, 65L, 65R, 84R
Problastomeryx, He1, 172L
Proboscidea, 156R, 160L, 161R, 162L (?pre-late Barstovian), 164R, 165L, 168R, 176L, 177L, 187R, 188L, 188R, 189L, 194R, 216R
Procadurcodon, ?Du–Ch?, 107R
Procamelus, Ba2–Hh1, ?2, 164R, 174R, 175L, 179R, 189L, 191L, 194R
Procaprolagus, Ui2–?Ch, 107R
Procastoroides, Bl1–2, 214R, 218L, 219L, 220L
    P. idahoensis, Bl2, BlV, 219L
    P. sweeti, Bl1, 219L
Procerberus, L–Pu3, 34, 43L, 43R, 44L, 46R
    P. formicarum, L–Pu1, 43R
Prochetodon, Ti3–Cf2, 33, 56L, 58L, 59R, 60L, 60R, 63L, 64R, 65L, 84R, 85L
Procynodictis, Ui2, 90L
Procyonidae, procyonid (carnivore), 166R, 185L, 186R
Procyoninae, 167R, 186R
Prodaphoenus, Ui2, 90L, 97R
Prodiacodon, Pu3–Wa3, 34, 43L, 46R, 49L, 51L, 51R, 53L, 56L, 57L, 58L, 59L, 59R, 60L, 60R, 63L, 64R, 65L, 65R
Prodipodomys, Hh3–Bl2, BlV, ?Ir1, 214R, 217R, 218L, 220L, 221L, 279L, 279R
Proheteromys, Wh, 145R
    P. nebraskensis, Wh, 145R
Prolagurus (Biharian), Europe, 249L
Prolimnocyon, ?To3–Br1, 39, 48R, 52R, 53L, 56L, 57L, 58L, 59L, 59R, 60L, 60R, 63L, 64R, 65L, 65R, 85R, 87R, 88L
Promartes, Ar2–4, 166L, 184R, 185L, 193R, 194L
Promerycochoerinae, 185L, 194L
Promerycochoerus, Ar1–4, 161L, 163L, 164L, 166L, 184R, 185L, 185R, 193R, 194L
    P. barbouri, Ar3, 164L
    P. carrikeri, Ar2–3, 166L
    P. (*Promerycochoerus*), Ar3–4, 194L
    P. (*Pseudopromerycochoerus*), Ar1–2, 163R, 184L
Prometheomyinae (rodent), 238R, 239L, 241R, 242L
Promimomys, Hh3, 22L, 183, 192L, 194R, 238R, 239L, 242L, 242R, 244R, 253L, 253R
    P. mimus, Hh3, 253L, 253R
Promioclaenus, Pu2–Ti3, 38, 43L, 46R, 49L, 51L, 51R, 52R, 53L, 54L, 56L, 57R, 58L, 58R
    P. acolytus, To3, 54L
Promylagaulus, Ar1, 164L, 165R, 184R
Proneofiber, Ir1, Ir1–II, 22L, 222R, 248R, 249L, 249R, 260L, 261L
    P. guildayi, Ir1, Ir1, 222R, 260L, 261L
Pronodens, Ar1, 163L, 163R

Pronothodectes, To3-Ti1?, 19R, 35, 48R, 49R, 52R, 54R, 56L, 57R
  P. jepi, To3, 49R
  P. matthewi, To3, 49R
Propalaeanodon, Ti5, 39, 56L, 60L
Propalaeosinopa, To3-Ti5, 34, 48R, 52R, 56L, 57R, 58L, 59L, 59R
Propliophenacomys, He3, 22L, 192L, 194R, 216L, 216R, 242L, 242R, 243R, 244R, 253R
  P. parkeri, He3, 216L, 216R, 243R, 253R
proscalopids, 89R
Proscalops, Wh-Ar1, 145R
  P. miocaenus, Wh, 145R
  P. tertius, Wh, 145R
Prosigmodon, Bl1–II, 254R, 279
Prosomys, Hh3, 242L
Prosthecion, Cf1, 38, 63L
Prosthennops, Ba2-Hh3, 157L, 170R, 189L, 190R, 191L, 194R, 214R, 216R, 279R
  P. kernensis, Hh1 or 2, 157L
Prosynthetoceras, Ar3-Ba3, 156R, 176L, 176R, 177L, 178R, 185L, 194L
Protapirus, Or-Ar4, 197R
Protentomodon, Cf1, 34, 59L, 63L
Proteryx, Wh, 145R
  P. bicuspis, Wh, 145R
  P. loomisi, Wh, 145R
Proteutherians, 34, 43R, 44L
Prothryptacodon, ?To2-To3, 36, 49L, 51L, 52R
Prothyracodon (= *Triplopus*), Ui, 89R
Protictis, To1-Ti5, Ui1, 39, 48R, 50R, 51L, 51R, 53L, 56L, 57R, 58L, 59L, 59R
Protitanotherium, Ui2, 89R, 90L
Protoceras, Wh-Ar3, 122R, 123L, 123R, 124L, 124R, 127R, 139R, 144R, 185L
  P. celer, Wh, 144R
Protoceratidae, protoceratids (artiodactyl), 89R, 144R, 166R, 174R, 178R, 185L, 190L, 192L, 192R, 195R
Protogonodon, 42R
"*Protohippus*," Ba1-Hh2, 164R, 169L, 170R, 176L, 189L, 191L, 194R
protolabine, protolabidine (camel), 159L, 167L, 176R, 185L, 185R
Protolabis, He1-Cl2, 169L, 173L, 186R, 190L, 194L, 194R
Protoreodon (= *Protagriochoerus*), Ui1-Du, 89L, 89R, 97R, 104R, 105R, 106R, 107R
Protoptychus, Ui1, 89R, 102R
Protosciurus, Ar1 or 2, 156L
  P. tecuyaensis, Ar1 or 2, 156L
Protoselene, Pu2-Ti3, 38, 43L, 46R, 49L, 50L, 51L, 51R, 53L, 56L, 57R, 58L, 58R
  P. bombadili, Pu1, 50L
  P. opistacus, ?To2-To3?, 50L
  P. (= *Dracoclaenus*) *griphus*, To1, 50L
Prototomus, Wa1-Br1, 18R, 85R
prototoptychids, 89R
Protungulatum, L-Pu3, 36, 43L, 43R, 46R
  P. donnae, L-Pu1, 43R
Protylopus, Ui-Du, 88L, 89R, 102R
Proviverra, Br2-Ui1, 88L
Pseudajidaumo, Ba2, 19L, 289L
  P. stirtoni, Ba2, 19L, 289L
Pseudaelurus, He2-Hh3, 168L, 183, 187L, 194L, 216R
Pseudhipparion, Ba3-Cl2, 169L, 173L, 189L, 194R
  P. retrusum, Ba3, 169L
Pseudoblastomeryx, Ar3, ?He1, 157R, 172L
  P. falkenbachi, ?Ar3 or 4, 157R
Pseudoceras, Ba3-Hh2, 169L, 175L, 179R, 181L, 183, 189L, 191L, 194R
Pseudocylindrodon, Ch1-2, 134R, 136L
Pseudocyclopidius, Or-Ar2, 145L, 163R
Pseudocynodictis, Wh-Ar1, 132R, 145L

Pseudocyon, Ba2–3, 169L, 183, 189L, 194R
Pseudodesmatochoerus, Ar3, 164L
  P. longiceps, Ar3, 164L
Pseudolabis, Wh-Ar1, 145R
  P. dakotensis, Wh, 145R
Pseudomesoreodon, Ar3, 164L
  ?*P. boulderensis*, Ar3, 164L
  P. rolli, Ar3, 164L
Pseudoparablastomeryx, Ba1–2, 189L
Pseudopromerycochoerus, Ar1, 193R
Pseudoprotoceras, Ch1–3, 134R
Pseudotheridomys, Ar2-He1, 166L, 183, 184R, 193R
Psittacotherium, To2-Ti5, 39, 48R, 51L, 53L, 56L, 57R, 58L, 59L, 59R, 84R, 85L
Pterodon, Du, 105R, 133R
Ptilodontidae, 33
Ptilodus, Pu2-Ti5, 33, 43L, 46R, 48R, 49L, 50L, 51L, 51R, 52R, 53L, 56L, 57R, 58L, 58R, 59L, 59R
  P. tsosiensis, Pu2, 50L
Purgatorius, ?L-Pu3, 35, 43L, 44R, 46R, 59L
  P. unio, Pu2, 46R
Ragnarok, L-Pu1, 36, 40R, 43L, 43R, 44L
  R. engdahli, Pu1, 40R
  R. harbichti, ?Pu1, 43R
  R. nordicum, Pu1, 44L
rabbit (lagomorph), 214R, 226R
Rakomeryx, Ba1, 162L, 165L, 188L, 194L
  R. kinseyi, Ba1, 165L
Ramoceros, Ba2–3, 169L, 173R
  R. osborni, Ba3, 173R
Rangifer, Ir1-Rct., 222L
Raphictis, Ti3, 39, 56L, 58R
Repomys, Hh3-BlIV, 159R
  R. gustelyi, Hh3, 159R
rhino, rhinoceratid, rhinoceros (perissodactyl), 135R, 166L, 168L, 169L, 175L, 175R, 176L, 177L, 178R, 185L, 186R, 187L, 192R, 195L, 216L
rhinocerotoid(s), 136L, 142L
rhynchorostrine gomphothere (proboscidean), 175L, 192L
Rhynchotherium, ?Ba2, ?Cl1, Hh3-Bl2, 160R, 173L, 175L, 181L, 192L, 195L, 217R, 218L, 279L, 279R
Rodentia, rodents, 19L, 21L, 55L, 56L, 60L, 60R, 61R, 62L, 63L, 63R, 64L, 66R, 101R, 108L, 120L, 121R, 136L, 140R, 142R, 157R, 163R, 166L, 167L, 168L, 168R, 171R, 176L, 184R, 185R, 187L, 188L, 191L, 214R, 216R, 217L, 218R, 219L, 219R, 221L, 222R, 223R, 225R, 226L, 226R, 227L, 236L, 236R, 238L, 238R, 240L, 240R, 241L, 241R, 250L, 286R
sabre-cat, saber-toothed cat (carnivore), 192L, 220L
Saiga, Rlb, 228L
Sanctimus, Ar1, 146L
Satherium, Bl1-III, 219L
Saxonella, Ti3, 36, 56L, 58R
Saxonellidae, 36
Scapanus, Bl2-Rct., 218R
Scenopagus, Wa1-Ui1, 88R, 89R, 97L
Schizodontomys, Ar4, 161R
Schizotheroides (= *Toxotherium*), Ch1, 136L
  S. jackwilsoni, Ch1, 136L
Sciuravidae, sciuravid, 85L
Sciuravus, Wa4-Ui1, 86R, 88L, 88R, 89R, 97L
Scottimus, ?Or-Wh, 143L
  S. exiguus, Or, 143L
  S. lophatus, Wh, 144L, 145R
selenodont artiodactyls, 89L, 89R, 97L
Semantorinae, phocid (carnivore), 186R
"*Serridentinus*" (= *Gomphotherium*), Ba2-Hh3, 173L
Sespia, Ar1–2, 157R, 163R, 165R, 171R
  S. californica, Ar1, 157R
  S. marianae, Ar1, 165R

Sewellelodon, Ar4, 161R
Shoshonius, Wa4-Br1, 86R, 87R, 88L
shrew (insectivore), 186R
Sicistinae (rodent), 184R
Sigmodon, Bl1-Rct., 214R, 217R, 218R, 226L, 261L
    S. curtisi, 226L
    S. hudspethensis, Bl2, 226L
    S. medius, Bl1, BlII or BlIII, 226L
    S. medius-minor, Bl1-?Ir1, 214R, 226L
    S. minor, Bl2, BlV, ?Ir1, 226L
Simidectes, Ui1-Du, 90L
Simimeryx, Du-Ch, 90L, 90R, 100R, 129L
Simocyon, Hh2, 183, 191L, 194R
Simocyoninae, procyonid (carnivore), 186R
Simpsonictis, To3-Ti2?, 39, 48R, 52R, 56L, 57R, 58L
Sinopa, Wa1, 84R
sloth (edentate), 158L, 169R, 170L, 170R, 174R, 175L, 180L, 191L, 192L
Smilodectes, Br1–3, 18R, 86L, 87R, 88L, 88R
    S. gracilis, Br2–3, 88L
    S. mcgrewi, Br1, 87R
Smilodon, Irl-RlbII, 21R, 214R, 220L, 220R, 223L, 226R, 279L
    S. fatalis, Ir3, RlbI, 21R, 223L, 223R, 226R
    S. gracilis, Ir2, IrII, 223L, 226R
    S. californicus, Rlb, RlbII, 226R
smilodontine, 192L
Soergelia, Ir1, 220L, 221L, 221R
Sorex, BlII-Rct., 226R
    S. cinereus, Ir2, IrII-Rct., 226R
Soricinae, soricine (soricids) (soricoid) (insectivore), 89R, 108L, 186R, 194L
Spanoxyodon (= *Chriacus*), 42R
Sparactolambda (= *Titanoides*), 55L
Spermophilus, Hh1-Rct., 157L, 216R
    S. (Otospermophilus) argonatus, Hh1, 157L
Sphenophalos, ?Hh1, Hh2-?3, 156L, 159R, 162L, 170R, 216L, 279R
    S. middleswarti, Hh2, 170R
squirrel, 158L, 187L
Stegomastodon, Bl1-Ir1, BlI-?IrI, 214R, 218L, 218R, 219L, 220R, 221L, 221R, 222R, 228L, 279L, 279R
Stelocyon, To3, 37, 49L, 53L
Stenomylinae, stenomyline (camel), 157R, 167L, 184R, 193R
Stenomylus, Ar2-He1, 164L, 166L, 166R, 184R, 186R, 193R, 194L
    S. hitchcocki, ?Ar3, 164L
Stilpnodon, To3, 34, 49L
Sthenictis, He2-Hh2, 168L, 183, 187L, 194L, 194R
Sthenodectes, Ui1–2, 104R
Stenopsochoerus (Pseudostenopsochoerus), Ch3-Or, 138L
    S. (P.) douglasensis, Ch3-Or, 138L
    S. (P.) chadronensis, Ch3-Or, 138L
Stibarus, Ch1-Wh, 145R
Strobodon, Ba3, 169L, 189L, 194R
Stygimys, L-To3, 33, 43L, 43R, 44L, 46R, 48L, 51L, 51R, 52R
    S. gratus, Pu1, 44L
    S. kuszmauli, L-?Pu1, 43R
Stylinodon, Wa4-Ui1, 84R, 106R
Stylinodontidae, 39
Subantilocapra, Hh3, 181L
Subhyracodon, Ch1-Ar1, 133L, 142L, 142R, 144R, 145L, 145R, 184R, 193R
    S. occidentalis, Or, 142L
    S. tridactylus, Wh, 144R
Sunkahetanka, Wh-Ar1, 145R
    S. sheffleri, Wh, 145R
Sylvilagus, Bl2, BlIV-Rct., 226L, 279L
Symbos, Rlb-Rct., 225L
    S. cavifrons, Rlb, 225L
Synaptomys, Bl2, BlV-Rct., 21L, 218L, 219L, 236R, 239R, 247L, 247R, 249L, 249R, 251L, 258L, 258R, 259L, 259R, 260L,

260R, 261L, 262R, 263L, 263R, 279L
S. ("*Metaxyomys*"), IrI, 22L, 250L, 260L, 260R
S. ("*M.*") *anzaensis*, IrI, 22L, 250L, 260L, 260R
S. (Mictomys), Bl2, BlV-Rct., 22L, 218L, 220L, 239R, 247R, 249L, 250L, 250R, 258R, 259L, 259R, 260L, 260R, 261L, 261R, 262R, 263L, 263R
    S. (M.) borealis, RlbII-Rct., 22R, 249L, 251L
    S. (M.) kansasensis, IrII, 22L, 249L, 250L, 260L, 261L, 261R, 262R
    S. (M.) landesi, BlV, 22L, 247R, 249L, 258R, 259R, 260L
    S. (M.) meltoni, IrII, 22L, 250L, 251L, 261L, 263L
    S. (M.) meltoni-borealis, RlbI, 263R
    S. (M.) vetus, BlV, 247R, 258R, 259L, 260L, 260R
    S. (Plioctomys), Bl2, BlV, 218L, 219L
    S. (Synaptomys), Bl1, BlV-Rct., 22L, 239R, 247R, 258R, 259R, 261L, 263L, 263R
    S. (S.) australis, Ir3, RlbI, 22R, 250R, 263R
    S. (S.) cooperi, Ir2, IrII-Rct., 22L, 250L, 261L, 263L
    S. (S.) rinkeri, BlV, 247R, 250L, 258R, 259R
Sylvilagus, BlV-Rct., 214L, 214R, 220L
Syndyoceras, Ar3–4, 166R, 185L, 194L
Synthetoceras, Cl1-Hh1, 174L, 177R, 190L, 194R
    S. tricornatus, ?Hh1, 179R
Synthetoceratinae, synthetoceratine protoceratid (artiodactyl), 166R, 185L, 194L
Systemodon (= *Homogalax*), 82L
Taeniodonta, taeniodonts, 39, 42L, 89R, 104R
Taeniolabis, Pu2-Pu3, 25L, 28, 33, 42R, 43L, 44L, 44R, 45L, 45R, 46L, 46R, 48R
    T. taoensis, Pu3, 25L, 43L, 44L, 44R, 45L, 45R, 46L, 46R
Taeniolabididae, taeniolabidid(s), 33, 68R
Tamias ateles, 13R
Taligrada, 42L
Talpavus, Wa2-Ui2, 89R
Talpinae, talpine moles (insectivore), 166L, 183, 184R, 193R
Talpohenach, To2, 35, 49L, 51L
Tanymykter, Ar4-He1, 157R, 185L, 185R, 194L
    T. brachyodontus, Ar4 or He1, 157R
tapir, 156R
tapiroid, 68L, 108L
Tapirus, ?Hh2-Rct., 170R
    ?*T. simpsoni*, Hh2, 170R
Tapocyon, Ui1-Du, 97L
Tardontia, Ba2, 160L
    T. nevadanus, Ba2, 160L
Taxidea, Hh3-Rct., 195L, 216R, 225L, 279L
    T. taxus, Rlb-Rct., 225L
Taxymys, Br2, 88L
Teilhardella (= *Apatemys*)
Teleoceras, He2-Hh3, 159R, 170R, 173L, 173R, 175L, 176R, 177L, 177R, 187L, 192R, 194L, 214R, 216R, 242R, 279R
    T. fossiger, ?Hh3, 159R
    T. hicksi, Hh1, 173R
    T. major, Cl1, 177R
teleoceratine rhino (artiodactyl), 169L
Teleodus (= *Duchesneodus*), Du, 90L, 100R, 101R, 105R, 107R
    "*T.*" *uintensis* [*Duchesneodus*], Du, 90L, 101R
Telmatherium, Br3-Du, 88L, 88R, 89L, 107R
Temnocyon, Ar1-4, 157R, 166R, 185L, 194L
Tenudomys, Ar1, 165R
Tetheopsis, Br3, 102R
Tetonius, Wa1-Wa3, 85L, 85R, 107L
    T. homunculus, Wa1–3, 85L
Tetraclaenodon, To2-To3, 38, 48L, 49L, 50L, 50R, 51L, 51R, 52L, 52R, 55L
Tetrameryx, Ir1, 220L
Texoceras, Hh1–3, 170L, 170R, 175L
Texomys, Ba1, 177L
Thangorodrim, Pu3, 36, 43L, 46R

Thinobadistes, Hh1–2, 175L, 180L, 181L, 191L, 194R
Thinocyon, Br2–3, 88L
Thomomys, Bl2, BlI-Rct., 218R, 254R, 257R, 279L
Thryptacodon, Ti1-Br1, 37, 55L, 56L, 57R, 58L, 59L, 59R, 60L, 60R, 62R, 63L, 64R, 65L, 65R, 84L, 87R, 88L
Thylacaelurus, Ui2-Du, 89R
Thylacodon, 43L
Ticholeptus, He2-Ba1, 161R, 162L, 164R, 173L, 187L, 188L, 194L, 194R
    T. obliquidens, Ba1, 161R, 162L
    T. zygomaticus, Ba1, 164R
Tillodon, Br2, 88R
Tillodontia, tillodonts, 38, 61R, 82R, 107R, 286R
Tillomys, Br1-Ui1?, 87L, 88L, 97L
Tillotherium (= *Trogosus*), Br2, 88L
Tinimomys, Cf2-Wa1, 35, 63L, 65L, 65R
Tinuviel, Pu3, 37, 43L, 46R
Titanoideidae, 38
Titanoides, Ti1-Cf1?, 29, 31, 38, 54L, 55L, 55R, 56L, 57R, 58L, 59L, 59R, 60L, 60R, 63L
    T. primaevus, 31
Titanotheriomys, Ch, 132L
titanothere(s), 88R, 100L, 101R, 105R, 107R, 108L, 121R, 133L, 135L, 135R, 137R, 138L, 138R, 139L, 139R
Titanotherium, 122R, 123L, 124L, 124R, 135R
Tomarctus, He1-Cl2, 156R, 158R, 160L, 161R, 162L, 164R, 168L, 169L, 172L, 178R, 186R, 190L, 194L, 194R
    T. hippophagus, ?He2-Ba1, 158R, 161R
    "T." kelloggi, Ba1-Ba2, 160L, 162L
    T. optatus, ?He2, 156R
    "T." robustus, Cl1, 159R
    T. rurestris, Ba1, 161R, 162L, 164R
Toromeryx, Ui2, 104R
Torrejonia, To2-To3, 35, 49L, 51L, 52R, 54R
Toxotherium, Ch1-Ch2, 136L
Tremarctos, ?Bl1, ?BlIII, Bl2, 218L
Tricentes, 42R
Trigonias, Ch, 132L, 133L
Trigonictis, Bl1-Ir1, BlI-?BlV, 183, 192R, 214R, 217L, 217R, 218R, 219L, 242R, 279L
Triisodon, To1-To2, 36, 49L, 50R, 51L, 51R
Trimylus, Or, 143L
    T. compressus, Or, 143L
Triplopus, Ui1-Du, 89L, 89R, 100R, 102R
Tritemnodon, Wa1-Br2, 84R, 88R
Trogolemur, Br2-Ui2, 89R
Trogomys, Ar4-He1, 186R, 194L
Trogosus, Br1–2, 18R, 86L, 87L, 87R, 88L, 88R, 97L, 105L, 107R
tylopod(s) camel (artiodactyl), 176L, 177R, 178R
Tytthaena, Ti3, 39, 56L, 58R
Uintacyon, Cf2-Ui2, 39, 63L, 64L, 65L, 65R, 84R, 85L, 104R
    U. rudis, 64L
Uintanius, Wa2-Ui1, 18R
Uintasorex, Wa4-Ui2, 88R, 97L

uintasoricines, 89R
uintatheres, 67L, 88R, 89R
Uintatheriidae, 38
Uintatherium, Br3-Ui1, 18R, 88L, 88R, 102R
ungulate(s), 68R, 166R, 182
Unuchinia, Ti2-Ti5, 34, 56L, 58L, 59L, 59R
Ursavus, He1-Ba3, 172L, 183, 186R, 189L, 194L, 194R
    U. pawniensis, Ba3, 173L
Ursidae, ursid (carnivore), 178R, 185L, 188L
Ursinae, ursine (carnivore), 186R
Ursus, Bl1, BlI-Rct., 183, 219L, 224R, 225L, 242R, 279L
    U. americanus, Rlb-Rct., 224R
    U. arctos, Rlb-Rct., 225L
Ustatochoerus, Ba2-Hh1, 157L, 159L, 159R, 162L, 169L, 170R, 171L, 173L, 173R, 189L, 190L, 194R
    U. californicus, Cl1-?2, 157L, 159R
    U. major, Cl2-?Hh1, 171L
    U. medius, ?Ba2, Ba3, 173L, 173R
    U. medius mohavensis (= *Mediochoerus*), Ba2, 159L
    U. profectus, ?Cl1, 159R
Utemylus, Ti4, 37, 56L, 59R
Vassacyon, Wa1-Br1, 85R
Villanyia, Triversa-Villanyian, Europe, 239R, 247L
Viverravidae, 39
Viverravus, Ti5-Ui2, 18R, 39, 56L, 59R, 60R, 63L, 64R, 65L, 65R, 84R, 85R, 97L
Vulpavus, Wa2-Br1, 39, 84R, 85L, 88L, 88R, 101R
    V. australis, Wa2–3, 101R
    V. canavus, Wa3–Br1, 20L
Vulpes, Hh1-Rct., 159R, 170L, 190R, 194R
Wasatchia, Wa1–4, 85R
Washakius, Br1-Ui1, 18R, 86L, 87L, 87R, 89R, 97L, 106R
wood rat (rodent), 238L
Worlandia, Cf2-Wa2, 35, 63L, 65L, 65R
Wortmania, Pu2-Pu3, 39, 42R, 43L, 46R
Xanoclomys, To3, 33, 49L, 53L
Xenacodon, Ti4, 35, 56L, 59R
Xenicohippus, Wa2–3, 85R
Xyronomys, Pu2-To3, 33, 43L, 46R, 48R, 52R
Yoderimys, Ch1–2, 132L, 133R, 134R, 135L
    Y. bumpi, Ch1, 133R, 135L
    Y. lustrorum, Ch1, 133R, 135L
Yumaceras, Cl2, Hh1–2, 170L, 170R, 171L, 173R, 174R, 175L, 179R, 190R, 194R
    Y. figginsi, Hh1, 173R
Ysengrinia, Ar4-He1, 167L, 183, 185L, 186R, 194L
Zanycteris, Ti3-Ti4, 33, 36, 43L, 46R, 48L, 52R, 56L, 58R, 59R
zapodid (rodent), 165R, 166L, 184R
Zapus, Bl2-Rct., 226R
    Z. hudsonius, Rlb-Rct., 226R
    Z. sandersi, Ir1, 226L
Zetamys, Ar1, 165R
Zodiolestes, Ar3, 166R, 183, 185L, 194L

SUBJECT INDEX

The following is a listing of important topics, geographical, formational, personal, and temporal names or units, exclusive of taxonomic entries. Names utilized only in bibliographic citations are not included here. Personal names and formal categories are capitalized. Page numbers in **boldface** show the location of original definitions, characterizations, or important concepts. L = left-hand column; R = right-hand column. If no letter is given, the page is not divided into columns.

Names of individual **local faunas** or **localities** are listed under those terms. If known, the correlation of a particular local fauna or locality to a subdivision of a mammal age is indicated by a number suffix that follows an abbreviation for the mammal age, based on the number of subdivisions for each mammal age utilized in the text. Thus, Pu1 is the first (chronologically oldest) subdivision of the Puercan mammal age (also known as the *Peradectes/Ectoconus* Interval-Zone; chap 3). Wa1 is the first subdivision of the Wasatchian mammal age (also known as the Sandcouleean subage; chap. 4). Ar1 is the oldest of four divisions of the Arikareean mammal age (and has no other name, except the somewhat cumbersome, early early Arikareean; chap. 6). Other mammal ages have comparable examples. Some remain undivided (e.g., Duchesnean, Orellan, Whitneyan), and that lack of subdivision has been followed here. Arabic numerals are used for subdivisions of the Blancan, Irvingtonian, and Rancholabrean mammal ages, after chap. 7. Roman numerals indicate subdivisions of those mammal ages after chap. 8. Irvingtonian 1, 2, 3 correspond respectively to Sappan, Cudahyan, and Sheridanian subages, as in chap. 7. Ir3 in chap. 7 is approximately the same interval as RlbI of chap 8.

18th International Geological Congress (1948), 213L
Absaroka Mountains, Wyoming, 78R, 97L, 106L, 108R
abundance-zones, 14L, 25R
"absolute dates," 3L, 3R
accurate, accuracy, 3L, 5L, 15R
acme datum, 214L
acme-zone, 25R, 63R, 65L, 65R

Adams County, Washington, 256L
Adelia, Nebraska, 124L
Adobe Town Member, Washakie Formation, Washakie Basin, Wyoming, 102R, 103L
Age of Mammals, 280L
Africa, ixL, 68L
Afton, Iowa, 213L
Aftonian (type section, glacial stage, High Plains), etc., 213L, 231R, 219R, 262L
Agate Fossil Beds National Monument, Nebraska, 166R
Age or age, viiL, viiiR, **xiiiL**, 10L, 10R, 15R, 26L
Agua Fria area, Brewster County, Texas, 104L
Ahearnian (subage, Chadronian), 130L
Ahearn Member, Chadron Formation, South Dakota, 129R, 133R, 134L, 134R, 135L, 135R, 136R, 137R, 148R
Alabama, 66R
Alachua Clays, Florida, 179L
Alachua County, Florida, 178L, 179R
Alachua Formation, Florida, 179R, 180L
Alameda County, California, 220L, 261L, 262L
Alamo Creek Basalt, Texas, 92, 104R
Alamosa, Colorado, 249R, 261R
Alamosa County, Colorado, 261R
Alamo Wash, New Mexico, 40L, 44R, 45L, 45R, 271R
Alaska, 215L, 219R, 222L, 224R, 225L, 227R, 228L, 238R, 240L, 251L
  unglaciated regions in, 224R, 227R
Alberta, Canada, 32, 40R, 52R, 53R, 54R, 57L, 58R, 59L, 211L, 222L, 224L, 290L
Aldrich Station Formation, Nevada, 160R
Alegria Formation, California, 100R
Allegany County, Maryland, 262R
allochthonous, **xiiiL**, 11L, 15R, 16L, 182R
Almagre beds, San Juan Basin, New Mexico, 82R, 105L
Almy Formation, Wyoming, 81L, 103R, 104L
alpine (European) Pleistocene subdivisions, 250L
alpine glaciation (pre-Pleistocene), 219R
alternating field (AF) demagnetization, 273R, 277L
alternating triangles (microtine rodent teeth), 238R, 245L
Alturas, California, 217L, 217R, 242R, 244L, 244R
Alturas Formation, California, 217L
Alum Bluff Group, Florida, Georgia, 179L, 180R
ambient magnetic field, 271L
America(n), 118R, 147L, 180L, 192R
American Museum of Natural History, 51R, 82R, 83L, 83R, 88L,

144R, 155L, 164L, 195L, 237R
ancestor-descendant relationships (microtine rodents), 236R, 250R
Animas Formation, Colorado, 53L
Antarctic (glaciation), 213L
Arkansas, 263L
Antelope County, Nebraska, 192L, 214L
Antelope Creek, Nebraska, 167R, 253R
    South Dakota, 90R
anteroconid complex (rodent teeth), 238L
Anza-Borrego Desert, California, 211L, 214L, 215L, 220R, 221L, 271R
Anza-Borrego sequence, California, 217R, 219L, 220R, 221L, 222L, 228L, 273R, 274R, 275L, 275R, 289R
Anza-Borrego State Park, California, 215R
Aphelops Draw, Nebraska, 171L
Appalachian mountains, 250R
Aquilapollenites extinction, 41R
Aquitanian Stage-Age, Europe, 147R
Archer, Florida, 179R
Archibald, J. D., xi, 24L
arctic grasslands, 236L
arctic steppe (expansion; microtine dispersals), 240L
arctic taxa, 222L, 224L, 236L, 248L
Ardath Shale, California, 98R
Argentina, 68L
Arikareean mammal age, faunas, rocks, 6L, 19L, 20R, 99R, 120R, 121L, 121R, 132R, 140L, 142L, 142R, 144R, 145L, 145R, 146L, 147R, 148L, 156L, 156R, 157R, 158R, 160R, 163L, 163R, 164L, 165L, 167R, 168R, 171R, 176L, 178L, 178R, 184L, 184R, 185L, 185R, 186L, 189L, 192R, 193L, 193R, 288L, 288R, 289L, 290L
    definition and characterization, **184L-185R**
    subdivisions, 184L-185R
Arikaree Group, 122R, 145R, 161L, 171R, 184L, 289L
Arizona, 156L, 192L, 211L, 214L, 215L, 216L, 216R, 217R, 218L, 218R, 220R, 243R, 244L, 244R, 246R, 247L, 247R, 248R, 250R, 254L, 257R, 258L, 258R, 259L, 260L, 262L, 264L, 271L, 271R, 277R, 278R, 279L, 289R
Arkansas, 223L
Armstrong County, Texas, 174L
Arroyo Eduardo, New Mexico, 40L
Arroyo Seco-Vallecito faunal transition, California, 215R
Arroyo Torrejon, New Mexico, 49L, 51L, 51R, 52L, 55R
arvicoline rodent zones, 219L
Ash B, White River Formation, Wyoming, 134R, 136L
Ash G, White River Formation, Wyoming, 138L
Ash J, White River Formation, Wyoming, 138L
Ash Hollow Canyon, Nebraska, 169R
Ash Hollow Formation, Nebraska, 159R, 162L, 169R, 170R, 171L, 173L, 174L, 177R, 179L, 182L, 188R, 189R, 191L, 198, 253R
Ash Springs Basalt Member, Chisos Formation, Texas, 92
Ashville, Florida, 179L, 180R
Asia, Asiatic, 19L, 50L, 61R, 67L, 67R, 90L, 129L, 133L, 227R, 237R, 239L, 240L, 240R, 242L, 248L, 249R, 250R, 262R, 280L, 286R, 288L
Assemblage-zones, **xiiiL**, 14L, 14R, 20R, 175R
Atlantic coast (coastal plain), 68L, 181R
atmospheric storm pattern (changes), 239R
Atwell Gulch Member, Wasatch Formation, Colorado, 61L, 101L
Australasia, ixL
autochthonous, **xiiiL**, 182R, 184R, 185R, 188L, 190L, 190R, 191R, 193L
Auversian Stage-Age, London and Paris basins, 101L
Aycross Formation, Wyoming, 78L, 85L, 87R, 91, 92, 93, 96R, 97L, 106L, 108R
Aztec, New Mexico, 52L
Baca Formation, New Mexico, 78R, 89L, 90R, 105R
Bad Lands of White River, 122L
Badwater area, Wyoming, 78R, 92, 93, 97R

Badwater Creek area, Wind River Basin, Wyoming, 89L, 98L, 128R
Baja California, 65R, 66R, 106R
Bakersfield, California, 156L
Bald Peak volcanics, California, 155R, 195
Bannock County, Idaho, 263R
Barrel Spring Arroyo (= De-na-zin wash), New Mexico, 40L
Barren Clays, Brule Formation, South Dakota, 123L, 123R, 124L
Barstow, California, 158R
Barstow Formation, California, 13R, 20R, 158L, 158R, 159L, 169L, 187L, 196, 289L, 289R, 290L
Barstovian mammal age, faunas, rocks, 13R, 19L, 20R, 156R, 158L, 158R, 159L, 160L, 163L, 164R, 165L, 176L, 176R, 177L, 179R, 180L, 180R, 186L, 187L, 187R, 188L, 189L, 189R, 190L, 193L, 193R, 194L, 194R, 289L, 289R, 290L
    definition and characterization, **187L-189L**
    subdivisions, 187L-189L
Barstow Syncline, California, 187L
Bartonian Stage-Age, London and Paris basins, 101L
Bashir, U.S.S.R., 238R
Basin and Range, Nevada, 160L
Bates Hole, Wyoming, 125L, 127L
Batesland Formation, South Dakota, 172L
Baylor County, Texas, 221R, 222R, 263L
Beaver County, Utah, 264L
Beaver Divide area, Wind River Basin, Wyoming, 78R, 89L, 98L, 125L, 127L, 133R, 149L
Beaver, Utah, 246R
Bed A (of Hayden = Titanotherium Bed), Chadron Formation, Nebraska, 122L, 122R
Bed B (of Hayden = Turtle and Oreodon Bed), Brule Formation, Nebraska and South Dakota, 122L
Bed C (of Hayden), ?Brule Formation, Nebraska and South Dakota, 122L
Bed D (of Hayden), ?Brule Formation (Arikaree Group), Nebraska, 122L, 122R
Bed E (of Hayden), ?Brule Formation, Nebraska and South Dakota, 122L, 122R
Bed F (of Hayden), "Pliocene Tertiary," Loup Fork, Nebraska, 122R
Bed H (of Hayden = Ogallala Group, in part), Nebraska, 122L
Bedrock Springs Formation, California, 159R
Bee County, Texas, 176L, 177L
Belgium, 67L
bell-shaped curve, 11R, 12R
Bennett County, South Dakota, 167R, 172L
benthonic foraminiferal stages (zones), 154L, 176R
Berkeley Hills, California, 155R
Bering land bridge, 221L
Beringia, 222L, **225L**, 228L, 240L, 247L, 247R, 248L, 249R, 250L
Bering Strait, 248L
Betonnie-Tsosie Arroyo, New Mexico, 40L, 44R, 46L, 48L, 48R, 50R
Bidahochi Formation, Arizona, 156L
Big Basin Member, John Day Formation, Oregon, 161L
Big Bend area, Texas, 54L, 57L, 58L, 59R, 61L, 65R
Big Bend National Park, Texas, 78L, 104L
Big Blue Formation, California, 156R
Bighorn (Big Horn) Basin, Wyoming, 19R, 58L, 59L, 59R, 61L, 62L, 63L, 64R, 65R, 66R, 69L, 78L, 80L, 81L, 82L, 82R, 83R, 86L, 86R, 87R, 101L, 105R, 106L, 106R, 108L, 108R, 271R
Bighorn Mountains, Wyoming, 98L
Bighorn River, Wyoming, 106L
Bighorn "Wasatch," Wyoming, 81R, 82L
Big Bad Lands, Big Badlands, South Dakota, 124L, 124R, 131R, 171R
Big Bend, Texas, 271R
Big Island Tuff, Wyoming, 94
Big Sand Draw Sandstone Lentil, White River Formation, Wyoming, 133R, 134L
Big Sandy area, Wyoming, 78L
Big Springs Ranch, Kansas, 224L

Biharian (mammal age; Europe), 222R, 248L, 249L, 249R, 250L
biochron, biochrons, xiiiL, 1R, 15L, 155L, 189L, 193R, 238L, 285L
biochronologic unit, etc., xiiiL, 25L, 26L, 26R, 42R, 47L, 56R, 61L, 119R, 120L, 153R, 155L, 157R, 164L, 181R, 182R, 184R, 185L, 188R, 190R, 192R, 193L, 249R, 269R, 278R, 289L, 289R
biochronology, viiR, xiiiL, 6R, 9L, 22R, 26L, 42L, 87L, 105L, 120R, 121R, 125L, 128R, 132L, 133L, 140R, 153L, 153R, 154L, 155L, 162R, 163R, 165L, 174L, 179L, 181R, 182L, 182R, 184L, 187R, 190L, 193L, 193R, 236L, 237L, 239L, 252R, 269L, 270R, 279R, 280R, 288L
biogeographic provinces; see faunal provinces
Biohorizon A, Willwood Formation (Wasatchian), Wyoming, 19R, 86L
Biohorizon B, Willwood Formation (Wasatchian), Wyoming, 19R
Biohorizon C, Willwood Formation (Wasatchian), Wyoming, 19R, 20L
biome, 180R
biostratigraphic unit, and biostratigraphic, xiiiR, 9R, 10L, 10R, 11L, 12L, 15L, 15R, 20L, 49R, 56R, 79R, 80L, 86R, 90L, 106R, 108L, 109L, 119L, 119R, 121R, 128R, 133L, 137L, 139R, 140L, 140R, 142L, 143L, 144L, 144R, 145R, 147R, 154R, 156L, 157R, 159L, 160R, 161R, 163R, 165L, 165R, 166R, 173L, 174L, 175L, 176R, 179L, 181R, 182R, 184R, 188L, 214R, 215R, 216L, 217L, 219L, 226R, 227R, 271L, 278R, 279R, 280L, 287R, 288R
biostratigraphy, xiiiR, 2R, 6R, 9L, 9R, 10L, 11L, 16R, 20L, 22R, 23L, 26L, 40L, 42L, 68R, 90R, 120R, 156L, 161L, 162R, 163L, 175R, 178L, 179L, 184L, 185R, 193L, 214L, 228L, 288L, 289L, 290L
biozone, xiiiR, 10L, 10R, 15L, 15R
Birch Hills Dacite, Wyoming, 92
Bishop Ash, western United States, 261R, 264L
Bison Basin, Wyoming, 58R, 59R
Bitter Creek, Wyoming, 65L, 78L, 102L
Bjork, P. R., xi, 118R
Black, C. C., xi, 77L
Black Hills, South Dakota, 124L, 125L
Black Peaks, Texas, 52R
Black Peaks Formation, Texas, 54L, 55R, 61L, 104L, 108R
Black Peaks paleomagnetic sequence, 55R
Blacksforkian subage (Br2, Bridger A, B) of the Bridgerian mammal age, 88R, 287L, 287R
Black's Fork Member, Bridger Formation (Bridger A, B), Wyoming, 83L, 87L
Blancan "interglacial" interval, 219R
Blancan/Irvingtonian boundary, transition, 214R, 217R, 220R, 221L, 222R, 248L
    approximates the Pliocene/Pleistocene boundary, 221L
    approximates the Villanyian/Biharian boundary, 222R
Blancan mammal age, faunas, rocks, 18L, 20R, 21L, 21R, 22L, 22R, 157L, 181L, 181R, 192R, 211L, 213R, 214L, 214R, 215L, 215R, 217L, 217R, 218L, 218R, 219L, 219R, 220L, 220R, 221L, 222L, 223R, 226L, 226R, 240R, 241L, 242R, 243L, 243R, 244L, 244R, 245L, 245R, 246L, 246R, 247L, 247R, 248L, 248R, 250L, 252L, 254R, 255L, 256L, 256R, 257R, 259L, 260R, 264L, 279R, 289R, 290L
    definition and characterization, 215L-220L
    subdivisions, 218R-220L
Blanco Formation, Texas, 219L
Blue Point Conglomerate Member, Wiggins Formation, Wyoming, 92, 95
Bone Valley Formation, Florida, 179L, 180L, 180R, 181L
Book Cliffs area, Wyoming, 78L, 101L
boundary stratotype, 214L
Box Butte County, Nebraska, 167L, 167R, 187L
Box Butte Formation, Nebraska, 168L, 168R, 178R, 186R
Box Butte Member, Sheep Creek Formation, Nebraska, 167R
Box Butte Table, Nebraska, 167L, 167R
Box Elder County, Utah, 263R

Bown, T. M., xi, 77R
Bracks Rhyolite, Texas, 104R, 134R, 136L, 148R
Branch Canyon Formation, California, 158L
Brazil, 68L
Brea Canyon, California, 99R
Brennan Basin Member, Duchesne River Formation (Ui1/Du), Utah, 84L, 89R, 90L, 101R
Brewster County, Texas, 104L
Brice Canyon Locality (Tiffanian, Ti5), Wyoming, 30
Bridge Creek Flora, Oregon, 148R, 197
Bridger A-E, 83L, 83R, 88L, 88R, 94, 102R, 103R, 287R
Bridger Group, 83L
Bridger Formation, Green River Basin, Wyoming, 78L, 78R, 79R, 82R, 83L, 83R, 84L, 87L, 88L, 88R, 95, 103L, 287R
Bridgerian mammal age, faunas, rocks, 77R, 78R, 80R, 82R, 83L, 85L, 85R, 86R, 87L, 87R, 88L, 88R, 89L, 90R, 91, 92, 93, 94, 95, 96L, 96R, 97L, 97R, 98L, 99L, 101L, 101R, 102L, 102R, 103L, 103R, 104L, 104R, 105L, 105R, 106L, 106R, 107R, 108L 108R, 286R, 287L, 278R, 290L
    definition and characterization, 88L-88R
    subdivisions, 88L-88R
Bridgerian/Uintan boundary, 88R, 89L, 106R, 107L, 108R, 287L
Bridger series, 83L
Brite Ignimbrite, Texas, 136L, 148R
British Columbia, 78L, 90R, 107R
Brooksville, Florida, 178L
Brougher Dacite, Nevada, 196
Brown County, Nebraska, 169R, 256R
browsing to grazing transition (rodents; Pleistocene), 226L
Brule Clay, South Dakota, 124L
Brule A, 138L, 139L
Brule B, 138L
Brule Formation, South Dakota, Nebraska, Wyoming, 119L, 120R, 121L, 124L, 124R, 125R, 127L, 128L, 132L, 137R, 138L, 138R, 139L, 139R, 140L, 141L, 143L, 143R, 144L, 145R, 165R, 171R
Brule Indians, Indian Reservation, South Dakota, 124L
Bruneau Formation, Idaho, 221L
Brunhes Chron, Normal Magnetic Polarity Chron, 21R, 216L, 223L, 223R, 227R, 249R, 273R, 277R
Buck Hill Group, Texas, 104L
Buckshot Ignimbrite, Texas, 93, 104R, 148R
Bugcreekian mammal age, faunas, rocks, 41L
Bug Creek faunal-facies, 41L
Bug Creek-like locality, 42L
Bug Creek sequence, Montana, 41L, 42L
Buginstav Basin, Mongolia, 67R
Bulldog Hollow Member, Fowkes Formation, Utah, 95
Bunophorus Interval-Zone (Wasatchian, Wa2), Wyoming, 19R, 20L, 287L
Bureau of Economic Geology, Texas, 175R
Burge Member, Valentine Formation, Nebraska, 169L, 189R
Butler, R. F., xi, 269
Butler Springs area, Kansas, 224L
Cabbage Patch beds, Montana, 163L, 163R, 164R
Cady Mountains, California, 158R, 196
Calabria, Italy, 214L
Calabrian Stage, Italy, 213L, 213R, 214L
calcareous nannoplankton, 214L
calibration, 3R, 154L, 154R, 155L, 179L, 183, 269L, 270L, 271L, 278L, 278R, 280L, 285R
    Aquitanian Stage-Age, base (22–23 Ma), 147R
    Arikareean (28, 29–20 Ma), 183
    Arikareean, base (28–29 Ma), 147R, 148L, 183
    Arikareean/Hemingfordian boundary (ca. 20 Ma), 183
    Barstovian (16.5–11.5 Ma), 183
    Barstovian/Clarendonian boundary (11.5 Ma), 183
    Blancan (ca. 4.5–1.9 Ma), 183, 217R
    Blancan/Hemphillian boundary (4.5 Ma), 183

Blancan/Irvingtonian boundary (ca. 1.6–1.9 Ma; 1.88–1.72 Ma), 217R, 220R, 221L
Bridgerian (51–48 Ma), 96L, 97L, 103R
Chadronian (38–31 Ma), 134R, 136L, 140L, 147R
Clarendonian (ca. 11.5–9 Ma), 183
Clarendonian/Hemphillian boundary (ca. 8.5–9 Ma), 183, 241R
Duchesnean (42–38 Ma), 96L, 98L, 101R, 102L
Duchesnean/Orellan boundary (ca. 38 Ma), 148L
earth's magnetic field, last 4 Ma, 270L
Eocene/Oligocene boundary (37 Ma), 147R
Gauss/Gilbert boundary (3.35 Ma), 270L
Hemingfordian (ca. 20–16.5 Ma), 183
Hemingfordian/Barstovian boundary (16.5 Ma), 183
Hemphillian (ca. 9–4.5 Ma), 183
Hemphillian/Blancan boundary (4.5 Ma), 181R, 183, 216L
Oligocene/Miocene boundary (22–23 Ma), 147R
Orellan-Whitneyan interval (31–28 Ma), 140L
Uintan (48–42 Ma), 96L, 97L, 103L
Villanyian/Biharian boundary (ca. 1.8 Ma), 222R
Wasatchian (57.5–51 Ma), 96L, 103R
Caliente Formation, California, 157R, 158L, 196, 289L, 290L
Caliente Range, California, 157R, 158L
California, 2L, 5R, 13R, 18L, 19L, 20L, 32, 66R, 78R, 84L, 89L, 90R, 96L, 98L, 98R, 99L, 99R, 100L, 106R, 108R, 120L, 128L, 146L, 146R, 154L, 155R, 156L, 157L, 157R, 158L, 162L, 168R, 170L, 184R, 187L, 187R, 188L, 190L, 192L, 192R, 195L, 195R, 211L, 214L, 214R, 215R, 216L, 216R, 217L, 217R, 219R, 220L, 220R, 222L, 223R, 224R, 240L, 242R, 243R, 244L, 244R, 245R, 246L, 246R, 247L, 248R, 249L, 249R, 252L, 254L, 256R, 257R, 260L, 260R, 261R, 262L, 264L, 271R, 278R, 286R, 289L, 289R, 290L
California Academy of Sciences, San Francisco, 237R
California Coast Ranges, 155R, 156R, 188L
Cambridge, Nebraska, 170L
Camp Pendleton Marine Corps Base, California, 99L
Camp San Onofre, California, 99L
Canada, 83L, 83R, 107R, 108L, 177R, 220L, 240R, 241L
Canadian plains, 249R
Canadian River, Texas, 174R, 175L
Canadian Rockies (mountains), 247R
Canadian Shield, 219R
Canoe Formation, Texas, 104L
Capote Mountain Tuff, Texas, 127R, 136L
Cap Rock Member, Ash Hollow Formation, Nebraska, 169R, 170L, 174L, 189R, 198, 253L
carbon-14 (radioisotopic dating method), 225L, 225R
carbonate (isotopic) composition, 248L
Caribbean averaged composite core (Pleistocene), 250L, 251L
Carlsbad, California, 99L
Carnegie Museum of Natural History, 86L, 89L, 162R, 237R
Carter Canyon Ash, Nebraska, 149L
Carter Mountain, Wyoming, 85L, 92, 93, 95, 106L, 106R
Carthage Coal Field, New Mexico, 105R
Cascade Range, Oregon, 161R
Castle Butte, South Dakota, 171R
Cathedral Bluffs Tongue, Wasatch Formation, Washakie Basin, Wyoming, 78L, 78R, 85L, 87L, 87R, 102L, 105L
   Green River Basin, Wyoming, 87L, 96L, 103R
cave fauna, 225L
Cedar Creek beds, Colorado, 172L
Cedar Creek Member, White River Formation, Colorado, 128L, 140R, 143R, 143R, 172R
Cedar Mountain Member, Bridger Formation (Bridger E), Wyoming, 83L, 88L
Cedar Mountain, Nevada, 160L, 160R
Cedar Pass, Big Badlands, South Dakota, 171L
Cedar Point, Nebraska, 169R
Cedar Ridge, Wyoming, 98L
cement (in re-entrant angles of microtine rodent teeth), 219L, 219R,

225R, 260L
Cenozoic Era, rocks, faunas, viiL, viiiR, ixL, 1L, 1R, 4L, 5R, 6R, 7L, 15L, 20R, 21R, 22R, 23L, 24L, 40R, 68L, 77L, 165L, 191L, 219L, 219R, 228L, 269L, 270L, 270R, 271L, 271R, 272L, 275L, 278L, 279L, 279R, 285R, 289L
Central America(n), 61R, 176L
Central and Eastern Wind River Basin, 97R
Cernaysian mammal age, faunas, rocks, 67L, 67R
Cerrotejonian Stage-Age, California, 2L, 18L, 20R, 155R, 157L, 158L, 159R, 190L
   Nevada, 160R
Cerro Toledo ash, Tule Formation, Texas, 221R
Cerro Toledo B ash, Kansas, 222R
Cerro Toledo Rhyolite, New Mexico, 221R
Chadron A (Lower Chadron), 129R, 133R, 135L
Chadron B (Middle Chadron), 129R, 135R, 137L, 138L
Chadron-Brule contact, 137R
Chadron C (Upper Chadron), 129R, 137L, 137R, 138L, 142R
Chadron, Nebraska, 124L
Chadron Formation, Nebraska and South Dakota, 120R, 121L, 122L, 122R, 124L, 124R, 125L, 125R, 127L, 127R, 129L, 129R, 131R, 132L, 133R, 135L, 135R, 136R, 137L, 137R, 138L, 138R, 139L, 139R, 142L, 142R, 146L, 146R, 288L
Chadronian mammal age, faunas, rocks, 6L, 20L, 20R, 84R, 85L, 89R, 90L, 93, 100L, 104R, 105R, 107R, 109R, 118L, 119L, 119R, 120L, 120R, 121L, 121R, 124R, 125R, 127L, 128L, 128R, 129L, 129R, 131R, 132L, 132R, 133L, 133R, 133L, 133R, 134L, 135L, 135R, 136L, 136R, 137L, 137R, 138L, 138R, 139L, 139R, 140L, 142L, 142R, 143L, 143R, 144R, 145L, 146L, 146R, 147L, 147R, 160R, 287R, 288R, 290L
   definition and characterization, **129R–133L**
   subdivisions, 132R–138R
Chadronian/Orellan boundary, 119L, 133L, 137L, 138R, 143R
Chadron, Nebraska, 129R
Chadronian-Whitneyan interval, 128L
Chadron sands, Nebraska, 124L
Cha-ling Basin, China, 67R
Chambers Tuff, Texas, 95, 104R, 127R, 134R, 135L
Chamita Formation, New Mexico, 271R
Chanac Formation, California, 157L
Chapadmalalan (mammal age, = ca. late Blancan), South America, 218L
Chappo Member, Wasatch Formation, Fossil Basin, Wyoming, 54L, 61L
character displacement (*Sigmodon*), 226L
characterize, characterization, 10R, 14R, 15R, 16R, 18R, 21L, 25L, 25R, 26L, 50L, 68R, 161L, 181R, 182R, 184R, 185R, 186R, 187L, 188R, 189L, 189R, 191R, 193R, 214R, 221L, 223R, 240L, 241L, 251L, 277R, 285R, 287R
Chattahootchee, Florida, 178R
chemical remanent magnetization (CRM), 273L, 273R
Cherry County, Nebraska, 198, 259R
Cheyenne County, Nebraska, 191R
Chihuahua, Mexico, 128L, 143L, 216L, 243R, 244R, 254L
Chi-jiang Basin, China, 67R
China, 18R, 61R, 67R, 68L, 68R
Chinji-Kamlial magnetic polarity sequence, Pakistan, 282
Chinji village, Pakistan, 280L, 282
Chipola Formation, Florida, 178R, 179L, 198
Chisos Formation, Texas, 92, 104R
Choctawhatchee Formation, Florida, 180R
Chron, chrons, **xiiiR**, 4R, 10R, 15R, 21L, 22R, 270L, 277L, 277R
chronocline, 219R, 225R
chronofauna, chronofaunal, 6L, 120R, 121L, 167R, 168L, 168R, 169L, 169R, 170R, 173R, 175L, 176L, 177L, 177R, 180R, 182L, 186R, 187R, 189L, 189R, 190L, 190R, 191L, 192L, 193L, 193R, 287R, 288L, 288R
"chronofaunal creep," 287R, 288L
chronological, chronology, **xiiiR**, 165L, 213L, 215L, 222L, 228L,

237L, 269L, 278R, 279R, 280L, 286R
chronometric, 15L, 22R
chronostratigraphic unit, stage, or zone, **xiiiR**, 9L, 10L, 10R, 11R,
    15R, 16L, 16R, 18L, 18R, 68R, 158R, 161L, 185R, 190R, 213R
chronostratigraphy, **xivL**, 2R, 4R, 9R, 10L, 11L, 14L, 15L, 23L
chronozone, **xivL**, 10L, 10R, 15L, 15R, 18L
Church Buttes Station, Wyoming, 83L
Churcher, C. S., xi, 211
Cimarron River, Oklahoma Panhandle, 173R
Clarendon, Texas, 173R, 174L, 174R, 189R
Clarendon beds, Texas, 155R, 169L, 174L, 177R, 189R
Clarendonian chronofauna, 177R, 179R, 191L, 192L
Clarendonian-Hemphillian boundary, 289L
Clarendonian mammal age, faunas, and rocks, 13R, 18L, 20R,
    157L, 159R, 160L, 160R, 162L, 163L, 164R, 168R, 170L,
    173R, 174L, 174R, 175L, 177L, 177R, 179R, 180L, 180R,
    188L, 189L, 189R, 190L, 190R, 191L, 192L, 193L, 194R, 241L,
    253R, 289L, 290L
    definition and characterization, **189R–190R**
    subdivisions, 190L-190R
Clark County, Mississippi, 107R
Clark Fork fauna, 60R
Clarkforkian mammal age, faunas, and rocks, 18L, 19R, 24L, 24R,
    25L, 26L, 26R, 42L, 53L, 55L, 60L-66R, 67R, 68R, 69L, 85L,
    85R, 90R, 96R, 101L, 102L, 103L, 105R, 106L, 106R, 108L,
    108R, 285R, 286L, 286R, 290L
    definition and characterization, **62L-63L**
    zonation, 63L-63R
Clarkforkian Stage-Age, 19L, 286R
Clarkforkian/Wasatchian boundary, 62R, 107L, 108L
Clark Fork Member (and faunal zone) Polecat Bench Formation,
    Clark's Fork Basin, Wyoming, 60R, 61L
Clark Fork Valley, Montana, 163L, 164L, 164R
Clark's Fork Basin, Wyoming, 20L, 26L, 52L, 53R, 54L, 55R, 56L,
    56R, 59R, 60L, 60R, 61L, 61R, 62L, 62R, 63L, 64L, 64R, 65R,
    66R, 69L, 78L, 106L, 276R, 280L, 283, 286L, 287L
    Montana, 64L
Clark's Fork fauna, Wyoming, 53L, 53R
Clarkston Basin, Montana, 127R, 128L
Clarno Formation, Oregon, 78R, 107R, 127R, 128L, 133R, 146R,
    148R
classification, 238L,
    magnetic polarity samples, 273R, 275L
Clemens, W. A., xi, 24R
climate, warm, 221L, 227R
climatic criteria (not unique in age designation), 213R, 214R
climatic cycle, 220L
climatic deterioration (Pleistocene), 213L, 213R
climatic fluctuations (difficult to recognize or date), 224L
Climbing Arrow Formation, Montana, 127R
Climbing Arrow Member, Renova Formation, Montana, 78R, 106R
clines, geographic, temporal, 224R
Coalinga, California, 156R
Coal Valley Formation, Nevada, 160R, 197
Cochise County, Arizona, 257R, 259L, 260L
Cochiti subchron (of Gilbert Chron), 215R, 217L, 217R, 243L, 243R,
    245L, 255L, 256L, 277R
Cochrane, Alberta, 52R
Coffee Ranch, Texas, 173R, 174R
cold climate (Pleistocene), 211R, 213L, 227R, 240L, 251L, 251R
    correlated with microtine rodent immigration, 240L, 251L, 251R
cold climate cycles (pre-Nebraskan glaciation), 219R
Coldwater Sandstone, California, 99R, 100L, 100R
Cold Spring Post Office, Montana, 164L
Cold Spring, Texas, 175R, 177L
Colmena Tuff, Texas, 104R
Colorado, 20L, 29, 40L, 41L, 41R, 43R, 44L, 45L, 46L, 52R, 53L,
    56R, 59L, 59R, 62L, 64L, 65L, 65R, 78L, 80R, 83L, 83R, 84L,
    85R, 87R, 89L, 95, 101L, 102L, 104R, 105L, 107L, 125L,

127R, 128L, 137L, 138R, 140R, 143L, 143R, 145L, 149L,
    167R, 168L, 171L, 172L, 173L, 173R, 177L, 186L, 187R, 188R,
    189L, 218L, 249R, 250L, 250R, 261R, 286L, 287L, 287R, 289L
Colorado Piedmont, 125L
Colorado River Valley, 101L
Colton Formation, Utah, 78L, 101L
Columbia Basalt Group, Oregon, 161R
Columbia Plateau, North America, 154L, 160R, 164L, 164R, 165L,
    165R, 168R, 185R, 188L, 190L, 191L, 192R
Commission on Mediterranean Neogene, 241L, 242L
composite sequence of seafloor magnetic anomaly patterns, 270L
Concurrent-range zone (includes several named units) **xivL**, 10L, 14R,
    16L, 20R, 161L, 161R, 185R
congregation, 10L
Conservation and Survey Division, State of Nebraska, 195R
Continental Divide, 51R, 163L, 163R, 164L, 185R
Continental fault, Wyoming, 103R
continental glaciation (pre-Pleistocene), 213L, 219R, 248L, 257L
continental ice sheet, 224R, 248L, 251L, 251R, 252L
Contra Costa County, California, 254L
cool ocean temperatures (inception ca. 3 Ma), 248L
Cooper Creek area or basin, Wyoming, 78L, 107L
Cope, E. D., 80R, 81L
Copemys longidens Assemblage-Zone (Barstovian, Ba3), California,
    19L
Copemys russelli Assemblage-Zone (Barstovian, Ba3), California, 19L
Cordilleran Corridor (dispersal, Alaska to midcontinent), 224R, 245R,
    247L, 256L
Cordilleran ice sheet, 224R, 248L, 249R
core 5-A-75, type area Aftonian glacial stage, 213L
Cornell Dam Member, Valentine Formation, Nebraska, 168R, 169L,
    188R
Corral Bluffs section, Denver Formation, Colorado, 45L, 46L
correlate, correlation, viiL, viiR, viiiL, **xivL**, 10L, 11R, 12R, 14L,
    14R, 15L, 16L, 16R, 22R, 24R, 25L, 26L, 26R, 42R, 90R,
    153R, 161R, 182R, 184L, 187L, 187R, 188L, 188R, 190R,
    191R, 193L, 193R, 213R, 215L, 215R, 218R, 219L, 221R,
    224L, 225R, 226R, 227R, 236R, 239R, 240L, 240R, 241L,
    248L, 249L, 250L, 252L, 269L, 219L, 270L, 271L, 277R, 279L,
    279R, 285R, 286R, 288R, 289L, 289R
Cosy Dell Shale, California, 99R, 100L
Cottonwood Creek, Wyoming, 97R
Coryphodon zone, 81L
Coyote Creek flora, 96R
Crawfish Draw, Texas, 215L
Crawford, Nebraska, 138L
Crazyjohnsonian (subage of Chadronian), 130L
Crazy Johnson Member, Chadron Formation, South Dakota, 129R,
    133R, 135R, 136R, 137L, 137R
Crazy Mountain Field (or Basin), Montana, 47L, 49R, 50L, 51R, 52R,
    53R, 54L, 54R, 56R, 57L, 57R, 69L
Cretaceous Period, age, faunas, and rocks, 5R, 24R, 41L, 41R, 42L,
    42R, 104R, 270L, 271L, 277L
Cretaceous/Paleocene boundary, 42L, 41R, 66L
Cretaceous/Tertiary boundary, 41L, 270L
Crooked Creek Formation, Kansas, 222R
Crooked River, Oregon, 161R
Crookston Bridge Member, Valentine Formation, Nebraska, 168R,
    169L, 188R, 189L, 189R
Crosby County, Texas, 215L
cryogenic magetometer, 273L
Csarnotan, European mammal age, 242R, 244R, 245L
Cuba (and Cuba Mesa), New Mexico, 40L, 47L
Cuba Mesa Member, San Jose Formation, New Mexico, 105L
Cuba Mesa Sandstone Member, San Jose Formation, New Mexico,
    53L
Cub Creek, Wyoming, 54L, 55R
Cub Mountain Formation, New Mexico, 78R
Cuchara Formation, Huerfano Basin, Colorado, 78L

Cudahy ash (= Pearlette Type O), Great Plains, 262L
Cudahyan subage (Ir2) of the Irvingtonian mammal age, faunas, rocks, 21R, 223L
Cupidinimus nebraskensis (= *C. lindsayi*), Assemblage-Zone (Barstovian, Ba1), California, 19L
Cuisian Stage or Substage (London and Paris basins), 66L, 66R
Cuyama Badlands, California, 13R, 158L, 271R
Cuyama Valley, California, 157R
Cypress Hills Formation, Saskatchewan, 127R, 133R, 138L
Cypress Hills, Saskatchewan, 68R, 107R, 136L
Czechoslovakia, 221R
Czechoslovakian Geological Survey, Prague, 237R
Dallas, Texas, 195L
Danian Stage, Belgium, 67L
Dano-Montian Stage, Europe, 68L
Danville, California, 156L
Davis Ash, Ash Hollow Formation, Nebraska, 198
Dawes County, Nebraska, 168R, 187L
Dawson, M. R., xi, 77L
Deadman Pass Till, California (2.7–3.0 Ma), 219R
Death Valley, California, 146R
Debeque Formation, Colorado, 78L, 101L
declination (magnetic), 275L, 276R
decrease in size (temporal trend), 222L, 224R, 226L
Deep Creek Tuff, John Day Formation, Oregon, 161L
Deep River beds, Montana, 163L
Deep River Formation, Montana, 163R, 164L
deep sea deposits: show cooling trend, 248L
    glacial-interglacial alternations, 227R, 252R
    sampling pattern (magnetic polarity stratigraphy), 275R
    uniform depositional rates, 236L
Deer Butte Formation, Oregon, 161R
Deer Lodge Valley, Montana, 163L, 163R, 164L, 164R
define, definition, 2R, 10R, 11R, 13L, 14R, 15R, 21L, 25L, 26L, 40R, 55L, 56R, 58L, 61L, 62L, 63R, 64R, 68R, 161L, 182R, 183, 184L, 184R, 185L, 186R, 187L, 188L, 188R, 189L, 189R, 190L, 190R, 191R, 193R, 213L, 213R, 214R, 220R, 240R, 252L, 279R, 285R, 286L, 287L, 287R, 289L, 290L
    base defines boundary, 15L, 15R, 50L, 51L, 51R, 55L, 57L, 57R, 58L, 59L, 59R, 60L, 61R, 64L, 64R, 182R, 213L, 213R, 287L
    based on a single taxon, 10R, 12L, 12R, 13L, 15R, 16R, 19L, 42L, 43L, 44R, 47L, 48L, 50L, 51L, 51R, 55L, 57L, 57R, 58L, 59L, 59R, 60L, 61L, 64L, 64R, 182R
    based on a number of taxa, 10R, 14R, 15R, 16L, 16R, 18R, 55L, 63R
deglaciation (end of Pleistocene; diachronous), 225R
Deltatherium Chronozone or Zone (Torrejonian, To2), New Mexico, 28, 46R, 49L
De-na-zin wash (= Barrel Spring Arroyo), New Mexico, 40L, 44R, 45L, 45R, 47R, 50R
De-na-zin section, New Mexico, 48L
dental root fusion, reduction, loss, increase (Pleistocene rodents), 225R, 226L
dentine tracts (in rodent teeth), 219R, 225R, 226L, 246L, 246R, 247L, 255R, 257L, 257R, 258L, 258R
Denver Basin, Colorado, 45L
Denver, Colorado, 195L, 241L, 244R, 246R
Denver Formation, Denver Basin, Colorado, 40L, 41R, 45L
depositional (detrital) remanent magnetization (DRM), 271L, 273L, 273R
De Soto County, Florida, 180L
Devensian (= Eemsian) interglacial (Europe), 223R
Devil's Graveyard Formation, Texas, 104L
Devil's Gulch Member, Valentine Formation, Nebraska, 169L, 189R
Devonshire, England, 251L
Diablo Range, California, 156R
Diceratherium zone, 161L
diphyly, 237R
Diplacodon-Epihippus zone, 83R

dirk-tooth cat (carnivore), 219L
Disaster Peak Member, Mehrten Formation, California, 170L
dischroneity (in faunal correlation), 215L, 218R
Discoaster sublodoensis Concurrent-range Zone, 98R
disharmonious faunas (taxa are ecologically incongruent; Pleistocene), 224L, 227L
dispersal, 5R, 6L, 15R, 19L, 24R, 66L, 182R, 215L, 225R, 227R, 228L, 239R, 240L, 244L, 246R, 247L, 248L, 248R, 249L, 249R, 250L, 251L, 251R, 269L, 270L, 278R, 280L
Divide, Montana, 164L
Dogtown Member, Torreya Formation, Florida, 178R
"Domengine Stage," California, 98R, 99L
Doniphan County, Kansas, 222R, 261L
Donley County, Texas, 173R, 174L, 189R
Douglas Creek Member, Green River Formation, Utah, 101R
Douglas, Wyoming, 125L, 138L
Downs, Theodore, xi, 211
Dragon Canyon, Utah, 271R
Dragonian mammal age, rocks, faunas, 24L, 47L, 47R, 48L, 48R, 49L, 50L, 50R, 67R, 286L
Drewsey Formation, Oregon, 162L, 197
Drinkwater Basalt, Oregon, 197
Drummond, Montana, 163L
Dry Gulch Creek Member, Duchesne River Formation, Utah, 84L, 90L, 93, 101R, 148R, 287R
DSDP (Deep Sea Drilling Project) Core 34, 254L
Duchesnean mammal age, rocks, faunas, 6L, 77R, 79L, 80R, 88L, 89R, 92, 93, 95, 96L, 98L, 100R, 101L, 102L, 104R, 105R, 106R, 107R, 108L, 109L, 120L, 128R, 129L, 129R, 134L, 134R, 146R, 147L, 147R, 286R, 287L, 287R, 288L, 288R, 290L
    definition and characterization, **90L-90R**
    subage of the Chadronian mammal age, 287R
Duchesnean/Chadronian boundary, 128R, 135R, 147L, 147R
Duchesnean-Chadronian interval, 129L
Duchesne Formation, Utah, 84L
Duchesne River Formation, Utah, 78R, 89R, 90L, 93, 94, 98L, 100R, 101R, 107R, 129L, 133R, 134R, 146R, 148R, 287L, 287R, 288L
Dunbar Creek Formation, Montana, 127R, 128L
Dunbar Creek Member, Renova Formation, Jefferson Basin, Montana, 128L
Eagle Crags Ash, Nebraska, 198
early Chadronian, 133R–135L
early Orellan, 138R
early Wasatchian (Sandcouleean and Graybullian), 86L
East Coast, 6L, 7L
East Fork Basin, Wyoming, 89L, 97L
East Fork River, Wyoming, 78R
East Walker River, Nevada, 160R
Echols County, Georgia, 179L
ecological shift (promotes speciation), 220R
ecological subzone, 121L
ecosystem, 121L, 121R
Ectoconus/Taeniolabis taoensis Interval-Zone (Puercan, Pu2), 43L, **44R–46R**
Ectoconus zone (Puercan, Pu2), 28, 44R
Eemian (= Devensian) interglacial stage; Europe, 223R
Elk Creek facies (Fort Union Formation), 82L
Ellesmere Island, Canada, 83L, 83R, 108L
Ellis County, Oklahoma, 174R, 175L
Ellsworth County, Kansas, 263R
El Paso Mountains or Range, California, 159L
Elster (glacial stage, Europe), 221R, 224L
emmigrant, 185R
Emry, R. J., xi, 118L
endemic, endemism, 214R, 217R, 219R, 237L, 239L, 239R, 240L, 242L, 242R, 245L, 245R, 246L, 247L, 247R, 249L, 250L, 251R, 252L, 288R, 290L
England, 18R

Entoptychus-Gregorymys Concurrent Range-Zone (Arikareean, Ar2–4), Oregon to Great Plains, 19L, 161L, 163R, 164L, 172L, 181L, 185R, 288R
environmental zonation, 211L
Eobasileus-Dolichorhinus zone, 83R
Eocene/Oligocene boundary, 134L, 147L, 147R
Eocene Series-Epoch, rocks, faunas, 2R, 5R, 6L, 7L, 19L, 24L, 24R, 53L, 62L, 66L, 66R, 68L, 77R, 79L, 79R, 80L, 80R, 82L, 82R, 83R, 84L, 84R, 90L, 90R, 92, 93, 96L, 98L, 98R, 99L, 99R, 100L, 100R, 101R, 103L, 104L, 104R, 105R, 106L, 106R, 133L, 134R, 146R, 147L, 147R, 276R, 280L, 286R
Eon, 10R
Eonothem, 10R
episodic record, 182L
Epoch (see also under individual units), 10R
equable Pleistocene climates, 227R
Era (see also under individual units), 10R
Erathem, 10R, 15L
Ertemte, Mongolia, 239L, 241R
Esmeralda County, Nevada, 160L
Esmeralda Formation, Nevada, 160L, 197
Etchegoin Formation, California, 157L, 157R
Eurasia(n), eurasiatic, 18R, 121L, 132R, 180L, 182L, 185L, 190L, 191L, 192R, 193L, 217L, 218L, 220R, 221L, 222R, 223R, 224R, 238R, 251L, 289L
Eureka Sound Formation, Canada, 108L
Europe, European, 5L, 6L, 6R, 18R, 19L, 21R, 24R, 41L, 41R, 66L, 66R, 67L, 67R, 68L, 84R, 90R, 96L, 98R, 101L, 118R, 133L, 146R, 147L, 147R, 211R, 213R, 221R, 222R, 223R, 224L, 236R, 237L, 238R, 239L, 239R, 240L, 241L, 242L, 242R, 244R, 245L, 247L, 248L, 249L, 250L, 250R, 251L, 251R, 278L, 280L, 286R
eustatic, 227R
Evanston area, Wyoming, 78L, 103L
Evanston Formation, Fossil Basin, Wyoming, 54L
Event (microtine rodent), 1–10, 239L, 239R
evolution, 10L, 219R, 225R, 226L, 226R, 228L, 236L, 237L, 239L, 239R, 240L, 242R, 243L, 243R, 244L, 245L, 246L, 246R, 249L, 251R, 252L, 252R, 255L, 255R, 256R, 257R, 258L, 260L, 269L, 271L, 278R, 280L, 280R, 290L
rapid rate, microtine rodents vs. horses and elephants, 240L
temporal subdivision based on evolution in:
  Allophaiomys, 250L
  Bison, 224R, 226R
  Blarina, 226R
  Canis, 226R
  Copemys, 19L
  Cosomys, 22L, 243L, 244L, 244R, 256L
  Felidae, 226R
  Hibbardomys, 226L
  Mammuthus, 226R
  microtine rodents, 236R, 237R, 239L, 239R, 243L, 243R, 246L, 251R, 252L, 255R, 256R, 260L
  Microtus, 226L, 251R
  Microtus pennsylvanicus, 226L
  Mictomys, 249L, 250L
  Ogmodontomys, 22L, 226L, 243L, 244R, 245L, 246L
  Ondatra, 226L, 247R, 249L, 250L, 260L
  Onychomys, 226L
  Ophiomys, 22L, 226L, 243L, 244R, 245L, 245R, 246R, 247L, 258L
  packrats, 226R, 227L
  Pelycodus, 19R
  Pitymys, 226L
  Plesiadapis, 25R, 55R, 56R, 57R, 58L, 59L, 59R, 60L, 60R, 63L, 63R, 64L, 64R, 65L, 66R
  Pliophenacomys, 22L, 226L, 243R, 244R, 244L, 246L, 246R
  Pliopotamys, 245R, 246R, 247R
  Proneofiber-Neofiber, 250L

rabbits, 226R
Sigmodon, 226L
Sorex cinereus, 226R
Synaptomys, 250L
Zapus, 226R
evolutionary first occurrence, 4L, 15R, 16L, 16R, 19R, 20L, 25R, 48L, 64L, 218L, 220R
extinction datum, extinction, 20L, 218L, 218R, 220L, 221L, 223R, 225L, 226L, 228L, 239R, 246R, 249L, 250L, 258L, 262L, 287R, 288L
causes (Pleistocene megafauna; 9,400–12,700 yrs. ago), 225L, 225R
differential, Beringia vs. southern North America, 225L
extrapolate, extrapolation, 4R, 5L, 7L, 270L, 285R
Fauna, faunal, **xivL**, 155L, 175R, 221L, 228L, 251L, 278R, 279L, 279R, 287R
datum events, 278R, 279L, 279R, 280L
hiatus, 285R, 286L, 289L
provinces, 182L, 185R, 189L, 190L, 193L, 193R, 218R, 225L, 236R, 240R, 247L, 249R, 252L, 255R
shifts (with shifting Pleistocene ice sheets), etc., 227L, 240R
turnover, 280L
Faunule, faunules, **xivL**, 187R
fecundity and evolutionary rates: in microtine rodents, 240L
in horses, 240L
in elephants, 240L
Fejfar, Oldrich, 237R
Feltz Ranch, Nebraska, 169R
Field Museum of Natural History, 101L
Fields, R. W., xi, 153
first appearance datum (FAD), 16L, 20L, 21L, 54R, 60L, 61R, 214L, 215L, 218L, 219L, 220R, 225L, 278R
differential, Beringia vs. southern North America, 225L
Fisherian statistics (magnetic polarity stratigraphy), 275R
fission-track (ages), 15L, 148L, 149L, 154R, 165L, 170L, 183, 195R, 196, 198, 213L, 215L, 216L, 217R, 219L, 222R, 228L
Flagstaff Limestone, Wyoming, 101L, 101R
Flagstaff Rim, Wyoming, 125L, 127L, 132L, 133R, 134L, 134R, 135L, 136L, 136R, 137L, 138L, 149L, 271R
Fleming Foundation, Texas, 176L, 176R, 177L
Flint Creek beds, Montana, 164R
Flint Creek Valley, Montana, 163L, 164L
Florida, 128R, 176L, 177R, 178L, 178R, 179L, 179R, 180L, 180R, 181L, 186L, 190L, 191L, 192L, 192R, 193L, 193R, 213L, 214L, 215L, 218L, 218R, 219L, 220L, 222L, 225L, 225R, 227R
Florida Geological Survey, 179L
Flynn, J. J., xi, 77L
forest communities, 227R
Fort Laramie, 122L
Fort Peck, Montana, 271R
Fort Union Formation (= Polecat Bench Formation), Clark's Fork Basin, Wyoming, 19L, 40L, 53R, 61L, 62L, 78L, 105R, 286L
Bighorn Basin, Wyoming, 53R, 106L
Fossil Basin, Wyoming, 47R
Montana, 53R
North Dakota, 107L
Washakie Basin, Wyoming, 47R, 61L, 102L
Wind River Basin, Wyoming, 54L, 97R
Fort Union Group, Bison Basin, Wyoming, 54L
Fossil Basin, Wyoming, 54L, 57L, 78L, 82R, 103L
"fossiliferous tuff member," Barstow Formation, California, 187L, 188L
Fowkes Formation, Utah, 78R, 95
Wyoming, 81L, 81R, 82L, 103R, 104L
Fraction Tuff, Nevada, 196
France, 66L, 67L, 98R, 214R, 242L, 247L, 269R
Franklin County, Washington, 254L
Frederick, Oklahoma, 221L
Fremont County, Wyoming, 149L

Friars Formation, California, 78R, 89L, 98R, 99L
Frick Collection or Laboratory (American Museum of Natural History), 144R, 155L, 158R, 162R, 167R, 172R, 173L, 174L, 174R, 175L, 176R, 237R
Frontier County, Nebraska, 170L
fuller's earth pits, Florida, 178R, 179L
Gadsden County, Florida, 178R
Galisteo Formation, New Mexico, 78R, 90R, 105L, 105R
Galusha, Theodore, xi, 87R, 88L, 88R, 153
Garden County, Nebraska, 198
Gardnerbuttean subage (Br1), of the Bridgerian mammal age, 82L, 86R, 87R, 97R, 101R, 105L, 287L
    "substage" of Wasatchian, 86R, 87R, 287L
Garlock fault, California, 159L, 159R
Gate Canyon, Utah, 94
Gateway, Oregon, 161R
Gauss Chron, Magnetic Chron or Normal Chron, 21L, 215R, 216L, 217R, 218L, 247R, 256L, 257L, 257R, 258L, 270L, 271L, 277R
Gauss/Matuyama boundary, 215R, 218L, 219L, 247R, 256L, 258R, 259R
geocentric dipole (magnetic polarity stratigraphy), 275L
    calculation, 275L
geochron, xivL, 1R, 118R, 181R, 184R, 186R, 188R, 189L, 191R, 285L
geochronologic unit, etc., xivL, 9L, 10R, 25L, 108L, 153R, 154R, 155L, 160L, 193L, 213R, 225, 289R
geochronology, viiL, viiiL, xivL, 6R, 15L, 118L, 165L, 177R, 181R, 211L, 215L, 228L, 228R, 278R
geochronologists, viiiL
geological shift (promotes speciation), 220R
Geological Society of America, 195L
geomagnetic stratigraphy (see magnetostratigraphy)
Georgia, 179L, 180R
Gering-Brule contact, 165R
Gering Formation, Nebraska, 149L, 157R, 163R, 165L, 165R, 166L, 171R, 184R, 184R, 197, 198
"Geringian" mammal age, 184R
Germany, 221R, 248L
Gilbert Chron; Reversed Chron, 215R, 216L, 216R, 217L, 217R, 242R, 243L, 243R, 244L, 245L, 253R, 254L, 255L, 256L, 271L, 277R
Gilchrist County, Florida, 178R
Gill Breccia, Texas, 95, 104R
Gingerich, P. D., xi, 2R, 19L, 19R, 24L
glacial, glaciation (pre-Pleistocene; Pleistocene), 213L, 219R, 220L, 221L, 223R, 225R, 227L, 249L
glacial climates, 227L, 227R, 228L, 251L
glacioeustatic sea level changes, Florida, 213L, 220L, 227R
glacial-interglacial correlations, environments, sequences, 223R, 225R, 227L, 227R, 228L
glacial stages (North America), 222L, 224L, 227R
Glenns Ferry Formation, Idaho, 215R, 278R, 289R
"Glutton Stratum," England, 251L
Goliad County, Texas, 176L, 177L
Goliad Formation, Texas, 176L, 177L
Golden Valley Formation, North Dakota, 78L, 107L
Golz, D. J., xi, 77R
Gooding County, Idaho, 253L
Goodnight beds, Texas, 174L, 174R
Goodnight, Texas, 174L
Goshen County, Wyoming, 166R
Goshen Hole, Wyoming, 133L
Gosiute Lake, Wyoming, 102R
gradual (evolution), viiR, 12R, 15R, 16L, 240
Graham County, Arizona, 258R
Granger Mountain Locality (Clarkforkian, Cf3), 30
Granger, Walter, 51R, 53L
Granite County, Montana, 163L
Granite Mountains, Wyoming, 125L

granivorous diet (Pleistocene rodents), 225L
Grant County, Washington, 253R
grass-eating (rodent), 238L
"Gray Bull beds," Willwood Formation, Big Horn Basin, 78L, 81L
Graybullian subage (Wa2) of the Wasatchian mammal age, 20L, 82L, 82R, 86L, 105L, 105R, 106L, 287L
grazing (rodents; Pleistocene), 226L
Great Basin, North America, 154L, 156R, 157L, 158L, 160L, 162L, 162R, 165L, 169R, 187R, 188L, 191L, 192L, 192R, 193R
Great Divide Basin, Wyoming, 82R, 102L, 125L, 125R
"Great Lignite Basin," 122L
Great Plains, North America, 20L, 120L, 146R, 154R, 157L, 157R, 158L, 159L, 160R, 161L, 161R, 162L, 162R, 163L, 163R, 164L, 164R, 165L, 165R, 166R, 168L, 168R, 169R, 170L, 171L, 172L, 173L, 176L, 176R, 177L, 179R, 180L, 180R, 182L, 184L, 184R, 185L, 185R, 186L, 186R, 187L, 187R, 188L, 188R, 189L, 189R, 190L, 191L, 191R, 192L, 193L, 193R, 194R, 215L, 216L, 217L, 218L, 219L, 220L, 220R, 222L, 222R, 223R, 224L, 224R, 227R, 241R, 244L, 244R, 245R, 246L, 246R, 247L, 247R, 248R, 249L, 249R, 250L, 250R, 255R, 256R, 260L, 289L
Great Valley, California, 156L
Green and Brown Member, Wagon Bed Formation, Wyoming, 98L
Greenlee County, Arizona, 264L
Green River Basin, Wyoming, 61L, 65L, 77R, 78L, 79R, 82R, 83L, 83R, 85R, 86R, 88L, 95, 96R, 97L, 102R, 103L, 103R, 104L
Green River fish beds, 103R
Green River Formation, Colorado, 83R, 95
    Utah, 78R, 87R, 94, 101R
    Wyoming, 82R, 87L, 93, 94, 95, 102L, 102R, 103L, 103R
Green Valley Formation, California, 155R, 196
Greenwood Canyon, Nebraska, 170L
Grenwich meridian, 275L
Grimes County, Texas, 175R, 176L
Guaje ash, Texas, 219L
Guanajuato, Mexico, 108L
Gulf Coast, North America, 6L, 20R, 154L, 154R, 175R, 176L, 176R, 177L, 177R, 178R, 179L, 180L, 182L, 186L, 186R, 188L, 188R, 189L, 192L, 193L, 194R
habitat invasion (Sigmodon), 226L
Hagerman, Idaho, 215R, 245L
Halfway Draw Tuff, Wind River Formation, Wyoming, 92
Halfway Member, Duchesne River Formation, Utah, 84R, 93, 94
Hannold Hill Formation, Big Bend area, Texas, 78L, 104L
Haplomylus-Ectocion, Range-Zone (Wasatchian), Wyoming, 19L, 20L, 287
Hardscrabble Creek, Wyoming, 96R
Harington, C. R., xi, 211
Harlan County, Nebraska, 222R, 248R, 261L
Harney County, Oregon, 253R
harmonious faunas (taxa are ecologically congruent; Pleistocene), 227L
Harrison Formation, Nebraska, 163R, 164L, 166L, 166R, 167R, 168L, 171R, 178L, 184L, 185L, 198
    South Dakota, 171L, 171R
"Harrisonian" mammal age, 184R, 186L
Harrison County, Iowa, 263L
Harrison, Nebraska, 127L, 166L
Hart Draw, Kansas, 255R
Hartford Ash, Great Plains, 213L, 221R
Hartville uplift, Wyoming, 166L, 166R
Hat Creek breaks, Wyoming, 166R
Hawks Butte, Wyoming, 93
Hawthorn Formation, Florida, 178L, 178R, 179L, 180L
Hayden, F. V., 80R, 81L
Hay Springs, Nebraska, 223R
Haystack Mountain, Wyoming, 102R
Haystack Valley Member, John Day Formation, Oregon, 161L
Hector Formation, California, 158R, 196, 289R, 290L
helium-uranium age, 179L

Hell Creek faunal-facies, 41L
Hell Creek Formation, Montana, 41L, 42L, 69L, 271R
Helvas Canyon Member, Gering Formation, Nebraska, 197
Helvas Canyon, Nebraska, 149L
Hemingford Group, Nebraska, 185R, 186L, 186R
Hemingfordian mammal age, faunas, and rocks, 19L, 156R, 157R,
    158L, 158R, 160R, 163L, 167R, 168L, 172R, 178R, 179L,
    184L, 185R, 186L, 186R, 187L, 187R, 189L, 193L, 194L, 289L
  definition and characterization, **185R–187L**
  subdivisions, 185R–187L
Hemithlaeus zone, 44R, 45R
Hemphill beds, Texas, 175L, 191L, 191R, 198
Hemphill County, Texas, 173R, 174R, 175L, 190R
Hemphillian/Blancan boundary, 181R, 183, 216L, 217L
Hemphillian/Clarendonian faunal change (8.5 Ma), 241R
Hemphillian mammal age, faunas, rocks, 20R, 21R, 155R, 156R,
    157L, 158L, 159R, 160R, 162L, 162R, 163L, 164R, 168R,
    169R, 170L, 170R, 171L, 173R, 174R, 177R, 178L, 179R,
    180R, 181L, 181R, 182L, 188L, 190L, 190R, 191L, 191R,
    192L, 192R, 193L, 193R, 211R, 214R, 216L, 216R, 217L,
    217R, 219L, 240L, 241L, 242L, 242R, 243R, 253L, 254L, 256R,
    279L, 279R, 288R, 289L, 289R, 290L
  definition and characterization, **190R–192R**
  subdivisions, 191L–192R
"Hemphill member of the Ogallala," 190R
Hendry Ranch Member, Wagon Bed Formation, Wyoming, 78R, 92,
    98R
Heptodon beds, 86L
Heptodon Range-Zone (Wasatchian), Wyoming, 20L, 287L
herbivorous (rodents), 238L
Hernando County, Florida, 178L
heterochroneity, 108L
Hiawatha Member, Wasatch Formation, Wyoming, 82R
Higgins, Texas, 174R, 175L, 181L
high elevation (glaciation), 213L
highest stratigraphic datum (HSD), 278R, 279L
high-horned (ovibovini), 221L
high latitude (glaciation), 213L
high-level shorelines, Florida, 178L, 227R
High Plains, North America, 125L, 176R, 189L, 213R
Hoback Basin, Wyoming, 26R, 53R, 58R, 59R, 61L, 62L, 64L, 65L,
    78L, 83R, 103L, 104L
Hoback Formation, Hoback Basin, Wyoming, 26R, 53R
Holarctic(a), 68L, 176R, 221R, 236L, 237R, 238L, 238R, 239L,
    239R, 240L, 245L, 248L, 250L, 251L
Holocene, 224L, 224R, 225R, 251L, 251R
  refugium (end of Pleistocene), 225R
Homogalax beds, 86L
homotaxial, homotaxis, 120L, 129L, 134R, 164R
homotaxy, viiR, **xivL**
Hooker County, Nebraska, 259R
Horned Toad Formation, California, 159R
Horsebench Sandstone, Utah, 94
Horse Heaven Mining District, Oregon, 148R
Horsetail Creek Member, White River Formation, Colorado, 137L,
    138R
Huerfano A (Lysitean-Gardnerbuttean; Wa3, Wa4, Br1), Colorado,
    105L
Huerfano B (earliest Bridgerian, Br1), 87L, 87R, 97R
Huerfano Basin, Colorado, 78L, 80L, 83L, 85R, 86R, 87L, 87R, 88L,
    104R, 286R
Huerfano Formation, Colorado, 85R, 87R, 105L
Huerfano Valley, Colorado, 105L
Huckleberry Ridge Ash (= Pearlette type B), West Coast and Great
    Plains, 214L, 217R, 220R, 222R
Humboldt County, California, 261R
Hungary, 236R
Hunt Creek, Wyoming, 54L
Hunter Wash, New Mexico, 271R

Huxley, T. H., viiR
hyphenated double species, 237R
hypsodont horses, 168L
  rhinos, 168L
  rodents, 219R, 225R, 226L
  proboscideans, 226R
Iceland, 213L, 248L
ice rafting: Antarctic, 213L
  North Pacific, 249R, 252L
ice sheets (absent Northern Hemisphere, 3.2–3.5 Ma), 219R
ice-transported; see ice rafting
Idaho, 161L, 163R, 185R, 211L, 215L, 215R, 218L, 221L, 241L,
    245L, 246L, 247L, 247R, 250R, 253L, 255L, 256L, 257R, 258L,
    258R, 259L, 259R, 263R, 271R, 278R, 288R, 289R
Idaho State University, Pocatello, 237R
Illinoian glacial stage, 223R, 224L, 224R, 226L, 252L
immigrants, immigration, 6L, 6R, 15R, 19L, 21L, 21R, 22L, 22R,
    61R, 166R, 167L, 167R, 169R, 170L, 170R, 171L, 175L, 178R, 179R,
    181L, 182L, 182R, 183, 185L, 186R, 187L, 188L, 189L, 190L,
    190R, 191L, 191R, 192L, 192R, 193L, 193R, 214R, 217R,
    218L, 218R, 219L, 219R, 220L, 220R, 221L, 222L, 222R,
    223R, 224R, 225L, 227R, 228L, 236L, 237L, 239L, 239R,
    240L, 241R, 242L, 242R, 244R, 245L, 247L, 249R, 250R,
    251R, 252L, 253L, 253R, 254R, 256L, 258L, 258R, 260L,
    261L, 262L, 263R, 264L, 280L, 286R, 287R, 288L, 288R,
    289L, 290L
Imola, Italy, 213R
Imperial Formation, California, 215R
inclination (magnetic), 275L, 276R
increase in size (temporal trend), 224R, 249L
increase in crown height and complexity (rodent teeth), 238L, 246L
Indian Canyon, Utah, 94
Indian Meadows Formation, Wind River Basin, Wyoming, 78L, 96R,
    97R
INQUA Congress, 214L
insectivory (diet, Pleistocene rodents), 226L, 226R
intercontinental correlations, 66L, 67L
intercontinental dispersal, 5R, 6L, 19L, 24R, 66L, 182R, 190L, 191L,
    192L, 192R, 221L, 271L, 280L
interglacial (oceanic temperatures, 3.2–3.5 Ma), 219R
interglacial climates, 227R, 262L
interglacial stages (North America), 222L, 223R, 224L, 227L
International Stratigraphic Guide, 9R, 25L
International Union of Geological Sciences Subcommission on Geo-
    chronology, 79L
interpolate, interpolation, 4R, 5L
interval chronology, 3L
Interval-Zone, interval-zone, interval zones or subzones, **xivR**, 11L,
    19R, 20L, 22R, 25L, 25R, 43L, 44R, 45R, 46L, 48L, 49L, 49R,
    60L, 60R, 63L, 63R
  Cf1, 60L, 60R, 63L, 63R, 64L, 67L
  Ti6, 56L, 56R, 60L, 60R, 63R, 64L, 69L
  To4, 49L, 49R
    rejected, but may exist, 49R
  To3/Ti1 boundary, 54R
  To3, 48R, 49L, 49R, 50L, **51R–53L**, 52L, 52R, 55R
  To2/To3 boundary, 48L, 52L
  To2, 48R, 49L, 49R, 50L, **51L–51R**, 52L
  To1/To2 boundary, 48R, 50L
  To1, 48R, 49L, **50L–51L**, 67R, 286L
  Pu3/To1 boundary, 47R, 28L
  Pu3, 43L, **44R–46R**, 48R, 286L
  Pu2/Pu3 boundary, 46L
  Pu2, 43L, **44R–46R**, 286
  Pu1/Pu2 boundary, 44L, 46L
  Pu1, 25R, **43L–44R**, 286L
intraspecific level (microevolutionary changes), 224R
invasion(s) (see immigration)
Inyo County, California, 257R, 262L

Iowa, 219R, 220L, 222L, 224L, 248L, 249L, 250L, 252L, 262L, 263L
Iowa Till, 220L
Irish Rock, Wyoming, 92
Irvington, California, 220L
Irvingtonian mammal age, faunas, and rocks, 18L, 21L, 21R, 22L, 22R, 211L, 213R, 214L, 214R, 215L, 216L, 218L, 218R, 220L, 220R, 221L, 221R, 222L, 222R, 223L, 223R, 224L, 226L, 226R, 240R, 241L, 241R, 247L, 248L, 248R, 249L, 249R, 250L, 250R, 251L, 252L, 252R, 260L, 260R, 261L, 261R, 262R, 264R, 279L, 290L
  definition and characterization, **220L–223L**
  subdivisions, 222R–223L
Ischia, Italy, 211R
isochroneity, 119R
isochronous, 4R, 10R, 11L, 15R, 16R, 20L, 20R, 119R
isothermal remanent magnetization (IRM), 272R, 277L
isotopic (oceanic ratios, composition, climatic correlation), 219R, 236L
Italy, Italian, 211R, 213L, 213R
Italian Neogene, 213L
Jackass Butte, Idaho, 259L
Jackson, Wyoming, 252R
Jackson Bluff Formation, Florida, 180R
Japan, 269R
Jaramillo subchron (of Matuyama Chron), 215R, 220L, 249R, 261R
Jefferson Basin, Montana, 127R, 128L
Jefferson County, Florida, 179L
Jefferson County, Oregon, 161R
Jefferson River Valley, Montana, 164L, 164R, 165L
Jemez Mountains, New Mexico, 221L
Jewel County, Kansas, 221R
John Day Basin (or region), Oregon, 162L, 162R, 163L
John Day Formation, Oregon, 13R, 19L, 20R, 127R, 128L, 140R, 142R, 145L, 146R, 148L, 160L, 160R, 161L, 161R, 163R, 185R, 197, 288R, 289L
John Day River (and Valley), Oregon, 160R, 161R
Johns Hopkins University, 86R
Johnson Member, Snake Creek Formation, Nebraska, 170R
Johnson, N. M., xii, 22R, 269
"Judith River," 122L
Juncal Formation, California, 99R
Juntura Basin, Oregon, 162L
Juntura Formation, Oregon, 162L, 197
Kaena subchron (of the Gauss magnetic chron), 215R, 257R
K-Ar, 3L, 4L, 4R, 15L, 79L, 148R, 149L, 156L, 183, 214R, 215R, 216L, 217R, 221L, 236L, 236R, 237L, 240L, 241L, 244R, 245L, 252L, 270L
Kansan (glacial stage), High Plains, 213L, 213R, 219R (0.6–1.2 Ma), 223R, 224L, 250L, 250R, 252L, 261L
Kansas, 211L, 214L, 215L, 216L, 216R, 217L, 217R, 218L, 220R, 221R, 222L, 222R, 223L, 224L, 226R, 227L, 243L, 243R, 244L, 244R, 246L, 246R, 247L, 248R, 249L, 250L, 254L, 255L, 256L, 257L, 259R, 261L, 263L, 263R, 264L, 271R, 277R
Kazakh S.S.R., 238R
Keith County, Nebraska, 253L
Kemmerer, Wyoming, 103R
Kern County, California, 256R
Kern River Formation, California, 157L
Kettleman Hills, California, 256R
Kimball County, Nebraska, 191R
"Kimballian Provincial Age," Nebraska, 191R
Kimball Formation, Nebraska, 170L, 182L, 191R
Kimberly Member, John Day Formation, Oregon, 161L
Kimbetoh, New Mexico, 40L
Kimbetoh Arroyo, New Mexico, 40L, 44R, 46L, 48L, 48R, 50L, 52L, 276R
Kinney Rim, Wyoming, 94
Kinney Rim Member, Washakie Formation, Washakie Basin, Wyoming, 78L, 102R
Kingman County, Kansas, 259R
Kishenehn Formation, British Columbia, 90R
Kissinger Lakes flora, Wyoming, 93, 95
Knight Formation, Wyoming, 81L, 81R, 82R, 103R, 104L
Knox County, Nebraska, 198
  Texas, 221R, 222R, 253R, 261L, 263L
Kramer beds, California, 158R
Krause, D.W., xii, 24R
Krishtalka, Leonard, xii, 77L
Kutz Canyon section (Torrejonian), San Juan Basin, New Mexico, 48R, 49L, 50R, 51L, 51R, 52L, 55R
LaBarge area, Wyoming, 64R, 78L, 103L
Lake County, Oregon, 253L
Lambdotherium Concurrent Range-Zone (Wasatchian, Wa4), Wyoming, 19L, 20L, 87R, 97R, 287L
Lambdotherium "zone" or level, 19L, 81R, 86R
Lance fauna, 40R
Lancian/Puercan boundary, 40R, 41L, 42L, 66L
Lancian mammal age, faunas, and rocks, 40R, 41L, 41R, 42L, 42R, 44L, 44R, 50L
Lancian "stage," 40R
Laney Shale Member, Green River Formation, Wyoming, 94, 95, 102R, 103L
Langford Formation, Wyoming, 91, 92
La Jolla Formation, California, 98R
Lapara Member, Goliad Formation, Texas, 177L, 177R
LaPoint Member, Duchesne River Formation, Utah, 78R, 90L, 93, 94, 98L, 100R, 101R, 129L, 133R, 148R, 287R
Laramie Basin, Wyoming, 78L, 83L, 84L, 84R, 107L
Laramie Range, Wyoming, 125L
Largo beds, San Juan Basin, New Mexico, 82R, 105L
Las Posas Hills, California, 157R
last appearance datum (LAD), 45R, 214L, 215L, 218L, 218R, 220L, 222R, 278R
late Chadronian, 137L–138R
Late Cretaceous, 40R, 42L, 50R, 256L, 278L
Late Cretaceous/Tertiary boundary, 41L, 270L
late Wasatchian (Lostcabinian), 86R, 97R
Laucomer Member, Snake Creek Formation, Nebraska, 170R
Lava Creek B (type O Pearlette ash), Texas, 221R, 223L
Lava Mountain Quadrangle, Wyoming, 96L
Lava Mountains, California, 159L
Lawlor Tuff, California, 156L
Le Castella, Italy, 214L
Leidy, Joseph, 80R
Lemhi Valley, Idaho, 163R
Leon County, Florida, 178L
Leptauchenia Beds, layer, 122R, 144L
Le Puy, France, 214R
Levy County, Florida, 159R
Lignites et Grès du Soissonais (Sparnacian and Cuisian), Paris Basin, France, 66L
Lillegraven, J. H., xii, 77R
Lima, Montana, 128L
Lincoln County, Kansas, 263L, 264L
  Nevada, 256L
  Texas, 259L
Lineage-Zone (includes named entities), lineage-zone or lineage-zones, **xivR**, 11L, 22R, 25R, 29R, 49R, 54R, 55R, 56L, 56R, 57R, 58L, 58R, 59L, 59R, 60L, 67L, 286R
  Cf3, **65L**, 65R, 69L
  Cf2, 60L, **64R**, 65L, 66R, 67L, 67R
  Ti6-Cf1, 56L, 56R, **60L**, 60R, 63L, 63R, 64R, 67L, 67R, 286R
  Ti5, 54L, 56L, 56R, 59L, **59R**, 60L
  Ti4, 55R, 56R, **59L**, 286L
  Ti3, 55R, 56R, **58L**, 58R, 59L
  Ti2, 55R, 56R, **57R**, 58L, 58R, 59R
  Ti1/Ti2 boundary, 57R, 69L

Ti1, 25R, 29R, 49R, 54L, 55R, 56R, **57L**, 57R, 58R, 286
Lind Coulee, Washington, 242R
Lindsay, E. H., xii, 2R, 22R, 24L, 211, 269
Lipscomb County, Texas, 174R
Lisbon Formation, Mississippi, 107R, 108L
lithologic unit, **xivR**, 61L, 143R, 144L, 145R, 180R
lithology, **xivR**, 214L, 273L
lithostratigraphic unit, etc., **xivR**, 77L, 79R, 86R, 118R, 119L, 120R, 124R, 125R, 128R, 129L, 139R, 140L, 143R, 144L, 145R, 147R, 168L, 175R, 180L, 184R, 186L, 189L
lithostratigraphy, **xivR**, 6R, 22R, 83L, 101R, 169L, 175R
Little Mountain flora, Wyoming, 95
Little Mountain Tuff, Wilkins Peak Member, Green River Formation, Wyoming, 93
Llajas Formation, California, 99R
Llano Estacado, Texas, 173R
Llaves Member, San Jose Formation, New Mexico, 105L
Local Fauna(s) [and Faunas], **xivR**, 155L
  111 Ranch Local Fauna (Blancan, Bl2), Arizona, 212, 218L, 271R
  Adams Local Fauna (Irvingtonian, Ir3), Kansas, 212, 223L, 224L, 271R
  Agate Springs Local Fauna (Arikareean, Ar4), Nebraska 166R, 167L, 184L, 185L, 199L
  Aiken Hill Local Fauna (Arikareean, Ar4), Texas, 176L, 199L
  Airstrip Local Fauna (?Duchesnean or Chadronian, Ch1), Texas, 109L, 136L, 137L
  Alamosa Local Fauna (Irvingtonian, IrII), Colorado, 250L
  American Falls Local Fauna (Rancholabrean, Rlb), Idaho, 212
  Anceney Local Fauna (Barstovian, Ba2), Montana, 165L, 199R
  Angel Peak Local Fauna (Torrejonian, To2), New Mexico, 51L
  Angus Local Fauna (Irvingtonian, Ir3, RlbI), Nebraska, 212, 223L, 263R
  Anita Local Fauna (?Blancan, ?Bl2 or ?Irvingtonian, ?Ir1), Arizona, 212, 218R, 220R
  Antelope Hills Local Fauna (Barstovian, Ba2), Montana, 164R, 199R
  Aphelops Draw Fauna (Hemphillian, Hh1-Hh2), Nebraska, 171L, 191L, 199R
  Aries Local Fauna (Irvingtonian, Ir1, IrI), Kansas, 212, 222R, 248R
  Arondelli-Triversa Fauna (Villafranchian), Italy, 245L, 247L
  Arnett Local Fauna (Hemphillian, Hh1), Oklahoma, 174R, 175L, 179R, 199R
  Arredondo Local Fauna (Rancholabrean, Rlb), Florida, 212
  Arroyo Seco Local Fauna (Blancan, Bl1-2, BlV), California, 212, 215R, 217R, 218L, 271R
  Ash Hollow Fauna or faunas, Nebraska, 164R, 189R
  Ash Springs Local Fauna (Chadronian, Ch2), Texas, 136L, 136R, 137L
  Ashville Local Fauna (Barstovian, Ba3), Florida, 199R
  Axtel Local Fauna (Hemphillian, Hh3), Texas, 271R
  Bangtail Local Fauna (Tiffanian, Ti1), Montana, 31, 53R, 57L
  Barker's Ranch Local Fauna (Hemingfordian, He2), California, 156R, 199R
  Barstow Fauna (Barstovian, Ba2), California, 156R, 158L, 159L, 160L, 187L, 187R, 188L, 188R, 189L, 199R
  Bartlett Mountain Local Fauna (Hemphillian, Hh1), Oregon, 162L, 197, 199R, 253
  Bear Creek Local Fauna (originally Tiffanian, now Clarkforkian, Cf1), Montana, 30, 53R, 61L, 62L, 64L
  Bear Tooth Local Fauna (Hemphillian, Hh3), Nebraska, 169R, 199R
  Beaver Local Fauna (Blancan, BlV), Utah, 264L
  Beck Ranch Local Fauna (Blancan, Bl1; BlIII), Texas, 212, 217R, 245R, 255R, 257L
  Bender Local Fauna (Bl1, BlIII), Kansas, 212, 218L, 219L, 255R, 256R, 257R, 258L, 271R
  Benson Local Fauna (Blancan, Bl1, BlIV), Arizona, 212, 216L, 217R, 257R, 264L, 271R, 277R
  Berends Local Fauna (Irvingtonian, Ir3), Oklahoma, 212, 223L
  Bert Creek Local Fauna (Barstovian, Ba3, or Clarendonian, Cl1),

  Montana, 164R, 199R
  Big Spring Canyon Local Fauna (Clarendonian, Cl1), South Dakota, 169R, 189R, 199R
  Big Springs Local Fauna (Blancan, Bl2), Nebraska, 212, 214L
  Biharian Fauna, Europe, 213R
  Black Butte Local Fauna (Clarendonian, Cl2), Oregon, 158R, 162L, 199R
  Black Butte Mine Fauna (Arikareean, Ar3), California, 158R, 196, 199R
  Black Hawk Ranch Local Fauna (Montediablan, = ca. Clarendonian, Cl2), California, 155R, 199R
  Blacktail Deer Creek Local Fauna (Arikareean, Ar3), Montana, 164L, 199R
  Black Peaks Fauna (Tiffanian, Ti1), Texas, 54R
  Blanco Local Fauna (= Mt. Blanco L.F.; Blancan, Bl2, BlV), Texas, 212, 215L, 217R, 218L, 218R, 219L
  Bone Valley Fauna (= Upper Bone Valley Fauna; Hemphillian, Hh3), Florida, 180L
  Borchers Local Fauna (Blancan, Bl2, BlV or Irvingtonian, Ir1, IrI), Kansas, 212, 214L, 217R, 218L, 218R, 219L, 220R, 221L, 222R, 226L, 247R, 248R, 259R, 260L, 271R
  Boron Local Fauna (Hemingfordian, He1), California, 158R, 186R, 196, 199R
  Box Butte Fauna (Hemingfordian, He2), Nebraska, 168L, 186R
  Box T Local Fauna (Hemphillian, Hh2), Oklahoma, 179R, 199R
  Boyle Ditch Local Fauna (Blancan, BlIV), Wyoming, 258R
  Bradenton Local Fauna (Rancholabrean, Rbl), Florida, 212
  Brady Pocket Local Fauna (Clarendonian, Cl1), Nevada, 162L, 199R
  Brea Canyon Local Fauna (Uintan, Ui2), California, 100R
  Bridge Ranch Local Fauna (Barstovian, Ba3), Texas, 177R, 199R
  Broadwater Local Fauna (Blancan, Bl2, BlIV), Nebraska, 212, 219L, 219R, 258L
  Brooksville Local Fauna (Arikareean, Ar3), Florida, 178L, 199R
  Buda Local Fauna (Arikareean, Ar3), Florida, 178L, 199R
  Buis Ranch Local Fauna (Hh3, Bll), Oklahoma, 212, 216L, 216R
  Burge Fauna (Barstovian, Ba3), Nebraska, 159R, 164R, 177R, 188R, 189L, 189R, 199R
  Burkeville Fauna (Barstovian, Ba2), Texas, 176L, 176R, 178R, 199R
  Butler Spring Local Fauna (Rancholabrean), Kansas, 212, 224L, 271R
  Buttonwillow Local Fauna (Blancan, BlIII), California, 245R, 256R
  Cabbage Patch local faunas (Arikareean, Ar1-2), Montana, 164L, 199R
  Calgary 2E Local Fauna (Torrejonian, To2?-3?), Alberta, 32, 49R, 51L
  California Wash Local Fauna (Blancan, Bl2, BlV), Arizona, 212, 220R, 247R, 259L, 271R
  Cambridge Local Fauna (Hemphillian, Hh2), Nebraska, 170L, 170R, 191R, 199R
  Camel Canyon Local Fauna (Hemphillian, Hh3), Arizona, 271R
  Camrose Local Fauna (Rancholabrean, Rbl), Alberta, 212
  Candelaria Local Fauna (Uintan, Ui2), Texas, 78R, 93, 95, 104R
  Canyon Ferry Fauna (Arikareean, ?Ar3), Montana, 163R
  Cape Deceit Local Fauna (Blancan, BlV, or Irvingtonian, Ir1), Alaska, 222L, 223L
  Capps Pit Local Fauna (Hemphillian, Hh1), Texas, 174R, 190R, 199R
  Cedar Mountain Local Fauna (Clarendonian, Cl1), Nevada, 160L, 160R, 199R
  Cedar Point Local Fauna (Tiffanian, Ti3), Wyoming, 31, 58R
  Cedar Ridge Local Fauna (Whitneyan), Wyoming, 128R
  Cedar Run Local Fauna (Arikareean, Ar4), Texas, 176L, 199R
  Centerville Beach Local Fauna (Irvingtonian, IrI), California, 249R, 261R
  Cerrillos Local Fauna (Wasatchian, ?Wa3), New Mexico, 105R
  Chamita Local Fauna (Hemphillian, Hh2), New Mexico, 279L
  Christian Ranch Local fauna (Hemphillian, Hh3), Texas, 174R,

179R, 192L, 199R

Christmas Valley Local Fauna (Hemphillian, Hh3), Oregon, 253L

Circle Local Fauna (Tiffanian, Ti4), Montana, 31, 53R, 58R

Cita Canyon Fauna (Blancan, Bl2, BlV), Texas (see Upper Cita Canyon; Lower Cita Canyon local faunas), 212, 247R, 259R, 271R

Clarendon Fauna (Clarendonian, Cl1 and 2), Texas, 174L, 180R, 189R, 190R, 199R

Clarendon Local Fauna (Clarendonian, Cl1), Texas, 189R

Coal Valley Fauna (Cerrotejonian, = ca. Clarendonian, Cl1), Nevada, 160R, 199R

Cochrane I Local Fauna (Tiffanian, Ti1), Alberta, 32, 54R, 57L

Cochrane II Local Fauna (Tiffanian, Ti1), Alberta, 32, 54R, 57L

Cochrane Local Fauna (Rancholabrean, Rlb), Alberta, 212

Coffee Ranch Local Fauna (Hemphillian, Hh3), Texas, 159R, 171L, 174R, 179R, 191R, 192L, 199R, 271R, 279

Commanche Point Local Fauna (Barstovian, Ba3), California, 156R, 190L

Concha Local Fauna (Blancan, Bl1, BlI), Chihuahua, Mexico, 216L, 216R, 217L, 243R, 244R, 254L

Conard Fissure Local Fauna (Irvingtonian, Ir2, IrII), Arkansas, 212, 222L, 223L, 263L

Cold Spring Fauna (Barstovian, Ba3), Texas, 175R, 176L, 176R, 180L, 189L

Cold Spring Local Fauna (Barstovian, Ba3), Texas, 175R, 177L, 179L

Coleman IIA Local Fauna (Irvingtonian, Ir2), Florida, 212, 222L

Commanche Point Local Fauna (Cerrotejonian, = ca. Clarendonian, Cl1), California, 156R, 199R

Cook Ranch Local Fauna (Orellan), Montana, 128L, 143L

Coso Mountains Local Fauna, California, Bl2, BlIV, 212, 257R

County Line Local Fauna (Irvingtonian, IrII), Iowa, 263L

Courtland Canal Local Fauna (Irvingtonian, Ir1), Kansas, 212, 221R

Cragin Quarry equivalent fauna, Kansas, 212, 224L

Cragin Quarry Local Fauna (Rancholabrean), Kansas, 212, 224L, 271R

Cronese Local Fauna (Barstovian, Ba3), California, 159L, 188L, 199R

Csarnotan faunas, Europe, 245L

Cub Creek Local Fauna (Torrejonian, To3), Wyoming, 30, 49R, 51R, 52R, 54L

Cudahy Local Fauna (Irvingtonian, Ir2, IrII), Kansas, 212, 213L, 222R, 223L, 226R, 250L, 262L, 263L, 271R

Cudahy Local Fauna equivalent, Texas, 212

Cumberland Cave Local Fauna (Irvingtonian, Ir2, IrII), Maryland, 212, 221R, 222L, 223L, 262R

Curtis Ranch Local Fauna (Irvingtonian, Ir1, IrI), Arizona, 212, 216L, 220R, 221L, 222L, 226L, 248R, 260L, 271R

Dad Local Fauna (Wasatchian, Wa4), Wyoming, 102L

Dalton Local Fauna (Hemphillian, Hh1), Nebraska, 170L, 200L

Deep River Fauna (Hemingfordian, Hh2 - Barstovian, Ba1), Montana, 187R, 200L

Deep River Formation (Arikareean, Ar1), Montana, 163L, 163R

Deer Lodge Fauna (Hemphillian, Hh1), Montana, 164R, 200L

Deer Park Local Fauna (Bl2, BlIII), Kansas, 212, 219L, 245R, 255R, 256R

Delmont Local Fauna (Blancan, Bl2), South Dakota, 212

Devil's Den Local Fauna (Holocene), Florida, 225R

Devil's Gulch Mbr., Valentine Formation, fauna of (Barstovian, Ba3), Nebraska, 188R, 200L

Devil's Nest Airport Local Fauna (Hemphillian, Hh3), Nebraska, 212, 216R, 253R

Dixon Local Fauna (Blancan, Bl2, BlV), Kansas, 212, 218L, 219L, 220L, 245R, 259R

Doby Springs Local Fauna (Rancholabrean, RlB), Oklahoma, 212

Dome Spring Fauna (Barstovian, Ba1), California, 158L, 196, 200L

Donnelly Ranch Local Fauna (Blancan, Bl2), Colorado, 212, 218L

Donnybrook Local Fauna (Torrejonian, To3?), North Dakota, 31, 51R

Dove Springs Fauna (Montediablan, = ca. Clarendonian, Cl2), California, 159R, 200L

Downey Dump Local Fauna (Irvingtonian, RlbI), Idaho, 263R

Dragon Local Fauna (Torrejonian, To1), Utah, 29, 43R, 47L, 47R, 48L, 50L, 50R

Drinkwater Local Fauna (Hemphillian, Hh1), Oregon, 162L, 200L

Duchesne River Fauna (Duchesnean), Utah, 129L

Duck Creek Local Fauna (Rancholabrean, Rlb), Kansas, 212

Duncan Local Fauna (Blancan, ?BlIII), Arizona, 245R, 258L, **264L**

Eagle Nest Local Fauna (Tiffanian, Ti1), Wyoming, 54L

Easley Ranch Local Fauna (Rancholabrean, Rbl), Texas, 212

El Casco Local Fauna (Irvingtonian, IrI), California, 249L, 260L

El Tajo de Tequixquiac Local Fauna (Rancholabrean), Mexico, 241R

Empress Local Fauna (Rancholabrean, Rlb), Alberta, 212

Etouaires Local Fauna (Villafranchian), France, 247L

Eubanks Fauna (Barstovian, Ba1), Colorado, 173L, 200L

Eubanks Fauna (Barstovian, Ba1), Colorado, 173L, 200L

Farish Ranch Local Fauna (Clarendonian, Cl1), Texas, 177R, 200L

"Feldt Ranch" Local Fauna (= Feltz Ranch L. F.), Nebraska, 169R

Feltz Ranch Local Fauna (Hemphillian, Hh1-2), Nebraska, 169R, 170L, 173R, 198, 200L

Fish Lake Valley Fauna (Clarendonian, Cl1), Nevada, 160L, 189R, 200L

Fish Lake Valley Local Fauna (Clarendonian, Cl1), Nevada, 160L, 160R, 200L

Flat Iron Butte Local Fauna (Blancan, BlIV), Idaho, 212, 215R, 245R, 258L

Flat Tire Local Fauna (Blancan, Bl2), Arizona, 212, 218L

Flint Creek Fauna (Barstovian, Ba1), Montana, 162L, 164R, 200L

Flint Hill Local Fauna (Hemingfordian, He1), South Dakota, 172L, 186L, 200L

Formosovka 2, Russia, ca. 8 Ma, 238R

Fort Logan Fauna (Arikareean, Ar1 or 2), Montana, 163L, 200L

Four Mile Local Fauna (Wasatchian, Wa1-2), Colorado, 102L, 107L

Fox Canyon Local Fauna (Blancan, Bl1, BlIII), Kansas, 212, 216R, 217L, 217R, 219L, 243L, 243R, 244L, 244R, 246L, 255L, 277R

Frank Ranch Local Fauna (Barstovian, Ba1), Montana, 164R, 200L

Ft. Qu'Apelle Local Fauna (Rancholabrean, Rlb), Saskatchewan, 212

Fyllan Cave Local Fauna (Irvingtonian, IrII), Texas, 262R

Garbani Local Fauna (Puercan, Pu3?), Montana, 31, 45R, 46L

Garvin Farm Local Fauna (Arikareean, Ar4 - Hemingfordian, He1), Texas, 178R, 186L, 200L

Garvin Gully Fauna (Arikareean, Ar4-Hemingfordian, He1), Texas, 176L, 200L

Gashato Fauna, Mongolia, 68L

Gas Tank Hill Local Fauna (= Flagstaff Peak Locality; Puercan, Pu2?), Utah, 28, 45L, 46L

Gering Formation, fauna of (Arikareean, Ar1), Nebraska, 165R, 184R, 200L

Gidley Local Fauna (Torrejonian, To3), Montana, 31, 49R, 50L, 51R, 57L

Gilliland Local Fauna (Irvingtonian, Ir1, IrI), Texas, 212, 218R, 221R, 222L, 222R, 228L, 261L

Goodnight Fauna (Hemphillian, Hh3), Texas, 174R, 200L

Goodrich Local Fauna (Barstovian, Ba3), Texas, 177L, 200L

Gordon Local Fauna (Irvingtonian, Ir3), Nebraska, 212, 223L

Grand View Local Fauna (Blancan, Bl2, BlV or Irvingtonian, Ir1, IrI), Idaho, 212, 215R, 217R, 218L, 218R, 219L, 247R, 257R, 258L, 259L, 271R

Green Hills Fauna (Barstovian, Ba1), California, 158L, 159L, 168R, 187L, 187R, 200L

Hagerman Local Fauna (Blancan, Bl1, BlIII), Idaho, 212, 215R, 217L, 217R, 218L, 218R, 219L, 255L, 255R, 256L, 256R, 257R, 259L

Haile XIVA Local Fauna (Rancholabrean, Rlb), Florida, 212

Haile XVA Local Fauna (Blancan, Bl2), Florida, 212, 218L

Haile XVIA Local Fauna (Irvingtonian, Ir1), Florida, 212, 218R

Hainin Local Fauna (Montian Stage), Belgium, 67L

Halfway Fauna, Duchesne River Formation, Uinta Basin (Uintan, Ui2), 78R, 84L, 84R, 90L, 101R, 104R, 129L

Hall Ash Local Fauna, Kansas, 212

Harbicht Hill Local Fauna (Lancian), Montana, 44L

Hares Local Fauna (Torrejonian, To3?), North Dakota, 31, 51R

Harrison Formation, fauna of (Arikareean, Ar3), Nebraska, 166L, 167L, 185L, 200L

Hart Draw Local Fauna (Blancan, BIII), Kansas, 255R, 256L, 257L, 258L

Haymaker's Orchard Local Fauna (Blancan, B11, BIII), Washington, 217L, 243L, 254R

Hay Springs Local Fauna (Irvingtonian, Ir3; RlbI), Nebraska, 212, 223L, 263R

Hell's Hollow Local Fauna (Puercan, Pu1), Montana, 31, 43R, 44L

Hemme Hills Local Fauna (Hemphillian, Hh3), California, 155R, 196, 200L

Hemphill Local Fauna (Hemphillian, Hh1), Texas, 190R, 191R

Hidden Treasure Spring Local Fauna (Hemingfordian, He2), California, 158L, 200L

Higgins Local Fauna (Hemphillian, Hh1–2), Oklahoma, 174R, 175L, 190R, 191R, 200L

Hill-Shuler Fauna (Rancholabrean, Rlb), Texas, 212

Holloman Local Fauna (Irvingtonian, Ir1), Oklahoma, 212, 221L

Horse Quarry Local Fauna (Blancan, Bl2), Idaho, 212

Howard Ranch Local Fauna (Rancholabrean, Rlb), Texas, 212

Hudspeth Local Fauna (Blancan, Bl2), Texas, 212, 218L

Ingleside Local Fauna (Rancholabrean, Rbl), Texas, 212

Inglis IA Local Fauna (?Irvingtonian, ?Ir1), Florida, 212, 218R, 222L

Iron Canyon Fauna (Clarendonian, Cl1), California, 159L

Irvington Local Fauna (Irvingtonian, Ir1), California, 212, 221R, 222L, 223L, 261R, 271R

Itaboraí Fauna (Riochican), Brazil, 68L

Jackass Butte Local Fauna (Blancan, Bl2), Idaho, 212

Java Local Fauna (Irvingtonian, Ir1, IrI), South Dakota, 212, 222R, 262R, **264R**

Jinglebob Local Fauna (Rancholabrean, Rlb), Kansas, 212

John Day "Fauna" (Arikareean, Ar1–4; Hemingfordian, He1), Oregon, 160R, 200L

Jones Fauna (Rancholabrean, Rlb), Kansas, 212

Kanopolis Local Fauna (Irvingtonian, Ir3; RlbI), Kansas, 212, 223L, 263R

Keefe Canyon Local Fauna (Blancan, Bl1) Kansas, 212, 219L

Keefer Hill Local Fauna (Tiffanian, Ti1), Wyoming, 30, 54L, 54R, 57L

Kelley Road Local Fauna (Hemphillian, Hh1 equiv.), Wyoming, 241R, 252R

Kennesaw Local Fauna (Barstovian, Ba3), Colorado, 173R, 200L

Kentuck Local Fauna (Irvingtonian, Ir1), Kansas, 212, 222R, 261L

Kettleman Hills Local Fauna (Blancan, BlIII), California, 245R

Kimball Fauna (Hemphillian, Hh1), Nebraska, 162L, 170L, 170R, 173R, 191R, 200L

Labahia Mission Local Fauna (Hemphillian, Hh1–2), Texas, 176L, 177R, 200L

LaBarge fauna (Wasatchian, Wa4), Wyoming, 103L

Lapara Creek Fauna (Barstovian, Ba3, - Clarendonian, Cl1), Texas, 176L, 177L, 177R, 200L

LaPoint Local Fauna (Duchesnean), Utah, 79L, 84L, 146R

Laudate Local Fauna (Torrejonian, To2?), California, 32, 51L

Lava Mountains Fauna (Hemphillian, Hh1), California, 159R, 200L

Layer Cake Local Fauna (Blancan, Bl1), California, 212, 215R, 216R, 217L, 217R, 271R

Le Coupet Local Fauna (Villanyian), France, 248L

Lind Coulee Local Fauna (Hemphillian, Hh3), Washington, 242R, 243R, 244R, 253R

Lisco Local Fauna (Blancan, Bl2), Nebraska, 212, 219L

Little Egypt Local Fauna (Chadronian, Ch1), Texas, 109L, 134L, 134R, 135L

Littleton Local Fauna (Puercan, Pu1), Colorado, 29, 43R, 44L

Lloyd Local Fauna (Torrejonian, To3?), North Dakota, 31, 51R

Logan Mine Fauna (Arikareean, Ar4), California, 158R, 200R

Love Bone Bed Local Fauna (Clarendonian, Cl2), Florida, 179R, 200L

Lower Bone Valley Fauna (Hemphillian, Hh1), Florida, 200R

Lower Cady Mountain Local Fauna (Hemingfordian, He1), California, 158R, 200R

Lower Cita Canyon Local Fauna (Blancan, Bl2, ?BlV), Texas, 218L, 259R

Lower Rosebud Fauna (Arikareean, Ar2–3), South Dakota, 176L, 200R

Lower Snake Creek Fauna (Barstovian, Ba1), Nebraska, 159L, 161R, 162L, 168R, 173L, 176R, 177L, 186R, 187R, 200R

Mailbox Local Fauna (Hemphillian, Hh3), Nebraska, 192L, 253L

Manatee Local Fauna (Hemphillian, Hh2), Florida, 180R, 200R

Mantua Lentil Local Fauna (Puercan, Pu1), Wyoming, 30, 40L, 43L, 44L

Marsland Fauna (Arikareean, Ar4), Nebraska, 164L, 167L, 167R, 178L, 185L, 185R, 200R

Martin-Anthony Local Fauna (Arikareean, Ar3), Florida, 178L, 200R

Martin Canyon Fauna (Hemingfordian, He1), Colorado, 172R, 200R

Mascall Fauna (Barstovian, Ba1), Oregon, 161R, 162L, 162R, 164R, 187R, 200R

Matthews Ranch Fauna (Cerrotejonian, = ca. Clarendonian, Cl1), California, 158L, 200R

Maxum Local Fauna (Blancan, Bl1, BlI), California, 156L, 200R, 243L, 254L

Mayflower Mine Local Fauna (Clarendonian, Cl2), Montana, 164R, 200R

McCarty's Mountain Local Fauna (Chadronian, Ch1), Montana, 136L

McGehee Local Fauna (Hemphillian, Hh1), Florida, 179R, 180L, 180R, 200R

McKanna Spring Fauna (Barstovian, Ba1), Montana, 162L, 165L, 200R

McKay Reservoir Local Fauna (Hemphillian, Hh3), Oregon, 192L, 200R, 253L

McRay Wash Fauna, Arizona, 212

Medicine Hat sequence, faunas of (Irvingtonian, Ir2 - Rancholabrean, Rlb2), Alberta, 212, 222L

Melbourne Local Fauna (Rancholabrean, Rlb), Florida, 212

Mendevil Ranch Local Fauna (Blancan, Bl2, BlIV), Arizona, 212, 246R, 257R

Mesa de Maya Local Fauna (Rancholabrean, Rlb), Colorado, 212

Midway Fauna (Hemingfordian, He2), Florida, 178R, 179L, 200R

Mink Creek Local Fauna, (Chadronian, Ch2), Wyoming, 149R

Minnechaduza Fauna (Clarendonian, Cl1), Nebraska, 159R, 164R, 169R, 170R, 174L, 177R, 180R, 200R

Mixon Local Fauna (Bone Bed Local Fauna; Hemphillian, Hh1), Florida, 179R, 180L, 191L, 200

Modesto Reservoir Local Fauna (Hemphillian, Hh3), California, 192L, 200R

Monroe Creek Formation, fauna of, (Arikareean, Ar2), Nebraska, 166L, 184R

Moore Pit Local Fauna (Rancholabrean, Rlb), Texas, 212

Moscow Local Fauna (Barstovian, Ba1), Texas, 176R, 177L, 200R

Mount Coupet Local Fauna (Villafranchian), France, 214R

Mount Eden Local Fauna (Hemphillian, Hh3), California, 159R, 192L, 200R

Mt. (Mount) Blanco Local Fauna (Blancan, Bl2, BlV), Texas, 215L, 218L, 271R

Mt. (or Mount) Scott Local Fauna (Rancholabrean, RlbII), Kansas, 212, 224L, 226R, 271R

Mulholland Fauna (Hemphillian, Hh2), California, 155R, 200R

Mullen I Fauna (Blancan, Bl2, BlV), Nebraska, 212, 219L, 259R

Mullen II Local Fauna (Irvingtonian, Ir2), Nebraska, 212

Murietta Local Fauna (Irvingtonian, IrII), California, 264L

Nash Local Fauna (Irvingtonian, Ir1), Kansas, 212, 222R

Nettle Spring Fauna (Montediablan, = ca. Clarendonian, Cl2), California, 158L, 200R

Newberry Fauna (Arikareean, Ar3–4), Florida, 178L

New Fork Fauna (Wasatchian, Wa4–?Br1), Wyoming, 103L

Nightingale Road Local Fauna (Clarendonian, Cl2), Nevada, 162L

Nine Foot Rapids Local Fauna (Blancan, BlV), Idaho, 215R, 259L, 259R

Niobrara River Fauna (Barstovian, Ba3), Nebraska, 169L, 188R, 189L, 189R, 200R

Norden Bridge Local Fauna (Barstovian, Ba2), Nebraska, 168R, 169L, 182L, 188R, 200R

North Boulder Valley Fauna (Arikareean, Ar3 or ?4), Montana, 164L, 165L, 200R

North Coalinga Local Fauna (Barstovian, Ba2), California, 156R, 200R

North Livermore Ave. Local Fauna (Irvingtonian, IrII), California, 262L

North Silver Star Triangle local faunas (Hemphillian, Hh1), Montana, 200R

North Tejon Hills Fauna (Montediablan, = ca. Clarendonian, Cl2), California, 157L, 200R

Old Wagonroad Local Fauna (Clarendonian, Cl1), Montana, 164R, 200R

Old Windmill Local Fauna (Clarendonian, Cl1), Montana, 164R, 200R

Olive Local Fauna (Tiffanian, Ti4), Montana, 53R

Olive Dell Local Fauna (Irvingtonian, IrII), California, 261R

O'Neill Local Fauna (Torrejonian, To3), New Mexico, 28, 51R

Optima Local Fauna (Hemphillian, Hh3), Oklahoma, 171L, 179R, 191R, 200R

Oshkosh Local Fauna (Hemphillian, Hh1–2), Nebraska, 170L, 200R

Otis Basin Local Fauna (Hemphillian, Hh1–2), Oregon, 162L, 200R

Panaca Local Fauna (Blancan, BlIII), Nevada, 245R, 246L, 256L

Pawnee Creek Fauna (Hemingfordian, He2 - Barstovian, Ba1–2), Colorado, 172R, 173L, 173R, 187R, 201L

Pearson Ranch Fauna (Duchesnean), California, 100R

Phillips Ranch Local Fauna (Hemingfordian, He2), California, 158L, 201L

Phosphate Company Pit No. 2 (Arikareean, Ar4), Florida, 178L

Pilgrim Creek Local Fauna (Chadronian, Ch2), Wyoming, 131

Pinole Local Fauna (Hemphillian, Hh3), California, 155R, 156L, 159R, 201L, 212, 216L

Pipestone Springs Local Fauna (Chadronian, Ch2), Montana, 127R, 129L, 135R, 136L, 136R, 137L, 137R, 138L

Podlesice Fauna (Turolian), Poland, 242L

Point Blank Fauna (Barstovian, Ba1), Texas, 176L, 176R, 201L

Police Point Local Fauna (Tiffanian, Ti3?), Alberta, 32, 53R, 58R

Port Kennedy Cave Local Fauna (Irvingtonian, ?Ir1 or 2), Pennsylvania, 212, 222L, 223L

Porvenir Local Fauna (Chadronian, Ch1), Texas, 78R, 104R, 109L, 133R, 134L, 134R, 135L, 146R

Purgatory Hill Local Fauna (Puercan, Pu3?), Montana, 31, 45R, 46L

Pyramid Hill Local Fauna (Arikareean, Ar3), California, 156R, 201L

Quarry A Local Fauna (Hemingfordian, He1), Colorado, 172R, 186L, 201L

Quartz Basin Local Fauna (Barstovian, Ba2), Oregon, 162L, 201L

Quincy Local Fauna (Hemingfordian, He2), Florida, 179L

Rainbow Beach Fauna, Idaho, 212

Rancho Gaitan Local Fauna (Chadronian, Ch1), Chihuahua, Mexico, 143L

Rancho La Brea Local Fauna (Rancholabrean, Rlb; RlbII), California, 212, 223R

Randlett Fauna, Duchesne River Formation, Uinta Basin (Uintan, Ui2), Utah, 78R, 84R, 84R, 90L, 101R, 104R, 129L

Rattlesnake Fauna (Hemphillian, Hh1–2), Oregon, 162R, 191L,

201L

Rebielice Fauna (Villafranchian), Poland, 247R

Red Basin Local Fauna (Barstovian, Ba2), Oregon, 162L, 201L

Red Corral Local Fauna (Blancan, Bl1), Texas, 212

Reddick Local Fauna (Rancholabrean, Rlb), Florida, 212

Redington Local Fauna (Hemphillian, Hh3), Arizona, 192L, 201L, 271R, 279L

Red Light Local Fauna (Blancan, Bl2), Texas, 212, 218L

Rexroad Local Fauna (Blancan, Bl1, BlII-III), Kansas, 212, 216R, 217R, 218L, 219L, 226L, 243L, 243R, 244L, 246L, 255L, 255R, 256L, 256R, 271R, 277R

Rezabek Local Fauna (Irvingtonian, Ir3, RlbI), Kansas, 212, 223L, 264L

Ricardo Fauna (Clarendonian, Cl1), California, 158L, 159R, 189R, 201L

Rincon Local Fauna (= Yepomera Local Fauna; Hemphillian, Hh3), Chihuahua, Mexico, 271R

Rizzi Ranch Local Fauna (Arikareean, Ar1 or 2), Nevada, 160R, 201L

Robert Local Fauna (Rancholabrean), Kansas, 212, 224L

Roca Neyra Local Fauna (Villanyian), France, 247L, 248L

Roche Percée Local Fauna (Tiffanian, Ti4), Saskatchewan, 32, 53R, 59R

Rock Bench Local Fauna (Torrejonian, To3), Polecat Bench, Wyoming, 30, 47L, 49R, 51R, 54L

Rock Creek Local Fauna (Irvingtonian, Ir1), Texas, 212, 218R, 221L, 221R

Rome Fauna (Hemphillian, Hh1), Oregon, 201L, 253L

Runningwater Fauna (Hemingfordian, He1), Nebraska, 167R, 186L, 201L

Rushville Local Fauna (Irvingtonian, Ir3), Nebraska, 212, 223L

Sam Houston Local Fauna (Barstovian, Ba3), Texas, 177L, 201L

Sandahl Local Fauna (Irvingtonian, Ir3; RlbI), Kansas, 212, 223L, 263R

Sand Canyon Fauna (Barstovian, Ba3), Colorado, 173R, 201L

Sand Coulee fauna (Wasatchian, Wa1), Wyoming, 86L

Sand Draw Local Fauna (Blancan, Bl2, BlIII), Nebraska, 212, 219L, 219R, 243R, 245R, 246L, 246R, 255R, 256R

Sanders Local Fauna (Blancan, Bl2, BlIV), Kansas, 212, 219L, 219R, 246R, 255R, 256L, 258L

Sand Point Local Fauna (Blancan, Bl2, BlIV), Idaho, 212, 215R, 245R, 246R, 257R, 258L

Sand Wash fauna (Uintan, Ui1), Wyoming, 89L, 107L

Santa Fe River IB Local Fauna (Blancan, Bl2), Florida, 212, 218L, 218R, 220L

Sant Ranch Local Fauna (Barstovian, Ba1), Montana, 164R, 201L

Santee Local Fauna (Hemphillian, Hh3), Nebraska, 192L, 201L, 212, 216L, 243R, 244R, 253R

Sappa Local Fauna (Irvingtonian, Ir1, IrI), Nebraska, 212, 222R, 248L, 261L

Saskatoon Local Fauna (Rancholabrean, Rlb), Saskatchewan, 212

Saw Rock Canyon Local Fauna (?Hemphillian or ?Blancan, Hh3, BlI), Kansas, 212, 216L, 216R, 243L, 243R, 244R, 254L

SB-1A Local Fauna (Arikareean, Ar3), Florida, 178L

Seaboard Local Fauna (Hemingfordian, He1), Florida, 178L, 178R, 201L

Seger Local Fauna (Blancan, Ba2), Kansas, 212

Seneca Local Fauna (Blancan, Bl2), Nebraska, 212, 219L

Sequence Canyon Fauna (Hemphillian, Hh2–3), California, 158L, 201L

Serendipity Local Fauna (Uintan, Ui2), Texas, 104L, 104R

Sharktooth Hill Local Fauna (Barstovian, Ba2), California, 156R, 201L

Sheep Creek Fauna (Hemingfordian, He2), Nebraska, 158R, 168L, 168R, 185R, 186L, 187L, 187R, 201L

Silver Coulee Local Fauna (Tiffanian), Montana, 53R

Skull Ridge Member, Tesuque Formation (Barstovian, Ba1), New Mexico, 168R

Skull Springs Fauna (Barstovian, Ba2), Oregon, 162L, 168R, 201L

Slaton Local Fauna (Irvingtonian, Ir3, RlbI), Texas, 212, 223L
Smiths Valley Fauna (Hemphillian, Hh1–2), Nevada, 160R, 162L, 191L, 197, 201L
Snake Creek Fauna (Clarendonian, Cl2), Nebraska, 170R, 201L
Snowville Local Fauna (Irvingtonian, RlbI), Utah, 263R
South Tejon Hills Fauna (Cerrotejonian, = ca. Clarendonian, Cl1), California, 157L, 201L
Stewart Spring Fauna (Barstovian, Ba2), Nevada, 160L, 201L
Sucker Creek Fauna (Barstovian, Ba2), Oregon, 162L, 201L
Swan Hills Local Fauna (Site 1; Tiffanian, Ti4), Alberta, 32, 53R, 59L
Swift Current Creek Fauna (Uintan, Ui2), Saskatchewan, 107R
Sycamore Creek Fauna (Cerrotejonian, = ca. Clarendonian, Cl1), California, 155R, 201L
Tapo Canyon Local Fauna (Uintan, Ui2), California, 100R
Tapo Ranch Local Fauna (Uintan, Ui2), California, 100R
Taunton Local Fauna (Blancan, BlIII), Washington, 212, 256L
Tavenner Ranch Local Faunas (Arikareean), Montana, 201L
Teewinot Local Fauna (Hemphillian), Wyoming, 241R
Tehama Local Fauna (Blancan, Bl1), California, 212
Thayne Local Fauna (Blancan, BlV), Wyoming, 247R, 259L
Thomas Farm Local Fauna (Hemingfordian, He1), Florida, 178R, 186L, 201L
Thompson Creek Local Fauna (Chadronian, Ch2), Montana, 129L
Thousand Creek Fauna (Hemphillian, Hh1–2), Nevada, 162L, 191L, 201L
Tiffany Local Fauna (Tiffanian, Ti4), Colorado, 53L
Tonque Local Fauna (Duchesnean), New Mexico, 90R, 105R
Tonopah Local Fauna (Barstovian, Ba2), Nevada, 160L, 201L
Trinity River Local Fauna (Barstovian, Ba1), Texas, 176R, 177L, 201L
Tusker Local Fauna (Blancan, Bl2, BlV or Irvingtonian, Ir1), Arizona, 212, 220R, 247R, 258R
Two Mile Bar Local Fauna (Barstovian, Ba3), California, 156R
Unnamed fauna, lower Sharps Formation (Arikareean, Ar1), South Dakota, 201L
Unnamed fauna, Murphy Member, Snake Creek Formation (Clarendonian, Cl1), Nebraska, 201L
Unnamed local fauna (Irvingtonian, Ir1), Texas, 212
Unnamed local fauna, Martin Canyon beds (Hemingfordian, He1), Colorado, 201L
Upper Alturas Local Fauna (Blancan, Bl1, BlI), California, 242R, 243R, 244L, 244R, 254L
Upper Bone Valley Fauna (Hemphillian, Hh3), Florida, 181L, 181R, 192L, 192R, 201R
Upper Cady Mountain Local Fauna (Hemingfordian, He2), California, 158R, 201R
Upper Cita Canyon Local Fauna (Blancan, Bl2, BlV), Texas, 218L, 220L, 259L
Upper Dry Canyon Fauna (Barstovian, Ba1), California, 158L, 201R
Upper Rosebud Fauna (= Wounded Knee-Rosebud Fauna) (Arikareean, Ar4), South Dakota, 201R
Upper Tecopa Local Fauna (Irvingtonian, IrII), California, 262L
Uptegrove Local Fauna (Hemphillian, Hh3), Nebraska, 170L, 191R, 201R
Valentine Fauna (Barstovian, Ba2–3), Nebraska, 164R, 173R, 187R, 188R, 189R
Vallecito Creek Fauna (Blancan, Bl2-Irvingtonian, Ir1, IrI), California, 212, 215R, 217R, 220R, 221R, 222L, 260R, 271R
Vendargues Fauna (Turolian), France, 242L
Vera Local Fauna (Irvingtonian, Ir2, IrII), Texas, 212, 222R, 263L
Verde Local Fauna (Blancan, Bl1, BlI), Arizona, 212, 216L, 216R, 217L, 243R, 244L, 246R, 254L
Vero Local Fauna (Rancholabrean, Rlb), Florida, 212
Vialette Local Fauna (Villafranchian), Europe, 245L, 247L
Villafranchian Fauna, Italy, 213R
Villanyian Fauna, Europe, 213R
Vim-Peetz Local Fauna (Barstovian, Ba3), Colorado, 173R, 201L
Virgin Valley Fauna (Barstovian, Ba1), Nevada, 187R, 201L

Wagonroad Local Fauna (Puercan, Pu3?), Utah, 28, 45L, 46L, 47R, 50L
Walbeck Local Fauna (late middle Paleocene), Germany, 67L
Warm Springs Local Fauna (Hemingfordian, He1), Oregon, 161R, 186R, 201R
Warren Local Fauna (Hemphillian, Hh3), California, 159R, 192L, 201R
Wathena Local Fauna (Irvingtonian, Ir1, IrI), Kansas, 212, 222R, 261L
Wellsch Valley Local Fauna (Irvingtonian, Ir1, IrI) Saskatchewan, 212, 218R, 220L, 221L, 221R, 228L, 241R, 248R, 249L, 260R
Wewela Local Fauna (Arikareean, Ar2), South Dakota, 166L, 171R, 201R
Whistler Squat Local Fauna (Uintan, Ui1), Texas, 104L, 104R, 107L
White Bluffs Local Fauna (Blancan, Bl1, BlI), Washington, 212, 216R, 217L, 217R, 218R, 243L, 244L, 254R
White Cone Local Fauna (Hemphillian, Hh3), Arizona, 156L, 201R, 271R
White Rock Local Fauna (Blancan, Bl2, BlV), Kansas, 212, 218L, 219L, 220L, 255R, 259R
Wikieup Local Fauna (Hemphillian, Hh3), Arizona, 192L, 201R, 271R, 279L
Wildhorse Butte Local Fauna (Blancan, BlV), Idaho, 212, 258R
Williston IIIA Local Fauna (Rancholabrean, Rlb), Florida, 212
Wilson Valley Local Fauna (Irvingtonian, IrII), Kansas, 263L
Woody Local Fauna (Arikareean, Ar3), California, 156R, 201R
Wolf Ranch Local Fauna (Blancan, Bl2), Arizona, 212, 218L, 271R
Wounded Knee-Harrison Fauna (Arikareean, Ar3), South Dakota, 171L, 201R
Wounded Knee-Monroe Creek Fauna (Arikareean, Ar2), South Dakota, 171L, 171R, 172L, 184R, 201R
Wounded Knee-Rosebud Fauna (Arikareean, Ar4), South Dakota, 166L, 172L, 185L, 185R, 201R
Wounded Knee-Sharps Fauna (Arikareean, Ar1), South Dakota, 145L, 165R, 171R, 184R, 201R
Yepomera Local Fauna (Hemphillian, Hh3), Mexico, 192L, 201R, 216R, 217L, 243R, 254R
Yoder Local Fauna (Chadronian, Ch1), Wyoming, 133R, 134L, 134R, 135L, 136L
ZX Bar Local Fauna (Hemphillian, Hh3), Nebraska, 170R, 201R
Locality (some lithostratigraphic units do not specify individual localities):
7-UP Butte Locality (Tiffanian, Ti2), Montana, 31
"A" sites, Caliente Formation (Arikareean, Ar3, to early Hemingfordian, He1), California, 157R, 199L
Agate Springs Quarry (Arikareean, Ar4), Nebraska, 167L, 185L, 198
Adair Ranch Quarry (Hemphillian, Hh1), Oklahoma, 174R, 199L
Airport Locality (Tiffanian, Ti4), Wyoming, 30, 59L
Alberta Core Hole 66-1 (Torrejonian, To2?), Alberta, 32, 40R
Aletomeryx Quarry (Hemingfordian, He1), Nebraska, 167R, 199L
Alexander Locality (Puercan, Pu1), Colorado, 29, 44L
American Museum of Natural History Quarry 7 (Clarendonian, Cl2), Nebraska, 170R, 199R
Animas River Valley sites (Torrejonian, To2–3), New Mexico, 28
Annex Locality (Tiffanian, Ti3), Texas, 28, 58R
Aycross Formation, Big Horn Basin (Bridgerian, Br1–2), Wyoming, 78L
Aycross Formation, Togwotee Summit, Togwotee Pass (Bridgerian, Br1–2), Wyoming, 78L
Aycross Formation, Wind River Basin (Bridgerian, Br1–2), Wyoming, 78L
Bab's Basin Locality (Torrejonian, To2), New Mexico, 28, 52L
Baca Formation (Duchesnean), New Mexico, 78R
Balzac West Locality (Torrejonian, To2?), Alberta, 32
Bangtail Locality (Tiffanian, Ti1), Montana, 57L
Bayfield Locality (Tiffanian, Ti5), Colorado, 28, 59R
Battle Mountain Locality (Tiffanian, Ti3), Wyoming, 30, 53R, 58R

Bechtold Locality or Site (Puercan, Pu3?), Montana, 31, 40R, 45R, 46L

Big Multi Locality (Clarkforkian, Cf2), Wyoming, 29, 61L, 65L

Big Pocket Locality (= KU loc. 13) (Torrejonian, To2), New Mexico, 28, 52L

Bison Basin Saddle Locality (Tiffanian, Ti2), 58L

Biscuit Butte Locality (Puercan, Pu3?), Montana, 31

Biscuit Springs Locality (Puercan, Pu3?), Montana, 31

Black Peaks Formation, Big Bend National Park (?Clarkforkian, Cf3; Wasatchian, Wa1), Texas, 104L

Black Stripe Site (Puercan, Pu2?), New Mexico, 28

Black Toe Site (Puercan, Pu2?), New Mexico, 28

Bob's Jaw Locality (Torrejonian, To2), New Mexico, 28, 50R

Bone Bed A, Tepee Trail Formation, Wind River Basin (Uintan, Ui1), Wyoming, 78R, 89L, 97L, 99L

Box T Quarry (Hemphillian, Hh2), Texas, 174R, 175L, 180L, 181L, 191L, 191R

Brea Canyon localities (Uintan, Ui2), California, 78R, 99L

Brice Canyon Locality (Tiffanian, Ti5), Wyoming, 30

Bridgeport quarries (Hemingfordian, He1), Nebraska, 167R, 199R

Brisbane Locality (Tiffanian, Ti3), North Dakota, 32, 53R, 58R

Buckman Hollow Locality (Clarkforkian, Cf2), Wyoming, 29, 64R, 65R

Bug Creek Anthills Locality (age disputed), Montana, 41R, 42L

Burge Quarry (Barstovian, Ba3), Nebraska, 169L

Burkeville site (Barstovian, Ba2), Texas, 176R

Butte Locality (Tiffanian, Ti2), Montana, 58L

California Institute of Technology localities
    150 (Duchesnean), 84L
    292 (Uintan-Chadronian), 100L, 100R
    315 (Hemingfordian, He2), 158L, 199R
    322 (Barstovian, Ba1), 158L, 199R
    323 (Barstovian, Ba1), 158L, 199R

California Wash faunal site (Blancan, Bl2, BlV), Arizona, 216L

Calgary 7E Locality (Torrejonian, To3), 32

Campbell Pit (Hemphillian, Hh3), Oklahoma, 175L, 199R

Camp San Onofre, Santiago Formation (Uintan, U12), southern California, 78R, 99L

Canyon Ferry sites (Orellan), Montana, 143L

Canyon Ski Quarry (Tiffanian, Ti4), Alberta, 32

Carthage Coal Field (Duchesnean), New Mexico, 78R

Cathedral Bluffs Tongue, Wasatch Formation, Washakie Basin (Wasatchian, Wa4 - Bridgerian, Br1), Wyoming, 78L

Cathedral Bluffs Tongue, Wasatch Formation, Green River Basin (Wasatchian, Wa4 - Bridgerian, Br1), Wyoming, 78L

Cedar Point Quarry (Tiffanian, Ti3), Wyoming, 31, 53R, 58R

Chambers Tuff (see Colmena and Chambers tuffs), 78R

Chadronia Pocket (Chadronian, Ch3), Nebraska, 138L

Chappo Type Locality (Tiffanian, Ti3), Wyoming, 29, 54L, 58R

Chono-Chariach 2 (Pontian), Mongolia, 238R

Christian Place Quarry (Hemphillian, Hh3), Texas, 174R

Christian Ranch Pit 2 (Hemphillian, Hh3), Texas, 174R

City Waterworks site (Hemingfordian, He1), Florida, 178L, 199R

Cleopatra Reservoir Quarry (Clarkforkian, Cf2), Wyoming, 31

Climbing Arrow Formation, Shoddy Springs area (Uintan, Ui2 - Chadronian), Montana, 78R

Coffee Ranch Quarry (Hemphillian, Hh3), Texas, 175L, 190R, 198, 200R

Cole Highway Pit (Clarendonian, Cl2?), Texas, 174R, 190R

Colmena and Chambers tuffs, Candelaria and Porvenir faunas (Duchesnean), Texas, 78R

Colton Formation, Book Cliffs area, Uinta Basin (Wasatchian), Utah, 78L

Coprolite Point Locality (Torrejonian, To3), New Mexico, 28, 51R, 52L

Corral Bluffs Locality (Puercan, Pu2?-3?), Colorado, 29

Crock Tooth Quarry (Tiffanian, Ti4), Wyoming, 31, 58R

Crooked River sites (Barstovian, Ba1), Oregon, 161R

Crookston Bridge Quarry (Barstovian, Ba3), Nebraska, 169L, 200L

Cub Mountain Formation (Duchesnean), New Mexico, 78R

Cuchara Formation, Huerfano Basin (Wasatchian, Wa4), Colorado, 78L

Dalton Quarry (Hemphillian, Hh1), Nebraska, 170L

Debeque Formation, Rifle area, Piceance Basin (Clarkforkian - Wasatchian, Wa2), Colorado, 78L

Dell Creek Quarry (Tiffanian, Ti5), Wyoming, 30, 53R, 59R

Dick's Dig Site (Torrejonian, To1), New Mexico, 28

Dinohyus Site (Arikareean, Ar?), Texas, 200L

Divide Quarry (Tiffanian, Ti4), Wyoming, 31, 58R, 59L

Douglass Quarry (Tiffanian, Ti1), Montana, 31, 54L, 54R, 55L, 57L

Dry Creek Prospect A (Hemingfordian, He2), Nebraska, 168L

Eastern Tornillo Flats Washing Site (Tiffanian, Ti3?), Texas, 28

Emerald Lake assemblage (Chadronian), Wyoming, 149L

Erickson's Landing Locality (Tiffanian, Ti3), Alberta, 32, 53R

Etchegoin Formation sites (Hemphillian), California, 200L

Flat Iron Butte Local Fauna (Blancan, BlIII), Idaho, 215R

Flint Hill Quarry (Hemingfordian, He1), South Dakota, 167R, 172L

Fort Union and Willwood formations, Clark's Fork Basin (Wasatchian, Wa1), Wyoming, 78L

Foster Gulch Locality (Clarkforkian, Cf2), Wyoming, 31, 61L, 64R

Foster Gulch Oil Well no. 1 Locality (Clarkforkian, Cf1), 31

Fowkes Formation (Bridgerian, Br3), Utah, 78R

Four Mile area (Wasatchian, Wa1–2), Washakie Basin, Colorado, 78L

Franimys Hill Locality (Clarkforkian, Cf2), Wyoming, 30

Franklin Phosphate Pit No. 2 (Arikareean, Ar4), Florida, 200L

Friars Formation (Uintan, Ui1), southern California, 78R

Fritz Quarry (Tiffanian, Ti5), Wyoming, 30

Galisteo Formation (Duchesnean), New Mexico, 78R

Garbani Quarry (Puercan, Pu3?), Montana, 31, 45R, 46L

Garvin Farm sites (Hemingfordian, He1), Texas, 175R

Gateway sites (Barstovian, Ba1), Oregon, 161R

Gidley Horse Quarry (Clarendonian, Cl2), Texas, 174L, 188R, 200L

Gidley Quarry (Torrejonian, To3), Montana, 54L, 57

Golden Valley Formation (Wasatchian, Wa2), North Dakota, 78L

Goler Formation sites (Torrejonian, To2), California, 47R, 51L

Gordon Creek Quarry (Barstovian, Ba3), Nebraska, 169L, 200L

Granger Mountain Locality (Clarkforkian, Cf3), 30

"Gray Bull beds," Willwood Formation, Big Horn Basin (Wasatchian, Wa2), Wyoming, 78L

Green River Formation (Bridgerian, Br3, - Duchesnean, Du), central Utah, 78R

Guymon Quarry (Hemphillian, Hh3), Oklahoma, 175L, 200L

Hancock Quarry, Clarno Formation (Duchesnean), Oregon, 78R, 107R

Hannold Hill Formation, Big Bend National Park (Wasatchian, Wa2), Texas, 78L

Harper Quarry (Arikareean, Ar4), Nebraska, 167L

Hemicyon Quarry (Barstovian, Ba3), California, 196

"*Hesperopithecus*" site (Clarendonian, Cl2), Nebraska, 170L, 200L

"Hh" sites, Caliente Formation (Hemphillian, Hh2–3), California, 158L, 200L

Highway Blowout Locality (Tiffanian, Ti2), Montana, 31, 58L

Hollow Locality of La Barge Creek (Clarkforkian), Wyoming, 61L

Holly's Microsite (Clarkforkian, Cf2), Wyoming, 30

Horse and Mastodon Quarry (Barstovian, Ba2), Colorado, 173L, 200L

Horsethief Canyon localities (Torrejonian, To1?), Montana, 31

Indian Meadows Formation, Wind River Basin (Wasatchian, Wa2–3), Wyoming, 78L

Jackson (Hemphillian, Hh1), Wyoming, 252R

Jepsen Quarry (Tiffanian, Ti3), Wyoming, 31

Jepsen Valley Locality (Tiffanian, Ti5), Wyoming, 30

Jimmy Camp Creek Locality (Puercan, Pu2?–3?), Colorado, 29

Jim Woodruf Dam site (Hemingfordian, He1), Florida, 178L, 200L

Joe's Bone Bed (Tiffanian, Ti5), Texas, 28, 54L, 55R, 59R

Judson Locality (Tiffanian, Ti3), North Dakota, 32, 53R, 58R

Kat Quarry (Clarendonian, Cl2), Nebraska, 169R, 174L, 191L, 200L

Keefer Hill Locality (Tiffanian; Ti1), Wyoming, 54L, 54R, 55L, 57L

Kern River Formation sites (Hemphillian, Hh1 or 2), California, 200L

Kew Quarry, (Arikareean, Ar1), California, 157R, 184R, 200L

Kinney Rim Member, Washakie Formation, Washakie Basin (Bridgerian, Br2), Wyoming, 78L, 102R

Krause Quarry (Clarkforkian, Cf2), Wyoming, 30

KU localities, New Mexico, 52L
  9 (Torrejonian, To3), 28, 51R, 52L
  13 (Torrejonian, To2), 52L
  15 (Torrejonian, To3?), 52L

L-41, Aycross Formation, Togwotee Pass (Wasatchian, Wa4), Wyoming, 78L, 93, 96R, 97L

Laguna Riviera, Santiago Formation (Uintan, Ui2), southern California, 78R, 99L

LaPoint Member, Duchesne River Formation, Uinta Basin (Duchesnean), Utah, 78R, 98L, 129L

Lebo Quarry (Torrejonian), Crazy Mountain Field, Montana, 47L

Ledge Creek (Chadronian), Wyoming, 136L

Ledge Locality (Tiffanian, Ti3), Wyoming, 29, 54L, 58R

Leidy Quarry (Puercan, Pu1), Wyoming, 31, 40R, 43R

Lemoyne (Hemphillian, Hh1), Nebraska, 253L

Leptarctus Quarry (Clarendonian, Cl2), Nebraska, 169R, 191L, 200R

Limestone Corner (BlIII), Nevada, 256L

Little Muddy Creek Locality (Tiffanian, Ti1), Wyoming, 29, 54L, 57L

Little Pocket Locality (Torrejonian, To3), New Mexico, 28, 51R

Little Sand Coulee Quarry (Clarkforkian, Cf1), Wyoming, 30

Locality 1, Wagon Bed Formation, Badwater area, Wind River Basin (Uintan, Ui2), Wyoming, 78R

Locality 5, Hendry Ranch Member, Badwater area, Wind River Basin (Uintan, Ui2), Wyoming, 78R, 98L

Locality 5, Tabernacle Butte (Bridgerian, Br3), Wyoming, 85L

Locality 5A, Hendry Ranch Member, Badwater area, Wind River Basin (Uintan, Ui2), Wyoming, 98L

Locality 6, Hendry Ranch Member, Badwater area, Wind River Basin (Uintan, Ui2), Wyoming, 78R, 98L

Locality 7, Hendry Ranch Member, Badwater area, Wind River Basin (Uintan, Ui2), Wyoming, 78R, 98L

Locality 17 (Bridgerian, Br2) Wagon Bed Formation, Badwater area, Wind River Basin, Wyoming, 78L, 85L, 98L

Locality 18 (Bridgerian, Br2) Wagon Bed Formation, Badwater area, Wind River Basin, Wyoming, 78L, 98L

Locality 20, Hendry Ranch Member, Badwater area, Wind River Basin (Duchesnean), Wyoming, 78R, 90R, 92, 98L, 106R

Locality 68 (Tiffanian, Ti1), Montana, 54L, 57L

Long Draw Quarry (Tiffanian, Ti4), Wyoming, 30, 53R

"Lost Cabin beds," Willwood Formation, Big Horn Basin (Wasatchian, Wa4), Wyoming, 78L

Lost Cabin Member, Wind River Formation, Wind River Basin (Wasatchian, Wa4 - Bridgerian, Br1), Wyoming, 78L

Love Bone Bed (Clarendonian, Cl2), Florida, 179R, 180R, 200R

Love Quarry (Tiffanian, Ti3), Wyoming, 30, 53R

Lower Adobe Town Member, Washakie Formation, Washakie Basin (Uintan, Ui1), Wyoming, 78R

Lower Blacks Fork Member, Bridger Formation, Green River Basin (Bridgerian, Br2), Wyoming, 78L

Lower Bridger Formation, New Fork-Big Sandy area, Green River Basin (Bridgerian, Br2), Wyoming, 78L

Lower Cady Mountains Local Fauna (Hemingfordian, He1), California, 158R, 196R

Lower Hagerman (Blancan, BlII), Idaho, 255L

Lower Huerfano Formation, Huerfano Basin (Wasatchian, Wa4), Colorado, 78L

Lower Kutz Canyon sites (Torrejonian, To1), New Mexico, 28

Lower Sand Draw Locality (Tiffanian, Ti4), Wyoming, 31

Lower variegated beds, Togwotee Pass (Wasatchian, Wa1 or Wa2), Wyoming, 78L

"Low" Locality (Ti6-Cf1?), Wyoming, 30, 61L

"Lysite beds," Willwood Formation, Bighorn Basin (Wasatchian, Wa3), Wyoming, 78L

Lysite Member, Wind River Formation, Wind River Basin (Wasatchian, Wa3), Wyoming, 78L, 86R

MacAdams Quarry (Clarendonian, Cl1), Texas, 174L, 177R, 200R

"Malcolm's Locality" (Tiffanian, Ti4), Wyoming, 30, 54L, 59L

Mammalon Hill Locality (Puercan, Pu2?), New Mexico, 28

Mason Pocket Quarry (Tiffanian, Ti4), Colorado, 28, 53L, 56L, 59L, 286L

McKeever Ranch localities (Puercan, Pu1), Montana, 31, 43R, 44L

Medicine Rocks 1 Locality (Torrejonian, To3), Montana, 31, 51R

Mehling Site (Torrejonian, To3), Montana, 31

Melville Locality (Tiffanian, Ti3), Montana, 31

Miami Quarry (Hemphillian, Hh3), Texas, 175R, 200R

Middle Sand Draw Locality (Tiffanian, Ti5), 31

Miller Pit (Hemphillian, Hh3), Oklahoma, 175L, 200R

Mission Valley Formation (Uintan, Ui1), southern California, 78R

Mixon's Bone Bed (Hemphillian, Hh1), Florida, 179R, 180L

Mosquito Gulch localities (Torrejonian, To1?), Montana, 31

Myton Member, Uinta Formation, Uinta Basin (Uintan, Ui2), Utah, 78R, 90L

Nation Pit (Hemphillian, Hh3), Oklahoma, 175L, 200R

New Taeniodont Site (Ti-Cf), Texas, 28

New Year Quarry (Barstovian, Ba2), California, 196

Norden Bridge Quarry (Barstovian, Ba3), Nebraska, 169L, 200R

North Livermore Avenue (Irvingtonian, IrII), California, 249R, 252R

Nut Bed, Clarno Formation (Uintan, Ui1), Oregon, 78R, 107R

Observation Quarry (Barstovian, Ba1), Nebraska, 168R, 177L

Old Crow River locality 11A (Irvingtonian), Yukon Territory, 221R

"Older Black Hawk Ranch faunule" (Cerrotejonian, = ca. Clarendonian, Cl1), California, 155R

Olive Locality (Tiffanian, Ti4), Montana, 31, 59L

Optima Quarry (Hemphillian, Hh3), Oklahoma, 175L, 200R

Oreodon Quarry (Barstovian, Ba1), California, 196

Oreodont Site (Arikareean, Ar3), Florida, 178L, 200R

Orinda Formation sites (Cerrotejonian, = ca. Clarendonian, Cl1), California, 155R

Olyor Suite, (Irvingtonian equivalent; U.S.S.R.), 221R

Paint Creek Locality (Clarkforkian, Cf2), Wyoming, 30

Pearson Ranch (C.I.T. locality 150; Duchesnean), southern California, 78R, 90R

Peterson's Quarry A (Arikareean, Ar3), Nebraska, 166R

Petropavlosk, Siberia (ca. 8 Ma), 238R

Phil's Hill Locality (Clarkforkian, Cf2), Wyoming, 30

Pine Cree Park Locality (Puercan, Pu2?), Saskatchewan, 32

Port of Entry Pit (Hemphillian, Hh1), Oklahoma, 174R, 201L

Post Ranch faunal horizon (Blancan, BlI, BlIV), Arizona, 216L

Powder Wash sites, Green River formation, Uinta Basin (Bridgerian, Br2), Utah, 78L, 101R

Powerline Locality (Torrejonian, To1), New Mexico, 28

Plateau Valley Locality (Clarkforkian, Cf2?), Colorado, 28, 61L, 65L, 65R, 101L

Princeton Quarry (Tiffanian, Ti5), Wyoming, 30, 59R, 62L

Princeton Locality (Bridgerian, Br2), British Columbia, 78L, 107R

Pruett Formation (Uintan, Ui1), Texas, 78R

Pumpkin Buttes (Wasatchian), Wyoming, 107L

Quarry A (Hemingfordian, He1), Colorado, 167R, 172L, 172R, 201L

Rabbit Hole (Hemphillian, Hh1), Nevada, 253L

Railway Quarry (Barstovian, Ba3), Nebraska, 169L, 201L

Rainbow Valley Locality (Clarkforkian, Cf3), Wyoming, 30

Ray's Bone Bed (Tiffanian, Ti3), Texas, 28, 54L, 58R

RAV W-1 Locality (Puercan, Pu2?), Saskatchewan, 32, 45R, 46L

"Red Deer" Locality (Tiffanian, Ti3), Alberta, 32

Red Division Quarry (Hemingfordian, He2), California, 158R, 187L, 201L
Reed and Longnecker locality 20 (Hemphillian, Hh3), Texas, 175L
Rexroad 3 (Blancan, BlIII), Kansas, 255L, 256R
Ries Locality (Clarkforkian, Cf2), Wyoming, 31, 61L, 64R
Riverdale Locality (Tiffanian, Ti4?), North Dakota, 32, 59L
Roche Percée localities (Tiffanian, Ti4), Saskatchewan, 59L
Rock Bench Quarry (Torrejonian, To3), Polecat Bench, Wyoming, 30, 47L, 49R, 51R, 54L
Rodent Locality, Hendry Ranch Member, Badwater area, Wind River Basin (Duchesnean), Wyoming, 78R, 98L
Rodent Quarry (BlIII), Nevada, 256L
"Rohrer" Locality (Ti6-Cf1), Wyoming, 30, 61L
Rough Gulch Locality (Clarkforkian, Cf2), Wyoming, 31, 61L, 64R
Saddle Annex Locality (Tiffanian, Ti3), Wyoming, 29, 58R
Saddle Locality (Tiffanian, Ti2), Wyoming, 29, 54L, 58L
Sand Draw Anthill Locality (Tiffanian, Ti4), Wyoming, 31
San Jose Formation, San Juan Basin (Wasatchian, Wa4), New Mexico, 78L
Saunders Creek Locality (Tiffanian, Ti1?), Alberta, 32
Scarritt Quarry (Tiffanian, Ti2), Montana, 31, 57L, 57R, 58L, 59R
Schaff Quarry (Tiffanian, Ti5), Wyoming, 30, 53R
Schiebout-Reeves Quarry (UT loc. 41274; Tiffanian, Ti1), Texas, 28, 54L, 54R, 55R, 57L
Seaboard Air Line Railway Company site (Hemingfordian, He1), Florida, 178L
Seaboard Well Locality (Tiffanian, Ti3), Wyoming, 30
Sebits Ranch locality (Hemphillian, Hh1), Texas, 174R
Sespe Formation sites (Arikareean, Ar1 or 2), California, 201L
Shutt Ranch (Irvingtonian, IrI), California, 260R
Siesta Formation sites (Montediablan, = ca. Clarendonian, Cl2), California, 155R, 201L
Silberling Quarry (Torrejonian, To3), Montana, 31, 54L
Sinclair and Granger Loc. 10 (lower part; Torrejonian, To2), New Mexico, 28
Sinclair and Granger Loc. 10 (upper part; Torrejonian, To3), New Mexico, 28
Sinclair and Granger Loc. 11 (Torrejonian, To3), New Mexico, 28
Slim Buttes Formation (Duchesnean), South Dakota, 78R
South Kutz Canyon sites (Torrejonian, To3), New Mexico, 28
South Table Mountain Locality (Puercan, Pu1), Colorado, 29
Southwall Site (Cf-Wa), Texas, 28, 65R, 66R
State Line Quarry (Bridgerian, Br3), Utah, 95
Stenomylus Quarry (Arikareean, Ar3), Nebraska, 166R
Stroud Claim (Hh1), Idaho, 241R, 253L
Sunbrite ash mine (Irvingtonian, IrII), Kansas, 263L
Sunday Locality (Tiffanian, Ti5), Wyoming, 31
Survey Quarry (Barstovian, Ba1), Nebraska, 168R, 201L
Swain Quarry (Torrejonian, To3?), Wyoming, 29, 51R
Swan Hills Site 1 (Tiffanian, Ti4), Alberta, 32, 59L
Swift Current Creek beds, Cypress Hills (Uintan, Ui2), Saskatchewan, 78R
Syndyoceras Quarry, (Arikareean, Ar3), Nebraska, 166R
Tatman Formation, western Bighorn Basin (Bridgerian), Wyoming, 78L
Tapo Canyon localities (Uintan, Ui2), California, 78R, 99L
Taylor Mount Locality (Torrejonian, To2), New Mexico, 28
Tecuya Formation sites (Arikareean, Ar1 or 2), California, 201L
Titanoides Locality (Tiffanian, Ti5), Wyoming, 29, 54L, 59R
Titus Canyon Local Fauna (Chadronian), California, 146R
Trinity River Quarry (Barstovian, Ba1), Texas, 176R
Tsentas' microsite (Torrejonian, To3), New Mexico, 28
Twin Buttes Member, Bridger Formation, Green River Basin (Bridgerian, Br3), Wyoming, 78R
Twin Creek Locality (Tiffanian, Ti3), Wyoming, 29, 54L
UADW (University of Alberta) localities, Alberta, 32, 58R
    UADW-1 (Tiffanian, Ti3), 32, 58R
    UADW-2 (Tiffanian, Ti3), 32, 58R
UALP (University of Arizona) localities, New Mexico, 48L, 50R

7595 (Torrejonian, To3), 52L
75139 (Torrejonian, To1), 50R
7650 (Torrejonian, To3), 52L
7691 (Puercan, Pu3), 48L
77114 (Torrejonian, To1), 48L, 52L
7782 (Torrejonian, To1), 48L
7896 (Torrejonian, To1), 50R
7899 (Torrejonian, To1?), 50R
UC (University of California, Berkeley) localities, 160L
Nevada, 160L
    2027 (Barstovian, Ba2), 160L
    V-5570 (Barstovian, Ba2), 160L
    V-5915 (Barstovian, Ba2), 160L
    V-6020 (Barstovian, Ba2), 160L
UC (University of Colorado) localities, Colorado, 105L
    Huerfano VIII (Lysitean, Wa3), 105L
    Huerfano IX (Lysitean, Wa3), 105L
    Huerfano XII (Lysitean, Wa3), 105L
    Huerfano IV (Lostcabinian, Wa4), 105L
    Huerfano VI (Lostcabinian, Wa4), 105L
    Huerfano XI (Lostcabinian, Wa4), 105L
    Huerfano VII (Gardnerbuttean, Br1), 105L
UM (University of Michigan) Sub-Wy localities, Colorado, 105L
    I, (Gardnerbuttean, Br1), 105L
    II, (Gardnerbuttean, Br1), 105L
    III, (Gardnerbuttean, Br1), 105L
    V, (Garnerbuttean, Br1), 105L
    Wyoming, 30, 54L, 104L
    2 (Wasatchian, Wa2), 104L
    7 (Clarkforkian, Cf2), 30, 104L
    10 (Clarkforkian, Cf2), 30, 104L
    16 (Wasatchian, Wa2), 104L
    20 (Clarkforkian, Cf2), 30, 104L
    23 (Wasatchian, Wa3), 104L
    27 (Wasatchian, Wa3), 104L
    28 (Wasatchian, Wa2), 104L
    29 (Wasatchian, Wa2), 104L
    263 (Tiffanian, Ti2), 30, 54L
UNM (U.S. National Museum) Locality 113 (Torrejonian), New Mexico, 52L
Upper Adobe Town Member, Washakie Formation, Washakie Basin (Uintan, Ui1), Wyoming, 78R
Upper Blacks Fork Member, Bridger Formation, Green River Basin (Bridgerian, Br2), Wyoming, 78L
Upper Bridger Formation, Tabernacle Butte, Green River Basin (Bridgerian, Br3), Wyoming, 78R
Upper Cady Mountains Local Fauna (Hemingfordian, He2), California, 158R
Upper Huerfano Formation, Huerfano Basin (Wasatchian, Wa4 - Bridgerian, Br1), Colorado, 78L
Upper Sand Draw Locality (Clarkforkian, Cf2), 31
UT (University of Texas) localities, Texas, 54L, 54R, 55R
    40147 (Tiffanian, Ti3), 55R
    41217 (Tiffanian, Ti3), 55R
    41274 (Tiffanian, ?Ti1), 54L, 54R, 55R
UTBEG (University of Texas Bureau of Economic Geology) localities, Texas,
    30895 (Hemphillian, Hh1), 177R
    30896 (Clarendonian, Cl1), 177R
    31057 (Barstovian, Ba1), 176R
    31081 (Clarendonian, Cl1), 177R
    31132 (Clarendonian, Cl1), 177R
    31183 (Barstovian, Ba3), 177L
    31190 (Barstovian, Ba1), 176L
    31191 (Barstovian, Ba3), 177L
    31200 (Barstovian, Ba3), 177L
    31242 (Barstovian, Ba1), 176L
    31243 (Barstovian, Ba1), 176L

40225 (Arikareean, Ar4), 176L
UW (University of Wyoming) localities, Wyoming, 29, 59R
  V77009–10, 77012, 77014, 78055 (Torrejonian, To3?), 29
  V77005–08, 77013, 77015–16, 77061 (Tiffanian, Ti1), 29
  V76008, 77059–60, 78052–54 (Tiffanian, Ti5), 29
Vedder site (Hemingfordian, He2), California, 158L, 201R
Virgil Clark Pit (Hemphillian, Hh3), Texas, 175L, 201R
Wagon Bed localities, Wagon Bed Formation, Beaver Divide area, Wind River Basin (Uintan), Wyoming, 78R
Wagonhound Member, Uinta Formation, Uinta Basin (Uintan, Ui1), Utah, 78R, 89R
Wannagan Creek Quarry (Tiffanian, Ti4), North Dakota, 31
Wasatch Formation, Bitter Creek area, Washakie Basin (Wasatchian, Wa2), Wyoming, 78L
Wasatch Formation, Evanston area, Green River Basin (Wasatchian, Wa3), Wyoming, 78L
Wasatch Formation, Fossil Basin (Wasatchian, Wa2), Wyoming, 78L
Wasatch Formation, Four Mile area, Washakie Basin (Wasatchian, Wa1), Wyoming, 78L
Wasatch Formation, LaBarge area, Green River Basin (Wasatchian, Wa3), Wyoming, 78L
"Wasatch" Formation, Powder River Basin (Wasatchian, Wa1), Wyoming, 78L
Wasatch Formation and Pass Peak Formation, Hoback Basin (Wasatchian, Wa2), Wyoming, 78L
West Bijou Creek-1 Locality (Puercan, Pu2–3?), Colorado, 29, 46L
West End Locality (Tiffanian, Ti3), Wyoming, 29, 58R
West Kutz Canyon sites (Torrejonian, To2), New Mexico, 28
Whistler Squat #2 Quarry (Uintan, Ui1), Texas, 93
Wind River Formation, Boysen Reservoir area, Wind River Basin (Wasatchian, Wa4 - Bridgerian, Br1), Wyoming, 78L
Wiggins Formation, Owl Creek area, Absaroka Mountains (Uintan, Ui1), Wyoming, 78R
"Wind River" Formation, Cooper Creek area, Laramie Basin (Wasatchian, Wa2), Wyoming, 78L
Withlacootchee River Site 4A (Hemphillian), Hh2, Florida, 181L, 191L, 201R
Witter Quarry (Tiffanian, Ti4), Wyoming, 31, 53R, 58R, 59L
White Site (Tiffanian, Ti2), Montana, 31, 58L
Windmill Hill Locality (Duchesnean), New Mexico, 78R
Wood Locality, Hendry Ranch Member, Badwater area, Wind River Basin (Duchesnean), Wyoming, 78R, 93, 98L
Worm Coulee #5 Locality (Puercan, Pu1), Montana, 31
Xmas Quarry (Clarendonian, Cl2), Nebraska, 169R, 174L, 191L
Yellow Sand Hill localities (Puercan, Pu3?), Montana, 31
local magnetic stratigraphy, 276L
Logan County, Colorado, 167R, 172L, 173L, 173R
London Clay (Sparnacian/Cuisian), England, 66L, 66R
Los Angeles County Natural History Museum, 237R
Lost Cabin beds (and *Lambdotherium* level, Wa4), 81R, 82L, 82R
Lost Cabin Member of Wind River Formation, Wind River Basin, Wyoming, 20L, 78L, 86R, 87R, 95, 97R, 105R
Lost Cabin Formation, 82L
Lostcabinian/Gardnerbuttean boundary, 86R, 87R
  = Wasatchian/Bridgerian boundary, 86R, 87R
Lostcabinian subage (Wa4) of the Wasatchian mammal age, 20L, 82L, 86L, 86R, 87L, 88L, 97L, 98L, 102L, 103L, 105L, 106L, 107L, 287L
Lost Creek Tuff, Wyoming, 91
Louisiana, 176R
Loup Fork, Niobrara River, Nebraska, 122R
"Loup Fork Beds or Formation," Nebraska, 122R, 172R
low-crowned teeth (microtine rodents), 238R
low sea levels (correspond to Pleistocene glacial periods, Florida), 227R
  promote trans-Beringian dispersal of microtine rodents, 239R
Lower Adobe Town Member, Washakie Formation, Wyoming, 78R
Lower Blacks Fork Member, Bridger Formation, Green River Basin, Wyoming, 78L
Lower Bone Valley Formation, Florida, 180L, 180R
Lower Bridger Formation, New Fork-Big Sandy area, Green River Basin, Wyoming, 78L
Lower Chadron, 129R
Lower John Day Formation, Oregon, 161L
Lower Nodular Layer or Zone, Brule Formation, South Dakota, 124L, 141L
Lower *Oreodon* Beds, Brule Formation, South Dakota, 123R, 140L
Lower *Oreodon* Banded Silts, South Dakota, 124R
Lower Purplish White Layer, Chadron Formation, Nebraska, 131L
Lower Rosebud Beds (or Formation), South Dakota, 166L, 171L, 172L
Lower Snake Creek beds (= Olcott Formation), Nebraska, 168R, 186R
Lower variegated beds or sequence, Togwotee Pass, 78L, 96R
lowest stratigraphic datum (LSD), 220R, 278R, 279R
Ludian Stage-Age, London and Paris basins, 101L
Ludlow Formation, Montana, 46L
Lundelius, E. L., Jr., xii, 211
Lusk, Wyoming, 166R
Lutetian Stage-Age, Paris Basin, France, 98R, 99R, 100R
  Mississippi, 107R
"Lysite beds," Willwood Formation, Bighorn Basin, 78L, 81R
Lysite Formation, 82L
Lysite Member of Wind River Formation, Wind River Basin, Wyoming, 20L, 78L, 86L, 97R, 105R
Lysite Mountain, Wyoming, 93
Lysitean subage (Wa3) of the Wasatchian mammal age, 20L, 82L, 86L, 86R, 97L, 105L, 105R, 106L, 287L
Ma (Megannum in the radioisotopic time scale), **xivR**, 3L, 3R, 4L, 4R, 13R, 21L, 21R, 90R, 96R, 97L, 97R, 102L, 103L, 103R, 104L, 104R, 134R, 136L, 147R, 148L, 149L, 159L, 161L, 162L, 176R, 179L, 181R, 191L, 191R, 213L, 213R, 214L, 215R, 216L, 216R, 217R, 218L, 218R, 219R, 220L, 220R, 221L, 221R, 222L, 222R, 223L, 223R, 237R, 238L, 238R, 239L, 239R, 240L, 241L, 242L, 242R, 243L, 243R, 244L, 244R, 245L, 245R, 246L, 246R, 247L, 248L, 248R, 251R, 252L, 285R, 286R, 287R, 288R, 289R, 290L
Macdonald, J. R., xii, 153
McGee Till, California, 219R, 220L
McKenna, M. C., xii, 77R
McKeever Ranch localities (Puercan, Pu1), Montana, 31, 43R, 44L
McPherson County, Kansas, 222R, 261L, 263R
Madison Valley beds, Montana, 164R, 165L
magnetic anomaly time scale; see magnetic polarity time scale
magnetic overprint, 272R
magnetic polarity chron (or anomaly), **xivR**
  chron 5N (V), 277R, 279L
  chron 6N, 242L, 279L
  chron 9N, 109L, 277L, 278L
  chron 12N, 109L
  chron 13N, 109L
  chron 15N, 109L
  chron 16N, 109L
  chron 20R, 108R
  chron 20N, 108R
  chron 21R, 108R
  chron 21N, 108R
  chron 22R, 108R
  chron 24R, 55R, 63L, 108L, 108R, 285R
  chron 25R, 55R, 56L
  chron 25N, 55R, 56L, 63L, 108L, 278L
  chron 26R, 49R, 55R, 56L
  chron 26N, 55R, 56L, 278L
  chron 27R, 48R, 49R, 50R, 51L, 52L, 55R
  chron 27N, 48R, 49R, 52L, 52R, 55R
  chron 28R, 48R
  chron 28N, 48L, 48R, 50R, 52L
  chron 29R, 41R, 42R, 44L, 270L, 285R

chron 29N, 42R, 44L, 46L, 48L
chron 30N, 278L
chron 31N, 278L
magnetic polarity epochs (= chrons), events (= subchrons), 270L
magnetic polarity stratigraphy, 4R, 15L, 20L, 108L, 119R, 215L, 269L, 271L
    correlation to MPTS, 277L, 277R, 278L
    development, theory, application, limitations, **269L–280R**
    fingerprints, 278L
    necessity for long stratigraphic sequences, 277L
    sampling procedures, 273R–275R
    self-reversals of polarity, 269R
    single sample imparts no time information, 277L
magnetic polarity time scale, MPTS, 4L, 21L, 22R, 23L, 44L, 79R, 108R, 215L, 271L, 277R, 278L, 279R, 288R,
    incomplete, based on sea floor record, 270L
magnetostratigraphic, magnetostratigraphy, 4R, 22R, 26L, 26R, 42R, 46L, 55R, 69L, 90R, 96L, 108L, 108R, 119R, 128R, 154R, 155L, 162L, 214L, 215R, 216L, 217R, 218L, 220R, 222L, 228L, 236L, 236R, 237L, 240R, 241L, 243R, 246R, 249L, 252L, 252R, 254L, 254R, 255L, 256L, 270L, 270R, 271L, 271R, 272L, 273L, 276L, 276R, 277L, 277R, 278L, 278R, 279L, 279R, 280L, 280R, 285L, 286L, 286R, 288L, 288R, 289R
Mahogany Oil Shale, Utah, 94, 101R
Mahogany Tuff, Utah, 94, 95
Malheur County, Oregon, 253L
Malibu Coast (fault), California, 99R
mammal age(s), viiiR, ixL, **xivR**, 1R, 3L, 4L, 5L, 5R, 6L, 7L, 9L, 19L, 19R, 20L, 21L, 21R, 22L, 22R, 24L, 24R, 25L, 25R, 26L, 26R, 40L, 42L, 47L, 118L, 181R, 182L, 183, 199L, 240L, 279R, 285L, 285R, 286L, 286R, 287L, 287R, 288L, 288R
    (cover all of Tertiary time), 2R, 118L, 118R, 145R, 181R, 285L, 285R
    (not necessarily coextensive with their types), 2L, 118R, 139R, 181R
    (limits between them somewhat flexible), 2L, 181R
    (most precisely dated boundary), 225R
    (purely temporal significance), 2R, 118L, 181R
    (recognition of ages beyond lithostratigraphic limits), 118R
    (type of each age belongs to it), 118R
Mammoth subchron (of Gauss Chron), 257R
Manatee County, Florida, 180R
Mantuan mammal age, faunas, rocks, 24L, 41L, 43L, 286L
Mariano Mesa, New Mexico, 90R, 105R
Marion County, Florida, 180R
Marsh, O. C., 80R, 81L
Marsland Formation, Nebraska, 158R, 166L, 166R, 167L, 168L, 172L, 184L, 185L, 185R, 186L, 198
"Marslandian" mammal age, 186L
Marsland, Nebraska, 167L, 167R
Marsland-Runningwater chronofauna, 168L
Martin Canyon beds, Colorado, 167R, 172L, 172R, 173R
Martin Canyon, Colorado, 172L, 172R
Maryland, 221R, 223L, 249R, 262R
Mascall Formation, Oregon, 161R, 162L
"Mascallian" mammal age, 186L, 187R, 188L
Matilija Sandstone, California, 99R
Matthew, W. D., 1L, 2L, 9L
Matuyama/Brunhes boundary, 261R
Matuyama Chron, Magnetic Chron or Reversed Chron, 21L, 215R, 216L, 217R, 218L, 219L, 220L, 220R, 221L, 223L, 249R, 259L, 260L, 260R, 261L, 271L, 277L
Mauer subage of Steinheimian mammal age, Europe, 251L
Meade County, Kansas, 211L, 215L, 220R, 222R, 224L, 243L, 255L, 255R, 256L, 258L, 259R, 263L, 271R
medial Chadronian, 135L–137L, 138R
medial Wasatchian (Lysitean), 86L, 97R
Medicine Hat, Alberta, 211L, 224L, 290L
Medicine Rocks area, Montana, 58L

Mehrten Formation, California, 157L, 170L
"Member C," Alegria Formation, California, 100R
Meniscomys Concurrent Range-Zone (Arikareean, Ar1–2), Oregon to Great Plains, 19L, 160L, 161L, 163R, 165R, 166L, 172L, 185R, 288R
Merritt Dam Member, Ash Hollow Formation, Nebraska, 169R
Mesa Falls ash (type S Pearlette ash), Nebraska, 222R
Messinian Stage, Europe, 242R, 245L
Mesozoic Era, rocks and faunas, 77L
Metarhinus zone, 83R
Mexico, 108L, 156L, 192L, 215L, 215R, 216L, 227R, 240R, 241R, 243R, 250R, 262L
Miami, Texas, 173R
microtine grade (tooth morphology), 238L, 239L
microtine immigration events, 22L, 22R
Miocene Series-Epoch, rocks, faunas, 3R, 5L, 6L, 6R, 7L, 18L, 20R, 23L, 100L, 122R, 147R, 148L, 153L, 154R, 164R, 176L, 178L, 182L, 187R, 190L, 192L, 193L, 211L, 213L, 237L, 241L, 278L, 280R, 288R, 289L, 289R
microtine faunas, 240L
microtine rodent events 1–10, 239L, 239R
midcontinent area (North America), 222L, 224L
Middle Chadron, 129R, 135R, 138L
Middle John Day Formation, Oregon, 163R
Middle *Oreodon* Beds, Brule Formation, South Dakota, 124R, 140L
Middle Sand Draw Locality (Tiffanian, Ti5), 31
Midway, Florida, 178R
Mindel (glacial stage, Europe), 221R, 224L
Mineral County, Nevada, 160L
Mission Valley Formation, California, 78R, 89L, 98R, 99L
Mississippi, 84L, 107R, 108L, 215L
Mississippi River, 249R
Missouri River, Montana, 163R
Mitchell Pass Member, Gering Formation, Nebraska, 197
Moffat County, Colorado, 102L
Modoc County, California, 254L
Mohnian Stage-Age, California, 155R
Mojave, California, 159R
Mojave Desert, California, 158L, 158R, 159L, 159R, 192L, 289R
Moliner Member, Wasatch Formation, Colorado, 101L
Mongolia, 67R, 68L, 133L, 238R, 239L
Monroe Creek Canyon, Nebraska, 166L, 171R
Monroe Creek Formation, Nebraska, 157R, 166L, 166R, 167R, 184R, 185L
    South Dakota, 163R, 171
    Wyoming, 184R
Montana, 30, 31, 40R, 41L, 43R, 44L, 45L, 45R, 46L, 47L, 49R, 50L, 50R, 51R, 52R, 53R, 54L, 56R, 57L, 57R, 58L, 58R, 59L, 61L, 61R, 64L, 69L, 78R, 84L, 90R, 106R, 120L, 125L, 127R, 135R, 136L, 136R, 137L, 137R, 143L, 149L, 161R, 162R, 163L, 163R, 164L, 164R, 185R, 192R, 271R, 286L, 288R
Montediablan Stage-Age, California, 2L, 18L, 20R, 155R, 157L, 159R, 162L, 190R
Montian Stage or Substage, Belgium, 67L, 68L
Moraga Formation, California, 195
Morocco, 68L
Morrill County, Nebraska, 167R, 258L
morph, morphs, 11L, 11R, 12L, 12R, 13R, 14L
Moulton Sandstone Member, Oakville Formation, Texas, 176L
Mount Diablo, California, 155R, 156L
M.Y. (or m.y., or m.y.b.p.), **xivR**, 3R, 4R, 16L, 20L, 148L, 155R, 193L, 237R
Muddy Creek, Wyoming, 166L
Mud Hills, California, 158R, 159L, 196
Mulberry Creek, Texas, 174L
Mulholland Formation, California, 155R, 191L
Murphy Member, Snake Creek Formation, Nebraska, 170R
Mylagaulodon Concurrent Range-Zone (late Arikareean, Ar4 - early Hemingfordian, He1), Oregon to Great Plains, North America,

19L, 161L, 288R
Myton Member, Uinta Formation (Uinta C), Utah, 78R, 84L, 89R, 90L, 99L, 100R, 101R
N.A. Arvicoline Zones, 214L
Nacimiento Formation, San Juan Basin, New Mexico, 40L, 42R, 45R, 46L, 47L, 47R, 49L, 50R, 52L, 52R, 53L, 275L, 276L
Nao-mu-gen area, China, 67R
nannofossil zones, 66R
  N9, 66R
  N10, 66R
Nan-xiong Basin, China, 67R
Naran Bulak Formation, Mongolia, 68L
"Narizian" West Coast benthonic foraminiferal assemblage, 98R
National Museum of Canada, 107R
natural remanent magnetization (NRM), 273L, 273R
Nearctic(a), 222L
Nebraska, 6L, 19L, 20L, 109L, 119L, 120R, 122R, 123R, 124R, 125L, 127L, 127R, 128L, 129L, 129R, 132L, 132R, 133R, 135L, 135R, 137L, 137R, 138L, 138R, 139L, 139R, 140L, 141R, 143L, 144L, 144R, 146L, 149L, 156R, 157R, 158R, 159L, 159R, 161R, 162L, 163R, 164L, 164R, 165R, 166L, 166R, 167R, 168R, 169R, 170L, 170R, 171L, 171R, 172L, 173L, 173R, 174L, 176L, 176R, 177L, 177R, 178L, 178R, 179L, 182L, 184L, 184R, 185R, 188R, 189L, 189R, 190L, 191L, 191R, 192L, 195R, 211L, 214L, 216L, 222L, 222R, 223L, 223R, 238R, 241R, 242L, 243L, 245R, 246L, 246R, 249L, 253L, 253R, 256R, 258L, 258R, 259R, 261L, 262L, 263R, 287R, 288R, 289L
Nebraska Geological Survey core 5-A-75, 213L
Nebraskan (glacial stage, High Plains), 213L, 213R, 219R, 248L, 249L, 249R, 250L, 252L
Nebraskan-Kansan sequence (contains seven tills), 213L
Neogene, 176R, 179L, 181R, 213L, 241L, 276R, 278R, 280R
neomammalogist, 11L, 11R
neotropical, neotropics, 182L, 191L, 192L, 192R
Nevada, 16R, 159R, 160L, 162L, 192R, 241R, 245R, 247L, 249R, 250L, 253L, 256L, 262L
Navasota, Texas, 175R
Newberry, Florida, 178L
Newer Pliocene, 211R
New Fork-Big Sandy area, Wyoming, 78L
New Fork Tongue, Wasatch Formation, Green River Basin, Wyoming, 87L, 87R
New Jersey, 83R, 107R
New Mexico, 40L, 41L, 41R, 42R, 44R, 45L, 45R, 46L, 47L, 47R, 50R, 51L, 52R, 53L, 55R, 78R, 80R, 81L, 82R, 84L, 84R, 89L, 90R, 104R, 105L, 105R, 154L, 168R, 221R, 271R, 275L, 276R, 277R, 280L, 286L
Newton County, Arkansas, 263L
  Texas, 176R
New World, 6L, 132R, 213L
New Zealand (glaciation), 213L
Niland Tongue, Wasatch Formation, Washakie Basin, Wyoming, 102L
Niobrara County, Wyoming, 127L, 127R, 139L, 141R, 166L, 166R
Niobrara, Nebraska, 122L
Niobrara River, Nebraska, 122L, 122R, 166R, 167R, 168L, 168R, 170R
nonglacial faunal sequence (Pleistocene), 224R
nonglaciated areas (Pleistocene), 227L
  problems in correlation to glacial sequence, 227L, 227R, 228L
North America, North American, viiiL, viiiR, ixL, 1L, 2R, 3L, 6L, 6R, 7L, 9L, 11L, 15L, 18L, 18R, 19L, 20R, 21L, 21R, 23L, 24L, 24R, 26L, 40R, 41L, 41R, 49R, 60R, 62L, 66L, 66R, 67L, 67R, 68L, 68R, 69L, 77L, 80L, 80R, 84L, 90R, 96L, 106R, 108L, 118L, 120L, 120R, 128R, 129L, 132L, 133L, 146L, 146R, 147L, 147R, 148L, 153L, 154L, 155R, 158L, 161L, 162R, 167L, 169L, 170L, 172L, 173L, 178L, 178R, 181L, 182L, 182R, 183, 185R, 187R, 190L, 190R, 192L, 193L, 199L, 213L, 213R, 214L, 214R, 215L, 217R, 218L, 219L, 219R, 220L, 221L, 221R,

222L, 222R, 223R, 224R, 225L, 227R, 237L, 238R, 239L, 239R, 240R, 241L, 242R, 244R, 245L, 246L, 247L, 248L, 248R, 249L, 251L, 251R, 258R, 262R, 270R, 271L, 271R, 278R, 279R, 280L, 285L, 287R, 289R
North American Commission on Stratigraphic Nomenclature, xiii, 9R
North American Land Mammal Ages, 128R, 147L, 147R, 214R
"North American Oligocene," 146R
"North American Provincial Ages," 118R, 120R, 124R, 181R, 182R, 184L
North American Stratigraphic Code, 9R, 25L
North Atlantic (ocean), 248L
North Boulder River (Valley), Montana, 164L, 165L
North Dakota, 20L, 31, 58R, 59L, 78L, 83L, 107L, 125L, 128L, 143L
Northern Hemisphere, 219R, 251R
North European Pleistocene subdivisions, 250L
North Fork of Owl Creek, Wyoming, 97R
North Horn Formation, Wasatch Plateau, Utah, 40L, 42R, 45L, 46L, 47L, 47R, 48L, 48R
  magnetic polarity sequence of, 47R
North Pacific (ocean), 248L, 249R
North Platte River, Nebraska, 122L, 125L, 144L, 168L
North Silver Star Triangle, Montana, 165L
Northwestern Wind River Basin, 96L
Northwest Territories, Canada, 108L
Norwood Tuff, Utah, 148L
Nuckolls County, Nebraska, 263R
Nunivak subchron, 216R, 243L, 244L, 254L, 255L
Oakville Formation, Texas, 175R, 176L
Ocala Arch, Florida, 178R, 179L, 180L
Oceanside, California, 99L
Ojo Alamo, New Mexico, 40L
Ojo Encino, New Mexico (= Arroyo Torrejon), 49L, 51L, 51R, 52L
Ogallala Formation, Nebraska, 169R, 191R, 198
Ogallala Group, Great Plains, 122L, 122R, 169R, 173L, 177L, 187R, 189L, 190R
Ogallala, Nebraska, 169R
Oklahoma, 173R, 174R, 190R, 191R, 192L, 221L, 222L
Oklahoma Panhandle, 173R, 175L, 190R, 192L, 193L, 222R
Olcott Formation, Nebraska, 168R, 170R, 173L, 186R
Olcott Hill, Nebraska, 170R
Older Pliocene, 211R
Olduvai subchron (of Matuyama Chron), 214L, 216R, 217R, 218L, 218R, 220L, 220R, 221L, 248L, 248R, 249L, 249R, 260L, 260R, 277R
Old World, 5L, 5R, 6L, 21L, 51L, 132R, 181L, 190L, 237L
Oligocene Series-Epoch, rocks and faunas, 5R, 6L, 18L, 20R, 84R, 93, 97R, 106R, 128L, 129R, 134R, 146R, 147L, 147R, 148L, 153L, 154L, 193L, 280R, 287R
Opal, Wyoming, 83L, 88R
Operculinoides Zone, Texas, 176R
Opdyke, N. D., xii, 22R, 269
Oppel-zone, **xvL**, 10L, 14R, 16L
ordinal chronology, 3L
Oregon, 78R, 107R, 127L, 128L, 133R, 142R, 146L, 149L, 160R, 161L, 161R, 162R, 163R, 168R, 185R, 192R, 238R, 241R, 242L, 253L, 288R, 289L
Orella A (basal Orella Member), Brule Formation, Nebraska, 139L, 140L
Orella B, Orella Member, Brule Formation, Nebraska, 140L
Orella C, Orella Member, Brule Formation, Nebraska, 140L
Orella C (uppermost Orella Member), Brule Formation, Nebraska, 140L
Orella Member, Brule Formation, Nebraska, South Dakota, Wyoming, 119L, 120R, 124R, 127R, 128L, 133L, **139L**, 139R, 140L, 141R, 143L, 143R
Orellan mammal age, faunas, rocks, 20R, 118L, 119L, 119R, 120R, 121L, 121R, 124R, 127L, 128L, 128R, 132L, 133L, 135L, 138L, 138R, 139R, 140L, 140R, 141R, 142L, 142R, 143L, 143R, 144L, 144R, 145L, 146L, 146R, 148L, 163L, 287R,

288R, 290L
definition and characterization, **139L–143L**
Orella, Nebraska, 139L, 139R
Orellan/Whitneyan boundary, 119L, 143L, 143R, 144L
Oreodon Beds, Oreodon beds, Oreodon Beds, Brule Formation, Nebraska, South Dakota, 122R, 123L, 123R, 124R, 139R, 142R
Oreodon layer, 122R, 123L, 123R
Oreodon (Lower), (Middle), (Upper), 124L, 140L
Oreodon series, 124L
oreodont faunal zones A, B, C, D, Brule Formation, Nebraska, 140L
Original continuity (of strata), principle of, 10L
Original horizontality, principle of, 10L
Osborn, Henry Fairfield (or H.F.), ixR, 1L, 2L, 9L
Ouarzazte Basin, Morocco, 68L
Owl Creek, Wyoming, 78R, 97L, 97R, 106R
Owl Creek Mountains, Wyoming, 98L
Owyhee Basalt, Columbia Basalt Group, Oregon, 161R, 162L, 197
Owyhee County, Idaho, 257R, 258L, 258R, 259L
overprint (magnetic), 272R
oxygen isotope ratios, deep sea cores, 219R, 250L, 251L, 251R, 252L
  stages, 250L, 251L, 251R, 252L
Ozark Mountains, 227R
Pacific Coast benthonic foraminiferal stages, 154L
Pacific Coast, Pacific Northwest, North America, 156L, 157L, 158L, 159R, 169L, 190L, 211L, 217R, 241R, 244L, 245R, 247L, 250L, 255R, 256R
Pacific Creek Tuff Member, Trout Peak Trachyandesite, Wyoming, 91
Pakistan, 270R, 277L, 277R, 280L, 281, 282
Palaearctic(a), 132R, 133L, 222L
paleobiogeography, 226R
Paleocene/Eocene boundary, 42L, 55R, 66L, 66R, 67L, 67R, 104L
Paleocene Series-Epoch, rocks, and faunas, 2R, 5R, 19L, 24L, 24R, 41R, 42L, 53R, 55R, 56R, 59L, 60R, 61R, 62L, 66L, 66R, 67L, 67R, 68L, 68R, 275L, 276L, 277L, 285R
paleoequator (magnetic determination), 275L
Paleogene, 108L, 147L, 276R, 280R
paleomagnetic (see magnetostratigraphic)
paleontological correlation, viiL, 10L
Paleontological Society (Vertebrate Section), 118L
Paleozoic (clasts), 97R
Palaeosyops borealis Assemblage-Zone (Bridgerian, Br1), 86R, 87L, 97R
Palm Springs Formation, California, 215R, 248R, 278R
palynological evidence (Pleistocene floras), 227L, 227R
Panamanian land bridge, 21L, 218L
Pantolambda Chronozone or Zone, 46R, 49L
Pantolambda/Plesiadapis praecursor Interval-Zone (Torrejonian, To3), 49L, 49R, **51R–53L**, 52L, 52R, 55R
Paris Basin, France, 66L, 66R, 67
parkland communities (Pleistocene floras), 227R
Pasco area, Washington, 245L
Paskapoo Formation, Alberta, 53R
Pass Peak Formation, Wyoming, 78L, 104L
Pawnee Buttes, Colorado, 172R, 173L
Pawnee Creek beds, Colorado, 172R
Pawnee Creek Formation, Colorado, 169L, 172R, 173L, 173R, 182L, 187R, 188R, 189L
Peanutpeekian (subage of Chadronian mammal age), 130L
Peanut Peak Member, Chadron Formation, South Dakota, 129R, 135R, 136R, 137L, 137R, 138L, 142R
Pearlette restricted (ash) (= Type O; Lava Creek B), High Plains, 213L, 224L
"Pearlette-type" ash, High Plains, 213L, 219R, 220R, 228L
Pearlette type B ash (= Huckleberry Ridge ash), 217R, 222R, 248R, 262L, 264L
Pearlette type O ash (= Lava Creek B ash), 221R, 223L, 224L, 249R, 250L, 262L
Pearlette type S ash (= Mesa Falls ash), 222R, 248R, 249R
Pennsylvania, 223L

Peoa, Utah, 128L
Peradectes/Ectoconus Interval-Zone (Puercan, Pu1), 25R, 40R, **43L–44R**
Periptychus-Loxolophus Chronozone, 48L, 49L
Periptychus site (Torrejonian, To1?), New Mexico, 28
Periptychus/Tetraclaenodon Interval-Zone (Torrejonian, To1), 48L, 49L, **50L–51L**
permafrost (geologically first), 248L
Permian, 121L
Pershing County, Nevada, 253L
Phenacodus-Ectocion Acme-Zone (Clarkforkian, Cf3), 25R, 63R, 64R, **65L–65R**, 69L
phosphate (mining) districts, Florida, 180L, 181L
phylogenetic, phylogeny, 224R, 226R, 237L, 238L
Piceance Basin, Colorado, 78L, 83R, 101L
Picture Gorge Basalt, Columbia Basalt Group, Oregon, 161R, 162L, 197
Picture Gorge Ignimbrite, John Day Formation, Oregon, 161L, 197
Pilgrim Creek, Wyoming, 93
Pine Grove Hills, Nevada, 160R
Pine Mountain, California, 100L
Pine Ridge escarpment, Nebraska, 125L, 144L, 166R
Pine Ridge Indian Reservation, South Dakota, 124L, 171L, 171R, 172L
Pinnacle Buttes area, Wyoming, 91
Pinole Tuff, California, 155R, 195, 196
Pinyon Peak, Wyoming, 92
Pinyon Conglomerate, Wyoming, 92
planktonic foraminiferal zonation, 154L, 181R, 278R
Planktonic Foraminiferal Zone, 66L, 66R, 176R, 179L, 214L
  N22, 214L
  N13, 176R
  N9, 176R
  N8, 179L
  N7, 179L
  N6, 179L
  N5, 179L
  P9, 66L
  P7, 66L, 66R
  P6b, 66R
  P6a, 66R
  P5, 66R
Plateau Valley area, Colorado, 62L, 64L, 65L
Pleistocene Series-Epoch, rocks and faunas, viiiL, ixL, 6R, 21L, 192L, 211L, 211R, 213L, 213R, 214L, 214R, 215L, 219R, 220L, 222L, 222R, 224L, 225R, 226R, 227L, 227R, 228L, 238R, 241L, 289R
Plesiadapis anceps/P. rex Lineage-Zone (Tiffanian, Ti2), 25R, 55R, 56R, **57R**
Plesiadapis cookei Lineage-Zone (Clarkforkian, Cf2), 63L, 63R, **64R–65L**, 66R
Plesiadapis cookei Zone (middle Clarkforkian), 66R
Plesiadapis churchilli/P. simonsi Lineage-Zone (Tiffanian, Ti4), 25R, 55R, 56R, **59L**
Plesiadapis gingerichi Zone (early Clarkforkian), 66R
Plesiadapis gingerichi/P. cookei Lineage-Zone (Ti6-Cf1), 56L, 56R, **60L**, 60R, 63L, 63R, 64L
Plesiadapis gingerichi/Rodentia Interval-Subzone (Ti6), 56L, 56R, **60L**, 63R, 69L
Plesiadapis praecursor/P. anceps Lineage-Zone (Tiffanian, Ti1), 25R, 55R, **56R**
Plesiadapis rex/P. churchilli Lineage-Zone (Ti3), 54L, 55R, 56R, **58L**
Plesiadapis russelli Zone (early Sparnacian = early Ypresian, early Eocene), 66R
Plesiadapis simonsi/P. gingerichi Lineage-Zone (Ti5), 54L, 56L, 56R, **59L, 59R**
Plesiadapis tricuspidens Zone (latest Thanetian, late Paleocene), 66R
Pleurolicus Partial Range-Zone, 161L
Pliocene-Pleistocene boundary, 213R, 214L, 221L

Pliocene-Pleistocene Commission, 18th International Geological Congress, 213L
Pliocene Series-Epoch, rocks, and faunas, 5L, 6L, 6R, 21L, 122L, 122R, 153L, 181R, 211L, 211R, 213L, 214L, 214R, 215L, 220L, 289R
Pliohippus Draw, Nebraska, 170R
plus or minus (±) factor in radioisotopic ages, 3L, 3R, 5L, 41L
Point Conception, California, 100R
Poland, 242L
polarity reversals, 236L, 273R, 276L
Polecat Bench Formation (see Fort Union Formation)
Polecat Bench, Wyoming, 53R, 54L, 57R, 58L, 60R, 61L, 62L, 286R
Poleslide Member, Brule Formation, South Dakota, 119L, 124R, 125R, 127L, 127R, 128L, 139R, 143R, 144L, 144R, 145R
Polk County, Florida, 180L, 181L
Polk County, Texas, 176R, 177L
polyphyletic (microtine rodents), 239L
Porcupine Hills Formation (Torrejonian), Alberta, 47R, 51L
Potamides matsoni Zone, Texas, 176R
potassium-argon (K-Ar), 3L, 4L, 228L
Potwar Plateau, Pakistan, 280L, 281, 282
Powder River Basin, Wyoming, 78L, 83L, 107L, 125L
Powder Wash, Green River Formation, Uinta Basin, Utah, 78L, 101R
Powell County, Montana, 163L
Prairie Dog Town Fork of the Red River, Texas, 174L
Priabonian Stage-Age, Paris Basin, France, 99R, 101L
Precambrian (clasts), 97R
precision, 3L, 5L, 13L, 15L, 15R, 25L, 40L, 184L, 193R, 236L, 275R
  in magnetic polarity stratigraphy results, 275R
  in microtine events, 239L, 252L, 252R
pre-Nebraskan glaciation, etc., 219R, 220L
pre-Pleistocene glaciation, etc., 213L, 213R, 214R
Presidio County, Texas, 104L
Princeton, British Columbia, 107R
Princeton University, 57L
prismatic cusps (microtine rodent teeth), 238L, 238R
Promerycochoerus zone, 161L
Pronothodectes jepi "interval-zone (Torrejonian, "To4" = To3), 49R
Protoceras Beds, Protoceras Beds, 122R, 123L, 123R, 139R, 144L
provincialism (faunal), 120L, 240R, 241L, 255R, 258L
Pruett Formation or Tuff, Texas, 78R, 89L, 93, 104L
Pseudadjidaumo stirtoni Assemblage-Zone (Barstovian, Ba2), California, 19L, 289L
Puercan mammal age, faunas, rocks, 19R, 24L, 24R, 25L, 25R, 26L, 26R, **40–43**, 44L, 44R, 45L, 45R, 47L, 47R, 49R, 50L, 50R, 53R, 66L, 67R, 68R, 69L, 285R, 286L, 286R, 290
  definition and characterization, **42L–43L**
  zonation, 43L–46R
"Puercan marls" (Torrejonian, To2 or 3), New Mexico, 28, 47L
Puercan through Clarkforkian fossil mammal localities, 28–32
"Puerco" Formation, San Juan Basin, New Mexico, 40L, 47L, 50R
Puercan/Torrejonian boundary, 47R, 48R, 68R
Pumpkin Buttes, Wyoming, 125L
punctuational (evolution), viiR, 12R, 15R, 16L
Punta Prieta, Baja California del Norte, 106R
Purdy Basin, Wyoming, 96R
Qian-shan Basin, China, 67R
Quaternary Period, 2R, 5L, 5R, 159L, 211L, 214L, 228L
Quaternary mammal ages, 1L
racemization (of proteins; dating method), 228L
radiocarbon (age determinations), 223R, 225L, 225R, 227L, 228L
  caution in using, 225R
  correlation to glacial changes, 227L
radioisotopic, radioisotopic time scale, 3L, 3R, 4L, 4R, 5R, 7L, 21L, 22R, 23L, 69L, 79L, 79R, 90R, 96L, 96R, 105L, 108L, 109L, 119L, 119R, 146R, 147R, 148L, 154R, 155L, 157R, 158R, 160L, 160R, 162L, 165L, 170L, 179L, 191L, 191R, 195R, 214L, 215L, 216L, 217R, 218R, 219R, 228L, 236L, 269L, 277R,

278L, 278R, 285R, 286R, 288L, 288R, 289R
"radioisotopic time" and "real time," 3R
radiometric (see radioisotopic)
Rancholabrean mammal age, faunas, rocks, 18L, 21R, 22L, 214R, 215L, 220L, 222L, 223R, 224L, 224R, 225L, 226R, 227L, 240R, 241L, 241R, 250R, 251L, 251R, 252L, 289R, 290L
  definition and characterization, **223R–225R**
  subdivisions, 224L–225R
Randall County, Texas, 259L
Randsburg mining district, California, 159R
Range-zone (includes various entities), range-zones, xvL, 11L, 22R, 25L
ratio reversal datum, 214L
Rattlesnake Formation, Oregon, 161R, 162L, 197
Rattlesnake Hills, Wyoming, 95
Ravenscrag Formation, Saskatchewan, 40R, 46L, 53R
  Alberta, 53R
Raymond Hill (fault), California, 99R
Recent (geochronological age), 211R, 214R, 220L, 226R, 227R, 240R
Red Creek, Wyoming, 96R
Redington Gap, Nebraska, 165R
Red River, Texas Panhandle, 173R, 174L
Red Valley Member, Box Butte Formation, Nebraska, 168L
Regina Member, San Jose Formation, New Mexico, 105L
Refugian (benthonic foraminiferal) "Stage," California, 100R, 146R
refugium, 181L, 227R, 241L
relict population, 220L, 241L
Relizian Stage-Age, California, 156R
Relizian/Luisian boundary, 156R
remanent magnetization, 216L, 271L, 272R, 277L
Renova Formation, Montana, 106R, 127R, 128L, 164L, 165L
Rensberger, J. W., xii, 2L, 19L, 153
Repenning, C. A., xii, 236
Republic County, Kansas, 259L
Republican River, Nebraska, 170L, 173R
resolving power of mammalian biostratigraphy, 290L
Reunion subchron, 259L, 260R
Rexroad Formation, Kansas, 219L
Rexroadian/Senecan boundary, 21L, 219L
Rexroadian subage of the Blancan mammal age, Bl1–2 (in part), faunas, rocks, 21L, 219L
Ricardo Formation, California, 159L, 159R, 196
Rifle area, Wyoming, 78L
Ringold Basin, Washington, 242R
Ringold Formation, Washington, 217L, 242R, 243L, 254R, 271R
Riochican mammal age, faunas, rocks, 68L
Rio Chico Formation, Argentina, 68L
Rio de Janeiro, Brazil, 68L
Rio Grande Rift, New Mexico, 104R, 105R
Rio Puerco, New Mexico, 40L
Riverside County, California, 260L
Robin's Egg Blue Tuff, Wyoming, 95, 103L
Rock Springs Uplift, Wyoming, 59L, 59R
Rockyford Ash Member, Sharps Formation, South Dakota, 145R, 171L
Rocky Mountain region, Rockies, 79R, 99L, 100L, 156R, 161R, 162R, 182L, 185R, 188R, 191L, 193R, 241L, 246L, 247L, 247R, 248L, 249L, 249R, 249R, 250L, 250R, 251L
Rodentia/*Plesiadapis cookei* Interval-Subzone (Clarkforkian, Cf1), 63L, 63R, 67L
Rodeo syncline, California, 155R
Romania, 221R
rooted cheek teeth (primitive microtines), 238R, 249L
rootless cheek teeth (advanced microtines), 248L, 249L, 258R
Rosebud Beds, South Dakota, 171L
Rosebud Formation, Nebraska, 168R, 184L
  South Dakota, 171L, 171R, 172L, 184L
Rosebud Indian Reservation, South Dakota, 171L, 172L
Rosebud, South Dakota, 171R

Rose Canyon Shale Member, La Jolla Formation, California, 98R
Rose, K. D., xii, 24R
Roundhouse Rock, Nebraska, 149L
Royal Ontario Museum, Canada, 107R
Runningwater Formation, Nebraska, 158R, 161R, 167L, 167R, 172L, 176L, 178R, 186L
Running Water (Niobrara River), Nebraska, 122L
Ruscinian Stage, faunas, Europe, 241L, 245L
Russia, 238R, 242L
Russell, L. S., xii, 118L
Sables de Bracheux (Thanetian), Paris Basin, France, 66L
Saddleback Basalt, California, 196
Salamanca Formation, Argentina, 68L
Salt Fork of Red River, Texas, 174L
San Andreas fault, California, 156L, 157R
San Antonio Range, Nevada, 160L
San Bernardino County, California, 187L
Sand Canyon, Colorado, 173R
Sand Canyon beds, Nebraska, 168R
Sand Canyon Member, Sheep Creek Formation, Nebraska, 168R, 198
Sandcouleean subage (Wa1) of the Wasatchian mammal age, 20L, 86L, 105R, 287L
Sand Coulee beds, 82L, 106L
Sand Creek facies (of Fort Union Formation), 82L
Sand Draw Anthill Locality (Tiffanian, Ti4), Wyoming, 31
San Diego, California, 98R, 99L, 100L, 100R, 260R
San Diego County, California, 99L
Sand Wash Basin, Colorado, 78R, 88L, 89L, 102L, 103L, 107L
San Emigdio Range, California, 156L, 196
San Francisco Bay area, 155R, 156L, 262L
Sangamonian (interglacial stage, North America), 223R, 224L
San Jacinto County, Texas, 175R, 176L, 177L, 261R
San Joaquin Basin, California, 157L
San Joaquin Formation, California, 157R, 256R
San Joaquin Valley, California, 156L, 156R, 157L
San Jose Formation, New Mexico, 53L, 78L, 82R, 104R, 105L
San Juan Basin, Colorado, 59R
San Juan Basin, New Mexico, 40L, 41L, 41R, 44L, 44R, 45L, 45R, 46L, 47L, 47R, 48L, 50L, 50R, 51L, 51R, 52L, 52R, 53L, 55R, 69L, 78L, 81L, 82R, 105L, 271R, 275L, 276R, 277L, 280L, 283, 286L
San Pablo Formation, California, 155R
San Pedro Valley (and sequence), Arizona, 211L, 214L, 215L, 216L, 218L, 218R, 219L, 220R, 221L, 228L, 246R, 271L, 271R, 273R, 274L, 277R, 278R, 289R
San Simon Valley, Arizona, 271R
Sanpete County, Utah, 101R
Sanpeteol, Utah, 94
Santa Ana Mountains, California, 99L, 99R
Santa Barbara, California, 99R
Santa Fe Group, New Mexico, 154L
"Santa Margarita" Formation, California, 156R, 157L
Santa Maria di Catanzaro, Italy, 213R, 214L
Santa Monica Mountains, California, 99R
Santee, Nebraska, 191R
Santiago Creek, California, 99L
Santiago Formation, California, 78R, 99L, 99R
Sappan subage (Ir1) of the Irvingtonian mammal age, faunas, rocks, 21R, 222R, 223L
Saskatchewan, 45L, 45R, 46L, 59L, 78L, 84L, 85L, 107L, 120L, 127R, 128L, 133R, 136L, 138L, 218R, 220L, 221L, 248R, 249L, 249R, 260R
Saskatchewan Museum of Natural History, Canada, 107R
savanna, 182L
Scenic Member, Brule Formation, South Dakota, 119L, 121L, 124R, 127L, 127R, 128L, 132R, 140R, 141L, 141R, 143L, 143R
Scenic/Poleslide boundary, Brule Formation, South Dakota, 143R
Schultz, G. E., xii, 21
Scott, W. B., 80R

Scottsbluff, Nebraska, 165L
Scripps Formation, California, 98R, 100L
Scurry County, Texas, 257L
sea floor magnetic anomaly patterns, 270L
    spreading, world's oceans, 270L
    incomplete record of magnetic polarity reversals, 270L
sea level changes, Florida, 180R, 181L, 181R
Seaman Hills, Wyoming, 139L
Sebits Ranch, Texas, 174R
secondary component of magnetization, 273R
    impossible to completely remove, 273R
Second Purplish White Layer, Chadron Formation, Nebraska, 131L
sedimentation rates, 216L
seed eating (microtine rodents), 238L
Semken, H. S., xii, 211
Senecan subage (Bl2) of the Blancan mammal age, faunas, rocks, 21L, 21R, 22R, 219L
Sentinel Butte Formation, North Dakota, 53R
Sentinel Butte Shale Member, Fort Union Formation, North Dakota, 107L
Series (relationship to Epoch), 10R
Sespe Creek, California, 100L, 100R
Sespe Formation, California, 78R, 84L, 84R, 90R, 99L, 99R, 100L, 100R, 101L, 146L, 157R
sexual dimorphism, 224R
Seward County, Kansas, 243L, 254R
Shara Murun Formation, Mongolia, 133L
Shark River Marls, New Jersey, 107R
Sharps Formation, South Dakota, 145R, 146L, 157R, 163R, 165R, 166L, 171L, 171R
Sheep Creek Formation, Nebraska, 167R, 168L, 168R, 186R, 198
"Sheepcreekian" mammal age, 186L, 187R
Sheep Creek, Nebraska, 168L, 170L
Sheridan County, Nebraska, 167R, 223L, 223R, 263R
Sheridanian subage (Ir3) of the Irvingtonian mammal age, faunas, rocks, 21R, 222R, 223L
Sheridan Pass Quadrangle, Wyoming, 96R
Shi-men Basin, China, 67R
Shire Member, Wasatch Formation, Colorado, 101R
Shirley Basin, Wyoming, 107L, 107R
Shoddy Springs, Montana, 78R, 90R, 106R
Shoshonian subage, earliest Uintan mammal age, 106R, 107L
Shotgun Butte, Wyoming, 97R
Shotgun Member, Fort Union Formation, Wind River Basin, Wyoming, 54L
Siberia, 221R, 238R, 248L
Sidney Gravel, Nebraska, 170L
Sidufjall (C^1) subchron, 216R, 243L, 254L, 254R
Siebert Tuff, Nevada, 160L
Sierra Madre (fault), California, 99R
Sierran glacial event, California, 219R
Sierra Nevada Mountains, California, Nevada, 156L, 157L, 159L, 170L, 213L, 219R
Siesta Formation, California, 195
Simi Anticline, California, 99R, 100L
Simi Valley, California, 99R, 157R
Simmler Formation, California, 157R
sink hole faunas (Pleistocene), 225L
Sioux County, Nebraska, 127R, 139L, 166L, 166R, 168L
Siwalik Group, Pakistan, 270R, 277R, 278R, 280L, 281
Six Mile Creek Formation, Montana, 164R, 165L
Skinner, M. F., xii, 153
Skull Ridge Member, Tesuque Formation, New Mexico, 168R
Slim Buttes, South Dakota, 143L
Slim Buttes Formation, South Dakota, 78R, 107R, 149R
Smith, William, viiL, 2L, 10L
Smith (= Deep) River, Montana, 163R
Smiths Valley beds, Nevada, 160R
Snake Creek, Nebraska, 168L, 170R

Snake Creek Formation, Nebraska, 170R
Snake River Plain, basin, Idaho, 211L, 215L, 215R, 219L, 245L, 245R, 246R, 247L, 247R, 257R, 258L, 289R
Society of Vertebrate Paleontology, 118L, 195L
South America(n), ixL, 68L, 68R, 218L, 219L, 222L, 289L
southern hemisphere (glaciation), 213L
Southern San Joaquin Valley, California, 156L
South Carolina, 66R
South Dakota, 6L, 19L, 20L, 78R, 84L, 90R, 107R, 119L, 120R, 124L, 124R, 125L, 125R, 127L, 128L, 129L, 129R, 131R, 132L, 132R, 133R, 134L, 135L, 135R, 136R, 137L, 137R, 138L, 138R, 139R, 141L, 141R, 143L, 143R, 144L, 144R, 145L, 145R, 146L, 149L, 149R, 161R, 163R, 165R, 166L, 167R, 169R, 171L, 184R, 185L, 186L, 190L, 193L, 222R, 262R, 287L, 288L, 288R
South Dakota School of Mines and Technology, 137L
Southern Plains, North America, 179R
South Mountain, California, 157R
South Saskatchewan River, Alberta, 224L
South Table Mountain, Colorado, 44L
South Townsend Basin, Montana, 127R, 128L
Sparnacian Stage (London and Paris basins), 18R, 66L, 66R
species concept, 11L, 11R, 12L, 12R, 13L, 13R, 14L, 15R, 16L, 19R
spinner magnetometer, 273L
spring (hole) faunas (Pleistocene), 225L
St. (or Saint) David Formation, Arizona, 216L, 221R, 278R, 289R
St. Helens ash, Washington, 243R
Stadium Conglomerate, California, 98R
Stage, stage, or stages, xvL, 10R, 15L, 15R, 18L, 25L, 285R
Stanislaus County, California, 170L
Starr Flat Member, Duchesne River Formation, Utah, 84L
stasis, 220R
State University of New York at Stony Brook, 57L, 58R
Stattenville, Florida, 180R
Steinheimian mammal age, Europe, 250L, 250R, 251L, 251R
Steno, Nicholas, 10L
steppe types (microtines), 237L
Stinking Water flora, Oregon, 197
stratigraphy, stratigraphic, viiL, viiR, viiiL, ix, xvL, 11R, 12L, 12R, 13L, 14L, 15L, 15R, 16L, 16R, 18L, 19L, 20R, 21L, 25L, 47L, 48L, 61L, 153L, 154L, 157L, 158R, 159L, 160L, 161L, 162R, 163R, 165L, 165R, 167L, 167R, 168L, 174L, 174R, 175R, 176R, 177R, 178R, 180L, 181R, 182L, 185R, 191L, 191R, 192R, 215L, 215R, 216L, 221R, 237L, 241L, 248R, 270R, 271L, 271R, 272L, 276L, 276R, 277R, 278R, 279L, 279R, 285L, 285R, 286L, 287L, 287R, 288L, 288R, 289L, 289R, 290L
Stucky, R. K., xii, 77R
subage, 18L, 20L, 21L, 285R, 287L, 288L, 289R
subchron, 270L
Sucker Creek Formation, Oregon, 161R
superposed, superposition(al), 186R, 188L, 191R, 192R, 211L, 214R, 224L, 241L, 269L
Superposition, principle of, 10L
Suwanee County, Florida, 178L
Swanscombe subage of Steiheimian mammal age, Europe, 251L
Swift Current, Saskatchewan, 221L
Sylvan Pass, Wyoming, 95
synchronous, 16R, 25L, 188L
Systemodon (= Homogalax) beds, 81R
Tabernacle Butte, Wyoming, 78R, 87L, 95, 103R
taxonomic, taxonomy, 224R, 226L, 238L, 288L, 289L
Taeniolabis taoensis/Periptychus Interval-Zone (Puercan, Pu3), 43L, 44R–46R
Taeniolabis zone (Puercan, Pu3), New Mexico, 28, 44R, 48L
Tallahassee, Florida, 178L
Tamiami Formation, Florida, 180R
Tan-tou Basin, China, 67R
Tapicitos Member, San Jose Formation, New Mexico, 105L
Tassajara Formation, California, 155R, 156L

Tatman Formation, western Big Horn Basin, Wyoming, 78L, 106L
Taubach subage of Steinheimian mammal age, Europe, 251L
Taunton, Washington, 255L
Tavenner Ranch, Montana, 163R
Tawney Tuff Member, Green River Formation, Utah, 94
Taylor, B. E., xii, 153
Tecolote Tunnel, California, 99R, 100L
Tecopa Lake beds, California, 262L
Tecuya Formation, California, 156L, 196
Tedford, R. H., xii, 153
Teewinot Formation, Wyoming, 241R
Tegelen warm period (interglacial), 248L
Tehachapi Mountains, California, 158L, 159R
Tejon Hills, California, 156R
"Tejon Stage," California, 99R
Tepee Trail Formation, Wyoming, 78R, 89L, 91, 92, 93, 97L, 97R, 98L, 99L, 106L, 106R, 108R
Temblor Formation, California, 156L, 156R
temperate grasslands, 236L
temporal ranges for Puercan through Clarkforkian mammals, 33–39
temporal unit, 61L
temporal resolution, 236L, 252L
Tepatate Formation, Baja California, 106R
tephrochronologic, tephrochronology, 21R, 22R, 23L, 221R, 228L, 236L, 236R, 241L, 252L
Tertiary Period, rocks and faunas, 2R, 5L, 5R, 41L, 102R, 118L, 120L, 120R, 121R, 122R, 133L, 143R, 146L, 147L, 147R, 155L, 156L, 158L, 160L, 162R, 163L, 164L, 164R, 168L, 168R, 173R, 174L, 175R, 177L, 177R, 179L, 180L, 181R, 228L, 269L, 270L, 278L, 287L
Tesuque Formation, New Mexico, 168L
Teton County, Wyoming, 252R, 258R
Tetraclaenodon/Pantolambda Interval-Zone (Torrejonian, To2), 49L, 50R, 51L–51R, 52L
Texas, 52R, 54L, 54R, 55R, 57L, 58L, 59R, 65R, 66R, 78L, 78R, 83L, 83R, 84L, 84R, 89L, 92, 96L, 98L, 104L, 107L, 108R, 109L, 120L, 127L, 128L, 133R, 134L, 135L, 136L, 137L, 138L, 149L, 159R, 173R, 174L, 175R, 177R, 178R, 180L, 180R, 186L, 189L, 189R, 190L, 190R, 191R, 192L, 193L, 195L, 216L, 217R, 218L, 218R, 221R, 222L, 222R, 223L, 245R, 255R, 257L, 259L, 261L, 262R, 263L, 271R, 288L, 289L
Texas A&M College, 175R
Texas Coastal Plain, 175R, 178R
Texas County, Oklahoma, 175L
Texas Memorial Museum, 175R
Texas Panhandle, 155R, 173R, 174L, 174R, 175R, 179L, 181L, 188L, 190R, 191L, 192L, 215L, 222R
Textularia Zone, Texas, 176R
Thanetian Stage-Age, London and Paris basins, 66L, 67L, 67R, 96L
thermal demagnetization, 273L, 277L
Three Forks Basin, Montana, 106R, 128L
Thvera (C_2) normal subchron (Gilbert Reversed Chron), 242R, 243R, 253R
Tiffanian mammal age, faunas, rocks, 19R, 24L, 25L, 43L, 47L, 49R, 52R, 53L, 53R, 54L, 54R, 55L, 55R, 56L, 56R, 57L, 57R, 58L, 58R, 59L, 60L, 61L, 62L, 62R, 63R, 65R, 67L, 67R, 69L, 85R, 88L, 101L, 108L, 286L, 286R, 290L
  definition and characterization, 55L–56L
  zonation, 56L
Tiffanian/Clarkforkian boundary, 55L, 60L, 60R, 61L, 62L, 63L, 64L, 64R, 67L, 67R, 69L, 107L
Tiffany beds, 53L
Tiffany, Colorado, 53L
till (glacial; Pleistocene), 213L, 213R
Tipton Tongue, Green River Formation, Wyoming, 82R, 102L
Titanotherium Beds, Titanotherium Beds, Nebraska, 122R, 123L, 124L, 124R, 129L
Titus Canyon, California, 128L
Toadstool Park, Nebraska, 139L

Togwotee Pass, Wyoming, 53R, 61L, 62L, 64L, 64R, 83L, 96R, 97L
Togwotee Summit, Wyoming, 78L, 97L
Tongue River Formation, Montana, 53R
　South Dakota, 53R
Tonopah Mining District, Nevada, 160L
Tonopah, Nevada, 160L
Toringian mammal age (Steinheimian and Recent), Europe, 251L
Tornillo Flats, Big Bend area, Texas, 54L
Tornetown Cave, England, 251L
Torrejon Arroyo, San Juan Basin, New Mexico, 271R
"Torrejon" formation, San Juan Basin, New Mexico, 2L, 47L
Torrejonian mammal age, faunas, rocks, 2L, 19R, 24L, 25L, 26R,
　40L, 42R, 46R, 47L, 47R, 48L, 48R, 49L, 49R, 50L, 51R, 52L,
　52R, 53L, 53R, 54L, 54R, 55L, 55R, 56L, 67L, 67R, 69L,
　285R, 286L, 286R, 290L
　definition and characterization, **48L-49L**
　zonation, 49L-53L
Torrejonian/Tiffanian boundary, 52R, 54L, 54R, 55L, 69L
Torreya Formation, Florida, 178L, 178R, 179L
Tortonian Stage, Europe, 242L
transberingian dispersals, 215L
"Transition Stage," California, 98R, 99L, 100L
Trans-Pecos, Texas, 120L, 127R, 128L, 133R, 135L, 137L, 138L,
　149L, 288L
Transverse Ranges, California, 157R
Travertins Anciens de Sezanne (Thanetian), Paris Basin, France, 66L
Travis County, Texas, 262R
Tripod Peak Quadrangle, Wyoming, 96R
Tropico Group, California, 158R
Trout Peak Formation or Trachyandesite, Wyoming, 92, 95, 106R
Truckee Formation, Nevada, 162L
Tule Formation, Texas, 218R, 221R
Tullock Formation, Montana, 40L, 42R, 45R, 47L, 50R
tundra (paleoenvironment), 222L
Turnbull, W. D., xii, 77L
Turtle Butte Formation, South Dakota, 171R
Tuolomne County, California, 157L
Turpan Basin, China, 67R
Turtle and Oreodon Bed (= Hayden's Bed B), White River Group,
　Great Plains, 122L
Turtle Buttes Formation, South Dakota, 145L
Turtle Cove Member, John Day Formation, Oregon, 161L
Turtle-*Oreodon* Beds, 122R
Twinbuttean subage (Br3, Bridger C, D) of the Bridgerian mammal
　age, 88R, 287R
Twin Buttes Member, Bridger Formation (Bridger C, D), Wyoming,
　78R
Twin Falls County, Idaho, 255L, 256L
Twin Sisters Pumice Conglomerate Bed, Nebraska, 149L, 197
"Two Ocean Formation," Wyoming, 91
Type B ash (Pearlette; Huckleberry Ridge), High Plains to California,
　213L, 214L, 217R, 222R, 224L, 228L
Type O ash (Pearlette restricted; Lava Creek B), High Plains, 213L,
　223L, 224L, 249L, 250L
Type S ash (Pearlette = Mesa Falls ash), High Plains, 222R, 248R,
　249R
typology, typological hiatus or overlap, 186L, 187L, 285R, 286L,
　286R, 289L, 289R
Uinta A-C, 83R, 84L, 89L, 89R, 97L, 99L, 101R, 102R, 108R, 287L
Uinta Basin, Utah, 77R, 78L, 78R, 80L, 83R, 84L, 85L, 85R, 89L,
　90L, 101L, 101R, 102R
Uinta Formation, Utah, 78R, 83R, 84L, 88L, 89L, 90L, 94, 99L,
　100R, 101R, 121L, 129L, 287R
Uintan/Chadronian boundary, 90L
Uintan-Duchesnean, 90R
Uintan/Duchesnean boundary, 90L, 108R, 287L
Uintan mammal age, faunas, rocks, 77R, 79L, 80L, 83R, 84L, 84R,
　85L, 85R, 88L, 89L, 89R, 91, 92, 93, 95, 96L, 97L, 97R, 98L,
　99L, 99R, 100L, 100R, 101L, 103L, 104L, 104R, 107L, 107R,

　108L, 108R, 109L, 120L, 129L, 134R, 146L, 146R, 147L, 286R,
　287L, 287R, 290
　definition and characterization, **89R-90L**
　subdivisions, 89R-90L
"Ulatisian" West Coast benthonic foraminiferal assemblage, 98R
Umatilla County, Oregon, 253L
United States, 1L, 24R, 106R, 186L, 190L, 192L, 192R, 193L, 215L,
　215R, 218R, 219R, 236R, 239L, 239R, 240L, 240R, 241L,
　241R, 242L, 242R, 244L, 244R, 245R, 246L, 247L, 247R,
　249L, 249R, 250R, 251L, 251R, 252L, 252R, 255R, 258L,
　262L, 288R
units A to H, Brule Formation, Slim Buttes, South Dakota, 128L,
　143R, 144L
University of Arizona, 238L
University of California, 238L
University of Colorado, 101L
University of Florida, 181L
University of Kansas, 172L, 172R, 238L
University of Michigan, 104L, 162R, 238L
University of Montana, 162R
University of Nebraska, 140L, 167R, 238L
University of Oklahoma, 174R
University of Oregon, 238L
University of Texas, 175R
University of Washington, 238L
Upper Adobe Town Member, Washakie Formation, Wyoming, 78R
Upper and Middle *Oreodon* beds, 139R
Upper Blacks Fork Member, Bridger Formation, Green River Basin,
　Wyoming, 78L
Upper Bone Valley Formation, Florida, 180L, 180R
Upper Chadron, South Dakota, 129R, 137L
Upper Harrison Formation, Nebraska, 166L, 166R, 167L, 167R,
　184L, 185L, 185R, 198
Upper Huerfano Formation, Huerfano Basin, Colorado, 78L
Upper John Day Formation, Oregon, 161L
Upper Nodular Layer, Brule Formation, South Dakota, 124R
Upper *Oreodon* Beds, Brule Formation, South Dakota, 123R, 124R,
　140L
upper purplish white ash, Orella type locality, Nebraska, 139L
upper purplish white layer, Chadron Formation, Nebraska, 127L, 139L
"upper purplish white ash," Seaman Hills, Wyoming, 139L
Upper Rosebud Beds, South Dakota, 171L, 172L
upper variegated unit, Wyoming, 96R
U.S. Borax and Chemical Company, California, 158R
U.S. Geological Survey, 83R, 84L, 86R, 101L, 104L, 107L, 195R,
　237R
U.S. National Museum, 83L, 238L
U.S.S.R., 221R
Utah, 28, 40L, 42R, 43R, 45L, 46L, 47L, 47R, 48L, 48R, 50L, 50R,
　78R, 80R, 81L, 83L, 83R, 84L, 89L, 90L, 94, 99L, 100R, 101L,
　101R, 104R, 107L, 108L, 128L, 129L, 133R, 149L, 246R,
　250L, 250R, 263R, 264L, 271R
UTBEG (University of Texas Bureau of Economic Geology), 175R
Val di Noto, Italy, 211R
Valentine Formation, Nebraska, 156R, 159L, 168R, 169L, 169R,
　173L, 173R, 179L, 179R, 180L, 188R, 189L, 189R
"Valentinian" mammal age, faunas, rocks, 20R, 188R, 189L
Valley of Mexico, 241R
Vaqueros Formation, California, 157R
Ventura, California, 157R
Ventura Basin, California, 157R
Ventura County, California, 99L, 99R
vertebrate paleontologist, viiiL, viiiR, 3L, 24R, 77L, 182R
vertebrate paleontology, viiiR, 14L, 195L, 228R
Vertebrate Paleontology, Section of the Paleontological Society, 1L,
　181R
Vieja area, Presidio County, Texas, 104L
"Vieja Formation," 134L
Vieja Group, Texas, 104R, 120L, 127R, 133R, 134L, 135L, 136L,

137L, 138L, 146R
Villafrancha d'Asti, Italy, 213R
Villafranchian Stage, rocks, faunas (Europe), 21L, 213L, 213R, 214R, 245L, 247L
Villanyian (mammal age; Europe), 222R, 247L, 248L
virtual geomagnetic pole (VGP), 275L, 276R, 277L
viscous remanent magnetization, 273R
Vista area, California, 99L
Vista Member, White River Formation, Colorado, 127R, 128L, 143R
Vrica, Italy, 214L
Wagon Bed Formation, Wyoming, 78R, 90R, 92, 95, 98L, 107R
Wagonhound Member, Uinta Formation (Uinta A, B, Ui1), Utah, 78R, 89R, 101R
Wahsatch, 82R
Walker County, Texas, 176L
Walworth County, South Dakota, 222R, 262R
Wapiti Formation, Wyoming, 106L
Warm Springs, Oregon, 161R
"warm" (faunal climate adaptation), 224L
Wasatch "beds," 81L
Wasatch Formation, Green River Basin, Wyoming, 77R
   Hoback Basin, Wyoming, 104L
   Piceance Basin, Colorado, 101L
   Powder River Basin, Wyoming, 107L
   Washakie Basin, Wyoming, 78L, 82R, 102L, 103R, 104L
   Wind River Basin, Wyoming, 81L
   Uinta Basin, Utah, 101R
"Wasatch Formation," Powder River Basin, Wyoming, 78L
Wasatch Group, 80R, 103R, 104L
   type locality, 81L
Wasatchian/Bridgerian boundary, 87L, 87R, 93, 102L, 108R
Wasatchian mammal age, faunas, rocks, 18L, 19R, 20L, 53L, 60R, 62L, 62R, 63R, 65L, 66R, 67L, 67R, 77R, 79L, 80R, 82L, 82R, 83L, 84R, 85L, 85R, 86R, 87L, 87R, 90R, 91, 92, 93, 95, 96L, 96R, 97L, 98L, 101L, 101R, 102L, 103R, 104L, 105L, 105R, 106L, 106R, 107L, 107R, 108L, 108R, 286R, 287L, 290L
   definition and characterization, **84R–86R**
   subdivisions, 86L–86R
Wasatchian Stage-Age, 18L, 18R, 19L, 87R, 286R
Wasatch Plateau, 69L
   (Cretaceous/Tertiary boundary), 41R
Wasatch Station, Weber Canyon, Summit County, Utah, 81L
Washakie A-B, 102R
Washakie Basin, Wyoming, 47R, 51R, 61L, 65L, 78L, 78R, 82R, 83R, 84L, 85L, 85R, 86R, 87L, 87R, 89L, 94, 102L, 102R, 103L, 106L, 108R, 271R, 286R
Washakie Formation, Colorado, Wyoming, 78L, 78R, 82R, 84L, 95, 102L, 108R
Washakie Needles Dacite, Wyoming, 92
Washington, 216R, 217L, 218R, 242R, 243L, 244L, 244R, 245L, 246L, 253R, 254R, 255L, 256L
Washington County, Texas, 175R, 176L
Wassuk Group, Nevada, 197
Wavy Tuff Member, Green River Formation, Utah, 94
Webb, S. D., xii, 153, 211
Weld County, Colorado, 172L, 172R
Welded Tuff of Devine Canyon, Drewsey Formation, Oregon, 197
West Coast, North America, 6L, 7R, 154L, 157R, 159R, 249R
Western Interior, 55R, 56R, 66R, 69L, 85L, 86R
Western Nevada, 159R
West Fork of Gallegos Canyon, New Mexico (Puercan, Pu3?), 28, 40L, 44R, 45L, 46L
West, R. M., xii, 77L
West Texas, 104L
West Walker River, Nevada, 160R
Whistler, D. P., xii, 153
White Bluffs, Washington, 243L
White Mesa, New Mexico, 105R
Whitney Member, Brule Formation, Nebraska, South Dakota, Wyom-

ing, 119L, 120R, 124R, 127R, 128L, 128R, **139L**, 139R, 143R, 144L, 144R, 145R, 146L
Whitneyan mammal age, faunas, rocks, 6L, 20L, 20R, 109L, 118L, 119L, 119R, 120L, 120R, 121L, 121R, 124R, 125R, 127R, 128L, 128R, 139R, 140L, 142R, 143L, 143R, 144L, 144R, 145L, 145R, 146L, 146R, 147L, 148L, 163L, 184L, 184R, 193L, 287R, 288L, 288R, 290L
   definition and characterization, **143L–145R**
Whitneyan/Arikareean boundary, 145L, 146L
White Pass Bentonite, Wyoming, 93, 96R
White River chronofauna, 121L, 129L, 145R
"White River Basin," 122L
White River beds, beds A-H, deposits, faunas, 122L, 124R, 125L, 125R, 127R, 129L, 171L
White River Formation, Colorado Dakotas, Nebraska, Wyoming, 122L, 125L, 127L, 132L, 133R, 134R, 135L, 136L, 136R, 137L, 138L, 143R, 144R, 148R, 149R, 171L, 172L, 172R, 173L, 173R
White River Group, 20L, 119R, 121L, 122R, 123R, 124L, 125L, 127R, 143L, 146R, 147L, 171L, 172L, 287R, 288L, 288R
White River "Oligocene," 146R
Wiggins Fork area, Wyoming, 91
Wiggins Formation, Wyoming, 78R, 91, 92, 93, 95, 97R, 98L, 106R
Wildcat Ridge, Nebraska, 165L, 165R
Wilkins Peak Member, Green River Formation, Wyoming, 93, 94, 96L, 102L, 103R
Williston Basin, North Dakota, 58R, 59L
Williston, Florida, 179R
Willwood Formation, Bighorn Basin, Wyoming, 19L, 19R, 20L, 61L, 62L, 82L, 87R, 91, 102L, 105R, 106L
   Clark's Fork Basin, Wyoming, 78L, 286R
Wilson Canyon, Nevada, 160R
Wind River Basin, Wyoming, 20L, 54L, 54R, 57L, 59L, 78L, 78R, 80L, 81L, 81R, 82L, 83R, 84R, 85R, 86L, 86R, 87L, 88L, 96L, 96R, 97L, 98L, 101L, 103L, 105L, 107L, 108R, 125L, 128R, 286R
Wind River Formation, Wind River Basin, Wyoming, 78L, 82L, 85L, 86R, 87R, 92, 95, 97L, 98L, 105R
"Wind River" Formation, Cooper Creek area, Laramie Basin, Wyoming, 78L, 96R, 107L
   Shirley Basin, Wyoming, 107L, 107R
Wisconsinan glaciation, 223R, 224L, 224R, 225L, 225R, 227L, 251R, 252L
Withlacoochee River, Florida, 180R
Wood committee, Wood, H. E., II, et al. 1941, etc., viiiR, 2L, 2R, 24L, 24R, 40R, 48L, 48R, 50L, 50R, 55L, 61L, 62L, 62R, 77L, 77R, 118L, 119L, 124R, 128L, 129L, 132L, 132R, 147L, 148L, 181R, 182R, 184L, 185L, 185R, 186L, 186R, 187L, 187R, 188R, 189R, 190R, 191L, 191R, 192R, 193R, 194L, 194R
Woodburne, M. O., vii, xiii, 1, 9, 18, 285
Wortman, J. L., 80R
Wounded Knee-Sharps, xii, 145L
Wray, Colorado, 173R
Wyoming, 2R, 19R, 20L, 26L, 29, 30, 31, 43R, 47L, 52L, 52R, 53L, 53R, 54L, 54R, 55R, 57L, 57R, 58L, 58R, 59L, 59R, 60R, 61L, 62L, 62R, 64L, 64R, 65L, 65R, 69L, 80R, 81L, 82L, 82R, 83L, 84R, 88R, 89L, 90R, 92, 96L, 98L, 102R, 103R, 104L, 105R, 106R, 107L, 108L, 109L, 120R, 125L, 127L, 127R, 128L, 128R, 129R, 132L, 133R, 134R, 135L, 135R, 136L, 136R, 137L, 137R, 138L, 138R, 139L, 139R, 141R, 143L, 144L, 144R, 145L, 149L, 166L, 166R, 184R, 193L, 238R, 241L, 245R, 246R, 247R, 252R, 258R, 259L, 271R, 276R, 280L, 283, 286L, 286R
Xuan-cheng Basin, China, 67R
Yapavai County, Arizona, 216R
Yellowstone National Park, 83L, 84L, 98L, 149L, 217R
Yellowstone Plateau, 79L, 96L, 103R
Yepomera, Mexico, 254L
Yoder Formation, Wyoming, 129R
Yorktown Formation, Atlantic coastal plain, 181R

Ypresian Stage (London and Paris basins), 66R, 96L, 99R
Yukon (Territory), 215L, 221R, 224R, 225L, 227R
Zakrzewski, R. J., xii, 211
Zemorrian (benthonic foraminiferal) "Stage," California, 146R
zones, 11L, 14L, 14R, 20R, 25L, 26L, 26R, 80L, 285R, 286L, 286R, 287L, 287R, 288R, 289L, 289R, 290L (see also below, and under named units)
boundaries defined, 2L, 11L, 12L, 13L, 15L, 16L, 16R, 19R, 25R, 42L, 43L, 44R, 47R, 48L, 50L, 51L, 51R, 55L, 55R, 56R, 57L, 57R, 58L, 59L, 59R, 60L, 185R, 219R
zoogeographic, zoogeography, 182L, 221R

Designer: U.C. Press Staff
Compositor: Prestige Typography
Text: 10/12 Times Roman
Display: Times Roman
Printer: Malloy Lithographing, Inc.
Binder: John H. Dekker & Sons